The Official
SCRABBLE®
Players
Dictionary

PUBLISHED BY POCKET BOOKS NEW YORK

POCKET BOOKS, a Simon & Schuster division of
GULF & WESTERN CORPORATION
1230 Avenue of the Americas, New York, N.Y. 10020

Copyright © 1978 by Selchow & Righter Company

Published by arrangement with G. & C. Merriam Company
Library of Congress Catalog Card Number: 78-3681

ISBN: 0-671-83146-1

First Pocket Books printing October, 1979

10   9   8   7   6   5   4   3

POCKET and colophon are trademarks of Simon & Schuster.

Printed in the U.S.A.

REFACE ● This word book has been long awaited by lovers of the SCRABBLE® Brand crossword games, and Scrabble® Crossword Game Players, Inc., a subsidiary of Selchow & Righter Co., is very pleased to present it to them. All who have looked for a guide to settle challenges that arise in the course of play now have one of authority. This is the dictionary of first reference for all official SCRABBLE® Players crossword game tournaments.

It is important to remember that The Official Scrabble® Players Dictionary was edited solely with this limited purpose in mind. It is not intended to serve as a general dictionary of English; thus, such important features of general dictionaries as definitions of multiple senses, pronunciation respellings, etymologies, and usage labels are omitted.

The plan of the dictionary and the policies that governed its editing were developed under the direction of Scrabble® Crossword Game Players, Inc. The finished manuscript was prepared for the typesetter and the dictionary was seen into print by members of the Editorial Department of G. & C. Merriam Company under the supervision of James G. Lowe, Associate Editor.

The detailed organization and special features of the dictionary are explained in the Introduction which immediately follows. It should be read with care by all who use the dictionary. Now that this work is available, we are confident that it will afford satisfaction and enjoyment to SCRABBLE® crossword game players everywhere.

Scrabble® Crossword Game Players, Inc.

NTRODUCTION • **MAIN ENTRIES** • Main entries are listed in boldface type and are set flush with the left-hand margin of each column. Except for an occasional cross-reference (such as **GUNFOUGHT** past tense of gunfight), main entries contain from two to eight letters since words within this range are considered to be most useful to SCRABBLE® crossword game players. Only words that are permissible in SCRABBLE® crossword games are included in this dictionary. Thus, proper names, words requiring hyphens or apostrophes, words considered foreign, and abbreviations have been omitted. Because dictionaries have different standards for selecting entries, several current desk dictionaries were consulted in preparing the list of main entries for this book in order to insure a wider range of entries than any single dictionary of that kind offers. Words that exceed eight letters in length and are not inflected forms of words entered in this dictionary should be looked up in a desk dictionary such as Webster's New Collegiate Dictionary. No attempt was made to omit obsolete, archaic, slang, or nonstandard words since they are permitted by the rules of the game. All variant forms of a main entry are shown at their own alphabetical places and defined in terms of the principal form.

RUN-ON ENTRIES • A main entry may be followed by one or more derivatives in boldface type with a different part-of-speech label. These are run-on entries. Run-on entries are not defined since their meanings are readily derivable from the meaning of the root word.

JOYOUS	*adj* joyful **JOYOUSLY** *adv*
KNOW	*v* KNEW, KNOWN, KNOWING, KNOWS to have a true understanding of **KNOWABLE** *adj*

No entry has been run on at another if it would fall alphabetically more than two places from the entry. **When you do not find a word at its own place, it is always wise to check several entries above and below to see if it is run on.**

CROSS-REFERENCES • A cross-reference is a main entry that is an inflected form (such as the plural form of a noun, the past tense form of a verb, or the comparative form of an adjective) of another word. An inflected form is entered as a main entry only if it undergoes a spelling change in addition to or instead of suffixation *and* if it falls alphabetically three or more places away from the root word.

For example, in the entries reproduced below **GAGGED** is a main entry because it involves a spelling change (the final -*g* of *gag* is doubled) besides the addition of the -*ed* ending and because it falls alphabetically three or more places away from the entry **GAG**. On the other hand, *gags* is not a main entry because it involves no spelling change beyond the addition of the ending -*s*. Equally, while **GAGING** is a main entry, *gaged* is not, because, even though it involves a spelling change (the final -*e* of *gage* is dropped) beyond the addition of the -*ed* ending, it would not fall three or more places from **GAGE**.

GAG	*v* GAGGED, GAGGING, GAGS to stop up the mouth
GAGA	*adj* crazy
GAGE	*v* GAGED, GAGING, GAGES to pledge as security
GAGER	*n* pl. -S gauger
GAGGED	past tense of gag
GAGGER	*n* pl. -S one that gags
GAGGING	present participle of gag
GAGGLE	*v* -GLED, -GLING, -GLES to cackle
GAGING	present participle of gage

This policy is intended to make the word desired as easy to find as possible without wasting space. Nevertheless, many inflected forms will appear only at the main entry.

Users of the book should always look at several entries above and below the expected place if they do not find the desired word as a main entry.

Cross-reference entries for present tense third person singular forms of verbs use the abbreviation "sing."

PARTS OF SPEECH ● An italic label indicating a part of speech follows each main entry except cross-references (such as **JOLLIED, JOLLIER, JOLLIES, JOLLIEST**), for which the label is given at the root word. The eight traditional parts of speech are indicated as follows:

n	noun	*pron*	pronoun
v	verb	*prep*	preposition
adj	adjective	*conj*	conjunction
adv	adverb	*interj*	interjection

The label *n/pl* is given to two kinds of nouns. One is the plural noun that has no singular form.

VIBES   *n/pl* a percussion instrument

The other is the plural noun of which the singular is not entered in this dictionary. Singular forms are omitted if they contain more than eight letters.

ROSTELLA   *n/pl* small, beaklike structures

Rostellum, the singular form, has nine letters and is not entered.

When a word can be used as more than one part of speech, each part of speech is entered separately if the inflected forms are not spelled alike. For example, both the adjective *lazy* and the verb *lazy* are entered because the inflected forms vary.

LAZY   *adj* LAZIER, LAZIEST disinclined
                to work or exertion

LAZY   *v* LAZIED, LAZYING, LAZIES to
                move or lie lazily

On the other hand, the verb *suit* is entered while the noun *suit* is not because the inflected form *suits* at the verb is spelled the same as the plural form of the noun. In a dictionary for SCRABBLE® crossword game players, entry of the noun is therefore redundant. Homographs (words spelled alike) which may be used as the same part of speech are treated in the same way. For example, *lepton* is entered as a noun twice because the plurals are spelled differently.

LEPTON   *n* pl. -TA a monetary unit of
                Greece

LEPTON   *n* pl. -S an atomic
                particle . . .

If both plurals were spelled alike, only one *lepton* would be entered in this dictionary. In this way the dictionary includes as many different spellings as possible yet avoids wasting space with repeated entry of words spelled in the same way. The SCRABBLE® crossword game player, after all, needs only one entry to justify his play.

INFLECTED FORMS ●   Inflected forms include the past tense, past participle, present participle, and present tense third person singular of verbs, the plural of nouns, and the comparative and superlative of adjectives and adverbs. They are shown in capital letters immediately following the part-of-speech label. Irregular inflected forms are listed as main entries when they fail three or more alphabetical places away from the root word (see **Cross-References** above). All inflected forms are allowable as entries in SCRABBLE® crossword games.

The principal parts of the majority of verbs are shown as -ED, -ING, -S (or -ES when applicable). This indicates that the past tense and past participle are formed simply by adding *-ed* to the entry word, that the present participle is formed simply by adding *-ing* to the entry word, and that the present third person singular is formed simply by adding *-s* (or *-es*) to the entry word.

TALK   *v* -ED, -ING, -S to communicate
                by speaking

When inflection of an entry word involves any spelling change in addition to the suffixal ending (such as the dropping of a final -*e*, the doubling of a final consonant, or the changing of a final -*y* to -*i*-) or when the inflection is irregular, the inflected forms given indicate such changes.

WASTE   *v* WASTED, WASTING, WASTES to use thoughtlessly

DIM   *v* DIMMED, DIMMING, DIMS to make dim

TRY   *v* TRIED, TRYING, TRIES to attempt

RISE   *v* ROSE, RISEN, RISING, RISES to move upward

For verbs of more than one syllable either the last syllable or the last two syllables are shown.

ABDICATE   *v* -CATED, -CATING, -CATES to give up formally

BEGIN   *v* -GAN, -GUN, -GINNING, -GINS to start

The plurals of nouns are preceded by the abbreviation "pl." Most plurals are shown as -S (or -ES when applicable) to indicate that the plural is formed simply by adding the given suffix to the entry word.

VINTNER   *n* pl. -S a wine merchant

When pluralizing a noun involves any spelling change in addition to the suffixal ending (such as the changing of a final -*y* to -*i*- or a final -*f* to -*v*-) or when the plural is irregular, the plural form shown indicates such change.

BEVY   *n* pl. BEVIES a group

LEAF   *n* pl. LEAVES a usually green, flattened organ of vascular plants

CHILD   *n* pl. CHILDREN a young person

In such cases involving polysyllabic nouns at least the last syllable is shown.

SUDATORY   *n* pl. -RIES a hot-air bath for inducing sweating

For the sake of clarity, two groups of nouns that are confusing to many, those ending in -*o* and those ending in -*y*, are always indicated in this dictionary by showing at least the last syllable, even though no spelling change is involved.

RONDO   *n* pl. -DOS a type of musical composition

SAWNEY   *n* pl. -NEYS a foolish person

Variant plurals are shown wherever they add another word permissible in SCRABBLE® crossword games.

GLOSSA   *n* pl. -SAE or -SAS the tongue

Plurals which have the same form as the singular are shown only when they are the only plural for that entry. This is done to show that for the entry in question it is not permissible to add *-s* (or *-es*) to the singular to create a plural.

HAIKU   *n* pl. HAIKU a Japanese poem
CALENDS   *n* pl. CALENDS the first day of
               the Roman month

Otherwise, they are omitted and only the plural with the inflection is shown.

DEER   *n* pl. -S a ruminant mammal

The comparative and superlative forms of adjectives and adverbs are shown, when applicable, immediately following the part-of-speech label. Any spelling changes are indicated in the forms shown.

WEAK   *adj* WEAKER, WEAKEST lacking
               strength
OFTEN   *adv* -ENER, -ENEST frequently
BALKY   *adj* BALKIER, BALKIEST
               stubborn . . .

Not all adjectives or adverbs can be inflected, and only those inflected forms shown are acceptable. None of the adjectives and adverbs listed as run-on entries in this dictionary have inflected forms.

DEFINITIONS ●

In most cases, only one very brief definition is given for each main entry since definitions do not play a significant role in the SCRABBLE® crossword game. This definition serves only to orient the player in a general way to a single meaning of the word. It is not intended to have all the precision and detail of a definition in a good general dictionary.

When a word consisting of eight letters or less appears in a definition but is not an entry in this dictionary, it is glossed in parentheses. For example, at the entry for the verb *bomb,* the noun "bombs" is used in the definition and is glossed because the noun *bomb* is not a separate entry.

BOMB   *v* -ED, -ING, -S to attack with
               bombs (explosive projectiles)

A main entry that is a variant form of another entry is defined in terms of the most common form, which is entered and defined at its own alphabetical place.

AMPOULE *n* pl. -S ampule
AMPUL *n* pl. -S ampule
AMPULE *n* pl. -S a small glass vial

SCRABBLE® crossword game players in Canada will be pleased to learn that variant forms such as *honour, centre,* and *cheque,* which are often omitted from general dictionaries, have also been included in this book.

LISTS OF UNDEFINED WORDS ● Lists of undefined words

appear after the entries of the prefixes **RE-** and **UN-**. These words are not defined because they are self-explanatory: their meanings are simply the sum of a meaning of the prefix combined with a meaning of the root word. All of their inflected forms are given, however.

AA	*n* pl. -S rough, cindery lava	**ABATOR**	*n* pl. -S one that unlawfully seizes an inheritance
AAH	*v* -ED, -ING, -S to exclaim in amazement, joy, or surprise	**ABATTIS**	*n* pl. -TISES abatis
AAL	*n* pl. -S an East Indian shrub	**ABATTOIR**	*n* pl. -S a slaughterhouse
AALII	*n* pl. -S a tropical tree	**ABAXIAL**	*adj* situated away from the axis
AARDVARK	*n* pl. -S an African mammal	**ABAXILE**	*adj* abaxial
AARDWOLF	*n* pl. -WOLVES an African mammal	**ABBACY**	*n* pl. -CIES the office of an abbot
AASVOGEL	*n* pl. -S a vulture	**ABBATIAL**	*adj* pertaining to an abbot
ABA	*n* pl. -S a sleeveless garment worn by Arabs	**ABBE**	*n* pl. -S an abbot
		ABBESS	*n* pl. -ES the female superior of a convent of nuns
ABACA	*n* pl. -S a Philippine plant		
ABACK	*adv* toward the back	**ABBEY**	*n* pl. -BEYS a monastery or convent
ABACUS	*n* pl. -CI or -CUSES a calculating device	**ABBOT**	*n* pl. -S the superior of a monastery
ABAFT	*adv* toward the stern	**ABBOTCY**	*n* pl. -CIES abbacy
ABAKA	*n* pl. -S abaca	**ABDICATE**	*v* -CATED, -CATING, -CATES to give up formally
ABALONE	*n* pl. -S an edible shellfish		
ABAMP	*n* pl. -S abampere	**ABDOMEN**	*n* pl. -MENS or -MINA the body cavity containing the viscera
ABAMPERE	*n* pl. -S a unit of electric current		
ABANDON	*v* -ED, -ING, -S to leave or give up completely	**ABDUCE**	*v* -DUCED, -DUCING, -DUCES to abduct
ABASE	*v* ABASED, ABASING, ABASES to lower in rank, prestige, or esteem **ABASEDLY** *adv*	**ABDUCENS**	*n* pl. -CENTES a cranial nerve
		ABDUCENT	*adj* serving to abduct
		ABDUCING	present participle of abduce
ABASER	*n* pl. -S one that abases	**ABDUCT**	*v* -ED, -ING, -S to draw away from the original position
ABASH	*v* -ED, -ING, -ES to make ashamed or embarrassed		
		ABDUCTOR	*n* pl. -ES or -S an abducent muscle
ABASING	present participle of abase		
ABATE	*v* ABATED, ABATING, ABATES to reduce in degree or intensity **ABATABLE** *adj*	**ABEAM**	*adv* at right angles to the keel of a ship
		ABED	*adv* in bed
ABATER	*n* pl. -S one that abates	**ABELE**	*n* pl. -S a Eurasian tree
ABATIS	*n* pl. -TISES a barrier made of felled trees	**ABELMOSK**	*n* pl. -S a tropical herb

ABERRANT	n pl. -S a deviant	**ABLINGS**	adv ablins
ABET	v ABETTED, ABETTING, ABETS to encourage and support	**ABLINS**	adv perhaps
		ABLOOM	adj blooming
ABETMENT	n pl. -S the act of abetting	**ABLUENT**	n pl. -S a cleansing agent
ABETTAL	n pl. -S abetment	**ABLUSH**	adj blushing
ABETTED	past tense of abet	**ABLUTED**	adj washed clean
ABETTER	n pl. -S abettor	**ABLUTION**	n pl. -S a washing
ABETTING	present participle of abet	**ABLY**	adv in an able manner
ABETTOR	n pl. -S one that abets	**ABMHO**	n pl. -MHOS a unit of electrical conductance
ABEYANCE	n pl. -S temporary inactivity		
ABEYANCY	n pl. -CIES abeyance	**ABNEGATE**	v -GATED, -GATING, -GATES to deny to oneself
ABEYANT	adj marked by abeyance		
ABFARAD	n pl. -S a unit of capacitance	**ABNORMAL**	n pl. -S a mentally deficient person
ABHENRY	n pl. -RIES or -RYS a unit of inductance		
		ABO	n pl. ABOS an aborigine (an original inhabitant)
ABHOR	v -HORRED, -HORRING, -HORS to loathe		
		ABOARD	adv into, in, or on a ship, train, or airplane
ABHORRER	n pl. -S one that abhors		
ABIDANCE	n pl. -S the act of abiding	**ABODE**	v ABODED, ABODING, ABODES to forebode
ABIDE	v ABODE or ABIDED, ABIDING, ABIDES to accept without objection		
		ABOHM	n pl. -S a unit of electrical resistance
ABIDER	n pl. -S one that abides		
ABIGAIL	n pl. -S a lady's maid	**ABOIDEAU**	n pl. -DEAUS or -DEAUX a type of dike
ABILITY	n pl. -TIES the quality of being able to do something		
		ABOIL	adj boiling
ABIOSIS	n pl. -OSES absence of life **ABIOTIC** adj	**ABOITEAU**	n pl. -TEAUS or -TEAUX aboideau
ABJECT	adj sunk to a low condition **ABJECTLY** adv	**ABOLISH**	v -ED, -ING, -ES to do away with
		ABOLLA	n pl. -LAE a cloak worn in ancient Rome
ABJURE	v -JURED, -JURING, -JURES to renounce under oath		
		ABOMA	n pl. -S a South American snake
ABJURER	n pl. -S one that abjures		
ABLATE	v -LATED, -LATING, -LATES to remove by cutting	**ABOMASAL**	adj pertaining to the abomasum
		ABOMASUM	n pl. -SA the fourth stomach of a ruminant
ABLATION	n pl. -S surgical removal of a bodily part		
		ABOMASUS	n pl. -MASI abomasum
ABLATIVE	n pl. -S a grammatical case	**ABOON**	adv above
ABLAUT	n pl. -S a patterned change in root vowels of verb forms	**ABORAL**	adj situated away from the mouth **ABORALLY** adv
ABLAZE	adj being on fire		
ABLE	adj ABLER, ABLEST having sufficient power, skill, or resources	**ABORNING**	adv while being born
		ABORT	v -ED, -ING, -S to bring forth a fetus prematurely
ABLE	n pl. -S a communications code word for the letter A		
		ABORTER	n pl. -S one that aborts
ABLEGATE	n pl. -S a papal envoy	**ABORTION**	n pl. -S induced expulsion of a nonviable fetus
ABLER	comparative of able		
		ABORTIVE	adj failing to succeed
ABLEST	superlative of able	**ABOUGHT**	past tense of aby and abye
		ABOULIA	n pl. -S abulia **ABOULIC** adj

ABOUND   v -ED, -ING, -S to have a large number or amount

ABOUT   adv approximately

ABOVE   n pl. -S something that is above (in a higher place)

ABRADANT   n pl. -S an abrasive

ABRADE   v ABRADED, ABRADING, ABRADES to wear away by friction

ABRADER   n pl. -S a tool for abrading

ABRASION   n pl. -S the act of abrading

ABRASIVE   n pl. -S an abrading substance

ABREACT   v -ED, -ING, -S to release repressed emotions by reliving the original traumatic experience

ABREAST   adv side by side

ABRI   n pl. -S a bomb shelter

ABRIDGE   v ABRIDGED, ABRIDGING, ABRIDGES to reduce the length of

ABRIDGER   n pl. -S one that abridges

ABROACH   adj astir

ABROAD   adv out of one's own country

ABROGATE   v -GATED, -GATING, -GATES to abolish by authoritative action

ABRUPT   adj -RUPTER, -RUPTEST rudely brief **ABRUPTLY** adv

ABSCESS   v -ED, -ING, -ES to form an abscess (a localized collection of pus surrounded by inflamed tissue)

ABSCISE   v -SCISED, -SCISING, -SCISES to cut off

ABSCISIN   n pl. -S a regulatory substance found in plants

ABSCISSA   n pl. -SAS or -SAE a particular geometric coordinate

ABSCOND   v -ED, -ING, -S to depart suddenly and secretly

ABSENCE   n pl. -S the state of being away

ABSENT   v -ED, -ING, -S to take or keep away

ABSENTEE   n pl. -S one that is not present

ABSENTER   n pl. -S one that absents himself

ABSENTLY   adv in an inattentive manner

ABSINTH   n pl. -S absinthe

ABSINTHE   n pl. -S a bitter liqueur

ABSOLUTE   adj -LUTER, -LUTEST free from restriction

ABSOLUTE   n pl. -S something that is absolute

ABSOLVE   v -SOLVED, -SOLVING, -SOLVES to free from the consequences of an action

ABSOLVER   n pl. -S one that absolves

ABSONANT   adj unreasonable

ABSORB   v -ED, -ING, -S to take up or in

ABSORBER   n pl. -S one that absorbs

ABSTAIN   v -ED, -ING, -S to refrain voluntarily

ABSTERGE   v -STERGED, -STERGING, -STERGES to cleanse by wiping

ABSTRACT   adj -STRACTER, -STRACTEST difficult to understand

ABSTRACT   v -ED, -ING, -S to take away

ABSTRICT   v -ED, -ING, -S to form by cutting off

ABSTRUSE   adj -STRUSER, -STRUSEST difficult to understand

ABSURD   adj -SURDER, -SURDEST ridiculously incongruous or unreasonable **ABSURDLY** adv

ABSURD   n pl. -S the condition in which man exists in an irrational and meaningless universe

ABUBBLE   adj bubbling

ABULIA   n pl. -S loss of will power **ABULIC** adj

ABUNDANT   adj present in great quantity

ABUSE   v ABUSED, ABUSING, ABUSES to use wrongly or improperly **ABUSABLE** adj

ABUSER   n pl. -S one that abuses

ABUSIVE   adj characterized by wrong or improper use

ABUT   v ABUTTED, ABUTTING, ABUTS to touch along a border

ABUTILON   n pl. -S a flowering plant

ABUTMENT   n pl. -S something that abuts

ABUTTAL   n pl. -S an abutment

ABUTTED   past tense of abut

ABUTTER   n pl. -S one that abuts

ABUTTING   present participle of abut

ABUZZ   adj buzzing

ABVOLT   n pl. -S a unit of electromotive force

ABWATT   n pl. -S a unit of power

ABY   v ABOUGHT, ABYING, ABYS to pay the penalty for

ABYE	v ABOUGHT, ABYING, ABYES to aby
ABYSM	n pl. -S an abyss
ABYSMAL	adj immeasurably deep
ABYSS	n pl. -ES a bottomless chasm **ABYSSAL** adj
ACACIA	n pl. -S a flowering tree or shrub
ACADEME	n pl. -S a place of instruction
ACADEMIA	n pl. -S scholastic life or environment
ACADEMIC	n pl. -S a college student or teacher
ACADEMY	n pl. -MIES a secondary school
ACAJOU	n pl. -S a tropical tree
ACALEPH	n pl. -LEPHAE or -LEPHS a jellyfish
ACALEPHE	n pl. -S acaleph
ACANTHUS	n pl. -THI or -THUSES a prickly herb
ACARI	pl. of acarus
ACARID	n pl. -S any of an order of arachnids
ACARIDAN	n pl. -S acarid
ACARINE	n pl. -S acarid
ACAROID	adj resembling an acarid
ACARPOUS	adj not producing fruit
ACARUS	n pl. -RI a mite
ACAUDAL	adj having no tail
ACAUDATE	adj acaudal
ACAULINE	adj having no stem
ACAULOSE	adj acauline
ACAULOUS	adj acauline
ACCEDE	v -CEDED, -CEDING, -CEDES to consent
ACCEDER	n pl. -S one that accedes
ACCENT	v -ED, -ING, -S to pronounce with prominence
ACCENTOR	n pl. -S a songbird
ACCEPT	v -ED, -ING, -S to receive willingly
ACCEPTEE	n pl. -S one that is accepted
ACCEPTER	n pl. -S one that accepts
ACCEPTOR	n pl. -S accepter
ACCESS	v -ED, -ING, -ES to get at
ACCIDENT	n pl. -S an unexpected or unintentional occurrence
ACCIDIE	n pl. -S acedia
ACCLAIM	v -ED, -ING, -S to shout approval of
ACCOLADE	n pl. -S an expression of praise
ACCORD	v -ED, -ING, -S to bring into agreement
ACCORDER	n pl. -S one that accords
ACCOST	v -ED, -ING, -S to approach and speak to first
ACCOUNT	v -ED, -ING, -S to give an explanation
ACCOUTER	v -ED, -ING, -S to equip
ACCOUTRE	v -TRED, -TRING, -TRES to accouter
ACCREDIT	v -ED, -ING, -S to give official authorization to
ACCRETE	v -CRETED, -CRETING, -CRETES to grow together
ACCRUAL	n pl. -S the act of accruing
ACCRUE	v -CRUED, -CRUING, -CRUES to come as an increase or addition
ACCURACY	n pl. -CIES the quality of being accurate
ACCURATE	adj free from error
ACCURSED	adj damnable
ACCURST	adj accursed
ACCUSAL	n pl. -S the act of accusing
ACCUSANT	n pl. -S an accuser
ACCUSE	v -CUSED, -CUSING, -CUSES to make an assertion against
ACCUSER	n pl. -S one that accuses
ACCUSTOM	v -ED, -ING, -S to make familiar
ACE	v ACED, ACING, ACES to score a point against in a single stroke
ACEDIA	n pl. -S apathy
ACELDAMA	n pl. -S a place of bloodshed
ACENTRIC	adj having no center
ACEQUIA	n pl. -S an irrigation ditch or canal
ACERATE	adj acerose
ACERATED	adj acerose
ACERB	adj ACERBER, ACERBEST sour
ACERBATE	v -BATED, -BATING, -BATES to make sour
ACERBIC	adj acerb
ACERBITY	n pl. -TIES sourness
ACEROLA	n pl. -S a West Indian shrub
ACEROSE	adj needle-shaped
ACEROUS	adj acerose

ACERVATE *adj* growing in compact clusters

ACERVULI *n/pl* spore-producing organs of certain fungi

ACESCENT *n* pl. -S something that is slightly sour

ACETA pl. of acetum

ACETAL *n* pl. -S a flammable liquid

ACETAMID *n* pl. -S an amide of acetic acid

ACETATE *n* pl. -S a salt of acetic acid **ACETATED** *adj*

ACETIC *adj* pertaining to vinegar

ACETIFY *v* -FIED, -FYING, -FIES to convert into vinegar

ACETONE *n* pl. -S a flammable liquid **ACETONIC** *adj*

ACETOSE *adj* acetous

ACETOUS *adj* tasting like vinegar

ACETOXYL *n* pl. -S a univalent radical

ACETUM *n* pl. -TA vinegar

ACETYL *n* pl. -S a univalent radical **ACETYLIC** *adj*

ACHE *v* ACHED, ACHING, ACHES to suffer a dull, continuous pain

ACHENE *n* pl. -S a type of fruit **ACHENIAL** *adj*

ACHIER comparative of achy

ACHIEST superlative of achy

ACHIEVE *v* ACHIEVED, ACHIEVING, ACHIEVES to carry out successfully

ACHIEVER *n* pl. -S one that achieves

ACHINESS *n* pl. -ES the state of being achy

ACHING present participle of ache

ACHINGLY *adv* in an aching manner

ACHIOTE *n* pl. -S a yellowish red dye

ACHOO *interj* ahchoo

ACHROMAT *n* pl. -S a type of lens

ACHROMIC *adj* having no color

ACHY *adj* ACHIER, ACHIEST aching

ACICULA *n* pl. -LAE or -LAS a needlelike part or process **ACICULAR** *adj*

ACID *n* pl. -S a type of chemical compound

ACIDHEAD *n* pl. -S one who uses LSD

ACIDIC *adj* sour

ACIDIFY *v* -FIED, -FYING, -FIES to convert into an acid

ACIDITY *n* pl. -TIES sourness

ACIDLY *adv* sourly

ACIDNESS *n* pl. -ES acidity

ACIDOSIS *n* pl. -DOSES an abnormal condition of the blood **ACIDOTIC** *adj*

ACIDY *adj* sour

ACIERATE *v* -ATED, -ATING, -ATES to turn into steel

ACIFORM *adj* needle-shaped

ACING present participle of ace

ACINUS *n* pl. -NI a small, saclike division of a gland **ACINAR, ACINIC, ACINOSE, ACINOUS** *adj*

ACLINIC *adj* having no inclination

ACME *n* pl. -S the highest point **ACMATIC, ACMIC** *adj*

ACNE *n* pl. -S a skin disease **ACNED** *adj*

ACNODE *n* pl. -S an element of a mathematical set that is isolated from the other elements

ACOCK *adj* cocked

ACOLD *adj* cold

ACOLYTE *n* pl. -S an assistant

ACONITE *n* pl. -S a poisonous herb **ACONITIC** *adj*

ACONITUM *n* pl. -S aconite

ACORN *n* pl. -S the fruit of the oak tree

ACOUSTIC *n* pl. -S a hearing aid

ACQUAINT *v* -ED, -ING, -S to cause to know

ACQUEST *n* pl. -S something acquired

ACQUIRE *v* -QUIRED, -QUIRING, -QUIRES to come into possession of

ACQUIRER *n* pl. -S one that acquires

ACQUIT *v* -QUITTED, -QUITTING, -QUITS to free or clear from a charge of fault or crime

ACRASIN *n* pl. -S a substance secreted by the cells of a slime mold

ACRE *n* pl. -S a unit of area

ACREAGE *n* pl. -S area in acres

ACRED *adj* owning many acres

ACRID *adj* -RIDER, -RIDEST sharp and harsh to the taste or smell

ACRIDINE *n* pl. -S a chemical compound

ACRIDITY *n* pl. -TIES the state of being acrid

ACRIDLY *adv* in an acrid manner

ACRIMONY *n pl.* -NIES sharpness or bitterness of speech or temper

ACROBAT *n pl.* -S one skilled in feats of agility and balance

ACRODONT *n pl.* -S an animal having rootless teeth

ACROGEN *n pl.* -S a plant growing at the apex only

ACROLEIN *n pl.* -S a flammable liquid

ACROLITH *n pl.* -S a type of statue

ACROMION *n pl.* -MIA the outward end of the shoulder blade **ACROMIAL** *adj*

ACRONIC *adj* occurring at sunset

ACRONYM *n pl.* -S a word formed from the initials of a compound term or series of words

ACROSS *prep* from one side of to the other

ACROSTIC *n pl.* -S a poem in which certain letters taken in order form a word or phrase

ACROTISM *n pl.* -S weakness of the pulse **ACROTIC** *adj*

ACRYLATE *n pl.* -S an acrylic

ACRYLIC *n pl.* -S a type of resin

ACT *v* -ED, -ING, -S to do something

ACTA *n/pl* recorded proceedings

ACTABLE *adj* suitable for performance on the stage

ACTIN *n pl.* -S a protein in muscle tissue

ACTINAL *adj* having tentacles

ACTING *n pl.* -S the occupation of an actor

ACTINIA *n pl.* -IAE or -IAS a marine animal

ACTINIAN *n pl.* -S actinia

ACTINIC *adj* pertaining to actinism

ACTINIDE *n pl.* -S any of a series of radioactive elements

ACTINISM *n pl.* -S the property of radiant energy that effects chemical changes

ACTINIUM *n pl.* -S a radioactive element

ACTINOID *n pl.* -S an actinide

ACTINON *n pl.* -S an isotope of radon

ACTION *n pl.* -S the process of acting

ACTIVATE *v* -VATED, -VATING, -VATES to set in motion

ACTIVE *n pl.* -S a participating member of an organization

ACTIVELY *adv* with activity

ACTIVISM *n pl.* -S a doctrine that emphasizes direct and decisive action

ACTIVIST *n pl.* -S an advocate of activism

ACTIVITY *n pl.* -TIES brisk action or movement

ACTOR *n pl.* -S a theatrical performer **ACTORISH** *adj*

ACTRESS *n pl.* -ES a female actor

ACTUAL *adj* existing in fact **ACTUALLY** *adv*

ACTUARY *n pl.* -ARIES a statistician who computes insurance risks and premiums

ACTUATE *v* -ATED, -ATING, -ATES to set into action or motion

ACTUATOR *n pl.* -S one that actuates

ACUATE *adj* sharp

ACUITY *n pl.* -ITIES sharpness

ACULEATE *adj* having a sting

ACUMEN *n pl.* -S mental keenness

ACUTANCE *n pl.* -S a measure of photographic clarity

ACUTE *adj* ACUTER, ACUTEST marked by sharpness or severity **ACUTELY** *adv*

ACUTE *n pl.* -S a type of accent mark

ACYCLIC *adj* not cyclic

ACYL *n pl.* -S a univalent radical

ACYLATE *v* -ATED, -ATING, -ATES to introduce acyl into

AD *n pl.* -S an advertisement

ADAGE *n pl.* -S a traditional saying expressing a common observation **ADAGIAL** *adj*

ADAGIO *n pl.* -GIOS a musical composition or movement played in a slow tempo

ADAMANCE *n pl.* -S adamancy

ADAMANCY *n pl.* -CIES unyielding hardness

ADAMANT *n pl.* -S an extremely hard substance

ADAMSITE *n pl.* -S a lung-irritating gas

ADAPT *v* -ED, -ING, -S to make suitable

ADAPTER *n pl.* -S one that adapts

ADAPTION *n pl.* -S the act of adapting **ADAPTIVE** *adj*

ADAPTOR   *n* pl. -S adapter

ADAXIAL   *adj* situated on the same side as

ADD   *v* -ED, -ING, -S to combine or join so as to bring about an increase **ADDABLE** *adj*

ADDAX   *n* pl. -ES a large antelope

ADDEDLY   *adv* additionally

ADDEND   *n* pl. -S a number to be added to another

ADDENDUM   *n* pl. -DA something added or to be added

ADDER   *n* pl. -S a venomous snake

ADDIBLE   *adj* capable of being added

ADDICT   *v* -ED, -ING, -S to devote or surrender to something habitually or compulsively

ADDITION   *n* pl. -S something added

ADDITIVE   *n* pl. -S a substance added to another to impart desirable qualities

ADDLE   *v* -DLED, -DLING, -DLES to confuse

ADDRESS   *v* -DRESSED or -DREST, -DRESSING, -DRESSES to speak to

ADDUCE   *v* -DUCED, -DUCING, -DUCES to bring forward as evidence

ADDUCENT   *adj* serving to adduct

ADDUCER   *n* pl. -S one that adduces

ADDUCING   present participle of adduce

ADDUCT   *v* -ED, -ING, -S to draw toward the main axis

ADDUCTOR   *n* pl. -S an adducent muscle

ADEEM   *v* -ED, -ING, -S to take away

ADENINE   *n* pl. -S an alkaloid

ADENITIS   *n* pl. -TISES inflammation of a lymph node

ADENOID   *n* pl. -S an enlarged lymphoid growth behind the pharynx

ADENOMA   *n* pl. -MAS or -MATA a tumor of glandular origin

ADENYL   *n* pl. -S a univalent radical

ADEPT   *adj* ADEPTER, ADEPTEST highly skilled **ADEPTLY** *adv*

ADEPT   *n* pl. -S an adept person

ADEQUACY   *n* pl. -CIES the state of being adequate

ADEQUATE   *adj* sufficient for a specific requirement

ADHERE   *v* -HERED, -HERING, -HERES to become or remain attached or close to something

ADHEREND   *n* pl. -S the surface to which an adhesive adheres

ADHERENT   *n* pl. -S a supporter

ADHERER   *n* pl. -S one that adheres

ADHERING   present participle of adhere

ADHESION   *n* pl. -S the act of adhering

ADHESIVE   *n* pl. -S a substance that causes adhesion

ADHIBIT   *v* -ED, -ING, -S to take or let in

ADIEU   *n* pl. ADIEUS or ADIEUX a farewell

ADIOS   *interj* — used to express farewell

ADIPOSE   *n* pl. -S animal fat **ADIPIC** *adj*

ADIPOSIS   *n* pl. -POSES obesity

ADIPOUS   *adj* pertaining to adipose

ADIT   *n* pl. -S an entrance

ADJACENT   *adj* next to

ADJOIN   *v* -ED, -ING, -S to lie next to

ADJOINT   *n* pl. -S a type of mathematical matrix

ADJOURN   *v* -ED, -ING, -S to suspend until a later time

ADJUDGE   *v* -JUDGED, -JUDGING, -JUDGES to determine judicially

ADJUNCT   *n* pl. -S something attached in a subordinate position

ADJURE   *v* -JURED, -JURING, -JURES to command solemnly

ADJURER   *n* pl. -S one that adjures

ADJUROR   *n* pl. -S adjurer

ADJUST   *v* -ED, -ING, -S to bring to a more satisfactory state

ADJUSTER   *n* pl. -S one that adjusts

ADJUSTOR   *n* pl. -S adjuster

ADJUTANT   *n* pl. -S an assistant

ADJUVANT   *n* pl. -S an assistant

ADMAN   *n* pl. -MEN a man employed in the advertising business

ADMASS   *adj* pertaining to a society strongly influenced by advertising

ADMIRAL   *n* pl. -S a high-ranking naval officer

ADMIRE   *v* -MIRED, -MIRING, -MIRES to regard with wonder, pleasure, and approval

ADMIRER   *n* pl. -S one that admires

ADMIT   *v* -MITTED, -MITTING, -MITS to allow to enter

ADMITTER   *n* pl. -S one that admits

ADMIX   *n* -MIXED or -MIXT, -MIXING, -MIXES to mix

ADMONISH   *n* -ED, -ING, -ES to reprove mildly or kindly

ADNATE   *adj* joined to another part or organ

ADNATION   *n* pl. -S the state of being adnate

ADNEXA   *n/pl* conjoined anatomical parts **ADNEXAL** *adj*

ADNOUN   *n* pl. -S an adjective when used as a noun

ADO   *n* pl. ADOS bustling excitement

ADOBE   *n* pl. -S an unburnt, sun-dried brick

ADOPT   *v* -ED, -ING, -S to take into one's family by legal means

ADOPTEE   *n* pl. -S one that is adopted

ADOPTER   *n* pl. -S one that adopts

ADOPTION   *n* pl. -S the act of adopting **ADOPTIVE** *adj*

ADORABLE   *adj* worthy of being adored **ADORABLY** *adv*

ADORE   *v* ADORED, ADORING, ADORES to love deeply

ADORER   *n* pl. -S one that adores

ADORN   *v* -ED, -ING, -S to add something to for the purpose of making more attractive

ADORNER   *n* pl. -S one that adorns

ADOWN   *adv* downward

ADOZE   *adj* dozing

ADRENAL   *n* pl. -S an endocrine gland

ADRIFT   *adj* drifting

ADROIT   *adj* ADROITER, ADROITEST skillful **ADROITLY** *adv*

ADSCRIPT   *n* pl. -S a distinguishing symbol written after another character

ADSORB   *v* -ED, -ING, -S to gather on a surface in a condensed layer

ADULARIA   *n* pl. -S a mineral

ADULATE   *v* -LATED, -LATING, -LATES to praise excessively

ADULATOR   *n* pl. -S one that adulates

ADULT   *n* pl. -S a fully developed individual

ADULTERY   *n* pl. -TERIES voluntary sexual intercourse between a married person and someone other than his or her spouse

ADULTLY   *adv* in a manner typical of an adult

ADUMBRAL   *adj* shadowy

ADUNC   *adj* bent inward

ADUNCATE   *adj* adunc

ADUNCOUS   *adj* adunc

ADUST   *adj* scorched

ADVANCE   *v* -VANCED, -VANCING, -VANCES to move or cause to move ahead

ADVANCER   *n* pl. -S one that advances

ADVENT   *n* pl. -S arrival

ADVERB   *n* pl. -S a word used to modify the meaning of a verb, adjective, or other adverb

ADVERSE   *adj* acting in opposition

ADVERT   *v* -ED, -ING, -S to call attention

ADVICE   *n* pl. -S recommendation regarding a decision or course of conduct

ADVISE   *v* -VISED, -VISING, -VISES to give advice to

ADVISEE   *n* pl. -S one that is advised

ADVISER   *n* pl. -S one that advises

ADVISING   present participle of advise

ADVISOR   *n* pl. -S adviser

ADVISORY   *n* pl. -RIES a report giving information

ADVOCACY   *n* pl. -CIES the act of advocating

ADVOCATE   *v* -CATED, -CATING, -CATES to speak in favor of

ADVOWSON   *n* pl. -S the right of presenting a nominee to a vacant church office

ADYNAMIA   *n* pl. -S lack of physical strength **ADYNAMIC** *adj*

ADYTUM   *n* pl. -TA an inner sanctuary in an ancient temple

ADZ   *n* pl.-ES a cutting tool

ADZE   *n* pl. -S adz

AE   *adj* one

AECIA   pl. of aecium

AECIAL   *adj* pertaining to an aecium

AECIDIUM   *n* pl. -IA an aecium

AECIUM   *n* pl. -IA a spore-producing organ of certain fungi

AEDES   *n* pl. AEDES any of a genus of mosquitoes

AEDILE   *n* pl. -S a magistrate of ancient Rome

AEDINE   *adj* pertaining to an aedes

AEGIS   *n* pl. -GISES protection

AENEOUS   *adj* having a greenish gold color

AENEUS   *adj* aeneous

AEOLIAN   *adj* eolian

AEON   *n* pl. -S eon

AEONIAN   *adj* eonian

AEONIC   *adj* eonian

AERATE   *v* -ATED, -ATING, -ATES to supply with air

AERATION   *n* pl. -S the act of aerating

AERATOR   *n* pl. -S one that aerates

AERIAL   *n* pl. -S a metallic apparatus for sending and receiving electromagnetic waves

AERIALLY   *adv* in a manner pertaining to the air

AERIE   *n* pl. -S a bird's nest built high on a mountain or cliff **AERIED** *adj*

AERIER   comparative of aery

AERIES   pl. of aery

AERIEST   superlative of aery

AERIFORM   *adj* having the form of air

AERIFY   *v* -FIED, -FYING, -FIES to aerate

AERILY   *adv* in an aery manner

AERO   *adj* pertaining to aircraft

AEROBE   *n* pl. -S an organism that requires oxygen to live **AEROBIC** *adj*

AEROBIUM   *n* pl. -BIA aerobe

AERODUCT   *n* pl. -S a type of jet engine

AERODYNE   *n* pl. -S an aircraft that is heavier than air

AEROFOIL   *n* pl. -S airfoil

AEROGEL   *n* pl. -S a highly porous solid

AEROGRAM   *n* pl. -S an airmail letter

AEROLITE   *n* pl. -S a meteorite containing more stone than iron

AEROLITH   *n* pl. -S aerolite

AEROLOGY   *n* pl. -GIES the study of the atmosphere

AERONAUT   *n* pl. -S one who operates an airship

AERONOMY   *n* pl. -MIES the study of the upper atmosphere

AEROSOL   *n* pl. -S a gaseous suspension of fine solid or liquid particles

AEROSTAT   *n* pl. -S an aircraft that is lighter than air

AERUGO   *n* pl. -GOS a green film that forms on copper

AERY   *adj* AERIER, AERIEST airy

AERY   *n* pl. AERIES aerie

AESTHETE   *n* pl. -S esthete

AESTIVAL   *adj* estival

AETHER   *n* pl. -S the upper region of the atmosphere **AETHERIC** *adj*

AFAR   *n* pl. -S a great distance

AFEARD   *adj* afraid

AFEARED   *adj* afeard

AFF   *adv* off

AFFABLE   *adj* easy to talk to **AFFABLY** *adv*

AFFAIR   *n* pl. -S anything done or to be done

AFFAIRE   *n* pl. -S a brief amorous relationship

AFFECT   *v* -ED, -ING, -S to give a false appearance of

AFFECTER   *n* pl. -S one that affects

AFFERENT   *adj* conducting toward an organ or part

AFFIANCE   *v* -ANCED, -ANCING, -ANCES to betroth

AFFIANT   *n* pl. -S one who makes a written declaration under oath

AFFICHE   *n* pl. -S a poster

AFFINE   *n* pl. -S a relative by marriage

AFFINED   *adj* closely related

AFFINELY   *adv* in the manner of a type of mathematical mapping

AFFINITY   *n* pl. -TIES a natural attraction or inclination

AFFIRM   *v* -ED, -ING, -S to state positively

AFFIRMER   *n* pl. -S one that affirms

AFFIX   *v* -ED, -ING, -ES to attach

AFFIXAL   *adj* pertaining to a prefix or suffix

AFFIXER   *n* pl. -S one that affixes

AFFIXIAL   *adj* affixal

AFFLATUS   *n pl.* -ES a creative inspiration

AFFLICT   *v* -ED, -ING, -S to distress with mental or physical pain

AFFLUENT   *n pl.* -S a stream that flows into another

AFFLUX   *n pl.* -ES a flowing toward a point

AFFORD   *v* -ED, -ING, -S to have sufficient means for

AFFOREST   *v* -ED, -ING, -S to convert into forest

AFFRAY   *v* -ED, -ING, -S to frighten

AFFRAYER   *n pl.* -S one that affrays

AFFRIGHT   *v* -ED, -ING, -S to frighten

AFFRONT   *v* -ED, -ING, -S to insult openly

AFFUSION   *n pl.* -S an act of pouring a liquid on

AFGHAN   *n pl.* -S a woolen blanket or shawl

AFGHANI   *n pl.* -S a monetary unit of Afghanistan

AFIELD   *adv* in the field

AFIRE   *adj* being on fire

AFLAME   *adj* flaming

AFLOAT   *adj* floating

AFLUTTER   *adj* nervously excited

AFOOT   *adv* on foot

AFORE   *adv* before

AFOUL   *adj* entangled

AFRAID   *adj* filled with apprehension

AFREET   *n pl.* -S an evil spirit in Arabic mythology

AFRESH   *adv* anew

AFRIT   *n pl.* -S afreet

AFT   *adv* toward the stern

AFTER   *prep* behind in place or order

AFTERS   *n/pl* dessert

AFTERTAX   *adj* remaining after payment of taxes

AFTMOST   *adj* nearest the stern

AFTOSA   *n pl.* -S a disease of hoofed mammals

AGA   *n pl.* -S a high-ranking Turkish military officer

AGAIN   *adv* once more

AGAINST   *prep* in opposition to

AGALLOCH   *n pl.* -S the fragrant wood of a tropical tree

AGALWOOD   *n pl.* -S agalloch

AGAMA   *n pl.* -S a tropical lizard

AGAMETE   *n pl.* -S an asexual reproductive cell

AGAMIC   *adj* asexual

AGAMOUS   *adj* agamic

AGAPE   *n pl.* -PAE or -PAI the love of God for mankind **AGAPEIC** *adj*

AGAR   *n pl.* -S a viscous substance obtained from certain seaweeds

AGARIC   *n pl.* -S any of a family of fungi

AGATE   *n pl.* -S a variety of quartz **AGATOID** *adj*

AGATIZE   *v* -IZED, -IZING, -IZES to cause to resemble agate

AGAVE   *n pl.* -S a tropical plant

AGAZE   *adj* gazing

AGE   *v* AGED, AGING or AGEING, AGES to grow old

AGEDLY   *adv* oldly

AGEDNESS   *n pl.* -ES oldness

AGEE   *adv* to one side

AGEING   *n pl.* -S aging

AGELESS   *adj* never growing old

AGELONG   *adj* lasting for a long time

AGENCY   *n pl.* -CIES an organization that does business for others

AGENDA   *n pl.* -S a list of things to be done

AGENDUM   *n pl.* -S an item on an agenda

AGENE   *n pl.* -S a chemical compound used in bleaching flour

AGENESIA   *n pl.* -S agenesis

AGENESIS   *n pl.* AGENESES absence or imperfect development of a bodily part **AGENETIC** *adj*

AGENIZE   *v* -NIZED, -NIZING, -NIZES to treat with agene

AGENT   *n pl.* -S one who is authorized to act for another **AGENTIAL** *adj*

AGENTRY   *n pl.* -RIES the office or duties of an agent

AGER   *n pl.* -S one that ages

AGERATUM   *n pl.* -S a flowering plant

AGGER   *n pl.* -S a mound of earth used as a fortification

AGGIE   *n pl.* -S a type of playing marble

AGGRADE   *v* -GRADED, -GRADING, -GRADES to fill with detrital material

AGGRESS   v -ED, -ING, -ES to commit the first act of hostility

AGGRIEVE   v -GRIEVED, -GRIEVING, -GRIEVES to distress

AGHA   n pl. -S aga

AGHAST   adj shocked by something horrible

AGILE   adj able to move quickly and easily **AGILELY** adv

AGILITY   n pl. -TIES the quality of being agile

AGIN   prep against

AGING   n pl. -S the process of growing old

AGINNER   n pl. -S one that is against change

AGIO   n pl. AGIOS a premium paid for the exchange of one currency for another

AGIOTAGE   n pl. -S the business of a broker

AGIST   v -ED, -ING, -S to feed and take care of for a fee, as livestock

AGITATE   v -TATED, -TATING, -TATES to move with a violent, irregular action **AGITABLE** adj

AGITATO   adj fast and stirring — used as a musical direction

AGITATOR   n pl. -S one that agitates

AGITPROP   n pl. -S pro-Communist propaganda

AGLARE   adj glaring

AGLEAM   adj gleaming

AGLEE   adv agley

AGLET   n pl. -S a metal sheath at the end of a lace

AGLEY   adv awry

AGLIMMER   adj glimmering

AGLITTER   adj glittering

AGLOW   adj glowing

AGLY   adv agley

AGLYCON   n pl. -S a type of chemical compound

AGLYCONE   n pl. -S aglycon

AGMA   n pl. -S eng

AGMINATE   adj clustered together

AGNAIL   n pl. -S a piece of loose skin at the base of a fingernail

AGNATE   n pl. -S a relative on the father's side **AGNATIC** adj

AGNATION   n pl. -S the relationship of agnates

AGNIZE   n -NIZED, -NIZING, -NIZES to acknowledge

AGNOMEN   n pl. -MINA or -MENS an additional name given to an ancient Roman

AGNOSTIC   n pl. -S one who disclaims any knowledge of God

AGO   adv in the past

AGOG   adv in a state of eager curiosity

AGON   n pl. -S or -ES the dramatic conflict between the main characters in a Greek play

AGONAL   adj pertaining to agony

AGONE   adv ago

AGONES   a pl. of agon

AGONIC   adj not forming an angle

AGONIES   pl. of agony

AGONISE   v -NISED, -NISING, -NISES to agonize

AGONIST   n pl. -S one that is engaged in a struggle

AGONIZE   v -NIZED, -NIZING, -NIZES to suffer extreme pain

AGONY   n pl. -NIES extreme pain

AGORA   n pl. -RAS or -RAE a marketplace in ancient Greece

AGORA   n pl. AGOROT or AGOROTH a monetary unit of Israel

AGOUTI   n pl. -S or -ES a burrowing rodent

AGOUTY   n pl.- TIES agouti

AGRAFE   n pl -S agraffe

AGRAFFE   n pl. -S an ornamental clasp

AGRAPHA   n/pl the sayings of Jesus not found in the Bible

AGRAPHIA   n pl. -S a mental disorder marked by inability to write **AGRAPHIC** adj

AGRARIAN   n pl. -S one who favors equal distribution of land

AGREE   v AGREED, AGREEING, AGREES to have the same opinion

AGRESTAL   adj growing wild

AGRESTIC   adj rural

AGRIMONY   n pl. -NIES a perennial herb

AGROLOGY   n pl. -GIES the science of soils in relation to crops

AGRONOMY *n* pl. -MIES the application of scientific principles to the cultivation of land

AGROUND *adv* on the ground

AGUE *n* pl. -S a malarial fever **AGUELIKE, AGUISH** *adj* **AGUISHLY** *adv*

AGUEWEED *n* pl. -S a flowering plant

AH *interj* — used to express delight, relief, or contempt

AHA *interj* — used to express surprise, triumph, or derision

AHCHOO *interj* — used to represent the sound of a sneeze

AHEAD *adv* at or to the front

AHEM *interj* — used to attract attention

AHIMSA *n* pl. -S the Hindu principle of nonviolence

AHOLD *n* pl. -S a hold or grasp of something

AHORSE *adv* on a horse

AHOY *interj* — used in hailing a ship or person

AHULL *adj* abandoned and flooded, as a ship

AI *n* pl. -S a three-toed sloth

AIBLINS *adv* ablins

AID *v* -ED, -ING, -S to help

AIDE *n* pl. -S an assistant

AIDER *n* pl. -S one that aids

AIDFUL *adj* helpful

AIDLESS *adj* helpless

AIDMAN *n* pl. -MEN a corpsman

AIGLET *n* pl. -S an aglet

AIGRET *n* pl. -S aigrette

AIGRETTE *n* pl. -S a tuft of feathers worn as a head ornament

AIGUILLE *n* pl. -S a sharp, pointed mountain peak

AIKIDO *n* pl. -DOS a Japanese art of self-defense

AIL *v* -ED, -ING, -S to cause pain or discomfort to

AILERON *n* pl. -S a movable control surface on an airplane wing

AILMENT *n* pl. -S a physical or mental disorder

AIM *v* -ED, -ING, -S to direct toward a specified object or goal

AIMER *n* pl. -S one that aims

AIMFUL *adj* full of purpose **AIMFULLY** *adv*

AIMLESS *adj* lacking direction or purpose

AIN *n* pl. -S ayin

AINE *adj* elder or eldest

AINEE *adj* aine

AINSELL *n* pl. -S own self

AIR *v* -ED, -ING, -S to expose to the air (the mixture of gases that surrounds the earth)

AIR *adv* AIRER, AIREST early

AIRBOAT *n* pl. -S a boat used in swampy areas

AIRBORNE *adj* flying

AIRBOUND *adj* stopped up by air

AIRBRUSH *v* -ED, -ING, -ES to apply in a fine spray by compressed air, as paint

AIRBURST *n* pl. -S an explosion in the air

AIRBUS *n* pl. -BUSES or -BUSSES a passenger airplane

AIRCOACH *n* pl. -ES the cheaper class of accommodations in commercial aircraft

AIRCRAFT *n* pl. AIRCRAFT any machine or device capable of flying

AIRCREW *n* pl. -S the crew of an aircraft

AIRDROME *n* pl. -S an airport

AIRDROP *v* -DROPPED, -DROPPING, -DROPS to drop from an aircraft

AIRFIELD *n* pl. -S an airport

AIRFLOW *n* pl. -S a flow of air

AIRFOIL *n* pl. -S a part of an aircraft designed to provide lift or control

AIRFRAME *n* pl. -S the framework and external covering of an airplane

AIRGLOW *n* pl. -S a glow in the upper atmosphere

AIRHEAD *n* pl. -S an area in hostile territory secured by paratroops

AIRIER comparative of airy

AIRIEST superlative of airy

AIRILY *adv* in an airy manner

AIRINESS *n* pl. -ES the state of being airy

AIRING *n* pl. -S an exposure to the air

AIRLESS *adj* having no air

AIRLIFT *v* -ED, -ING, -S to transport by airplane

AIRLIKE *adj* resembling air

AIRLINE *n* pl. -S an air transportation system

AIRLINER *n* pl. -S a large passenger aircraft

AIRMAIL *v* -ED, -ING, -S to send mail by airplane

AIRMAN *n* pl. -MEN an aviator

AIRN *n* pl. -S iron

AIRPARK *n* pl. -S a small airport

AIRPLANE *n* pl. -S a winged aircraft propelled by jet engines or propellers

AIRPORT *n* pl. -S a tract of land maintained for the landing and takeoff of aircraft

AIRPOST *n* pl. -S a system of conveying mail by airplane

AIRPROOF *v* -ED, -ING, -S to make impermeable to air

AIRSCREW *n* pl. -S an airplane propeller

AIRSHIP *n* pl. -S a lighter-than-air aircraft having propulsion and steering systems

AIRSICK *adj* nauseated from flying in an airplane

AIRSPACE *n* pl. -S the portion of the atmosphere above a particular land area

AIRSPEED *n* pl. -S the speed of an aircraft with relation to the air

AIRSTRIP *n* pl. -S a runway

AIRT *v* -ED, -ING, -S to guide

AIRTH *v* -ED, -ING, -S to airt

AIRTIGHT *adj* not allowing air to escape or enter

AIRWARD *adv* toward the sky

AIRWAVE *n* pl. -S the medium of radio and television transmission

AIRWAY *n* pl. -WAYS a passageway in which air circulates

AIRWISE *adj* skillful in aviation

AIRWOMAN *n* pl. -WOMEN a female aviator

AIRY *adj* AIRIER, AIRIEST having the nature of air

AISLE *n* pl. -S a passageway between sections of seats **AISLED** *adj*

AIT *n* pl. -S a small island

AITCH *n* pl. -ES the letter H

AIVER *n* pl. -S a draft horse

AJAR *adj* partly open

AJEE *adv* agee

AJIVA *n* pl. -S inanimate matter

AJOWAN *n* pl. -S the fruit of an Egyptian plant

AKEE *n* pl. -S a tropical tree

AKELA *n* pl. -S a leader of a cub scout pack

AKENE *n* pl. -S achene

AKIMBO *adj* having hands on hips and elbows bent outward

AKIN *adj* related by blood

AKVAVIT *n* pl. -S aquavit

ALA *n* pl. ALAE a wing or winglike part

ALACK *interj* — used to express sorrow or regret

ALACRITY *n* pl. -TIES cheerful promptness

ALAE pl. of ala

ALAMEDA *n* pl. -S a shaded walkway

ALAMO *n* pl. -MOS a softwood tree

ALAMODE *n* pl. -S a silk fabric

ALAN *n* pl. -S a large hunting dog

ALAND *n* pl. -S alan

ALANE *adj* alone

ALANG *adv* along

ALANIN *n* pl. -S alanine

ALANINE *n* pl. -S an amino acid

ALANT *n* pl. -S alan

ALANYL *n* pl. -S a univalent radical

ALAR *adj* pertaining to wings

ALARM *v* -ED, -ING, -S to frighten by a sudden revelation of danger

ALARMISM *n* pl. -S the practice of alarming others needlessly

ALARMIST *n* pl. -S one who alarms others needlessly

ALARUM *v* -ED, -ING, -S to alarm

ALARY *adj* alar

ALAS *interj* — used to express sorrow or regret

ALASKA *n* pl. -S a heavy fabric

ALASTOR *n* pl. -S an avenging deity in Greek tragedy

ALATE *adj* having wings

ALATED *adj* alate

ALATION *n* pl. -S the state of having wings

ALB *n* pl. -S a long-sleeved vestment

ALBA n pl. -S the white substance of the brain

ALBACORE n pl. -S a marine food fish

ALBATA n pl. -S an alloy of copper, nickel, and zinc

ALBEDO n pl. -S the ratio of the light reflected by a planet to that received by it

ALBEIT conj although

ALBICORE n pl. -S albacore

ALBINAL adj albinic

ALBINIC adj pertaining to albinism

ALBINISM n pl. -S the condition of being an albino

ALBINO n pl. -NOS an organism lacking normal pigmentation

ALBITE n pl. -S a mineral **ALBITIC** adj

ALBUM n pl. -S a book for preserving photographs or stamps

ALBUMEN n pl. -S the white of an egg

ALBUMIN n pl. -S a simple protein

ALBUMOSE n pl. -S a proteose

ALBURNUM n pl. -S sapwood

ALCADE n pl. -S alcalde

ALCAHEST n pl. -S alkahest

ALCAIC n pl. -S a type of verse form

ALCAIDE n pl. -S the commander of a Spanish fortress

ALCALDE n pl. -S the mayor of a Spanish town

ALCAYDE n pl. -S alcaide

ALCAZAR n pl. -S a Spanish fortress or palace

ALCHEMY n pl. -MIES a medieval form of chemistry **ALCHEMIC** adj

ALCHYMY n pl. -MIES alchemy

ALCIDINE adj pertaining to a family of seabirds

ALCOHOL n pl. -S a flammable liquid

ALCOVE n pl. -S a recessed section of a room **ALCOVED** adj

ALDEHYDE n pl. -S a type of chemical compound

ALDER n pl. -S a shrub or small tree

ALDERMAN n pl. -MEN a member of a municipal legislative body

ALDOL n pl. -S a chemical compound

ALDOLASE n pl. -S an enzyme

ALDOSE n pl. -S a type of sugar

ALDRIN n pl. -S an insecticide

ALE n pl. -S an alcoholic beverage

ALEATORY adj pertaining to luck

ALEC n pl. -S a herring

ALEE adv toward the side of a vessel sheltered from the wind

ALEF n pl. -S aleph

ALEGAR n pl. -S sour ale

ALEHOUSE n pl. -S a tavern where ale is sold

ALEMBIC n pl. -S an apparatus formerly used in distilling

ALEPH n pl. -S a Hebrew letter

ALERT adj ALERTER, ALERTEST ready for sudden action **ALERTLY** adv

ALERT v -ED, -ING, -S to warn

ALEURON n pl. -S aleurone

ALEURONE n pl. -S protein matter found in the seeds of certain plants

ALEVIN n pl. -S a young fish

ALEWIFE n pl. -WIVES a marine fish

ALEXIA n pl. -S a cerebral disorder marked by the loss of the ability to read

ALEXIN n pl. -S a substance in the blood that aids in the destruction of bacteria

ALEXINE n pl. -S alexin

ALFA n pl. -S a communications code word for the letter A

ALFAKI n pl. -S alfaqui

ALFALFA n pl. -S a plant cultivated for use as hay and forage

ALFAQUI n pl. -S a teacher of Muslim law

ALFAQUIN n pl. -S alfaqui

ALFORJA n pl. -S a leather bag

ALFRESCO adv outdoors

ALGA n pl. -GAE or -GAS any of a group of primitive aquatic plants **ALGAL** adj

ALGAROBA n pl. -S the mesquite

ALGEBRA n pl. -S a branch of mathematics

ALGERINE n pl. -S a woolen fabric

ALGICIDE n pl. -S a substance used to kill algae

ALGID adj cold

ALGIDITY n pl. -TIES coldness

ALGIN   *n* pl. -S a viscous substance obtained from certain algae

ALGINATE   *n* pl. -S a chemical salt

ALGOID   *adj* resembling algae

ALGOLOGY   *n* pl. -GIES the study of algae

ALGOR   *n* pl. -S coldness

ALGORISM   *n* pl. -S the Arabic system of arithmetic notation

ALGUM   *n* pl. -S almug

ALIAS   *n* pl. -ES an assumed name

ALIBI   *v* -BIED, -BIING, -BIES or -BIS to make excuses for oneself

ALIBLE   *adj* nourishing

ALIDAD   *n* pl. -S alidade

ALIDADE   *n* pl. -S a device used in angular measurement

ALIEN   *v* -ED, -ING, -S to transfer to another, as property

ALIENAGE   *n* pl. -S the state of being foreign

ALIENATE   *v* -ATED, -ATING, -ATES to make indifferent or unfriendly

ALIENEE   *n* pl. -S one to whom property is transferred

ALIENER   *n* pl. -S alienor

ALIENISM   *n* pl. -S alienage

ALIENIST   *n* pl. -S a physician who treats mental disorders

ALIENLY   *adv* in a foreign manner

ALIENOR   *n* pl. S one that transfers property

ALIF   *n* pl. -S an Arabic letter

ALIFORM   *adj* shaped like a wing

ALIGHT   *v* ALIGHTED or ALIT, ALIGHTING, ALIGHTS to come down from something

ALIGN   *v* -ED, -ING, -S to arrange in a straight line

ALIGNER   *n* pl. -S one that aligns

ALIKE   *adj* having close resemblance

ALIMENT   *v* -ED, -ING, -S to nourish

ALIMONY   *n* pl. -NIES an allowance paid to a woman by her divorced husband

ALINE   *v* ALINED, ALINING, ALINES to align

ALINER   *n* pl. -S aligner

ALIPED   *n* pl. -S an animal having a membrane connecting the toes

ALIQUANT   *adj* not dividing evenly into another number

ALIQUOT   *n* pl. -S a number that divides evenly into another

ALIST   *adj* leaning to one side

ALIT   a past tense of alight

ALIUNDE   *adv* from a source extrinsic to the matter at hand

ALIVE   *adj* having life

ALIYAH   *n* pl. -S the immigration of Jews to Israel

ALIZARIN   *n* pl. -S a red dye

ALKAHEST   *n* pl. -S the hypothetical universal solvent sought by alchemists

ALKALI   *n* pl. -LIES or -LIS a type of chemical compound **ALKALIC** *adj*

ALKALIFY   *v* -FIED, -FYING, -FIES to alkalize

ALKALIN   *adj* alkaline

ALKALINE   *adj* containing an alkali

ALKALISE   *v* -LISED, -LISING, -LISES to alkalize

ALKALIZE   *v* -LIZED, -LIZING, -LIZES to convert into an alkali

ALKALOID   *n* pl. -S a type of chemical compound

ALKANE   *n* pl. -S a type of chemical compound

ALKANET   *n* pl. -S a European plant

ALKENE   *n* pl. -S a type of chemical compound

ALKINE   *n* pl. -S alkyne

ALKOXY   *adj* containing a univalent radical composed of alkyl united with oxygen

ALKYD   *n* pl. -S a synthetic resin

ALKYL   *n* pl. -S a univalent radical **ALKYLIC** *adj*

ALKYLATE   *v* -ATED, -ATING, -ATES to combine with alkyl

ALKYNE   *n* pl. -S a type of chemical compound

ALL   *n* pl. -S everything that one has

ALLANITE   *n* pl. -S a mineral

ALLAY   *v* -ED, -ING, -S to reduce in intensity or severity

ALLAYER   *n* pl. -S one that allays

ALLEGE   *v* -LEGED, -LEGING, -LEGES to assert without proof or before proving

ALLEGER *n pl.* -S one that alleges

ALLEGORY *n pl.* -RIES a story presenting a moral principle

ALLEGRO *n pl.* -GROS a musical passage played in rapid tempo

ALLELE *n pl.* -S any of several forms of a gene **ALLELIC** *adj*

ALLELISM *n pl.* -S the state of possessing alleles

ALLELUIA *n pl.* -S a song of praise to God

ALLERGEN *n pl.* -S a substance capable of inducing an allergy

ALLERGIC *adj* pertaining to allergy

ALLERGIN *n pl.* -S allergen

ALLERGY *n pl.* -GIES a state of hypersensitive reaction to certain things

ALLEY *n pl.* -LEYS a narrow passageway

ALLEYWAY *n pl.* -WAYS an alley

ALLHEAL *n pl.* -S a medicinal herb

ALLIABLE *adj* capable of being allied

ALLIANCE *n pl.* -S an association formed to further the common interests of its members

ALLIED past tense of ally

ALLIES present 3d person sing. of ally

ALLIUM *n pl.* -S a bulbous herb

ALLOBAR *n pl.* -S a change in barometric pressure

ALLOCATE *v* -CATED, -CATING, -CATES to set apart for a particular purpose

ALLOD *n pl.* -S allodium

ALLODIUM *n pl.* -DIA land held in absolute ownership **ALLODIAL** *adj*

ALLOGAMY *n pl.* -MIES fertilization of a flower by pollen from another

ALLONGE *n pl.* -S an addition to a document

ALLONYM *n pl.* -S the name of one person assumed by another

ALLOPATH *n pl.* -S one who treats diseases by producing effects incompatible with those of the disease

ALLOT *v* -LOTTED, -LOTTING, -LOTS to give as a share or portion

ALLOTTEE *n pl.* -S one to whom something is allotted

ALLOTTER *n pl.* -S one that allots

ALLOTTING present participle of allot

ALLOTYPE *n pl.* -S a type of antibody

ALLOTYPY *n pl.* -TYPIES the condition of being an allotype

ALLOVER *n pl.* -S a fabric having a pattern extending over the entire surface

ALLOW *v* -ED, -ING, -S to put no obstacle in the way of

ALLOXAN *n pl.* -S a chemical compound

ALLOY *v* -ED, -ING, -S to combine to form an alloy (a homogenous mixture of metals)

ALLSEED *n pl.* -S a plant having many seeds

ALLSPICE *n pl.* -S a tropical tree

ALLUDE *v* -LUDED, -LUDING, -LUDES to make an indirect reference

ALLURE *v* -LURED, -LURING, -LURES to attract with something desirable

ALLURER *n pl.* -S one that allures

ALLUSION *n pl.* -S the act of alluding **ALLUSIVE** *adj*

ALLUVIA *a pl.* of alluvium

ALLUVIAL *n pl.* -S soil composed of alluvium

ALLUVION *n pl.* -S alluvium

ALLUVIUM *n pl.* -VIA or -VIUMS detrital material deposited by running water

ALLY *v* -LIED, -LYING, -LIES to unite in a formal relationship

ALLYL *n pl.* -S a univalent radical **ALLYLIC** *adj*

ALMA *n pl.* -S almah

ALMAGEST *n pl.* -S a medieval treatise on astrology or alchemy

ALMAH *n pl.* -S an Egyptian girl who sings and dances professionally

ALMANAC *n pl.* -S an annual publication containing general information

ALME *n pl.* -S almah

ALMEH *n pl.* -S almah

ALMEMAR *n pl.* -S a bema

ALMIGHTY *adj* having absolute power over all

ALMNER *n pl.* -S almoner

ALMOND *n pl.* -S the edible nut of a small tree

ALMONER *n pl.* -S one that distributes alms

ALMONRY *n pl.* -RIES a place where alms are distributed

ALMOST *adv* very nearly

ALMS *n pl.* ALMS money or goods given to the poor

ALMSMAN *n pl.* -MEN one who receives alms

ALMUCE *n pl.* -S a hooded cape

ALMUD *n pl.* -S a Spanish unit of capacity

ALMUDE *n pl.* -S almud

ALMUG *n pl.* -S a precious wood mentioned in the Bible

ALNICO *n pl.* -COES a magnetic alloy

ALODIUM *n pl.* -DIA allodium **ALODIAL** *adj*

ALOE *n pl.* -S an African plant **ALOETIC** *adj*

ALOFT *adv* in or into the air

ALOGICAL *adj* being outside the bounds of that to which logic can apply

ALOHA *n pl.* -S love — used as a greeting or farewell

ALOIN *n pl.* -S a laxative

ALONE *adj* apart from others

ALONG *adv* onward

ALOOF *adj* distant in interest or feeling **ALOOFLY** *adv*

ALOPECIA *n pl.* -S baldness **ALOPECIC** *adj*

ALOUD *adv* audibly

ALOW *adv* in or to a lower position

ALP *n pl.* -S a high mountain

ALPACA *n pl.* -S a ruminant mammal

ALPHA *n pl.* -S a Greek letter

ALPHABET *v* -ED, -ING, -S to arrange in the customary order of the letters of a language

ALPHORN *n pl.* -S a wooden horn used by Swiss herdsmen

ALPHOSIS *n pl.* -SISES lack of skin pigmentation

ALPHYL *n pl.* -S a univalent radical

ALPINE *n pl.* -S a plant native to high mountain regions

ALPINELY *adv* in a lofty manner

ALPINISM *n pl.* -S mountain climbing

ALPINIST *n pl.* -S a mountain climber

ALREADY *adv* by this time

ALRIGHT *adj* satisfactory

ALSIKE *n pl.* -S a European clover

ALSO *adv* in addition

ALT *n pl.* -S a high-pitched musical note

ALTAR *n pl.* -S a raised structure used in worship

ALTER *v* -ED, -ING, -S to make different

ALTERANT *n pl.* -S something that alters

ALTERER *n pl.* -S one that alters

ALTHAEA *n pl.* -S althea

ALTHEA *n pl.* -S a flowering plant

ALTHO *conj* although

ALTHORN *n pl.* S a brass wind instrument

ALTHOUGH *conj* despite the fact that

ALTITUDE *n pl.* -S the vertical elevation of an object above a given level

ALTO *n pl.* -TOS a low female singing voice

ALTRUISM *n pl.* -S selfless devotion to the welfare of others

ALTRUIST *n pl.* -S one that practices altruism

ALUDEL *n pl.* -S a pear-shaped vessel

ALULA *n pl.* -LAE a tuft of feathers on the first digit of a bird's wing **ALULAR** *adj*

ALUM *n pl.* -S a chemical compound

ALUMIN *n pl.* -S alumina

ALUMINA *n pl.* -S an oxide of aluminum

ALUMINE *n pl.* -S alumina

ALUMINUM *n pl.* -S a metallic element **ALUMINIC** *adj*

ALUMNA *n pl.* -NAE a female graduate

ALUMNUS *n pl.* -NI a male graduate

ALUMROOT *n pl.* -S a flowering plant

ALUNITE *n pl.* -S a mineral

ALVEOLAR *n pl.* -S a sound produced with the tongue touching a place just behind the front teeth

ALVEOLUS *n pl.* -LI a small anatomical cavity

ALVINE *adj* pertaining to the abdomen and lower intestines

ALWAY *adv* always

ALWAYS *adv* at all times

ALYSSUM *n pl.* -S a flowering plant

AM present 1st person sing. of be

AMA *n pl.* -S amah

AMADAVAT *n pl.* -S an Asian songbird

AMADOU *n* pl. -S a substance prepared from fungi for use as tinder

AMAH *n* pl. -S an Oriental nurse

AMAIN *adv* with full strength

AMALGAM *n* pl. -S an alloy of mercury with another metal

AMANDINE *adj* prepared with almonds

AMANITA *n* pl. -S any of a genus of poisonous fungi

AMARANTH *n* pl. -S a flowering plant

AMARELLE *n* pl. -S a variety of sour cherry

AMARNA *adj* pertaining to a certain historical period of ancient Egypt

AMASS *v* -ED, -ING, -ES to gather

AMASSER *n* pl. -S one that amasses

AMATEUR *n* pl. -S one that engages in an activity for pleasure

AMATIVE *adj* amorous

AMATOL *n* pl. -S a powerful explosive

AMATORY *adj* pertaining to sexual love

AMAZE *v* AMAZED, AMAZING, AMAZES to overwhelm with surprise or wonder **AMAZEDLY** *adv*

AMAZON *n* pl. -S a tall, powerful woman

AMBAGE *n* pl. -S a winding path

AMBARI *n* pl. -S ambary

AMBARY *n* pl. -RIES an East Indian plant

AMBEER *n* pl. -S tobacco juice

AMBER *n* pl. -S a fossil resin

AMBEROID *n* pl. -S ambroid

AMBERY *n* pl. -BERIES ambry

AMBIANCE *n* pl. -S ambience

AMBIENCE *n* pl. -S the character, mood, or atmosphere of a place or situation

AMBIENT *n* pl. -S ambience

AMBIT *n* pl. -S the external boundary of something

AMBITION *v* -ED, -ING, -S to seek with eagerness

AMBIVERT *n* pl. -S a person whose personality type is intermediate between introvert and extravert

AMBLE *v* -BLED, -BLING, -BLES to saunter

AMBLER *n* pl. -S one that ambles

AMBO *n* pl. AMBOS or AMBONES a pulpit in an early Christian church

AMBOINA *n* pl. -S amboyna

AMBOYNA *n* pl. -S the mottled wood of an Indonesian tree

AMBRIES pl. of ambry

AMBROID *n* pl. -S a synthetic amber

AMBROSIA *n* pl. -S the food of the Greek and Roman gods

AMBRY *n* pl. -BRIES a recess in a church wall for sacred vessels

AMBSACE *n* pl. -S bad luck

AMBULANT *adj* ambulating

AMBULATE *v* -LATED, -LATING, -LATES to move or walk about

AMBUSH *v* -ED, -ING, -ES to attack from a concealed place

AMBUSHER *n* pl. -S one that ambushes

AMEBA *n* pl. -BAS or -BAE amoeba **AMEBAN, AMEBIC, AMEBOID** *adj*

AMEBEAN *adj* alternately responding

AMEER *n* pl. -S amir

AMEERATE *n* pl. -S amirate

AMELCORN *n* pl. -S a variety of wheat

AMEN *n* pl. -S a word used at the end of a prayer to express agreement

AMENABLE *adj* capable of being persuaded **AMENABLY** *adv*

AMEND *v* -ED, -ING, -S to improve

AMENDER *n* pl. -S one that amends

AMENITY *n* pl. -TIES the quality of being pleasant or agreeable

AMENT *n* pl. -S a mentally deficient person

AMENTIA *n* pl. -S mental deficiency

AMERCE *v* AMERCED, AMERCING, AMERCES to punish by imposing an arbitrary fine

AMERCER *n* pl. -S one that amerces

AMESACE *n* pl. -S ambsace

AMETHYST *n* pl. -S a variety of quartz

AMI *n* pl. -S a friend

AMIA *n* pl. -S a freshwater fish

AMIABLE *adj* having a pleasant disposition **AMIABLY** *adv*

AMIANTUS *n* pl. -ES a variety of asbestos

AMICABLE *adj* friendly **AMICABLY** *adv*

AMICE *n* pl. -S a vestment worn about the neck and shoulders

AMID *n* pl. -S amide

AMIDASE *n* pl. -S an enzyme

AMIDE *n* pl. -S a type of chemical compound **AMIDIC** *adj*

AMIDIN *n* pl. -S the soluble matter of starch

AMIDO *adj* containing an amido united with an acid radical

AMIDOGEN *n* pl. -S a univalent chemical radical

AMIDOL *n* pl. -S a chemical compound

AMIDSHIP *adv* toward the middle of a ship

AMIDST *prep* in tho midat of

AMIE *n* pl. -S a female friend

AMIGA *n* pl. -S a female friend

AMIGO *n* pl. -GOS a friend

AMIN *n* pl. -S amine

AMINE *n* pl. -S a type of chemical compound **AMINIC** *adj*

AMINITY *n* pl. -TIES the state of being an amine

AMINO *adj* containing an amine united with a nonacid radical

AMIR *n* pl. -S a Muslim prince or governor

AMIRATE *n* pl. -S the rank of an amir

AMISS *adj* being out of proper order

AMITOSIS *n* pl. -TOSES a type of cell division **AMITOTIC** *adj*

AMITROLE *n* pl. -S an herbicide

AMITY *n* pl. -TIES friendship

AMMETER *n* pl. -S an instrument for measuring amperage

AMMINE *n* pl. -S a type of chemical compound

AMMINO *adj* pertaining to an ammine

AMMO *n* pl. -MOS ammunition

AMMOCETE *n* pl. -S the larva of a lamprey

AMMONAL *n* pl. -S a powerful explosive

AMMONIA *n* pl. -S a pungent gas

AMMONIAC *n* pl. -S a gum resin

AMMONIC *adj* pertaining to ammonia

AMMONIFY *v* -FIED, FYING, -FIES to treat with ammonia

AMMONITE *n* pl. -S the coiled shell of an extinct mollusk

AMMONIUM *n* pl. -S a univalent chemical radical

AMMONOID *n* pl. -S ammonite

AMNESIA *n* pl. -S loss of memory

AMNESIAC *n* pl. -S one suffering from amnesia

AMNESIC *n* pl. -S amnesiac

AMNESTIC *adj* pertaining to amnesia

AMNESTY *v* -TIED, -TYING, -TIES to pardon

AMNION *n* pl. -NIONS or -NIA a membranous sac enclosing an embryo **AMNIC, AMNIONIC, AMNIOTIC** *adj*

AMNIOTE *n* pl. -S a vertebrate that develops an amnion during the embryonic stage

AMOEBA *n* pl. -BAS or -BAE a unicellular microscopic organism **AMOEBAN, AMOEBIC, AMOEBOID** *adj*

AMOEBEAN *adj* amebean

AMOK *n* pl. -S a murderous frenzy

AMOLE *n* pl. -S a plant root used as a substitute for soap

AMONG *prep* in the midst of

AMONGST *prep* among

AMORAL *adj* lacking a sense of right and wrong **AMORALLY** *adv*

AMORETTO *n* pl. -TI or -TOS a cupid

AMORINO *n* pl. -NI an amoretto

AMORIST *n* pl. -S a lover

AMOROSO *adv* tenderly — used as a musical direction

AMOROUS *adj* pertaining to love

AMORT *adj* being without life

AMORTISE *v* -TISED, TISING, TISES to amortize

AMORTIZE *v* -TIZED, TIZING, -TIZES to liquidate gradually, as a debt

AMOTION *n* pl. -S the removal of a corporate officer from his office

AMOUNT *v* -ED, -ING, -S to combine to yield a sum

AMOUR *n* pl. -S a love affair

AMP *n* pl. -S ampere

AMPERAGE *n* pl. -S the strength of an electric current expressed in amperes

AMPERE *n* pl. -S a unit of electric current strength

AMPHIBIA *n/pl* organisms adapted for life both on land and in water

AMPHIOXI *n/pl* lancelets

AMPHIPOD *n* pl. -S a small crustacean

AMPHORA   *n* pl. -RAE or -RAS a narrow-necked jar used in ancient Greece **AMPHORAL** *adj*

AMPLE   *adj* -PLER, -PLEST abundant **AMPLY** *adv*

AMPLIFY   *v* -FIED, FYING, FIES to make larger or more powerful

AMPOULE   *n* pl. -S ampule

AMPUL   *n* pl. -S ampule

AMPULE   *n* pl. -S a small glass vial

AMPULLA   *n* pl. -LAE a globular bottle used in ancient Rome **AMPULLAR** *adj*

AMPUTATE   *v* -TATED, -TATING, -TATES to cut off by surgical means

AMPUTEE   *n* pl. -S one that has had a limb amputated

AMREETA   *n* pl. -S amrita

AMRITA   *n* pl. -S a beverage that bestows immortality in Hindu mythology

AMTRAC   *n* pl. -S a military vehicle equipped to move on land and water

AMTRACK   *n* pl. -S amtrac

AMU   *n* pl. -S a unit of mass

AMUCK   *n* pl. -S amok

AMULET   *n* pl. -S an object worn to protect against evil or injury

AMUSE   *v* AMUSED, AMUSING, AMUSES to occupy pleasingly **AMUSABLE** *adj* **AMUSEDLY** *adv*

AMUSER   *n* pl. -S one that amuses

AMUSIVE   *adj* amusing

AMYGDALA   *n* pl. -LAE an almond-shaped anatomical part

AMYGDALE   *n* pl. -S amygdule

AMYGDULE   *n* pl. -S a small gas bubble in lava

AMYL   *n* pl. -S a univalent radical

AMYLASE   *n* pl. -S an enzyme

AMYLENE   *n* pl. -S a flammable liquid

AMYLIC   *adj* pertaining to amyl

AMYLOID   *n* pl. -S a hard protein deposit resulting from degeneration of tissue

AMYLOSE   *n* pl. -S the relatively soluble component of starch

AMYLUM   *n* pl. -S starch

AN   *indefinite article* — used before words beginning with a vowel sound

ANA   *n* pl. -S a collection of miscellaneous information about a particular subject

ANABAENA   *n* pl. -S a freshwater alga

ANABAS   *n* pl. -ES a freshwater fish

ANABASIS   *n* pl. -ASES a military advance

ANABATIC   *adj* pertaining to rising wind currents

ANABLEPS   *n* pl. -ES a freshwater fish

ANABOLIC   *adj* pertaining to a process by which food is built up into protoplasm

ANACONDA   *n* pl. -S a large snake

ANADEM   *n* pl. -S a wreath for the head

ANAEMIA   *n* pl. -S anemia **ANAEMIC** *adj*

ANAEROBE   *n* pl. -S an organism that does not require oxygen to live

ANAGLYPH   *n* pl. -S a type of carved ornament

ANAGOGE   *n* pl. -S a spiritual interpretation of words **ANAGOGIC** *adj*

ANAGOGY   *n* pl. -GIES anagoge

ANAGRAM   *v* -GRAMMED, -GRAMMING, -GRAMS to transpose the letters of a word or phrase to form a new one

ANAL   *adj* pertaining to the anus

ANALCIME   *n* pl. -S analcite

ANALCITE   *n* pl. -S a mineral

ANALECTA   *n/pl* analects

ANALECTS   *n/pl* selections from a literary work or group of works

ANALEMMA   *n* pl. -MAS or -MATA a type of graduated scale

ANALGIA   *n* pl. -S inability to feel pain

ANALITY   *n* pl. -TIES a type of psychological state

ANALLY   *adv* at or through the anus

ANALOG   *n* pl. -S analogue

ANALOGIC   *adj* pertaining to an analogy

ANALOGUE   *n* pl. -S something that bears an analogy to something else

ANALOGY   *n* pl. -GIES resemblance in some respects between things otherwise unlike

ANALYSE   *v* -LYSED, -LYSING, -LYSES to analyze

ANALYSER   *n* pl. -S analyzer

ANALYSIS   *n* pl. -YSES the separation of a whole into its parts

ANALYST *n* pl. -S one that analyzes

ANALYTIC *adj* pertaining to analysis

ANALYZE *v* -LYZED, LYZING, -LYZES to subject to analysis

ANALYZER *n* pl. -S one that analyzes

ANANKE *n* pl. -S a compelling necessity in ancient Greek religion

ANAPAEST *n* pl. -S anapest

ANAPEST *n* pl. -S a type of metrical foot

ANAPHASE *n* pl. -S a stage of mitosis

ANAPHORA *n* pl. -S the repetition of a word or phrase at the beginning of several successive verses or sentences

ANARCH *n* pl. -S an advocate of anarchy

ANARCHY *n* pl. -CHIES absence of government **ANARCHIC** *adj*

ANASARCA *n* pl. -S a form of dropsy

ANATASE *n* pl. -S a mineral

ANATHEMA *n* pl. -MAS or -MATA a formal ecclesiastical ban or curse

ANATOMY *n* pl. -MIES the structure of an organism **ANATOMIC** *adj*

ANATOXIN *n* pl. -S a toxoid

ANATTO *n* pl. -TOS annatto

ANCESTOR *n* pl. -S a person from whom one is descended

ANCESTRY *n* pl. -TRIES a line or body of ancestors

ANCHOR *v* -FD, -ING, -S to secure by means of an anchor (a device for holding a floating vessel in place)

ANCHORET *n* pl. -S a recluse

ANCHOVY *n* pl. -VIES a small food fish

ANCHUSA *n* pl. -S a hairy-stemmed plant

ANCHUSIN *n* pl. -S a red dye

ANCIENT *adj* -CIENTER, -CIENTEST of or pertaining to time long past

ANCIENT *n* pl. -S one who lived in ancient times

ANCILLA *n* pl. -LAE or -LAS a helper

ANCON *n* pl. -ES the elbow **ANCONAL, ANCONEAL, ANCONOID** *adj*

ANCONE *n* pl. -S ancon

ANCRESS *n* pl. -ES a female recluse

AND *n* pl. -S an added condition or stipulation

ANDANTE *n* pl. -S a moderately slow musical passage

ANDESITE *n* pl. -S a volcanic rock

ANDESYTE *n* pl. -S andesite

ANDIRON *n* pl. -S a metal support for holding wood in a fireplace

ANDROGEN *n* pl. -S a male sex hormone

ANDROID *n* pl. -S a synthetic man

ANE *n* pl. -S one

ANEAR *v* -ED, -ING, -S to approach

ANECDOTE *n* pl. -DOTES or -DOTA a brief story

ANECHOIC *adj* neither having nor producing echoes

ANELE *v* ANELED, ANELING, ANELES to anoint

ANEMIA *n* pl. -S a disorder of the blood **ANEMIC** *adj*

ANEMONE *n* pl. -S a flowering plant

ANENST *prep* anent

ANENT *prep* in regard to

ANERGIA *n* pl. -S anergy

ANERGY *n* pl. -GIES lack of energy **ANERGIC** *adj*

ANEROID *n* pl. -S a type of barometer

ANESTRUS *n* pl. -TRI a period of sexual dormancy

ANETHOL *n* pl. -S anethole

ANETHOLE *n* pl. -S a chemical compound

ANEURISM *n* pl. -S aneurysm

ANEURYSM *n* pl. -S an abnormal blood-filled dilation of a blood vessel

ANEW *adv* once more

ANGA *n* pl. -S any of the eight practices of yoga

ANGARIA *n* pl. -S angary

ANGARY *n* pl. -RIES the right of a warring state to seize neutral property

ANGEL *n* pl. -S a winged celestial being **ANGELIC** *adj*

ANGELICA *n* pl. -S an aromatic herb

ANGELUS *n* pl. -ES a Roman Catholic prayer

ANGER *v* -ED, -ING, -S to make angry

ANGERLY *adv* in an angry manner

ANGINA *n* pl. -S a disease marked by spasmodic attacks of intense pain **ANGINAL, ANGINOSE, ANGINOUS** *adj*

ANGIOMA *n* pl. -MAS or -MATA a tumor composed of blood or lymph vessels

ANGLE

ANGLE	v -GLED, -GLING, -GLES to fish with a hook and line
ANGLEPOD	n pl. -S a flowering plant
ANGLER	n pl. -S one that angles
ANGLICE	adv in readily understood English
ANGLING	n pl. -S the sport of fishing
ANGORA	n pl. -S the long, silky hair of a domestic goat
ANGRY	adj -GRIER, -GRIEST feeling strong displeasure or hostility **ANGRILY** adv
ANGST	n pl. -S a feeling of anxiety or dread
ANGSTROM	n pl. -S a unit of length
ANGUINE	adj resembling a snake
ANGUISH	v -ED, -ING, -ES to suffer extreme pain
ANGULAR	adj having sharp corners
ANGULATE	v -LATED, -LATING, -LATES to make angular
ANGULOSE	adj angular
ANGULOUS	adj angular
ANHINGA	n pl. -S an aquatic bird
ANI	n pl. -S a tropical American bird
ANIL	n pl. -S a West Indian shrub
ANILE	adj resembling an old woman
ANILIN	n pl. -S aniline
ANILINE	n pl. -S a chemical compound
ANILITY	n pl. -TIES the state of being anile
ANIMA	n pl. -S the soul
ANIMAL	n pl. -S a living organism typically capable of voluntary motion and sensation
ANIMALLY	adv physically
ANIMATE	v -MATED, -MATING, -MATES to give life to
ANIMATER	n pl. -S animator
ANIMATO	adv in a lively manner — used as a musical direction
ANIMATOR	n pl. -S one that animates
ANIME	n pl. -S a resin obtained from a tropical tree
ANIMI	n pl. -S anime
ANIMISM	n pl. -S the belief that souls may exist apart from bodies
ANIMIST	n pl. -S an adherent of animism
ANIMUS	n pl. -ES a feeling of hostility
ANION	n pl. -S a negatively charged ion **ANIONIC** adj
ANISE	n pl. -S a North African plant
ANISEED	n pl. -S the seed of the anise used as a flavoring
ANISETTE	n pl. -S a liqueur flavored with aniseed
ANISIC	adj pertaining to an anise
ANISOLE	n pl. -S a chemical compound
ANKERITE	n pl. -S a mineral
ANKH	n pl. -S an Egyptian symbol of enduring life
ANKLE	n pl. -S the joint connecting the foot and the leg
ANKLET	n pl. -S an ornament for the ankle
ANKUS	n pl. -ES an elephant goad
ANKUSH	n pl. -ES ankus
ANKYLOSE	v -LOSED, -LOSING, -LOSES to unite or grow together, as the bones of a joint
ANLACE	n pl. -S a medieval dagger
ANLAGE	n pl. -GEN or -GES the initial cell structure from which an embryonic organ develops
ANLAS	n pl. -ES anlace
ANNA	n pl. -S a former coin of India and Pakistan
ANNAL	n pl. -S a record of a single year
ANNALIST	n pl. -S a historian
ANNATES	n/pl the first year's revenue of a bishop paid to the pope
ANNATTO	n pl. -TOS a yellowish-red dye
ANNEAL	v -ED, -ING, -S to toughen
ANNEALER	n pl. -S one that anneals
ANNELID	n pl. -S any of a phylum of segmented worms
ANNEX	v -ED, -ING, -ES to add or attach
ANNEXE	n pl. -S something added or attached
ANNOTATE	v -TATED, -TATING, -TATES to furnish with critical or explanatory notes
ANNOUNCE	v -NOUNCED, -NOUNCING, -NOUNCES to make known publicly
ANNOY	v -ED, -ING, -S to be troublesome to
ANNOYER	n pl. -S one that annoys

ANNUAL   *n* pl. -S a publication issued once a year

ANNUALLY   *adv* once a year

ANNUITY   *n* pl. -TIES an allowance or income paid at regular intervals

ANNUL   *v* -NULLED, -NULLING, -NULS to make or declare void or invalid

ANNULAR   *adj* shaped like a ring

ANNULATE   *adj* composed of or furnished with rings

ANNULET   *n* pl. -S a small ring

ANNULI   a pl. of annulus

ANNULLED   past tense of annul

ANNULLING   present participle of annul

ANNULUS   *n* pl. -LI or -LUSES a ring or ringlike part **ANNULOSE** *adj*

ANOA   *n* pl. -S a wild ox

ANODE   *n* pl. -S a positively charged electrode **ANODAL, ANODIC** *adj* **ANODALLY** *adv*

ANODIZE   *v* -IZED, -IZING, -IZES to coat with a protective film by chemical means

ANODYNE   *n* pl. -S a medicine that relieves pain **ANODYNIC** *adj*

ANOINT   *v* -ED, -ING, -S to apply oil to as a sacred rite

ANOINTER   *n* pl. -S one that anoints

ANOLE   *n* pl. -S a tropical lizard

ANOLYTE   *n* pl. -S the part of an electricity-conducting solution nearest the anode

ANOMALY   *n* pl. -LIES a deviation from the common rule, type, or form

ANOMIE   *n* pl. -S a collapse of the social structures governing a given society **ANOMIC** *adj*

ANOMY   *n* pl. -MIES anomie

ANON   *adv* at another time

ANONYM   *n* pl. -S a false or assumed name

ANOOPSIA   *n* pl. -S a visual defect

ANOPIA   *n* pl. -S anoopsia

ANOPSIA   *n* pl. -S anoopsia

ANORAK   *n* pl. -S a parka

ANORETIC   *adj* lacking appetite

ANOREXIA   *n* pl. -S loss of appetite

ANOREXY   *n* pl. -OREXIES anorexia

ANORTHIC   *adj* denoting a certain type of crystal system

ANOSMIA   *n* pl. -S loss of the sense of smell **ANOSMIC** *adj*

ANOTHER   *adj* one more

ANOXEMIA   *n* pl. -S a disorder of the blood **ANOXEMIC** *adj*

ANOXIA   *n* pl. -S absence of oxygen **ANOXIC** *adj*

ANSA   *n* pl. -SAE the projecting part of Saturn's rings

ANSATE   *adj* having a handle

ANSATED   *adj* ansate

ANSERINE   *n* pl. -S a chemical compound

ANSEROUS   *adj* silly

ANSWER   *v* -ED, -ING, -S to say, write, or act in return

ANSWERER   *n* pl. -S one that answers

ANT   *n* pl. -S a small insect

ANTA   *n* pl. -TAE or -TAS a pilaster formed at the termination of a wall

ANTACID   *n* pl. -S a substance that neutralizes acid

ANTALGIC   *n* pl. -S an anodyne

ANTE   *v* ANTED or ANTEED, ANTEING, ANTES to put a fixed stake into the pot before the cards are dealt in poker

ANTEATER   *n* pl. -S any of several mammals that feed on ants

ANTECEDE   *v* -CEDED, -CEDING, -CEDES to precede

ANTED   a past tense of ante

ANTEDATE   *v* -DATED, -DATING, -DATES to be of an earlier date than

ANTEFIX   *n* pl. -FIXES or -FIXA an upright ornament at the eaves of a tiled roof

ANTELOPE   *n* pl. -S a ruminant mammal

ANTENNA   *n* pl. -NAE or -NAS a sensory appendage on the head of an insect, myriapod, or crustacean **ANTENNAL** *adj*

ANTEPAST   *n* pl. -S an appetizer

ANTERIOR   *adj* situated in or toward the front

ANTEROOM   *n* pl. -S a waiting room

ANTETYPE   *n* pl. -S an earlier form

ANTEVERT   *v* -ED, -ING, -S to displace by tipping forward

ANTHELIA   *n/pl* halolike areas seen in the sky opposite the sun

ANTHELIX n pl. -LICES the inner curved ridge on the cartilage of the external ear

ANTHEM v -ED, -ING, -S to praise in a song

ANTHEMIA n/pl decorative floral patterns used in Greek art

ANTHER n pl. -S the pollen-bearing part of a stamen **ANTHERAL** adj

ANTHERID n pl. -S a male reproductive organ of certain plants

ANTHESIS n pl. -THESES the full bloom of a flower

ANTHILL n pl. -S a mound formed by ants in building their nest

ANTHODIA n/pl flower heads of certain plants

ANTHOID adj resembling a flower

ANTHRAX n pl. -THRACES an infectious disease

ANTI n pl. -S one that is opposed

ANTIAR n pl. -S an arrow poison

ANTIARIN n pl. -S antiar

ANTIBODY n pl. -BODIES a body protein that produces immunity against certain microorganisms or toxins

ANTIC v -TICKED, -TICKING, -TICS to act in a clownish manner

ANTICK v -ED, -ING, -S to antic

ANTICLY adv in a clownish manner

ANTIDOTE n pl. -S a remedy to counteract the effects of a poison

ANTIFAT adj preventing the formation of fat

ANTIGEN n pl. -S a substance that stimulates the production of antibodies

ANTIGENE n pl. -S antigen

ANTIHERO n pl. -ROES a protagonist who is notably lacking in heroic qualities

ANTIKING n pl. -S a usurping king

ANTILOG n pl. -S the number corresponding to a given logarithm

ANTILOGY n pl. -GIES a contradiction in terms or ideas

ANTIMASK n pl. -S a comic performance between the acts of a masque

ANTIMERE n pl. -S a part of an organism symmetrical with a part on the opposite side of the main axis

ANTIMONY n pl. -NIES a metallic element

ANTING n pl. -S the deliberate placing, by certain birds, of living ants among the feathers

ANTINODE n pl. -S a region between adjacent nodes

ANTINOMY n pl. -MIES a contradiction between two seemingly valid principles

ANTIPHON n pl. -S a psalm or hymn sung responsively

ANTIPODE n pl. -S an exact opposite

ANTIPOLE n pl. -S the opposite pole

ANTIPOPE n pl. -S one claiming to be pope in opposition to the one chosen by church law

ANTIPYIC n pl. -S a medicine that prevents the formation of pus

ANTIQUE v -TIQUED, TIQUING, TIQUES to give an appearance of age to

ANTIQUER n pl. -S one that antiques

ANTIRUST n pl. -S something that prevents rust

ANTISERA n/pl serums that contain antibodies

ANTISKID adj designed to prevent skidding

ANTISMOG adj designed to reduce pollutants that cause smog

ANTITANK adj designed to combat tanks

ANTITAX adj opposing taxes

ANTITYPE n pl. -S an opposite type

ANTIWAR adj opposing war

ANTLER n pl. -S the horn of an animal of the deer family **ANTLERED** adj

ANTLIKE adj resembling an ant

ANTLION n pl. -S a predatory insect

ANTONYM n pl. -S a word opposite in meaning to another

ANTONYMY n pl. -MIES the state of being an antonym

ANTRA pl. of antrum

ANTRAL adj pertaining to an antrum

ANTRE n pl. -S a cave

ANTRORSE adj directed forward or upward

ANTRUM n pl. -TRA a cavity in a bone

ANURAN n pl. -S a frog or toad

ANURESIS n pl. -RESES inability to urinate **ANURETIC** adj

ANURIA   *n pl.* -S absence of urine **ANURIC** *adj*

ANUROUS   *adj* having no tail

ANUS   *n pl.* -ES the excretory opening at the end of the alimentary canal

ANVIL   *v* -VILED, -VILING, -VILS or -VILLED, -VILLING, -VILS to shape on an anvil (a heavy iron block)

ANVILTOP   *n pl.* -S an anvil-shaped cloud mass

ANXIETY   *n pl.* -ETIES painful or apprehensive uneasiness of mind

ANXIOUS   *adj* full of anxiety

ANY   *adj* one, no matter which

ANYBODY   *n pl.* -BODIES a person of some importance

ANYHOW   *adv* in any way

ANYMORE   *adv* at the present time

ANYONE   *pron* any person

ANYPLACE   *adv* in any place

ANYTHING   *n pl.* -S a thing of any kind

ANYTIME   *adv* at any time

ANYWAY   *adv* in any way

ANYWAYS   *adv* anyway

ANYWHERE   *n pl.* -S any place

ANYWISE   *adv* in any way

AORIST   *n pl.* -S a verb tense **AORISTIC** *adj*

AORTA   *n pl.* -TAS or -TAE a main artery **AORTAL, AORTIC** *adj*

AOUDAD   *n pl.* -S a wild sheep

APACE   *adv* swiftly

APACHE   *n pl.* -S a Parisian gangster

APAGOGE   *n pl.* -S establishment of a thesis by showing its contrary to be absurd **APAGOGIC** *adj*

APANAGE   *n pl.* -S appanage

APAREJO   *n pl.* -JOS a type of saddle

APART   *adv* not together

APATETIC   *adj* having coloration serving as natural camouflage

APATHY   *n pl.* -THIES lack of emotion

APATITE   *n pl.* -S a mineral

APE   *v* APED, APING, APES to mimic

APEAK   *adv* in a vertical position

APEEK   *adv* apeak

APELIKE   *adj* resembling an ape (a large, tailless primate)

APER   *n pl.* -S one that apes

APERCU   *n pl.* -S a brief summary

APERIENT   *n pl.* -S a mild laxative

APERITIF   *n pl.* -S an alcoholic drink taken before a meal

APERTURE   *n pl.* -S an opening

APERY   *n pl.* -ERIES the act of aping

APETALY   *n pl.* -ALIES the state of having no petals

APEX   *n pl.* APEXES or APICES the highest point

APHAGIA   *n pl.* -S inability to swallow

APHANITE   *n pl.* -S an igneous rock

APHASIA   *n pl.* -S loss of the ability to use words

APHASIAC   *n pl.* -S one suffering from aphasia

APHASIC   *n pl.* -S aphasiac

APHELION   *n pl.* -ELIA the point in a planetary orbit farthest from the sun **APHELIAN** *adj*

APHESIS   *n pl.* -ESES the loss of an unstressed vowel from the beginning of a word **APHETIC** *adj*

APHID   *n pl.* -S any of a family of small, soft-bodied insects

APHIDIAN   *n pl.* -S an aphid

APHIS   *n pl.* APHIDES an aphid

APHOLATE   *n pl.* -S a chemical used to control houseflies

APHONIA   *n pl.* -S loss of voice

APHONIC   *n pl.* -S one affected with aphonia

APHORISE   *v* -RISED, -RISING, -RISES to aphorize

APHORISM   *n pl.* -S a brief statement of a truth or principle

APHORIST   *n pl.* -S one that aphorizes

APHORIZE   *v* -RIZED, -RIZING, -RIZES to write or speak in aphorisms

APHOTIC   *adj* lacking light

APHTHA   *n pl.* -THAE a small blister in the mouth or stomach **APHTHOUS** *adj*

APHYLLY   *n pl.* -LIES the state of being leafless

APIAN   *adj* pertaining to bees

APIARIAN   *n pl.* -S an apiarist

APIARIST	*n pl.* -S a person who raises bees
APIARY	*n pl.* -ARIES a place where bees are kept
APICAL	*adj* situated at the apex **APICALLY** *adv*
APICES	a *pl.* of apex
APICULUS	*n pl.* -LI a sharp point at the end of a leaf
APIECE	*adv* for each one
APIMANIA	*n pl.* -S an excessive interest in bees
APING	present participle of ape
APIOLOGY	*n pl.* -GIES the study of bees
APISH	*adj* slavishly or foolishly imitative **APISHLY** *adv*
APLASIA	*n pl.* -S defective development of an organ or part
APLASTIC	*adj* not plastic
APLENTY	*adj* being in sufficient quantity
APLITE	*n pl.* -S a fine-grained rock **APLITIC** *adj*
APLOMB	*n pl.* -S self-confidence
APNEA	*n pl.* -S temporary cessation of respiration **APNEAL, APNEIC** *adj*
APNOEA	*n pl.* -S apnea **APNOEAL, APNOEIC** *adj*
APOCARP	*n pl.* -S a fruit having separated carpels
APOCARPY	*n pl.* -PIES the state of being an apocarp
APOCOPE	*n pl.* -S an omission of the last sound of a word **APOCOPIC** *adj*
APOCRINE	*adj* pertaining to a type of gland
APODAL	*adj* having no feet or footlike appendages
APODOSIS	*n pl.* -OSES the main clause of a conditional sentence
APODOUS	*adj* apodal
APOGAMY	*n pl.* -MIES a form of plant reproduction **APOGAMIC** *adj*
APOGEE	*n pl.* -S the point in the orbit of a celestial body which is farthest from the earth **APOGEAL, APOGEAN, APOGEIC** *adj*
APOLLO	*n pl.* -LOS a handsome young man
APOLOG	*n pl.* -S apologue
APOLOGAL	*adj* pertaining to an apologue
APOLOGIA	*n pl.* -GIAS or -GIAE a formal justification or defense
APOLOGUE	*n pl.* -S an allegory
APOLOGY	*n pl.* -GIES an expression of regret for some error or offense
APOLUNE	*n pl.* -S the point in the orbit of a celestial body which is farthest from the moon
APOMICT	*n pl.* -S an organism produced by apomixis
APOMIXIS	*n pl.* -MIXES a type of reproductive process
APOPHYGE	*n pl.* -S a concave curve in a column
APOPLEXY	*n pl.* -PLEXIES a sudden loss of sensation and muscular control
APORT	*adv* on or toward the left side of a ship
APOSTACY	*n pl.* -CIES apostasy
APOSTASY	*n pl.* -SIES an abandonment of one's faith or principles
APOSTATE	*n pl.* -S one who commits apostasy
APOSTIL	*n pl.* -S a marginal note
APOSTLE	*n pl.* -S a disciple sent forth by Christ to preach the gospel
APOTHECE	*n pl.* -S a spore-producing organ of certain fungi
APOTHEGM	*n pl.* -S a maxim
APOTHEM	*n pl.* -S the perpendicular from the center to any side of a regular polygon
APPAL	*v* -PALLED, -PALLING, -PALS to appall
APPALL	*v* -ED, -ING, -S to fill with horror or dismay
APPANAGE	*n pl.* -S land or revenue granted to a member of a royal family
APPARAT	*n pl.* -S a political organization
APPAREL	*v* -ELED, -ELING, -ELS or -ELLED, -ELLING, -ELS to provide with outer garments
APPARENT	*adj* easily seen
APPEAL	*v* -ED, -ING, -S to make an earnest request
APPEALER	*n pl.* -S one that appeals
APPEAR	*v* -ED, -ING, -S to come into view
APPEASE	*v* -PEASED, -PEASING, -PEASES to bring to a state of peace or contentment

APPEASER *n* pl. -S one that appeases

APPEL *n* pl. -S a feint in fencing

APPELLEE *n* pl. -S the defendant in a type of judicial proceeding

APPELLOR *n* pl. -S a confessed criminal who accuses an accomplice

APPEND *v* -ED, -ING, -S to add as a supplement

APPENDIX *n* pl. -DIXES or -DICES a collection of supplementary material at the end of a book

APPESTAT *n* pl. -S the mechanism in the central nervous system that regulates appetite

APPETENT *adj* marked by strong desire

APPETITE *n* pl. -S a desire for food or drink

APPLAUD *v* -ED, -ING, -S to express approval by clapping the hands

APPLAUSE *n* pl. -S the sound made by persons applauding

APPLE *n* pl. -S an edible fruit

APPLIER *n* pl. -S one that applies

APPLIQUE *v* -QUED, -QUEING, -QUES to apply as a decoration to a larger surface

APPLY *v* -PLIED, -PLYING, -PLIES to bring into contact with something

APPOINT *v* -ED, -ING, -S to name or assign to a position or office

APPOSE *v* -POSED, -POSING, -POSES to place side by side

APPOSER *n* pl. -S one that apposes

APPOSITE *adj* relevant

APPRAISE *v* -PRAISED, -PRAISING, -PRAISES to set a value on

APPRISE *v* -PRISED, -PRISING, -PRISES to notify

APPRISER *n* pl. -S one that apprises

APPRIZE *v* -PRIZED, -PRIZING, -PRIZES to appraise

APPRIZER *n* pl. -S one that apprizes

APPROACH *v* -ED, -ING, -ES to come near or nearer to

APPROVAL *n* pl. -S the act of approving

APPROVE *v* -PROVED, -PROVING, -PROVES to regard favorably

APPROVER *n* pl. -S one that approves

APPULSE *n* pl. -S the approach of one moving body toward another

APRAXIA *n* pl. -S loss of the ability to perform coordinated movements **APRACTIC, APRAXIC** *adj*

APRICOT *n* pl. -S an edible fruit

APRON *v* -ED, -ING, -S to provide with an apron (a garment worn to protect one's clothing)

APROPOS *adj* relevant

APSE *n* pl. -S a domed, semicircular projection of a building **APSIDAL** *adj*

APSIS *n* pl. -SIDES an apse

APT *adj* APTER, APTEST suitable

APTERAL *adj* apterous

APTEROUS *adj* having no wings

APTERYX *n* pl. -ES the kiwi

APTITUDE *n* pl. -S an ability

APTLY *adv* in an apt manner

APTNESS *n* pl. -ES the quality of being apt

APYRASE *n* pl. -S an enzyme

APYRETIC *adj* having no fever

AQUA *n* pl. AQUAE or AQUAS water

AQUACADE *n* pl. -S a swimming and diving exhibition

AQUANAUT *n* pl. -S a scuba diver trained to live in underwater installations

AQUARIA a pl. of aquarium

AQUARIAL *adj* pertaining to an aquarium

AQUARIAN *n* pl. -S a member of the old sects that used water rather than wine in religious ceremonies

AQUARIST *n* pl. -S one who keeps an aquarium

AQUARIUM *n* pl. -IUMS or -IA a water-filled enclosure in which aquatic animals are kept

AQUATIC *n* pl. -S an organism living or growing in or near water

AQUATINT *v* -ED, -ING, -S to etch, using a certain process

AQUATONE *n* pl. -S a type of printing process

AQUAVIT *n* pl. -S a Scandinavian liquor

AQUEDUCT *n* pl. -S a water conduit

AQUEOUS *adj* pertaining to water

AQUIFER *n* pl. -S a water-bearing rock formation

AQUILINE *adj* curving like an eagle's beak

AQUIVER	*adj* quivering
AR	*n* pl. -S the letter R
ARABESK	*n* pl. -S a design of intertwined floral figures
ARABIZE	*v* -IZED, -IZING, -IZES to cause to acquire Arabic customs
ARABLE	*n* pl. -S land suitable for cultivation
ARACEOUS	*adj* belonging to the arum family of plants
ARACHNID	*n* pl. -S any of a class of segmented invertebrate animals
ARAK	*n* pl. -S arrack
ARANEID	*n* pl. -S a spider
ARAPAIMA	*n* pl. -S a large food fish
ARAROBA	*n* pl. -S a Brazilian tree
ARBALEST	*n* pl. -S a type of crossbow
ARBALIST	*n* pl. -S arbalest
ARBITER	*n* pl. -S one chosen or appointed to judge a disputed issue **ARBITRAL** *adj*
ARBOR	*n* pl. -S a shady garden shelter
ARBOR	*n* pl. -ES a tree
ARBOREAL	*adj* living in trees
ARBORED	*adj* having trees
ARBORETA	*n/pl* places for the study and exhibition of trees
ARBORIST	*n* pl. -S a tree specialist
ARBORIZE	*v* -IZED, -IZING, -IZES to form many branches
ARBOROUS	*adj* pertaining to trees
ARBOUR	*n* pl. -S a shady garden shelter **ARBOURED** *adj*
ARBUSCLE	*n* pl. -S a dwarf tree
ARBUTE	*n* pl. -S an evergreen tree **ARBUTEAN** *adj*
ARBUTUS	*n* pl. -ES an evergreen tree
ARC	*v* ARCED, ARCING, ARCS or ARCKED, ARCKING, ARCS to move in a curved course
ARCADE	*v* -CADED, -CADING, -CADES to provide with an arcade (a series of arches)
ARCADIA	*n* pl. -S a region of simple pleasure and quiet
ARCADIAN	*n* pl. -S one who lives in an arcadia
ARCADING	*n* pl. -S an arcade
ARCANE	*adj* mysterious
ARCANUM	*n* pl. -NA a mystery
ARCATURE	*n* pl. -S a small arcade
ARCH	*v* -ED, -ING, -ES to bend like an arch (a curved structure spanning an opening)
ARCHAIC	*adj* pertaining to an earlier time
ARCHAISE	*v* -ISED, -ISING, -ISES to archaize
ARCHAISM	*n* pl. -S an archaic word, idiom, or expression
ARCHAIST	*n* pl. -S one that archaizes
ARCHAIZE	*v* -IZED, -IZING, -IZES to use archaisms
ARCHDUKE	*n* pl. -S an Austrian prince
ARCHER	*n* pl. -S one that shoots with a bow and arrow
ARCHERY	*n* pl. -CHERIES the sport of shooting with a bow and arrow
ARCHIL	*n* pl. -S orchil
ARCHINE	*n* pl. -S a Russian unit of linear measure
ARCHING	*n* pl. -S a series of arches
ARCHIVE	*v* -CHIVED, -CHIVING, -CHIVES to file in an archive (a place where records are kept) **ARCHIVAL** *adj*
ARCHLY	*adv* slyly
ARCHNESS	*n* pl. -ES slyness
ARCHON	*n* pl. -S a magistrate of ancient Athens
ARCHWAY	*n* pl. -WAYS a passageway under an arch
ARCIFORM	*adj* having the form of an arch
ARCKED	a past tense of arc
ARCKING	a present participle of arc
ARCO	*adv* with the bow — used as a direction to players of stringed instruments
ARCTIC	*n* pl. -S a warm, waterproof overshoe
ARCUATE	*adj* curved like a bow
ARCUATED	*adj* arcuate
ARCUS	*n* pl. -ES an arch-shaped cloud
ARDEB	*n* pl. -S an Egyptian unit of capacity
ARDENCY	*n* pl. -CIES ardor
ARDENT	*adj* characterized by intense emotion **ARDENTLY** *adv*
ARDOR	*n* pl. -S intensity of emotion
ARDOUR	*n* pl. -S ardor

ARDUOUS   *adj* involving great labor or hardship

ARE   *n pl.* -S a unit of surface measure

AREA   *n pl.* AREAE a section of the cerebral cortex having a specific function

AREA   *n pl.* -S a particular extent of space or surface **AREAL** *adj* **AREALLY** *adv*

AREAWAY   *n pl.* -WAYS a sunken area leading to a basement entrance

ARECA   *n pl.* -S a tropical tree

AREIC   *adj* pertaining to a region of the earth contributing little surface drainage

ARENA   *n pl.* -S an enclosed area for contests

ARENOSE   *adj* sandy

ARENOUS   *adj* arenose

AREOLA   *n pl.* -LAE or -LAS a small space in a network of leaf veins **AREOLAR, AREOLATE** *adj*

AREOLE   *n pl.* -S areola

AREOLOGY   *n pl.* -GIES the study of the planet Mars

ARETE   *n pl.* -S a sharp mountain ridge

ARETHUSA   *n pl.* -S a flowering plant

ARF   *interj* — used to express the bark of a dog

ARGAL   *n pl.* -S argol

ARGALI   *n pl.* -S a wild sheep

ARGENT   *n pl.* -S silver **ARGENTAL, ARGENTIC** *adj*

ARGENTUM   *n pl.* -S silver

ARGIL   *n pl.* -S a white clay

ARGINASE   *n pl.* -S an enzyme

ARGININE   *n pl.* -S an amino acid

ARGLE   *v* -GLED, -GLING, -GLES to argue

ARGOL   *n pl.* -S a crust deposited in wine casks during aging

ARGON   *n pl.* -S a gaseous element

ARGONAUT   *n pl.* -S a marine mollusk

ARGOSY   *n pl.* -SIES a large merchant ship

ARGOT   *n pl.* -S a specialized vocabulary **ARGOTIC** *adj*

ARGUABLE   *adj* capable of being argued about **ARGUABLY** *adv*

ARGUE   *v* -GUED, -GUING, -GUES to present reasons for or against

ARGUER   *n pl.* -S one that argues

ARGUFIER   *n pl.* -S one that argufies

ARGUFY   *v* -FIED, -FYING, -FIES to argue stubbornly

ARGUING   present participle of argue

ARGUMENT   *n pl.* -S a discussion involving differing points of view

ARGUS   *n pl.* -ES an East Indian pheasant

ARGYLE   *n pl.* -S a knitting pattern

ARGYLL   *n pl.* -S argyle

ARHAT   *n pl.* -S a Buddhist who has attained nirvana

ARIA   *n pl.* -S an elaborate melody for a single voice

ARID   *adj* -IDER, -IDEST extremely dry **ARIDLY** *adv*

ARIDITY   *n pl.* -TIES the state of being arid

ARIDNESS   *n pl.* -ES aridity

ARIEL   *n pl.* -S an African gazelle

ARIETTA   *n pl.* -S a short aria

ARIETTE   *n pl.* -S arietta

ARIGHT   *adv* rightly; correctly

ARIL   *n pl.* -S an outer covering of certain seeds **ARILED, ARILLATE, ARILLOID** *adj*

ARILLODE   *n pl.* -S a type of aril

ARIOSE   *adj* characterized by melody

ARIOSO   *n pl.* -SOS or -SI a musical passage resembling an aria

ARISE   *v* AROSE, ARISEN, ARISING, ARISES to get up

ARISTA   *n pl.* -TAE or -TAS a bristlelike structure or appendage **ARISTATE** *adj*

ARK   *n pl.* -S a large boat

ARLES   *n/pl* money paid to bind a bargain

ARM   *v* -ED, -ING, -S to supply with weapons

ARMADA   *n pl.* -S a fleet of warships

ARMAMENT   *n pl.* -S a military force equipped for war

ARMATURE   *v* -TURED, -TURING, -TURES to furnish with armor

ARMBAND   *n pl.* -S a band worn around an arm (an upper appendage of the human body)

ARMCHAIR n pl. -S a chair with armrests

ARMER n pl. -S one that arms

ARMET n pl. -S a medieval helmet

ARMFUL n pl. ARMFULS or ARMSFUL as much as the arm can hold

ARMHOLE n pl. -S an opening for the arm in a garment

ARMIES pl. of army

ARMIGER n pl. -S one who carries the armor of a knight

ARMIGERO n pl. -GEROS armiger

ARMILLA n pl. -LAE or -LAS a thin membrane around the stem of certain fungi

ARMING n pl. -S the act of one that arms

ARMLESS adj having no arms

ARMLET n pl. -S an armband

ARMLIKE adj resembling an arm

ARMLOAD n pl. -S an armful

ARMOIRE n pl. -S a large, ornate cabinet

ARMONICA n pl. -S a type of musical instrument

ARMOR v -ED, -ING, -S to furnish with armor (a defensive covering for the body)

ARMORER n pl. -S one that makes or repairs armor

ARMORIAL n pl. -S a treatise on heraldry

ARMORY n pl. -MORIES a place where weapons are stored

ARMOUR v -ED, -ING, -S to armor

ARMOURER n pl. -S armorer

ARMOURY n pl. -MOURIES armory

ARMPIT n pl. -S the hollow under the arm at the shoulder

ARMREST n pl. -S a support for the arm

ARMSFUL a pl. of armful

ARMURE n pl. -S a woven fabric

ARMY n pl. -MIES a large body of men trained and armed for war

ARMYWORM n pl. -S a destructive moth larva

ARNATTO n pl. -TOS annatto

ARNICA n pl. -S a perennial herb

ARNOTTO n pl. -TOS a tropical tree

AROID n pl. -S a flowering plant

AROINT v -ED, -ING, -S to drive away

AROMA n pl. -S a pleasant odor

AROMATIC n pl. -S a fragrant plant or substance

AROSE past tense of arise

AROUND prep on all sides of

AROUSAL n pl. -S the act of arousing

AROUSE v AROUSED, AROUSING, AROUSES to stimulate

AROUSER n pl. -S one that arouses

AROYNT v -ED, -ING, -S to aroint

ARPEGGIO n pl. -GIOS a technique of playing a musical chord

ARPEN n pl. -S arpent

ARPENT n pl. -S an old French unit of area

ARQUEBUS n pl. -ES an early portable firearm

ARRACK n pl. -S an Oriental liquor

ARRAIGN v -ED, -ING, -S to call before a court of law to answer an indictment

ARRANGE v -RANGED, -RANGING, -RANGES to put in definite or proper order

ARRANGER n pl. -S one that arranges

ARRANT adj outright **ARRANTLY** adv

ARRAS n pl. ARRAS a tapestry **ARRASED** adj

ARRAY v -ED, -ING, -S to place in proper or desired order

ARRAYAL n pl. -S the act of arraying

ARRAYER n pl. -S one that arrays

ARREAR n pl. -S an unpaid and overdue debt

ARREST v -ED, -ING, -S to seize and hold by legal authority

ARRESTEE n pl. -S one that is arrested

ARRESTER n pl. -S one that arrests

ARRESTOR n pl. -S arrester

ARRHIZAL adj rootless

ARRIS n pl. -RISES a ridge formed by the meeting of two surfaces

ARRIVAL n pl. -S the act of arriving

ARRIVE v -RIVED, -RIVING, -RIVES to reach a destination

ARRIVER n pl. -S one that arrives

ARROBA n pl. -S a Spanish unit of weight

ARROGANT adj overly convinced of one's own worth or importance

ARROGATE v -GATED, -GATING, -GATES to claim or take without right

ARROW   *v* -ED, -ING, -S to indicate the proper position of by means of a linear figure with a wedge-shaped end

ARROWY   *adj* moving swiftly

ARROYO   *n pl.* -ROYOS a brook or creek

ARSE   *n pl.* -S the buttocks — usually considered vulgar

ARSENAL   *n pl.* -S a collection or supply of weapons

ARSENATE   *n pl.* -S a chemical salt

ARSENIC   *n pl.* -S a metallic element

ARSENIDE   *n pl.* -S an arsenic compound

ARSENITE   *n pl.* -S a chemical salt

ARSENO   *adj* containing a certain bivalent chemical radical

ARSENOUS   *adj* pertaining to arsenic

ARSHIN   *n pl.* -S archine

ARSINE   *n pl.* -S a poisonous gas

ARSINO   *adj* containing a certain univalent chemical radical

ARSIS   *n pl.* ARSES the unaccented part of a musical measure

ARSON   *n pl.* -S the malicious or fraudulent burning of property **ARSONOUS** *adj*

ARSONIST   *n pl.* -S one that commits arson

ART   *n pl.* -S an esthetically pleasing and meaningful arrangement of elements

ARTAL   *a pl.* of rotl

ARTEFACT   *n pl.* -S artifact

ARTEL   *n pl.* -S a collective farm in Russia

ARTERIAL   *n pl.* -S a type of highway

ARTERY   *n pl.* -TERIES a vessel that carries blood away from the heart

ARTFUL   *adj* crafty **ARTFULLY** *adv*

ARTICLE   *v* -CLED, -CLING, -CLES to charge with specific offenses

ARTIER   comparative of arty

ARTIEST   superlative of arty

ARTIFACT   *n pl.* -S an object made by man

ARTIFICE   *n pl.* -S a clever stratagem

ARTILY   *adv* in an arty manner

ARTINESS   *n pl.* -ES the quality of being arty

ARTISAN   *n pl.* -S a trained or skilled workman

ARTIST   *n pl.* -S one who practices one of the fine arts

ARTISTE   *n pl.* -S a skilled public performer

ARTISTIC   *adj* characteristic of art

ARTISTRY   *n pl.* -RIES artistic quality or workmanship

ARTLESS   *adj* lacking cunning or guile

ARTWORK   *n pl.* -S illustrative or decorative work in printed matter

ARTY   *adj* ARTIER, ARTIEST showily or pretentiously artistic

ARUM   *n pl.* -S a flowering plant

ARUSPEX   *n pl.* -PICES haruspex

ARVAL   *adj* pertaining to plowed land

ARVO   *n pl.* -VOS afternoon

ARYL   *n pl.* -S a univalent radical

ARYTHMIA   *n pl.* -S an irregularity in the rhythm of the heartbeat **ARYTHMIC** *adj*

AS   *adv* to the same degree

ASARUM   *n pl.* -S a perennial herb

ASBESTOS   *n pl.* -ES a mineral **ASBESTIC** *adj*

ASBESTUS   *n pl.* -ES asbestos

ASCARID   *n pl.* -S a parasitic worm

ASCARIS   *n pl.* -RIDES ascarid

ASCEND   *v* -ED, -ING, -S to go or move upward

ASCENDER   *n pl.* -S one that ascends

ASCENT   *n pl.* -S the act of ascending

ASCESIS   *n pl.* -CESES the conduct of an ascetic

ASCETIC   *n pl.* -S one who practices extreme self-denial for religious reasons

ASCI   pl. of ascus

ASCIDIAN   *n pl.* -S a small marine animal

ASCIDIUM   *n pl.* -DIA a flask-shaped plant appendage

ASCITES   *n pl.* ASCITES accumulation of serous fluid in the abdomen **ASCITIC** *adj*

ASCOCARP   *n pl.* -S a spore-producing organ of certain fungi

ASCORBIC   *adj* relieving scurvy

ASCOT   *n pl.* -S a broad neck scarf

ASCRIBE   *v* -CRIBED, -CRIBING, -CRIBES to attribute to a specified cause, source, or origin

ASCUS *n pl.* ASCI a spore sac in certain fungi

ASDIC *n pl.* -S sonar

ASEA *adv* at sea

ASEPSIS *n pl.* -SEPSES the condition of being aseptic

ASEPTIC *adj* free from germs

ASEXUAL *adj* occurring or performed without sexual action

ASH *v* -ED, -ING, -ES to convert into ash (the residue of a substance that has been burned)

ASHAMED *adj* feeling shame, guilt, or disgrace

ASHCAN *n pl.* -S a metal receptacle for garbage

ASHEN *adj* consisting of ashes

ASHIER comparative of ashy

ASHIEST superlative of ashy

ASHLAR *v* -ED, -ING, -S to build with squared stones

ASHLER *v* -ED, -ING, -S to ashlar

ASHLESS *adj* having no ashes

ASHMAN *n pl.* -MEN one who collects and removes ashes

ASHORE *adv* toward or on the shore

ASHPLANT *n pl.* -S a walking stick

ASHRAM *n pl.* -S a secluded dwelling of a Hindu sage

ASHTRAY *n pl.* -TRAYS a receptacle for tobacco ashes

ASHY *adj* ASHIER, ASHIEST covered with ashes

ASIDE *n pl.* -S a comment by an actor intended to be heard by the audience but not the other actors

ASININE *adj* obstinately stupid or silly

ASK *v* -ED, -ING, -S to put a question to

ASKANCE *adv* with a side glance

ASKANT *adv* askance

ASKER *n pl.* -S one that asks

ASKESIS *n pl.* ASKESES ascesis

ASKEW *adv* to one side

ASKING *n pl.* -S the act of one who asks

ASLANT *adj* slanting

ASLEEP *adj* sleeping

ASLOPE *adj* sloping

ASOCIAL *adj* avoiding the company of others

ASP *n pl.* -S a venomous snake

ASPECT *n pl.* -S appearance of something to the eye or mind

ASPEN *n pl.* -S any of several poplars

ASPER *n pl.* -S a Turkish money of account

ASPERATE *v* -ATED, ATING, -ATES to make uneven

ASPERGES *n pl.* ASPERGES a Roman Catholic rite

ASPERITY *n pl.* -TIES acrimony

ASPERSE *v* -PERSED, -PERSING, -PERSES to spread false charges against

ASPERSER *n pl.* -S one that asperses

ASPERSOR *n pl.* -S asperser

ASPHALT *v* -ED, -ING, -S to coat with asphalt (a substance used for paving and roofing)

ASPHERIC *adj* varying slightly from an exactly spherical shape

ASPHODEL *n pl.* -S a flowering plant

ASPHYXIA *n pl.* -S unconsciousness caused by lack of oxygen

ASPHYXY *n pl.* -PHYXIES asphyxia

ASPIC *n pl.* -S the asp

ASPIRANT *n pl.* -S one that aspires

ASPIRATA *n pl.* -TAE a type of plosive

ASPIRATE *v* -RATED, -RATING, -RATES to pronounce with an initial release of breath

ASPIRE *v* -PIRED, -PIRING, PIRES to have an earnest desire or ambition

ASPIRER *n pl.* -S an aspirant

ASPIRIN *n pl.* -S a pain reliever

ASPIRING present participle of aspire

ASPIS *n pl.* -PISES aspic

ASPISH *adj* resembling an asp

ASQUINT *adv* with a sidelong glance

ASRAMA *n pl.* -S ashram

ASS *n pl.* -ES a hoofed mammal

ASSAGAI *v* -GAIED, -GAIING, -GAIS to pierce with a light spear

ASSAI *n pl.* -S a tropical tree

ASSAIL *v* -ED, -ING, -S to attack

ASSAILER *n pl.* -S one that assails

ASSASSIN   *n* pl. -S a murderer

ASSAULT   *v* -ED, -ING, -S to attack

ASSAY   *v* -ED, -ING, -S to attempt

ASSAYER   *n* pl. -S one that assays

ASSEGAI   *v* -GAIED, -GAIING, -GAIS to assagai

ASSEMBLE   *v* -BLED, -BLING, -BLES to come or bring together

ASSEMBLY   *n* pl. -BLIES the act of assembling

ASSENT   *v* -ED, -ING, -S to express agreement

ASSENTER   *n* pl. -S one that assents

ASSENTOR   *n* pl. -S assenter

ASSERT   *v* -ED, -ING, -S to state positively

ASSERTER   *n* pl. -S one that asserts

ASSERTOR   *n* pl. -S asserter

ASSESS   *v* -ED, -ING, -ES to estimate the value of for taxation

ASSESSOR   *n* pl. -S one that assesses

ASSET   *n* pl. -S a useful quality or thing

ASSIGN   *v* -ED, -ING, -S to set apart for a particular purpose

ASSIGNAT   *n* pl. -S one of the notes issued as currency by the French revolutionary government

ASSIGNEE   *n* pl. -S one to whom property or right is legally transferred

ASSIGNER   *n* pl. -S one that assigns

ASSIGNOR   *n* pl. -S one who legally transfers property or right

ASSIST   *v* -ED, -ING, -S to give aid or support to

ASSISTER   *n* pl. -S one that assists

ASSISTOR   *n* pl. -S assister

ASSIZE   *n* pl. -S a session of a legislative or judicial body

ASSLIKE   *adj* resembling an ass

ASSOIL   *v* -ED, -ING, -S to pardon

ASSONANT   *n* pl. -S a word or syllable that resembles another in sound

ASSORT   *v* -ED, -ING, -S to distribute into groups according to kind or class

ASSORTER   *n* pl. -S one that assorts

ASSUAGE   *v* -SUAGED, -SUAGING, -SUAGES to make less severe

ASSUME   *v* -SUMED, -SUMING, SUMES to take on

ASSUMER   *n* pl. -S one that assumes

ASSURE   *v* -SURED, -SURING, -SURES to insure

ASSURED   *n* pl. -S an insured person

ASSURER   *n* pl. -S one that assures

ASSURING   present participle of assure

ASSUROR   *n* pl. -S assurer

ASSWAGE   *v* -SWAGED, -SWAGING, -SWAGES to assuage

ASTASIA   *n* pl. -S inability to stand resulting from muscular incoordination

ASTATIC   *adj* unstable

ASTATINE   *n* pl. -S a radioactive element

ASTER   *n* pl. -S a flowering plant

ASTERIA   *n* pl. -S a gemstone cut to exhibit asterism

ASTERISK   *v* -ED, -ING, -S to mark with an asterisk (a star-shaped printing mark)

ASTERISM   *n* pl. -S a property of certain minerals of showing a starlike luminous figure

ASTERN   *adv* at or toward the rear of a ship

ASTERNAL   *adj* not connected to the sternum

ASTEROID   *n* pl. -S a type of celestial body

ASTHENIA   *n* pl. -S lack of strength

ASTHENIC   *n* pl. -S a slender, lightly muscled person

ASTHENY   *n* pl. -NIES asthenia

ASTHMA   *n* pl. -S a respiratory disease

ASTIR   *adj* moving about

ASTOMOUS   *adj* having no stomata

ASTONISH   *v* -ED, -ING, -ES to fill with sudden wonder or surprise

ASTONY   *v* -TONIED, -TONYING, -TONIES to astonish

ASTOUND   *v* -ED, -ING, -S to amaze

ASTRAGAL   *n* pl. -S a convex molding

ASTRAL   *n* pl. -S a type of oil lamp

ASTRALLY   *adv* in a stellar manner

ASTRAY   *adv* off the right course

ASTRICT   *v* -ED, -ING, -S to restrict

ASTRIDE   *adv* with one leg on each side

ASTRINGE   *v* -TRINGED, -TRINGING, -TRINGES to bind or draw together

ASTUTE *adj* shrewd **ASTUTELY** *adv*

ASTYLAR *adj* having no columns

ASUNDER *adv* into pieces

ASWARM *adj* swarming

ASWIRL *adj* swirling

ASWOON *adj* swooning

ASYLUM *n* pl. -LUMS or -LA an institution for the care of the mentally ill or aged

ASYNDETA *n/pl* omissions of certain conjunctions

AT *prep* in the position of

ATABAL *n* pl. -S a type of drum

ATAGHAN *n* pl. -S yataghan

ATALAYA *n* pl. -S a watchtower

ATAMAN *n* pl. -S a hetman

ATAMASCO *n* pl. -COS a flowering plant

ATARAXIA *n* pl. -S peace of mind

ATARAXIC *n* pl. -S a drug that relieves nervous tension

ATARAXY *n* pl. -RAXIES ataraxia

ATAVIC *adj* pertaining to a remote ancestor

ATAVISM *n* pl. -S the reappearance of a genetic characteristic after several generations of absence

ATAVIST *n* pl. -S an individual displaying atavism

ATAXIA *n* pl. -S loss of muscular coordination

ATAXIC *n* pl. -S one suffering from ataxia

ATAXY *n* pl. ATAXIES ataxia

ATE *n* pl. -S blind impulse or reckless ambition that drives one to ruin

ATECHNIC *adj* lacking technical knowledge

ATELIC *adj* pertaining to a type of verb form

ATELIER *n* pl. -S a workshop or studio

ATHANASY *n* pl. -SIES immortality

ATHEISM *n* pl. -S the belief that there is no God

ATHEIST *n* pl. -S a believer in atheism

ATHELING *n* pl. -S an Anglo-Saxon prince or nobleman

ATHENEUM *n* pl. -S a literary institution

ATHEROMA *n* pl. -MAS or -MATA a disease of the arteries

ATHIRST *adj* having a strong desire

ATHLETE *n* pl. -S one skilled in feats of physical strength and agility **ATHLETIC** *adj*

ATHODYD *n* pl. -S a type of jet engine

ATHWART *adv* from side to side

ATILT *adj* being in a tilted position

ATINGLE *adj* tingling

ATLAS *n* pl. ATLANTES or ATLASES a male figure used as a supporting column

ATLATL *n* pl. -S a device for throwing a spear or dart

ATMA *n* pl. -S atman

ATMAN *n* pl. -S the individual soul in Hinduism

ATOLL *n* pl. -S a ring-shaped coral island

ATOM *n* pl. -S the smallest unit of an element **ATOMIC, ATOMICAL** *adj*

ATOMICS *n/pl* the science dealing with atoms

ATOMISE *v* -ISED, -ISING, -ISES to atomize

ATOMISM *n* pl. -S the theory that the universe is composed of simple, indivisible, minute particles

ATOMIST *n* pl. -S an adherent of atomism

ATOMIZE *v* -IZED, -IZING, -IZES to reduce to a fine spray

ATOMIZER *n* pl. -S a device for atomizing liquids

ATOMY *n* pl. -MIES a tiny particle

ATONAL *adj* lacking tonality **ATONALLY** *adv*

ATONE *v* ATONED, ATONING, ATONES to make amends or reparation **ATONABLE** *adj*

ATONER *n* pl. -S one that atones

ATONIC *n* pl. -S an unaccented syllable or word

ATONING present participle of atone

ATONY *n* pl. -NIES muscular weakness

ATOP *adj* being on or at the top

ATOPY *n* pl. -PIES a type of allergy **ATOPIC** *adj*

ATRAZINE *n* pl. -S an herbicide

ATREMBLE *adj* trembling

ATRESIA *n* pl. -S absence or closure of a natural bodily passage

ATRIA a pl. of atrium

ATRIAL	*adj* pertaining to an atrium	**ATTORNEY**	*n pl.* -NEYS a lawyer
ATRIP	*adj* aweigh	**ATTRACT**	*v* -ED, -ING, -S to cause to approach or adhere
ATRIUM	*n pl.* ATRIA or ATRIUMS the main room of an ancient Roman house	**ATTRITE**	*adj* attrited
ATROCITY	*n pl.* -TIES a heinous act	**ATTRITED**	*adj* worn down by rubbing
ATROPHIA	*n pl.* S a wasting away of the body or any of its parts **ATROPHIC** *adj*	**ATTUNE**	*v* -TUNED, -TUNING, -TUNES to bring into harmony
ATROPHY	*v* -PHIED, -PHYING, -PHIES to waste away	**ATWAIN**	*adv* in two
		ATWEEN	*prep* between
ATROPIN	*n pl.* -S atropine	**ATWITTER**	*adj* twittering
ATROPINE	*n pl.* -S a poisonous alkaloid	**ATYPIC**	*adj* atypical
ATROPISM	*n pl.* -S atropine poisoning	**ATYPICAL**	*adj* not typical
ATTACH	*v* -ED, -ING, -ES to connect as an associated part	**AUBADE**	*n pl.* -S a morning song
		AUBERGE	*n pl.* -S an inn
ATTACHE	*n pl.* -S a diplomatic official	**AUBURN**	*n pl.* -S a reddish brown color
ATTACHER	*n pl.* -S one that attaches	**AUCTION**	*v* -ED, -ING, -S to sell publicly to the highest bidder
ATTACK	*v* -ED, -ING, -S to set upon violently	**AUDACITY**	*n pl.* -TIES boldness
ATTACKER	*n pl.* -S one that attacks	**AUDAD**	*n pl.* -S aoudad
ATTAIN	*v* -ED, -ING, -S to gain or achieve by mental or physical effort	**AUDIBLE**	*n pl.* -S a type of play in football
		AUDIBLY	*adv* in a way so as to be heard
ATTAINER	*n pl.* -S one that attains	**AUDIENCE**	*n pl.* -S a group of listeners or spectators
ATTAINT	*v* -ED, -ING, -S to disgrace	**AUDIENT**	*n pl.* -S one that hears
ATTAR	*n pl.* -S a fragrant oil	**AUDILE**	*n pl.* -S one whose mental imagery is chiefly auditory
ATTEMPER	*v* -ED, -ING, -S to modify the temperature of		
ATTEMPT	*v* -ED, -ING, -S to make an effort to do or accomplish	**AUDING**	*n pl.* -S the process of hearing, recognizing, and interpreting a spoken language
ATTEND	*v* -ED, -ING, -S to be present at	**AUDIO**	*n pl.* -DIOS sound reception or transmission
ATTENDEE	*n pl.* -S an attender		
ATTENDER	*n pl.* -S one that attends	**AUDIT**	*v* -ED, -ING, -S to examine with intent to verify
ATTENT	*adj* heedful		
ATTEST	*v* -ED, -ING, -S to affirm to be true or genuine	**AUDITION**	*v* -ED, -ING, -S to give a trial performance
ATTESTER	*n pl.* -S one that attests	**AUDITIVE**	*n pl.* -S an auditory
ATTESTOR	*n pl.* -S attester	**AUDITOR**	*n pl.* -S one that audits
ATTIC	*n pl.* -S a story or room directly below the roof of a house	**AUDITORY**	*n pl.* -RIES a group of listeners
		AUGEND	*n pl.* -S a number to which another is to be added
ATTICISM	*n pl.* -S a concise and elegant expression	**AUGER**	*n pl.* -S a tool for boring
ATTICIST	*n pl.* -S one who uses atticisms	**AUGHT**	*n pl.* -S a zero
ATTIRE	*v* -TIRED, -TIRING, -TIRES to clothe	**AUGITE**	*n pl.* -S a mineral **AUGITIC** *adj*
		AUGMENT	*v* -ED, -ING, -S to increase
ATTITUDE	*n pl.* -S a state of mind with regard to some matter	**AUGUR**	*v* -ED, -ING, -S to foretell from omens
ATTORN	*v* -ED, -ING, -S to acknowledge a new owner as one's landlord	**AUGURAL**	*adj* pertaining to augury
		AUGURER	*n pl.* -S one that augurs

AUGURY *n* pl. -RIES the practice of auguring

AUGUST *adj* -GUSTER, -GUSTEST inspiring reverence or admiration **AUGUSTLY** *adv*

AUK *n* pl. -S a diving seabird

AUKLET *n* pl. -S a small auk

AULD *adj* AULDER, AULDEST old

AULIC *adj* pertaining to a royal court

AUNT *n* pl. -S the sister of one's father or mother

AUNTHOOD *n* pl. -S the state of being an aunt

AUNTIE *n* pl. -S aunt

AUNTLIKE *adj* resembling an aunt

AUNTLY *adj* -LIER, -LIEST of or suggesting an aunt

AUNTY *n* pl. AUNTIES aunt

AURA *n* pl. -RAS or -RAE an invisible emanation

AURAL *adj* pertaining to the ear **AURALLY** *adv*

AURAR pl. of eyrir

AURATE *adj* having ears

AURATED *adj* aurate

AUREATE *adj* golden

AUREI pl. of aureus

AUREOLA *n* pl. -LAS or -LAE a halo

AUREOLE *v* -OLED, -OLING, -OLES to surround with a halo

AURES pl. of auris

AUREUS *n* pl. -REI a gold coin of ancient Rome

AURIC *adj* pertaining to gold

AURICLE *n* pl. -S an ear or ear-shaped part **AURICLED** *adj*

AURICULA *n* pl. -LAS or -LAE an auricle

AURIFORM *adj* ear-shaped

AURIS *n* pl. AURES the ear

AURIST *n* pl. -S a specialist in diseases of the ear

AUROCHS *n* pl. -ES an extinct European ox

AURORA *n* pl. -RAS or -RAE the rising light of the morning **AURORAL**, **AUROREAN** *adj*

AUROUS *adj* pertaining to gold

AURUM *n* pl. -S gold

AUSPEX *n* pl. -PICES a soothsayer of ancient Rome

AUSPICE *n* pl. -S a favorable omen

AUSTERE *adj* -TERER, -TEREST grave in disposition or appearance

AUSTRAL *adj* pertaining to the south

AUTACOID *n* pl. -S a hormone

AUTARCHY *n* pl. -CHIES absolute rule or power

AUTARKY *n* pl. -KIES national economic self-sufficiency **AUTARKIC**, **AUTARKIK** *adj*

AUTECISM *n* pl. -S the development of the entire life cycle of a parasitic fungus on a single host

AUTHOR *v* -ED, -ING, -S to write

AUTISM *n* pl. -S extreme withdrawal into fantasy **AUTISTIC** *adj*

AUTO *v* -ED, -ING, -S to ride in an automobile

AUTOBAHN *n* pl. -BAHNS or -BAHNEN a German superhighway

AUTOBUS *n* pl. -SES or -SSES a bus

AUTOCADE *n* pl. -S a procession of automobiles

AUTOCOID *n* pl. -S autacoid

AUTOCRAT *n* pl. -S an absolute ruler

AUTODYNE *n* pl. -S a type of electrical circuit

AUTOGAMY *n* pl. -MIES fertilization of a flower by its own pollen

AUTOGENY *n* pl. -NIES the production of living organisms from inanimate matter

AUTOGIRO *n* pl. -ROS a type of airplane

AUTOGYRO *n* pl. -ROS autogiro

AUTOLYZE *v* -LYZED, -LYZING, -LYZES to break down tissue by the action of self-contained enzymes

AUTOMATA *n/pl* robots

AUTOMATE *v* -MATED, -MATING, -MATES to convert to a system of automatic control

AUTONOMY *n* pl. -MIES the state of being self-governing

AUTOPSIC *adj* pertaining to an autopsy

AUTOPSY *v* -SIED, -SYING, -SIES to examine a dead body to determine the cause of death

AUTOSOME *n* pl. -S a type of chromosome

AUTOTOMY *n* pl. -MIES the shedding of a damaged body part

AUTOTYPE *n* pl. -S a type of photographic process

AUTOTYPY *n* pl. -TYPIES autotype

AUTUMN *n* pl. -S a season of the year **AUTUMNAL** *adj*

AUTUNITE *n* pl. -S a mineral

AUXESIS *n* pl. AUXESES an increase in cell size without cell division

AUXETIC *n* pl. -S a substance that promotes auxesis

AUXIN *n* pl. -S a substance used to regulate plant growth **AUXINIC** *adj*

AVA *adv* at all

AVAIL *v* -ED, -ING, -S to be of use or advantage to

AVARICE *n* pl. -S greed

AVAST *interj* — used as a command to stop

AVATAR *n* pl. -S the incarnation of a Hindu deity

AVAUNT *interj* — used as an order of dismissal

AVE *n* pl. -S an expression of greeting or farewell

AVELLAN *adj* having the four arms shaped like filberts — used of a heraldic cross

AVELLANE *adj* avellan

AVENGE *v* AVENGED, AVENGING, AVENGES to exact retribution for

AVENGER *n* pl. -S one that avenges

AVENS *n* pl. -ES a perennial herb

AVENTAIL *n* pl. -S ventail

AVENUE *n* pl. -S a wide street

AVER *v* AVERRED, AVERRING, AVERS to declare positively

AVERAGE *v* -AGED, -AGING, -AGES to calculate the arithmetic mean of

AVERMENT *n* pl. -S the act of averring

AVERRED past tense of aver

AVERRING present participle of aver

AVERSE *adj* opposed; reluctant **AVERSELY** *adv*

AVERSION *n* pl. -S a feeling of repugnance **AVERSIVE** *adj*

AVERT *v* -ED, -ING, -S to turn away

AVGAS *n* pl. -GASES or -GASSES gasoline for airplanes

AVIAN *n* pl. -S a bird

AVIANIZE *v* -IZED, -IZING, -IZES to make less severe by repeated culture in a chick embryo, as a virus

AVIARIST *n* pl. -S the keeper of an aviary

AVIARY *n* pl. -ARIES a large enclosure for live birds

AVIATE *v* -ATED, -ATING, -ATES to fly an aircraft

AVIATION *n* pl. -S the act of aviating

AVIATOR *n* pl. -S one that aviates

AVIATRIX *n* pl. -TRICES or -TRIXES a female aviator

AVICULAR *adj* pertaining to birds

AVID *adj* eager

AVIDIN *n* pl. -S a protein found in egg white

AVIDITY *n* pl. -TIES the state of being avid

AVIDLY *adv* in an avid manner

AVIDNESS *n* pl. -ES avidity

AVIFAUNA *n* pl. -NAS or -NAE the bird life of a particular region

AVIGATOR *n* pl. -S one that navigates aircraft

AVION *n* pl. -S an airplane

AVIONICS *n/pl* the science of electronics applied to aviation **AVIONIC** *adj*

AVISO *n* pl. -SOS advice

AVO *n* pl. AVOS a monetary unit of Macao

AVOCADO *n* pl. -DOS or -DOES the edible fruit of a tropical tree

AVOCET *n* pl. -S a shore bird

AVODIRE *n* pl. -S an African tree

AVOID *v* -ED, -ING, -S to keep away from

AVOIDER *n* pl. -S one that avoids

AVOSET *n* pl. -S avocet

AVOUCH *v* -ED, -ING, -ES to affirm

AVOUCHER *n* pl. -S one that avouches

AVOW *v* -ED, -ING, -S to declare openly **AVOWABLE** *adj* **AVOWABLY, AVOWEDLY** *adv*

AVOWAL *n* pl. -S an open declaration

AVOWER *n* pl. -S one that avows

AVULSE *v* AVULSED, AVULSING, AVULSES to tear off forcibly

AVULSION *n* pl. -S the act of avulsing

AW *interj* — used to express protest, disgust, or disbelief

AWA *adv* away

AWAIT *v* -ED, -ING, -S to wait for

AWAITER *n pl.* -S one that awaits

AWAKE *v* AWAKED or AWOKE, AWOKEN, AWAKING, AWAKES to wake up

AWAKEN *v* -ED, -ING, -S to awake

AWAKENER *n pl.* -S one that awakens

AWAKING present participle of awake

AWARD *v* -ED, -ING, -S to grant as due or merited

AWARDEE *n pl.* -S one that is awarded something

AWARDER *n pl.* -S one that awards

AWARE *adj* having perception or knowledge

AWASH *adj* covered with water

AWAY *adv* from a certain place

AWAYNESS *n pl.* -ES the state of being distant

AWE *v* AWED, AWING or AWEING, AWES to inspire with awe (reverential fear)

AWEARY *adj* weary

AWEATHER *adv* toward the windward side of a vessel

AWED past tense of awe

AWEE *adv* awhile

AWEIGH *adj* hanging just clear of the bottom — used of an anchor

AWELESS *adj* lacking awe

AWESOME *adj* inspiring awe

AWFUL *adj* -FULLER, -FULLEST extremely bad or unpleasant **AWFULLY** *adv*

AWHILE *adv* for a short time

AWHIRL *adj* whirling

AWING a present participle of awe

AWKWARD *adj* -WARDER, -WARDEST lacking skill, dexterity, or grace

AWL *n pl.* -S a pointed tool for making small holes

AWLESS *adj* aweless

AWLWORT *n pl* -S an aquatic plant

AWMOUS *n pl.* AWMOUS alms

AWN *n pl.* -S a bristlelike appendage of certain grasses **AWNED, AWNLESS, AWNY** *adj*

AWNING *n pl.* -S a rooflike canvas cover **AWNINGED** *adj*

AWOKE a past tense of awake

AWOKEN a past participle of awake

AWOL *n pl.* -S one who is absent without leave

AWRY *adv* with a turn or twist to one side

AX *v* -ED, -ING, -ES to work on with an ax (a type of cutting tool)

AXAL *adj* axial

AXE *v* AXED, AXING, AXES to ax

AXEL *n pl.* -S a jump in figure skating

AXEMAN *n pl.* -MEN axman

AXENIC *adj* free from germs

AXES pl. of axis

AXIAL *adj* pertaining to or forming an axis **AXIALLY** *adv*

AXIALITY *n pl.* -TIES the state of being axial

AXIL *n pl.* -S the angle between the upper side of a leaf and its supporting stem

AXILE *adj* axial

AXILLA *n pl.* -LAE or -LAS the armpit

AXILLAR *n pl.* -S a feather on the undersurface of a bird's wing

AXILLARY *n pl.* -LARIES an axillar

AXING present participle of axe

AXIOLOGY *n pl.* -GIES the study of values and value judgments

AXIOM *n pl.* -S a self-evident truth

AXIS *n pl.* AXES a straight line about which a body rotates **AXISED** *adj*

AXIS *n pl.* AXISES an Asian deer

AXITE *n pl.* -S a fiber of an axon

AXLE *n pl.* -S a shaft upon which a wheel revolves **AXLED** *adj*

AXLETREE *n pl.* -S a type of axle

AXLIKE *adj* resembling an ax

AXMAN *n pl.* -MEN one who wields an ax

AXOLOTL *n pl.* -S a salamander of Mexico and western United States

AXON *n pl.* -S the central procoss of a neuron **AXONAL, AXONIC** *adj*

AXONE *n pl.* -S axon

AXOPLASM *n pl.* -S the protoplasm of an axon

AXSEED *n pl.* -S a European herb

AY   *n* pl. AYS aye

AYAH   *n* pl. -S a native maid or nurse in India

AYE   *n* pl. -S an affirmative vote

AYIN   *n* pl. -S a Hebrew letter

AZALEA   *n* pl. -S a flowering shrub

AZAN   *n* pl. -S a Muslim call to prayer

AZIDE   *n* pl. -S a type of chemical compound **AZIDO** *adj*

AZIMUTH   *n* pl. -S an angle of horizontal deviation

AZINE   *n* pl. -S a type of chemical compound

AZO   *adj* containing nitrogen

AZOIC   *adj* pertaining to geologic periods that precede the appearance of life

AZOLE   *n* pl. -S a type of chemical compound

AZON   *n* pl. -S a radio-controlled aerial bomb

AZONAL   *adj* pertaining to a type of a soil group

AZONIC   *adj* not restricted to any particular zone

AZOTE   *n* pl. -S nitrogen **AZOTED** *adj*

AZOTEMIA   *n* pl. -S an excess of nitrogenous substances in the blood **AZOTEMIC** *adj*

AZOTH   *n* pl. -S mercury

AZOTIC   *adj* pertaining to azote

AZOTISE   *v* -TISED, -TISING, -TISES to azotize

AZOTIZE   *v* -TIZED, -TIZING, -TIZES to treat with nitrogen

AZOTURIA   *n* pl. -S an excess of nitrogenous substances in the urine

AZURE   *n* pl. -S a blue color

AZURITE   *n* pl. -S a mineral

AZYGOS   *n* pl. -ES an azygous anatomical part

AZYGOUS   *adj* not being one of a pair

B 3

BA	n pl. -S the eternal soul, in Egyptian mythology	**BABYISH**	adj resembling a baby
		BACCA	n pl. -CAE a berry
BAA	v -ED, -ING, -S to bleat	**BACCARA**	n pl. -S baccarat
BAAL	n pl. -S or -IM a false god	**BACCARAT**	n pl. -S a card game
BAALISM	n pl. -S the worship of a baal	**BACCATE**	adj pulpy like a berry
BABA	n pl. -S a rum cake	**BACCATED**	adj baccate
BABASSU	n pl. -S a palm tree	**BACCHANT**	n pl. -S or -ES a carouser
BABBITT	v -ED, -ING, -S to line with a type of metal	**BACCHIC**	adj riotous
		BACCHIUS	n pl. -CHII a type of metrical foot
BABBLE	v -BLED, -BLING, -BLES to talk idly or excessively	**BACH**	v -ED, -ING, -ES to live as a bachelor
BABBLER	n pl. -S one that babbles		
BABBLING	n pl. -S idle talk	**BACHELOR**	n pl. -S an unmarried man
BABBOOL	n pl. -S babul	**BACILLAR**	adj rod-shaped
BABE	n pl. -S a baby	**BACILLUS**	n pl. -LI any of a class of rod-shaped bacteria
BABEL	n pl. -S confusion		
BABESIA	n pl. -S a parasitic protozoan	**BACK**	v -ED, -ING, -S to support
BABICHE	n pl. -S rawhide thongs	**BACKACHE**	n pl. -S a pain in the back
BABIED	past tense of baby	**BACKBEND**	n pl. -S an acrobatic feat
BABIES	present 3d person sing. of baby	**BACKBITE**	v -BIT, -BITTEN, -BITING, -BITES to slander
BABIRUSA	n pl. -S a wild pig	**BACKBONE**	n pl. -S the spine
BABKA	n pl. -S a coffee cake	**BACKDOOR**	adj secretive
BABOO	n pl. -BOOS a Hindu gentleman	**BACKDROP**	n pl. -S a stage setting
BABOOL	n pl. -S babul	**BACKER**	n pl. -S a supporter
BABOON	n pl. -S a large ape	**BACKFILL**	v -ED, -ING, -S to refill
BABU	n pl. -S baboo	**BACKFIRE**	v -FIRED, -FIRING, -FIRES to result in undesirable consequences
BABUL	n pl. -S a North African tree		
BABUSHKA	n pl. -S a woman's scarf		
BABY	v -BIED, -BYING, -BIES to coddle	**BACKHAND**	v -ED, -ING, -S to strike with the back of the hand
BABYHOOD	n pl. -S the state of being a baby (an infant)	**BACKHOE**	n pl. -S an excavating machine
		BACKING	n pl. -S support

BACKLASH v -ED, -ING, -ES to cause a reaction

BACKLESS adj having no back

BACKLIST n pl. -S a publisher's list of older book titles

BACKLIT adj illuminated from behind

BACKLOG v -LOGGED, -LOGGING, -LOGS to accumulate

BACKMOST adj hindmost

BACKOUT n pl. -S a reversal of launching procedures

BACKPACK v -ED, -ING, -S to hike with a pack on one's back

BACKREST n pl. -S a back support

BACKSAW n pl. -S a type of saw

BACKSEAT n pl. -S a rear seat

BACKSET n pl. -S a setback

BACKSIDE n pl. -S the hind part

BACKSLAP v -SLAPPED, -SLAPPING, -SLAPS to show much approval

BACKSLID past tense of backslide (to revert to sin)

BACKSPIN n pl. -S a backward rotation

BACKSTAY n pl. -STAYS a support for a mast

BACKSTOP v -STOPPED, -STOPPING, -STOPS to bolster

BACKUP n pl. -S a substitute

BACKWARD adv toward the back

BACKWASH v -ED, -ING, -ES to spray water backward

BACKWOOD adj uncouth

BACKYARD n pl. -S an area at the rear of a house

BACON n pl. -S a side of a pig cured and smoked

BACTERIA n/pl microscopic organisms

BACTERIN n pl. -S a vaccine prepared from dead bacteria

BACULINE adj pertaining to a rod

BAD adj WORSE, WORST not good in any way

BAD n pl. -S something that is bad

BADDIE n pl. -S a bad person

BADDY n pl. -DIES baddie

BADE past tense of bid

BADGE v BADGED, BADGING, BADGES to supply with an insignia

BADGER v -ED, -ING, -S to harass

BADGERLY adj bothersome

BADGING present participle of badge

BADINAGE v -NAGED, -NAGING, -NAGES to banter

BADLAND n pl. -S a barren, hilly area

BADLY adv in a bad manner

BADMAN n pl. -MEN an outlaw

BADMOUTH v -ED, -ING, -S to criticize

BADNESS n pl. -ES the state of being bad

BAFF v -ED, -ING, -S to strike under a golf ball

BAFFIES pl. of baffy

BAFFLE v -FLED, -FLING, -FLES to confuse

BAFFLER n pl. -S one that baffles

BAFFY n pl. -FIES a wooden golf club

BAG v BAGGED, BAGGING, BAGS to put into a bag (a flexible container)

BAGASS n pl. -ES bagasse

BAGASSE n pl. -S crushed sugarcane

BAGEL n pl. -S a ring-shaped roll

BAGFUL n pl. -BAGFULS or BAGSFUL as much as a bag will hold

BAGGAGE n pl. -S luggage

BAGGED past tense of bag

BAGGIE n pl. -S the stomach

BAGGING n pl. -S material for making bags

BAGGY adj -GIER, -GIEST loose-fitting
BAGGILY adv

BAGMAN n pl. -MEN a traveling salesman

BAGNIO n pl. -NIOS a brothel

BAGPIPE n pl. -S a wind instrument

BAGPIPER n pl. -S one that plays bagpipes

BAGSFUL a pl. of bagful

BAGUET n pl. -S baguette

BAGUETTE n pl. -S a rectangular gem

BAGWIG n pl. -S a type of wig

BAGWORM n pl. -S the larva of certain moths

BAH interj — an exclamation of disgust

BAHADUR n pl. -S a Hindu title of respect

BAHT n pl. -S a monetary unit of Thailand

BAIDARKA n pl. -S bidarka

BAIL   v -ED, -ING, -S to transfer property temporarily **BAILABLE** adj

BAILEE   n pl. -S a person to whom property is bailed

BAILER   n pl. -S bailor

BAILEY   n pl. -LEYS an outer castle wall

BAILIE   n pl. -S a Scottish magistrate

BAILIFF   n pl. -S a court officer

BAILMENT   n pl. -S the act of bailing

BAILOR   n pl. -S a person who bails property to another

BAILOUT   n pl. -S the act of parachuting from an aircraft

BAILSMAN   n pl. -MEN one who provides security for another

BAIRN   n pl. -S a child **BAIRNISH** adj

BAIRNLY   adj -LIER, -LIEST childish

BAIT   v -ED, -ING, -S to lure

BAITER   n pl. -S one that baits

BAITH   adj both

BAIZA   n pl. -S a monetary unit of Oman

BAIZE   n pl. -S a green, woolen fabric

BAKE   v BAKED, BAKING, BAKES to prepare food in an oven

BAKEMEAT   n pl. -S a pastry

BAKER   n pl. -S one that bakes

BAKERY   n pl. -ERIES a place where baked goods are sold

BAKESHOP   n pl. -S a bakery

BAKING   n pl. -S a quantity baked

BAKLAVA   n pl. -S a Turkish pastry

BAKLAWA   n pl. -S baklava

BAKSHISH   v -ED, -ING, -ES to give a tip

BAL   n pl. -S a balmoral

BALANCE   v -ANCED, -ANCING, -ANCES to weigh

BALANCER   n pl. -S one that balances

BALAS   n pl. -ES a red variety of spinel

BALATA   n pl. -S a tropical tree

BALBOA   n pl. -S a monetary unit of Panama

BALCONY   n pl. -NIES an elevated platform

BALD   adj BALDER, BALDEST lacking hair

BALD   v -ED, -ING, -S to become bald

BALDHEAD   n pl. -S a bald person

BALDISH   adj somewhat bald

BALDLY   adv in a plain and blunt manner

BALDNESS   n pl. -ES the state of being bald

BALDPATE   n pl. -S a baldhead

BALDRIC   n pl. -S a shoulder belt

BALDRICK   n pl. -S baldric

BALE   v BALED, BALING, BALES to form into tightly compressed bundles

BALEEN   n pl. -S whalebone

BALEFIRE   n pl. -S a bonfire

BALEFUL   adj menacing

BALER   n pl. -S one that bales

BALING   present participle of bale

BALISAUR   n pl. -S a long-tailed badger

BALK   v -ED, -ING, -S to stop short and refuse to proceed

BALKER   n pl. -S one that balks

BALKLINE   n pl. -S the starting line in track events

BALKY   adj BALKIER, BALKIEST stubborn **BALKILY** adv

BALL   v -ED, -ING, -S to form into a ball (a spherical object)

BALLAD   n pl. -S a narrative poem or song **BALLADIC** adj

BALLADE   n pl. -S a type of poem

BALLADRY   n pl. -RIES ballad poetry

BALLAST   v -ED, -ING, -S to stabilize

BALLER   n pl. -S one that balls

BALLET   n pl. -S a classical dance form **BALLETIC** adj

BALLISTA   n pl. -TAE an ancient weapon

BALLON   n pl. -S lightness of movement

BALLONET   n pl. -S a small balloon

BALLONNE   n pl. -S a ballet jump

BALLOON   v -ED, -ING, -S to swell out

BALLOT   v -ED, -ING, -S to vote

BALLOTER   n pl. -S one that ballots

BALLROOM   n pl. -S a large room for dancing

BALLY   adj damned

BALLYHOO   v -ED, -ING, -S to promote by uproar

BALLYRAG   v -RAGGED, -RAGGING, -RAGS to bullyrag

BALM   n pl. -S a fragrant resin **BALMLIKE** adj

BALMORAL   *n pl.* -S a type of shoe

BALMY   *adj* BALMIER, BALMIEST mild **BALMILY** *adv*

BALNEAL   *adj* pertaining to baths

BALONEY   *n pl.* -NEYS bologna

BALSA   *n pl.* -S a tropical tree

BALSAM   *v* -ED, -ING, -S to anoint with balsam (an aromatic, resinous substance)

BALSAMIC   *adj* containing balsam

BALUSTER   *n pl.* -S a railing support

BAMBINO   *n pl.* -NOS or -NI a baby

BAMBOO   *n pl.* -BOOS a tropical grass

BAN   *v* BANNED, BANNING, BANS to prohibit

BAN   *n pl.* BANI a Rumanian coin

BANAL   *adj* ordinary **BANALLY** *adv*

BANALITY   *n pl.* -TIES something banal

BANANA   *n pl.* -S an edible fruit

BANAUSIC   *adj* practical

BANCO   *n pl.* -COS a bet in certain gambling games

BAND   *v* -ED, -ING, -S to decorate with flexible strips of material

BANDAGE   *v* -DAGED, -DAGING, -DAGES to cover a wound with a strip of cloth

BANDAGER   *n pl.* -S one that bandages

BANDANA   *n pl.* -S bandanna

BANDANNA   *n pl.* -S a large, colored handkerchief

BANDBOX   *n pl.* -ES a lightweight box

BANDEAU   *n pl.* -DEAUX or -DEAUS a headband

BANDER   *n pl.* -S one that bands

BANDEROL   *n pl.* -S a streamer

BANDIED   past tense of bandy

BANDIES   present 3d person sing. of bandy

BANDIT   *n pl.* -DITS or -DITTI a robber

BANDITRY   *n pl.* -TRIES robbery by bandits

BANDOG   *n pl.* -S a watchdog

BANDORA   *n pl.* -S bandore

BANDORE   *n pl.* -S an ancient lute

BANDSMAN   *n pl.* -MEN a member of a musical band

BANDY   *v* -DIED, -DYING, -DIES to throw to and fro

BANE   *v* BANED, BANING, BANES to kill with poison

BANEFUL   *adj* poisonous

BANG   *v* -ED, -ING, -S to hit sharply

BANGER   *n pl.* -S a sausage

BANGKOK   *n pl.* -S a straw hat

BANGLE   *n pl.* -S a bracelet

BANGTAIL   *n pl.* -S a racehorse

BANI   pl. of ban

BANIAN   *n pl.* -S a Hindu merchant

BANING   present participle of bane

BANISH   *v* -ED, -ING, -ES to expel

BANISHER   *n pl.* -S one that banishes

BANISTER   *n pl.* -S a handrail

BANJO   *n pl.* -JOS or -JOES a musical instrument

BANJOIST   *n pl.* -S one who plays the banjo

BANK   *v* -ED, -ING, -S to keep money in a bank (an institution dealing in money matters) **BANKABLE** *adj*

BANKBOOK   *n pl.* -S a depositor's book

BANKER   *n pl.* -S one who works in a bank

BANKING   *n pl.* -S the business of a bank

BANKNOTE   *n pl.* -S a promissory note

BANKROLL   *v* -ED, -ING, -S to supply the capital for

BANKRUPT   *v* -ED, -ING, -S to impoverish

BANKSIA   *n pl.* -S an Australian plant

BANKSIDE   *n pl.* -S the slope of a river bank

BANNED   past tense of ban

BANNER   *n pl.* -S a flag

BANNERET   *n pl.* -S a small banner

BANNEROL   *n pl.* -S a banderol

BANNET   *n pl.* -S a bonnet

BANNING   present participle of ban

BANNOCK   *n pl.* -S a type of cake

BANNS   *n/pl* a marriage notice

BANQUET   *v* -ED, -ING, -S to feast

BANSHEE   *n pl.* -S a female spirit

BANSHIE   *n pl.* -S banshee

BANTAM   *n pl.* -S a small fowl

BANTER   *v* -ED, -ING, -S to exchange mildly teasing remarks

BANTERER *n pl.* -S one that banters

BANTLING *n pl.* -S a very young child

BANYAN *n pl.* -S an East Indian tree

BANZAI *n pl.* -S a Japanese battle cry

BAOBAB *n pl.* -S a tropical tree

BAPTISE *v* -TISED, -TISING, -TISES to baptize

BAPTISIA *n pl.* -S a flowering plant

BAPTISM *n pl.* -S a Christian ceremony

BAPTIST *n pl.* -S one who baptizes

BAPTIZE *v* -TIZED, -TIZING, -TIZES to administer baptism to

BAPTIZER *n pl.* -S a baptist

BAR *v* BARRED, BARRING, BARS to exclude

BARATHEA *n pl.* -S a silk fabric

BARB *v* -ED, -ING, -S to furnish with a barb (a sharp projection)

BARBAL *adj* pertaining to the beard

BARBARIC *adj* uncivilized

BARBASCO *n pl.* -COS a tropical tree

BARBATE *adj* bearded

BARBE *n pl.* -S a medieval cloth headdress

BARBECUE *v* -CUED, -CUING, -CUES to cook over live coals or an open fire

BARBEL *n pl.* -S an organ of a fish

BARBELL *n pl.* -S an exercise apparatus

BARBER *v* -ED, -ING, -S to cut hair

BARBERRY *n pl.* -RIES a shrub

BARBET *n pl.* -S a tropical bird

BARBETTE *n pl.* -S a platform

BARBICAN *n pl.* -S an outer fortification

BARBICEL *n pl.* -S a part of a feather

BARBITAL *n pl.* -S a sedative

BARBLESS *adj* having no barbs

BARBULE *n pl.* -S a small barb

BARBUT *n pl.* -S a type of helmet

BARBWIRE *n pl.* -S barbed wire

BARD *v* -ED, -ING, -S to armor a horse

BARDE *v* BARDED, BARDING, BARDES to bard

BARDIC *adj* poetic

BARE *adj* BARER, BAREST naked

BARE *v* BARED, BARING, BARES to expose

BAREBACK *adv* without a saddle

BAREFIT *adj* barefoot

BAREFOOT *adj* being without shoes

BAREGE *n pl.* -S a sheer fabric

BAREHEAD *adv* without a hat

BARELY *adv* scarcely

BARENESS *n pl.* -ES the state of being bare

BARER comparative of bare

BARESARK *n pl.* -S an ancient warrior

BAREST superlative of bare

BARF *v* -ED, -ING, -S to vomit

BARFLY *n pl.* -FLIES a drinker who frequents bars

BARGAIN *v* -ED, -ING, -S to discuss terms for selling or buying

BARGE *v* BARGED, BARGING, BARGES to move by barge (a long, large boat)

BARGEE *n pl.* -S a bargeman

BARGEMAN *n pl.* -MEN the master or a crew member of a barge

BARGHEST *n pl.* -S a goblin

BARGING present participle of barge

BARGUEST *n pl.* -S barghest

BARHOP *v* -HOPPED, -HOPPING, -HOPS to visit a number of bars during an evening

BARIC *adj* pertaining to barium

BARILLA *n pl.* -S a chemical compound

BARING present participle of bare

BARITE *n pl.* -S a mineral

BARITONE *n pl.* -S a male singing voice

BARIUM *n pl.* -S a metallic element

BARK *v* -ED, -ING, -S to cry like a dog

BARKEEP *n pl.* -S a bartender

BARKER *n pl.* -S one that barks

BARKLESS *adj* having no bark; unable to bark.

BARKY *adj* BARKIER, BARKIEST covered with bark (tough outer covering of a root or stem)

BARLEDUC *n pl.* -S a fruit jam

BARLESS *adj* having no restraints

BARLEY *n pl.* -LEYS a cereal grass

BARLOW *n pl.* -S a jackknife

BARM *n pl.* -S the foam on malt liquors

BARMAID *n pl.* -S a female bartender

BARMAN *n* pl. -MEN a male bartender

BARMIE *adj* barmy

BARMY *adj* BARMIER, BARMIEST full of barm; frothy

BARN *n* pl. -S a large storage building

BARNACLE *n* pl. -S a shellfish

BARNY *adj* BARNIER, BARNIEST resembling a barn in size, shape, or smell

BARNYARD *n* pl. -S a yard near a barn

BAROGRAM *n* pl. -S a barometric reading

BARON *n* pl. -S a lower member of nobility

BARONAGE *n* pl. -S the rank of a baron

BARONESS *n* pl. -ES the wife of a baron

BARONET *n* pl. -S the holder of a rank below that of a baron

BARONG *n* pl. -S a broad knife

BARONIAL *adj* pertaining to a baron

BARONNE *n* pl. -S a baroness

BARONY *n* pl. -ONIES the domain of a baron

BAROQUE *n* pl. -S an ornate object

BAROUCHE *n* pl. -S a type of carriage

BARQUE *n* pl. -S a sailing vessel

BARRABLE *adj* capable of being barred

BARRACK *v* -ED, -ING, -S to shout boisterously

BARRAGE *v* -RAGED, -RAGING, -RAGES to subject to a massive attack

BARRANCA *n* pl. -S a steep ravine

BARRANCO *n* pl. -COS barranca

BARRATER *n* pl. -S barrator

BARRATOR *n* pl. -S one who commits barratry

BARRATRY *n* pl. -TRIES fraud committed by a master or crew of a ship

BARRE *v* BARRED, BARRING, BARRES to play a type of guitar chord

BARRED past tense of bar

BARREL *v* -RELED, -RELING, -RELS or -RELLED, -RELLING, -RELS to move fast

BARREN *adj* -RENER, -RENEST unproductive **BARRENLY** *adv*

BARREN *n* pl. -S a tract of barren land

BARRET *n* pl. -S a flat cap

BARRETOR *n* pl. -S barrator

BARRETRY *n* pl. -TRIES barratry

BARRETTE *n* pl. -S a hair clip

BARRIER *n* pl. -S an obstacle

BARRING present participle of bar and barre

BARRIO *n* pl. -RIOS a district

BARROOM *n* pl. -S a room where liquor is sold

BARROW *n* pl. -S a type of cart

BARSTOOL *n* pl. -S a stool in a barroom

BARTEND *v* -ED, -ING, -S to tend a barroom

BARTER *v* -ED, -ING, -S to trade

BARTERER *n* pl. -S one that barters

BARTISAN *n* pl. -S bartizan

BARTIZAN *n* pl. -S a small turret

BARWARE *n* pl. -S barroom equipment

BARYE *n* pl. -S a unit of pressure

BARYON *n* pl. -S an atomic particle **BARYONIC** *adj*

BARYTA *n* pl. -S a compound of barium **BARYTIC** *adj*

BARYTE *n* pl. -S a barite

BARYTONE *n* pl. -S baritone

BASAL *adj* pertaining to the foundation **BASALLY** *adv*

BASALT *n* pl. -S a volcanic rock **BASALTIC** *adj*

BASALTES *n* pl. BASALTES unglazed stoneware

BASCULE *n* pl. -S a type of seesaw

BASE *adj* BASER, BASEST morally low

BASE *v* BASED, BASING, BASES to found

BASEBALL *n* pl. -S a type of ball

BASEBORN *adj* of low birth

BASED past tense of base

BASING present participle of base

BASELESS *adj* having no foundation

BASELINE *n* pl. -S a line at either end of a court in certain sports

BASELY *adv* in a base manner

BASEMAN *n* pl. -MEN a certain player in baseball

BASEMENT *n* pl. -S the part of a building below ground level

BASENESS *n* pl. -ES the state of being base

BASENJI *n* pl. -S a barkless dog

BASER	comparative of base
BASES	pl. of basis
BASEST	superlative of base
BASH	v -ED, -ING, -ES to smash
BASHAW	n pl. -S a pasha
BASHER	n pl. -S one that bashes
BASHFUL	adj shy; timid
BASHLYK	n pl. -S a cloth hood
BASIC	n pl. -S a fundamental
BASICITY	n pl. -TIES the state of being alkaline
BASIDIUM	n pl. -IA a structure on a fungus **BASIDIAL** adj
BASIFIER	n pl. -S one that basifies
BASIFY	v -FIED, -FYING, -FIES to alkalize
BASIL	n pl. -S an aromatic herb
BASILAR	adj basal
BASILARY	adj basilar
BASILIC	adj pertaining to a basilica
BASILICA	n pl. -CAS or -CAE an ancient Roman building
BASILISK	n pl. -S a fabled serpent
BASIN	n pl. -S an enclosed body of water **BASINAL, BASINED** adj
BASINET	n pl. -S a medieval helmet
BASION	n pl. -S a part of the skull
BASIS	n pl. BASES the foundation of something
BASK	v -ED, -ING, -S to lie in a pleasant warmth
BASKET	n pl. -S a wooden container
BASKETRY	n pl. -RIES basket weaving
BASOPHIL	n pl. -S a type of cell
BASQUE	n pl. -S a bodice
BASS	n pl. -ES an edible fish
BASSET	v -SETED, -SETING, -SETS or -SETTED, -SETTING, -SETS to outcrop
BASSI	a pl. of basso
BASSINET	n pl. -S a basket used as a baby's crib
BASSIST	n pl. -S a person who plays a double bass
BASSLY	adv in a low-pitched manner
BASSNESS	n pl. -ES the state of being low in pitch
BASSO	n pl. -SOS or -SI a low-pitched singer

BASSOON	n pl. -S a low-pitched instrument
BASSWOOD	n pl. -S a linden tree
BASSY	adj low in pitch
BAST	n pl. -S a woody fiber
BASTARD	n pl. -S an illegitimate child
BASTARDY	n pl. -TARDIES the state of being a bastard
BASTE	v BASTED, BASTING, BASTES to sew loosely together
BASTER	n pl. -S one that bastes
BASTILE	n pl. -S bastille
BASTILLE	n pl. -S a prison
BASTING	n pl. -S the thread used by a baster
BASTION	n pl. -S a fortified place
BAT	v BATTED, BATTING, BATS to hit a baseball
BATBOY	n pl. -BOYS a boy who minds baseball equipment
BATCH	v -ED, -ING, -ES to bring together
BATCHER	n pl. -S one that batches
BATE	v BATED, BATING, BATES to reduce the force of
BATEAU	n pl. -TEAUX a flat-bottomed boat
BATFISH	n pl. -ES a batlike fish
BATFOWL	v -ED, -ING, -S to catch birds at night
BATH	n pl. -S a washing
BATHE	v BATHED, BATHING, BATHES to wash
BATHER	n pl. -S one that bathes
BATHETIC	adj trite
BATHING	present participle of bathe
BATHLESS	adj not having had a bath
BATHOS	n pl. -ES triteness
BATHROBE	n pl. -S a housecoat
BATHROOM	n pl. -S a room in which to bathe
BATHTUB	n pl. -S a tub in which to bathe
BATHYAL	adj pertaining to deep water
BATIK	n pl. -S a dyeing process
BATING	present participle of bate
BATISTE	n pl. -S a sheer fabric
BATLIKE	adj resembling a bat (a flying mammal)

BATMAN   n pl. -MEN an orderly

BATON   n pl. -S a short rod

BATSMAN   n pl. -MEN one who bats

BATT   n pl. -S a sheet of cotton

BATTALIA   n pl. -S a military unit

BATTEAU   n pl. -TEAUX bateau

BATTED   past tense of bat

BATTEN   v -ED, -ING, -S to fasten with strips of wood

BATTENER   n pl. -S one that battens

BATTER   v -ED, -ING, -S to beat repeatedly

BATTERIE   n pl. -S a ballet movement

BATTERY   n pl. -TERIES a device for generating an electric current

BATTIER   comparative of batty

BATTIEST   superlative of batty

BATTIK   n pl. -S batik

BATTING   n pl. -S a batt

BATTLE   v -TLED, -TLING, -TLES to fight

BATTLER   n pl. -S one that battles

BATTU   adj pertaining to a ballet movement

BATTUE   n pl. -S a type of hunt

BATTY   adj -TIER, -TIEST crazy

BATWING   adj shaped like a bat's wing

BAUBEE   n pl. -S bawbee

BAUBLE   n pl. -S a cheap trinket

BAUD   n pl. -S a unit of data transmission speed

BAUDEKIN   n pl. -S a brocaded fabric

BAUDRONS   n pl. -ES a cat

BAULK   v -ED, -ING, -S to balk

BAULKY   adj BAULKIER, BAULKIEST balky

BAUSOND   adj having white marks

BAUXITE   n pl. -S an ore of aluminum BAUXITIC adj

BAWBEE   n pl. -S a Scottish coin

BAWCOCK   n pl. -S a fine fellow

BAWD   n pl. -S a madman

BAWDIER   comparative of bawdy

BAWDIES   pl. of bawdy

BAWDIEST   superlative of bawdy

BAWDILY   adv in a bawdy manner

BAWDRIC   n pl. -S baldric

BAWDRY   n pl. -RIES obscenity

BAWDY   adj BAWDIER, BAWDIEST obscene

BAWDY   n pl. BAWDIES obscene language

BAWL   v -ED, -ING, -S to cry loudly

BAWLER   n pl. -S one that bawls

BAWSUNT   adj bausond

BAWTIE   n pl. -S a dog

BAWTY   n pl. -TIES bawtie

BAY   v -ED, -ING, -S to howl

BAYADEER   n pl. -S bayadere

BAYADERE   n pl. -S a dancing girl

BAYAMO   n pl. -MOS a strong wind

BAYARD   n pl. -S a horse

BAYBERRY   n pl. -RIES a berry tree

BAYONET   v -NETED, -NETING, -NETS or -NETTED, -NETTING, -NETS to stab with a dagger-like weapon

BAYOU   n pl. -S a marshy body of water

BAYWOOD   n pl. -S a coarse mahogany

BAZAAR   n pl. -S a marketplace

BAZAR   n pl. -S bazaar

BAZOOKA   n pl. -S a small rocket launcher

BDELLIUM   n pl. -S a gum resin

BE   v present sing. 1st person AM, 2d ARE or ART, 3d IS, past sing. 1st and 3d persons WAS, 2d WERE or WAST or WERT, past participle BEEN, present participle BEING to have actuality

BEACH   v -ED, -ING, -ES to drive ashore

BEACHBOY   n pl. -BOYS a male beach attendant

BEACHY   adj BEACHIER, BEACHIEST sandy or pebbly

BEACON   v -ED, -ING, -S to warn or guide

BEAD   v -ED, -ING, -S to adorn with beads (round pieces of glass)

BEADIER   comparative of beady

BEADIEST   superlative of beady

BEADILY   adv in a beady manner

BEADING   n pl. -S beaded material

BEADLE   n pl. -S a parish official

BEADLIKE   adj beady

BEADMAN   n pl. -MEN beadsman

BEADROLL   n pl. -S a list of names

BEADSMAN *n* pl. -MEN one who prays for another

BEADWORK *n* pl. -S beading

BEADY *adj* BEADIER, BEADIEST resembling beads

BEAGLE *n* pl. -S a small hound

BEAK *n* pl. -S a bird's bill **BEAKED, BEAKLESS, BEAKLIKE** *adj*

BEAKER *n* pl. -S a large cup

BEAKY *adj* BEAKIER, BEAKIEST resembling a beak

BEAM *v* -ED, -ING, -S to emit in beams (rays of light)

BEAMIER comparative of beamy

BEAMIEST superlative of beamy

BEAMILY *adv* in a beamy manner

BEAMISH *adj* cheerful

BEAMLESS *adj* having no beam

BEAMLIKE *adj* resembling a beam

BEAMY *adj* BEAMIER, BEAMIEST beaming

BEAN *v* -ED, -ING, -S to hit on the head

BEANBAG *n* pl. -S a small cloth bag

BEANBALL *n* pl. -S a baseball thrown at the head

BEANERY *n* pl. -ERIES a cheap restaurant

BEANIE *n* pl. -S a small cap

BEANLIKE *adj* resembling a bean

BEANO *n* pl. BEANOS a form of bingo

BEANPOLE *n* pl. -S a thin pole

BEAR *v* BORE, BORNE or BORN, BEARING, BEARS to endure **BEARABLE** *adj* **BEARABLY** *adv*

BEARCAT *n* pl. -S a small mammal

BEARD *v* -ED, -ING, -S to oppose boldly

BEARER *n* pl. -S one that bears

BEARING *n* pl. -S demeanor

BEARISH *adj* resembling a bear (a large mammal)

BEARLIKE *adj* bearish

BEARSKIN *n* pl. -S the skin of a bear

BEAST *n* pl. -S an animal

BEASTIE *n* pl. -S a tiny animal

BEASTLY *adj* -LIER, -LIEST resembling a beast

BEAT *v* BEAT, BEATEN, BEATING, BEATS to strike repeatedly **BEATABLE** *adj*

BEATER *n* pl. -S one that beats

BEATIFIC *adj* blissful

BEATIFY *v* -FIED, -FYING, -FIES to make happy

BEATING *n* pl. -S a defeat

BEATLESS *adj* having no rhythm

BEATNIK *n* pl. -S a nonconformist

BEAU *n* pl. BEAUX or BEAUS a boyfriend **BEAUISH** *adj*

BEAUT *n* pl. -S something beautiful

BEAUTIFY *v* -FIED, -FYING, -FIES to make beautiful

BEAUTY *n* pl. -TIES one that is lovely

BEAUX a pl. of beau

BEAVER *v* -ED, -ING, -S to work hard

BEBEERU *n* pl. -S a tropical tree

BEBLOOD *v* -ED, ING, -S to cover with blood

BEBOP *n* pl. -S a type of jazz

BEBOPPER *n* pl. -S one that likes bebop

BECALM *v* -ED, -ING, -S to make calm

BECAME past tense of become

BECAP *v* -CAPPED, -CAPPING, CAPS to put a cap on

BECARPET *v* -ED, -ING, -S to cover with a carpet

BECAUSE *conj* for the reason that

BECHALK *v* -ED, -ING, -S to cover with chalk

BECHAMEL *n* pl. -S a white sauce

BECHANCE *v* -CHANCED, -CHANCING, -CHANCES to befall

BECHARM *v* -ED, -ING, -S to hold under a spell

BECK *v* -ED, -ING, -S to beckon

BECKET *n* pl. -S a securing rope

BECKON *v* -ED, -ING, -S to signal by sign or gesture

BECKONER *n* pl. -S one that beckons

BECLAMOR *v* -ED, -ING, -S to clamor loudly

BECLASP *v* -ED, -ING, -S to embrace

BECLOAK *v* -ED, -ING, -S to place a cloak on

BECLOG *v* -CLOGGED, -CLOGGING, -CLOGS to clog thoroughly

BECLOTHE   *v* -CLOTHED, -CLOTHING, -CLOTHES to clothe

BECLOUD   *v* -ED, -ING, -S to make cloudy

BECLOWN   *v* -ED, -ING, -S to cause to appear ridiculous

BECOME   *v* -CAME, -COMING, -COMES to come to be

BECOMING   *n* pl. -S a process of change

BECOWARD   *v* -ED, -ING, -S to accuse of cowardice

BECRAWL   *v* -ED, -ING, -S to crawl over

BECRIME   *v* -CRIMED, -CRIMING, -CRIMES to make guilty of a crime

BECROWD   *v* -ED, -ING, -S to crowd closely

BECRUST   *v* -ED, -ING, -S to cover with a crust

BECUDGEL   *v* -GELLED, -GELLING, -GELS or -GELED, -GELING, -GELS to cudgel thoroughly

BECURSE   *v* -CURSED or -CURST, -CURSING, -CURSES to curse severely

BED   *v* BEDDED, BEDDING, BEDS to provide with a bed (a piece of furniture used for sleeping)

BEDABBLE   *v* -BLED, -BLING, -BLES to soil

BEDAMN   *v* -ED, -ING, -S to swear at

BEDARKEN   *v* -ED, -ING, -S to darken

BEDAUB   *v* -ED, -ING, -S to besmear

BEDAZZLE   *v* -ZLED, -ZLING, -ZLES to confuse

BEDBUG   *n* pl. -S a bloodsucking insect

BEDCHAIR   *n* pl. -S a chair near a bed

BEDCOVER   *n* pl. -S a cover for a bed

BEDDED   past tense of bed

BEDDER   *n* pl. -S one that makes up beds

BEDDING   *n* pl. -S material for making up a bed

BEDEAFEN   *v* -ED, -ING, -S to deafen

BEDECK   *v* -ED, -ING, -S to clothe with finery

BEDEL   *n* pl. -S an English university officer

BEDELL   *n* pl. -S bedel

BEDEMAN   *n* pl. -MEN beadsman

BEDESMAN   *n* pl. -MEN beadsmen

BEDEVIL   *v* -ILED, -ILING, -ILS or -ILLED, -ILLING, -ILS to harass

BEDEW   *v* -ED, -ING, -S to wet with dew

BEDFAST   *adj* confined to bed

BEDFRAME   *n* pl. -S the frame of a bed

BEDGOWN   *n* pl. -S a dressing gown

BEDIAPER   *v* -ED, -ING, -S to ornament with a kind of design

BEDIGHT   *v* -ED, -ING, -S to bedeck

BEDIM   *v* -DIMMED, -DIMMING, -DIMS to make dim

BEDIMPLE   *v* -PLED, -PLING, -PLIES to dimple

BEDIRTY   *v* -DIRTIED, -DIRTYING, -DIRTIES to make dirty

BEDIZEN   *v* -ED, -ING, -S to dress gaudily

BEDLAM   *n* pl. -S confusion

BEDLAMP   *n* pl. -S a lamp near a bed

BEDLESS   *adj* having no bed

BEDLIKE   *adj* resembling a bed

BEDMAKER   *n* pl. -S one that makes beds

BEDMATE   *n* pl. -S a bed companion

BEDOTTED   *adj* covered with dots

BEDOUIN   *n* pl. -S a nomadic Arab

BEDPAN   *n* pl. -S a toilet pan

BEDPLATE   *n* pl. -S a frame support

BEDPOST   *n* pl. -S a post of a bed

BEDQUILT   *n* pl. -S a quilt for a bed

BEDRAIL   *n* pl. -S a board at the side of a bed

BEDRAPE   *v* -DRAPED, -DRAPING, -DRAPES to drape

BEDRENCH   *v* -ED, -ING, -ES to drench thoroughly

BEDRID   *adj* bedfast

BEDRIVEL   *v* -ELLED, -ELLING, -ELS or -ELED, -ELING, -ELS to cover with saliva

BEDROCK   *n* pl. -S the rock under soil

BEDROLL   *n* pl. -S a portable roll of bedding

BEDROOM   *n* pl. -S a room for sleeping

BEDRUG   *v* -DRUGGED, -DRUGGING, -DRUGS to make sleepy

BEDSIDE   *n* pl. -S the side of a bed

BEDSONIA   *n* pl. -S a virus

BEDSORE   *n* pl. -S a type of sore

BEDSTAND   *n* pl. -S a table next to a bed

BEDSTEAD   *n* pl. -S a support for a bed

BEDSTRAW   *n* pl. -S a woody herb

BEDTICK   *n* pl. -S the cloth case of a mattress

BEDTIME *n* pl. -S a time for going to bed

BEDUIN *n* pl. -S bedouin

BEDUMB *v* -ED, -ING, -S to render speechless

BEDUNCE *v* -DUNCED, -DUNCING, -DUNCES to make a dunce of

BEDWARD *adv* toward bed

BEDWARDS *adv* bedward

BEDWARF *v* -ED, -ING, -S to cause to appear small by comparison

BEE *n* pl. -S a winged insect

BEEBEE *n* pl. -S a pellet

BEEBREAD *n* pl. -S a pollen mixture

BEECH *n* pl. -ES a type of tree **BEECHEN** *adj*

BEECHNUT *n* pl. -S the nut of a beech

BEECHY *adj* BEECHIER, BEECHIEST abounding in beeches

BEEF *n* pl. BEEFS or BEEVES a steer or cow fattened for food

BEEF *v* -ED, -ING, -S to add bulk to

BEEFCAKE *n* pl. -S pictures of male physiques

BEEFIER comparative of beefy

BEEFIEST superlative of beefy

BEEFILY *adv* in a beefy manner

BEEFLESS *adj* being without beef

BEEFWOOD *n* pl. -S a hardwood tree

BEEFY *adj* BEEFIER, BEEFIEST brawny

BEEHIVE *n* pl. -S a hive for bees

BEELIKE *adj* resembling a bee

BEELINE *n* pl. -S a direct route

BEEN past participle of be

BEEP *v* -ED, -ING, -S to honk a horn

BEEPER *n* pl. -S a signaling device

BEER *n* pl. -S an alcoholic beverage

BEERY *adj* BEERIER, BEERIEST affected by beer

BEESWAX *n* pl. -ES a type of wax

BEESWING *n* pl. -S a crust that forms on old wines

BEET *n* pl. -S a garden plant

BEETLE *v* -TLED, -TLING, -TLES to jut out

BEETROOT *n* pl. -S the root of the beet

BEEVES a pl. of beef

BEFALL *v* -FELL, -FALLEN, -FALLING, -FALLS to happen to

BEFINGER *v* -ED, -ING, -S to touch all over

BEFIT *v* -FITTED, -FITTING, -FITS to be suitable to

BEFLAG *v* -FLAGGED, -FLAGGING, -FLAGS to deck with flags

BEFLEA *v* -ED, -ING, -S to infest with fleas

BEFLECK *v* -ED, -ING, -S to fleck

BEFLOWER *v* -ED, -ING, -S to cover with flowers

BEFOG *v* -FOGGED, -FOGGING, -FOGS to envelop in fog

BEFOOL *v* -ED, -ING, -S to deceive

BEFORE *adv* previously

BEFOUL *v* -ED, -ING, -S to foul

BEFOULER *n* pl. -S one that befouls

BEFRET *v* -FRETTED, -FRETTING, -FRETS to gnaw

BEFRIEND *v* -ED, -ING, -S to act as a friend to

BEFRINGE *v* -FRINGED, -FRINGING, -FRINGES to border with a fringe

BEFUDDLE *v* -DLED, -DLING, -DLES to confuse

BEG *v* BEGGED, BEGGING, BEGS to plead

BEGALL *v* -ED, -ING, -S to make sore by rubbing

BEGAN past tense of begin

BEGAZE *v* -GAZED, -GAZING, -GAZES to gaze at

BEGET *v* -GOT or -GAT, -GOTTEN, -GETTING, -GETS to cause to exist

BEGETTER *n* pl. -S one that begets

BEGGAR *v* -ED, -ING, -S to impoverish

BEGGARLY *adj* very poor

BEGGARY *n* pl. -GARIES extreme poverty

BEGGED past tense of beg

BEGGING present participle of beg

BEGIN *v* -GAN, -GUN, -GINNING, -GINS to start

BEGINNER *n* pl. -S one that begins

BEGIRD *v* -GIRT or -GIRDED, -GIRDING, -GIRDS to surround

BEGIRDLE *v* -DLED -DLING, -DLES to surround

BEGLAD *v* -GLADDED, -GLADDING, -GLADS to gladden

BEGLOOM *v* -ED, -ING, -S to make gloomy

BEGONE *interj* — used as an order of dismissal

BEGONIA *n pl.* -S a tropical herb

BEGORAH *interj* begorra

BEGORRA *interj* — used as a mild oath

BEGORRAH *interj* begorra

BEGOT a past tense of beget

BEGOTTEN past participle of beget

BEGRIM *v* -GRIMMED, -GRIMMING, -GRIMS to begrime

BEGRIME *v* -GRIMED, -GRIMING, -GRIMES to dirty

BEGROAN *v* -ED, -ING, -S to groan at

BEGRUDGE *v* -GRUDGED, -GRUDGING, -GRUDGES to concede reluctantly

BEGUILE *v* -GUILED, -GUILING, -GUILES to deceive

BEGUILER *n pl.* -S one that beguiles

BEGUINE *n pl.* -S a lively dance

BEGULF *v* -ED, -ING, -S to engulf

BEGUM *n pl.* -S a Muslim lady of high rank

BEGUN past participle of begin

BEHALF *n pl.* -HALVES interest, support, or benefit

BEHAVE *v* -HAVED, -HAVING, -HAVES to act properly

BEHAVER *n pl.* -S one that behaves

BEHAVIOR *n pl.* -S demeanor

BEHEAD *v* -ED, -ING, -S to cut off the head of

BEHELD past tense of behold

BEHEMOTH *n pl.* -S a large beast

BEHEST *n pl.* -S a command

BEHIND *n pl.* -S the buttocks

BEHOLD *v* -HELD, -HOLDING, -HOLDS to view

BEHOLDEN *adj* indebted

BEHOLDER *n pl.* -S one that beholds

BEHOOF *n pl.* -HOOVES use, advantage, or benefit

BEHOOVE *v* -HOOVED, -HOOVING, -HOOVES to be proper for

BEHOVE *v* -HOVED, -HOVING, -HOVES to behoove

BEHOWL *v* -ED, -ING, -S to howl at

BEIGE *n pl.* -S a tan color

BEIGY *adj* of the color beige

BEING *n pl.* -S somthing that exists

BEJEWEL *v* -ELED, -ELING, -ELS or -ELLED, -ELLING, -ELS to adorn with jewels

BEJUMBLE *v* -BLED, -BLING, -BLES to jumble

BEKISS *v* -ED, -ING, -ES to cover with kisses

BEKNIGHT *v* -ED, -ING, -S to raise to knighthood

BEKNOT *v* -KNOTTED, -KNOTTING, -KNOTS to tie in knots

BEL *n pl.* -S a unit of power

BELABOR *v* -ED, -ING, -S to discuss for an absurd amount of time

BELABOUR *v* -ED, -ING, -S to belabor

BELACED *adj* adorned with lace

BELADY *v* -DIED, -DYING, -DIES to apply the title of lady to

BELATED *adj* late or too late

BELAUD *v* -ED, -ING, -S to praise

BELAY *v* -ED, -ING, -S to fasten a rope

BELCH *v* -ED, -ING, -ES to expel gas through the mouth

BELCHER *n pl.* -S one that belches

BELDAM *n pl.* -S an old woman

BELDAME *n pl.* -S beldam

BELEAP *v* -LEAPT or -LEAPED, -LEAPING, -LEAPS to leap upon

BELFRY *n pl.* -FRIES a bell tower
BELFRIED *adj*

BELGA *n pl.* -S a former Belgian monetary unit

BELIE *v* -LIED, -LYING, -LIES to misrepresent

BELIEF *n pl.* -S acceptance of the truth or actuality of something

BELIER *n pl.* -S one that belies

BELIEVE *v* -LIEVED, -LIEVING, -LIEVES to accept as true or real

BELIEVER *n pl.* -S one that believes

BELIKE *adv* perhaps

BELIQUOR *v* -ED, -ING, -S to soak with liquor

BELITTLE *v* -TLED, -TLING, -TLES to disparage

BELIVE *adv* in due time

BELL *v* -ED, -ING, -S to provide with a bell (a ringing device)

BELLBIRD *n pl.* -S a tropical bird

BELLBOY *n pl.* -BOYS a hotel's errand boy

BELLE *n pl.* -S an attractive woman

BELLEEK *n pl.* -S a very thin translucent porcelain

BELLHOP *n pl.* -S a bellboy

BELLIED past tense of belly

BELLIES present 3d person sing. of belly

BELLMAN *n pl.* -MEN a town crier

BELLOW *v* -ED, -ING, -S to shout in a deep voice

BELLOWER *n pl.* -S one that bellows

BELLPULL *n pl.* -S a cord pulled to ring a bell

BELLWORT *n pl.* -S a flowering plant

BELLY *v* -LIED, -LYING, -LIES to swell out

BELLYFUL *n pl.* -S an excessive amount

BELONG *v* -ED, -ING, -S to be a member of

BELOVED *n pl.* -S one who is loved

BELOW *n pl.* -S something that is beneath

BELT *v* -ED, -ING, -S to fasten with a belt (a strap or band worn around the waist)

BELTLESS *adj* having no belt

BELTING *n pl.* -S material for belts

BELTLINE *n pl.* -S the waistline

BELTWAY *n pl.* -WAYS a highway around an urban area

BELUGA *n pl.* -S a white sturgeon

BELYING present participle of belie

BEMA *n pl.* -MATA or -MAS a platform in a synagogue

BEMADAM *v* -ED, -ING, -S to call by the title of madam

BEMADDEN *v* -ED, -ING, -S to madden

BEMEAN *v* -ED, -ING, -S to debase

BEMINGLE *v* -GLED, -GLING, -GLES to mix together

BEMIRE *v* -MIRED, -MIRING, -MIRES to soil with mud

BEMIST *v* -ED, -ING, -S to envelop in a mist

BEMIX *v* -MIXED or -MIXT, -MIXING, -MIXES to mix thoroughly

BEMOAN *v* -ED, -ING, -S to lament

BEMOCK *v* -ED, -ING, -S to mock

BEMUDDLE *v* -DLED, -DLING, -DLES to confuse completely

BEMURMUR *v* -ED, -ING, -S to murmur at

BEMUSE *v* -MUSED, -MUSING, -MUSES to confuse

BEMUZZLE *v* -ZLED, -ZLING, -ZLES to muzzle

BEN *n pl.* -S an inner room

BENAME *v* -NAMED, -NEMPT or -NEMPTED, -NAMING, -NAMES to name

BENCH *v* -ED, -ING, -ES to take a player out of a game

BENCHER *n pl.* -S a magistrate

BEND *v* BENT or BENDED, BENDING, BENDS to curve **BENDABLE** *adj*

BENDAY *v* -ED, -ING, -S to reproduce using a certain process

BENDEE *n pl.* -S bendy

BENDER *n pl.* -S one that bends

BENDWAYS *adv* bendwise

BENDWISE *adv* diagonally

BENDY *n pl.* -DYS okra

BENE *n pl.* -S benne

BENEATH *prep* under

BENEDICK *n pl.* -S benedict

BENEDICT *n pl.* -S a newly married man

BENEFIC *adj* kindly

BENEFICE *v* -FICED, -FICING, -FICES to endow with land

BENEFIT *v* -FITED, -FITING, -FITS or -FITTED, -FITTING, -FITS to be helpful or useful to

BENEMPT a past participle of bename

BENEMPTED a past participle of bename

BENIGN *adj* kind **BENIGNLY** *adv*

BENISON *n pl.* -S a blessing

BENJAMIN *n pl.* -S benzoin

BENNE *n pl.* -S the sesame plant

BENNET *n pl.* -S a perennial herb

BENNI *n pl.* -S benne

BENNY *n pl.* -NIES an amphetamine tablet

BENT *n pl.* -S an inclination

BENTHAL *adj* benthic

BENTHIC *adj* pertaining to oceanic depths

BENTHOS *n pl.* -ES benthic sea life

BENTWOOD n pl. -S wood bent for use in furniture

BENUMB v -ED, -ING, -S to make numb

BENZAL adj pertaining to a certain chemical group

BENZENE n pl. -S a volatile liquid

BENZIDIN n pl. -S a hydrocarbon

BENZIN n pl. -S benzine

BENZINE n pl. -S a volatile liquid

BENZOATE n pl. -S a chemical salt

BENZOIN n pl. -S a gum resin **BENZOIC** adj

BENZOL n pl. -S a benzene

BENZOLE n pl. -S benzol

BENZOYL n pl. -S a univalent chemical radical

BENZYL n pl. -S a univalent chemical radical **BENZYLIC** adj

BEPAINT v -ED, -ING, -S to tinge

BEPIMPLE v -PLED, -PLING, -PLES to cover with pimples

BEQUEATH v -ED, -ING, -S to grant by testament

BEQUEST n pl. -S a legacy

BERASCAL v -ED, -ING, -S to accuse of being a rascal

BERAKE v -RAKED, -RAKING, -RAKES to rake all over

BERATE v -RATED, -RATING, -RATES to scold severely

BERBERIN n pl. -S a medicinal alkaloid

BERCEUSE n pl. -S a lullaby

BEREAVE v -REAVED or -REFT, -REAVING, -REAVES to deprive

BEREAVER n pl. -S one that bereaves

BERET n pl. -S a soft, flat cap

BERETTA n pl. -S biretta

BERG n pl. -S an iceberg

BERGAMOT n pl. -S a citrus tree

BERHYME v -RHYMED, -RHYMING, -RHYMES to compose in rhyme

BERIBERI n pl. -S a thiamine deficiency disease

BERIME v -RIMED, -RIMING, -RIMES to berhyme

BERINGED adj adorned with rings

BERLIN n pl. -S a type of carriage

BERLINE n pl. -S a limousine

BERM n pl. -S a ledge

BERME n pl. -S berm

BERNICLE n pl. -S a wild goose

BEROBED adj wearing a robe

BEROUGED adj obviously or thickly rouged

BERRETTA n pl. -S biretta

BERRY v -RIED, -RYING, -RIES to produce berries (fleshy fruits)

BERSEEM n pl. -S a clover

BERSERK n pl. -S a fierce warrior

BERTH v -ED, -ING, -S to provide with a mooring

BERTHA n pl. -S a wide collar

BERYL n pl. -S a green mineral **BERYLINE** adj

BESCORCH v -ED, -ING, -ES to scorch

BESCOUR v -ED, -ING, -S to scour thoroughly

BESCREEN v -ED, -ING, -S to screen

BESEECH v -SOUGHT or -SEECHED, -SEECHING, -SEECHES to implore

BESEEM v -ED, -ING, -S to be suitable

BESET v -SET, -SETTING, -SETS to assail

BESETTER n pl. -S one that besets

BESHADOW v -ED, -ING, -S to cast a shadow on

BESHAME v -SHAMED, -SHAMING, -SHAMES to put to shame

BESHIVER v -ED, -ING, -S to break into small pieces

BESHOUT v -ED, -ING, -S to shout at

BESHREW v -ED, -ING, -S to curse

BESHROUD v -ED, -ING, -S to cover

BESIDE prep next to

BESIDES adv in addition

BESIEGE v -SIEGED, -SIEGING, -SIEGES to surround

BESIEGER n pl. -S one that besieges

BESLAVED adj filled with slaves

BESLIME v -SLIMED, -SLIMING, -SLIMES to cover with slime

BESMEAR v -ED, -ING, -S to smear over

BESMILE v -SMILED, -SMILING, -SMILES to smile on

BESMIRCH v -ED, -ING, -ES to dirty

BESMOKE v -SMOKED, -SMOKING, -SMOKES to soil with smoke

BESMOOTH v -ED, -ING, -S to smooth

BESMUDGE v -SMUDGED, -SMUDGING, -SMUDGES to smudge

BESMUT v -SMUTTED, -SMUTTING, -SMUTS to blacken with smut

BESNOW v -ED, -ING, -S to cover with snow

BESOM n pl. -S a broom

BESOOTHE v -SOOTHED, -SOOTHING -SOOTHES to soothe

BESOT v -SOTTED, -SOTTING, -SOTS to stupefy

BESOUGHT a past tense of beseech

BESPEAK v -SPOKE or -SPAKE, -SPOKEN, -SPEAKING, -SPEAKS to claim in advance

BESPOUSE v -SPOUSED, -SPOUSING, -SPOUSES to marry

BESPREAD v -SPREAD, -SPREADING, -SPREADS to spread over

BESPRENT adj sprinkled over

BEST v -ED, -ING, -S to outdo

BESTEAD v -ED, -ING, -S to help

BESTIAL adj pertaining to beasts

BESTIARY n pl. -ARIES a collection of animal fables

BESTIR v -STIRRED, -STIRRING, -STIRS to rouse

BESTOW v -ED, -ING, -S to present as a gift

BESTOWAL n pl. -S a gift

BESTREW v -STREWED, -STREWN, -STREWING, -STREWS to scatter

BESTRIDE v -STRODE or -STRID, -STRIDDEN, -STRIDING, -STRIDES to straddle

BESTROW v -STROWED, -STROWN, -STROWING, -STROWS to bestrew

BESTUD v -STUDDED, -STUDDING, -STUDS to dot

BESWARM v -ED, -ING, -S to swarm all over

BET v BET or BETTED, BETTING, BETS to wager

BETA n pl. -S a Greek letter

BETAINE n pl. -S an alkaloid

BETAKE v -TOOK, -TAKEN, -TAKING, -TAKES to cause to go

BETATRON n pl. -S an electron accelerator

BETATTER v -ED, -ING, -S to tatter

BETAXED adj burdened with taxes

BETEL n pl. -S a climbing plant

BETELNUT n pl. -S a seed chewed as a stimulant

BETH n pl. -S a Hebrew letter

BETHANK v -ED, -ING, -S to thank

BETHEL n pl. -S a holy place

BETHINK v -THOUGHT, -THINKING, -THINKS to consider

BETHORN v -ED, -ING, -S to fill with thorns

BETHUMP v -ED, -ING, -S to thump soundly

BETIDE v -TIDED, -TIDING, -TIDES to befall

BETIME adv betimes

BETIMES adv soon

BETISE n pl. -S stupidity

BETOKEN v -ED, -ING, -S to indicate

BETON n pl. -S a type of concrete

BETONY n pl. -NIES a European herb

BETOOK past tense of betake

BETRAY v -ED, -ING, -S to aid an enemy of

BETRAYAL n pl. -S the act of betraying

BETRAYER n pl. -S one that betrays

BETROTH v -ED, -ING, -S to engage to marry

BETTA n pl. -S a freshwater fish

BETTED a past tense of bet

BETTER v -ED, -ING, -S to improve

BETTING present participle of bet

BETTOR n pl. -S one that bets

BETWEEN prep in the space that separates

BETWIXT prep between

BEUNCLED adj having many uncles

BEVATRON n pl. -S a proton accelerator

BEVEL v -ELED, -ELING, -ELS or -ELLED, -ELLING, -ELS to cut at an angle

BEVELER n pl. -S one that bevels

BEVELLER n pl. -S beveler

BEVELLING a present participle of bevel

BEVERAGE n pl. -S a liquid for drinking

BEVIES pl. of bevy

BEVOMIT v -ED, -ING, -S to vomit all over

BEVOR n pl. -S a piece of armor for the lower face

BEVY n pl. BEVIES a group

BEWAIL   v -ED, -ING, -S to lament

BEWAILER   n pl. -S one that bewails

BEWARE   v -WARED, -WARING, -WARES to be careful

BEWEARY   v -WEARIED, -WEARYING, -WEARIES to make weary

BEWEEP   v -WEPT, -WEEPING, -WEEPS to lament

BEWIG   v -WIGGED, -WIGGING, -WIGS to adorn with a wig

BEWILDER   v -ED, -ING, -S to confuse

BEWINGED   adj having wings

BEWITCH   v -ED, -ING, -ES to affect by witchcraft or magic

BEWORM   v -ED, -ING, -S to infest with worms

BEWORRY   v -RIED, -RYING, -RIES to worry

BEWRAP   v -WRAPPED or -WRAPT, -WRAPPING, -WRAPS to wrap completely

BEWRAY   v -ED, -ING, -S to divulge

BEWRAYER   n pl. -S one that bewrays

BEY   n pl. BEYS a Turkish ruler

BEYLIC   n pl. -S the domain of a bey

BEYLIK   n pl. -S beylic

BEYOND   n pl. -S something that lies farther ahead

BEZANT   n pl. -S a coin of ancient Rome

BEZEL   n pl. -S a slanted surface

BEZIL   n pl. -S bezel

BEZIQUE   n pl. -S a card game

BEZOAR   n pl. -S a gastric mass

BEZZANT   n pl. -S bezant

BHAKTA   n pl. -S one who practices bhakti

BHAKTI   n pl. -S a selfless devotion to a deity in Hinduism

BHANG   n pl. -S the hemp plant

BHEESTIE   n pl. -S bheesty

BHEESTY   n pl. -TIES a water carrier

BHISTIE   n pl. -S bheesty

BHOOT   n pl. -S bhut

BHUT   n pl. -S a small whirlwind

BI   n pl. -S a bisexual

BIACETYL   n pl. -S a chemical flavor enhancer

BIALY   n pl. -ALYS an onion roll

BIANNUAL   adj occurring twice a year

BIAS   v -ASED, -ASING, -ASES or -ASSED, -ASSING -ASSES to prejudice **BIASEDLY** adv

BIASNESS   n pl. -ES the state of being slanted

BIATHLON   n pl. -S an athletic contest

BIAXAL   adj biaxial

BIAXIAL   adj having two axes

BIB   v BIBBED, BIBBING, BIBS to tipple

BIBASIC   adj dibasic

BIBB   n pl. -S a mast support

BIBBED   past tense of bib

BIBBER   n pl. -S a tippler

BIBBERY   n pl. -BERIES the act of bibbing

BIBBING   present participle of bib

BIBCOCK   n pl. -S a type of faucet

BIBELOT   n pl. -S a trinket

BIBLE   n pl. -S an authoritative publication **BIBLICAL** adj

BIBLESS   adj having no bib (a cloth covering)

BIBLIKE   adj resembling a bib

BIBULOUS   adj given to drinking

BICARB   n pl. -S sodium bicarbonate

BICE   n pl. -S a blue or green pigment

BICEPS   n pl. -ES an arm muscle

BICHROME   adj two-colored

BICKER   v -ED, -ING, -S to argue

BICKERER   n pl. -S one that bickers

BICOLOR   n pl. -S something having two colors

BICOLOUR   n pl. -S bicolor

BICONVEX   adj convex on both sides

BICORN   adj having two horns

BICORNE   n pl. -S a type of hat

BICRON   n pl. -S one billionth of a meter

BICUSPID   n pl. -S a tooth

BICYCLE   v -CLED, -CLING, -CLES to ride a bicycle (a two-wheeled vehicle)

BICYCLER   n pl. -S one that bicycles

BICYCLIC   adj having two cycles

BICYCLING   present participle of bicycle

BID   v BADE, BIDDEN, BIDDING, BIDS to make a bid (an offer of a price)

BIDARKA   n pl. -S an Eskimo canoe

BIDARKEE n pl. -S bidarka

BIDDABLE adj obedient **BIDDABLY** adv

BIDDEN past participle of bid

BIDDER n pl. -S one that bids

BIDDING n pl. -S a command

BIDDY n pl. -DIES a hen

BIDE v BIDED or BODE, BIDING, BIDES to wait

BIDENTAL adj having two teeth

BIDER n pl. -S one that bides

BIDET n pl. -S a low basin used for washing

BIDING present participle of bide

BIELD v -ED, -ING, -S to shelter

BIENNIAL n pl. -S an event that occurs every two years

BIENNIUM n pl. -NIA or -NIUMS a period of two years

BIER n pl. -S a coffin stand

BIFACIAL adj having two faces

BIFF v -ED, -ING, -S to hit

BIFFIN n pl. -S a cooking apple

BIFFY n pl. -FIES a toilet

BIFID adj divided into two parts **BIFIDLY** adv

BIFIDITY n pl. -TIES the state of being bifid

BIFILAR adj having two threads

BIFLEX adj bent in two places

BIFOCAL n pl. -S a type of lens

BIFOLD adj twofold

BIFORATE adj having two perforations

BIFORKED adj divided into two branches

BIFORM adj having two forms

BIFORMED adj biform

BIG adj BIGGER, BIGGEST of considerable size

BIGAMIES pl. of bigamy

BIGAMIST n pl. -S one who commits bigamy

BIGAMOUS adj guilty of bigamy

BIGAMY n pl. -MIES the crime of being married to two people simultaneously

BIGAROON n pl. -S a type of cherry

BIGEMINY n pl. -NIES the state of having a double pulse

BIGEYE n pl. -S a marine fish

BIGGER comparative of big

BIGGEST superlative of big

BIGGETY adj biggity

BIGGIE n pl. -S one that is big

BIGGIN n pl. -S a house

BIGGING n pl. -S biggin

BIGGISH adj somewhat big

BIGGITY adj conceited

BIGHEAD n pl. -S a disease of animals

BIGHORN n pl. -S a wild sheep

BIGHT v -ED, -ING, -S to fasten with a loop of rope

BIGLY adv in a big manner

BIGMOUTH n pl. -S a talkative person

BIGNESS n pl. -ES the state of being big

BIGNONIA n pl. -S a climbing plant

BIGOT n pl. -S a prejudiced person

BIGOTED adj intolerant

BIGOTRY n pl. -RIES prejudice

BIGWIG n pl. -S an important person

BIHOURLY adj occurring every two hours

BIJOU n pl. -JOUX or -JOUS a jewel

BIJUGATE adj two-paired

BIJUGOUS adj bijugate

BIKE v BIKED, BIKING, BIKES to bicycle

BIKER n pl. -S one that bikes

BIKEWAY n pl. -WAYS a route for bikes

BIKING present participle of bike

BIKINI n pl. -S a type of bathing suit **BIKINIED** adj

BILABIAL n pl. -S a sound articulated with both lips

BILANDER n pl. -S a small ship

BILBERRY n pl. -RIES an edible berry

BILBO n pl. -BOS or -BOES a finely tempered sword

BILBOA n pl. -S bilbo

BILE n pl. -S a fluid secreted by the liver

BILGE v BILGED, BILGING, BILGES to spring a leak

BILGY adj BILGIER, BILGIEST smelling like seepage

BILIARY adj pertaining to bile

BILINEAR adj pertaining to two lines

BILIOUS adj pertaining to bile

BILK   *v* -ED, -ING, -S to cheat

BILKER   *n* pl. -S one that bilks

BILL   *v* -ED, -ING, -S to present a statement of costs to **BILLABLE** *adj*

BILLBUG   *n* pl. -S a weevil

BILLER   *n* pl. -S one that bills

BILLET   *v* -ED, -ING, -S to lodge soldiers

BILLETER   *n* pl. -S one that billets

BILLFISH   *n* pl. -ES a fish with long, slender jaws

BILLFOLD   *n* pl. -S a wallet

BILLHEAD   *n* pl. -S a letterhead

BILLHOOK   *n* pl. -S a cutting tool

BILLIARD   *n* pl. -S a carom shot in billiards

BILLIE   *n* pl. -S a comrade

BILLIES   pl. of billy

BILLING   *n* pl. -S the relative position in which a performer is listed

BILLION   *n* pl. -S a number

BILLON   *n* pl. -S an alloy of silver and copper

BILLOW   *v* -ED, -ING, -S to swell

BILLOWY   *adj* -LOWIER, -LOWIEST swelling; surging

BILLY   *n* pl. -LIES a short club

BILLYCAN   *n* pl. -S a pot for heating water

BILOBATE   *adj* having two lobes

BILOBED   *adj* bilobate

BILSTED   *n* pl. -S a hardwood tree

BILTONG   *n* pl. -S dried and cured meat

BIMA   *n* pl. -S bema

BIMAH   *n* pl. -S bema

BIMANOUS   *adj* two-handed

BIMANUAL   *adj* done with two hands

BIMENSAL   *adj* occurring every two months

BIMESTER   *n* pl. -S a two-month period

BIMETAL   *n* pl. -S something composed of two metals

BIMETHYL   *n* pl. -S ethane

BIMODAL   *adj* having two statistical modes

BIN   *v* BINNED, BINNING, BINS to store in a large receptacle

BINAL   *adj* twofold

BINARY   *n* pl. -RIES a combination of two things

BINATE   *adj* growing in pairs **BINATELY** *adv*

BINAURAL   *adj* hearing with both ears

BIND   *v* BOUND, BINDING, BINDS to tie or secure **BINDABLE** *adj*

BINDER   *n* pl. -S one that binds

BINDERY   *n* pl. -ERIES a place where books are bound

BINDING   *n* pl. -S the cover and fastenings of a book

BINDLE   *n* pl. -S a bundle

BINDWEED   *n* pl. -S a twining plant

BINE   *n* pl. -S a twining plant stem

BINGE   *n* pl. -S a drunken carousal

BINGO   *n* pl. -GOS a game of chance

BINIT   *n* pl. -S a unit of computer information

BINNACLE   *n* pl. -S a compass stand

BINNED   past tense of bin

BINNING   present participle of bin

BINOCLE   *n* pl. -S a binocular

BINOMIAL   *n* pl. -S an algebraic expression

BINT   *n* pl. -S a woman

BIO   *n* pl. BIOS a biography

BIOASSAY   *v* -ED, -ING, -S to find the strength of a substance

BIOCIDE   *n* pl. -S a substance destructive to living organisms **BIOCIDAL** *adj*

BIOCLEAN   *adj* free of harmful organisms

BIOCYCLE   *n* pl. -S a life-supporting region

BIOGEN   *n* pl. -S a hypothetical protein molecule

BIOGENIC   *adj* produced by living organisms

BIOGENY   *n* pl. -NIES the development of life from preexisting life

BIOHERM   *n* pl. -S a mass of marine fossils

BIOLOGIC   *n* pl. -S a drug obtained from an organic source

BIOLOGY   *n* pl. -GIES the science of life

BIOLYSIS   *n* pl. -YSES death **BIOLYTIC** *adj*

BIOMASS   *n* pl. -ES an amount of living matter

BIOME   *n* pl. -S an ecological community

BIOMETRY   *n* pl. -TRIES the statistical study of biological data

BIONICS *n/pl* a science joining biology and electronics **BIONIC** *adj*

BIONOMY *n* pl. -MIES ecology **BIONOMIC** *adj*

BIONT *n* pl. -S a living organism **BIONTIC** *adj*

BIOPLASM *n* pl. -S living matter

BIOPSY *n* pl. -SIES the examination of tissue **BIOPSIC, BIOPTIC** *adj*

BIOSCOPE *n* pl. -S an early movie projector

BIOSCOPY *n* pl. -PIES a type of medical examination

BIOTA *n* pl. -S the flora and fauna of a region

BIOTIC *adj* pertaining to life

BIOTICAL *adj* biotic

BIOTICS *n/pl* a life science

BIOTIN *n* pl. -S a B vitamin

BIOTITE *n* pl. -S a form of mica **BIOTITIC** *adj*

BIOTOPE *n* pl. -S a stable habitat

BIOTRON *n* pl. -S a climate control chamber

BIOTYPE *n* pl. -S a group of genetically similar organisms **BIOTYPIC** *adj*

BIOVULAR *adj* derived from two ova

BIPACK *n* pl. -S a pair of films

BIPAROUS *adj* producing offspring in pairs

BIPARTED *adj* having two parts

BIPARTY *adj* of two parties

BIPED *n* pl. -S a two-footed animal **BIPEDAL** *adj*

BIPHENYL *n* pl. -S a hydrocarbon

BIPLANE *n* pl. -S a type of airplane

BIPOD *n* pl. -S a two-legged support

BIPOLAR *adj* having two poles

BIRACIAL *adj* including members of two races

BIRADIAL *adj* having dual symmetry

BIRAMOSE *adj* biramous

BIRAMOUS *adj* divided into two branches

BIRCH *v* -ED, -ING, -ES to whip

BIRCHEN *adj* made of birch wood

BIRD *v* -ED, -ING, -S to hunt birds (winged, warm-blooded vertebrates)

BIRDBATH *n* pl. -S a bath for birds

BIRDCAGE *n* pl. -S a cage for birds

BIRDCALL *n* pl. -S the call of a bird

BIRDER *n* pl. -S a bird hunter

BIRDFARM *n* pl. -S an aircraft carrier

BIRDIE *v* BIRDIED, BIRDIEING, BIRDIES to shoot in one stroke under par in golf

BIRDLIKE *adj* resembling a bird

BIRDLIME *v* -LIMED, -LIMING, -LIMES to trap small birds

BIRDMAN *n* pl. -MEN one who keeps birds

BIRDSEED *n* pl. -S a mixture of seeds used for feeding birds

BIRDSEYE *n* pl. -S a flowering plant

BIREME *n* pl. -S an ancient galley

BIRETTA *n* pl. -S a cap worn by clergymen

BIRK *n* pl. -S a birch tree

BIRKIE *n* pl. -S a lively person

BIRL *v* -ED, -ING, -S to rotate a floating log

BIRLE *v* BIRLED, BIRLING, BIRLES to carouse

BIRLER *n* pl. -S one that birls

BIRLING *n* pl. -S a lumberjack's game

BIRR *v* -ED, -ING, -S to make a whirring noise

BIRRETTA *n* pl. -S biretta

BIRSE *n* pl. -S a bristle

BIRTH *v* -ED, -ING, -S to originate

BIRTHDAY *n* pl. -DAYS an anniversary of a birth

BIS *adv* twice

BISCUIT *n* pl. -S a small cake of shortened bread

BISE *n* pl. -S a cold wind

BISECT *v* -ED, -ING, -S to cut into two parts

BISECTOR *n* pl. -S something that bisects

BISEXUAL *n* pl. -S one who is attracted to both sexes

BISHOP *v* -ED, -ING, -S to appoint as a bishop (the head of a diocese)

BISK *n* pl. -S bisque

BISMUTH *n* pl. -S a metallic element

BISNAGA *n* pl. -S a type of cactus

BISON *n* pl. -S an ox-like animal

BISQUE *n* pl. -S a thick soup

BISTATE *adj* pertaining to two states

BISTER n pl. -S a brown pigment **BISTERED** adj

BISTORT n pl. -S a perennial herb

BISTOURY n pl. -RIES a surgical knife

BISTRE n pl. -S bister **BISTRED** adj

BISTRO n pl. -TROS a small tavern **BISTROIC** adj

BIT v BITTED, BITTING, BITS to restrain

BITABLE adj capable of being bitten

BITCH v -ED, -ING, -ES to complain

BITCHERY n pl. -ERIES bitchy behavior

BITCHY adj BITCHIER, BITCHIEST malicious **BITCHILY** adv

BITE v BIT, BITTEN, BITING, BITES to seize with the teeth **BITEABLE** adj

BITER n pl. -S one that bites

BITEWING n pl. -S a dental X-ray film

BITING present participle of bite

BITINGLY adv sarcastically

BITSTOCK n pl. -S a brace on a drill

BITSY adj tiny

BITT v -ED, -ING, -S to secure a cable

BITTE interj please

BITTED past tense of bit

BITTEN a past participle of bite

BITTER adj -TERER, -TEREST having a disagreeable taste **BITTERLY** adv

BITTER v -ED, -ING, -S to make bitter

BITTERN n pl. -S a wading bird

BITTIER comparative of bitty

BITTIEST superlative of bitty

BITTING n pl. -S an indentation in a key

BITTOCK n pl. -S a small amount

BITTY adj -TIER, -TIEST fragmented

BITUMEN n pl. -S an asphalt

BIVALENT n pl. -S a pair of chromosomes

BIVALVE n pl. -S a bivalved mollusk

BIVALVED adj having a two-valved shell

BIVINYL n pl. -S a flammable gas

BIVOUAC v -OUACKED, -OUACKING, -OUACKS or -OUACS to make a camp

BIWEEKLY n pl. -LIES a publication issued every two weeks

BIYEARLY adj occurring every two years

BIZARRE n pl. -S a strangely striped flower

BIZE n pl. -S bise

BIZNAGA n pl. -S bisnaga

BIZONE n pl. -S two combined zones **BIZONAL** adj

BLAB v BLABBED, BLABBING, BLABS to talk idly

BLABBER v -ED, -ING, -S to blab

BLABBY adj talkative

BLACK adj BLACKER, BLACKEST being of the darkest color

BLACK v -ED, -ING, -S to make black

BLACKBOY n pl. -BOYS an Australian plant

BLACKCAP n pl. -S a small European bird

BLACKEN v -ED, -ING, -S to make black

BLACKFIN n pl. -S a food fish

BLACKFLY n pl. -FLIES a biting fly

BLACKGUM n pl. -S a tupelo

BLACKING n pl. -S black shoe polish

BLACKISH adj somewhat black

BLACKLEG n pl. -S a cattle disease

BLACKLY adv in a black manner

BLACKOUT n pl. -S a light failure

BLACKTOP v -TOPPED, -TOPPING, -TOPS to pave with asphalt

BLADDER n pl. -S a saclike receptacle **BLADDERY** adj

BLADE n pl. -S a cutting edge **BLADED** adj

BLAE adj bluish-black

BLAH n pl. -S nonsense

BLAIN n pl. -S a blister

BLAMABLE adj being at fault **BLAMABLY** adv

BLAME v BLAMED, BLAMING, BLAMES to find fault with

BLAMEFUL adj blamable

BLAMER n pl. -S one that blames

BLAMING present participle of blame

BLANCH v -ED, -ING, -ES to whiten

BLANCHER n pl. -S a whitener

BLAND adj BLANDER, BLANDEST soothing **BLANDLY** adv

BLANDISH v -ED, -ING, -ES to coax by flattery

BLANK	*adj* BLANKER, BLANKEST empty	**BLEAK**	*adj* BLEAKER, BLEAKEST dreary
BLANK	*v* -ED, -ING, -S to delete	**BLEAK**	*n* pl. -S a freshwater fish
BLANKET	*v* -ED, -ING, -S to cover uniformly	**BLEAKISH**	*adj* somewhat bleak
		BLEAKLY	*adv* in a bleak manner
BLANKLY	*adv* in a blank manner	**BLEAR**	*v* -ED, -ING, -S to dim
BLARE	*v* BLARED, BLARING, BLARES to sound loudly	**BLEARY**	*adj* BLEARIER, BLEARIEST dimmed **BLEARILY** *adv*
BLARNEY	*v* -NEYED, -NEYING, -NEYS to beguile with flattery	**BLEAT**	*v* -ED, -ING, -S to utter the cry of a sheep
BLASE	*adj* indifferent	**BLEATER**	*n* pl. -S one that bleats
BLAST	*v* -ED, -ING, -S to use an explosive	**BLEB**	*n* pl. -S a blister **BLEBBY** *adj*
BLASTEMA	*n* pl. -MAS or -MATA a region of embryonic cells	**BLEED**	*v* BLED, BLEEDING, BLEEDS to lose blood
BLASTER	*n* pl. -S one that blasts	**BLEEDER**	*n* pl. -S one that bleeds
BLASTIE	*n* pl. -S a dwarf	**BLEEDING**	*n* pl. -S the act of losing blood
BLASTIER	comparative of blasty	**BLELLUM**	*n* pl. -S a babbler
BLASTIEST	superlative of blasty	**BLEMISH**	*v* -ED, -ING, -ES to mar
BLASTING	*n* pl. -S the act of one that blasts	**BLENCH**	*v* -ED, -ING, -ES to flinch
		BLENCHER	*n* pl. -S one that blenches
BLASTOFF	*n* pl. -S the launching of a rocket	**BLEND**	*v* BLENDED or BLENT, BLENDING, BLENDS to mix smoothly and inseparably together
BLASTOMA	*n* pl. -MAS or -MATA a type of tumor		
BLASTULA	*n* pl. -LAS or -LAE an early embryo	**BLENDE**	*n* pl. -S a shiny mineral
		BLENDER	*n* pl. -S one that blends
BLASTY	*adj* BLASTIER, BLASTIEST gusty	**BLENNY**	*n* pl. -NIES a marine fish
		BLENT	a past tense of blend
BLAT	*v* BLATTED, BLATTING, BLATS to bleat	**BLESBOK**	*n* pl. -S a large antelope
		BLESBUCK	*n* pl. -S blesbok
BLATANCY	*n* pl. -CIES something blatant	**BLESS**	*v* BLESSED or BLEST, BLESSING, BLESSES to sanctify
BLATANT	*adj* obvious		
BLATE	*adj* timid	**BLESSED**	*adj* -EDER, -EDEST holy
BLATHER	*v* -ED, -ING, -S to talk foolishly	**BLESSER**	*n* pl. -S one that blesses
BLATTED	past tense of blat	**BLESSING**	*n* pl. -S a prayer
BLATTER	*v* -ED, -ING, -S to chatter	**BLEST**	a past tense of bless
BLATTING	present participle of blat	**BLET**	*n* pl. -S a decay of fruit
BLAUBOK	*n* pl. -S an extinct antelope	**BLETHER**	*v* -ED, -ING, -S to blather
BLAW	*v* BLAWED, BLAWN, BLAWING, BLAWS to blow	**BLEW**	past tense of blow
		BLIGHT	*v* -ED, -ING, -S to cause decay
BLAZE	*v* BLAZED, BLAZING, BLAZES to burn brightly	**BLIGHTER**	*n* pl. -S one that blights
		BLIGHTY	*n* pl. BLIGHTIES a wound causing one to be sent home to England
BLAZER	*n* pl. -S a lightweight jacket		
BLAZON	*v* -ED, -ING, -S to proclaim		
BLAZONER	*n* pl. -S one that blazons	**BLIMEY**	*interj* — used as an expression of surprise
BLAZONRY	*n* pl. -RIES a great display		
BLEACH	*v* -ED, -ING, -ES to whiten	**BLIMP**	*n* pl. -S a nonrigid aircraft **BLIMPISH** *adj*
BLEACHER	*n* pl. -S one that bleaches		

BLIMY	*interj* blimey	**BLOND**	*n* pl. -S a blond person
BLIN	*n* pl. BLINI or BLINIS a blintze	**BLONDE**	*n* pl. -S blond
BLIND	*adj* BLINDER, BLINDEST sightless	**BLONDISH**	*adj* somewhat blond
BLIND	*v* -ED, -ING, -S to make sightless	**BLOOD**	*v* -ED, -ING, -S to stain with blood (the fluid circulated by the heart)
BLINDAGE	*n* pl. -S a protective screen	**BLOODFIN**	*n* pl. -S a freshwater fish
BLINDER	*n* pl. -S an obstruction to sight	**BLOODIED**	past tense of bloody
BLINDLY	*adv* in a blind manner	**BLOODIER**	comparative of bloody
BLINI	a pl. of blin	**BLOODIES**	present 3d person sing. of bloody
BLINIS	a pl. of blin	**BLOODIEST**	superlative of bloody
BLINK	*v* -ED, -ING, -S to open and shut the eyes	**BLOODILY**	*adv* in a bloody manner
BLINKARD	*n* pl. -S one who habitually blinks	**BLOODING**	*n* pl. -S a fox hunting ceremony
BLINKER	*v* -ED, -ING, -S to put blinders on	**BLOODRED**	*adj* of the color of blood
BLINTZ	*n* pl. -ES blintze	**BLOODY**	*adj* BLOODIER, BLOODIEST stained with blood
BLINTZE	*n* pl. -S a thin pancake	**BLOODY**	*v* BLOODIED, BLOODYING, BLOODIES to make bloody
BLIP	*v* BLIPPED, BLIPPING, BLIPS to remove sound from a videotape	**BLOOM**	*v* -ED, -ING, -S to bear flowers
BLISS	*n* pl. -ES happiness **BLISSFUL** *adj*	**BLOOMER**	*n* pl. -S a blooming plant
BLISTER	*v* -ED, -ING, -S to cause blisters (skin swellings)	**BLOOMERY**	*n* pl. -ERIES a furnace for smelting iron
BLISTERY	*adj* having blisters	**BLOOMY**	*adj* BLOOMIER, BLOOMIEST covered with flowers
BLITE	*n* pl. -S an annual herb	**BLOOP**	*v* -ED, -ING, -S to hit a short fly ball
BLITHE	*adj* BLITHER, BLITHEST merry **BLITHELY** *adv*	**BLOOPER**	*n* pl. -S a public blunder
BLITHER	*v* -ED, -ING, -S to blather	**BLOSSOM**	*v* -ED, -ING, -S to bloom
BLITZ	*v* -ED, -ING, -ES to subject to a sudden attack	**BLOSSOMY**	*adj* having blossoms
BLIZZARD	*n* pl. -S a heavy snowstorm	**BLOT**	*v* BLOTTED, BLOTTING, BLOTS to spot or stain
BLOAT	*v* -ED, -ING, -S to swell	**BLOTCH**	*v* -ED, -ING, -ES to mark with large spots
BLOATER	*n* pl. -S a smoked herring	**BLOTCHY**	*adj* BLOTCHIER, BLOTCHIEST blotched
BLOB	*v* BLOBBED, BLOBBING, BLOBS to splotch	**BLOTLESS**	*adj* spotless
BLOC	*n* pl. -S a coalition	**BLOTTED**	past tense of blot
BLOCK	*v* -ED, -ING, -S to obstruct	**BLOTTER**	*n* pl. -S a piece of ink-absorbing paper
BLOCKADE	*v* -ADED, -ADING, -ADES to block	**BLOTTIER**	comparative of blotty
BLOCKAGE	*n* pl. -S the act of blocking	**BLOTTIEST**	superlative of blotty
BLOCKER	*n* pl. -S one that blocks	**BLOTTING**	present participle of blot
BLOCKISH	*adj* blocky	**BLOTTO**	*adj* drunk
BLOCKY	*adj* BLOCKIER, BLOCKIEST short and stout	**BLOTTY**	*adj* -TIER, -TIEST spotty
BLOKE	*n* pl. -S a fellow	**BLOUSE**	*v* BLOUSED, BLOUSING, BLOUSES to hang loosely
BLOND	*adj* BLONDER, BLONDEST light-colored	**BLOUSON**	*n* pl. -S a woman's garment

BLOUSY *adj* BLOUSIER, BLOUSIEST blowsy **BLOUSILY** *adv*

BLOW *v* BLEW, BLOWN, BLOWING, BLOWS to drive or impel by a current of air

BLOWBACK *n* pl. -S an escape of gases

BLOWBY *n* pl. -BYS leakage of exhaust fumes

BLOWER *n* pl. -S one that blows

BLOWFISH *n* pl. -ES a marine fish

BLOWFLY *n* pl. -FLIES a type of fly

BLOWGUN *n* pl. -S a tube through which darts may be blown

BLOWHARD *n* pl. -S a braggart

BLOWHOLE *n* pl. -S an air or gas vent

BLOWIER comparative of blowy

BLOWIEST superlative of blowy

BLOWN past participle of blow

BLOWOFF *n* pl. -S the expelling of gas

BLOWOUT *n* pl. -S a sudden rupture

BLOWPIPE *n* pl. -S a blowgun

BLOWSED *adj* blowsy

BLOWSY *adj* -SIER, -SIEST slovenly **BLOWSILY** *adv*

BLOWTUBE *n* pl. -S a blowgun

BLOWUP *n* pl. -S an explosion

BLOWY *adj* BLOWIER, BLOWIEST windy

BLOWZED *adj* blowzy

BLOWZY *adj* -ZIER, -ZIEST blowsy **BLOWZILY** *adv*

BLUBBER *v* -ED, -ING, -S to weep noisily

BLUBBERY *adj* fat; swollen

BLUCHER *n* pl. -S a half boot

BLUDGEON *v* -ED, -ING, -S to hit with a club

BLUE *adj* BLUER, BLUEST having the color of the clear sky

BLUE *v* BLUED, BLUEING or BLUING, BLUES to make blue

BLUEBALL *n* pl. -S a medicinal herb

BLUEBELL *n* pl. -S a flowering plant

BLUEBILL *n* pl. -S the scaup duck

BLUEBIRD *n* pl. -S a songbird

BLUEBOOK *n* pl. -S an examination booklet

BLUECAP *n* pl. -S a flowering plant

BLUECOAT *n* pl. -S a policeman

BLUED past tense of blue

BLUEFIN *n* pl. -S a large tuna

BLUEFISH *n* pl. -ES a marine fish

BLUEGILL *n* pl. -S an edible sunfish

BLUEGUM *n* pl. -S a timber tree

BLUEHEAD *n* pl. -S a marine fish

BLUEING *n* pl. -S bluing

BLUEISH *adj* bluish

BLUEJACK *n* pl. -S an oak tree

BLUEJAY *n* pl. -JAYS a corvine bird

BLUELINE *n* pl. -S a line that divides a hockey rink

BLUELY *adv* in a blue manner

BLUENESS *n* pl. -ES the state of being blue

BLUENOSE *n* pl. -S a puritanical person

BLUER comparative of blue

BLUESMAN *n* pl. -MEN one who plays the blues

BLUEST superlative of blue

BLUESTEM *n* pl. -S a prairie grass

BLUESY *adj* resembling the blues (a musical form)

BLUET *n* pl. -S a meadow flower

BLUEWEED *n* pl. -S a bristly weed

BLUEWOOD *n* pl. -S a shrub

BLUEY *n* pl. BLUEYS a bag of clothing carried in travel

BLUFF *v* -ED, -ING, -S to mislead

BLUFF *adj* BLUFFER, BLUFFEST having a broad front **BLUFFLY** *adv*

BLUFFER *n* pl. -S one that bluffs

BLUING *n* pl. -S a fabric coloring

BLUISH *adj* somewhat blue

BLUME *v* BLUMED, BLUMING, BLUMES to blossom

BLUNDER *v* -ED, -ING, -S to make a mistake

BLUNGE *v* BLUNGED, BLUNGING, BLUNGES to mix clay with water

BLUNGER *n* pl. -S one that blunges

BLUNT *adj* BLUNTER, BLUNTEST not sharp or pointed **BLUNTLY** *adv*

BLUNT *v* -ED, -ING, -S to make blunt

BLUR *v* BLURRED, BLURRING, BLURS to make unclear

BLURB *n* pl. -S a note on a book jacket

BLURRY *adj* -RIER, -RIEST unclear **BLURRILY** *adv*

BLURT	v -ED, -ING, -S to speak abruptly
BLURTER	n pl. -S one that blurts
BLUSH	v -ED, -ING, -ES to become red
BLUSHER	n pl. -S one that blushes
BLUSHFUL	adj of a red color
BLUSTER	v -ED, -ING, -S to blow violently
BLUSTERY	adj windy
BLYPE	n pl. -S a shred
BO	n pl. BOS a pal
BOA	n pl. -S a large snake
BOAR	n pl. -S a male pig
BOARD	v -ED, -ING, -S to take meals for a fixed price
BOARDER	n pl. -S one that boards
BOARDING	n pl. -S a surface of wooden boards
BOARDMAN	n pl. -MEN a board member
BOARFISH	n pl. -ES a marine fish
BOARISH	adj swinish; coarse
BOART	n pl. -S a bort
BOAST	v -ED, -ING, -S to brag
BOASTER	n pl. -S one that boasts
BOASTFUL	adj given to boasting
BOAT	v -ED, -ING, -S to travel by boat (watercraft) **BOATABLE** adj
BOATBILL	n pl. -S a wading bird
BOATEL	n pl. -S a waterside hotel
BOATER	n pl. -S one that boats
BOATING	n pl. -S the sport of traveling by boat
BOATLOAD	n pl. -S the amount that a boat holds
BOATMAN	n pl. -MEN one who works on boats
BOATSMAN	n pl. -MEN boatman
BOATYARD	n pl. -S a marina
BOB	v BOBBED, BOBBING, BOBS to move up and down
BOBBER	n pl. -S one that bobs
BOBBERY	n pl. -BERIES a disturbance
BOBBIES	pl. of bobby
BOBBIN	n pl. -S a thread holder
BOBBINET	n pl. -S a machine-made net
BOBBING	present participle of bob
BOBBLE	v -BLED, -BLING, -BLES to fumble

BOBBY	n pl. -BIES a policeman
BOBCAT	n pl. -S a lynx
BOBECHE	n pl. -S a glass collar on a candle holder
BOBOLINK	n pl. -S a songbird
BOBSLED	v -SLEDDED, -SLEDDING, -SLEDS to ride on a bobsled (a racing sled)
BOBSTAY	n pl. -STAYS a steadying rope
BOBTAIL	v -ED, -ING, -S to cut short
BOBWHITE	n pl. -S a game bird
BOCACCIO	n pl. -CIOS a rockfish
BOCCE	n pl. -S boccie
BOCCI	n pl. -S boccie
BOCCIA	n pl. -S boccie
BOCCIE	n pl. -S an Italian bowling game
BOCHE	n pl. -S a German — a derogatory term
BOCK	n pl. -S a dark beer
BOD	n pl. -S a body
BODE	v BODED, BODING, BODES to be an omen of
BODEGA	n pl. -S a grocery store
BODEMENT	n pl. -S an omen
BODICE	n pl. -S a corset
BODIED	past tense of body
BODIES	present 3d person sing. of body
BODILESS	adj lacking material form
BODILY	adj of the body
BODING	n pl. -S an omen
BODINGLY	adv ominously
BODKIN	n pl. -S a sharp instrument
BODY	v BODIED, BODYING, BODIES to give form to
BODYSURF	v -ED, -ING, -S to ride a wave without a surfboard
BODYWORK	n pl. -S a vehicle body
BOEHMITE	n pl. -S a mineral
BOFF	n pl. -S a hearty laugh
BOFFIN	n pl. -S a scientific expert
BOFFO	n pl. -FOS a boff
BOFFOLA	n pl. -S a boff
BOG	v BOGGED, BOGGING, BOGS to impede
BOGAN	n pl. -S a backwater or tributary
BOGBEAN	n pl. -S a marsh plant

BOGEY	*v* -GEYED, -GEYING, -GEYS to shoot in one stroke over par in golf	**BOLIVAR**	*n* pl. -S or -ES a unit of Venezuelan currency
BOGEYMAN	*n* pl. -MEN a terrifying creature	**BOLIVIA**	*n* pl. -S a soft fabric
BOGGED	past tense of bog	**BOLL**	*v* -ED, -ING, -S to form pods
BOGGIER	comparative of boggy	**BOLLARD**	*n* pl. -S a thick post on a ship or wharf
BOGGIEST	superlative of boggy	**BOLLIX**	*v* -ED, -ING, -ES to bungle
BOGGING	present participle of bog	**BOLLOX**	*v* -ED, -ING, -ES to bollix
BOGGISH	*adj* boggy	**BOLLWORM**	*n* pl. -S the larva of a certain moth
BOGGLE	*v* -GLED, -GLING, -GLES to hesitate	**BOLO**	*n* pl. -LOS a machete
BOGGLER	*n* pl. -S one that causes another to boggle	**BOLOGNA**	*n* pl. -S a seasoned sausage
BOGGY	*adj* -GIER, -GIEST marshy	**BOLONEY**	*n* pl. -NEYS bologna
BOGIE	*n* pl. -S bogy	**BOLSON**	*n* pl. -S a flat arid valley
BOGIES	pl. of bogy	**BOLSTER**	*v* -ED, -ING, -S to support
BOGLE	*n* pl. -S a bogy	**BOLT**	*v* -ED, -ING, -S to sift
BOGUS	*adj* not genuine; fake	**BOLTER**	*n* pl. -S a sifting machine
BOGWOOD	*n* pl. -S preserved tree wood	**BOLTHEAD**	*n* pl. -S a matrass
BOGY	*n* pl. -GIES a goblin	**BOLTONIA**	*n* pl. -S a perennial herb
BOGYISM	*n* pl. -S behavior characteristic of a bogy	**BOLTROPE**	*n* pl. -S a rope sewn to a sail
BOGYMAN	*n* pl. -MEN bogeyman	**BOLUS**	*n* pl. -ES a large pill
BOHEA	*n* pl. -S a black tea	**BOMB**	*v* -ED, -ING, -S to attack with bombs (explosive projectiles)
BOHEMIA	*n* pl. -S a community of bohemians	**BOMBARD**	*v* -ED, -ING, -S to bomb
BOHEMIAN	*n* pl. -S an unconventional person	**BOMBAST**	*n* pl. -S pompous language
		BOMBE	*n* pl. -S a frozen dessert
BOHUNK	*n* pl. -S an unskilled laborer	**BOMBER**	*n* pl. -S one that bombs
BOIL	*v* -ED, -ING, -S to vaporize liquid **BOILABLE** *adj*	**BOMBLOAD**	*n* pl. -S the quantity of bombs being carried
BOILER	*n* pl. -S a vessel for boiling	**BOMBYCID**	*n* pl. -S a moth
BOITE	*n* pl. -S a nightclub	**BOMBYX**	*n* pl. -ES a silkworm
BOLA	*n* pl. -S a throwing weapon	**BONACI**	*n* pl. -S an edible fish
BOLAR	*adj* pertaining to bole	**BONANZA**	*n* pl. -S a rich mine
BOLAS	*n* pl. -ES bola	**BONBON**	*n* pl. -S a sugared candy
BOLD	*adj* BOLDER, BOLDEST daring **BOLDLY** *adv*	**BOND**	*v* -ED, -ING, -S to join together **BONDABLE** *adj*
BOLDFACE	*v* -FACED, -FACING, -FACES to print in thick type	**BONDAGE**	*n* pl. -S slavery
BOLDNESS	*n* pl. -ES the quality of being bold	**BONDER**	*n* pl. -S one that bonds
		BONDMAID	*n* pl. -S a female slave
BOLE	*n* pl. -S a fine clay	**BONDMAN**	*n* pl. -MEN a male slave
BOLERO	*n* pl. -ROS a Spanish dance	**BONDSMAN**	*n* pl. -MEN bondman
BOLETE	*n* pl. -S boletus	**BONDUC**	*n* pl. -S a prickly seed
BOLETUS	*n* pl. -TUSES or -TI a fungus	**BONE**	*v* BONED, BONING, BONES to debone
BOLIDE	*n* pl. -S an exploding meteor	**BONEFISH**	*n* pl. -ES a slender marine fish
		BONEHEAD	*n* pl. -S a stupid person

BONELESS   *adj* having no bones (hard connective tissue)

BONER   *n* pl. -S a blunder

BONESET   *n* pl. -S a perennial herb

BONEY   *adj* BONIER, BONIEST bony

BONEYARD   *n* pl. -S a junkyard

BONFIRE   *n* pl. -S an open fire

BONG   *v* -ED, -ING, -S to make a deep, ringing sound

BONGO   *n* pl. -GOS or -GOES a small drum

BONGOIST   *n* pl. -S a bongo player

BONHOMIE   *n* pl. -S friendliness

BONIER   comparative of bony or boney

BONIEST   superlative of bony or boney

BONIFACE   *n* pl. -S an innkeeper

BONINESS   *n* pl. -ES the state of being bony

BONING   present participle of bone

BONITA   *n* pl. -S bonito

BONITO   *n* pl. -TOS or -TOES a marine food fish

BONKERS   *adj* crazy

BONNE   *n* pl. -S a housemaid

BONNET   *v* -ED, -ING, -S to provide with a bonnet (a type of hat)

BONNIE   *adj* bonny

BONNOCK   *n* pl. -S bannock

BONNY   *adj* -NIER, -NIEST pretty
BONNILY *adv*

BONSAI   *n* pl. BONSAI a potted shrub that has been dwarfed

BONSPELL   *n* pl. -S bonspiel

BONSPIEL   *n* pl. -S a curling match or tournament

BONTEBOK   *n* pl. -S an antelope

BONUS   *n* pl. -ES an additional payment

BONY   *adj* BONIER, BONIEST full of bones

BONZE   *n* pl. -S a Buddhist monk

BONZER   *adj* very good

BOO   *v* -ED, -ING, -S to cry "boo"

BOOB   *n* pl. -S a dolt

BOOBOO   *n* pl. -BOOS a mistake

BOOBY   *n* pl. -BIES a dolt

BOODLE   *v* -DLED, -DLING, -DLES to take bribes

BOODLER   *n* pl. -S one that boodles

BOOGER   *n* pl. -S a bogeyman

BOOGIE   *n* pl. -S a jazz form

BOOGYMAN   *n* pl. -MEN bogeyman

BOOHOO   *v* -ED, -ING, -S to weep noisily

BOOK   *v* -ED, -ING, -S to engage services

BOOKCASE   *n* pl. -S a case which holds books (literary volumes)

BOOKEND   *n* pl. -S a support for a row of books

BOOKER   *n* pl. -S one that books

BOOKIE   *n* pl. -S a bet taker

BOOKING   *n* pl. -S an engagement

BOOKISH   *adj* pertaining to books

BOOKLET   *n* pl. -S a small book

BOOKLORE   *n* pl. -S book learning

BOOKMAN   *n* pl. -MEN a scholar

BOOKMARK   *n* pl. -S a marker for finding a place in a book

BOOKRACK   *n* pl. -S a support for an open book

BOOKREST   *n* pl. -S a bookrack

BOOKSHOP   *n* pl. -S a store where books are sold

BOOKWORM   *n* pl. -S an avid book reader

BOOM   *v* -ED, -ING, -S to make a deep, resonant sound

BOOMER   *n* pl. -S one that booms

BOOMIER   comparative of boomy

BOOMIEST   superlative of boomy

BOOMKIN   *n* pl. -S a bumkin

BOOMLET   *n* pl. -S a small increase in prosperity

BOOMTOWN   *n* pl. -S a prospering town

BOOMY   *adj* BOOMIER, BOOMIEST prospering

BOON   *n* pl. -S a timely benefit

BOONIES   *n/pl* a backwoods area

BOOR   *n* pl. -S a rude person

BOORISH   *adj* rude

BOOST   *v* -ED, -ING, -S to support

BOOSTER   *n* pl. -S one that boosts

BOOT   *v* -ED, -ING, -S to provide with boots (protective coverings for the feet)

BOOTEE   *n* pl. -S a baby's boot

BOOTERY   *n* pl. -ERIES a shoe store

BOOTH   *n* pl. -S a small enclosure

BOOTIE   *n* pl. -S bootee

BOOTIES   pl. of booty

BOOTJACK   *n* pl. -S a device for pulling off boots

BOOTLACE   *n* pl. -S a shoelace

BOOTLEG   *v* -LEGGED, -LEGGING, -LEGS to smuggle

BOOTLESS   *adj* useless

BOOTLICK   *v* -ED, -ING, -S to flatter servilely

BOOTY   *n* pl. -TIES a rich gain or prize

BOOZE   *v* BOOZED, BOOZING, BOOZES to drink liquor excessively

BOOZER   *n* pl. -S one that boozes

BOOZY   *adj* BOOZIER, BOOZIEST drunken **BOOZILY** *adv*

BOP   *v* BOPPED, BOPPING, BOPS to hit or strike

BOPPER   *n* pl. -S a bebopper

BORA   *n* pl. -S a cold wind

BORACES   a pl. of borax

BORACIC   *adj* boric

BORACITE   *n* pl. -S a mineral

BORAGE   *n* pl. -S a medicinal herb

BORANE   *n* pl. -S a chemical compound

BORATE   *n* pl. -S a salt of boric acid **BORATED** *adj*

BORAX   *n* pl. -RAXES or -RACES a white crystalline compound

BORAZON   *n* pl. -S a hard boron compound

BORDEL   *n* pl. -S a brothel

BORDELLO   *n* pl. -LOS a brothel

BORDER   *v* -ED, -ING, -S to put a border (an edge) on

BORDERER   *n* pl. -S one that borders

BORDURE   *n* pl. -S a border around a shield

BORE   *v* BORED, BORING, BORES to pierce with a rotary tool

BOREAL   *adj* pertaining to the north

BORECOLE   *n* pl. -S kale

BORED   past tense of bore

BOREDOM   *n* pl. -S tedium

BORER   *n* pl. -S one that bores

BORIC   *adj* pertaining to boron

BORIDE   *n* pl. -S a boron compound

BORING   *n* pl. -S an inner cavity

BORINGLY   *adv* tediously

BORN   *adj* having particular qualities from birth

BORNE   a past participle of bear

BORNEOL   *n* pl. -S an alcohol

BORNITE   *n* pl. -S an ore of copper

BORON   *n* pl. -S a nonmetallic element **BORONIC** *adj*

BOROUGH   *n* pl. -S an incorporated town

BORROW   *v* -ED, -ING, -S to take on loan

BORROWER   *n* pl. -S one that borrows

BORSCH   *n* pl. -ES borscht

BORSCHT   *n* pl. -S a beet soup

BORSHT   *n* pl. -S borscht

BORSTAL   *n* pl. -S a reformatory

BORT   *n* pl. -S a low-quality diamond **BORTY** *adj*

BORTZ   *n* pl. -ES bort

BORZOI   *n* pl. -S a Russian hound

BOSCAGE   *n* pl. -S a thicket

BOSCHBOK   *n* pl. -S bushbuck

BOSH   *n* pl. -ES nonsense

BOSHBOK   *n* pl. -S bushbuck

BOSHVARK   *n* pl. -S a wild hog

BOSK   *n* pl. -S a small wooded area

BOSKAGE   *n* pl. -S boscage

BOSKER   *adj* fine; very good

BOSKET   *n* pl. -S a thicket

BOSKY   *adj* BOSKIER, BOSKIEST wooded; bushy

BOSOM   *v* -ED, -ING, -S to embrace

BOSOMY   *adj* swelling outward

BOSON   *n* pl. -S an atomic particle

BOSQUE   *n* pl. -S bosk

BOSQUET   *n* pl. -S basket

BOSS   *v* -ED, -ING, -ES to supervise

BOSSDOM   *n* pl. -S the domain of a political boss

BOSSIER   comparative of bossy

BOSSIES   pl. of bossy

BOSSISM   *n* pl. -S control by political bosses

BOSSY   *adj* BOSSIER, BOSSIEST domineering **BOSSILY** *adv*

BOSSY   *n* pl. BOSSIES a cow

BOSTON   *n* pl. -S a card game

BOSUN *n* pl. -S a boatswain

BOT *n* pl. -S the larva of a botfly

BOTANIC *adj* pertaining to botany

BOTANIES pl. of botany

BOTANISE *v* -NISED, -NISING, -NISES to botanize

BOTANIST *n* pl. -S one skilled in botany

BOTANIZE *v* -NIZED, -NIZING, -NIZES to study plants

BOTANY *n* pl. -NIES the science of plants

BOTCH *v* -ED, -ING, -ES to bungle

BOTCHER *n* pl. -S one that botches

BOTCHERY *n* pl. -ERIES something botched

BOTCHY *adj* BOTCHIER, BOTCHIEST badly done **BOTCHILY** *adv*

BOTEL *n* pl. -S a boatel

BOTFLY *n* pl. -FLIES a type of fly

BOTH *adj* being the two

BOTHER *v* -ED, -ING, -S to annoy

BOTONEE *adj* having arms ending in a trefoil — used of a heraldic cross

BOTONNEE *adj* botonee

BOTRYOID *adj* resembling a cluster of grapes

BOTRYOSE *adj* botryoid

BOTT *n* pl. -S bot

BOTTLE *v* -TLED, -TLING, -TLES to put into a bottle (a rigid container)

BOTTLER *n* pl. -S one that bottles

BOTTOM *v* -ED, -ING, -S to comprehend

BOTTOMER *n* pl. -S one that bottoms

BOTTOMRY *n* pl. -RIES a maritime contract

BOTULIN *n* pl. -S a nerve poison

BOTULISM *n* pl. -S botulin poisoning

BOUCLE *n* pl. -S a knitted fabric

BOUDOIR *n* pl. -S a woman's bedroom

BOUFFANT *n* pl. -S a woman's hairdo

BOUFFE *n* pl. -S a comic opera

BOUGH *n* pl. -S a tree branch **BOUGHED** *adj*

BOUGHPOT *n* pl. -S a large vase

BOUGHT past tense of buy

BOUGHTEN *adj* purchased

BOUGIE *n* pl. -S a wax candle

BOUILLON *n* pl. -S a clear soup

BOULDER *n* pl. -S a large rock **BOULDERY** *adj*

BOULE *n* pl. -S buhl

BOULLE *n* pl. -S buhl

BOUNCE *v* BOUNCED, BOUNCING, BOUNCES to spring back

BOUNCER *n* pl. -S one that bounces

BOUNCY *adj* BOUNCIER, BOUNCIEST tending to bounce **BOUNCILY** *adv*

BOUND *v* -ED, -ING, -S to leap

BOUNDARY *n* pl. -ARIES a dividing line

BOUNDEN *adj* obliged

BOUNDER *n* pl. -S one that bounds

BOUNTY *n* pl. -TIES a reward **BOUNTIED** *adj*

BOUQUET *n* pl. -S a bunch of flowers

BOURBON *n* pl. -S a whiskey

BOURDON *n* pl. -S a part of a bagpipe

BOURG *n* pl. -S a medieval town

BOURGEON *v* -ED, -ING, -S to burgeon

BOURN *n* pl. -S a stream

BOURNE *n* pl. -S bourn

BOURREE *n* pl. -S an old French dance

BOURSE *n* pl. -S a stock exchange

BOURTREE *n* pl. -S a European tree

BOUSE *v* BOUSED, BOUSING, BOUSES to haul by means of a tackle

BOUSOUKI *n* pl. -KIA or -KIS bouzouki

BOUSY *adj* boozy

BOUT *n* pl. -S a contest

BOUTIQUE *n* pl. -S a small shop

BOUZOUKI *n* pl. -KIA or KIS a stringed musical instrument

BOVID *n* pl. -S a bovine

BOVINE *n* pl. -S an ox-like animal

BOVINELY *adj* stolidly

BOVINITY *n* pl. -TIES the state of being a bovine

BOW *v* -ED, -ING, -S to bend forward

BOWEL *v* -ELED, -ELING, -ELS or -ELLED, -ELLING, -ELS to disbowel

BOWER *v* -ED, -ING, -S to embower

BOWERY *n* -ERIES a colonial Dutch farm

BOWFIN *n* pl. -S a freshwater fish

BOWFRONT *adj* having a curved front

BOWHEAD   n pl. -S an arctic whale

BOWING   n pl. -S the technique of managing the bow of a stringed instrument

BOWINGLY   adv in a bowing manner

BOWKNOT   n pl. -S a type of knot

BOWL   v -ED, -ING, -S to play at bowling

BOWLDER   n pl. -S boulder

BOWLEG   n pl. -S an outwardly curved leg

BOWLER   n pl. -S one that bowls

BOWLESS   adj being without an archery bow

BOWLFUL   n pl. -S as much as a bowl can hold

BOWLIKE   adj curved

BOWLINE   n pl. -S a type of knot

BOWLING   n pl. -S a game in which balls are rolled at objects

BOWLLIKE   adj concave

BOWMAN   n pl. -MEN an archer

BOWPOT   n pl. -S boughpot

BOWSE   v BOWSED, BOWSING, BOWSES to bouse

BOWSHOT   n pl. -S the distance an arrow is shot

BOWSPRIT   n pl. -S a ship's spar

BOWWOW   n pl. -S the bark of a dog

BOWYER   n pl. -S a maker of archery bows

BOX   v -ED, -ING, -ES to put in a box (a rectangular container)

BOXBERRY   n pl. -RIES an evergreen plant

BOXCAR   n pl. -S a roofed freight car

BOXER   n pl. -S one that packs boxes

BOXFISH   n pl. -ES a marine fish

BOXFUL   n pl. -S as much as a box can hold

BOXHAUL   v -ED, -ING, -S to veer a ship around

BOXIER   comparative of boxy

BOXIEST   superlative of boxy

BOXINESS   n pl. -ES the state of being boxy

BOXING   n pl. -S a casing

BOXLIKE   adj resembling a box

BOXTHORN   n pl. -S a thorny shrub

BOXWOOD   n pl. -S an evergreen shrub

BOXY   adj BOXIER, BOXIEST resembling a box

BOY   n pl. BOYS a male child

BOYAR   n pl. -S a former Russian aristocrat

BOYARD   n pl. -S boyar

BOYARISM   n pl. -S the rule of boyars

BOYCOTT   v -ED, -ING, -S to refuse to buy

BOYHOOD   n pl. -S the state of being a boy

BOYISH   adj resembling a boy **BOYISHLY** adv

BOYLA   n pl. -S a witch doctor

BOYO   n pl. BOYOS a boy

BOZO   n pl. -ZOS a fellow

BRA   n pl. -S a brassiere

BRABBLE   v -BLED, -BLING, -BLES to quarrel noisily

BRABBLER   n pl. -S one that brabbles

BRACE   v BRACED, BRACING, BRACES to support

BRACELET   n pl. -S a wrist ornament

BRACER   n pl. -S one that braces

BRACERO   n pl. -ROS a Mexican laborer

BRACH   n pl. -ES a hound bitch

BRACHET   n pl. -S a brach

BRACHIAL   n pl. -S a part of the arm

BRACHIUM   n pl. -IA the upper part of arm

BRACING   n pl. -S a brace or reinforcement

BRACKEN   n pl. -S a large fern

BRACKET   v -ED, -ING, -S to classify

BRACKISH   adj salty

BRACT   n pl. -S a leaflike plant part **BRACTEAL, BRACTED** adj

BRACTLET   n pl. -S a small bract

BRAD   v BRADDED, BRADDING, BRADS to fasten with thin nails

BRADAWL   n pl. -S a type of awl

BRADOON   n pl. -S bridoon

BRAE   n pl. -S a hillside

BRAG   adj BRAGGER, BRAGGEST first-rate

BRAG   v BRAGGED, BRAGGING, BRAGS to speak vainly of one's deeds

BRAGGART   n pl. -S one who brags

BRAGGER   n pl. -S a braggart

BRAGGEST superlative of brag

BRAGGING present participle of brag

BRAGGY *adj* -GIER, -GIEST tending to brag

BRAHMA *n* pl. -S a large domestic fowl

BRAID *v* -ED, -ING, -S to weave together

BRAIDER *n* pl. -S one that braids

BRAIDING *n* pl. -S something made of braided material

BRAIL *v* -ED, -ING, -S to haul in a sail

BRAILLE *v* BRAILLED, BRAILLING, BRAILLES to write in braille (raised writing for the blind)

BRAIN *v* -ED, -ING, -S to hit on the head

BRAINIER comparative of brainy

BRAINIEST superlative of brainy

BRAINILY *adv* in a brainy manner

BRAINISH *adj* impetuous

BRAINPAN *n* pl. -S the skull

BRAINY *adj* BRAINIER, BRAINIEST smart

BRAISE *v* BRAISED, BRAISING, BRAISES to cook in fat

BRAIZE *n* pl. -S a marine fish

BRAKE *v* BRAKED, BRAKING, BRAKES to slow down or stop

BRAKEAGE *n* pl. -S the act of braking

BRAKEMAN *n* pl. -MEN a trainman

BRAKING present participle of brake

BRAKY *adj* BRAKIER, BRAKIEST abounding in shrubs or ferns

BRAMBLE *v* -BLED, -BLING, -BLES to gather berries

BRAMBLY *adj* -BLIER, -BLIEST prickly

BRAN *v* BRANNED, BRANNING, BRANS to soak in water mixed with bran (the outer coat of cereals)

BRANCH *v* -ED, -ING, -ES to form branches (offshoots)

BRANCHIA *n* pl. -CHIAE a respiratory organ of aquatic animals

BRANCHY *adj* BRANCHIER, BRANCHIEST having many branches

BRAND *v* -ED, -ING, -S to mark with a hot iron

BRANDER *n* pl. -S one that brands

BRANDISH *v* -ED, -ING, -ES to wave menacingly

BRANDY *v* -DIED, -DYING, -DIES to mix with brandy (a liquor)

BRANK *n* pl. -S a device used to restrain the tongue

BRANNED past tense of bran

BRANNER *n* pl. -S one that brans

BRANNING present participle of bran

BRANNY *adj* -NIER, -NIEST containing bran

BRANT *n* pl. -S a wild goose

BRANTAIL *n* pl. -S a singing bird

BRASH *adj* BRASHER, BRASHEST rash; hasty **BRASHLY** *adv*

BRASH *n* pl. -ES a mass of fragments

BRASHY *adj* BRASHIER, BRASHIEST brash

BRASIER *n* pl. -S brazier

BRASIL *n* pl. -S brazil

BRASILIN *n* pl. -S brazilin

BRASS *n* pl. -ES an alloy of copper and zinc

BRASSAGE *n* pl. -S a fee for coining money

BRASSARD *n* pl. -S an insignia

BRASSART *n* pl. -S brassard

BRASSICA *n* pl. -S a tall herb

BRASSIE *n* pl. -S a golf club

BRASSISH *adj* resembling brass

BRASSY *adj* BRASSIER, BRASSIEST resembling brass **BRASSILY** *adv*

BRAT *n* pl. -S a spoiled child **BRATTISH** *adj*

BRATTICE *v* -TICED, -TICING, -TICES to partition

BRATTLE *v* -TLED, -TLING, -TLES to clatter

BRATTY *adj* -TIER, -TIEST resembling a brat

BRAUNITE *n* pl. -S a mineral

BRAVA *n* pl. -S a shout of approval

BRAVADO *n* pl. -DOS or -DOES false bravery

BRAVE *adj* BRAVER, BRAVEST showing courage **BRAVELY** *adv*

BRAVE *v* BRAVED, BRAVING, BRAVES to face with courage

BRAVER *n* pl. -S one that braves

BRAVERY *n* pl. -ERIES courage

BRAVEST superlative of brave

BRAVING present participle of brave

BRAVO	*n* pl. -VOS or -VOES a hired killer
BRAVO	*v* -ED, -ING, -ES to applaud by shouting "bravo"
BRAVURA	*n* pl. -RAS or -RE fine musical technique
BRAW	*adj* BRAWER, BRAWEST splendid
BRAWL	*v* -ED, -ING, -S to fight
BRAWLER	*n* pl. -S a fighter
BRAWLIE	*adv* splendidly
BRAWLY	*adj* BRAWLIER, BRAWLIEST inclined to brawl
BRAWN	*n* pl. -S muscular strength
BRAWNY	*adj* BRAWNIER, BRAWNIEST muscular **BRAWNILY** *adv*
BRAWS	*n/pl* fine clothes
BRAXY	*n* pl. BRAXIES a fever of sheep
BRAY	*v* BRAYED, BRAYING, BRAYS to utter a harsh cry
BRAYER	*n* pl. -S a roller used to spread ink
BRAZA	*n* pl. -S a Spanish unit of length
BRAZE	*v* BRAZED, BRAZING, BRAZES to solder together
BRAZEN	*v* -ED, -ING, -S to face boldly
BRAZENLY	*adv* boldly
BRAZER	*n* pl. -S one that brazes
BRAZIER	*n* pl. -S one who works in brass
BRAZIL	*n* pl. -S a dyewood
BRAZILIN	*n* pl. -S a chemical compound
BRAZING	present participle of braze
BREACH	*v* -ED, -ING, -ES to break through
BREACHER	*n* pl. -S one that breaches
BREAD	*v* -ED, -ING, -S to cover with bread crumbs
BREADNUT	*n* pl. -S a tropical fruit
BREADTH	*n* pl. -S width
BREAK	*v* BROKE, BROKEN, BREAKING, BREAKS to reduce to fragments
BREAKAGE	*n* pl. -S the act of breaking
BREAKER	*n* pl. -S one that breaks
BREAKING	*n* pl. -S the change of a pure vowel to a diphthong
BREAKOUT	*n* pl. -S an escape
BREAKUP	*n* pl. -S the act of breaking up
BREAM	*v* -ED, -ING, -S to clean a ship's bottom

BREAST	*v* -ED, -ING, -S to confront boldly
BREATH	*n* pl. -S air inhaled and exhaled
BREATHE	*v* BREATHED, BREATHING, BREATHES to inhale and exhale air
BREATHER	*n* pl. -S one that breathes
BREATHY	*adj* BREATHIER, BREATHIEST marked by loud breathing
BRECCIA	*n* pl. -S a type of rock **BRECCIAL** *adj*
BRECHAM	*n* pl. -S a collar for a horse
BRECHAN	*n* pl. -S brecham
BRED	past tense of breed
BREDE	*n* pl. -S a braid
BREE	*n* pl. -S broth
BREECH	*v* -ED, -ING, -ES to clothe with breeches (trousers)
BREED	*v* BRED, BREEDING, BREEDS to cause to give birth
BREEDER	*n* pl. -S one that breeds
BREEDING	*n* pl. -S upbringing
BREEKS	*n/pl* breeches
BREEZE	*v* BREEZED, BREEZING, BREEZES to move swiftly
BREEZY	*adj* BREEZIER, BREEZIEST windy **BREEZILY** *adv*
BREGMA	*n* pl. -MATA a junction point of the skull **BREGMATE** *adj*
BRENT	*n* pl. -S brant
BRETHREN	*a* pl. of brother
BREVE	*n* pl. -S a symbol used to indicate a short vowel
BREVET	*v* -VETED, -VETING, -VETS or -VETTED, -VETTING, -VETS to confer an honorary rank upon
BREVETCY	*n* pl. -CIES an honorary rank
BREVIARY	*n* pl. -RIES a prayer book
BREVIER	*n* pl. -S a size of type
BREVITY	*n* pl. -TIES shortness of duration
BREW	*v* -ED, -ING, -S to make beer or the like
BREWAGE	*n* pl. -S a brewed beverage
BREWER	*n* pl. -S one that brews
BREWERY	*n* pl. -ERIES a place for brewing
BREWING	*n* pl. -S a quantity brewed at one time
BREWIS	*n* pl. BREWISES broth
BRIAR	*n* pl. -S brier **BRIARY** *adj*

BRIARD	*n* pl. -S a large dog	**BRIMFULL**	*adj* brimful
BRIBE	*v* BRIBED, BRIBING, BRIBES to practice bribery **BRIBABLE** *adj*	**BRIMLESS**	*adj* having no brim (an upper edge)
BRIBER	*n* pl. -S one that bribes	**BRIMMED**	past tense of brim
BRIBERY	*n* pl. -ERIES an act of influencing corruptly	**BRIMMER**	*n* pl. -S a brimming cup or glass
BRIBING	present participle of bribe	**BRIMMING**	present participle of brim
BRICK	*v* -ED, -ING, -S to build with bricks (blocks of clay)	**BRIN**	*n* pl. -S a rib of a fan
		BRINDED	*adj* brindled
BRICKBAT	*n* pl. -S a piece of brick	**BRINDLE**	*n* pl. -S a brindled color
BRICKLE	*adj* brittle	**BRINDLED**	*adj* streaked
BRICKY	*adj* BRICKIER, BRICKIEST made of bricks	**BRINE**	*v* BRINED, BRINING, BRINES to treat with brine (salted water)
BRICOLE	*n* pl. -S a cushion shot in billiards	**BRINER**	*n* pl. -S one that brines
BRIDAL	*n* pl. -S a wedding	**BRING**	*v* BROUGHT, BRINGING, BRINGS to take with oneself to a place
BRIDALLY	*adv* in a manner befitting a bride		
BRIDE	*n* pl. -S a woman just married or about to be married	**BRINGER**	*n* pl. -S one that brings
		BRINIER	comparative of briny
BRIDGE	*v* BRIDGED, BRIDGING, BRIDGES to connect	**BRINIES**	pl. of briny
		BRINIEST	superlative of briny
BRIDGING	*n* pl. -S a bracing	**BRINISH**	*adj* resembling brine
BRIDLE	*v* -DLED, -DLING, -DLES to control with a restraint	**BRINK**	*n* pl. -S an extreme edge
		BRINY	*n* pl. BRINIES the sea
BRIDLER	*n* pl. -S one that bridles	**BRINY**	*adj* BRINIER, BRINIEST salty
BRIDOON	*n* pl. -S a device used to control a horse	**BRIO**	*n* pl. BRIOS liveliness
		BRIOCHE	*n* pl. -S a rich roll
BRIE	*n* pl. -S bree	**BRIONY**	*n* pl. -NIES bryony
BRIEF	*adj* BRIEFER, BRIEFEST short	**BRIQUET**	*v* -QUETTED, -QUETTING, -QUETS to mold into small bricks
BRIEF	*v* -ED, ING, -S to summarize		
BRIEFER	*n* pl. -S one that briefs		
BRIEFING	*n* pl. -S a short lecture	**BRISANCE**	*n* pl. -S the shattering effect of an explosive **BRISANT** *adj*
BRIEFLY	*adv* in a brief manner		
BRIER	*n* pl. -S a thorny shrub **BRIERY** *adj*	**BRISK**	*adj* BRISKER, BRISKEST lively
		BRISK	*v* -ED, -ING, -S to make brisk
BRIG	*n* pl. -S a two-masted ship	**BRISKET**	*n* pl. -S the breast of an animal
BRIGADE	*v* -GADED, -GADING, -GADES to group together	**BRISKLY**	*adv* in a brisk manner
		BRISLING	*n* pl. -S a small herring
BRIGAND	*n* pl. -S a bandit	**BRISTLE**	*v* -TLED, -TLING, -TLES to rise stiffly
BRIGHT	*adj* BRIGHTER, BRIGHTEST emitting much light **BRIGHTLY** *adv*		
		BRISTLY	*adj* -TLIER, -TLIEST stiffly erect
		BRISTOL	*n* pl. -S a smooth cardboard
BRIGHT	*n* pl. -S a light-hued tobacco	**BRIT**	*n* pl. -S a young herring
BRIGHTEN	*v* -ED, -ING, -S to make bright	**BRITCHES**	*n/pl* breeches; trousers
BRILL	*n* pl. -S an edible flatfish	**BRITSKA**	*n* pl. -S an open carriage
BRIM	*v* BRIMMED, BRIMMING, BRIMS to fill to the top	**BRITT**	*n* pl. -S brit
		BRITTLE	*adj* -TLER, -TLEST likely to break
BRIMFUL	*adj* ready to overflow		

BRITTLE   v -TLED, -TLING, -TLES to become brittle

BRITZKA   n pl. -S britska

BRITZSKA   n pl. -S britska

BROACH   v -ED, -ING, -ES to pierce so as to withdraw a liquid

BROACHER   n pl. -S one that broaches

BROAD   adj BROADER, BROADEST wide

BROAD   n pl. -S an expansion of a river

BROADAX   n pl. -ES a broad-edged ax

BROADAXE   n pl. -S broadax

BROADEN   v -ED, -ING, -S to make broad

BROADISH   adj somewhat broad

BROADLY   adv in a broad manner

BROCADE   v -CADED, -CADING, -CADES to weave with a raised design

BROCATEL   n pl. -S a heavy fabric

BROCCOLI   n pl. -S a vegetable related to the cabbage

BROCHE   adj brocaded

BROCHURE   n pl. -S a pamphlet

BROCK   n pl. -S a badger

BROCKAGE   n pl. -S an imperfectly minted coin

BROCKET   n pl. -S a small, red deer

BROCOLI   n pl. -S broccoli

BROGAN   n pl. -S a heavy shoe

BROGUE   n pl. -S an Irish accent

BROGUERY   n pl. -ERIES the use of an Irish accent

BROGUISH   adj resembling a brogue

BROIDER   v -ED, -ING, -S to adorn with needlework

BROIDERY   n pl. -DERIES the act of broidering

BROIL   v -ED, -ING, -S to cook by direct heat

BROILER   n pl. -S a device for broiling

BROKAGE   n pl. -S the business of a broker

BROKE   past tense of break

BROKEN   adj shattered **BROKENLY** adv

BROKER   n pl. -S an agent who buys and sells stocks

BROLLY   n pl. -LIES an umbrella

BROMAL   n pl. -S a medicinal liquid

BROMATE   v -MATED, -MATING, -MATES to combine with bromine

BROME   n pl. -S a tall grass

BROMELIN   n pl. -S an enzyme

BROMIC   adj containing bromine

BROMID   n pl. -S bromide

BROMIDE   n pl. -S a bromine compound

BROMIDIC   adj commonplace; trite

BROMIN   n pl. -S bromine

BROMINE   n pl. -S a volatile liquid element

BROMISM   n pl. -S a diseased condition of the skin

BROMO   n pl. -MOS a medicinal compound

BRONC   n pl. -S bronco

BRONCHI   pl. of bronchus

BRONCHIA   n/pl the main air passages of the lungs

BRONCHO   n pl. -CHOS bronco

BRONCHUS   n pl. -CHI a tracheal branch

BRONCO   n pl. -COS a wild horse

BRONZE   v BRONZED, BRONZING, BRONZES to make brown or tan

BRONZER   n pl. -S one that bronzes

BRONZING   n pl. -S a brownish coloring

BRONZY   adj BRONZIER, BRONZIEST of a brownish color

BROO   n pl. BROOS a bree

BROOCH   n pl. -ES a decorative pin

BROOD   v -ED, -ING, -S to ponder gloomily

BROODER   n pl. -S one that broods

BROODY   adj BROODIER, BROODIEST tending to brood

BROOK   v -ED, -ING, -S to tolerate

BROOKITE   n pl. -S a mineral

BROOKLET   n pl. -S a small brook or creek

BROOM   v -ED, -ING, -S to sweep

BROOMY   adj BROOMIER, BROOMIEST abounding in broom (a type of shrub)

BROSE   n pl. -S a porridge

BROSY   adj smeared with brose

BROTH   n pl. -S a thin clear soup

BROTHEL   n pl. -S a house of prostitution

BROTHER   n pl. -S or BRETHREN a male sibling

BROTHER   v -ED, -ING, -S to treat like a brother

BROTHY   adj resembling broth

BROUGHAM   *n* pl. -S a type of carriage

BROUGHT   past tense of bring

BROUHAHA   *n* pl. -S an uproar

BROW   *n* pl. -S the forehead

BROWBEAT   *v* -BEAT, -BEATEN, -BEATING, -BEATS to intimidate

BROWLESS   *adj* lacking eyebrows

BROWN   *adj* BROWNER, BROWNEST of a dark color

BROWN   *v* -ED, -ING, -S to make brown

BROWNIE   *n* pl. -S a small sprite

BROWNIER   comparative of browny

BROWNIEST   superlative of browny

BROWNISH   *adj* somewhat brown

BROWNOUT   *n* pl. -S a power reduction

BROWNY   *adj* BROWNIER, BROWNIEST somewhat brown

BROWSE   *v* BROWSED, BROWSING, BROWSES to look at casually

BROWSER   *n* pl. -S one that browses

BRUCELLA   *n* pl. -LAE or -LAS any of a genus of harmful bacteria

BRUCIN   *n* pl. -S brucine

BRUCINE   *n* pl. -S a poisonous alkaloid

BRUGH   *n* pl. -S a borough

BRUIN   *n* pl. -S a bear

BRUISE   *v* BRUISED, BRUISING, BRUISES to injure without breaking the surface of the skin

BRUISER   *n* pl. -S a big, husky man

BRUIT   *v* -ED, -ING, -S to spread news of

BRUITER   *n* pl. -S one that bruits

BRULOT   *n* pl. -S a biting fly

BRULYIE   *n* pl. -S a noisy quarrel

BRULZIE   *n* pl. -S brulyie

BRUMAL   *adj* wintry

BRUMBY   *n* pl. -BIES a wild horse

BRUME   *n* pl. -S fog **BRUMOUS** *adj*

BRUNCH   *v* -ED, -ING, -ES to eat a late morning meal

BRUNET   *n* pl. -S a dark-haired male

BRUNETTE   *n* pl. -S a dark-haired female

BRUNIZEM   *n* pl. -S a prairie soil

BRUNT   *n* pl. -S the main impact

BRUSH   *v* -ED, -ING, -ES to touch lightly

BRUSHER   *n* pl. -S one that brushes

BRUSHIER   comparative of brushy

BRUSHIEST   superlative of brushy

BRUSHOFF   *n* pl. -S an abrupt dismissal

BRUSHUP   *n* pl. -S a quick review

BRUSHY   *adj* BRUSHIER, BRUSHIEST shaggy; rough

BRUSK   *adj* BRUSKER, BRUSKEST brusque

BRUSQUE   *adj* BRUSQUER, BRUSQUEST abrupt in manner

BRUT   *adj* very dry

BRUTAL   *adj* cruel; savage **BRUTALLY** *adv*

BRUTE   *v* BRUTED, BRUTING, BRUTES to shape a diamond by rubbing it with another diamond

BRUTELY   *adv* in a brutal manner

BRUTIFY   *v* -FIED, -FYING, -FIES to make brutal

BRUTING   present participle of brute

BRUTISH   *adj* brutal

BRUTISM   *n* pl. -S the state of being brutal

BRUXISM   *n* pl. -S a nervous grinding of the teeth

BRYOLOGY   *n* pl. -GIES the study of mosses

BRYONY   *n* pl. -NIES a climbing plant

BRYOZOAN   *n* pl. -S a type of small aquatic animal

BUB   *n* pl. -S young fellow

BUBAL   *n* pl. -S a large antelope

BUBALE   *n* pl. -S bubal

BUBALINE   *adj* pertaining to the bubal

BUBALIS   *n* pl. -LISES bubal

BUBBIES   pl. of bubby

BUBBLE   *v* -BLED, -BLING, -BLES to form bubbles (bodies of gas contained within a liquid)

BUBBLER   *n* pl. -S a drinking fountain

BUBBLY   *n* pl. -BLIES champagne

BUBBLY   *adj* -BLIER, -BLIEST full of bubbles

BUBBY   *n* pl. -BIES a breast — often considered vulgar

BUBINGA   *n* pl. -S an African tree

BUBO   *n* pl. -BOES a swelling of a lymph gland **BUBOED** *adj*

BUBONIC   *adj* pertaining to a bubo

BUCCAL   *adj* pertaining to the cheek **BUCCALLY** *adv*

BUCK   v -ED, -ING, -S to leap forward and upward suddenly

BUCKAROO   n pl. -ROOS a cowboy

BUCKAYRO   n pl. -ROS buckaroo

BUCKBEAN   n pl. -S a marsh plant

BUCKEEN   n pl. -S a poor man who acts as if wealthy

BUCKER   n pl. -S a bucking horse

BUCKEROO   n pl. -ROOS buckaroo

BUCKET   v -ED, -ING, -S to hurry

BUCKEYE   n pl. -S a nut-bearing tree

BUCKISH   adj foppish

BUCKLE   v -LED, -LING, -LES to bend under pressure

BUCKLER   v -ED, -ING, -S to shield

BUCKO   n pl. BUCKOES a bully

BUCKRA   n pl. -S a white man — often used disparagingly

BUCKRAM   v -ED, -ING, -S to stiffen

BUCKSAW   n pl. -S a wood-cutting saw

BUCKSHEE   n pl. -S something extra obtained free

BUCKSHOT   n pl. -S a large lead shot

BUCKSKIN   n pl. -S the skin of a male deer

BUCKTAIL   n pl. -S a fishing lure

BUCOLIC   n pl. -S a pastoral poem

BUD   v BUDDED, BUDDING, BUDS to put forth buds (undeveloped plant parts)

BUDDER   n pl. -S one that buds

BUDDIES   pl. of buddy

BUDDING   adj being in an early stage of development

BUDDLE   n pl. -S an apparatus on which crushed ore is washed

BUDDLEIA   n pl. -S a tropical shrub

BUDDY   n pl. -DIES a good friend

BUDGE   v BUDGED, BUDGING, BUDGES to move slightly

BUDGER   n pl. -S one that budges

BUDGET   v -ED, -ING, -S to estimate expenditures

BUDGETER   n pl. -S one that budgets

BUDGIE   n pl. -S a small parrot

BUDGING   present participle of budge

BUDLESS   adj being without buds

BUDLIKE   adj resembling a bud

BUFF   v -ED, -ING, -S to polish
BUFFABLE adj

BUFFALO   n pl. -LOES or -LOS an ox-like animal

BUFFALO   v -ED, -ING, -ES to intimidate

BUFFER   v -ED, -ING, -S to cushion

BUFFET   v -ED, -ING, -S to hit sharply

BUFFETER   n pl. -S one that buffets

BUFFIER   comparative of buffy

BUFFIEST   superlative of buffy

BUFFO   n pl. -FI or -FOS an operatic clown

BUFFOON   n pl. -S a clown

BUFFY   adj BUFFIER, BUFFIEST of a yellowish-brown color

BUG   v BUGGED, BUGGING, BUGS to annoy

BUGABOO   n pl. -BOOS a bugbear

BUGBANE   n pl. -S a perennial herb

BUGBEAR   n pl. -S an object or source of dread

BUGEYE   n pl. -S a small boat

BUGGED   past tense of bug

BUGGER   v -ED, -ING, -S to commit sodomy with — usually considered vulgar

BUGGERY   n pl. -GERIES sodomy

BUGGING   present participle of bug

BUGGY   n pl. -GIES a light carriage

BUGGY   adj -GIER, -GIEST infested with bugs

BUGHOUSE   n pl. -S an insane asylum

BUGLE   v -GLED, -GLING, -GLES to play a bugle (a brass wind instrument)

BUGLER   n pl. -S one that plays a bugle

BUGLOSS   n pl. -ES a coarse plant

BUGSEED   n pl. -S an annual herb

BUGSHA   n pl. -S buqsha

BUHL   n pl. -S a style of furniture decoration

BUHLWORK   n pl. -S buhl

BUHR   n pl. -S a heavy stone

BUILD   v BUILT or BUILDED, BUILDING, BUILDS to construct

BUILDER   n pl. -S one that builds

BUILDING   n pl. -S something that is built

BUILDUP   n pl. -S an accumulation

BUILT	a past tense of build
BUIRDLY	adj burly
BULB	n pl. -S an underground bud **BULBAR, BULBED** adj
BULBEL	n pl. -S bulbil
BULBIL	n pl. -S a small bulb
BULBOUS	adj bulb-shaped; bulging
BULBUL	n pl. -S a songbird
BULGE	v BULGED, BULGING, BULGES to swell out
BULGER	n pl. -S a golf club
BULGUR	n pl. -S crushed wheat
BULGY	adj BULGIER, BULGIEST bulging
BULIMIA	n pl. -S insatiable appetite **BULIMIC, BULIMIAC** adj
BULK	v -ED, -ING, -S to gather into a mass
BULKAGE	n pl. -S a peristaltic stimulant
BULKHEAD	n pl. -S an upright partition in a ship
BULKY	adj BULKIER, BULKIEST massive **BULKILY** adv
BULL	v -ED, -ING, -S to push ahead
BULLA	n pl. -LAE a large blister
BULLACE	n pl. -S a purple plum
BULLATE	adj having a blistered appearance
BULLBAT	n pl. -S a nocturnal bird
BULLDOG	v -DOGGED, -DOGGING, -DOGS to throw a steer
BULLDOZE	v -DOZED, -DOZING, -DOZES to bully
BULLET	v -ED, -ING, -S to move swiftly
BULLETIN	v -ED, -ING, -S to issue a news item
BULLFROG	n pl. -S a large frog
BULLHEAD	n pl. -S a freshwater catfish
BULLHORN	n pl. -S an electric megaphone
BULLIED	past tense of bully
BULLIER	comparative of bully
BULLIES	present 3d person sing. of bully
BULLIEST	superlative of bully
BULLION	n pl. -S uncoined gold or silver
BULLISH	adj stubborn
BULLNECK	n pl. -S a thick neck
BULLNOSE	n pl. -S a disease of swine
BULLOCK	n pl. -S a castrated bull **BULLOCKY** adj
BULLOUS	adj resembling bullae
BULLPEN	n pl. -S an enclosure for bulls
BULLPOUT	n pl. -S a bullhead
BULLRING	n pl. -S a bullfight arena
BULLRUSH	n pl. -ES bulrush
BULLSHIT	v -SHITTED, -SHITTING, -SHITS to mislead — usually considered vulgar
BULLWEED	n pl. -S knapweed
BULLWHIP	v -WHIPPED, -WHIPPING, -WHIPS to strike with a long whip
BULLY	v -LIED, -LYING, -LIES to treat abusively
BULLY	adj -LIER, -LIEST wonderful
BULLYBOY	n pl. -BOYS a ruffian
BULLYRAG	v -RAGGED, -RAGGING, -RAGS to bully
BULRUSH	n pl. -ES a tall marsh plant
BULWARK	v -ED, -ING, -S to fortify with a defensive wall
BUM	v BUMMED, BUMMING, BUMS to live idly
BUMBLE	v -BLED, -BLING, -BLES to bungle
BUMBLER	n pl. -S one that bumbles
BUMBLING	n pl. -S an instance of clumsiness
BUMBOAT	n pl. -S a boat used to peddle wares to larger ships
BUMF	n pl. -S paperwork
BUMKIN	n pl. -S a ship's spar
BUMMED	past tense of bum
BUMMER	n pl. -S one that bums
BUMMING	present participle of bum
BUMP	v -ED, -ING, -S to knock against
BUMPER	v -ED, -ING, -S to fill to the brim
BUMPKIN	n pl. -S an unsophisticated rustic
BUMPY	adj BUMPIER, BUMPIEST of uneven surface **BUMPILY** adv
BUN	n pl. -S a small bread roll
BUNCH	v -ED, -ING, -ES to group together
BUNCHY	adj BUNCHIER, BUNCHIEST clustered **BUNCHILY** adv
BUNCO	v -ED, -ING, -S to swindle
BUNCOMBE	n pl. -S nonsense
BUND	n pl. -S a political association

BUNDIST *n pl.* -S a member of a bund

BUNDLE *v* -DLED, -DLING, -DLES to fasten a group of objects together

BUNDLER *n pl.* -S one that bundles

BUNDLING *n pl.* -S a former courtship custom

BUNG *v* -ED, -ING, -S to plug with a cork or stopper

BUNGALOW *n pl.* -S a small cottage

BUNGHOLE *n pl.* -S a hole in a keg or barrel

BUNGLE *v* -GLED, -GLING, -GLES to work, make, or do clumsily

BUNGLER *n pl.* -S one that bungles

BUNGLING *n pl.* -S an instance of clumsiness

BUNION *n pl.* -S a painful swelling of the foot

BUNK *v* -ED, -ING, -S to go to bed

BUNKER *v* -ED, -ING, -S to store in a large bin

BUNKMATE *n pl.* -S a person with whom sleeping quarters are shared

BUNKO *v* -ED, -ING, -S to bunco

BUNKUM *n pl.* -S nonsense

BUNN *n pl.* -S bun

BUNNY *n pl.* -NIES a rabbit

BUNT *v* -ED, -ING, -S to butt

BUNTER *n pl.* -S one that bunts

BUNTING *n pl.* -S a fabric used for flags

BUNTLINE *n pl.* -S a rope used to haul up a sail

BUNYA *n pl.* -S an evergreen tree

BUOY *v* -ED, -ING, -S to mark with a buoy (a warning float)

BUOYAGE *n pl.* -S a group of buoys

BUOYANCE *n pl.* -S buoyancy

BUOYANCY *n pl.* -CIES the tendency to float

BUOYANT *adj* having buoyancy

BUQSHA *n pl.* -S a monetary unit of Yemen

BUR *v* BURRED, BURRING, BURS to burr

BURA *n pl.* -S buran

BURAN *n pl.* -S a violent windstorm

BURBLE *v* -BLED, -BLING, -BLES to speak quickly and excitedly

BURBLER *n pl.* -S one that burbles

BURBLY *adj* -BLIER, -BLIEST burbling

BURBOT *n pl.* -S a freshwater fish

BURD *n pl.* -S a maiden

BURDEN *v* -ED, -ING, -S to load heavily

BURDENER *n pl.* -S one that burdens

BURDIE *n pl.* -S burd

BURDOCK *n pl.* -S a coarse weed

BUREAU *n pl.* -REAUS or -REAUX a chest of drawers

BURET *n pl.* -S burette

BURETTE *n pl.* -S a measuring tube

BURG *n pl.* -S a city or town

BURGAGE *n pl.* -S a feudal tenure

BURGEE *n pl.* -S a small flag

BURGEON *v* -ED, -ING, -S to develop rapidly

BURGER *n pl.* -S a hamburger

BURGESS *n pl.* -ES a citizen of an English borough

BURGH *n pl.* -S a Scottish borough **BURGHAL** *adj*

BURGHER *n pl.* -S a citizen of a borough

BURGLAR *n pl.* -S one who commits burglary

BURGLARY *n pl.* -GLARIES a felonious theft

BURGLE *v* -GLED, -GLING, -GLES to commit burglary

BURGONET *n pl.* -S an open helmet

BURGOO *n pl.* -GOOS a thick oatmeal

BURGOUT *n pl.* -S burgoo

BURGRAVE *n pl.* -S a German nobleman

BURGUNDY *n pl.* -DIES a red wine

BURIAL *n pl.* -S the act of burying

BURIED past tense of bury

BURIER *n pl.* -S one that buries

BURIES present 3d person sing. of bury

BURIN *n pl.* -S an engraving tool

BURKE *v* BURKED, BURKING, BURKES to murder by suffocation

BURKER *n pl.* -S one that burkes

BURKITE *n pl.* -S a burker

BURL *v* -ED, -ING, -S to finish cloth by removing lumps

BURLAP *n pl.* -S a coarse fabric

BURLER *n pl.* -S one that burls

BURLESK *n pl.* -S a type of stage show

BURLEY *n pl.* -LEYS a light tobacco

BURLY *adj* -LIER, -LIEST heavy and muscular **BURLILY** *adv*

BURN *v* BURNED or BURNT, BURNING, BURNS to destroy by fire **BURNABLE** *adj*

BURNER *n* pl. -S one that burns

BURNET *n* pl. -S a perennial herb

BURNIE *n* pl. -S a brooklet

BURNING *n* pl. -S the firing of ceramic materials

BURNISH *v* -ED, -ING, -ES to polish

BURNOOSE *n* pl. -S a hooded cloak

BURNOUS *n* pl. -ES burnoose

BURNOUT *n* pl. -S a destructive fire

BURNT a past tense of burn

BURP *v* -ED, -ING, -S to belch

BURR *v* -ED, -ING, -S to remove a rough edge from

BURRED past tense of bur

BURRER *n* pl. -S one that burrs

BURRIER comparative of burry

BURRIEST superlative of burry

BURRING present participle of bur

BURRO *n* pl. -ROS a small donkey

BURROW *v* -ED, -ING, -S to dig a hole or tunnel in the ground

BURROWER *n* pl. -S one that burrows

BURRY *adj* -RIER, -RIEST prickly

BURSA *n* pl. -SAS or -SAE a bodily pouch **BURSAL** *adj*

BURSAR *n* pl. -S a college treasurer

BURSARY *n* pl. -RIES a college treasury

BURSATE *adj* pertaining to a bursa

BURSE *n* pl. -S a small bag or pouch

BURSEED *n* pl. -S a coarse weed

BURSITIS *n* pl. -TISES inflammation of a bursa

BURST *v* BURST or BURSTED, BURSTING, BURSTS to break open suddenly or violently

BURSTER *n* pl. -S one that bursts

BURSTONE *n* pl. -S a heavy stone

BURTHEN *v* -ED, -ING, -S to burden

BURTON *n* pl. -S a hoisting tackle

BURWEED *n* pl. -S a coarse weed

BURY *v* BURIED, BURYING, BURIES to put in the ground and cover with earth

BUS *v* BUSED, BUSING, BUSES or BUSSED, BUSSING, BUSSES to transport by bus (a large motor vehicle)

BUSBOY *n* pl. -BOYS a waiter's assistant

BUSBY *n* pl. -BIES a tall fur hat

BUSH *v* -ED, -ING, -ES to cover with bushes (shrubs)

BUSHBUCK *n* pl. -S a small antelope

BUSHEL *v* -ELED, -ELING, -ELS or -ELLED, -ELLING, -ELS to mend clothing

BUSHELER *n* pl. -S one that bushels

BUSHER *n* pl. -S a minor league baseball player

BUSHFIRE *n* pl. -S a fire in a wooded area

BUSHGOAT *n* pl. -S a bushbuck

BUSHIDO *n* pl. -DOS the code of the samurai

BUSHIER comparative of bushy

BUSHIEST superlative of bushy

BUSHILY *adv* in a bushy manner

BUSHING *n* pl. -S a lining for a hole

BUSHLAND *n* pl. -S unsettled forest land

BUSHLESS *adj* having no bushes

BUSHLIKE *adj* resembling a bush

BUSHMAN *n* pl. -MEN a woodsman

BUSHTIT *n* pl. -S a titmouse

BUSHY *adj* BUSHIER, BUSHIEST covered with bushes

BUSIED past tense of busy

BUSIER comparative of busy

BUSIES present 3d person sing. of busy

BUSIEST superlative of busy

BUSILY *adv* in a busy manner

BUSINESS *n* pl. -ES an occupation, profession, or trade

BUSING *n* pl. -S the act of transporting by bus

BUSK *v* -ED, -ING, -S to prepare

BUSKER *n* pl. -S a roaming entertainer

BUSKIN *n* pl. -S a high shoe **BUSKINED** *adj*

BUSMAN *n* pl. -MEN a bus operator

BUSS *v* -ED, -ING, -ES to kiss

BUSSED a past tense of bus

BUSSES a present 3d person sing. of bus

BUSSING   *n* pl. -S busing

BUST   *v* -ED, -ING, -S to burst

BUSTARD   *n* pl. -S a game bird

BUSTER   *n* pl. -S one that breaks up something

BUSTIC   *n* pl. -S a tropical tree

BUSTLE   *v* -TLED, -TLING, -TLES to move energetically

BUSTY   *adj* BUSIER, BUSIEST full-bosomed

BUSULFAN   *n* pl. -S a medicine

BUSY   *adj* BUSIER, BUSIEST occupied

BUSY   *v* BUSIED, BUSYING, BUSIES to make busy

BUSYBODY   *n* pl. -BODIES a nosy person

BUSYNESS   *n* pl. -ES the state of being busy

BUSYWORK   *n* pl. -S active but valueless work

BUT   *n* pl. -S a flatfish

BUTANE   *n* pl. -S a flammable gas

BUTANOL   *n* pl. -S a flammable alcohol

BUTANONE   *n* pl. -S a flammable ketone

BUTCH   *n* pl. -ES a lesbian with mannish traits

BUTCHER   *v* -ED, -ING, -S to slaughter

BUTCHERY   *n* pl. -ERIES wanton or cruel killing

BUTENE   *n* pl. -S butylene

BUTEO   *n* pl. -TEOS a hawk

BUTLER   *n* pl. -S a male servant

BUTLERY   *n* pl. -LERIES a storage room

BUTT   *v* -ED, -ING, -S to hit with the head

BUTTALS   *n/pl* boundary lines

BUTTE   *n* pl. -S an isolated hill

BUTTER   *v* -ED, -ING, -S to spread with butter (a milk product)

BUTTERY   *adj* -TERIER, -TERIEST containing butter

BUTTERY   *n* pl. -TERIES a wine cellar

BUTTIES   pl. of butty

BUTTOCK   *n* pl. -S either of the two rounded parts of the rump

BUTTON   *v* -ED, -ING, -S to fasten with a button (a small disk)

BUTTONER   *n* pl. -S one that buttons

BUTTONY   *adj* resembling a button

BUTTRESS   *v* -ED, -ING, -ES to prop up

BUTTY   *n* pl. -TIES a fellow workman

BUTUT   *n* pl. -S a unit of Gambian currency

BUTYL   *n* pl. -S a hydrocarbon radical

BUTYLATE   *v* -ATED, -ATING, -ATES to add a butyl to

BUTYLENE   *n* pl. -S a gaseous hydrocarbon

BUTYRAL   *n* pl. -S a chemical compound

BUTYRATE   *n* pl. -S a chemical salt

BUTYRIC   *adj* derived from butter

BUTYRIN   *n* pl. -S a chemical compound

BUTYROUS   *adj* resembling butter

BUTYRYL   *n* pl. -S a radical of butyric acid

BUXOM   *adj* -OMER, -OMEST heathily plump **BUXOMLY** *adv*

BUY   *v* BOUGHT, BUYING, BUYS to purchase **BUYABLE** *adj*

BUYER   *n* pl. -S one that buys

BUZZ   *v* -ED, -ING, -ES to make a vibrating sound

BUZZARD   *n* pl. -S a large bird of prey

BUZZER   *n* pl. -S a signaling device

BUZZWIG   *n* pl. -S a large, thick wig

BUZZWORD   *n* pl. -S a word used to impress someone

BWANA   *n* pl. -S master; boss

BY   *n* pl. BYS a pass in certain card games

BYE   *n* pl. -S a side issue

BYELAW   *n* pl. -S bylaw

BYGONE   *n* pl. -S a past occurrence

BYLAW   *n* pl. -S a secondary law

BYLINE   *v* -LINED, -LINING, -LINES to write under a byline (a line giving the author's name)

BYLINER   *n* pl. -S one that writes under a byline

BYNAME   *n* pl. -S a secondary name

BYPASS   *v* -ED, -ING, -ES to avoid by going around

BYPAST   *adj* past; gone by

BYPATH   *n* pl. -S an indirect road

BYPLAY   *n* pl. -PLAYS secondary action

BYRE   *n* pl. -S a cowshed

BYRL   *v* -ED, -ING, -S to birle

BYRNIE   *n* pl. -S an armored shirt

BYROAD   *n* pl. -S a side road

BYSSUS   *n* pl. BYSSUSES or BYSSI a fine linen

BYSTREET   *n* pl. -S a side street

BYTALK   *n* pl. -S small talk

BYTE   *n* pl. -S a group of adjacent binary digits

BYWAY   *n* pl. -WAYS a side road

BYWORD   *n* pl. -S a well-known saying

BYWORK   *n* pl. -S work done during leisure time

BYZANT   *n* pl. -S bezant

CAB	*n* pl. -S a taxicab	**CABOB**	*n* pl. -S kabob
CABAL	*v* -BALLED, -BALLING, -BALS to conspire	**CABOCHED**	*adj* full-faced — used of an animal's head in heraldry
CABALA	*n* pl. -S an occult or secret doctrine	**CABOCHON**	*n* pl. -S a precious stone
CABALISM	*n* pl. -S adherence to a cabala	**CABOODLE**	*n* pl. -S a collection
CABALIST	*n* pl. -S one who practices cabalism	**CABOOSE**	*n* pl. -S the last car of a freight train
CABALLED	past tense of cabal	**CABOSHED**	*adj* caboched
CABALLING	present participle of cabal	**CABOTAGE**	*n* pl. -S coastal trade
CABANA	*n* pl. -S a small cabin	**CABRESTA**	*n* pl. -S cabestro
CABARET	*n* pl. -S a music hall	**CABRESTO**	*n* pl. -TOS cabestro
CABBAGE	*v* -BAGED, -BAGING, -BAGES to steal	**CABRETTA**	*n* pl. -S a soft leather
CABBALA	*n* pl. -S cabala	**CABRILLA**	*n* pl. -S a sea bass
CABBALAH	*n* pl. -S cabala	**CABRIOLE**	*n* pl. -S a curved furniture leg
CABBIE	*n* pl. -S cabby	**CABSTAND**	*n* pl. -S a place where cabs await hire
CABBY	*n* pl. -BIES a driver of a cab	**CACAO**	*n* pl. -CAOS a tropical tree
CABER	*n* pl. -S a heavy pole thrown as a trial of strength	**CACHALOT**	*n* pl. -S a large whale
CABESTRO	*n* pl. -TROS a lasso	**CACHE**	*v* CACHED, CACHING, CACHES to store in a hiding place
CABEZON	*n* pl. -S a large, edible fish	**CACHEPOT**	*n* pl. -S an ornamental container for a flowerpot
CABEZONE	*n* pl. -S cabezon	**CACHET**	*n* pl. -S an official seal
CABILDO	*n* pl. -DOS a town council	**CACHEXIA**	*n* pl. -S general ill health **CACHEXIC** *adj*
CABIN	*v* -ED, -ING, -S to live in a cabin (a roughly built house)	**CACHEXY**	*n* pl. -CHEXIES cachexia
CABINET	*n* pl. -S a piece of furniture with shelves and drawers	**CACHING**	present participle of cache
CABLE	*v* -BLED, -BLING, -BLES to fasten with a cable (a heavy rope)	**CACHOU**	*n* pl. -S catechu
		CACHUCHA	*n* pl. -S a Spanish dance
CABLET	*n* pl. -S a small cable	**CACIQUE**	*n* pl. -S a tropical oriole
CABLEWAY	*n* pl. -WAYS a suspended cable	**CACKLE**	*v* -LED, -LING, -LES to make the sound of a hen
CABMAN	*n* pl. -MEN a driver of a cab	**CACKLER**	*n* pl. -S one that cackles

CACODYL	n pl. -S a poisonous liquid		**CAFE**	n pl. -S a restaurant
CACOMIXL	n pl. -S a raccoon-like mammal		**CAFFEIN**	n pl. -S caffeine
CACTUS	n pl. -TI or -TUSES a plant native to arid regions **CACTOID** adj		**CAFFEINE**	n pl. -S a bitter alkaloid used as a stimulant
CAD	n pl. -S an ungentlemanly man		**CAFTAN**	n pl. -S a full-length tunic
CADASTER	n pl. -S a public record of land ownership		**CAGE**	v CAGED, CAGING, CAGES to confine
CADASTRE	n pl. -S cadaster		**CAGELING**	n pl. -S a caged bird
CADAVER	n pl. -S a corpse		**CAGEY**	adj CAGIER, CAGIEST shrewd and careful
CADDICE	n pl. -S caddis		**CAGIER**	comparative of cagy
CADDIE	v -DIED, -DYING, -DIES to serve as a golfer's assistant		**CAGIEST**	superlative of cagy
CADDIS	n pl. -DISES a coarse woolen fabric		**CAGILY**	adv in a cagey manner
CADDISH	adj resembling a cad		**CAGINESS**	n pl. -ES the quality of being cagey
CADDY	v -DIED, -DYING, -DIES to caddie		**CAGING**	present participle of cage
CADE	n pl. -S a European shrub		**CAGY**	adj CAGIER, CAGIEST cagey
CADELLE	n pl. -S a small, black beetle		**CAHIER**	n pl. -S a notebook
CADENCE	v -DENCED, -DENCING, -DENCES to make rhythmic		**CAHOOT**	n pl. -S partnership
			CAHOW	n pl. -S a sea bird
CADENCY	n pl. -CIES a rhythm		**CAID**	n pl. -S a Muslim leader
CADENT	adj having rhythm		**CAIMAN**	n pl. -S a tropical reptile
CADENZA	n pl. -S an elaborate musical passage		**CAIN**	n pl. -S kain
			CAIQUE	n pl. -S a long, narrow rowboat
CADET	n pl. -S a student at a military school		**CAIRD**	n pl. -S a gypsy
CADGE	v CADGED, CADGING, CADGES to get by begging		**CAIRN**	n pl. -S a mound of stones set up as a memorial **CAIRNED, CAIRNY** adj
CADGER	n pl. -S one that cadges		**CAISSON**	n pl. -S a watertight chamber
CADGY	adj cheerful		**CAITIFF**	n pl. -S a despicable person
CADI	n pl. -S a Muslim judge		**CAJAPUT**	n pl. -S cajeput
CADMIUM	n pl. -S a metallic element **CADMIC** adj		**CAJEPUT**	n pl. -S an Australian tree
CADRE	n pl. -S a nucleus of trained personnel		**CAJOLE**	v -JOLED, -JOLING, -JOLES to persuade by flattery
CADUCEUS	n pl. -CEI a heraldic wand or staff **CADUCEAN** adj		**CAJOLER**	n pl. -S one that cajoles
			CAJOLERY	n pl. -ERIES persuasion by flattery
CADUCITY	n pl. -TIES senility		**CAJOLING**	present participle of cajole
CADUCOUS	adj transitory; perishable		**CAJON**	n pl. -ES a steep-sided canyon
CAECUM	n pl. -CA cecum **CAECAL** adj **CAECALLY** adv		**CAJUPUT**	n pl. -S cajeput
CAEOMA	n pl. -S a spore-forming organ of a fungus		**CAKE**	v CAKED, CAKING, CAKES to form into a hardened mass
CAESIUM	n pl. -S cesium		**CAKEWALK**	v -ED, -ING, -S to step stylishly
CAESTUS	n pl. -ES cestus		**CALABASH**	n pl. -ES a gourd
CAESURA	n pl. -RAS or -RAE a pause in a line of verse **CAESURAL, CAESURIC** adj		**CALADIUM**	n pl. -S a tropical plant
			CALAMAR	n pl. -S calamary
			CALAMARY	n pl. -MARIES a squid

CALAMI pl. of calamus

CALAMINE v -MINED, -MINING, -MINES to apply an ointment for skin ailments

CALAMINT n pl. -S a perennial herb

CALAMITE n pl. -S an extinct treelike plant

CALAMITY n pl. -TIES a grievous misfortune

CALAMUS n pl. -MI a marsh plant

CALANDO adj gradually diminishing

CALASH n pl. -ES a light carriage

CALATHOS n pl. -THI a fruit basket

CALATHUS n pl. -THI calathos

CALCANEA n/pl calcanei

CALCANEI n/pl bones of the heel

CALCAR n pl. -CARIA an anatomical projection

CALCAR n pl. -S a type of oven

CALCEATE adj wearing shoes

CALCES a pl. of calx

CALCIC adj pertaining to lime or calcium

CALCIFIC adj containing salts of calcium

CALCIFY v -FIED, -FYING, -FIES to harden

CALCINE v -CINED, -CINING, -CINES to reduce to a calx by heat

CALCITE n pl. -S a mineral CALCITIC adj

CALCIUM n pl. -S a metallic element

CALCSPAR n pl. -S a calcite

CALCTUFA n pl. -S a mineral deposit

CALCTUFF n pl. -S calctufa

CALCULUS n pl. -LI or -LUSES a branch of mathematics

CALDERA n pl. -S a large crater

CALDRON n pl. -S a large kettle or boiler

CALECHE n pl. -S calash

CALENDAL adj pertaining to calends

CALENDAR v -ED, -ING, -S to schedule

CALENDER v -ED, -ING, -S to smooth by pressing between rollers

CALENDS n pl. -S the first day of the Roman month

CALESA n pl. -S a calash

CALF n pl. CALVES or CALFS a young cow or bull CALFLIKE adj

CALFSKIN n pl. -S the skin of a calf

CALIBER n pl. -S the diameter of a gun barrel

CALIBRE n pl. -S caliber CALIBRED adj

CALICES pl. of calix

CALICHE n pl. -S a mineral deposit

CALICLE n pl. -S a cup-shaped, anatomical structure

CALICO n pl. -COES or -COS a cotton fabric

CALIF n pl. -S caliph

CALIFATE n pl. -S the domain of a calif

CALIPASH n pl. -ES an edible part of a turtle

CALIPEE n pl. -S an edible part of a turtle

CALIPER v -ED, -ING, -S to use a type of measuring device

CALIPH n pl. -S a Muslim leader CALIPHAL adj

CALISAYA n pl. -S the medicinal bark of the cinchona

CALIX n pl. -LICES a cup

CALK v -ED, -ING, -S to caulk

CALKER n pl. -S one that calks

CALKIN n pl. -S a gripping projection on a horseshoe

CALL v -ED, -ING, -S to summon CALLABLE adj

CALLA n pl. -S a tropical plant

CALLAN n pl. -S callant

CALLANT n pl. -S a lad

CALLBACK n pl. -S a recall of a defective product

CALLBOY n pl. -BOYS a bellboy

CALLER n pl. -S one that calls

CALLET n pl. -S a prostitute

CALLING n pl. -S a vocation or profession

CALLIOPE n pl. -S a keyboard musical instrument

CALLIPEE n pl. -S calipee

CALLIPER v -ED, -ING, -S to caliper

CALLOSE n pl. -S a part of a plant cell wall

CALLOUS v -ED, -ING, -ES to make or become hard

CALLOW adj -LOWER, -LOWEST immature

CALLUS v -ED, -ING, -ES to form a hard growth

CALM adj CALMER, CALMEST free from agitation CALMLY adv

CALM v -ED, -ING, -S to make calm

CALMNESS *n* pl. -ES the state of being calm

CALOMEL *n* pl. -S a chemical compound used as a purgative

CALORIC *n* pl. -S heat

CALORIE *n* pl. -S a unit of heat

CALORY *n* pl. -RIES calorie

CALOTTE *n* pl. -S a skullcap

CALOYER *n* pl. -S a monk of the Eastern Church

CALPAC *n* pl. -S a sheepskin hat

CALPACK *n* pl. -S calpac

CALQUE *v* CALQUED, CALQUING, CALQUES to model a word's meaning upon that of an analogous word in another language

CALTHROP *n* pl. -S caltrop

CALTRAP *n* pl. -S caltrop

CALTROP *n* pl. -S a spiny plant

CALUMET *n* pl. -S a ceremonial pipe

CALUMNY *n* pl. -NIES a false and malicious accusation

CALUTRON *n* pl. -S a device used for separating isotopes

CALVADOS *n* pl. -ES a dry apple brandy

CALVARIA *n* pl. -S the dome of the skull

CALVARY *n* pl. -RIES a representation of the Crucifixion

CALVE *v* CALVED, CALVING, CALVES to give birth to a calf

CALVES a pl. of calf

CALX *n* pl. -ES or CALCES a mineral residue

CALYCATE *adj* calycine

CALYCEAL *adj* calycine

CALYCES a pl. of calyx

CALYCINE *adj* pertaining to a calyx

CALYCLE *n* pl. -S an outer calyx

CALYCULI *n/pl* small, cup-shaped structures

CALYPSO *n* pl. -SOS or -SOES an improvised song

CALYPTER *n* pl. -S calyptra

CALYPTRA *n* pl. -S a hood-shaped organ of flowers

CALYX *n* pl. -LYXES or -LYCES the outer protective covering of a flower

CAM *n* pl. -S a rotating or sliding piece of machinery

CAMAIL *n* pl. -S a piece of armor for the neck **CAMAILED** *adj*

CAMAS *n* pl. -ES camass

CAMASS *n* pl. -ES a perennial herb

CAMBER *v* -ED, -ING, -S to arch slightly

CAMBIA a pl. of cambium

CAMBIAL *adj* pertaining to cambium

CAMBISM *n* pl. -S the theory and practice of exchange in commerce

CAMBIST *n* pl. -S a dealer in bills of exchange

CAMBIUM *n* pl. -BIUMS or -BIA a layer of plant tissue

CAMBOGIA *n* pl. -S a gum resin

CAMBRIC *n* pl. -S a fine linen

CAME *n* pl. -S a leaden window rod

CAMEL *n* pl. -S a large, humped mammal

CAMELEER *n* pl. -S a camel driver

CAMELIA *n* pl. -S camellia

CAMELLIA *n* pl. -S a tropical shrub

CAMEO *v* -ED, -ING, -S to portray in sharp, delicate relief

CAMERA *n* pl. -ERAS or -ERAE a judge's chamber **CAMERAL** *adj*

CAMION *n* pl. -S a military truck

CAMISA *n* pl. -S a shirt or chemise

CAMISADE *n* pl. -S camisado

CAMISADO *n* pl. -DOS or -DOES an attack made at night

CAMISE *n* pl. -S a loose shirt or gown

CAMISIA *n* pl. -S camise

CAMISOLE *n* pl. -S a brief negligee

CAMLET *n* pl. -S a durable fabric

CAMOMILE *n* pl. -S a medicinal herb

CAMORRA *n* pl. -S an unscrupulous secret society

CAMP *v* -ED, -ING, -S to live in the open

CAMPAGNA *n* pl. -PAGNE a flat, open plain

CAMPAIGN *v* -ED, -ING, -S to conduct a series of operations to reach a specific goal

CAMPER *n* pl. -S one that camps

CAMPFIRE *n* pl. -S an outdoor fire

CAMPHENE *n* pl. -S camphine

CAMPHINE	*n pl.* -S an explosive liquid
CAMPHOL	*n pl.* -S borneol
CAMPHOR	*n pl.* -S a volatile compound
CAMPI	pl. of campo
CAMPIER	comparative of campy
CAMPIEST	superlative of campy
CAMPILY	*adv* in a campy manner
CAMPING	*n pl.* -S the act of living outdoors
CAMPION	*n pl.* -S an herb
CAMPO	*n pl.* -PI an open space in a town
CAMPO	*n pl.* -POS a level, grassy plain
CAMPONG	*n pl.* -S kampong
CAMPOREE	*n pl.* -S a gathering of Boy Scouts
CAMPSITE	*n pl.* -S an area suitable for camping
CAMPUS	*n pl.* -ES the grounds of a school
CAMPY	*adj* CAMPIER, CAMPIEST comically exaggerated
CAMSHAFT	*n pl.* -S a shaft fitted with cams
CAN	*v* CANNED, CANNING, CANS to put in a can (a cylindrical container)
CAN	*v* present sing. 2d person CAN or CANST, past sing. 2d person COULD, COULDEST, or COULDST — used as an auxiliary to express ability
CANAILLE	*n pl.* -S the common people
CANAKIN	*n pl.* -S cannikin
CANAL	*v* -NALLED, -NALLING, -NALS or -NALED, -NALING, -NALS to dig an artificial waterway through
CANALISE	*v* -ISED, -ISING, -ISES to canalize
CANALIZE	*v* -IZED, -IZING, -IZES to canal
CANALLED	a past tense of canal
CANALLER	*n pl.* -S a freight boat
CANALLING	a present participle of canal
CANAPE	*n pl.* -S a food served before a meal
CANARD	*n pl.* -S a false story
CANARY	*n pl.* -NARIES a songbird
CANASTA	*n pl.* -S a card game
CANCAN	*n pl.* -S a dance marked by high kicking
CANCEL	*v* -CELLED, -CELLING, -CELS or -CELED, -CELING, -CELS to annul
CANCELER	*n pl.* -S one that cancels
CANCER	*n pl.* -S a malignant growth
CANCHA	*n pl.* -S a jai alai court
CANCROID	*n pl.* -S a skin cancer
CANDELA	*n pl.* -S a unit of luminous intensity
CANDENT	*adj* glowing
CANDID	*adj* -DIDER, -DIDEST frank and sincere
CANDID	*n pl.* -S an unposed photograph
CANDIDA	*n pl.* -S a parasitic fungus
CANDIDLY	*adv* in a candid manner
CANDIED	past tense of candy
CANDIES	present 3d person sing. of candy
CANDLE	*v* -DLED, -DLING, -DLES to examine eggs in front of a light
CANDLER	*n pl.* -S one that candles
CANDOR	*n pl.* -S frankness; sincerity
CANDOUR	*n pl.* -S candor
CANDY	*v* -DIED, -DYING, -DIES to coat with sugar
CANE	*v* CANED, CANING, CANES to beat with a rod
CANELLA	*n pl.* -S a medicinal tree bark
CANER	*n pl.* -S one that canes
CANEWARE	*n pl.* -S a yellowish stoneware
CANFIELD	*n pl.* -S a card game
CANFUL	*n pl.* CANFULS or CANSFUL as much as a can holds
CANGUE	*n pl.* -S an ancient Chinese punishing device
CANIKIN	*n pl.* -S cannikin
CANINE	*n pl.* -S a dog
CANING	present participle of cane
CANINITY	*n pl.* -TIES the state of being a canine
CANISTER	*n pl.* -S a small, metal box
CANITIES	*n pl.* CANITIES the turning gray of the hair
CANKER	*v* -ED, -ING, -S to affect with ulcerous sores
CANNA	*n pl.* -S a tropical plant
CANNABIC	*adj* pertaining to cannabis
CANNABIN	*n pl.* -S a resin extracted from cannabis

CANNABIS   *n* pl. -BISES hemp

CANNED   past tense of can

CANNEL   *n* pl. -S an oily, compact coal

CANNELON   *n* pl. -S a stuffed roll

CANNER   *n* pl. -S one that cans food

CANNERY   *n* pl. -NERIES a place where food is canned

CANNIBAL   *n* pl. -S one who eats his own kind

CANNIE   *adj* -NIER, -NIEST canny

CANNIER   comparative of canny

CANNIEST   superlative of canny

CANNIKIN   *n* pl. -S a small can or cup

CANNILY   *adv* in a canny manner

CANNING   *n* pl. -S the business of preserving food in airtight containers

CANNON   *v* -ED, -ING, -S to fire a cannon (a heavy firearm)

CANNONRY   *n* pl. -RIES artillery

CANNOT   the negative form of can

CANNULA   *n* pl. -LAS or -LAE a tube inserted into a bodily cavity **CANNULAR** *adj*

CANNY   *adj* -NIER, -NIEST prudent

CANOE   *v* -NOED, -NOEING, -NOES to paddle a canoe (a light, slender boat)

CANOEIST   *n* pl. -S one who canoes

CANON   *n* pl. -S a law decreed by a church council **CANONIC** *adj*

CANONESS   *n* pl. -ES a woman who lives according to a canon

CANONISE   *v* -ISED, -ISING, -ISES to canonize

CANONIST   *n* pl. -S a specialist in canon law

CANONIZE   *v* -IZED, -IZING, -IZES to declare to be a saint

CANONRY   *n* pl. -RIES a clerical office

CANOPY   *v* -PIED, -PYING, -PIES to cover from above

CANOROUS   *adj* melodic

CANSFUL   a pl. of canful

CANSO   *n* pl. -SOS a love song

CANST   a present 2d person sing. of can

CANT   *v* -ED, -ING, -S to tilt or slant

CANTALA   *n* pl. -S a tropical plant

CANTATA   *n* pl. -S a vocal composition

CANTDOG   *n* pl. -S a device used to move logs

CANTEEN   *n* pl. -S a small container for carrying water

CANTER   *v* -ED, -ING, -S to ride a horse at a moderate pace

CANTHUS   *n* pl. -THI a corner of the eye **CANTHAL** *adj*

CANTIC   *adj* slanted

CANTICLE   *n* pl. -S a hymn

CANTINA   *n* pl. -S a saloon

CANTLE   *n* pl. -S the rear part of a saddle

CANTO   *n* pl. -TOS a division of a long poem

CANTON   *v* -ED, -ING, -S to divide into cantons (districts)

CANTONAL   *adj* pertaining to a canton

CANTOR   *n* pl. -S a religious singer

CANTRAIP   *n* pl. -S cantrip

CANTRAP   *n* pl. -S cantrip

CANTRIP   *n* pl. -S a magic spell

CANTUS   *n* pl. CANTUS a style of church music

CANTY   *adj* cheerful

CANULA   *n* pl. -LAS or -LAE cannula

CANULATE   *v* -LATED, -LATING, -LATES to insert a canula into

CANVAS   *v* -ED, -ING, -ES to canvass

CANVASER   *n* pl. -S one that canvases

CANVASS   *v* -ED, -ING, -ES to examine thoroughly

CANYON   *n* pl. -S a deep valley with steep sides

CANZONA   *n* pl. -S canzone

CANZONE   *n* pl. -NI or -NES a form of lyric poetry

CANZONET   *n* pl. -S a short song

CAP   *v* CAPPED, CAPPING, CAPS to provide with a cap (a type of head covering)

CAPABLE   *adj* -BLER, -BLEST having ability **CAPABLY** *adv*

CAPACITY   *n* pl. -TIES the ability to receive or contain

CAPE   *n* pl. -S a sleeveless garment **CAPED** *adj*

CAPELAN   *n* pl. -S capelin

CAPELET   *n* pl. -S a small cape

CAPELIN *n pl.* -S a small, edible fish

CAPER *v* -ED, -ING, -S to frolic

CAPERER *n pl.* -S one that capers

CAPESKIN *n pl.* -S a soft leather

CAPEWORK *n pl.* -S a bullfighting technique

CAPFUL *n pl.* -S as much as a cap can hold

CAPH *n pl.* -S kaph

CAPIAS *n pl.* -ES a judicial writ

CAPITA *pl.* of caput

CAPITAL *n pl.* -S the upper part of a column

CAPITATE *adj* head-shaped

CAPITOL *n pl.* -S a building occupied by a state legislature

CAPITULA *n/pl* flower clusters

CAPLESS *adj* being without a cap

CAPLIN *n pl.* -S capelin

CAPMAKER *n pl.* -S one that makes caps

CAPO *n pl.* -POS a pitch raising device for fretted instruments

CAPON *n pl.* -S a gelded rooster

CAPONIER *n pl.* -S a type of defense

CAPONIZE *v* -IZED, -IZING, -IZES to geld a rooster

CAPORAL *n pl.* -S a coarse tobacco

CAPOTE *n pl.* -S a hooded cloak or overcoat

CAPOUCH *n pl.* -ES capuche

CAPPED past tense of cap

CAPPER *n pl.* -S a capmaker

CAPPING *n pl.* -S a wax covering in a honeycomb

CAPRIC *adj* pertaining to a goat

CAPRICCI *n/pl* caprices

CAPRICE *n pl.* -S a whim

CAPRIFIG *n pl.* -S a European tree

CAPRINE *adj* capric

CAPRIOLE *v* -OLED, -OLING, -OLES to leap

CAPSICIN *n pl.* -S a liquid used as a flavoring

CAPSICUM *n pl.* -S a tropical herb

CAPSID *n pl.* -S the outer shell of a virus particle **CAPSIDAL** *adj*

CAPSIZE *v* -SIZED, -SIZING, -SIZES to overturn

CAPSTAN *n pl.* -S a machine used to hoist weights

CAPSTONE *n pl.* -S the top stone of a structure

CAPSULAR *adj* enclosed and compact

CAPSULE *v* -SULED, -SULING, -SULES to condense into a brief form

CAPTAIN *v* -ED, -ING, -S to lead or command

CAPTAN *n pl.* -S a fungicide

CAPTION *v* -ED, -ING, -S to provide with a title

CAPTIOUS *adj* tending to find fault

CAPTIVE *n pl.* -S a prisoner

CAPTOR *n pl.* -S one who takes or holds a captive

CAPTURE *v* -TURED, -TURING, -TURES to take by force or cunning

CAPTURER *n pl.* -S one that captures

CAPUCHE *n pl.* -S a hood or cowl **CAPUCHED** *adj*

CAPUCHIN *n pl.* -S a long-tailed monkey

CAPUT *n pl.* CAPITA a head or head-like part

CAPYBARA *n pl.* -S a large rodent

CAR *n pl.* -S an automobile

CARABAO *n pl.* -BAOS a water buffalo

CARABID *n pl.* -S a predatory beetle

CARABIN *n pl.* -S carbine

CARABINE *n pl.* -S carbine

CARACAL *n pl.* -S an African lynx

CARACARA *n pl.* -S a large hawk

CARACK *n pl.* -S carrack

CARACOL *v* -COLLED, -COLLING, -COLS to caracole

CARACOLE *v* -COLED, -COLING, -COLES to perform a half turn on a horse

CARACUL *n pl.* -S karakul

CARAFE *n pl.* -S a glass bottle

CARAGANA *n pl.* -S an Asian shrub

CARAGEEN *n pl.* -S an edible seaweed

CARAMEL *n pl.* -S a chewy candy

CARANGID *n pl.* -S a marine fish

CARAPACE *n pl.* -S a hard, protective outer covering

CARAPAX *n pl.* -ES carapace

CARASSOW *n pl.* -S curassow

CARAT *n pl.* -S a unit of weight for gems

CARATE *n pl.* -S a tropical skin disease

CARAVAN *v* -VANED, -VANING, -VANS or -VANNED, -VANNING, -VANS to travel in a group

CARAVEL *n* pl. -S a small sailing ship

CARAWAY *n* pl. -WAYS an herb used in cooking

CARBAMIC *adj* pertaining to a type of acid

CARBAMYL *n* pl. -S a chemical radical

CARBARN *n* pl. -S a garage for buses

CARBARYL *n* pl. -S an insecticide

CARBIDE *n* pl. -S a carbon compound

CARBINE *n* pl. -S a light rifle

CARBINOL *n* pl. -S an alcohol

CARBON *n* pl. -S a nonmetallic element **CARBONIC** *adj*

CARBONYL *n* pl. -S a chemical compound

CARBORA *n* pl. -S a wood-boring worm

CARBOXYL *n* pl. -S a univalent acid radical

CARBOY *n* pl. -BOYS a bottle enclosed in a protective basket **CARBOYED** *adj*

CARBURET *v* -RETED, -RETING, -RETS or -RETTED, -RETTING, -RETS to combine chemically with carbon

CARCAJOU *n* pl. -S a carnivorous mammal

CARCANET *n* pl. -S a jeweled necklace

CARCASE *n* pl. -S carcass

CARCASS *n* pl. -ES the body of a dead animal

CARCEL *n* pl. -S a unit of illumination

CARD *v* -ED, -ING, -S to provide with a card (a stiff piece of paper)

CARDAMOM *n* pl. -S a tropical herb

CARDAMON *n* pl. -S cardamom

CARDAMUM *n* pl. -S cardamom

CARDCASE *n* pl. -S a case for holding cards

CARDER *n* pl. -S one that does carding

CARDIA *n* pl. -DIAS or -DIAE an opening of the esophagus

CARDIAC *n* pl. -S a person with a heart disorder

CARDIGAN *n* pl. -S a type of sweater

CARDINAL *n* pl. -S a high-ranking official of the Roman Catholic Church

CARDING *n* pl. -S the process of combing and cleaning cotton fibers; cleaned and combed fibers

CARDIOID *n* pl. -S a heart-shaped curve

CARDITIS *n* pl. -TISES inflammation of the heart **CARDITIC** *adj*

CARDOON *n* pl. -S a perennial plant

CARE *v* CARED, CARING, CARES to be concerned or interested

CAREEN *v* -ED, -ING, -S to lurch while moving

CAREENER *n* pl. -S one that careens

CAREER *v* -ED, -ING, -S to go at full speed

CAREERER *n* pl. -S one that careers

CAREFREE *adj* being without worry or anxiety

CAREFUL *adj* -FULLER, -FULLEST cautious

CARELESS *adj* inattentive; negligent

CARER *n* pl. -S one that cares

CARESS *v* -ED, -ING, -ES to touch lovingly

CARESSER *n* pl. -S one that caresses

CARET *n* pl. -S a proofreaders' symbol

CAREWORN *adj* haggard

CAREX *n* pl. CARICES a marsh plant

CARFARE *n* pl. -S payment for a bus or car ride

CARFUL *n* pl. -S as much as a car can hold

CARGO *n* pl. -GOS or -GOES conveyed merchandise

CARHOP *n* pl. -S a waitress at a drive-in restaurant

CARIBE *n* pl. -S the piranha

CARIBOU *n* pl. -S a large deer

CARICES pl. of carex

CARIES *n* pl. CARIES tooth decay **CARIED** *adj*

CARILLON *v* -LONNED, -LONNING, -LONS to play a set of bells

CARINA *n* pl. -NAS or -NAE a carinate anatomical part **CARINAL** *adj*

CARINATE *adj* shaped like the keel of a ship

CARING present participle of care

CARIOCA *n* pl. -S a South American dance

CARIOLE *n* pl. -S a small, open carriage

CARIOUS *adj* decayed

CARK *v* -ED, -ING, -S to worry

CARL *n* pl. -S a peasant

CARLE *n* pl. -S carl

CARLESS *adj* being without a car

CARLIN	*n* pl. -S an old woman
CARLINE	*n* pl. -S carling
CARLING	*n* pl. -S a beam supporting a ship's deck
CARLISH	*adj* resembling a carl
CARLOAD	*n* pl. -S as much as a car can hold
CARMAKER	*n* pl. -S an automobile manufacturer
CARMAN	*n* pl. -MEN a streetcar driver
CARMINE	*n* pl. -S a vivid red color
CARN	*n* pl. -S cairn
CARNAGE	*n* pl. -S great and bloody slaughter
CARNAL	*adj* pertaining to bodily appetites **CARNALLY** *adv*
CARNAUBA	*n* pl. -S a palm tree
CARNEY	*n* pl. -NEYS carny
CARNIE	*n* pl. -S carny
CARNIES	pl. of carny
CARNIFY	*v* -FIED, -FYING, -FIES to form into flesh
CARNIVAL	*n* pl. -S a traveling amusement show
CARNY	*n* pl. -NIES a carnival
CAROACH	*n* pl. -ES caroche
CAROB	*n* pl. -S an evergreen tree
CAROCH	*n* pl. -ES caroche
CAROCHE	*n* pl. -S a stately carriage
CAROL	*v* -OLED, -OLING, -OLS or -OLLED, -OLLING, -OLS to sing joyously
CAROLER	*n* pl. -S one that carols
CAROLI	a pl. of carolus
CAROLLED	a past tense of carol
CAROLLER	*n* pl. -S caroler
CAROLLING	a present participle of carol
CAROLUS	*n* pl. -LUSES or -LI an old English coin
CAROM	*v* -ED, -ING, -S to collide with and rebound
CAROTENE	*n* pl. -S a plant pigment
CAROTID	*n* pl. -S an artery in the neck
CAROTIN	*n* pl. -S carotene
CAROUSAL	*n* pl. -S a boisterous drinking party
CAROUSE	*v* -ROUSED, -ROUSING, -ROUSES to engage in a carousal
CAROUSEL	*n* pl. -S an amusement park ride
CAROUSER	*n* pl. -S one that carouses
CAROUSING	present participle of carouse
CARP	*v* -ED, -ING, -S to find fault unreasonably
CARPAL	*n* pl. -S carpale
CARPALE	*n* pl. -LIA a bone of the wrist
CARPEL	*n* pl. -S a simple pistil
CARPER	*n* pl. -S one that carps
CARPET	*v* -ED, -ING, -S to cover a floor with a heavy fabric
CARPI	pl. of carpus
CARPING	*n* pl. -S the act of one who carps
CARPORT	*n* pl. -S a shelter for a car
CARPUS	*n* pl. -PI the wrist
CARRACK	*n* pl. -S a type of merchant ship
CARREL	*n* pl. -S a desk in a library stack for solitary study
CARRELL	*n* pl. -S carrel
CARRIAGE	*n* pl. -S a wheeled, horse-drawn vehicle
CARRIED	past tense of carry
CARRIER	*n* pl. -S one that carries
CARRIES	present 3d person sing. of carry
CARRIOLE	*n* pl. -S cariole
CARRION	*n* pl. -S dead and putrefying flesh
CARRITCH	*n* pl. -ES a religious handbook
CARROCH	*n* pl. -ES caroche
CARROM	*v* -ED, -ING, -S to carom
CARROT	*n* pl. -S an edible orange root
CARROTIN	*n* pl. -S carotene
CARROTY	*adj* -ROTIER, -ROTIEST resembling a carrot in color
CARRY	*v* -RIED, -RYING, -RIES to convey from one place to another
CARRYALL	*n* pl. -S a light covered carriage
CARRYON	*n* pl. -S a small piece of luggage
CARRYOUT	*n* pl. -S a take-out order of food
CARSE	*n* pl. -S low, fertile land along a river
CARSICK	*adj* nauseated from riding in a car

CART	v -ED, -ING, -S to convey in a cart (a two-wheeled vehicle) **CARTABLE** adj	**CASEOSE**	n pl. -S a proteose
		CASEOUS	adj cheesy
CARTAGE	n pl. -S the act of carting	**CASERN**	n pl. -S a barracks for soldiers
CARTE	n pl. -S a menu	**CASERNE**	n pl. -S casern
CARTEL	n pl. -S a business organization	**CASETTE**	n pl. -S cassette
CARTER	n pl. -S one that carts	**CASEWORK**	n pl. -S a form of social work
CARTLOAD	n pl. -S as much as a cart can hold	**CASEWORM**	n pl. -S an insect larva
CARTON	v -ED, -ING, -S to pack in a cardboard box	**CASH**	v -ED, -ING, -ES to convert into cash (ready money) **CASHABLE** adj
CARTOON	v -ED, -ING, -S to sketch a humorous representation of	**CASHAW**	n pl. -S cushaw
CARTOP	adj able to fit on top of a car	**CASHBOOK**	n pl. S a book of monetary records
CARTOUCH	n pl. -ES a scroll-like tablet	**CASHBOX**	n pl. -ES a container for money
CARUNCLE	n pl. -S a fleshy outgrowth	**CASHEW**	n pl. -S a nut-bearing tree
CARVE	v CARVED, CARVING, CARVES to form by cutting	**CASHIER**	v -ED, -ING, -S to dismiss in disgrace
CARVEL	n pl. -S caravel	**CASHLESS**	adj having no cash
CARVEN	adj carved	**CASHMERE**	n pl. -S a fine wool
CARVER	n pl. -S one that carves	**CASHOO**	n pl. -SHOOS catechu
CARVING	n pl. -S a carved figure or design	**CASIMERE**	n pl. -S a woolen fabric
CARYATID	n pl. -S or -ES a sculptured female figure used as a column	**CASIMIRE**	n pl. -S casimere
CARYOTIN	n pl. -S karyotin	**CASING**	n pl. -S a protective outer covering
CASA	n pl. -S a dwelling	**CASINO**	n pl. -NOS a gambling room
CASABA	n pl. -S a variety of melon	**CASK**	v -ED, -ING, -S to store in a cask (a strong barrel)
CASAVA	n pl. -S cassava		
CASCABEL	n pl. -S the rear part of a cannon	**CASKET**	v -ED, -ING, -S to place in a burial case
CASCABLE	n pl. -S cascabel	**CASKY**	adj resembling a cask
CASCADE	v -CADED, -CADING, -CADES to fall like a waterfall	**CASQUE**	n pl. -S a helmet **CASQUED** adj
CASCARA	n pl. -S a medicinal tree bark	**CASSABA**	n pl. -S casaba
CASE	v CASED, CASING, CASES to put in a case (a container or receptacle)	**CASSAVA**	n pl. -S a tropical plant
		CASSETTE	n pl. -S a small case containing audiotape or videotape
CASEASE	n pl. -S an enzyme	**CASSIA**	n pl. -S a variety of cinnamon
CASEATE	v -ATED, -ATING, -ATES to become cheesy	**CASSINO**	n pl. -NOS a card game
		CASSIS	n pl. -SISES a European bush
CASEBOOK	n pl. -S a law textbook	**CASSOCK**	n pl. -S a long garment worn by clergymen
CASED	past tense of case	**CAST**	v CAST, CASTING, CASTS to throw with force
CASEFY	v -FIED, -FYING, -FIES to caseate		
CASEIN	n pl. -S a milk protein **CASEIC** adj	**CASTANET**	n pl. -S a rhythm instrument
		CASTAWAY	n pl. -WAYS an outcast
CASEMATE	n pl. -S a bombproof shelter	**CASTE**	n pl. -S a system of distinct social classes
CASEMENT	n pl. -S a type of window	**CASTEISM**	n pl. -S the use of a caste system

CASTER *n pl.* -S a small, swiveling wheel

CASTING *n pl.* -S something made in a mold

CASTLE *v* -TLED, -TLING, -TLES to make a certain move in chess

CASTOFF *n pl.* -S a discarded person or thing

CASTOR *n pl.* -S caster

CASTRATE *v* -TRATED, -TRATING, -TRATES to remove the testes of

CASTRATO *n pl.* -TI a singer castrated in boyhood

CASUAL *n pl.* -S one who works occasionally

CASUALLY *adv* informally

CASUALTY *n pl.* -TIES a victim of war or disaster

CASUIST *n pl.* -S one who resolves ethical problems

CASUS *n pl.* CASUS a legal occurrence or event

CAT *v* CATTED, CATTING, CATS to hoist an anchor to the cathead

CATACOMB *n pl.* -S an underground cemetery

CATALASE *n pl.* -S an enzyme

CATALO *n pl.* -LOS or -LOES a hybrid between a buffalo and a cow

CATALOG *v* -ED, -ING, -S to classify information descriptively

CATALPA *n pl.* -S a tree

CATALYST *n pl.* -S a substance that accelerates a chemical reaction

CATALYZE *v* -LYZED, -LYZING, -LYZES to act as a catalyst

CATAMITE *n pl.* -S a boy used in sodomy

CATAPULT *v* -ED, -ING, -S to hurl through the air

CATARACT *n pl.* -S a tremendous waterfall

CATARRH *n pl.* -S inflammation of a mucous membrane

CATBIRD *n pl.* -S a songbird

CATBOAT *n pl.* -S a small sailboat

CATBRIER *n pl.* -S a thorny vine

CATCALL *v* -ED, -ING, -S to deride by making shrill sounds

CATCH *v* CAUGHT, CATCHING, CATCHES to capture after pursuit

CATCHALL *n pl.* -S a container for odds and ends

CATCHER *n pl.* -S one that catches

CATCHFLY *n pl.* -FLIES an insect-catching plant

CATCHUP *n pl.* -S ketchup

CATCHY *adj* CATCHIER, CATCHIEST pleasing and easily remembered

CATE *n pl.* -S a choice food

CATECHIN *n pl.* -S a chemical used in dyeing

CATECHOL *n pl.* -S a chemical used in photography

CATECHU *n pl.* -S a resin used in tanning

CATEGORY *n pl.* -RIES a division in any system of classification

CATENA *n pl.* -NAS or -NAE a closely linked series

CATENARY *n pl.* -NARIES a mathematical curve

CATENATE *v* -NATED, -NATING, -NATES to link together

CATENOID *n pl.* -S a geometric surface

CATER *v* -ED, -ING, -S to provide food and service for

CATERAN *n pl.* -S a brigand

CATERER *n pl.* -S one that caters

CATERESS *n pl.* -ES a woman who caters

CATFACE *n pl.* -S a deformity of fruit

CATFALL *n pl.* -S an anchor line

CATFISH *n pl.* -ES a scaleless, large-headed fish

CATGUT *n pl.* -S a strong cord

CATHEAD *n pl.* -S a beam projecting from a ship's bow

CATHECT *v* -ED, -ING, -S to invest with psychic energy

CATHEDRA *n pl.* -DRAS or -DRAE a bishop's throne

CATHETER *n pl.* -S a medical instrument

CATHEXIS *n pl.* -THEXES the concentration of psychic energy on a person or idea

CATHODE *n pl.* -S a negatively charged electrode **CATHODIC** *adj*

CATHOLIC *adj* universal

CATHOUSE *n pl.* -S a brothel

CATION *n pl.* -S a positively charged ion **CATIONIC** *adj*

CATKIN *n pl.* -S a flower cluster

CATLIKE *adj* resembling a cat; stealthy; silent

CATLIN	*n* pl. -S catling	**CAULKING**	*n* pl. -S the material used to caulk
CATLING	*n* pl. -S a surgical knife	**CAUSABLE**	*adj* capable of being caused
CATMINT	*n* pl. -S catnip	**CAUSAL**	*n* pl. -S a word expressing cause or reason
CATNAP	*v* -NAPPED, -NAPPING, -NAPS to doze	**CAUSALLY**	*adv* by way of causing
CATNAPER	*n* pl. -S one that steals cats	**CAUSE**	*v* CAUSED, CAUSING, CAUSES to bring about
CATNIP	*n* pl. -S an aromatic herb	**CAUSER**	*n* pl. -S one that causes
CATSPAW	*n* pl. -S a light wind	**CAUSERIE**	*n* pl. -S an informal conversation
CATSUP	*n* pl. -S ketchup	**CAUSEWAY**	*v* -ED, -ING, -S to build a raised roadway over
CATTAIL	*n* pl. -S a marsh plant	
CATTALO	*n* pl. -LOS or -LOES catalo	**CAUSEY**	*n* pl. -SEYS a paved road
CATTED	past tense of cat	**CAUSING**	present participle of cause
CATTIE	*n* pl. -S an Asian unit of weight	**CAUSTIC**	*n* pl. -S a corrosive substance
CATTIER	comparative of catty	**CAUTERY**	*n* pl. -TERIES something used to destroy tissue
CATTIEST	superlative of catty	
CATTILY	*adv* in a catty manner	**CAUTION**	*v* -ED, -ING, -S to warn
CATTING	present participle of cat	**CAUTIOUS**	*adj* exercising prudence to avoid danger
CATTISH	*adj* catty	
CATTLE	*n/pl* domesticated bovines	**CAVALERO**	*n* pl. -ROS a horseman
CATTLEYA	*n* pl. -S a tropical orchid	**CAVALIER**	*v* -ED, -ING, -S to behave haughtily
CATTY	*adj* -TIER, -TIEST catlike; spiteful	
		CAVALLA	*n* pl. -S a large food fish
CATWALK	*n* pl. -S a narrow walkway	**CAVALLY**	*n* pl. -LIES cavalla
CAUCUS	*v* -CUSED, -CUSING, -CUSES or -CUSSED, -CUSSING, -CUSSES to hold a political meeting	**CAVALRY**	*n* pl. -RIES a mobile army unit
		CAVATINA	*n* pl. -NAS or -NE a simple song
CAUDAD	*adv* toward the tail	**CAVE**	*v* CAVED, CAVING, CAVES to hollow out
CAUDAL	*adj* taillike **CAUDALLY** *adv*	
CAUDATE	*adj* having a tail	**CAVEAT**	*n* pl. -S a legal warning
CAUDATED	*adj* caudate	**CAVEATOR**	*n* pl. -S one that files a caveat
CAUDEX	*n* pl. -DICES or -DEXES the woody base of some plants	**CAVED**	past tense of cave
		CAVEFISH	*n* pl. -ES a sightless fish
CAUDILLO	*n* pl. -LLOS a military dictator	**CAVELIKE**	*adj* resembling a cave (an underground chamber)
CAUDLE	*n* pl. -S a warm beverage	
CAUGHT	past tense of catch	**CAVEMAN**	*n* pl. -MEN a cave dweller
CAUL	*n* pl. -S a fetal membrane	**CAVER**	*n* pl. -S one that caves
CAULD	*n* pl. -S cold	**CAVERN**	*v* -ED, -ING, -S to hollow out
CAULDRON	*n* pl. -S caldron	**CAVETTO**	*n* pl. -TOS or -TI a concave molding
CAULES	pl. of caulis	
CAULICLE	*n* pl. -S a small stem	**CAVIAR**	*n* pl. -S the roe of sturgeon
CAULINE	*adj* pertaining to a stem	**CAVIARE**	*n* pl. -S caviar
CAULIS	*n* pl. -LES a plant stem	**CAVICORN**	*adj* having hollow horns
CAULK	*v* -ED, -ING, -S to make the seams of a ship watertight	**CAVIE**	*n* pl. -S a hencoop
		CAVIES	pl. of cavy
CAULKER	*n* pl. -S one that caulks	**CAVIL**	*v* -ILED, -ILING, -ILS or -ILLED, -ILLING, -ILS to carp

CAVILER *n* pl. -S one that cavils

CAVILLER *n* pl. -S caviler

CAVILLING a present participle of cavil

CAVING present participle of cave

CAVITARY *adj* pertaining to the formation of cavities in tissue

CAVITATE *v* -TATED, -TATING, -TATES to form cavities

CAVITY *n* pl. -TIES an unfilled space within a mass **CAVITIED** *adj*

CAVORT *v* -ED, -ING, -S to frolic

CAVORTER *n* pl. -S one that cavorts

CAVY *n* pl. -VIES a short-tailed rodent

CAW *v* -ED, -ING, -S to utter the sound of a crow

CAY *n* pl. CAYS a small, low island

CAYENNE *n* pl. -S a hot seasoning **CAYENNED** *adj*

CAYMAN *n* pl. -S caiman

CAYUSE *n* pl. -S an Indian pony

CAZIQUE *n* pl. -S cacique

CEASE *v* CEASED, CEASING, CEASES to stop

CEBID *n* pl. -S ceboid

CEBOID *n* pl. -S one of a family of monkeys

CECUM *n* pl. CECA a bodily cavity with one opening **CECAL** *adj* **CECALLY** *adv*

CEDAR *n* pl. -S an evergreen tree **CEDARN** *adj*

CEDE *v* CEDED, CEDING, CEDES to yield

CEDER *n* pl. -S one that cedes

CEDI *n* pl. -S a monetary unit of Ghana

CEDILLA *n* pl. -S a pronunciation mark

CEDING present participle of cede

CEDULA *n* pl. -S a Philippine tax

CEE *n* pl. -S the letter C

CEIBA *n* pl. -S a tropical tree

CEIL *v* -ED, -ING, -S to furnish with a ceiling

CEILER *n* pl. -S one that ceils

CEILING *n* pl. -S the overhead lining of a room

CEINTURE *n* pl. -S a belt for the waist

CELADON *n* pl. -S a pale green color

CELEB *n* pl. -S a celebrity; a famous person

CELERIAC *n* pl. -S a variety of celery

CELERITY *n* pl. -TIES swiftness

CELERY *n* pl. -ERIES a plant with edible stalks

CELESTA *n* pl. -S a keyboard instrument

CELESTE *n* pl. -S celesta

CELIAC *adj* pertaining to the abdomen

CELIBACY *n* pl. -CIES abstention from sexual intercourse

CELIBATE *n* pl. -S one who lives a life of celibacy

CELL *v* -ED, -ING, -S to store in a honeycomb

CELLA *n* pl. -LAE the interior of an ancient temple

CELLAR *v* -ED, ING, -S to store in an underground room

CELLARER *n* pl. -S the steward of a monastery

CELLARET *n* pl. -S a cabinet for wine bottles

CELLIST *n* pl. -S one who plays the cello

CELLO *n* pl. -LOS or -LI a stringed musical instrument

CELLULAR *adj* pertaining to a cell (a basic unit of life)

CELLULE *n* pl. -S a small cell

CELOM *n* pl. -LOMS or -LOMATA coelom

CELT *n* pl. -S a primitive ax

CEMBALO *n* pl. -LI or -LOS a harpsichord

CEMENT *v* -ED, -ING, -S to bind firmly

CEMENTER *n* pl. -S one that cements

CEMENTUM *n* pl. -TA the hard tissue covering the roots of the teeth

CEMETERY *n* pl. -TERIES a burial ground

CENACLE *n* pl. -S a small dining room

CENOBITE *n* pl. -S a member of a religious order

CENOTAPH *n* pl. -S an empty tomb

CENOTE *n* pl. -S a sinkhole in limestone

CENSE *v* CENSED, CENSING, CENSES to perfume with incense

CENSER *n* pl. -S a vessel for burning incense

CENSOR *v* -ED, -ING, -S to delete an objectionable word or passage

CENSUAL	*adj* pertaining to the act of censusing	**CENTURY**	*n* pl. -RIES a period of 100 years
CENSURE	*v* -SURED, -SURING, -SURES to criticize severely	**CEORL**	*n* pl. -S a freeman of low birth **CEORLISH** *adj*
CENSURER	*n* pl. -S one that censures	**CEPHALAD**	*adv* toward the head
CENSUS	*n* -ED, -ING, -ES to take an official count of	**CEPHALIC**	*adj* pertaining to the head
CENT	*n* pl. -S the 100th part of a dollar	**CEPHALIN**	*n* pl. -S a bodily chemical
CENTAL	*n* pl. -S a unit of weight	**CERAMAL**	*n* pl. -S a heat-resistant alloy
CENTARE	*n* pl. -S a measure of land area	**CERAMIC**	*n* pl. -S an item made of baked clay
CENTAUR	*n* pl. -S a mythological creature	**CERAMIST**	*n* pl. -S one who makes ceramics
CENTAURY	*n* pl. -RIES a medicinal herb	**CERASTES**	*n* pl. CERASTES a venomous snake
CENTAVO	*n* pl. -VOS a coin of various Spanish-American nations	**CERATE**	*n* pl. -S a medicated ointment
CENTER	*v* -ED, -ING, -S to place at the center (the midpoint)	**CERATED**	*adj* covered with wax
CENTESIS	*n* pl. -TESES a surgical puncture	**CERATIN**	*n* pl. -S keratin
CENTIARE	*n* pl. -S centare	**CERATOID**	*adj* hornlike
CENTILE	*n* pl. -S a value of a statistical variable	**CERCARIA**	*n* pl. -IAE or -IAS a parasitic worm
CENTIME	*n* pl. -S the 100th part of a franc	**CERCIS**	*n* pl. -CISES a shrub
CENTIMO	*n* pl. -MOS any of various small coins	**CERCUS**	*n* pl. CERCI a sensory appendage of an insect
CENTNER	*n* pl. -S a unit of weight	**CERE**	*v* CERED, CERING, CERES to wrap in a waxy cloth
CENTO	*n* pl. -TONES or -TOS a literary work made up of parts from other works	**CEREAL**	*n* pl. -S a food made from grain
		CEREBRAL	*n* pl. -S a kind of consonant
CENTRA	a pl. of centrum	**CEREBRUM**	*n* pl. -BRUMS or -BRA a part of the brain **CEREBRIC** *adj*
CENTRAL	*n* pl. -S a telephone exchange	**CERED**	past tense of cere
CENTRAL	*adj* -TRALER, -TRALEST situated at, in, or near the center	**CEREMENT**	*n* pl. -S a waxy cloth
CENTRE	*n* -TRED, -TRING, -TRES to center	**CEREMONY**	*n* pl. -NIES a formal observance
		CEREUS	*n* pl. -ES a tall cactus
CENTRIC	*adj* situated at the center	**CERIA**	*n* pl. -S a chemical compound
CENTRING	*n* pl. -S a temporary framework for an arch	**CERIC**	*adj* containing cerium
		CERING	present participle of cere
CENTRISM	*n* pl. -S moderate political philosophy	**CERIPH**	*n* pl. -S serif
		CERISE	*n* pl. -S a red color
CENTRIST	*n* pl. -S an advocate of centrism	**CERITE**	*n* pl. -S a mineral
CENTROID	*n* pl. -S the center of mass of an object	**CERIUM**	*n* pl. -S a metallic element
		CERMET	*n* pl. -S ceramal
CENTRUM	*n* pl. -TRUMS or -TRA the body of a vertebra	**CERNUOUS**	*adj* drooping or nodding
CENTUM	*n* pl. -S one hundred	**CERO**	*n* pl. CEROS a large food fish
CENTUPLE	*v* -PLED, -PLING, -PLES to increase a hundredfold	**CEROTIC**	*adj* pertaining to beeswax
		CEROTYPE	*n* pl. -S a process of engraving using wax
		CEROUS	*adj* pertaining to cerium

CERTAIN *adj* -TAINER, -TAINEST absolutely confident

CERTES *adv* in truth

CERTIFY *v* -FIED, -FYING, -FIES to confirm

CERULEAN *n pl.* -S a blue color

CERUMEN *n pl.* -S a waxy secretion of the ear

CERUSE *n pl.* -S a lead compound

CERUSITE *n pl.* -S a lead ore

CERVELAT *n pl.* -S a smoked sausage

CERVICAL *adj* pertaining to the cervix

CERVINE *adj* pertaining to deer

CERVIX *n pl.* -VICES or -VIXES the neck

CESAREAN *n pl.* -S a method of child delivery

CESARIAN *n pl.* -S cesarean

CESIUM *n pl.* -S a metallic element

CESS *v* -ED, -ING, -ES to tax or assess

CESSION *n pl.* -S the act of ceding

CESSPIT *n pl.* -S a cesspool

CESSPOOL *n pl.* -S a covered well or pit for sewage

CESTA *n pl.* -S a basket used in jai alai

CESTI pl. of cestus

CESTODE *n pl.* -S a tapeworm

CESTOID *n pl.* -S cestode

CESTOS *n pl.* -TOI cestus

CESTUS *n pl.* -TI a belt or girdle

CESTUS *n pl.* -ES a hand covering for ancient Roman boxers

CESURA *n pl.* -RAS or -RAE caesura

CETACEAN *n pl.* -S an aquatic mammal

CETANE *n pl.* -S a diesel fuel

CETE *n pl.* -S a group of badgers

CETOLOGY *n pl.* -GIES the study of whales

CHABOUK *n pl.* -S a type of whip

CHABUK *n pl.* -S chabouk

CHACMA *n pl.* -S a large baboon

CHACONNE *n pl.* -S an ancient dance

CHAD *n pl.* -S a scrap of paper **CHADLESS** *adj*

CHADARIM a pl. of cheder

CHAETA *n pl.* -TAE a bristle or seta **CHAETAL** *adj*

CHAFE *v* CHAFED, CHAFING, CHAFES to warm by rubbing

CHAFER *n pl.* -S a large beetle

CHAFF *v* -ED, -ING, -S to poke fun at

CHAFFER *v* -ED, -ING, -S to bargain or haggle

CHAFFY *adj* CHAFFIER, CHAFFIEST worthless

CHAFING present participle of chafe

CHAGRIN *v* -GRINED, -GRINING, -GRINS or -GRINNED, -GRINNING, -GRINS to humiliate

CHAIN *v* -ED, -ING, -S to bind with a chain (a series of connected rings)

CHAINE *n pl.* -S a series of ballet turns

CHAINMAN *n pl.* -MEN a surveyor's assistant who uses a measuring chain

CHAIR *v* -ED, -ING, -S to install in office

CHAIRMAN *n pl.* -MEN the presiding officer of a meeting

CHAIRMAN *v* -MANED, -MANING, -MANS or -MANNED, -MANNING, -MANS to act as chairman of

CHAISE *n pl.* -S a light carriage

CHALAH *n pl.* -LAHS, -LOTH or -LOT, challah

CHALAZA *n pl.* -ZAS or -ZAE a band of tissue in an egg **CHALAZAL** *adj*

CHALCID *n pl.* -S a tiny fly

CHALDRON *n pl.* -S a unit of dry measure

CHALEH *n pl.* -S challah

CHALET *n pl.* -S a Swiss cottage

CHALICE *n pl.* -S a drinking cup **CHALICED** *adj*

CHALK *v* -ED, -ING, -S to mark with chalk (a soft limestone)

CHALKY *adj* CHALKIER, CHALKIEST resembling chalk

CHALLAH *n pl.* -LAHS, -LOTH, or -LOT a kind of bread

CHALLIE *n pl.* -S challis

CHALLIES pl. of chally

CHALLIS *n pl.* -LISES a light fabric

CHALLOT a pl. of challah

CHALLOTH a pl. of challah

CHALLY *n pl.* -LIES challis

CHALONE *n pl.* -S a hormone

CHALOT — a pl. of chalah

CHALOTH — a pl. of chalah

CHALUTZ — n pl. -LUTZIM halutz

CHAM — n pl. -S a khan

CHAMADE — n pl. -S a signal made with a drum

CHAMBER — v -ED, -ING, -S to put in a chamber (a room)

CHAMBRAY — n pl. -BRAYS a fine fabric

CHAMFER — v -ED, -ING, -S to groove

CHAMFRON — n pl. -S armor for a horse's head

CHAMISE — n pl. -S chamiso

CHAMISO — n pl. -SOS a flowering shrub

CHAMMY — v -MIED, -MYING, -MIES to chamois

CHAMOIS — n pl. -OIX a soft leather

CHAMOIS — v -ED, -ING, -ES to prepare leather like chamois

CHAMP — v -ED, -ING, -S to chew noisily

CHAMPAC — n pl. -S champak

CHAMPAK — n pl. -S an East Indian tree

CHAMPER — n pl. -S one that champs

CHAMPION — v -ED, -ING, -S to defend or support

CHAMPY — adj broken up by the trampling of beasts

CHANCE — v CHANCED, CHANCING, CHANCES to risk

CHANCEL — n pl. -S an area around a church altar

CHANCERY — n pl. -CERIES a court of public record

CHANCIER — comparative of chancy

CHANCIEST — superlative of chancy

CHANCILY — adv in a chancy manner

CHANCING — present participle of chance

CHANCRE — n pl. -S a hard-based sore

CHANCY — adj CHANCIER, CHANCIEST risky

CHANDLER — n pl. -S a dealer in provisions

CHANFRON — n pl. -S chamfron

CHANG — n pl. -S a cattie

CHANGE — v CHANGED, CHANGING, CHANGES to make different

CHANGER — n pl. -S one that changes

CHANNEL — v -NELED, -NELING, -NELS or -NELLED, -NELLING, -NELS to direct along some desired course

CHANSON — n pl. -S a song

CHANT — v -ED, -ING, -S to sing

CHANTAGE — n pl. -S blackmail

CHANTER — n pl. -S one that chants

CHANTEY — n pl. -TEYS a sailor's song

CHANTIES — pl. of chanty

CHANTOR — n pl. -S chanter

CHANTRY — n pl. -TRIES an endowment given to a church

CHANTY — n pl. -TIES chantey

CHAOS — n pl. -ES a state of total disorder; a confused mass CHAOTIC adj

CHAP — v CHAPPED or CHAPT, CHAPPING, CHAPS to split, crack, or redden

CHAPBOOK — n pl. -S a small book of popular tales

CHAPE — n pl. -S a part of a scabbard

CHAPEAU — n pl. -PEAUX or -PEAUS a hat

CHAPEL — n pl. -S a place of worship

CHAPERON — v -ED, -ING, -S to accompany

CHAPITER — n pl. -S the capital of a column

CHAPLAIN — n pl. -S a clergyman attached to a chapel

CHAPLET — n pl. -S a wreath for the head

CHAPMAN — n pl. -MEN a peddler

CHAPPED — a past tense of chap

CHAPPING — present participle of chap

CHAPT — a past tense of chap

CHAPTER — v -ED, -ING, -S to divide a book into main sections

CHAQUETA — n pl. -S a jacket worn by cowboys

CHAR — v CHARRED, CHARRING, CHARS to burn slightly

CHARACID — n pl. -S characin

CHARACIN — n pl. -S a tropical fish

CHARADE — n pl. -S a word represented by pantomime

CHARAS — n pl. -ES hashish

CHARCOAL — v -ED, -ING, -S to blacken with charcoal (a dark, porous carbon)

CHARD — n pl. -S a variety of beet

CHARE v CHARED, CHARING, CHARES to do small jobs

CHARGE v CHARGED, CHARGING, CHARGES to accuse formally

CHARGER n pl. -S one that charges

CHARIER comparative of chary

CHARIEST superlative of chary

CHARILY adv in a chary manner

CHARING present participle of chare

CHARIOT v -ED, -ING, -S to ride in a type of cart

CHARISM n pl. -S charisma

CHARISMA n pl. -MATA a special magnetic appeal

CHARITY n pl. -TIES something given to the needy

CHARK v -ED, -ING, -S to char

CHARKA n pl. -S charkha

CHARKHA n pl. -S a spinning wheel

CHARLADY n pl. -DIES a cleaning woman

CHARLOCK n pl. -S a troublesome weed

CHARM v -ED, -ING, -S to attract irresistibly

CHARMER n pl. -S one that charms

CHARMING adj -INGER, -INGEST pleasing

CHARNEL n pl. -S a room where corpses are placed

CHARPAI n pl. -S charpoy

CHARPOY n pl. -POYS a bed used in India

CHARQUI n pl. -S a type of meat **CHARQUID** adj

CHARR n pl. -S a small-scaled trout

CHARRED past tense of char

CHARRIER comparative of charry

CHARRIEST superlative of charry

CHARRING present participle of char

CHARRO n pl. -ROS a cowboy

CHARRY adj -RIER, -RIEST resembling charcoal

CHART v -ED, -ING, -S to map out

CHARTER v -ED, -ING, -S to lease or hire

CHARTIST n pl. -S a stock market specialist

CHARY adj CHARIER, CHARIEST cautious

CHASE v CHASED, CHASING, CHASES to pursue

CHASER n pl. -S one that chases

CHASING n pl. -S a design engraved on metal

CHASM n pl. -S a deep cleft in the earth **CHASMAL, CHASMED, CHASMIC, CHASMY** adj

CHASSE v CHASSED, CHASSEING, CHASSES to perform a dance movement

CHASSEUR n pl. -S a cavalry soldier

CHASSIS n pl. CHASSIS the frame of a car

CHASTE adj CHASTER, CHASTEST morally pure **CHASTELY** adv

CHASTEN v -ED, -ING, -S to chastise

CHASTISE v -TISED, -TISING, -TISES to discipline by punishment

CHASTITY n pl. -TIES moral purity

CHASUBLE n pl. -S a sleeveless vestment

CHAT v CHATTED, CHATTING, CHATS to converse informally

CHATEAU n pl. -TEAUX or -TEAUS a large country house

CHATTEL n pl. -S a slave

CHATTER v -ED, -ING, -S to talk rapidly and trivially **CHATTERY** adj

CHATTING present participle of chat

CHATTY adj -TIER, -TIEST talkative **CHATTILY** adv

CHAUFER n pl. -S chauffer

CHAUFFER n pl. -S a small furnace

CHAUNT v -ED, -ING, -S to chant

CHAUNTER n pl. -S one that chaunts

CHAUSSES n/pl medieval armor

CHAW v -ED, -ING, -S to chew

CHAWER n pl. -S one that chaws

CHAYOTE n pl. -S a tropical vine

CHAZAN n pl. -ZANS or -ZANIM a cantor

CHAZZEN n pl. -ZENS or -ZENIM chazan

CHEAP adj CHEAPER, CHEAPEST inexpensive

CHEAP n pl. -S a market

CHEAPEN v -ED, -ING, -S to make cheap

CHEAPIE n pl. -S one that is cheap

CHEAPISH adj somewhat cheap

CHEAPLY adv in a cheap manner

CHEAT v -ED, -ING, -S to defraud

CHEATER n pl. -S one that cheats

CHEBEC n pl. -S a small bird

CHECHAKO *n* pl. -KOS a newcomer

CHECK *v* -ED, -ING, -S to inspect

CHECKER *v* -ED, -ING, -S to mark with squares

CHECKOFF *n* pl. -S a method of collecting union dues

CHECKOUT *n* pl. -S a test of a machine

CHECKROW *v* -ED, -ING, -S to plant in rows which divide the land into squares

CHECKUP *n* pl. -S an examination

CHEDDAR *n* pl. -S a type of cheese

CHEDDITE *n* pl. -S cheddite

CHEDER *n* pl. CHADARIM or CHEDERS heder

CHEDITE *n* pl. -S an explosive

CHEEK *v* -ED, -ING, -S to speak impudently to

CHEEKFUL *n* pl. -S the amount held in one's cheek

CHEEKY *adj* CHEEKIER, CHEEKIEST impudent **CHEEKILY** *adv*

CHEEP *v* -ED, -ING, -S to chirp

CHEEPER *n* pl. -S one that cheeps

CHEER *v* -ED, -ING, -S to applaud with shouts of approval

CHEERER *n* pl. -S one that cheers

CHEERFUL *adj* -FULLER, -FULLEST full of spirits

CHEERIER comparative of cheery

CHEERIEST superlative of cheery

CHEERILY *adv* in a cheery manner

CHEERIO *n* pl. -IOS a greeting

CHEERO *n* pl. CHEEROS cheerio

CHEERY *adj* CHEERIER, CHEERIEST cheerful

CHEESE *v* CHEESED, CHEESING, CHEESES to stop

CHEESY *adj* CHEESIER, CHEESIEST resembling cheese (a food made from milk curds) **CHEESILY** *adv*

CHEETAH *n* pl. -S a swift-running wildcat

CHEF *n* pl. -S a chief cook

CHEFDOM *n* pl. -S the status or function of a chef

CHEGOE *n* pl. -S chigoe

CHELA *n* pl. -LAE a pincerlike claw

CHELA *n* pl. -S a pupil of a guru

CHELATE *v* -LATED, -LATING, -LATES to subject a compound to combination with a metal ion

CHELATOR *n* pl. -S one that chelates

CHELOID *n* pl. -S keloid

CHEMIC *n* pl. -S a chemist

CHEMICAL *n* pl. -S a substance obtained by a process of chemistry (the science of the various properties and transformations of substances)

CHEMISE *n* pl. -S a loose dress

CHEMISM *n* pl. -S chemical attraction

CHEMIST *n* pl. -S one versed in chemistry

CHEMURGY *n* pl. -GIES a branch of applied chemistry

CHENILLE *n* pl. -S a soft fabric

CHENOPOD *n* pl. -S a flowering plant

CHEQUE *n* pl. -S a written order directing a bank to pay money

CHEQUER *v* -ED, -ING, -S to checker

CHERISH *v* -ED, -ING, -ES to hold dear

CHEROOT *n* pl. -S a square-cut cigar

CHERRY *n* pl. -RIES a fruit

CHERT *n* pl. -S a compact rock

CHERTY *adj* CHERTIER, CHERTIEST resembling chert

CHERUB *n* pl. -UBS or -UBIM an angel **CHERUBIC** *adj*

CHERVIL *n* pl. -S an aromatic herb

CHESS *n* pl. -ES a weed

CHESSMAN *n* pl. -MEN one of the pieces used in chess (a board game for two players)

CHEST *n* pl. -S a part of the body **CHESTED** *adj*

CHESTFUL *n* pl. -S as much as a chest or box can hold

CHESTNUT *n* pl. -S an edible nut

CHESTY *adj* CHESTIER, CHESTIEST proud

CHETAH *n* pl. -S cheetah

CHETH *n* pl. -S heth

CHEVALET *n* pl. -S a part of a stringed instrument

CHEVERON *n* pl. -S chevron

CHEVIED past tense of chevy

CHEVIES present 3d person sing. of chevy

CHEVIOT	n pl. -S a coarse fabric	**CHIEL**	n pl. -S chield
CHEVRON	n pl. -S a V-shaped pattern	**CHIELD**	n pl. -S a young man
CHEVY	v CHEVIED, CHEVYING, CHEVIES to chase about	**CHIFFON**	n pl. -S a sheer fabric
		CHIGETAI	n pl. -S a wild ass
CHEW	v -ED, -ING, -S to crush or grind with the teeth **CHEWABLE** adj	**CHIGGER**	n pl. -S a parasitic mite
		CHIGNON	n pl. -S a woman's hairdo
CHEWER	n pl. -S one that chews	**CHIGOE**	n pl. -S a tropical flea
CHEWINK	n pl. -S a common finch	**CHILD**	n pl. CHILDREN a young person
CHEWY	adj CHEWIER, CHEWIEST not easily chewed	**CHILDBED**	n pl. -S the state of a woman giving birth
CHEZ	prep at the home of	**CHILDE**	n pl. -S a youth of noble birth
CHI	n pl. -S a Greek letter	**CHILDING**	adj pregnant
CHIA	n pl. -S a Mexican herb	**CHILDISH**	adj resembling a child
CHIAO	n pl. CHIAO a monetary unit of China	**CHILDLY**	adj -LIER, -LIEST resembling a child
CHIASM	n pl. -S chiasma	**CHILDREN**	pl. of child
CHIASMA	n pl. -MATA or -MAS an anatomical junction **CHIASMAL**, **CHIASMIC** adj	**CHILE**	n pl. -S chili
		CHILI	n pl. -ES a hot pepper
CHIASMUS	n pl. -MI a reversal of word order between parallel phrases **CHIASTIC** adj	**CHILIAD**	n pl. -S a group of one thousand
		CHILIASM	n pl. -S a religious doctrine
		CHILIAST	n pl. -S a supporter of chiliasm
CHIAUS	n pl. -ES a Turkish messenger	**CHILL**	v -ED, -ING, -S to make cold
CHIBOUK	n pl. -S a tobacco pipe	**CHILL**	adj CHILLER, CHILLEST cool
CHIC	n pl. -S elegance	**CHILLER**	n pl. -S one that chills
CHICANE	v -CANED, -CANING, -CANES to trick	**CHILLI**	n pl. -ES chili
		CHILLUM	n pl. -S a part of a water pipe
CHICANER	n pl. -S one that chicanes	**CHILLY**	adj CHILLIER, CHILLIEST cool **CHILLILY** adv
CHICCORY	n pl. -RIES chicory		
CHICHI	n pl. -S elaborate ornamentation	**CHILOPOD**	n pl. -S a multi-legged insect
CHICK	n pl. -S a young bird	**CHIMAERA**	n pl. -S a marine fish
CHICKEN	v -ED, -ING, -S to lose one's nerve	**CHIMAR**	n pl. -S chimere
		CHIMB	n pl. -S the rim of a cask
CHICKPEA	n pl. -S an Asian herb	**CHIMBLEY**	n pl. -BLEYS chimley
CHICLE	n pl. -S a tree gum	**CHIMBLY**	n pl. -BLIES chimley
CHICLY	adv in an elegant manner	**CHIME**	v CHIMED, CHIMING, CHIMES to ring harmoniously
CHICNESS	n pl. -ES elegance		
CHICO	n pl. -COS a prickly shrub	**CHIMER**	n pl. -S one that chimes
CHICORY	n pl. -RIES a perennial herb	**CHIMERA**	n pl. -S an imaginary monster
CHIDE	v CHIDED or CHID, CHIDDEN, CHIDING, CHIDES to scold	**CHIMERE**	n pl. -S a bishop's robe
		CHIMERIC	adj imaginary; unreal
CHIDER	n pl. -S one that chides	**CHIMING**	present participle of chime
CHIEF	adj CHIEFER, CHIEFEST highest in authority	**CHIMLA**	n pl. -S chimley
		CHIMLEY	n pl. -LEYS a chimney
CHIEF	n pl. -S the person highest in authority	**CHIMNEY**	n pl. -NEYS a flue
CHIEFDOM	n pl. -S the domain of a chief	**CHIMP**	n pl. -S a chimpanzee
CHIEFLY	adv above all		

CHIN	v CHINNED, CHINNING, CHINS to hold with the chin (the lower part of the face)
CHINA	n pl. -S fine porcelain ware
CHINBONE	n pl. -S the lower jaw
CHINCH	n pl. -ES a bedbug
CHINCHY	adj CHINCHIER, CHINCHIEST stingy
CHINE	v CHINED, CHINING, CHINES to cut through the backbone of
CHINK	v -ED, -ING, -S to fill cracks or fissures in
CHINKY	adj CHINKIER, CHINKIEST full of cracks
CHINLESS	adj lacking a chin
CHINNED	past tense of chin
CHINNING	present participle of chin
CHINO	n pl. -NOS a strong fabric
CHINONE	n pl. -S quinone
CHINOOK	n pl. -S a warm wind
CHINTS	n pl. -ES chintz
CHINTZ	n pl. -ES a cotton fabric
CHINTZY	adj CHINTZIER, CHINTZIEST gaudy; cheap
CHIP	v CHIPPED, CHIPPING, CHIPS to break a small piece from
CHIPMUCK	n pl. -S a chipmunk
CHIPMUNK	n pl. -S a small rodent
CHIPPED	past tense of chip
CHIPPER	v -ED, -ING, -S to chirp
CHIPPIE	n pl. -S chippy
CHIPPING	present participle of chip
CHIPPY	n pl. -PIES a prostitute
CHIRK	v -ED, -ING, -S to make a shrill noise
CHIRK	adj CHIRKER, CHIRKEST cheerful
CHIRM	v -ED, -ING, -S to chirp
CHIRO	n pl. -ROS a marine fish
CHIRP	v -ED, -ING, -S to utter a short, shrill sound
CHIRPER	n pl. -S one that chirps
CHIRPY	adj CHIRPIER, CHIRPIEST cheerful **CHIRPILY** adv
CHIRR	v -ED, -ING, -S to make a harsh, vibrant sound
CHIRRE	v CHIRRED, CHIRRING, CHIRRES to chirr

CHIRRUP	v -ED, -ING, -S to chirp repeatedly **CHIRRUPY** adj
CHISEL	v -ELED, -ELING, -ELS or -ELLED, -ELLING, -ELS to use a chisel (a cutting tool)
CHISELER	n pl. -S one that chisels
CHIT	n pl. -S a short letter
CHITAL	n pl. CHITAL an Asian deer
CHITCHAT	v -CHATTED, -CHATTING, -CHATS to indulge in small talk
CHITIN	n pl. -S the main component of insect shells
CHITLIN	n pl. -S chitling
CHITLING	n pl. -S a part of the small intestine of swine
CHITON	n pl. -S a tunic worn in ancient Greece
CHITTER	v -ED, -ING, -S to twitter
CHITTY	n pl. -TIES a chit
CHIVALRY	n pl. -RIES knightly behavior and skill
CHIVAREE	v -REED, -REEING, -REES to perform a mock serenade
CHIVARI	v -ED, -ING, -S to chivaree
CHIVE	n pl. -S an herb used as a seasoning
CHIVVY	v -VIED, -VYING, -VIES to chevy
CHIVY	v CHIVIED, CHIVYING, CHIVIES to chevy
CHLAMYS	n pl. -MYSES or -MYDES a garment worn in ancient Greece
CHLORAL	n pl. -S a chemical compound
CHLORATE	n pl. -S a chemical salt
CHLORDAN	n pl. -S a toxic compound of chlorine
CHLORIC	adj pertaining to chlorine
CHLORID	n pl. -S chloride
CHLORIDE	n pl. -S a chlorine compound
CHLORIN	n pl. -S chlorine
CHLORINE	n pl. -S a gaseous element
CHLORITE	n pl. -S a mineral group
CHLOROUS	adj pertaining to chlorine
CHOCK	v -ED, -ING, -S to secure with a wedge of wood or metal
CHOICE	n pl. -S one that is chosen
CHOICE	adj CHOICER, CHOICEST of fine quality **CHOICELY** adv
CHOIR	v -ED, -ING, -S to sing in unison

CHOIRBOY *n* pl. -BOYS a boy who sings in a body of church singers

CHOKE *v* CHOKED, CHOKING, CHOKES to impede the breathing of

CHOKER *n* pl. -S one that chokes

CHOKEY *adj* CHOKIER, CHOKIEST choky

CHOKING present participle of choke

CHOKY *adj* CHOKIER, CHOKIEST tending to cause choking

CHOLATE *n* pl. -S a chemical salt

CHOLER *n* pl. -S anger

CHOLERA *n* pl. -S an acute disease

CHOLERIC *adj* bad-tempered

CHOLINE *n* pl. -S a B vitamin

CHOLLA *n* pl. -S a treelike cactus

CHOMP *v* -ED, -ING, -S to champ

CHON *n* pl. CHON a monetary unit of South Korea

CHOOSE *v* CHOSE, CHOSEN, CHOOSING, CHOOSES to take by preference

CHOOSER *n* pl. -S one that chooses

CHOOSEY *adj* CHOOSIER, CHOOSIEST choosy

CHOOSING present participle of choose

CHOOSY *adj* CHOOSIER, CHOOSIEST hard to please

CHOP *v* CHOPPED, CHOPPING, CHOPS to sever with a sharp tool

CHOPIN *n* pl. -S chopine

CHOPINE *n* pl. -S a type of shoe

CHOPPED past tense of chop

CHOPPER *n* pl. -S one that chops

CHOPPING present participle of chop

CHOPPY *adj* CHOPPIER, CHOPPIEST full of short, rough waves **CHOPPILY** *adv*

CHORAGUS *n* pl. -GI or -GUSES the leader of a chorus or choir **CHORAGIC** *adj*

CHORAL *n* pl. -S chorale

CHORALE *n* pl. -S a hymn that is sung in unison

CHORALLY *adv* harmoniously

CHORD *v* -ED, -ING, -S to play a chord (a combination of three or more musical tones)

CHORDAL *adj* pertaining to a chord

CHORDATE *n* pl. -S any of a large phylum of animals

CHORE *v* CHORED, CHORING, CHORES to do small jobs

CHOREA *n* pl. -S a nervous disorder **CHOREAL, CHOREIC** *adj*

CHOREGUS *n* pl. -GI or -GUSES choragus

CHOREMAN *n* pl. -MEN a menial worker

CHOREOID *adj* resembling chorea

CHORIAL *adj* pertaining to the chorion

CHORIAMB *n* pl. -S a type of metrical foot

CHORIC *adj* pertaining to a chorus

CHORINE *n* pl. -S a chorus girl

CHORING present participle of chore

CHORIOID *n* pl. -S choroid

CHORION *n* pl. -S an embryonic membrane

CHORIZO *n* pl. -ZOS a highly seasoned sausage

CHOROID *n* pl. -S a membrane of the eye

CHORTLE *v* -TLED, -TLING, -TLES to chuckle with glee

CHORTLER *n* pl. -S one that chortles

CHORUS *v* -RUSED, -RUSING, -RUSES or -RUSSED, -RUSSING, -RUSSES to sing in unison

CHOSE *n* pl. -S an item of personal property

CHOSEN past participle of choose

CHOTT *n* pl. -S a saline lake

CHOUGH *n* pl. -S a crow-like bird

CHOUSE *v* CHOUSED, CHOUSING, CHOUSES to swindle

CHOUSER *n* pl. -S one that chouses

CHOUSH *n* pl. -ES chiaus

CHOUSING present participle of chouse

CHOW *v* -ED, -ING, -S to eat

CHOWCHOW *n* pl. -S a relish of mixed pickles in mustard

CHOWDER *v* -ED, -ING, -S to make a thick soup of

CHOWSE *v* CHOWSED, CHOWSING, CHOWSES to chouse

CHOWTIME *n* pl. -S mealtime

CHRESARD *n* pl. -S the available water of the soil

CHRISM *n* pl. -S a consecrated oil **CHRISMAL** *adj*

CHRISMON *n* pl. -MA or -MONS a Christian monogram

CHRISOM *n* pl. -S chrism

CHRISTEN	v -ED, -ING, -S to baptize	**CHUGGER**	n pl. -S one that chugs
CHRISTIE	n pl. -S christy	**CHUKAR**	n pl. -S a game bird
CHRISTY	n pl. -TIES a skiing turn	**CHUKKA**	n pl. -S a type of boot
CHROMA	n pl. -S the purity of a color	**CHUKKAR**	n pl. -S chukker
CHROMATE	n pl. -S a chemical salt	**CHUKKER**	n pl. -S a period of play in polo
CHROME	v CHROMED, CHROMING, CHROMES to plate with chromium	**CHUM**	v CHUMMED, CHUMMING, CHUMS to be close friends with someone
CHROMIC	adj pertaining to chromium	**CHUMMY**	adj -MIER, -MIEST friendly CHUMMILY adv
CHROMIDE	n pl. -S a tropical fish		
CHROMING	present participle of chrome	**CHUMP**	v -ED, -ING, -S to munch
CHROMITE	n pl. -S a chromium ore	**CHUMSHIP**	n pl. -S friendship
CHROMIUM	n pl. -S a metallic element	**CHUNK**	v -ED, -ING, -S to make a dull explosive sound
CHROMIZE	v -MIZED, -MIZING, -MIZES to chrome		
CHROMO	n pl. -MOS a type of color picture	**CHUNKY**	adj CHUNKIER, CHUNKIEST stocky CHUNKILY adv
CHROMOUS	adj pertaining to chromium	**CHUNTER**	v -ED, -ING, -S to mutter
CHROMYL	adj containing chromium	**CHURCH**	v -ED, -ING, -ES to bring to church (a building for Christian worship)
CHRONAXY	n pl. -AXIES the time required to excite a nerve cell electrically		
CHRONIC	n pl. -S one that suffers from a long-lasting disease	**CHURCHLY**	adj -LIER, -LIEST pertaining to a church
		CHURCHY	adj CHURCHIER, CHURCHIEST churchly
CHRONON	n pl. -S a hypothetical unit of time		
CHTHONIC	adj pertaining to the gods of the underworld	**CHURL**	n pl. -S a rude person CHURLISH adj
		CHURN	v -ED, -ING, -S to stir briskly in order to make butter
CHUB	n pl. -S a freshwater fish		
CHUBASCO	n pl. -COS a violent thunderstorm	**CHURNER**	n pl. -S one that churns
		CHURNING	n pl. -S the butter churned at one time
CHUBBY	adj -BIER, -BIEST plump CHUBBILY adv		
		CHURR	v -ED, -ING, -S to make a vibrant sound
CHUCK	v -ED, -ING, -S to throw		
CHUCKIES	pl. of chucky	**CHUTE**	v CHUTED, CHUTING, CHUTES to convey by chute (a vertical passage)
CHUCKLE	v -LED, -LING, -LES to laugh quietly		
		CHUTIST	n pl. -S a parachutist
CHUCKLER	n pl. -S one that chuckles	**CHUTNEE**	n pl. -S chutney
CHUCKY	n pl. CHUCKIES a little chick	**CHUTNEY**	n pl. -NEYS a sweet and sour sauce
CHUDDAH	n pl. -S chuddar		
CHUDDAR	n pl. -S a large, square shawl	**CHUTZPA**	n pl. -S chutzpah
CHUDDER	n pl. -S chuddar	**CHUTZPAH**	n pl. -S supreme self-confidence
CHUFA	n pl. -S a European sedge		
CHUFF	adj CHUFFER, CHUFFEST gruff	**CHYLE**	n pl. -S a digestive fluid CHYLOUS adj
CHUFF	v -ED, -ING, -S to chug		
CHUFFY	adj -FIER, -FIEST plump	**CHYME**	n pl. -S semi-digested food
CHUG	v CHUGGED, CHUGGING, CHUGS to move with a dull explosive sound	**CHYMIC**	n pl. -S chemic
		CHYMIST	n pl. -S chemist
		CHYMOSIN	n pl. -S rennin
		CHYMOUS	adj pertaining to chyme

CIAO   *interj* — used as an expression of greeting and farewell

CIBOL   *n pl.* -S a variety of onion

CIBORIUM   *n pl.* -RIA a vessel for holding holy bread

CIBOULE   *n pl.* -S cibol

CICADA   *n pl.* -DAS or -DAE a winged insect

CICALA   *n pl.* -LAS or -LE cicada

CICATRIX   *n pl.* -TRICES scar tissue

CICELY   *n pl.* -LIES a fragrant herb

CICERO   *n pl.* -ROS a unit of measure in printing

CICERONE   *n pl.* -NES or -NI a tour guide

CICHLID   *n pl.* -LIDS or -LIDAE a tropical fish

CICISBEO   *n pl.* -BEI a lover of a married woman

CICOREE   *n pl.* -S a perennial herb

CIDER   *n pl.* -S the juice pressed from apples

CIGAR   *n pl.* -S a roll of tobacco leaf for smoking

CIGARET   *n pl.* -S a narrow roll of finely cut tobacco for smoking

CILANTRO   *n pl.* -TROS an herb used in cooking

CILIA   pl. of cilium

CILIARY   *adj* pertaining to cilia

CILIATE   *n pl.* -S one of a class of ciliated protozoans

CILIATED   *adj* having cilia

CILICE   *n pl.* -S a coarse cloth

CILIUM   *n pl.* CILIA a short, hairlike projection

CIMEX   *n pl.* -MICES a bedbug

CINCH   *v* -ED, -ING, -ES to girth

CINCHONA   *n pl.* -S a Peruvian tree

CINCTURE   *v* -TURED, -TURING, -TURES to gird or encircle

CINDER   *v* -ED, -ING, -S to reduce to cinders (ashes)

CINDERY   *adj* containing cinders

CINE   *n pl.* -S a motion picture

CINEAST   *n pl.* -S a devotee of motion pictures

CINEASTE   *n pl.* -S cineast

CINEMA   *n pl.* -S a motion-picture theater

CINEOL   *n pl.* -S a liquid used as an antiseptic

CINEOLE   *n pl.* -S cineol

CINERARY   *adj* used for cremated ashes

CINERIN   *n pl.* -S a compound used in insecticides

CINGULUM   *n pl.* -LA an anatomical band or girdle

CINNABAR   *n pl.* -S the principal ore of mercury

CINNAMON   *n pl.* -S a spice obtained from tree bark **CINNAMIC** *adj*

CINNAMYL   *n pl.* -S a chemical used to make soap

CINQUAIN   *n pl.* -S a stanza of five lines

CINQUE   *n pl.* -S the number five

CION   *n pl.* -S a cutting from a plant or tree

CIPHER   *v* -ED, -ING, -S to solve problems in arithmetic

CIPHONY   *n pl.* -NIES the electronic scrambling of voice transmissions

CIPOLIN   *n pl.* -S a type of marble

CIRCA   *prep* about; around

CIRCLE   *v* -CLED, -CLING, -CLES to move or revolve around

CIRCLER   *n pl.* -S one that circles

CIRCLET   *n pl.* -S a small ring or ring-shaped object

CIRCLING   present participle of circle

CIRCUIT   *v* -ED, -ING, -S to move around

CIRCUITY   *n pl.* -ITIES lack of straightforwardness

CIRCULAR   *n pl.* -S a leaflet intended for wide distribution

CIRCUS   *n pl.* -ES a public entertainment **CIRCUSY** *adj*

CIRQUE   *n pl.* -S a deep, steep-walled basin

CIRRATE   *adj* having cirri

CIRRI   pl. of cirrus

CIRRIPED   *n pl.* -S any of an order of crustaceans

CIRROSE   *adj* cirrous

CIRROUS   *adj* having cirri

CIRRUS   *n pl.* -RI a tendril or similar part

CIRSOID   *adj* varicose

CISCO   *n pl.* -COS or -COES a freshwater fish

CISLUNAR *adj* situated between the earth and the moon

CISSOID *n* pl. -S a type of geometric curve

CIST *n* pl. -S a prehistoric stone coffin

CISTERN *n* pl. -S a water tank

CISTERNA *n* pl. -NAE a fluid-containing sac

CISTRON *n* pl. -S a segment of DNA

CITABLE *adj* citeable

CITADEL *n* pl. -S a fortress or stronghold

CITATION *n* pl. -S the act of citing **CITATORY** *adj*

CITE *v* CITED, CITING, CITES to quote as an authority or example

CITEABLE *adj* suitable for citation

CITER *n* pl. -S one that cites

CITHARA *n* pl. -S an ancient stringed instrument

CITHER *n* pl. -S cittern

CITHERN *n* pl. -S cittern

CITHREN *n* pl. -S cittern

CITIED *adj* having cities

CITIES pl. of city

CITIFY *v* -FIED, -FYING, -FIES to urbanize

CITING present participle of cite

CITIZEN *n* pl. -S a resident of a city or town

CITOLA *n* pl. -S a cittern

CITOLE *n* pl. -S citola

CITRAL *n* pl. -S a lemon flavoring

CITRATE *n* pl. -S a salt of citric acid **CITRATED** *adj*

CITREOUS *adj* having a lemonlike color

CITRIC *adj* derived from citrus fruits

CITRIN *n* pl. -S a citric vitamin

CITRINE *n* pl. -S a variety of quartz

CITRON *n* pl. -S a lemonlike fruit

CITROUS *adj* pertaining to a citrus tree

CITRUS *n* pl. -ES any of a genus of tropical, fruit-bearing trees

CITTERN *n* pl. -S a pear-shaped guitar

CITY *n* pl. CITIES a large town

CITYFIED *adj* having the customs and manners of city people

CITYWARD *adv* toward the city

CIVET *n* pl. -S a catlike mammal

CIVIC *adj* pertaining to a city

CIVICISM *n* pl. -S a system of government based upon individual rights

CIVICS *n/pl* the science of civic affairs

CIVIE *n* pl. -S civvy

CIVIL *adj* pertaining to citizens

CIVILIAN *n* pl. -S a nonmilitary person

CIVILISE *v* -LISED, -LISING, -LISES to civilize

CIVILITY *n* pl. -TIES courtesy; politeness

CIVILIZE *v* -LIZED, -LIZING, -LIZES to bring out of savagery

CIVILLY *adv* politely

CIVISM *n* pl. -S good citizenship

CIVVY *n* pl. -VIES a civilian

CLABBER *v* -ED, -ING, -S to curdle

CLACH *n* pl. -S clachan

CLACHAN *n* pl. -S a hamlet

CLACK *v* -ED, -ING, -S to make an abrupt, dry sound

CLACKER *n* pl. -S one that clacks

CLAD *v* CLAD, CLADDING, CLADS to coat one metal over another

CLADDING *n* pl. -S something that overlays

CLADODE *n* pl. -S a leaflike part of a stem

CLAG *v* CLAGGED, CLAGGING, CLAGS to clog

CLAIM *v* -ED, -ING, -S to demand as one's due

CLAIMANT *n* pl. -S one that asserts a right or title

CLAIMER *n* pl. -S one that claims

CLAM *v* CLAMMED, CLAMMING, CLAMS to dig for clams (bivalve mollusks)

CLAMANT *adj* noisy

CLAMBAKE *n* pl. -S a beach picnic

CLAMBER *v* -ED, -ING, -S to climb awkwardly

CLAMMED past tense of clam

CLAMMING present participle of clam

CLAMMY *adj* CLAMMIER, CLAMMIEST cold and damp **CLAMMILY** *adv*

CLAMOR *v* -ED, -ING, -S to make loud outcries

CLAMORER *n* pl. -S one that clamors

CLAMOUR *v* -ED, -ING, -S to clamor

CLAMP v -ED, -ING, -S to fasten with a clamp (a securing device)

CLAMPER n pl. -S a device worn on shoes to prevent slipping on ice

CLAMWORM n pl. -S a marine worm

CLAN n pl. -S a united group of families

CLANG v -ED, -ING, -S to ring loudly

CLANGOR v -ED, -ING, -S to clang repeatedly

CLANGOUR v -ED, -ING, -S to clangor

CLANK v -ED, -ING, -S to make a sharp, metallic sound

CLANNISH adj characteristic of a clan

CLANSMAN n pl. -MEN a member of a clan

CLAP v CLAPPED or CLAPT, CLAPPING, CLAPS to strike one palm against the other

CLAPPER n pl. -S one that claps

CLAPTRAP n pl. -S pretentious language

CLAQUE n pl. -S a group of hired applauders

CLAQUER n pl. -S claqueur

CLAQUEUR n pl. -S a member of a claque

CLARENCE n pl. -S a closed carriage

CLARET n pl. -S a dry red wine

CLARIES pl. of clary

CLARIFY v -FIED, -FYING, -FIES to make clear

CLARINET n pl. -S a woodwind instrument

CLARION v -ED, -ING, -S to proclaim by blowing a medieval trumpet

CLARITY n pl. -TIES the state of being clear

CLARKIA n pl. -S an annual herb

CLARO n pl. -ROS or -ROES a mild cigar

CLARY n pl. CLARIES an aromatic herb

CLASH v -ED, -ING, -ES to conflict or disagree

CLASHER n pl. -S one that clashes

CLASP v CLASPED or CLASPT, CLASPING, CLASPS to embrace tightly

CLASPER n pl. -S one that clasps

CLASS v -ED, -ING, -ES to classify

CLASSER n pl. -S one that classes

CLASSES pl. of classis

CLASSIC n pl. -S a work of enduring excellence

CLASSIER comparative of classy

CLASSIEST superlative of classy

CLASSIFY v -FIED, -FYING, -FIES to arrange according to characteristics

CLASSIS n pl. CLASSES a governing body in certain churches

CLASSY adj CLASSIER, CLASSIEST stylish; elegant **CLASSILY** adv

CLAST n pl. -S a fragment of rock

CLASTIC n pl. -S a rock made up of other rocks

CLATTER v -ED, -ING, -S to move with a rattling noise

CLATTERY adj having a rattling noise

CLAUCHT a past tense of cleek

CLAUGHT v -ED, -ING, -S to clutch

CLAUSE n pl. -S a distinct part of a composition **CLAUSAL** adj

CLAVATE adj shaped like a club

CLAVE a past tense of cleave

CLAVER v -ED, -ING, -S to gossip

CLAVICLE n pl. -S a bone of the shoulder

CLAVIER n pl. -S a keyboard instrument

CLAW v -ED, -ING, -S to scratch with claws (sharp, curved toenails)

CLAWER n pl. -S one that claws

CLAWLESS adj having no claws

CLAXON n pl. -S klaxon

CLAY v -ED, -ING, -S to treat with clay (a fine-grained, earthy material)

CLAYBANK n pl. -S a yellow-brown color

CLAYEY adj CLAYIER, CLAYIEST resembling clay

CLAYISH adj resembling or containing clay

CLAYLIKE adj resembling clay

CLAYMORE n pl. -S a type of sword

CLAYPAN n pl. -S a shallow natural depression

CLAYWARE n pl. -S pottery

CLEAN adj CLEANER, CLEANEST free from dirt or stain

CLEAN v -ED, -ING, -S to rid of dirt or stain

CLEANER n pl. -S one that cleans

CLEANLY *adj* -LIER, -LIEST habitually clean

CLEANSE *v* CLEANSED, CLEANSING, CLEANSES to clean

CLEANSER *n* pl. -S one that cleanses

CLEANUP *n* pl. -S an act of cleaning

CLEAR *adj* CLEARER, CLEAREST clean and pure

CLEAR *v* -ED, -ING, -S to remove obstructions

CLEARER *n* pl. -S one that clears

CLEARING *n* pl. -S an open space

CLEARLY *adv* in a clear manner

CLEAT *v* -ED, -ING, -S to strengthen with a strip of wood or iron

CLEAVAGE *n* pl. -S the act of cleaving

CLEAVE *v* CLEAVED, CLEFT, CLOVE or CLAVE, CLOVEN, CLEAVING, CLEAVES to split or divide

CLEAVER *n* pl. -S a heavy knife

CLEEK *v* CLAUGHT or CLEEKED, CLEEKING, CLEEKS to clutch

CLEF *n* pl. -S a musical symbol

CLEFT *n* pl. -S a space or opening made by cleavage

CLEMATIS *n* pl. -TISES a flowering vine

CLEMENCY *n* pl. -CIES mercy

CLEMENT *adj* merciful

CLENCH *v* -ED, -ING, -ES to grasp firmly

CLEOME *n* pl. -S a tropical plant

CLEPE *v* CLEPED or CLEPT, CLEPING, CLEPES to call by name

CLERGY *n* pl. -GIES the body of men ordained for religious service

CLERIC *n* pl. -S a member of the clergy

CLERICAL *n* pl. -S a cleric

CLERID *n* pl. -S a predatory beetle

CLERIHEW *n* pl. -S a humorous poem

CLERISY *n* pl. -SIES the well-educated class

CLERK *v* -ED, -ING, -S to serve as a clerk (an office worker)

CLERKDOM *n* pl. -S the status or function of a clerk

CLERKISH *adj* resembling or suitable to a clerk

CLERKLY *adj* -LIER, -LIEST pertaining to a clerk

CLEVEITE *n* pl. -S a radioactive mineral

CLEVER *adj* -ERER, -EREST mentally keen **CLEVERLY** *adv*

CLEVIS *n* pl. -ISES a metal fastening device

CLEW *v* -ED, -ING, -S to roll into a ball

CLICHE *n* pl. -S a trite expression **CLICHED** *adj*

CLICK *v* -ED, -ING, -S to make a short, sharp sound

CLICKER *n* pl. -S one that clicks

CLIENT *n* pl. -S a customer **CLIENTAL** *adj*

CLIFF *n* pl. -S a high, steep face of rock

CLIFFY *adj* CLIFFIER, CLIFFIEST abounding in cliffs

CLIFT *n* pl. -S cliff

CLIMATE *n* pl. -S the weather conditions characteristic of an area **CLIMATAL, CLIMATIC** *adj*

CLIMAX *v* -ED, -ING, -ES to reach a high or dramatic point

CLIMB *v* CLIMBED or CLOMB, CLIMBING, CLIMBS to ascend

CLIMBER *n* pl. -S one that climbs

CLIME *n* pl. -S climate

CLINAL *adj* pertaining to a cline

CLINALLY *adv* in a clinal manner

CLINCH *v* -ED, -ING, -ES to settle a matter decisively

CLINCHER *n* pl. -S a decisive fact or remark

CLINE *n* pl. -S a series of changes within a species

CLING *v* CLUNG, CLINGING, CLINGS to adhere closely

CLING *v* -ED, -ING, -S to make a high-pitched ringing sound

CLINGER *n* pl. -S one that clings

CLINGY *adj* CLINGIER, CLINGIEST adhesive

CLINIC *n* pl. -S a medical facility **CLINICAL** *adj*

CLINK *v* -ED, -ING, -S to make a soft, sharp, ringing sound

CLINKER *v* -ED, -ING, -S to form fused residue in burning

CLIP *v* CLIPPED, CLIPT, CLIPPING, CLIPS to trim by cutting

CLIPPER *n* pl. -S one that clips

CLIPPING *n pl.* -S something that is clipped out or off

CLIPT a past participle of clip

CLIQUE *v* CLIQUED, CLIQUING, CLIQUES to form a clique (an exclusive group of persons)

CLIQUEY *adj* CLIQUIER, CLIQUIEST inclined to form cliques

CLIQUISH *adj* cliquey

CLIQUY *adj* CLIQUIER, CLIQUIEST cliquey

CLITELLA *n/pl* regions in the body walls of certain annelids

CLITORIS *n pl.* -RISES a sex organ CLITORAL, CLITORIC *adj*

CLIVERS *n pl.* CLIVERS an annual herb

CLOACA *n pl.* -ACAE a sewer CLOACAL *adj*

CLOAK *v* -ED, -ING, -S to conceal

CLOBBER *v* -ED, -ING, -S to trounce

CLOCHE *n pl.* -S a bell-shaped hat

CLOCK *v* -ED, -ING, -S to time with a stopwatch

CLOCKER *n pl.* -S one that clocks

CLOD *n pl.* -S a dolt CLODDISH *adj*

CLODDY *adj* -DIER, -DIEST lumpy

CLODPATE *n pl.* -S a stupid person

CLODPOLE *n pl.* -S clodpate

CLODPOLL *n pl.* -S clodpate

CLOG *v* CLOGGED, CLOGGING, CLOGS to block up or obstruct

CLOGGY *adj* -GIER, -GIEST clogging or able to clog

CLOISTER *v* -ED, -ING, -S to seclude

CLOMB a past tense of climb

CLOMP *v* -ED, -ING, -S to walk heavily and clumsily

CLON *n pl.* -S a group of asexually derived organisms CLONAL *adj* CLONALLY *adv*

CLONE *v* CLONED, CLONING, CLONES to reproduce by asexual means

CLONIC *adj* pertaining to clonus

CLONISM *n pl.* -S the condition of having clonus

CLONK *v* -ED, -ING, -S to make a dull thumping sound

CLONUS *n pl.* -ES a form of muscular spasm

CLOOT *n pl.* -S a cloven hoof

CLOP *v* CLOPPED, CLOPPING, CLOPS to make the sound of a hoof striking pavement

CLOSE *adj* CLOSER, CLOSEST near CLOSELY *adv*

CLOSE *v* CLOSED, CLOSING, CLOSES to block against entry or passage CLOSABLE *adj*

CLOSEOUT *n pl.* -S a clearance sale

CLOSER *n pl.* -S one that closes

CLOSEST superlative of close

CLOSET *v* -ED, -ING, -S to enclose in a private room

CLOSING *n pl.* -S a concluding part

CLOSURE *v* -SURED, -SURING, -SURES to cloture

CLOT *v* CLOTTED, CLOTTING, CLOTS to form into a clot (a thick mass)

CLOTH *n pl.* -S fabric

CLOTHE *v* CLOTHED or CLAD, CLOTHING, CLOTHES to provide with clothing

CLOTHIER *n pl.* -S one who makes or sells clothing

CLOTHING *n pl.* -S wearing apparel

CLOTTED past tense of clot

CLOTTING present participle of clot

CLOTTY *adj* tending to clot

CLOTURE *v* -TURED, -TURING, -TURES to end a debate by calling for a vote

CLOUD *v* -ED, -ING, -S to cover with clouds (masses of visible vapor)

CLOUDLET *n pl.* -S a small cloud

CLOUDY *adj* CLOUDIER, CLOUDIEST overcast with clouds CLOUDILY *adv*

CLOUGH *n pl.* -S a ravine

CLOUR *v* -ED, -ING, -S to knock or bump

CLOUT *v* -ED, -ING, -S to hit with the hand

CLOUTER *n pl.* -S one that clouts

CLOVE *n pl.* -S a spice

CLOVEN *adj* split; divided

CLOVER *n pl.* -S a plant

CLOWDER *n pl.* -S a group of cats

CLOWN *v* -ED, -ING, -S to act like a clown (a humorous performer)

CLOWNERY	*n* pl. -ERIES clownish behavior
CLOWNISH	*adj* resembling or befitting a clown
CLOY	*v* -ED, -ING, -S to gratify beyond desire
CLOZE	*adj* pertaining to a type of reading comprehension test
CLUB	*v* CLUBBED, CLUBBING, CLUBS to form a club (an organized group of persons)
CLUBABLE	*adj* sociable
CLUBBER	*n* pl. -S a member of a club
CLUBBING	present participle of club
CLUBBY	*adj* -BIER, -BIEST characteristic of a club
CLUBFOOT	*n* pl. -FEET a deformed foot
CLUBHAND	*n* pl. -S a deformed hand
CLUBHAUL	*v* -ED, -ING, -S to put a vessel about
CLUBMAN	*n* pl. -MEN a male member of a club
CLUBROOT	*n* pl. -S a plant disease
CLUCK	*v* -ED, -ING, -S to make the sound of a hen
CLUE	*v* CLUED, CLUEING or CLUING, CLUES to give guiding information
CLUMBER	*n* pl. -S a stocky spaniel
CLUMP	*v* -ED, -ING, -S to form into a thick mass
CLUMPISH	*adj* resembling a clump (a thick mass)
CLUMPY	*adj* CLUMPIER, CLUMPIEST lumpy
CLUMSY	*adj* -SIER, -SIEST awkward **CLUMSILY** *adv*
CLUNG	past tense of cling
CLUNK	*v* -ED, -ING, -S to thump
CLUNKER	*n* pl. -S a jalopy
CLUPEID	*n* pl. -S a fish of the herring family
CLUPEOID	*n* pl. -S a clupeid
CLUSTER	*v* -ED, -ING, -S to form into a cluster (a group of similar objects)
CLUSTERY	*adj* pertaining to a cluster
CLUTCH	*v* -ED, -ING, -ES to grasp and hold tightly
CLUTCHY	*adj* tending to clutch
CLUTTER	*v* -ED, -ING, -S to pile in a disorderly state
CLYPEUS	*n* pl. CLYPEI a shield-like structure **CLYPEAL, CLYPEATE** *adj*
CLYSTER	*n* pl. -S an enema
COACH	*v* -ED, -ING, -ES to tutor or train
COACHER	*n* pl. -S one that coaches
COACHMAN	*n* pl. -MEN one who drives a coach or carriage
COACT	*v* -ED, -ING, -S to act together
COACTIVE	*adj* mutually active
COACTION	*n* pl. -S joint action
COADMIRE	*v* -MIRED, -MIRING, -MIRES to admire together
COADMIT	*v* -MITTED, -MITTING, -MITS to admit several things equally
COAEVAL	*n* pl. -S coeval
COAGENCY	*n* pl. -CIES a joint agency
COAGENT	*n* pl. -S a person, force, or other agent working together with another
COAGULUM	*n* pl. -LA or -LUMS a clot
COAL	*v* -ED, -ING, -S to supply with coal (a carbon fuel)
COALA	*n* pl. -S koala
COALBIN	*n* pl. -S a bin for storing coal
COALBOX	*n* pl. -ES a box for storing coal
COALER	*n* pl. -S one that supplies coal
COALESCE	*v* -ALESCED, -ALESCING, -ALESCES to blend
COALFISH	*n* pl. -ES a blackish fish
COALHOLE	*n* pl. -S a compartment for storing coal
COALIFY	*v* -FIED, -FYING, -FIES to convert into coal
COALLESS	*adj* lacking coal
COALPIT	*n* pl. -S a pit from which coal is obtained
COALSACK	*n* pl. -S a dark region of the Milky Way
COALSHED	*n* pl. -S a shed for storing coal
COALYARD	*n* pl. -S a yard for storing coal
COAMING	*n* pl. -S a raised border
COANNEX	*v* -ED, -ING, -ES to annex jointly
COAPPEAR	*v* -ED, -ING, -S to appear together or at the same time
COAPT	*v* -ED, -ING, -S to fit together and make fast
COARSE	*adj* COARSER, COARSEST rough **COARSELY** *adv*

COARSEN *v* -ED, -ING, -S to make coarse

COASSIST *v* -ED, -ING, -S to assist jointly

COASSUME *v* -SUMED, -SUMING, -SUMES to assume together

COAST *v* -ED, -ING, -S to slide down a hill

COASTAL *adj* pertaining to or located near a seashore

COASTER *n* pl. -S a sled

COASTING *n* pl. -S coastal trade

COAT *v* -ED, -ING, -S to cover with a coat (an outer garment)

COATEE *n* pl. -S a small coat

COATER *n* pl. -S one that coats

COATI *n* pl. -S a tropical mammal

COATING *n* pl. -S a covering layer

COATLESS *adj* lacking a coat

COATRACK *n* pl. -S a rack or stand for coats

COATROOM *n* pl. -S a room for storing coats

COATTAIL *n* pl. -S the back lower portion of a coat

COATTEND *v* -ED, -ING, -S to attend together

COATTEST *v* -ED, -ING, -S to attest jointly

COAUTHOR *v* -ED, -ING, -S to write together

COAX *v* -ED, -ING, -ES to cajole

COAXAL *adj* coaxial

COAXER *n* pl. -S one that coaxes

COAXIAL *adj* having a common axis

COB *n* pl. -S a corncob

COBALT *n* pl. -S a metallic element **COBALTIC** *adj*

COBB *n* pl. -S a sea gull

COBBER *n* pl. -S a comrade

COBBIER comparative of cobby

COBBIEST superlative of cobby

COBBLE *v* -BLED, -BLING, -BLES to mend

COBBLER *n* pl. -S a mender of shoes

COBBY *adj* -BIER, -BIEST stocky

COBIA *n* pl. -S a large game fish

COBLE *n* pl. -S a small fishing boat

COBNUT *n* pl. -S an edible nut

COBRA *n* pl. -S a venomous snake

COBWEB *v* -WEBBED, -WEBBING, -WEBS to cover with cobwebs (spider webs)

COBWEBBY *adj* -BIER, -BIEST covered with cobwebs

COCA *n* pl. -S a South American shrub

COCAIN *n* pl. -S cocaine

COCAINE *n* pl. -S a narcotic alkaloid

COCCAL *adj* pertaining to a coccus

COCCI pl. of coccus

COCCIC *adj* coccal

COCCID *n* pl. -S an insect

COCCIDIA *n/pl* parasitic protozoans

COCCOID *n* pl. -S a spherical cell or body

COCCUS *n* pl. COCCI a spherical bacterium **COCCOUS** *adj*

COCCYX *n* pl. -CYGES or -CYXES a bone of the spine

COCHAIR *v* -ED, -ING, -S to serve jointly as chairman of

COCHIN *n* pl. -S a large domestic chicken

COCHLEA *n* pl. -CHLEAE or -CHLEAS a part of the ear **COCHLEAR** *adj*

COCINERA *n* pl. -S a cook

COCK *v* -ED, -ING, -S to tilt to one side

COCKADE *n* pl. -S an ornament worn on a hat **COCKADED** *adj*

COCKATOO *n* pl. -TOOS a parrot

COCKBILL *v* -ED, -ING, -S to raise the yardarm on a ship

COCKBOAT *n* pl. -S a small boat

COCKCROW *n* pl. -S daybreak

COCKER *v* -ED, -ING, -S to pamper

COCKEREL *n* pl. -S a young rooster

COCKEYE *n* pl. -S a squinting eye **COCKEYED** *adj*

COCKIER comparative of cocky

COCKIEST superlative of cocky

COCKILY *adv* in a cocky manner

COCKISH *adj* cocky

COCKLE *v* -LED, -LING, -LES to wrinkle or pucker

COCKLIKE *adj* resembling a rooster

COCKLOFT *n* pl. -S a small attic

COCKNEY *n* pl. -NEYS a resident of the East End of London

COCKPIT *n* pl. -S a pilot's compartment in certain airplanes

COCKSHUT *n* pl. -S the close of day

COCKSHY *n pl.* -SHIES a target in a throwing contest

COCKSPUR *n pl.* -S a thorny plant

COCKSURE *adj* certain

COCKTAIL *v* -ED, -ING, -S to drink alcoholic beverages

COCKUP *n pl.* -S a turned-up part of something

COCKY *adj* COCKIER, COCKIEST arrogantly self-confident

COCO *n pl.* -COS a tall palm tree

COCOA *n pl.* -S chocolate

COCOANUT *n pl.* -S coconut

COCOBOLA *n pl.* -S cocobolo

COCOBOLO *n pl.* -LOS a tropical tree

COCOMAT *n pl.* -S a matting made from coir

COCONUT *n pl.* -S the fruit of the coco

COCOON *v* -ED, -ING, -S to wrap or envelop tightly

COCOTTE *n pl.* -S a prostitute

COCREATE *v* -ATED, -ATING, -ATES to create together

COD *n pl.* -S a marine food fish

CODA *n pl.* -S a passage at the end of a musical composition

CODABLE *adj* capable of being coded

CODDER *n pl.* -S a cod fisherman

CODDLE *v* -DLED, -DLING, -DLES to pamper

CODDLER *n pl.* -S one that coddles

CODE *v* CODED, CODING, CODES to convert into symbols

CODEBTOR *n pl.* -S one that shares a debt

CODEIA *n pl.* -S codeine

CODEIN *n pl.* -S codeine

CODEINA *n pl.* -S codeine

CODEINE *n pl.* -S a narcotic alkaloid

CODELESS *adj* being without a set of laws

CODEN *n pl.* -S a coding classification

CODER *n pl.* -S one that codes

CODERIVE *v* -RIVED, -RIVING, -RIVES to derive jointly

CODEX *n pl.* -DICES an ancient manuscript

CODFISH *n pl.* -ES the cod

CODGER *n pl.* -S an old man

CODICES pl. of codex

CODICIL *n pl.* -S a supplement to a will

CODIFIER *n pl.* -S one that codifies

CODIFY *v* -FIED, -FYING, -FIES to arrange or systematize

CODING present participle of code

CODLIN *n pl.* -S codling

CODLING *n pl.* -S an unripe apple

CODON *n pl.* -S a triplet of nucleotides (basic components of DNA)

CODPIECE *n pl.* -S a cover for the crotch in men's breeches

COED *n pl.* -S a female student

COEDITOR *n pl.* -S one who edits with another person

COEFFECT *n pl.* -S an accompanying effect

COELIAC *adj* celiac

COELOM *n pl.* -LOMS or -LOMATA a body cavity in some animals **COELOMIC** *adj*

COELOME *n pl.* -S coelom

COEMBODY *v* -BODIED, -BODYING, -BODIES to embody jointly

COEMPLOY *v* -ED, -ING, -S to employ together

COEMPT *v* -ED, -ING, -S to buy up the entire supply of a product

COENACT *v* -ED, -ING, -S to enact jointly or at the same time

COENAMOR *v* -ED, -ING, -S to inflame with mutual love

COENDURE *v* -DURED, -DURING, -DURES to endure together

COENURE *n pl.* -S coenurus

COENURUS *n pl.* -RI a tapeworm larva

COENZYME *n pl.* -S a substance necessary for the functioning of certain enzymes

COEQUAL *n pl.* -S one who is equal with another

COEQUATE *v* -QUATED, -QUATING, -QUATES to equate with something else

COERCE *v* -ERCED, -ERCING, -ERCES to compel by force or threat

COERCER *n pl.* -S one that coerces

COERCION *n pl.* -S the act of coercing

COERCIVE *adj* serving to coerce

COERECT *v* -ED, -ING, -S to erect together

COEVAL *n pl.* -S one of the same era or period as another

COEVALLY *adv* contemporarily

COEXERT *v* -ED, -ING, -S to exert jointly

COEXIST *v* -ED, -ING, -S to exist together

COEXTEND *v* -ED, -ING, -S to extend through the same space or time as another

COFACTOR *n pl.* -S a coenzyme

COFF *v* COFT, COFFING, COFFS to buy

COFFEE *n pl.* -S an aromatic, mildly stimulating beverage

COFFER *v* -ED, -ING, -S to put in a strongbox

COFFIN *v* -ED, -ING, -S to put in a coffin (a burial case)

COFFING present participle of coff

COFFLE *v* -FLED, -FLING, -FLES to chain slaves together

COFFRET *n pl.* -S a small strongbox

COFT past tense of coff

COG *v* COGGED, COGGING, COGS to cheat at dice

COGENCY *n pl.* -CIES the state of being cogent

COGENT *adj* convincing **COGENTLY** *adv*

COGGED past tense of cog

COGGING present participle of cog

COGITATE *v* -TATED, -TATING, -TATES to ponder

COGITO *n pl.* -TOS a philosophical principle

COGNAC *n pl.* -S a brandy

COGNATE *n pl.* -S one that is related to another

COGNISE *v* -NISED, -NISING, -NISES to cognize

COGNIZE *v* -NIZED, -NIZING, -NIZES to become aware of in one's mind

COGNIZER *n pl.* -S one that cognizes

COGNOMEN *n pl.* -MENS or -MINA a family name

COGNOVIT *n pl.* -S a written admission of liability

COGON *n pl.* -S a tall tropical grass

COGWAY *n pl.* -WAYS a railway operating on steep slopes

COGWHEEL *n pl.* -S a toothed wheel

COHABIT *v* -ED, -ING, -S to live together as man and wife while unmarried

COHEIR *n pl.* -S a joint heir

COHERE *v* -HERED, -HERING, -HERES to stick together

COHERENT *adj* sticking together

COHERER *n pl.* -S a device used to detect radio waves

COHERING present participle of cohere

COHESION *n pl.* -S the act or state of cohering **COHESIVE** *adj*

COHO *n pl.* -HOS a small salmon

COHOBATE *v* -BATED, -BATING, -BATES to distill again

COHOG *n pl.* -S a quahog

COHORT *n pl.* -S a companion or associate

COHOSH *n pl.* -ES a medicinal plant

COHUNE *n pl.* -S a palm tree

COIF *v* -ED, -ING -S to style the hair

COIFFE *v* COIFFED, COIFFING, COIFFES to coif

COIFFEUR *n pl.* -S a male hairdresser

COIFFURE *v* -FURED, -FURING, -FURES to coif

COIGN *v* -ED, -ING, -S to quoin

COIGNE *v* COIGNED, COIGNING, COIGNES to quoin

COIL *v* -ED, -ING, -S to wind in even rings

COILER *n pl.* -S one that coils

COIN *v* -ED, -ING, -S to make coins (metal currency) **COINABLE** *adj*

COINAGE *n pl.* -S the act of making coins

COINCIDE *v* -CIDED, -CIDING, -CIDES to be in the same place

COINER *n pl.* -S one that coins

COINFER *v* -FERRED, -FERRING, -FERS to infer jointly

COINHERE *v* -HERED, -HERING, -HERES to inhere jointly

COINMATE *n pl.* -S a fellow inmate

COINSURE *v* -SURED, -SURING, -SURES to insure with another

COINTER *v* -TERRED, -TERRING, -TERS to bury together

COIR *n pl.* -S a fiber obtained from coconut husks

COISTREL *n pl.* -S a knave

COISTRIL *n pl.* -S coistrel

COITION *n pl.* -S coitus

COITUS *n pl.* -ES sexual intercourse **COITAL** *adj* **COITALLY** *adv*

COKE	v COKED, COKING, COKES to change into a carbon fuel
COL	n pl. -S a depression between two mountains
COLA	n pl. -S a carbonated beverage
COLANDER	n pl. -S a kitchen utensil for draining off liquids
COLD	adj COLDER, COLDEST having little or no warmth
COLD	n pl. -S the relative lack of heat; a chill
COLDISH	adj somewhat cold
COLDLY	adv in a cold manner
COLDNESS	n pl. -ES the state of being cold
COLE	n pl. -S a plant of the cabbage family
COLESEED	n pl. -S colza
COLESLAW	n pl. -S a salad made of shredded raw cabbage
COLESSEE	n pl. -S a joint lessee
COLESSOR	n pl. -S a joint lessor
COLEUS	n pl. -ES a tropical plant
COLEWORT	n pl. -S cole
COLIC	n pl. -S acute abdominal pain
COLICIN	n pl. -S an antibacterial substance
COLICINE	n pl. -S colicin
COLICKY	adj pertaining to or associated with colic
COLIES	pl. of coly
COLIFORM	n pl. -S a bacillus of the colon
COLIN	n pl. -S the bobwhite
COLINEAR	adj lying in the same straight line
COLISEUM	n pl. -S a large structure for public entertainment
COLISTIN	n pl. -S an antibiotic
COLITIS	n pl. -TISES inflammation of the colon COLITIC adj
COLLAGE	n pl. -S a kind of artistic composition
COLLAGEN	n pl. -S a protein
COLLAPSE	v -LAPSED, -LAPSING, -LAPSES to crumble suddenly
COLLAR	v -ED, -ING, -S to provide with a collar (something worn around the neck)
COLLARD	n pl. -S a variety of kale
COLLARET	n pl. -S a small collar

COLLATE	v -LATED, -LATING, -LATES to compare critically
COLLATOR	n pl. -S one that collates
COLLECT	v -ED, -ING, -S to bring together in a group
COLLEEN	n pl. -S an Irish girl
COLLEGE	n pl. -S a school of higher learning
COLLEGER	n pl. -S a student supported by funds from his college
COLLEGIA	n/pl soviet executive councils
COLLET	v -ED, -ING, -S to set a gem in a rim or ring
COLLIDE	v -LIDED, -LIDING, -LIDES to come together with violent impact
COLLIE	n pl. -S a large dog
COLLIED	past tense of colly
COLLIER	n pl. -S a coal miner
COLLIERY	n pl. -LIERIES a coal mine
COLLIES	present 3d person sing. of colly
COLLINS	n pl. -ES an alcoholic beverage
COLLOGUE	v -LOGUED, -LOGUING, -LOGUES to conspire
COLLOID	n pl. -S a type of chemical suspension
COLLOP	n pl. -S a small portion of meat
COLLOQUY	n pl. -QUIES a conversation
COLLUDE	v -LUDED, -LUDING, -LUDES to conspire
COLLUDER	n pl. -S one that colludes
COLLUVIA	n/pl rock debris
COLLY	v -LIED, -LYING, -LIES to blacken with coal dust
COLLYRIA	n/pl medicinal lotions
COLOCATE	v -CATED, -CATING, -CATES to place two or more housing units in close proximity
COLOG	n pl. -S the logarithm of the reciprocal of a number
COLOGNE	n pl. -S a scented liquid COLOGNED adj
COLON	n pl. -S a section of the large intestine
COLON	n pl. -ES a monetary unit of Costa Rica
COLONEL	n pl. -S a military officer
COLONI	pl. of colonus
COLONIAL	n pl. -S a citizen of a colony

COLONIC *adj* pertaining to the colon

COLONIES pl. of colony

COLONISE *v* -NISED, -NISING, -NISES to colonize

COLONIST *n* pl. -S one who settles a colony

COLONIZE *v* -NIZED, -NIZING, -NIZES to establish a colony

COLONUS *n* pl. -NI a freeborn serf

COLONY *n* pl. -NIES a group of emigrants living in a new land

COLOPHON *n* pl. -S an inscription placed at the end of a book

COLOR *v* -ED, -ING, -S to give color (a visual attribute of objects) to

COLORADO *adj* of medium strength and color — used of cigars

COLORANT *n* pl. -S a pigment or dye

COLORED *n* pl. -S a nonwhite person

COLORER *n* pl. -S one that colors

COLORFUL *adj* full of color

COLORING *n* pl. -S appearance in regard to color

COLORISM *n* pl. -S coloring

COLORIST *n* pl. -S a person skilled in the use of color

COLOSSAL *adj* gigantic

COLOSSUS *n* pl. -LOSSI or -LOSSUSES a gigantic statue

COLOTOMY *n* pl. -MIES a surgical incision of the colon

COLOUR *v* -ED, -ING, -S to color

COLOURER *n* pl. -S colorer

COLPITIS *n* pl. -TISES a vaginal inflammation

COLT *n* pl. -S a young male horse COLTISH *adj*

COLTER *n* pl. -S a blade on a plow

COLUBRID *n* pl. -S any of a large family of snakes

COLUGO *n* pl. -GOS a small mammal

COLUMBIC *adj* pertaining to niobium

COLUMEL *n* pl. -S a small column-like anatomical part

COLUMN *n* pl. -S a vertical cylindrical support COLUMNAL, COLUMNAR, COLUMNED *adj*

COLURE *n* pl. -S an astronomical circle

COLY *n* pl. COLIES an African bird

COLZA *n* pl. -S a plant of the cabbage family

COMA *n* pl. -S a condition of prolonged unconsciousness

COMA *n* pl. -MAE a tuft of silky hairs

COMAKER *n* pl. -S one who assumes financial responsibility for another's default

COMAL *adj* comose

COMATE *n* pl. -S a companion

COMATIC *adj* having blurred vision as a result of coma

COMATIK *n* pl. -S komatik

COMATOSE *adj* affected with coma

COMATULA *n* pl. -LAE a marine animal

COMB *v* -ED, -ING, -S to arrange or clean with a comb (a toothed instrument)

COMBAT *v* -BATED, -BATING, -BATS or -BATTED, -BATTING, -BATS to fight against

COMBATER *n* pl. -S one that combats

COMBE *n* pl. -S a narrow valley

COMBER *n* pl. -S one that combs

COMBINE *v* -BINED, -BINING, -BINES to blend

COMBINER *n* pl. -S one that combines

COMBINGS *n/pl* hair removed by a comb

COMBINING present participle of combine

COMBLIKE *adj* resembling a comb

COMBO *n* pl. -BOS a small jazz band

COMBUST *v* -ED, -ING, -S to burn

COME *v* CAME, COMING, COMES or COMETH to move toward something or someone

COMEBACK *n* pl. -S a return to former prosperity

COMEDIAN *n* pl. -S a humorous entertainer

COMEDIC *adj* pertaining to comedy

COMEDIES pl. of comedy

COMEDO *n* pl. -DOS or -DONES a skin blemish

COMEDOWN *n* pl. -S a drop in status

COMEDY *n* pl. -DIES a humorous play, movie, or other work

COMELY *adj* -LIER, -LIEST pleasing to look at COMELILY *adv*

COMER *n* pl. -S one showing great promise

COMET *n* pl. -S a celestial body **COMETARY** *adj*

COMETH a present 3d person sing. of come

COMETHER *n* pl. -S an affair or matter

COMETIC *adj* pertaining to a comet

COMFIER comparative of comfy

COMFIEST superlative of comfy

COMFIT *n* pl. -S a candy

COMFORT *v* -ED, -ING, -S to soothe in time of grief

COMFREY *n* pl. -FREYS a coarse herb

COMFY *adj* -FIER, -FIEST comfortable

COMIC *n* pl. -S a comedian

COMICAL *adj* funny

COMING *n* pl. -S arrival

COMITIA *n* pl. COMITIA a public assembly in ancient Rome **COMITIAL** *adj*

COMITY *n* pl. -TIES civility

COMMA *n* pl. -MAS or -MATA a fragment of a few words or feet in ancient prosody

COMMAND *v* -ED, -ING, -S to direct with authority

COMMANDO *n* pl. -DOES or -DOS a military unit

COMMATA a pl. of comma

COMMENCE *v* -MENCED, -MENCING, -MENCES to begin

COMMEND *v* -ED, -ING, -S to praise

COMMENT *v* -ED, -ING, -S to remark

COMMERCE *v* -MERCED, -MERCING, -MERCES to commune

COMMIE *n* pl. -S a Communist

COMMIES pl. of commy

COMMIT *v* -MITTED, -MITTING, -MITS to do, perform, or perpetrate

COMMIX *v* -MIXED or -MIXT, -MIXING, -MIXES to mix together

COMMODE *n* pl. -S a cabinet

COMMON *adj* -MONER, -MONEST ordinary

COMMON *n* pl. -S a tract of publicly used land

COMMONER *n* pl. -S one of the common people

COMMONLY *adv* in a common manner

COMMOVE *v* -MOVED, -MOVING, -MOVES to move violently

COMMUNAL *adj* belonging to a community; public

COMMUNE *v* -MUNED, -MUNING, -MUNES to converse intimately

COMMUTE *v* -MUTED, -MUTING, -MUTES to exchange

COMMUTER *n* pl. -S one that commutes

COMMY *n* pl. -MIES commie

COMOSE *adj* bearing a tuft of silky hairs

COMOUS *adj* comose

COMP *v* -ED, -ING, -S to play a jazz accompaniment

COMPACT *adj* -PACTER, -PACTEST closely and firmly united

COMPACT *v* -ED, -ING, -S to pack closely together

COMPADRE *n* pl. -S a close friend

COMPANY *v* -NIED, -NYING, -NIES to associate with

COMPARE *v* -PARED, -PARING, -PARES to represent as similar

COMPARER *n* pl. -S one that compares

COMPART *v* -ED, -ING, -S to divide into parts

COMPASS *v* -ED, -ING, -ES to go around

COMPEER *v* -ED, -ING, -S to equal or match

COMPEL *v* -PELLED, -PELLING, -PELS to urge forcefully

COMPEND *n* pl. -S a brief summary

COMPERE *v* -PERED, -PERING, -PERES to act as master of ceremonies

COMPETE *v* -PETED, -PETING, -PETES to vie

COMPILE *v* -PILED, -PILING, -PILES to collect into a volume

COMPILER *n* pl. -S one that compiles

COMPLAIN *v* -ED, -ING, -S to express discontent

COMPLEAT *adj* highly skilled

COMPLECT *v* -ED, -ING, -S to weave together

COMPLETE *adj* -PLETER, -PLETEST having all necessary parts

COMPLETE *v* -PLETED, -PLETING, -PLETES to bring to an end

COMPLEX *adj* -PLEXER, -PLEXEST complicated

COMPLEX *v* -ED, -ING, -ES to make complex

COMPLICE *n* pl. -S an associate

COMPLIED past tense of comply

COMPLIER *n* pl. -S one that complies

COMPLIES present 3d person sing. of comply

COMPLIN *n* pl. -S compline

COMPLINE *n* pl. -S the last liturgical prayer of the day

COMPLOT *v* -PLOTTED, -PLOTTING, -PLOTS to conspire

COMPLY *v* -PLIED, -PLYING, -PLIES to obey

COMPO *n* pl. -POS a mixed substance

COMPONE *adj* compony

COMPONY *adj* composed of squares of alternating colors

COMPORT *v* -ED, -ING -S to conduct oneself in a certain way

COMPOSE *v* -POSED, -POSING, -POSES to form the substance of

COMPOSER *n* pl. -S one that writes music

COMPOST *v* -ED, -ING, -S to fertilize

COMPOTE *n* pl. -S fruit stewed in syrup

COMPOUND *v* -ED, -ING, -S to add to

COMPRESS *v* -ED, -ING, -ES to compact

COMPRISE *v* -PRISED, -PRISING, -PRISES to include or contain

COMPRIZE *v* -PRIZED, -PRIZING, -PRIZES to comprise

COMPT *v* -ED, -ING, -S to count

COMPUTE *v* -PUTED, -PUTING, -PUTES to determine by mathematical means

COMPUTER *n* pl. -S a machine that computes automatically

COMRADE *n* pl. -S a close friend

COMTE *n* pl. -S a French nobleman

CON *v* CONNED, CONNING, CONS to study carefully

CONATION *n* pl. -S the inclination to act purposefully **CONATIVE** *adj*

CONATUS *n* pl. CONATUS an effort

CONCAVE *v* -CAVED, -CAVING, -CAVES to make concave (curving inward)

CONCEAL *v* -ED, -ING, -S to keep from sight or discovery

CONCEDE *v* -CEDED, -CEDING, -CEDES to acknowledge as true

CONCEDER *n* pl. -S one that concedes

CONCEIT *v* -ED, -ING, -S to imagine

CONCEIVE *v* -CEIVED, -CEIVING, -CEIVES to understand

CONCENT *n* pl. -S harmony

CONCEPT *n* pl. -S a general idea

CONCERN *v* -ED, -ING, -S to be of interest to

CONCERT *v* -ED, -ING, -S to plan

CONCERTO *n* pl. -TOS or -TI a musical composition

CONCH *n* pl. -S or -ES a marine mollusk

CONCHA *n* pl. -CHAE an anatomical shell-like structure **CONCHAL** *adj*

CONCHOID *n* pl. -S a type of geometric curve

CONCHY *n* pl. -CHIES a conscientious objector

CONCISE *adj* -CISER, -CISEST succinct

CONCLAVE *n* pl. -S a secret meeting

CONCLUDE *v* -CLUDED, -CLUDING, -CLUDES to finish

CONCOCT *v* -ED, -ING, -S to prepare by combining ingredients

CONCORD *n* pl. -S a state of agreement

CONCRETE *v* -CRETED, -CRETING, -CRETES to solidify

CONCUR *v* -CURRED, -CURRING, -CURS to agree

CONCUSS *v* -ED, -ING, -ES to injure the brain by a violent blow

CONDEMN *v* -ED, -ING, -S to criticize severely

CONDENSE *v* -DENSED, -DENSING, -DENSES to compress

CONDIGN *adj* deserved; appropriate

CONDOLE *v* -DOLED, -DOLING, -DOLES to mourn

CONDOLER *n* pl. -S one that condoles

CONDOM *n* pl. -S a prophylactic

CONDONE *v* -DONED, -DONING, -DONES to forgive or overlook

CONDONER *n* pl. -S one that condones

CONDOR *n* pl. -S or -ES a coin of Chile

CONDUCE *v* -DUCED, -DUCING, -DUCES to contribute to a result

CONDUCER *n* pl. -S one that conduces

CONDUCT *v* -ED, -ING, -S to lead or guide

CONDUIT *n* pl. -S a channel or pipe for conveying fluids

CONDYLE *n* pl. -S a protuberance on a bone **CONDYLAR** *adj*

CONE   v CONED, CONING, CONES to shape like a cone (a geometric solid)

CONELRAD   n pl. -S a system of defense in the event of air attack

CONENOSE   n pl. -S a bloodsucking insect

CONEPATE   n pl. -S a skunk

CONEPATL   n pl. -S conepate

CONEY   n pl. -NEYS cony

CONFAB   v -FABBED, -FABBING, FABS to chat

CONFECT   v -ED, -ING, -S to prepare from various ingredients

CONFER   v -FERRED, -FERRING, -FERS to bestow

CONFEREE   n pl. -S one upon whom something is conferred

CONFERVA   n pl. -VAE or -VAS a freshwater alga

CONFESS   v -ED, -ING, -ES to acknowledge or disclose

CONFETTO   n pl. -TI a bonbon

CONFIDE   v -FIDED, -FIDING, -FIDES to reveal in trust or confidence

CONFIDER   n pl. -S one that confides

CONFINE   v -FINED, -FINING, -FINES to shut within an enclosure

CONFINER   n pl. -S one that confines

CONFIRM   v -ED, -ING, -S to assure the validity of

CONFLATE   v -FLATED, -FLATING, -FLATES to blend

CONFLICT   v -ED, -ING, -S to come into opposition

CONFLUX   n pl. -ES a flowing together of streams

CONFOCAL   adj having the same focus or foci

CONFORM   v -ED, -ING, -S to become the same or similar

CONFOUND   v -ED, -ING, -S to confuse

CONFRERE   n pl. -S a colleague

CONFRONT   v -ED, -ING, -S to face defiantly

CONFUSE   v -FUSED, -FUSING, -FUSES to mix up mentally

CONFUTE   v -FUTED, -FUTING, -FUTES to disprove

CONFUTER   n pl. -S one that confutes

CONGA   v -ED, -ING, -S to perform a Latin American dance

CONGE   n pl. -S permission to depart

CONGEAL   v -ED, -ING, -S to change from a fluid to a solid

CONGEE   v -GEED, -GEEING, -GEES to bow politely

CONGENER   n pl. -S one of the same kind or class

CONGER   n pl. -S a marine eel

CONGEST   v -ED, -ING, -S to fill to excess

CONGIUS   n pl. -GII an ancient unit of measure

CONGLOBE   v -GLOBED, -GLOBING, -GLOBES to become a globule

CONGO   n pl. -GOS congou

CONGO   n pl. -GOES an eellike amphibian

CONGOU   n pl. -S a Chinese tea

CONGRESS   v -ED, -ING, -ES to assemble together

CONI   pl. of conus

CONIC   n pl. -S a geometric curve

CONICAL   adj shaped like a cone

CONICITY   n pl. -TIES the state of being conical

CONIDIUM   n pl. -NIDIA a fungus spore CONIDIAL, CONIDIAN adj

CONIES   pl. of cony

CONIFER   n pl. -S an evergreen tree

CONIINE   n pl. -S a poisonous alkaloid

CONIN   n pl. -S coniine

CONINE   n pl. -S coniine

CONING   present participle of cone

CONIUM   n pl. -S a poisonous herb

CONJOIN   v -ED, -ING, -S to join together CONJOINT adj

CONJUGAL   adj pertaining to marriage

CONJUNCT   n pl. -S one that is joined with another

CONJURE   v -JURED, -JURING, -JURES to summon a spirit

CONJURER   n pl. -S a sorcerer

CONJUROR   n pl. -S conjurer

CONK   v -ED, -ING, -S to hit on the head

CONKER   n pl. -S a chestnut used in a British game

CONKY   adj full of a tree fungus

CONN   v -ED, -ING, -S to direct the steering of a ship

CONNATE   adj innate

CONNECT v -ED, -ING, -S to join together

CONNED past tense of con

CONNER n pl. -S one that cons

CONNING present participle of con

CONNIVE v -NIVED, -NIVING, -NIVES to feign ignorance of wrongdoing

CONNIVER n pl. -S one that connives

CONNOTE v -NOTED, -NOTING, -NOTES to imply another meaning besides the literal one

CONODONT n pl. -S a fossil

CONOID n pl. -S a geometric solid **CONOIDAL** adj

CONQUER v -ED, -ING, -S to overcome by force

CONQUEST n pl. -S the act of conquering

CONQUIAN n pl. -S a card game

CONSENT v -ED, -ING, -S to permit or approve

CONSERVE v -SERVED, -SERVING, -SERVES to protect from loss or depletion

CONSIDER v -ED, -ING, -S to think about

CONSIGN v -ED, -ING, -S to give over to another's care

CONSIST v -ED, -ING, -S to be made up or composed

CONSOL n pl. -S a government bond

CONSOLE v -SOLED, -SOLING, -SOLES to comfort

CONSOLER n pl. -S one that consoles

CONSOMME n pl. -S a clear soup

CONSORT v -ED, -ING, -S to keep company

CONSPIRE v -SPIRED, -SPIRING, -SPIRES to plan secretly with another

CONSTANT n pl. -S something that does not vary

CONSTRUE v -STRUED, -STRUING, -STRUES to interpret

CONSUL n pl. -S an official serving abroad **CONSULAR** adj

CONSULT v -ED, -ING, -S to ask an opinion of

CONSUME v -SUMED, -SUMING, -SUMES to use up

CONSUMER n pl. -S one that consumes

CONTACT v -ED, -ING, -S to communicate with

CONTAGIA n/pl causative agents of infectious diseases

CONTAIN v -ED, -ING, -S to hold within

CONTE n pl. -S a short story

CONTEMN v -ED, -ING, -S to scorn

CONTEMPT n pl. -S the feeling of one who views something as mean, vile, or worthless

CONTEND v -ED, -ING, -S to vie

CONTENT v -ED, -ING, -S to satisfy

CONTEST v -ED, -ING, -S to compete for

CONTEXT n pl. -S the part of a discourse in which a particular word or phrase appears

CONTINUA n/pl mathematical sets

CONTINUE v -UED, -UING, -UES to go on with

CONTINUO n pl. -UOS a type of intrumental part

CONTO n pl. -TOS a Portuguese money of account

CONTORT v -ED, -ING, -S to twist out of shape

CONTOUR v -ED, -ING, -S to make the outline of

CONTRA prep against

CONTRACT v -ED, -ING, -S to decrease in size or volume

CONTRAIL n pl. -S a visible trail of water vapor from an aircraft

CONTRARY n pl. -TRARIES an opposite

CONTRAST v -ED, -ING, -S to place in opposition to set off differences

CONTRITE adj deeply sorry for one's sins

CONTRIVE v -TRIVED, -TRIVING, -TRIVES to devise

CONTROL v -TROLLED, -TROLLING, -TROLS to exercise authority over

CONTUSE v -TUSED, -TUSING, -TUSES to bruise

CONUS n pl. CONI an anatomical part in mammals

CONVECT v -ED, -ING, -S to transfer heat by a process of circulation

CONVENE v -VENED, -VENING, -VENES to assemble

CONVENER n pl. -S one that convenes

CONVENT v -ED, -ING, -S to convene

CONVERGE v -VERGED, -VERGING, -VERGES to come together

CONVERSE v -VERSED, -VERSING, -VERSES to speak together

CONVERT v -ED, -ING, -S to change into another form

CONVEX n pl. -ES a surface or body that is convex (curving outward)

CONVEXLY adv in a convex manner

CONVEY v -ED, -ING, -S to transport

CONVEYER n pl. -S one that conveys

CONVEYOR n pl. -S conveyer

CONVICT v -ED, -ING, -S to prove guilty

CONVINCE v -VINCED, -VINCING, -VINCES to cause to believe something

CONVOKE v -VOKED, -VOKING, -VOKES to cause to assemble

CONVOKER n pl. -S one that convokes

CONVOLVE v -VOLVED, -VOLVING, -VOLVES to roll together

CONVOY v -ED, -ING, -S to escort

CONVULSE v -VULSED, -VULSING, -VULSES to shake violently

CONY n pl. CONIES a rabbit

COO v COOED, COOING, COOS to make the sound of a dove

COOCH n pl. -ES a sinuous dance

COOEE v COOEED, COOEEING, COOEES to cry out shrilly

COOER n pl. -S one that coos

COOEY v -EYED, -EYING, -EYS to cooee

COOF n pl. -S a dolt

COOINGLY adv in the manner of cooing doves; affectionately

COOK v -ED, -ING, -S to prepare food by heating **COOKABLE** adj

COOKBOOK n pl. -S a book of recipes

COOKER n pl. -S one that cooks

COOKERY n pl. -ERIES the art of cooking

COOKEY n pl. -EYS cookie

COOKIE n pl. -S a small, flat cake

COOKIES pl. of cooky

COOKING n pl. -S the act of one that cooks

COOKLESS adj having no person that cooks

COOKOUT n pl. -S a meal eaten and prepared outdoors

COOKSHOP n pl. -S a shop that sells cooked food

COOKWARE n pl. -S utensils used in cooking

COOKY n pl. COOKIES cookie

COOL adj COOLER, COOLEST moderately cold

COOL v -ED, -ING, -S to make less warm

COOLANT n pl. -S a fluid used to cool engines

COOLER n pl. -S something that cools

COOLIE n pl. -S an Oriental laborer

COOLIES pl. of cooly

COOLISH adj somewhat cool

COOLLY adv in a cool manner

COOLNESS n pl. -ES the state of being cool

COOLY n pl. COOLIES coolie

COOMB n pl. -S combe

COOMBE n pl. -S combe

COON n pl. -S a raccoon

COONCAN n pl. -S conquian

COONSKIN n pl. -S the pelt of a raccoon

COONTIE n pl. -S a tropical plant

COOP v -ED, -ING, -S to confine

COOPER v -ED, -ING, -S to make or mend barrels

COOPERY n pl. -ERIES the trade of coopering

COOPT v -ED, -ING, -S to elect or appoint

COOPTION n pl. -S the act of coopting

COOT n pl. -S an aquatic bird

COOTIE n pl. -S a body louse

COP v COPPED, COPPING, COPS to steal

COPAIBA n pl. -S a resin

COPAL n pl. -S a resin

COPALM n pl. -S a hardwood tree

COPARENT n pl. -S a fellow parent

COPASTOR n pl. -S one that shares the duties of a pastor

COPATRON n pl. -S a fellow patron

COPE v COPED, COPING, COPES to contend or strive

COPECK n pl. -S kopeck

COPEMATE n pl. -S an antagonist

COPEN n pl. -S a blue color

COPEPOD n pl. -S a minute crustacean

COPER n pl. -S a horse dealer

COPIED past tense of copy

COPIER n pl. -S one that copies

COPIES present 3d person sing. of copy

COPIHUE *n* -pl. -S a climbing vine

COPILOT *n* pl. -S a pilot who assists the pilot in command

COPING *n* pl. -S the top part of a wall

COPIOUS *adj* abundant

COPLANAR *adj* lying in the same plane

COPLOT *v* -PLOTTED, -PLOTTING, -PLOTS to plot together

COPPED past tense of cop

COPPER *v* -ED, -ING, -S to cover with copper (a metallic element)

COPPERAH *n* pl. -S copra

COPPERAS *n* pl. -ES a compound used in making inks

COPPERY *adj* resembling copper

COPPICE *n* pl. -S a thicket COPPICED *adj*

COPPING present participle of cop

COPPRA *n* pl. -S copra

COPRA *n* pl. -S dried coconut meat

COPRAH *n* pl. -S copra

COPREMIA *n* pl. -S a form of blood poisoning COPREMIC *adj*

COPSE *n* pl. -S a coppice

COPTER *n* pl. -S a helicopter

COPULA *n* pl. -LAS or -LAE something that links COPULAR *adj*

COPULATE *v* -LATED, -LATING, -LATES to engage in coitus

COPY *v* COPIED, COPYING, COPIES to imitate

COPYBOOK *n* pl. -S a book used in teaching penmanship

COPYBOY *n* pl. -BOYS an office boy

COPYCAT *v* -CATTED, -CATTING, -CATS to imitate

COPYDESK *n* pl. -S an editor's desk in a newspaper office

COPYHOLD *n* pl. -S a type of ownership of land

COPYIST *n* pl. -S an imitator

COQUET *v* -QUETTED, -QUETTING, -QUETS to flirt

COQUETRY *n* pl. -TRIES flirtatious behavior

COQUETTE *v* -QUETTED, -QUETTING, -QUETTES to coquet

COQUILLE *n* pl. -S a cooking utensil

COQUINA *n* pl. -S a small marine clam

COQUITO *n* pl. -TOS a palm tree

CORACLE *n* pl. -S a small boat

CORACOID *n* pl. -S a bone of the shoulder girdle

CORAL *n* pl. -S a mass of marine animal skeletons

CORANTO *n* pl. -TOS or -TOES courante

CORBAN *n* pl. -S an offering to God

CORBEIL *n* pl. -S a sculptured fruit basket

CORBEL *v* -BELED, -BELING, -BELS or -BELLED, -BELLING, -BELS to provide a wall with a bracket

CORBIE *n* pl. -S a raven or crow

CORBINA *n* pl. -S a food and game fish

CORBY *n* pl. CORBIES corbie

CORD *v* -ED, -ING, -S to fasten with a cord (a thin rope)

CORDAGE *n* pl. -S the amount of wood in an area

CORDATE *adj* heart-shaped

CORDER *n* pl. -S one that cords

CORDIAL *n* pl. -S a liqueur

CORDITE *n* pl. -S an explosive powder

CORDLESS *adj* having no cord

CORDLIKE *adj* resembling a cord

CORDOBA *n* pl. -S a monetary unit of Nicaragua

CORDON *v* -ED, -ING, -S to form a barrier around

CORDOVAN *n* pl. -S a fine leather

CORDUROY *v* -ED, -ING, -S to build a type of road

CORDWAIN *n* pl. -S cordovan

CORDWOOD *n* pl. -S wood used for fuel

CORE *v* CORED, CORING, CORES to remove the core (the central part) of

COREDEEM *v* -ED, -ING, -S to redeem jointly

COREIGN *n* pl. -S a joint reign

CORELATE *v* -LATED, -LATING, -LATES to place into mutual or reciprocal relation

CORELESS *adj* having no core

COREMIUM *n* pl. -MIA an organ of certain fungi

CORER *n* pl. -S a utensil for coring apples

CORF *n* pl. CORVES a wagon used in a mine

CORGI *n* pl. -S a short-legged dog

CORING present participle of core

CORIUM   *n* pl. -RIA a skin layer

CORK   *v* -ED, -ING, -S to stop up

CORKAGE   *n* pl. -S a charge for wine in a restaurant

CORKER   *n* pl. -S one that corks

CORKIER   comparative of corky

CORKIEST   superlative of corky

CORKLIKE   *adj* resembling cork (a porous tree bark)

CORKWOOD   *n* pl. -S a small tree

CORKY   *adj* CORKIER, CORKIEST corklike

CORM   *n* pl. -S a stem of certain plants **CORMOID, CORMOUS, CORMLIKE** *adj*

CORMEL   *n* pl. -S a small corm

CORN   *v* -ED, -ING, -S to preserve with salt

CORNBALL   *n* pl. -S a hick

CORNCAKE   *n* pl. -S a cake made of cornmeal

CORNCOB   *n* pl. -S the woody core of an ear of corn

CORNCRIB   *n* pl. -S a building in which corn is stored

CORNEA   *n* pl. -S a part of the eye **CORNEAL** *adj*

CORNEL   *n* pl. -S a hardwood tree or shrub

CORNEOUS   *adj* of a hornlike texture

CORNER   *v* -ED, -ING, -S to gain control of

CORNET   *n* pl. -S a trumpetlike instrument

CORNETCY   *n* -CIES a rank in the British cavalry

CORNFED   *adj* fed on corn

CORNHUSK   *n* pl. -S the husk covering an ear of corn

CORNICE   *v* -NICED, -NICING, -NICES to decorate with a molding

CORNICHE   *n* pl. -S a road built along a cliff

CORNICLE   *n* pl. -S a part of an aphid

CORNIER   comparative of corny

CORNIEST   superlative of corny

CORNILY   *adv* in a corny manner

CORNMEAL   *n* pl. -S meal made from corn

CORNU   *n* pl. -NUA a hornlike bone formation **CORNUAL** *adj*

CORNUS   *n* pl. -ES a cornel

CORNUTE   *adj* horn-shaped

CORNUTED   *adj* cornute

CORNUTO   *n* pl. -TOS the husband of an unfaithful wife

CORNY   *adj* CORNIER, CORNIEST trite

CORODY   *n* pl. -DIES an allowance of food or clothes

COROLLA   *n* pl. -S a protective covering of a flower

CORONA   *n* pl. -NAS or -NAE a luminous circle around a celestial body

CORONACH   *n* pl. -S a dirge

CORONAL   *n* pl. -S a wreath worn on the head

CORONARY   *n* pl. -NARIES an artery supplying blood to the heart

CORONEL   *n* pl. -S coronal

CORONER   *n* pl. -S an officer who investigates questionable deaths

CORONET   *n* pl. -S a small crown

COROTATE   *v* -TATED, -TATING, -TATES to rotate together

CORPORA   pl. of corpus

CORPORAL   *n* pl. -S a military rank

CORPS   *n* pl. CORPS a military unit

CORPSE   *n* pl. -S a dead body

CORPSMAN   *n* pl. -MEN an enlisted man trained to give minor medical treatment

CORPUS   *n* pl. -PORA a human or animal body

CORRADE   *v* -RADED, -RADING, -RADES to erode

CORRAL   *v* -RALLED, -RALLING, -RALS to place livestock in an enclosure

CORRECT   *v* -ED, -ING, -S to make free from error

CORRECT   *adj* -RECTER, -RECTEST free from error

CORRIDA   *n* pl. -S a bullfight

CORRIDOR   *n* pl. -S a narrow hallway

CORRIE   *n* pl. -S a cirque

CORRIVAL   *n* pl. -S a rival or opponent

CORRODE   *v* -RODED, -RODING, -RODES to eat away gradually

CORRODY   *n* pl. -DIES corody

CORRUPT   *adj* -RUPTER, -RUPTEST dishonest and venal

CORRUPT   *v* -ED, -ING, -S to subvert the honesty or integrity of

CORSAC   *n* pl. -S an Asian fox

CORSAGE   *n* pl. -S a small bouquet of flowers

CORSAIR   *n* pl. -S a pirate

CORSE   *n* pl. -S a corpse

CORSELET   *n* pl. -S a piece of body armor

CORSET   *v* -ED, -ING, -S to fit with a corset (a supporting undergarment)

CORSLET   *n* pl. -S corselet

CORTEGE   *n* pl. -S a retinue

CORTEX   *n* pl. -TICES or -TEXES the outer layer of an organ **CORTICAL** *adj*

CORTIN   *n* pl. -S a hormone

CORTISOL   *n* pl. -S a hormone

CORUNDUM   *n* pl. -S a hard mineral

CORVEE   *n* pl. -S an obligation to perform feudal service

CORVES   pl. of corf

CORVET   *n* pl. -S a corvette

CORVETTE   *n* pl. -S a swift warship

CORVINA   *n* pl. -S corbina

CORVINE   *adj* pertaining or belonging to the crow family of birds

CORYMB   *n* pl. -S a flower cluster **CORYMBED** *adj*

CORYPHEE   *n* pl. -S a ballet dancer

CORYZA   *n* pl. -S a head cold **CORYZAL** *adj*

COS   *n* pl. -ES a variety of lettuce

COSEC   *n* pl. -S cosecant

COSECANT   *n* pl. -S a trigonometric function of an angle

COSET   *n* pl. -S a mathematical subset

COSEY   *n* pl. -SEYS a cozy

COSH   *v* -ED, -ING, -ES to bludgeon

COSHER   *v* -ED, -ING, -S to coddle

COSIE   *n* pl. -S a cozy

COSIER   comparative of cosy

COSIES   pl. of cosy

COSIEST   superlative of cosy

COSIGN   *v* -ED, -ING, -S to sign jointly

COSIGNER   *n* pl. -S one that cosigns

COSILY   *adv* in a cosy manner

COSINE   *n* pl. -S a trigonometric function of an angle

COSINESS   *n* pl. -ES coziness

COSMETIC   *n* pl. -S a beauty preparation

COSMIC   *adj* pertaining to the cosmos

COSMICAL   *adj* cosmic

COSMISM   *n* pl. -S a philosophical theory

COSMIST   *n* pl. -S a supporter of cosmism

COSMOS   *n* pl. -ES the universe regarded as an orderly system

COSS   *n* pl. COSS kos

COSSACK   *n* pl. -S a Russian cavalryman

COSSET   *v* -ED, -ING, -S to fondle

COST   *v* COST or COSTED, COSTING, COSTS to estimate a price for production of

COSTA   *n* pl. -TAE a rib **COSTAL** *adj*

COSTAR   *v* -STARRED, -STARRING, -STARS to star with another actor

COSTARD   *n* pl. -S a large cooking apple

COSTATE   *adj* having a rib or ribs

COSTER   *n* pl. -S a hawker of fruit or vegetables

COSTIVE   *adj* constipated

COSTLESS   *adj* free of charge

COSTLY   *adj* -LIER, -LIEST expensive

COSTMARY   *n* pl. -MARIES an herb used in salads

COSTREL   *n* pl. -S a flask

COSTUME   *v* -TUMED, -TUMING, -TUMES to supply with a costume (a style of dress)

COSTUMER   *n* pl. -S one that costumes

COSTUMEY   *adj* of or pertaining to a costume

COSTUMING   present participle of costume

COSY   *adj* COSIER, COSIEST cozy

COSY   *n* pl. COSIES a cozy

COT   *n* pl. -S a light, narrow bed

COTAN   *n* pl. -S a trigonometric function of an angle

COTE   *v* COTED, COTING, COTES to pass by

COTEAU   *n* pl. -TEAUX the higher ground of a region

COTENANT   *n* pl. -S one who is a tenant with another in the same place

COTERIE   *n* pl. -S a clique

COTHURN   *n* pl. -S a buskin worn by ancient Roman actors

COTHURNI   *n/pl* cothurns

COTIDAL *adj* indicating coincidence of the tides

COTILLON *n pl.* -S a ballroom dance

COTING present participle of cote

COTQUEAN *n pl.* -S a vulgar woman

COTTA *n pl.* -TAE or -TAS a short surplice

COTTAGE *n pl.* -S a small house **COTTAGEY** *adj*

COTTAGER *n pl.* -S one that lives in a cottage

COTTAR *n pl.* -S cotter

COTTER *n pl.* -S a tenant farmer

COTTIER *n pl.* -S cotter

COTTON *v* -ED, -ING, -S to take a liking

COTTONY *adj* resembling cotton (a soft, fibrous material)

COTYLOID *adj* cup-shaped

COTYPE *n pl.* -S a taxonomic type

COUCH *v* -ED, -ING, -ES to put into words

COUCHANT *adj* lying down

COUCHER *n pl.* -S one that couches

COUCHING *n pl.* -S a form of embroidery

COUDE *adj* pertaining to a type of telescope

COUGAR *n pl.* -S a mountain lion

COUGH *v* -ED, -ING, -S to expel air from the lungs noisily

COUGHER *n pl.* -S one that coughs

COULD past tense of can

COULDEST a past 2d person sing. of can

COULDST a past 2d person sing. of can

COULEE *n pl.* -S a small ravine

COULISSE *n pl.* -S a side scene of a theater stage

COULOIR *n pl.* -S a deep gorge or gully

COULOMB *n pl.* -S an electrical measure

COULTER *n pl.* -S colter

COUMARIN *n pl.* -S a chemical compound **COUMARIC** *adj*

COUMAROU *n pl.* -S the seed of a tropical tree

COUNCIL *n pl.* -S a group of persons appointed for a certain function

COUNSEL *v* -SELED, -SELING, -SELS or -SELLED, -SELLING, -SELS to advise

COUNT *v* -ED, -ING, -S to list or mention the units of one by one to ascertain the total

COUNTER *v* -ED, -ING, -S to oppose

COUNTESS *n pl.* -ES a noblewoman

COUNTIAN *n pl.* -S a resident of a county

COUNTRY *n pl.* -TRIES the territory of a nation

COUNTY *n pl.* -TIES an administrative division of a state

COUP *v* -ED, -ING, -S to overturn

COUPE *n pl.* -S an automobile with two doors

COUPLE *v* -PLED, -PLING, -PLES to unite in pairs

COUPLER *n pl.* -S one that couples

COUPLET *n pl.* -S a pair of successive lines of verse

COUPLING *n pl.* -S a joining device

COUPON *n pl.* -S a certificate entitling the holder to certain benefits

COURAGE *n pl.* -S the quality that enables one to face danger fearlessly; spirit

COURANT *n pl.* -S courante

COURANTE *n pl.* -S an old, lively dance

COURANTO *n pl.* -TOS or -TOES courante

COURIER *n pl.* -S a messenger

COURLAN *n pl.* -S a wading bird

COURSE *v* COURSED, COURSING, COURSES to cause hounds to chase game

COURSER *n pl.* -S one that courses

COURSING *n pl.* -S the pursuit of game by hounds

COURT *v* -ED, -ING, -S to woo

COURTESY *v* -SIED, -SYING, -SIES to curtsy

COURTIER *n pl.* -S one who attends a royal court

COURTLY *adj* -LIER, -LIEST stately

COUSCOUS *n pl.* -ES a North African cereal

COUSIN *n pl.* -S a child of one's aunt or uncle **COUSINLY** *adj*

COUSINRY *n pl.* -RIES cousins collectively

COUTEAU *n pl.* -TEAUX a knife

COUTER *n pl.* -S a piece of armor for the elbow

COUTH *adj* COUTHER, COUTHEST sophisticated

COUTH *n pl.* -S refinement

COUTHIE	*adj* COUTHIER, COUTHIEST friendly	**COWHERB**	*n* pl. -S an annual herb
COUTURE	*n* pl. -S the business of dressmaking	**COWHERD**	*n* pl. -S one who tends cattle
COUVADE	*n* pl. -S a primitive birth ritual	**COWHIDE**	*v* -HIDED, -HIDING, -HIDES to flog with a leather whip
COVALENT	*adj* sharing electron pairs	**COWIER**	comparative of cowy
COVE	*v* COVED, COVING, COVES to curve over or inward	**COWIEST**	superlative of cowy
		COWINNER	*n* pl. -S one of two or more winners
COVEN	*n* pl. -S a group of thirteen witches	**COWL**	*v* -ED, -ING, -S to cover with a hood
COVENANT	*v* -ED, -ING, -S to enter into a binding agreement	**COWLICK**	*n* pl. -S a lock of unruly hair
COVER	*v* -ED, -ING, -S to place something over or upon	**COWLING**	*n* pl. -S a covering for an aircraft engine
COVERAGE	*n* pl. -S the extent to which something is covered	**COWMAN**	*n* pl. -MEN one who owns cattle
COVERALL	*n* pl. -S a one-piece work garment	**COWORKER**	*n* pl. -S a fellow worker
		COWPAT	*n* pl. -S a dropping of cow dung
COVERER	*n* pl. -S one that covers	**COWPEA**	*n* pl. -S a black-eyed pea
COVERING	*n* pl. -S something that covers	**COWPOKE**	*n* pl. -S a cowboy
COVERLET	*n* pl. -S a bed covering	**COWPOX**	*n* pl. -ES a cattle disease
COVERLID	*n* pl. -S a coverlet	**COWRIE**	*n* pl. -S cowry
COVERT	*n* pl. -S a hiding place	**COWRY**	*n* pl. -RIES a glossy seashell
COVERTLY	*adv* secretly	**COWSHED**	*n* pl. -S a shelter for cows
COVET	*v* -ED, -ING, -S to desire greatly	**COWSKIN**	*n* pl. -S the hide of a cow
COVETER	*n* pl. -S one that covets	**COWSLIP**	*n* pl. -S a flowering plant
COVETOUS	*adj* excessively desirous	**COWY**	*adj* COWIER, COWIEST suggestive of a cow
COVEY	*n* pl. -EYS a flock of birds	**COX**	*v* -ED, -ING, -ES to coxswain
COVING	*n* pl. -S a concave molding	**COXA**	*n* pl. COXAE the hip or hip joint COXAL *adj*
COW	*n* pl. -S or KINE a farm animal		
COW	*v* -ED, -ING, -S to intimidate	**COXALGIA**	*n* pl. -S pain in the hip COXALGIC *adj*
COWAGE	*n* pl. -S a tropical vine		
COWARD	*n* pl. -S one who lacks courage	**COXALGY**	*n* pl. -GIES coxalgia
COWARDLY	*adj* lacking courage	**COXCOMB**	*n* pl. -S a conceited dandy
COWBANE	*n* pl. -S a poisonous plant	**COXSWAIN**	*v* -ED, -ING, -S to steer a racing rowboat
COWBELL	*n* pl. -S a bell around a cow's neck		
		COY	*adj* COYER, COYEST shy
COWBERRY	*n* pl. -RIES a pasture shrub	**COY**	*v* -ED, -ING, -S to caress
COWBIND	*n* pl. -S a species of bryony	**COYISH**	*adj* somewhat coy
COWBIRD	*n* pl. -S a blackbird	**COYLY**	*adv* in a coy manner
COWBOY	*n* pl. -BOYS a ranch worker	**COYNESS**	*n* pl. -ES the state of being coy
COWEDLY	*adv* in a cowed manner	**COYOTE**	*n* pl. -S a small wolf
COWER	*v* -ED, -ING, -S to cringe	**COYPOU**	*n* pl. -S coypu
COWFISH	*n* pl. -ES an aquatic mammal	**COYPU**	*n* pl. -S an aquatic rodent
COWGIRL	*n* pl. -S a female ranch worker	**COZ**	*n* pl. COZES or COZZES a cousin
COWHAGE	*n* pl. -S cowage		
COWHAND	*n* pl. -S a cowboy	**COZEN**	*v* -ED, -ING, -S to deceive
		COZENAGE	*n* pl. -S the practice of cozening

COZENER *n pl.* -S one that cozens

COZEY *n pl.* -ZEYS cozy

COZIE *n pl.* -S cozy

COZIER comparative of cozy

COZIES pl. of cozy

COZINESS *n pl.* -ES the state of being cozy

COZY *adj* COZIER, COZIEST snug and comfortable **COZILY** *adv*

COZY *n pl.* -ZIES a covering for a teapot

COZZES a pl. of coz

CRAAL *v* -ED, -ING, -S to kraal

CRAB *v* CRABBED, CRABBING, CRABS to complain

CRABBER *n pl.* -S one that crabs

CRABBY *adj* -BIER, -BIEST grumpy

CRABWISE *adv* sideways

CRACK *v* -ED, -ING, -S to break without dividing into parts

CRACKER *n pl.* -S a thin, crisp biscuit

CRACKING *n pl.* -S a chemical process

CRACKLE *v* -LED, -LING, -LES to make a succession of snapping sounds

CRACKLY *adj* -LIER, -LIEST brittle

CRACKNEL *n pl.* -S a hard, crisp biscuit

CRACKPOT *n pl.* -S an eccentric person

CRACKUP *n pl.* -S a collision

CRACKY *interj* — used to express surprise

CRADLE *v* -DLED, -DLING, -DLES to nurture during infancy

CRADLER *n pl.* -S one that cradles

CRAFT *v* -ED, -ING, -S to make by hand

CRAFTY *adj* CRAFTIER, CRAFTIEST skillful in deceiving **CRAFTILY** *adv*

CRAG *n pl.* -S a rough rock **CRAGGED** *adj*

CRAGGY *adj* -GIER, -GIEST full of crags **CRAGGILY** *adv*

CRAGSMAN *n pl.* -MEN one who climbs crags

CRAKE *n pl.* -S a small, harsh-voiced bird

CRAM *v* CRAMMED, CRAMMING, CRAMS to fill or pack tightly

CRAMBE *n pl.* -S an annual herb

CRAMBO *n pl.* -BOS or -BOES a word game

CRAMMED past tense of cram

CRAMMER *n pl.* -S one that crams

CRAMMING present participle of cram

CRAMOISY *n pl.* -SIES crimson cloth

CRAMP *v* -ED, -ING, -S to restrain or confine

CRAMPIT *n pl.* -S a piece of equipment used in curling

CRAMPON *n pl.* -S a device for raising heavy objects

CRAMPOON *n pl.* -S crampon

CRANCH *v* -ED, -ING, -S to craunch

CRANE *v* CRANED, CRANING, CRANES to stretch out one's neck

CRANIA a pl. of cranium

CRANIAL *adj* pertaining to the skull

CRANIATE *n pl.* -S one that has a skull

CRANING present participle of crane

CRANIUM *n pl.* -NIUMS or -NIA the skull

CRANK *v* -ED, -ING, -S to start manually

CRANK *adj* CRANKER, CRANKEST lively

CRANKIER comparative of cranky

CRANKIEST superlative of cranky

CRANKILY *adv* in a cranky manner

CRANKLE *v* -KLED, -KLING, -KLES to crinkle

CRANKLY *adv* in a crank manner

CRANKOUS *adj* cranky

CRANKPIN *n pl.* -S the handle of a crank

CRANKY *adj* CRANKIER, CRANKIEST grumpy

CRANNIED *adj* having crannies

CRANNIES pl. of cranny

CRANNOG *n pl.* -S an artificial island

CRANNOGE *n pl.* -S crannog

CRANNY *n pl.* -NIES a crevice

CRAP *v* CRAPPED, CRAPPING, CRAPS to defecate — usually considered vulgar

CRAPE *v* CRAPED, CRAPING, CRAPES to crepe

CRAPPER *n pl.* -S a toilet — usually considered vulgar

CRAPPIE *n pl.* -S an edible fish

CRAPPING present participle of crap

CRAPPY *adj* -PIER, -PIEST markedly inferior in quality

CRASES pl. of crasis

CRASH *v* -ED, -ING,- ES to collide noisily

CRASHER *n* pl. -S one that crashes

CRASIS *n* pl. CRASES a vowel contraction

CRASS *adj* CRASSER, CRASSEST grossly vulgar or stupid **CRASSLY** *adv*

CRATCH *n* pl. -ES a manger

CRATE *v* CRATED, CRATING, CRATES to put in a packing box

CRATER *v* -ED, -ING, -S to form cavities in a surface

CRATON *n* pl. -S a part of the earth's crust **CRATONIC** *adj*

CRAUNCH *v* -ED, -ING, -ES to crunch

CRAVAT *n* pl. -S a necktie

CRAVE *v* CRAVED, CRAVING, CRAVES to desire greatly

CRAVEN *v* -ED, -ING, -S to make cowardly

CRAVENLY *adv* in a cowardly manner

CRAVER *n* pl. -S one that craves

CRAVING *n* pl. -S a great desire

CRAW *n* pl. -S the stomach of certain animals

CRAWDAD *n* pl. -S a crayfish

CRAWFISH *v* -ED, -ING, -ES to back out or retreat

CRAWL *v* -ED, -ING, -S to move with the body on or near the ground

CRAWLER *n* pl. -S one that crawls

CRAWLWAY *n* pl. -WAYS a small, low tunnel

CRAWLY *adj* CRAWLIER, CRAWLIEST creepy

CRAYFISH *n* pl. -ES a crustacean

CRAYON *v* -ED, -ING, -S to use a drawing implement

CRAZE *v* CRAZED, CRAZING, CRAZES to make insane

CRAZY *adj* -ZIER, -ZIEST insane **CRAZILY** *adv*

CREAK *v* -ED, -ING, -S to squeak

CREAKY *adj* CREAKIER, CREAKIEST creaking **CREAKILY** *adv*

CREAM *v* -ED, -ING, -S to form cream (a part of milk)

CREAMER *n* pl. -S a cream pitcher

CREAMERY *n* pl. -ERIES a dairy

CREAMY *adj* CREAMIER, CREAMIEST rich in cream **CREAMILY** *adv*

CREASE *v* CREASED, CREASING, CREASES to make a fold or wrinkle in

CREASER *n* pl. -S one that creases

CREASY *adj* CREASIER, CREASIEST having folds or wrinkles

CREATE *v* -ATED, -ATING, -ATES to cause to exist

CREATIN *n* pl. -S creatine

CREATINE *n* pl. -S a chemical compound

CREATION *n* pl. -S something created

CREATIVE *adj* having the ability to create

CREATOR *n* pl. -S one that creates

CREATURE *n* pl. -S a living being

CRECHE *n* pl. -S a day nursery

CREDAL *adj* pertaining to a creed

CREDENCE *n* pl. -S belief

CREDENDA *n/pl* articles of faith

CREDENT *adj* believing

CREDENZA *n* pl. -S a piece of furniture

CREDIBLE *adj* believable **CREDIBLY** *adv*

CREDIT *v* -ED, -ING, -S to accept as true

CREDITOR *n* pl. -S one to whom money is owed

CREDO *n* pl. -DOS a creed

CREED *n* pl. -S a statement of belief **CREEDAL** *adj*

CREEK *n* pl. -S a watercourse smaller than a river

CREEL *n* pl. -S a fish basket

CREEP *v* CREPT, CREEPING, CREEPS to crawl

CREEPAGE *n* pl. -S gradual movement

CREEPER *n* pl. -S one that creeps

CREEPIE *n* pl. -S a low stool

CREEPY *adj* CREEPIER, CREEPIEST repugnant **CREEPILY** *adv*

CREESE *n* pl. -S kris

CREESH *v* -ED, -ING, -ES to grease

CREMAINS *n/pl* the ashes of a cremated body

CREMATE *v* -MATED, -MATING, -MATES to reduce to ashes by burning

CREMATOR *n* pl. -S one that cremates

CREME *n* pl. -S cream

CRENATE *adj* having an edge with rounded projections

CRENATED *adj* crenate

CRENEL *v* -ELED, -ELING, -ELS or -ELLED, -ELLING, -ELS to provide with crenelles

CRENELLE *n* pl. -S a rounded projection

CREODONT *n* pl. -S an extinct carnivore

CREOLE *n* pl. -S a type of mixed language

CREOSOL *n* pl. -S a chemical compound

CREOSOTE *v* -SOTED, -SOTING, -SOTES to treat with a wood preservative

CREPE *v* CREPED, CREPING, CREPES to frizz the hair

CREPEY *adj* CREPIER, CREPIEST crinkly

CREPT past tense of creep

CREPY *adj* CREPIER, CREPIEST crepey

CRESCENT *n* pl. -S the figure of the moon in its first or last quarter

CRESIVE *adj* increasing

CRESOL *n* pl. -S a chemical disinfectant

CRESS *n* pl. -ES a plant used in salads

CRESSET *n* pl. -S a metal cup for burning oil

CREST *v* -ED, -ING, -S to reach a crest (a peak)

CRESTAL *adj* pertaining to a crest

CRESTING *n* pl. -S a decorative coping

CRESYL *n* pl. -S tolyl

CRESYLIC *adj* pertaining to cresol

CRETIC *n* pl. -S a type of metrical foot

CRETIN *n* pl. -S an idiot

CRETONNE *n* pl. -S a heavy fabric

CREVALLE *n* pl. -S a food and game fish

CREVASSE *v* -VASSED, -VASSING, -VASSES to fissure

CREVICE *n* pl. -S a cleft **CREVICED** *adj*

CREW *v* -ED, -ING, -S to serve aboard a ship

CREWEL *n* pl. -S a woolen yarn

CREWLESS *adj* being without any crewmen

CREWMAN *n* pl. -MEN one who serves on a ship

CRIB *v* CRIBBED, CRIBBING, CRIBS to confine closely

CRIBBAGE *n* pl. -S a card game

CRIBBER *n* pl. -S one that cribs

CRIBBING *n* pl. -S a supporting framework

CRIBBLED *adj* covered with dots

CRIBROUS *adj* pierced with small holes

CRIBWORK *n* pl. -S a framework of logs

CRICETID *n* pl. -S a small rodent

CRICK *v* -ED, -ING, -S to cause a spasm of the neck

CRICKET *v* -ED, -ING, -S to play cricket (a ball game)

CRICOID *n* pl. -S a cartilage of the larynx

CRIED past tense of cry

CRIER *n* pl. -S one that cries

CRIES present 3d person sing. of cry

CRIME *n* pl. -S a violation of the law

CRIMINAL *n* pl. -S one who has committed a crime

CRIMMER *n* pl. -S krimmer

CRIMP *v* -ED, -ING, -S to pleat

CRIMPER *n* pl. -S one that crimps

CRIMPLE *v* -PLED, -PLING, -PLES to wrinkle

CRIMPY *adj* CRIMPIER, CRIMPIEST wavy

CRIMSON *v* -ED, -ING, -S to make crimson (a red color)

CRINGE *v* CRINGED, CRINGING, CRINGES to shrink in fear

CRINGER *n* pl. -S one that cringes

CRINGLE *n* pl. -S a small loop of rope

CRINITE *n* pl. -S a fossil crinoid

CRINKLE *v* -KLED, -KLING, -KLES to wrinkle

CRINKLY *adj* -KLIER, -KLIEST crinkled

CRINOID *n* pl. -S a marine animal

CRINUM *n* pl. -S a tropical herb

CRIOLLO *n* pl. -LLOS a person of Spanish ancestry

CRIPPLE *v* -PLED, -PLING, -PLES to disable or impair

CRIPPLER *n* pl. -S one that cripples

CRIS *n* pl. -ES kris

CRISIS *n* pl. CRISES a crucial turning point **CRISIC** *adj*

CRISP *adj* CRISPER, CRISPEST brittle

CRISP *v* -ED, -ING, -S to make crisp

CRISPATE *adj* curled

CRISPEN *v* -ED, -ING, -S to make crisp

CRISPER *n* pl. -S one that crisps

CRISPLY	adv in a crisp manner	**CROPLAND**	n pl. -S farmland
CRISPY	adj CRISPIER, CRISPIEST crisp **CRISPILY** adv	**CROPLESS**	adj being without crops (agricultural produce)
CRISSUM	n pl. CRISSA a region of feathers on a bird **CRISSAL** adj	**CROPPED**	past tense of crop
CRISTA	n pl. -TAE a part of a cell	**CROPPER**	n pl. -S one that crops
CRISTATE	adj having a projection on the head	**CROPPING**	present participle of crop
		CROQUET	v -ED, -ING, -S to drive a ball away in a certain game
CRITERIA	n/pl standards of judgment	**CROQUIS**	n pl. CROQUIS a sketch
CRITIC	n pl. -S one who judges the merits of something **CRITICAL** adj	**CRORE**	n pl. -S a monetary unit of India
		CROSIER	n pl. -S a bishop's staff
CRITIQUE	v -TIQUED, -TIQUING, -TIQUES to judge as a critic	**CROSS**	v -ED, -ING, -ES to intersect
		CROSS	adj CROSSER, CROSSEST ill-tempered **CROSSLY** adv
CRITTER	n pl. -S a creature		
CRITTUR	n pl. -S critter	**CROSSARM**	n pl. -S a horizontal bar
CROAK	v -ED, -ING, -S to utter a low, hoarse sound	**CROSSBAR**	v -BARRED, -BARRING, -BARS to fasten with crossarms
CROAKER	n pl. -S one that croaks	**CROSSBOW**	n pl. -S a kind of weapon
CROAKY	adj CROAKIER, CROAKIEST low and hoarse **CROAKILY** adv	**CROSSCUT**	v -CUT, -CUTTING, -CUTS to cut across
CROCEIN	n pl. -S a red dye	**CROSSE**	n pl. -S a lacrosse stick
CROCEINE	n pl. -S crocein	**CROSSER**	n pl. -S one that crosses
CROCHET	v -ED, -ING, -S to do a type of needlework	**CROSSING**	n pl. -S an intersection
		CROSSLET	n pl. -S a heraldic symbol
CROCI	a pl. of crocus	**CROSSTIE**	n pl. -S a transverse beam
CROCINE	adj pertaining to the crocus	**CROSSWAY**	n pl. -WAYS a road that crosses another road
CROCK	v -ED, -ING, -S to stain or soil		
CROCKERY	n pl. -ERIES pottery	**CROTCH**	n pl. -ES an angle formed by two diverging parts **CROTCHED** adj
CROCKET	n pl. -S an architectural ornament		
CROCOITE	n pl. -S a mineral	**CROTCHET**	n pl. -S a small hook
CROCUS	n pl. -CUSES or -CI a flowering plant	**CROTON**	n pl. -S a tropical plant
		CROUCH	v -ED, -ING, -ES to stoop
CROFT	n pl. -S a small tenant farm	**CROUP**	n pl. -S a disease of the throat
CROFTER	n pl. -S a tenant farmer	**CROUPE**	n pl. -S the rump of certain animals
CROJIK	n pl. -S a triangular sail		
CROMLECH	n pl. -S a dolmen	**CROUPIER**	n pl. -S an attendant in a casino
CRONE	n pl. -S a withered old woman	**CROUPOUS**	adj pertaining to croup
CRONY	n pl. CRONIES a close friend	**CROUPY**	adj CROUPIER, CROUPIEST affected with croup **CROUPILY** adv
CRONYISM	n pl. -S a kind of political favoritism		
		CROUSE	adj lively **CROUSELY** adv
CROOK	v -ED, -ING, -S to bend	**CROUTON**	n pl. -S a small cube of toasted bread
CROOKED	adj -EDER, -EDEST dishonest		
CROON	v -ED, -ING, -S to sing softly	**CROW**	v -ED, -ING, -S to boast
CROONER	n pl. -S one that croons	**CROWBAR**	n pl. -S a steel bar used as a lever
CROP	v CROPPED, CROPPING, CROPS to cut off short		

CROWD v -ED, -ING, -S to press into an insufficient space

CROWDER n pl. -S one that crowds

CROWDIE n pl. -S crowdy

CROWDY n pl. -DIES porridge

CROWER n pl. -S one that crows

CROWFOOT n pl. -FOOTS or -FEET a flowering plant

CROWN v -ED, -ING, -S to supply with a crown (a royal headpiece)

CROWNER n pl. -S a coroner

CROWNET n pl. -S a coronet

CROWSTEP n pl. S a step on top of a wall

CROZE n pl. -S a tool used in barrel-making

CROZER n pl. -S a croze

CROZIER n pl. -S a crosier

CRUCES a pl. of crux

CRUCIAL adj of supreme importance

CRUCIAN n pl. -S a European fish

CRUCIATE adj cross-shaped

CRUCIBLE n pl. -S a heat-resistant vessel

CRUCIFER n pl. -S one who carries a cross

CRUCIFIX n pl. -ES a cross bearing an image of Christ

CRUCIFY v -FIED, -FYING, -FIES to put to death on a cross

CRUD v CRUDDED, CRUDDING, CRUDS to curd

CRUDDY adj trashy

CRUDE adj CRUDER, CRUDEST unrefined **CRUDELY** adv

CRUDE n pl. -S unrefined petroleum

CRUDITY n pl. -TIES the state of being crude

CRUEL adj CRUELER, CRUELEST or CRUELLER, CRUELLEST indifferent to the pain of others **CRUELLY** adv

CRUELTY n pl. -TIES a cruel act

CRUET n pl. -S a glass bottle

CRUISE v CRUISED, CRUISING, CRUISES to sail about touching at several ports

CRUISER n pl. -S a boat that cruises

CRULLER n pl. -S a small sweet cake

CRUMB v -ED, -ING, -S to break into crumbs (small pieces)

CRUMBER n pl. -S one that crumbs

CRUMBIER comparative of crumby

CRUMBIEST superlative of crumby

CRUMBLE v -BLED, -BLING, -BLES to break into small pieces

CRUMBLY adj -BLIER, -BLIEST easily crumbled

CRUMBY adj CRUMBIER, CRUMBIEST full of crumbs

CRUMMIE n pl. -S a cow with crooked horns

CRUMMY adj -MIER, -MIEST of little or no value

CRUMP v -ED, -ING, -S to crunch

CRUMPET n pl. -S a small cake cooked on a griddle

CRUMPLE v -PLED, -PLING, -PLES to wrinkle

CRUMPLY adj full of wrinkles

CRUNCH v -ED, -ING, -ES to chew with a crackling sound

CRUNCHER n pl. -S one that crunches

CRUNCHY adj CRUNCHIER, CRUNCHIEST crisp

CRUNODE n pl. -S a point at which a curve crosses itself **CRUNODAL** adj

CRUOR n pl. -S clotted blood

CRUPPER n pl. -S the rump of a horse

CRURAL adj pertaining to the thigh or leg

CRUS n pl. CRURA a part of the leg

CRUSADE v -SADED, -SADING, -SADES to engage in a holy war

CRUSADER n pl. -S one that crusades

CRUSADO n pl. -DOES or -DOS a Portuguese coin

CRUSE n pl. -S a small bottle

CRUSET n pl. -S a melting pot

CRUSH v -ED, -ING, -ES to press or squeeze out of shape

CRUSHER n pl. -S one that crushes

CRUSILY adj covered with crosslets

CRUST v -ED, -ING, -S to form a crust (an outer surface)

CRUSTAL adj pertaining to the crust of the earth

CRUSTOSE adj forming a thin, brittle crust

CRUSTY adj CRUSTIER, CRUSTIEST surly **CRUSTILY** adv

CRUTCH v -ED, -ING, -ES to prop up or support

CRUX	*n* pl. CRUXES or CRUCES a basic or decisive point	**CUBIFORM**	*adj* shaped like a cube
CRUZADO	*n* pl. -DOES or -DOS crusado	**CUBING**	present participle of cube
CRUZEIRO	*n* pl. -ROS a monetary unit of Brazil	**CUBISM**	*n* pl. -S a style of art **CUBISTIC** *adj*
CRWTH	*n* pl. -S an ancient stringed musical instrument	**CUBIST**	*n* pl. -S an adherent of cubism
CRY	*v* CRIED, CRYING, CRIES to weep **CRYINGLY** *adv*	**CUBIT**	*n* pl. -S an ancient measure of length **CUBITAL** *adj*
CRYBABY	*n* pl. -BIES a person who cries easily	**CUBOID**	*n* pl. -S a bone of the foot **CUBOIDAL** *adj*
CRYOGEN	*n* pl. -S a substance for producing low temperatures	**CUCKOLD**	*v* -ED, -ING, -S to make a cuckold (a cornuto) of
CRYOGENY	*n* pl. -NIES a branch of physics	**CUCKOO**	*v* -ED, -ING, -S to repeat monotonously
CRYOLITE	*n* pl. -S a mineral	**CUCUMBER**	*n* pl. -S a garden vegetable
CRYONICS	*n/pl* the practice of freezing dead bodies for future revival **CRYONIC** *adj*	**CUCURBIT**	*n* pl. -S a gourd
		CUD	*n* pl. -S a portion of food to be chewed again
CRYOSTAT	*n* pl. -S a refrigerating device	**CUDBEAR**	*n* pl. -S a red dye
CRYOTRON	*n* pl. -S an electronic device	**CUDDIE**	*n* pl. -S cuddy
CRYPT	*n* pl. -S a burial vault **CRYPTAL** *adj*	**CUDDIES**	pl. of cuddy
CRYPTIC	*adj* mysterious	**CUDDLE**	*v* -DLED, -DLING, -DLES to hug tenderly
CRYPTO	*n* pl. -TOS one who belongs secretly to a group	**CUDDLY**	*adj* -DLIER, -DLIEST fit for cuddling
CRYSTAL	*n* pl. -S a transparent mineral	**CUDDY**	*n* pl. -DIES a donkey
CTENIDIA	*n/pl* comblike anatomical structures	**CUDGEL**	*v* -ELED, -ELING, -ELS or -ELLED, -ELLING, -ELS to beat with a heavy club
CTENOID	*adj* comblike		
CUB	*n* pl. -S the young of certain animals	**CUDGELER**	*n* pl. -S one that cudgels
CUBAGE	*n* pl. -S cubature	**CUDWEED**	*n* pl. -S a perennial herb
CUBATURE	*n* pl. -S cubical content	**CUE**	*v* CUED, CUING or CUEING, CUES to give a signal to an actor
CUBBISH	*adj* resembling a cub		
CUBBY	*n* pl. -BIES a small, enclosed space	**CUESTA**	*n* pl. -S a type of land elevation
CUBE	*v* CUBED, CUBING, CUBES to form into a cube (a regular solid)	**CUFF**	*v* -ED, -ING, -S to furnish with a cuff (a part of a sleeve)
		CUFFLESS	*adj* having no cuff
CUBEB	*n* pl. -S a woody vine	**CUIF**	*n* pl. -S coof
CUBER	*n* pl. -S a device that cubes meat	**CUING**	a present participle of cue
CUBIC	*n* pl. -S a mathematical equation or expression	**CUIRASS**	*v* -ED, -ING, -ES to cover with a type of armor
CUBICAL	*adj* shaped like a cube	**CUISH**	*n* pl. -ES cuisse
CUBICITY	*n* pl. -TIES the state of being cubical	**CUISINE**	*n* pl. -S a style of cooking
CUBICLE	*n* pl. -S a small chamber	**CUISSE**	*n* pl. -S a piece of armor for the thigh
CUBICLY	*adv* in the form of a cube	**CUITTLE**	*v* -TLED, -TLING, -TLES to coax
CUBICULA	*n/pl* burial chambers	**CUKE**	*n* pl. -S a cucumber
		CULCH	*n* pl. -ES an oyster bed

CULET   *n pl.* -S a piece of armor for the lower back

CULEX   *n pl.* CULICES a mosquito

CULICID   *n pl.* -S a culicine

CULICINE   *n pl.* -S a mosquito

CULINARY   *adj* pertaining to cookery

CULL   *v* -ED, -ING, -S to select from others

CULLAY   *n pl.* -LAYS quillai

CULLER   *n pl.* -S one that culls

CULLET   *n pl.* -S broken glass gathered for remelting

CULLIED   past tense of cully

CULLIES   present 3d person sing. of cully

CULLION   *n pl.* -S a vile fellow

CULLIS   *n pl.* -LISES a gutter in a roof

CULLY   *v* -LIED, -LYING, -LIES to trick

CULM   *v* -ED, -ING, -S to form a hollow stem

CULOTTE   *n pl.* -S a divided skirt

CULPA   *n pl.* -PAE negligence for which one is liable

CULPABLE   *adj* deserving blame or censure CULPABLY *adv*

CULPRIT   *n pl.* -S one that is guilty

CULT   *n pl.* -S a religious society CULTIC *adj*

CULTCH   *n pl.* -ES culch

CULTI   a pl. of cultus

CULTIGEN   *n pl.* -S a cultivar

CULTISM   *n pl.* -S devotion to a cult

CULTIST   *n pl.* -S a member of a cult

CULTIVAR   *n pl.* -S a variety of plant originating under cultivation

CULTRATE   *adj* sharp-edged and pointed

CULTURAL   *adj* produced by breeding

CULTURE   *v* -TURED, -TURING, -TURES to make fit for raising crops

CULTUS   *n pl.* -TUSES or -TI a cult

CULVER   *n pl.* -S a pigeon

CULVERIN   *n pl.* -S a medieval musket

CULVERT   *n pl.* -S a conduit

CUM   *prep* together with

CUMARIN   *n pl.* -S coumarin

CUMBER   *v* -ED, -ING, -S to hinder

CUMBERER   *n pl.* -S one that cumbers

CUMBROUS   *adj* unwieldy

CUMIN   *n pl.* -S a plant used in cooking

CUMMER   *n pl.* -S a godmother

CUMMIN   *n pl.* -S cumin

CUMQUAT   *n pl.* -S kumquat

CUMSHAW   *n pl.* -S a gift

CUMULATE   *v* -LATED, -LATING, -LATES to heap

CUMULUS   *n pl.* -LI a type of cloud CUMULOUS *adj*

CUNDUM   *n pl.* -S condom

CUNEAL   *adj* cuneate

CUNEATE   *adj* wedge-shaped; triangular

CUNEATED   *adj* cuneate

CUNEATIC   *adj* cuneate

CUNIFORM   *n pl.* -S wedge-shaped writing characters

CUNNER   *n pl.* -S a marine fish

CUNNING   *adj* -NINGER, -NINGEST crafty

CUNNING   *n pl.* -S skill in deception

CUNT   *n pl.* -S the female pudendum — usually considered obscene

CUP   *v* CUPPED, CUPPING, CUPS to place in a cup (a small, open container)

CUPBOARD   *n pl.* -S a cabinet

CUPCAKE   *n pl.* -S a small cake

CUPEL   *v* -PELED, -PELING, -PELS or -PELLED, -PELLING, -PELS to refine gold or silver in a cuplike vessel

CUPELER   *n pl.* -S cupeller

CUPELLER   *n pl.* -S one that cupels

CUPFUL   *n pl.* CUPFULS or CUPSFUL as much as a cup can hold

CUPID   *n pl.* -S a naked, winged representation of the Roman god of love

CUPIDITY   *n pl.* -TIES greed; lust

CUPLIKE   *adj* resembling a cup

CUPOLA   *v* -ED, -ING, -S to shape like a dome

CUPPA   *n pl.* -S a cup of tea

CUPPED   past tense of cup

CUPPER   *n pl.* -S one that performs cupping

CUPPING   *n pl.* -S an archaic medical process

CUPPY adj -PIER, PIEST cuplike

CUPREOUS adj containing copper

CUPRIC adj containing copper

CUPRITE n pl. -S an ore of copper

CUPROUS adj containing copper

CUPRUM n pl. -S copper

CUPSFUL a pl. of cupful

CUPULA n pl. -LAE a cup-shaped anatomical structure

CUPULAR adj cupulate

CUPULATE adj cup-shaped

CUPULE n pl. -S a cup-shaped anatomical structure

CUR n pl. -S a mongrel dog

CURABLE adj capable of being cured **CURABLY** adv

CURACAO n pl. -S a type of liqueur

CURACOA n pl. -S curacao

CURACY n pl. -CIES the office of a curate

CURAGH n pl. -S currach

CURARA n pl. -S curare

CURARE n pl. -S an arrow poison

CURARI n pl. -S curare

CURARINE n pl. -S a poisonous alkaloid

CURARIZE v -RIZED, -RIZING, -RIZES to poison with curare

CURASSOW n pl. -S a turkey-like bird

CURATE n pl. -S a clergyman in charge of a parish

CURATIVE n pl. -S something that cures

CURATOR n pl. -S a museum manager

CURB v -ED, -ING, -S to restrain **CURBABLE** adj

CURBER n pl. -S one that curbs

CURBING n pl. -S a concrete border along a street

CURCH n pl. -ES a kerchief

CURCULIO n pl. -LIOS a weevil

CURCUMA n pl. -S a tropical plant

CURD v -ED, -ING, -S to curdle

CURDIER comparative of curdy

CURDIEST superlative of curdy

CURDLE v -DLED, -DLING, -DLES to congeal

CURDLER n pl. -S one that curdles

CURDY adj CURDIER, CURDIEST curdled

CURE v CURED, CURING, CURES to restore to health

CURELESS adj not curable

CURER n pl. -S one that cures

CURET n pl. -S a surgical instrument

CURETTE v -RETTED, -RETTING, -RETTES to treat with a curet

CURING present participle of cure

CURF n pl. -S an incision made by a cutting tool

CURFEW n pl. -S a regulation concerning the hours which one may keep

CURIA n pl. -RIAE a court of justice **CURIAL** adj

CURIE n pl. -S a unit of radioactivity

CURIO n pl. -RIOS an unusual art object

CURIOSA n/pl pornographic books

CURIOUS adj -OUSER, -OUSEST eager for information

CURITE n pl. -S a radioactive mineral

CURIUM n pl. -S a radioactive element

CURL v -ED, -ING, -S to form into ringlets

CURLER n pl. -S one that curls

CURLEW n pl. -S a shore bird

CURLICUE v -CUED, -CUING, -CUES to decorate with curlicues (fancy spiral figures)

CURLING n pl. -S a game played on ice

CURLY adj CURLIER, CURLIEST tending to curl **CURLILY** adv

CURLYCUE n pl. -S curlicue

CURN n pl. -S grain

CURR v -ED, -ING, -S to purr

CURRACH n pl. -S a coracle

CURRAGH n pl. -S currach

CURRAN n pl. -S curn

CURRANT n pl. -S an edible berry

CURRENCY n pl. -CIES money

CURRENT n pl. -S a continuous flow

CURRICLE n pl. -S a light carriage

CURRIE v -RIED, -RYING, -RIES to prepare food a certain way

CURRIED past tense of curry

CURRIER n pl. -S one that curries leather

CURRIERY	*n* pl. -ERIES the shop of a currier
CURRISH	*adj* resembling a cur
CURRY	*v* -RIED, -RYING, -RIES to prepare leather for use or sale
CURRYING	present participle of currie
CURSE	*v* CURSED or CURST, CURSING, CURSES to wish evil upon
CURSED	*adj* CURSEDER, CURSEDEST wicked **CURSEDLY** *adv*
CURSER	*n* pl. -S one that curses
CURSING	present participle of curse
CURSIVE	*n* pl. -S a style of print
CURSORY	*adj* hasty and superficial
CURST	a past tense of curse
CURT	*adj* CURTER, CURTEST abrupt
CURTAIL	*v* -ED, -ING, -S to cut short
CURTAIN	*v* -ED, -ING, -S to provide with a hanging piece of fabric
CURTAL	*n* pl. -S an animal with a clipped tail
CURTALAX	*n* pl. -ES a cutlass
CURTATE	*adj* shortened
CURTESY	*n* pl. -SIES a type of legal tenure
CURTLY	*adv* in a curt manner
CURTNESS	*n* pl. -ES the quality of being curt
CURTSEY	*v* -ED, -ING, -S to curtsy
CURTSY	*v* -SIED, -SYING, -SIES to bow politely
CURULE	*adj* of the highest rank
CURVE	*v* CURVED, CURVING, CURVES to deviate from straightness
CURVET	*v* -VETED, -VETING, -VETS or -VETTED, -VETTING, -VETS to prance
CURVEY	*adj* CURVIER, CURVIEST curvy
CURVING	present participle of curve
CURVY	*adj* CURVIER, CURVIEST curved
CUSCUS	*n* pl. -ES an arboreal mammal
CUSEC	*n* pl. -S a volumetric unit of flow of liquids
CUSHAT	*n* pl. -S a pigeon
CUSHAW	*n* pl. -S a variety of squash
CUSHIER	comparative of cushy
CUSHIEST	superlative of cushy
CUSHILY	*adj* in a cushy manner

CUSHION	*v* -ED, -ING, -S to pad with soft material
CUSHIONY	*adj* soft
CUSHY	*adj* CUSHIER, CUSHIEST easy
CUSK	*n* pl. -S a marine food fish
CUSP	*n* pl. -S a pointed end **CUSPATE, CUSPATED, CUSPED** *adj*
CUSPID	*n* pl. -S a pointed tooth
CUSPIDAL	*adj* having a cusp
CUSPIDOR	*n* pl. -S a spittoon
CUSPIS	*n* pl. -PIDES a cusp
CUSS	*v* -ED, -ING, -ES to curse
CUSSEDLY	*adv* in a cranky manner
CUSSER	*n* pl. -S one that cusses
CUSSO	*n* pl. -SOS an Ethiopian tree
CUSSWORD	*n* pl. -S a profane or obscene word
CUSTARD	*n* pl. -S a dessert
CUSTODES	pl. of custos
CUSTODY	*n* pl. -DIES guardianship
CUSTOM	*n* pl. -S a habitual practice
CUSTOMER	*n* pl. -S one who buys something
CUSTOS	*n* pl. -TODES a guardian or keeper
CUSTUMAL	*n* pl. -S a written record of laws and customs
CUT	*v* CUT, CUTTING, CUTS to divide into parts with a sharp-edged instrument
CUTAWAY	*n* pl. -AWAYS a type of coat
CUTBACK	*n* pl. -S a reduction
CUTCH	*n* pl. -ES catechu
CUTCHERY	*n* pl. -CHERIES a judicial office in India
CUTDOWN	*n* pl. -S a reduction
CUTE	*adj* CUTER, CUTEST pleasingly attractive **CUTELY** *adv*
CUTENESS	*n* pl. -ES the quality of being cute
CUTES	a pl. of cutis
CUTEST	superlative of cute
CUTESY	*adj* -SIER, -SIEST self-consciously cute
CUTEY	*n* pl. -TEYS cutie
CUTGRASS	*n* pl. -ES a swamp grass
CUTICLE	*n* pl. -S the epidermis

CUTICULA *n* pl. -LAE the outer hard covering of an insect

CUTIE *n* pl. -S a cute person

CUTIN *n* pl. -S a waxy substance found on plants

CUTINISE *v* -ISED, -ISING, -ISES to cutinize

CUTINIZE *v* -IZED, -IZING, -IZES to become coated with cutin

CUTIS *n* pl. -TES or -TISES the corium

CUTLAS *n* pl. -ES cutlass

CUTLASS *n* pl. -ES a short sword

CUTLER *n* pl. -S one who sells and repairs cutting tools

CUTLERY *n* pl. -LERIES the occupation of a cutler

CUTLET *n* pl. -S a slice of meat

CUTLINE *n* pl. -S a caption

CUTOFF *n* pl. -S the point at which something terminates

CUTOUT *n* pl. -S something cut out

CUTOVER *adj* cleared of trees

CUTPURSE *n* pl. -S a pickpocket

CUTTABLE *adj* capable of being cut

CUTTAGE *n* pl. -S a means of plant propagation

CUTTER *n* pl. -S one that cuts

CUTTING *n* pl. -S a section cut from a plant

CUTTLE *v* -TLED, -TLING, -TLES to fold cloth in a particular fashion

CUTTY *n* pl. -TIES a thickset girl

CUTUP *n* pl. -S a mischievous person

CUTWATER *n* pl. -S the front part of a ship's prow

CUTWORK *n* pl. -S a type of embroidery

CUTWORM *n* pl. -S a caterpillar

CUVETTE *n* pl. -S a small tube or vessel

CWM *n* pl. -S a cirque

CYAN *n* pl. -S a blue color

CYANAMID *n* pl. -S a chemical compound

CYANATE *n* pl. -S a chemical salt

CYANIC *adj* blue or bluish

CYANID *n* pl. -S a compound of cyanogen

CYANIDE *v* -NIDED, -NIDING, -NIDES to treat an ore with cyanid

CYANIN *n* pl. -S cyanine

CYANINE *n* pl. -S a blue dye

CYANITE *n* pl. -S a mineral **CYANITIC** *adj*

CYANO *adj* pertaining to cyanogen

CYANOGEN *n* pl. -S a reactive compound of carbon and nitrogen

CYANOSIS *n* pl. -NOSES bluish discoloration of the skin **CYANOSED, CYANOTIC** *adj*

CYBORG *n* pl. -S a human linked to a mechanical device for life support

CYCAD *n* pl. -S a tropical plant

CYCAS *n* pl. -ES a tropical plant

CYCASIN *n* pl. -S a sugar derivative

CYCLAMEN *n* pl. -S a flowering plant

CYCLASE *n* pl. -S an enzyme

CYCLE *v* -CLED, -CLING, -CLES to ride a bicycle

CYCLECAR *n* pl. -S a type of motor vehicle

CYCLER *n* pl. -S a cyclist

CYCLIC *adj* moving in complete circles **CYCLICLY** *adv*

CYCLICAL *adj* cyclic

CYCLING *n* pl. -S the act of riding a bicycle

CYCLIST *n* pl. -S one who rides a bicycle

CYCLITOL *n* pl. -S a chemical compound

CYCLIZE *v* -CLIZED, -CLIZING, -CLIZES to form one or more rings in a chemical compound

CYCLO *n* pl. -CLOS a three-wheeled motor vehicle

CYCLOID *n* pl. -S a geometric curve

CYCLONE *n* pl. -S a rotating system of winds **CYCLONAL, CYCLONIC** *adj*

CYCLOPS *n* pl. CYCLOPS a freshwater animal

CYCLOSIS *n* pl. -CLOSES the circulation of protoplasm within a cell

CYDER *n* pl. -S cider

CYESIS *n* pl. CYESES pregnancy

CYGNET *n* pl. -S a young swan

CYLINDER *v* -ED, -ING, -S to furnish with a cylinder (a chamber in an engine)

CYLIX *n* pl. CYLICES kylix

CYMA *n* pl. -MAS or -MAE a curved molding

CYMAR *n* pl. -S simar

CYMATIUM	*n* pl. -TIA a cyma
CYMBAL	*n* pl. -S a percussion instrument
CYMBALER	*n* pl. -S one that plays the cymbals
CYMBLING	*n* pl. -S cymling
CYME	*n* pl. -S a flower cluster
CYMENE	*n* pl. -S a hydrocarbon
CYMLIN	*n* pl. -S cymling
CYMLING	*n* pl. -S a variety of squash
CYMOGENE	*n* pl. -S a volatile compound
CYMOID	*adj* resembling a cyma
CYMOL	*n* pl. -S cymene
CYMOSE	*adj* resembling a cyme **CYMOSELY** *adv*
CYMOUS	*adj* cymose
CYNIC	*n* pl. -S a cynical person
CYNICAL	*adj* distrusting the motives of others
CYNICISM	*n* pl. -S cynical quality
CYNOSURE	*n* pl. -S a center of attraction
CYPHER	*v* -ED, -ING, -S to cipher
CYPRES	*n* pl. -ES a legal doctrine
CYPRESS	*n* pl. -ES a thin fabric
CYPRIAN	*n* pl. -S a prostitute
CYPRINID	*n* pl. -S a small freshwater fish
CYPRUS	*n* pl. -ES cypress
CYPSELA	*n* pl. -LAE an achene in certain plants

CYST	*n* pl. -S a sac
CYSTEIN	*n* pl. -S cysteine
CYSTEINE	*n* pl. -S an amino acid
CYSTIC	*adj* pertaining to a cyst
CYSTINE	*n* pl. -S an amino acid
CYSTITIS	*n* pl. -TITIDES inflammation of the urinary bladder
CYSTOID	*n* pl. -S a cyst-like structure
CYTASTER	*n* pl. -S a structure formed in a cell during mitosis
CYTIDINE	*n* pl. -S a compound containing cytosine
CYTOGENY	*n* pl. -NIES the formation of cells
CYTOLOGY	*n* pl. -GIES a study of cells
CYTON	*n* pl. -S the body of a nerve cell
CYTOSINE	*n* pl. -S a component of DNA and RNA
CZAR	*n* pl. -S an emperor or king
CZARDAS	*n* pl. CZARDAS a Hungarian dance
CZARDOM	*n* pl. -S the domain of a czar
CZAREVNA	*n* pl. -S the daughter of a czar
CZARINA	*n* pl. -S the wife of a czar
CZARISM	*n* pl. -S autocratic government
CZARIST	*n* pl. -S a supporter of czarism
CZARITZA	*n* pl. -S a czarina

DA	*prep* of; from — used in names
DAB	*v* DABBED, DABBING, DABS to touch lightly
DABBER	*n pl.* -S one that dabs
DABBLE	*v* -BLED, -BLING, -BLES to splash
DABBLER	*n pl.* -S one that dabbles
DABBLING	*n pl.* -S a superficial interest
DABCHICK	*n pl.* -S a small grebe
DABSTER	*n pl.* -S a bungler
DACE	*n pl.* -S a freshwater fish
DACHA	*n pl.* -S a Russian cottage
DACKER	*v* -ED, -ING, -S to waver
DACOIT	*n pl.* -S a bandit in India
DACOITY	*n pl.* -COITIES robbery by dacoits
DACTYL	*n pl.* -S a type of metrical foot
DACTYLIC	*n pl.* -S a verse consisting of dactyls
DACTYLUS	*n pl.* -LI a leg joint of certain insects
DAD	*n pl.* -S father
DADA	*n pl.* -S an artistic and literary movement
DADAISM	*n pl.* -S the dada movement
DADAIST	*n pl.* -S a follower of dadaism
DADDLE	*v* -DLED, -DLING, -DLES to diddle
DADDY	*n pl.* -DIES father
DADO	*v* -ED, -ING, -ES or -S to set into a groove
DAEDAL	*adj* skillful
DAEMON	*n pl.* -S demon **DAEMONIC** *adj*
DAFF	*v* -ED, -ING, -S to thrust aside
DAFFODIL	*n pl.* -S a flowering plant
DAFFY	*adj* -FIER, -FIEST silly
DAFT	*adj* DAFTER, DAFTEST insane **DAFTLY** *adv*
DAFTNESS	*n pl.* -ES the quality of being daft
DAG	*n pl.* -S a hanging end or shred
DAGGER	*v* -ED, -ING, -S to stab with a small knife
DAGGLE	*v* -GLED, -GLING, -GLES to drag in mud
DAGLOCK	*n pl.* -S a dirty or tangled lock of wool
DAGO	*n pl.* -GOS or -GOES an Italian or Spaniard — a derogatory term
DAGOBA	*n pl.* -S a Buddhist shrine
DAH	*n pl.* -S a dash in Morse code
DAHABEAH	*n pl.* -S a large passenger boat
DAHABIAH	*n pl.* -S dahabeah
DAHABIEH	*n pl.* -S dahabeah
DAHABIYA	*n pl.* -S dahabeah
DAHLIA	*n pl.* -S a flowering plant
DAHOON	*n pl.* -S an evergreen tree
DAIKER	*v* -ED, -ING, -S to dacker
DAILY	*n pl.* -LIES a newspaper published every weekday
DAIMEN	*adj* occasional
DAIMIO	*n pl.* -MIOS a former Japanese nobleman
DAIMON	*n pl.* -S or -ES an attendant spirit **DAIMONIC** *adj*
DAIMYO	*n pl.* -MYOS daimio

DAINTY   *n pl.* -TIES something delicious

DAINTY   *adj* -TIER, -TIEST delicately pretty **DAINTILY** *adv*

DAIQUIRI   *n pl.* -S a cocktail

DAIRY   *n pl.* DAIRIES an establishment dealing in milk products

DAIRYING   *n pl.* -S the business of a dairy

DAIRYMAN   *n pl.* -MEN a man who works in or owns a dairy

DAIS   *n pl.* -ISES a raised platform

DAISHIKI   *n pl.* -S dashiki

DAISY   *n pl.* -SIES a flowering plant **DAISIED** *adj*

DAK   *n pl.* -S transportation by relays of men and horses

DAKERHEN   *n pl.* -S a European bird

DAKOIT   *n pl.* -S dacoit

DAKOITY   *n pl.* -TIES dacoity

DALAPON   *n pl.* -S an herbicide used on unwanted grasses

DALASI   *n pl.* DALASI a unit of Gambian currency

DALE   *n pl.* -S a valley

DALESMAN   *n pl.* -MEN one living in a dale

DALETH   *n pl.* -S a Hebrew letter

DALLES   *n/pl* rapids

DALLIER   *n pl.* -S one that dallies

DALLY   *v* -LIED, -LYING, -LIES to waste time

DALMATIC   *n pl.* -S a wide-sleeved vestment

DALTONIC   *adj* pertaining to a form of color blindness

DAM   *v* DAMMED, DAMMING, DAMS to build a barrier to obstruct the flow of water

DAMAGE   *v* -AGED, -AGING, -AGES to injure

DAMAGER   *n pl.* -S one that damages

DAMAN   *n pl.* -S a small mammal

DAMAR   *n pl.* -S dammar

DAMASK   *v* -ED, -ING, -S to weave with elaborate design

DAME   *n pl.* -S a matron

DAMEWORT   *n pl.* -S a flowering plant

DAMMED   past tense of dam

DAMMAR   *n pl.* -S a hard resin

DAMMER   *n pl.* -S dammar

DAMMING   present participle of dam

DAMN   *v* -ED, -ING, -S to curse

DAMNABLE   *adj* detestable **DAMNABLY** *adv*

DAMNDEST   *n pl.* -S utmost

DAMNED   *adj* DAMNEDER, DAMNEDEST or DAMNDEST damnable

DAMNER   *n pl.* -S one that damns

DAMNIFY   *v* -FIED, -FYING, -FIES to cause loss or damage to

DAMOSEL   *n pl.* -S damsel

DAMOZEL   *n pl.* -S damsel

DAMP   *adj* DAMPER, DAMPEST moist

DAMP   *v* -ED, -ING, -S to moisten

DAMPEN   *v* -ED, -ING, -S to moisten

DAMPENER   *n pl.* -S one that dampens

DAMPER   *n pl.* -S one that damps

DAMPISH   *adj* somewhat damp

DAMPLY   *adv* in a damp manner

DAMPNESS   *n pl.* -ES the state of being damp

DAMSEL   *n pl.* -S a maiden

DAMSON   *n pl.* -S a small purple plum

DANCE   *v* DANCED, DANCING, DANCES to move rhythmically to music

DANCER   *n pl.* -S one that dances

DANDER   *v* -ED, -ING, -S to stroll

DANDIER   comparative of dandy

DANDIES   pl. of dandy

DANDIEST   superlative of dandy

DANDIFY   *v* -FIED, -FYING, -FIES to cause to resemble a dandy

DANDILY   *adv* in a dandy manner

DANDLE   *v* -DLED, -DLING, -DLES to fondle

DANDLER   *n pl.* -S one that dandles

DANDRIFF   *n pl.* -S dandruff

DANDRUFF   *n pl.* -S a scurf that forms on the scalp

DANDY   *adj* -DIER, -DIEST fine

DANDY   *n pl.* -DIES a man who is overly concerned about his appearance

DANDYISH   *adj* suggestive of a dandy

DANDYISM   *n pl.* -S the style or conduct of a dandy

DANEGELD   *n pl.* -S an annual tax in medieval England

DANEWEED   *n pl.* -S a danewort

DANEWORT   *n pl.* -S a flowering plant

DANG   v -ED, -ING, -S to damn

DANGER   v -ED, -ING, -S to endanger

DANGLE   v -GLED, -GLING, -GLES to hang loosely

DANGLER   n pl. -S one that dangles

DANIO   n pl. -NIOS an aquarium fish

DANK   adj DANKER, DANKEST unpleasantly damp **DANKLY** adv

DANKNESS   n pl. -ES the state of being dank

DANSEUR   n pl. -S a male ballet dancer

DANSEUSE   n pl. -S a female ballet dancer

DAP   v DAPPED, DAPPING, DAPS to dip lightly or quickly into water

DAPHNE   n pl. -S a flowering shrub

DAPHNIA   n pl. -S a minute freshwater crustacean

DAPPED   past tense of dap

DAPPER   adj -PERER, -PEREST neat and trim in appearance

DAPPING   present participle of dap

DAPPLE   v -PLED, -PLING, -PLES to mark with spots

DAPPERLY   adv in a dapper manner

DARB   n pl. -S something considered extraordinary

DARBIES   n/pl handcuffs

DARE   v DARED or DURST, DARING, DARES to have the necessary courage

DAREFUL   adj brave

DARER   n pl. -S one that dares

DARESAY   v to venture to say — DARESAY is the only form of this verb; it is not conjugated

DARIC   n pl. -S an ancient Persian coin

DARING   n pl. -S bravery

DARINGLY   adv in a brave manner

DARIOLE   n pl. -S a type of pastry

DARK   adj DARKER, DARKEST having little or no light

DARK   v -ED, -ING, -S to darken

DARKEN   v -ED, -ING, -S to make dark

DARKENER   n pl. -S one that darkens

DARKEY   n pl. -EYS darky

DARKIE   n pl. -S darky

DARKIES   pl. of darky

DARKISH   adj somewhat dark

DARKLE   v -KLED, -KLING, -KLES to become dark

DARKLY   adv -LIER, -LIEST in a dark manner

DARKNESS   n pl. -ES the state of being dark

DARKROOM   n pl. -S a room in which film is processed

DARKSOME   adj dark

DARKY   n pl. DARKIES a black person — a derogatory term

DARLING   n pl. -S a much-loved person

DARN   v -ED, -ING, -S to mend with interlacing stitches

DARNDEST   n pl. -S damndest

DARNED   adj DARNEDER, DARNEDEST or DARNDEST damned

DARNEL   n pl. -S an annual grass

DARNER   n pl. -S one that darns

DARNING   n pl. -S things darned or to be darned

DART   v -ED, -ING, -S to move suddenly or swiftly

DARTER   n pl. -S one that darts

DARTLE   v -TLED, -TLING, -TLES to dart repeatedly

DASH   v -ED, -ING, -ES to strike violently

DASHEEN   n pl. -S a tropical plant

DASHER   n pl. -S one that dashes

DASHIER   comparative of dashy

DASHIEST   superlative of dashy

DASHIKI   n pl. -S an African tunic

DASHPOT   n pl. -S a shock absorber

DASHY   adj DASHIER, DASHIEST stylish

DASSIE   n pl. -S a hyrax

DASTARD   n pl. -S a base coward

DASYURE   n pl. -S a flesh-eating mammal

DATA   a pl. of datum

DATARY   n pl. -RIES a cardinal in the Roman Catholic Church

DATCHA   n pl. -S dacha

DATE   v DATED, DATING, DATES to determine or record the date of **DATABLE, DATEABLE** adj

DATEDLY   adv in an old-fashioned manner

DATELESS   adj having no date

DATELINE   v -LINED, -LINING, -LINES to provide a news story with a line giving its date and place of origin

DATER   n pl. -S one that dates

DATING   present participle of date

DATIVE   n pl. -S a grammatical case **DATIVAL** adj **DATIVELY** adv

DATO   n pl. -TOS datto

DATTO   n pl. -TOS a Philippine tribal chief

DATUM   n pl. -TA or -TUMS something used as a basis for calculating

DATURA   n pl. -S a flowering plant **DATURIC** adj

DAUB   v -ED, -ING, -S to smear

DAUBE   n pl. -S a braised meat stew

DAUBER   n pl. -S one that daubs

DAUBERY   n pl. -ERIES a bad or inexpert painting

DAUBRY   n pl. -RIES daubery

DAUBY   adj DAUBIER, DAUBIEST smeary

DAUGHTER   n pl. -S a female child

DAUNDER   v -ED, -ING, -S to dander

DAUNT   v -ED, -ING, -S to intimidate

DAUNTER   n pl. -S one that daunts

DAUPHIN   n pl. -S the eldest son of a French king

DAUPHINE   n pl. -S the wife of a dauphin

DAUT   v -ED, -ING, -S to fondle

DAUTIE   n pl. -S a small pet

DAVEN   v -ED, -ING, -S to utter Jewish prayers

DAVIT   n pl. -S a hoisting device on a ship

DAVY   n pl. -VIES a safety lamp

DAW   v DAWED, DAWEN, DAWING, DAWS to dawn

DAWDLE   v -DLED, -DLING, -DLES to waste time

DAWDLER   n pl. -S one that dawdles

DAWEN   past participle of daw

DAWK   n pl. -S dak

DAWN   v -ED, -ING, -S to begin to grow light in the morning

DAWNLIKE   adj suggestive of daybreak

DAWT   v -ED, -ING, -S to daut

DAWTIE   n pl. -S dautie

DAY   n pl. DAYS the time between sunrise and sunset

DAYBED   n pl. -S a couch that can be converted into a bed

DAYBOOK   n pl. -S a diary

DAYBREAK   n pl. -S the first appearance of light in the morning

DAYDREAM   v -DREAMED or -DREAMT, -DREAMING, -DREAMS to fantasize

DAYFLY   n pl. -FLIES a mayfly

DAYGLOW   n pl. -S airglow seen during the day

DAYLIGHT   v -LIGHTED or -LIT, -LIGHTING, -LIGHTS to illuminate with the light of day

DAYLILY   n pl. -LILIES a flowering plant

DAYLONG   adj lasting all day

DAYMARE   n pl. -S a nightmarish fantasy experienced while awake

DAYROOM   n pl. -S a room for reading and recreation

DAYSIDE   n pl. -S the sun side of a planet or the moon

DAYSMAN   n pl. -MEN an arbiter

DAYSTAR   n pl. -S a planet visible in the east just before sunrise

DAYTIME   n pl. -S day

DAZE   v DAZED, DAZING, DAZES to stun **DAZEDLY** adv

DAZZLE   v -ZLED, -ZLING, -ZLES to blind by bright light

DAZZLER   n pl. -S one that dazzles

DE   prep of; from — used in names and phrases

DEACON   v -ED, -ING, -S to read a hymn aloud

DEACONRY   n pl. -RIES a clerical office

DEAD   adj DEADER, DEADEST deprived of life

DEAD   n pl. -S the period of greatest intensity

DEADBEAT   n pl. -S a loafer

DEADEN   v -ED, -ING, -S to diminish the sensitivity or vigor of

DEADENER   n pl. -S one that deadens

DEADEYE   n pl. -S an expert marksman

DEADFALL   n pl. -S a type of animal trap

DEADHEAD   v -ED, -ING, -S to travel without freight

DEADLIER   comparative of deadly

DEADLIEST   superlative of deadly

DEADLINE   n pl. -S a time limit

DEADLOCK *v* -ED, -ING, -S to come to a standstill

DEADLY *adj* -LIER, -LIEST fatal

DEADNESS *n* pl. -ES the state of being dead

DEADPAN *v* -PANNED, -PANNING, -PANS to act without emotion

DEADWOOD *n* pl. -S a reinforcement in a ship's keel

DEAERATE *v* -ATED, -ATING, -ATES to remove air or gas from

DEAF *adj* DEAFER, DEAFEST lacking the sense of hearing

DEAFEN *v* -ED, -ING, -S to make deaf

DEAFISH *adj* somewhat deaf

DEAFLY *adv* in a deaf manner

DEAFNESS *n* pl. -ES the state of being deaf

DEAIR *v* -ED, -ING, -S to remove air from

DEAL *v* DEALT, DEALING, DEALS to trade or do business

DEALATE *n* pl. -S an insect divested of its wings **DEALATED** *adj*

DEALER *n* pl. -S one that deals

DEALFISH *n* pl. -ES a marine fish

DEALING *n* pl. -S a business transaction

DEALT past tense of deal

DEAN *v* -ED, -ING, -S to serve as dean (the head of a faculty)

DEANERY *n* pl. -ERIES the office of a dean

DEANSHIP *n* pl. -S deanery

DEAR *adj* DEARER, DEAREST greatly loved

DEAR *n* pl. -S a loved one

DEARIE *n* pl. -S deary

DEARIES pl. of deary

DEARLY *adv* in a dear manner

DEARNESS *n* pl. -ES the state of being dear

DEARTH *n* pl. -S scarcity

DEARY *n* pl. DEARIES darling

DEASH *v* -ED, -ING, -ES to remove ash from

DEASIL *adv* clockwise

DEATH *n* pl. -S the end of life

DEATHBED *n* pl. -S the bed on which a person dies

DEATHCUP *n* pl. -S a poisonous mushroom

DEATHFUL *adj* fatal

DEATHLY *adj* fatal

DEATHY *adj* deathly

DEAVE *v* DEAVED, DEAVING, DEAVES to deafen

DEB *n* pl. -S a debutante

DEBACLE *n* pl. -S a sudden collapse

DEBAR *v* -BARRED, -BARRING, -BARS to exclude

DEBARK *v* -ED, -ING, -S to unload from a ship

DEBASE *v* -BASED, -BASING, -BASES to lower in character, quality, or value

DEBASER *n* pl. -S one that debases

DEBATE *v* -BATED, -BATING, -BATES to argue about

DEBATER *n* pl. -S one that debates

DEBAUCH *v* -ED, -ING, -ES to corrupt

DEBILITY *n* pl. -TIES weakness

DEBIT *v* -ED, -ING, -S to charge with a debt

DEBONAIR *adj* suave

DEBONE *v* -BONED, -BONING, -BONES to remove the bones from

DEBONER *n* pl. -S a bone remover

DEBOUCH *v* -ED, -ING, -ES to march into the open

DEBOUCHE *n* pl. -S an opening for the passage of troops

DEBRIEF *v* -ED, -ING, -S to question after a mission

DEBRIS *n* pl. DEBRIS fragments or scattered remains

DEBRUISE *v* -BRUISED, -BRUISING, -BRUISES to cross a coat of arms

DEBT *n* pl. -S something that is owed **DEBTLESS** *adj*

DEBTOR *n* pl. -S one who owes something to another

DEBUG *v* -BUGGED, -BUGGING, -BUGS to remove insects from

DEBUNK *v* -ED, -ING, -S to expose the sham or falseness of

DEBUNKER *n* pl. -S one that debunks

DEBUT *v* -ED, -ING, -S to make one's first public appearance

DEBUTANT *n* pl. -S one who is debuting

DEBYE *n* pl. -S a unit of measure for electric dipole moments

DECADE   *n* pl. -S a period of ten years **DECADAL** *adj*

DECADENT   *n* pl. -S one in a state of mental or moral decay

DECAGON   *n* pl. -S a ten-sided polygon

DECAGRAM   *n* pl. -S dekagram

DECAL   *n* pl. -S a picture or design made to be transferred to specially prepared paper

DECAMP   *v* -ED, -ING, -S to depart from a camping ground

DECANAL   *adj* pertaining to a dean

DECANE   *n* pl. -S a hydrocarbon

DECANT   *v* -ED, -ING, -S to pour from one container into another

DECANTER   *n* pl. -S a decorative bottle

DECAPOD   *n* pl. -S a ten-legged crustacean

DECARE   *n* pl. -S dekare

DECAY   *v* -ED, -ING, -S to decompose

DECAYER   *n* pl. -S one that decays

DECEASE   *v* -CEASED, -CEASING, -CEASES to die

DECEDENT   *n* pl. -S a deceased person

DECEIT   *n* pl. -S the act of deceiving

DECEIVE   *v* -CEIVED, -CEIVING, -CEIVES to mislead by falsehood

DECEIVER   *n* pl. -S one that deceives

DECEMVIR   *n* pl. -VIRS or -VIRI one of a body of ten Roman magistrates

DECENARY   *n* pl. -RIES a tithing

DECENCY   *n* pl. -CIES the state of being decent

DECENNIA   *n/pl* decades

DECENT   *adj* -CENTER, -CENTEST conforming to recognized standards of propriety **DECENTLY** *adv*

DECENTER   *v* -ED, -ING, -S to put out of center

DECENTRE   *v* -TRED, -TRING, -TRES to decenter

DECERN   *v* -ED, -ING, -S to decree by judicial sentence

DECIARE   *n* pl. -S a metric unit of area

DECIBEL   *n* pl. -S a unit of sound intensity

DECIDE   *v* -CIDED, -CIDING, -CIDES to make a choice or judgment

DECIDER   *n* pl. -S one that decides

DECIDUA   *n* pl. -UAS or -UAE a mucous membrane of the uterus **DECIDUAL** *adj*

DECIGRAM   *n* pl. -S one tenth of a gram

DECILE   *n* pl. -S a statistical interval

DECIMAL   *n* pl. -S a fraction whose denominator is some power of ten

DECIMATE   *v* -MATED, -MATING, -MATES to destroy a large part of

DECIPHER   *v* -ED, -ING, -S to determine the meaning of

DECISION   *n* pl. -S the act of deciding

DECISIVE   *adj* conclusive

DECK   *v* -ED, -ING, -S to adorn

DECKEL   *n* pl. -S deckle

DECKER   *n* pl. -S something having a specified number of levels, floors, or layers

DECKHAND   *n* pl. -S a seaman who performs manual duties

DECKING   *n* pl. -S material for a ship's deck

DECKLE   *n* pl. -S a frame used in making paper by hand

DECLAIM   *v* -ED, -ING, -S to speak formally

DECLARE   *v* -CLARED, -CLARING, -CLARES to make known clearly

DECLARER   *n* pl. -S one that declares

DECLASS   *v* -ED, -ING, -ES to lower in status

DECLASSE   *adj* lowered in status

DECLINE   *v* -CLINED, -CLINING, -CLINES to refuse

DECLINER   *n* pl. -S one that declines

DECOCT   *v* -ED, -ING, -S to extract the flavor of by boiling

DECODE   *v* -CODED, -CODING, -CODES to convert a coded message into plain language

DECODER   *n* pl. -S one that decodes

DECOLOR   *v* -ED, -ING, -S to deprive of color

DECOLOUR   *v* -ED, -ING, -S to decolor

DECOR   *n* pl. -S style or mode of decoration

DECORATE   *v* -RATED, -RATING, -RATES to adorn

DECOROUS   *adj* proper

DECORUM   *n* pl. -S conformity to social conventions

DECOY   *v* -ED, -ING, -S to lure into a trap

DECOYER *n* pl. -S one that decoys

DECREASE *v* -CREASED, -CREASING, -CREASES to diminish

DECREE *v* -CREED, -CREEING, -CREES to order or establish by law or edict

DECREER *n* pl. -S one that decrees

DECREPIT *adj* worn out by long use

DECRETAL *n* pl. -S a papal edict

DECRIAL *n* pl. -S the act of decrying

DECRIED past tense of decry

DECRIER *n* pl. -S one that decries

DECROWN *v* -ED, -ING, -S to deprive of a crown; depose

DECRY *v* -CRIED, -CRYING, -CRIES to denounce

DECRYPT *v* -ED, -ING, -S to decode

DECUMAN *adj* extremely large

DECUPLE *v* -PLED, -PLING, -PLES to increase tenfold

DECURION *n* pl. -S a commander of a decury

DECURVE *v* -CURVED, -CURVING, -CURVES to curve downward

DECURY *n* pl. -RIES a group of ten soldiers in ancient Rome

DEDAL *adj* daedal

DEDANS *n* pl. DEDANS a gallery for tennis spectators

DEDICATE *v* -CATED, -CATING, -CATES to set apart for some special use

DEDUCE *v* -DUCED, -DUCING, -DUCES to infer

DEDUCT *v* -ED, -ING, -S to subtract

DEE *n* pl. -S the letter D

DEED *v* -ED, -ING, -S to transfer by deed (a legal document)

DEEDLESS *adj* being without deeds

DEEDY *adj* DEEDIER, DEEDIEST industrious

DEEJAY *n* pl. -JAYS a disc jockey

DEEM *v* -ED, -ING, -S to hold as an opinion

DEEMSTER *n* pl. -S a judicial officer of the Isle of Man

DEEP *adj* DEEPER, DEEPEST extending far down from a surface

DEEP *n* pl. -S a place or thing of great depth

DEEPEN *v* -ED, -ING, -S to make deep

DEEPENER *n* pl. -S one that deepens

DEEPLY *adv* at or to a great depth

DEEPNESS *n* pl. -ES the quality of being deep

DEER *n* pl. -S a ruminant mammal

DEERFLY *n* pl. -FLIES a bloodsucking fly

DEERSKIN *n* pl. -S the skin of a deer

DEERWEED *n* pl. -S a bushlike herb

DEERYARD *n* pl. -S an area where deer herd in winter

DEEWAN *n* pl. -S dewan

DEFACE *v* -FACED, -FACING, -FACES to mar the appearance of

DEFACER *n* pl. -S one that defaces

DEFAME *v* -FAMED, -FAMING, -FAMES to attack the good name of

DEFAMER *n* pl. -S one that defames

DEFAT *v* -FATTED, -FATTING, -FATS to remove fat from

DEFAULT *v* -ED, -ING, -S to fail to do something required

DEFEAT *v* -ED, -ING, -S to win victory over

DEFEATER *n* pl. -S one that defeats

DEFECATE *v* -CATED, -CATING, -CATES to discharge feces

DEFECT *v* -ED, -ING, -S to desert an allegiance

DEFECTOR *n* pl. -S one that defects

DEFENCE *n* pl. -S something that defends

DEFEND *v* -ED, -ING, -S to protect

DEFENDER *n* pl. -S one that defends

DEFENSE *v* -FENSED, -FENSING, -FENSES to guard against a specific attack

DEFER *v* -FERRED, -FERRING, -FERS to postpone

DEFERENT *n* pl. -S an imaginary circle around the earth

DEFERRAL *n* pl. -S the act of deferring

DEFERRED past tense of defer

DEFERRER *n* pl. -S one that defers

DEFERRING present participle of defer

DEFI *n* pl. -S a challenge

DEFIANCE *n* pl. -S bold opposition

DEFIANT *adj* showing defiance

DEFICIT *n* pl. -S a shortage

DEFIED	past tense of defy
DEFIER	n pl. -S one that defies
DEFIES	present 3d person sing. of defy
DEFILADE	v -LADED, -LADING, -LADES to shield from enemy fire
DEFILE	v -FILED, -FILING, -FILES to make dirty
DEFILER	n pl. -S one that defiles
DEFINE	v -FINED, -FINING, -FINES to state the meaning of
DEFINER	n pl. -S one that defines
DEFINITE	adj known for certain
DEFLATE	v -FLATED, -FLATING, -FLATES to release the air or gas from
DEFLATOR	n pl. -S one that deflates
DEFLEA	v -ED, -ING, -S to rid of fleas
DEFLECT	v -ED, -ING, -S to turn aside
DEFLEXED	adj bent downward
DEFLOWER	v -ED, -ING, -S to deprive of flowers
DEFOAM	v -ED, -ING, -S to remove foam from
DEFOAMER	n pl. -S one that defoams
DEFOG	v -FOGGED, -FOGGING, -FOGS to remove fog from
DEFOGGER	n pl. -S one that defogs
DEFORCE	v -FORCED, -FORCING, -FORCES to withhold by force
DEFOREST	v -ED, -ING, -S to clear of forests
DEFORM	v -ED, -ING, -S to spoil the form of
DEFORMER	n pl. -S one that deforms
DEFRAUD	v -ED, -ING, -S to swindle
DEFRAY	v -ED, -ING, -S to pay
DEFRAYAL	n pl. -S the act of defraying
DEFRAYER	n pl. -S one that defrays
DEFROCK	v -ED, -ING, -S to unfrock
DEFROST	v -ED, -ING, -S to remove frost from
DEFT	adj DEFTER, DEFTEST skillful **DEFTLY** adv
DEFTNESS	n pl. -ES the quality of being deft
DEFUNCT	adj deceased
DEFUSE	v -FUSED, -FUSING, -FUSES to remove the fuse from
DEFUZE	v -FUZED, -FUZING, -FUZES to defuse

DEFY	v -FIED, -FYING, -FIES to resist openly and boldly
DEGAGE	adj free and relaxed in manner
DEGAME	n pl. -S a tropical tree
DEGAMI	n pl. -S degame
DEGAS	v -GASSED, -GASSING, -GASSES or -GASES to remove gas from
DEGASSER	n pl. -S one that degasses
DEGAUSS	v -ED, -ING, -ES to demagnetize
DEGERM	v -ED, -ING, -S to remove germs from
DEGLAZE	v -GLAZED, -GLAZING, -GLAZES to remove the glaze from
DEGRADE	v -GRADED, -GRADING, -GRADES to debase
DEGRADER	n pl. -S one that degrades
DEGREASE	v -GREASED, -GREASING, -GREASES to remove the grease from
DEGREE	n pl. -S one of a series of stages **DEGREED** adj
DEGUM	v -GUMMED, -GUMMING, -GUMS to free from gum
DEGUST	v -ED, -ING, -S to taste with pleasure
DEHISCE	v -HISCED, -HISCING, -HISCES to split open
DEHORN	v -ED, -ING, -S to deprive of horns
DEHORNER	n pl. -S one that dehorns
DEHORT	v -ED, -ING, -S to try to dissuade
DEI	prep of; from — used in names
DEICE	v -ICED, -ICING, -ICES to free from ice
DEICER	n pl. -S one that deices
DEICIDE	n pl. -S the killing of a god **DEICIDAL** adj
DEICTIC	adj proving directly
DEIFIC	adj godlike
DEIFICAL	adj deific
DEIFIED	past tense of deify
DEIFIER	n pl. -S one that deifies
DEIFORM	adj having the form of a god
DEIFY	v -FIED, -FYING, -FIES to make a god of
DEIGN	v -ED, -ING, -S to lower oneself to do something
DEIL	n pl. -S the devil

DEIONIZE v -IZED, -IZING, -IZES to remove ions from

DEISM n pl. -S a religious philosophy

DEIST n pl. -S an adherent of deism **DEISTIC** adj

DEITY n pl. -TIES a god or goddess

DEJECT v -ED, -ING, -S to depress

DEJECTA n/pl excrements

DEJEUNER n pl. -S a late breakfast

DEKAGRAM n pl. -S a measure equal to ten grams

DEKARE n pl. -S a measure equal to ten ares

DEKE v DEKED, DEKING, DEKES to feint in hockey

DEL n pl. -S an operator in differential calculus

DELAINE n pl. -S a wool fabric

DELATE v -LATED, -LATING, -LATES to accuse

DELATION n pl. -S the act of delating

DELATOR n pl. -S one that delates

DELAY v -ED, -ING, -S to put off to a later time

DELAYER n pl. -S one that delays

DELE v DELED, DELEING, DELES to delete

DELEAD v -ED, -ING, -S to remove lead from

DELEGACY n pl. -CIES the act of delegating

DELEGATE v -GATED, -GATING, -GATES to appoint as one's representative

DELETE v -LETED, -LETING, -LETES to remove written or printed matter

DELETION n pl. -S the act of deleting

DELF n pl. -S delft

DELFT n pl. -S an earthenware

DELI n pl. DELIS a delicatessen

DELICACY n pl. -CIES a choice food

DELICATE n pl. -S a delicacy

DELICT n pl. -S an offense against civil law

DELIGHT v -ED, -ING, -S to give great pleasure to

DELIME v -LIMED, -LIMING, -LIMES to free from lime

DELIMIT v -ED, -ING, -S to mark the boundaries of

DELIRIUM n pl. -IUMS or -IA wild excitement

DELIST v -ED, -ING, -S to remove from a list

DELIVER v -ED, -ING, -S to take to the intended recipient

DELIVERY n pl. -ERIES the act of delivering

DELL n pl. -S a small, wooded valley

DELLY n pl. DELLIES deli

DELOUSE v -LOUSED, -LOUSING, -LOUSES to remove lice from

DELTA n pl. -S an alluvial deposit at the mouth of a river **DELTAIC, DELTIC** adj

DELTOID n pl. -S a shoulder muscle

DELUDE v -LUDED, -LUDING, -LUDES to mislead the mind or judgment of

DELUDER n pl. -S one that deludes

DELUGE v -UGED, -UGING, -UGES to flood

DELUSION n pl. -S the act of deluding

DELUSIVE adj tending to delude

DELUSORY adj delusive

DELUSTER v -ED, -ING, -S to lessen the sheen of

DELUXE adj of special elegance or luxury

DELVE v DELVED, DELVING, DELVES to search in depth

DELVER n pl. -S one that delves

DEMAGOG n pl. -S an unethical leader

DEMAGOGY n pl. -GOGIES the rule of a demagog

DEMAND v -ED, -ING, -S to ask for with authority

DEMANDER n pl. -S one that demands

DEMARCHE n pl. -S a procedure

DEMARK v -ED, -ING, -S to delimit

DEMAST v -ED, -ING, -S to strip masts from

DEME n pl. -S a Greek district

DEMEAN v -ED, -ING, -S to conduct oneself in a particular manner

DEMEANOR n pl. -S the manner in which one conducts oneself

DEMENT v -ED, -ING, -S to make insane

DEMENTIA n pl. -S mental illness

DEMERIT v -ED, -ING, -S to lower in rank or status

DEMESNE n pl. -S the legal possession of land as one's own

DEMIES pl. of demy

DEMIGOD n pl. -S a lesser god

DEMIJOHN n pl. -S a narrow-necked jug

DEMILUNE n pl. -S a half-moon

DEMIREP n pl. -S a prostitute

DEMISE v -MISED, -MISING, -MISES to bequeath

DEMIT v -MITTED, -MITTING, -MITS to resign

DEMIURGE n pl. -S a magistrate of ancient Greece

DEMIVOLT n pl. -S a half turn made by a horse

DEMO n pl. DEMOS a demonstration

DEMOB v -MOBBED, -MOBBING, -MOBS to discharge from military service

DEMOCRAT n pl. -S one who believes in political and social equality

DEMODE adj demoded

DEMODED adj out-of-date

DEMOLISH v -ED, -ING, -ES to destroy

DEMON n pl. -S an evil spirit

DEMONESS n pl. -ES a female demon

DEMONIAC n pl. -S one regarded as possessed by a demon

DEMONIAN adj demonic

DEMONIC adj characteristic of a demon

DEMONISE v -ISED, -ISING, -ISES to demonize

DEMONISM n pl. -S belief in demons

DEMONIST n pl. -S one who believes in demons

DEMONIZE v -IZED, -IZING, -IZES to make a demon of

DEMOS n pl. -ES the people of an ancient Greek state

DEMOTE v -MOTED, -MOTING, -MOTES to lower in rank or grade

DEMOTIC adj pertaining to a simplified form of ancient Egyptian writing

DEMOTICS n/pl the study of people in society

DEMOTING present participle of demote

DEMOTION n pl. -S the act of demoting

DEMOTIST n pl. -S a student of demotic writings

DEMOUNT v -ED, -ING, -S to remove from a mounting

DEMPSTER n pl. -S a deemster

DEMUR v -MURRED, -MURRING, -MURS to object

DEMURE adj -MURER, -MUREST shy and modest **DEMURELY** adv

DEMURRAL n pl. -S the act of demurring

DEMURRED past tense of demur

DEMURRER n pl. -S one that demurs

DEMURRING present participle of demur

DEMY n pl. -MIES a size of paper

DEN v DENNED, DENNING, DENS to live in a lair

DENARIUS n pl. DENARII a coin of ancient Rome

DENARY adj containing ten

DENATURE v -TURED, -TURING, -TURES to deprive of natural qualities

DENAZIFY v -FIED, -FYING, -FIES to rid of Nazism

DENDRITE n pl. -S a branched part of a nerve cell

DENDROID adj shaped like a tree

DENDRON n pl. -S a dendrite

DENE n pl. -S a valley

DENGUE n pl. -S a tropical disease

DENIABLE adj capable of being denied **DENIABLY** adv

DENIAL n pl. -S the act of denying

DENIED past tense of deny

DENIER n pl. -S one that denies

DENIES present 3d person sing. of deny

DENIM n pl. -S a durable fabric

DENIZEN v -ED, -ING, -S to make a citizen of

DENNED past tense of den

DENNING present participle of den

DENOTE v -NOTED, -NOTING, -NOTES to indicate **DENOTIVE** adj

DENOUNCE v -NOUNCED, -NOUNCING, -NOUNCES to condemn openly

DENSE adj DENSER, DENSEST compact **DENSELY** adv

DENSIFY v -FIED, -FYING, -FIES to make denser

DENSITY n pl. -TIES the state of being dense

DENT v -ED, -ING, -S to make a depression in

DENTAL n pl. -S a dentally produced sound

DENTALIA *n/pl* mollusks with long, tapering shells

DENTALLY *adv* with the tip of the tongue against the upper front teeth

DENTATE *adj* having teeth

DENTATED *adj* dentate

DENTICLE *n* pl. -S a small tooth

DENTIL *n* pl. -S a small rectangular block

DENTIN *n* pl. -S the hard substance forming the body of a tooth **DENTINAL** *adj*

DENTINE *n* pl. -S dentin

DENTIST *n* pl. -S one who treats the teeth

DENTOID *adj* resembling a tooth

DENTURE *n* pl. -S a set of teeth **DENTURAL** *adj*

DENUDATE *v* -DATED, -DATING, -DATES to denude

DENUDE *v* -NUDED, -NUDING, -NUDES to strip of all covering

DENUDER *n* pl. -S one that denudes

DENY *v* -NIED, -NYING, -NIES to declare to be untrue

DEODAND *n* pl. -S property forfeited to the crown under a former English law

DEODAR *n* pl. -S an East Indian cedar

DEODARA *n* pl. -S deodar

DEPAINT *v* -ED, -ING, -S to depict

DEPART *v* -ED, -ING, -S to go away

DEPEND *v* -ED, -ING, -S to rely

DEPERM *v* -ED, -ING, -S to demagnetize

DEPICT *v* -ED, -ING, -S to portray

DEPICTER *n* pl. -S one that depicts

DEPICTOR *n* pl. -S depicter

DEPILATE *v* -LATED, -LATING, -LATES to remove hair from

DEPLANE *v* -PLANED, -PLANING, -PLANES to get off an airplane

DEPLETE *v* -PLETED, -PLETING, -PLETES to lessen or exhaust the supply of

DEPLORE *v* -PLORED, -PLORING, -PLORES to regret strongly

DEPLORER *n* pl. -S one that deplores

DEPLOY *v* -ED, -ING, -S to position troops for battle

DEPLUME *v* -PLUMED, -PLUMING, -PLUMES to deprive of feathers

DEPOLISH *v* -ED, -ING, -ES to remove the gloss or polish of

DEPONE *v* -PONED, -PONING, -PONES to testify under oath

DEPONENT *n* pl. -S one that depones

DEPORT *v* -ED, -ING, -S to expel from a country

DEPORTEE *n* pl. -S one who is deported

DEPOSAL *n* pl. -S the act of deposing

DEPOSE *v* -POSED, -POSING, -POSES to remove from office

DEPOSER *n* pl. -S one that deposes

DEPOSIT *v* -ED, -ING, -S to place

DEPOT *n* pl. -S a railroad or bus station

DEPRAVE *v* -PRAVED, -PRAVING, -PRAVES to corrupt in morals

DEPRAVER *n* pl. -S one that depraves

DEPRESS *v* -ED, -ING, -ES to make sad

DEPRIVAL *n* pl. -S the act of depriving

DEPRIVE *v* -PRIVED, -PRIVING, -PRIVES to take something away from

DEPRIVER *n* pl. -S one that deprives

DEPSIDE *n* pl. -S an aromatic compound

DEPTH *n* pl. -S deepness

DEPURATE *v* -RATED, -RATING, -RATES to free from impurities

DEPUTE *v* -PUTED, -PUTING, -PUTES to delegate

DEPUTIZE *v* -TIZED, -TIZING, -TIZES to appoint as a deputy

DEPUTY *n* pl. -TIES one appointed to act for another

DERAIGN *v* -ED, -ING, -S to dispute a claim

DERAIL *v* -ED, -ING, -S to run off the rails of a track

DERANGE *v* -RANGED, -RANGING, -RANGES to disorder

DERAT *v* -RATTED, -RATTING, -RATS to rid of rats

DERAY *n* pl. -RAYS disorderly revelry

DERBY *n* pl. -BIES a type of hat

DERE *adj* dire

DERELICT *n* pl. -S something abandoned

DERIDE *v* -RIDED, -RIDING, -RIDES to ridicule

DERIDER *n* pl. -S one that derides

DERINGER *n pl.* -S a short-barreled pistol

DERISION *n pl.* -S the act of deriding

DERISIVE *adj* expressing derision

DERISORY *adj* derisive

DERIVATE *n pl.* -S something derived

DERIVE *v* -RIVED, -RIVING, -RIVES to obtain or receive from a source

DERIVER *n pl.* -S one that derives

DERM *n pl.* -S derma

DERMA *n pl.* -S a layer of the skin **DERMAL** *adj*

DERMIS *n pl.* -MISES derma **DERMIC** *adj*

DERMOID *adj* resembling skin

DERNIER *adj* last

DEROGATE *v* -GATED, -GATING, -GATES to detract

DERRICK *n pl.* -S a hoisting apparatus

DERRIERE *n pl.* -S the buttocks

DERRIS *n pl.* -RISES a climbing plant

DERRY *n pl.* -RIES a meaningless word used as part of a chorus in old songs

DERVISH *n pl.* -ES a member of a Muslim religious order

DES *prep* of the — used in names

DESALT *v* -ED, -ING, -S to remove the salt from

DESALTER *n pl.* -S one that desalts

DESAND *v* -ED, -ING, -S to remove sand from

DESCANT *v* -ED, -ING, -S to sing

DESCEND *v* -ED, -ING, -S to come or go down

DESCENT *n pl.* -S the act of descending

DESCRIBE *v* -SCRIBED, -SCRIBING, -SCRIBES to give a verbal account of

DESCRIER *n pl.* -S one that descries

DESCRY *v* -SCRIED, -SCRYING, -SCRIES to discern

DESELECT *v* -ED, -ING, -S to dismiss from a training program

DESERT *v* -ED, -ING, -S to abandon

DESERTER *n pl.* -S one that deserts

DESERTIC *adj* arid and barren

DESERVE *v* -SERVED, -SERVING, -SERVES to be entitled to or worthy of

DESERVER *n pl.* -S one that deserves

DESEX *v* -ED, -ING, -ES to castrate or spay

DESIGN *v* -ED, -ING, -S to conceive and plan out

DESIGNEE *n pl.* -S one who is designated

DESIGNER *n pl.* -S one that designs

DESILVER *v* -ED, -ING, -S to remove the silver from

DESINENT *adj* terminating

DESIRE *v* -SIRED, -SIRING, -SIRES to wish for

DESIRER *n pl.* -S one that desires

DESIROUS *adj* desiring

DESIST *v* -ED, -ING, -S to cease doing something

DESK *n pl.* -S a writing table

DESKMAN *n pl.* -MEN one who works at a desk

DESMAN *n pl.* -S an aquatic mammal

DESMID *n pl.* -S a freshwater alga

DESMOID *n pl.* -S a very hard tumor

DESOLATE *v* -LATED, -LATING, -LATES to lay waste

DESORB *v* -ED, -ING, -S to remove by the reverse of absorption

DESPAIR *v* -ED, -ING, -S to lose all hope

DESPATCH *v* -ED, -ING, -ES to dispatch

DESPISE *v* -SPISED, -SPISING, -SPISES to loathe

DESPISER *n pl.* -S one that despises

DESPITE *v* -SPITED, -SPITING, -SPITES to treat with contempt

DESPOIL *v* -ED, -ING, -S to plunder

DESPOND *v* -ED, -ING, -S to lose spirit or hope

DESPOT *n pl.* -S a tyrant **DESPOTIC** *adj*

DESSERT *n pl.* -S something served as the last course of a meal

DESTAIN *v* -ED, -ING, -S to remove stain from

DESTINE *v* -TINED, -TINING, -TINES to determine beforehand

DESTINY *n pl.* -NIES the fate or fortune to which one is destined

DESTRIER *n pl.* -S a war horse

DESTROY *v* -ED, -ING, -S to damage beyond repair or renewal

DESTRUCT *v* -ED, -ING, -S to destroy

DESUGAR *v* -ED, -ING, -S to remove sugar from

DESULFUR v -ED, -ING, -S to free from sulfur

DETACH v -ED, -ING, -ES to unfasten and separate

DETACHER n pl. -S one that detaches

DETAIL v -ED, -ING, -S to report with complete particulars

DETAILER n pl. -S one that details

DETAIN v -ED, -ING, -S to hold in custody

DETAINEE n pl. -S one who is detained

DETAINER n pl. -S the unlawful withholding of another's property

DETECT v -ED, -ING, -S to discover or perceive

DETECTER n pl. -S detector

DETECTOR n pl. -S one that detects

DETENT n pl. -S a mechanical device that either stops or releases a movement

DETENTE n pl. -S an easing of international tension

DETER v -TERRED, -TERRING, -TERS to stop from proceeding

DETERGE v -TERGED, -TERGING, -TERGES to cleanse

DETERGER n pl. -S one that deterges

DETERRED past tense of deter

DETERRER n pl. -S one that deters

DETERRING present participle of deter

DETEST v -ED, -ING, -S to dislike intensely

DETESTER n pl. -S one that detests

DETHRONE v -THRONED, -THRONING, -THRONES to remove from a throne

DETICK v -ED, -ING, -S to remove ticks from

DETICKER n pl. -S one that deticks

DETINUE n pl. -S an action to recover property wrongfully detained

DETONATE v -NATED, -NATING, -NATES to cause to explode

DETOUR v -ED, -ING, -S to take an indirect route

DETOXIFY v -FIED, -FYING, -FIES to remove a toxin from

DETRACT v -ED, -ING, -S to take away

DETRAIN v -ED, -ING, -S to get off a railroad train

DETRITUS n pl. DETRITUS particles of rock DETRITAL adj

DETRUDE v -TRUDED, -TRUDING, -TRUDES to thrust out

DEUCE v DEUCED, DEUCING, DEUCES to bring a tennis score to a tie

DEUCEDLY adv extremely

DEUTERIC adj pertaining to heavy hydrogen

DEUTERON n pl. -S an atomic particle

DEUTZIA n pl. -S an ornamental shrub

DEV n pl. -S deva

DEVA n pl. -S a Hindu god

DEVALUE v -UED, -UING, -UES to lessen the worth of

DEVEIN v -ED, -ING, -S to remove the dorsal vein from

DEVEL v -ED, -ING, -S to strike forcibly

DEVELOP v -ED, -ING, -S to bring to a more advanced or effective state

DEVELOPE v -OPED, -OPING, -OPES to develop

DEVEST v -ED, -ING, -S to divest

DEVIANCE n pl. -S the behavior of a deviant

DEVIANCY n pl. -CIES deviance

DEVIANT n pl. -S one that deviates from a norm

DEVIATE v -ATED, -ATING, -ATES to turn aside from a course or norm

DEVIATOR n pl. -S one that deviates

DEVICE n pl. -S something devised or constructed for a specific purpose

DEVIL v -ILED, -ILING, -ILS or -ILLED, -ILLING, -ILS to prepare food with pungent seasoning

DEVILISH adj fiendish

DEVILKIN n pl. -S a small demon

DEVILLED a past tense of devil

DEVILLING a present participle of devil

DEVILRY n pl. -RIES deviltry

DEVILTRY n pl. -TRIES mischief

DEVIOUS adj indirect

DEVISAL n pl. -S the act of devising

DEVISE v -VISED, -VISING, -VISES to form in the mind

DEVISEE n pl. -S one to whom a will is made

DEVISER   *n* pl. -S one that devises

DEVISING   present participle of devise

DEVISOR   *n* pl. -S one who makes a will

DEVOICE   *v* -VOICED, -VOICING, -VOICES to unvoice

DEVOID   *adj* completely lacking

DEVOIR   *n* pl. -S an act of civility or respect

DEVOLVE   *v* -VOLVED, -VOLVING, -VOLVES to transfer from one person to another

DEVON   *n* pl. -S one of a breed of small, hardy cattle

DEVOTE   *v* -VOTED, -VOTING, -VOTES to give oneself wholly to

DEVOTEE   *n* pl. -S an ardent follower or supporter

DEVOTION   *n* pl. -S the act of devoting

DEVOUR   *v* -ED, -ING, -S to eat up voraciously

DEVOURER   *n* pl. -S one that devours

DEVOUT   *adj* pious DEVOUTLY *adv*

DEW   *v* -ED, -ING, -S to wet with dew (condensed moisture)

DEWAN   *n* pl. -S an official in India

DEWATER   *v* -ED, -ING, -S to remove water from

DEWAX   *v* -ED, -ING, -ES to remove wax from

DEWBERRY   *n* pl. -RIES an edible berry

DEWCLAW   *n* pl. -S a vestigial toe

DEWDROP   *n* pl. -S a drop of dew

DEWFALL   *n* pl. -S the formation of dew

DEWIER   comparative of dewy

DEWIEST   superlative of dewy

DEWILY   *adv* in a dewy manner

DEWINESS   *n* pl. -ES the state of being dewy

DEWLAP   *n* pl. -S a fold of loose skin under the neck

DEWLESS   *adj* having no dew

DEWOOL   *v* -ED, -ING, -S to remove the wool from

DEWORM   *v* -ED, -ING, -S to rid of worms

DEWY   *adj* DEWIER, DEWIEST moist with dew

DEX   *n* pl. -ES a sulfate used as a central nervous system stimulant

DEXIES   *n/pl* tablets of dex

DEXTER   *adj* situated on the right

DEXTRAL   *adj* pertaining to the right

DEXTRAN   *n* pl. -S a substance used as a plasma substitute

DEXTRIN   *n* pl. -S a substance used as an adhesive

DEXTRINE   *n* pl. -S dextrin

DEXTRO   *adj* turning to the right

DEXTROSE   *n* pl. -S a form of glucose

DEXTROUS   *adj* adroit

DEY   *n* pl. DEYS a former North African ruler

DEZINC   *v* -ZINCKED, -ZINCKING, -ZINCS or -ZINCED, -ZINCING, -ZINCS to remove zinc from

DHAK   *n* pl. -S an Asian tree

DHARMA   *n* pl. -S conformity to Hindu law DHARMIC *adj*

DHARNA   *n* pl. -S a form of protest in India

DHOLE   *n* pl. -S a wild dog of India

DHOOLY   *n* pl. -LIES dooly

DHOORA   *n* pl. -S durra

DHOOTI   *n* pl. -S dhoti

DHOOTIE   *n* pl. -S dhoti

DHOTI   *n* pl. -S a loincloth worn by Hindu men

DHOURRA   *n* pl. -S durra

DHOW   *n* pl. -S an Arabian sailing vessel

DHURNA   *n* pl. -S dharna

DHUTI   *n* pl. -S dhoti

DIABASE   *n* pl. -S an igneous rock DIABASIC *adj*

DIABETES   *n* pl. DIABETES a metabolic disorder

DIABETIC   *n* pl. -S one who has diabetes

DIABLERY   *n* pl. -RIES sorcery

DIABOLIC   *adj* devilish

DIABOLO   *n* pl. -LOS a game requiring manual dexterity

DIACETYL   *n* pl. -S biacetyl

DIACID   *n* pl. -S a type of acid DIACIDIC *adj*

DIACONAL   *adj* pertaining to a deacon

DIADEM   *v* -ED, -ING, -S to adorn with a crown

DIAGNOSE v -NOSED, -NOSING, -NOSES to recognize a disease by its signs and symptoms

DIAGONAL n pl. -S an oblique line

DIAGRAM v -GRAMED, -GRAMING, -GRAMS or -GRAMMED, -GRAMMING, -GRAMS to illustrate by a diagram (a graphic design)

DIAGRAPH n pl. -S a drawing device

DIAL v DIALED, DIALING, DIALS or DIALLED, DIALLING, DIALS to manipulate a calibrated disk

DIALECT n pl. -S a regional variety of a language

DIALER n pl. -S one that dials

DIALING n pl. -S the measurement of time by sundials

DIALIST n pl. -S a dialer

DIALLAGE n pl. -S a mineral

DIALLED a past tense of dial

DIALLEL adj pertaining to a genetic crossing

DIALLER n pl. -S dialer

DIALLING n pl. -S dialing

DIALLIST n pl. -S dialist

DIALOG v -LOGGED, -LOGGING, -LOGS to dialogue

DIALOGER n pl. -S one that dialogs

DIALOGIC adj conversational

DIALOGUE v -LOGUED, -LOGUING, -LOGUES to converse

DIALYSE v -LYSED, -LYSING, -LYSES to dialyze

DIALYSER n pl. -S dialyzer

DIALYSIS n pl. -YSES the separation of substances in a solution by diffusion through a membrane

DIALYTIC adj pertaining to dialysis

DIALYZE v -LYZED, -LYZING, -LYZES to subject to dialysis

DIALYZER n pl. -S an apparatus used for dialysis

DIAMETER n pl. -S a straight line passing through the center of a circle and ending at the periphery

DIAMIDE n pl. -S a chemical compound

DIAMIN n pl. -S diamine

DIAMINE n pl. -S a chemical compound

DIAMOND v -ED, -ING, -S to adorn with diamonds (precious gems)

DIANTHUS n pl. -ES an ornamental herb

DIAPASON n pl. -S a burst of harmonious sound

DIAPAUSE v -PAUSED, -PAUSING, -PAUSES to undergo dormancy

DIAPER v -ED, -ING, -S to put a diaper (a baby's breechcloth) on

DIAPHONE n pl. -S a low-pitched foghorn

DIAPHONY n pl. -NIES organum

DIAPIR n pl. -S a bend in a layer of rock DIAPIRIC adj

DIAPSID adj pertaining to a type of reptile

DIARCHY n pl. -CHIES a government with two rulers DIARCHIC adj

DIARIES pl. of diary

DIARIST n pl. -S one who keeps a diary

DIARRHEA n pl. -S an intestinal disorder

DIARY n pl. -RIES a personal journal

DIASPORA n pl. -S migration

DIASPORE n pl. -S a mineral

DIASTASE n pl. -S an enzyme

DIASTEMA n pl. -MATA a space between teeth

DIASTER n pl. -S a stage in mitosis DIASTRAL adj

DIASTOLE n pl. -S the normal rhythmical dilation of the heart

DIATOM n pl. -S any of a class of algae

DIATOMIC adj composed of two atoms

DIATONIC adj pertaining to a type of musical scale

DIATRIBE n pl. -S a bitter and abusive criticism

DIAZEPAM n pl. -S a tranquilizer

DIAZIN n pl. -S diazine

DIAZINE n pl. -S a chemical compound

DIAZO adj containing a certain chemical group

DIAZOLE n pl. -S a chemical compound

DIB v DIBBED, DIBBING, DIBS to fish by letting the bait bob lightly on the water

DIBASIC adj having two replaceable hydrogen atoms

DIBBER n pl. -S a planting implement

DIBBING present participle of dib

DIBBLE v -BLED, -BLING, -BLES to dib

DIBBLER n pl. -S one that dibbles

DIBBUK	*n* pl. -BUKS or -BUKIM dybbuk
DICAST	*n* pl. -S a judge of ancient Athens **DICASTIC** *adj*
DICE	*v* DICED, DICING, DICES to cut into small cubes
DICENTRA	*n* pl. -S a perennial herb
DICER	*n* pl. -S a device that dices food
DICEY	*adj* DICIER, DICIEST dangerous
DICHASIA	*n/pl* flower clusters
DICHOTIC	*adj* affecting the two ears differently
DICHROIC	*adj* having two colors
DICIER	comparative of dicey
DICIEST	superlative of dicey
DICING	present participle of dice
DICK	*n* pl. -S a detective
DICKENS	*n* pl. -ES devil
DICKER	*v* -ED, -ING, -S to bargain
DICKEY	*n* pl. -EYS a blouse front
DICKIE	*n* pl. -S dickey
DICKY	*n* pl. DICKIES dickey
DICLINY	*n* pl. -NIES the state of having stamens and pistils in separate flowers
DICOT	*n* pl. -S a plant with two seed leaves
DICOTYL	*n* pl. -S dicot
DICROTAL	*adj* dicrotic
DICROTIC	*adj* having a double pulse beat
DICTA	a pl. of dictum
DICTATE	*v* -TATED, -TATING, -TATES to read aloud for recording
DICTATOR	*n* pl. -S one that dictates
DICTION	*n* pl. -S choice and use of words in speech or writing
DICTUM	*n* pl. -TA or -TUMS an authoritative statement
DICYCLIC	*adj* having two maxima of population each year
DICYCLY	*n* pl. -CLIES the state of being dicyclic
DID	a past tense of do
DIDACT	*n* pl. -S a didactic person
DIDACTIC	*adj* instructive
DIDACTYL	*adj* having two digits at the end of each limb
DIDAPPER	*n* pl. -S a dabchick
DIDDLE	*v* -DLED, -DLING, -DLES to swindle
DIDDLER	*n* pl. -S one that diddles
DIDIES	pl. of didy
DIDO	*n* pl. -DOS or -DOES a mischievous act
DIDST	a past tense of do
DIDY	*n* pl. -DIES a diaper
DIDYMIUM	*n* pl. -S a mixture of rare-earth elements
DIDYMOUS	*adj* occurring in pairs
DIDYNAMY	*n* pl. -MIES the state of having four stamens in pairs of unequal length
DIE	*v* DIED, DYING, DIES to cease living
DIE	*v* DIED, DIEING, DIES to cut with a die (a device for shaping material)
DIEBACK	*n* pl. -S a gradual dying of plant shoots
DIECIOUS	*adj* dioicous
DIED	past tense of die
DIEHARD	*n* pl. -S a stubborn person
DIEL	*adj* involving a full day
DIELDRIN	*n* pl. -S an insecticide
DIEMAKER	*n* pl. -S one that makes dies
DIENE	*n* pl. -S a chemical compound
DIERESIS	*n* pl. DIERESES the separation of two vowels into two syllables **DIERETIC** *adj*
DIES	present 3d person sing. of die
DIESEL	*n* pl. -S a type of engine
DIESIS	*n* pl. DIESES a reference mark in printing
DIESTER	*n* pl. -S a type of chemical compound
DIESTOCK	*n* pl. -S a frame for holding dies
DIESTRUM	*n* pl. -S diestrus
DIESTRUS	*n* pl. -ES a period of sexual inactivity
DIET	*v* -ED, -ING, -S to regulate one's daily sustenance
DIETARY	*n* pl. -ETARIES a system of dieting
DIETER	*n* pl. -S one that diets
DIETETIC	*adj* pertaining to diet
DIFFER	*v* -ED, -ING, -S to be unlike
DIFFRACT	*v* -ED, -ING, -S to separate into parts

DIFFUSE   v -FUSED, -FUSING, -FUSES to spread widely or thinly

DIFFUSER   n pl. -S one that diffuses

DIFFUSOR   n pl. -S diffuser

DIG   v DUG or DIGGED, DIGGING, DIGS to break up, turn over, or remove earth

DIGAMIST   n pl. -S one who practices digamy

DIGAMMA   n pl. -S a Greek letter

DIGAMY   n pl. -MIES a second legal marriage **DIGAMOUS** adj

DIGEST   v -ED, -ING, -S to render food usable for the body

DIGESTER   n pl. -S an apparatus in which substances are softened or decomposed

DIGESTOR   n pl. -S digester

DIGGED   a past tense of dig

DIGGER   n pl. -S one that digs

DIGGING   present participle of dig

DIGGINGS   n/pl an excavation site

DIGHT   v -ED, -ING, -S to adorn

DIGIT   n pl. -S a finger or toe

DIGITAL   n pl. -S a piano key

DIGITATE   adj having digits

DIGITIZE   v -TIZED, -TIZING, -TIZES to put data into digital notation

DIGLOT   n pl. -S a bilingual book or edition

DIGNIFY   v -FIED, -FYING, -FIES to add dignity to

DIGNITY   n pl. -TIES stateliness and nobility of manner

DIGOXIN   n pl. -S a poisonous steroid

DIGRAPH   n pl. -S a pair of letters representing a single speech sound

DIGRESS   v -ED, -ING, -ES to stray from the main topic

DIHEDRAL   n pl. -S a dihedron

DIHEDRON   n pl. -S a figure formed by two intersecting planes

DIHYBRID   n pl. -S an offspring of parents differing in two pairs of genes

DIHYDRIC   adj containing two hydroxyl radicals

DIKDIK   n pl. -S a small antelope

DIKE   v DIKED, DIKING, DIKES to furnish with an embankment

DIKER   n pl. -S one that dikes

DIKTAT   n pl. -S a harsh settlement imposed on a defeated nation

DILATANT   n pl. -S a dilator

DILATATE   adj dilated

DILATE   v -LATED, -LATING, -LATES to make wider or larger

DILATER   n pl. -S dilator

DILATION   n pl. -S the act of dilating

DILATIVE   adj tending to dilate

DILATOR   n pl. -S one that dilates

DILATORY   adj tending to delay

DILDO   n pl. -DOS an object used as a penis substitute

DILDOE   n pl. -S dildo

DILEMMA   n pl. -S a perplexing situation **DILEMMIC** adj

DILIGENT   adj persevering

DILL   n pl. -S an annual herb

DILLY   n pl. DILLIES something remarkable

DILUENT   n pl. -S a diluting substance

DILUTE   v -LUTED, -LUTING, -LUTES to thin or reduce the concentration of

DILUTER   n pl. -S one that dilutes

DILUTION   n pl. -S the act of diluting

DILUTIVE   adj tending to dilute

DILUTOR   n pl. -S diluter

DILUVIA   a pl. of diluvium

DILUVIAL   adj pertaining to a flood

DILUVIAN   adj diluvial

DILUVION   n pl. -S diluvium

DILUVIUM   n pl. -VIA or -VIUMS coarse rock material deposited by glaciers

DIM   adj DIMMER, DIMMEST obscure

DIM   v DIMMED, DIMMING, DIMS to make dim

DIME   n pl. -S a coin of the United States

DIMER   n pl. -S a molecule composed of two identical molecules

DIMERIC   adj dimerous

DIMERISM   n pl. -S the state of being dimerous

DIMERIZE   v -IZED, -IZING, -IZES to form a dimer

DIMEROUS   adj composed of two parts

DIMETER   *n* pl. -S a verse of two metrical feet

DIMETHYL   *n* pl. -S ethane

DIMETRIC   *adj* pertaining to a type of crystal system

DIMINISH   *v* -ED, -ING, -ES to lessen

DIMITY   *n* pl. -TIES a cotton fabric

DIMLY   *adv* in a dim manner

DIMMABLE   *adj* capable of being dimmed

DIMMED   past tense of dim

DIMMER   *n* pl. -S a device for varying the intensity of illumination

DIMMEST   superlative of dim

DIMMING   present participle of dim

DIMNESS   *n* pl. -ES the state of being dim

DIMORPH   *n* pl. -S either of two distinct forms

DIMOUT   *n* pl. -S a condition of partial darkness

DIMPLE   *v* -PLED, -PLING, -PLES to mark with indentations

DIMPLY   *adj* -PLIER, -PLIEST dimpled

DIMWIT   *n* pl. -S a dunce

DIN   *v* DINNED, DINNING, DINS to make a loud noise

DINAR   *n* pl. -S an ancient gold coin of Muslim areas

DINDLE   *v* -DLED, -DLING, -DLES to tingle

DINE   *v* DINED, DINING, DINES to eat dinner

DINER   *n* pl. -S one that dines

DINERIC   *adj* pertaining to the interface between two immiscible liquids

DINERO   *n* pl. -ROS a former silver coin of Peru

DINETTE   *n* pl. -S a small dining room

DING   *v* -ED, -ING, -S to ring

DINGBAT   *n* pl. -S a typographical ornament

DINGDONG   *v* -ED, -ING, -S to make a ringing sound

DINGEY   *n* pl. -GEYS dinghy

DINGHY   *n* pl. -GHIES a small boat

DINGIER   comparative of dingy

DINGIEST   superlative of dingy

DINGILY   *adv* in a dingy manner

DINGLE   *n* pl. -S a dell

DINGO   *n* pl. -GOES a wild dog of Australia

DINGUS   *n* pl. -ES a gadget or object whose name is unknown or forgotten

DINGY   *n* pl. -GIES dinghy

DINGY   *adj* DINGIER, DINGIEST grimy

DINING   present participle of dine

DINK   *v* -ED, -ING, -S to adorn

DINKEY   *n* pl. -KEYS a small locomotive

DINKIER   comparative of dinky

DINKIES   pl. of dinky

DINKIEST   superlative of dinky

DINKLY   *adv* neatly

DINKUM   *adj* genuine

DINKY   *n* pl. -KIES dinkey

DINKY   *adj* -KIER, -KIEST small

DINNED   past tense of din

DINNER   *n* pl. -S the main meal of the day

DINNING   present participle of din

DINOSAUR   *n* pl. -S one of a group of extinct reptiles

DINT   *v* -ED, -ING, -S to dent

DIOBOL   *n* pl. -S a coin of ancient Greece

DIOBOLON   *n* pl. -S diobol

DIOCESAN   *n* pl. -S a bishop

DIOCESE   *n* pl. -S an ecclesiastical district

DIODE   *n* pl. -S a type of electron tube

DIOECISM   *n* pl. -S the state of being dioicous

DIOICOUS   *adj* unisexual

DIOL   *n* pl. -S a chemical compound

DIOLEFIN   *n* pl. -S a hydrocarbon

DIOPSIDE   *n* pl. -S a mineral

DIOPTASE   *n* pl. -S a mineral

DIOPTER   *n* pl. -S a measure of refractive power **DIOPTRAL** *adj*

DIOPTRE   *n* pl. -S diopter

DIOPTRIC   *adj* aiding the vision by refraction

DIORAMA   *n* pl. -S a three-dimensional exhibit **DIORAMIC** *adj*

DIORITE   *n* pl. -S an igneous rock **DIORITIC** *adj*

DIOXANE   *n* pl. -S a flammable liquid

DIOXID *n* pl. -S dioxide

DIOXIDE *n* pl. -S a type of oxide

DIP *v* DIPPED or DIPT, DIPPING, DIPS to immerse briefly into a liquid

DIPHASE *adj* having two phases

DIPHASIC *adj* diphase

DIPHENYL *n* pl. -S biphenyl

DIPLEGIA *n* pl. -S paralysis of the same part on both sides of the body

DIPLEX *adj* pertaining to the simultaneous transmission or reception of two radio signals

DIPLOE *n* pl. -S a bony tissue of the cranium **DIPLOIC** *adj*

DIPLOID *n* pl. -S a cell having the basic chromosome number doubled

DIPLOIDY *n* pl. -DIES the condition of being a diploid

DIPLOMA *n* pl. -MAS or -MATA a certificate of an academic degree

DIPLOMA *v* -ED, -ING, -S to furnish with a diploma

DIPLOMAT *n* pl. -S a governmental official

DIPLONT *n* pl. -S an organism having a particular chromosomal structure

DIPLOPIA *n* pl. -S double vision **DIPLOPIC** *adj*

DIPLOPOD *n* pl. -S a multi-legged insect

DIPLOSIS *n* pl. -LOSES a method of chromosome formation

DIPNOAN *n* pl. -S a lungfish

DIPODY *n* pl. -DIES a dimeter **DIPODIC** *adj*

DIPOLE *n* pl. -S a pair of equal and opposite electric charges **DIPOLAR** *adj*

DIPPABLE *adj* capable of being dipped

DIPPED a past tense of dip

DIPPER *n* pl. -S one that dips

DIPPING present participle of dip

DIPPY *adj* -PIER, -PIEST foolish

DIPSAS *n* pl. DIPSADES a fabled serpent

DIPSTICK *n* pl. -S a measuring rod

DIPT a past tense of dip

DIPTERA pl. of dipteron

DIPTERAL *adj* having two rows or columns

DIPTERAN *n* pl. -S a two-winged fly

DIPTERON *n* pl. -TERA dipteran

DIPTYCA *n* pl. -S diptych

DIPTYCH *n* pl. -S an ancient writing tablet

DIQUAT *n* pl. -S an herbicide

DIRDUM *n* pl. -S blame

DIRE *adj* DIRER, DIREST disastrous

DIRECT *v* -ED, -ING, -S to control or conduct the affairs of

DIRECT *adj* -RECTER, -RECTEST straightforward **DIRECTLY** *adv*

DIRECTOR *n* pl. -S one that directs

DIREFUL *adj* dreadful

DIRELY *adv* in a dire manner

DIRENESS *n* pl. -ES the state of being dire

DIRER comparative of dire

DIREST superlative of dire

DIRGE *n* pl. -S a funeral song **DIRGEFUL** *adj*

DIRHAM *n* pl. -S a monetary unit of Morocco

DIRIMENT *adj* nullifying

DIRK *v* -ED, -ING, -S to stab with a small knife

DIRL *v* -ED, -ING, -S to tremble

DIRNDL *n* pl. -S a woman's dress

DIRT *n* pl. -S earth or soil

DIRTY *adj* DIRTIER, DIRTIEST unclean **DIRTILY** *adv*

DIRTY *v* DIRTIED, DIRTYING, DIRTIES to make dirty

DISABLE *v* -ABLED, -ABLING, -ABLES to render incapable or unable

DISABUSE *v* -ABUSED, -ABUSING, -ABUSES to free from false or mistaken ideas

DISAGREE *v* -AGREED, -AGREEING, -AGREES to differ in opinion

DISALLOW *v* -ED, -ING, -S to refuse to allow

DISANNUL *v* -NULLED, -NULLING, -NULS to annul

DISARM *v* -ED, -ING, -S to deprive of weapons

DISARMER *n* pl. -S one that disarms

DISARRAY *v* -ED, -ING, -S to disorder

DISASTER *n* pl. -S a calamity

DISAVOW *v* -ED, -ING, -S to disclaim responsibility for

DISBAND   v -ED, -ING, -S to break up

DISBAR   v -BARRED, -BARRING, -BARS to expel from the legal profession

DISBOSOM   v -ED, -ING, -S to confess

DISBOUND   adj not having a binding

DISBOWEL   v -ELED, -ELING, -ELS or -ELLED, -ELLING, -ELS to remove the intestines of

DISBUD   v -BUDDED, -BUDDING, -BUDS to remove buds from

DISBURSE   v -BURSED, -BURSING, BURSES to pay out

DISC   v -ED, -ING, -S to disk

DISCANT   v -ED, -ING, -S to descant

DISCARD   v -ED, -ING, -S to throw away

DISCASE   v -CASED, -CASING, -CASES to remove the case of

DISCEPT   v -ED, -ING, -S to debate

DISCERN   v -ED, -ING, -S to perceive

DISCI   a pl. of discus

DISCIPLE   v -PLED, -PLING, -PLES to cause to become a follower

DISCLAIM   v -ED, -ING, -S to renounce any claim to or connection with

DISCLIKE   adj disklike

DISCLOSE   v -CLOSED, -CLOSING, -CLOSES to reveal

DISCO   n pl. -COS a discotheque

DISCOID   n pl. -S a disk

DISCOLOR   v -ED, -ING, -S to alter the color of

DISCORD   v -ED, -ING, -S to disagree

DISCOUNT   v -ED, -ING, -S to reduce the price of

DISCOVER   v -ED, -ING, -S to gain sight or knowledge of

DISCREET   adj -CREETER, -CREETEST tactful

DISCRETE   adj separate

DISCROWN   v -ED, -ING, -S to deprive of a crown

DISCUS   n pl. -CUSES or -CI a disk hurled in athletic competition

DISCUSS   v -ED, -ING, -ES to talk over or write about

DISDAIN   v -ED, -ING, -S to scorn

DISEASE   v -EASED, -EASING, -EASES to make unhealthy

DISENDOW   v -ED, -ING, -S to deprive of endowment

DISEUSE   n pl. -S a female entertainer

DISFAVOR   v -ED, -ING, -S to regard with disapproval

DISFROCK   v -ED, -ING, -S to unfrock

DISGORGE   v -GORGED, -GORGING, -GORGES to vomit

DISGRACE   v -GRACED, -GRACING, -GRACES to bring shame or discredit upon

DISGUISE   v -GUISED, -GUISING, -GUISES to alter the appearance of

DISGUST   v -ED, -ING, -S to cause nausea or loathing in

DISH   v -ED, -ING, -ES to put into a dish (a concave vessel)

DISHELM   v -ED, -ING, -S to deprive of a helmet

DISHERIT   v -ED, -ING, -S to deprive of an inheritance

DISHEVEL   v -ELED, -ELING, -ELS or -ELLED, -ELLING, -ELS to make messy

DISHFUL   n pl. -S as much as a dish can hold

DISHIER   comparative of dishy

DISHIEST   superlative of dishy

DISHLIKE   adj resembling a dish

DISHONOR   v -ED, -ING, -S to deprive of honor

DISHPAN   n pl. -S a pan for washing dishes

DISHRAG   n pl. -S a cloth for washing dishes

DISHWARE   n pl. -S tableware used in serving food

DISHY   adj DISHIER, DISHIEST attractive

DISINTER   v -TERRED, -TERRING, -TERS to exhume

DISJECT   v -ED, -ING, -S to disperse

DISJOIN   v -ED, -ING, -S to separate

DISJOINT   v -ED, -ING, -S to put out of order

DISJUNCT   n pl. -S an alternative in a logical disjunction

DISK   v -ED, -ING, -S to break up land with a type of farm implement

DISKLIKE   adj resembling a disk (a flat, circular plate)

DISLIKE *v* -LIKED, -LIKING, -LIKES to regard with aversion

DISLIKER *n* pl. -S one that dislikes

DISLIMN *v* -ED, -ING, -S to make dim

DISLODGE *v* -LODGED, -LODGING, -LODGES to remove from a firm position

DISLOYAL *adj* not loyal

DISMAL *n* pl. -S a track of swampy land

DISMAL *adj* -MALER, -MALEST cheerless and depressing **DISMALLY** *adv*

DISMAST *v* -ED, -ING, -S to remove the mast of

DISMAY *v* -ED, -ING, -S to deprive of courage or resolution

DISME *n* pl. -S a former coin of the United States

DISMISS *v* -ED, -ING, -ES to permit or cause to leave

DISMOUNT *v* -ED, -ING, -S to get down from an elevated position

DISOBEY *v* -ED, -ING, -S to fail to obey

DISOMIC *adj* having a number of chromosomes duplicated

DISORDER *v* -ED, -ING, -S to put out of order

DISOWN *v* -ED, -ING, -S to deny the ownership of

DISPART *v* -ED, -ING, -S to separate

DISPATCH *v* -ED, -ING, -ES to send off with speed

DISPEL *v* -PELLED, -PELLING, -PELS to drive off in various directions

DISPEND *v* -ED, -ING, -S to squander

DISPENSE *v* -PENSED, -PENSING, -PENSES to distribute

DISPERSE *v* -PERSED, -PERSING, -PERSES to scatter

DISPIRIT *v* -ED, -ING, -S to lower in spirit

DISPLACE *v* -PLACED, -PLACING, -PLACES to remove from the usual or proper place

DISPLANT *v* -ED, -ING, -S to dislodge

DISPLAY *v* -ED, -ING, -S to make evident or obvious

DISPLODE *v* -PLODED, -PLODING, -PLODES to explode

DISPLUME *v* -PLUMED, -PLUMING, -PLUMES to deplume

DISPORT *v* -ED, -ING, -S to amuse oneself

DISPOSAL *n* pl. -S the act of disposing

DISPOSE *v* -POSED, -POSING, -POSES to put in place

DISPOSER *n* pl. -S one that disposes

DISPREAD *v* -SPREAD, -SPREADING, -SPREADS to spread out

DISPRIZE *v* -PRIZED, -PRIZING, -PRIZES to disdain

DISPROOF *n* pl. -S the act of disproving

DISPROVE *v* -PROVED, -PROVEN, -PROVING, -PROVES to refute

DISPUTE *v* -PUTED, -PUTING, -PUTES to argue about

DISPUTER *n* pl. -S one that disputes

DISQUIET *v* -ED, -ING, -S to deprive of quiet, rest, or peace

DISRATE *v* -RATED, -RATING, -RATES to lower in rating or rank

DISROBE *v* -ROBED, -ROBING, -ROBES to undress

DISROBER *n* pl. -S one that disrobes

DISROOT *v* -ED, -ING, -S to uproot

DISRUPT *v* -ED, -ING, -S to throw into confusion

DISSAVE *v* -SAVED, -SAVING, -SAVES to use savings for current expenses

DISSEAT *v* -ED, -ING, -S to unseat

DISSECT *v* -ED, -ING, -S to cut apart for scientific examination

DISSEISE *v* -SEISED, -SEISING, -SEISES to deprive

DISSEIZE *v* -SEIZED, -SEIZING, -SEIZES to disseise

DISSENT *v* -ED, -ING, -S to disagree

DISSERT *v* -ED, -ING, -S to discuss in a learned or formal manner

DISSERVE *v* -SERVED, -SERVING, -SERVES to treat badly

DISSEVER *v* -ED, -ING, -S to sever

DISSOLVE *v* -SOLVED, -SOLVING, -SOLVES to make into a solution

DISSUADE *v* -SUADED, -SUADING, -SUADES to persuade not to do something

DISTAFF *n* pl. -TAFFS or -TAVES a type of staff

DISTAIN *v* -ED, -ING, -S to stain

DISTAL *adj* located far from the point of origin **DISTALLY** *adv*

DISTANCE   *v* -TANCED, -TANCING, -TANCES to leave behind

DISTANT   *adj* far off or apart

DISTASTE   *v* -TASTED, -TASTING, -TASTES to dislike

DISTAVES   a pl. of distaff

DISTEND   *v* -ED, -ING, -S to swell

DISTENT   *adj* distended

DISTICH   *n* pl. -S a couplet

DISTIL   *v* -TILLED, -TILLING, TILS to distill

DISTILL   *v* -ED, -ING, -S to extract by vaporization and condensation

DISTINCT   *adj* -TINCTER, -TINCTEST clearly different

DISTOME   *n* pl. -S a parasitic flatworm

DISTORT   *v* -ED, -ING, -S to twist or bend out of shape

DISTRACT   *v* -ED, -ING, -S to divert the attention of

DISTRAIN   *v* -ED, -ING, -S to seize and hold property as security

DISTRAIT   *adj* absentminded

DISTRESS   *v* -ED, -ING, -ES to cause anxiety or suffering to

DISTRICT   *v* -ED, -ING, -S to divide into localities

DISTRUST   *v* -ED, -ING, -S to have no trust in

DISTURB   *v* -ED, -ING, -S to interrupt the quiet, rest, or peace of

DISULFID   *n* pl. -S a chemical compound

DISUNION   *n* pl. -S the state of being disunited

DISUNITE   *v* -UNITED, -UNITING, -UNITES to separate

DISUNITY   *n* pl. -TIES lack of unity

DISUSE   *v* -USED, -USING, -USES to stop using

DISVALUE   *v* -UED, -UING, -UES to treat as of little value

DISYOKE   *v* -YOKED, -YOKING, -YOKES to free from a yoke

DIT   *n* pl. -S a dot in Morse code

DITA   *n* pl. -S a Philippine tree

DITCH   *v* -ED, -ING, -ES to dig a long, narrow excavation in the ground

DITCHER   *n* pl. -S one that ditches

DITE   *n* pl. -S a small amount

DITHEISM   *n* pl. -S belief in two coequal gods

DITHEIST   *n* pl. -S an adherent of ditheism

DITHER   *v* -ED, -ING, -S to act nervously or indecisively

DITHERY   *adj* nervously excited

DITHIOL   *adj* containing two chemical groups both of which include sulfur and hydrogen

DITTANY   *n* pl. -NIES a perennial herb

DITTO   *v* ED, -ING, -S to repeat

DITTY   *n* pl. -TIES a short, simple song

DIURESIS   *n* pl. DIURESES excessive discharge of urine

DIURETIC   *n* pl. -S a drug which increases urinary discharge

DIURNAL   *n* pl. -S a diary

DIURON   *n* pl. -S an herbicide

DIVA   *n* pl. -S a distinguished female operatic singer

DIVAGATE   *v* -GATED, -GATING, -GATES to wander

DIVALENT   *adj* having a valence of two

DIVAN   *n* pl. -S a sofa or couch

DIVE   *v* DIVED or DOVE, DIVING, DIVES to plunge headfirst into water

DIVER   *n* pl. -S one that dives

DIVERGE   *v* -VERGED, -VERGING, -VERGES to move in different directions from a common point

DIVERSE   *adj* different

DIVERT   *v* -ED, -ING, -S to turn aside

DIVERTER   *n* pl. -S one that diverts

DIVEST   *v* -ED, -ING, -S to strip or deprive of anything

DIVIDE   *v* -VIDED, -VIDING, -VIDES to separate into parts, areas, or groups

DIVIDEND   *n* pl. -S a quantity to be divided

DIVIDER   *n* pl. -S one that divides

DIVIDING   present participle of divide

DIVIDUAL   *adj* capable of being divided

DIVINE   *v* -VINED, -VINING, -VINES to foretell by occult means

DIVINE   *adj* -VINER, -VINEST pertaining to or characteristic of a god **DIVINELY** *adv*

DIVINER   *n* pl. -S one that divines

DIVING   present participle of dive

DIVINING present participle of divine

DIVINISE v -NISED, -NISING, -NISES to divinize

DIVINITY n pl. -TIES the state of being divine

DIVINIZE v -NIZED, -NIZING, -NIZES to make divine

DIVISION n pl. -S the act of dividing

DIVISIVE adj causing disunity or dissension

DIVISOR n pl. -S a number by which a dividend is divided

DIVORCE v -VORCED, -VORCING, -VORCES to terminate the marriage contract between

DIVORCEE n pl. -S a divorced woman

DIVORCER n pl. -S one that divorces

DIVORCING present participle of divorce

DIVOT n pl. -S a piece of turf

DIVULGE v -VULGED, -VULGING, -VULGES to reveal

DIVULGER n pl. -S one that divulges

DIVVY v -VIED, -VYING, -VIES to divide

DIWAN n pl. -S dewan

DIXIT n pl. -S a statement

DIZEN v -ED, -ING, -S to dress in fine clothes

DIZYGOUS adj developed from two fertilized ova

DIZZY adj -ZIER, -ZIEST having a sensation of whirling **DIZZILY** adv

DIZZY v -ZIED, -ZYING, -ZIES to make dizzy

DJEBEL n pl. -S jebel

DJELLABA n pl. -S a long hooded garment

DJIN n pl. -S jinni

DJINN n pl. -S jinni

DJINNI n pl. DJINN jinni

DJINNY n pl. DJINN jinni

DO v DID or DIDST, DONE, DOING, present sing. 2d person DO, DOEST or DOST, 3d person DOES, DOETH or DOTH to begin and carry through to completion

DO n pl. DOS the first tone of the diatonic musical scale

DOABLE adj able to be done

DOAT v -ED, -ING, -S to dote

DOBBER n pl. -S a float for a fishing line

DOBBIN n pl. -S a farm horse

DOBBY n pl. -BIES a fool

DOBIE n pl. -S adobe

DOBIES pl. of doby

DOBLA n pl. -S a former gold coin of Spain

DOBLON n pl. -S or -ES a former gold coin of Spain and Spanish America

DOBRA n pl. -S a former gold coin of Portugal

DOBSON n pl. -S an aquatic insect larva

DOBY n pl. -BIES dobie

DOC n pl. -S doctor

DOCENT n pl. -S a college or university lecturer

DOCETIC adj pertaining to a religious doctrine

DOCILE adj easily trained **DOCILELY** adv

DOCILITY n pl. -TIES the quality of being docile

DOCK v -ED, -ING, -S to bring into a dock (a wharf)

DOCKAGE n pl. -S a charge for the use of a dock

DOCKER n pl. -S a dock worker

DOCKET v -ED, -ING, -S to supply with an identifying statement

DOCKHAND n pl. -S a docker

DOCKLAND n pl. -S the part of a port occupied by docks

DOCKSIDE n pl. -S the area adjacent to a dock

DOCKYARD n pl. -S a shipyard

DOCTOR v -ED, -ING, -S to treat medically

DOCTORAL adj pertaining to a doctor

DOCTRINE n pl. -S a belief or set of beliefs taught or advocated

DOCUMENT v -ED, -ING, -S to support by conclusive information or evidence

DODDER v -ED, -ING, -S to totter

DODDERER n pl. -S one that dodders

DODDERY adj feeble

DODGE v DODGED, DODGING, DODGES to evade

DODGER n pl. -S one that dodges

DODGERY n pl. -ERIES evasion

DODGING	present participle of dodge	**DOGGONE**	v -GONED, -GONING, -GONES to damn
DODGY	adj DODGIER, DODGIEST evasive	**DOGGONE**	adj -GONER, -GONEST damned
DODO	n pl. -DOES or -DOS an extinct flightless bird	**DOGGONED**	adj -GONEDER, -GONEDEST damned
DODOISM	n pl. -S a stupid remark	**DOGGONING**	present participle of doggone
DOE	n pl. -S a female deer	**DOGGREL**	n pl. -S doggerel
DOER	n pl. -S one that does something	**DOGGY**	n pl. -GIES a small dog
DOES	a present 3d person sing. of do	**DOGGY**	adj -GIER, -GIEST resembling or suggestive of a dog
DOESKIN	n pl. -S the skin of a doe	**DOGHOUSE**	n pl. -S a shelter for a dog
DOEST	a present 2d person sing. of do	**DOGIE**	n pl. -S a stray calf
DOETH	a present 3d person sing. of do	**DOGIES**	pl. of dogy
DOFF	v -ED, -ING, -S to take off	**DOGLEG**	v -LEGGED, -LEGGING, -LEGS to move along a bent course
DOFFER	n pl. -S one that doffs	**DOGLIKE**	adj resembling a dog
DOG	v DOGGED, DOGGING, DOGS to follow after like a dog (a domesticated, carnivorous mammal)	**DOGMA**	n pl. -MAS or -MATA a principle or belief put forth as authoritative DOGMATIC adj
DOGBANE	n pl. -S a perennial herb	**DOGNAP**	v -NAPED, -NAPING, -NAPS or -NAPPED, -NAPPING, -NAPS to steal a dog
DOGBERRY	n pl. -RIES a wild berry		
DOGCART	n pl. -S a one-horse carriage	**DOGNAPER**	n pl. -S one that dognaps
DOGDOM	n pl. -S the world of dogs	**DOGSBODY**	n pl. -BODIES a menial worker
DOGE	n pl. -S the chief magistrate in the former republics of Venice and Genoa	**DOGSLED**	n pl. -S a sled drawn by dogs
		DOGTOOTH	n pl. -TEETH a cuspid
DOGEDOM	n pl. -S the domain of a doge	**DOGTROT**	v -TROTTED, -TROTTING, -TROTS to move at a steady trot
DOGESHIP	n pl. -S the office of a doge		
DOGEY	n pl. -GEYS dogie	**DOGVANE**	n pl. -S a small vane
DOGFACE	n pl. -S a soldier in the U.S. Army	**DOGWATCH**	n pl. -ES a short period of watch duty on a ship
DOGFIGHT	v -FOUGHT, -FIGHTING, -FIGHTS to engage in an aerial battle	**DOGWOOD**	n pl. -S a tree
		DOGY	n pl. -GIES dogie
DOGFISH	n pl. -ES a small shark	**DOILED**	adj dazed
DOGGED	past tense of dog	**DOILY**	n pl. -LIES a small napkin
DOGGEDLY	adv stubbornly	**DOING**	n pl. -S an action
DOGGER	n pl. -S a fishing vessel	**DOIT**	n pl. -S a former Dutch coin
DOGGEREL	n pl. -S trivial, awkwardly written verse	**DOITED**	adj old and feeble
DOGGERY	n pl. -GERIES surly behavior	**DOJO**	n pl. -JOS a school that teaches judo or karate
DOGGIE	n pl. -S doggy	**DOL**	n pl. -S a unit of pain intensity
DOGGIER	comparative of doggy	**DOLCE**	n pl. -CI a soft-toned organ stop
DOGGIES	pl. of doggy	**DOLDRUMS**	n/pl a state of inactivity or stagnation
DOGGIEST	superlative of doggy		
DOGGING	present participle of dog	**DOLE**	v DOLED, DOLING, DOLES to distribute in small portions
DOGGISH	adj doglike		
DOGGO	adv in hiding	**DOLEFUL**	adj -FULLER, -FULLEST mournful
		DOLERITE	n pl. -S a variety of basalt

DOLESOME *adj* doleful

DOLING present participle of dole

DOLL *v* -ED, -ING, -S to dress stylishly

DOLLAR *n* pl. -S a monetary unit of the United States

DOLLIED past tense of dolly

DOLLIES present 3d person sing. of dolly

DOLLISH *adj* pretty

DOLLOP *n* pl. -S a serving

DOLLY *v* -LIED, -LYING, -LIES to move on a wheeled platform

DOLMAN *n* pl. -S a Turkish robe

DOLMEN *n* pl. -S a prehistoric monument

DOLOMITE *n* pl. -S a mineral

DOLOR *n* pl. -S grief

DOLOROSO *adj* having a mournful musical quality

DOLOROUS *adj* mournful

DOLOUR *n* pl. -S dolor

DOLPHIN *n* pl. -S a marine mammal

DOLT *n* pl. -S a stupid person **DOLTISH** *adj*

DOM *n* pl. -S a title given to certain monks

DOMAIN *n* pl. -S an area of control

DOMAL *adj* domical

DOME *v* DOMED, DOMING, DOMES to cover with a dome (a rounded roof)

DOMELIKE *adj* resembling a dome

DOMESDAY *n* pl. -DAYS doomsday

DOMESTIC *n* pl. -S a household servant

DOMIC *adj* domical

DOMICAL *adj* shaped like a dome

DOMICIL *v* -ED, -ING, -S to domicile

DOMICILE *v* -CILED, -CILING, -CILES to establish a residence

DOMINANT *n* pl. -S a controlling genetic character

DOMINATE *v* -NATED, -NATING, -NATES to control

DOMINE *n* pl. -S master

DOMINEER *v* -ED, -ING, -S to tyrannize

DOMING present participle of dome

DOMINICK *n* pl. -S one of an American breed of chickens

DOMINIE *n* pl. -S a clergyman

DOMINION *n* pl. -S supreme authority

DOMINIUM *n* pl. -S the right of ownership and control of property

DOMINO *n* pl. -NOES or -NOS a small mask

DON *v* DONNED, DONNING, DONS to put on

DONA *n* pl. -S a Spanish lady

DONATE *v* -NATED, -NATING, -NATES to contribute

DONATION *n* pl. -S something donated

DONATIVE *n* pl. -S a donation

DONATOR *n* pl. -S a donor

DONE past tense of do

DONEE *n* pl. -S a recipient of a gift

DONENESS *n* pl. -ES the state of being cooked enough

DONG *n* pl. -S a deep sound like that of a large bell

DONGOLA *n* pl. -S a type of leather

DONJON *n* pl. -S the main tower of a castle

DONKEY *n* pl. -KEYS the domestic ass

DONNA *n* pl. DONNAS or DONNE an Italian lady

DONNED past tense of don

DONNEE *n* pl. -S the set of assumptions upon which a story proceeds

DONNERD *adj* donnered

DONNERED *adj* dazed

DONNERT *adj* donnered

DONNING present participle of don

DONNISH *adj* scholarly

DONOR *n* pl. -S one that donates

DONSIE *adj* unlucky

DONSY *adj* donsie

DONUT *n* pl. -S doughnut

DONZEL *n* pl. -S a young squire

DOODAD *n* pl. -S a dingus

DOODLE *v* -DLED, -DLING, -DLES to draw or scribble aimlessly

DOODLER *n* pl. -S one that doodles

DOOLEE *n* pl. -S a stretcher for the sick or wounded

DOOLIE *n* pl. -S doolee

DOOLY *n* pl. -LIES doolee

DOOM *v* -ED, -ING, -S to destine to an unhappy fate

DOOMFUL *adj* ominous

DOOMSDAY *n pl.* -DAYS judgment day

DOOMSTER *n pl.* -S a judge

DOOR *n pl.* -S a movable barrier for opening and closing an entranceway

DOORBELL *n pl.* -S a bell at a door

DOORJAMB *n pl.* -S a vertical piece at the side of a doorway

DOORKNOB *n pl.* -S a handle for opening a door

DOORLESS *adj* having no door

DOORMAN *n pl.* -MEN the door attendant of a building

DOORMAT *n pl.* -S a mat placed in front of a door

DOORNAIL *n pl.* -S a large-headed nail

DOORPOST *n pl.* -S a doorjamb

DOORSILL *n pl.* -S the sill of a door

DOORSTEP *n pl.* -S a step leading to a door

DOORSTOP *n pl.* -S a wedge for holding a door open

DOORWAY *n pl.* -WAYS the entranceway to a room or building

DOORYARD *n pl.* -S a yard in front of a house

DOOZER *n pl.* -S an extraordinary one of its kind

DOOZY *n pl.* -ZIES doozer

DOPA *n pl.* -S an amino acid

DOPAMINE *n pl.* -S a form of dopa

DOPANT *n pl.* -S an impurity added to a pure substance

DOPE *v* DOPED, DOPING, DOPES to give a narcotic to

DOPER *n pl.* -S one that dopes

DOPESTER *n pl.* -S a forecaster of the outcome of sports events or other contests

DOPEY *adj* DOPIER, DOPIEST lethargic; stupid

DOPIER comparative of dopy

DOPIEST superlative of dopy

DOPINESS *n pl.* -ES the state of being dopey

DOPING present participle of dope

DOPY *adj* DOPIER, DOPIEST dopey

DOR *n pl.* -S a black European beetle

DORADO *n pl.* -DOS a marine fish

DORBUG *n pl.* -S a dor

DORHAWK *n pl.* -S a nocturnal bird

DORIES pl. of dory

DORM *n pl.* -S a dormitory

DORMANCY *n pl.* -CIES the state of being dormant

DORMANT *adj* lying asleep

DORMER *n pl.* -S a type of window

DORMICE pl. of dormouse

DORMIE *adj* being ahead by as many holes in golf as remain to be played

DORMIENT *adj* dormant

DORMIN *n pl.* -S a plant hormone

DORMOUSE *n pl.* -MICE a small rodent

DORMY *adj* dormie

DORNECK *n pl.* -S dornick

DORNICK *n pl.* -S a heavy linen fabric

DORNOCK *n pl.* -S dornick

DORP *n pl.* -S a village

DORPER *n pl.* -S one of a breed of mutton-producing sheep

DORR *n pl.* -S dor

DORSA pl. of dorsum

DORSAD *adv* dorsally

DORSAL *n pl.* -S a dorsally located anatomical part

DORSALLY *adv* toward the back

DORSER *n pl.* -S dosser

DORSUM *n pl.* -SA the back

DORTY *adj* sullen

DORY *n pl.* -RIES a flat-bottomed boat

DOSAGE *n pl.* -S the amount of medicine to be given

DOSE *v* DOSED, DOSING, DOSES to give a specified quantity of medicine to

DOSER *n pl.* -S one that doses

DOSS *v* -ED, -ING, -ES to sleep in any convenient place

DOSSAL *n pl.* -S an ornamental cloth hung behind an altar

DOSSEL *n pl.* -S dossal

DOSSER *n pl.* -S a basket carried on the back

DOSSERET *n pl.* -S a block resting on the capital of a column

DOSSIER	*n* pl. -S a file of papers on a single subject	**DOUBTER**	*n* pl. -S one that doubts
DOSSIL	*n* pl. -S a cloth roll for wiping ink	**DOUBTFUL**	*adj* uncertain
DOST	a present 2d person sing. of do	**DOUCE**	*adj* sedate **DOUCELY** *adv*
DOT	*v* DOTTED, DOTTING, DOTS to cover with dots (tiny round marks)	**DOUCEUR**	*n* pl. -S a gratuity
		DOUCHE	*v* DOUCHED, DOUCHING, DOUCHES to cleanse with a jet of water
DOTAGE	*n* pl. -S a state of senility	**DOUGH**	*n* pl. -S a flour mixture
DOTAL	*adj* pertaining to a dowry	**DOUGHBOY**	*n* pl. -BOYS an infantryman
DOTARD	*n* pl. -S a senile person **DOTARDLY** *adj*	**DOUGHIER**	comparative of doughy
DOTATION	*n* pl. -S an endowment	**DOUGHIEST**	superlative of doughy
DOTE	*v* DOTED, DOTING, DOTES to show excessive affection	**DOUGHNUT**	*n* pl. -S a ring-shaped cake
		DOUGHT	a past tense of dow
DOTER	*n* pl. -S one that dotes	**DOUGHTY**	*adj* -TIER, -TIEST courageous
DOTH	a present 3d person sing. of do	**DOUGHY**	*adj* DOUGHIER, DOUGHIEST resembling dough
DOTIER	comparative of doty		
DOTIEST	superlative of doty	**DOUMA**	*n* pl. -S duma
DOTING	present participle of dote	**DOUR**	*adj* DOURER, DOUREST sullen
DOTINGLY	*adv* in an excessively affectionate manner	**DOURA**	*n* pl. -S durra
		DOURAH	*n* pl. -S durra
DOTTED	past tense of dot	**DOURINE**	*n* pl. -S a disease of horses
DOTTEL	*n* pl. -S dottle	**DOURLY**	*adv* in a dour manner
DOTTER	*n* pl. -S one that dots	**DOURNESS**	*n* pl. -ES the state of being dour
DOTTEREL	*n* pl. -S a shore bird	**DOUSE**	*v* DOUSED, DOUSING, DOUSES to plunge into water
DOTTIER	comparative of dotty		
DOTTIEST	superlative of dotty	**DOUSER**	*n* pl. -S one that douses
DOTTILY	*adv* in a dotty manner	**DOUZEPER**	*n* pl. -S one of twelve legendary knights
DOTTING	present participle of dot		
DOTTLE	*n* pl. -S a mass of half-burnt pipe tobacco	**DOVE**	*n* pl. -S a bird of the pigeon family
DOTTREL	*n* pl. -S dotterel	**DOVECOT**	*n* pl. -S dovecote
DOTTY	*adj* -TIER, -TIEST crazy	**DOVECOTE**	*n* pl. -S a roost for domesticated pigeons
DOTY	*adj* DOTIER, DOTIEST stained by decay	**DOVEKEY**	*n* pl. -KEYS dovekie
DOUBLE	*v* -BLED, -BLING, -BLES to make twice as great	**DOVEKIE**	*n* pl. -S a seabird
		DOVELIKE	*adj* resembling or suggestive of a dove
DOUBLER	*n* pl. -S one that doubles	**DOVEN**	*v* -ED, -ING, -S to daven
DOUBLET	*n* pl. -S a close-fitting jacket	**DOVETAIL**	*v* -ED, -ING, -S to fit together closely
DOUBLING	present participle of double		
DOUBLOON	*n* pl. -S a former Spanish gold coin	**DOVISH**	*adj* not warlike
DOUBLURE	*n* pl. -S the lining of a book cover	**DOW**	*v* DOWED or DOUGHT, DOWING, DOWS to prosper
DOUBLY	*adv* to twice the degree	**DOWABLE**	*adj* entitled to an endowment
DOUBT	*v* -ED, -ING, -S to be uncertain about	**DOWAGER**	*n* pl. -S a dignified elderly woman

DOWDY	*adj* DOWDIER, DOWDIEST lacking in stylishness or neatness **DOWDILY** *adv* **DOWDYISH** *adj*
DOWDY	*n pl.* DOWDIES a dowdy woman
DOWEL	*v* -ELED, -ELING, -ELS or -ELLED, -ELLING, -ELS to fasten with wooden pins
DOWER	*v* -ED, -ING, -S to provide with a dowry
DOWERY	*n pl.* -ERIES dowry
DOWIE	*adj* dreary
DOWN	*v* -ED, -ING, -S to cause to fall
DOWNBEAT	*n pl.* -S the first beat of a musical measure
DOWNCAST	*n pl.* -S an overthrow or ruin
DOWNCOME	*n pl.* -S downfall
DOWNER	*n pl.* -S a depressant drug
DOWNFALL	*n pl.* -S a sudden fall
DOWNHAUL	*n pl.* -S a rope for hauling down sails
DOWNHILL	*n pl.* -S a downward slope
DOWNIER	comparative of downy
DOWNIEST	superlative of downy
DOWNPLAY	*v* -ED, -ING, -S to de-emphasize
DOWNPOUR	*n pl.* -S a heavy rain
DOWNTIME	*n pl.* -S the time when a machine or factory is inactive
DOWNTOWN	*n pl.* -S the business district of a city
DOWNTROD	*adj* oppressed
DOWNTURN	*n pl.* -S a downward turn
DOWNWARD	*adv* from a higher to a lower place
DOWNWIND	*adv* in the direction that the wind blows
DOWNY	*adj* DOWNIER, DOWNIEST soft
DOWRY	*n pl.* -RIES the money or property a wife brings to her husband at marriage
DOWSABEL	*n pl.* -S a sweetheart
DOWSE	*v* DOWSED, DOWSING, DOWSES to search for underground water with a divining rod
DOWSER	*n pl.* -S one that dowses
DOXIE	*n pl.* -S doxy
DOXOLOGY	*n pl.* -GIES a hymn or verse of praise to God
DOXY	*n pl.* DOXIES a doctrine

DOYEN	*n pl.* -S the senior member of a group
DOYENNE	*n pl.* -S a female doyen
DOYLEY	*n pl.* -LEYS doily
DOYLY	*n pl.* -LIES doily
DOZE	*v* DOZED, DOZING, DOZES to sleep lightly
DOZEN	*v* -ED, -ING, -S to stun
DOZENTH	*n pl.* -S twelfth
DOZER	*n pl.* -S one that dozes
DOZILY	*adv* in a dozy manner
DOZINESS	*n pl.* -ES the state of being dozy
DOZING	present participle of doze
DOZY	*adj* DOZIER, DOZIEST drowsy
DRAB	*adj* DRABBER, DRABBEST cheerless
DRAB	*v* DRABBED, DRABBING, DRABS to consort with prostitutes
DRABBET	*n pl.* -S a coarse linen fabric
DRABBLE	*v* -BLED, -BLING, -BLES to draggle
DRABLY	*adv* in a drab manner
DRABNESS	*n pl.* -ES the quality of being drab
DRACAENA	*n pl.* -S a tropical plant
DRACHM	*n pl.* -S a unit of weight
DRACHMA	*n pl.* -MAS, -MAE or -MAI a Greek coin
DRACONIC	*adj* pertaining to a dragon
DRAFF	*n pl.* -S the damp remains of malt after brewing
DRAFFISH	*adj* draffy
DRAFFY	*adj* DRAFFIER, DRAFFIEST worthless
DRAFT	*v* -ED, -ING, -S to conscript for military service
DRAFTEE	*n pl.* -S one that is drafted
DRAFTER	*n pl.* -S one that drafts
DRAFTING	*n pl.* -S mechanical drawing
DRAFTY	*adj* DRAFTIER, DRAFTIEST having or exposed to currents of air **DRAFTILY** *adv*
DRAG	*v* DRAGGED, DRAGGING, DRAGS to pull along the ground
DRAGEE	*n pl.* -S a sugarcoated candy
DRAGGER	*n pl.* -S one that drags
DRAGGIER	comparative of draggy

DRAGGIEST superlative of draggy

DRAGGING present participle of drag

DRAGGLE v -GLED, -GLING, -GLES to make wet and dirty

DRAGGY adj -GIER, -GIEST sluggish

DRAGLINE n pl. -S a line used for dragging

DRAGNET n pl. -S a net for trawling

DRAGOMAN n pl. -MANS or -MEN an interpreter in Near Eastern countries

DRAGON n pl. -S a mythical, serpentlike monster

DRAGONET n pl. -S a marine fish

DRAGOON v -ED, -ING, -S to harass by the use of troops

DRAGROPE n pl. -S a rope used for dragging

DRAGSTER n pl. -S a vehicle used in drag racing

DRAIL n pl. -S a heavy fishhook

DRAIN v -ED, -ING, -S to draw off a liquid

DRAINAGE n pl. -S the act of draining

DRAINER n pl. -S one that drains

DRAKE n pl. -S a male duck

DRAM v DRAMMED, DRAMMING, DRAMS to tipple

DRAMA n pl. -S a composition written for theatrical performance

DRAMATIC adj pertaining to drama

DRAMMED past tense of dram

DRAMMING present participle of dram

DRAMMOCK n pl. -S raw oatmeal mixed with cold water

DRAMSHOP n pl. -S a barroom

DRANK past tense of drink

DRAPE v DRAPED, DRAPING, DRAPES to arrange in graceful folds **DRAPABLE** adj

DRAPER n pl. -S a dealer in cloth

DRAPERY n pl. -ERIES cloth arranged in graceful folds

DRAPING present participle of drape

DRASTIC adj extremely severe

DRAT v DRATTED, DRATTING, DRATS to damn

DRAUGHT v -ED, -ING, -S to draft

DRAUGHTY adj DRAUGHTIER, DRAUGHTIEST drafty

DRAVE a past tense of drive

DRAW v DREW, DRAWN, DRAWING, DRAWS to move by pulling **DRAWABLE** adj

DRAWBACK n pl. -S a hindrance

DRAWBAR n pl. -S a railroad coupler

DRAWBORE n pl. -S a hole for joining a mortise and tenon

DRAWDOWN n pl. -S a lowering of a water level

DRAWEE n pl. -S the person on whom a bill of exchange is drawn

DRAWER n pl. -S one that draws

DRAWING n pl. -S a portrayal in lines of a form or figure

DRAWL v -ED, -ING, -S to speak slowly with vowels greatly prolonged

DRAWLER n pl. -S one that drawls

DRAWLY adj DRAWLIER, DRAWLIEST marked by drawling

DRAWN past participle of draw

DRAWTUBE n pl. -S a tube that slides within another tube

DRAY v -ED, -ING, -S to transport by dray (a low, strong cart)

DRAYAGE n pl. -S transportation by dray

DRAYMAN n pl. -MEN one who drives a dray

DREAD v -ED, -ING, -S to fear greatly

DREADFUL n pl. -S a publication containing sensational material

DREAM v DREAMED or DREAMT, DREAMING, DREAMS to have a dream (a series of images occurring during sleep)

DREAMER n pl. -S one that dreams

DREAMFUL adj dreamy

DREAMT a past tense of dream

DREAMY adj DREAMIER, DREAMIEST full of dreams **DREAMILY** adv

DREAR adj dreary

DREARY adj DREARIEST, DREARIER dismal **DREARILY** adv

DREARY n pl. DREARIES a dismal person

DRECK n pl. -S rubbish

DREDGE v DREDGED, DREDGING, DREDGES to clear with a scooping device

DREDGER n pl. -S one that dredges

DREDGING n pl. -S matter that is dredged up

DREE   v DREED, DREEING, DREES to suffer

DREG   n pl. -S the sediment of liquors **DREGGISH** adj

DREGGY   adj -GIER, -GIEST full of dregs

DREICH   adj dreary

DREIDEL   n pl. -S a spinning toy

DREIDL   n pl. -S dreidel

DREIGH   adj dreich

DREK   n pl. -S dreck

DRENCH   v -ED, -ING, -ES to wet thoroughly

DRENCHER   n pl. -S one that drenches

DRESS   v DRESSED or DREST, DRESSING, DRESSES to put clothes on

DRESSAGE   n pl. -S the training of a horse in obedience and deportment

DRESSER   n pl. -S one that dresses

DRESSING   n pl. -S material applied to cover a wound

DRESSY   adj DRESSIER, DRESSIEST stylish **DRESSILY** adv

DREST   a past tense of dress

DREW   past tense of draw

DRIB   v DRIBBED, DRIBBING, DRIBS to drip

DRIBBLE   v -BLED, -BLING, -BLES to drivel

DRIBBLER   n pl. -S one that dribbles

DRIBBLET   n pl. -S driblet

DRIBBLING   present participle of dribble

DRIBLET   n pl. -S a small drop of liquid

DRIED   past tense of dry

DRIER   n pl. -S one that dries

DRIES   present 3d person sing. of dry

DRIEST   a superlative of dry

DRIFT   v -ED, -ING, -S to move along in a current

DRIFTAGE   n pl. -S the act of drifting

DRIFTER   n pl. -S one that drifts

DRIFTPIN   n pl. -S a metal rod for securing timbers

DRIFTY   adj DRIFTIER, DRIFTIEST full of drifts (masses of wind-driven snow)

DRILL   v -ED, -ING, -S to bore a hole in

DRILLER   n pl. -S one that drills

DRILLING   n pl. -S a heavy twilled cotton fabric

DRILY   adv dryly

DRINK   v DRANK, DRUNK, DRINKING, DRINKS to swallow liquid

DRINKER   n pl. -S one that drinks

DRIP   v DRIPPED or DRIPT, DRIPPING, DRIPS to fall in drops

DRIPLESS   adj designed not to drip

DRIPPER   n pl. -S something from which a liquid drips

DRIPPING   n pl. -S juice drawn from meat during cooking

DRIPPY   adj -PIER, -PIEST very wet

DRIPT   a past tense of drip

DRIVE   v DROVE or DRAVE, DRIVEN, DRIVING, DRIVES to urge or propel forward **DRIVABLE** adj

DRIVEL   v -ELED, -ELING, -ELS or -ELLED, -ELLING, -ELS to let saliva flow from the mouth

DRIVELER   n pl. -S one that drivels

DRIVEN   past participle of drive

DRIVER   n pl. -S one that drives

DRIVEWAY   n pl. -WAYS a private road providing access to a building

DRIVING   present participle of drive

DRIZZLE   v -ZLED, -ZLING, -ZLES to rain lightly

DRIZZLY   adj -ZLIER, -ZLIEST characterized by light rain

DROGUE   n pl. -S a canvas bag dragged behind a ship to reduce drifting

DROIT   n pl. -S a legal right

DROLL   adj DROLLER, DROLLEST comical

DROLL   v -ED, -ING, -S to jest

DROLLERY   n pl. -ERIES something droll

DROLLY   adv in a droll manner

DROMON   n pl. -S dromond

DROMOND   n pl. -S a large fast-sailing medieval galley

DRONE   v DRONED, DRONING, DRONES to make a continuous low sound

DRONER   n pl. -S one that drones

DRONGO   n pl. -GOS a tropical bird

DRONING   present participle of drone

DRONISH   adj habitually lazy

DROOL   v -ED, -ING, -S to drivel

DROOP   v -ED, -ING, -S to hang downward

DROOPY   adj DROOPIER, DROOPIEST drooping **DROOPILY** adv

DROP   v DROPPED or DROPT, DROPPING, DROPS to fall in drops (globules)

DROPHEAD   n pl. -S a convertible car

DROPKICK   n pl. -S a type of kick in football

DROPLET   n pl. -S a tiny drop

DROPOUT   n pl. -S one who quits school prematurely

DROPPED   past tense of drop

DROPPER   n pl. -S a tube for dispensing liquid in drops

DROPPING   n pl. -S something that has been dropped

DROPSHOT   n pl. -S a type of shot in tennis

DROPSY   n pl. -SIES an excessive accumulation of serous fluid **DROPSIED** adj

DROPT   a past tense of drop

DROPWORT   n pl. -S a perennial herb

DROSERA   n pl. -S a sundew

DROSHKY   n pl. -KIES an open carriage

DROSKY   n pl. -KIES droshky

DROSS   n pl. -ES waste matter

DROSSY   adj DROSSIER, DROSSIEST worthless

DROUGHT   n pl. -S a dry period

DROUGHTY   adj DROUGHTIER, DROUGHTIEST dry

DROUK   v -ED, -ING, -S to drench

DROUTH   n pl. -S drought

DROUTHY   adj DROUTHIER, DROUTHIEST droughty

DROVE   v DROVED, DROVING, DROVES to drive cattle or sheep

DROVER   n pl. -S a driver of cattle or sheep

DROWN   v -ED, -ING, -S to suffocate in water

DROWND   v -ED, -ING, -S to drown

DROWNER   n pl. -S one that drowns

DROWSE   v DROWSED, DROWSING, DROWSES to doze

DROWSY   adj DROWSIER, DROWSIEST sleepy **DROWSILY** adv

DRUB   v DRUBBED, DRUBBING, DRUBS to beat severely

DRUBBER   n pl. -S one that drubs

DRUBBING   n pl. -S a severe beating

DRUDGE   v DRUDGED, DRUDGING, DRUDGES to do hard, menial, or tedious work

DRUDGER   n pl. -S one that drudges

DRUDGERY   n pl. -ERIES hard, menial, or tedious work

DRUDGING   present participle of drudge

DRUG   v DRUGGED, DRUGGING, DRUGS to affect with a medicinal substance

DRUGGET   n pl. -S a coarse woolen fabric

DRUGGIST   n pl. -S a pharmacist

DRUID   n pl. -S one of an ancient Celtic order of priests **DRUIDIC** adj

DRUIDESS   n pl. -ES a female druid

DRUIDISM   n pl. -S the religious system of the druids

DRUM   v DRUMMED, DRUMMING, DRUMS to beat a drum (a percussion instrument)

DRUMBEAT   n pl. -S the sound of a drum

DRUMBLE   v -BLED, -BLING, -BLES to move slowly

DRUMFIRE   n pl. -S heavy, continuous gunfire

DRUMFISH   n pl. -ES a fish that makes a drumming sound

DRUMHEAD   n pl. -S the material stretched over the end of a drum

DRUMLIER   comparative of drumly

DRUMLIEST   superlative of drumly

DRUMLIKE   adj resembling the head of a drum

DRUMLIN   n pl. -S a long hill of glacial drift

DRUMLY   adj -LIER, -LIEST dark and gloomy

DRUMMED   past tense of drum

DRUMMER   n pl. -S one that drums

DRUMMING   present participle of drum

DRUMROLL   n pl. -S a roll played on a drum

DRUNK   adj DRUNKER, DRUNKEST intoxicated

DRUNK   n pl. -S a drunken person

DRUNKARD   n pl. -S one who is habitually drunk

DRUNKEN   adj drunk

DRUPE   n pl. -S a fleshy fruit

DRUPELET   n pl. -S a small drupe

DRUSE *n* pl. -S a crust of small crystals lining a rock cavity

DRUTHERS *n/pl* one's preference

DRY *adj* DRIER, DRIEST or DRYER, DRYEST having no moisture

DRY *v* DRIED, DRYING, DRIES to make dry **DRYABLE** *adj*

DRY *n* pl. DRYS a prohibitionist

DRYAD *n* pl. -S or -ES a nymph of the woods **DRYADIC** *adj*

DRYER *n* pl. -S drier

DRYLOT *n* pl. -S an enclosure for livestock

DRYLY *adv* in a dry manner

DRYNESS *n* pl. -ES the state of being dry

DRYPOINT *n* pl. -S a method of engraving

DUAD *n* pl. -S a pair

DUAL *n* pl. -S a linguistic form

DUALISM *n* pl. -S a philosophical theory

DUALIST *n* pl. -S an adherent of dualism

DUALITY *n* pl. -TIES the state of being twofold

DUALIZE *v* -IZED, -IZING, -IZES to make twofold

DUALLY *adv* in two ways

DUB *v* DUBBED, DUBBING, DUBS to confer knighthood on

DUBBER *n* pl. -S one that dubs

DUBBIN *n* pl. -S material for softening and waterproofing leather

DUBBING *n* pl. -S dubbin

DUBIETY *n* pl. -ETIES the state of being dubious

DUBIOUS *adj* doubtful

DUBONNET *n* pl. -S a red color

DUC *n* pl. -S a duke

DUCAL *adj* pertaining to a duke **DUCALLY** *adv*

DUCAT *n* pl. -S any of several gold coins formerly used in Europe

DUCE *n* pl. DUCES or DUCI a leader

DUCHESS *n* pl. -ES the wife or widow of a duke

DUCHY *n* pl. DUCHIES the domain of a duke

DUCI a pl. of duce

DUCK *v* -ED, -ING, -S to lower quickly

DUCKBILL *n* pl. -S a platypus

DUCKER *n* pl. -S one that ducks

DUCKIE *adj* ducky

DUCKIER comparative of ducky

DUCKIES pl. of ducky

DUCKIEST superlative of ducky

DUCKLING *n* pl. -S a young duck

DUCKPIN *n* pl. -S a type of bowling pin

DUCKTAIL *n* pl. -S a style of haircut

DUCKWEED *n* pl. -S an aquatic plant

DUCKY *adj* DUCKIER, DUCKIEST excellent

DUCKY *n* pl. DUCKIES a darling

DUCT *v* -ED, -ING, -S to convey through a duct (a tubular passage)

DUCTILE *adj* easily molded or shaped

DUCTING *n* pl. -S a system of ducts

DUCTLESS *adj* being without a duct

DUCTULE *n* pl. -S a small duct

DUD *n* pl. -S a bomb that fails to explode

DUDDIE *adj* ragged

DUDDY *adj* duddie

DUDE *n* pl. -S a dandy

DUDEEN *n* pl. -S a short tobacco pipe

DUDGEON *n* pl. -S a feeling of resentment

DUDISH *adj* resembling a dude

DUDISHLY *adv* in the manner of a dude

DUE *n* pl. -S something that is owed

DUECENTO *n* pl. -TOS the thirteenth century

DUEL *v* DUELED, DUELING, DUELS or DUELLED, DUELLING, DUELS to fight formally

DUELER *n* pl. -S one that duels

DUELIST *n* pl. -S a dueler

DUELLED a past tense of duel

DUELLER *n* pl. -S dueler

DUELLI a pl. of duello

DUELLING a present participle of duel

DUELLIST *n* pl. -S duelist

DUELLO *n* pl. -LOS or -LI the art of dueling; a duel

DUENDE *n* pl. -S charisma

DUENESS *n* pl. -ES the state of being owed

DUENNA *n* pl. -S a governess

DUET   *v* DUETTED, DUETTING, DUETS to perform a duet (a musical composition for two)

DUETTIST   *n pl.* -S a participant in a duet

DUFF   *n pl.* -S a thick pudding

DUFFEL   *n pl.* -S a coarse woolen fabric

DUFFER   *n pl.* -S a clumsy person

DUFFLE   *n pl.* -S duffel

DUG   *n pl.* -S the teat or udder of a female mammal

DUGONG   *n pl.* -S an aquatic mammal

DUGOUT   *n pl.* -S a canoe made by hollowing out a log

DUI   a *pl.* of duo

DUIKER   *n pl.* -S a small antelope

DUIT   *n pl.* -S doit

DUKE   *n pl.* -S a high-ranking nobleman

DUKEDOM   *n pl.* -S duchy

DULCET   *n pl.* -S a soft-toned organ stop

DULCETLY   *adv* melodiously

DULCIANA   *n pl.* -S a soft-toned organ stop

DULCIFY   *v* -FIED, -FYING, -FIES to sweeten

DULCIMER   *n pl.* -S a stringed musical instrument

DULCINEA   *n pl.* -S a sweetheart

DULIA   *n pl.* -S veneration given to saints

DULL   *adj* DULLER, DULLEST mentally slow **DULLY** *adv*

DULL   *v* -ED, -ING, -S to make less sharp

DULLARD   *n pl.* -S a dolt

DULLISH   *adj* somewhat dull

DULLNESS   *n pl.* -ES the state of being dull

DULNESS   *n pl.* -ES dullness

DULSE   *n pl.* -S an edible seaweed

DULY   *adv* rightfully

DUMA   *n pl.* -S a Russian council

DUMB   *adj* DUMBER, DUMBEST incapable of speech **DUMBLY** *adv*

DUMB   *v* -ED, -ING, -S to make silent

DUMBBELL   *n pl.* -S a weight lifted for muscular exercise

DUMBNESS   *n pl.* -ES the state of being dumb

DUMDUM   *n pl.* -S a type of bullet

DUMFOUND   *v* -ED, -ING, -S to astonish

DUMKA   *n pl.* -KY a Slavic folk ballad

DUMMKOPF   *n pl.* -S a dolt

DUMMY   *v* -MIED, -MYING, -MIES to make a representation of

DUMP   *v* -ED, -ING, -S to let fall heavily

DUMPCART   *n pl.* -S a type of cart

DUMPER   *n pl.* -S one that dumps

DUMPIER   comparative of dumpy

DUMPIEST   superlative of dumpy

DUMPILY   *adv* in a dumpy manner

DUMPING   *n pl.* -S the selling of large quantities of goods at below the market price

DUMPISH   *adj* sad

DUMPLING   *n pl.* -S a ball of dough cooked with stew or soup

DUMPY   *adj* DUMPIER, DUMPIEST short and thick

DUN   *v* DUNNED, DUNNING, DUNS to make demands upon for payment of a debt

DUN   *adj* DUNNER, DUNNEST of a dull brown color

DUNCE   *n pl.* -S a stupid person DUNCICAL, DUNCISH *adj*

DUNCH   *n pl.* -ES a push

DUNE   *n pl.* -S a hill of sand DUNELIKE *adj*

DUNELAND   *n pl.* -S an area having many dunes

DUNG   *v* -ED, -ING, -S to fertilize with manure

DUNGAREE   *n pl.* -S a coarse cotton fabric

DUNGEON   *n pl.* -S an underground prison

DUNGHILL   *n pl.* -S a heap of manure

DUNGY   *adj* DUNGIER, DUNGIEST filthy

DUNITE   *n pl.* -S an igneous rock DUNITIC *adj*

DUNK   *v* -ED, -ING, -S to dip into liquid

DUNKER   *n pl.* -S one that dunks

DUNLIN   *n pl.* -S a wading bird

DUNNAGE   *n pl.* -S packing material used to protect cargo

DUNNED   past tense of dun

DUNNER   comparative of dun

DUNNESS   *n pl.* -ES the state of being dun

DUNNEST   superlative of dun

DUNNING   present participle of dun

DUNNITE   *n* pl. -S an explosive

DUNT   *v* -ED, -ING, -S to strike with a heavy blow

DUO   *n* pl. DUOS or DUI an instrumental duet

DUODENUM   *n* pl. -DENA or -DENUMS the first portion of the small intestine **DUODENAL** *adj*

DUOLOG   *n* pl. -S duologue

DUOLOGUE   *n* pl. -S a conversation between two persons

DUOMO   *n* pl. -MOS or -MI a cathedral

DUOPOLY   *n* pl. -LIES the market condition existing when there are two sellers only

DUOPSONY   *n* pl. -NIES the market condition existing when there are two buyers only

DUOTONE   *n* pl. -S an illustration in two tones

DUP   *v* DUPPED, DUPPING, DUPS to open

DUPE   *v* DUPED, DUPING, DUPES to deceive **DUPABLE** *adj*

DUPER   *n* pl. -S one that dupes

DUPERY   *n* pl. -ERIES the act of duping

DUPING   present participle of dupe

DUPLE   *adj* having two parts or elements

DUPLEX   *v* -ED, -ING, -ES to make duple

DUPLEXER   *n* pl. -S an electronic switching device

DUPPED   past tense of dup

DUPPING   present participle of dup

DURA   *n* pl. -S durra

DURABLE   *adj* able to withstand wear or decay **DURABLY** *adv*

DURABLES   *n/pl* durable goods

DURAL   *adj* of the dura mater (a brain membrane)

DURAMEN   *n* pl. -S the central wood of a tree

DURANCE   *n* pl. -S restraint by or as if by physical force

DURATION   *n* pl. -S continuance in time

DURATIVE   *n* pl. -S a type of verb

DURBAR   *n* pl. -S the court of a native ruler in India

DURE   *v* DURED, DURING, DURES to endure

DURESS   *n* pl. -ES compulsion by threat

DURIAN   *n* pl. -S an East Indian tree

DURING   *prep* throughout the duration of

DURION   *n* pl. -S durian

DURMAST   *n* pl. -S a European oak

DURN   *v* -ED, -ING, -S to damn

DURNED   *adj* DURNEDER, DURNEDEST or DURNDEST damned

DURO   *n* pl. -ROS a Spanish silver dollar

DUROC   *n* pl. -S a large red hog

DURR   *n* pl. -S durra

DURRA   *n* pl. -S a cereal grain

DURST   a past tense of dare

DURUM   *n* pl. -S a kind of wheat

DUSK   *v* -ED, -ING, -S to become dark

DUSKISH   *adj* dusky

DUSKY   *adj* DUSKIER, DUSKIEST somewhat dark **DUSKILY** *adv*

DUST   *v* -ED, -ING, -S to make free of dust (minute particles of matter)

DUSTBIN   *n* pl. -S a trash can

DUSTER   *n* pl. -S one that dusts

DUSTHEAP   *n* pl. -S a pile of trash

DUSTIER   comparative of dusty

DUSTIEST   superative of dusty

DUSTILY   *adv* in a dusty manner

DUSTLESS   *adj* being without dust

DUSTLIKE   *adj* resembling dust

DUSTMAN   *n* pl. -MEN a trashman

DUSTPAN   *n* pl. -S a pan for holding swept dust

DUSTRAG   *n* pl. -S a rag used for dusting

DUSTUP   *n* pl. -S an argument

DUSTY   *adj* DUSTIER, DUSTIEST full of dust

DUTCH   *adv* with each person paying for himself

DUTCHMAN   *n* pl. -MEN something used to hide structural defects

DUTEOUS   *adj* dutiful

DUTIABLE   *adj* subject to import tax

DUTIFUL   *adj* obedient

DUTY   *n* pl. -TIES a moral or legal obligation

DUUMVIR   *n* pl. -VIRS or -VIRI a magistrate of ancient Rome

DUVETINE   *n* pl. -S duvetyn

DUVETYN   *n* pl. -S a soft fabric

DUVETYNE   *n* pl. -S duvetyn

DWARF   *adj* DWARFER, DWARFEST extremely small

DWARF   *n* pl. DWARFS or DWARVES an extremely small person

DWARF   *v* -ED, -ING, -S to cause to appear small

DWARFISH   *adj* resembling a dwarf

DWARFISM   *n* pl. -S a condition of stunted growth

DWARVES   a pl. of dwarf

DWELL   *v* DWELT or DWELLED, DWELLING, DWELLS to reside

DWELLER   *n* pl. -S one that dwells

DWELLING   *n* pl. -S a place of residence

DWELT   a past tense of dwell

DWINDLE   *v* -DLED, -DLING, -DLES to decrease steadily

DWINE   *v* DWINED, DWINING, DWINES to pine or waste away

DYABLE   *adj* dyeable

DYAD   *n* pl. -S a pair of units

DYADIC   *n* pl. -S a sum of mathematical dyads

DYARCHY   *n* pl. -CHIES diarchy **DYARCHIC** *adj*

DYBBUK   *n* pl. -BUKS or -BUKIM a wandering soul in Jewish folklore

DYE   *v* DYED, DYEING, DYES to treat with a dye (a coloring material or matter)

DYEABLE   *adj* capable of being dyed

DYEING   *n* pl. -S something colored with a dye

DYER   *n* pl. -S one that dyes

DYESTUFF   *n* pl. -S a material yielding or used as a dye

DYEWEED   *n* pl. -S a shrub that yields a yellow dye

DYEWOOD   *n* pl. -S a wood used as a dyestuff

DYING   *n* pl. -S a passing out of existence

DYKE   *v* DYKED, DYKING, DYKES to dike

DYNAMIC   *n* pl. -S a physical force

DYNAMISM   *n* pl. -S a theory that explains the universe in terms of force or energy

DYNAMIST   *n* pl. -S an adherent of dynamism

DYNAMITE   *v* -MITED, -MITING, -MITES to blow up with a powerful explosive

DYNAMO   *n* pl. -MOS a generator

DYNAST   *n* pl. -S a ruler

DYNASTY   *n* pl. -TIES a succession of rulers from the same line of descent **DYNASTIC** *adj*

DYNATRON   *n* pl. -S a type of electron tube

DYNE   *n* pl. -S a unit of force

DYNODE   *n* pl. -S a type of electrode

DYSGENIC   *adj* causing the deterioration of hereditary qualities

DYSLEXIA   *n* pl. -S impairment of the ability to read **DYSLEXIC** *adj*

DYSPEPSY   *n* pl. -SIES indigestion

DYSPNEA   *n* pl. -S labored breathing **DYSPNEAL, DYSPNEIC** *adj*

DYSPNOEA   *n* pl. -S dyspnea **DYSPNOIC** *adj*

DYSTAXIA   *n* pl. -S a form of muscular tremor

DYSTOCIA   *n* pl. -S difficult labor and delivery in childbirth

DYSTONIA   *n* pl. -S a condition of disordered tonicity of muscle tissue

DYSTOPIA   *n* pl. -S a wretched place

DYSURIA   *n* pl. -S painful urination **DYSURIC** *adj*

DYVOUR   *n* pl. -S one who is bankrupt

EACH *adj* being one of two or more distinct individuals

EAGER *adj* -GERER, -GEREST impatiently longing **EAGERLY** *adv*

EAGER *n* pl. -S eagre

EAGLE *n* pl. -S a large bird of prey

EAGLET *n* pl. -S a young eagle

EAGRE *n* pl. -S a tidal flood

EANLING *n* pl. -S yeanling

EAR *n* pl. -S the organ of hearing

EARACHE *n* pl. -S a pain in the ear

EARDROP *n* pl. -S an earring

EARDRUM *n* pl. -S the tympanic membrane

EARED *adj* having ears

EARFLAP *n* pl. -S a part of a cap designed to cover the ears

EARFUL *n* pl. -S a flow of information

EARING *n* pl. -S a line on a ship

EARL *n* pl. -S a British nobleman

EARLAP *n* pl. -S an earflap

EARLDOM *n* pl. -S the rank of an earl

EARLESS *adj* lacking ears

EARLIER comparative of early

EARLIEST superlative of early

EARLOBE *n* pl. -S a part of the ear

EARLOCK *n* pl. -S a curl of hair by the ear

EARLSHIP *n* pl. -S earldom

EARLY *adv* -LIER, -LIEST near the beginning of a period of time or a series of events

EARMARK *v* -ED, -ING, -S to designate for a specific use

EARMUFF *n* pl. -S one of a pair of ear coverings

EARN *v* -ED, -ING, -S to gain or deserve for one's labor or service

EARNER *n* pl. -S one that earns

EARNEST *n* pl. -S a down payment

EARNINGS *n/pl* something earned

EARPHONE *n* pl. -S a listening device worn over the ear

EARPIECE *n* pl. -S an earphone

EARPLUG *n* pl. -S a plug for the ear

EARRING *n* pl. -S an ornament for the earlobe

EARSHOT *n* pl. -S the range within which sound can be heard

EARSTONE *n* pl. -S an otolith

EARTH *v* -ED, -ING, -S to cover with earth (soil)

EARTHEN *adj* made of earth

EARTHIER comparative of earthy

EARTHIEST superlative of earthy

EARTHILY *adv* in an earthy manner

EARTHLY *adj* -LIER, -LIEST worldly

EARTHMAN *n* pl. -MEN a person from the planet earth

EARTHNUT *n* pl. -S a European herb

EARTHPEA *n* pl. -S a twining plant

EARTHSET *n* pl. -S the setting of the earth as seen from the moon

EARTHY *adj* EARTHIER, EARTHIEST composed of, resembling, or suggestive of earth

EARWAX *n* pl. -ES cerumen

EARWIG *v* -WIGGED, -WIGGING, -WIGS to insinuate against in secret

EARWORM *n* pl. -S a bollworm

EASE *v* EASED, EASING, EASES to give rest of relief to

EASEFUL *adj* restful

EASEL *n* pl. -S a three-legged frame

EASEMENT *n* pl. -S relief

EASIER comparative of easy

EASIES pl. of easy

EASIEST superlative of easy

EASILY *adv* without difficulty

EASINESS *n* pl. -ES the state of being easy

EASING present participle of ease

EAST *n* pl. -S a cardinal point of the compass

EASTER *n* pl. -S a wind or storm from the east

EASTERLY *n* pl. -LIES a wind from the east

EASTERN *adj* being to, toward, or in the east

EASTING *n* pl. -S a movement toward the east

EASTWARD *n* pl. -S a direction toward the east

EASY *adj* EASIER, EASIEST not difficult

EASY *n* pl. EASIES a communications code word for the letter E

EAT *v* ATE or ET, EATEN, EATING, EATS to consume food

EATABLE *n* pl. -S an edible

EATER *n* pl. -S one that eats

EATERY *n* pl. -ERIES a lunchroom

EATH *adj* easy

EATING *n* pl. -S the act of consuming food

EAU *n* pl. EAUX water

EAVE *n* pl. -S the lower projecting edge of a roof **EAVED** *adj*

EBB *v* -ED, -ING, -S to recede

EBBET *n* pl. -S a common green newt

EBON *n* pl. -S ebony

EBONIES pl. of ebony

EBONISE *v* -ISED, -ISING, -ISES to ebonize

EBONITE *n* pl. -S a hard rubber

EBONIZE *v* -IZED, -IZING, -IZES to stain black in imitation of ebony

EBONY *n* pl. -NIES a hard, heavy wood

ECARTE *n* pl. -S a card game

ECAUDATE *adj* having no tail

ECBOLIC *n* pl. -S a type of drug

ECCLESIA *n* pl. -SIAE an assembly in ancient Greece

ECCRINE *adj* producing secretions externally

ECDYSIS *n* pl. -DYSES the shedding of an outer layer of skin **ECDYSIAL** *adj*

ECDYSON *n* pl. -S ecdysone

ECDYSONE *n* pl. -S an insect hormone

ECESIS *n* pl. -SISES the establishment of a plant or animal in a new environment

ECHARD *n* pl. -S the water in the soil not available to plants

ECHE *v* ECHED, ECHING, ECHES to increase

ECHELON *v* -ED, -ING, -S to group in a particular formation

ECHIDNA *n* pl. -NAS or -NAE a spiny anteater

ECHINATE *adj* spiny

ECHING present participle of eche

ECHINOID *n* pl. -S a spiny marine animal

ECHINUS *n* pl. -NI echinoid

ECHO *v* -ED, -ING, -ES to produce an echo (a repetition of sound by reflection of sound waves)

ECHOER *n* pl. -S one that echoes

ECHOEY *adj* full of echoes

ECHOIC *adj* resembling an echo

ECHOISM *n* pl. -S the formation of words in imitation of sounds

ECHOLESS *adj* producing no echo

ECLAIR *n* pl. -S a type of pastry

ECLAT *n* pl. -S brilliance

ECLECTIC *n* pl. -S one who draws his beliefs from various sources

ECLIPSE *v* ECLIPSED, ECLIPSING, ECLIPSES to obscure

ECLIPSIS *n* pl. -SES or -SISES an ellipsis

ECLIPTIC *n* pl. -S an astronomical plane

ECLOGITE *n* pl. -S a type of rock

ECLOGUE *n* pl. -S a pastoral poem

ECLOSION   n pl. -S the emergence of an insect larva from an egg

ECOLE   n pl. -S a French school

ECOLOGY   n pl. -GIES an environmental science **ECOLOGIC** adj

ECONOMIC   adj pertaining to financial matters

ECONOMY   n pl. -MIES thrift

ECOTONE   n pl. -S a type of ecological zone **ECOTONAL** adj

ECOTYPE   n pl. -S a subspecies adapted to specific environmental conditions **ECOTYPIC** adj

ECRASEUR   n pl. -S a surgical instrument

ECRU   n pl. -S a yellowish brown color

ECSTASY   n pl. -SIES a state of exaltation

ECSTATIC   n pl. -S one that is subject to ecstasies

ECTASIS   n pl. -TASES the lengthening of a usually short syllable **ECTATIC** adj

ECTHYMA   n pl. -MATA a virus disease

ECTODERM   n pl. -S the outermost germ layer of an embryo

ECTOMERE   n pl. -S a cell that develops into ectoderm

ECTOPIA   n pl. -S congenital displacement of parts or organs **ECTOPIC** adj

ECTOSARC   n pl. -S the outermost layer of protoplasm of certain protozoans

ECTOZOAN   n pl. -S ectozoon

ECTOZOON   n pl. -ZOA a parasite on the body of an animal

ECTYPE   n pl. -S a copy **ECTYPAL** adj

ECU   n pl. -S an old French coin

ECUMENIC   adj universal

ECZEMA   n pl. -S a skin disease

EDACIOUS   adj voracious

EDACITY   n pl. -TIES gluttony

EDAPHIC   adj pertaining to the soil

EDDO   n pl. -DOES a tropical plant

EDDY   v -DIED, -DYING, -DIES to move against the main current

EDEMA   n pl. -MAS or -MATA an excessive accumulation of serous fluid

EDENTATE   n pl. -S a toothless mammal

EDGE   v EDGED, EDGING, EDGES to provide with an edge (a bounding or dividing line)

EDGELESS   adj lacking an edge

EDGER   n pl. -S a tool used to trim a lawn's edge

EDGEWAYS   adv edgewise

EDGEWISE   adv sideways

EDGIER   comparative of edgy

EDGIEST   superlative of edgy

EDGILY   adv in an edgy manner

EDGINESS   n pl. -ES the state of being edgy

EDGING   n pl. -S something that forms or serves as an edge

EDGY   adj EDGIER, EDGIEST tense, nervous, or irritable

EDH   n pl. -S an Old English letter

EDIBLE   n pl. -S something fit to be eaten

EDICT   n pl. -S an authoritative order having the force of law **EDICTAL** adj

EDIFICE   n pl. -S a building

EDIFIER   n pl. -S one that edifies

EDIFY   v -FIED, -FYING, -FIES to enlighten

EDILE   n pl. -S a aedile

EDIT   v -ED, -ING, -S to correct and prepare for publication **EDITABLE** adj

EDITION   n pl. -S a particular series of printed material

EDITOR   n pl. -S one that edits

EDITRESS   n pl. -ES a female editor

EDUCABLE   n pl. -S a mildly retarded person

EDUCATE   v -CATED, -CATING, -CATES to teach

EDUCATOR   n pl. -S one that educates

EDUCE   v EDUCED, EDUCING, EDUCES to draw forth or bring out **EDUCIBLE** adj

EDUCT   n pl. -S something educed

EDUCTION   n pl. -S the act of educing **EDUCTIVE** adj

EDUCTOR   n pl. -S one that educes

EEL   n pl. -S a snakelike fish

EELGRASS   n pl. -ES an aquatic plant

EELIER   comparative of eely

EELIEST   superlative of eely

EELLIKE   adj resembling an eel

EELPOUT   n pl. -S a marine fish

EELWORM *n* pl. -S a small roundworm

EELY *adj* EELIER, EELIEST resembling an eel

EERIE *adj* -RIER, -RIEST weird **EERILY** *adv*

EERINESS *n* pl. -ES the state of being eerie

EERY *adj* -RIER, -RIEST eerie

EF *n* pl. -S the letter F

EFF *n* pl. -S ef

EFFABLE *adj* capable of being uttered or expressed

EFFACE *v* -FACED, -FACING, -FACES to rub or wipe out

EFFACER *n* pl. -S one that effaces

EFFECT *v* -ED, -ING, -S to bring about

EFFECTER *n* pl. -S effector

EFFECTOR *n* pl. -S a bodily organ that responds to a nerve impulse

EFFENDI *n* pl. -S a Turkish title of respect

EFFERENT *n* pl. -S an organ or part conveying nervous impulses to an effector

EFFETE *adj* exhausted of vigor or energy **EFFETELY** *adv*

EFFICACY *n* pl. -CIES effectiveness

EFFIGY *n* pl. -GIES a likeness or representation

EFFLUENT *n* pl. -S an outflow

EFFLUVIA *n/pl* byproducts in the form of waste

EFFLUX *n* pl. -ES an outflow

EFFORT *n* pl. -S a deliberate exertion

EFFULGE *v* -FULGED, -FULGING, -FULGES to shine forth

EFFUSE *v* -FUSED, -FUSING, -FUSES to pour forth

EFFUSION *n* pl. -S an outpouring of emotion

EFFUSIVE *adj* pouring forth

EFT *n* pl. -S a newt

EFTSOON *adv* soon afterward

EFTSOONS *adv* eftsoon

EGAD *interj* — used as a mild oath

EGADS *interj* egad

EGAL *adj* equal

EGALITE *n* pl. -S equality

EGER *n* pl. -S eagre

EGEST *v* -ED, -ING, -S to discharge from the body

EGESTA *n/pl* egested matter

EGESTION *n* pl. -S the act of egesting **EGESTIVE** *adj*

EGG *v* -ED, -ING, -S to incite or urge

EGGAR *n* pl. -S egger

EGGCUP *n* pl. -S a cup from which an egg is eaten

EGGER *n* pl. -S a kind of moth

EGGHEAD *n* pl. -S an intellectual

EGGNOG *n* pl. -S a beverage

EGGPLANT *n* pl. -S a perennial herb yielding edible fruit

EGGSHELL *n* pl. -S the hard exterior of a bird's egg

EGIS *n* pl. EGISES aegis

EGLATERE *n* pl. -S a wild rose

EGO *n* pl. EGOS the conscious self

EGOISM *n* pl. -S extreme devotion to self-interest

EGOIST *n* pl. -S one who practices egoism **EGOISTIC** *adj*

EGOMANIA *n* pl. -S extreme egotism

EGOTISM *n* pl. -S self-conceit

EGOTIST *n* pl. -S a conceited person

EGRESS *v* -ED, -ING, -ES to go out

EGRET *n* pl. -S a wading bird

EH *interj* — used to express doubt or surprise

EIDE pl. of eidos

EIDER *n* pl. -S a large sea duck

EIDETIC *adj* pertaining to vivid recall

EIDOLON *n* pl. -LONS or -LA a phantom

EIDOS *n* pl. EIDE an essence

EIGHT *n* pl. -S a number

EIGHTEEN *n* pl. -S a number

EIGHTH *n* pl. -S one of eight equal parts

EIGHTHLY *adv* in the eighth place

EIGHTVO *n* pl. -VOS octavo

EIGHTY *n* pl. EIGHTIES a number

EIKON *n* pl. -S or -ES icon

EINKORN *n* pl. -S a variety of wheat

EIRENIC *adj* irenic

EITHER *adj* being one or the other

EJECT *v* -ED, -ING, -S to throw out forcibly

EJECTA	*n/pl* ejected material
EJECTION	*n* pl. -S the act of ejecting
EJECTIVE	*n* pl. -S a sound produced with air compressed above the closed glottis
EJECTOR	*n* pl. -S one that ejects
EKE	*v* EKED, EKING, EKES to supplement with great effort
EKISTICS	*n/pl* a science dealing with human habitats **EKISTIC** *adj*
EKTEXINE	*n* pl. -S an outer layer of the exine
EL	*n* pl. -S an elevated railroad or train
ELAIN	*n* pl. -S olein
ELAN	*n* pl. -S enthusiasm
ELAND	*n* pl. -S a large antelope
ELAPHINE	*adj* pertaining to a genus of deer
ELAPID	*n* pl. -S a venomous snake
ELAPINE	*adj* pertaining to a family of snakes
ELAPSE	*v* ELAPSED, ELAPSING, ELAPSES to pass away
ELASTASE	*n* pl. -S an enzyme
ELASTIC	*n* pl. -S a stretchable material
ELASTIN	*n* pl. -S a bodily protein
ELATE	*v* ELATED, ELATING, ELATES to raise the spirits of **ELATEDLY** *adv*
ELATER	*n* pl. -S a click beetle
ELATERID	*n* pl. -S an elater
ELATERIN	*n* pl. -S a chemical compound
ELATING	present participle of elate
ELATION	*n* pl. -S a feeling of great joy
ELATIVE	*n* pl. -S an adjectival form in some languages
ELBOW	*v* -ED, -ING, -S to jostle
ELD	*n* pl. -S old age
ELDER	*n* pl. -S an older person
ELDERLY	*adj* rather old
ELDEST	*adj* oldest
ELDRICH	*adj* eldritch
ELDRITCH	*adj* weird
ELECT	*v* -ED, -ING, -S to select by vote for an office
ELECTION	*n* pl. -S the act of electing
ELECTIVE	*n* pl. -S an optional course of study
ELECTOR	*n* pl. -S one that elects
ELECTRET	*n* pl. -S a type of nonconductor
ELECTRIC	*n* pl. -S something run by electricity
ELECTRO	*v* -ED, -ING, -S to make a metallic copy of a page of type for printing
ELECTRON	*n* pl. -S an atomic particle
ELECTRUM	*n* pl. -S an alloy of gold and silver
ELEGANCE	*n* pl. -S tasteful opulence
ELEGANCY	*n* pl. -CIES elegance
ELEGANT	*adj* tastefully opulent
ELEGIAC	*n* pl. -S a type of verse
ELEGIES	pl. of elegy
ELEGISE	*v* -GISED, -GISING, -GISES to elegize
ELEGIST	*n* pl. -S one that writes elegies
ELEGIT	*n* pl. -S a type of judicial writ
ELEGIZE	*v* -GIZED, -GIZING, -GIZES to write an elegy
ELEGY	*n* pl. -GIES a mournful poem for one who is dead
ELEMENT	*n* pl. -S any of a class of substances that cannot be separated into simpler substances by chemical means
ELEMI	*n* pl. -S a fragrant resin
ELENCHUS	*n* pl. -CHI a logical refutation **ELENCHIC, ELENCTIC** *adj*
ELEPHANT	*n* pl. -S a large mammal
ELEVATE	*v* -VATED, -VATING, -VATES to raise
ELEVATOR	*n* pl. -S one that elevates
ELEVEN	*n* pl. -S a number
ELEVENTH	*n* pl. -S one of eleven equal parts
ELEVON	*n* pl. -S a type of airplane control surface
ELF	*n* pl. ELVES a small, often mischievous fairy
ELFIN	*n* pl. -S an elf
ELFISH	*adj* resembling an elf **ELFISHLY** *adv*
ELFLOCK	*n* pl. -S a lock of tangled hair
ELHI	*adj* pertaining to school grades 1 through 12
ELICIT	*v* -ED, -ING, -S to educe
ELICITOR	*n* pl. -S one that elicits

ELIDE   *v* ELIDED, ELIDING, ELIDES to omit **ELIDIBLE** *adj*

ELIGIBLE   *n* pl. -S one that is qualified to be chosen

ELIGIBLY   *adv* in a qualified manner

ELISION   *n* pl. -S the act of eliding

ELITE   *n* pl. -S a socially superior group

ELITISM   *n* pl. -S belief in rule by an elite

ELITIST   *n* pl. -S an adherent of elitism

ELIXIR   *n* pl. -S a medicinal beverage

ELK   *n* pl. -S a large deer

ELKHOUND   *n* pl. -S a hunting dog

ELL   *n* pl. -S the letter L

ELLIPSE   *n* pl. -S a type of plane curve

ELLIPSIS   *n* pl. -LIPSES an omission of a word or words in a sentence

ELLIPTIC   *adj* having the shape of an ellipse

ELM   *n* pl. -S a deciduous tree

ELMY   *adj* -MIER, -MIEST abounding in elms

ELODEA   *n* pl. -S an aquatic herb

ELOIGN   *v* -ED, -ING, -S to remove to a distant place

ELOIGNER   *n* pl. -S one that eloigns

ELOIN   *v* -ED, -ING, -S to eloign

ELOINER   *n* pl. -S one that eloins

ELONGATE   *v* -GATED, -GATING, -GATES to lengthen

ELOPE   *v* ELOPED, ELOPING, ELOPES to run off secretly to be married

ELOPER   *n* pl. -S one that elopes

ELOQUENT   *adj* fluent and convincing in speech

ELSE   *adv* in a different place, time, or way

ELUANT   *n* pl. -S a solvent

ELUATE   *n* pl. -S the material obtained by eluting

ELUDE   *v* ELUDED, ELUDING, ELUDES to evade

ELUDER   *n* pl. -S one that eludes

ELUENT   *n* pl. -S eluant

ELUSION   *n* pl. -S the act of eluding

ELUSIVE   *adj* tending to elude

ELUSORY   *adj* elusive

ELUTE   *v* ELUTED, ELUTING, ELUTES to remove by means of a solvent

ELUTION   *n* pl. -S the act of eluting

ELUVIA   a pl. of eluvium

ELUVIAL   *adj* pertaining to an eluvium

ELUVIATE   *v* -ATED, -ATING, -ATES to undergo a transfer of materials in the soil

ELUVIUM   *n* pl. -VIA or -VIUMS a soil deposit

ELVER   *n* pl. -S a young eel

ELVES   pl. of elf

ELVISH   *adj* elfish **ELVISHLY** *adv*

ELYSIAN   *adj* delightful

ELYTRON   *n* pl. -TRA a hardened forewing of certain insects **ELYTROID,** **ELYTROUS** *adj*

ELYTRUM   *n* pl. -TRA elytron

EM   *n* pl. -S the letter M

EMACIATE   *v* -ATED, -ATING, -ATES to make thin

EMANATE   *v* -NATED, -NATING, -NATES to send forth

EMANATOR   *n* pl. -S one that emanates

EMBALM   *v* -ED, -ING, -S to treat so as to protect from decay

EMBALMER   *n* pl. -S one that embalms

EMBANK   *v* -ED, -ING, -S to confine or protect with a raised structure

EMBAR   *v* -BARRED, -BARRING, -BARS to imprison

EMBARGO   *v* -ED, -ING, -ES to restrain trade by a governmental order

EMBARK   *v* -ED, -ING, -S to make a start

EMBARRED   past tense of embar

EMBARRING   present participle of embar

EMBASSY   *n* pl. -SIES the headquarters of an ambassador

EMBATTLE   *v* -TLED, -TLING, -TLES to prepare for battle

EMBAY   *v* -ED, -ING, -S to enclose in a bay

EMBED   *v* -BEDDED, -BEDDING, -BEDS to fix firmly into a surrounding mass

EMBER   *n* pl. -S a glowing fragment from a fire

EMBEZZLE   *v* -ZLED, -ZLING, -ZLES to appropriate fraudulently to one's own use

EMBITTER   *v* -ED, -ING, -S to make bitter

EMBLAZE   *v* -BLAZED, -BLAZING, -BLAZES to set on fire

EMBLAZER   *n* pl. -S one that emblazes

EMBLAZON   *v* -ED, -ING, -S to decorate with brilliant colors

EMBLEM   *v* -ED, -ING, -S to represent with an emblem (a graphical symbol)

EMBODIER   *n* pl. -S one that embodies

EMBODY   *v* -BODIED, -BODYING, -BODIES to provide with a body

EMBOLDEN   *v* -ED, -ING, -S to instill with courage

EMBOLI   pl. of embolus

EMBOLIES   pl. of emboly

EMBOLISM   *n* pl. -S the obstruction of a blood vessel by an embolus **EMBOLIC** *adj*

EMBOLUS   *n* pl. -LI an abnormal particle circulating in the blood

EMBOLY   *n* pl. -LIES a phase of embryonic growth

EMBORDER   *v* -ED, -ING, -S to provide with a border

EMBOSK   *v* -ED, -ING, -S to conceal with foliage

EMBOSOM   *v* -ED, -ING, -S to embrace

EMBOSS   *v* -ED, -ING, -ES to decorate with raised designs

EMBOSSER   *n* pl. -S one that embosses

EMBOW   *v* -ED, -ING, -S to arch

EMBOWEL   *v* -ELED, -ELING, -ELS or -ELLED, -ELLING, -ELS to disbowel

EMBOWER   *v* -ED, -ING, -S to surround with foliage

EMBRACE   *v* -BRACED, -BRACING, -BRACES to hug

EMBRACER   *n* pl. -S one that embraces

EMBROIL   *v* -ED, -ING, -S to involve in conflict

EMBROWN   *v* -ED, -ING, -S to make brown

EMBRUE   *v* -BRUED, -BRUING, -BRUES to imbrue

EMBRUTE   *v* -BRUTED, -BRUTING, -BRUTES to imbrute

EMBRYO   *n* pl. -BRYOS an organism in its early stages of development **EMBRYOID** *adj*

EMBRYON   *n* pl. -S an embryo

EMCEE   *v* -CEED, -CEEING, -CEES to serve as master of ceremonies

EME   *n* pl. -S an uncle

EMEER   *n* pl. -S emir

EMEERATE   *n* pl. -S emirate

EMEND   *v* -ED, -ING, -S to correct

EMENDATE   *v* -DATED, -DATING, -DATES to emend

EMENDER   *n* pl. -S one that emends

EMERALD   *n* pl. -S a green gem

EMERGE   *v* EMERGED, -EMERGING, EMERGES to come out into view

EMERGENT   *n* pl. -S a type of aquatic plant

EMERITA   *adj* retired but retaining an honorary title — used of a woman

EMERITUS   *n* pl. -ITI a retired person who retains an honorary title

EMEROD   *n* pl. -S a tumor

EMEROID   *n* pl. -S emerod

EMERSED   *adj* standing out of water

EMERSION   *n* pl. -S the act of emerging

EMERY   *n* pl. -ERIES a granular corundum

EMESIS   *n* pl. EMESES the act of vomiting

EMETIC   *n* pl. -S a substance which induces vomiting

EMETIN   *n* pl. -S emetine

EMETINE   *n* pl. -S an alkaloid

EMEU   *n* pl. -S emu

EMEUTE   *n* pl. -S a riot

EMIGRANT   *n* pl. -S one that emigrates

EMIGRATE   *v* -GRATED, -GRATING, -GRATES to leave one country or region to settle in another

EMIGRE   *n* pl. -S an emigrant

EMINENCE   *n* pl. -S high station or rank

EMINENCY   *n* pl. -CIES eminence

EMINENT   *adj* of high station or rank

EMIR   *n* pl. -S an Arab chieftain or prince

EMIRATE   *n* pl. -S the rank of an emir

EMISSARY   *n* pl. -SARIES a person sent on a mission

EMISSION   *n* pl. -S the act of emitting **EMISSIVE** *adj*

EMIT   *v* EMITTED, EMITTING, EMITS to send forth

EMITTER   *n* pl. -S one that emits

EMMER   *n* pl. -S a type of wheat

EMMET   *n* pl. -S an ant

EMODIN   *n* pl. -S a chemical compound

EMOTE   v EMOTED, EMOTING, EMOTES to express emotion in an exaggerated manner

EMOTER   n pl. -S one that emotes

EMOTION   n pl. -S an affective state of consciousness

EMOTIVE   adj pertaining to emotion

EMPALE   v -PALED, -PALING, -PALES to impale

EMPALER   n pl. -S one that empales

EMPANEL   v -ELED, -ELING, -ELS or -ELLED, -ELLING, -ELS to impanel

EMPATHY   n pl. -THIES imaginative identification with another's thoughts and feelings **EMPATHIC** adj

EMPEROR   n pl. -S the ruler of an empire

EMPERY   n pl. -PERIES absolute dominion

EMPHASIS   n pl. -PHASES special significance imparted to something

EMPHATIC   adj strongly expressive

EMPIRE   n pl. -S a major political unit

EMPIRIC   n pl. -S one who relies on practical experience

EMPLACE   v -PLACED, -PLACING, -PLACES to position

EMPLANE   v -PLANED, -PLANING, -PLANES to enplane

EMPLOY   v -ED, -ING, -S to hire

EMPLOYE   n pl. -S employee

EMPLOYEE   n pl. -S a person who is employed

EMPLOYER   n pl. -S one that employs

EMPOISON   v -ED, -ING, -S to embitter

EMPORIUM   n pl. -RIUMS or -RIA a trading or market center

EMPOWER   v -ED, -ING, -S to give legal power to

EMPRESS   n pl. -ES a female ruler of an empire

EMPRISE   n pl. -S an adventurous undertaking

EMPRIZE   n pl. -S emprise

EMPTIED   past tense of empty

EMPTIER   n pl. -S one that empties

EMPTIES   present 3d person sing. of empty

EMPTIEST   superlative of empty

EMPTILY   adv in an empty manner

EMPTINGS   n/pl emptins

EMPTINS   n/pl a liquid leavening

EMPTY   adj -TIER, -TIEST containing nothing

EMPTY   v -TIED, -TYING, -TIES to remove the contents of

EMPURPLE   v -PLED, -PLING, -PLES to tinge with purple

EMPYEMA   n pl. -EMATA or -EMAS a collection of pus in a body cavity **EMPYEMIC** adj

EMPYREAL   adj pertaining to the sky

EMPYREAN   n pl. -S the highest heaven

EMU   n pl. -S a large, flightless bird

EMULATE   v -LATED, -LATING, -LATES to try to equal or surpass

EMULATOR   n pl. -S one that emulates

EMULOUS   adj eager to equal or surpass another

EMULSIFY   v -FIED, -FYING, -FIES to make into an emulsion

EMULSION   n pl. -S a type of liquid mixture **EMULSIVE** adj

EMULSOID   n pl. -S a liquid dispersed in another liquid

EMYD   n pl. -S a freshwater tortoise

EMYDE   n pl. -S emyd

EN   n pl. -S the letter N

ENABLE   v -BLED, -BLING, -BLES to make possible

ENABLER   n pl. -S one that enables

ENACT   v -ED, -ING, -S to make into a law

ENACTIVE   adj having the power to enact

ENACTOR   n pl. -S one that enacts

ENACTORY   adj pertaining to the enactment of law

ENAMEL   v -ELED, -ELING, -ELS or -ELLED, -ELLING, -ELS to cover with a hard, glossy surface

ENAMELER   n pl. -S one that enamels

ENAMINE   n pl. -S a type of amine

ENAMOR   v -ED, -ING, -S to inspire with love

ENAMOUR   v -ED, -ING, -S to enamor

ENATE   n pl. -S a relative on the mother's side **ENATIC** adj

ENATION   n pl. -S an outgrowth from the surface of an organ

ENCAENIA *n/pl* annual university ceremonies

ENCAGE *v* -CAGED, -CAGING, -CAGES to confine in a cage

ENCAMP *v* -ED, -ING, -S to set up a camp

ENCASE *v* -CASED, -CASING, -CASES to enclose in a case

ENCASH *v* -ED, -ING, -ES to cash

ENCEINTE *n* pl. -S an encircling fortification

ENCHAIN *v* -ED, -ING, -S to bind with chains

ENCHANT *v* -ED, -ING, -S to delight

ENCHASE *v* -CHASED, -CHASING, -CHASES to place in an ornamental setting

ENCHASER *n* pl. -S one that enchases

ENCHORIC *adj* belonging to a particular country

ENCINA *n* pl. -S an evergreen oak **ENCINAL** *adj*

ENCIPHER *v* -ED, -ING, -S to write in characters of hidden meaning

ENCIRCLE *v* -CLED, -CLING, -CLES to form a circle around

ENCLASP *v* -ED, -ING, -S to embrace

ENCLAVE *n* pl. -S a territorial unit enclosed within foreign territory

ENCLITIC *n* pl. -S a word pronounced as part of the preceding word

ENCLOSE *v* -CLOSED, -CLOSING, -CLOSES to close in on all sides

ENCLOSER *n* pl. -S one that encloses

ENCODE *v* -CODED, -CODING, -CODES to put into code

ENCODER *n* pl. -S one that encodes

ENCOMIUM *n* pl. -MIUMS or -MIA a eulogy

ENCORE *v* -CORED, -CORING, -CORES to call for the reappearance of a performer

ENCROACH *v* -ED, -ING, -ES to advance beyond the proper limits

ENCRUST *v* -ED, -ING, -S to cover with a crust

ENCRYPT *v* -ED, -ING, -S to encipher

ENCUMBER *v* -ED, -ING, -S to hinder in action or movement

ENCYCLIC *n* pl. -S a letter addressed by the pope to the bishops of the world

ENCYST *v* -ED, -ING, -S to enclose in a cyst

END *v* -ED, -ING, -S to terminate

ENDAMAGE *v* -AGED, -AGING, -AGES to damage

ENDAMEBA *n* pl. -BAS or -BAE a parasitic ameba

ENDANGER *v* -ED, -ING, -S to imperil

ENDARCH *adj* formed from the center outward

ENDARCHY *n* pl. -CHIES the condition of being endarch

ENDBRAIN *n* pl. -S a part of the brain

ENDEAR *v* -ED, -ING, -S to make dear or beloved

ENDEAVOR *v* -ED, -ING, -S to make an effort

ENDEMIAL *adj* peculiar to a country or people

ENDEMIC *n* pl. -S an endemial disease

ENDEMISM *n* pl. -S the state of being endemial

ENDER *n* pl. -S one that ends something

ENDERMIC *adj* acting by absorption through the skin

ENDEXINE *n* pl. -S an inner layer of the exine

ENDING *n* pl. -S a termination

ENDITE *v* -DITED, -DITING, -DITES to indite

ENDIVE *n* pl. -S an herb cultivated as a salad plant

ENDLEAF *n* pl. -LEAVES an endpaper

ENDLESS *adj* enduring forever

ENDLONG *adv* lengthwise

ENDMOST *adj* farthest

ENDOCARP *n* pl. -S the inner layer of a pericarp

ENDODERM *n* pl. -S the innermost germ layer of an embryo

ENDOGAMY *n* pl. -MIES marriage within a particular group

ENDOGEN *n* pl. -S a type of plant

ENDOGENY *n* pl. -NIES growth from within

ENDOPOD *n* pl. -S a branch of a crustacean limb

ENDORSE *v* -DORSED, -DORSING, -DORSES to sign the back of a negotiable document

ENDORSEE *n* pl. -S one to whom a document is transferred by endorsement

ENDORSER *n* pl. -S one that endorses

ENDORSING present participle of endorse

ENDORSOR n pl. -S endorser

ENDOSARC n pl. -S a portion of a cell

ENDOSMOS n pl. -ES a form of osmosis

ENDOSOME n pl. -S a cellular particle

ENDOSTEA n/pl bone membranes

ENDOW v -ED, -ING, -S to provide with something

ENDOWER n pl. -S one that endows

ENDOZOIC adj involving passage through an animal

ENDPAPER n pl. -S a sheet of paper used in bookbinding

ENDPLATE n pl. -S a type of nerve terminal

ENDRIN n pl. -S an insecticide

ENDUE v -DUED, -DUING, -DUES to provide with some quality or gift

ENDURE v -DURED, -DURING, -DURES to last

ENDURO n pl. -DUROS a long race

ENDWAYS adv endwise

ENDWISE adv lengthwise

ENEMA n pl. -MAS or -MATA a liquid injected into the rectum

ENEMY n pl. -MIES one that is antagonistic toward another

ENERGID n pl. -S a nucleus and the body of cytoplasm with which it interacts

ENERGIES pl. of energy

ENERGISE v -GISED, -GISING, -GISES to energize

ENERGIZE v -GIZED, -GIZING, -GIZES to give energy to

ENERGY n -GIES the capacity for vigorous activity

ENERVATE v -VATED, -VATING, -VATES to deprive of strength or vitality

ENFACE v -FACED, -FACING, -FACES to write on the front of

ENFEEBLE v -BLED, -BLING, -BLES to make feeble

ENFEOFF v -ED, -ING, -S to invest with a feudal estate

ENFETTER v -ED, -ING, -S to enchain

ENFEVER v -ED, -ING, -S to fever

ENFILADE v -LADED, -LADING, -LADES to direct heavy gunfire along the length of

ENFIN adv finally

ENFLAME v -FLAMED, -FLAMING, -FLAMES to inflame

ENFOLD v -ED, -ING, -S to envelop

ENFOLDER n pl. -S one that enfolds

ENFORCE v -FORCED, -FORCING, -FORCES to compel obedience to

ENFORCER n pl. -S one that enforces

ENFRAME v -FRAMED, -FRAMING, -FRAMES to frame

ENG n pl. -S a phonetic symbol

ENGAGE v -GAGED, -GAGING, -GAGES to employ

ENGAGER n pl. -S one that engages

ENGENDER v -ED, -ING, -S to bring into existence

ENGILD v -ED, -ING, -S to brighten

ENGINE v -GINED, -GINING, -GINES to equip with machinery

ENGINEER v -ED, -ING, -S to carry through or manage by contrivance

ENGINERY n pl. -RIES machinery

ENGINING present participle of engine

ENGINOUS adj ingenious

ENGIRD v -GIRT or -GIRDED, -GIRDING, -GIRDS to gird

ENGIRDLE v -DLED, -DLING, -DLES to engird

ENGLISH v -ED, -ING, -ES to cause a billiard ball to spin around its vertical axis

ENGLUT v -GLUTTED, -GLUTTING, -GLUTS to gulp down

ENGORGE v -GORGED, -GORGING, -GORGES to fill with blood

ENGRAFT v -ED, -ING, -S to graft for propagation

ENGRAIL v -ED, -ING, -S to ornament the edge of with curved indentations

ENGRAIN v -ED, -ING, -S to ingrain

ENGRAM n pl. -S the durable mark caused by a stimulus upon protoplasm

ENGRAMME n pl. -S engram

ENGRAVE v -GRAVED, -GRAVING, -GRAVES to form by incision

ENGRAVER n pl. -S one that engraves

ENGROSS v -ED, -ING, -ES to occupy completely

ENGULF v -ED, -ING, -S to surround completely

ENHALO   *v* -ED, -ING, -ES to surround with a halo

ENHANCE   *v* -HANCED, -HANCING, -HANCES to raise to a higher degree

ENHANCER   *n pl.* -S one that enhances

ENIGMA   *n pl.* -MAS or -MATA something that is hard to understand or explain

ENISLE   *v* -ISLED, -ISLING, -ISLES to isolate

ENJAMBED   *adj* marked by the continuation of a sentence from one line of a poem to the next

ENJOIN   *v* -ED, -ING, -S to command

ENJOINER   *n pl.* -S one that enjoins

ENJOY   *v* -ED, -ING, -S to receive pleasure from

ENJOYER   *n pl.* -S one that enjoys

ENKINDLE   *v* -DLED, -DLING, -DLES to set on fire

ENLACE   *v* -LACED, -LACING, -LACES to bind with laces

ENLARGE   *v* -LARGED, -LARGING, -LARGES to make or become larger

ENLARGER   *n pl.* -S a device used to enlarge photographs

ENLIST   *v* -ED, -ING, -S to engage for military service

ENLISTEE   *n pl.* -S one that is enlisted

ENLISTER   *n pl.* -S one that enlists

ENLIVEN   *v* -ED, -ING, -S to make lively

ENMESH   *v* -ED, -ING, -ES to ensnare or entangle in a net

ENMITY   *n pl.* -TIES hostility

ENNEAD   *n pl.* -S a group of nine
     ENNEADIC *adj*

ENNEAGON   *n pl.* -S a nonagon

ENNOBLE   *v* -BLED, -BLING, -BLES to make noble

ENNOBLER   *n pl.* -S one that ennobles

ENNUI   *n pl.* -S a feeling of weariness and discontent

ENNUYE   *adj* oppressed with ennui

ENNUYEE   *adj* ennuye

ENOL   *n pl.* -S a chemical compound
     ENOLIC *adj*

ENOLASE   *n pl.* -S an enzyme

ENOLOGY   *n pl.* -GIES oenology

ENORM   *adj* enormous

ENORMITY   *n pl.* -TIES a grave offense against decency

ENORMOUS   *adj* huge

ENOSIS   *n pl.* -SISES union

ENOUGH   *n pl.* -S a sufficient supply

ENOUNCE   *v* ENOUNCED, ENOUNCING, ENOUNCES to announce

ENOW   *n pl.* -S enough

ENPLANE   *v* -PLANED, -PLANING, -PLANES to board an airplane

ENQUIRE   *v* -QUIRED, -QUIRING, -QUIRES to inquire

ENQUIRY   *n pl.* -RIES inquiry

ENRAGE   *v* -RAGED, -RAGING, -RAGES to make very angry

ENRAPT   *adj* rapt

ENRAVISH   *v* -ED, -ING, -ES to delight greatly

ENRICH   *v* -ED, -ING, -ES to add desirable elements to

ENRICHER   *n pl.* -S one that enriches

ENROBE   *v* -ROBED, -ROBING, -ROBES to dress

ENROBER   *n pl.* -S one that enrobes

ENROL   *v* -ROLLED, -ROLLING, -ROLS to enroll

ENROLL   *v* -ED, -ING, -S to enter the name of in a register, record, or roll

ENROLLEE   *n pl.* -S one that is enrolled

ENROLLER   *n pl.* -S one that enrolls

ENROLLING   present participle of enrol

ENROOT   *v* -ED, -ING, -S to implant

ENS   *n pl.* ENTIA an entity

ENSAMPLE   *n pl.* -S an example

ENSCONCE   *v* -SCONCED, -SCONCING, -SCONCES to settle securely or comfortably

ENSCROLL   *v* -ED, -ING, -S to write on a scroll

ENSEMBLE   *n pl.* -S a group of complementary parts

ENSERF   *v* -ED, -ING, -S to make a serf of

ENSHEATH   *v* -ED, -ING, -S to enclose in a sheath

ENSHRINE   *v* -SHRINED, -SHRINING, -SHRINES to place in a shrine

ENSHROUD   *v* -ED, -ING, -S to conceal

ENSIFORM   *adj* sword-shaped

ENSIGN   *n pl.* -S a navy officer

ENSIGNCY   *n* pl. -CIES the rank of an ensign

ENSILAGE   *v* -LAGED, -LAGING, -LAGES to ensile

ENSILE   *v* -SILED, -SILING, -SILES to store in a silo

ENSKY   *v* -SKIED or -SKYED, -SKYING, -SKIES to raise to the skies

ENSLAVE   *v* -SLAVED, -SLAVING, -SLAVES to make a slave of

ENSLAVER   *n* pl. -S one that enslaves

ENSNARE   *v* -SNARED, -SNARING, -SNARES to trap

ENSNARER   *n* pl. -S one that ensnares

ENSNARL   *v* -ED, -ING, -S to tangle

ENSORCEL   *v* -ED, -ING, -S to bewitch

ENSOUL   *v* -ED, -ING, -S to endow with a soul

ENSPHERE   *v* -SPHERED, -SPHERING, -SPHERES to enclose in a sphere

ENSUE   *v* -SUED, -SUING, -SUES to occur afterward or as a result

ENSURE   *v* -SURED, -SURING, -SURES to make certain

ENSURER   *n* pl. -S one that ensures

ENSWATHE   *v* -SWATHED, -SWATHING, -SWATHES to swathe

ENTAIL   *v* -ED, -ING, -S to restrict the inheritance of to a specified line of heirs

ENTAILER   *n* pl. -S one that entails

ENTAMEBA   *n* pl. -BAE or -BAS endameba

ENTANGLE   *v* -TANGLED, -TANGLING, -TANGLES to tangle

ENTASIA   *n* pl. -S spasmodic contraction of a muscle

ENTASIS   *n* pl. -TASES a slight convexity in a column **ENTASTIC** *adj*

ENTELLUS   *n* pl. -ES a hanuman

ENTENTE   *n* pl. -S an agreement between nations

ENTER   *v* -ED, -ING, -S to come or go into

ENTERA   *a* pl. of enteron

ENTERAL   *adj* enteric

ENTERER   *n* pl. -S one that enters

ENTERIC   *adj* pertaining to the enteron

ENTERON   *n* pl. -TERONS or -TERA the alimentary canal

ENTHALPY   *n* pl. -PIES a thermodynamic measure

ENTHETIC   *adj* introduced from outside

ENTHRAL   *v* -THRALLED, -THRALLING, -THRALS to enthrall

ENTHRALL   *v* -ED, -ING, -S to charm

ENTHRONE   *v* -THRONED, -THRONING, -THRONES to place on a throne

ENTHUSE   *v* -THUSED, -THUSING, -THUSES to show enthusiasm

ENTIA   pl. of ens

ENTICE   *v* -TICED, -TICING, -TICES to allure

ENTICER   *n* pl. -S one that entices

ENTIRE   *n* pl. -S the whole of something

ENTIRELY   *adv* completely

ENTIRETY   *n* pl. -TIES completeness

ENTITLE   *v* -TLED, -TLING, -TLES to give a title to

ENTITY   *n* pl. -TIES something that has a real existence

ENTODERM   *n* pl. -S endoderm

ENTOIL   *v* -ED, -ING, -S to entrap

ENTOMB   *v* -ED, -ING, -S to place in a tomb

ENTOPIC   *adj* situated in the normal place

ENTOZOA   *a* pl. of entozoan and pl. of entozoon

ENTOZOAL   *adj* entozoic

ENTOZOAN   *n* pl. -ZOANS or -ZOA an entozoic parasite

ENTOZOIC   *adj* living within an animal

ENTOZOON   *n* pl. -ZOA entozoan

ENTRAILS   *n/pl* the internal organs

ENTRAIN   *v* -ED, -ING, -S to board a train

ENTRANCE   *v* -TRANCED, -TRANCING, -TRANCES to fill with delight or wonder

ENTRANT   *n* pl. -S one that enters

ENTRAP   *v* -TRAPPED, -TRAPPING, -TRAPS to trap

ENTREAT   *v* -ED, -ING, -S to ask for earnestly

ENTREATY   *n* pl. -TREATIES an earnest request

ENTREE   *n* pl. -S the principal dish of a meal

ENTRENCH   *v* -ED, -ING, -ES to establish firmly

ENTREPOT   *n* pl. -S a warehouse

ENTRESOL *n* pl. -S a mezzanine

ENTRIES pl. of entry

ENTROPY *n* pl. -PIES a thermodynamic measure

ENTRUST *v* -ED, -ING, -S to give over for safekeeping

ENTRY *n* pl. -TRIES a place of entrance

ENTRYWAY *n* pl. -WAYS a passage serving as an entrance

ENTWINE *v* -TWINED, -TWINING, -TWINES to twine around

ENTWIST *v* -ED, -ING, -S to twist together

ENURE *v* -URED, -URING, -URES to inure

ENURESIS *n* pl. -SISES involuntary urination **ENURETIC** *adj*

ENVELOP *v* -ED, -ING, -S to cover completely

ENVELOPE *n* pl. -S a paper container

ENVENOM *v* -ED, -ING, -S to put venom into

ENVIABLE *adj* desirable **ENVIABLY** *adv*

ENVIED past tense of envy

ENVIER *n* pl. -S one that envies

ENVIES present 3d person sing. of envy

ENVIOUS *adj* resentful and desirous of another's possessions or qualities

ENVIRON *v* -ED, -ING, -S to encircle

ENVISAGE *v* -AGED, -AGING, -AGES to form a mental image of

ENVISION *v* -ED, -ING, -S to envisage

ENVOI *n* pl. -S the closing of a poem or prose work

ENVOY *n* pl. -VOYS a representative

ENVY *v* -VIED, -VYING, -VIES to be envious of

ENWHEEL *v* -ED, -ING, -S to encircle

ENWIND *v* -WOUND, -WINDING, -WINDS to wind around

ENWOMB *v* -ED, -ING, -S to enclose as if in a womb

ENWRAP *v* -WRAPPED, -WRAPPING, -WRAPS to envelop

ENZOOTIC *n* pl. -S a type of animal disease

ENZYM *n* pl. -S enzyme

ENZYME *n* pl. -S a complex protein **ENZYMIC** *adj*

EOBIONT *n* pl. -S a type of basic organism

EOHIPPUS *n* pl. -ES an extinct horse

EOLIAN *adj* pertaining to the wind

EOLIPILE *n* pl. -S a type of engine

EOLITH *n* pl. -S a prehistoric stone tool **EOLITHIC** *adj*

EOLOPILE *n* pl. -S eolipile

EON *n* pl. -S an indefinitely long period of time

EONIAN *adj* everlasting

EONISM *n* pl. -S adoption of the dress and mannerisms of the opposite sex

EOSIN *n* pl. -S a red dye **EOSINIC** *adj*

EOSINE *n* pl. -S eosin

EPACT *n* pl. -S the difference between the lengths of the solar and lunar years

EPARCH *n* pl. -S the head of an eparchy

EPARCHY *n* pl. -CHIES a district of modern Greece

EPAULET *n* pl. -S a shoulder ornament

EPEE *n* pl. -S a type of sword

EPEEIST *n* pl. -S one who fences with an epee

EPEIRIC *adj* pertaining to vertical movement of the earth's crust

EPERGNE *n* pl. -S an ornamental dish

EPHA *n* pl. -S ephah

EPHAH *n* pl. -S a Hebrew unit of dry measure

EPHEBE *n* pl. -S ephebus **EPHEBIC** *adj*

EPHEBOS *n* pl. -BOI ephebus

EPHEBUS *n* pl. -BI a young man of ancient Greece

EPHEDRA *n* pl. -S a desert shrub

EPHEDRIN *n* pl. -S an alkaloid used to treat allergies

EPHEMERA *n* pl. -ERAS or -ERAE something of very short life or duration

EPHOD *n* pl. -S an ancient Hebrew vestment

EPHOR *n* pl. -ORS or -ORI a magistrate of ancient Greece **EPHORAL** *adj*

EPHORATE *n* pl. -S the office of ephor

EPIBLAST *n* pl. -S the ectoderm

EPIBOLY *n* pl. -LIES the growth of one part around another **EPIBOLIC** *adj*

EPIC n pl. -S a long narrative poem **EPICAL** adj **EPICALLY** adv

EPICALYX n pl. -LYXES or -LYCES a set of bracts close to and resembling a calyx

EPICARP n pl. -S the outer layer of a pericarp

EPICEDIA n/pl funeral songs

EPICENE n pl. -S one having both male and female characteristics

EPICLIKE adj resembling an epic

EPICOTYL n pl. -S a part of a plant embryo

EPICURE n pl. -S a gourmet

EPICYCLE n pl. -S a circle that rolls on the circumference of another circle

EPIDEMIC n pl. -S a rapid spread of a disease

EPIDERM n pl. -S the outer layer of skin

EPIDOTE n pl. -S a mineral **EPIDOTIC** adj

EPIDURAL adj situated on the membrane that encloses the brain

EPIFAUNA n pl. -FAUNAE or -FAUNAS fauna living on a hard sea floor

EPIFOCAL adj pertaining to the point of origin of an earthquake

EPIGEAL adj epigeous

EPIGEAN adj epigeous

EPIGENE adj occurring near the surface of the earth

EPIGENIC adj pertaining to change in the mineral character of a rock

EPIGEOUS adj growing on or close to the ground

EPIGON n pl. -S epigone

EPIGONE n pl. -S an inferior imitator **EPIGONIC** adj

EPIGONUS n pl. -NI epigone

EPIGRAM n pl. -S a brief, witty remark

EPIGRAPH n pl. -S an engraved inscription

EPIGYNY n pl. -NIES the state of having floral organs near the top of the ovary

EPILEPSY n pl. -SIES a disorder of the nervous system

EPILOG n pl. -S a concluding section

EPILOGUE v -LOGUED, -LOGUING, -LOGUES to provide with a concluding section

EPIMER n pl. -S a type of sugar compound **EPIMERIC** adj

EPIMERE n pl. -S a part of an embryo

EPIMYSIA n/pl muscle sheaths

EPINAOS n pl. -NAOI a rear vestibule

EPINASTY n pl. -TIES a downward bending of plant parts

EPIPHANY n pl. -NIES an appearance of a deity

EPIPHYTE n pl. -S a plant growing upon another plant

EPISCIA n pl. -S a tropical herb

EPISCOPE n pl. -S a type of projector

EPISODE n pl. -S an incident in the course of a continuous experience **EPISODIC** adj

EPISOME n pl. -S a genetic determinant **EPISOMAL** adj

EPISTASY n pl. -SIES a suppression of genetic effect

EPISTLE n pl. -S a long or formal letter

EPISTLER n pl. -S one that writes epistles

EPISTYLE n pl. -S a part of a classical building

EPITAPH n pl. -S an inscription on a tomb

EPITASIS n pl. -ASES the main part of a classical drama

EPITAXY n pl. -TAXIES a type of crystalline growth

EPITHET n pl. -S a term used to characterize a person or thing

EPITOME n pl. -S a typical or ideal example **EPITOMIC** adj

EPIZOA pl. of epizoon

EPIZOIC adj living on the body of an animal

EPIZOISM n pl. -S the state of being epizoic

EPIZOITE n pl. -S an epizoic organism

EPIZOON n pl. -ZOA an epizoic parasite

EPIZOOTY n pl. -TIES a type of animal disease

EPOCH n pl. -S a particular period of time **EPOCHAL** adj

EPODE n pl. -S a type of poem

EPONYM n pl. -S the person for whom something is named **EPONYMIC** adj

EPONYMY n pl. -MIES the derivation of an eponymic name

EPOPEE n pl. -S an epic poem

EPOPOEIA n pl. -S epopee

EPOS n pl. -ES an epic poem

EPOXIDE	*n* pl. -S an epoxy compound
EPOXY	*v* EPOXIED or EPOXYED, EPOXYING, EPOXIES to glue with epoxy (a type of resin)
EPSILON	*n* pl. -S a Greek letter
EQUABLE	*adj* not changing or varying greatly **EQUABLY** *adv*
EQUAL	*adj* having the same capability, quantity, or effect as another
EQUAL	*v* EQUALED, EQUALING, EQUALS or EQUALLED, EQUALLING, EQUALS to be equal to
EQUALISE	*v* -ISED, -ISING, -ISES to equalize
EQUALITY	*n* pl. -TIES the state of being equal
EQUALIZE	*v* -IZED, -IZING, -IZES to make equal
EQUALLED	a past tense of equal
EQUALLING	a past participle of equal
EQUALLY	*adv* in an equal manner
EQUATE	*v* EQUATED, EQUATING, EQUATES to make equal
EQUATION	*n* pl. -S the act of equating
EQUATOR	*n* pl. -S the great circle of the earth
EQUERRY	*n* pl. -RIES an officer in charge of the care of horses
EQUINE	*n* pl. -S a horse
EQUINELY	*adv* in a horselike manner
EQUINITY	*n* pl. -TIES the state of being like a horse
EQUINOX	*n* pl. -ES a point on the celestial sphere
EQUIP	*v* EQUIPPED, EQUIPPING, EQUIPS to provide with whatever is needed
EQUIPAGE	*n* pl. -S a carriage
EQUIPPER	*n* pl. -S one that equips
EQUIPPING	present participle of equip
EQUISETA	*n/pl* rushlike plants
EQUITANT	*adj* overlapping
EQUITES	*n/pl* a privileged military class of ancient Rome
EQUITY	*n* pl. -TIES fairness or impartiality
EQUIVOKE	*n* pl. -S a play on words
ER	*interj* — used to express hesitation
ERA	*n* pl. -S an epoch
ERADIATE	*v* -ATED, -ATING, -ATES to radiate
ERASE	*v* ERASED, ERASING, ERASES to rub or scrape out **ERASABLE** *adj*
ERASER	*n* pl. -S one that erases
ERASION	*n* pl. -S the act of erasing
ERASURE	*n* pl. -S erasion
ERBIUM	*n* pl. -S a metallic element
ERE	*prep* previous to; before
ERECT	*v* -ED, -ING, -S to build
ERECTER	*n* pl. -S erector
ERECTILE	*adj* capable of being raised upright
ERECTION	*n* pl. -S the act of erecting
ERECTIVE	*adj* tending to erect
ERECTLY	*adv* in an upright manner
ERECTOR	*n* pl. -S one that erects
ERELONG	*adv* soon
EREMITE	*n* pl. -S a hermit **EREMITIC** *adj*
EREMURUS	*n* pl. -URI a perennial herb
ERENOW	*adv* before this time
EREPSIN	*n* pl. -S a mixture of enzymes in the small intestine
ERETHISM	*n* pl. -S abnormal irritability **ERETHIC** *adj*
EREWHILE	*adv* some time ago
ERG	*n* pl. -S a unit of work or energy
ERGASTIC	*adj* constituting the nonliving by-products of protoplasmic activity
ERGATE	*n* pl. -S a worker ant
ERGO	*conj* therefore
ERGODIC	*adj* pertaining to the probability that any state will recur
ERGOT	*n* pl. -S a fungus **ERGOTIC** *adj*
ERGOTISM	*n* pl. -S poisoning produced by eating ergot-infected grain
ERICA	*n* pl. -S a shrub of the heath family
ERICOID	*adj* resembling heath
ERIGERON	*n* pl. -S an herb
ERINGO	*n* pl. -GOES or -GOS eryngo
ERISTIC	*n* pl. -S an expert in debate
ERLKING	*n* pl. -S an evil spirit of Germanic folklore
ERMINE	*n* pl. -S the fur of certain weasels **ERMINED** *adj*

ERN *n* pl. -S erne

ERNE *n* pl. -S a sea eagle

ERODE *v* ERODED, ERODING, ERODES to wear away by constant friction

ERODENT *adj* erosive

ERODIBLE *adj* erosible

ERODING present participle of erode

EROGENIC *adj* arousing sexual desire

EROS *n* pl. -ES sexual desire

EROSE *adj* uneven **EROSELY** *adv*

EROSIBLE *adj* capable of being eroded

EROSION *n* pl. -S the act of eroding

EROSIVE *adj* causing erosion

EROTIC *n* pl. -S an amatory poem **EROTICAL** *adj*

EROTICA *n/pl* literature or art dealing with sexual love

EROTISM *n* pl. -S sexual excitement

ERR *v* -ED, -ING, -S to make a mistake

ERRANCY *n* pl. -CIES an instance of erring

ERRAND *n* pl. -S a short trip made for a particular purpose

ERRANT *n* pl. -S a wanderer

ERRANTLY *adv* in a wandering manner

ERRANTRY *n* pl. -RIES the state of wandering

ERRATA *n* pl. -S a list of printing errors

ERRATIC *n* pl. -S an eccentric person

ERRATUM *n* pl. -TA a printing error

ERRHINE *n* pl. -S a substance that promotes nasal discharge

ERRINGLY *adv* in a mistaken manner

ERROR *n* pl. -S a mistake

ERS *n* pl. -ES ervil

ERSATZ *n* pl. -ES a substitute

ERST *adv* formerly

ERUCT *v* -ED, -ING, -S to belch

ERUCTATE *v* -TATED, -TATING, -TATES to eruct

ERUDITE *adj* scholarly

ERUGO *n* pl. -GOS aerugo

ERUMPENT *adj* bursting forth

ERUPT *v* -ED, -ING, -S to burst forth

ERUPTION *n* pl. -S the act of erupting

ERUPTIVE *n* pl. -S a type of rock

ERVIL *n* pl. -S a European vetch

ERYNGO *n* pl. -GOES or -GOS a medicinal herb

ERYTHEMA *n* pl. -S a redness of the skin

ERYTHRON *n* pl. -S a bodily organ consisting of the red blood cells

ES *n* pl. ESES ess

ESCALADE *v* -LADED, -LADING, -LADES to enter by means of ladders

ESCALATE *v* -LATED, -LATING, -LATES to increase

ESCALLOP *v* -ED, -ING, -S to scallop

ESCALOP *v* -ED, -ING, -S to escallop

ESCAPADE *n* pl. -S a reckless adventure

ESCAPE *v* -CAPED, -CAPING, -CAPES to get away

ESCAPEE *n* pl. -S one that has escaped

ESCAPER *n* pl. -S one that escapes

ESCAPING present participle of escape

ESCAPISM *n* pl. -S the avoidance of reality by diversion of the mind

ESCAPIST *n* pl. -S one given to escapism

ESCAR *n* pl. -S esker

ESCARGOT *n* pl. -S an edible snail

ESCAROLE *n* pl. -S a variety of endive

ESCARP *v* -ED, -ING, -S to cause to slope steeply

ESCHALOT *n* pl. -S a shallot

ESCHAR *n* pl. -S a hard, dry scab

ESCHEAT *v* -ED, -ING, -S to confiscate

ESCHEW *v* -ED, -ING, -S to avoid

ESCHEWAL *n* pl. -S the act of eschewing

ESCOLAR *n* pl. -S a food fish

ESCORT *v* -ED, -ING, -S to accompany

ESCOT *v* -ED, -ING, -S to provide support for

ESCROW *v* -ED, -ING, -S to place in the custody of a third party

ESCUAGE *n* pl. -S scutage

ESCUDO *n* pl. -DOS a monetary unit of Portugal

ESCULENT *n* pl. -S something that is edible

ESERINE *n* pl. -S a toxic alkaloid

ESKAR *n* pl. -S esker

ESKER *n* pl. -S a narrow ridge of gravel and sand

ESOPHAGI *n/pl* tubes connecting the mouth to the stomach

ESOTERIC *adj* designed for a select few

ESPALIER *v* -ED, -ING, -S to furnish with a trellis

ESPANOL *n* pl. -ES a native of Spain

ESPARTO *n* pl. -TOS a perennial grass

ESPECIAL *adj* special

ESPIAL *n* pl. -S the act of espying

ESPIED past tense of espy

ESPIEGLE *adj* playful

ESPIES present 3d person sing. of espy

ESPOUSAL *n* pl. -S a marriage ceremony

ESPOUSE *v* -POUSED, -POUSING, -POUSES to marry

ESPOUSER *n* pl. -S one that espouses

ESPRESSO *n* pl. -SOS a strong coffee

ESPRIT *n* pl. -S spirit

ESPY *v* -PIED, -PYING, -PIES to catch sight of

ESQUIRE *v* -QUIRED, -QUIRING, -QUIRES to escort

ESS *n* pl. -ES the letter S

ESSAY *v* -ED, -ING, -S to try

ESSAYER *n* pl. -S one that essays

ESSAYIST *n* pl. -S a writer of essays (prose compositions)

ESSENCE *n* pl. -S a fundamental nature or quality

ESSOIN *n* pl. -S an excuse

ESSONITE *n* pl. -S a variety of garnet

ESTANCIA *n* pl. -S a cattle ranch

ESTATE *v* -TATED, -TATING, -TATES to provide with landed property

ESTEEM *v* -ED, -ING, -S to have a high opinion of

ESTER *n* pl. -S a type of chemical compound

ESTERASE *n* pl. -S a type of enzyme

ESTERIFY *v* -FIED, -FYING, -FIES to convert into an ester

ESTHESIA *n* pl. -S the ability to receive sensation

ESTHESIS *n* pl. -THESISES or -THESES esthesia

ESTHETE *n* pl. -S an esthetic person

ESTHETIC *adj* keenly appreciative of the beautiful

ESTIMATE *v* -MATED, -MATING, -MATES to make an approximate judgment of

ESTIVAL *adj* pertaining to summer

ESTIVATE *v* -VATED, -VATING, -VATES to spend the summer

ESTOP *v* -TOPPED, -TOPPING, -TOPS to impede by estoppel

ESTOPPEL *n* pl. -S a legal restraint preventing a person from contradicting his own previous statement

ESTOVERS *n/pl* necessities allowed by law

ESTRAGON *n* pl. -S tarragon

ESTRAL *adj* estrous

ESTRANGE *v* -TRANGED, -TRANGING, -TRANGES to alienate

ESTRAY *v* -ED, -ING, -S to stray

ESTREAT *v* -ED, -ING, -S to copy from court records for use in prosecution

ESTRIN *n* pl. -S estrone

ESTRIOL *n* pl. -S an estrogen

ESTROGEN *n* pl. -S any of a group of female hormones promoting or producing estrus

ESTRONE *n* pl. -S an estrogen

ESTROUS *adj* pertaining to estrus

ESTRUAL *adj* estrous

ESTRUM *n* pl. -S estrus

ESTRUS *n* pl. -ES the period of heat in female mammals

ESTUARY *n* pl. -ARIES an inlet of the sea at a river's lower end

ESURIENT *adj* greedy

ET a past tense of eat

ETA *n* pl. -S a Greek letter

ETAGERE *n* pl. -S an ornamental stand

ETAMIN *n* pl. -S etamine

ETAMINE *n* pl. -S a loosely woven fabric

ETAPE *n* pl. -S a warehouse

ETATISM *n* pl. -S state socialism **ETATIST** *adj*

ETCETERA *n* pl. -S a number of additional items

ETCH *v* -ED, -ING, -ES to engrave with acid

ETCHER *n* pl. -S one that etches

ETCHING *n* pl. -S an etched design

ETERNAL	n pl. -S something lasting forever
ETERNE	adj everlasting
ETERNISE	v -NISED, -NISING, -NISES to eternize
ETERNITY	n pl. -TIES infinite time
ETERNIZE	v -NIZED, -NIZING, -NIZES to make everlasting
ETESIAN	n pl. -S an annually recurring wind
ETH	n pl. -S edh
ETHANE	n pl. -S a gaseous hydrocarbon
ETHANOL	n pl. -S an alcohol
ETHENE	n pl. -S ethylene
ETHER	n pl. -S a volatile liquid used as an anesthetic **ETHERIC** adj
ETHEREAL	adj airy
ETHERIFY	v -FIED, -FYING, -FIES to convert into ether
ETHERISH	adj resembling ether
ETHERIZE	v -IZED, -IZING, -IZES to treat with ether
ETHIC	n pl. -S a body of moral principles
ETHICAL	n pl. -S a drug sold by prescription only
ETHICIAN	n pl. -S an ethicist
ETHICIST	n pl. -S a specialist in ethics
ETHICIZE	v -CIZED, -CIZING, -CIZES to make ethical
ETHINYL	n pl. -S ethynyl
ETHION	n pl. -S a pesticide
ETHMOID	n pl. -S a bone of the nasal cavity
ETHNARCH	n pl. -S the ruler of a people or province
ETHNIC	n pl. -S a member of a particular ethnos **ETHNICAL** adj
ETHNOS	n pl. -ES a group of people who share a common and distinctive culture
ETHOLOGY	n pl. -GIES the study of animal behavior
ETHOS	n pl. -ES the fundamental character of a culture
ETHOXY	adj pertaining to ethoxyl
ETHOXYL	n pl. -S a univalent chemical radical
ETHYL	n pl. -S a univalent chemical radical
ETHYLATE	v -ATED, -ATING, -ATES to introduce the ethyl group into
ETHYLENE	n pl. -S a flammable gas
ETHYLIC	adj pertaining to ethyl
ETHYNE	n pl. -S a flammable gas
ETHYNYL	n pl. -S a univalent chemical radical
ETIOLATE	v -LATED, -LATING, -LATES to whiten
ETIOLOGY	n pl. -GIES the study of the causes of diseases
ETNA	n pl. -S a container for heating liquids
ETOILE	n pl. -S a star
ETUDE	n pl. -S a piece of music for the practice of a point of technique
ETUI	n pl. -S a case for holding small articles
ETWEE	n pl. -S etui
ETYMON	n pl. -MA or -MONS the earliest known form of a word
EUCAINE	n pl. -S an anesthetic
EUCALYPT	n pl. -S an evergreen tree
EUCHARIS	n pl. -RISES a flowering plant
EUCHRE	v -CHRED, -CHRING, -CHRES to prevent from winning three tricks in euchre (a card game)
EUCLASE	n pl. -S a mineral
EUCRITE	n pl. -S a type of meteorite **EUCRITIC** adj
EUDAEMON	n pl. -S eudemon
EUDEMON	n pl. -S a good spirit
EUGENICS	n/pl the science of hereditary improvement **EUGENIC** adj
EUGENIST	n pl. -S a student of eugenics
EUGENOL	n pl. -S an aromatic liquid
EUGLENA	n pl. -S a freshwater protozoan
EULACHAN	n pl. -S eulachon
EULACHON	n pl. -S a marine food fish
EULOGIA	n pl. -GIAE holy bread
EULOGIA	n pl. -S a blessing
EULOGISE	v -GISED, -GISING, -GISES to eulogize
EULOGIST	n pl. -S one that eulogizes
EULOGIUM	n pl. -GIA or -GIUMS a eulogy
EULOGIZE	v -GIZED, -GIZING, -GIZES to praise highly
EULOGY	n pl. -GIES a formal expression of high praise

EUNUCH — *n pl.* -S a castrated man

EUONYMUS — *n pl.* -ES any of a genus of shrubs or small trees

EUPATRID — *n pl.* -RIDS or -RIDAE an aristocrat of ancient Athens

EUPEPSIA — *n pl.* -S good digestion **EUPEPTIC** *adj*

EUPEPSY — *n pl.* -SIES eupepsia

EUPHENIC — *adj* dealing with biological improvement

EUPHONY — *n pl.* -NIES pleasant sound **EUPHONIC** *adj*

EUPHORIA — *n pl.* -S a feeling of well-being **EUPHORIC** *adj*

EUPHOTIC — *adj* pertaining to the upper layer of a body of water

EUPHRASY — *n pl.* -SIES an annual herb

EUPHROE — *n pl.* -S a device used to adjust a shipboard awning

EUPHUISM — *n pl.* -S an artificially elegant style of speech or writing

EUPHUIST — *n pl.* -S one given to euphuism

EUPLOID — *n pl.* -S a cell having three or more identical genomes

EUPLOIDY — *n pl.* -DIES the state of being a euploid

EUPNEA — *n pl.* -S normal breathing **EUPNEIC** *adj*

EUPNOEA — *n pl.* -S eupnea **EUPNOEIC** *adj*

EUREKA — *interj* — used to express triumph upon discovering something

EURIPUS — *n pl.* -PI a swift sea channel

EURO — *n pl.* EUROS a large kangaroo

EUROPIUM — *n pl.* -S a metallic element

EURYTHMY — *n pl.* -MIES harmony of movement or structure

EUSTACY — *n pl.* -CIES a worldwide change in sea level **EUSTATIC** *adj*

EUSTELE — *n pl.* -S a plant part

EUTAXY — *n pl.* -TAXIES good order

EUTECTIC — *n pl.* -S an alloy that has the lowest possible melting point

EUTROPHY — *n pl.* -PHIES healthful nutrition

EUXENITE — *n pl.* -S a mineral

EVACUANT — *n pl.* -S a cathartic medicine

EVACUATE — *v* -ATED, -ATING, -ATES to remove from a dangerous area

EVACUEE — *n pl.* -S one that is evacuated

EVADE — *v* EVADED, EVADING, EVADES to escape or avoid by cleverness or deceit **EVADABLE, EVADIBLE** *adj*

EVADER — *n pl.* -S one that evades

EVALUATE — *v* -ATED, -ATING, -ATES to determine the value of

EVANESCE — *v* -NESCED, -NESCING, -NESCES to fade away

EVANGEL — *n pl.* -S a preacher of the gospel

EVANISH — *v* -ED, -ING, -ES to vanish

EVASION — *n pl.* -S the act of evading

EVASIVE — *adj* tending to evade

EVE — *n pl.* -S evening

EVECTION — *n pl.* -S irregularity in the moon's motion

EVEN — *adj* EVENER, EVENEST flat and smooth

EVEN — *v* -ED, -ING, -S to make even

EVENER — *n pl.* -S one that evens

EVENFALL — *n pl.* -S twilight

EVENING — *n pl.* -S the latter part of the day and early part of the night

EVENLY — *adv* in an even manner

EVENNESS — *n pl.* -ES the state of being even

EVENSONG — *n pl.* -S an evening prayer service

EVENT — *n pl.* -S something that occurs

EVENTFUL — *adj* momentous

EVENTIDE — *n pl.* -S evening

EVENTUAL — *adj* occurring at a later time

EVER — *adv* at all times

EVERMORE — *adv* forever

EVERSION — *n pl.* -S the act of everting

EVERT — *v* -ED, -ING, -S to turn outward or inside out

EVERTOR — *n pl.* -S a muscle that turns a part outward

EVERY — *adj* each without exception

EVERYDAY — *adj* ordinary

EVERYMAN — *n pl.* -MEN the typical or ordinary man

EVERYONE — *pron* every person

EVERYWAY — *adv* in every way

EVICT — *v* -ED, -ING, -S to expel by legal process

EVICTEE — *n pl.* -S one that is evicted

EVICTION   n pl. -S the act of evicting

EVICTOR   n pl. -S one that evicts

EVIDENCE   v -DENCED, -DENCING, -DENCES to indicate clearly

EVIDENT   adj clear to the vision or understanding

EVIL   adj EVILER, EVILEST or EVILLER, EVILLEST morally bad

EVIL   n pl. -S something that is evil

EVILDOER   n pl. -S one that does evil

EVILLER   a comparative of evil

EVILLEST   a superlative of evil

EVILLY   adv in an evil manner

EVILNESS   n pl. -ES the quality of being evil

EVINCE   v EVINCED, EVINCING, EVINCES to show clearly **EVINCIVE** adj

EVITE   v EVITED, EVITING, EVITES to avoid **EVITABLE** adj

EVOCABLE   adj capable of being evoked

EVOCATOR   n pl. -S one that evokes

EVOKE   v EVOKED, EVOKING, EVOKES to call forth

EVOKER   n pl. -S an evocator

EVOLUTE   n pl. -S a type of geometric curve

EVOLVE   v EVOLVED, EVOLVING, EVOLVES to develop

EVOLVER   n pl. -S one that evolves

EVONYMUS   n pl. -ES euonymus

EVULSION   n pl. -S the act of pulling out

EVZONE   n pl. -S a Greek soldier

EWE   n pl. -S a female sheep

EWER   n pl. -S a large pitcher

EX   n pl. -ES the letter X

EXACT   adj -ACTER, -ACTEST precise

EXACT   v -ED, -ING, -S to force the payment or yielding of

EXACTA   n pl. -S a type of horse racing bet

EXACTER   n pl. -S one that exacts

EXACTION   n pl. -S the act of exacting

EXACTLY   adv in an exact manner

EXACTOR   n pl. -S exacter

EXALT   v -ED, -ING, -S to raise

EXALTER   n pl. -S one that exalts

EXAM   n pl. -S an examination

EXAMEN   n pl. -S a critical study

EXAMINE   v -INED, -INING, -INES to inspect

EXAMINEE   n pl. -S one that is taking an examination

EXAMINER   n pl. -S one that examines

EXAMINING   present participle of examine

EXAMPLE   v -PLED, -PLING, -PLES to show by representation

EXANTHEM   n pl. -S a skin eruption

EXARCH   n pl. -S the ruler of a province in the Byzantine Empire **EXARCHAL** adj

EXARCHY   n pl. -CHIES the domain of an exarch

EXCAVATE   v -VATED, -VATING, -VATES to dig out

EXCEED   v -ED, -ING, -S to go beyond

EXCEEDER   n pl. -S one that exceeds

EXCEL   v -CELLED, -CELLING, -CELS to surpass others

EXCEPT   v -ED, -ING, -S to leave out

EXCERPT   v -ED, -ING, -S to pick out a passage from for quoting

EXCESS   n pl. -ES an overabundance

EXCHANGE   v -CHANGED, -CHANGING, -CHANGES to give and receive reciprocally

EXCIDE   v -CIDED, -CIDING, -CIDES to excise

EXCIPLE   n pl. -S a rim around the hymenium of various lichens

EXCISE   v -CISED, -CISING, -CISES to remove by cutting out

EXCISION   n pl. -S the act of excising

EXCITANT   n pl. -S a stimulant

EXCITE   v -CITED, -CITING, -CITES to arouse the emotions of

EXCITER   n pl. -S one that excites

EXCITON   n pl. -S an energy level of a crystal

EXCITOR   n pl. -S exciter

EXCLAIM   v -ED, -ING, -S to cry out suddenly

EXCLAVE   n pl. -S a portion of a country which is isolated in foreign territory

EXCLUDE   v -CLUDED, -CLUDING, -CLUDES to shut out

EXCLUDER   n pl. -S one that excludes

EXCRETA   n/pl excreted matter **EXCRETAL** adj

EXCRETE   *v* -CRETED, -CRETING, -CRETES to separate and eliminate from an organic body

EXCRETER   *n* pl. -S one that excretes

EXCUSE   *v* -CUSED, -CUSING, -CUSES to apologize for

EXCUSER   *n* pl. -S one that excuses

EXEC   *n* pl. -S an executive officer

EXECRATE   *v* -CRATED, -CRATING, -CRATES to curse

EXECUTE   *v* -CUTED, -CUTING, -CUTES to carry out

EXECUTER   *n* pl. -S executor

EXECUTOR   *n* pl. -S one that executes

EXEDRA   *n* pl. -DRAE a curved outdoor bench

EXEGESIS   *n* pl. -GESES critical explanation or analysis **EXEGETIC** *adj*

EXEGETE   *n* pl. -S one skilled in exegesis

EXEMPLAR   *n* pl. -S one that is worthy of being copied

EXEMPLUM   *n* pl. -PLA an example

EXEMPT   *v* -ED, -ING, -S to free from an obligation required of others

EXEQUY   *n* pl. -QUIES a funeral procession **EXEQUIAL** *adj*

EXERCISE   *v* -CISED, -CISING, -CISES to make use of

EXERGUE   *n* pl. -S a space on a coin **EXERGUAL** *adj*

EXERT   *v* -ED, -ING, -S to put into action

EXERTION   *n* pl. -S the act of exerting

EXERTIVE   *adj* tending to exert

EXHALANT   *n* pl. -S something that exhales

EXHALE   *v* -HALED, -HALING, -HALES to expel air or vapor

EXHALENT   *n* pl. -S exhalant

EXHAUST   *v* -ED, -ING, -S to use up

EXHIBIT   *v* -ED, -ING, -S to present for public viewing

EXHORT   *v* -ED, -ING, -S to advise urgently

EXHORTER   *n* pl. -S one that exhorts

EXHUME   *v* -HUMED, -HUMING, -HUMES to dig out of the earth

EXHUMER   *n* pl. -S one that exhumes

EXIGENCE   *n* pl. -S exigency

EXIGENCY   *n* pl. -CIES urgency

EXIGENT   *adj* urgent

EXIGIBLE   *adj* liable to be demanded

EXIGUITY   *n* pl. -ITIES the state of being exiguous

EXIGUOUS   *adj* meager

EXILE   *v* -ILED, -ILING, -ILES to banish from one's own country

EXILIAN   *adj* exilic

EXILIC   *adj* pertaining to exile (banishment from one's own country)

EXIMIOUS   *adj* excellent

EXINE   *n* pl. -S the outer layer of certain spores

EXIST   *v* -ED, -ING, -S to be

EXISTENT   *n* pl. -S something that exists

EXIT   *v* -ED, -ING, -S to go out

EXOCARP   *n* pl. -S the epicarp

EXOCRINE   *n* pl. -S an external secretion

EXODERM   *n* pl. -S the ectoderm

EXODOS   *n* pl. -DOI a concluding dramatic scene

EXODUS   *n* pl. -ES a movement away

EXOERGIC   *adj* releasing energy

EXOGAMY   *n* pl. -MIES marriage outside of a particular group **EXOGAMIC** *adj*

EXOGEN   *n* pl. -S a type of plant

EXORABLE   *adj* persuadable

EXORCISE   *v* -CISED, -CISING, -CISES to free of an evil spirit

EXORCISM   *n* pl. -S the act of exorcising

EXORCIST   *n* pl. -S one who practices exorcism

EXORCIZE   *v* -CIZED, -CIZING, -CIZES to exorcise

EXORDIUM   *n* pl. -DIUMS or -DIA a beginning **EXORDIAL** *adj*

EXOSMOSE   *n* pl. -S a form of osmosis **EXOSMIC** *adj*

EXOSPORE   *n* pl. -S the outer coat of a spore

EXOTERIC   *adj* suitable for the public

EXOTIC   *n* pl. -S something from another part of the world

EXOTICA   *n/pl* things excitingly different or unusual

EXOTISM   *n* pl. -S an exotic

EXOTOXIN   *n* pl. -S an excreted toxin **EXOTOXIC** *adj*

EXPAND   v -ED, -ING, -S to increase in size or volume

EXPANDER   n pl. -S one that expands

EXPANSE   n pl. -S a wide, continuous area

EXPECT   v -ED, -ING, -S to anticipate

EXPEDITE   v -DITED, -DITING, -DITES to speed up the progress of

EXPEL   v -PELLED, -PELLING, -PELS to force out

EXPELLEE   n pl. -S a deportee

EXPELLER   n pl. -S one that expels

EXPELLING   present participle of expel

EXPEND   v -ED, -ING, -S to use up

EXPENDER   n pl. -S one that expends

EXPENSE   v -PENSED, -PENSING, -PENSES to charge with costs

EXPERT   v -ED, -ING, -S to serve as an authority

EXPERTLY   adv skillfully

EXPIABLE   adj capable of being expiated

EXPIATE   v -ATED, ATING, -ATES to atone for

EXPIATOR   n pl. -S one that expiates

EXPIRE   v -PIRED, -PIRING, -PIRES to come to an end

EXPIRER   n pl. -S one that expires

EXPIRY   n pl. -RIES a termination

EXPLAIN   v -ED, -ING, -S to make plain or understandable

EXPLANT   v -ED, -ING, -S to remove from the natural site of growth and place in a medium

EXPLICIT   n pl. -S a statement formerly used at the close of a book

EXPLODE   v -PLODED, -PLODING, -PLODES to blow up

EXPLODER   n pl. -S one that explodes

EXPLOIT   v -ED, -ING, -S to take advantage of

EXPLORE   v -PLORED, -PLORING, -PLORES to travel through for the purpose of discovery

EXPLORER   n pl. -S one that explores

EXPO   n pl. -POS a public exhibition

EXPONENT   n pl. -S one who expounds

EXPORT   v -ED, -ING, -S to send to other countries for commercial purposes

EXPORTER   n pl. -S one that exports

EXPOSAL   n pl. -S an exposure

EXPOSE   v -POSED, -POSING, -POSES to lay open to view

EXPOSER   n pl. -S one that exposes

EXPOSIT   v -ED, -ING, -S to expound

EXPOSURE   n pl. -S the act of exposing

EXPOUND   v -ED, -ING, -S to explain in detail

EXPRESS   v -ED, -ING, -ES to set forth in words

EXPULSE   v -PULSED, -PULSING, -PULSES to expel

EXPUNGE   v -PUNGED, PUNGING, -PUNGES to delete

EXPUNGER   n pl. -S one that expunges

EXSCIND   v -ED, -ING, -S to cut out

EXSECANT   n pl. -S a trigonometric function of an angle

EXSECT   v -ED, -ING, -S to cut out

EXSERT   v -ED, -ING, -S to thrust out

EXTANT   adj still in existence

EXTEND   v -ED, -ING, -S to stretch out to full length

EXTENDER   n pl. -S a substance added to another substance

EXTENSOR   n pl. -S a muscle that extends a limb

EXTENT   n pl. -S the range over which something extends

EXTERIOR   n pl. -S a part or surface that is outside

EXTERN   n pl. -S a nonresident of an institution

EXTERNAL   n pl. -S an exterior

EXTERNE   n pl. -S extern

EXTINCT   v -ED, -ING, -S to extinguish

EXTOL   v -TOLLED, -TOLLING, -TOLS to praise highly

EXTOLL   v -ED, -ING, -S to extol

EXTOLLER   n pl. -S one that extols

EXTOLLING   present participle of extol

EXTORT   v -ED, -ING, -S to obtain from a person by violence or intimidation

EXTORTER   n pl. -S one that extorts

EXTRA   n pl. -S something additional

EXTRACT   v -ED, -ING, -S to pull or draw out

EXTRADOS   n pl. -ES the outer curve of an arch

EXTREMA   pl. of extremum

EXTREME   *adj* -TREMER, -TREMEST existing in a very high degree

EXTREME   *n* pl. -S the highest degree

EXTREMUM   *n* pl. -MA a maximum or a minimum of a mathematical function

EXTRORSE   *adj* facing outward

EXTRUDE   *v* -TRUDED, -TRUDING, -TRUDES to force, thrust, or push out

EXTRUDER   *n* pl. -S one that extrudes

EXUDATE   *n* pl. -S an exuded substance

EXUDE   *v* -UDED, -UDING, -UDES to ooze forth

EXULT   *v* -ED, -ING, -S to rejoice greatly

EXULTANT   *adj* exulting

EXURB   *n* pl. -S a residential area lying beyond the suburbs of a city **EXURBAN** *adj*

EXURBIA   *n* pl. -S an exurb

EXUVIATE   *v* -ATED, -ATING, -ATES to molt

EXUVIUM   *n* pl. -VIAE or -VIA the molted covering of an animal **EXUVIAL** *adj*

EYAS   *n* pl. -ES a young hawk

EYE   *v* EYED, EYING or EYEING, EYES to watch closely **EYEABLE** *adj*

EYE   *n* pl. EYES, EYEN or EYNE the organ of sight

EYEBALL   *v* -ED, -ING, -S to eye

EYEBEAM   *n* pl. -S a glance

EYEBOLT   *n* pl. -S a type of bolt or screw

EYEBROW   *n* pl. -S the ridge over the eye

EYECUP   *n* pl. -S a cup used for applying lotions to the eyes

EYED   past tense of eye

EYEDNESS   *n* pl. -ES preference for the use of one eye over the other

EYEFUL   *n* pl. -S a complete view

EYEGLASS   *n* pl. -ES a lens used to aid vision

EYEHOLE   *n* pl. -S a small opening

EYEHOOK   *n* pl. -S a type of hook

EYELASH   *n* pl. -ES a hair growing on the edge of an eyelid

EYELESS   *adj* lacking eyes

EYELET   *v* -LETTED, -LETTING, -LETS to make a small hole in

EYELID   *n* pl. -S the lid of skin that can be closed over an eyeball

EYELIKE   *adj* resembling an eye

EYELINER   *n* pl. -S makeup for the eyes

EYEN   a pl. of eye

EYEPIECE   *n* pl. -S the lens or lens group nearest the eye in an optical instrument

EYEPOINT   *n* pl. -S the point at which an eye is placed in using an optical instrument

EYER   *n* pl. -S one that eyes

EYESHADE   *n* pl. -S a visor for shading the eyes

EYESHOT   *n* pl. -S the range of vision

EYESIGHT   *n* pl. -S the ability to see

EYESOME   *adj* pleasant to look at

EYESORE   *n* pl. -S something offensive to the sight

EYESPOT   *n* pl. -S a simple visual organ of lower animals

EYESTALK   *n* pl. -S a stalklike structure with an eye at its tip

EYESTONE   *n* pl. -S a disk used to remove foreign matter from the eye

EYETOOTH   *n* pl. -TEETH a cuspid

EYEWASH   *n* pl. -ES an eye lotion

EYEWATER   *n* pl. -S an eyewash

EYEWINK   *n* pl. -S a wink of the eye

EYING   a present participle of eye

EYNE   a pl. of eye

EYRA   *n* pl. -S a wild cat of tropical America

EYRE   *n* pl. -S a journey

EYRIE   *n* pl. -S aerie

EYRIR   *n* pl. AURAR a monetary unit of Iceland

EYRY   *n* pl. -RIES aerie

FA	*n* pl. -S the fourth tone of the diatonic musical scale	**FACIES**	*n* pl. FACIES general appearance
FABLE	*v* -BLED, -BLING, -BLES to compose or tell fictitious tales	**FACILE**	*adj* easily achieved or performed **FACILELY** *adv*
FABLER	*n* pl. -S one that fables	**FACILITY**	*n* pl. -TIES the quality of being facile
FABLIAU	*n* pl. -AUX a short metrical tale popular in medieval France	**FACING**	*n* pl. -S a lining at the edge of a garment
FABLING	present participle of fable	**FACT**	*n* pl. -S something known with certainty **FACTFUL** *adj*
FABRIC	*n* pl. -S a woven, felted, or knitted material	**FACTION**	*n* pl. -S a clique within a larger group
FABULAR	*adj* legendary	**FACTIOUS**	*adj* promoting dissension
FABULIST	*n* pl. -S a liar	**FACTOR**	*v* -ED, -ING, -S to express as a product of two or more quantities
FABULOUS	*adj* almost unbelievable		
FACADE	*n* pl. -S the front of a building	**FACTORY**	*n* pl. -RIES a building or group of buildings in which goods are manufactured
FACE	*v* FACED, FACING, FACES to oppose or meet defiantly **FACEABLE** *adj*		
		FACTOTUM	*n* pl. -S a person employed to do many kinds of work
FACEDOWN	*adv* with the front part down		
FACELESS	*adj* lacking personal distinction or identity	**FACTUAL**	*adj* pertaining to facts
		FACTURE	*n* pl. -S the act of making something
FACER	*n* pl. -S one that faces		
FACET	*v* -ETED, -ETING, -ETS or -ETTED, -ETTING, -ETS to cut small plane surfaces on	**FACULA**	*n* pl. -LAE an unusually bright spot on the sun's surface **FACULAR** *adj*
FACETE	*adj* witty **FACETELY** *adv*	**FACULTY**	*n* pl. -TIES an inherent power or ability
FACETIAE	*n/pl* witty sayings or writings		
FACETTED	past tense of facet	**FAD**	*n* pl. -S a practice or interest that enjoys brief popularity
FACETTING	present participle of facet		
FACEUP	*adv* with the front part up	**FADABLE**	*adj* capable of fading
FACIA	*n* pl. -S fascia	**FADDIER**	comparative of faddy
FACIAL	*n* pl. -S a treatment for the face	**FADDIEST**	superlative of faddy
FACIALLY	*adv* with respect to the face	**FADDISH**	*adj* inclined to take up fads
FACIEND	*n* pl. -S a number to be multiplied by another		

FADDISM   n pl. -S inclination to take up fads

FADDIST   n pl. -S a faddish person

FADDY   adj -DIER, -DIEST faddish

FADE   v FADED, FADING, FADES to lose color or brightness **FADEDLY** adv

FADEAWAY   n pl. -AWAYS a type of pitch in baseball

FADELESS   adj not fading

FADER   n pl. -S one that fades

FADGE   v FADGED, FADGING, FADGES to succeed

FADING   n pl. -S an Irish dance

FADO   n pl. -DOS a Portuguese folk song

FAECES   n/pl feces **FAECAL** adj

FAENA   n pl. -S a series of passes made by a matador in a bullfight

FAERIE   n pl. -S a fairy

FAERY   n pl. -ERIES faerie

FAG   v FAGGED, FAGGING, FAGS to make weary by hard work

FAGGOT   v -ED, -ING, -S to fagot

FAGIN   n pl. -S a person who instructs others in crime

FAGOT   v -ED, -ING, -S to bind together into a bundle

FAGOTER   n pl. -S one that fagots

FAGOTING   n pl. -S a type of embroidery

FAHLBAND   n pl. -S a band or stratum of rock impregnated with metallic sulfides

FAIENCE   n pl. -S a variety of glazed pottery

FAIL   v -ED, -ING, -S to be unsuccessful in an attempt

FAILING   n pl. -S a minor fault or weakness

FAILLE   n pl. -S a woven fabric

FAILURE   n pl. -S the act of failing

FAIN   adj FAINER, FAINEST glad

FAINEANT   n pl. -S a lazy person

FAINT   v -ED, -ING, -S to lose consciousness

FAINT   adj FAINTER, FAINTEST lacking strength or vigor

FAINTER   n pl. -S one that faints

FAINTISH   adj somewhat faint

FAINTLY   adv in a faint manner

FAIR   adj FAIRER, FAIREST free from bias, dishonesty, or injustice

FAIR   v -ED, -ING, -S to make smooth

FAIRIES   pl. of fairy

FAIRING   n pl. -S a structure on an aircraft serving to reduce drag

FAIRISH   adj moderately good

FAIRLEAD   n pl. -S a device used to hold a ship's rigging in place

FAIRLY   adv in a fair manner

FAIRNESS   n pl. -ES the quality of being fair

FAIRWAY   n pl. -WAYS the mowed part of a golf course between tee and green

FAIRY   n pl. FAIRIES an imaginary supernatural being

FAIRYISM   n pl. -S the quality of being like a fairy

FAITH   v -ED, -ING, -S to believe or trust

FAITHFUL   n pl. -S a loyal follower or member

FAITOUR   n pl. -S an impostor

FAKE   v FAKED, FAKING, FAKES to contrive and present as genuine

FAKEER   n pl. -S fakir

FAKER   n pl. -S one that fakes

FAKERY   n pl. -ERIES the practice of faking

FAKING   present participle of fake

FAKIR   n pl. -S a Hindu ascetic

FALBALA   n pl. -S a trimming for a woman's garment

FALCATE   adj curved and tapering to a point

FALCATED   adj falcate

FALCHION   n pl. -S a broad-bladed sword

FALCON   n pl. -S a bird of prey

FALCONER   n pl. -S one that hunts with hawks

FALCONET   n pl. -S a small falcon

FALCONRY   n pl. -RIES the sport of hunting with falcons

FALDERAL   n pl. -S nonsense

FALDEROL   n pl. -S falderal

FALL   v FELL, FALLEN, FALLING, FALLS to descend under the force of gravity

FALLACY   n pl. -CIES a false idea

FALLAL *n* pl. -S a showy article of dress

FALLBACK *n* pl. -S an act of retreating

FALLEN past participle of fall

FALLER *n* pl. -S one that falls

FALLFISH *n* pl. -ES a freshwater fish

FALLIBLE *adj* capable of erring **FALLIBLY** *adv*

FALLOFF *n* pl. -S a decline in quantity or quality

FALLOUT *n* pl. -S radioactive debris resulting from a nuclear explosion

FALLOW *v* -ED, -ING, -S to plow and leave unseeded

FALSE *adj* FALSER, FALSEST contrary to truth or fact **FALSELY** *adv*

FALSETTO *n* pl. -TOS an artificially high voice

FALSIE *n* pl. -S a pad worn within a brassiere

FALSIFY *v* -FIED, -FYING, -FIES to represent falsely

FALSITY *n* pl. -TIES something false

FALTBOAT *n* pl. -S a collapsible boat resembling a kayak

FALTER *v* -ED, -ING, -S to hesitate

FALTERER *n* pl. -S one that falters

FAME *v* FAMED, FAMING, FAMES to make famous

FAMELESS *adj* not famous

FAMILIAL *adj* pertaining to a family

FAMILIAR *n* pl. -S a close friend or associate

FAMILY *n* pl. -LIES a group of persons related by blood or marriage

FAMINE *n* pl. -S a widespread scarcity of food

FAMING present participle of fame

FAMISH *v* -ED, -ING, -ES to suffer extreme hunger

FAMOUS *adj* well-known **FAMOUSLY** *adv*

FAMULUS *n* pl. -LI a servant or attendant

FAN *v* FANNED, FANNING, FANS to cool or refresh with a fan (a device for putting air into motion)

FANATIC *n* pl. -S a zealot

FANCIED past tense of fancy

FANCIER *n* pl. -S one that has a special liking for something

FANCIES present 3d person sing. of fancy

FANCIFUL *adj* unrealistic

FANCY *adj* -CIER, -CIEST ornamental **FANCILY** *adv*

FANCY *v* -CIED, -CYING, -CIES to take a liking to

FANDANGO *n* pl. -GOS a lively Spanish dance

FANDOM *n* pl. -S an aggregate of enthusiastic devotees

FANE *n* pl. -S a temple

FANEGA *n* pl. -S a Spanish unit of dry measure

FANEGADA *n* pl. -S a Spanish unit of area

FANFARE *n* pl. -S a short, lively musical flourish

FANFARON *n* pl. -S a braggart

FANFOLD *n* pl. -S a type of writing pad or tablet

FANG *n* pl. -S a long, pointed tooth **FANGED, FANGLESS, FANGLIKE** *adj*

FANGA *n* pl. -S fanega

FANION *n* pl. -S a small flag

FANJET *n* pl. -S a type of jet engine

FANLIGHT *n* pl. -S a type of window

FANLIKE *adj* resembling a fan

FANNED past tase of fan

FANNER *n* pl. -S one that fans

FANNING present participle of fan

FANNY *n* pl. -NIES the buttocks

FANO *n* pl. FANOS a fanon

FANON *n* pl. -S a cape worn by the pope

FANTAIL *n* pl. -S a fan-shaped tail or end

FANTASIA *n* pl. -S a free-form musical composition

FANTASIE *n* pl. -S a fantasia

FANTASIED past tense of fantasy

FANTASIES present 3d person sing. of fantasy

FANTASM *n* pl. -S phantasm

FANTAST *n* pl. -S an impractical person

FANTASY *v* -SIED, -SYING, -SIES to imagine

FANTOD *n* pl. -S an emotional outburst

FANTOM *n* pl. -S phantom

FANUM *n* pl. -S fanon

FANWISE *adj* spread out like an open fan

FANWORT *n* pl. -S an aquatic plant

FAQIR *n* pl. -S fakir

FAQUIR *n* pl. -S fakir

FAR *adv* FARTHER, FARTHEST or FURTHER, FURTHEST at or to a great distance

FARAD *n* pl. -S a unit of electrical capacitance

FARADAIC *adj* faradic

FARADAY *n* pl. -DAYS a unit of electricity

FARADIC *adj* pertaining to a type of electric current

FARADISE *v* -DISED, -DISING, -DISES to faradize

FARADISM *n* pl. -S the use of faradic current for therapeutic purposes

FARADIZE *v* -DIZED, -DIZING, -DIZES to treat by faradism

FARAWAY *adj* distant

FARCE *v* FARCED, FARCING, FARCES to fill out with witty material

FARCER *n* pl. -S farceur

FARCEUR *n* pl. -S a joker

FARCI *adj* stuffed with finely chopped meat

FARCICAL *adj* absurd

FARCIE *adj* farci

FARCING present participle of farce

FARCY *n* pl. -CIES a disease of horses

FARD *v* -ED, -ING, -S to apply cosmetics to

FARDEL *n* pl. -S a bundle

FARE *v* FARED, FARING, FARES to get along

FARER *n* pl. -S a traveler

FAREWELL *v* -ED, -ING, -S to say goodby

FARFAL *n* pl. FARFAL farfel

FARFEL *n* pl. -S noodles in the form of small pellets or granules

FARINA *n* pl. -S a fine meal made from cereal grain

FARING present participle of fare

FARINHA *n* pl. -S a meal made from the root of the cassava

FARINOSE *adj* resembling farina

FARL *n* pl. -S a thin oatmeal cake

FARLE *n* pl. -S farl

FARM *v* -ED, -ING, -S to manage and cultivate as a farm (a tract of land devoted to agriculture) FARMABLE *adj*

FARMER *n* pl. -S one that farms

FARMHAND *n* pl. -S a farm laborer

FARMING *n* pl. -S the business of operating a farm

FARMLAND *n* pl. -S cultivated land

FARMYARD *n* pl. -S an area surrounded by farm buildings

FARNESOL *n* pl. -S an alcohol used in perfumes

FARNESS *n* pl. -ES the state of being far off or apart

FARO *n* pl. FAROS a card game

FAROUCHE *adj* sullenly shy

FARRAGO *n* pl. -GOES a confused mixture

FARRIER *n* pl. -S one that shoes horses

FARRIERY *n* pl. -ERIES the trade of a farrier

FARROW *v* -ED, -ING, -S to give birth to a litter of pigs

FART *v* -ED, -ING, -S to expel gas through the anus — usually considered vulgar

FARTHER a comparative of far

FARTHEST a superlative of far

FARTHING *n* pl. -S a former British coin

FASCES *n* pl. FASCES an ancient Roman symbol of power

FASCIA *n* pl. -CIAE or -CIAS a broad and distinct band of color FASCIAL, FASCIATE *adj*

FASCICLE *n* pl. -S a small bundle

FASCINE *n* pl. -S a bundle of sticks used in building fortifications

FASCISM *n* pl. -S an oppressive political system

FASCIST *n* pl. -S an advocate of fascism

FASH *v* -ED, -ING, -ES to annoy

FASHION *v* -ED, -ING, -S to give a particular shape or form to

FASHIOUS *adj* annoying

FAST *adj* FASTER, FASTEST moving or able to move quickly

FAST *v* -ED, -ING, -S to abstain from eating

FASTBACK *n* pl. -S a type of automobile roof

FASTBALL   *n* pl. -S a type of pitch in baseball

FASTEN   *v* -ED, -ING, -S to secure

FASTENER   *n* pl. -S one that fastens

FASTING   *n* pl. -S abstention from eating

FASTNESS   *n* pl. -ES the quality of being fast

FASTUOUS   *adj* arrogant

FAT   *adj* FATTER, FATTEST having an abundance of flesh

FAT   *v* FATTED, FATTING, FATS to make fat

FATAL   *adj* causing or capable of causing death

FATALISM   *n* pl. -S the doctrine that all events are predetermined

FATALIST   *n* pl. -S a believer in fatalism

FATALITY   *n* pl. -TIES a death resulting from an unexpected occurrence

FATALLY   *adv* in a fatal manner

FATBACK   *n* pl. -S a marine fish

FATBIRD   *n* pl. -S a wading bird

FATE   *v* FATED, FATING, FATES to destine

FATEFUL   *adj* decisively important

FATHEAD   *n* pl. -S a dolt

FATHER   *v* -ED, -ING, -S to cause to exist

FATHERLY   *adj* paternal

FATHOM   *v* -ED, -ING, -S to understand

FATIDIC   *adj* pertaining to prophecy

FATIGUE   *v* -TIGUED, -TIGUING, -TIGUES to weary

FATING   present participle of fate

FATLESS   *adj* having no fat

FATLIKE   *adj* resembling fat

FATLING   *n* pl. -S a young animal fattened for slaughter

FATLY   *adv* in the manner of one that is fat

FATNESS   *n* pl. -ES the state of being fat

FATSO   *n* pl. -SOES or -SOS a fat person

FATSTOCK   *n* pl. -S livestock that is fat and ready for market

FATTED   past tense of fat

FATTEN   *v* -ED, -ING, -S to make fat

FATTENER   *n* pl. -S one that fattens

FATTER   comparative of fat

FATTEST   superlative of fat

FATTIER   comparative of fatty

FATTIES   pl. of fatty

FATTIEST   superlative of fatty

FATTILY   *adv* in a fatty manner

FATTING   present participle of fat

FATTISH   *adj* somewhat fat

FATTY   *adj* -TIER, -TIEST greasy; oily

FATTY   *n* pl. -TIES one that is fat

FATUITY   *n* pl. -ITIES something foolish or stupid

FATUOUS   *adj* smugly stupid

FAUBOURG   *n* pl. -S a suburb

FAUCAL   *n* pl. -S a sound produced in the fauces

FAUCES   *n/pl* the passage from the mouth to the pharynx

FAUCET   *n* pl. -S a device for controlling the flow of liquid from a pipe

FAUCIAL   *adj* pertaining to the fauces

FAUGH   *interj* — used to express disgust

FAULD   *n* pl. -S a piece of armor below the breastplate

FAULT   *v* -ED, -ING, -S to criticize

FAULTY   *adj* FAULTIER, FAULTIEST imperfect FAULTILY *adv*

FAUN   *n* pl. -S a woodland deity of Roman mythology FAUNLIKE *adj*

FAUNA   *n* pl. -NAS or -NAE the animal life of a particular region FAUNAL *adj* FAUNALLY *adv*

FAUTEUIL   *n* pl. -S an armchair

FAUVE   *n* pl. -S a fauvist

FAUVISM   *n* pl. -S a movement in painting

FAUVIST   *n* pl. -S an advocate of fauvism

FAVELA   *n* pl. -S a slum area

FAVONIAN   *adj* pertaining to the west wind

FAVOR   *v* -ED, -ING, -S to regard with approval

FAVORER   *n* pl. -S one that favors

FAVORITE   *n* pl. -S a person or thing preferred above all others

FAVOUR   *v* -ED, -ING, -S to favor

FAVOURER   *n* pl. -S favorer

FAVUS   *n* pl. -ES a skin disease

FAWN   *v* -ED, -ING, -S to seek notice or favor by servile demeanor

FAWNER *n* pl. -S one that fawns

FAWNLIKE *adj* resembling a young deer

FAWNY *adj* FAWNIER, FAWNIEST of a yellowish-brown color

FAX *v* -ED, -ING, -ES to reproduce by electronic means

FAY *v* -ED, -ING, -S to join closely

FAYALITE *n* pl. -S a mineral

FAZE *v* FAZED, FAZING, FAZES to disturb the composure of

FAZENDA *n* pl. -S a Brazilian plantation

FEAL *adj* loyal

FEALTY *n* pl. -TIES loyalty

FEAR *v* -ED, -ING, -S to be afraid of

FEARER *n* pl. -S one that fears

FEARFUL *adj* -FULLER, -FULLEST afraid

FEARLESS *adj* unafraid

FEARSOME *adj* frightening

FEASANCE *n* pl. -S the performance of a condition, obligation, or duty

FEASE *v* FEASED, FEASING, FEASES to faze

FEASIBLE *adj* capable of being done FEASIBLY *adv*

FEAST *v* -ED, -ING, -S to eat sumptuously

FEASTER *n* pl. -S one that feasts

FEASTFUL *adj* festive

FEAT *n* pl. -S a notable act or achievement

FEAT *adj* FEATER, FEATEST skillful

FEATHER *v* -ED, -ING, -S to cover with feathers (horny structures that form the principal covering of birds)

FEATHERY *adj* -ERIER, -ERIEST resembling feathers

FEATLY *adj* -LIER, -LIEST graceful

FEATURE *v* -TURED, -TURING, -TURES to give special prominence to

FEAZE *v* FEAZED, FEAZING, FEAZES to faze

FEBRIFIC *adj* feverish

FEBRILE *adj* feverish

FECAL *adj* pertaining to feces

FECES *n/pl* bodily waste discharged through the anus

FECIAL *n* pl. -S fetial

FECK *n* pl. -S value

FECKLESS *adj* worthless

FECKLY *adv* almost

FECULA *n* pl. -LAE fecal matter

FECULENT *adj* foul with impurities

FECUND *adj* fruitful

FED *n* pl. -S a federal agent

FEDAYEE *n* pl. -YEEN an Arab commando

FEDERACY *n* pl. -CIES an alliance

FEDERAL *n* pl. -S a supporter of a type of central government

FEDERATE *v* -ATED, -ATING, -ATES to unite in an alliance

FEDORA *n* pl. -S a type of hat

FEE *v* FEED, FEEING, FEES to pay a fee (a fixed charge) to

FEEBLE *adj* -BLER, -BLEST weak FEEBLY *adv*

FEEBLISH *adj* somewhat feeble

FEED *v* FED, FEEDING, FEEDS to give food to FEEDABLE *adj*

FEEDBACK *n* pl. -S the return of a portion of the output to the input

FEEDBAG *n* pl. -S a bag for feeding horses

FEEDBOX *n* pl. -ES a box for animal feed

FEEDER *n* pl. -S one that feeds

FEEDLOT *n* pl. -S a plot of land on which livestock is fattened

FEEL *v* FELT, FEELING, FEELS to perceive through the sense of touch

FEELER *n* pl. -S a tactile organ

FEELESS *adj* requiring no fee

FEELING *n* pl. -S the function or power of perceiving by touch

FEET pl. of foot FEETLESS *adj*

FEEZE *v* FEEZED, FEEZING, FEEZES to faze

FEIGN *v* -ED, -ING, -S to pretend

FEIGNER *n* pl. -S one that feigns

FEINT *v* -ED, -ING, -S to make a deceptive movement

FEIRIE *adj* nimble

FEIST *n* pl. -S a small dog of mixed breed

FEISTY *adj* FEISTIER, FEISTIEST full of nervous energy

FELDSPAR *n* pl. -S a mineral

FELICITY *n* pl. -TIES happiness

FELID *n pl.* -S a feline

FELINE *n pl.* -S an animal of the cat family

FELINELY *adv* in a catlike manner

FELINITY *n pl.* -TIES the quality of being catlike

FELL *v* -ED, -ING, -S to cause to fall

FELL *adj* FELLER, FELLEST cruel

FELLA *n pl.* -S a man or boy

FELLABLE *adj* capable of being felled

FELLAH *n pl.* -LAHS, -LAHIN, or -LAHEEN a peasant or laborer in Arab countries

FELLATIO *n pl.* -TIOS oral stimulation of the penis

FELLER *n pl.* -S one that fells

FELLIES *pl.* of felly

FELLNESS *n pl.* -ES extreme cruelty

FELLOE *n pl.* -S the rim of a wheel

FELLOW *v* -ED, -ING, -S to produce an equal to

FELLOWLY *adj* friendly

FELLY *n pl.* -LIES a felloe

FELON *n pl.* -S a person who has committed a felony

FELONRY *n pl.* -RIES the whole class of felons

FELONY *n pl.* -NIES a grave crime

FELSITE *n pl.* -S an igneous rock **FELSITIC** *adj*

FELSPAR *n pl.* -S feldspar

FELSTONE *n pl.* -S felsite

FELT *v* -ED, -ING, -S to mat together

FELTING *n pl.* -S felted material

FELUCCA *n pl.* -S a swift sailing vessel

FELWORT *n pl.* -S a flowering plant

FEMALE *n pl.* -S an individual that bears young or produces ova

FEME *n pl.* -S a wife

FEMINACY *n pl.* -CIES the state of being a female

FEMINIE *n/pl* women collectively

FEMININE *n pl.* -S a word or form having feminine gender

FEMINISE *v* -NISED, -NISING, -NISES to feminize

FEMINISM *n pl.* -S a doctrine advocating rights for women equal to those of men

FEMINIST *n pl.* -S a supporter of feminism

FEMINITY *n pl.* -TIES the quality of being womanly

FEMINIZE *v* -NIZED, -NIZING, -NIZES to make womanly

FEMME *n pl.* -S a woman

FEMORAL *adj* pertaining to the femur

FEMUR *n pl.* -MURS or -MORA a bone of the leg

FEN *n pl.* -S a marsh

FENAGLE *v* -GLED, -GLING, -GLES to finagle

FENCE *v* FENCED, FENCING, FENCES to practice the art of fencing

FENCER *n pl.* -S one that fences

FENCIBLE *n pl.* -S a soldier enlisted for home service only

FENCING *n pl.* -S the art of using a sword in attack and defense

FEND *v* -ED, -ING, -S to ward off

FENDER *n pl.* -S a metal guard over the wheel of a motor vehicle **FENDERED** *adj*

FENESTRA *n pl.* -TRAE a small anatomical opening

FENNEC *n pl.* -S an African fox

FENNEL *n pl.* -S a perennial herb

FENNY *adj* marshy

FEOD *n pl.* -S a fief

FEODARY *n pl.* -RIES a vassal

FEOFF *v* -ED, -ING, -S to grant a fief to

FEOFFEE *n pl.* -S one to whom a fief is granted

FEOFFER *n pl.* -S one that grants a fief to another

FEOFFOR *n pl.* -S feoffer

FER *prep* for

FERACITY *n pl.* -TIES the state of being fruitful

FERAL *adj* wild

FERBAM *n pl.* -S a fungicide

FERE *n pl.* -S a companion

FERETORY *n pl.* -RIES a receptacle in which sacred relics are kept

FERIA *n pl.* -RIAS or -RIAE a weekday of a church calendar on which no feast is celebrated **FERIAL** *adj*

FERINE *adj* feral

FERITY *n pl.* -TIES wildness

FERLIE   *n* pl. -S a strange sight

FERLY   *n* pl. -LIES ferlie

FERMATA   *n* pl. -TAS or -TE the sustaining of a musical note, chord, or rest beyond its written time value

FERMENT   *v* -ED, -ING, -S to undergo a type of chemical reaction

FERMI   *n* pl. -S a unit of length

FERMION   *n* pl. -S a type of atomic particle

FERMIUM   *n* pl. -S a radioactive element

FERN   *n* pl. -S a flowerless vascular plant **FERNLESS, FERNLIKE** *adj*

FERNERY   *n* pl. -ERIES a place in which ferns are grown

FERNY   *adj* **FERNIER, FERNIEST** abounding in ferns

FEROCITY   *n* pl. -TIES fierceness

FERRATE   *n* pl. -S a chemical salt

FERREL   *v* -RELED, -RELING, -RELS or -RELLED, -RELLING, -RELS ferrule

FERREOUS   *adj* containing iron

FERRET   *v* -ED, -ING, -S to search out by careful investigation

FERRETER   *n* pl. -S one that ferrets

FERRETY   *adj* suggestive of a ferret (a polecat)

FERRIAGE   *n* pl. -S transportation by ferry

FERRIC   *adj* pertaining to iron

FERRIED   past tense of ferry

FERRIES   present 3d person sing. of ferry

FERRITE   *n* pl. -S a magnetic substance **FERRITIC** *adj*

FERRITIN   *n* pl. -S a protein that contains iron

FERROUS   *adj* pertaining to iron

FERRULE   *v* -RULED, -RULING, -RULES to furnish with a metal ring or cap to prevent splitting

FERRUM   *n* pl. -S iron

FERRY   *v* -RIED, -RYING, -RIES to transport by ferry (a type of boat)

FERRYMAN   *n* pl. -MEN one who operates a ferry

FERTILE   *adj* capable of reproducing

FERULA   *n* pl. -LAE or -LAS a flat piece of wood

FERULE   *v* -ULED, -ULING, -ULES to ferrule

FERVENCY   *n* pl. -CIES fervor

FERVENT   *adj* marked by fervor

FERVID   *adj* fervent **FERVIDLY** *adv*

FERVOR   *n* pl. -S great warmth or intensity

FERVOUR   *n* pl. -S fervor

FESCUE   *n* pl. -S a perennial grass

FESS   *v* -ED, -ING, -ES to confess

FESSE   *n* pl. -S a horizontal band across the middle of a heraldic shield

FESSWISE   *adv* horizontally

FESTAL   *adj* festive **FESTALLY** *adv*

FESTER   *v* -ED, -ING, -S to generate pus

FESTIVAL   *n* pl. -S a day or time of celebration

FESTIVE   *adj* of or befitting a festival

FESTOON   *v* -ED, -ING, -S to hang decorative chains or strips on

FET   *v* **FETTED, FETTING, FETS** to fetch

FETA   *n* pl. -S a Greek cheese

FETAL   *adj* pertaining to a fetus

FETATION   *n* pl. -S the development of a fetus

FETCH   *v* -ED, -ING, -ES to go after and bring back

FETCHER   *n* pl. -S one that fetches

FETE   *v* **FETED, FETING, FETES** to honor with a celebration

FETERITA   *n* pl. -S a cereal grass

FETIAL   *n* pl. -S a priest of ancient Rome

FETIALIS   *n* pl. -LES fetial

FETICH   *n* pl. -ES fetish

FETICIDE   *n* pl. -S the killing of a fetus

FETID   *adj* having an offensive odor **FETIDLY** *adv*

FETING   present participle of fete

FETISH   *n* pl. -ES an object believed to have magical power

FETLOCK   *n* pl. -S a joint of a horse's leg

FETOLOGY   *n* pl. -GIES the branch of medicine dealing with the fetus

FETOR   *n* pl. -S an offensive odor

FETTED   past tense of fet

FETTER   *v* -ED, -ING, -S to shackle

FETTERER *n* pl. -S one that fetters

FETTING present participle of fet

FETTLE *v* -TLED, -TLING, -TLES to cover the hearth of with fettling

FETTLING *n* pl. -S loose material thrown on the hearth of a furnace to protect it

FETUS *n* pl. -ES the unborn organism carried within the womb in the later stages of its development

FEU *v* -ED, -ING, -S to grant land to under Scottish feudal law

FEUAR *n* pl. -S one granted land under Scottish feudal law

FEUD *v* -ED, -ING, -S to engage in a feud (a bitter, continuous hostility)

FEUDAL *adj* pertaining to a political and economic system of medieval Europe **FEUDALLY** *adv*

FEUDARY *n* pl. -RIES a vassal

FEUDIST *n* pl. -S one that feuds

FEVER *v* -ED, -ING, -S to affect with fever (abnormal elevation of the body temperature)

FEVERFEW *n* pl. -S a perennial herb

FEVERISH *adj* having a fever

FEVEROUS *adj* feverish

FEW *adj* FEWER, FEWEST amounting to or consisting of a small number

FEWNESS *n* pl. -ES the state of being few

FEWTRILS *n/pl* things of little value

FEY *adj* FEYER, FEYEST crazy

FEYNESS *n* pl. -ES the state of being fey

FEZ *n* pl. FEZZES or FEZES a brimless cap worn by men in the Near East **FEZZED** *adj*

FIACRE *n* pl. -S a small carriage

FIANCE *n* pl. -S a man engaged to be married

FIANCEE *n* pl. -S a woman engaged to be married

FIAR *n* pl. -S the holder of a type of absolute ownership of land under Scottish law

FIASCO *n* pl. -COES or -CHI a wine bottle

FIASCO *n* pl. -COES or -COS a complete failure

FIAT *n* pl. -S an authoritative order

FIB *v* FIBBED, FIBBING, FIBS to tell a trivial lie

FIBBER *n* pl. -S one that fibs

FIBER *n* pl. -S a thread or threadlike object or structure **FIBERED** *adj*

FIBERIZE *v* -IZED, -IZING, -IZES to break into fibers

FIBRE *n* pl. -S fiber

FIBRIL *n* pl. -S a small fiber

FIBRILLA *n* pl. -LAE a fibril

FIBRIN *n* pl. -S an insoluble protein

FIBROID *n* pl. -S a fibroma

FIBROIN *n* pl. -S an insoluble protein

FIBROMA *n* pl. -MAS or -MATA a benign tumor composed of fibrous tissue

FIBROSIS *n* pl. -BROSES the development of excess fibrous tissue in a bodily organ **FIBROTIC** *adj*

FIBROUS *adj* containing, consisting of, or resembling fibers

FIBULA *n* pl. -LAE or -LAS a bone of the leg **FIBULAR** *adj*

FICE *n* pl. -S a feist

FICHE *n* pl. -S a sheet of microfilm

FICHU *n* pl. -S a woman's scarf

FICIN *n* pl. -S an enzyme

FICKLE *adj* -LER, -LEST not constant or loyal

FICO *n* pl. -COES something of little worth

FICTILE *adj* moldable

FICTION *n* pl. -S a literary work whose content is produced by the imagination

FICTIVE *adj* imaginary

FID *n* pl. -S a square bar used as a support for a topmast

FIDDLE *v* -DLED, -DLING, -DLES to play a violin

FIDDLER *n* pl. -S one that fiddles

FIDEISM *n* pl. -S reliance on faith rather than reason

FIDEIST *n* pl. -S a believer in fideism

FIDELITY *n* pl. -TIES loyalty

FIDGE *v* FIDGED, FIDGING, FIDGES to fidget

FIDGET *v* -ED, -ING, -S to move nervously or restlessly

FIDGETER *n* pl. -S one that fidgets

FIDGETY	*adj* nervously restless
FIDGING	present participle of fidge
FIDO	*n* pl. -DOS a defective coin
FIDUCIAL	*adj* based on faith or trust
FIE	*interj* — used to express disapproval
FIEF	*n* pl. -S a feudal estate
FIEFDOM	*n* pl. -S a fief
FIELD	*v* -ED, -ING, -S to play as a fielder
FIELDER	*n* pl. -S one that catches or picks up a ball in play
FIEND	*n* pl. -S a demon
FIENDISH	*adj* extremely wicked or cruel
FIERCE	*adj* FIERCER, FIERCEST violently hostile or aggressive FIERCELY *adv*
FIERY	*adj* -ERIER, -ERIEST intensely hot FIERILY *adv*
FIESTA	*n* pl. -S a festival
FIFE	*v* FIFED, FIFING, FIFES to play a fife (a high-pitched flute)
FIFER	*n* pl. -S one that plays a fife
FIFTEEN	*n* pl. -S a number
FIFTH	*n* pl. -S one of five equal parts
FIFTHLY	*adv* in the fifth place
FIFTIETH	*n* pl. -S one of fifty equal parts
FIFTY	*n* pl. -TIES a number
FIG	*v* FIGGED, FIGGING, FIGS to adorn
FIGEATER	*n* pl. -S a large beetle
FIGHT	*v* FOUGHT, FIGHTING, FIGHTS to attempt to defeat an adversary
FIGHTER	*n* pl. -S one that fights
FIGHTING	*n* pl. -S the act of one that fights
FIGMENT	*n* pl. -S a product of mental invention
FIGULINE	*n* pl. -S a piece of pottery
FIGURAL	*adj* consisting of human or animal forms
FIGURANT	*n* pl. -S a ballet dancer who dances only in groups
FIGURATE	*adj* having a definite shape
FIGURE	*v* -URED, -URING, -URES to compute
FIGURER	*n* pl. -S one that figures
FIGURINE	*n* pl. -S a small statue

FIGURING	present participle of figure
FIGWORT	*n* pl. -S a flowering plant
FIL	*n* pl. -S a coin of Iraq and Jordan
FILA	pl. of filum
FILAGREE	*v* -GREED, -GREEING, -GREES to filigree
FILAMENT	*n* pl. -S a very thin thread or threadlike structure
FILAR	*adj* pertaining to a thread
FILAREE	*n* pl. -S a European weed
FILARIA	*n* pl. -IAE a parasitic worm FILARIAL, FILARIAN *adj*
FILARIID	*n* pl. -S filaria
FILATURE	*n* pl. -S the reeling of silk from cocoons
FILBERT	*n* pl. -S the edible nut of a European shrub
FILCH	*v* -ED, -ING, -ES to steal
FILCHER	*n* pl. -S one that filches
FILE	*v* FILED, FILING, FILES to remove with a file (an abrading tool)
FILEFISH	*n* pl. -ES a marine fish
FILEMOT	*adj* of a brownish yellow color
FILER	*n* pl. -S one that files
FILET	*v* -ED, -ING, -S to fillet
FILIAL	*adj* pertaining to a son or daughter FILIALLY *adv*
FILIATE	*v* -ATED, -ATING, -ATES to bring into close association
FILIBEG	*n* pl. -S a pleated skirt worn by Scottish Highlanders
FILICIDE	*n* pl. -S the killing of one's child
FILIFORM	*adj* shaped like a filament
FILIGREE	*v* -GREED, -GREEING, -GREES to adorn with intricate ornamental work
FILING	*n* pl. -S a particle removed by a file
FILISTER	*n* pl. -S a groove on a window frame
FILL	*v* -ED, -ING, -S to put as much as can be held into
FILLE	*n* pl. -S a girl
FILLER	*n* pl. -S one that fills
FILLET	*v* -ED, -ING, -S to cut boneless slices from
FILLIES	pl. of filly

FILLING   *n* pl. -S that which is used to fill something

FILLIP   *v* -ED, -ING, -S to strike sharply

FILLY   *n* pl. -LIES a young female horse

FILM   *v* -ED, -ING, -S to cover with a film (a thin layer or coating)

FILMCARD   *n* pl. -S a fiche

FILMDOM   *n* pl. -S the motion-picture industry

FILMGOER   *n* pl. -S one that goes to see motion pictures

FILMIC   *adj* pertaining to motion pictures

FILMIER   comparative of filmy

FILMIEST   superlative of filmy

FILMILY   *adv* in a filmy manner

FILMLAND   *n* pl. -S filmdom

FILMSET   *v* -SET, -SETTING, -SETS to photoset

FILMY   *adj* FILMIER, FILMIEST resembling or covered with film; hazy

FILOSE   *adj* resembling a thread

FILTER   *v* -ED, -ING, -S to pass through a filter (a device for removing suspended matter)

FILTERER   *n* pl. -S one that filters

FILTH   *n* pl. -S foul or dirty matter

FILTHY   *adj* FILTHIER, FILTHIEST offensively dirty **FILTHILY** *adv*

FILTRATE   *v* -TRATED, -TRATING, -TRATES to filter

FILUM   *n* pl. -LA a threadlike anatomical structure

FIMBLE   *n* pl. -S the male hemp plant

FIMBRIA   *n* pl. -BRIAE a fringe or fringe-like structure **FIMBRIAL** *adj*

FIN   *v* FINNED, FINNING, FINS to equip with fins (external paddle-like structures)

FINABLE   *adj* subject to the payment of a fine

FINAGLE   *v* -GLED, -GLING, -GLES to obtain by trickery

FINAGLER   *n* pl. -S one that finagles

FINAL   *n* pl. -S the last examination of an academic course

FINALE   *n* pl. -S a close or termination of something

FINALIS   *n* pl. -LES a type of tone in medieval music

FINALISM   *n* pl. -S the doctrine that all events are determined by ultimate purposes

FINALIST   *n* pl. -S a contestant who reaches the last part of a competition

FINALITY   *n* pl. -TIES the state of being conclusive

FINALIZE   *v* -IZED, -IZING, -IZES to put into finished form

FINALLY   *adv* at the end

FINANCE   *v* -NANCED, -NANCING, -NANCES to supply the money for

FINBACK   *n* pl. -S the rorqual

FINCH   *n* pl. -ES a small bird

FIND   *v* FOUND, FINDING, FINDS to come upon after a search

FINDER   *n* pl. -S one that finds

FINDING   *n* pl. -S something that is found

FINE   *adj* FINER, FINEST of excellent quality

FINE   *v* FINED, FINING, FINES to subject to a fine (a monetary penalty)

FINEABLE   *adj* finable

FINELY   *adv* in a fine manner

FINENESS   *n* pl. -ES the quality of being fine

FINER   comparative of fine

FINERY   *n* pl. -ERIES elaborate adornment

FINESPUN   *adj* developed with extreme care

FINESSE   *v* -NESSED, -NESSING, -NESSES to bring about by adroit maneuvering

FINEST   superlative of fine

FINFISH   *n* pl. -ES a true fish

FINFOOT   *n* pl. -S an aquatic bird

FINGER   *v* -ED, -ING, -S to touch with the fingers (the terminating members of the hand)

FINGERER   *n* pl. -S one that fingers

FINIAL   *n* pl. -S a crowning ornament **FINIALED** *adj*

FINICAL   *adj* finicky

FINICKIN   *adj* finicky

FINICKY	*adj* -ICKIER, -ICKIEST difficult to please
FINIKIN	*adj* finicky
FINIKING	*adj* finicky
FINING	*n* pl. -S the clarifying of wines
FINIS	*n* pl. -NISES the end
FINISH	*v* -ED, -ING, -ES to bring to an end
FINISHER	*n* pl. -S one that finishes
FINITE	*n* pl. -S something that is finite (having definite limits)
FINITELY	*adv* to a finite extent
FINITUDE	*n* pl. -S the state of being finite
FINK	*v* -ED, -ING, -S to inform to the police
FINLESS	*adj* having no fins
FINLIKE	*adj* resembling a fin
FINMARK	*n* pl. -S a monetary unit of Finland
FINNED	past tense of fin
FINNIER	comparative of finny
FINNIEST	superlative of finny
FINNING	present participle of fin
FINNICKY	*adj* -NICKIER, -NICKIEST finicky
FINNMARK	*n* pl. -S finmark
FINNY	*adj* -NIER, -NIEST having or characterized by fins
FINOCHIO	*n* pl. -CHIOS a perennial herb
FIORD	*n* pl. -S fjord
FIPPLE	*n* pl. -S a plug of wood at the mouth of certain wind instruments
FIQUE	*n* pl. -S a tropical plant
FIR	*n* pl. -S an evergreen tree
FIRE	*v* FIRED, FIRING, FIRES to project by discharging from a gun
FIREARM	*n* pl. -S a weapon from which a shot is discharged by gunpowder
FIREBALL	*n* pl. -S a luminous meteor
FIREBIRD	*n* pl. -S a brightly colored bird
FIREBOAT	*n* pl. -S a boat equipped with fire-fighting apparatus
FIREBOMB	*v* -ED, -ING, -S to attack with incendiary bombs
FIREBOX	*n* pl. -ES a chamber in which fuel is burned
FIREBRAT	*n* pl. -S a small, wingless insect
FIREBUG	*n* pl. -S an arsonist
FIRECLAY	*n* pl. -CLAYS a heat-resistant clay
FIRED	past tense of fire
FIREDAMP	*n* pl. -S a combustible gas
FIREDOG	*n* pl. -S an andiron
FIREFANG	*v* -ED, -ING, -S to decompose by oxidation
FIREFLY	*n* pl. -FLIES a luminous insect
FIREHALL	*n* pl. -S a fire station
FIRELESS	*adj* having no fire
FIRELOCK	*n* pl. -S a type of gun
FIREMAN	*n* pl. -MEN a man employed to extinguish fires
FIREPAN	*n* pl. -S an open pan for holding live coals
FIREPINK	*n* pl. -S a flowering plant
FIREPLUG	*n* pl. -S a hydrant
FIRER	*n* pl. -S one that fires
FIREROOM	*n* pl. -S a room containing a ship's boilers
FIRESIDE	*n* pl. -S the area immediately surrounding a fireplace
FIRETRAP	*n* pl. -S a building that is likely to catch on fire
FIREWEED	*n* pl. -S a perennial herb
FIREWOOD	*n* pl. -S wood used as fuel
FIREWORK	*n* pl. -S a device for producing a striking display of light or a loud noise
FIREWORM	*n* pl. -S a glowworm
FIRING	*n* pl. -S the process of maturing ceramic products by heat
FIRKIN	*n* pl. -S a British unit of capacity
FIRM	*adj* FIRMER, FIRMEST unyielding to pressure
FIRM	*v* -ED, -ING, -S to make firm
FIRMAN	*n* pl. -S an edict issued by a Middle Eastern sovereign
FIRMER	*n* pl. -S a woodworking tool
FIRMLY	*adv* in a firm manner
FIRMNESS	*n* pl. -ES the state of being firm
FIRN	*n* pl. -S neve
FIRRY	*adj* abounding in firs
FIRST	*n* pl. -S something that precedes all others
FIRSTLY	*adv* before all others
FIRTH	*n* pl. -S an inlet of the sea

FISC	*n* pl. -S a state or royal treasury
FISCAL	*n* pl. -S a public prosecutor
FISCALLY	*adv* with regard to financial matters
FISH	*v* -ED, -ING, -ES to catch or try to catch fish (cold-blooded aquatic vertebrates)
FISHABLE	*adj* suitable for fishing
FISHBOLT	*n* pl. -S a type of bolt
FISHBONE	*n* pl. -S a bone of a fish
FISHBOWL	*n* pl. -S a bowl in which live fish are kept
FISHER	*n* pl. -S one that fishes
FISHERY	*n* pl. -ERIES a place for catching fish
FISHEYE	*n* pl. -S a suspicious stare
FISHGIG	*n* pl. -S a pronged implement for spearing fish
FISHHOOK	*n* pl. -S a barbed hook for catching fish
FISHIER	comparative of fishy
FISHIEST	superlative of fishy
FISHILY	*adv* in a fishy manner
FISHING	*n* pl. -S the occupation or pastime of catching fish
FISHLESS	*adj* having no fish
FISHLIKE	*adj* resembling a fish
FISHLINE	*n* pl. -S a line used in fishing
FISHMEAL	*n* pl. -S ground dried fish
FISHNET	*n* pl. -S a net for catching fish
FISHPOLE	*n* pl. -S a fishing rod
FISHPOND	*n* pl. -S a pond abounding in edible fish
FISHTAIL	*v* -ED, -ING, -S to have the rear end of a moving vehicle slide from side to side
FISHWAY	*n* pl. -WAYS a device for enabling fish to pass around a dam
FISHWIFE	*n* pl. -WIVES a woman who sells fish
FISHY	*adj* FISHIER, FISHIEST of or resembling a fish
FISSATE	*adj* deeply split
FISSILE	*adj* capable of being split
FISSION	*v* -ED, -ING, -S to split into parts
FISSIPED	*n* pl. -S a mammal that has separated toes
FISSURE	*v* -SURED, -SURING, -SURES to split

FIST	*v* -ED, -ING, -S to strike with the fist (the hand closed tightly)
FISTFUL	*n* pl. -S a handful
FISTIC	*adj* pertaining to pugilism
FISTNOTE	*n* pl. -S a part of a text to which attention is drawn by an index mark
FISTULA	*n* pl. -LAE or -LAS a duct formed by the imperfect closing of a wound **FISTULAR** *adj*
FIT	*adj* FITTER, FITTEST healthy
FIT	*v* FITTED, FITTING, FITS to bring to a required form and size
FITCH	*n* pl. -ES a polecat
FITCHEE	*adj* fitchy
FITCHET	*n* pl. -S a fitch
FITCHEW	*n* pl. -S a fitch
FITCHY	*adj* having the arms ending in a point — used of a heraldic cross
FITFUL	*adj* recurring irregularly **FITFULLY** *adv*
FITLY	*adv* in a fit manner
FITMENT	*n* pl. -S equipment
FITNESS	*n* pl. -ES the state of being fit
FITTABLE	*adj* capable of being fitted
FITTED	past tense of fit
FITTER	*n* pl. -S one that fits
FITTEST	superlative of fit
FITTING	*n* pl. -S a small often standardized accessory part
FIVE	*n* pl. -S a number
FIVEFOLD	*adj* five times as great
FIVEPINS	*n/pl* a bowling game
FIVER	*n* pl. -S a five-dollar bill
FIX	*v* FIXED or FIXT, FIXING, FIXES to repair **FIXABLE** *adj*
FIXATE	*v* -ATED, -ATING, -ATES to make stable or stationary
FIXATIF	*n* pl. -S fixative
FIXATION	*n* pl. -S the act of fixating
FIXATIVE	*n* pl. -S a substance for preserving paintings or drawings
FIXEDLY	*adv* firmly
FIXER	*n* pl. -S one that fixes
FIXINGS	*n/pl* accompaniments to the main dish of a meal
FIXITY	*n* pl. -TIES stability
FIXT	a past tense of fix

FIXTURE   *n pl.* -S a permanent part or appendage of a house

FIXURE   *n pl.* -S firmness

FIZ   *n pl.* FIZZES a hissing or sputtering sound

FIZGIG   *n pl.* -S fishgig

FIZZ   *v* -ED, -ING, -ES to make a hissing or sputtering sound

FIZZER   *n pl.* -S one that fizzes

FIZZES   pl. of fiz

FIZZLE   *v* -ZLED, -ZLING, -ZLES to fizz

FIZZY   *adj* FIZZIER, FIZZIEST fizzing

FJELD   *n pl.* -S a high, barren plateau

FJORD   *n pl.* -S a narrow inlet of the sea between steep cliffs

FLAB   *n pl.* -S flabby body tissue

FLABBY   *adj* -BIER, -BIEST flaccid **FLABBILY** *adv*

FLABELLA   *n/pl* fan-shaped anatomical structures

FLACCID   *adj* lacking firmness

FLACK   *n pl.* -S a press agent

FLACON   *n pl.* -S a small stoppered bottle

FLAG   *v* FLAGGED, FLAGGING, FLAGS to mark with a flag (a piece of cloth used as a symbol)

FLAGELLA   *n/pl* long, slender plant shoots

FLAGGER   *n pl.* -S one that flags

FLAGGING   *n pl.* -S a type of pavement

FLAGGY   *adj* -GIER, -GIEST drooping

FLAGLESS   *adj* having no flag

FLAGMAN   *n pl.* -MEN one who carries a flag

FLAGON   *n pl.* -S a large bulging bottle

FLAGPOLE   *n pl.* -S a pole on which a flag is displayed

FLAGRANT   *adj* extremely or deliberately conspicuous

FLAGSHIP   *n pl.* -S a ship bearing the flag of a fleet

FLAIL   *v* -ED, -ING, -S to swing freely

FLAIR   *n pl.* -S a natural aptitude

FLAK   *n pl.* FLAK antiaircraft fire

FLAKE   *v* FLAKED, FLAKING, FLAKES to peel off in flakes (flat, thin pieces)

FLAKER   *n pl.* -S one that flakes

FLAKY   *adj* FLAKIER, FLAKIEST resembling flakes **FLAKILY** *adv*

FLAM   *v* FLAMMED, FLAMMING FLAMS to deceive

FLAMBE   *v* -BEED, -BEING, -BES to douse with a liqueur and ignite

FLAMBEAU   *n pl.* -BEAUX or -BEAUS a flaming torch

FLAMBEE   *adj* flaming

FLAME   *v* FLAMED, FLAMING, FLAMES to burn brightly

FLAMEN   *n pl.* -MENS or -MINES a priest of ancient Rome

FLAMENCO   *n pl.* -COS a strongly rhythmic style of dancing

FLAMEOUT   *n pl.* -S a failure of a jet engine in flight

FLAMER   *n pl.* -S one that flames

FLAMIER   comparative of flamy

FLAMIEST   superlative of flamy

FLAMINES   a pl. of flamen

FLAMING   present participle of flame

FLAMINGO   *n pl.* -GOS or -GOES a wading bird

FLAMMED   past tense of flam

FLAMMING   present participle of flam

FLAMY   *adj* FLAMIER, FLAMIEST flaming

FLAN   *n pl.* -S or -ES a type of custard

FLANCARD   *n pl.* -S a piece of armor for the side of a horse

FLANERIE   *n pl.* -S idleness

FLANEUR   *n pl.* -S an idler

FLANGE   *v* FLANGED, FLANGING, FLANGES to provide with a protecting rim

FLANGER   *n pl.* -S one that flanges

FLANK   *v* -ED, -ING, -S to be located at the side of

FLANKER   *n pl.* -S one that flanks

FLANNEL   *v* -NELED, -NELING, -NELS or -NELLED, -NELLING, -NELS to cover with flannel (a soft fabric)

FLAP   *v* FLAPPED, FLAPPING, FLAPS to wave up and down

FLAPJACK   *n pl.* -S a pancake

FLAPLESS   *adj* having no flap (a flat appendage)

FLAPPED   past tense of flap

FLAPPER   *n pl.* -S one that flaps

FLAPPING   present participle of flap

FLAPPY   *adj* -PIER, -PIEST flapping

FLARE	v FLARED, FLARING, FLARES to burn with a bright, wavering light	**FLATWARE**	n pl. -S tableware that is fairly flat
FLASH	v -ED, -ING, -ES to send forth a sudden burst of light	**FLATWASH**	n pl. -ES flatwork
		FLATWAYS	adv flatwise
FLASHER	n pl. -S one that flashes	**FLATWISE**	adv with the flat side in a particular position
FLASHGUN	n pl. -S a photographic apparatus		
FLASHING	n pl. -S sheet metal used in waterproofing a roof	**FLATWORK**	n pl. -S laundry that can be ironed mechanically
		FLATWORM	n pl. -S a flat-bodied worm
FLASHY	adj FLASHIER, FLASHIEST gaudy **FLASHILY** adv	**FLAUNT**	v -ED, -ING, -S to exhibit in a gaudy manner
FLASK	n pl. -S a narrow-necked container	**FLAUNTER**	n pl. -S one that flaunts
FLASKET	n pl. -S a small flask	**FLAUNTY**	adj FLAUNTIER, FLAUNTIEST gaudy
FLAT	adj FLATTER, FLATTEST having a smooth or even surface	**FLAUTIST**	n pl. -S flutist
FLAT	v FLATTED, FLATTING, FLATS to flatten	**FLAVIN**	n pl. -S a yellow pigment
		FLAVINE	n pl. -S flavin
FLATBED	n pl. -S a type of truck or trailer	**FLAVONE**	n pl. -S a chemical compound
FLATBOAT	n pl. -S a flat-bottomed boat	**FLAVONOL**	n pl. -S a derivative of flavone
FLATCAP	n pl. -S a type of hat	**FLAVOR**	v -ED, -ING, -S to give flavor (distinctive taste) to
FLATCAR	n pl. -S a railroad car without sides or roof	**FLAVORER**	n pl. -S one that flavors
FLATFISH	n pl. -ES any of an order of marine fishes	**FLAVORY**	adj full of flavor
FLATFOOT	n pl. -FEET a foot condition	**FLAVOUR**	v -ED, -ING, -S to flavor
FLATFOOT	v -ED, -ING, -S to walk with a dragging gait	**FLAVOURY**	adj flavory
		FLAW	v -ED, -ING, -S to produce a flaw (an imperfection) in
FLATHEAD	n pl. -S a marine food fish	**FLAWLESS**	adj having no flaw
FLATIRON	n pl. -S a device for pressing clothes	**FLAWY**	adj FLAWIER, FLAWIEST full of flaws
FLATLAND	n pl. -S land lacking significant variation in elevation	**FLAX**	n pl. -ES an annual herb
		FLAXEN	adj of a pale yellow color
FLATLET	n pl. -S a type of apartment	**FLAXSEED**	n pl. -S the seed of flax
FLATLING	adv with a flat side or edge	**FLAXY**	adj FLAXIER, FLAXIEST flaxen
FLATLY	adv in a flat manner	**FLAY**	v -ED, -ING, -S to strip off the skin of
FLATNESS	n pl. -ES the state of being flat		
FLATTED	past tense of flat	**FLAYER**	n pl. -S one that flays
FLATTEN	v -ED, -ING, -S to make or become flat	**FLEA**	n pl. -S a parasitic insect
		FLEABAG	n pl. -S an inferior hotel
FLATTER	v -ED, -ING, -S to praise excessively	**FLEABANE**	n pl. -S a flowering plant
FLATTERY	n pl. -TERIES the act of flattering	**FLEABITE**	n pl. -S the bite of a flea
		FLEAM	n pl. -S a surgical instrument
FLATTEST	superlative of flat	**FLEAWORT**	n pl. -S a European herb
FLATTING	present participle of flat	**FLECHE**	n pl. -S a steeple
FLATTISH	adj somewhat flat	**FLECK**	v -ED, -ING, -S to mark with flecks (tiny streaks or spots)
FLATTOP	n pl. -S an aircraft carrier		
FLATUS	n pl. -ES intestinal gas	**FLECKY**	adj flecked

FLECTION   n pl. -S the act of bending

FLED   past tense of flee

FLEDGE   v FLEDGED, FLEDGING, FLEDGES to furnish with feathers

FLEDGY   adj FLEDGIER, FLEDGIEST covered with feathers

FLEE   v FLED, FLEEING, FLEES to run away

FLEECE   v FLEECED, FLEECING, FLEECES to remove the coat of wool from

FLEECER   n pl. -S one that fleeces

FLEECH   v -ED, -ING, -ES to coax

FLEECING   present participle of fleece

FLEECY   adj FLEECIER, FLEECIEST woolly FLEECILY adv

FLEER   v -ED, -ING, -S to deride

FLEET   adj FLEETER, FLEETEST swift FLEETLY adv

FLEET   v -ED, -ING, -S to move swiftly

FLEISHIG   adj made of meat or meat products

FLEMISH   v -ED, -ING, -ES to coil rope in a certain manner

FLENCH   v -ED, -ING, -ES to flense

FLENSE   v FLENSED, FLENSING, FLENSES to strip the blubber or skin from

FLENSER   n pl. -S one that flenses

FLESH   v -ED, -ING, -ES to plunge into the flesh (soft body tissue)

FLESHER   n pl. -S one that removes flesh from animal hides

FLESHIER   comparative of fleshy

FLESHIEST   superlative of fleshy

FLESHING   n pl. -S the distribution of the lean and fat on an animal

FLESHLY   adj -LIER, -LIEST pertaining to the body

FLESHPOT   n pl. -S a pot for cooking meat

FLESHY   adj FLESHIER, FLESHIEST having much flesh

FLETCH   v -ED, -ING, -ES to fledge

FLETCHER   n pl. -S one that makes arrows

FLEURY   adj having the arms terminating in three leaves — used of a heraldic cross

FLEW   n pl. -S a fishing net

FLEX   v -ED, -ING, -ES to bend

FLEXIBLE   adj capable of being bent FLEXIBLY adv

FLEXILE   adj flexible

FLEXION   n pl. -S flection

FLEXOR   n pl. -S a muscle that serves to bend a bodily part

FLEXUOSE   adj flexuous

FLEXUOUS   adj winding

FLEXURE   n pl. -S the act of bending FLEXURAL adj

FLEY   v -ED, -ING, -S to frighten

FLIC   n pl. -S a Parisian policeman

FLICHTER   v -ED, -ING, -S to flicker

FLICK   v -ED, -ING, -S to strike with a quick, light blow

FLICKER   v -ED, -ING, -S to move waveringly

FLICKERY   adj flickering

FLIED   a past tense of fly

FLIER   n pl. -S one that flies

FLIES   present 3d person sing. of fly

FLIEST   superlative of fly

FLIGHT   v -ED, -ING, -S to fly in a flock

FLIGHTY   adj FLIGHTIER, FLIGHTIEST fickle

FLIMFLAM   v -FLAMMED, -FLAMMING, -FLAMS to swindle

FLIMSY   adj -SIER, -SIEST lacking solidity or strength FLIMSILY adv

FLIMSY   n pl. -SIES a thin paper

FLINCH   v -ED, -ING, -ES to shrink back involuntarily

FLINCHER   n pl. -S one that flinches

FLINDER   n pl. -S a small fragment

FLING   v FLUNG, FLINGING, FLINGS to throw with force

FLINGER   n pl. -S one that flings

FLINT   v -ED, -ING, -S to provide with flint (a spark-producing rock)

FLINTY   adj FLINTIER, FLINTIEST resembling flint FLINTILY adv

FLIP   v FLIPPED, FLIPPING, FLIPS to throw with a brisk motion

FLIP   adj FLIPPER, FLIPPEST flippant

FLIPPANT   adj impudent

FLIPPED   past tense of flip

FLIPPER   n pl. -S a broad, flat limb adapted for swimming

FLIPPEST	superlative of flip	**FLOODWAY**	n pl. -WAYS an overflow channel
FLIPPING	present participle of flip	**FLOOEY**	adj awry
FLIRT	v -ED, -ING, -S to behave amorously without serious intent	**FLOOR**	v -ED, -ING, -S to provide with a floor (the level base of a room)
FLIRTER	n pl. -S one that flirts	**FLOORAGE**	n pl. -S floor space
FLIRTY	adj FLIRTIER, FLIRTIEST given to flirting	**FLOORER**	n pl. -S one that floors
FLIT	v FLITTED, FLITTING, FLITS to move lightly and swiftly	**FLOORING**	n pl. -S a floor
		FLOOSY	n pl. -SIES floozy
FLITCH	v -ED, -ING, -ES to cut into strips	**FLOOZIE**	n pl. -S floozy
FLITE	v FLITED, FLITING, FLITES to quarrel	**FLOOZY**	n pl. -ZIES a prostitute
FLITTED	past tense of flit	**FLOP**	v FLOPPED, FLOPPING, FLOPS to fall heavily and noisily
FLITTER	v -ED, -ING, -S to flutter	**FLOPOVER**	n pl. -S a defect in television reception
FLITTING	present participle of flit	**FLOPPER**	n pl. -S one that flops
FLIVVER	n pl. -S an old, battered car	**FLOPPING**	present participle of flop
FLOAT	v -ED, -ING, -S to rest or remain on the surface of a liquid	**FLOPPY**	adj -PIER, -PIEST soft and flexible FLOPPILY adv
FLOATAGE	n pl. -S flotage	**FLORA**	n pl. -RAS or -RAE the plant life of a particular region
FLOATER	n pl. -S one that floats	**FLORAL**	adj pertaining to flowers FLORALLY adv
FLOATY	adj FLOATIER, FLOATIEST tending to float	**FLORENCE**	n pl. -S florin
FLOC	v FLOCCED, FLOCCING, FLOCS to aggregate into floccules	**FLORET**	n pl. -S a small flower
		FLORID	adj ruddy FLORIDLY adv
FLOCCI	pl. of floccus	**FLORIGEN**	n pl. -S a plant hormone
FLOCCOSE	adj having woolly tufts	**FLORIN**	n pl. -S a former gold coin of Europe
FLOCCULE	n pl. -S a tuft-like mass	**FLORIST**	n pl. -S a grower or seller of flowers
FLOCCULI	n/pl small, loosely aggregated masses	**FLORUIT**	n pl. -S a period of flourishing
FLOCCUS	n pl. FLOCCI a floccule	**FLOSS**	n pl. -ES a soft, light fiber
FLOCK	v -ED, -ING, -S to gather or move in a crowd	**FLOSSIE**	n pl. -S a floozy
FLOCKING	n pl. -S a velvety design in short fibers on cloth or paper	**FLOSSY**	adj FLOSSIER, FLOSSIEST resembling floss
FLOCKY	adj FLOCKIER, FLOCKIEST woolly	**FLOTA**	n pl. -S a fleet of Spanish ships
FLOE	n pl. -S a large mass of floating ice	**FLOTAGE**	n pl. -S the act of floating
FLOG	v FLOGGED, FLOGGING, FLOGS to beat with a whip or rod	**FLOTILLA**	n pl. -S a fleet of ships
		FLOTSAM	n pl. -S floating wreckage of a ship or its cargo
FLOGGER	n pl. -S one that flogs	**FLOUNCE**	v FLOUNCED, FLOUNCING, FLOUNCES to move with exaggerated motions
FLOGGING	n pl. -S a whipping		
FLONG	n pl. -S a sheet of a certain type of paper	**FLOUNCY**	adj FLOUNCIER, FLOUNCIEST flouncing
FLOOD	v -ED, -ING, -S to inundate	**FLOUNDER**	v -ED, -ING, -S to struggle clumsily
FLOODER	n pl. -S one that floods		
FLOODLIT	adj illuminated by floodlights		

FLOUR v -ED, -ING, -S to cover with flour (a finely ground meal of grain)

FLOURISH v -ED, -ING, -ES to thrive

FLOURY adj resembling flour

FLOUT v -ED, -ING, -S to treat with contempt

FLOUTER n pl. -S one that flouts

FLOW v -ED, -ING, -S to move steadily and smoothly along

FLOWAGE n pl. -S the act of flowing

FLOWER v -ED, -ING, -S to put forth flowers (reproductive structures of seed-bearing plants)

FLOWERER n pl. -S a plant that flowers at a certain time

FLOWERET n pl. -S a floret

FLOWERY adj -ERIER, -ERIEST abounding in flowers

FLOWN a past participle of fly

FLU n pl. -S a virus disease

FLUB v FLUBBED, FLUBBING, FLUBS to bungle

FLUBDUB n pl. -S pretentious nonsense

FLUE n pl. -S an enclosed passageway for directing a current **FLUED** adj

FLUENCY n pl. -CIES the quality of being fluent

FLUENT adj spoken or written with effortless ease **FLUENTLY** adv

FLUERICS n/pl fluidics **FLUERIC** adj

FLUFF v -ED, -ING, -S to make fluffy

FLUFFY adj FLUFFIER, FLUFFIEST light and soft **FLUFFILY** adv

FLUID n pl. -S a substance that tends to flow **FLUIDAL** adj

FLUIDICS n/pl a branch of mechanical engineering **FLUIDIC** adj

FLUIDISE v -ISED, -ISING, -ISES to fluidize

FLUIDITY n pl. -TIES the quality of being able to flow

FLUIDIZE v -IZED, -IZING, -IZES to cause to flow like a fluid

FLUIDLY adv with fluidity

FLUIDRAM n pl. -S a unit of liquid capacity

FLUKE v FLUKED, FLUKING, FLUKES to obtain by chance

FLUKEY adj FLUKIER, FLUKIEST fluky

FLUKY adj FLUKIER, FLUKIEST happening by or depending on chance

FLUME v FLUMED, FLUMING, FLUMES to convey by means of an artificial water channel

FLUMMERY n pl. -MERIES a sweet dessert

FLUMMOX v -ED, -ING, -ES to confuse

FLUMP v -ED, -ING, -S to fall heavily

FLUNG past tense of fling

FLUNK v -ED, -ING, -S to fail an examination or course

FLUNKER n pl. -S one that flunks

FLUNKEY n pl. -KEYS flunky

FLUNKY n pl. -KIES a servile follower

FLUOR n pl. -S fluorite **FLUORIC** adj

FLUORENE n pl. -S a chemical compound

FLUORID n pl. -S fluoride

FLUORIDE n pl. -S a compound of fluorine

FLUORIN n pl. -S fluorine

FLUORINE n pl. -S a gaseous element

FLUORITE n pl. -S a mineral

FLURRY v -RIED, -RYING, -RIES to confuse

FLUSH adj FLUSHER, FLUSHEST ruddy

FLUSH v -ED, -ING, -ES to blush

FLUSHER n pl. -S one that flushes

FLUSTER v -ED, -ING, -S to put into a state of nervous confusion

FLUTE v FLUTED, FLUTING, FLUTES to play on a flute (a woodwind instrument)

FLUTER n pl. -S a flutist

FLUTIER comparative of fluty

FLUTIEST superlative of fluty

FLUTING n pl. -S a series of parallel grooves

FLUTIST n pl. -S one who plays the flute

FLUTTER v -ED, -ING, -S to wave rapidly and irregularly

FLUTTERY adj marked by fluttering

FLUTY adj FLUTIER, FLUTIEST resembling a flute in sound

FLUVIAL adj pertaining to a river

FLUX v -ED, -ING, -ES to melt

FLUXION n pl. -S the act of flowing

FLUYT n pl. -S a type of ship

FLY	v FLEW, FLOWN, FLYING, FLIES to move through the air	**FOAMY**	adj FOAMIER, FOAMIEST covered with foam
FLY	v FLIED, FLYING, FLIES to hit a ball high into the air in baseball	**FOB**	v FOBBED, FOBBING, FOBS to deceive
FLY	adj FLIER, FLIEST clever	**FOCAL**	adj pertaining to a focus
FLYABLE	adj suitable for flying	**FOCALISE**	v -ISED, -ISING, -ISES to focalize
FLYAWAY	n pl. -AWAYS one that is elusive	**FOCALIZE**	v -IZED, -IZING, -IZES to focus
FLYBELT	n pl. -S an area infested with tsetse flies	**FOCALLY**	adv with regard to focus
FLYBLOW	v -BLEW, -BLOWN, -BLOWING, -BLOWS to taint	**FOCUS**	n pl. -CUSES or -CI a point at which rays converge or from which they diverge
FLYBOAT	n pl. -S a small, fast boat	**FOCUS**	v -CUSED, -CUSING, -CUSES or -CUSSED, -CUSSING, -CUSSES to bring to a focus
FLYBY	n pl. -BYS a flight of aircraft close to a specified place		
FLYER	n pl. -S flier	**FOCUSER**	n pl. -S one that focuses
FLYING	n pl. -S the operation of an aircraft	**FODDER**	v -ED, -ING, -S to feed with coarse food
FLYLEAF	n pl. -LEAVES a blank leaf at the beginning or end of a book	**FODGEL**	adj plump
FLYMAN	n pl. -MEN a stage worker in a theater	**FOE**	n pl. -S an enemy
		FOEHN	n pl. -S a warm, dry wind
FLYOVER	n pl. -S a flight of aircraft over a specific location	**FOEMAN**	n pl. -MEN an enemy in war
		FOETAL	adj fetal
FLYPAPER	n pl. -S paper designed to catch or kill flies	**FOETID**	adj fetid
		FOETOR	n pl. -S fetor
FLYPAST	n pl. -S a flyby	**FOETUS**	n pl. -ES fetus
FLYSCH	n pl. -ES a sandstone deposit	**FOG**	v FOGGED, FOGGING, FOGS, to cover with fog (condensed water vapor near the earth's surface)
FLYSPECK	v -ED, -ING, -S to mark with minute spots		
FLYTE	v FLYTED, FLYTING, FLYTES to flite	**FOGBOUND**	adj surrounded by fog
		FOGBOW	n pl. -S a nebulous arc of light sometimes seen in a fog
FLYTIER	n pl. -S a maker of fishing flies		
FLYTING	n pl. -S a dispute in verse form	**FOGDOG**	n pl. -S a fogbow
FLYTRAP	n pl. -S a trap for catching flies	**FOGEY**	n pl. -GEYS fogy
FLYWAY	n pl. -WAYS an established air route of migratory birds	**FOGFRUIT**	n pl. -S a flowering plant
		FOGGAGE	n pl. -S a second growth of grass
FLYWHEEL	n pl. -S a heavy disk used in machinery		
		FOGGED	past tense of fog
FOAL	v -ED, -ING, -S to give birth to a horse	**FOGGER**	n pl. -S one that fogs
		FOGGING	present participle of fog
FOAM	v -ED, -ING, -S to form foam (a light, bubbly, gas and liquid mass)	**FOGGY**	adj -GIER, -GIEST filled with fog FOGGILY adv
		FOGHORN	n pl. -S a horn sounded in a fog to give warning
FOAMER	n pl. -S one that foams		
FOAMIER	comparative of foamy	**FOGIE**	n pl. -S fogy
FOAMIEST	superlative of foamy	**FOGLESS**	adj having no fog
FOAMILY	adv in a foamy manner	**FOGY**	n pl. -GIES an old-fashioned person FOGYISH adj
FOAMLESS	adj being without foam		
FOAMLIKE	adj resembling foam	**FOGYISM**	n pl. -S old-fashioned behavior

FOH _interj_ faugh

FOHN _n_ pl. -S foehn

FOIBLE _n_ pl. -S a minor weakness

FOIL _v_ -ED, -ING, -S to prevent the success of **FOILABLE** _adj_

FOILSMAN _n_ pl. -MEN a fencer

FOIN _v_ -ED, -ING, -S to thrust with a pointed weapon

FOISON _n_ pl. -S strength

FOIST _v_ -ED, -ING, -S to force upon slyly

FOLACIN _n_ pl. -S a B vitamin

FOLATE _n_ pl. -0 folacin

FOLD _v_ -ED, -ING, -S to lay one part over another part of **FOLDABLE** _adj_

FOLDAWAY _adj_ designed to fold out of the way

FOLDBOAT _n_ pl. -S a faltboat

FOLDER _n_ pl. -S one that folds

FOLDEROL _n_ pl. -S falderal

FOLDOUT _n_ pl. -S a gatefold

FOLIA a pl. of folium

FOLIAGE _n_ pl. -S the growth of leaves of a plant **FOLIAGED** _adj_

FOLIAR _adj_ pertaining to a leaf

FOLIATE _v_ -ATED, -ATING, -ATES to hammer into thin plates

FOLIO _v_ -ED, -ING, -S to number the pages of

FOLIOSE _adj_ having leaves

FOLIOUS _adj_ foliose

FOLIUM _n_ pl. -LIA or -LIUMS a thin layer

FOLK _n_ pl. -S a people or tribe

FOLKISH _adj_ characteristic of the common people

FOLKLIKE _adj_ folkish

FOLKLORE _n_ pl. -S the lore of a people

FOLKMOOT _n_ pl. -S a general assembly of the people in early England

FOLKMOT _n_ pl. -S folkmoot

FOLKMOTE _n_ pl. -S folkmoot

FOLKSY _adj_ FOLKSIER, FOLKSIEST friendly **FOLKSILY** _adv_

FOLKTALE _n_ pl. -S a tale forming part of the oral tradition of a people

FOLKWAY _n_ pl. -WAYS a traditional custom of a people

FOLLICLE _n_ pl. -S a small bodily cavity

FOLLIES pl. of folly

FOLLIS _n_ pl. -LES a coin of ancient Rome

FOLLOW _v_ -ED, -ING, -S to come or go after

FOLLOWER _n_ pl. -S one that follows

FOLLY _n_ pl. -LIES a foolish idea or action

FOMENT _v_ -ED, -ING, -S to promote the development of

FOMENTER _n_ pl. -S one that foments

FON _n_ pl. -S foehn

FOND _adj_ FONDER, FONDEST having an affection

FOND _v_ -ED, -ING, -S to display affection

FONDANT _n_ pl. -S a soft, creamy candy

FONDLE _v_ -DLED, -DLING, -DLES to caress

FONDLER _n_ pl. -S one that fondles

FONDLING _n_ pl. -S one that is fondled

FONDLY _adv_ in a fond manner

FONDNESS _n_ pl. -ES affection

FONDU _n_ pl. -S fondue

FONDUE _n_ pl. -S a dish of melted cheese

FONT _n_ pl. -S a receptacle for the water used in baptism **FONTAL** _adj_

FONTANEL _n_ pl. -S a space in the fetal and infantile skull

FONTINA _n_ pl. -S an Italian cheese

FOOD _n_ pl. -S a substance taken into the body to maintain life and growth **FOODLESS** _adj_

FOOFARAW _n_ pl. -S excessive ornamentation

FOOL _v_ -ED, -ING, -S to deceive

FOOLERY _n_ pl. -ERIES foolish behavior or speech

FOOLFISH _n_ pl. -ES a marine fish

FOOLISH _adj_ -ISHER, -ISHEST lacking good sense or judgment

FOOLSCAP _n_ pl. -S a paper size

FOOT _n_ pl. FEET the terminal part of the leg on which the body stands and moves

FOOT _v_ -ED, -ING, -S to walk

FOOTAGE _n_ pl. -S a length or quantity expressed in feet

FOOTBALL _n_ pl. -S a type of ball

FOOTBATH *n* pl. -S a bath for the feet

FOOTBOY *n* pl. -BOYS a serving boy

FOOTER *n* pl. -S one that walks

FOOTFALL *n* pl. -S the sound of a footstep

FOOTGEAR *n* pl. -S footwear

FOOTHILL *n* pl. -S a low hill at the foot of higher hills

FOOTHOLD *n* pl. -S a secure support for the feet

FOOTIER comparative of footy

FOOTIEST superlative of footy

FOOTING *n* pl. -S a foothold

FOOTLE *v* -TLED, -TLING, -TLES to waste time

FOOTLER *n* pl. -S one that footles

FOOTLESS *adj* having no feet

FOOTLIKE *adj* resembling a foot

FOOTLING present participle of footle

FOOTMAN *n* pl. -MEN a male servant

FOOTMARK *n* pl. -S a mark left by the foot on a surface

FOOTNOTE *v* -NOTED, -NOTING, -NOTES to furnish with explanatory notes

FOOTPACE *n* pl. -S a walking pace

FOOTPAD *n* pl. -S one who robs a pedestrian

FOOTPATH *n* pl. -S a path for pedestrians

FOOTRACE *n* pl. -S a race run on foot

FOOTREST *n* pl. -S a support for the feet

FOOTROPE *n* pl. -S a rope used in sailing

FOOTSIE *n* pl. -S a flirting game played with the feet

FOOTSLOG *v* -SLOGGED, -SLOGGING, -SLOGS to march through mud

FOOTSORE *adj* having sore or tired feet

FOOTSTEP *n* pl. -S a step with the foot

FOOTWALL *n* pl. -S the layer of rock beneath a vein of ore

FOOTWAY *n* pl. -WAYS a footpath

FOOTWEAR *n* pl. -S wearing apparel for the feet

FOOTWORK *n* pl. -S the use of the feet

FOOTWORN *adj* footsore

FOOTY *adj* -TIER, -TIEST paltry

FOOZLE *v* -ZLED, -ZLING, -ZLES to bungle

FOOZLER *n* pl. -S one that foozles

FOP *v* FOPPED, FOPPING, FOPS to deceive

FOPPERY *n* pl. -PERIES foppish behavior

FOPPISH *adj* characteristic of a dandy

FOR *prep* directed or sent to

FORA a pl. of forum

FORAGE *v* -AGED, -AGING, -AGES to search about

FORAGER *n* pl. -S one that forages

FORAM *n* pl. -S a marine rhizopod

FORAMEN *n* pl. -MINA or -MENS a small anatomical opening

FORAY *v* -ED, -ING, -S to raid

FORAYER *n* pl. -S one that forays

FORB *n* pl. -S an herb other than grass

FORBAD a past tense of forbid

FORBADE a past tense of forbid

FORBEAR *v* -BORE, -BORNE, -BEARING, -BEARS to refrain from

FORBID *v* -BADE or -BAD, -BIDDEN, -BIDDING, -BIDS to command not to do something

FORBIDAL *n* pl. -S the act of forbidding

FORBODE *v* -BODED, -BODING, -BODES to forebode

FORBORE past tense of forbear

FORBORNE past participle of forbear

FORBY *prep* close by

FORBYE *prep* forby

FORCE *v* FORCED, FORCING, FORCES to overcome resistance by the exertion of strength **FORCEDLY** *adv*

FORCEFUL *adj* strong

FORCEPS *n* pl. -CIPES an instrument for seizing and holding objects

FORCER *n* pl. -S one that forces

FORCIBLE *adj* effected by force **FORCIBLY** *adv*

FORCING present participle of force

FORCIPES pl. of forceps

FORD *v* -ED, -ING, -S to cross by wading **FORDABLE** *adj*

FORDLESS *adj* unable to be forded

FORDO *v* -DID, -DONE, -DOING, -DOES to destroy

FORE *n* pl. -S the front part of something

FOREARM *v* -ED, -ING, -S to arm in advance

FOREBAY *n pl.* -BAYS a reservoir from which water is taken to run equipment

FOREBEAR *n pl.* -S an ancestor

FOREBODE *v* -BODED, -BODING, -BODES to indicate in advance

FOREBODY *n pl.* -BODIES the forward part of a ship

FOREBOOM *n pl.* -S the boom of a ship's foremast

FOREBY *prep* forby

FOREBYE *prep* forby

FORECAST *v* -ED, -ING, -S to estimate or calculate in advance

FOREDATE *v* -DATED, -DATING, -DATES to antedate

FOREDECK *n pl.* -S the forward part of a ship's deck

FOREDO *v* -DID, -DONE, -DOING, -DOES to fordo

FOREDOOM *v* -ED, -ING, -S to doom in advance

FOREFACE *n pl.* -S the front part of the head of a quadruped

FOREFEEL *v* -FELT, -FEELING, -FEELS to have a premonition of

FOREFEND *v* -ED, -ING, -S to forfend

FOREFOOT *n pl.* -FEET one of the front feet of an animal

FOREGO *v* -WENT, -GONE, -GOING, -GOES to go before

FOREGOER *n pl.* -S one that foregoes

FOREGUT *n pl.* -S the front part of the embryonic alimentary canal

FOREHAND *n pl.* -S a type of tennis stroke

FOREHEAD *n pl.* -S the part of the face above the eyes

FOREHOOF *n pl.* -HOOFS or -HOOVES the hoof of a forefoot

FOREIGN *adj* situated outside a place or country

FOREKNOW *v* -KNEW, -KNOWN, -KNOWING, -KNOWS to know in advance

FORELADY *n pl.* -DIES a woman who supervises workers

FORELAND *n pl.* -S a projecting mass of land

FORELEG *n pl.* -S one of the front legs of an animal

FORELIMB *n pl.* -S a foreleg

FORELOCK *n pl.* -S a lock of hair growing over the forehead

FOREMAN *n pl.* -MEN a man who supervises workers

FOREMAST *n pl.* -S the forward mast of a ship

FOREMILK *n pl.* -S the milk secreted immediately after childbirth

FOREMOST *adj* first in position

FORENAME *n pl.* -S a first name

FORENOON *n pl.* -S the period of daylight before noon

FORENSIC *n pl.* -S an argumentative exercise

FOREPART *n pl.* -S the front part

FOREPAST *adj* already in the past

FOREPAW *n pl.* -S the paw of a foreleg

FOREPEAK *n pl.* -S the forward part of a ship's hold

FOREPLAY *n pl.* -PLAYS erotic stimulation preceding sexual intercourse

FORERANK *n pl.* -S the first rank

FORERUN *v* -RAN, -RUNNING, -RUNS to run in advance of

FORESAID *adj* previously said

FORESAIL *n pl.* -S the lowest sail on a foremast

FORESEE *v* -SAW, -SEEN, -SEEING, -SEES to see in advance

FORESEER *n pl.* -S one that foresees

FORESHOW *v* -SHOWED, -SHOWN, -SHOWING, -SHOWS to show in advance

FORESIDE *n pl.* -S the front side

FORESKIN *n pl.* -S the prepuce

FOREST *v* -ED, -ING, -S to convert into a forest (a densely wooded area)

FORESTAL *adj* of or pertaining to a forest

FORESTAY *n pl.* -STAYS a wire or rope used to support a foremast

FORESTER *n pl.* -S one skilled in forestry

FORESTRY *n pl.* -RIES the science of planting and managing forests

FORETELL *v* -TOLD, -TELLING, -TELLS to tell of or about in advance

FORETIME *n pl.* -S the past

FORETOP *n pl.* -S a forelock

FOREVER *n pl.* -S an indefinite length of time

FOREWARN v -ED, -ING, -S to warn in advance

FOREWENT past tense of forego

FOREWING n pl. -S an anterior wing of an insect

FOREWORD n pl. -S an introductory statement

FOREWORN adj forworn

FOREYARD n pl. -S the lowest yard on a foremast

FORFEIT v -ED, -ING, -S to lose as a penalty

FORFEND v -ED, -ING, -S to protect

FORGAT a past tense of forget

FORGAVE past tense of forgive

FORGE v FORGED, FORGING, FORGES to fashion or reproduce for fraudulent purposes

FORGER n pl. -S one that forges

FORGERY n pl. -ERIES the act of forging

FORGET v -GOT or -GAT, -GOTTEN, -GETTING, -GETS to fail to remember

FORGING n pl. -S a forgery

FORGIVE v -GAVE, -GIVEN, -GIVING, -GIVES to pardon

FORGIVER n pl. -S one that forgives

FORGO v -WENT, -GONE, -GOING, -GOES to refrain from

FORGOER n pl. -S one that forgoes

FORGOT a past tense of forget

FORGOTTEN past participle of forget

FORINT n pl. -S a monetary unit of Hungary

FORJUDGE v -JUDGED, -JUDGING, -JUDGES to deprive by judgment of a court

FORK v -ED, -ING, -S to work with a fork (a pronged implement) FORKEDLY adv

FORKER n pl. -S one that forks

FORKFUL n pl. FORKFULS or FORKSFUL as much as a fork will hold

FORKIER comparative of forky

FORKIEST superlative of forky

FORKLESS adj having no fork

FORKLIFT n pl. -S a machine for lifting and carrying loads

FORKLIKE adj resembling a fork

FORKSFUL a pl. of forkful

FORKY adj FORKIER, FORKIEST resembling a fork

FORLORN adj -LORNER, -LORNEST dreary

FORM v -ED, -ING, -S to produce FORMABLE adj

FORMAL n pl. -S a social event that requires evening dress

FORMALIN n pl. -S an aqueous solution of formaldehyde

FORMALLY adv in a prescribed or customary manner

FORMANT n pl. -S a characteristic component of the quality of a speech sound

FORMAT v -MATTED, -MATTING, -MATS to produce in a specified style

FORMATE n pl. -S a chemical salt

FORME n pl. -S an assemblage of printing type secured in a metal frame

FORMEE adj having the arms narrow at the center and expanding toward the ends — used of a heraldic cross

FORMER n pl. -S one that forms

FORMERLY adv previously

FORMFUL adj exhibiting good form

FORMIC adj pertaining to ants

FORMLESS adj lacking structure

FORMOL n pl. -S formalin

FORMULA n pl. -LAS or -LAE an exact method for doing something

FORMYL n pl. -S a univalent chemical radical

FORNIX n pl. -NICES an arched anatomical structure FORNICAL adj

FORRADER adv further ahead

FORRIT adv toward the front

FORSAKE v -SOOK, -SAKEN, -SAKING, -SAKES to quit or leave entirely

FORSAKER n pl. -S one that forsakes

FORSOOTH adv in truth

FORSPENT adj worn out

FORSWEAR v -SWORE, -SWORN, -SWEARING, -SWEARS to deny under oath

FORT n pl. -S a fortified enclosure or structure

FORTE n pl. -S a strong point

FORTH	adv onward in time, place, or order	
FORTIES	pl. of forty	
FORTIETH	n pl. -S one of forty equal parts	
FORTIFY	v -FIED, -FYING, -FIES to strengthen against attack	
FORTIS	n pl. -TES a consonant pronounced with relatively strong release of breath	
FORTRESS	v -ED, -ING, -ES to fortify	
FORTUITY	n pl. -ITIES an accidental occurrence	
FORTUNE	v -TUNED, -TUNING, -TUNES to endow with wealth	
FORTY	n pl. -TIES a number	
FORUM	n pl. -RUMS or -RA a public meeting place	
FORWARD	adj -WARDER, -WARDEST being at or near a point in advance	
FORWARD	v -ED, -ING, -S to help onward	
FORWENT	past tense of forgo	
FORWHY	adv for what reason	
FORWORN	adj worn out	
FORZANDO	n pl. -DOS sforzato	
FOSS	n pl. -ES fosse	
FOSSA	n pl. -SAE an anatomical depression FOSSATE adj	
FOSSE	n pl. -S a ditch	
FOSSETTE	n pl. -S a small fossa	
FOSSICK	v -ED, -ING, -S to search for gold	
FOSSIL	n pl. -S the remains of an animal or plant preserved in the earth's crust	
FOSTER	v -ED, -ING, -S to promote the growth of	
FOSTERER	n pl. -S one that fosters	
FOU	adj drunk	
FOUGHT	past tense of fight	
FOUGHTEN	adj exhausted especially from fighting	
FOUL	adj FOULER, FOULEST offensive to the senses	
FOUL	v -ED, -ING, -S to make foul	
FOULARD	n pl. -S a soft fabric	
FOULING	n pl. -S a deposit or crust	
FOULLY	adv in a foul manner	
FOULNESS	n pl. -ES the state of being foul	
FOUND	v -ED, -ING, -S to establish	

FOUNDER	v -ED, -ING, -S to become disabled
FOUNDRY	n pl. -RIES an establishment in which metal is cast
FOUNT	n pl. -S a fountain
FOUNTAIN	v -ED, -ING, -S to flow like a fountain (a spring of water)
FOUR	n pl. -S a number
FOURCHEE	adj having the end of each arm forked — used of a heraldic cross
FOURFOLD	adj four times as great
FOURGON	n pl. -S a wagon for carrying baggage
FOURSOME	n pl. -S a group of four
FOURTEEN	n pl. -S a number
FOURTH	n pl. -S one of four equal parts
FOURTHLY	adv in the fourth place
FOVEA	n pl. -VEAE a shallow anatomical depression FOVEAL, FOVEATE, FOVEATED adj
FOVEOLA	n pl. -LAE or -LAS a small fovea FOVEOLAR adj
FOVEOLE	n pl. -S a foveola
FOVEOLET	n pl. -S a foveola
FOWL	v -ED, -ING, -S to hunt birds
FOWLER	n pl. -S one that fowls
FOWLING	n pl. -S the hunting of birds
FOWLPOX	n pl. -ES a virus disease of poultry
FOX	v -ED, -ING, -ES to outwit
FOXFIRE	n pl. -S a glow produced by certain fungi on decaying wood
FOXFISH	n pl. -ES a large shark
FOXGLOVE	n pl. -S a flowering plant
FOXHOLE	n pl. -S a small pit used for cover in a battle zone
FOXHOUND	n pl. -S a hunting dog
FOXIER	comparative of foxy
FOXIEST	superlative of foxy
FOXILY	adv in a foxy manner
FOXINESS	n pl. -ES the state of being foxy
FOXING	n pl. -S a piece of material used to cover the upper portion of a shoe
FOXLIKE	adj resembling a fox (a carnivorous mammal)
FOXSKIN	n pl. -S the skin of a fox
FOXTAIL	n pl. -S the tail of a fox

FOXY   *adj* FOXIER, FOXIEST crafty

FOY   *n* pl. -S a farewell feast or gift

FOYER   *n* pl. -S an entrance room or hall

FOZINESS   *n* pl. -ES the state of being fozy

FOZY   *adj* -ZIER, -ZIEST too ripe

FRACAS   *n* pl. -ES a brawl

FRACTED   *adj* broken

FRACTION   *v* -ED, -ING, -S to divide into portions

FRACTUR   *n* pl. -S fraktur

FRACTURE   *v* -TURED, -TURING, -TURES to break

FRAE   *prep* from

FRAENUM   *n* pl. -NA or -NUMS frenum

FRAG   *v* FRAGGED, FRAGGING, FRAGS to injure with a type of grenade

FRAGGING   *n* pl. -S the act of one that frags

FRAGILE   *adj* easily broken or damaged

FRAGMENT   *v* -ED, -ING, -S to break into pieces

FRAGRANT   *adj* having a pleasant odor

FRAIL   *adj* FRAILER, FRAILEST fragile **FRAILLY** *adv*

FRAIL   *n* pl. -S a basket for holding dried fruits

FRAILTY   *n* pl. -TIES a weakness of character

FRAISE   *n* pl. -S a barrier of pointed stakes

FRAKTUR   *n* pl. -S a style of type

FRAME   *v* FRAMED, FRAMING, FRAMES to construct by putting together the various parts **FRAMABLE** *adj*

FRAMER   *n* pl. -S one that frames

FRANC   *n* pl. -S a monetary unit of France

FRANCIUM   *n* pl. -S a radioactive element

FRANK   *adj* FRANKER, FRANKEST honest and unreserved in speech

FRANK   *v* -ED, -ING, -S to mark (a piece of mail) for free delivery

FRANKER   *n* pl. -S one that franks

FRANKEST   superlative of frank

FRANKLIN   *n* pl. -S a medieval English landowner

FRANKLY   *adv* in a frank manner

FRANTIC   *adj* wildly excited

FRAP   *v* FRAPPED, FRAPPING, FRAPS to bind firmly

FRAPPE   *n* pl. -S a partly frozen drink

FRAT   *n* pl. -S a college fraternity

FRATER   *n* pl. -S a comrade

FRAUD   *n* pl. -S trickery

FRAUGHT   *v* -ED, -ING, -S to load down

FRAULEIN   *n* pl. -S a German governess

FRAY   *v* -ED, -ING, -S to wear off by rubbing

FRAYING   *n* pl. -S something worn off by rubbing

FRAZZLE   *v* -ZLED, -ZLING, -ZLES to fray

FREAK   *v* -ED, -ING, -S to streak with color

FREAKIER   comparative of freaky

FREAKIEST   superlative of freaky

FREAKILY   *adv* in a freaky manner

FREAKISH   *adj* unusual

FREAKOUT   *n* pl. -S an event marked by wild excitement

FREAKY   *adj* FREAKIER, FREAKIEST freakish

FRECKLE   *v* -LED, -LING, -LES to mark with freckles (small, brownish spots)

FRECKLY   *adj* -LIER, -LIEST marked with freckles

FREE   *adj* FREER, FREEST not subject to restriction or control

FREE   *v* FREED, FREEING, FREES to make free

FREEBEE   *n* pl. -S freebie

FREEBIE   *n* pl. -S something given or received without charge

FREEBOOT   *v* -ED, -ING, -S to plunder

FREEBORN   *adj* born free

FREED   past tense of free

FREEDMAN   *n* pl. -MEN a man who has been freed from slavery

FREEDOM   *n* pl. -S the state of being free

FREEFORM   *adj* having a free flowing design or shape

FREEHAND   *adj* drawn by hand without mechanical aids

FREEHOLD   *n* pl. -S a form of tenure of real property

FREELOAD   *v* -ED, -ING, -S to live at the expense of others

FREELY   *adv* in a free manner

FREEMAN   *n pl.* -MEN one who is free

FREENESS   *n pl.* -ES freedom

FREER   *n pl.* -S one that frees

FREESIA   *n pl.* -S an African herb

FREEST   superlative of free

FREEWAY   *n pl.* -WAYS an express highway

FREEWILL   *adj* voluntary

FREEZE   *v* FROZE, FROZEN, FREEZING, FREEZES to become hardened into a solid body by loss of heat

FREEZER   *n pl.* -S an apparatus for freezing food

FREIGHT   *v* -ED, -ING, -S to load with goods for transportation

FREMD   *adj* strange

FREMITUS   *n pl.* -ES a palpable vibration

FRENA   a *pl.* of frenum

FRENCH   *v* -ED, -ING, -ES to cut into thin strips before cooking

FRENETIC   *n pl.* -S a frantic person

FRENULUM   *n pl.* -LA a frenum

FRENUM   *n pl.* -NA or -NUMS a connecting fold of membrane

FRENZILY   *adv* in a frantic manner

FRENZY   *v* -ZIED, -ZYING, -ZIES to make frantic

FREQUENT   *adj* -QUENTER, -QUENTEST occurring again and again

FREQUENT   *v* -ED, -ING, -S to be in or at often

FRERE   *n pl.* -S brother

FRESCO   *v* -ED, -ING, -ES or -S to paint on a surface of plaster

FRESCOER   *n pl.* -S one that frescoes

FRESH   *adj* FRESHER, FRESHEST new

FRESH   *v* -ED, -ING, -ES to freshen

FRESHEN   *v* -ED, -ING, -S to make or become fresh

FRESHET   *n pl.* -S a sudden overflow of a stream

FRESHLY   *adv* in a fresh manner

FRESHMAN   *n pl.* -MEN a first-year student

FRESNEL   *n pl.* -S a unit of frequency

FRET   *v* FRETTED, FRETTING, FRETS to worry

FRETFUL   *adj* inclined to fret

FRETLESS   *adj* having no fretwork

FRETSAW   *n pl.* -S a narrow-bladed saw

FRETSOME   *adj* fretful

FRETTED   past tense of fret

FRETTING   present participle of fret

FRETTY   *adj* -TIER, -TIEST fretful

FRETWORK   *n pl.* -S ornamental work consisting of interlacing parts

FRIABLE   *adj* easily crumbled

FRIAR   *n pl.* -S a member of a religious order **FRIARLY** *adj*

FRIARY   *n pl.* -ARIES a monastery of friars

FRIBBLE   *v* -BLED, -BLING, -BLES to act foolishly

FRIBBLER   *n pl.* -S one that fribbles

FRICANDO   *n pl.* -DOES a roasted loin of veal

FRICTION   *n pl.* -S the rubbing of one body against another

FRIDGE   *n pl.* -S a refrigerator

FRIED   past tense of fry

FRIEND   *v* -ED, -ING, -S to enter into a warm association with

FRIENDLY   *adj* -LIER, -LIEST inclined to approve, help, or support

FRIENDLY   *n pl.* -LIES one who is friendly

FRIER   *n pl.* -S fryer

FRIES   present 3d person sing. of fry

FRIEZE   *n pl.* -S a coarse woolen fabric

FRIG   *v* FRIGGED, FRIGGING, FRIGS to copulate — usually considered vulgar

FRIGATE   *n pl.* -S a sailing vessel

FRIGHT   *v* -ED, -ING, -S to frighten

FRIGHTEN   *v* -ED, -ING, -S to make afraid

FRIGID   *adj* very cold **FRIGIDLY** *adv*

FRIJOL   *n pl.* -ES a bean used as food

FRIJOLE   *n pl.* -S frijol

FRILL   *v* -ED, -ING, -S to provide with a frill (an ornamental ruffled edge)

FRILLER   *n pl.* -S one that frills

FRILLING   *n pl.* -S an arrangement of frills

FRILLY   *adj* FRILLIER, FRILLIEST having frills

FRINGE   *v* FRINGED, FRINGING, FRINGES to provide with a fringe (an ornamental border)

FRINGY   *adj* FRINGIER, FRINGIEST resembling a fringe

FRIPPERY   *n* pl. -PERIES excessive ornamentation

FRISE   *n* pl. -S frieze

FRISETTE   *n* pl. -S frizette

FRISEUR   *n* pl. -S a hairdresser

FRISK   *v* -ED, -ING, -S to move or leap about playfully

FRISKER   *n* pl. -S one that frisks

FRISKET   *n* pl. -S a frame used to protect paper in a printing press

FRISKY   *adj* FRISKIER, FRISKIEST lively and playful **FRISKILY** *adv*

FRISSON   *n* pl. -S a shudder

FRIT   *v* FRITTED, FRITTING, FRITS to fuse into a vitreous substance

FRITH   *n* pl. -S firth

FRITT   *v* -ED, -ING, -S to frit

FRITTED   past tense of frit

FRITTER   *v* -ED, -ING, -S to squander little by little

FRITTING   present participle of frit

FRIVOL   *v* -OLED, -OLING, -OLS or -OLLED, -OLLING, -OLS to behave playfully

FRIVOLER   *n* pl. -S one that frivols

FRIZ   *n* pl. -ES a tight curl

FRIZ   *v* -ED, -ING, -ES to frizz

FRIZER   *n* pl. -S frizzer

FRIZETTE   *n* pl. -S a frizzed fringe of hair

FRIZZ   *n* pl. -ES friz

FRIZZ   *v* -ED, -ING, -ES to form into small, tight curls

FRIZZER   *n* pl. -S one that frizzes

FRIZZIER   comparative of frizzy

FRIZZIEST   superlative of frizzy

FRIZZILY   *adv* in a frizzy manner

FRIZZLE   *v* -ZLED, -ZLING, -ZLES to frizz

FRIZZLER   *n* pl. -S one that frizzles

FRIZZLY   *adj* -ZLIER, -ZLIEST frizzy

FRIZZY   *adj* FRIZZIER, FRIZZIEST tightly curled

FRO   *adv* away

FROCK   *v* -ED, -ING, -S to clothe in a long, loose outer garment

FROE   *n* pl. -S a cleaving tool

FROG   *v* FROGGED, FROGGING, FROGS to hunt frogs (web-footed, tailless amphibians)

FROGEYE   *n* pl. -S a plant disease **FROGEYED** *adj*

FROGFISH   *n* pl. -ES a marine fish

FROGGED   past tense of frog

FROGGING   present participle of frog

FROGGY   *adj* -GIER, -GIEST abounding in frogs

FROGLIKE   *adj* resembling a frog

FROGMAN   *n* pl. -MEN a person equipped for extended periods of underwater swimming

FROLIC   *v* -ICKED, -ICKING, -ICS to play and run about merrily **FROLICKY** *adj*

FROM   *prep* starting at

FROMAGE   *n* pl. -S cheese

FROMENTY   *n* pl. -TIES frumenty

FROND   *n* pl. -S a type of leaf **FRONDED, FRONDOSE** *adj*

FRONDEUR   *n* pl. -S a rebel

FRONS   *n* pl. FRONTES the upper anterior portion of an insect's head

FRONT   *v* -ED, -ING, -S to provide with a front (a forward part)

FRONT   *adj* FRONTER articulated at the front of the oral passage

FRONTAGE   *n* pl. -S the front of a building or lot

FRONTAL   *n* pl. -S a bone of the skull

FRONTES   pl. of frons

FRONTIER   *n* pl. -S a border between two countries

FRONTLET   *n* pl. -S a decorative band worn across the forehead

FRONTON   *n* pl. -S a jai alai arena

FRORE   *adj* frozen

FROSH   *n* pl. FROSH a freshman

FROST   *v* -ED, -ING, -S to cover with frost (a deposit of minute ice crystals)

FROSTBIT   *adj* injured by extreme cold

FROSTED   *n* pl. -S a type of milk shake

FROSTING   *n* pl. -S icing

FROSTY   *adj* FROSTIER, FROSTIEST covered with frost **FROSTILY** *adv*

FROTH   *v* -ED, -ING, -S to foam

FROTHY *adj* FROTHIER, FROTHIEST foamy **FROTHILY** *adv*

FROTTAGE *n* pl. -S masturbation by rubbing against another person

FROTTEUR *n* pl. -S one who practices frottage

FROUFROU *n* pl. -S a rustling sound

FROUNCE *v* FROUNCED, FROUNCING, FROUNCES to pleat

FROUZY *adj* -ZIER, -ZIEST frowzy

FROW *n* pl. -S froe

FROWARD *adj* disobedient

FROWN *v* -ED, -ING, S to contract the brow in displeasure

FROWNER *n* pl. -S one that frowns

FROWSTY *adj* -TIER, -TIEST musty

FROWSY *adj* -SIER, -SIEST frowzy

FROWZY *adj* -ZIER, -ZIEST unkempt **FROWZILY** *adv*

FROZE past tense of freeze

FROZEN *adj* very cold **FROZENLY** *adv*

FRUCTIFY *v* -FIED, -FYING, -FIES to bear fruit

FRUCTOSE *n* pl. -S a sugar found in various fruits

FRUG *v* FRUGGED, FRUGGING, FRUGS to perform a type of vigorous dance

FRUGAL *adj* thrifty **FRUGALLY** *adv*

FRUIT *v* -ED, -ING, -S to bear fruit (usually edible reproductive bodies of a seed plant)

FRUITAGE *n* pl. -S the process of bearing fruit

FRUITER *n* pl. -S one that grows or sells fruit

FRUITFUL *adj* -FULLER, -FULLEST producing abundantly

FRUITIER comparative of fruity

FRUITIEST superlative of fruity

FRUITION *n* pl. -S the accomplishment of something desired

FRUITLET *n* pl. -S a small fruit

FRUITY *adj* FRUITIER, FRUITIEST suggestive of fruit

FRUMENTY *n* pl. -TIES a dish of wheat boiled in milk and sweetened with sugar

FRUMP *n* pl. -S a dowdy woman **FRUMPISH** *adj*

FRUMPY *adj* FRUMPIER, FRUMPIEST dowdy **FRUMPILY** *adv*

FRUSTA a pl. of frustum

FRUSTULE *n* pl. -S the shell of a diatom

FRUSTUM *n* pl. -TA or -TUMS a part of a conical solid

FRY *v* FRIED, FRYING, FRIES to cook over direct heat in hot fat or oil

FRYER *n* pl. -S one that fries

FRYPAN *n* pl. -S a pan for frying food

FUB *v* FUBBED, FUBBING, FUBS to fob

FUBSY *adj* FUBSIER, FUBSIEST chubby and somewhat squat

FUCHSIA *n* pl. -S a flowering shrub

FUCHSIN *n* pl. -S a red dye

FUCHSINE *n* pl. -S fuchsin

FUCI a pl. of fucus

FUCK *v* -ED, -ING, -S to copulate — usually considered obscene

FUCOID *n* pl. -S a brown seaweed **FUCOIDAL** *adj*

FUCOSE *n* pl. -S a type of sugar

FUCOUS *adj* of or pertaining to fucoids

FUCUS *n* pl. -CI or -CUSES any of a genus of brown algae

FUD *n* pl. -S an old-fashioned person

FUDDLE *v* -DLED, -DLING, -DLES to confuse

FUDGE *v* FUDGED, FUDGING, FUDGES to falsify

FUEHRER *n* pl. -S fuhrer

FUEL *v* -ELED, -ELING, -ELS or -ELLED, -ELLING, -ELS to provide with fuel (material used to produce energy)

FUELER *n* pl. -S one that fuels

FUELLER *n* pl. -S fueler

FUELLING a present participle of fuel

FUG *v* FUGGED, FUGGING, FUGS to make stuffy and odorous

FUGACITY *n* pl. -TIES lack of enduring qualities

FUGAL *adj* being in the style of a fugue **FUGALLY** *adv*

FUGATO *n* pl. -TOS a fugal composition

FUGGED past tense of fug

FUGGING present participle of fug

FUGGY *adj* -GIER, -GIEST stuffy and odorous

FUGIO *n* pl. -GIOS a former coin of the United States

FUGITIVE *n* pl. -S one who flees

FUGLE *v* -GLED, -GLING, -GLES to lead

FUGLEMAN *n* pl. -MEN a leader

FUGUE *v* FUGUED, FUGUING, FUGUES to compose a fugue (a type of musical composition)

FUGUIST *n* pl. -S one who composes fugues

FUHRER *n* pl. -S a leader

FUJI *n* pl. -S a silk fabric

FULCRUM *n* pl. -CRUMS or -CRA a support for a lever

FULFIL *v* -FILLED, -FILLING, -FILS to fulfill

FULFILL *v* -ED, -ING, -S to bring about the accomplishment of

FULGENT *adj* shining brightly

FULGID *adj* fulgent

FULHAM *n* pl. -S a loaded die

FULL *adj* FULLER, FULLEST filled completely

FULL *v* -ED, -ING, -S to shrink and thicken, as cloth

FULLAM *n* pl. -S fulham

FULLBACK *n* pl. -S an offensive back in football

FULLER *v* -ED, -ING, -S to groove with a type of hammer

FULLERY *n* pl. -ERIES a place for fulling cloth

FULLFACE *n* pl. -S a heavy-faced type

FULLNESS *n* pl. -ES the state of being full

FULLY *adv* in a full manner

FULMAR *n* pl. -S an arctic seabird

FULMINE *v* -MINED, -MINING, -MINES to explode loudly

FULMINIC *adj* highly explosive

FULNESS *n* pl. -ES fullness

FULSOME *adj* repulsive

FULVOUS *adj* of a brownish yellow color

FUMARASE *n* pl. -S an enzyme

FUMARATE *n* pl. -S a chemical salt

FUMARIC *adj* pertaining to a certain acid

FUMAROLE *n* pl. -S a hole from which volcanic vapors issue

FUMATORY *n* pl. -RIES a fumigation chamber

FUMBLE *v* -BLED, -BLING, -BLES to handle clumsily

FUMBLER *n* pl. -S one that fumbles

FUME *v* FUMED, FUMING, FUMES to give off fumes (gaseous exhalations)

FUMELESS *adj* having no fumes

FUMELIKE *adj* resembling fumes

FUMER *n* pl. -S one that fumes

FUMET *n* pl. -S the odor of meat while cooking

FUMETTE *n* pl. -S fumet

FUMIER comparative of fumy

FUMIEST superlative of fumy

FUMIGANT *n* pl. -S a substance used in fumigating

FUMIGATE *v* -GATED, -GATING, -GATES to subject to fumes in order to destroy pests

FUMING present participle of fume

FUMITORY *n* pl. -RIES a climbing plant

FUMULUS *n* pl. -LI a thin cloud

FUMY *adj* FUMIER, FUMIEST producing or full of fumes

FUN *v* FUNNED, FUNNING, FUNS to act playfully

FUNCTION *v* -ED, -ING, -S to be in action

FUNCTOR *n* pl. -S one that functions

FUND *v* -ED, -ING, -S to provide money for

FUNDUS *n* pl. -DI the inner basal surface of a bodily organ **FUNDIC** *adj*

FUNERAL *n* pl. -S a ceremony held for a dead person

FUNERARY *adj* pertaining to a funeral

FUNEREAL *adj* funerary

FUNEST *adj* portending death or evil

FUNFAIR *n* pl. -S an amusement park

FUNGAL *n* pl. -S a fungus

FUNGI *a* pl. of fungus

FUNGIBLE *n* pl. -S something that may be exchanged for an equivalent unit of the same class

FUNGIC *adj* fungous

FUNGO *n* pl. -GOES a fly ball hit to a fielder for practice in baseball

FUNGOID *n* pl. -S a growth resembling a fungus

FUNGOUS	*adj* pertaining to a fungus
FUNGUS	*n* pl. -GI or -GUSES any of a major group of lower plants
FUNICLE	*n* pl. -S a cordlike anatomical structure
FUNICULI	*n/pl* funicles
FUNK	*v* -ED, -ING, -S to shrink back in fear
FUNKER	*n* pl. -S one that funks
FUNKIA	*n* pl. -S a flowering plant
FUNKY	*adj* FUNKIER, FUNKIEST having an offensive odor
FUNNED	past tense of fun
FUNNEL	*v* -NELED, -NELING, -NELS or -NELLED, -NELLING, -NELS to pass through a funnel (a cone-shaped utensil)
FUNNING	present participle of fun
FUNNY	*adj* -NIER, -NIEST causing laughter or amusement **FUNNILY** *adv*
FUNNY	*n* pl. -NIES a comic strip
FUNNYMAN	*n* pl. -MEN a comedian
FUR	*v* FURRED, FURRING, FURS to cover with fur (a dressed animal pelt)
FURAN	*n* pl. -S a flammable liquid
FURANE	*n* pl. -S furan
FURANOSE	*n* pl. -S a type of sugar
FURBELOW	*v* -ED, -ING, -S to decorate with ruffles
FURBISH	*v* -ED, -ING, -ES to polish
FURCATE	*v* -CATED, -CATING, -CATES to divide into branches
FURCRAEA	*n* pl. -S a tropical plant
FURCULA	*n* pl. -LAE a forked bone **FURCULAR** *adj*
FURCULUM	*n* pl. -LA a furcula
FURFUR	*n* pl. -ES dandruff
FURFURAL	*n* pl. -S a chemical compound
FURFURAN	*n* pl. -S furan
FURIBUND	*adj* furious
FURIES	pl. of fury
FURIOSO	*adv* with great force — used as a musical direction
FURIOUS	*adj* extremely angry
FURL	*v* -ED, -ING, -S to roll up **FURLABLE** *adj*
FURLER	*n* pl. -S one that furls

FURLESS	*adj* having no fur
FURLONG	*n* pl. -S a unit of distance
FURLOUGH	*v* -ED, -ING, -S to grant a leave of absence to
FURMENTY	*n* pl. -TIES frumenty
FURMETY	*n* pl. -TIES frumenty
FURMITY	*n* pl. -TIES frumenty
FURNACE	*v* -NACED, -NACING, -NACES to subject to heat
FURNISH	*v* -ED, -ING, -ES to equip
FUROR	*n* pl. -S an uproar
FURORE	*n* pl. -S furor
FURRED	past tense of fur
FURRIER	*n* pl. -S one that deals in furs
FURRIERY	*n* pl. -ERIES the business of a furrier
FURRIEST	superlative of furry
FURRILY	*adv* in a furry manner
FURRINER	*n* pl. -S a foreigner
FURRING	*n* pl. -S a trimming or lining of fur
FURROW	*v* -ED, -ING, -S to make furrows (narrow depressions) in
FURROWER	*n* pl. -S one that furrows
FURROWY	*adj* marked by furrows
FURRY	*adj* -RIER, -RIEST covered with fur
FURTHER	*v* -ED, -ING, -S to help forward
FURTHEST	a superlative of far
FURTIVE	*adj* stealthy
FURUNCLE	*n* pl. -S a painful swelling of the skin
FURY	*n* pl. -RIES violent anger
FURZE	*n* pl. -S a spiny shrub
FURZY	*adj* FURZIER, FURZIEST abounding in furze
FUSAIN	*n* pl. -S a fine charcoal used in drawing
FUSCOUS	*adj* of a dusky color
FUSE	*v* FUSED, FUSING, FUSES to equip with a fuse (a detonating device)
FUSEE	*n* pl. -S a large-headed friction match
FUSEL	*n* pl. -S an oily liquid
FUSELAGE	*n* pl. -S the body of an airplane
FUSELESS	*adj* lacking a fuse

FUSIBLE   *adj* capable of being melted
FUSIBLY *adv*

FUSIFORM   *adj* tapering toward each end

FUSIL   *n* pl. -S a type of musket

FUSILE   *adj* formed by melting

FUSILEER   *n* pl. -S fusilier

FUSILIER   *n* pl. -S a soldier armed with a fusil

FUSING   present participle of fuse

FUSION   *n* pl. -S the act of melting together

FUSS   *v* -ED, -ING, -ES to be overly concerned with small details

FUSSER   *n* pl. -S one that fusses

FUSSPOT   *n* pl. -S a fusser

FUSSY   *adj* FUSSIER, FUSSIEST overly concerned with small details
FUSSILY *adv*

FUSTIAN   *n* pl. -S a cotton fabric

FUSTIC   *n* pl. -S a tropical tree

FUSTY   *adj* -TIER, -TIEST musty
FUSTILY *adv*

FUTHARC   *n* pl. -S futhark

FUTHARK   *n* pl. -S an ancient alphabet

FUTHORC   *n* pl. -S futhark

FUTHORK   *n* pl. -S futhark

FUTILE   *adj* having no useful result
FUTILELY *adv*

FUTILITY   *n* pl. -TIES the quality of being futile

FUTTOCK   *n* pl. -S a curved timber in the frame of a wooden ship

FUTURE   *n* pl. -S the time yet to come
FUTURAL *adj*

FUTURISM   *n* pl. -S an artistic and literary movement

FUTURIST   *n* pl. -S an advocate of futurism

FUTURITY   *n* pl. -TIES the future

FUZE   *v* FUZED, FUZING, FUZES to fuse

FUZEE   *n* pl. -S fusee

FUZIL   *n* pl. -S fusil

FUZING   present participle of fuze

FUZZ   *v* -ED, -ING, -ES to become fuzzy

FUZZY   *adj* FUZZIER, FUZZIEST blurry
FUZZILY *adv*

FYCE   *n* pl. -S feist

FYKE   *n* pl. -S a bag-shaped fishnet

FYLFOT   *n* pl. -S a swastika

FYTTE   *n* pl. -S a division of a poem or song

GAB   *v* GABBED, GABBING, GABS to chatter

GABBARD   *n pl.* -S a barge

GABBART   *n pl.* -S gabbard

GABBED   past tense of gab

GABBER   *n pl.* -S one that gabs

GABBING   present participle of gab

GABBLE   *v* -BLED, -BLING, -BLES to jabber

GABBLER   *n pl.* -S one that gabbles

GABBRO   *n pl.* -BROS a type of rock **GABBROIC, GABBROID** *adj*

GABBY   *adj* -BIER, -BIEST talkative

GABELLE   *n pl.* -S a tax on salt **GABELLED** *adj*

GABFEST   *n pl.* -S an informal gathering for general talk

GABIES   pl. of gaby

GABION   *n pl.* -S a type of basket

GABLE   *v* -BLED, -BLING, -BLES to form a triangular section of a wall

GABOON   *n pl.* -S a spittoon

GABY   *n pl.* -BIES a dolt

GAD   *v* GADDED, GADDING, GADS to roam about restlessly

GADABOUT   *n pl.* -S one that gads about

GADARENE   *adj* headlong

GADDED   past tense of gad

GADDER   *n pl.* -S one that gads about

GADDI   *n pl.* -S a hassock

GADDING   present participle of gad

GADFLY   *n pl.* -FLIES a biting fly

GADGET   *n pl.* -S a mechanical device **GADGETY** *adj*

GADGETRY   *n pl.* -RIES the devising or constructing of gadgets

GADI   *n pl.* -S gaddi

GADID   *n pl.* -S gadoid

GADOID   *n pl.* -S a type of fish

GADROON   *n pl.* -S a band of fluted or reeded molding

GADWALL   *n pl.* -S a wild duck

GADZOOKS   *interj* — used as a mild oath

GAE   *v* GAED, GANE, GAUN, GAES to go

GAFF   *v* -ED, -ING, -S to catch a fish with a sharp hook

GAFFE   *n pl.* -S a social blunder

GAFFER   *n pl.* -S an old man

GAG   *v* GAGGED, GAGGING, GAGS to stop up the mouth

GAGA   *adj* crazy

GAGE   *v* GAGED, GAGING, GAGES to pledge as security

GAGER   *n pl.* -S gauger

GAGGED   past tense of gag

GAGGER   *n pl.* -S one that gags

GAGGING   present participle of gag

GAGGLE   *v* -GLED, -GLING, -GLES to cackle

GAGING   present participle of gage

GAGMAN   *n pl.* -MEN one who writes jokes

GAGSTER   *n pl.* -S a gagman

GAHNITE   *n pl.* -S a mineral

GAIETY   *n pl.* -ETIES festive activity

GAILY *adv* in a gay manner

GAIN *v* -ED, -ING, -S to acquire **GAINABLE** *adj*

GAINER *n* pl. -S one that gains

GAINFUL *adj* profitable

GAINLESS *adj* profitless

GAINLY *adj* -LIER, -LIEST graceful

GAINSAY *v* -SAID, -SAYING, -SAYS to deny

GAINST *prep* against

GAIT *v* -ED, -ING, -S to train a horse to move in a particular way

GAITER *n* pl. -S a covering for the lower leg

GAL *n* pl. -S a girl

GALA *n* pl. -S a celebration

GALACTIC *adj* pertaining to a galaxy

GALAGO *n* pl. -GOS a small primate

GALAH *n* pl. -S a cockatoo

GALANGAL *n* pl. -S a medicinal plant

GALATEA *n* pl. -S a strong cotton fabric

GALAVANT *v* -ED, -ING, -S to gad about

GALAX *n* pl. -ES an evergreen herb

GALAXY *n* pl. -AXIES a large system of celestial bodies

GALBANUM *n* pl. -S a gum resin

GALE *n* pl. -S a strong wind

GALEA *n* pl. -LEAE or -LEAS a helmet-shaped anatomical part **GALEATE, GALEATED** *adj*

GALENA *n* pl. -S the principal ore of lead **GALENIC** *adj*

GALENITE *n* pl. -S galena

GALERE *n* pl. -S a group of people having a common quality

GALILEE *n* pl. -S a type of porch

GALIOT *n* pl. -S galliot

GALIPOT *n* pl. -S a type of turpentine

GALIVANT *v* -ED, -ING, -S to gad about

GALL *v* -ED, -ING, -S to vex or irritate

GALLANT *v* -ED, -ING, -S to court a woman

GALLATE *n* pl. -S a chemical salt

GALLEASS *n* pl. -ES a large war galley

GALLEIN *n* pl. -S a green dye

GALLEON *n* pl. -S a large sailing vessel

GALLERY *v* -LERIED, -LERYING, -LERIES to provide with a long covered area

GALLETA *n* pl. -S a perennial grass

GALLEY *n* pl. -LEYS a long, low medieval ship

GALLFLY *n* pl. -FLIES a small insect

GALLIARD *n* pl. -S a lively dance

GALLIASS *n* pl. -ES galleass

GALLIC *adj* containing gallium

GALLICAN *adj* pertaining to a French religious movement

GALLIED past tense of gally

GALLIES present 3d person sing. of gally

GALLIOT *n* pl. -S a small galley

GALLIPOT *n* pl. -S a small earthen jar

GALLIUM *n* pl. -S a metallic element

GALLNUT *n* pl. -S an abnormal swelling of plant tissue

GALLON *n* pl. -S a unit of liquid measure

GALLOON *n* pl. -S an ornamental braid

GALLOOT *n* pl. -S galoot

GALLOP *v* -ED, -ING, -S to ride a horse at full speed

GALLOPER *n* pl. -S one that gallops

GALLOUS *adj* containing gallium

GALLOWS *n* pl. -ES a structure used for hanging a condemned person

GALLUS *n* pl. -ES a suspender for trousers **GALLUSED** *adj*

GALLY *v* -LIED, -LYING, -LIES to frighten

GALOOT *n* pl. -S an awkward or uncouth person

GALOP *n* pl. -S a lively dance

GALOPADE *n* pl. -S a galop

GALORE *n* pl. -S abundance

GALOSH *n* pl. -ES an overshoe **GALOSHED** *adj*

GALOSHE *n* pl. -S galosh

GALUMPH *v* -ED, -ING, -S to move clumsily

GALVANIC *adj* pertaining to a direct electric current

GALYAC *n* pl. -S galyak

GALYAK *n* pl. -S a fur made from lambskin

GAM *v* GAMMED, GAMMING, GAMS to visit socially

GAMASHES *n/pl* boots worn by horseback riders

GAMB *n* pl. -S a leg

GAMBA *n* pl. -S a bass viol

GAMBADE *n* pl. -S a gambado

GAMBADO *n* pl. -DOES or -DOS a leap made by a horse

GAMBE *n* pl. -S gamb

GAMBESON *n* pl. -S a medieval coat

GAMBIA *n* pl. -S gambier

GAMBIER *n* pl. -S an extract obtained from an Asian vine

GAMBIR *n* pl. -S gambier

GAMBIT *n* pl. -S a type of chess opening

GAMBLE *v* -BLED, -BLING, -BLES to play a game of chance for money or valuables

GAMBLER *n* pl. -S one that gambles

GAMBOGE *n* pl. -S a gum resin

GAMBOL *v* -BOLED, -BOLING, -BOLS or -BOLLED, -BOLLING, -BOLS to leap about playfully

GAMBREL *n* pl. -S a part of a horse's leg

GAMBUSIA *n* pl. -S a small fish

GAME *adj* GAMER, GAMEST plucky

GAME *v* GAMED, GAMING, GAMES to gamble

GAMECOCK *n* pl. -S a rooster trained for fighting

GAMELAN *n* pl. -S a type of orchestra

GAMELIKE *adj* similar to a game (a contest governed by a set of rules)

GAMELY *adv* in a game manner

GAMENESS *n* pl. -ES the quality of being game

GAMER comparative of game

GAMESOME *adj* playful

GAMEST superlative of game

GAMESTER *n* pl. -S a gambler

GAMETE *n* pl. -S a mature reproductive cell **GAMETIC** *adj*

GAMEY *adj* GAMIER, GAMIEST gamy

GAMIC *adj* requiring fertilization

GAMIER comparative of gamy

GAMIEST superlative of gamy

GAMILY *adv* in a game manner

GAMIN *n* pl. -S an urchin

GAMINE *n* pl. -S a tomboy

GAMINESS *n* pl. -ES the quality of being gamy

GAMING *n* pl. -S the practice of gambling

GAMMA *n* pl. -S a Greek letter

GAMMADIA *n/pl* Greek ornamental designs

GAMMED past tense of gam

GAMMER *n* pl. -S an old woman

GAMMING present participle of gam

GAMMON *v* -ED, -ING, -S to mislead by deceptive talk

GAMMONER *n* pl. -S one that gammons

GAMODEME *n* pl. -S a somewhat isolated breeding community of organisms

GAMP *n* pl. -S a large umbrella

GAMUT *n* pl. -S an entire range

GAMY *adj* GAMIER, GAMIEST plucky

GAN past tense of gin

GANDER *v* -ED, -ING, -S to wander

GANE past participle of gae

GANEF *n* pl. -S a thief

GANEV *n* pl. -S ganef

GANG *v* -ED, -ING, -S to form into a gang (a group)

GANGER *n* pl. -S a foreman of a gang of laborers

GANGLAND *n* pl. -S the criminal underworld

GANGLIA a pl. of ganglion

GANGLIAL *adj* gangliar

GANGLIAR *adj* pertaining to a ganglion

GANGLIER comparative of gangly

GANGLIEST superlative of gangly

GANGLING *adj* awkwardly tall and lanky

GANGLION *n* pl. -GLIA or -GLIONS a group of nerve cells

GANGLY *adj* -GLIER, -GLIEST gangling

GANGPLOW *n* pl. -S an agricultural implement

GANGREL *n* pl. -S a vagabond

GANGRENE *v* -GRENED, -GRENING, -GRENES to suffer the loss of tissue in part of the body

GANGSTER *n* pl. -S a member of a criminal gang

GANGUE *n* pl. -S the worthless rock in which valuable minerals are found

GANGWAY *n* pl. -WAYS a passageway

GANISTER   *n* pl. -S a type of rock

GANJA   *n* pl. -S cannabis used for smoking

GANNET   *n* pl. -S a large seabird

GANOF   *n* pl. -S ganef

GANOID   *n* pl. -S a type of fish

GANTLET   *v* -ED, -ING, -S to overlap railroad tracks

GANTLINE   *n* pl. -S a rope on a ship

GANTLOPE   *n* pl. -S a former military punishment

GANTRY   *n* pl. -TRIES a structure for supporting railroad signals

GANYMEDE   *n* pl. -S a youth who serves liquors

GAOL   *v* -ED, -ING, -S to jail

GAOLER   *n* pl. -S jailer

GAP   *v* GAPPED, GAPPING, GAPS to make an opening in

GAPE   *v* GAPED, GAPING, GAPES to stare with open mouth

GAPER   *n* pl. -S one that gapes

GAPESEED   *n* pl. -S something that causes wonder

GAPEWORM   *n* pl. -S a worm that causes a disease of young birds

GAPING   present participle of gape

GAPINGLY   *adv* in a gaping manner

GAPOSIS   *n* pl. -SISES a gap in a row of buttons or snaps

GAPPED   past tense of gap

GAPPING   present participle of gap

GAPPY   *adj* -PIER, -PIEST having openings

GAPY   *adj* infested with gapeworms

GAR   *v* GARRED, GARRING, GARS to cause or compel

GARAGE   *v* -RAGED, -RAGING, -RAGES to put in a garage (a car shelter)

GARB   *v* -ED, -ING, -S to clothe

GARBAGE   *n* pl. -S food waste

GARBANZO   *n* pl. -ZOS a chickpea

GARBLE   *v* -BLED, -BLING, -BLES to distort the meaning of

GARBLER   *n* pl. -S one that garbles

GARBLESS   *adj* being without clothing

GARBOARD   *n* pl. -S a plank on a ship's bottom

GARBOIL   *n* pl. -S turmoil

GARCON   *n* pl. -S a waiter

GARDANT   *adj* turned directly toward the observer — used of a heraldic animal

GARDEN   *v* -ED, -ING, -S to cultivate a plot of ground

GARDENER   *n* pl. -S one that gardens

GARDENIA   *n* pl. -S a tropical shrub or tree

GARDYLOO   *interj* — used as a warning cry

GARFISH   *n* pl. -ES a freshwater fish

GARGANEY   *n* pl. -NEYS a small duck

GARGET   *n* pl. -S mastitis of domestic animals **GARGETY** *adj*

GARGLE   *v* -GLED, -GLING, -GLES to rinse the mouth or throat

GARGLER   *n* pl. -S one that gargles

GARGOYLE   *n* pl. -S an ornamental figure

GARISH   *adj* gaudy **GARISHLY** *adv*

GARLAND   *v* -ED, -ING, -S to deck with wreaths of flowers

GARLIC   *n* pl. -S an herb used in cooking **GARLICKY** *adj*

GARMENT   *v* -ED, -ING, -S to clothe

GARNER   *v* -ED, -ING, -S to gather and store

GARNET   *n* pl. -S a mineral

GARNISH   *v* -ED, -ING, -ES to decorate

GAROTE   *v* -ROTED, -ROTING, -ROTES to garrote

GAROTTE   *v* -ROTTED, -ROTTING, -ROTTES to garrote

GAROTTER   *n* pl. -S one that garottes

GARPIKE   *n* pl. -S a garfish

GARRED   past tense of gar

GARRET   *n* pl. -S an attic

GARRING   present participle of gar

GARRISON   *v* -ED, -ING, -S to assign to a military post

GARRON   *n* pl. -S a small, sturdy horse

GARROTE   *v* -ROTED, -ROTING, -ROTES to execute by strangling

GARROTER   *n* pl. -S one that garrotes

GARROTTE   *v* -ROTTED, -ROTTING, -ROTTES to garrote

GARTER   *v* -ED, -ING, -S to fasten with an elastic band

GARTH   *n* pl. -S a yard or garden

GARVEY   *n* pl. -VEYS a small scow

GAS	v GASSED, GASSING, GASES or GASSES to supply with gas (a substance capable of indefinite expansion)	**GASTRAL**	adj pertaining to the stomach
		GASTREA	n pl. -S gastraea
		GASTRIC	adj pertaining to the stomach
GASALIER	n pl. -S gaselier	**GASTRIN**	n pl. -S a hormone
GASBAG	n pl. -S a bag for holding gas	**GASTRULA**	n pl. -LAS or -LAE a metazoan embryo
GASCON	n pl. -S a boaster		
GASELIER	n pl. -S a gaslight chandelier	**GASWORKS**	n pl. GASWORKS a factory where gas is produced
GASEOUS	adj pertaining to gas		
GASH	v -ED, -ING, -ES to make a long deep cut in	**GAT**	n pl. -S a pistol
		GATE	v GATED, GATING, GATES to supply with a gate (a movable barrier)
GASH	adj GASHER, GASHEST knowing		
GASHOUSE	n pl. -S a gasworks		
GASIFIED	past tense of gasify	**GATEFOLD**	n pl. -S a folded insert in a book or magazine
GASIFIER	n pl. -S one that gasifies		
GASIFORM	adj having the form of gas	**GATELESS**	adj lacking a gate
GASIFY	v -IFIED, -IFYING, -IFIES to convert into gas	**GATELIKE**	adj resembling a gate
		GATEMAN	n pl. -MEN a person in charge of a gate
GASKET	n pl. -S packing for making something fluid-tight		
		GATEPOST	n pl. -S a post from which a gate is hung
GASKIN	n pl. -S a part of a horse's leg		
GASKING	n pl. -S a gasket	**GATEWAY**	n pl. -WAYS a passage that may be closed by a gate
GASLESS	adj having no gas		
GASLIGHT	n pl. -S light made by burning gas	**GATHER**	v -ED, -ING, -S to bring together into one place or group
GASLIT	adj illuminated by gaslight	**GATHERER**	n pl. -S one that gathers
GASMAN	n pl. -MEN an employee of a gas company	**GATING**	present participle of gate
		GAUCHE	adj GAUCHER, GAUCHEST lacking social grace GAUCHELY adv
GASOGENE	n pl. -S gazogene		
GASOLENE	n pl. -S gasoline	**GAUCHO**	n pl. -CHOS a cowboy of the South American pampas
GASOLIER	n pl. -S gaselier		
GASOLINE	n pl. -S a liquid fuel	**GAUD**	n pl. -S a showy ornament
GASP	v -ED, -ING, -S to breathe convulsively	**GAUDERY**	n pl. -ERIES finery
		GAUDY	adj GAUDIER, GAUDIEST tastelessly showy GAUDILY adv
GASPER	n pl. -S a cigarette		
GASSED	past tense of gas	**GAUDY**	n pl. -DIES a festival
GASSER	n pl. -S one that gasses	**GAUFFER**	v -ED, -ING, -S to goffer
GASSES	a present 3d person sing. of gas	**GAUGE**	v GAUGED, GAUGING, GAUGES to measure precisely
GASSING	n pl. -S a poisoning by noxious gas		
		GAUGER	n pl. -S one that gauges
GASSY	adj -SIER, -SIEST containing gas	**GAULT**	n pl. -S a heavy, thick clay soil
		GAUM	v -ED, -ING, -S to smear
GAST	v -ED, -ING, -S to scare	**GAUN**	present participle of gae
GASTIGHT	adj not allowing gas to escape or enter	**GAUNT**	adj GAUNTER, GAUNTEST emaciated GAUNTLY adv
GASTNESS	n pl. -ES fright	**GAUNTLET**	v -ED, -ING, -S to gantlet
GASTRAEA	n pl. -S a type of metazoan	**GAUNTRY**	n pl. -TRIES gantry
		GAUR	n pl. -S a wild ox

GAUSS *n pl.* -ES a unit of magnetic induction

GAUZE *n pl.* -S a transparent fabric

GAUZY *adj* GAUZIER, GAUZIEST resembling gauze **GAUZILY** *adv*

GAVAGE *n pl.* -S introduction of material into the stomach by a tube

GAVE past tense of give

GAVEL *v* -ELED, -ELING, -ELS or -ELLED, -ELLING, -ELS to signal for attention or order by use of a gavel (a small mallet)

GAVELOCK *n pl.* -S a crowbar

GAVIAL *n pl.* -S a large reptile

GAVOT *n pl.* -S a French dance

GAVOTTE *v* -VOTTED, -VOTTING, -VOTTES to dance a gavot

GAWK *v* -ED, -ING, -S to stare stupidly

GAWKER *n pl.* -S one that gawks

GAWKIER comparative of gawky

GAWKIES pl. of gawky

GAWKISH *adj* gawky

GAWKY *adj* GAWKIER, GAWKIEST awkward **GAWKILY** *adv*

GAWKY *n pl.* GAWKIES an awkward person

GAWSIE *adj* well-fed and healthy looking

GAWSY *adj* gawsie

GAY *adj* GAYER, GAYEST merry

GAY *n pl.* GAYS a homosexual

GAYAL *n pl.* -S a domesticated ox

GAYETY *n pl.* -ETIES gaiety

GAYLY *adv* in a gay manner

GAYNESS *n pl.* -ES gaiety

GAYWINGS *n pl.* GAYWINGS a perennial herb

GAZABO *n pl.* -BOS or -BOES a fellow

GAZE *v* GAZED, GAZING, GAZES to look intently

GAZEBO *n pl.* -BOS or -BOES a roofed structure open on the sides

GAZELLE *n pl.* -S a small antelope

GAZER *n pl.* -S one that gazes

GAZETTE *v* -ZETTED, -ZETTING, -ZETTES to announce in an official journal

GAZING present participle of gaze

GAZOGENE *n pl.* -S an apparatus for carbonating liquids

GAZPACHO *n pl.* -CHOS a cold, spicy soup

GEAR *v* -ED, -ING, -S to provide with gears (toothed machine parts)

GEARBOX *n pl.* -ES an automotive transmission

GEARCASE *n pl.* -S a casing for gears

GEARING *n pl.* -S a system of gears

GEARLESS *adj* being without gears

GECK *v* -ED, -ING, -S to mock

GECKO *n pl.* GECKOS or GECKOES a small lizard

GED *n pl.* -S a food fish

GEE *v* GEED, GEEING, GEES to turn to the right

GEEGAW *n pl.* -S gewgaw

GEEK *n pl.* -S a carnival performer

GEEPOUND *n pl.* -S a unit of mass

GEESE pl. of goose

GEEST *n pl.* -S old alluvial matter

GEEZER *n pl.* -S an eccentric man

GEISHA *n pl.* -S a Japanese girl trained to entertain

GEL *v* GELLED, GELLING, GELS to become like jelly **GELABLE** *adj*

GELADA *n pl.* -S a baboon

GELANT *n pl.* -S gellant

GELATE *v* -ATED, -ATING, -ATES to gel

GELATIN *n pl.* -S a glutinous substance

GELATINE *n pl.* -S gelatin

GELATION *n pl.* -S the process of gelling

GELD *v* -ED, -ING, -S to castrate

GELDER *n pl.* -S one that gelds

GELDING *n pl.* -S a castrated animal

GELEE *n pl.* -S a cosmetic gel

GELID *adj* icy **GELIDLY** *adv*

GELIDITY *n pl.* -TIES iciness

GELLANT *n pl.* -S a substance used to produce gelling

GELLED past tense of gel

GELLING present participle of gel

GELSEMIA *n/pl* medicinal plant roots

GELT *n pl.* -S money

GEM *v* GEMMED, GEMMING, GEMS to adorn with gems (precious stones)

GEMINAL *adj* of or pertaining to two substituents on the same atom

GEMINATE *v* -NATED, -NATING, -NATES to arrange in pairs

GEMLIKE *adj* resembling a gem

GEMMA *n* pl. -MAE an asexual reproductive structure

GEMMATE *v* -MATED, -MATING, -MATES to produce gemmae

GEMMED past tense of gem

GEMMIER comparative of gemmy

GEMMIEST superlative of gemmy

GEMMILY *adv* in a manner suggesting a gem

GEMMING present participle of gem

GEMMULE *n* pl. -S a small gemma

GEMMY *adj* -MIER, -MIEST resembling a gem

GEMOLOGY *n* pl. -GIES the science of gems

GEMOT *n* pl. -S a public meeting in Anglo-Saxon England

GEMOTE *n* pl. -S gemot

GEMSBOK *n* pl. -S a large antelope

GEMSBUCK *n* pl. -S gemsbok

GEMSTONE *n* pl. -S a precious stone

GENDARME *n* pl. -S a policeman

GENDER *v* -ED, -ING, -S to engender

GENE *n* pl. -S a hereditary unit

GENERA a pl. of genus

GENERAL *n* pl. -S a military officer

GENERATE *v* -ATED, -ATING, -ATES to bring into existence

GENERIC *n* pl. -S a type of drug

GENEROUS *adj* willing to give

GENESIS *n* pl. GENESES an origin

GENET *n* pl. -S a carnivorous mammal

GENETIC *adj* pertaining to genetics

GENETICS *n/pl* the science of heredity

GENETTE *n* pl. -S genet

GENEVA *n* pl. -S a liquor

GENIAL *adj* having a pleasant or friendly manner **GENIALLY** *adv*

GENIC *adj* pertaining to genes

GENIE *n* pl. -S jinni

GENII a pl. of genius

GENIP *n* pl. -S a tropical tree

GENIPAP *n* pl. -S a tropical tree

GENITAL *adj* pertaining to reproduction

GENITALS *n/pl* the sexual organs

GENITIVE *n* pl. -S a grammatical case

GENITOR *n* pl. -S a male parent

GENITURE *n* pl. -S birth

GENIUS *n* pl. GENIUSES or GENII an exceptional natural aptitude

GENOA *n* pl. -S a triangular sail

GENOCIDE *n* pl. -S the deliberate extermination of a national or racial group

GENOM *n* pl. -S genome

GENOME *n* pl. -S a haploid set of chromosomes **GENOMIC** *adj*

GENOTYPE *n* pl. -S the genetic constitution of an organism

GENRE *n* pl. -S a type or kind

GENRO *n* pl. -ROS a group of elder statesmen in Japan

GENS *n* pl. GENTES a type of clan

GENSENG *n* pl. -S ginseng

GENT *n* pl. -S a gentleman

GENTEEL *adj* -TEELER, -TEELEST well-bred or refined

GENTES pl. of gens

GENTIAN *n* pl. -S a flowering plant

GENTIL *adj* kind

GENTILE *n* pl. -S a non-Jewish person

GENTLE *adj* -TLER, -TLEST mild **GENTLY** *adv*

GENTLE *v* -TLED, -TLING, -TLES to tame

GENTRICE *n* pl. -S good breeding

GENTRY *n* pl. -TRIES people of high social class

GENU *n* pl. GENUA the knee

GENUINE *adj* authentic

GENUS *n* pl. GENERA or GENUSES a kind, sort, or class

GEODE *n* pl. -S a type of rock

GEODESIC *n* pl. -S a geometric line

GEODESY *n* pl. -SIES geographical surveying

GEODETIC *adj* pertaining to geodesy

GEODIC *adj* of or pertaining to a geode

GEODUCK *n* pl. -S a large, edible clam

GEOGNOSY *n* pl. -SIES a branch of geology

GEOID *n* pl. -S a hypothetical surface of the earth **GEOIDAL** *adj*

GEOLOGER *n* pl. -S a specialist in geology

GEOLOGY *n* pl. -GIES the science that deals with the origin and structure of the earth **GEOLOGIC** *adj*

GEOMANCY *n* pl. -CIES a method of foretelling the future by geographical features

GEOMETER *n* pl. -S a specialist in geometry

GEOMETRY *n* pl. -TRIES a branch of mathematics

GEOPHAGY *n* pl. -GIES the practice of eating earthy substances

GEOPHONE *n* pl. -S a device that detects vibrations in the earth

GEOPHYTE *n* pl. -S a plant having underground buds

GEOPONIC *adj* pertaining to farming

GEORGIC *n* pl. -S a poem about farming

GEOTAXIS *n* pl. -TAXES the movement of an organism in response to gravity

GERAH *n* pl. -S a Hebrew unit of weight

GERANIAL *n* pl. -S citral

GERANIOL *n* pl. -S an alcohol used in perfumes

GERANIUM *n* pl. -S a flowering plant

GERARDIA *n* pl. -S an herb

GERBERA *n* pl. -S an herb

GERBIL *n* pl. -S a burrowing rodent

GERBILLE *n* pl. -S gerbil

GERENT *n* pl. -S a ruler or manager

GERENUK *n* pl. -S a long-necked antelope

GERM *n* pl. -S a microorganism that causes disease

GERMAN *n* pl. -S an elaborate dance

GERMANE *adj* relevant

GERMANIC *adj* containing germanium (a metallic element)

GERMEN *n* pl. -MENS or -MINA something that serves as an origin

GERMFREE *adj* free from germs

GERMIER comparative of germy

GERMIEST superlative of germy

GERMINA a pl. of germen

GERMINAL *adj* being in the earliest stage of development

GERMY *adj* GERMIER, GERMIEST full of germs

GERONTIC *adj* pertaining to old age

GERUND *n* pl. -S a verbal noun

GESSO *n* pl. -SOES a plaster mixture

GEST *n* pl. -S a feat

GESTALT *n* pl. -STALTS or -STALTEN a unified whole

GESTAPO *n* pl. -POS a secret-police organization

GESTATE *v* -TATED, -TATING, -TATES to carry in the uterus during pregnancy

GESTE *n* pl. -S gest

GESTIC *adj* pertaining to bodily motion

GESTICAL *adj* gestic

GESTURAL *adj* pertaining to or consisting of gestures (expressive bodily motions)

GESTURE *v* -TURED, -TURING, -TURES to express by bodily motion

GESTURER *n* pl. -S one that gestures

GET *v* GOT, GOTTEN, GETTING, GETS to obtain or acquire **GETABLE, GETTABLE** *adj*

GETAWAY *n* pl. -AWAYS an escape

GETTER *v* -ED, -ING, -S to purify with a chemically active substance

GETTING present participle of get

GETUP *n* pl. -S a costume

GEUM *n* pl. -S a perennial herb

GEWGAW *n* pl. -S a showy trinket

GEY *adv* very

GEYSER *n* pl. -S a spring that ejects jets of hot water and steam

GHARRI *n* pl. -S gharry

GHARRY *n* pl. -RIES a carriage used in India

GHAST *adj* ghastly

GHASTFUL *adj* frightful

GHASTLY *adj* -LIER, -LIEST terrifying

GHAT *n* pl. -S a passage leading down to a river

GHAUT *n* pl. -S ghat

GHAZI *n* pl. -S or -ES a Muslim war hero

GHEE *n* pl. -S a kind of liquid butter made in India

GHERAO *v* -ED, -ING, -ES to coerce by physical means

GHERKIN *n* pl. -S a small cucumber

GHETTO *v* -ED, -ING, -S or -ES to isolate in a slum

GHI *n* pl. -S ghee

GHIBLI   *n* pl. -S a hot desert wind

GHILLIE   *n* pl. -S a type of shoe

GHOST   *v* -ED, -ING, -S to haunt

GHOSTLY   *adj* -LIER, -LIEST spectral

GHOSTY   *adj* GHOSTIER, GHOSTIEST ghostly

GHOUL   *n* pl. -S a demon GHOULISH *adj*

GHYLL   *n* pl. -S a ravine

GIANT   *n* pl. -S a person or thing of great size

GIANTESS   *n* pl. -ES a female giant

GIANTISM   *n* pl. -S the condition of being a giant

GIAOUR   *n* pl. -S a non-Muslim

GIB   *v* GIBBED, GIBBING, GIBS to fasten with a wedge of wood or metal

GIBBER   *v* -ED, -ING, -S to jabber

GIBBET   *v* -BETED, -BETING, -BETS or -BETTED, -BETTING, -BETS to execute by hanging

GIBBING   present participle of gib

GIBBON   *n* pl. -S an arboreal ape

GIBBOSE   *adj* gibbous

GIBBOUS   *adj* irregularly rounded

GIBBSITE   *n* pl. -S a mineral

GIBE   *v* GIBED, GIBING, GIBES to jeer GIBINGLY *adv*

GIBER   *n* pl. -S one that gibes

GIBLET   *n* pl. -S an edible part of a fowl

GID   *n* pl. -S a disease of sheep

GIDDAP   *interj* — used as a command to a horse to go faster

GIDDY   *adj* -DIER, -DIEST dizzy GIDDILY *adv*

GIDDY   *v* -DIED, -DYING, -DIES to make giddy

GIE   *v* GIED, GIEN, GIEING, GIES to give

GIFT   *v* -ED, -ING, -S to present with a gift (something given without charge)

GIFTEDLY   *adv* in a talented manner

GIFTLESS   *adj* being without a gift

GIG   *v* GIGGED, GIGGING, GIGS to catch fish with a pronged spear

GIGA   *n* pl. GIGHE a gigue

GIGABIT   *n* pl. -S a unit of information

GIGANTIC   *adj* huge

GIGAS   *adj* pertaining to variations in plant development

GIGATON   *n* pl. -S a unit of weight

GIGAWATT   *n* pl. -S a unit of power

GIGGED   past tense of gig

GIGGING   present participle of gig

GIGGLE   *v* -GLED, -GLING, -GLES to laugh in a silly manner

GIGGLER   *n* pl. -S one that giggles

GIGGLY   *adj* -GLIER, -GLIEST tending to giggle

GIGHE   pl. of giga

GIGLET   *n* pl. -S a playful girl

GIGLOT   *n* pl. -S giglet

GIGOLO   *n* pl. -LOS a man supported financially by a woman

GIGOT   *n* pl. -S a leg of lamb

GIGUE   *n* pl. -S a lively dance

GILBERT   *n* pl. -S a unit of magnetomotive force

GILD   *v* GILDED or GILT, GILDING, GILDS to cover with a thin layer of gold

GILDER   *n* pl. -S one that gilds

GILDHALL   *n* pl. -S a town hall

GILDING   *n* pl. -S the application of gilt

GILL   *v* -ED, -ING, -S to catch fish with a type of net

GILLER   *n* pl. -S one that gills

GILLIE   *n* pl. -S ghillie

GILLNET   *v* -NETTED, -NETTING, -NETS to gill

GILLY   *v* -LIED, -LYING, -LIES to transport on a type of wagon

GILT   *n* pl. -S the gold with which something is gilded

GILTHEAD   *n* pl. -S a marine fish

GIMBAL   *v* -BALED, -BALING, -BALS or -BALLED, -BALLING, -BALS to support on a set of rings

GIMCRACK   *n* pl. -S a gewgaw

GIMEL   *n* pl. -S a Hebrew letter

GIMLET   *n* -ED, -ING, -S to pierce with a boring tool

GIMMAL   *n* pl. -S a pair of interlocked rings

GIMMICK   *v* -ED, -ING, -S to provide with a gimmick (a novel or tricky feature)

GIMMICKY *adj* having or being like a gimmick

GIMP *v* -ED, -ING, -S to limp

GIMPY *adj* GIMPIER, GIMPIEST limping

GIN *v* GINNED, GINNING, GINS to remove seeds from cotton

GIN *v* GAN, GUNNEN, GINNING, GINS to begin

GINGAL *n* pl. -S jingal

GINGALL *n* pl. -S jingal

GINGELEY *n* pl. -LEYS gingelly

GINGELI *n* pl. -S gingelly

GINGELLY *n* pl. -LIES the sesame seed or its oil

GINGELY *n* pl. -LIES gingelly

GINGER *v* -ED, -ING, -S to flavor with ginger (a pungent spice)

GINGERLY *adv* in a careful manner

GINGERY *adj* having the characteristics of ginger

GINGHAM *n* pl. -S a cotton fabric

GINGILI *n* pl. -LIS gingelly

GINGIVA *n* pl. -VAE the fleshy tissue that surrounds the teeth **GINGIVAL** *adj*

GINGKO *n* pl. -KOES ginkgo

GINK *n* pl. -S a fellow

GINKGO *n* pl. -GOES an ornamental tree

GINNED past tense of gin

GINNER *n* pl. -S one that gins cotton

GINNING *n* pl. -S cotton as it comes from a gin

GINNY *adj* GINNIER, GINNIEST affected with gin (a strong liquor)

GINSENG *n* pl. -S a perennial herb

GIP *v* GIPPED, GIPPING, GIPS to gyp

GIPON *n* pl. -S jupon

GIPPER *n* pl. -S one that gips

GIPPING present participle of gip

GIPSY *v* -SIED, -SYING, -SIES to gypsy

GIRAFFE *n* pl. -S a long-necked mammal

GIRASOL *n* pl. -S a variety of opal

GIRASOLE *n* pl. -S girasol

GIRD *v* GIRDED or GIRT, GIRDING, GIRDS to surround

GIRDER *n* pl. -S a horizontal support

GIRDLE *v* -DLED, -DLING, -DLES to encircle with a belt

GIRDLER *n* pl. -S one that girdles

GIRL *n* pl. -S a female child

GIRLHOOD *n* pl. -S the state of being a girl

GIRLIE *n* pl. -S a girl

GIRLISH *adj* of, pertaining to, or having the characteristics of a girl

GIRLY *adj* featuring scantily clothed women

GIRN *v* -ED, -ING, -S to snarl

GIRO *n* pl. -ROS an autogiro

GIRON *n* pl. -S gyron

GIROSOL *n* pl. -S girasol

GIRSH *n* pl. -ES qursh

GIRT *v* -ED, -ING, -S to gird

GIRTH *v* -ED, -ING, -S to encircle

GISARME *n* pl. -S a medieval weapon

GISMO *n* pl. -MOS a gadget

GIST *n* pl. -S the main point of a matter

GIT *interj* — used as an order of dismissal

GITANO *n* pl. -NOS a Spanish gypsy

GITTERN *n* pl. -S a medieval guitar

GIVE *v* GAVE, GIVEN, GIVING, GIVES to transfer freely to another's possession **GIVEABLE** *adj*

GIVEAWAY *n* pl. -AWAYS something given away free of charge

GIVEN *n* pl. -S something assigned as a basis for a calculation

GIVER *n* pl. -S one that gives

GIVING present participle of give

GIZMO *n* pl. -MOS gismo

GIZZARD *n* pl. -S a digestive organ

GJETOST *n* pl. -S a hard brown cheese

GLABELLA *n* pl. -BELLAE the smooth area between the eyebrows

GLABRATE *adj* glabrous

GLABROUS *adj* smooth

GLACE *v* -CEED, -CEING, -CES to cover with icing

GLACIAL *adj* of or pertaining to glaciers

GLACIATE *v* -ATED, -ATING, -ATES to cover with glaciers

GLACIER *n* pl. -S a huge mass of ice

GLACIS *n* pl. -CISES a slope

GLAD   adj GLADDER, GLADDEST feeling pleasure

GLAD   v GLADDED, GLADDING, GLADS to gladden

GLADDEN   v -ED, -ING, -S to make glad

GLADDER   comparative of glad

GLADDEST   superlative of glad

GLADDING   present participle of glad

GLADE   n pl. -S an open space in a forest

GLADIATE   adj shaped like a sword

GLADIER   comparative of glady

GLADIEST   superlative of glady

GLADIOLA   n pl. -S a flowering plant

GLADIOLI   n/pl segments of the sternum

GLADLY   adv -LIER, -LIEST in a glad manner

GLADNESS   n pl. -ES the state of being glad

GLADSOME   adj -SOMER, -SOMEST glad

GLADY   adj GLADIER, GLADIEST having glades

GLAIKET   adj glaikit

GLAIKIT   adj foolish

GLAIR   v -ED, -ING, -S to coat with egg white

GLAIRE   v GLAIRED, GLAIRING, GLAIRES to glair

GLAIRY   adj GLAIRIER, GLAIRIEST resembling egg white

GLAIVE   n pl. -S a sword GLAIVED adj

GLAMOR   n pl. -S alluring attractiveness

GLAMOUR   v -ED, -ING, -S to bewitch

GLANCE   v GLANCED, GLANCING, GLANCES to look quickly

GLAND   n pl. -S a secreting organ

GLANDERS   n/pl a disease of horses

GLANDULE   n pl. -S a small gland

GLANS   n pl. GLANDES the tip of the penis or clitoris

GLARE   v GLARED, GLARING, GLARES to shine with a harshly brilliant light

GLARY   adj GLARIER, GLARIEST glaring

GLASS   v -ED, -ING, -ES to encase in glass (a transparent substance)

GLASSFUL   n pl. -FULS as much as a drinking glass will hold

GLASSIE   n pl. -S a type of playing marble

GLASSIER   comparative of glassy

GLASSIEST   superlative of glassy

GLASSILY   adv in a glassy manner

GLASSINE   n pl. -S a type of paper

GLASSMAN   n pl. -MEN a glazier

GLASSY   adj GLASSIER, GLASSIEST resembling glass

GLAUCOMA   n pl. -S a disease of the eye

GLAUCOUS   adj bluish green

GLAZE   v GLAZED, GLAZING, GLAZES to fit windows with glass panes

GLAZER   n pl. -S a glazier

GLAZIER   n pl. -S one that glazes

GLAZIERY   n pl. -ZIERIES the work of a glazier

GLAZING   n pl. -S glaziery

GLAZY   adj GLAZIER, GLAZIEST covered with a smooth, glossy coating

GLEAM   v -ED, -ING, -S to shine with a soft radiance

GLEAMY   adj GLEAMIER, GLEAMIEST gleaming

GLEAN   v -ED, -ING, -S to gather little by little

GLEANER   n pl. -S one that gleans

GLEANING   n pl. -S something that is gleaned

GLEBA   n pl. -BAE a spore-bearing mass of some fungi

GLEBE   n pl. -S the soil or earth

GLED   n pl. -S glede

GLEDE   n pl. -S a bird of prey

GLEE   n pl. -S an unaccompanied song

GLEED   n pl. -S a glowing coal

GLEEFUL   adj merry

GLEEK   v -ED, -ING, -S to gibe

GLEEMAN   n pl. -MEN a minstrel

GLEESOME   adj gleeful

GLEET   v -ED, -ING, -S to discharge mucus from the urethra

GLEETY   adj GLEETIER, GLEETIEST resembling mucus

GLEG   adj alert GLEGLY adv

GLEGNESS   n pl. -ES alertness

GLEN   n pl. -S a small valley GLENLIKE adj

GLENOID   adj having the shallow or slightly cupped form of a bone socket

GLEY *n pl.* GLEYS a soil layer

GLIADIN *n pl.* -S a simple protein

GLIADINE *n pl.* -S gliadin

GLIAL *adj* pertaining to the supporting tissue of the central nervous system

GLIB *adj* GLIBBER, GLIBBEST fluent **GLIBLY** *adv*

GLIBNESS *n pl.* -ES the quality of being glib

GLIDE *v* GLIDED, GLIDING, GLIDES to move effortlessly

GLIDER *n pl.* -S a type of aircraft

GLIFF *n pl.* -S a brief moment

GLIM *n pl.* -S a light or lamp

GLIME *v* GLIMED, GLIMING, GLIMES to glance slyly

GLIMMER *v* -ED, -ING, -S to shine faintly or unsteadily

GLIMPSE *v* GLIMPSED, GLIMPSING, GLIMPSES to see for an instant

GLIMPSER *n pl.* -S one that glimpses

GLINT *v* -ED, -ING, -S to glitter

GLIOMA *n pl.* -MAS or -MATA a type of tumor

GLISSADE *v* -SADED, -SADING, -SADES to perform a gliding dance step

GLISTEN *v* -ED, -ING, -S to shine by reflection

GLISTER *v* -ED, -ING, -S to glisten

GLITCH *n pl.* -ES a malfunction

GLITTER *v* -ED, -ING, -S to sparkle

GLITTERY *adj* glittering

GLOAM *n pl.* -S twilight

GLOAMING *n pl.* -S twilight

GLOAT *v* -ED, -ING, -S to regard with great or excessive satisfaction

GLOATER *n pl.* -S one that gloats

GLOB *n pl.* -S a rounded mass

GLOBAL *adj* spherical **GLOBALLY** *adv*

GLOBATE *adj* spherical

GLOBATED *adj* spherical

GLOBE *v* GLOBED, GLOBING, GLOBES to form into a perfectly round body

GLOBIN *n pl.* -S a simple protein

GLOBOID *n pl.* -S a spheroid

GLOBOSE *adj* spherical

GLOBOUS *adj* spherical

GLOBULAR *adj* spherical

GLOBULE *n pl.* -S a small spherical mass

GLOBULIN *n pl.* -S a simple protein

GLOCHID *n pl.* -S a barbed hair on some plants

GLOGG *n pl.* -S an alcoholic beverage

GLOM *v* GLOMMED, GLOMMING, GLOMS to steal

GLOMUS *n pl.* -MERA a type of vascular tuft

GLOOM *v* -ED, -ING, -S to become dark

GLOOMFUL *adj* gloomy

GLOOMING *n pl.* -S gloaming

GLOOMY *adj* GLOOMIER, GLOOMIEST dismally dark **GLOOMILY** *adv*

GLOP *n pl.* -S a messy mass or mixture

GLORIA *n pl.* -S a halo

GLORIED past tense of glory

GLORIES present 3d person sing. of glory

GLORIFY *v* -FIED, -FYING, -FIES to bestow honor or praise on

GLORIOLE *n pl.* -S a halo

GLORIOUS *adj* magnificent

GLORY *v* -RIED, -RYING, -RIES to rejoice proudly

GLOSS *v* -ED, -ING, -ES to make lustrous

GLOSSA *n pl.* -SAE or -SAS the tongue **GLOSSAL** *adj*

GLOSSARY *n pl.* -RIES a list of terms and their definitions

GLOSSEME *n pl.* -S the smallest linguistic unit that signals a meaning

GLOSSER *n pl.* -S one that glosses

GLOSSIES pl. of glossy

GLOSSINA *n pl.* -S a tsetse fly

GLOSSY *adj* GLOSSIER, GLOSSIEST lustrous **GLOSSILY** *adv*

GLOSSY *n pl.* GLOSSIES a type of photograph

GLOST *n pl.* -S pottery that has been coated with a glassy surface

GLOTTIS *n pl.* -TISES or -TIDES the opening between the vocal cords **GLOTTAL, GLOTTIC** *adj*

GLOUT *v* -ED, -ING, -S to scowl

GLOVE	v GLOVED, GLOVING, GLOVES to furnish with gloves (hand coverings)		**GLYCERIN**	n pl. -S a glycerol **GLYCERIC** adj
GLOVER	n pl. -S a maker or seller of gloves		**GLYCEROL**	n pl. -S a syrupy alcohol
GLOW	v -ED, -ING, -S to emit light and heat		**GLYCERYL**	n pl. -S a radical derived from glycerol
GLOWER	v -ED, -ING, -S to scowl		**GLYCIN**	n pl. -S a compound used in photography
GLOWFLY	n pl. -FLIES a firefly		**GLYCINE**	n pl. -S an amino acid
GLOWWORM	n pl. -S a luminous insect		**GLYCOGEN**	n pl. -S a carbohydrate
GLOXINIA	n pl. -S a tropical plant		**GLYCOL**	n pl. -S an alcohol **GLYCOLIC** adj
GLOZE	v GLOZED, GLOZING, GLOZES to explain away		**GLYCONIC**	n pl. -S a type of verse line
GLUCAGON	n pl. -S a hormone		**GLYCOSYL**	n pl. -S a radical derived from glucose
GLUCINUM	n pl. -S a metallic element **GLUCINIC** adj		**GLYCYL**	n pl. -S a radical derived from glycine
GLUCOSE	n pl. -S a sugar **GLUCOSIC** adj		**GLYPH**	n pl. -S an ornamental groove **GLYPHIC** adj
GLUE	v GLUED, GLUING or GLUEING, GLUES to fasten with glue (an adhesive substance)		**GLYPTIC**	n pl. -S the art or process of engraving on gems
GLUELIKE	adj resembling glue		**GNAR**	v GNARRED, GNARRING, GNARS to snarl
GLUER	n pl. -S one that glues			
GLUEY	adj GLUIER, GLUIEST resembling glue **GLUILY** adv		**GNARL**	v -ED, -ING, -S to twist into a state of deformity
GLUING	present participle of glue		**GNARLY**	adj GNARLIER, GNARLIEST gnarled
GLUM	adj GLUMMER, GLUMMEST being in low spirits **GLUMLY** adv		**GNARR**	v -ED, -ING, -S to gnar
GLUME	n pl. -S a bract on grassy plants		**GNARRED**	past tense of gnar
			GNARRING	present participle of gnar
GLUMNESS	n pl. -ES the state of being glum		**GNASH**	v -ED, -ING, -ES to grind the teeth together
GLUMPY	adj GLUMPIER, GLUMPIEST glum **GLUMPILY** adv		**GNAT**	n pl. -S a small winged insect
			GNATHAL	adj gnathic
GLUNCH	v -ED, -ING, -ES to frown		**GNATHIC**	adj of or pertaining to the jaw
GLUT	v GLUTTED, GLUTTING, GLUTS to feed or fill to excess		**GNATHION**	n pl. -S the tip of the chin
GLUTEAL	adj of or pertaining to the buttock muscles		**GNATHITE**	n pl. -S a jawlike appendage of an insect
GLUTEI	pl. of gluteus		**GNATLIKE**	adj resembling a gnat
GLUTELIN	n pl. -S a plant protein		**GNATTY**	adj -TIER, -TIEST infested with gnats
GLUTEN	n pl. -S a tough elastic plant protein substance		**GNAW**	v GNAWED, GNAWN, GNAWING, GNAWS to wear away by persistent biting **GNAWABLE** adj
GLUTEUS	n pl. -TEI a buttock muscle			
GLUTTED	past tense of glut		**GNAWER**	n pl. -S one that gnaws
GLUTTING	present participle of glut		**GNAWING**	n pl. -S a persistent dull pain
GLUTTON	n pl. -S a person who eats to excess		**GNAWN**	a past participle of gnaw
			GNEISS	n pl. -ES a type of rock **GNEISSIC** adj
GLUTTONY	n pl. -TONIES excessive eating		**GNOCCHI**	n/pl dumplings made of pasta
GLYCAN	n pl. -S a carbohydrate		**GNOME**	n pl. -S a dwarf

GNOMIC   *adj* resembling or containing aphorisms

GNOMICAL   *adj* gnomic

GNOMISH   *adj* resembling a gnome

GNOMIST   *n* pl. -S a writer of aphorisms

GNOMON   *n* pl. -S a part of a sundial **GNOMONIC** *adj*

GNOSIS   *n* pl. GNOSES mystical knowledge

GNOSTIC   *adj* possessing knowledge

GNU   *n* pl. -S a large antelope

GO   *v* WENT, GONE, GOING, GOES to move along

GOA   *n* pl. -S an Asian gazelle

GOAD   *v* -ED, -ING, -S to drive animals with a goad (a pointed stick)

GOADLIKE   *adj* resembling a goad

GOAL   *v* -ED, -ING, -S to score a goal (a point-scoring play in some games)

GOALIE   *n* pl. -S a player who defends against goals

GOALLESS   *adj* having no goal

GOALPOST   *n* pl. -S a post that marks a boundary of the scoring area in some games

GOAT   *n* pl. -S a horned mammal

GOATEE   *n* pl. -S a small pointed beard **GOATEED** *adj*

GOATFISH   *n* pl. -ES a tropical fish

GOATHERD   *n* pl. -S one who tends goats

GOATISH   *adj* resembling a goat

GOATLIKE   *adj* goatish

GOATSKIN   *n* pl. -S the hide of a goat

GOB   *v* GOBBED, GOBBING, GOBS to fill a mine pit with waste material

GOBAN   *n* pl. -S gobang

GOBANG   *n* pl. -S a Japanese game

GOBBED   past tense of gob

GOBBET   *n* pl. -S a piece of raw meat

GOBBING   present participle of gob

GOBBLE   *v* -BLED, -BLING, -BLES to eat hastily

GOBBLER   *n* pl. -S a male turkey

GOBIES   pl. of goby

GOBIOID   *n* pl. -S a fish of the goby family

GOBLET   *n* pl. -S a drinking vessel

GOBLIN   *n* pl. -S an evil or mischievous creature

GOBO   *n* pl. -BOS or -BOES a device used to shield a microphone from extraneous sounds

GOBONEE   *adj* gobony

GOBONY   *adj* compony

GOBY   *n* pl. GOBIES a small fish

GOD   *v* GODDED, GODDING, GODS to treat as a god (a supernatural being)

GODCHILD   *n* pl. -CHILDREN one whom a person sponsors at baptism

GODDAM   *v* -DAMMED, -DAMMING, -DAMS goddamn

GODDAMN   *v* -ED, -ING, -S to damn

GODDED   past tense of god

GODDESS   *n* pl. -ES a female god

GODDING   present participle of god

GODHEAD   *n* pl. -S godhood

GODHOOD   *n* pl. -S the state of being a god

GODLESS   *adj* worshiping no god

GODLIER   comparative of godly

GODLIEST   superlative of godly

GODLIKE   *adj* divine

GODLING   *n* pl. -S a lesser god

GODLY   *adj* -LIER, -LIEST pious **GODLILY** *adv*

GODOWN   *n* pl. -S an oriental warehouse

GODROON   *n* pl. -S gadroon

GODSEND   *n* pl. -S an unexpected boon

GODSHIP   *n* pl. -S the rank of a god

GODSON   *n* pl. -S a male godchild

GODWIT   *n* pl. -S a wading bird

GOER   *n* pl. -S one that goes

GOETHITE   *n* pl. -S an ore of iron

GOFFER   *v* -ED, -ING, -S to press ridges or pleats into

GOGGLE   *v* -GLED, -GLING, -GLES to stare with wide eyes

GOGGLER   *n* pl. -S one that goggles

GOGGLY   *adj* -GLIER, -GLIEST wide-eyed

GOGLET   *n* pl. -S a long-necked jar

GOGO   *n* pl. -GOS a discotheque

GOING   *n* pl. -S an advance toward an objective

GOITER   *n* pl. -S an enlargement of the thyroid gland **GOITROUS** *adj*

GOITRE n pl. -S goiter

GOLCONDA n pl. -S a source of great wealth

GOLD n pl. -S a precious metallic element

GOLD adj GOLDER, GOLDEST golden

GOLDARN n pl. -S an expression of anger

GOLDBUG n pl. -S a gold beetle

GOLDEN adj -ENER, -ENEST of the color of gold GOLDENLY adv

GOLDEYE n pl. -S a freshwater fish

GOLDFISH n pl. -ES a freshwater fish

GOLDURN n pl. -S goldarn

GOLEM n pl. -S a legendary creature

GOLF v -ED, -ING, -S to play golf (a type of ball game)

GOLFER n pl. -S one that golfs

GOLFING n pl. -S the game of golf

GOLGOTHA n pl. -S a place of burial

GOLIARD n pl. -S a wandering student

GOLLIWOG n pl. -S a grotesque doll

GOLLY interj — used as a mild oath

GOLOSH n pl. -ES galosh

GOMBO n pl. -BOS gumbo

GOMBROON n pl. -S a kind of Persian pottery

GOMERAL n pl. -S a fool

GOMEREL n pl. -S gomeral

GOMERIL n pl. -S gomeral

GOMUTI n pl. -S a palm tree

GONAD n pl. -S a sex gland GONADAL, GONADIAL, GONADIC adj

GONDOLA n pl. -S a long, narrow boat

GONE adj departed

GONENESS n pl. -ES a state of exhaustion

GONER n pl. -S one who is in a hopeless situation

GONFALON n pl. -S a banner

GONFANON n pl. -S gonfalon

GONG v -ED, -ING, -S to make the sound of a gong (a disk-shaped percussion instrument)

GONGLIKE adj resembling a gong

GONIA pl. of gonion and of gonium

GONIDIUM n pl. -IA an asexual reproductive cell GONIDIAL, GONIDIC adj

GONIF n pl. -S ganef

GONION n pl. -NIA a part of the lower jaw

GONIUM n pl. -NIA an immature reproductive cell

GONOCYTE n pl. -S a cell that produces gametes

GONOF n pl. -S ganef

GONOPH n pl. -S ganef

GONOPORE n pl. -S a genital pore

GOO n pl. GOOS a sticky or viscid substance

GOOBER n pl. -S a peanut

GOOD adj BETTER, BEST having positive or desirable qualities

GOOD n pl. -S something that is good

GOODBY n pl. -BYS goodbye

GOODBYE n pl. -S a concluding remark or gesture at parting

GOODIES pl. of goody

GOODISH adj somewhat good

GOODLY adj -LIER, -LIEST of pleasing appearance

GOODMAN n pl. -MEN the master of a household

GOODNESS n pl. -ES the state of being good

GOODWIFE n pl. -WIVES the mistress of a household

GOODWILL n pl. -S an attitude of friendliness

GOODY n pl. GOODIES a desirable food

GOOEY adj GOOIER, GOOIEST sticky or viscid

GOOF v -ED, -ING, -S to blunder

GOOFBALL n pl. -S a sleeping pill

GOOFY adj GOOFIER, GOOFIEST silly GOOFILY adv

GOOGLY n pl. -GLIES a type of bowled ball in cricket

GOOGOL n pl. -S an enormous number

GOOIER comparative of gooey

GOOIEST superlative of gooey

GOOK n pl. -S goo GOOKY adj

GOON n pl. -S a hired thug

GOONEY n pl. -NEYS an albatross

GOONIE n pl. -S gooney

GOONY n pl. -NIES gooney

GOOP n pl. -S a boor

GOORAL n pl. -S goral

GOOSE   *n pl.* GEESE a swimming bird

GOOSE   *v* GOOSED, GOOSING, GOOSES to poke between the buttocks

GOOSEY   *adj* GOOSIER, GOOSIEST goosy

GOOSY   *adj* GOOSIER, GOOSIEST resembling a goose

GOPHER   *n pl.* -S a burrowing rodent

GOR   *interj* — used as a mild oath

GORAL   *n pl.* -S a goat antelope

GORBELLY   *n pl.* -LIES a potbelly

GORBLIMY   *interj* blimey

GORCOCK   *n pl.* -S the male red grouse

GORE   *v* GORED, GORING, GORES to pierce with a horn or tusk

GORGE   *v* GORGED, GORGING, GORGES to stuff with food **GORGEDLY** *adv*

GORGEOUS   *adj* beautiful

GORGER   *n pl.* -S one that gorges

GORGERIN   *n pl.* -S a part of a column

GORGET   *n pl.* -S a piece of armor for the throat **GORGETED** *adj*

GORGING   present participle of gorge

GORGON   *n pl.* -S an ugly woman

GORHEN   *n pl.* -S the female red grouse

GORIER   comparative of gory

GORIEST   superlative of gory

GORILLA   *n pl.* -S a large ape

GORILY   *adv* in a gory manner

GORINESS   *n pl.* -ES the state of being gory

GORING   present participle of gore

GORMAND   *n pl.* -S gourmand

GORSE   *n pl.* -S furze

GORSY   *adj* GORSIER, GORSIEST abounding in gorse

GORY   *adj* GORIER, GORIEST bloody

GOSH   *interj* — used as an exclamation of surprise

GOSHAWK   *n pl.* -S a large hawk

GOSLING   *n pl.* -S a young goose

GOSPEL   *n pl.* -S the message concerning Christ, the kingdom of God, and salvation

GOSPELER   *n pl.* -S one that teaches the gospel

GOSPORT   *n pl.* -S a communication device in an airplane

GOSSAMER   *n pl.* -S a fine film of cobwebs

GOSSAN   *n pl.* -S a type of decomposed rock

GOSSIP   *v* -SIPED, -SIPING, -SIPS or -SIPPED, -SIPPING, -SIPS to talk idly about the affairs of others

GOSSIPER   *n pl.* -S one that gossips

GOSSIPRY   *n pl.* -RIES the practice of gossiping

GOSSIPY   *adj* inclined to gossip

GOSSOON   *n pl.* -S a boy

GOSSYPOL   *n pl.* -S a toxic pigment

GOT   past tense of get

GOTHIC   *n pl.* -S a style of printing

GOTHITE   *n pl.* -S goethite

GOTTEN   past participle of get

GOUACHE   *n pl.* -S a method of painting

GOUGE   *v* GOUGED, GOUGING, GOUGES to cut or scoop out

GOUGER   *n pl.* -S one that gouges

GOULASH   *n pl.* -ES a beef stew

GOURAMI   *n pl.* -S a food fish

GOURD   *n pl.* -S a hard-shelled fruit

GOURDE   *n pl.* -S a monetary unit of Haiti

GOURMAND   *n pl.* -S one who loves to eat

GOURMET   *n pl.* -S a connoisseur of fine food and drink

GOUT   *n pl.* -S a metabolic disease

GOUTY   *adj* GOUTIER, GOUTIEST affected with gout **GOUTILY** *adv*

GOVERN   *v* -ED, -ING, -S to rule or direct

GOVERNOR   *n pl.* -S one that governs

GOWAN   *n pl.* -S a daisy **GOWANED, GOWANY** *adj*

GOWD   *n pl.* -S gold

GOWK   *n pl.* -S a fool

GOWN   *v* -ED, -ING, -S to dress in a gown (a long, loose outer garment)

GOWNSMAN   *n pl.* -MEN a professional or academic person

GOX   *n pl.* -ES gaseous oxygen

GOY   *n pl.* GOYIM or GOYS a non-Jewish person **GOYISH** *adj*

GRAAL   *n pl.* -S grail

GRAB   *v* GRABBED, GRABBING, GRABS to grasp suddenly

GRABBER   *n pl.* -S one that grabs

GRABBIER   comparative of grabby

GRABBIEST superlative of grabby

GRABBING present participle of grab

GRABBLE v -BLED, -BLING, -BLES to grope

GRABBLER n pl. -S one that grabbles

GRABBY adj -BIER, -BIEST tending to grab

GRABEN n pl. -S a depression of the earth's crust

GRACE v GRACED, GRACING, GRACES to give beauty to

GRACEFUL adj -FULLER, -FULLEST having beauty of form or movement

GRACILE adj gracefully slender

GRACILIS n pl. -LES a thigh muscle

GRACING present participle of grace

GRACIOSO n pl. -SOS a clown in Spanish comedy

GRACIOUS adj marked by kindness and courtesy

GRACKLE n pl. -S a blackbird

GRAD n pl. -S a graduate

GRADATE v -DATED, -DATING, -DATES to change by degrees

GRADE v GRADED, GRADING, GRADES to arrange in steps or degrees GRADABLE adj

GRADER n pl. -S one that grades

GRADIENT n pl. -S a rate of inclination

GRADIN n pl. -S a gradine

GRADINE n pl. -S one of a series of steps

GRADING present participle of grade

GRADUAL n pl. -S a hymn sung in alternate parts

GRADUAND n pl. -S one who is about to graduate

GRADUATE v -ATED, -ATING, -ATES to receive an academic degree or diploma

GRADUS n pl. -ES a dictionary of prosody

GRAECIZE v -CIZED, -CIZING, -CIZES to grecize

GRAFFITO n pl. -TI an inscription or drawing made on a rock or wall

GRAFT v -ED, -ING, -S to unite with a growing plant by insertion

GRAFTAGE n pl. -S the process of grafting

GRAFTER n pl. -S one that grafts

GRAHAM adj made of whole wheat flour

GRAIL n pl. -S the cup used by Christ at the Last Supper

GRAIN v -ED, -ING, -S to form into small particles

GRAINER n pl. -S one that grains

GRAINY adj GRAINIER, GRAINIEST granular

GRAM pl. -S a unit of mass and weight

GRAMA n pl. -S a pasture grass

GRAMARY n pl. -RIES gramarye

GRAMARYE n pl. -S occult learning; magic

GRAMERCY n pl. -CIES an expression of gratitude

GRAMMAR n pl. -S the study of the formal features of a language

GRAMME n pl. -S gram

GRAMP n pl. -S grandfather

GRAMPUS n pl. -ES a marine mammal

GRANA pl. of granum

GRANARY n pl. -RIES a storehouse for grain

GRAND adj GRANDER, GRANDEST large and impressive

GRAND n pl. -S a type of piano

GRANDAD n pl. -S granddad

GRANDAM n pl. -S a grandmother

GRANDAME n pl. -S grandam

GRANDDAD n pl. -S a grandfather

GRANDEE n pl. -S man of high social position

GRANDEUR n pl. -S the state of being grand

GRANDLY adv in a grand manner

GRANDMA n pl. -S a grandmother

GRANDPA n pl. -S a grandfather

GRANDSIR n pl. -S a grandfather

GRANDSON n pl. -S a son of one's son or daughter

GRANGE n pl. -S a farm

GRANGER n pl. -S a farmer

GRANITE n pl. -S a type of rock GRANITIC adj

GRANNIE n pl. -S granny

GRANNY n pl. -NIES a grandmother

GRANT v -ED, -ING, -S to bestow upon

GRANTEE n pl. -S one to whom something is granted

GRANTER n pl. -S one that grants

GRANTOR	*n pl.* -S granter	**GRAVE**	*adj* GRAVER, GRAVEST extremely serious
GRANULAR	*adj* composed of granules		
GRANULE	*n pl.* -S a small particle	**GRAVE**	*v* GRAVED, GRAVEN, GRAVING, GRAVES to engrave
GRANUM	*n pl.* GRANA a part of a plant chloroplast	**GRAVEL**	*v* -ELED, -ELING, -ELS or -ELLED, -ELLING, -ELS to pave with gravel (a mixture of rock fragments)
GRAPE	*n pl.* -S an edible berry		
GRAPERY	*n pl.* -ERIES a vinery		
GRAPH	*v* -ED, -ING, -S to represent by means of a diagram	**GRAVELLY**	*adj* containing gravel
		GRAVELY	*adv* in a grave manner
GRAPHEME	*n pl.* -S a unit of a writing system	**GRAVEN**	past participle of grave
		GRAVER	*n pl.* -S an engraver
GRAPHIC	*n pl.* -S a product of the art of representation	**GRAVEST**	superlative of grave
		GRAVID	*adj* pregnant GRAVIDLY *adv*
GRAPHITE	*n pl.* -S a variety of carbon	**GRAVIDA**	*n pl.* -DAS or -DAE a pregnant woman
GRAPIER	comparative of grapy		
GRAPIEST	superlative of grapy	**GRAVIES**	pl. of gravy
GRAPLIN	*n pl.* -S a grapnel	**GRAVING**	present participle of grave
GRAPLINE	*n pl.* -S a graplin	**GRAVITON**	*n pl.* -S a hypothetical particle
GRAPNEL	*n pl.* -S a type of anchor		
GRAPPA	*n pl.* -S an Italian brandy	**GRAVITY**	*n pl.* -TIES the force of attraction toward the earth's center
GRAPPLE	*v* -PLED, -PLING, -PLES to struggle or contend		
		GRAVURE	*n pl.* -S a printing process
GRAPPLER	*n pl.* -S one that grapples	**GRAVY**	*n pl.* -VIES a sauce of the fat and juices from cooked meat
GRAPY	*adj* GRAPIER, GRAPIEST resembling grapes		
		GRAY	*adj* GRAYER, GRAYEST of a color between white and black
GRASP	*v* -ED, -ING, -S to seize firmly with the hand		
		GRAY	*v* -ED, -ING, -S to make gray
GRASPER	*n pl.* -S one that grasps	**GRAYBACK**	*n pl.* -S a gray bird
GRASS	*v* -ED, -ING, -ES to cover with grass (herbaceous plants)	**GRAYFISH**	*n pl.* -ES a dogfish
		GRAYISH	*adj* somewhat gray
GRASSY	*adj* GRASSIER, GRASSIEST of, resembling, or pertaining to grass GRASSILY *adv*	**GRAYLAG**	*n pl.* -S a wild goose
		GRAYLING	*n pl.* -S a food fish
GRAT	past tense of greet (to weep)	**GRAYLY**	*adv* in a gray manner
GRATE	*v* GRATED, GRATING, GRATES to reduce to shreds by rubbing	**GRAYNESS**	*n pl.* -ES the state of being gray
		GRAYOUT	*n pl.* -S a temporary blurring of vision
GRATEFUL	*adj* -FULLER, -FULLEST deeply thankful		
		GRAZE	*v* GRAZED, GRAZING, GRAZES to feed on growing grass GRAZABLE *adj*
GRATER	*n pl.* -S one that grates		
GRATIFY	*v* -FIED, -FYING, -FIES to satisfy	**GRAZER**	*n pl.* -S one that grazes
GRATIN	*n pl.* -S a type of food crust	**GRAZIER**	*n pl.* -S one that grazes cattle
GRATING	*n pl.* -S a network of bars covering an opening	**GRAZING**	*n pl.* -S land used for the feeding of animals
GRATIS	*adj* free of charge		
GRATUITY	*n pl.* -ITIES a gift of money	**GRAZIOSO**	*adj* graceful in style
GRAUPEL	*n pl.* -S precipitation consisting of granular snow pellets	**GREASE**	*v* GREASED, GREASING, GREASES to smear with grease (a lubricating substance)
GRAVAMEN	*n pl.* -MENS or -MINA the most serious part of an accusation		
		GREASER	*n pl.* -S one that greases

GREASY _adj_ GREASIER, GREASIEST containing or resembling grease **GREASILY** _adv_

GREAT _adj_ GREATER, GREATEST large

GREAT _n pl._ -S a distinguished or outstanding person

GREATEN _v_ -ED, -ING, -S to make greater

GREATLY _adv_ in a great manner

GREAVE _n pl._ -S a piece of armor for the leg **GREAVED** _adj_

GREBE _n pl._ -S a diving bird

GRECIZE _v_ -CIZED, -CIZING, -CIZES to provide with a Greek style

GREE _v_ GREED, GREEING, GREES to agree

GREED _n pl._ -S excessive desire for gain or wealth

GREEDY _adj_ GREEDIER, GREEDIEST marked by greed **GREEDILY** _adv_

GREEGREE _n pl._ -S grigri

GREEK _n pl._ GREEK something unintelligible

GREEN _adj_ GREENER, GREENEST of the color of growing foliage

GREEN _v_ -ED, -ING, -S to become green

GREENBUG _n pl._ -S a green aphid

GREENERY _n pl._ -ERIES green vegetation

GREENFLY _n pl._ -FLIES a green aphid

GREENIER comparative of greeny

GREENIEST superlative of greeny

GREENING _n pl._ -S a variety of apple

GREENISH _adj_ somewhat green

GREENLET _n pl._ -S a vireo

GREENLY _adv_ in a green manner

GREENTH _n pl._ -S verdure

GREENY _adj_ GREENIER, GREENIEST somewhat green

GREET _v_ -ED, -ING, -S to address in a friendly and courteous way

GREET _v_ GRAT, GRUTTEN, GREETING, GREETS to weep

GREETER _n pl._ -S one that greets

GREETING _n pl._ -S a salutation

GREGO _n pl._ -GOS a hooded coat

GREIGE _n pl._ -S fabric in an unfinished state

GREISEN _n pl._ -S a type of rock

GREMIAL _n pl._ -S a lap cloth used by a bishop during a service

GREMLIN _n pl._ -S a mischievous creature

GREMMIE _n pl._ -S an inexperienced surfer

GREMMY _n pl._ -MIES gremmie

GRENADE _n pl._ -S an explosive device

GREW past tense of grow

GREWSOME _adj_ -SOMER, -SOMEST gruesome

GREY _adj_ GREYER, GREYEST gray

GREY _v_ -ED, -ING, -S to gray

GREYHEN _n pl._ -S the female black grouse

GREYISH _adj_ grayish

GREYLAG _n pl._ -S graylag

GREYLY _adv_ grayly

GREYNESS _n pl._ -ES grayness

GRIBBLE _n pl._ -S a marine isopod

GRID _n pl._ -S a grating

GRIDDLE _v_ -DLED, -DLING, -DLES to cook on a flat pan

GRIDE _v_ GRIDED, GRIDING, GRIDES to scrape harshly

GRIDIRON _n pl._ -S a grate for broiling food

GRIEF _n pl._ -S intense mental distress

GRIEVANT _n pl._ -S one that submits a complaint for arbitration

GRIEVE _v_ GRIEVED, GRIEVING, GRIEVES to feel grief

GRIEVER _n pl._ -S one that grieves

GRIEVOUS _adj_ causing grief

GRIFF _n pl._ -S griffe

GRIFFE _n pl._ -S the offspring of a black person and a mulatto

GRIFFIN _n pl._ -S a mythological creature

GRIFFON _n pl._ -S griffin

GRIFT _v_ -ED, -ING, -S to swindle

GRIFTER _n pl._ -S a swindler

GRIG _n pl._ -S a lively person

GRIGRI _n pl._ -S a fetish or amulet

GRILL _v_ -ED, -ING, -S to broil on a gridiron

GRILLADE _n pl._ -S a dish of grilled meat

GRILLAGE _n pl._ -S a framework of timber

GRILLE _n pl._ -S a grating

GRILLER _n pl._ -S one that grills

GRILSE _n pl._ -S a young salmon

GRIM _adj_ GRIMMER, GRIMMEST stern and unrelenting

GRIMACE	v -MACED, -MACING, -MACES to contort the facial features	**GRIPY**	adj GRIPIER, GRIPIEST causing sharp pains in the bowels
GRIMACER	n pl. -S one that grimaces	**GRISEOUS**	adj grayish
GRIME	v GRIMED, GRIMING, GRIMES to make dirty	**GRISETTE**	n pl. -S a young French working-class girl
GRIMIER	comparative of grimy	**GRISKIN**	n pl. -S the lean part of a loin of pork
GRIMIEST	superlative of grimy		
GRIMILY	adv in a grimy manner	**GRISLY**	adj -LIER, -LIEST horrifying
GRIMING	present participle of grime	**GRISON**	n pl. -S a carnivorous mammal
GRIMLY	adv in a grim manner	**GRIST**	n pl. -S grain for grinding
GRIMMER	comparative of grim	**GRISTLE**	n pl. -S the tough part of meat
GRIMMEST	superlative of grim	**GRISTLY**	adj -TLIER, -TLIEST containing gristle
GRIMNESS	n pl. -ES the quality of being grim	**GRIT**	v GRITTED, GRITTING, GRITS to press the teeth together
GRIMY	adj GRIMIER, GRIMIEST dirty	**GRITH**	n pl. -S sanctuary for a limited period of time
GRIN	v GRINNED, GRINNING, GRINS to smile broadly	**GRITTY**	adj -TIER, -TIEST plucky **GRITTILY** adv
GRIND	v GROUND or GRINDED, GRINDING, GRINDS to wear, smooth, or sharpen by friction	**GRIVET**	n pl. -S a small monkey
GRINDER	n pl. -S one that grinds	**GRIZZLE**	v -ZLED, -ZLING, -ZLES to complain
GRINDERY	n pl. -ERIES a place where tools are ground	**GRIZZLER**	n pl. -S one that grizzles
GRINGO	n pl. -GOS a foreigner in Latin America — a derogatory term	**GRIZZLY**	adj -ZLIER, -ZLIEST grayish
		GRIZZLY	n pl. -ZLIES a large bear
GRINNED	past tense of grin	**GROAN**	v -ED, -ING, -S to utter a low, mournful sound
GRINNER	n pl. -S one that grins		
GRINNING	present participle of grin	**GROANER**	n pl. -S one that groans
GRIP	v GRIPPED or GRIPT, GRIPPING, GRIPS to grasp	**GROAT**	n pl. -S an old English coin
GRIPE	v GRIPED, GRIPING, GRIPES to grasp	**GROCER**	n pl. -S a dealer in foodstuffs and household supplies
GRIPER	n pl. -S one that gripes	**GROCERY**	n pl. -CERIES a grocer's store
GRIPEY	adj GRIPIER, GRIPIEST gripy	**GROG**	n pl. -S a mixture of liquor and water
GRIPIER	comparative of gripy		
GRIPIEST	superlative of gripy	**GROGGERY**	n pl. -GERIES a barroom
GRIPING	present participle of gripe	**GROGGY**	adj -GIER, -GIEST dazed **GROGGILY** adv
GRIPPE	n pl. -S a virus disease		
GRIPPED	a past tense of grip	**GROGRAM**	n pl. -S a coarse silk fabric
GRIPPER	n pl. -S one that grips	**GROGSHOP**	n pl. -S a groggery
GRIPPIER	comparative of grippy	**GROIN**	v -ED, -ING, -S to build with intersecting arches
GRIPPIEST	superlative of grippy		
GRIPPING	present participle of grip	**GROMMET**	n pl. -S a reinforcing ring of metal
GRIPPLE	adj greedy		
GRIPPY	adj GRIPPIER, GRIPPIEST affected with the grippe	**GROMWELL**	n pl. -S an herb
		GROOM	v -ED, -ING, -S to clean and care for
GRIPSACK	n pl. -S a valise		
GRIPT	a past tense of grip	**GROOMER**	n pl. -S one that grooms
		GROOVE	v GROOVED, GROOVING, GROOVES to form a groove (a long, narrow depression)

GROOVER   n pl. -S one that grooves

GROOVY   adj GROOVIER, GROOVIEST marvelous

GROPE   v GROPED, GROPING, GROPES to feel about with the hands

GROPER   n pl. -S one that gropes

GROSBEAK   n pl. -S a finch

GROSCHEN   n pl. GROSCHEN an Austrian coin

GROSS   adj GROSSER, GROSSEST flagrant

GROSS   v -ED, -ING, -ES to earn exclusive of deductions

GROSSER   n pl. -S a product yielding a large volume of business

GROSSLY   adv in a gross manner

GROSZ   n pl. GROSZY a Polish coin

GROT   n pl. -S a grotto

GROTTO   n pl. -TOES or -TOS a cave

GROUCH   v -ED, -ING, -ES to complain

GROUCHY   adj GROUCHIER, GROUCHIEST ill-tempered

GROUND   v -ED, -ING, -S to place on a foundation

GROUNDER   n pl. -S a type of batted baseball

GROUP   v -ED, -ING, -S to arrange in a group (an assemblage of persons or things)

GROUPER   n pl. -S a food fish

GROUPIE   n pl. -S a female follower of rock groups

GROUPING   n pl. -S a set of objects

GROUPOID   n pl. -S a type of mathematical set

GROUSE   v GROUSED, GROUSING, GROUSES to complain

GROUSER   n pl. -S one that grouses

GROUT   v -ED, -ING, -S to fill with a thin mortar

GROUTER   n pl. -S one that grouts

GROUTY   adj GROUTIER, GROUTIEST surly

GROVE   n pl. -S a small forested area **GROVED** adj

GROVEL   v -ELED, -ELING, -ELS or -ELLED, -ELLING, -ELS to crawl in an abject manner

GROVELER   n pl. -S one that grovels

GROW   v GREW, GROWN, GROWING, GROWS to cultivate **GROWABLE** adj

GROWER   n pl. -S one that grows

GROWL   v -ED, -ING, -S to utter a deep, harsh sound

GROWLER   n pl. -S one that growls

GROWLY   adj GROWLIER, GROWLIEST deep and harsh in speech

GROWN   adj mature

GROWNUP   n pl. -S a mature person

GROWTH   n pl. -S development

GROYNE   n pl. -S a structure built to protect a shore from erosion

GRUB   v GRUBBED, GRUBBING, GRUBS to dig

GRUBBER   n pl. -S one that grubs

GRUBBY   adj -BIER, -BIEST dirty **GRUBBILY** adv

GRUBWORM   n pl. -S the larva of some insects

GRUDGE   v GRUDGED, GRUDGING, GRUDGES to be unwilling to give or admit

GRUDGER   n pl. -S one that grudges

GRUEL   v -ELED, -ELING, -ELS or -ELLED, -ELLING, -ELS to disable by hard work

GRUELER   n pl. -S one that gruels

GRUELING   n pl. -S an exhausting experience

GRUELLED   a past tense of gruel

GRUELLER   n pl. -S grueler

GRUELLING   n pl. -S grueling

GRUESOME   adj -SOMER, -SOMEST repugnant

GRUFF   adj GRUFFER, GRUFFEST low and harsh in speech

GRUFF   v -ED, -ING, -S to utter in a gruff voice

GRUFFIER   comparative of gruffy

GRUFFIEST   superlative of gruffy

GRUFFILY   adv in a gruffy manner

GRUFFISH   adj somewhat gruff

GRUFFLY   adv in a gruff manner

GRUFFY   adj GRUFFIER, GRUFFIEST gruff

GRUGRU   n pl. -S a palm tree

GRUM   adj GRUMMER, GRUMMEST morose

GRUMBLE   v -BLED, -BLING, -BLES to mutter in discontent **GRUMBLY** adj

GRUMBLER   n pl. -S one that grumbles

GRUME   n pl. -S a thick, viscid substance

GRUMMER   comparative of grum

GRUMMEST   superlative of grum

GRUMMET   n pl. -S a grommet

GRUMOSE   adj grumous

GRUMOUS   adj consisting of clustered grains

GRUMP   v -ED, -ING, -S to complain

GRUMPHIE   n pl. -S a pig

GRUMPHY   n pl. GRUMPHIES grumphie

GRUMPISH   adj grumpy

GRUMPY   adj GRUMPIER, GRUMPIEST ill-tempered **GRUMPILY** adv

GRUNION   n pl. -S a small food fish

GRUNT   v -ED, -ING, -S to utter a deep, guttural sound

GRUNTER   n pl. -S one that grunts

GRUNTLE   v -TLED, -TLING, -TLES to put in a good humor

GRUSHIE   adj thriving

GRUTCH   v -ED, -ING, -ES to grudge

GRUTTEN   past participle of greet (to weep)

GRYPHON   n pl. -S griffin

GUACHARO   n pl. -ROS or -ROES a tropical bird

GUACO   n pl. -COS a tropical plant

GUAIAC   n pl. -S guaiacum

GUAIACOL   n pl. -S a chemical compound

GUAIACUM   n pl. -S a medicinal resin

GUAIOCUM   n pl. -S guaiacum

GUAN   n pl. -S a large bird

GUANACO   n pl. -COS a South American mammal

GUANASE   n pl. -S an enzyme

GUANIDIN   n pl. -S a chemical compound

GUANIN   n pl. -S guanine

GUANINE   n pl. -S a chemical compound

GUANO   n pl. -NOS the accumulated excrement of sea birds

GUAR   n pl. -S a drought-tolerant legume

GUARANI   n pl. -NIS or -NIES a monetary unit of Paraguay

GUARANTY   v -TIED, -TYING, -TIES to assume responsibility for the quality of

GUARD   v -ED, -ING, -S to protect

GUARDANT   n pl. -S a guardian

GUARDER   n pl. -S one that guards

GUARDIAN   n pl. -S one that guards

GUAVA   n pl. -S a tropical shrub

GUAYULE   n pl. -S a shrub that is a source of rubber

GUCK   n pl. -S a messy substance

GUDE   n pl. -S good

GUDGEON   v -ED, -ING, -S to dupe

GUENON   n pl. -S a long-tailed monkey

GUERDON   v -ED, -ING, -S to reward

GUERILLA   n pl. -S a member of a small independent band of soldiers

GUERNSEY   n pl. -SEYS a woolen shirt

GUESS   v -ED, -ING, -ES to form an opinion from little or no evidence

GUESSER   n pl. -S one that guesses

GUEST   v -ED, -ING, -S to appear as a visitor

GUFF   n pl. -S foolish talk

GUFFAW   v -ED, -ING, -S to laugh loudly

GUGGLE   v -GLED, -GLING, GLES to gurgle

GUGLET   n pl. -S goglet

GUID   n pl. -S good

GUIDANCE   n pl. -S advice

GUIDE   v GUIDED, GUIDING, GUIDES to show the way to **GUIDABLE** adj

GUIDER   n pl. -S one that guides

GUIDON   n pl. -S a small flag

GUILD   n pl. -S an association of people of the same trade

GUILDER   n pl. -S a monetary unit of the Netherlands

GUILE   v GUILED, GUILING, GUILES to beguile

GUILEFUL   adj cunning

GUILT   n pl. -S the fact of having committed an offense

GUILTY   adj GUILTIER, GUILTIEST worthy of blame for an offense **GUILTILY** adv

GUIMPE   n pl. -S a short blouse

GUINEA   n pl. -S a former British coin

GUIPURE   *n* pl. -S a type of lace

GUIRO   *n* pl. GUIRO a percussion instrument

GUISARD   *n* pl. -S a masker

GUISE   *v* GUISED, GUISING, GUISES to disguise

GUITAR   *n* pl. -S a stringed musical instrument

GUL   *n* pl. -S a design in oriental carpets

GULAR   *adj* of or pertaining to the throat

GULCH   *n* pl. -ES a deep, narrow ravine

GULDEN   *n* pl. -S a guilder

GULES   *n* pl. GULES the color red

GULF   *v* -ED, -ING, -S to swallow up

GULFIER   comparative of gulfy

GULFIEST   superlative of gulfy

GULFLIKE   *adj* resembling a deep chasm

GULFWEED   *n* pl. -S a brownish seaweed

GULFY   *adj* GULFIER, GULFIEST full of whirlpools

GULL   *v* -ED, -ING, -S to deceive

GULLABLE   *adj* gullible GULLABLY *adv*

GULLET   *n* pl. -S the throat

GULLEY   *n* pl. -LEYS a ravine

GULLIBLE   *adj* easily deceived GULLIBLY *adv*

GULLY   *v* -LIED, -LYING, -LIES to form ravines by the action of water

GULOSITY   *n* pl. -TIES gluttony

GULP   *v* -ED, -ING, -S to swallow rapidly

GULPER   *n* pl. -S one that gulps

GULPY   *adj* GULPIER, GULPIEST marked by gulping

GUM   *v* GUMMED, GUMMING, GUMS to smear, seal, or clog with gum (a sticky, viscid substance)

GUMBO   *n* pl. -BOS the okra plant

GUMBOIL   *n* pl. -S an abscess in the gum

GUMBOTIL   *n* pl. -S a sticky clay

GUMDROP   *n* pl. -S a chewy candy

GUMLESS   *adj* having no gum

GUMLIKE   *adj* resembling gum

GUMMA   *n* pl. -MAS or -MATA a soft tumor

GUMMED   past tense of gum

GUMMER   *n* pl. -S one that gums

GUMMIER   comparative of gummy

GUMMIEST   superlative of gummy

GUMMING   present participle of gum

GUMMITE   *n* pl. -S a mixture of various minerals

GUMMOSE   *adj* gummy

GUMMOSIS   *n* pl. -MOSES a disease of plants

GUMMOUS   *adj* gummy

GUMMY   *adj* -MIER, -MIEST resembling gum

GUMPTION   *n* pl. -S shrewdness

GUMSHOE   *v* -SHOED, -SHOEING, -SHOES to investigate stealthily

GUMTREE   *n* pl. -S a tree that yields gum

GUMWEED   *n* pl. -S a plant covered with a gummy substance

GUMWOOD   *n* pl. -S the wood of a gumtree

GUN   *v* GUNNED, GUNNING, GUNS to shoot with a gun (a portable firearm)

GUNBOAT   *n* pl. -S an armed vessel

GUNDOG   *n* pl. -S a hunting dog

GUNFIGHT   *v* -FOUGHT, -FIGHTING, -FIGHTS to fight with guns

GUNFIRE   *n* pl. -S the firing of guns

GUNFLINT   *n* pl. -S the flint in a flintlock

GUNFOUGHT   past tense of gunfight

GUNK   *n* pl. -S filthy, sticky, or greasy matter

GUNLESS   *adj* having no gun

GUNLOCK   *n* pl. -S the mechanism which ignites the charge of a gun

GUNMAN   *n* pl. -MEN one who is armed with a gun

GUNMETAL   *n* pl. -S a dark gray color

GUNNED   past tense of gun

GUNNEL   *n* pl. -S a marine fish

GUNNEN   past participle of gin

GUNNER   *n* pl. -S one that operates a gun

GUNNERY   *n* pl. -NERIES the use of guns

GUNNING   *n* pl. -S the sport of hunting with a gun

GUNNY   *n* pl. -NIES a coarse fabric

GUNPAPER   *n* pl. -S a type of explosive paper

GUNPLAY   *n* pl. -PLAYS the shooting of guns

GUNPOINT *n* pl. -S the point or aim of a gun

GUNROOM *n* pl. -S a room on a British warship

GUNSEL *n* pl. -S a gunman

GUNSHIP *n* pl. -S an armed helicopter

GUNSHOT *n* pl. -S a projectile fired from a gun

GUNSMITH *n* pl. -S one who makes or repairs firearms

GUNSTOCK *n* pl. -S the rear wooden part of a rifle

GUNWALE *n* pl. -S the upper edge of a ship's side

GUPPY *n* pl. -PIES a small, tropical fish

GURGE *v* GURGED, GURGING, GURGES to swirl

GURGLE *v* -GLED, -GLING, -GLES to flow unevenly

GURGLET *n* pl. -S goglet

GURNARD *n* pl. -S a marine fish

GURNET *n* pl. -S a gurnard

GURNEY *n* pl. -NEYS a wheeled cot

GURRY *n* pl. -RIES fish offal

GURSH *n* pl. -ES qursh

GURU *n* pl. -S a Hindu spiritual teacher

GURUSHIP *n* pl. -S the office of a guru

GUSH *v* -ED, -ING, -ES to flow forth forcefully

GUSHER *n* pl. -S a gushing oil well

GUSHY *adj* GUSHIER, GUSHIEST overly sentimental **GUSHILY** *adv*

GUSSET *v* -ED, -ING, -S to furnish with a reinforcing piece of material

GUST *v* -ED, -ING, -S to blow in gusts (sudden blasts of wind)

GUSTABLE *n* pl. -S a savory food

GUSTIER comparative of gusty

GUSTIEST superlative of gusty

GUSTILY *adv* in a gusty manner

GUSTLESS *adj* having no gusts

GUSTO *n* pl. -TOES vigorous enjoyment

GUSTY *adj* GUSTIER, GUSTIEST blowing in gusts

GUT *v* GUTTED, GUTTING, GUTS to remove the guts (intestines) of

GUTLESS *adj* lacking courage

GUTLIKE *adj* resembling guts

GUTSY *adj* GUTSIER, GUTSIEST brave

GUTTA *n* pl. -TAE a drop of liquid

GUTTATE *adj* resembling a drop

GUTTATED *adj* guttate

GUTTED past tense of gut

GUTTER *v* -ED, -ING, -S to form channels for draining off water

GUTTERY *adj* marked by extreme vulgarity or indecency

GUTTIER comparative of gutty

GUTTIEST superlative of gutty

GUTTING present participle of gut

GUTTLE *v* -TLED, -TLING, -TLES to eat rapidly

GUTTLER *n* pl. -S one that guttles

GUTTURAL *n* pl. -S a throaty sound

GUTTY *adj* -TIER, -TIEST marked by courage

GUY *v* -ED, -ING, -S to ridicule

GUYOT *n* pl. -S a flat-topped seamount

GUZZLE *v* -ZLED, -ZLING, -ZLES to drink rapidly

GUZZLER *n* pl. -S one that guzzles

GWEDUC *n* pl. -S geoduck

GWEDUCK *n* pl. -S geoduck

GYBE *v* GYBED, GYBING, GYBES to shift from side to side while sailing

GYM *n* pl. -S a room for athletic activities

GYMKHANA *n* pl. -S an athletic meet

GYMNASIA *n/pl* gyms

GYMNAST *n* pl. -S one who is skilled in physical exercises

GYNAECEA *n/pl* gynecia

GYNAECIA *n/pl* gynecia

GYNANDRY *n* pl. -DRIES the condition of having both male and female sexual organs

GYNARCHY *n* pl. -CHIES government by women

GYNECIA pl. of gynecium

GYNECIC *adj* pertaining to women

GYNECIUM *n* pl. -CIA the pistil of a flower

GYNECOID *adj* resembling a woman

GYNIATRY *n* pl. -TRIES the treatment of women's diseases

GYNOECIA *n/pl* gynecia

GYP   v GYPPED, GYPPING, GYPS to swindle

GYPPER   n pl. -S one that gyps

GYPSEIAN   adj of or pertaining to gypsies

GYPSEOUS   adj containing gypsum

GYPSUM   n pl. -S a mineral

GYPSY   v -SIED, -SYING, -SIES to live like a gypsy (a wanderer)

GYPSYDOM   n pl. -S the realm of gypsies

GYPSYISH   adj resembling a gypsy

GYPSYISM   n pl. -S the mode of life of gypsies

GYRAL   adj gyratory GYRALLY adv

GYRATE   v -RATED, -RATING, -RATES to revolve or rotate

GYRATION   n pl. -S the act of gyrating

GYRATOR   n pl. -S one that gyrates

GYRATORY   adj moving in a circle or spiral

GYRE   v GYRED, GYRING, GYRES to move in a circle or spiral

GYRENE   n pl. -S a marine

GYRI   pl. of gyrus

GYRING   present participle of gyre

GYRO   n pl. -ROS a gyroscope

GYROIDAL   adj spiral in arrangement

GYRON   n pl. -S a heraldic design

GYROSE   adj marked with wavy lines

GYROSTAT   n pl. -S a type of stabilizing device

GYRUS   n pl. -RI a ridge in the brain

GYVE   v GYVED, GYVING, GYVES to shackle

HA	*n* pl. -S a sound of surprise	**HACKLY**	*adj* -LIER, -LIEST jagged
HAAF	*n* pl. -S a deep-sea fishing ground	**HACKMAN**	*n* pl. -MEN a hackie
HAAR	*n* pl. -S a fog	**HACKNEY**	*v* -NEYED, -NEYING, -NEYS to make common
HABANERA	*n* pl. -S a Cuban dance	**HACKSAW**	*n* pl. -S a type of saw
HABDALAH	*n* pl. -S a Jewish ceremony	**HACKWORK**	*n* pl. -S artistic work done according to formula
HABILE	*adj* skillful	**HAD**	a past tense of have
HABIT	*v* -ED, -ING, -S to clothe or dress	**HADAL**	*adj* pertaining to deep parts of the ocean
HABITAN	*n* pl. -S a French settler	**HADARIM**	a pl. of heder
HABITANT	*n* pl. -S an inhabitant	**HADDEST**	a past 2d person sing. of have
HABITAT	*n* pl. -S the natural environment of an organism	**HADDOCK**	*n* pl. -S a food fish
HABITUAL	*adj* occurring frequently or constantly	**HADE**	*v* HADED, HADING, HADES to incline
HABITUDE	*n* pl. -S a usual course of action	**HADJ**	*n* pl. -ES a pilgrimage to Mecca
HABITUE	*n* pl. -S a frequent customer	**HADJEE**	*n* pl. -S hadji
HABITUS	*n* pl. HABITUS bodily build and constitution	**HADJI**	*n* pl. -S one who has made a hadj
HABU	*n* pl. -S a poisonous snake	**HADRON**	*n* pl. -S an elementary particle
HACEK	*n* pl. -S a mark placed over a letter to modify it	**HADRONIC** *adj*	
		HADST	a past 2d person sing. of have
HACHURE	*v* -CHURED, -CHURING, -CHURES to make a hatching on a map	**HAE**	*v* HAED, HAEN, HAEING, HAES to have
HACIENDA	*n* pl. -S an estate	**HAEM**	*n* pl. -S heme
HACK	*v* -ED, -ING, -S to cut or chop roughly	**HAEMAL**	*adj* hemal
		HAEMATAL	*adj* hemal
HACKBUT	*n* pl. -S a type of gun	**HAEMATIC**	*n* pl. -S hematic
HACKEE	*n* pl. -S a chipmunk	**HAEMATIN**	*n* pl. -S hematin
HACKER	*n* pl. -S one that hacks	**HAEMIC**	*adj* hemic
HACKIE	*n* pl. -S a taxicab driver	**HAEMIN**	*n* pl. -S hemin
HACKLE	*v* -LED, -LING, -LES to hack	**HAEMOID**	*adj* hemoid
HACKLER	*n* pl. -S one that hackles	**HAEN**	past participle of hae

HAERES	n pl. -REDES heres	**HAIRCUT**	n pl. -S a cutting of the hair
HAET	n pl. -S a small amount	**HAIRDO**	n pl. -DOS a style of wearing the hair
HAFFET	n pl. -S the cheekbone and temple	**HAIRED**	adj having hair
HAFFIT	n pl. -S haffet	**HAIRIER**	comparative of hairy
HAFIZ	n pl. HAFIS a Muslim who knows the Koran by heart	**HAIRIEST**	superlative of hairy
		HAIRLESS	adj having no hair
HAFNIUM	n pl. -S a metallic element	**HAIRLIKE**	adj resembling a hair
HAFT	v -ED, -ING, -S to supply with a handle	**HAIRLINE**	n pl. -S a very thin line
HAFTARAH	n pl. -RAHS, -ROTH or -ROT a biblical selection	**HAIRLOCK**	n pl. -S a lock of hair
		HAIRPIN	n pl. -S a hair fastener
HAFTER	n pl. -S one that hafts	**HAIRWORK**	n pl. -S the making of articles from hair
HAFTORAH	n pl. -RAHS, -ROTH or -ROT haftarah		
		HAIRWORM	n pl. -S a parasitic worm
HAG	v HAGGED, HAGGING, HAGS to hack	**HAIRY**	adj HAIRIER, HAIRIEST covered with hair
HAGADIC	adj haggadic		
HAGADIST	n pl. -S a haggadic scholar	**HAJ**	n pl. -ES hadj
HAGBERRY	n pl. -RIES a small cherry	**HAJI**	n pl. -S hadji
HAGBORN	adj born of a witch	**HAJJ**	n pl. -ES hadj
HAGBUSH	n pl. -ES a large tree	**HAJJI**	n pl. -S hadji
HAGBUT	n pl. -S hackbut	**HAKE**	n pl. -S a marine fish
HAGDON	n pl. -S a seabird	**HAKEEM**	n pl. -S hakim
HAGFISH	n pl. -ES an eellike fish	**HAKIM**	n pl. -S a Muslim physician
HAGGADIC	adj pertaining to the story of Exodus	**HALAKAH**	n pl. -KOTH or -KAHS the legal part of the Talmud
HAGGARD	n pl. -S an adult hawk	**HALAKIC**	adj pertaining to the halakah
HAGGED	past tense of hag	**HALAKIST**	n pl. -S a halakic writer
HAGGING	present participle of hag	**HALAKOTH**	a pl. of halakah
HAGGIS	n pl. -GISES a Scottish dish	**HALALA**	n pl. -S a Saudi Arabian coin
HAGGISH	adj resembling a hag	**HALALAH**	n pl. -S halala
HAGGLE	v -GLED, -GLING, -GLES to bargain	**HALATION**	n pl. -S a blurring of light in photographs
HAGGLER	n pl. -S one that haggles	**HALAVAH**	n pl. -S halvah
HAGRIDE	v -RODE, -RIDDEN, -RIDING, -RIDES to harass	**HALBERD**	n pl. -S an axlike weapon
		HALBERT	n pl. -S halberd
HAH	n pl. -S ha	**HALCYON**	n pl. -S a mythical bird
HAIK	n pl. HAIKS or HAIKA an outer garment worn by Arabs	**HALE**	adj HALER, HALEST healthy
		HALE	v HALED, HALING, HALES to compel to go
HAIKU	n pl. HAIKU a Japanese poem		
HAIL	v -ED, -ING, -S to welcome	**HALENESS**	n pl. -ES the state of being hale
HAILER	n pl. -S one that hails	**HALER**	n pl. -LERS or -LERU a Czechoslovakian coin
HAIR	n pl. -S a threadlike growth		
HAIRBALL	n pl. -S a ball of hair	**HALEST**	superlative of hale
HAIRBAND	n pl. -S a headband	**HALING**	present participle of hale
HAIRCAP	n pl. -S a hat	**HALF**	n pl. HALVES one of two equal parts

HALFBACK *n* pl. -S a member of the backfield in football

HALFBEAK *n* pl. -S a marine fish

HALFLIFE *n* pl. -LIVES a measure of radioactive decay

HALFNESS *n* pl. -ES the state of being half

HALFTIME *n* pl. -S an intermission in a football game

HALFTONE *n* pl. -S a shade between light and dark

HALFWAY *adj* being at a point in the middle

HALIBUT *n* pl. -S a flatfish

HALID *n* pl. -S halide

HALIDE *n* pl. -S a chemical compound

HALIDOM *n* pl. -S something holy

HALIDOME *n* pl. -S halidom

HALITE *n* pl. -S a mineral

HALITUS *n* pl. -ES an exhalation

HALL *n* pl. -S a large room for assembly

HALLAH *n* pl. -LAHS, -LOTH or -LOT challah

HALLEL *n* pl. -S a chant of praise

HALLIARD *n* pl. -S halyard

HALLMARK *v* -ED, -ING, -S to mark with an official stamp

HALLO *v* -ED, -ING, -S or -ES to shout

HALLOA *v* -ED, -ING, -S to hallo

HALLOO *v* -ED, -ING, -S to hallo

HALLOT a pl. of hallah

HALLOTH a pl. of hallah

HALLOW *v* -ED, -ING, -S to make holy

HALLOWER *n* pl. -S one that hallows

HALLUX *n* pl. -LUCES the big toe

HALLWAY *n* pl. -WAYS a hall

HALM *n* pl. -S haulm

HALO *v* -ED, -ING, -ES or -S to form a halo (a ring of light)

HALOGEN *n* pl. -S a nonmetallic element

HALOID *n* pl. -S a chemical salt

HALOLIKE *adj* resembling a halo

HALT *v* -ED, -ING, -S to stop

HALTER *v* -ED, -ING, -S to put restraint upon

HALTERE *n* pl. -S a pair of wings of an insect

HALTLESS *adj* not hesitant

HALUTZ *n* pl. -LUTZIM an Israeli farmer

HALVA *n* pl. -S halvah

HALVAH *n* pl. -S a Turkish confection

HALVE *v* HALVED, HALVING, HALVES to divide into two equal parts

HALVERS *n* pl. HALVERS half shares

HALVES pl. of half

HALYARD *n* pl. -S a line used to hoist a sail

HAM *v* HAMMED, HAMMING, HAMS to overact

HAMAL *n* pl. -S a porter in eastern countries

HAMARTIA *n* pl. -S a defect of character

HAMATE *n* pl. -S a wrist bone

HAMAUL *n* pl. -S a hamal

HAMBURG *n* pl. -S a patty of ground beef

HAME *n* pl. -S a part of a horse collar

HAMLET *n* pl. -S a small town

HAMMAL *n* pl. -S a hamal

HAMMED past tense of ham

HAMMER *v* -ED, -ING, -S to strike repeatedly

HAMMERER *n* pl. -S one that hammers

HAMMIER comparative of hammy

HAMMIEST superlative of hammy

HAMMILY *adv* in a hammy manner

HAMMING present participle of ham

HAMMOCK *n* pl. -S a hanging cot

HAMMY *adj* -MIER, -MIEST overly theatrical

HAMPER *v* -ED, -ING, -S to hinder

HAMPERER *n* pl. -S one that hampers

HAMSTER *n* pl. -S a burrowing rodent

HAMULUS *n* pl. -LI a small hook HAMULAR, HAMULATE, HAMULOSE, HAMULOUS *adj*

HAMZA *n* pl. -S an Arabic diacritical mark

HAMZAH *n* pl. -S hamza

HANAPER *n* pl. -S a wicker receptacle

HANCE *n* pl. -S a side of an arch

HAND *v* -ED, -ING, -S to present with the hand (the end of the forearm)

HANDBAG *n* pl. -S a small carrying bag

HANDBALL *n* pl. -S a small rubber ball

HANDBILL *n* pl. -S a circular

HANDBOOK *n* pl. -S a manual

HANDCAR *n* pl. -S a hand-operated railroad car

HANDCART *n* pl. -S a cart pushed by hand

HANDCUFF *v* -ED, -ING, -S to fetter with restraining cuffs

HANDFAST *v* -ED, -ING, -S to grip securely

HANDFUL *n* pl. HANDFULS or HANDSFUL as much as the hand can hold

HANDGRIP *n* pl. -S a grip by the hand or hands

HANDGUN *n* pl. -S a small firearm

HANDHOLD *n* pl. -S a handgrip

HANDICAP *v* -CAPPED, -CAPPING, -CAPS to hinder

HANDIER comparative of handy

HANDIEST superlative of handy

HANDILY *adv* in a handy manner

HANDLE *v* -DLED, -DLING, -DLES to touch with the hands

HANDLER *n* pl. -S one that handles

HANDLESS *adj* having no hands

HANDLIKE *adj* resembling a hand

HANDLING *n* pl. -S the manner in which something is handled

HANDLIST *n* pl. -S a reference list

HANDLOOM *n* pl. -S a manually operated loom

HANDMADE *adj* made by hand

HANDMAID *n* pl. -S a female servant

HANDOFF *n* pl. -S a play in football

HANDOUT *n* pl. -S something given out free

HANDPICK *v* -ED, -ING, -S to choose carefully

HANDRAIL *n* pl. -S a railing used for support

HANDSAW *n* pl. -S a saw used manually

HANDSEL *v* -SELED, -SELING, -SELS or -SELLED, -SELLING, -SELS to give a gift to

HANDSET *n* pl. -S a type of telephone

HANDSEWN *adj* sewn by hand

HANDSFUL a pl. of handful

HANDSOME *adj* -SOMER, -SOMEST attractive

HANDWORK *n* pl. -S manual labor

HANDWRIT *adj* written by hand

HANDY *adj* HANDIER, HANDIEST convenient for handling

HANDYMAN *n* pl. -MEN a man who does odd jobs

HANG *v* HUNG or HANGED, HANGING, HANGS to attach from above only HANGABLE *adj*

HANGAR *v* -ED, -ING, -S to place in an aircraft shelter

HANGBIRD *n* pl. -S a type of bird

HANGDOG *n* pl. -S a sneaky person

HANGER *n* pl. -S one that hangs

HANGFIRE *n* pl. -S a delay in detonation

HANGING *n* pl. -S an execution by strangling with a suspended noose

HANGMAN *n* pl. -MEN an executioner

HANGNAIL *n* pl. -S an agnail

HANGNEST *n* pl. -S a hangbird

HANGOUT *n* pl. -S a place often visited

HANGOVER *n* pl. -S the physical effects following a drinking binge

HANGTAG *n* pl. -S a type of tag used commercially

HANGUP *n* pl. -S an inhibition or obsession

HANK *v* -ED, -ING, -S to fasten a sail

HANKER *v* -ED, -ING, -S to long for

HANKERER *n* pl. -S one that hankers

HANKIE *n* pl. -S hanky

HANKY *n* pl. -KIES a handkerchief

HANSE *n* pl. -S a guild of merchants

HANSEL *v* -SELED, -SELING, -SELS or -SELLED, -SELLING, -SELS to handsel

HANSOM *n* pl. -S a light carriage

HANT *v* -ED, -ING, -S to haunt

HANTLE *n* pl. -S a large amount

HANUMAN *n* pl. -S an East Indian monkey

HAOLE *n* pl. -S one who is not a native Hawaiian

HAP *v* HAPPED, HAPPING, HAPS to happen

HAPAX *n* pl. -ES a word that occurs only once

HAPLESS *adj* luckless

HAPLITE *n* pl. -S aplite

HAPLOID *n* pl. -S a cell having only one set of chromosomes

HAPLOIDY *n* pl. -DIES the state of being a haploid

HAPLONT *n* pl. -S an organism having a particular chromosomal structure

HAPLOPIA *n* pl. -S normal vision

HAPLOSIS *n* pl. -LOSES the halving of the chromosome number

HAPLY *adv* by chance

HAPPED past tense of hap

HAPPEN *v* -ED, -ING, -S to occur

HAPPING present participle of hap

HAPPY *adj* -PIER, -PIEST marked by joy **HAPPILY** *adv*

HAPTEN *n* pl. -S a substance similar to an antigen **HAPTENIC** *adj*

HAPTENE *n* pl. -S hapten

HAPTIC *adj* pertaining to the sense of touch

HAPTICAL *adj* haptic

HARANGUE *v* -RANGUED, -RANGUING, -RANGUES to deliver a tirade to

HARASS *v* -ED, -ING, -ES to bother persistently

HARASSER *n* pl. -S one that harasses

HARBOR *v* -ED, -ING, -S to shelter

HARBORER *n* pl. -S one that harbors

HARBOUR *v* -ED, -ING, -S to harbor

HARD *adj* HARDER, HARDEST firm and unyielding

HARDBACK *n* pl. -S a hardcover book

HARDBALL *n* pl. -S baseball

HARDBOOT *n* pl. -S a horseman

HARDCASE *adj* tough

HARDCORE *adj* unyielding

HARDEN *v* -ED, -ING, -S to make hard

HARDENER *n* pl. -S one that hardens

HARDHACK *n* pl. -S a woody plant

HARDHAT *n* pl. -S a conservative

HARDHEAD *n* pl. -S a practical person

HARDIER comparative of hardy

HARDIES pl. of hardy

HARDIEST superlative of hardy

HARDILY *adv* in a hardy manner

HARDLY *adv* scarcely

HARDNESS *n* pl. -ES the state of being hard

HARDPAN *n* pl. -S a layer of hard subsoil

HARDS *n/pl* the coarse refuse of flax

HARDSET *adj* rigid

HARDSHIP *n* pl. -S a difficult, painful condition

HARDTACK *n* pl. -S a hard biscuit

HARDTOP *n* pl. -S a type of car

HARDWARE *n* pl. -S metal goods

HARDWOOD *n* pl. -S the hard, compact wood of various trees

HARDY *adj* -DIER, -DIEST very sturdy

HARDY *n* pl. -DIES a blacksmith's chisel

HARE *v* HARED, HARING, HARES to run

HAREBELL *n* pl. -S a perennial herb

HAREEM *n* pl. -S harem

HARELIKE *adj* resembling a hare (a long-eared mammal)

HARELIP *n* pl. -S a deformity of the upper lip

HAREM *n* pl. -S the section of a Muslim household reserved for women

HARIANA *n* pl. -S a breed of cattle

HARICOT *n* pl. -S the seed of various string beans

HARIJAN *n* pl. -S an outcaste in India

HARING present participle of hare

HARK *v* -ED, -ING, -S to listen to

HARKEN *v* -ED, -ING, -S to hearken

HARKENER *n* pl. -S one that harkens

HARL *n* pl. -S a herl

HARLOT *n* pl. -S a prostitute

HARLOTRY *n* pl. -RIES prostitution

HARM *v* -ED, -ING, -S to injure

HARMER *n* pl. -S one that harms

HARMFUL *adj* capable of harming

HARMIN *n* pl. -S harmine

HARMINE *n* pl. -S an alkaloid used as a stimulant

HARMLESS *adj* not harmful

HARMONIC *n* pl. -S an overtone

HARMONY *n* pl. -NIES agreement

HARNESS *v* -ED, -ING, -ES to put tackle on a draft animal

HARP *v* -ED, -ING, -S to play on a harp (a type of stringed musical instrument)

HARPER *n* pl. -S a harpist

HARPIES pl. of harpy

HARPIN	*n* pl. -S harping
HARPING	*n* pl. -S a wooden plank used in shipbuilding
HARPIST	*n* pl. -S one that plays the harp
HARPOON	*v* -ED, -ING, -S to strike with a harpoon
HARPY	*n* pl. -PIES a shrewish person
HARRIDAN	*n* pl. -S a haggard woman
HARRIED	past tense of harry
HARRIER	*n* pl. -S a hunting dog
HARRIES	present 3d person sing. of harry
HARROW	*v* -ED, -ING, -S to break up and level soil
HARROWER	*n* pl. -S one that harrows
HARRUMPH	*v* -ED, -ING, -S to make a guttural sound
HARRY	*v* -RIED, -RYING, -RIES to pillage
HARSH	*adj* HARSHER, HARSHEST severe
HARSHEN	*v* -ED, -ING, -S to make harsh
HARSHLY	*adv* in a harsh manner
HARSLET	*n* pl. -S haslet
HART	*n* pl. -S a male deer
HARTAL	*n* pl. -S a stoppage of work
HARUSPEX	*n* pl. -PICES a soothsayer of ancient Rome
HARVEST	*v* -ED, -ING, -S to gather a crop
HAS	a present 3d person sing. of have
HASH	*v* -ED, -ING, -ES to mince
HASHEESH	*n* pl. -ES hashish
HASHISH	*n* pl. -ES a mild narcotic
HASLET	*n* pl. -S the edible viscera of an animal
HASP	*v* -ED, -ING, -S to fasten with a clasp
HASSEL	*n* pl. -S an argument
HASSLE	*v* -SLED, -SLING, -SLES to argue
HASSOCK	*n* pl. -S a footstool
HAST	a present 2d person sing. of have
HASTATE	*adj* triangular
HASTE	*v* HASTED, HASTING, HASTES to hasten
HASTEFUL	*adj* hasty
HASTEN	*v* -ED, -ING, -S to hurry
HASTENER	*n* pl. -S one that hastens
HASTING	present participle of haste
HASTY	*adj* HASTIER, HASTIEST speedy **HASTILY** *adv*
HAT	*v* HATTED, HATTING, HATS to provide with a hat (a covering for the head)
HATABLE	*adj* hateable
HATBAND	*n* pl. -S a band worn on a hat
HATBOX	*n* pl. -ES a box for a hat
HATCH	*v* -ED, -ING, -ES to bring forth young from an egg
HATCHECK	*adj* pertaining to the checking of hats
HATCHEL	*v* -ELED, -ELING, -ELS or -ELLED, -ELLING, -ELS to separate flax fibers with a comb
HATCHER	*n* pl. -S one that hatches
HATCHERY	*n* pl. -ERIES a place for hatching eggs
HATCHET	*n* pl. -S a small ax
HATCHING	*n* pl. -S a series of lines used to show shading
HATCHWAY	*n* pl. -WAYS an opening in the deck of a ship
HATE	*v* HATED, HATING, HATES to despise
HATEABLE	*adj* meriting hatred
HATEFUL	*adj* detestable
HATER	*n* pl. -S one that hates
HATFUL	*n* pl. HATSFUL or HATFULS as much as a hat can hold
HATH	a present 3d person sing. of have
HATING	present participle of hate
HATLESS	*adj* lacking a hat
HATLIKE	*adj* resembling a hat
HATMAKER	*n* pl. -S one that makes hats
HATPIN	*n* pl. -S a pin for securing a hat
HATRACK	*n* pl. -S a rack for hats
HATRED	*n* pl. -S intense dislike or aversion
HATSFUL	a pl. of hatful
HATTED	past tense of hat
HATTER	*n* pl. -S a hatmaker
HATTERIA	*n* pl. -S a reptile
HATTING	present participle of hat
HAUBERK	*n* pl. -S a coat of armor
HAUGH	*n* pl. -S a low-lying meadow

HAUGHTY	*adj* -TIER, -TIEST arrogant	**HAWKMOTH**	*n pl.* -S a large moth
HAUL	*v* -ED, -ING, -S to pull with force	**HAWKNOSE**	*n pl.* -S a large, curved nose
HAULAGE	*n pl.* -S the act of hauling	**HAWKSHAW**	*n pl.* -S a detective
HAULER	*n pl.* -S one that hauls	**HAWKWEED**	*n pl.* -S a weedlike herb
HAULIER	*n pl.* -S hauler	**HAWSE**	*n pl.* -S a part of a ship's bow
HAULM	*n pl.* -S a plant stem	**HAWSER**	*n pl.* -S a mooring rope
HAULMY	*adj* HAULMIER, HAULMIEST having haulms	**HAWTHORN**	*n pl.* -S a thorny shrub
HAULYARD	*n pl.* -S halyard	**HAY**	*v* -ED, -ING, -S to convert into hay (grass, cut and dried for fodder)
HAUNCH	*n pl.* -ES the hindquarter **HAUNCHED** *adj*	**HAYCOCK**	*n pl.* -S a pile of hay
HAUNT	*v* -ED, -ING, -S to visit frequently	**HAYER**	*n pl.* -S one that hays
HAUNTER	*n pl.* -S one that haunts	**HAYFORK**	*n pl.* -S a tool for pitching hay
HAUSEN	*n pl.* -S a Russian sturgeon	**HAYING**	*n pl.* -S the season for harvesting hay
HAUSFRAU	*n pl.* -FRAUS or -FRAUEN a housewife	**HAYLAGE**	*n pl.* -S a type of hay
HAUTBOIS	*n pl.* HAUTBOIS hautboy	**HAYLOFT**	*n pl.* -S a loft for hay storage
HAUTBOY	*n pl.* -BOYS an oboe	**HAYMAKER**	*n pl.* -S one that makes hay
HAUTEUR	*n pl.* -S haughty manner or spirit	**HAYMOW**	*n pl.* -S a hayloft
HAVDALAH	*n pl.* -S habdalah	**HAYRACK**	*n pl.* -S a frame used in hauling hay
HAVE	*v* past 2d person sing. HAD, HADDEST or HADST, present participle HAVING, present 2d person sing. HAVE or HAST, 3d person sing. HAS or HATH to be in possession of	**HAYRICK**	*n pl.* -S a haystack
		HAYRIDE	*n pl.* -S a wagon ride
		HAYSEED	*n pl.* -S a bumpkin
		HAYSTACK	*n pl.* -S a pile of hay
HAVE	*n pl.* -S a wealthy person	**HAYWARD**	*n pl.* -S an officer who tends cattle
HAVELOCK	*n pl.* -S a covering for a cap	**HAYWIRE**	*n, pl.* -S wire used in baling hay
HAVEN	*v* -ED, -ING, -S to shelter	**HAZAN**	*n pl.* -ZANIM or -ZANS a cantor
HAVER	*v* -ED, -ING, -S to hem and haw	**HAZARD**	*v* -ED, -ING, -S to venture
HAVEREL	*n pl.* -S a fool	**HAZE**	*v* HAZED, HAZING, HAZES to subject to a humiliating initiation
HAVIOR	*n pl.* -S behavior		
HAVIOUR	*n pl.* -S havior	**HAZEL**	*n pl.* -S a shrub
HAVOC	*v* -OCKED, -OCKING, -OCS to destroy	**HAZELLY**	*adj* yellowish brown
		HAZELNUT	*n pl.* -S an edible nut
HAVOCKER	*n pl.* -S one that havocs	**HAZER**	*n pl.* -S one that hazes
HAW	*v* -ED, -ING, -S to turn left	**HAZIER**	comparative of hazy
HAWFINCH	*n pl.* -ES a Eurasian finch	**HAZIEST**	superlative of hazy
HAWK	*v* -ED, -ING, -S to peddle	**HAZILY**	*adv* in a hazy manner
HAWKBILL	*n pl.* -S a sea turtle	**HAZINESS**	*n pl.* -ES the state of being hazy
HAWKER	*n pl.* -S one that hawks	**HAZING**	*n pl.* -S an attempt to embarrass or ridicule
HAWKEY	*n pl.* -EYS a hawkie		
HAWKIE	*n pl.* -S a white-faced cow	**HAZY**	*adj* HAZIER, HAZIEST unclear
HAWKING	*n pl.* -S falconry	**HAZZAN**	*n pl.* HAZZANIM or HAZZANS hazan
HAWKISH	*adj* warlike		
HAWKLIKE	*adj* resembling a hawk (a bird of prey)	**HE**	*n pl.* -S a male person
		HEAD	*v* -ED, -ING, -S to be chief of

HEADACHE   *n* pl. -S a pain inside the head

HEADACHY   *adj* -ACHIER, -ACHIEST having a headache

HEADBAND   *n* pl. -S a band worn on the head

HEADER   *n* pl. -S a grain harvester

HEADGATE   *n* pl. -S a gate to control the flow of water

HEADGEAR   *n* pl. -S a covering for the head

HEADHUNT   *v* -ED, -ING, -S to seek out, decapitate, and preserve the heads of enemies

HEADIER   comparative of heady

HEADIEST   superlative of heady

HEADILY   *adv* in a heady manner

HEADING   *n* pl. -S a title

HEADLAMP   *n* pl. -S a light on the front of a car

HEADLAND   *n* pl. -S a cliff

HEADLESS   *adj* lacking a head

HEADLINE   *v* -LINED, -LINING, -LINES to provide with a title

HEADLOCK   *n* pl. -S a wrestling hold

HEADLONG   *adj* rash; impetuous

HEADMAN   *n* pl. -MEN a foreman

HEADMOST   *adj* foremost

HEADNOTE   *n* pl. -S a prefixed note

HEADPIN   *n* pl. -S a bowling pin

HEADRACE   *n* pl. -S a water channel

HEADREST   *n* pl. -S a support for the head

HEADROOM   *n* pl. -S clear vertical space

HEADSAIL   *n* pl. -S a type of sail

HEADSET   *n* pl. -S a pair of earphones

HEADSHIP   *n* pl. -S the position of a leader

HEADSMAN   *n* pl. -MEN an executioner

HEADSTAY   *n* pl. -STAYS a support for a ship's foremast

HEADWAY   *n* pl. -WAYS forward movement

HEADWIND   *n* pl. -S an oncoming wind

HEADWORD   *n* pl. -S a word put at the beginning

HEADWORK   *n* pl. -S mental work

HEADY   *adj* HEADIER, HEADIEST intoxicating

HEAL   *v* -ED, -ING, -S to make sound or whole **HEALABLE** *adj*

HEALER   *n* pl. -S one that heals

HEALTH   *n* pl. -S the physical condition of an organism

HEALTHY   *adj* HEALTHIER, HEALTHIEST having good health

HEAP   *v* -ED, -ING, -S to pile up

HEAR   *v* HEARD, HEARING, HEARS to perceive by the ear **HEARABLE** *adj*

HEARER   *n* pl. -S one that hears

HEARING   *n* pl. -S a preliminary examination

HEARKEN   *v* -ED, -ING, -S to listen to

HEARSAY   *n* pl. -SAYS secondhand information

HEARSE   *v* HEARSED, HEARSING, HEARSES to transport in a hearse (a vehicle for conveying corpses)

HEART   *v* -ED, -ING, -S to hearten

HEARTEN   *v* -ED, -ING, -S to give courage to

HEARTH   *n* pl. -S the floor of a fireplace

HEARTY   *adj* HEARTIER, HEARTIEST very friendly **HEARTILY** *adv*

HEARTY   *n* pl. HEARTIES a comrade

HEAT   *v* HEATED or HET, HEATING, HEATS to make hot **HEATABLE** *adj*

HEATEDLY   *adv* in an inflamed or excited manner

HEATER   *n* pl. -S an apparatus for heating

HEATH   *n* pl. -S an evergreen shrub

HEATHEN   *n* pl. -S an uncivilized person

HEATHER   *n* pl. -S an evergreen shrub **HEATHERY** *adj*

HEATHY   *adj* HEATHIER, HEATHIEST abounding in heath

HEATLESS   *adj* having no warmth

HEAUME   *n* pl. -S a medieval helmet

HEAVE   *v* HEAVED or HOVE, HEAVING, HEAVES to lift forcefully

HEAVEN   *n* pl. -S the sky

HEAVENLY   *adj* -LIER, -LIEST full of beauty and peace

HEAVER   *n* pl. -S one that heaves

HEAVIER   comparative of heavy

HEAVIES   pl. of heavy

HEAVING   present participle of heave

HEAVY   *adj* HEAVIER, HEAVIEST having much weight **HEAVILY** *adv*

HEAVY   *n* pl. HEAVIES a villain

HEAVYSET   *adj* solidly built; stocky

HEBDOMAD   *n* pl. -S the number seven

HEBETATE   *v* -TATED, -TATING, -TATES to make dull

HEBETIC   *adj* pertaining to puberty

HEBETUDE   *n* pl. -S mental dullness

HEBRAIZE   *v* -IZED, -IZING, -IZES to make Hebrew

HECATOMB   *n* pl. -S a great sacrifice or slaughter

HECK   *n* pl. -S hell

HECKLE   *v* -LED, -LING, -LES to harass a speaker

HECKLER   *n* pl. -S one that heckles

HECTARE   *n* pl. -S a unit of area

HECTIC   *adj* filled with turmoil **HECTICLY** *adv*

HECTICAL   *adj* hectic

HECTOR   *v* -ED, -ING, -S to bully

HEDDLE   *n* pl. -S a part of a loom

HEDER   *n* pl. HEDERS or HADARIM a Jewish school

HEDGE   *v* HEDGED, HEDGING, HEDGES to surround with a hedge

HEDGER   *n* pl. -S one that hedges

HEDGEHOG   *n* pl. -S a small mammal

HEDGEHOP   *v* -HOPPED, -HOPPING, -HOPS to fly near the ground

HEDGEPIG   *n* pl. -S a hedgehog

HEDGEROW   *n* pl. -S a row of bushes

HEDGING   present participle of hedge

HEDGY   *adj* HEDGIER, HEDGIEST abounding in hedges

HEDONIC   *adj* pertaining to pleasure

HEDONICS   *n/pl* a branch of psychology

HEDONISM   *n* pl. -S the pursuit of pleasure

HEDONIST   *n* pl. -S a follower of hedonism

HEED   *v* -ED, -ING, -S to pay attention to

HEEDER   *n* pl. -S one that heeds

HEEDFUL   *adj* paying close attention

HEEDLESS   *adj* paying little or no attention

HEEHAW   *v* -ED, -ING, -S to guffaw

HEEL   *v* -ED, -ING, -S to supply with a heel (the raised part of a shoe)

HEELBALL   *n* pl. -S a composition used for polishing

HEELER   *n* pl. -S one that puts heels on shoes

HEELING   *n* pl. -S the act of inclining laterally

HEELLESS   *adj* lacking heels

HEELPOST   *n* pl. -S a post fitted to the end of something

HEELTAP   *n* pl. -S material put on the heel of a shoe

HEEZE   *v* HEEZED, HEEZING, HEEZES to hoist

HEFT   *v* -ED, -ING, -S to lift up

HEFTER   *n* pl. -S one that hefts

HEFTY   *adj* HEFTIER, HEFTIEST heavy **HEFTILY** *adv*

HEGARI   *n* pl. -S a grain

HEGEMONY   *n* pl. -NIES great authority

HEGIRA   *n* pl. -S an exodus

HEGUMEN   *n* pl. -S the head of a monastery

HEGUMENE   *n* pl. -S the head of a nunnery

HEGUMENY   *n* pl. -NIES the office of a hegumen

HEIFER   *n* pl. -S a young cow

HEIGH   *interj* — used to attract attention

HEIGHT   *n* pl. -S the highest point

HEIGHTEN   *v* -ED, -ING, -S to raise

HEIGHTH   *n* pl. -S height

HEIL   *v* -ED, -ING, -S to salute

HEINIE   *n* pl. -S the buttocks

HEINOUS   *adj* very wicked

HEIR   *v* -ED, -ING, -S to inherit

HEIRDOM   *n* pl. -S heirship

HEIRESS   *n* pl. -ES a female inheritor

HEIRLESS   *adj* having no inheritors

HEIRLOOM   *n* pl. -S an inherited possession

HEIRSHIP   *n* pl. -S the right to inheritance

HEIST   *v* -ED, -ING, -S to steal

HEISTER   *n* pl. -S one that heists

HEJIRA   *n* pl. -S hegira

HEKTARE   *n* pl. -S hectare

HELD   past tense of hold

HELIAC   *adj* heliacal

HELIACAL   *adj* pertaining to the sun

HELIAST   *n* pl. -S an Athenian judge

HELICAL   *adj* shaped like a helix

HELICES a pl. of helix

HELICITY n pl. -TIES a component of a particle's spin

HELICOID n pl. -S a type of geometrical surface

HELICON n pl. -S a large bass tuba

HELICOPT v -ED, -ING, -S to travel by helicopter

HELIO n pl. -LIOS a signaling mirror

HELIPAD n pl. -S a heliport

HELIPORT n pl. -S an airport for helicopters

HELISTOP n pl. -S a hellport

HELIUM n pl. -S a gaseous element

HELIX n pl. -LIXES or -LICES something spiral in form

HELL v -ED, -ING, -S to behave raucously

HELLBENT adj stubbornly determined

HELLBOX n pl. -ES a printer's receptacle

HELLCAT n pl. -S a shrewish person

HELLER n pl. -S a hellion

HELLERI n pl. -ES a tropical fish

HELLERY n pl. -LERIES rough play

HELLFIRE n pl. -S the torment of hell

HELLHOLE n pl. -S a horrible place

HELLION n pl. -S a troublesome person

HELLISH adj horrible

HELLKITE n pl. -S a cruel person

HELLO v -ED, -ING, -ES or -S to greet

HELLUVA adj disagreeable

HELM v -ED, -ING, -S to steer a ship

HELMET v -ED, -ING, -S to supply with a helmet (a protective covering for the head)

HELMINTH n pl. -S a worm

HELMLESS adj lacking a helm (a steering system)

HELMSMAN n pl. -MEN one that steers a ship

HELOT n pl. -S a slave or serf

HELOTAGE n pl. -S helotism

HELOTISM n pl. -S slavery or serfdom

HELOTRY n pl. -RIES helotism

HELP v HELPED or HOLP, HOLPEN, HELPING, HELPS to give assistance to **HELPABLE** adj

HELPER n pl. -S one that helps

HELPFUL adj being of service or assistance

HELPING n pl. -S a portion of food

HELPLESS adj defenseless

HELPMATE n pl. -S a helpful companion

HELPMEET n pl. -S a helpmate

HELVE v HELVED, HELVING, HELVES to provide with a handle

HEM v HEMMED, HEMMING, HEMS to provide with an edge

HEMAGOG n pl. -S an agent that promotes blood flow

HEMAL adj pertaining to the blood

HEMATAL adj hemal

HEMATEIN n pl. -S a chemical compound

HEMATIC n pl. -S a medicine for a blood disease

HEMATIN n pl. -S heme

HEMATINE n pl. -S hematin

HEMATITE n pl. -S an ore or iron

HEMATOID adj resembling blood

HEMATOMA n pl. -MAS or -MATA a swelling filled with blood

HEME n pl. -S a component of hemoglobin

HEMIC adj hemal

HEMIN n pl. -S a chloride of heme

HEMIOLA n pl. -S a rhythmic alteration in music

HEMIPTER n pl. -S an insect

HEMLINE n pl. -S the bottom edge of a garment

HEMLOCK n pl. -S a poisonous herb

HEMMED past tense of hem

HEMMER n pl. -S one that hems

HEMMING present participle of hem

HEMOCOEL n pl. -S a body cavity

HEMOCYTE n pl. -S a blood cell

HEMOID adj hemal

HEMOLYZE v -LYZED, -LYZING, -LYZES to break down red blood cells

HEMOSTAT n pl. -S an instrument for reducing bleeding

HEMP n pl. -S a tall herb

HEMPEN adj made of hemp

HEMPIE adj HEMPIER, HEMPIEST hempy

HEMPIER comparative of hempy

HEMPIEST superlative of hempy

HEMPLIKE *adj* resembling hemp

HEMPSEED *n* pl. -S the seed of hemp

HEMPWEED *n* pl. -S a climbing plant

HEMPY *adj* HEMPIER, HEMPIEST mischievous

HEN *n* pl. -S a female chicken **HENLIKE** *adj*

HENBANE *n* pl. -S a poisonous herb

HENBIT *n* pl. -S a perennial herb

HENCE *adv* consequently

HENCHMAN *n* pl. -MEN an unscrupulous supporter

HENCOOP *n* pl. -S a cage for hens

HENEQUEN *n* pl. -S a fiber used to make ropes

HENEQUIN *n* pl. -S henequen

HENHOUSE *n* pl. -S a shelter for poultry

HENIQUEN *n* pl. -S henequen

HENNA *v* -ED, -ING, -S to dye with a reddish coloring

HENNERY *n* pl. -NERIES a poultry farm

HENPECK *v* -ED, -ING, -S to dominate by nagging

HENRY *n* pl. -RIES or -RYS a unit of inductance

HENT *v* -ED, -ING, -S to grasp

HEP *adj* hip

HEPARIN *n* pl. -S a biochemical

HEPATIC *n* pl. -S a drug acting on the liver

HEPATICA *n* pl. -CAS or -CAE a perennial herb

HEPATIZE *v* -TIZED, -TIZING, -TIZES to convert tissue into a firm mass

HEPATOMA *n* pl. -MAS or -MATA a tumor of the liver

HEPCAT *n* pl. -S a jazz enthusiast

HEPTAD *n* pl. -S a group of seven

HEPTAGON *n* pl. -S a seven-sided polygon

HEPTANE *n* pl. -S a hydrocarbon used as a solvent

HEPTARCH *n* pl. -S one of a group of seven rulers

HEPTOSE *n* pl. -S a chemical compound

HER *pron* the objective or possessive case of the pronoun she

HERALD *v* -ED, -ING, -S to proclaim

HERALDIC *adj* pertaining to heraldry

HERALDRY *n* pl. -RIES the art or science of armorial bearings

HERB *n* pl. -S a flowering plant with a nonwoody stem

HERBAGE *n* pl. -S nonwoody plant life

HERBAL *n* pl. -S a book about herbs and plants

HERBARIA *n/pl* collections of dried plants

HERBIER comparative of herby

HERBIEST superlative of herby

HERBLESS *adj* lacking herbs

HERBLIKE *adj* resembling an herb

HERBY *adj* HERBIER, HERBIEST abounding in herbs

HERCULES *n* pl. -LESES any man of great size and strength

HERD *v* -ED, -ING, -S to bring together in a herd (a group of animals)

HERDER *n* pl. -S one who tends a herd

HERDIC *n* pl. -S a type of carriage

HERDLIKE *adj* resembling a herd

HERDMAN *n* pl. -MEN herdsman

HERDSMAN *n* pl. -MEN a herder

HERE *n* pl. -S this place

HEREAT *adv* at this time

HEREAWAY *adv* in this vicinity

HEREBY *adv* by this means

HEREDES pl. of heres

HEREDITY *n* pl. -TIES the genetic transmission of characteristics

HEREIN *adv* in this

HEREINTO *adv* into this place

HEREOF *adv* of this

HEREON *adv* on this

HERES *n* pl. HEREDES an heir

HERESY *n* pl. -SIES a belief contrary to a church doctrine

HERETIC *n* pl. -S one that upholds heresy

HERETO *adv* to this matter

HERETRIX *n* pl. -TRIXES or -TRICES heritrix

HEREUNTO *adv* hereto

HEREUPON *adv* immediately following this

HEREWITH *adv* along with this

HERIOT *n* pl. -S a feudal tribute or payment

HERITAGE *n* pl. -S something that is inherited

HERITOR	*n* pl. -S one that inherits
HERITRIX	*n* pl. -TRIXES or -TRICES a female heritor
HERL	*n* pl. -S a feathered fishing lure
HERM	*n* pl. -S a type of statue
HERMA	*n* pl. -MAE or -MAI a herm **HERMAEAN** *adj*
HERMETIC	*adj* airtight
HERMIT	*n* pl. -S a recluse **HERMITIC** *adj*
HERMITRY	*n* pl. -RIES the state of being a hermit
HERN	*n* pl. -S a heron
HERNIA	*n* pl. -NIAS or -NIAE the protrusion of an organ through its surrounding wall **HERNIAL** *adj*
HERNIATE	*v* -ATED, -ATING, -ATES to protrude through an abnormal bodily opening
HERO	*n* pl. -ROES or -ROS one who shows great courage
HEROIC	*n* pl. -S an epic verse
HEROICAL	*adj* courageous; noble
HEROIN	*n* pl. -S an addictive narcotic
HEROINE	*n* pl. -S a brave woman
HEROISM	*n* pl. -S heroic behavior
HEROIZE	*v* -IZED, -IZING, -IZES to make heroic
HERON	*n* pl. -S a wading bird
HERONRY	*n* pl. -RIES a place where herons breed
HERPES	*n* pl. -PESES a skin infection **HERPETIC** *adj*
HERRING	*n* pl. -S a food fish
HERRY	*v* -RIED, -RYING, -RIES to harry
HERS	*pron* the possessive case of the pronoun she
HERSELF	*pron* a form of the 3d person sing. feminine pronoun
HERTZ	*n* pl. -ES a unit of frequency
HESITANT	*adj* tending to hesitate
HESITATE	*v* -TATED, -TATING, -TATES to hold back in uncertainty
HESSIAN	*n* pl. -S a coarse cloth
HESSITE	*n* pl. -S a mineral
HEST	*n* pl. -S a command
HET	a past tense of heat
HETAERA	*n* pl. -RAE or -RAS a concubine **HETAERIC** *adj*
HETAIRA	*n* pl. -RAI or -RAS hetaera
HETERO	*n* pl. -EROS a heterosexual
HETH	*n* pl. -S a Hebrew letter
HETMAN	*n* pl. -S a cossack leader
HEUCH	*n* pl. -S heugh
HEUGH	*n* pl. -S a steep cliff
HEW	*v* HEWED, HEWN, HEWING, HEWS to cut with an ax **HEWABLE** *adj*
HEWER	*n* pl. -S one that hews
HEX	*v* -ED, -ING, -ES to cast an evil spell upon
HEXAD	*n* pl. -S a group of six **HEXADIC** *adj*
HEXADE	*n* pl. -S hexad
HEXAGON	*n* pl. -S a polygon having six sides
HEXAGRAM	*n* pl. -S a six-pointed star
HEXAMINE	*n* pl. -S a chemical compound
HEXANE	*n* pl. -S a volatile liquid
HEXAPLA	*n* pl. -S an edition in which six texts are set in parallel columns **HEXAPLAR** *adj*
HEXAPOD	*n* pl. -S a six-legged insect
HEXAPODY	*n* pl. -DIES a line of verse with six feet
HEXARCHY	*n* pl. -CHIES a group of six separate states
HEXER	*n* pl. -S one that hexes
HEXEREI	*n* pl. -S witchcraft
HEXONE	*n* pl. -S a hydrocarbon solvent
HEXOSAN	*n* pl. -S a carbohydrate
HEXOSE	*n* pl. -S a simple sugar
HEXYL	*n* pl. -S a hydrocarbon radical
HEY	*interj* — used to attract attention
HEYDAY	*n* pl. -DAYS the period of one's greatest success
HEYDEY	*n* pl. -DEYS heyday
HI	*interj* — used as a greeting
HIATUS	*n* pl. -ES a gap or missing section **HIATAL** *adj*
HIBACHI	*n* pl. -S a cooking device
HIBERNAL	*adj* pertaining to winter
HIBISCUS	*n* pl. -ES a tropical plant
HIC	*interj* — used to represent a hiccup
HICCOUGH	*v* -ED, -ING, -S to hiccup

HICCUP	*v* -CUPED, -CUPING, -CUPS or -CUPPED, -CUPPING, -CUPS to make a peculiar-sounding, spasmodic inhalation
HICK	*n* pl. -S a rural person
HICKEY	*n* pl. -EYS a gadget
HICKORY	*n* pl. -RIES a hardwood tree
HID	a past tense of hide
HIDABLE	*adj* able to be hidden
HIDALGO	*n* pl. -GOS a minor Spanish nobleman
HIDDEN	*adj* concealed; obscure **HIDDENLY** *adv*
HIDE	*v* HID, HIDDEN, HIDING, HIDES to conceal
HIDE	*v* HIDED, HIDING, HIDES to flog
HIDEAWAY	*n* pl. -AWAYS a hideout
HIDELESS	*adj* lacking a skin
HIDEOUS	*adj* very ugly
HIDEOUT	*n* pl. -S a place of refuge
HIDER	*n* pl. -S one that hides
HIDING	*n* pl. -S a beating
HIDROSIS	*n* pl. -DROSES abnormal perspiration **HIDROTIC** *adj*
HIE	*v* HIED, HIEING or HYING, HIES to hurry
HIEMAL	*adj* pertaining to winter
HIERARCH	*n* pl. -S a religious leader
HIERATIC	*adj* pertaining to priests
HIGGLE	*v* -GLED, -GLING, -GLES to haggle
HIGGLER	*n* pl. -S one that higgles
HIGH	*adj* HIGHER, HIGHEST reaching far upward
HIGH	*n* pl. -S a high level
HIGHBALL	*v* -ED, -ING, -S to go at full speed
HIGHBORN	*adj* of noble birth
HIGHBOY	*n* pl. -BOYS a tall chest of drawers
HIGHBRED	*adj* highborn
HIGHBROW	*n* pl. -S a person who has superior tastes
HIGHBUSH	*adj* forming a tall bush
HIGHJACK	*v* -ED, -ING, -S to hijack
HIGHLAND	*n* pl. -S an elevated region
HIGHLY	*adv* to a high degree
HIGHNESS	*n* pl. -ES the state of being high
HIGHROAD	*n* pl. -S a highway
HIGHT	*v* -ED, -ING, -S to command
HIGHTAIL	*v* -ED, -ING, -S to retreat rapidly
HIGHTH	*n* pl. -S height
HIGHWAY	*n* pl. -WAYS a main road
HIJACK	*v* -ED, -ING, -S to seize a vehicle while in transit
HIJACKER	*n* pl. -S one that hijacks
HIJINKS	*n/pl* mischievous fun
HIKE	*v* HIKED, HIKING, HIKES to walk a long distance
HIKER	*n* pl. -S one that hikes
HILA	pl. of hilum
HILAR	*adj* pertaining to a hilum
HILARITY	*n* pl. -TIES noisy merriment
HILDING	*n* pl. -S a vile person
HILI	pl. of hilus
HILL	*v* -ED, -ING, -S to form into a hill (a rounded elevation)
HILLER	*n* pl. -S one that hills
HILLIER	comparative of hilly
HILLIEST	superlative of hilly
HILLO	*v* -ED, -ING, -S to hallo
HILLOA	*v* -ED, -ING, -S to hallo
HILLOCK	*n* pl. -S a small hill **HILLOCKY** *adj*
HILLSIDE	*n* pl. -S the side of a hill
HILLTOP	*n* pl. -S the top of a hill
HILLY	*adj* HILLIER, HILLIEST abounding in hills
HILT	*v* -ED, -ING, -S to provide with a hilt (a handle for a weapon)
HILTLESS	*adj* having no hilt
HILUM	*n* pl. HILA a small opening in a bodily organ
HILUS	*n* pl. HILI hilum
HIM	*pron* the objective case of the pronoun he
HIMATION	*n* pl. -MATIA or -MATIONS a loose outer garment
HIMSELF	*pron* a form of the 3d person sing. masculine pronoun
HIN	*n* pl. -S a Hebrew unit of liquid measure
HIND	*n* pl. -S a female red deer
HINDER	*v* -ED, -ING, -S to impede
HINDERER	*n* pl. -S one that hinders

HINDGUT	*n* pl. -S the rear part of the alimentary canal
HINDMOST	*adj* farthest to the rear
HINGE	*v* HINGED, HINGING, HINGES to attach a jointed device
HINGER	*n* pl. -S one that hinges
HINNY	*v* -NIED, -NYING, -NIES to whinny
HINT	*v* -ED, -ING, -S to suggest indirectly
HINTER	*n* pl. -S one that hints
HIP	*v* HIPPED, HIPPING, HIPS to build a type of roof
HIP	*adj* HIPPER, HIPPEST aware of the most current styles and trends
HIPBONE	*n* pl. -S a pelvic bone
HIPLESS	*adj* lacking a hip (the pelvic joint)
HIPLIKE	*adj* suggestive of a hip
HIPNESS	*n* pl. -ES the state of being hip
HIPPARCH	*n* pl. -S a cavalry commander in ancient Greece
HIPPED	past tense of hip
HIPPER	comparative of hip
HIPPEST	superlative of hip
HIPPING	present participle of hip
HIPPIE	*n* pl. -S a nonconformist
HIPPIER	comparative of hippy
HIPPIEST	superlative of hippy
HIPPISH	*adj* depressed; sad
HIPPO	*n* pl. -POS a hippopotamus
HIPPY	*adj* -PIER, -PIEST having big hips
HIPSHOT	*adj* lame; awkward
HIPSTER	*n* pl. -S one that is hip
HIRABLE	*adj* available for hire
HIRAGANA	*n* pl. -S a Japanese cursive script
HIRCINE	*adj* pertaining to a goat
HIRE	*v* HIRED, HIRING, HIRES to engage the services of for payment **HIREABLE** *adj*
HIRELING	*n* pl. -S one that works for money only
HIRER	*n* pl. -S one that hires
HIRING	present participle of hire
HIRPLE	*v* -PLED, -PLING, -PLES to limp

HIRSEL	*v* -SELED, -SELING, -SELS or -SELLED, -SELLING, -SELS to herd sheep
HIRSLE	*v* -SLED, -SLING, -SLES to slide along
HIRSUTE	*adj* hairy
HIRUDIN	*n* pl. -S an anticoagulant
HIS	*pron* the possessive form of the pronoun he
HISN	*pron* his
HISPID	*adj* covered with stiff hairs
HISS	*v* -ED, -ING, -ES to make a sibilant sound
HISSELF	*pron* himself
HISSER	*n* pl. -S one that hisses
HISSING	*n* pl. -S an object of scorn
HIST	*v* -ED, -ING, -S to hoist
HISTAMIN	*n* pl. -S an amine released in allergic reactions
HISTIDIN	*n* pl. -S an amino acid
HISTOGEN	*n* pl. -S interior plant tissue
HISTOID	*adj* pertaining to connective tissue
HISTONE	*n* pl. -S a simple protein
HISTORIC	*adj* important in history
HISTORY	*n* pl. -RIES a chronological record of past events
HIT	*v* HIT, HITTING, HITS to strike forcibly
HITCH	*v* -ED, -ING, -ES to fasten with a knot or hook
HITCHER	*n* pl. -S one that hitches
HITHER	*adv* toward this place
HITHERTO	*adv* up to now
HITLESS	*adj* being without a hit
HITTER	*n* pl. -S one that hits
HITTING	present participle of hit
HIVE	*v* HIVED, HIVING, HIVES to cause to enter a hive (a bee's nest)
HIVELESS	*adj* lacking a hive
HO	*interj* — used to express surprise
HOACTZIN	*n* pl. -S or -ES hoatzin
HOAGIE	*n* pl. -S a long sandwich
HOAGY	*n* pl. -GIES hoagie
HOAR	*n* pl. -S a white coating
HOARD	*v* -ED, -ING, -S to gather and store away

HOARDER   *n* pl. -S one that hoards

HOARDING   *n* pl. -S something hoarded

HOARIER   comparative of hoary

HOARIEST   superlative of hoary

HOARILY   *adv* in a hoary manner

HOARSE   *adj* HOARSER, HOARSEST low and rough in sound **HOARSELY** *adv*

HOARSEN   *v* -ED, -ING, -S to make hoarse

HOARY   *adj* HOARIER, HOARIEST white with age

HOATZIN   *n* pl. -S or -ES a tropical bird

HOAX   *v* -ED, -ING, -ES to deceive

HOAXER   *n* pl. -S one that hoaxes

HOB   *v* HOBBED, HOBBING, HOBS to furnish with hobnails

HOBBIES   pl. of hobby

HOBBLE   *v* -BLED, -BLING, -BLES to limp

HOBBLER   *n* pl. -S one that hobbles

HOBBY   *n* pl. -BIES a recreational pastime

HOBBYIST   *n* pl. -S one that pursues a hobby

HOBLIKE   *adj* suggestive of an elf

HOBNAIL   *n* pl. -S a short nail with a thick head

HOBNOB   *v* -NOBBED, -NOBBING, -NOBS to associate in a friendly way

HOBO   *v* -ED, -ING, -S or -ES to live like a hobo (a vagrant or tramp)

HOBOISM   *n* pl. -S the state of being a hobo

HOCK   *v* -ED, -ING, -S to pawn

HOCKER   *n* pl. -S one that hocks

HOCKEY   *n* pl. -EYS a game played on ice

HOCKSHOP   *n* pl. -S a pawnshop

HOCUS   *v* -CUSED, -CUSING, -CUSES or -CUSSED, -CUSSING, -CUSSES to deceive or cheat

HOD   *n* pl. -S a portable trough

HODAD   *n* pl. -S a nonsurfer

HODADDY   *n* pl. -DIES hodad

HODDEN   *n* pl. -S a coarse cloth

HODDIN   *n* pl. -S hodden

HOE   *v* HOED, HOEING, HOES to use a hoe (a gardening tool)

HOECAKE   *n* pl. -S a cornmeal cake

HOEDOWN   *n* pl. -S a square dance

HOELIKE   *adj* resembling a hoe

HOER   *n* pl. -S one that hoes

HOG   *v* HOGGED, HOGGING, HOGS to take more than one's share

HOGAN   *n* pl. -S a Navaho Indian dwelling

HOGBACK   *n* pl. -S a sharp ridge

HOGFISH   *n* pl. -ES a tropical fish

HOGG   *n* pl. -S a young sheep

HOGGED   past tense of hog

HOGGER   *n* pl. -S one that hogs

HOGGING   present participle of hog

HOGGISH   *adj* coarsely selfish

HOGLIKE   *adj* hoggish

HOGMANAY   *n* pl. -NAYS a Scottish celebration

HOGMANE   *n* pl. -S hogmanay

HOGMENAY   *n* pl. -NAYS hogmanay

HOGNOSE   *n* pl. -S a nonvenomous snake

HOGNUT   *n* pl. -S a hickory nut

HOGSHEAD   *n* pl. -S a large cask

HOGTIE   *v* -TIED, -TIEING or -TYING, -TIES to tie together the legs of

HOGWASH   *n* pl. -ES meaningless talk

HOGWEED   *n* pl. -S a coarse plant

HOICK   *v* -ED, -ING, -S to change directions abruptly

HOIDEN   *v* -ED, -ING, -S to hoyden

HOISE   *v* HOISED, HOISING, HOISES to hoist

HOIST   *v* -ED, -ING, -S to haul up by some mechanical means

HOISTER   *n* pl. -S one that hoists

HOKE   *v* HOKED, HOKING, HOKES to give false value to

HOKEY   *adj* false; contrived

HOKKU   *n* pl. HOKKU haiku

HOKUM   *n* pl. -S nonsense

HOKYPOKY   *n* pl. -KIES trickery

HOLARD   *n* pl. -S the total quantity of water in the soil

HOLD   *v* HELD, HOLDEN, HOLDING, HOLDS to maintain possession of **HOLDABLE** *adj*

HOLDALL   *n* pl. -S a carrying case

HOLDBACK   *n* pl. -S a restraining device

HOLDEN   a past participle of hold

HOLDER   *n* pl. -S one that holds

HOLDFAST *n pl.* -S a fastening device

HOLDING *n pl.* -S something held

HOLDOUT *n pl.* -S one who delays signing a contract

HOLDOVER *n pl.* -S something left over

HOLDUP *n pl.* -S a delay

HOLE *v* HOLED, HOLING, HOLES to make a hole (a cavity in a solid)

HOLELESS *adj* lacking a hole

HOLEY *adj* full of holes

HOLIBUT *n pl.* -S halibut

HOLIDAY *v* -ED, -ING, -S to take a vacation

HOLIER comparative of holy

HOLIES pl. of holy

HOLIEST superlative of holy

HOLILY *adv* in a holy manner

HOLINESS *n pl.* -ES the state of being holy

HOLING present participle of hole

HOLISM *n pl.* -S a philosophical theory

HOLIST *n pl.* -S one who adheres to the theory of holism **HOLISTIC** *adj*

HOLK *v* -ED, -ING, -S to howk

HOLLA *v* -ED, -ING, -S to hallo

HOLLAND *n pl.* -S a cotton fabric

HOLLER *v* -ED, -ING, -S to yell

HOLLO *v* -ED, -ING, -S or -ES to hallo

HOLLOA *v* -ED, -ING, -S to hallo

HOLLOO *v* -ED, -ING, -S to hallo

HOLLOW *adj* -LOWER, -LOWEST not solid **HOLLOWLY** *adv*

HOLLOW *v* -ED, -ING, -S to make hollow

HOLLY *n pl.* -LIES a tree

HOLM *n pl.* -S an island in a river

HOLMIUM *n pl.* -S a metallic element **HOLMIC** *adj*

HOLOGRAM *n pl.* -S a three-dimensional photograph

HOLOGYNY *n pl.* -NIES a trait transmitted solely in the female line

HOLOTYPE *n pl.* -S an animal or plant specimen

HOLOZOIC *adj* eating solid foods

HOLP a past tense of help

HOLPEN a past participle of help

HOLSTEIN *n pl.* -S a breed of cattle

HOLSTER *n pl.* -S a case for a pistol

HOLT *n pl.* -S a grove

HOLY *adj* -LIER, -LIEST having a divine nature or origin

HOLY *n pl.* -LIES a holy place

HOLYDAY *n pl.* -DAYS a religious holiday

HOLYTIDE *n pl.* -S a time of religious observance

HOMAGE *v* -AGED, -AGING, -AGES to pay tribute to

HOMAGER *n pl.* -S a feudal vassal

HOMBRE *n pl.* -S a fellow

HOMBURG *n pl.* -S a felt hat

HOME *v* HOMED, HOMING, HOMES to return to one's home (place of residence)

HOMEBODY *n pl.* -BODIES one who likes to stay at home

HOMEBRED *n pl.* -S a native athlete

HOMED past tense of home

HOMELAND *n pl.* -S one's native land

HOMELESS *adj* lacking a home

HOMELIKE *adj* suggestive of a home; comfortably familiar

HOMELY *adj* -LIER, -LIEST unattractive

HOMEMADE *adj* made at home

HOMER *v* -ED, -ING, -S to hit a home run

HOMEROOM *n pl.* -S the classroom where pupils report before classes begin

HOMESICK *adj* longing for home

HOMESITE *n pl.* -S a location for a house

HOMESPUN *n pl.* -S a loosely woven fabric

HOMETOWN *n pl.* -S the town of one's birth or residence

HOMEWARD *adv* toward home

HOMEWORK *n pl.* -S work done at home

HOMEY *adj* HOMIER, HOMIEST homelike

HOMICIDE *n pl.* -S the killing of one person by another

HOMIER comparative of homy

HOMIEST superlative of homy

HOMILIST *n pl.* -S one that delivers a homily

HOMILY *n pl.* -LIES a sermon

HOMINESS *n pl.* -ES the quality of being homey

HOMING present participle of home

HOMINIAN *n pl.* -S a hominid

HOMINID   *n* pl. -S a manlike creature

HOMINIES   pl. of hominy

HOMININE   *adj* characteristic of man

HOMINOID   *n* pl. -S a manlike animal

HOMINY   *n* pl. -NIES hulled and dried corn

HOMMOCK   *n* pl. -S a ridge in an ice field

HOMO   *n* pl. -MOS a homosexual

HOMOGAMY   *n* pl. -MIES the bearing of sexually similar flowers

HOMOGENY   *n* pl. -NIES correspondence in form or structure

HOMOGONY   *n* pl. -NIES the condition of having flowers with uniform stamens and pistils

HOMOLOG   *n* pl. -S something that exhibits homology

HOMOLOGY   *n* pl. -GIES similarity in structure due to origin

HOMONYM   *n* pl. -S a namesake

HOMONYMY   *n* pl. -MIES the condition of having the same name

HOMY   *adj* HOMIER, HOMIEST homey

HONAN   *n* pl. -S a fine silk

HONCHO   *n* pl. -CHOS a chief

HONDA   *n* pl. -S a part of a lariat

HONE   *v* HONED, HONING, HONES to sharpen

HONER   *n* pl. -S one that hones

HONEST   *adj* -ESTER, -ESTEST truthful **HONESTLY** *adv*

HONESTY   *n* pl. -TIES the quality of being honest

HONEWORT   *n* pl. -S a perennial herb

HONEY   *v* -EYED or -IED, -EYING, -EYS to sweeten with honey (a sweet, viscid fluid)

HONEYBEE   *n* pl. -S a type of bee

HONEYBUN   *n* pl. -S a sweetheart

HONEYDEW   *n* pl. -S a sweet fluid

HONEYFUL   *adj* containing much honey

HONG   *n* pl. -S a Chinese factory

HONIED   a past tense of honey

HONING   present participle of hone

HONK   *v* -ED, -ING, -S to emit a cry like that of a goose

HONKER   *n* pl. -S one that honks

HONKEY   *n* pl. -KEYS honkie

HONKIE   *n* pl. -S a white man — a derogatory term

HONKY   *n* pl. -KIES honkie

HONOR   *v* -ED, -ING, -S to treat with respect

HONORAND   *n* pl. -S one that receives an honor

HONORARY   *n* pl. -ARIES an honor society

HONOREE   *n* pl. -S one that receives an honor

HONORER   *n* pl. -S one that honors

HONOUR   *v* -ED, -ING, -S to honor

HONOURER   *n* pl. -S honorer

HOOCH   *n* pl. -ES cheap whiskey

HOOD   *v* -ED, -ING, -S to furnish with a hood (a covering for the head)

HOODIE   *n* pl. -S a gray crow of Europe

HOODLESS   *adj* lacking a hood

HOODLIKE   *adj* resembling a hood

HOODLUM   *n* pl. -S a thug

HOODOO   *v* -ED, -ING, -S to bring bad luck to

HOODWINK   *v* -ED, -ING, -S to trick

HOOEY   *n* pl. -EYS something false or nonsensical

HOOF   *v* -ED, -ING, -S to dance

HOOF   *n* pl. HOOVES or HOOFS the hard covering on the feet of certain animals

HOOFBEAT   *n* pl. -S the sound of hooves striking the ground

HOOFER   *n* pl. -S a professional dancer

HOOFLESS   *adj* lacking hooves

HOOFLIKE   *adj* resembling a hoof

HOOK   *v* -ED, -ING, -S to catch with a hook (a bent piece of metal)

HOOKA   *n* pl. -S hookah

HOOKAH   *n* pl. -S a water pipe

HOOKED   past tense of hook

HOOKER   *n* pl. a prostitute

HOOKEY   *n* pl. -EYS hooky

HOOKIER   comparative of hooky

HOOKIES   pl. of hooky

HOOKIEST   superlative of hooky

HOOKLESS   *adj* lacking a hook

HOOKLET   *n* pl. -S a small hook

HOOKLIKE   *adj* resembling a hook

HOOKNOSE   *n* pl. -S an aquiline nose

HOOKUP n pl. -S an electrical assemblage

HOOKWORM n pl. -S a parasitic worm

HOOKY n pl. HOOKIES truancy

HOOKY adj HOOKIER, HOOKIEST full of hooks

HOOLIE adj easy; slow

HOOLIGAN n pl. -S a hoodlum

HOOLY adj hoolie

HOOP v -ED, -ING, -S to fasten with a hoop (a circular band of metal)

HOOPER n pl. -S one that hoops

HOOPLA n pl. -S commotion

HOOPLESS adj lacking a hoop

HOOPLIKE adj suggestive of a hoop

HOOPOE n pl. -S a European bird

HOOPOO n pl. -POOS hoopoe

HOOPSTER n pl. -S a basketball player

HOORAH v -ED, -ING, -S to hurrah

HOORAY v -ED, -ING, -S to hurrah

HOOSEGOW n pl. -S a jail

HOOSGOW n pl. -S hoosegow

HOOT v -ED, -ING, -S to cry like an owl

HOOTCH n pl. -ES hooch

HOOTER n pl. -S one that hoots

HOOVES a pl. of hoof

HOP v HOPPED, HOPPING, HOPS to move by jumping on one foot

HOPE v HOPED, HOPING, HOPES to have a desire or expectation

HOPEFUL n pl. -S one that seems promising

HOPELESS adj despairing

HOPER n pl. -S one that hopes

HOPHEAD n pl. -S a drug addict

HOPING present participle of hope

HOPLITE n pl. -S a foot soldier of ancient Greece **HOPLITIC** adj

HOPPED past tense of hop

HOPPER n pl. -S one that hops

HOPPING present participle of hop

HOPPLE n -PLED, -PLING, -PLES to hobble

HOPSACK n pl. -S a coarse fabric

HOPTOAD n pl. -S a toad

HORA n pl. -S an Israeli dance

HORAH n pl. -S hora

HORAL adj hourly

HORARY adj hourly

HORDE v HORDED, HORDING, HORDES to gather in a large group

HORDEIN n pl. -S a simple protein

HORIZON n pl. -S the line where the sky seems to meet the earth

HORMONE n pl. -S a secretion of the endocrine organs **HORMONAL, HORMONIC** adj

HORN v -ED, -ING, -S to form a horn (a hard, bonelike projection of the head)

HORNBEAM n pl. -S a small tree

HORNBILL n pl. -S a large-billed bird

HORNBOOK n pl. -S a primer

HORNET n pl. -S a stinging insect

HORNFELS n pl. HORNFELS a silicate rock

HORNIER comparative of horny

HORNIEST superlative of horny

HORNILY adv in a horny manner

HORNITO n pl. -TOS a mound of volcanic matter

HORNLESS adj lacking a horn

HORNLIKE adj resembling a horn

HORNPIPE n pl. -S a musical instrument

HORNPOUT n pl. -S a catfish

HORNTAIL n pl. -S a wasplike insect

HORNWORM n pl. -S the larva of a hawkmoth

HORNWORT n pl. -S an aquatic herb

HORNY adj HORNIER, HORNIEST hornlike in hardness

HOROLOGE n pl. -S a timepiece

HOROLOGY n pl. -GIES the science of measuring time

HORRENT adj bristling; standing erect

HORRIBLE n pl. -S something that causes horror

HORRIBLY adv dreadfully

HORRID adj repulsive **HORRIDLY** adv

HORRIFIC adj causing horror

HORRIFY v -FIED, -FYING, -FIES to cause to feel horror

HORROR n pl. -S a feeling of intense fear or repugnance

HORSE v HORSED, HORSING, HORSES to provide with a horse (a large, hoofed mammal)

HORSECAR *n* pl. -S a streetcar drawn by a horse

HORSEFLY *n* pl. -FLIES a large fly

HORSEMAN *n* pl. -MEN one who rides a horse

HORSEY *adj* HORSIER, HORSIEST horsy

HORSIER comparative of horsy

HORSIEST superlative of horsy

HORSILY *adj* in a horsy manner

HORSING present participle of horse

HORST *n* pl. -S a portion of the earth's crust

HORSTE *n* pl. -S horst

HORSY *adj* HORSIER, HORSIEST resembling a horse

HOSANNA *v* -ED, -ING, -S to praise

HOSE *v* HOSED, HOSING, HOSES to spray with water

HOSE *n* pl. HOSEN stockings or socks

HOSEL *n* pl. -S a part of a golf club

HOSIER *n* pl. -S one that makes hose

HOSIERY *n* pl. -SIERIES hose

HOSING present participle of hose

HOSPICE *n* pl. -S a shelter

HOSPITAL *n* pl. -S a medical institution

HOSPITIA *n/pl* places of shelter

HOSPODAR *n* pl. -S a governor of a region under Turkish rule

HOST *v* -ED, -ING, -S to entertain socially

HOSTAGE *n* pl. -S a person held as security

HOSTEL *v* -ED, -ING, -S to stay at inns overnight while traveling

HOSTELER *n* pl. -S an innkeeper

HOSTELRY *n* pl. -RIES an inn

HOSTESS *v* -ED, -ING, -ES to act as a hostess (a woman who entertains socially)

HOSTILE *n* pl. -S an unfriendly person

HOSTLER *n* pl. -S a person who tends horses or mules

HOSTLY *adj* pertaining to one who hosts

HOT *adj* HOTTER, HOTTEST having a high temperature

HOT *v* HOTTED, HOTTING, HOTS to heat

HOTBED *n* pl. -S a bed of rich soil

HOTBLOOD *n* pl. -S a thoroughbred horse

HOTBOX *n* pl. -ES an overheated bearing of a railroad car

HOTCAKE *n* pl. -S a pancake

HOTCH *v* -ED, -ING, -ES to wiggle

HOTCHPOT *n* pl. -S the combining of properties in order to divide them equally among heirs

HOTDOG *v* -DOGGED, -DOGGING, -DOGS to perform in a showy manner

HOTEL *n* pl. -S a public lodging

HOTELIER *n* pl. -S a hotel manager

HOTELMAN *n* pl. -MEN a hotelier

HOTFOOT *v* -FOOTED, -FOOTING, -FOOTS to hurry

HOTHEAD *n* pl. -S a quick-tempered person

HOTHOUSE *n* pl. -S a heated greenhouse

HOTLY *adv* in a hot manner

HOTNESS *n* pl. -ES the state of being hot

HOTPRESS *v* -ED, -ING, -ES to subject to heat and pressure

HOTROD *n* pl. -S a car modified for high speeds

HOTSHOT *n* pl. -S a showily skillful person

HOTSPUR *n* pl. -S a hothead

HOTTED past tense of hot

HOTTER comparative of hot

HOTTEST superlative of hot

HOTTING present participle of hot

HOTTISH *adj* somewhat hot

HOUDAH *n* pl. -S howdah

HOUND *v* -ED, -ING, -S to pursue relentlessly

HOUNDER *n* pl. -S one that hounds

HOUR *n* pl. -S a period of sixty minutes

HOURI *n* pl. -S a beautiful maiden in Muslim belief

HOURLY *adj* occurring every hour

HOUSE *v* HOUSED, HOUSING, HOUSES to lodge in a house (a building in which people live)

HOUSEBOY *n* pl. -BOYS a male servant

HOUSEFLY *n* pl. -FLIES a common fly

HOUSEFUL *n* pl. -S as much as a house wi hold

HOUSEL *v* -SELED, -SELING, -SELS or -SELLED, -SELLING, -SELS to administer the Eucharist to

HOUSEMAN *n pl.* -MEN a male servant

HOUSER *n pl.* -S one who organizes housing projects

HOUSETOP *n pl.* -S the roof of a house

HOUSING *n pl.* -S any dwelling place

HOVE a past tense of heave

HOVEL *v* -ELED, -ELING, -ELS or -ELLED, -ELLING, -ELS to live in a small, miserable dwelling

HOVER *v* -ED, -ING, -S to hang suspended in the air

HOVERER *n pl.* -S something that hovers

HOW *n pl.* -S a method of doing something

HOWBEIT *adv* nevertheless

HOWDAH *n pl.* -S a seat on an elephant or camel for riders

HOWDIE *n pl.* -S a midwife

HOWDY *n pl.* -DIES howdie

HOWE *n pl.* -S a valley

HOWEVER *adv* nevertheless

HOWF *n pl.* -S a place frequently visited

HOWFF *n pl.* -S howf

HOWITZER *n pl.* -S a short cannon

HOWK *v* -ED, -ING, -S to dig

HOWL *v* -ED, -ING, -S to cry like a dog

HOWLER *n pl.* -S one that howls

HOWLET *n pl.* -S an owl

HOY *n pl.* HOYS a heavy barge or scow

HOYDEN *v* -ED, -ING, -S to act like a tomboy

HOYLE *n pl.* -S a rule book

HUARACHE *n pl.* -S a flat-heeled sandal

HUARACHO *n pl.* -CHOS huarache

HUB *n pl.* -S the center of a wheel

HUBBUB *n pl.* -S an uproar

HUBBY *n pl.* -BIES a husband

HUBCAP *n pl.* -S a covering for the hub of a wheel

HUBRIS *n pl.* -BRISES arrogance

HUCK *n pl.* -S a durable fabric

HUCKLE *n pl.* -S the hip

HUCKSTER *v* -ED, -ING, -S to peddle

HUDDLE *v* -DLED, -DLING, -DLES to crowd together

HUDDLER *n pl.* -S one that huddles

HUE *n pl.* -S color **HUED**, **HUELESS** *adj*

HUFF *v* -ED, -ING, -S to breathe heavily

HUFFISH *adj* sulky

HUFFY *adj* HUFFIER, HUFFIEST easily offended **HUFFILY** *adv*

HUG *v* HUGGED, HUGGING, HUGS to clasp tightly in the arms

HUGE *adj* HUGER, HUGEST very large **HUGELY** *adj*

HUGENESS *n pl.* -ES the quality of being huge

HUGEOUS *adj* huge

HUGER comparative of huge

HUGEST superlative of huge

HUGGABLE *adj* cuddlesome

HUGGED past tense of hug

HUGGER *n pl.* -S one that hugs

HUGGING present participle of hug

HUH *interj* — used to express surprise

HUIC *interj* — used to encourage hunting hounds

HULA *n pl.* -S a Hawaiian dance

HULK *v* -ED, -ING, -S to appear impressively large

HULKY *adj* HULKIER, HULKIEST massive

HULL *v* -ED, -ING, -S to remove the shell from a seed

HULLER *n pl.* -S one that hulls

HULLO *v* -ED, -ING, -S or -ES to hallo

HULLOA *v* -ED, -ING, -S to hallo

HUM *v* HUMMED, HUMMING, HUMS to sing without opening the lips or saying words

HUMAN *n pl.* -S a person

HUMANE *adj* -MANER, -MANEST compassionate **HUMANELY** *adv*

HUMANISE *v* -ISED, -ISING, -ISES to humanize

HUMANISM *n pl.* -S the quality of being human

HUMANIST *n pl.* -S one who studies human nature

HUMANITY *n pl.* -TIES the human race

HUMANIZE *v* -IZED, -IZING, -IZES to make human

HUMANLY *adv* in a human manner

HUMANOID n pl. -S something having human form

HUMATE n pl. -S a chemical salt

HUMBLE adj -BLER, -BLEST modest

HUMBLE v -BLED, -BLING, -BLES to reduce the pride of

HUMBLER n pl. -S one that humbles

HUMBLEST superlative of humble

HUMBLING present participle of humble

HUMBLY adv in a humble manner

HUMBUG v -BUGGED, -BUGGING, -BUGS to deceive

HUMDRUM n pl. -S a dull, boring person

HUMERAL n pl. -S a bone of the shoulder

HUMERUS n pl. -MERI the large bone of the upper arm

HUMIC adj derived from humus

HUMID adj having much humidity

HUMIDIFY v -FIED, -FYING, -FIES to make humid

HUMIDITY n pl. -TIES moisture of the air

HUMIDLY adv in a humid manner

HUMIDOR n pl. -S a cigar case

HUMIFIED adj converted into humus

HUMILITY n pl. -TIES the quality of being humble

HUMMABLE adj capable of being hummed

HUMMED past tense of hum

HUMMER n pl. -S one that hums

HUMMING present participle of hum

HUMMOCK n pl. -S a small hill **HUMMOCKY** adj

HUMOR v -ED, -ING, -S to indulge

HUMORAL adj pertaining to bodily fluids

HUMORFUL adj humorous

HUMORIST n pl. -S a humorous writer or entertainer

HUMOROUS adj funny; witty

HUMOUR v -ED, -ING, -S to humor

HUMP v -ED, -ING, -S to arch into a hump (a rounded protuberance)

HUMPBACK n pl. -S a humped back

HUMPH v -ED, -ING, -S to utter a grunt

HUMPLESS adj lacking a hump

HUMPY adj HUMPIER, HUMPIEST full of humps

HUMUS n pl. -ES decomposed organic matter

HUN n pl. -S a barbarous, destructive person

HUNCH v -ED, -ING, -ES to arch forward

HUNDRED n pl. -S a number

HUNG a past tense of hang

HUNGER v -ED, -ING, -S to crave

HUNGRY adj -GRIER, -GRIEST wanting food **HUNGRILY** adv

HUNK n pl. -S a large piece

HUNKER v -ED, -ING, -S to squat

HUNKY n pl. -KIES an unskilled laborer

HUNNISH adj resembling a hun

HUNT v -ED, -ING, -S to pursue for food or sport **HUNTABLE** adj **HUNTEDLY** adv

HUNTER n pl. -S one that hunts

HUNTING n pl. -S an instance of searching

HUNTRESS n pl. -ES a female hunter

HUNTSMAN n pl. -MEN a hunter

HUP interj — used to mark a marching cadence

HURDIES n/pl the buttocks

HURDLE v -DLED, -DLING, -DLES to jump over

HURDLER n pl. -S one that hurdles

HURDS n/pl hards

HURL v -ED, -ING, -S to throw with great force

HURLER n pl. -S one that hurls

HURLEY n pl. -LEYS hurling

HURLING n pl. -S an Irish game

HURLY n pl. -LIES commotion

HURRAH v -ED, -ING, -S to cheer

HURRAY v -ED, -ING, -S to hurrah

HURRIER n pl. -S one that hurries

HURRY v -RIED, -RYING, -RIES to move swiftly

HURT v HURT, HURTING, HURTS to injure

HURTER n pl. -S one that hurts

HURTFUL adj causing injury

HURTLE v -TLED, -TLING, -TLES to rush violently

HURTLESS adj harmless

HUSBAND v -ED, -ING, -S to spend wisely

HUSH v -ED, -ING, -ES to quiet **HUSHEDLY** adv

HUSHABY	*v* go to sleep — used imperatively to soothe a child
HUSHFUL	*adj* quiet
HUSK	*v* -ED, -ING, -S to remove the husk (the outer covering) from
HUSKER	*n* pl. -S one that husks
HUSKIER	comparative of husky
HUSKIES	pl. of husky
HUSKIEST	superlative of husky
HUSKILY	*adv* in a husky manner
HUSKING	*n* pl. -S a gathering of families to husk corn
HUSKLIKE	*adj* resembling a husk
HUSKY	*adj* -KIER, -KIEST hoarse
HUSKY	*n* pl. -KIES an Eskimo dog
HUSSAR	*n* pl. -S a cavalry soldier
HUSSY	*n* pl. -SIES a lewd woman
HUSTINGS	*n* pl. HUSTINGS a British court
HUSTLE	*v* -TLED, -TLING, -TLES to hurry
HUSTLER	*n* pl. -S one that hustles
HUSWIFE	*n* pl. -WIFES or -WIVES a sewing kit
HUT	*v* HUTTED, HUTTING, HUTS to live in a hut (a simple shelter)
HUTCH	*v* -ED, -ING, -ES to store away
HUTLIKE	*adj* resembling a hut
HUTMENT	*n* pl. -S a group of huts
HUTTED	past tense of hut
HUTTING	present participle of hut
HUTZPA	*n* pl. -S chutzpah
HUTZPAH	*n* pl. -S chutzpah
HUZZA	*v* -ED, -ING, -S to cheer
HUZZAH	*v* -ED, -ING, -S to huzza
HWAN	*n* pl. HWAN a monetary unit of South Korea
HYACINTH	*n* pl. -S a flowering plant
HYAENA	*n* pl. -S hyena **HYAENIC** *adj*
HYALIN	*n* pl. -S hyaline
HYALINE	*n* pl. -S a transparent substance
HYALITE	*n* pl. -S a colorless opal
HYALOGEN	*n* pl. -S a substance found in animal cells
HYALOID	*n* pl. -S a membrane of the eye
HYBRID	*n* pl. -S the offspring of genetically dissimilar parents
HYBRIS	*n* pl. -BRISES hubris

HYDATID	*n* pl. -S a cyst caused by a tapeworm
HYDRA	*n* pl. -DRAS or -DRAE a freshwater polyp
HYDRACID	*n* pl. -S an acid
HYDRAGOG	*n* pl. -S a purgative causing watery discharges
HYDRANT	*n* pl. -S an outlet from a water main
HYDRANTH	*n* pl. -S the oral opening of a hydra
HYDRASE	*n* pl. -S an enzyme
HYDRATE	*v* -DRATED, -DRATING, -DRATES to combine with water
HYDRATOR	*n* pl. -S one that hydrates
HYDRIA	*n* pl. -DRIAE a water jar
HYDRIC	*adj* pertaining to moisture
HYDRID	*n* pl. -S hydride
HYDRIDE	*n* pl. -S a chemical compound
HYDRO	*n* pl. -DROS electricity produced by waterpower
HYDROGEL	*n* pl. -S a colloid
HYDROGEN	*n* pl. -S a gaseous element
HYDROID	*n* pl. -S a polyp
HYDROMEL	*n* pl. -S a mixture of honey and water
HYDRONIC	*adj* pertaining to heating and cooling by water
HYDROPIC	*adj* affected with hydropsy
HYDROPS	*n* pl. -ES hydropsy
HYDROPSY	*n* pl. -SIES dropsy
HYDROSOL	*n* pl. -S an aqueous solution of a colloid
HYDROUS	*adj* containing water
HYDROXY	*adj* containing hydroxyl
HYDROXYL	*n* pl. -S the radical or group containing oxygen and hydrogen
HYENA	*n* pl. -S a wolflike mammal **HYENIC, HYENINE, HYENOID** *adj*
HYETAL	*adj* pertaining to rain
HYGEIST	*n* pl. -S an expert in hygiene
HYGIEIST	*n* pl. -S hygeist
HYGIENE	*n* pl. -S the science of health **HYGIENIC** *adj*
HYING	present participle of hie
HYLA	*n* pl. -S a tree frog

HYLOZOIC *adj* pertaining to the doctrine that life and matter are inseparable

HYMEN *n* pl. -S a vaginal membrane **HYMENAL** *adj*

HYMENEAL *n* pl. -S a wedding song or poem

HYMENIUM *n* pl. -NIA or -NIUMS a layer in certain fungi **HYMENIAL** *adj*

HYMN *v* -ED, -ING, -S to sing a hymn (a song of praise to God)

HYMNAL *n* pl. -S a book of hymns

HYMNARY *n* pl. -RIES a hymnal

HYMNBOOK *n* pl. -S a hymnal

HYMNIST *n* pl. -S one who composes hymns

HYMNLESS *adj* lacking a hymn

HYMNLIKE *adj* resembling a hymn

HYMNODY *n* pl. -DIES the singing of hymns

HYOID *n* pl. -S a bone of the tongue **HYOIDAL, HYOIDEAN** *adj*

HYOSCINE *n* pl. -S a sedative

HYP *n* pl. -S hypochondria

HYPE *n* pl. -S a deception

HYPERGOL *n* pl. -S a rocket fuel

HYPERON *n* pl. -S an atomic particle

HYPEROPE *n* pl. -S a farsighted person

HYPHA *n* pl. -PHAE a threadlike element of a fungus **HYPHAL** *adj*

HYPHEMIA *n* pl. -S deficiency of blood

HYPHEN *v* -ED, -ING, -S to connect words or syllables with a hyphen (a mark of punctuation)

HYPNIC *adj* pertaining to sleep

HYPNOID *adj* pertaining to hypnosis or sleep

HYPNOSIS *n* pl. -NOSES an artificially induced state resembling sleep

HYPNOTIC *n* pl. -S a sleep-inducing drug

HYPO *v* -ED, -ING, -S to inject with a hypodermic needle

HYPOACID *adj* having a lower than normal degree of acidity

HYPODERM *n* pl. -S a skin layer

HYPOGEAL *adj* underground

HYPOGEAN *adj* hypogeal

HYPOGENE *adj* formed underground

HYPOGEUM *n* pl. -GEA an underground chamber

HYPOGYNY *n* pl. -NIES the condition of having flowers with organs situated below the ovary

HYPONEA *n* pl. -S hyponoia

HYPONOIA *n* pl. -S dulled mental activity

HYPOPNEA *n* pl. -S abnormally shallow breathing

HYPOPYON *n* pl. -S an accumulation of pus in the eye

HYPOTHEC *n* pl. -S a type of mortgage

HYPOXIA *n* pl. -S a deficiency of oxygen in body tissue **HYPOXIC** *adj*

HYRACOID *n* pl. -S a hyrax

HYRAX *n* pl. -RAXES or -RACES a small, harelike mammal

HYSON *n* pl. -S a Chinese tea

HYSSOP *n* pl. -S a medicinal herb

HYSTERIA *n* pl. -S uncontrollable excitement or fear

HYSTERIC *n* pl. -S one who is subject to fits of hysteria

HYTE *adj* insane

IAMB *n pl.* -S a type of metrical foot

IAMBIC *n pl.* -S an iamb

IAMBUS *n pl.* -BUSES or -BI an iamb

IATRIC *adj* pertaining to medicine

IATRICAL *adj* iatric

IBEX *n pl.* IBEXES or IBICES a wild goat

IBIDEM *adv* in the same place

IBIS *n pl.* IBISES a wading bird

ICE *v* ICED, ICING, ICES to cover with ice (frozen water)

ICEBERG *n pl.* -S a large floating body of ice

ICEBLINK *n pl.* -S a glare over an ice field

ICEBOAT *n pl.* -S a vehicle that sails on ice

ICEBOUND *adj* surrounded by ice

ICEBOX *n pl.* -ES a cabinet for cooling food

ICECAP *n pl.* -S a covering of ice and snow

ICED past tense of ice

ICEFALL *n pl.* -S a kind of frozen waterfall

ICEHOUSE *n pl.* -S a building for storing ice

ICEKHANA *n pl.* -S an automotive event held on a frozen lake

ICELESS *adj* having no ice

ICELIKE *adj* resembling ice

ICEMAN *n pl.* -MEN a man who supplies ice

ICH *n pl.* ICHS a disease of certain fishes

ICHNITE *n pl.* -S a fossil footprint

ICHOR *n pl.* -S a watery discharge from a wound ICHOROUS *adj*

ICHTHYIC *adj* pertaining to fishes

ICICLE *n pl.* -S a hanging spike of ice ICICLED *adj*

ICIER comparative of icy

ICIEST superlative of icy

ICILY *adv* in an icy manner

ICINESS *n pl.* -ES the state of being icy

ICING *n pl.* -S a sweet mixture for covering cakes

ICKER *n pl.* -S a head of grain

ICKY *adj* ICKIER, ICKIEST repulsive

ICON *n pl.* -S or -ES a representation ICONIC, ICONICAL *adj*

ICTERIC *n pl.* -S a remedy for icterus

ICTERUS *n pl.* -ES a diseased condition of the liver

ICTUS *n pl.* -ES a recurring stress or beat in a poetical form ICTIC *adj*

ICY *adj* ICIER, ICIEST covered with ice

ID *n pl.* -S a part of the psyche

IDEA *n pl.* -S a conception existing in the mind IDEALESS *adj*

IDEAL *n pl.* -S a standard of perfection

IDEALISE *v* -ISED, -ISING, -ISES to idealize

IDEALISM *n pl.* -S the pursuit of noble goals

IDEALIST *n pl.* -S an adherent of idealism

IDEALITY *n pl.* -TIES the state of being perfect; something idealized

IDEALIZE *v* -IZED, -IZING, -IZES to regard as perfect

IDEALLY	*adv* perfectly
IDEALOGY	*n* pl. -GIES ideology
IDEATE	*v* -ATED, -ATING, -ATES to form an idea
IDEATION	*n* pl. -S the act of ideating
IDEATIVE	*adj* pertaining to ideation
IDEM	*adj* the same
IDENTIC	*adj* identical
IDENTIFY	*v* -FIED, -FYING, -FIES to establish the identity of
IDENTITY	*n* pl. -TIES the essential character of a person or thing
IDEOGRAM	*n* pl. -S a type of written symbol
IDEOLOGY	*n* pl. -GIES a systematic body of ideas
IDES	*n* pl. IDES a certain day in the ancient Roman calendar
IDIOCY	*n* pl. -CIES the condition of being an idiot
IDIOLECT	*n* pl. -S one's speech pattern
IDIOM	*n* pl. -S an expression peculiar to a language
IDIOT	*n* pl. -S a mentally deficient person **IDIOTIC** *adj*
IDIOTISM	*n* pl. -S idiocy
IDLE	*adj* IDLER, IDLEST inactive
IDLE	*v* IDLED, IDLING, IDLES to pass time idly
IDLENESS	*n* pl. -ES the state of being idle
IDLER	*n* pl. -S one that idles
IDLESSE	*n* pl. -S idleness
IDLEST	superlative of idle
IDLING	present participle of idle
IDLY	*adv* in an idle manner
IDOCRASE	*n* pl. -S a mineral
IDOL	*n* pl. -S an object of worship
IDOLATER	*n* pl. -S one that worships idols
IDOLATRY	*n* pl. -TRIES the worship of idols
IDOLISE	*v* -ISED, -ISING, -ISES to idolize
IDOLISER	*n* pl. -S one that idolises
IDOLISM	*n* pl. -S idolatry
IDOLIZE	*v* -IZED, -IZING, -IZES to worship
IDOLIZER	*n* pl. -S one that idolizes
IDONEITY	*n* pl. -TIES the state of being idoneous
IDONEOUS	*adj* suitable

IDYL	*n* pl. -S a poem or prose work depicting scenes of rural simplicity
IDYLIST	*n* pl. -S a writer of idyls
IDYLL	*n* pl. -S idyl **IDYLLIC** *adj*
IDYLLIST	*n* pl. -S idylist
IF	*n* pl. -S a possibility
IFFINESS	*n* pl. -ES the state of being iffy
IFFY	*adj* IFFIER, IFFIEST full of uncertainty
IGLOO	*n* pl. -LOOS an Eskimo dwelling
IGLU	*n* pl. -S igloo
IGNATIA	*n* pl. -S a medicinal seed
IGNEOUS	*adj* pertaining to fire
IGNIFY	*v* -FIED, -FYING, -FIES to burn
IGNITE	*v* -NITED, -NITING, -NITES to set on fire
IGNITER	*n* pl. -S one that ignites
IGNITION	*n* pl. -S the act of igniting
IGNITOR	*n* pl. -S igniter
IGNITRON	*n* pl. -S a type of rectifier tube
IGNOBLE	*adj* of low character **IGNOBLY** *adv*
IGNOMINY	*n* pl. -NIES disgrace or dishonor
IGNORANT	*adj* having no knowledge
IGNORE	*v* -NORED, -NORING, -NORES to refuse to notice
IGNORER	*n* pl. -S one that ignores
IGUANA	*n* pl. -S a tropical lizard
IGUANIAN	*n* pl. -S a lizard related to the iguana
IHRAM	*n* pl. -S the garb worn by Muslim pilgrims
IKEBANA	*n* pl. -S the Japanese art of flower arranging
IKON	*n* pl. -S icon
ILEA	pl. of ileum
ILEAC	*adj* pertaining to the ileum
ILEAL	*adj* ileac
ILEITIS	*n* pl. ILEITIDES inflammation of the ileum
ILEUM	*n* pl. ILEA a part of the small intestine
ILEUS	*n* pl. -ES intestinal obstruction
ILEX	*n* pl. -ES a holly
ILIA	pl. of ilium
ILIAC	*adj* pertaining to the ilium
ILIAD	*n* pl. -S a long poem

ILIAL   *adj* iliac

ILIUM   *n* pl. ILIA a bone of the pelvis

ILK   *n* pl. -S a class or kind

ILKA   *adj* each

ILL   *n* pl. -S an evil

ILLATION   *n* pl. -S the act of inferring

ILLATIVE   *n* pl. -S a word or phrase introducing an inference

ILLEGAL   *adj* prohibited by law

ILLICIT   *adj* not permitted

ILLINIUM   *n* pl. -S a radioactive element

ILLIQUID   *adj* not readily convertible into cash

ILLITE   *n* pl. -S a group of minerals **ILLITIC** *adj*

ILLNESS   *n* pl. -ES sickness

ILLOGIC   *n* pl. -S absence of logic

ILLUME   *v* -LUMED, -LUMING, -LUMES to illuminate

ILLUMINE   *v* -MINED, -MINING, -MINES to illuminate

ILLUSION   *n* pl. -S a false perception

ILLUSIVE   *adj* illusory

ILLUSORY   *adj* based on illusion

ILLUVIUM   *n* pl. -VIA or -VIUMS a type of material accumulated in soil **ILLUVIAL** *adj*

ILLY   *adv* badly

ILMENITE   *n* pl. -S a mineral

IMAGE   *v* -AGED, -AGING, -AGES to imagine

IMAGERY   *n* pl. -ERIES mental pictures

IMAGINAL   *adj* pertaining to an imago

IMAGINE   *v* -INED, -INING, -INES to form a mental picture of

IMAGINER   *n* pl. -S one that imagines

IMAGING   present participle of image

IMAGINING   present participle of imagine

IMAGISM   *n* pl. -S a movement in poetry

IMAGIST   *n* pl. -S an adherent of imagism

IMAGO   *n* pl. -GOES an adult insect

IMAM   *n* pl. -S a Muslim priest

IMAMATE   *n* pl. -S the office of an imam

IMARET   *n* pl. -S a Turkish inn

IMAUM   *n* pl. -S imam

IMBALM   *v* -ED, -ING, -S to embalm

IMBALMER   *n* pl. -S embalmer

IMBARK   *v* -ED, -ING, -S to embark

IMBECILE   *n* pl. -S a mentally deficient person

IMBED   *v* -BEDDED, -BEDDING, -BEDS to embed

IMBIBE   *v* -BIBED, -BIBING, -BIBES to drink

IMBIBER   *n* pl. -S one that imbibes

IMBITTER   *v* -ED, -ING, -S to embitter

IMBLAZE   *v* -BLAZED, -BLAZING, -BLAZES to emblaze

IMBODY   *v* -BODIED, -BODYING, -BODIES to embody

IMBOLDEN   *v* -ED, -ING, -S to embolden

IMBOSOM   *v* -ED, -ING, -S to embosom

IMBOWER   *v* -ED, -ING, -S to embower

IMBROWN   *v* -ED, -ING, -S to embrown

IMBRUE   *v* -BRUED, -BRUING, -BRUES to stain

IMBRUTE   *v* -BRUTED, -BRUTING, -BRUTES to make brutal

IMBUE   *v* -BUED, -BUING, -BUES to make thoroughly wet

IMID   *n* pl. -S imide

IMIDE   *n* pl. -S a chemical compound **IMIDIC** *adj*

IMIDO   *adj* containing an imide

IMINE   *n* pl. -S a chemical compound

IMINO   *adj* containing an imine

IMITABLE   *adj* capable of being imitated

IMITATE   *v* -TATED, -TATING, -TATES to behave in the same way as

IMITATOR   *n* pl. -S one that imitates

IMMANE   *adj* great in size

IMMANENT   *adj* existing within

IMMATURE   *n* pl. -S an individual that is not fully grown or developed

IMMENSE   *adj* -MENSER, -MENSEST great in size

IMMERGE   *v* -MERGED, -MERGING, -MERGES to immerse

IMMERSE   *v* -MERSED, -MERSING, -MERSES to plunge into a liquid

IMMESH   *v* -ED, -ING, -ES to enmesh

IMMIES   pl. of immy

IMMINENT   *adj* ready to take place

IMMINGLE   *v* -GLED, -GLING, -GLES to blend

IMMIX   *v* -ED, -ING, -ES to mix in

IMMOBILE *adj* incapable of being moved

IMMODEST *adj* not modest

IMMOLATE *v* -LATED, -LATING, -LATES to kill as a sacrifice

IMMORAL *adj* contrary to established morality

IMMORTAL *n pl.* -S one who is not subject to death

IMMOTILE *adj* lacking mobility

IMMUNE *n pl.* -S one who is protected from a disease

IMMUNISE *v* -NISED, -NISING, -NISES to immunize

IMMUNITY *n pl.* -TIES the state of being protected from a disease

IMMUNIZE *v* -NIZED, -NIZING, -NIZES to protect from a disease

IMMURE *v* -MURED, -MURING, -MURES to imprison

IMMY *n pl.* -MIES a type of playing marble

IMP *v* -ED, -ING, -S to graft feathers onto a bird's wing

IMPACT *v* -ED, -ING, -S to pack firmly together

IMPACTER *n pl.* -S one that impacts

IMPACTOR *n pl.* -S impacter

IMPAINT *v* -ED, -ING, -S to paint or depict

IMPAIR *v* -ED, -ING, -S to make worse

IMPAIRER *n pl.* -S one that impairs

IMPALA *n pl.* -S an African antelope

IMPALE *v* -PALED, -PALING, -PALES to pierce with a pointed object

IMPALER *n pl.* -S one that impales

IMPANEL *v* -ELED, -ELING, -ELS or -ELLED, -ELLING, -ELS to enter on a list for jury duty

IMPARITY *n pl.* -TIES lack of equality

IMPARK *v* -ED, -ING, -S to confine in a park

IMPART *v* -ED, -ING, -S to make known

IMPARTER *n pl.* -S one that imparts

IMPASSE *n pl.* -S a road or passage having no exit

IMPASTE *v* -PASTED, -PASTING, -PASTES to make into a paste

IMPASTO *n pl.* -TOS a painting technique

IMPAVID *adj* brave

IMPAWN *v* -ED, -ING, -S to pawn

IMPEACH *v* -ED, -ING, -ES to charge with misconduct in office

IMPEARL *v* -ED, -ING, -S to make pearly

IMPEDE *v* -PEDED, -PEDING, -PEDES to obstruct the progress of

IMPEDER *n pl.* -S one that impedes

IMPEL *v* -PELLED, -PELLING, -PELS to force into action

IMPELLER *n pl.* -S one that impels

IMPELLOR *n pl.* -S impeller

IMPEND *v* -ED, -ING, -S to be imminent

IMPERIA a *pl.* of imperium

IMPERIAL *n pl.* -S an emperor or empress

IMPERIL *v* -ILED, -ILING, -ILS or -ILLED, -ILLING, -ILS to place in jeopardy

IMPERIUM *n pl.* -RIUMS or -RIA absolute power

IMPETIGO *n pl.* -GOS a skin disease

IMPETUS *n pl.* -ES an impelling force

IMPHEE *n pl.* -S an African grass

IMPI *n pl.* -S a body of warriors

IMPIETY *n pl.* -TIES lack of piety

IMPING *n pl.* -S the process of grafting

IMPINGE *v* -PINGED, -PINGING, -PINGES to collide

IMPINGER *n pl.* -S one that impinges

IMPIOUS *adj* not pious

IMPISH *adj* mischievous **IMPISHLY** *adv*

IMPLANT *v* -ED, -ING, -S to set securely

IMPLEAD *v* -ED, -ING, -S to sue in a court of law

IMPLEDGE *v* -PLEDGED, -PLEDGING, -PLEDGES to pawn

IMPLICIT *adj* implied

IMPLIED past tense of imply

IMPLIES present 3d person sing. of imply

IMPLODE *v* -PLODED, -PLODING, -PLODES to collapse inward

IMPLORE *v* -PLORED, -PLORING, -PLORES to beg for urgently

IMPLORER *n pl.* -S one that implores

IMPLY *v* -PLIED, -PLYING, -PLIES to indicate or suggest indirectly

IMPOLICY *n pl.* -CIES an unwise course of action

IMPOLITE *adj* not polite

IMPONE   v -PONED, -PONING, -PONES to wager

IMPOROUS   adj extremely dense

IMPORT   v -ED, -ING, -S to bring into a country from abroad

IMPORTER   n pl. -S one that imports

IMPOSE   v -POSED, -POSING, -POSES to establish as compulsory

IMPOSER   n pl. -S one that imposes

IMPOST   v -ED, -ING, -S to determine customs duties

IMPOSTER   n pl. -S impostor

IMPOSTOR   n pl. -S one that poses as another for deceptive purposes

IMPOTENT   n pl. -S one that is powerless

IMPOUND   v -ED, -ING, -S to seize and retain in legal custody

IMPOWER   v -ED, -ING, -S to empower

IMPREGN   v -ED, -ING, -S to make pregnant

IMPRESA   n pl. -S a type of emblem

IMPRESE   n pl. -S impresa

IMPRESS   v -ED, -ING, -ES to affect strongly

IMPREST   n pl. -S a loan or advance of money

IMPRIMIS   adv in the first place

IMPRINT   v -ED, -ING, -S to produce a mark by pressure

IMPRISON   v -ED, -ING, -S to confine

IMPROPER   adj not proper

IMPROVE   v -PROVED, -PROVING, -PROVES to make better

IMPROVER   n pl. -S one that improves

IMPUDENT   adj offensively bold or disrespectful

IMPUGN   v -ED, -ING, -S to make insinuations against

IMPUGNER   n pl. -S one that impugns

IMPULSE   v -PULSED, -PULSING, -PULSES to give impetus to

IMPUNITY   n pl. -TIES exemption from penalty

IMPURE   adj not pure **IMPURELY** adv

IMPURITY   n pl. -TIES something that is impure

IMPUTE   v -PUTED, -PUTING, -PUTES to credit to a person or a cause

IMPUTER   n pl. -S one that imputes

IN   v INNED, INNING, INS to harvest

INACTION   n pl. -S lack of action

INACTIVE   adj not active

INANE   adj INANER, INANEST nonsensical **INANELY** adv

INANE   n pl. -S empty space

INANITY   n pl. -TIES something that is inane

INAPT   adj not apt **INAPTLY** adv

INARABLE   adj not arable

INARCH   v -ED, -ING, -ES to graft with in a certain way

INARM   v -ED, -ING, -S to encircle with the arms

INBEING   n pl. -S the state of being inherent

INBOARD   n pl. -S a type of boat motor

INBORN   adj existing in one from birth

INBOUND   adj approaching a destination

INBOUNDS   adj being within certain boundaries

INBREED   v -BRED, -BREEDING, -BREEDS to breed closely related stock

INBUILT   adj forming an integral part of a structure

INBURST   n pl. -S the act of bursting inward

INBY   adv inward

INBYE   adv inby

INCAGE   v -CAGED, -CAGING, -CAGES to encage

INCASE   v -CASED, -CASING, -CASES to encase

INCENSE   v -CENSED, -CENSING, -CENSES to make angry

INCEPT   v -ED, -ING, -S to take in

INCEPTOR   n pl. -S one that incepts

INCEST   n pl. -S sexual intercourse between closely related persons

INCH   v -ED, -ING, -ES to move very slowly

INCHMEAL   adv little by little

INCHOATE   adj being in an early stage

INCHWORM   n pl. -S a type of worm

INCIDENT   n pl. -S an event

INCIPIT   n pl. -S the opening words of a text

INCISE   v -CISED, -CISING, -CISES to cut into

INCISION   n pl. -S the act of incising

INCISIVE	*adj* penetrating
INCISOR	*n* pl. -S a cutting tooth
INCISORY	*adj* adapted for cutting
INCISURE	*n* pl. -S a notch or cleft of a body part
INCITANT	*n* pl. -S something that incites
INCITE	*v* -CITED, -CITING, -CITES to arouse to action
INCITER	*n* pl. -S one that incites
INCIVIL	*adj* discourteous
INCLASP	*v* -ED, -ING, -S to enclasp
INCLINE	*v* -CLINED, -CLINING, -CLINES to slant
INCLINER	*n* pl. -S one that inclines
INCLIP	*v* -CLIPPED, -CLIPPING, -CLIPS to clasp
INCLOSE	*v* -CLOSED, -CLOSING, -CLOSES to enclose
INCLOSER	*n* pl. -S one that incloses
INCLUDE	*v* -CLUDED, -CLUDING, -CLUDES to have as a part
INCOG	*n* pl. -S a disguised person
INCOME	*n* pl. -S a sum of money earned regularly
INCOMER	*n* pl. -S one that comes in
INCOMING	*n* pl. -S an arrival
INCONNU	*n* pl. -S a large food fish
INCONY	*adj* pretty
INCORPSE	*v* -CORPSED, -CORPSING, -CORPSES to become combined with
INCREASE	*v* -CREASED, -CREASING, -CREASES to make or become greater
INCREATE	*adj* not created
INCROSS	*n* pl. -ES an individual produced by inbreeding
INCRUST	*v* -ED, -ING, -S to encrust
INCUBATE	*v* -BATED, -BATING, -BATES to warm eggs for hatching
INCUBUS	*n* pl. -BI or -BUSES a demon
INCUDAL	*adj* pertaining to the incus
INCUDATE	*adj* incudal
INCUDES	pl. of incus
INCULT	*adj* uncultivated
INCUMBER	*v* -ED, -ING, -S to encumber
INCUR	*v* -CURRED, -CURRING, -CURS to bring upon oneself
INCURVE	*v* -CURVED, -CURVING, -CURVES to curve inward
INCUS	*n* pl. INCUDES a bone in the middle ear
INCUSE	*v* -CUSED, -CUSING, -CUSES to mark by stamping
INDABA	*n* pl. -S a meeting of South African tribes
INDAGATE	*v* -GATED, -GATING, -GATES to investigate
INDAMIN	*n* pl. -S indamine
INDAMINE	*n* pl. -S a chemical compound
INDEBTED	*adj* beholden
INDECENT	*adj* -CENTER, -CENTEST not decent
INDEED	*adv* in truth
INDENE	*n* pl. -S a hydrocarbon
INDENT	*v* -ED, -ING, -S to cut or tear irregularly
INDENTER	*n* pl. -S one that indents
INDENTOR	*n* pl. -S indenter
INDEVOUT	*adj* not devout
INDEX	*n* pl. INDEXES or INDICES a type of reference guide at the end of a book
INDEX	*v* -ED, -ING, -ES to provide with an index
INDEXER	*n* pl. -S one that indexes
INDICAN	*n* pl. -S a chemical compound
INDICANT	*n* pl. -S something that indicates
INDICATE	*v* -CATED, -CATING, -CATES to point out
INDICES	a pl. of index
INDICIA	*n* pl. -S a distinctive mark
INDICIUM	*n* pl. -S an indicia
INDICT	*v* -ED, -ING, -S to charge with a crime
INDICTEE	*n* pl. -S one that is indicted
INDICTER	*n* pl. -S one that indicts
INDICTOR	*n* pl. -S indicter
INDIGEN	*n* pl. -S indigene
INDIGENE	*n* pl. -S a native
INDIGENT	*n* pl. -S a needy person
INDIGN	*adj* disgraceful **INDIGNLY** *adv*
INDIGO	*n* pl. -GOS or -GOES a blue dye
INDIGOID	*n* pl. -S a blue dye
INDIRECT	*adj* not direct

INDITE   v -DITED, -DITING, -DITES to write or compose

INDITER   n pl. -S one that indites

INDIUM   n pl. -S a metallic element

INDOCILE   adj not docile

INDOL   n pl. -S indole

INDOLE   n pl. -S a chemical compound

INDOLENT   adj lazy

INDOOR   adj pertaining to the interior of a building

INDOORS   adv in or into a house

INDORSE   v -DORSED, -DORSING, -DORSES to endorse

INDORSEE   n pl. -S endorsee

INDORSER   n pl. -S endorser

INDORSING   present participle of indorse

INDORSOR   n pl. -S endorsor

INDOW   v -ED, -ING, -S to endow

INDOXYL   n -S a chemical compound

INDRAFT   n pl. -S an inward flow or current

INDRAWN   adj drawn in

INDRI   n pl. -S a short-tailed lemur

INDUCE   v -DUCED, -DUCING, -DUCES to influence into doing something

INDUCER   n pl. -S one that induces

INDUCT   v -ED, -ING, -S to bring into military service

INDUCTEE   n pl. -S one that is inducted

INDUCTOR   n pl. -S one that inducts

INDUE   v -DUED, -DUING, -DUES to endue

INDULGE   v -DULGED, -DULGING, -DULGES to yield to the desire of

INDULGER   n pl. -S one that indulges

INDULIN   n pl. -S induline

INDULINE   n pl. -S a blue dye

INDULT   n pl. -S a privilege granted by the pope

INDURATE   v -RATED, -RATING, -RATES to make hard

INDUSIUM   n pl. -SIA an enclosing membrane **INDUSIAL** adj

INDUSTRY   n pl. -TRIES a group of productive enterprises

INDWELL   v -DWELT, -DWELLING, -DWELLS to live within

INEARTH   v -ED, -ING, -S to bury

INEDIBLE   adj not fit to be eaten

INEDITA   n/pl unpublished literary works

INEDITED   adj not published

INEPT   adj not suitable **INEPTLY** adv

INEQUITY   n pl. -TIES unfairness

INERRANT   adj free from error

INERT   n pl. -S something that lacks active properties

INERTIA   n pl. -TIAS or -TIAE the tendency of a body to resist acceleration **INERTIAL** adj

INERTLY   adv inactively

INEXACT   adj not exact

INEXPERT   n pl. -S a novice

INFAMOUS   adj having a vile reputation

INFAMY   n pl. -MIES the state of being infamous

INFANCY   n pl. -CIES the state of being an infant

INFANT   n pl. -S a child in the earliest stages of life

INFANTA   n pl. -S a daughter of a Spanish or Portuguese monarch

INFANTE   n pl. -S a younger son of a Spanish or Portuguese monarch

INFANTRY   n pl. -TRIES a branch of the army composed of foot soldiers

INFARCT   n pl. -S an area of dead or dying tissue

INFARE   n pl. -S a reception for newlyweds

INFAUNA   n pl. -NAS or -NAE fauna living on a soft sea floor **INFAUNAL** adj

INFECT   v -ED, -ING, -S to contaminate with disease-producing germs

INFECTER   n pl. -S one that infects

INFECTOR   n pl. -S infecter

INFECUND   adj barren

INFEOFF   v -ED, -ING, -S to enfeoff

INFER   v -FERRED, -FERRING, -FERS to reach or derive by reasoning

INFERIOR   n pl. -S one of lesser rank

INFERNAL   adj pertaining to hell

INFERNO   n pl. -NOS a place that resembles or suggests hell

INFERRED   past tense of infer

INFERRER   n pl. -S one that infers

INFERRING   present participle of infer

INFEST *v* -ED, -ING, -S to overrun in large numbers

INFESTER *n* pl. -S one that infests

INFIDEL *n* pl. -S one who has no religious faith

INFIELD *n* pl. -S a part of a baseball field

INFINITE *n* pl. -S something that has no limits

INFINITY *n* pl. -TIES the state of having no limits

INFIRM *v* -ED, -ING, -S to weaken or destroy the validity of

INFIRMLY *adv* in a feeble manner

INFIX *v* -ED, -ING, -ES to implant

INFIXION *n* pl. -S the act of infixing

INFLAME *v* -FLAMED, -FLAMING, -FLAMES to set on fire

INFLAMER *n* pl. -S one that inflames

INFLATE *v* -FLATED, -FLATING, -FLATES to cause to expand by filling with gas or air

INFLATER *n* pl. -S one that inflates

INFLATOR *n* pl. -S inflater

INFLECT *v* -ED, -ING, -S to bend

INFLEXED *adj* bent inward

INFLICT *v* -ED, -ING, -S to cause to be endured; impose

INFLIGHT *adj* done during an air voyage

INFLOW *n* pl. -S the act of flowing in

INFLUENT *n* pl. -S a tributary

INFLUX *n* pl. -ES a flowing in

INFO *n* pl. -FOS information

INFOLD *v* -ED, -ING, -S to fold inward

INFOLDER *n* pl. -S one that infolds

INFORM *v* -ED, -ING, -S to supply with information

INFORMAL *adj* marked by the absence of formality or ceremony

INFORMER *n* pl. -S one that informs

INFRA *adv* below

INFRACT *v* -ED, -ING, -S to break a legal rule

INFRARED *n* pl. -S a part of the invisible spectrum

INFRINGE *v* -FRINGED, -FRINGING, -FRINGES to violate an oath or a law

INFRUGAL *adj* not frugal

INFUSE *v* -FUSED, -FUSING, -FUSES to permeate with something

INFUSER *n* pl. -S one that infuses

INFUSION *n* pl. -S the act of infusing

INFUSIVE *adj* capable of infusing

INGATE *n* pl. -S a channel by which molten metal enters a mold

INGATHER *v* -ED, -ING, -S to gather in

INGENUE *n* pl. -S a naive young woman

INGEST *v* -ED, -ING, -S to take into the body

INGESTA *n/pl* ingested material

INGLE *n* pl. -S a fire

INGOING *adj* entering

INGOT *v* -ED, -ING, -S to shape into a convenient form for storage

INGRAFT *v* -ED, -ING, -S to engraft

INGRAIN *v* -ED, -ING, -S to impress firmly on the mind

INGRATE *n* pl. -S an ungrateful person

INGRESS *n* pl. -ES the act of entering

INGROUP *n* pl. -S a group united by common interests

INGROWN *adj* grown into the flesh

INGROWTH *n* pl. -S growth inward

INGUINAL *adj* pertaining to the groin

INGULF *v* -ED, -ING, -S to engulf

INHABIT *v* -ED, -ING, -S to live in

INHALANT *n* pl. -S something that is inhaled

INHALE *v* -HALED, -HALING, -HALES to take into the lungs

INHALER *n* pl. -S one that inhales

INHAUL *n* pl. -S a line for bringing in a sail

INHAULER *n* pl. -S an inhaul

INHERE *v* -HERED, -HERING, -HERES to be inherent

INHERENT *adj* existing in something as an essential characteristic

INHERIT *v* -ED, -ING, -S to receive by legal succession

INHESION *n* pl. -S the state of inhering

INHIBIT *v* -ED, -ING, -S to restrain or hold back

INHUMAN *adj* lacking desirable human qualities

INHUMANE *adj* not humane

INHUME   v -HUMED, -HUMING, -HUMES to bury

INHUMER   n pl. -S one that inhumes

INIMICAL   adj unfriendly

INION   n pl. INIA a part of the skull

INIQUITY   n pl. -TIES a gross injustice

INITIAL   v -TIALED, -TIALING, -TIALS or -TIALLED, -TIALLING, -TIALS to mark with the first letters of one's name

INITIATE   v -ATED, -ATING, -ATES to originate

INJECT   v -ED, -ING, -S to force a fluid into

INJECTOR   n pl. -S one that injects

INJURE   v -JURED, -JURING, -JURES to do or cause injury to

INJURER   n pl. -S one that injures

INJURY   n pl. -RIES harm inflicted or suffered

INK   v -ED, -ING, -S to mark with ink (a colored fluid used for writing)

INKBERRY   n pl. -RIES a small shrub

INKBLOT   n pl. -S a blotted pattern of spilled ink

INKER   n pl. -S one that inks

INKHORN   n pl. -S a small container for ink

INKIER   comparative of inky

INKIEST   superlative of inky

INKINESS   n pl. -ES the state of being inky

INKLE   n pl. -S a tape used for trimming

INKLESS   adj being without ink

INKLIKE   adj resembling ink

INKLING   n pl. -S a slight suggestion

INKPOT   n pl. -S an inkwell

INKSTAND   n pl. -S an inkwell

INKWELL   n pl. -S a small container for ink

INKWOOD   n pl. -S an evergreen tree

INKY   adj INKIER, INKIEST resembling ink

INLACE   v -LACED, -LACING, -LACES to enlace

INLAID   past tense of inlay

INLAND   n pl. -S the interior of a region

INLANDER   n pl. -S one living in the interior of a region

INLAY   v -LAID, -LAYING, -LAYS to set into a surface

INLAYER   n pl. -S one that inlays

INLET   v -LET, -LETTING, -LETS to insert

INLIER   n pl. -S a type of rock formation

INLY   adv inwardly

INMATE   n pl. -S one who is confined to an institution

INMESH   v -ED, -ING, -ES to enmesh

INMOST   adj farthest within

INN   v -ED, -ING, -S to put up at an inn (a public lodging house)

INNARDS   n/pl the internal organs

INNATE   adj inborn INNATELY adv

INNED   past tense of in

INNER   n pl. -S something that is within

INNERLY   adv inwardly

INNERVE   v -NERVED, -NERVING, -NERVES to stimulate

INNING   n pl. -S a division of a baseball game

INNLESS   adj having no inns

INNOCENT   adj -CENTER, -CENTEST free from guilt or sin

INNOCENT   n pl. -S an innocent person

INNOVATE   v -VATED, -VATING, -VATES to introduce something new

INNUENDO   v -ED, -ING, -S or -ES to make a derogatory implication

INOCULUM   n pl. -LA or -LUMS the material used in an inoculation

INOSITE   n pl. -S inositol

INOSITOL   n pl. -S an alcohol found in plant and animal tissue

INPHASE   adj having matching electrical phases

INPOUR   v -ED, -ING, -S to pour in

INPUT   v -PUTTED, -PUTTING, -PUTS to enter data into a computer

INQUEST   n pl. -S a legal inquiry

INQUIET   v -ED, -ING, -S to disturb

INQUIRE   v -QUIRED, -QUIRING, -QUIRES to ask about

INQUIRER   n pl. -S one that inquires

INQUIRY   n pl. -RIES a question

INROAD   n pl. -S a hostile invasion

INRUSH   n pl. -ES a rushing in

INSANE   adj -SANER, -SANEST mentally unsound INSANELY adv

INSANITY *n* pl. -TIES the state of being insane; something utterly foolish

INSCRIBE *v* -SCRIBED, -SCRIBING, -SCRIBES to write or engrave as a lasting record

INSCROLL *v* -ED, -ING, -S to enscroll

INSCULP *v* -ED, -ING, -S to engrave

INSEAM *n* pl. -S an inner seam

INSECT *n* pl. -S any of a class of small invertebrate animals

INSECTAN *adj* pertaining to insects

INSECURE *adj* unsafe

INSERT *v* -ED, -ING, -S to put in

INSERTER *n* pl. -S one that inserts

INSET *v* -SETTED, -SETTING, -SETS to insert

INSETTER *n* pl. -S one that inserts

INSHEATH *v* -ED, -ING, -S to ensheath

INSHORE *adj* near the shore

INSHRINE *v* -SHRINED, -SHRINING, -SHRINES to enshrine

INSIDE *n* pl. -S something that lies within

INSIDER *n* pl. -S an accepted member of a clique

INSIGHT *n* pl. -S a perception of the inner nature of things

INSIGNE *n* pl. INSIGNIA an insignia

INSIGNIA *n* pl. -S an emblem of authority or honor

INSIPID *adj* dull and uninteresting

INSIST *v* -ED, -ING, -S to be resolute on some matter

INSISTER *n* pl. -S one that insists

INSNARE *v* -SNARED, -SNARING, -SNARES to ensnare

INSNARER *n* pl. -S ensnarer

INSOFAR *adv* to such an extent

INSOLATE *v* -LATED, -LATING, -LATES to expose to sunlight

INSOLE *n* pl. -S the inner sole of a boot or shoe

INSOLENT *n* pl. -S an extremely rude person

INSOMNIA *n* pl. -S chronic inability to sleep

INSOMUCH *adv* to such a degree

INSOUL *v* -ED, -ING, -S to ensoul

INSPAN *v* -SPANNED, -SPANNING, -SPANS to harness or yoke to a vehicle

INSPECT *v* -ED, -ING, -S to look carefully at or over

INSPHERE *v* -SPHERED, -SPHERING, -SPHERES to ensphere

INSPIRE *v* -SPIRED, -SPIRING, -SPIRES to animate the mind or emotions of

INSPIRER *n* pl. -S one that inspires

INSPIRIT *v* -ED, -ING, -S to fill with spirit or life

INSTABLE *adj* unstable

INSTAL *v* -STALLED, -STALLING, -STALS to install

INSTALL *v* -ED, -ING, -S to place in position for use

INSTANCE *v* -STANCED, -STANCING, -STANCES to cite as an example

INSTANCY *n* pl. -CIES urgency

INSTANT *n* pl. -S a very short time

INSTAR *v* -STARRED, -STARRING, -STARS to adorn with stars

INSTATE *v* -STATED, -STATING, -STATES to place in office

INSTEAD *adv* as a substitute or equivalent

INSTEP *n* pl. -S a part of the foot

INSTIL *v* -STILLED, -STILLING, -STILS to instill

INSTILL *v* -ED, -ING, -S to infuse slowly

INSTINCT *n* pl. -S an inborn behavioral pattern

INSTROKE *n* pl. -S an inward stroke

INSTRUCT *v* -ED, -ING, -S to supply with knowledge

INSULANT *n* pl. -S an insulating material

INSULAR *n* pl. -S an islander

INSULATE *v* -LATED, -LATING, -LATES to separate with nonconducting material

INSULIN *n* pl. -S a hormone

INSULT *v* -ED, -ING, -S to treat offensively

INSULTER *n* pl. -S one that insults

INSURANT *n* pl. -S one who is insured

INSURE *v* -SURED, -SURING, -SURES to guarantee against loss

INSURED *n* pl. -S one who is insured

INSURER   *n* pl. -S one that insures

INSURING   present participle of insure

INSWATHE   *v* -SWATHED, -SWATHING, -SWATHES to enswathe

INSWEPT   *adj* narrowed in front

INTACT   *adj* not damaged in any way

INTAGLIO   *n* pl. -GLIOS or -GLI an incised or sunken design

INTAKE   *n* pl. -S the act of taking in

INTARSIA   *n* pl. -S a decorative technique

INTEGER   *n* pl. -S a whole number

INTEGRAL   *n* pl. -S a total unit

INTEND   *v* -ED, -ING, -S to have as a specific aim or purpose

INTENDED   *n* pl. -S one's spouse to-be

INTENDER   *n* pl. -S one that intends

INTENSE   *adj* -TENSER, -TENSEST existing in an extreme degree

INTENT   *n* pl. -S a purpose

INTENTLY   *adv* in an unwavering manner

INTER   *v* -TERRED, -TERRING, -TERS to bury

INTERACT   *v* -ED, -ING, -S to act on each other

INTERCOM   *n* pl. -S a type of communication system

INTERCUT   *v* -CUT, -CUTTING, -CUTS to alternate camera shots

INTEREST   *v* -ED, -ING, -S to engage the attention of

INTERIM   *n* pl. -S an interval

INTERIOR   *n* pl. -S the inside

INTERLAP   *v* -LAPPED, -LAPPING, -LAPS to lap one over another

INTERLAY   *v* -LAID, -LAYING, -LAYS to place between

INTERMIT   *v* -MITTED, -MITTING, -MITS to stop temporarily

INTERMIX   *v* -ED, -ING, -ES to mix together

INTERN   *v* -ED, -ING, -S to confine during a war

INTERNAL   *n* pl. -S an inner attribute

INTERNE   *n* pl. -S a recent medical school graduate on a hospital staff

INTERNEE   *n* pl. -S one who has been interned

INTERRED   past tense of inter

INTERREX   *n* pl. -REGES a type of sovereign

INTERRING   present participle of inter

INTERSEX   *n* pl. -ES a person having characteristics of both sexes

INTERTIE   *n* pl. -S a type of electrical connection

INTERVAL   *n* pl. -S a space of time between periods or events

INTERWAR   *adj* happening between wars

INTHRAL   *v* -THRALLED, -THRALLING, -THRALS to enthrall

INTHRALL   *v* -ED, -ING, -S to enthrall

INTHRONE   *v* -THRONED, -THRONING, -THRONES to enthrone

INTIMA   *n* pl. -MAE or -MAS the innermost layer of an organ INTIMAL *adj*

INTIMACY   *n* pl. -CIES the state of being closely associated

INTIMATE   *v* -MATED, -MATING, -MATES to make known indirectly

INTIME   *adj* cozy

INTINE   *n* pl. -S the inner wall of a spore

INTITLE   *v* -TLED, -TLING, -TLES to entitle

INTITULE   *v* -ULED, -ULING, -ULES to entitle

INTO   *prep* to the inside of

INTOMB   *v* -ED, -ING, -S to entomb

INTONATE   *v* -NATED, -NATING, -NATES to intone

INTONE   *v* -TONED, -TONING, -TONES to speak in a singing voice

INTONER   *n* pl. -S one that intones

INTORT   *v* -ED, -ING, -S to twist inward

INTOWN   *adj* located in the center of a city

INTRADOS   *n* pl. -S the inner curve of an arch

INTRANT   *n* pl. -S an entrant

INTREAT   *v* -ED, -ING, -S to entreat

INTRENCH   *v* -ED, -ING, -ES to entrench

INTREPID   *adj* fearless

INTRIGUE   *v* -TRIGUED, -TRIGUING, -TRIGES to arouse the curiosity of

INTRO   *n* pl. -TROS an introduction

INTROFY   *v* -FIED, -FYING, -FIES to increase the wetting properties of

INTROIT   *n* pl. -S music sung at the beginning of a worship service

INTROMIT	v -MITTED, -MITTING, -MITS to put in	**INVERTOR**	n pl. -S a type of electrical device
INTRORSE	adj facing inward	**INVEST**	v -ED, -ING, -S to commit something of value for future profit
INTRUDE	v -TRUDED, -TRUDING, -TRUDES to thrust or force oneself in		
INTRUDER	n pl. -S one that intrudes	**INVESTOR**	n pl. -S one that invests
INTRUST	v -ED, -ING, -S to entrust	**INVIABLE**	adj not viable **INVIABLY** adv
INTUBATE	v -BATED, -BATING, -BATES to insert a tube into	**INVIRILE**	adj not virile
		INVISCID	adj not viscid
INTUIT	v -ED, -ING, -S to know without conscious reasoning	**INVITAL**	adj not vital
		INVITE	v -VITED, -VITING, -VITES to request the presence of
INTURN	n pl. -S a turning inward **INTURNED** adj		
INTWINE	v -TWINED, -TWINING, -TWINES to entwine	**INVITEE**	n pl. -S one that is invited
		INVITER	n pl. -S one that invites
INTWIST	v -ED, -ING, -S to entwist	**INVITING**	present participle of invite
INULASE	n pl. -S an enzyme	**INVOCATE**	v -CATED, -CATING, -CATES to invoke
INULIN	n pl. -S a chemical compound		
INUNDANT	adj inundating	**INVOICE**	v -VOICED, -VOICING, -VOICES to bill
INUNDATE	v -DATED, -DATING, -DATES to overwhelm with water		
		INVOKE	v -VOKED, -VOKING, -VOKES to appeal to for aid
INURBANE	adj not urbane		
INURE	v -URED, -URING, -URES to accustom to accept something undesirable	**INVOKER**	n pl. -S one that invokes
		INVOLUTE	v -LUTED, -LUTING, -LUTES to roll or curl up
INURN	v -ED, -ING, -S to put in an urn	**INVOLVE**	v -VOLVED, -VOLVING, -VOLVES to contain or include as a part
INUTILE	adj useless		
INVADE	v -VADED, -VADING, -VADES to enter for conquest or plunder		
		INVOLVER	n pl. -S one that involves
INVADER	n pl. -S one that invades	**INWALL**	v -ED, -ING, -S to surround with a wall
INVALID	v -ED, -ING, -S to disable physically		
		INWARD	adv toward the inside
INVAR	n pl. -S a steel alloy	**INWARDLY**	adv on the inside
INVASION	n pl. -S the act of invading **INVASIVE** adj	**INWARDS**	adv inward
		INWEAVE	v -WOVE or -WEAVED, -WOVEN, -WEAVING, -WEAVES to weave together
INVECTED	adj edged by convex curves		
INVEIGH	v -ED, -ING, -S to protest angrily		
INVEIGLE	v -GLED, -GLING, -GLES to induce by guile or flattery	**INWIND**	v -WOUND, -WINDING, -WINDS to enwind
		INWRAP	v -WRAPPED, -WRAPPING, -WRAPS to enwrap
INVENT	v -ED, -ING, -S to devise originally		
		IODATE	v -DATED, -DATING, -DATES to iodize
INVENTER	n pl. -S inventor		
INVENTOR	n pl. -S one that invents	**IODATION**	n pl. -S the act of iodating
INVERITY	n pl. -TIES lack of truth	**IODIC**	adj pertaining to iodine
INVERSE	n pl. -S something that is opposite	**IODID**	n pl. -S iodide
		IODIDE	n pl. -S a compound of iodine
INVERT	v -ED, -ING, -S to turn upside down	**IODIN**	n pl. -S iodine
		IODINATE	v -ATED, -ATING, -ATES to iodize
INVERTER	n pl. -S one that inverts	**IODINE**	n pl. -S a nonmetallic element

IODISM   *n pl.* -S iodine poisoning

IODIZE   *v* -DIZED, -DIZING, -DIZES to treat with iodine

IODIZER   *n pl.* -S one that iodizes

IODOFORM   *n pl.* -S an iodine compound

IODOL   *n pl.* -S an iodine compound

IODOPHOR   *n pl.* -S an iodine compound

IODOPSIN   *n pl.* -S a pigment in the retina

IODOUS   *adj* pertaining to iodine

IOLITE   *n pl.* -S a mineral

ION   *n pl.* -S an electrically charged atom

IONIC   *n pl.* -S a style of type

IONICITY   *n pl.* -TIES the state of existing as or like an ion

IONISE   *v* -ISED, -ISING, -ISES to ionize

IONIUM   *n pl.* -S an isotope of thorium

IONIZE   *v* -IZED, -IZING, -IZES to convert into ions

IONIZER   *n pl.* -S one that ionizes

IONOMER   *n pl.* -S a type of plastic

IONONE   *n pl.* -S a chemical compound

IOTA   *n pl.* -S a Greek letter

IOTACISM   *n pl.* -S excessive use of the letter iota

IPECAC   *n pl.* -S a medicinal plant

IPOMOEA   *n pl.* -S a flowering plant

IRACUND   *adj* easily angered

IRADE   *n pl.* -S a decree of a Muslim ruler

IRATE   *adj* IRATER, IRATEST angry **IRATELY** *adv*

IRE   *v* IRED, IRING, IRES to anger

IREFUL   *adj* angry **IREFULLY** *adv*

IRELESS   *adj* not angry

IRENIC   *adj* peaceful in purpose

IRENICAL   *adj* irenic

IRENICS   *n/pl* a branch of theology

IRIDES   *a pl.* of iris

IRIDIC   *adj* pertaining to iridium

IRIDIUM   *n pl.* -S a metallic element

IRING   present participle of ire

IRIS   *n pl.* IRISES or IRIDES a part of the eye

IRIS   *v* -ED, -ING, -ES to give the form of a rainbow to

IRITIS   *n pl.* -TISES inflammation of the iris **IRITIC** *adj*

IRK   *v* -ED, -ING, -S to annoy or weary

IRKSOME   *adj* tending to irk

IRON   *v* -ED, -ING, -S to furnish with iron (a metallic element)

IRONBARK   *n pl.* -S a timber tree

IRONCLAD   *n pl.* -S an armored warship

IRONE   *n pl.* -S an aromatic oil

IRONER   *n pl.* -S a machine for pressing clothes

IRONIC   *adj* pertaining to irony

IRONICAL   *adj* ironic

IRONIES   *pl.* of irony

IRONING   *n pl.* -S clothes pressed or to be pressed

IRONIST   *n pl.* -S one who uses irony

IRONLIKE   *adj* resembling iron

IRONNESS   *n pl.* -ES the state of being iron

IRONSIDE   *n pl.* -S a man of great strength

IRONWARE   *n pl.* -S articles made of iron

IRONWEED   *n pl.* -S a shrub

IRONWOOD   *n pl.* -S a hardwood tree

IRONWORK   *n pl.* -S objects made of iron

IRONY   *n pl.* -NIES the use of words to express the opposite of what is literally said

IRREAL   *adj* not real

IRRIGATE   *v* -GATED, -GATING, -GATES to supply with water by artificial means

IRRITANT   *n pl.* -S something that irritates

IRRITATE   *v* -TATED, -TATING, -TATES to excite to impatience or anger

IRRUPT   *v* -ED, -ING, -S to rush in forcibly

IS   present 3d person sing. of be

ISAGOGE   *n pl.* -S a type of introduction to a branch of study

ISAGOGIC   *n pl.* -S a branch of theology

ISARITHM   *n pl.* -S an isopleth

ISATIN   *n pl.* -S a chemical compound **ISATINIC** *adj*

ISATINE   *n pl.* -S isatin

ISBA   *n pl.* -S a Russian log hut

ISCHEMIA   *n pl.* -S a type of anemia **ISCHEMIC** *adj*

ISCHIUM   *n* pl. -CHIA a pelvic bone **ISCHIAL** *adj*

ISLAND   *v* -ED, -ING, -S to make into an island (a land area entirely surrounded by water)

ISLANDER   *n* pl. -S one that lives on an island

ISLE   *v* ISLED, ISLING, ISLES to place on an isle (a small island)

ISLELESS   *adj* lacking an isle

ISLET   *n* pl. -S a small island

ISLING   present participle of isle

ISM   *n* pl. -S a distinctive theory or doctrine

ISOBAR   *n* pl. -S a type of atom **ISOBARIC** *adj*

ISOBARE   *n* pl. -S isobar

ISOBATH   *n* pl. -S a line on a map connecting points of equal water depth

ISOCHEIM   *n* pl. -S a type of isotherm

ISOCHIME   *n* pl. -S isocheim

ISOCHOR   *n* pl. -S isochore

ISOCHORE   *n* pl. -S a curve used to show a relationship between pressure and temperature

ISOCHRON   *n* pl. -S a line on a chart connecting points representing the same time

ISOCLINE   *n* pl. -S a type of rock formation

ISOCRACY   *n* pl. -CIES a form of government

ISODOSE   *adj* pertaining to zones that receive equal doses of radiation

ISOGAMY   *n* pl. -MIES the fusion of two similar gametes

ISOGENIC   *adj* genetically similar

ISOGENY   *n* pl. -NIES the state of being of similar origin

ISOGLOSS   *n* pl. -ES a line on a map between linguistically varied areas

ISOGON   *n* pl. -S a polygon having equal angles

ISOGONAL   *n* pl. -S isogone

ISOGONE   *n* pl. -S a line on a map used to show characteristics of the earth's magnetic field

ISOGONIC   *n* pl. -S isogone

ISOGONY   *n* pl. -NIES an equivalent relative growth of parts

ISOGRAM   *n* pl. -S a line on a map connecting points of equal value

ISOGRAPH   *n* pl. -S a line on a map indicating areas that are linguistically similar

ISOGRIV   *n* pl. -S a line drawn on a map such that all points have equal grid variation

ISOHEL   *n* pl. -S a line on a map connecting points receiving equal sunshine

ISOHYET   *n* pl. -S a line on a map connecting points having equal rainfall

ISOLABLE   *adj* capable of being isolated

ISOLATE   *n* -LATED, -LATING, -LATES to set apart from others

ISOLATOR   *n* pl. -S one that isolates

ISOLEAD   *n* pl. -S a line on a ballistic graph

ISOLINE   *n* pl. -S an isogram

ISOLOG   *n* pl. -S isologue

ISOLOGUE   *n* pl. -S a type of chemical compound

ISOMER   *n* pl. -S a type of chemical compound **ISOMERIC** *adj*

ISOMETRY   *n* pl. -TRIES equality of measure

ISOMORPH   *n* pl. -S something similar to something else in form

ISONOMY   *n* pl. -MIES equality of civil rights **ISONOMIC** *adj*

ISOPHOTE   *n* pl. -S a curve on a chart joining points of equal light intensity

ISOPLETH   *n* pl. -S a type of isogram

ISOPOD   *n* pl. -S a kind of crustacean

ISOPODAN   *n* pl. -S an isopod

ISOPRENE   *n* pl. -S a volatile liquid

ISOSPIN   *n* pl. -S a type of quantum number

ISOSPORY   *n* pl. -RIES the condition of producing sexual or asexual spores of but one kind

ISOSTASY   *n* pl. -SIES the state of balance in the earth's crust

ISOTACH   *n* pl. -S a line on a map connecting points of equal wind velocity

ISOTHERE   *n* pl. -S a type of isotherm

ISOTHERM   *n* pl. -S a line on a map connecting points of equal mean temperature

ISOTONE	*n pl.* -S a type of atom
ISOTONIC	*adj* of equal tension
ISOTOPE	*n pl.* -S a form of an element **ISOTOPIC** *adj*
ISOTOPY	*n pl.* -PIES the state of being an isotope
ISOTROPY	*n pl.* -PIES the state of being identical in all directions
ISOTYPE	*n pl.* -S a type of diagram **ISOTYPIC** *adj*
ISOZYME	*n pl.* -S a type of enzyme **ISOZYMIC** *adj*
ISSEI	*n pl.* -S a Japanese immigrant to the United States
ISSUABLE	*adj* authorized for issuing **ISSUABLY** *adv*
ISSUANCE	*n pl.* -S the act of issuing
ISSUANT	*adj* coming forth
ISSUE	*v* -SUED, -SUING, -SUES to come forth
ISSUER	*n pl.* -S one that issues
ISTHMI	*a pl.* of isthmus
ISTHMIAN	*n pl.* -S a native of an isthmus
ISTHMIC	*adj* pertaining to an isthmus
ISTHMOID	*adj* isthmic
ISTHMUS	*n pl.* -MUSES or -MI a strip of land connecting two larger land masses
ISTLE	*n pl.* -S a strong fiber
IT	*pron* the 3d person sing. neuter pronoun
ITALIC	*n pl.* -S a style of print

ITCH	*v* -ED, -ING, -ES to have an uneasy or tingling skin sensation
ITCHING	*n pl.* -S an uneasy or tingling skin sensation
ITCHY	*adj* ITCHIER, ITCHIEST causing an itching sensation
ITEM	*v* -ED, -ING, -S to itemize
ITEMIZE	*v* -IZED, -IZING, -IZES to set down the particulars of
ITEMIZER	*n pl.* -S one that itemizes
ITERANCE	*n pl.* -S repetition
ITERANT	*adj* repeating
ITERATE	*v* -ATED, -ATING, -ATES to repeat
ITERUM	*adv* again; once more
ITHER	*adj* other
ITS	*pron* the possessive form of the pronoun it
ITSELF	*pron* a reflexive form of the pronoun it
IVIED	*adj* covered with ivy
IVORY	*n pl.* -RIES a hard white substance found in elephant tusks
IVY	*n pl.* IVIES a climbing vine **IVYLIKE** *adj*
IWIS	*adv* certainly
IXIA	*n pl.* -S a flowering plant
IXODID	*n pl.* -S a bloodsucking insect
IXTLE	*n pl.* -S istle
IZAR	*n pl.* -S an outer garment worn by Muslim women
IZZARD	*n pl.* -S the letter Z

JAB	v JABBED, JABBING, JABS to poke sharply
JABBER	v -ED, -ING, -S to talk rapidly
JABBERER	n pl. -S one that jabbers
JABBING	present participle of jab
JABIRU	n pl. -S a wading bird
JABOT	n pl. -S a decoration on a shirt
JACAL	n pl. -ES or -S a hut
JACAMAR	n pl. -S a tropical bird
JACANA	n pl. -S a wading bird
JACINTH	n pl. -S a variety of zircon
JACINTHE	n pl. -S an orange color
JACK	v -ED, -ING, -S to raise with a type of lever
JACKAL	n pl. -S a doglike mammal
JACKAROO	n pl. -ROOS jackeroo
JACKASS	n pl. -ES a male donkey
JACKBOOT	n pl. -S a heavy boot
JACKDAW	n pl. -S a crowlike bird
JACKER	n pl. -S one that jacks
JACKEROO	n pl. -ROOS an inexperienced ranch hand
JACKET	v -ED, -ING, -S to provide with a jacket (a short coat)
JACKFISH	n pl. -ES a food fish
JACKIES	pl. of jacky
JACKLEG	n pl. -S an unskilled worker
JACKPOT	n pl. -S a top prize or reward
JACKSTAY	n pl. -STAYS a rope on a ship
JACKY	n pl. JACKIES a sailor
JACOBIN	n pl. -S a pigeon
JACOBUS	n pl. -ES an old English coin
JACONET	n pl. -S a cotton cloth
JACQUARD	n pl. -S a fabric of intricate weave
JACULATE	v -LATED, -LATING, -LATES to throw
JADE	v JADED, JADING, JADES to weary **JADEDLY** adv
JADEITE	n pl. -S a mineral **JADITIC** adj
JADISH	adj worn-out **JADISHLY** adv
JAEGER	n pl. -S a hunter
JAG	v JAGGED, JAGGING, JAGS to cut unevenly
JAGER	n pl. -S jaeger
JAGG	v -ED, -ING, -S to jag
JAGGARY	n pl. -RIES jaggery
JAGGED	adj -GEDER, -GEDEST having a sharply uneven edge of surface **JAGGEDLY** adv
JAGGER	n pl. -S one that jags
JAGGERY	n pl. -GERIES a coarse, dark sugar
JAGGHERY	n pl. -GHERIES jaggery
JAGGING	present participle of jag
JAGGY	adj -GIER, -GIEST jagged
JAGLESS	adj smooth and even
JAGRA	n pl. -S jaggery
JAGUAR	n pl. -S a large feline animal
JAIL	v -ED, -ING, -S to put in jail (a place of confinement)
JAILBAIT	n pl. JAILBAIT a girl under the age of consent with whom sexual intercourse constitutes statutory rape
JAILBIRD	n pl. -S a prisoner

JAILER	*n pl.* -S a keeper of a jail
JAILOR	*n pl.* -S jailer
JAKE	*adj* all right; fine
JAKES	*n/pl* an outhouse
JALAP	*n pl.* -S a Mexican plant **JALAPIC** *adj*
JALAPIN	*n pl.* -S a medicinal substance contained in jalap
JALOP	*n pl.* -S jalap
JALOPPY	*n pl.* -PIES jalopy
JALOPY	*n pl.* -LOPIES a decrepit car
JALOUSIE	*n pl.* -S a type of window
JAM	*v* JAMMED, JAMMING, JAMS to force together tightly
JAMB	*v* -ED, -ING, -S to jam
JAMBE	*n pl.* -S a jambeau
JAMBEAU	*n pl.* -BEAUX a piece of armor for the leg
JAMBOREE	*n pl.* -S a noisy celebration
JAMMED	past tense of jam
JAMMER	*n pl.* -S one that jams
JAMMING	present participle of jam
JANE	*n pl.* -S a girl or woman
JANGLE	*v* -GLED, -GLING, -GLES to make a harsh, metallic sound
JANGLER	*n pl.* -S one that jangles
JANIFORM	*adj* hypocritical
JANISARY	*n pl.* -SARIES janizary
JANITOR	*n pl.* -S a maintenance man
JANIZARY	*n pl.* -ZARIES a Turkish soldier
JANTY	*adj* jaunty
JAPAN	*v* -PANNED, -PANNING, -PANS to coat with a glossy, black lacquer
JAPANIZE	*v* -NIZED, -NIZING, -NIZES to make Japanese
JAPANNER	*n pl.* -S one that japans
JAPANNING	present participle of japan
JAPE	*v* JAPED, JAPING, JAPES to mock
JAPER	*n pl.* -S one that japes
JAPERY	*n pl.* -ERIES mockery
JAPING	present participle of jape
JAPINGLY	*adv* in a japing manner
JAPONICA	*n pl.* -S an Asian shrub
JAR	*v* JARRED, JARRING, JARS to cause to shake
JARFUL	*n pl.* JARFULS or JARSFUL the quantity held by a jar (a cylindrical container)
JARGON	*v* -ED, -ING, -S to speak or write an obscure and often pretentious kind of language
JARGONEL	*n pl.* -S a variety of pear
JARGOON	*n pl.* -S a variety of zircon
JARINA	*n pl.* -S the hard seed of a palm tree
JARL	*n pl.* -S a Scandinavian nobleman
JARLDOM	*n pl.* -S the domain of a jarl
JAROSITE	*n pl.* -S a mineral
JAROVIZE	*v* -VIZED, -VIZING, -VIZES to hasten the flowering of a plant
JARRAH	*n pl.* -S an evergreen tree
JARRED	past tense of jar
JARRING	present participle of jar
JARSFUL	a pl. of jarful
JARVEY	*n pl.* -VEYS the driver of a carriage for hire
JASMINE	*n pl.* -S a climbing shrub
JASPER	*n pl.* -S a variety of quartz **JASPERY** *adj*
JASSID	*n pl.* -S any of a family of plant pests
JATO	*n pl.* -TOS a takeoff aided by jet propulsion
JAUK	*v* -ED, -ING, -S to dawdle
JAUNCE	*v* JAUNCED, JAUNCING, JAUNCES to prance
JAUNDICE	*v* -DICED, -DICING, -DICES to prejudice unfavorably
JAUNT	*v* -ED, -ING, -S to make a pleasure trip
JAUNTY	*adj* -TIER, -TIEST having a lively and self-confident manner **JAUNTILY** *adv*
JAUP	*v* -ED, -ING, -S to splash
JAVA	*n pl.* -S coffee
JAVELIN	*v* -ED, -ING, -S to pierce with a javelin (a light spear)
JAVELINA	*n pl.* -S a peccary
JAW	*v* -ED, -ING, -S to jabber
JAWAN	*n pl.* -S a soldier of India
JAWBONE	*v* -BONED, -BONING, -BONES to attempt to convince
JAWLIKE	*adj* resembling the jaw (the framework of the mouth)

JAWLINE *n* pl. -S the outline of the lower jaw

JAY *n* pl. JAYS a corvine bird

JAYBIRD *n* pl. -S a jay

JAYGEE *n* pl. -S a military officer

JAYVEE *n* pl. -S a junior varsity player

JAYWALK *v* -ED, -ING, -S to cross a street recklessly

JAZZ *v* -ED, -ING, -ES to enliven

JAZZER *n* pl. -S one that jazzes

JAZZMAN *n* pl. -MEN a type of musician

JAZZY *adj* JAZZIER, JAZZIEST lively **JAZZILY** *adv*

JEALOUS *adj* resentful of another's advantages

JEALOUSY *n* pl. -SIES a jealous feeling

JEAN *n* pl. -S a durable cotton fabric

JEBEL *n* pl. -S a mountain

JEE *v* JEED, JEEING, JEES to gee

JEEP *n* pl. -S a type of motor vehicle

JEEPERS *interj* — used as a mild oath

JEER *v* -ED, -ING, -S to mock

JEERER *n* pl. -S one that jeers

JEEZ *interj* — used as a mild oath

JEFE *n* pl. -S a chief

JEHAD *n* pl. -S jihad

JEHU *n* pl. -S a fast driver

JEJUNA pl. of jejunum

JEJUNAL *adj* pertaining to the jejunum

JEJUNE *adj* uninteresting; childish **JEJUNELY** *adv*

JEJUNITY *n* pl. -TIES something that is jejune

JEJUNUM *n* pl. -NA a part of the small intestine

JELL *v* -ED, -ING, -S to congeal

JELLIFY *v* -FIED, -FYING, -FIES to jelly

JELLY *v* -LIED, -LYING, -LIES to make into a jelly (a soft, semisolid substance)

JELUTONG *n* pl. -S a tropical tree

JEMADAR *n* pl. -S an officer in the army of India

JEMIDAR *n* pl. -S jemadar

JEMMY *v* -MIED, -MYING, -MIES to jimmy

JENNET *n* pl. -S a small horse

JENNY *n* pl. -NIES a female donkey

JEOPARD *v* -ED, -ING, -S to imperil

JEOPARDY *n* pl. -DIES risk of loss or injury

JERBOA *n* pl. -S a small rodent

JEREED *n* pl. -S a wooden javelin

JEREMIAD *n* pl. -S a tale of woe

JERID *n* pl. -S jereed

JERK *v* -ED, -ING, -S to move with a sharp, sudden motion

JERKER *n* pl. -S one that jerks

JERKIES pl. of jerky

JERKIN *n* pl. -S a sleeveless jacket

JERKY *adj* JERKIER, JERKIEST characterized by jerking movements **JERKILY** *adv*

JERKY *n* pl. -KIES dried and smoked meat

JEROBOAM *n* pl. -S a wine bottle

JERREED *n* pl. -S jereed

JERRICAN *n* pl. -S jerrycan

JERRID *n* pl. -S jereed

JERRY *n* pl. -RIES a German soldier

JERRYCAN *n* pl. -S a fuel container

JERSEY *n* pl. -SEYS a close-fitting knitted shirt **JERSEYED** *adj*

JESS *v* -ED, -ING, -ES to fasten straps around the legs of a hawk

JESSANT *adj* shooting forth

JESSE *v* JESSED, JESSING, JESSES to jess

JEST *v* -ED, -ING, -S to joke

JESTER *n* pl. -S one that jests

JESTFUL *adj* tending to jest

JESTING *n* pl. -S the act of one who jests

JESUIT *n* pl. -S a scheming person **JESUITIC** *adj*

JESUITRY *n* pl. -RIES an unethical principle or practice

JET *v* JETTED, JETTING, JETS to spurt forth in a stream

JETBEAD *n* pl. -S an ornamental shrub

JETE *n* pl. -S a ballet leap

JETLINER *n* pl. -S a type of aircraft

JETON *n* pl. -S jetton

JETPORT *n* pl. -S a type of airport

JETSAM *n* pl. -S goods cast overboard to lighten an imperiled vessel

JETSOM *n* pl. -S jetsam

JETTED past tense of jet

JETTIED   past tense of jetty

JETTIES   present 3d person sing. of jetty

JETTING   present participle of jet

JETTISON   *v* -ED, -ING, -S to cast overboard

JETTON   *n* pl. -S a piece used in counting

JETTY   *v* -TIED, -TYING, -TIES to jut

JEU   *n* pl. JEUX a game

JEW   *v* -ED, -ING, -S to bargain with — usually taken to be offensive

JEWEL   *v* -ELED, -ELING, -ELS or -ELLED, -ELLING, -ELS to adorn with jewels (precious stones)

JEWELER   *n* pl. -S a dealer or maker of jewelry

JEWELLER   *n* pl. -S jeweler

JEWELLING   a present participle of jewel

JEWELRY   *n* pl. -RIES an article or articles for personal adornment

JEWFISH   *n* pl. -ES a large marine fish

JEZAIL   *n* pl. -S a type of firearm

JEZEBEL   *n* pl. -S a scheming, wicked woman

JIB   *v* JIBBED, JIBBING, JIBS to refuse to proceed further

JIBB   *v* -ED, -ING, -S to shift from side to side while sailing

JIBBER   *n* pl. -S a horse that jibs

JIBBING   present participle of jib

JIBBOOM   *n* pl. -S a ship's spar

JIBE   *v* JIBED, JIBING, JIBES to gibe **JIBINGLY** *adv*

JIBER   *n* pl. -S one that jibes

JIFF   *n* pl. -S a jiffy

JIFFY   *n* pl. -FIES a short time

JIG   *v* JIGGED, JIGGING, JIGS to bob

JIGABOO   *n* pl. -BOOS a black person — often taken to be offensive

JIGGER   *n* pl. -S a small whiskey glass

JIGGERED   *adj* damned

JIGGING   present participle of jig

JIGGLE   *v* -GLED, -GLING, -GLES to shake lightly

JIGGLY   *adj* -GLIER, -GLIEST unsteady

JIGSAW   *v* -SAWED, -SAWN, -SAWING, -SAWS to cut with a type of saw

JIHAD   *n* pl. -S a Muslim holy war

JILL   *n* pl. -S a unit of liquid measure

JILLION   *n* pl. -S a very large number

JILT   *v* -ED, -ING, -S to reject a lover

JILTER   *n* pl. -S one that jilts

JIMINY   *interj* — used to express surprise

JIMJAMS   *n/pl* violent delirium

JIMMINY   *interj* jiminy

JIMMY   *v* -MIED, -MYING, -MIES to pry open with a crowbar

JIMP   *adj* JIMPER, JIMPEST natty **JIMPLY** *adv*

JIMPY   *adj* jimp

JIN   *n* pl. -S jinn

JINGAL   *n* pl. -S a heavy musket

JINGALL   *n* pl. -S jingal

JINGKO   *n* pl. -KOES ginkgo

JINGLE   *v* -GLED, -GLING, -GLES to make a tinkling sound

JINGLER   *n* pl. -S one that jingles

JINGLY   *adj* -GLIER, -GLIEST jingling

JINGO   *n* pl. -GOES a zealous patriot **JINGOISH** *adj*

JINGOISM   *n* pl. -S the spirit or policy of jingoes

JINGOIST   *n* pl. -S a jingo

JINK   *v* -ED, -ING, -S to move quickly out of the way

JINKER   *n* pl. -S one that jinks

JINN   *n* pl. -S a supernatural being in Muslim mythology

JINNEE   *n* pl. JINN jinn

JINNI   *n* pl. JINN jinn

JINX   *v* -ED, -ING, -ES to bring bad luck to

JIPIJAPA   *n* pl. -S a tropical plant

JITNEY   *n* pl. -NEYS a small bus

JITTER   *v* -ED, -ING, -S to fidget

JITTERY   *adj* extremely nervous

JIUJITSU   *n* pl. -S jujitsu

JIUJUTSU   *n* pl. -S jujitsu

JIVE   *v* JIVED, JIVING, JIVES to play jazz or swing music

JNANA   *n* pl. -S knowledge acquired through meditation

JO   *n* pl. JOES a sweetheart

JOANNES   *n* pl. JOANNES johannes

JOB   v JOBBED, JOBBING, JOBS to work by the piece

JOBBER   n pl. -S a pieceworker

JOBBERY   n pl. -BERIES corruption in public office

JOBBING   present participle of job

JOBLESS   adj having no job

JOCK   n pl. -S an athletic supporter

JOCKEY   v -EYED, -EYING, -EYS to maneuver for an advantage

JOCKO   n pl. JOCKOS a monkey

JOCOSE   adj humorous **JOCOSELY** adv

JOCOSITY   n pl. -TIES the state of being jocose

JOCULAR   adj given to joking

JOCUND   adj cheerful **JOCUNDLY** adv

JODHPUR   n pl. -S a type of boot

JOE   n pl. -S a fellow

JOEY   n pl. -EYS a young kangaroo

JOG   v JOGGED, JOGGING, JOGS to run at a slow, steady pace

JOGGER   n pl. -S one that jogs

JOGGLE   v -GLED, -GLING, -GLES to shake slightly

JOGGLER   n pl. -S one that joggles

JOHANNES   n pl. JOHANNES a Portuguese coin

JOHN   n pl. -S a toilet

JOHNBOAT   n pl. -S a narrow square-ended boat

JOHNNY   n pl. -NIES a sleeveless hospital gown

JOIN   v -ED, -ING, -S to unite **JOINABLE** adj

JOINDER   n pl. -S a joining of parties in a lawsuit

JOINER   n pl. -S a carpenter

JOINERY   n pl. -ERIES the trade of a joiner

JOINING   n pl. -S a juncture

JOINT   v -ED, -ING, -S to fit together by means of a junction

JOINTER   n pl. -S one that joints

JOINTLY   adv together

JOINTURE   v -TURED, -TURING, -TURES to set aside property as an inheritance

JOIST   v -ED, -ING, -S to support with horizontal beams

JOJOBA   n pl. -S a small tree

JOKE   v JOKED, JOKING, JOKES to say something amusing

JOKER   n pl. -S one that jokes

JOKESTER   n pl. -S a practical joker

JOKING   present participle of joke

JOKINGLY   adv in a joking manner

JOLE   n pl. -S jowl

JOLLIED   past tense of jolly

JOLLIER   comparative of jolly

JOLLIES   present 3d person sing. of jolly

JOLLIEST   superlative of jolly

JOLLIFY   v -FIED, -FYING, -FIES to make jolly

JOLLITY   n pl. -TIES mirth

JOLLY   adj -LIER, -LIEST cheerful **JOLLILY** adv

JOLLY   v -LIED, -LYING, -LIES to put in a good humor for one's own purposes

JOLT   v -ED, -ING, -S to jar or shake roughly

JOLTER   n pl. -S one that jolts

JOLTY   adj JOLTIER, JOLTIEST marked by a jolting motion **JOLTILY** adv

JONGLEUR   n pl. -S a minstrel

JONQUIL   n pl. -S a perennial herb

JORAM   n pl. -S a jorum

JORDAN   n pl. -S a type of container

JORUM   n pl. -S a large drinking bowl

JOSEPH   n pl. -S a woman's long cloak

JOSH   v -ED, -ING, -ES to tease

JOSHER   n pl. -S one that joshes

JOSS   n pl. -ES a Chinese idol

JOSTLE   v -TLED, -TLING, -TLES to bump or push roughly

JOSTLER   n pl. -S one that jostles

JOT   v JOTTED, JOTTING, JOTS to write down quickly

JOTA   n pl. -S a Spanish dance

JOTTING   n pl. -S a brief note

JOTTY   adj written down quickly

JOUK   v -ED, -ING, -S to dodge

JOULE   n pl. -S a unit of energy

JOUNCE   v JOUNCED, JOUNCING, JOUNCES to move roughly up and down

JOUNCY *adj* JOUNCIER, JOUNCIEST marked by a jouncing motion

JOURNAL *n* pl. -S a record of daily events

JOURNEY *v* -ED, -ING, -S to travel

JOUST *v* -ED, -ING, -S to engage in personal combat

JOUSTER *n* pl. -S one that jousts

JOVIAL *adj* good-humored **JOVIALLY** *adv*

JOVIALTY *n* pl. -TIES the quality or state of being jovial

JOW *v* -ED, -ING, -S to toll

JOWL *n* pl. -S the fleshy part under the lower jaw **JOWLED** *adj*

JOWLY *adj* JOWLIER, JOWLIEST having prominent jowls

JOY *v* -ED, -ING, -S to rejoice

JOYANCE *n* pl. -S gladness

JOYFUL *adj* -FULLER, -FULLEST happy **JOYFULLY** *adv*

JOYLESS *adj* being without gladness

JOYOUS *adj* joyful **JOYOUSLY** *adv*

JOYPOP *v* -POPPED, -POPPING, -POPS to use habit-forming drugs occasionally

JOYRIDE *n* pl. -S a ride taken for pleasure

JOYRIDER *n* pl. -S one that takes a joyride

JOYSTICK *n* pl. -S the control stick in an airplane

JUBA *n* pl. -S a lively dance

JUBBAH *n* pl. -S a loose outer garment

JUBE *n* pl. -S a platform in a church

JUBHAH *n* pl. -S jubbah

JUBILANT *adj* exultant

JUBILATE *v* -LATED, -LATING, -LATES to exult

JUBILE *n* pl. -S jubilee

JUBILEE *n* pl. -S a celebration

JUDAS *n* pl. -ES a peephole

JUDDER *v* -ED, -ING, -S to vibrate

JUDGE *v* JUDGED, JUDGING, JUDGES to decide on critically

JUDGER *n* pl. -S one that judges

JUDGMENT *n* pl. -S an authoritative opinion

JUDICIAL *adj* pertaining to courts of law

JUDO *n* pl. -DOS a form of jujitsu

JUDOIST *n* pl. -S one skilled in judo

JUDOKA *n* pl. -S a judoist

JUG *v* JUGGED, JUGGING, JUGS to put into a jug (a large, deep container with a narrow mouth and a handle)

JUGA a pl. of jugum

JUGAL *adj* pertaining to the cheek or cheekbone

JUGATE *adj* occurring in pairs

JUGFUL *n* pl. JUGFULS or JUGSFUL as much as a jug will hold

JUGGED past tense of jug

JUGGING present participle of jug

JUGGLE *v* -GLED, -GLING, -GLES to perform feats of manual dexterity

JUGGLER *n* pl. -S one that juggles

JUGGLERY *n* pl. -GLERIES the art of a juggler

JUGGLING *n* pl. -S jugglery

JUGHEAD *n* pl. -S a dolt

JUGSFUL a pl. of jugful

JUGULA pl. of jugulum

JUGULAR *n* pl. -S a vein of the neck

JUGULATE *v* -LATED, -LATING, -LATES to suppress a disease by extreme measures

JUGULUM *n* pl. -LA a part of a bird's neck

JUGUM *n* pl. -GA or -GUMS a pair of the opposite leaflets of a pinnate leaf

JUICE *v* JUICED, JUICING, JUICES to extract the juice (the liquid part of a fruit or vegetable) from

JUICER *n* pl. -S a juice extractor

JUICY *adj* JUICIER, JUICIEST full of juice **JUICILY** *adv*

JUJITSU *n* pl. -S a Japanese art of self-defense

JUJU *n* pl. -S an object regarded as having magical power

JUJUBE *n* pl. -S a fruit-flavored candy

JUJUISM *n* pl. -S the system of beliefs connected with jujus

JUJUIST *n* pl. -S a follower of jujuism

JUJUTSU *n* pl. -S jujitsu

JUKE *v* JUKED, JUKING, JUKES to fake out of position

JUKEBOX *n* pl. -ES a coin-operated phonograph

JULEP *n* pl. -S a sweet drink

JULIENNE *n* pl. -S a clear soup

JUMBLE *v* -BLED, -BLING, -BLES to mix in a disordered manner

JUMBLER *n* pl. -S one that jumbles

JUMBO *n* pl. -BOS a very large specimen of its kind

JUMBUCK *n* pl. -S a sheep

JUMP *v* -ED, -ING, -S to spring off the ground

JUMPER *n* pl. -S one that jumps

JUMPOFF *n* pl. -S a starting point

JUMPY *adj* JUMPIER, JUMPIEST nervous **JUMPILY** *adv*

JUN *n* pl. JUN a coin of North Korea

JUNCO *n* pl. -COS or -COES a small finch

JUNCTION *n* pl. -S a place where things join

JUNCTURE *n* pl. -S the act of joining

JUNGLE *n* pl. -S land covered with dense tropical vegetation

JUNGLY *adj* -GLIER, -GLIEST resembling a jungle

JUNIOR *n* pl. -S a person who is younger than another

JUNIPER *n* pl. -S an evergreen tree

JUNK *v* -ED, -ING, -S to discard as trash

JUNKER *n* pl. -S something ready for junking

JUNKET *v* -ED, -ING, -S to banquet

JUNKETER *n* pl. -S one that junkets

JUNKIE *n* pl. -S a drug addict

JUNKMAN *n* pl. -MEN one who buys and sells junk

JUNKY *adj* JUNKIER, JUNKIEST worthless

JUNKYARD *n* pl. -S a place where junk is stored

JUNTA *n* pl. -S a political or governmental council

JUNTO *n* pl. -TOS a political faction

JUPE *n* pl. -S a woman's jacket

JUPON *n* pl. -S a tunic

JURA pl. of jus

JURAL *adj* pertaining to law **JURALLY** *adv*

JURANT *n* pl. -S one that takes an oath

JURAT *n* pl. -S a statement on an affidavit

JURATORY *adj* pertaining to an oath

JUREL *n* pl. -S a food fish

JURIDIC *adj* pertaining to the law

JURIES pl. of jury

JURIST *n* pl. -S one versed in the law **JURISTIC** *adj*

JUROR *n* pl. -S a member of a jury

JURY *n* pl. -RIES a group of persons sworn to render a verdict

JURYMAN *n* pl. -MEN a juror

JUS *n* pl. JURA a legal right

JUSSIVE *n* pl. -S a word used to express command

JUST *v* -ED, -ING, -S to joust

JUST *adj* JUSTER, JUSTEST acting in conformity with what is morally good

JUSTER *n* pl. -S jouster

JUSTICE *n* pl. -S a judge

JUSTIFY *v* -FIED, -FYING, -FIES to show to be just, right, or valid

JUSTLE *v* -TLED, -TLING, -TLES to jostle

JUSTLY *adv* in a just manner

JUSTNESS *n* pl. -ES the quality of being just

JUT *v* JUTTED, JUTTING, JUTS to protrude

JUTE *n* pl. -S a strong, coarse fiber

JUTTY *v* -TIED, -TYING, -TIES to jut

JUVENAL *n* pl. -S a young bird's plumage

JUVENILE *n* pl. -S a young person

KA   *n* pl. -S the spiritual self of a human being in Egyptian religion

KAAS   *n* pl. KAAS kas

KAB   *n* pl. -S an ancient Hebrew unit of measure

KABAB   *n* pl. -S kabob

KABAKA   *n* pl. -S a Ugandan emperor

KABALA   *n* pl. -S cabala

KABAR   *n* pl. -S caber

KABAYA   *n* pl. -S a cotton jacket

KABBALA   *n* pl. -S cabala

KABBALAH   *n* pl. -S cabala

KABELJOU   *n* pl. -S a large food fish

KABIKI   *n* pl. -S a tropical tree

KABOB   *n* pl. -S cubes of meat cooked on a skewer

KABUKI   *n* pl. -S a form of Japanese theater

KACHINA   *n* pl. -S an ancestral spirit

KADDISH   *n* pl. -DISHIM a Jewish prayer

KADI   *n* pl. -S cadi

KAE   *n* pl. -S a bird resembling a crow

KAFFIR   *n* pl. -S kafir

KAFFIYEH   *n* pl. -S a large, square kerchief

KAFIR   *n* pl. -S a cereal grass

KAFTAN   *n* pl. -S caftan

KAGU   *n* pl. -S a flightless bird

KAHUNA   *n* pl. -S a medicine man

KAIAK   *n* pl. -S kayak

KAIF   *n* pl. -S kef

KAIL   *n* pl. -S kale

KAILYARD   *n* pl. -S kaleyard

KAIN   *n* pl. -S a tax paid in produce or livestock

KAINIT   *n* pl. -S kainite

KAINITE   *n* pl. -S a mineral salt

KAISER   *n* pl. -S an emperor

KAISERIN   *n* pl. -S a kaiser's wife

KAJEPUT   *n* pl. -S cajuput

KAKA   *n* pl. -S a parrot

KAKAPO   *n* pl. -POS a flightless parrot

KAKEMONO   *n* pl. -NOS a Japanese scroll

KAKI   *n* pl. -S a Japanese tree

KALAM   *n* pl. -S a type of Muslim theology

KALE   *n* pl. -S a variety of cabbage

KALENDS   *n* pl. KALENDS calends

KALEWIFE   *n* pl. -WIVES a female vegetable vendor

KALEYARD   *n* pl. -S a kitchen garden

KALIAN   *n* pl. -S a hookah

KALIF   *n* pl. -S caliph

KALIFATE   *n* pl. -S califate

KALIMBA   *n* pl. -S an African musical instrument

KALIPH   *n* pl. -S caliph

KALIUM   *n* pl. -S potassium

KALLIDIN   *n* pl. -S a hormone

KALMIA   *n* pl. -S an evergreen shrub

KALONG   *n* pl. -S a fruit-eating bat

KALPA   *n* pl. -S a period of time in Hindu religion

KALPAK   *n* pl. -S calpac

KALYPTRA *n* pl. -S a thin veil

KAMAAINA *n* pl. -S a longtime resident of Hawaii

KAMACITE *n* pl. -S an alloy of nickel and iron

KAMALA *n* pl. -S an Asian tree

KAME *n* pl. -S a mound of detrital material

KAMI *n* pl. KAMI a sacred power or force

KAMIK *n* pl. -S a type of boot

KAMIKAZE *n* pl. -S a plane to be flown in a suicide crash on a target

KAMPONG *n* pl. -S a small village

KAMSEEN *n* pl. -S khamsin

KAMSIN *n* pl. -S khamsin

KANA *n* pl. -S the Japanese syllabic script

KANE *n* pl. -S kain

KANGAROO *n* pl. -ROOS an Australian mammal

KANJI *n* pl. -S a system of Japanese writing

KANTAR *n* pl. -S a unit of weight

KANTELE *n* pl. -S a type of harp

KAOLIANG *n* pl. -S an Asian sorghum

KAOLIN *n* pl. -S a fine white clay KAOLINIC *adj*

KAOLINE *n* pl. -S kaolin

KAON *n* pl. -S a type of meson

KAPA *n* pl. -S a coarse cloth

KAPH *n* pl. -S a Hebrew letter

KAPOK *n* pl. -S a mass of silky fibers

KAPPA *n* pl. -S a Greek letter

KAPUT *adj* ruined

KAPUTT *adj* kaput

KARAKUL *n* pl. -S an Asian sheep

KARAT *n* pl. -S a unit of quality for gold

KARATE *n* pl. -S a Japanese art of self-defense

KARMA *n* pl. -S the force generated by a person's actions KARMIC *adj*

KARN *n* pl. -S a cairn

KAROO *n* pl. -ROOS karroo

KAROSS *n* pl. -ES an African garment

KARROO *n* pl. -ROOS a dry plateau

KARST *n* pl. -S a limestone region KARSTIC *adj*

KART *n* pl. -S a small motor vehicle

KARTING *n* pl. -S the sport of racing karts

KARYOTIN *n* pl. -S the nuclear material of a cell

KAS *n* pl. KAS a large cupboard

KASHA *n* pl. -S a cooked cereal

KASHER *v* -ED, -ING, -S to kosher

KASHMIR *n* pl. -S cashmere

KASHRUT *n* pl. -S kashruth

KASHRUTH *n* pl. -S the Jewish dietary laws

KAT *n* pl. -S an evergreen shrub

KATAKANA *n* pl. -S a Japanese syllabic symbol

KATHODE *n* pl. -S cathode KATHODAL, KATHODIC *adj*

KATION *n* pl. -S cation

KATYDID *n* pl. -S a grasshopper

KAURI *n* pl. -S a timber tree

KAURY *n* pl. -RIES kauri

KAVA *n* pl. -S a tropical shrub

KAVASS *n* pl. -ES a Turkish policeman

KAY *n* pl. KAYS the letter K

KAYAK *n* pl. -S an Eskimo canoe

KAYAKER *n* pl. -S one that rides in a kayak

KAYLES *n/pl* a British game

KAYO *v* -ED, -ING, -S or -ES to knock out

KAZOO *n* pl. -ZOOS a toy musical instrument

KEA *n* pl. -S a parrot

KEBAB *n* pl. -S kabob

KEBAR *n* pl. -S caber

KEBBIE *n* pl. -S a rough walking stick

KEBBOCK *n* pl. -S kebbuck

KEBBUCK *n* pl. -S a whole cheese

KEBLAH *n* pl. -S kiblah

KEBOB *n* pl. -S kabob

KECK *v* -ED, -ING, -S to retch

KECKLE *v* -LED, -LING, -LES to wind with rope to prevent chafing

KEDDAH *n* pl. -S an enclosure for elephants

KEDGE *v* KEDGED, KEDGING, KEDGES to move a vessel with the use of an anchor

KEDGEREE *n* pl. -S a food in India

KEEF   n pl. -S kef

KEEK   v -ED, -ING, -S to peep

KEEL   v -ED, -ING, -S to capsize

KEELAGE   n pl. -S the amount paid to keep a boat in a harbor

KEELBOAT   n pl. -S a freight boat

KEELHALE   v -HALED, -HALING, -HALES to keelhaul

KEELHAUL   v -ED, -ING, -S to rebuke severely

KEELLESS   adj having no keel (the main structural part of a ship)

KEELSON   n pl. -S a beam in a ship

KEEN   adj KEENER, KEENEST enthusiastic

KEEN   v -ED, -ING, -S to wail loudly over the dead

KEENER   n pl. -S one that keens

KEENLY   adv in a keen manner

KEENNESS   n pl. -ES sharpness

KEEP   v KEPT, KEEPING, KEEPS to continue to possess KEEPABLE adj

KEEPER   n pl. -S one that keeps

KEEPING   n pl. -S custody

KEEPSAKE   n pl. -S a memento

KEESHOND   n pl. -HONDS or -HONDEN a small, heavy-coated dog

KEESTER   n pl. -S keister

KEET   n pl. -S a young guinea fowl

KEEVE   n pl. -S a tub or vat

KEF   n pl. -S hemp smoked to produce euphoria

KEFIR   n pl. -S a fermented beverage made from cow's milk

KEG   n pl. -S a small barrel

KEGELER   n pl. -S kegler

KEGLER   n pl. -S a bowler

KEGLING   n pl. -S bowling

KEIR   n pl. -S a kier

KEISTER   n pl. -S the buttocks

KEITLOA   n pl. -S a rhinoceros

KELOID   n pl. -S a scar caused by excessive growth of fibrous tissue KELOIDAL adj

KELP   v -ED, -ING, -S to burn a type of seaweed

KELPIE   n pl. -S a water sprite

KELPY   n pl. -PIES kelpie

KELSON   n pl. -S keelson

KELTER   n pl. -S kilter

KELVIN   n pl. -S a unit of temperature

KEMP   n pl. -S a champion

KEMPT   adj neatly kept

KEN   v KENNED or KENT, KENNING, KENS to know

KENAF   n pl. -S an East Indian plant

KENCH   n pl. -ES a bin for salting fish

KENDO   n pl. -DOS a Japanese sport

KENNED   a past tense of ken

KENNEL   v -NELED, -NELING, -NELS or -NELLED, -NELLING, -NELS to keep in a shelter for dogs

KENNING   n pl. -S a metaphorical compound word or phrase

KENO   n pl. -NOS a game of chance

KENOSIS   n pl. -SISES the incarnation of Christ KENOTIC adj

KENOTRON   n pl. -S a type of diode

KENT   a past tense of ken

KEP   v KEPPED, KEPPEN or KIPPEN, KEPPING, KEPS to catch

KEPHALIN   n pl. -S cephalin

KEPI   n pl. -S a type of cap

KEPPED   past tense of kep

KEPPEN   a past participle of kep

KEPPING   present participle of kep

KEPT   past tense of keep

KERAMIC   n pl. -S ceramic

KERATIN   n pl. -S a fibrous protein

KERATOID   adj horny

KERATOMA   n pl. -MAS or -MATA a skin disease

KERATOSE   adj of or resembling horny tissue

KERB   v -ED, -ING, -S to provide with curbing

KERCHIEF   n pl. -CHIEFS or -CHIEVES a cloth worn as a head covering

KERCHOO   interj ahchoo

KERF   v -ED, -ING, -S to make an incision with a cutting tool

KERMES   n pl. KERMES a red dye

KERMESS   n pl. -ES kermis

KERMIS   n pl. -MISES a festival

KERN   v -ED, -ING, -S to be formed with a projecting typeface

KERNE n pl. -S a medieval foot soldier

KERNEL v -NELED, -NELING, -NELS or -NELLED, -NELLING, -NELS to envelop as a kernel (the inner part of a nut)

KERNITE n pl. -S a mineral

KEROGEN n pl. -S a substance found in shale

KEROSENE n pl. -S a fuel oil

KEROSINE n pl. -S kerosene

KERPLUNK adv with a muffled sound

KERRIA n pl. -S a Chinese shrub

KERRY n pl. -RIES one of an Irish breed of cattle

KERSEY n pl. -SEYS a woolen cloth

KERYGMA n pl. -MATA the preaching of the gospel

KESTREL n pl. -S a small falcon

KETCH n pl. -ES a sailing vessel

KETCHUP n pl. -S a spicy tomato sauce

KETENE n pl. -S a toxic gas

KETO adj of or pertaining to ketone

KETONE n pl. -S a type of chemical compound **KETONIC** adj

KETOSE n pl. -S a simple sugar

KETOSIS n pl. -TOSES a buildup of ketones in the body **KETOTIC** adj

KETTLE n pl. -S a vessel for boiling liquids

KEVEL n pl. -S a belaying cleat or peg

KEVIL n pl. -S kevel

KEX n pl. -ES a dry, hollow stalk

KEY v -ED, -ING, -S to provide with a key (a device used to turn the bolt in a lock)

KEYBOARD v -ED, -ING, -S to operate a machine by means of a keyset

KEYHOLE n pl. -S a hole for a key

KEYLESS adj being without a key

KEYNOTE v -NOTED, -NOTING, -NOTES to deliver the main speech at a function

KEYNOTER n pl. -S one that keynotes

KEYPUNCH v -ED, -ING, -ES to perforate with a machine

KEYSET n pl. -S a system of finger levers

KEYSTER n pl. -S keister

KEYSTONE n pl. -S the central stone of an arch

KEYWAY n pl. -WAYS a slot for a key

KEYWORD n pl. -S a significant word

KHADDAR n pl. -S cotton cloth

KHADI n pl. -S khaddar

KHAKI n pl. -S a durable cloth

KHALIF n pl. -S caliph

KHALIFA n pl. -S caliph

KHAMSEEN n pl. -S khamsin

KHAMSIN n pl. -S a hot, dry wind

KHAN n pl. -S an Asian ruler

KHANATE n pl. -S the domain of a khan

KHAT n pl. -S kat

KHAZEN n pl. -ZENS or -ZENIM hazzan

KHEDA n pl. -S keddah

KHEDAH n pl. -S keddah

KHEDIVE n pl. -S a Turkish viceroy **KHEDIVAL** adj

KHI n pl. -S chi

KHIRKAH n pl. -S a patchwork garment

KIANG n pl. -S a wild ass

KIAUGH n pl. -S trouble; worry

KIBBLE v -BLED, -BLING, -BLES to grind coarsely

KIBBUTZ n pl. -BUTZIM a collective farm in Israel

KIBE n pl. -S a sore caused by exposure to cold

KIBITZ v -ED, -ING, -ES to meddle

KIBITZER n pl. -S one that kibitzes

KIBLA n pl. -S kiblah

KIBLAH n pl. -S the direction toward which Muslims face while praying

KIBOSH v -ED, -ING, -ES to stop

KICK v -ED, -ING, -S to strike out with the foot or feet

KICKBACK n pl. -S a strong reaction

KICKER n pl. -S one that kicks

KICKOFF n pl. -S the kick that begins play in football

KICKSHAW n pl. -S a trifle or trinket

KICKUP n pl. -S a noisy argument

KID v KIDDED, KIDDING, KIDS to tease

KIDDER n pl. -S one that kids

KIDDIE *n pl.* -S a small child

KIDDIES *pl.* of kiddy

KIDDING present participle of kid

KIDDISH *adj* childish

KIDDO *n pl.* -DOS or -DOES — used as a form of familiar address

KIDDUSH *n pl.* -ES a Jewish prayer

KIDDY *n pl.* -DIES kiddie

KIDLIKE *adj* resembling a child

KIDNAP *v* -NAPED, -NAPING, -NAPS or -NAPPED, -NAPPING, -NAPS to take a person by force and often for ransom

KIDNAPER *n pl.* -S one that kidnaps

KIDNAPPER *n pl.* -S kidnaper

KIDNAPPING present participle of kidnap

KIDNEY *n pl.* -NEYS a bodily organ

KIDSKIN *n pl.* -S a type of leather

KIEF *n pl.* -S kef

KIELBASA *n pl.* -BASAS or -BASY a smoked sausage

KIER *n pl.* -S a vat for boiling and dyeing fabrics

KIESTER *n pl.* -S keister

KIF *n pl.* -S kef

KIKE *n pl.* -S a Jew — usually taken to be offensive

KILIM *n pl.* -S an oriental tapestry

KILL *v* -ED, -ING, -S to cause to die

KILLDEE *n pl.* -S killdeer

KILLDEER *n pl.* -S a wading bird

KILLER *n pl.* -S one that kills

KILLICK *n pl.* -S a small anchor

KILLING *n pl.* -S a sudden notable success

KILLJOY *n pl.* -JOYS one who spoils the fun of others

KILLOCK *n pl.* -S killick

KILN *v* -ED, -ING, -S to bake in a type of oven

KILO *n pl.* KILOS a kilogram or kilometer

KILOBAR *n pl.* -S a unit of atmospheric pressure

KILOBIT *n pl.* -S a unit of computer information

KILOGRAM *n pl.* -S a unit of mass and weight

KILOMOLE *n pl.* -S one thousand moles

KILORAD *n pl.* -S a unit of nuclear radiation

KILOTON *n pl.* -S a unit of weight

KILOVOLT *n pl.* -S a unit of electromotive force

KILOWATT *n pl.* -S a unit of power

KILT *v* -ED, -ING, -S to make creases or pleats in

KILTER *n pl.* -S good condition

KILTIE *n pl.* -S one who wears a kilt (a type of skirt)

KILTING *n pl.* -S an arrangement of kilt pleats

KILTY *n pl.* KILTIES kiltie

KIMONO *n pl.* -NOS a loose robe **KIMONOED** *adj*

KIN *n pl.* -S a group of persons of common ancestry

KINASE *n pl.* -S an enzyme

KIND *adj* KINDER, KINDEST having a gentle, giving nature

KIND *n pl.* -S a class of similar or related objects or individuals

KINDLE *v* -DLED, -DLING, -DLES to cause to burn

KINDLER *n pl.* -S one that kindles

KINDLESS *adj* lacking kindness

KINDLING *n pl.* -S material that is easily ignited

KINDLY *adj* -LIER, -LIEST kind

KINDNESS *n pl.* -ES the quality of being kind

KINDRED *n pl.* -S a natural grouping

KINE *n pl.* -S a type of television tube

KINEMA *n pl.* -S cinema

KINESICS *n/pl* the study of body motion in relation to communication

KINESIS *n pl.* -NESES a type of movement

KINETIC *adj* pertaining to motion

KINETICS *n/pl* a branch of science dealing with motion

KINETIN *n pl.* -S a substance that increases plant growth

KINFOLK *n/pl* relatives

KINFOLKS *n/pl* kinfolk

KING *v* -ED, -ING, -S to reign as king (a male monarch)

KINGBIRD *n pl.* -S an American bird

KINGBOLT *n pl.* -S a kingpin

KINGCUP *n* pl. -S a marsh plant

KINGDOM *n* pl. -S the area ruled by a king

KINGFISH *n* pl. -ES a marine food fish

KINGHOOD *n* pl. -S the office of a king

KINGLESS *adj* having no king

KINGLET *n* pl. -S a king who rules over a small area

KINGLIKE *adj* resembling a king

KINGLY *adj* -LIER, -LIEST of or befitting a king

KINGPIN *n* pl. -S a central bolt connecting an axle to a vehicle

KINGPOST *n* pl. -S a supporting structure of a roof

KINGSHIP *n* pl. -S the power or position of a king

KINGSIDE *n* pl. -S a part of a chessboard

KINGWOOD *n* pl. -S a hardwood tree

KININ *n* pl. -S a hormone

KINK *v* -ED, -ING, -S to form a tight curl or bend in

KINKAJOU *n* pl. -S an arboreal mammal

KINKY *adj* KINKIER, KINKIEST tightly curled **KINKILY** *adv*

KINO *n* pl. -NOS a gum resin

KINSFOLK *n/pl* kinfolk

KINSHIP *n* pl. -S relationship

KINSMAN *n* pl. -MEN a male relative

KIOSK *n* pl. -S an open booth

KIP *v* KIPPED, KIPPING, KIPS to sleep

KIPPEN a past participle of kep

KIPPER *v* -ED, -ING, -S to cure fish by salting and smoking

KIPPING present participle of kip

KIPSKIN *n* pl. -S an animal hide that has not been tanned

KIRIGAMI *n* pl. -S the Japanese art of folding paper

KIRK *n* pl. -S a church

KIRKMAN *n* pl. -MEN a member of a church

KIRMESS *n* pl. -ES kermis

KIRN *v* -ED, -ING, -S to churn

KIRSCH *n* pl. -ES a kind of brandy

KIRTLE *n* pl. -S a man's tunic or coat **KIRTLED** *adj*

KISHKA *n* pl. -S kishke

KISHKE *n* pl. -S a sausage

KISMAT *n* pl. -S kismet

KISMET *n* pl. -S destiny **KISMETIC** *adj*

KISS *v* -ED, -ING, -ES to touch with the lips as a sign of affection **KISSABLE** *adj* **KISSABLY** *adv*

KISSER *n* pl. -S one that kisses

KIST *n* pl. -S a chest, box, or coffin

KISTFUL *n* pl. -S as much as a kist can hold

KIT *v* KITTED, KITTING, KITS to equip

KITCHEN *n* pl. -S a room where food is cooked

KITE *v* KITED, KITING, KITES to obtain money or credit fraudulently

KITER *n* pl. -S one that kites

KITH *n* pl. -S one's friends and neighbors

KITHARA *n* pl. -S cithara

KITHE *v* KITHED, KITHING, KITHES to make known

KITING present participle of kite

KITLING *n* pl. -S a young animal

KITSCH *n* pl. -ES faddish art or literature **KITSCHY** *adj*

KITTED past tense of kit

KITTEL *n* pl. KITTEL a Jewish ceremonial robe

KITTEN *v* -ED, -ING, -S to bear kittens (young cats)

KITTIES pl. of kitty

KITTING present participle of kit

KITTLE *v* -TLED, -TLING, -TLES to tickle

KITTLE *adj* -TLER, -TLEST ticklish

KITTY *n* pl. -TIES a kitten or cat

KIVA *n* pl. -S an underground ceremonial chamber

KIWI *n* pl. -S a flightless bird

KLATCH *n* pl. -ES a social gathering

KLATSCH *n* pl. -ES klatch

KLAVERN *n* pl. -S a local branch of the Ku Klux Klan

KLAXON *n* pl. -S a low-pitched horn

KLEAGLE *n* pl. -S an official in the Ku Klux Klan

KLEPHT *n* pl. -S a Greek guerrilla **KLEPHTIC** *adj*

KLONG	*n* pl. -S a canal
KLOOF	*n* pl. -S a ravine
KLUDGE	*n* pl. -S a system composed of ill-fitting components
KLUTZ	*n* pl. -ES a clumsy person
KLUTZY	*adj* KLUTZIER, KLUTZIEST clumsy
KLYSTRON	*n* pl. -S a type of electron tube
KNACK	*v* -ED, -ING, -S to strike sharply
KNACKER	*n* pl. -S one that buys old livestock
KNACKERY	*n* pl. -ERIES the place of business of a knacker
KNAP	*v* KNAPPED, KNAPPING, KNAPS to strike sharply
KNAPPER	*n* pl. -S one that knaps
KNAPSACK	*n* pl. -S a bag carried on the back
KNAPWEED	*n* pl. -S a meadow plant
KNAR	*n* pl. -S a bump on a tree KNARRED, KNARRY *adj*
KNAVE	*n* pl. -S a dishonest person KNAVISH *adj*
KNAVERY	*n* pl. -ERIES trickery
KNAWEL	*n* pl. -S a Eurasian plant
KNEAD	*v* -ED, -ING, -S to work into a uniform mixture with the hands
KNEADER	*n* pl. -S one that kneads
KNEE	*v* KNEED, KNEEING, KNEES to strike with the knee (a joint of the leg)
KNEECAP	*n* pl. -S a bone at the front of the knee
KNEEHOLE	*n* pl. -S a space for the knees
KNEEL	*v* KNELT or KNEELED, KNEELING, KNEELS to rest on the knees
KNEELER	*n* pl. -S one that kneels
KNEEPAD	*n* pl. -S a covering for a knee
KNEEPAN	*n* pl. -S the kneecap
KNELL	*v* -ED, -ING, -S to sound a bell
KNELT	a past tense of kneel
KNEW	past tense of know
KNICKERS	*n/pl* loose-fitting pants gathered at the knee
KNIFE	*n* pl. KNIVES a sharp-edged instrument used for cutting
KNIFE	*v* KNIFED, KNIFING, KNIFES to cut with a knife
KNIFER	*n* pl. -S one that knifes
KNIGHT	*v* -ED, -ING, -S to make a knight (a medieval gentleman-soldier) of
KNIGHTLY	*adj* of or befitting a knight
KNISH	*n* pl. -ES dough stuffed with filling and fried
KNIT	*v* KNITTED, KNITTING, KNITS to make a fabric or garment by joining loops of yarn
KNITTER	*n* pl. -S one that knits
KNITTING	*n* pl. -S work done by a knitter
KNITWEAR	*n* pl. -S knitted clothing
KNIVES	pl. of knife
KNOB	*n* pl. -S a rounded protuberance KNOBBED, KNOBLIKE *adj*
KNOBBY	*adj* -BIER, -BIEST full of knobs
KNOCK	*v* -ED, -ING, -S to strike sharply
KNOCKER	*n* pl. -S one that knocks
KNOCKOFF	*n* pl. -S a copy that sells for less than the original
KNOCKOUT	*n* pl. -S a blow that induces unconsciousness
KNOLL	*v* -ED, -ING, -S to knell
KNOLLER	*n* pl. -S one that knolls
KNOLLY	*adj* hilly
KNOP	*n* pl. -S a knob KNOPPED *adj*
KNOSP	*n* pl. -S a knob
KNOT	*v* KNOTTED, KNOTTING, KNOTS to tie in a knot (a closed loop)
KNOTHOLE	*n* pl. -S a hole in a plank
KNOTLESS	*adj* having no knots
KNOTLIKE	*adj* resembling a knot
KNOTTER	*n* pl. -S one that knots
KNOTTY	*adj* -TIER, -TIEST full of knots KNOTTILY *adv*
KNOTWEED	*n* pl. -S a common weed
KNOUT	*v* -ED, -ING, -S to flog with a leather whip
KNOW	*v* KNEW, KNOWN, KNOWING, KNOWS to have a true understanding of KNOWABLE *adj*
KNOWER	*n* pl. -S one that knows
KNOWING	*adj* -INGER, -INGEST astute
KNOWING	*n* pl. -S knowledge
KNOWN	*n* pl. -S a mathematical quanity whose value is given

KNUCKLE   v -LED, -LING, -LES to hit with the knuckles (the joints of the fingers)

KNUCKLER   n pl. -S a type of baseball pitch

KNUCKLY   adj -LIER, -LIEST having prominent knuckles

KNUR   n pl. -S a bump on a tree

KNURL   v -ED, -ING, -S to make grooves or ridges in

KNURLY   adj KNURLIER, KNURLIEST gnarly

KOA   n pl. -S a timber tree

KOALA   n pl. -S an Australian mammal

KOAN   n pl. -S a paradox meditated on by Buddhist monks

KOBOLD   n pl. -S an elf

KOEL   n pl. -S an Australian bird

KOHL   n pl. -S a type of eye makeup

KOHLRABI   n pl. -ES a variety of cabbage

KOINE   n pl. -S a type of dialect

KOKANEE   n pl. -S a food fish

KOLA   n pl. -S cola

KOLACKY   n pl. KOLACKY a kind of pastry

KOLHOZ   n pl. -HOZY or -HOZES kolkhoz

KOLINSKI   n pl. -ES kolinsky

KOLINSKY   n pl. -SKIES an Asian mink

KOLKHOS   n pl. -KHOSY or -KHOSES kolkhoz

KOLKHOZ   n pl. -KHOZY or -KHOZES a collective farm in Russia

KOLKOZ   n pl. -KOZY or -KOZES kolkhoz

KOLO   n pl. -LOS a European folk dance

KOMATIK   n pl. -S an Eskimo sledge

KOMONDOR   n pl. -DORS, -DOROK, or -DOROCK a large, shaggy-coated dog

KOODOO   n pl. -DOOS kudu

KOOK   n pl. -S an eccentric person

KOOKIE   adj KOOKIER, KOOKIEST kooky

KOOKY   adj KOOKIER, KOOKIEST eccentric

KOP   n pl. -S a hill

KOPECK   n pl. -S a Russian coin

KOPEK   n pl. -S kopeck

KOPH   n pl. -S a Hebrew letter

KOPJE   n pl. -S a small hill

KOPPA   n pl. -S a Greek letter

KOPPIE   n pl. -S kopje

KOR   n pl. -S a Hebrew unit of measure

KORUNA   n pl. KORUNAS, KORUNY, or KORUN a monetary unit of Czechoslovakia

KOS   n pl. KOS a land measure in India

KOSHER   v -ED, -ING, -S to make fit to be eaten according to Jewish dietary laws

KOSS   n pl. KOSS kos

KOTO   n pl. -TOS a musical instrument

KOTOW   v -ED, -ING, -S to kowtow

KOTOWER   n pl. -S one that kotows

KOUMIS   n pl. -MISES koumiss

KOUMISS   n pl. -ES a beverage made from camel's milk

KOUMYS   n pl. -ES koumiss

KOUMYSS   n pl. -ES koumiss

KOUSSO   n pl. -SOS cusso

KOWTOW   v -ED, -ING, -S to behave in a servile manner

KOWTOWER   n pl. -S one that kowtows

KRAAL   v -ED, -ING, -S to pen in a type of enclosure

KRAFT   n pl. -S a strong paper

KRAIT   n pl. -S a venomous snake

KRAKEN   n pl. -S a legendary sea monster

KRATER   n pl. -S a type of vase

KRAUT   n pl. -S sauerkraut

KREMLIN   n pl. -S a Russian citadel

KREUTZER   n pl. -S an Austrian coin

KREUZER   n pl. -S kreutzer

KRILL   n pl. -S an aggregate of small marine crustaceans

KRIMMER   n pl. -S a kind of fur

KRIS   n pl. -ES a short sword

KRONA   n pl. KRONUR a monetary unit of Iceland

KRONA   n pl. KRONOR a monetary unit of Sweden

KRONE   n pl. KRONER a monetary unit of Denmark

KRONE   n pl. KRONEN a former monetary unit of Austria

KRONOR   pl. of krona

KRONUR   pl. of krona

KROON   *n* pl. KROONS or KROONI a former monetary unit of Estonia

KRUBI   *n* pl. -S a tropical plant

KRUBUT   *n* pl. -S krubi

KRULLER   *n* pl. -S cruller

KRYOLITE   *n* pl. -S cryolite

KRYOLITH   *n* pl. -S cryolite

KRYPTON   *n* pl. -S a gaseous element

KUCHEN   *n* pl. KUCHEN a coffee cake

KUDO   *n* pl. -DOS award; honor

KUDU   *n* pl. -S a large antelope

KUDZU   *n* pl. -S an Asian vine

KUE   *n* pl. -S the letter Q

KULAK   *n* pl. -LAKS or -LAKI a rich Russian peasant

KULTUR   *n* pl. -S culture; civilization

KUMISS   *n* pl. -ES koumiss

KUMMEL   *n* pl. -S a type of liqueur

KUMQUAT   *n* pl. -S a citrus fruit

KUMYS   *n* pl. -ES koumiss

KUNZITE   *n* pl. -S a mineral

KURBASH   *v* -ED, -ING, -ES to flog with a leather whip

KURGAN   *n* pl. -S a mound of earth over a grave

KURTA   *n* pl. -S a shirt worn in India

KURTOSIS   *n* pl. -SISES the relative degree of curvature in a statistical curve

KURU   *n* pl. -S a disease of the nervous system

KUSSO   *n* pl. -SOS cusso

KVAS   *n* pl. -ES kvass

KVASS   *n* pl. -ES a Russian beer

KVETCH   *v* -ED, -ING, -ES to complain

KWACHA   *n* pl. KWACHA a monetary unit of Zambia

KYACK   *n* pl. -S a packsack

KYANISE   *v* -ISED, -ISING, -ISES to kyanize

KYANITE   *n* pl. -S cyanite

KYANIZE   *v* -IZED, -IZING, -IZES to treat wood with a type of preservative

KYAR   *n* pl. -S coir

KYAT   *n* pl. -S a monetary unit of Burma

KYLIX   *n* pl. -LIKES a drinking vessel

KYMOGRAM   *n* pl. -S a record of fluid pressure

KYPHOSIS   *n* pl. -PHOSES abnormal curvature of the spine **KYPHOTIC** *adj*

KYRIE   *n* pl. -S a religious petition for mercy

KYTE   *n* pl. -S the stomach

KYTHE   *v* KYTHED, KYTHING, KYTHES to kithe

LA   n pl. -S the sixth tone of the diatonic musical scale

LAAGER   v -ED, -ING, -S to form a defensive encampment

LAB   n pl. -S a laboratory

LABARUM   n pl. -RA or -RUMS an ecclesiastical banner

LABDANUM   n pl. -S a fragrant resin

LABEL   v -BELED, -BELING, -BELS or -BELLED, -BELLING, -BELS to describe or designate

LABELER   n pl. -S one that labels

LABELLA   pl. of labellum

LABELLED   a past tense of label

LABELLER   n pl. -S labeler

LABELLING   a present participle of label

LABELLUM   n pl. -LA the lower petal of an orchid

LABIA   pl. of labium

LABIAL   n pl. -S a labially produced sound

LABIALLY   adv by means of the lips

LABIATE   n pl. -S a labiated plant

LABIATED   adj having corollas that are divided into two liplike parts

LABILE   adj likely to change

LABILITY   n pl. -TIES the state of being labile

LABIUM   n pl. -BIA a fold of the vulva

LABOR   v -ED, -ING, -S to work

LABORER   n pl. -S one that labors

LABORITE   n pl. -S a supporter of labor interests

LABOUR   v -ED, -ING, -S to labor

LABOURER   n pl. -S laborer

LABRA   a pl. of labrum

LABRET   n pl. -S an ornament worn in a perforation of the lip

LABROID   n pl. -S a marine fish

LABRUM   n pl. -BRA or -BRUMS a lip or liplike structure

LABURNUM   n pl. -S an ornamental tree

LAC   n pl. -S a resinous substance secreted by certain insects

LACE   v LACED, LACING, LACES to fasten by means of a lace (a cord for drawing together two edges)

LACELESS   adj lacking lace

LACELIKE   adj resembling lace

LACER   n pl. -S one that laces

LACERATE   v -ATED, -ATING, -ATES to tear roughly

LACERTID   n pl. -S a type of lizard

LACEWING   n pl. -S a winged insect

LACEWOOD   n pl. -S an Australian tree

LACEWORK   n pl. -S a delicate openwork fabric

LACEY   adj LACIER, LACIEST lacy

LACHES   n pl. LACHES undue delay in asserting a legal right

LACIER   comparative of lace

LACIEST   superlative of lace

LACILY   adv in a lacy manner

LACINESS   n pl. -ES the quality of being lacy

LACING   n pl. -S a contrasting marginal band of color

LACK	*v* -ED, -ING, -S to be without
LACKADAY	*interj* — used to express regret
LACKER	*v* -ED, -ING, -S to lacquer
LACKEY	*v* -ED, -ING, -S to act in a servile manner
LACONIC	*adj* using a minimum of words
LACONISM	*n pl.* -S brevity of expression
LACQUER	*v* -ED, -ING, -S to coat with a glossy substance
LACQUEY	*v* -ED, -ING, -S to lackey
LACRIMAL	*n pl.* -S a type of vase
LACROSSE	*n pl.* -S a type of ball game
LACTAM	*n pl.* -S a chemical compound
LACTARY	*adj* pertaining to milk
LACTASE	*n pl.* -S an enzyme
LACTATE	*v* -TATED, -TATING, -TATES to secrete milk
LACTEAL	*n pl.* -S a lymphatic vessel
LACTEAN	*adj* lacteous
LACTEOUS	*adj* resembling milk
LACTIC	*adj* derived from milk
LACTONE	*n pl.* -S any of a group of esters **LACTONIC** *adj*
LACTOSE	*n pl.* -S a lactic sugar
LACUNA	*n pl.* -NAE or -NAS an empty space or missing part **LACUNAL, LACUNARY, LACUNATE** *adj*
LACUNAR	*n pl.* -NARS or -NARIA a ceiling with recessed panels
LACUNE	*n pl.* -S lacuna
LACUNOSE	*adj* marked by shallow depressions
LACY	*adj* LACIER, LACIEST resembling lacework
LAD	*n pl.* -S a boy or youth
LADANUM	*n pl.* -S labdanum
LADDER	*v* -ED, -ING, -S to cause a run in a stocking
LADDIE	*n pl.* -S a lad
LADE	*v* LADED, LADEN, LADING, LADES to load with a cargo
LADEN	*v* -ED, -ING, -S to lade
LADER	*n pl.* -S one that lades
LADIES	pl. of lady
LADING	*n pl.* -S cargo; freight
LADINO	*n pl.* -NOS a fast-growing clover

LADLE	*v* -DLED, -DLING, -DLES to lift out with a ladle (a type of spoon)
LADLEFUL	*n pl.* -S as much as a ladle will hold
LADLER	*n pl.* -S one that ladles
LADRON	*n pl.* S ladrone
LADRONE	*n pl.* -S a thief
LADY	*n pl.* -DIES a woman of refinement and gentle manners
LADYBIRD	*n pl.* -S a ladybug
LADYBUG	*n pl.* -S a small beetle
LADYFISH	*n pl.* -ES a bonefish
LADYHOOD	*n pl.* -S the state of being a lady
LADYISH	*adj* somewhat ladylike
LADYKIN	*n pl.* -S a small lady
LADYLIKE	*adj* resembling or suitable to a lady
LADYLOVE	*n pl.* -S a sweetheart
LADYPALM	*n pl.* -S a palm tree
LADYSHIP	*n pl.* -S the condition of being a lady
LAEVO	*adj* levo
LAG	*v* LAGGED, LAGGING, LAGS to stay or fall behind
LAGAN	*n pl.* -S goods thrown into the sea with a buoy attached to enable recovery
LAGEND	*n pl.* -S lagan
LAGER	*v* -ED, -ING, -S to laager
LAGGARD	*n pl.* -S one that lags
LAGGED	past tense of lag
LAGGER	*n pl.* -S a laggard
LAGGING	*n pl.* -S an insulating material
LAGNAPPE	*n pl.* -S a small gift given to a customer with his purchase
LAGOON	*n pl.* -S a shallow body of water **LAGOONAL** *adj*
LAGUNA	*n pl.* -S lagoon
LAGUNE	*n pl.* -S lagoon
LAIC	*n pl.* -S a layman **LAICAL** *adj* **LAICALLY** *adv*
LAICH	*n pl.* -S laigh
LAICISE	*v* -ICISED, -ICISING, -ICISES to laicize
LAICISM	*n pl.* -S a political system free from clerical control

LAICIZE   v -ICIZED, -ICIZING, -ICIZES to free from clerical control

LAID   a past tense of lay

LAIGH   n pl. -S a lowland

LAIN   past participle of lie

LAIR   v -ED, -ING, -S to live in a lair (a wild animal's resting or dwelling place)

LAIRD   n pl. -S the owner of a landed estate **LAIRDLY** adj

LAITANCE   n pl. -S a milky deposit on the surface of fresh concrete

LAITH   adj loath **LAITHLY** adv

LAITY   n pl. -ITIES the nonclerical membership of a religious faith

LAKE   n pl. -S a sizable inland body of water

LAKED   adj subjected to the process of laking

LAKEPORT   n pl. -S a city located on the shore of a lake

LAKER   n pl. -S a lake fish

LAKESIDE   n pl. -S the land along the edge of a lake

LAKH   n pl. -S the sum of one hundred thousand

LAKING   n pl. -S the reddening of blood plasma by the release of hemoglobin from the red corpuscles

LAKY   adj LAKIER, LAKIEST of the color of blood

LALL   v -ED, -ING, -S to articulate the letter r as l

LALLAN   n pl. -S a lowland

LALLAND   n pl. -S a lowland

LALLYGAG   v -GAGGED, -GAGGING, -GAGS to dawdle

LAM   v LAMMED, LAMMING, LAMS to flee hastily

LAMA   n pl. -S a Buddhist monk

LAMASERY   n pl. -SERIES a monastery of lamas

LAMB   v -ED, -ING, -S to give birth to a lamb (a young sheep)

LAMBAST   v -ED, -ING, -S to lambaste

LAMBASTE   v -BASTED, -BASTING, -BASTES to beat severely

LAMBDA   n pl. -S a Greek letter **LAMBDOID** adj

LAMBENCY   n pl. -CIES the quality or an instance of being lambent

LAMBENT   adj flickering lightly and gently over a surface

LAMBER   n pl. -S a ewe that is lambing

LAMBERT   n pl. -S a unit of brightness

LAMBIE   n pl. -S a lambkin

LAMBKILL   n pl. -S an evergreen shrub

LAMBKIN   n pl. -S a small lamb

LAMBLIKE   adj resembling a lamb

LAMBSKIN   n pl. -S the skin of a lamb

LAME   adj LAMER, LAMEST physically disabled

LAME   v LAMED, LAMING, LAMES to make lame

LAMED   n pl. -S a Hebrew letter

LAMEDH   n pl. -S lamed

LAMELLA   n pl. -LAE or -LAS a thin plate, scale, or membrane **LAMELLAR** adj

LAMELY   adv in a lame manner

LAMENESS   n pl. -ES the state of being lame

LAMENT   v -ED, -ING, -S to express sorrow or regret for

LAMENTER   n pl. -S one that laments

LAMER   comparative of lame

LAMEST   superlative of lame

LAMIA   n pl. -MIAS or -MIAE a female demon

LAMINA   n pl. -NAE or -NAS a thin plate, scale, or layer **LAMINAL, LAMINAR, LAMINARY** adj

LAMINATE   v -NATED, -NATING, -NATES to compress into a thin plate

LAMING   present participle of lame

LAMINOSE   adj composed of laminae

LAMINOUS   adj laminose

LAMISTER   n pl. -S lamster

LAMMED   past tense of lam

LAMMING   present participle of lam

LAMP   v -ED, -ING, -S to look at

LAMPAD   n pl. -S a candlestick

LAMPAS   n pl. -ES inflammation of the roof of a horse's mouth

LAMPERS   n pl. -ES lampas

LAMPION   n pl. -S a type of light-generating device

LAMPOON   v -ED, -ING, -S to ridicule in a satirical composition

LAMPPOST *n* pl. -S a post supporting a streetlight

LAMPREY *n* pl. -PREYS an eellike fish

LAMPYRID *n* pl. -S any of a family of beetles

LAMSTER *n* pl. -S a fugitive

LANAI *n* pl. -S a veranda

LANATE *adj* covered with wool

LANATED *adj* lanate

LANCE *v* LANCED, LANCING, LANCES to pierce with a lance (a spearlike weapon)

LANCELET *n* pl. -S a small marine organism

LANCER *n* pl. -S a cavalryman armed with a lance

LANCET *n* pl. -S a narrow, pointed arch **LANCETED** *adj*

LANCIERS *n* pl. LANCIERS a French dance

LANCING present participle of lance

LAND *v* -ED, -ING, -S to set down upon land (solid ground)

LANDAU *n* pl. -S a type of carriage

LANDER *n* pl. -S one that lands

LANDFALL *n* pl. -S a sighting or approach to land

LANDFILL *n* pl. -S a system of waste disposal

LANDFORM *n* pl. -S a natural feature of the earth's surface

LANDING *n* pl. -S a place for discharging or taking on passengers or cargo

LANDLADY *n* pl. -DIES a female landlord

LANDLER *n* pl. -S a slow Austrian dance

LANDLESS *adj* owning no land

LANDLORD *n* pl. -S one who owns and rents out real estate

LANDMAN *n* pl. -MEN one who lives and works on land

LANDMARK *n* pl. -S an object that marks a boundary line

LANDMASS *n* pl. -ES a large area of land

LANDMEN pl. of landman

LANDSIDE *n* pl. -S a part of a plow

LANDSKIP *n* pl. -S landscape

LANDSLEIT pl. of landsman

LANDSLID past tense of landslide (to win an election by an overwhelming majority)

LANDSLIP *n* pl. -S the fall of a mass of earth

LANDSMAN *n* pl. LANDSLEIT a fellow Jew coming from one's own section of Eastern Europe

LANDSMAN *n* pl. -MEN landman

LANDWARD *adv* toward the land

LANE *n* pl. -S a narrow passageway

LANELY *adj* lonely

LANG *adj* long

LANGLAUF *n* pl. -S a cross-country ski run

LANGLEY *n* pl. -LEYS a unit of illumination

LANGRAGE *n* pl. -S a shot formerly used in naval warfare

LANGREL *n* pl. -S langrage

LANGSHAN *n* pl. -S any of a breed of large domestic fowl

LANGSYNE *n* pl. -S time long past

LANGUAGE *n* pl. -S a body of words and systems serving as a means of communication

LANGUE *n* pl. -S a type of language

LANGUET *n* pl. -S a tonguelike part

LANGUID *adj* lacking in vigor or vitality

LANGUISH *v* -ED, -ING, -ES to lose vigor or vitality

LANGUOR *n* pl. -S the state of being languid

LANGUR *n* pl. -S an Asian monkey

LANIARD *n* pl. -S lanyard

LANIARY *n* pl. -ARIES a cuspid

LANITAL *n* pl. -S a woollike fiber

LANK *adj* LANKER, LANKEST long and slender **LANKLY** *adv*

LANKNESS *n* pl. -ES the state of being lank

LANKY *adj* LANKIER, LANKIEST ungracefully tall and thin **LANKILY** *adv*

LANNER *n* pl. -S a falcon of Europe and Asia

LANNERET *n* pl. -S a male lanner

LANOLIN *n* pl. -S a fatty substance obtained from wool

LANOLINE *n* pl. -S lanolin

LANOSE *adj* lanate

LANOSITY *n* pl. -TIES the state of being lanose

LANTANA *n* pl. -S a tropical shrub

LANTERN   n pl. -S a protective case for a light

LANTHORN   n pl. -S a lantern

LANUGO   n pl. -GOS fine, soft hair

LANYARD   n pl. -S a fastening rope on a ship

LAP   v LAPPED, LAPPING, LAPS to fold over or around something

LAPBOARD   n pl. -S a flat board used as a table or desk

LAPDOG   n pl. -S a small dog

LAPEL   n pl. -S an extension of the collar of a garment LAPELLED adj

LAPFUL   n pl. -S as much as the lap can hold

LAPIDARY   n pl. -DARIES one who works with precious stones

LAPIDATE   v -DATED, -DATING, -DATES to hurl stones at

LAPIDES   pl. of lapis

LAPIDIFY   v -FIED, -FYING, -FIES to turn to stone

LAPIDIST   n pl. -S a lapidary

LAPILLUS   n pl. -LI a small fragment of lava

LAPIN   n pl. -S a rabbit

LAPIS   n pl. LAPIDES a stone

LAPIS   n pl. -PISES a mineral

LAPPED   past tense of lap

LAPPER   v -ED, -ING, -S to lopper

LAPPET   n pl. -S a decorative flap on a garment LAPPETED adj

LAPPING   present participle of lap

LAPSE   v LAPSED, LAPSING, LAPSES to fall from a previous standard LAPSABLE, LAPSIBLE adj

LAPSER   n pl. -S one that lapses

LAPSUS   n pl. LAPSUS a mistake

LAPWING   n pl. -S a shore bird

LAR   n pl. -ES or -S a tutelary god or spirit of an ancient Roman household

LARBOARD   n pl. -S the left-hand side of a ship

LARCENER   n pl. -S one that commits larceny

LARCENY   n pl. -NIES the felonious taking and removal of another's personal goods

LARCH   n pl. -ES a coniferous tree

LARD   v -ED, -ING, -S to coat with lard (the melted fat of hogs)

LARDER   n pl. -S a place where food is stored

LARDIER   comparative of lardy

LARDIEST   superlative of lardy

LARDLIKE   adj resembling lard

LARDON   n pl. -S a thin slice of bacon or pork

LARDOON   n pl. -S lardon

LARDY   adj LARDIER, LARDIEST resembling lard

LARES   a pl. of lar

LARGE   adj LARGER, LARGEST of considerable size or quantity LARGELY adv

LARGE   n pl. -S generosity

LARGESS   n pl. -ES generosity

LARGESSE   n pl. -S largess

LARGISH   adj somewhat large

LARGO   n pl. -GOS a slow musical movement

LARIAT   v -ED, -ING, -S to lasso

LARINE   adj resembling a gull

LARK   v -ED, -ING, -S to behave playfully

LARKER   n pl. -S one that larks

LARKIER   comparative of larky

LARKIEST   superlative of larky

LARKSOME   adj playful

LARKSPUR   n pl. -S a flowering plant

LARKY   adj LARKIER, LARKIEST playful

LARRIGAN   n pl. -S a type of moccasin

LARRIKIN   n pl. -S a rowdy

LARRUP   v -ED, -ING, -S to beat or thrash

LARRUPER   n pl. -S one that larrups

LARUM   n pl. -S an alarm

LARVA   n pl. -VAE or -VAS the immature form of various insects and animals when newly hatched LARVAL adj

LARYNX   n pl. LARYNGES or LARYNXES an organ of the respiratory tract LARYNGAL adj

LASAGNA   n pl. -S an Italian baked dish

LASAGNE   n pl. -S lasagna

LASCAR   n pl. -S an East Indian sailor

LASE   v LASED, LASING, LASES to function as a laser

LASER *n* pl. -S a device that amplifies light waves

LASH *v* -ED, -ING, -ES to strike with a whip

LASHER *n* pl. -S one that lashes

LASHING *n* pl. -S a flogging

LASHINS *n/pl* an abundance

LASHKAR *n* pl. -S lascar

LASING present participle of lase

LASS *n* pl. -ES a young woman

LASSIE *n* pl. -S a lass

LASSO *v* -ED, -ING, -S or -ES to catch with a lasso (a long rope with a running noose)

LASSOER *n* pl. -S one that lassos

LAST *v* -ED, -ING, -S to continue in existence

LASTER *n* pl. -S one that lasts

LASTING *n* pl. -S a durable fabric

LASTLY *adv* in conclusion

LAT *n* pl. LATS or LATI a former monetary unit of Latvia

LATAKIA *n* pl. -S a variety of Turkish tobacco

LATCH *v* -ED, -ING, -ES to close with a type of fastening device

LATCHET *n* pl. -S a thong used to fasten a shoe

LATCHKEY *n* pl. -KEYS a key for opening a latched door

LATE *adj* LATER, LATEST coming or occurring after the expected time

LATED *adj* belated

LATEEN *n* pl. -S a sailing vessel

LATEENER *n* pl. -S a lateen

LATELY *adv* not long ago

LATEN *v* -ED, -ING, -S to become late

LATENCY *n* pl. -CIES the state of being present but not manifest

LATENESS *n* pl. -ES the state of being late

LATENT *n* pl. -S a barely visible fingerprint that can be developed for study

LATENTLY *adv* dormantly

LATER comparative of late

LATERAD *adv* toward the side

LATERAL *v* -ED, -ING, -S to throw a sideward pass in football

LATERITE *n* pl. -S a type of soil

LATEST *n* pl. -S the most recent development

LATEWOOD *n* pl. -S a part of an annual ring of wood

LATEX *n* pl. LATICES or LATEXES a milky liquid of certain plants

LATH *v* -ED, -ING, -S to cover with laths (thin strips of wood)

LATHE *v* LATHED, LATHING, LATHES to cut or shape on a type of machine

LATHER *v* -ED, -ING, -S to cover with lather (a light foam)

LATHERER *n* pl. -S one that lathers

LATHERY *adj* covered with lather

LATHIER comparative of lathy

LATHIEST superlative of lathy

LATHING *n* pl. -S work made of or using laths

LATHWORK *n* pl. -S lathing

LATHY *adj* LATHIER, LATHIEST long and slender

LATI a pl. of lat

LATICES a pl. of latex

LATIGO *n* pl. -GOS or -GOES a strap used to fasten a saddle

LATINITY *n* pl. -TIES a manner of writing or speaking Latin

LATINIZE *v* -IZED, -IZING, -IZES to translate into Latin

LATISH *adj* somewhat late

LATITUDE *n* pl. -S freedom from narrow restrictions

LATOSOL *n* pl. -S a tropical soil

LATRIA *n* pl. -S the supreme worship given to God only, in Roman Catholicism

LATRINE *n* pl. -S a type of toilet

LATTEN *n* pl. -S a brass-like alloy

LATTER *adj* being the second mentioned of two

LATTERLY *adv* lately

LATTICE *v* -TICED, -TICING, -TICES to form a structure consisting of interlaced strips of material

LATTIN *n* pl. -S latten

LAUAN *n* pl. -S a Philippine timber

LAUD *v* -ED, -ING, -S to praise

LAUDABLE *adj* worthy of praise **LAUDABLY** *adv*

LAUDANUM *n pl.* -S a type of opium preparation

LAUDATOR *n pl.* -S a lauder

LAUDER *n pl.* -S one that lauds

LAUGH *v* -ED, -ING, -S to express emotion, typically mirth, by a series of inarticulate sounds

LAUGHER *n pl.* -S one that laughs

LAUGHING *n pl.* -S laughter

LAUGHTER *n pl.* -S the act or sound of one that laughs

LAUNCE *n pl.* -S a marine fish

LAUNCH *v* -ED, -ING, -ES to set in motion

LAUNCHER *n pl.* -S a launching device

LAUNDER *v* -ED, -ING, -S to wash clothes

LAUNDRY *n pl.* -DRIES a collection of clothes to be washed

LAURA *n pl.* -RAS or -RAE a type of monastery

LAUREATE *v* -ATED, -ATING, -ATES to laurel

LAUREL *v* -RELED, -RELING, -RELS or -RELLED, -RELLING, -RELS to crown with a wreath of evergreen leaves

LAUWINE *n pl.* -S an avalanche

LAVA *n pl.* -S molten rock that issues from a volcano

LAVABO *n pl.* -BOES or -BOS a ceremonial washing in certain Christian churches

LAVAGE *n pl.* -S a washing

LAVALAVA *n pl.* -S a Polynesian garment

LAVALIER *n pl.* -S a pendant worn on a chain around the neck

LAVALIKE *adj* resembling lava

LAVATION *n pl.* -S the act of washing

LAVATORY *n pl.* -RIES a room equipped with washing and toilet facilities

LAVE *v* LAVED, LAVING, LAVES to wash

LAVEER *v* -ED, -ING, -S to sail against the wind

LAVENDER *v* -ED, -ING, -S to sprinkle with a type of perfume

LAVER *n pl.* -S a vessel used for ancient Hebrew ceremonial washings

LAVEROCK *n pl.* -S a songbird

LAVING present participle of lave

LAVISH *adj* -ISHER, -ISHEST expending or giving in great amounts **LAVISHLY** *adv*

LAVISH *v* -ED, -ING, -ES to expend or give in great amounts

LAVISHER *n pl.* -S one that lavishes

LAVROCK *n pl.* -S laverock

LAW *v* -ED, -ING, -S to take a complaint to court for settlement

LAWFUL *adj* allowed by law (the body of rules governing the affairs of a community) **LAWFULLY** *adv*

LAWGIVER *n pl.* -S one who institutes a legal system

LAWINE *n pl.* -S lauwine

LAWING *n pl.* -S a bill for food or drink in a tavern

LAWLESS *adj* having no system of laws

LAWLIKE *adj* being like the law

LAWMAKER *n pl.* -S a legislator

LAWMAN *n pl.* -MEN a law-enforcement officer

LAWN *n pl.* -S an area of grass-covered land **LAWNY** *adj*

LAWSUIT *n pl.* -S a legal action

LAWYER *n pl.* -S a member of the legal profession **LAWYERLY** *adj*

LAX *adj* LAXER, LAXEST not strict or stringent

LAXATION *n pl.* -S the act of relaxing

LAXATIVE *n pl.* -S a drug that stimulates evacuation of the bowels

LAXITY *n pl.* -ITIES the state of being lax

LAXLY *adv* in a lax manner

LAXNESS *n pl.* -ES laxity

LAY *v* LAID or LAYED, LAYING, LAYS to deposit as a wager

LAYABOUT *n pl.* -S a lazy person

LAYAWAY *n pl.* -AWAYS an item that has been reserved with a down payment

LAYER *v* -ED, -ING, -S to form a layer (a single thickness, coating, or covering)

LAYERAGE *n pl.* -S a method of plant propagation

LAYERING *n pl.* -S layerage

LAYETTE *n pl.* -S an outfit of clothing and equipment for a newborn child

LAYMAN   *n* pl. -MEN a member of the laity

LAYOFF   *n* pl. -S the suspension or dismissal of employees

LAYOUT   *n* pl. -S an arrangement or plan

LAYOVER   *n* pl. -S a stopover

LAYWOMAN   *n* pl. -WOMEN a female member of the laity

LAZAR   *n* pl. -S a beggar afflicted with a loathsome disease

LAZARET   *n* pl. -S a hospital treating contagious diseases

LAZE   *v* LAZED, LAZING, LAZES to pass time lazily

LAZIED   past tense of lazy

LAZIER   comparative of lazy

LAZIES   present 3d person sing. of lazy

LAZIEST   superlative of lazy

LAZILY   *adv* in a lazy manner

LAZINESS   *n* pl. -ES the state of being lazy

LAZING   present participle of laze

LAZULI   *n* pl. -S a mineral

LAZULITE   *n* pl. -S a mineral

LAZURITE   *n* pl. -S a mineral

LAZY   *adj* LAZIER, LAZIEST disinclined to work or exertion

LAZY   *v* LAZIED, LAZYING, LAZIES to move or lie lazily

LAZYISH   *adj* somewhat lazy

LEA   *n* pl. -S a meadow

LEACH   *v* -ED, -ING, -ES to subject to the filtering action of a liquid

LEACHATE   *n* pl. -S a solution obtained by leaching

LEACHER   *n* pl. -S one that leaches

LEACHY   *adj* LEACHIER, LEACHIEST porous

LEAD   *v* LED, LEADING, LEADS to show the way to by going in advance

LEAD   *v* -ED, -ING, -S to cover with lead (a heavy metallic element)

LEADEN   *adj* oppressively heavy **LEADENLY** *adv*

LEADER   *n* pl. -S one that leads or guides

LEADIER   comparative of leady

LEADIEST   superlative of leady

LEADING   *n* pl. -S a covering or border of lead

LEADLESS   *adj* having no lead

LEADOFF   *n* pl. -S an opening play or move

LEADSMAN   *n* pl. -MEN a seaman who measures the depth of water

LEADWORK   *n* pl. -S something made of lead

LEADWORT   *n* pl. -S a tropical plant

LEADY   *adj* LEADIER, LEADIEST resembling lead

LEAF   *n* pl. LEAVES a usually green, flattened organ of vascular plants

LEAF   *v* -ED, -ING, -S to turn pages rapidly

LEAFAGE   *n* pl. -S foliage

LEAFIER   comparative of leafy

LEAFIEST   superlative of leafy

LEAFLESS   *adj* having no leaves

LEAFLET   *n* pl. -S a small printed sheet of paper

LEAFLIKE   *adj* resembling a leaf

LEAFWORM   *n* pl. -S a moth larva that feeds on leaves

LEAFY   *adj* LEAFIER, LEAFIEST covered with leaves

LEAGUE   *v* LEAGUED, LEAGUING, LEAGUES to come together for a common purpose

LEAGUER   *v* -ED, -ING, -S to besiege

LEAK   *v* -ED, -ING, -S to permit the escape of something through a breach or flaw

LEAKAGE   *n* pl. -S the act or an instance of leaking

LEAKER   *n* pl. -S one that leaks

LEAKLESS   *adj* designed not to leak

LEAKY   *adj* LEAKIER, LEAKIEST tending to leak **LEAKILY** *adv*

LEAL   *adj* loyal **LEALLY** *adv*

LEALTY   *n* pl. -TIES loyalty

LEAN   *v* LEANED or LEANT, LEANING, LEANS to deviate from a vertical position

LEAN   *adj* LEANER, LEANEST having little fat **LEANLY** *adv*

LEANING   *n* pl. -S a tendency

LEANNESS   *n* pl. -ES the state of being lean

LEANT   a past tense of lean

LEAP   *v* LEAPED or LEAPT, LEAPING, LEAPS to spring off the ground

LEAPER   *n* pl. -S one that leaps

LEAPFROG   *v* -FROGGED, -FROGGING, -FROGS to jump over with the legs wide apart

LEAPT   a past tense of leap

LEAR   *n* pl. -S learning

LEARIER   comparative of leary

LEARIEST   superlative of leary

LEARN   *v* LEARNED or LEARNT, LEARNING, LEARNS to gain knowledge by experience, instruction, or study

LEARNER   *n* pl. -S one that learns

LEARNING   *n* pl. -S acquired knowledge

LEARNT   a past tense of learn

LEARY   *adj* LEARIER, LEARIEST leery

LEASE   *v* LEASED, LEASING, LEASES to grant temporary use of in exchange for rent LEASABLE *adj*

LEASER   *n* pl. -S one that leases

LEASH   *v* -ED, -ING, -ES to restrain an animal with a line or thong

LEASING   *n* pl. -S a falsehood

LEAST   *n* pl. -S something that is smallest in size or degree

LEATHER   *v* -ED, -ING, -S to cover with leather (the dressed or tanned hide of an animal)

LEATHERN   *adj* made of leather

LEATHERY   *adj* resembling leather

LEAVE   *v* LEFT, LEAVING, LEAVES to go away from

LEAVED   *adj* having a leaf or leaves

LEAVEN   *v* -ED, -ING, -S to produce fermentation in

LEAVER   *n* pl. -S one that leaves

LEAVES   pl. of leaf

LEAVING   *n* pl. -S a leftover

LEAVY   *adj* LEAVIER, LEAVIEST leafy

LEBEN   *n* pl. -S a type of liquid food

LECH   *n* pl. -ES letch

LECHAYIM   *n* pl. -S lehayim

LECHER   *v* -ED, -ING, -S to engage in lechery

LECHERY   *n* pl. -ERIES excessive sexual indulgence

LECITHIN   *n* pl. -S any of a group of fatty substances found in plant and animal tissues

LECTERN   *n* pl. -S a reading desk

LECTION   *n* pl. -S a portion of sacred writing read in a church service

LECTOR   *n* pl. -S a low-ranking church officer

LECTURE   *v* -TURED, -TURING, -TURES to expound on a specific subject

LECTURER   *n* pl. -S one that lectures

LECYTHUS   *n* pl. -THI lekythos

LED   past tense of lead

LEDGE   *n* pl. -S a narrow, shelflike projection

LEDGER   *n* pl. -S an account book of final entry

LEDGY   *adj* LEDGIER, LEDGIEST abounding in ledges

LEE   *n* pl. -S shelter from the wind

LEEBOARD   *n* pl. -S a board attached to a sailing vessel to prevent leeway

LEECH   *v* -ED, -ING, -ES to cling to and feed upon or drain

LEEK   *n* pl. -S an herb used in cookery

LEER   *v* -ED, -ING, -S to look with a sideways glance

LEERY   *adj* LEERIER, LEERIEST suspicious LEERILY *adv*

LEET   *n* pl. -S a former English court for petty offenses

LEEWARD   *n* pl. -S the direction toward which the wind is blowing

LEEWAY   *n* pl. -WAYS the lateral drift of a ship

LEFT   *adj* LEFTER, LEFTEST pertaining to the side of the body to the north when one faces east

LEFT   *n* pl. -S the left side or hand

LEFTISM   *n* pl. -S a liberal political philosophy

LEFTIST   *n* pl. -S an advocate of leftism

LEFTOVER   *n* pl. -S an unused or unconsumed portion

LEFTWARD   *adv* toward the left

LEFTWING   *adj* favoring leftism

LEFTY   *n* pl. LEFTIES a left-handed person

LEG   *v* LEGGED, LEGGING, LEGS to move with the legs (appendages that serve as a means of support and locomotion)

LEGACY   *n* pl. -CIES something bequeathed

LEGAL	*n* pl. -S an authorized investment that may be made by investors such as savings banks
LEGALESE	*n* pl. -S the specialized language of lawyers
LEGALISE	*v* -ISED, -ISING, -ISES to legalize
LEGALISM	*n* pl. -S strict conformity to the law
LEGALIST	*n* pl. -S an adherent of legalism
LEGALITY	*n* pl. -TIES the condition of being lawful
LEGALIZE	*v* -IZED, -IZING, -IZES to make lawful
LEGALLY	*adv* in a lawful manner
LEGATE	*v* -GATED, -GATING, -GATES to bequeath
LEGATEE	*n* pl. -S the inheritor of a legacy
LEGATINE	*adj* pertaining to an official envoy
LEGATING	present participle of legate
LEGATION	*n* pl. -S the sending of an official envoy
LEGATO	*n* pl. -TOS a smooth and flowing musical style
LEGATOR	*n* pl. -S one that legates
LEGEND	*n* pl. -S an unverified story from earlier times
LEGENDRY	*n* pl. -RIES a collection of legends
LEGER	*n* pl. -S fishing bait made to lie on the bottom
LEGERITY	*n* pl. -TIES quickness of the mind or body
LEGES	pl. of lex
LEGGED	past tense of leg
LEGGIER	comparative of leggy
LEGGIEST	superlative of leggy
LEGGIN	*n* pl. -S legging
LEGGING	*n* pl. -S a covering for the leg
LEGGY	*adj* -GIER, -GIEST having long legs
LEGHORN	*n* pl. -S a smooth, plaited straw
LEGIBLE	*adj* capable of being read **LEGIBLY** *adv*
LEGION	*n* pl. -S a large military force
LEGIST	*n* pl. -S one learned or skilled in the law
LEGIT	*n* pl. -S legitimate drama
LEGLESS	*adj* having no legs
LEGLIKE	*adj* resembling a leg
LEGMAN	*n* pl. -MEN a newspaperman assigned to gather information
LEGROOM	*n* pl. -S space in which to extend the legs
LEGUME	*n* pl. -S a type of plant
LEGUMIN	*n* pl. -S a plant protein
LEGWORK	*n* pl. -S work that involves extensive walking
LEHAYIM	*n* pl. -S a traditional Jewish toast
LEHR	*n* pl. -S a type of oven
LEHUA	*n* pl. -S a tropical tree
LEI	*n* pl. -S a wreath of flowers
LEISTER	*v* -ED, -ING, -S to spear with a three-pronged fishing implement
LEISURE	*n* pl. -S freedom from the demands of work or duty **LEISURED** *adj*
LEK	*n* pl. -S a monetary unit of Albania
LEKYTHOS	*n* pl. -THOI an oil jar used in ancient Greece
LEKYTHUS	*n* pl. -THI lekythos
LEMAN	*n* pl. -S a lover
LEMMA	*n* pl. -MAS or -MATA a type of proposition in logic
LEMMING	*n* pl. -S a mouselike rodent
LEMNISCI	*n/pl* bands of nerve fibers
LEMON	*n* pl. -S a citrus fruit **LEMONISH, LEMONY** *adj*
LEMONADE	*n* pl. -S a beverage
LEMPIRA	*n* pl. -S a monetary unit of Honduras
LEMUR	*n* pl. -S an arboreal mammal related to the monkeys
LEMURES	*n/pl* the ghosts of the dead in ancient Roman religion
LEMUROID	*n* pl. -S a lemur
LEND	*v* LENT, LENDING, LENDS to give the temporary use of
LENDER	*n* pl. -S one that lends
LENES	pl. of lenis
LENGTH	*n* pl. -S the longer or longest dimension of an object
LENGTHEN	*v* -ED, -ING, -S to make or become longer
LENGTHY	*adj* LENGTHIER, LENGTHIEST very long
LENIENCE	*n* pl. -S leniency

LENIENCY   *n* pl. -CIES the quality of being lenient

LENIENT   *adj* gently tolerant

LENIS   *n* pl. LENES a speech sound pronounced with little or no aspiration

LENITIVE   *n* pl. -S a soothing medicine

LENITY   *n* pl. -TIES leniency

LENO   *n* pl. -NOS a style of weaving

LENS   *n* pl. -ES a piece of transparent material used in changing the convergence of light rays **LENSED, LENSLESS** *adj*

LENSE   *n* pl. -S lens

LENT   past tense of lend

LENTANDO   *adv* becoming slower — used as a musical direction

LENTEN   *adj* meager

LENTIC   *adj* pertaining to still water

LENTICEL   *n* pl. -S a mass of cells on a plant stem

LENTIGO   *n* pl. -TIGINES a freckle

LENTIL   *n* pl. -S a Eurasian annual plant

LENTISK   *n* pl. -S an evergreen tree

LENTO   *n* pl. -TOS a slow musical movement

LENTOID   *adj* lens-shaped

LEONE   *n* pl. -S a monetary unit of Sierra Leone

LEONINE   *adj* pertaining to a lion

LEOPARD   *n* pl. -S a large, carnivorous feline mammal

LEOTARD   *n* pl. -S a close-fitting garment

LEPER   *n* pl. -S one affected with leprosy

LEPIDOTE   *adj* covered with small scales

LEPORID   *n* pl. -S a gnawing mammal

LEPORINE   *adj* resembling a rabbit or hare

LEPROSE   *adj* leprous

LEPROSY   *n* pl. -SIES a chronic disease characterized by skin lesions and deformities

LEPROTIC   *adj* leprous

LEPROUS   *adj* affected with leprosy

LEPTON   *n* pl. -TA a monetary unit of Greece

LEPTON   *n* pl. -S an atomic particle **LEPTONIC** *adj*

LESBIAN   *n* pl. -S a female homosexual

LESION   *n* pl. -S an abnormal change in the structure of an organ or tissue

LESS   *adj* LESSER, LEAST not as great in quantity or degree

LESSEE   *n* pl. -S one to whom a lease is granted

LESSEN   *v* -ED, -ING, -S to make or become less

LESSER   *adj* not as large or important

LESSON   *v* -ED, -ING, -S to instruct

LESSOR   *n* pl. -S one that grants a lease

LEST   *conj* for fear that

LET   *v* LETTED, LETTING, LETS to hinder

LETCH   *n* pl. -ES a strong sexual craving

LETDOWN   *n* pl. -S a decrease

LETHAL   *n* pl. -S a death-causing genetic defect

LETHALLY   *adv* in a deadly manner

LETHARGY   *n* pl. -GIES drowsiness; sluggishness

LETHE   *n* pl. -S forgetfulness **LETHEAN** *adj*

LETTED   past tense of let

LETTER   *v* -ED, -ING, -S to mark with letters (written symbols representing speech sounds)

LETTERER   *n* pl. -S one that letters

LETTING   present participle of let

LETTUCE   *n* pl. -S an herb cultivated as a salad plant

LETUP   *n* pl. -S a lessening or relaxation

LEU   *n* pl. LEI a monetary unit of Rumania

LEUCEMIA   *n* pl. -S leukemia **LEUCEMIC** *adj*

LEUCIN   *n* pl. -S leucine

LEUCINE   *n* pl. -S an amino acid

LEUCITE   *n* pl. -S a mineral **LEUCITIC** *adj*

LEUCOMA   *n* pl. -S leukoma

LEUD   *n* pl. -S or -ES a feudal vassal

LEUKEMIA   *n* pl. -S a disease of the blood-forming organs

LEUKEMIC   *n* pl. -S one affected with leukemia

LEUKOMA   *n* pl. -S an opacity of the cornea

LEUKON *n* pl. -S a bodily organ consisting of the white blood cells

LEUKOSIS *n* pl. -KOSES leukemia **LEUKOTIC** *adj*

LEV *n* pl. LEVA a monetary unit of Bulgaria

LEVANT *v* -ED, -ING, -S to avoid a debt

LEVANTER *n* pl. -S an easterly Mediterranean wind

LEVATOR *n* pl. -ES or -S a muscle that raises an organ or part

LEVEE *v* LEVEED, LEVEEING, LEVEES to provide with an embankment

LEVEL *v* -ELED, -ELING, -ELS or -ELLED, -ELLING, -ELS to make even

LEVELER *n* pl. -S one that levels

LEVELLER *n* pl. -S leveler

LEVELLING present participle of level

LEVELLY *adv* in an even manner

LEVER *v* -ED, -ING, -S to move with a lever (a rigid body used to lift weight)

LEVERAGE *v* -AGED, -AGING, -AGES to provide with a type of economic advantage

LEVERET *n* pl. -S a young hare

LEVIABLE *adj* liable to be levied

LEVIED past tense of levy

LEVIER *n* pl. -S one that levies

LEVIES present 3d person sing. of levy

LEVIGATE *v* -GATED, -GATING, -GATES to reduce to a fine powder

LEVIN *n* pl. -S lightning

LEVIRATE *n* pl. -S the custom of marrying the widow of one's brother

LEVITATE *v* -TATED, -TATING, -TATES to rise and float in the air

LEVITY *n* pl. -TIES conduct characterized by a lack of seriousness

LEVO *adj* turning toward the left

LEVOGYRE *adj* turning toward the left

LEVULIN *n* pl. -S a chemical compound

LEVULOSE *n* pl. -S a very sweet sugar

LEVY *v* LEVIED, LEVYING, LEVIES to impose or collect by legal authority

LEWD *adj* LEWDER, LEWDEST obscene **LEWDLY** *adv*

LEWDNESS *n* pl. -ES the state of being lewd

LEWIS *n* pl. -ISES a hoisting device

LEWISITE *n* pl. -S a vesicant liquid

LEWISSON *n* pl. -S lewis

LEX *n* pl. LEGES law

LEXICAL *adj* pertaining to the words of a language

LEXICON *n* pl. -CA or -CONS a dictionary

LEY *n* pl. LEYS lea

LI *n* pl. -S a Chinese unit of distance

LIABLE *adj* subject or susceptible to something possible or likely

LIAISE *v* LIAISED, LIAISING, LIAISES to establish liaison

LIAISON *n* pl. -S a means for maintaining communication

LIANA *n* pl. -S a tropical vine

LIANE *n* pl. -S liana

LIANG *n* pl. -S a Chinese unit of weight

LIANOID *adj* pertaining to a liana

LIAR *n* pl. -S one that speaks falsely

LIARD *n* pl. -S a former silver coin of France

LIB *n* pl. -S liberation

LIBATION *n* pl. -S a ceremonial pouring of a liquid

LIBBER *n* pl. -S one that supports a liberation movement

LIBECCIO *n* pl. -CIOS a southwest wind

LIBEL *v* -BELED, -BELING, -BELS or -BELLED, -BELLING, -BELS to make or publish a defamatory statement about

LIBELANT *n* pl. -S a plaintiff in a type of lawsuit

LIBELEE *n* pl. -S a defendant in a type of lawsuit

LIBELER *n* pl. -S one that libels

LIBELIST *n* pl. -S a libeler

LIBELLED a past tense of libel

LIBELLEE *n* pl. -S libelee

LIBELLER *n* pl. -S libeler

LIBELLING a present participle of libel

LIBELOUS *adj* defamatory

LIBER *n* pl. LIBRI or LIBERS a book of public records

LIBERAL *n* pl. -S a person favorable to progress or reform

LIBERATE	*v* -ATED, -ATING, -ATES to set free
LIBERTY	*n* pl. -TIES the state of being free
LIBIDO	*n* pl. -DOS the energy derived from instinctual biological drives
LIBRA	*n* pl. -BRAE an ancient Roman unit of weight
LIBRA	*n* pl. -S a former gold coin of Peru
LIBRARY	*n* pl. -BRARIES a place where literary materials are kept for reading and reference
LIBRATE	*v* -BRATED, -BRATING, -BRATES to move from side to side
LIBRETTO	*n* pl. -TOS or -TI the text of an opera
LIBRI	a pl. of liber
LICE	pl. of louse
LICENCE	*v* -CENCED, -CENCING, -CENCES to license
LICENCEE	*n* pl. -S licensee
LICENCER	*n* pl. -S licenser
LICENSE	*v* -CENSED, -CENSING, -CENSES to issue or grant authoritative permission to
LICENSEE	*n* pl. -S one that is licensed
LICENSER	*n* pl. -S one that licenses
LICENSOR	*n* pl. -S licenser
LICHEE	*n* pl. -S litchi
LICHEN	*v* -ED, -ING, -S to cover with lichens (flowerless plants)
LICHENIN	*n* pl. -S a chemical compound
LICHI	*n* pl. -S litchi
LICHT	*v* -ED, -ING, -S to light
LICHTLY	*adv* lightly
LICIT	*adj* lawful LICITLY *adv*
LICK	*v* -ED, -ING, -S to pass the tongue over the surface of
LICKER	*n* pl. -S one that licks
LICKING	*n* pl. -S a thrashing or beating
LICKSPIT	*n* pl. -S a fawning person
LICORICE	*n* pl. -S a perennial herb
LICTOR	*n* pl. -S a magistrate's attendant in ancient Rome
LID	*v* LIDDED, LIDDING, LIDS to provide with a lid (a movable cover)
LIDAR	*n* pl. -S an electronic locating device
LIDLESS	*adj* having no lid
LIDO	*n* pl. -DOS a fashionable beach resort
LIE	*v* LIED, LYING, LIES to speak falsely
LIE	*v* LAY, LAIN, LYING, LIES to be in or get into a horizontal position
LIED	*n* pl. LIEDER a German song
LIEF	*adj* LIEFER, LIEFEST willing LIEFLY *adv*
LIEGE	*n* pl. -S a feudal lord
LIEGEMAN	*n* pl. -MEN a feudal vassal
LIEN	*n* pl. -S a legal right to hold or sell a debtor's property
LIENABLE	*adj* capable of being subjected to a lien
LIENAL	*adj* pertaining to the spleen
LIENTERY	*n* pl. -TERIES a form of diarrhea
LIER	*n* pl. -S one that lies or reclines
LIERNE	*n* pl. -S a connecting part in Gothic vaulting
LIEU	*n* pl. -S place; stead
LIEVE	*adv* LIEVER, LIEVEST gladly
LIFE	*n* pl. LIVES the quality that distinguishes animals and plants from inanimate matter
LIFEBOAT	*n* pl. -S a small rescue boat
LIFEFUL	*adj* full of life
LIFELESS	*adj* having no life
LIFELIKE	*adj* resembling a living thing
LIFELINE	*n* pl. -S a rope used to aid a person in distress
LIFELONG	*adj* lasting for a lifetime
LIFER	*n* pl. -S a prisoner serving a life sentence
LIFETIME	*n* pl. -S the period of living existence
LIFEWAY	*n* pl. -WAYS a way of living
LIFEWORK	*n* pl. -S the major work of one's lifetime
LIFT	*v* -ED, -ING, -S to move to a higher position LIFTABLE *adj*
LIFTER	*n* pl. -S one that lifts
LIFTMAN	*n* pl. -MEN an elevator operator
LIFTOFF	*n* pl. -S the vertical takeoff of a rocket
LIGAMENT	*n* pl. -S a band of firm, fibrous tissue
LIGAN	*n* pl. -S lagan

LIGAND *n* pl. -S a type of ion or molecule

LIGASE *n* pl. -S an enzyme

LIGATE *v* -GATED, -GATING, -GATES to bind

LIGATION *n* pl. -S the act of ligating **LIGATIVE** *adj*

LIGATURE *v* -TURED, -TURING, -TURES to ligate

LIGHT *adj* LIGHTER, LIGHTEST having little weight

LIGHT *v* LIGHTED or LIT, LIGHTING, LIGHTS to illuminate

LIGHTEN *v* -ED, -ING, -S to reduce the weight of

LIGHTER *v* -ED, -ING, -S to convey in a type of barge

LIGHTFUL *adj* brightly illuminated

LIGHTING *n* pl. -S illumination

LIGHTISH *adj* somewhat light

LIGHTLY *adv* to a moderate degree

LIGNEOUS *adj* of or resembling wood

LIGNIFY *v* -FIED, -FYING, -FIES to convert into wood

LIGNIN *n* pl. -S an essential part of woody tissue

LIGNITE *n* pl. -S a type of coal **LIGNITIC** *adj*

LIGROIN *n* pl. -S a flammable liquid

LIGROINE *n* pl. -S ligroin

LIGULA *n* pl. -LAE or -LAS a strap-shaped organ or part **LIGULAR, LIGULATE, LIGULOID** *adj*

LIGULE *n* pl. -S a strap-shaped plant part

LIGURE *n* pl. -S a precious stone

LIKABLE *adj* pleasant

LIKE *v* LIKED, LIKING, LIKES to find pleasant

LIKE *adj* LIKER, LIKEST possessing the same or almost the same characteristics

LIKEABLE *adj* likable

LIKED past tense of like

LIKELY *adj* -LIER, -LIEST probable

LIKEN *v* -ED, -ING, -S to represent as similar

LIKENESS *n* pl. -ES a pictorial representation

LIKER *n* pl. -S one that likes

LIKEST superlative of like

LIKEWISE *adv* in a similar manner

LIKING *n* pl. -S a feeling of attraction or affection

LIKUTA *n* pl. MAKUTA a monetary unit of Zaire

LILAC *n* pl. -S a flowering shrub

LILIED *adj* covered with lilies

LILLIPUT *n* pl. -S a very small person

LILT *v* -ED, -ING, -S to sing or speak rhythmically

LILY *n* pl. LILIES a flowering plant **LILYLIKE** *adj*

LIMA *n* pl. -S the edible seed of a tropical American plant

LIMACINE *adj* resembling a type of mollusk

LIMACON *n* pl. -S a type of geometric curve

LIMAN *n* pl. -S a lagoon

LIMB *v* -ED, -ING, -S to cut off the arms or legs of

LIMBA *n* pl. -S an African tree

LIMBATE *adj* having an edge of a different color

LIMBECK *n* pl. -S alembic

LIMBER *adj* -BERER, -BEREST flexible **LIMBERLY** *adv*

LIMBER *v* -ED, -ING, -S to make flexible

LIMBI a pl. of limbus

LIMBIC *adj* pertaining to a system of the brain

LIMBIER comparative of limby

LIMBIEST superlative of limby

LIMBLESS *adj* having no arms or legs

LIMBO *n* pl. -BOS a condition of oblivion or neglect

LIMBUS *n* pl. -BUSES or -BI a distinctive border

LIMBY *adj* LIMBIER, LIMBIEST having many large branches

LIME *v* LIMED, LIMING, LIMES to treat with lime (a calcium compound)

LIMEADE *n* pl. -S a beverage

LIMEKILN *n* pl. -S a furnace in which shells are burned to produce lime

LIMELESS *adj* having no lime

LIMEN *n* pl. -MENS or -MINA a sensory threshold

LIMERICK	*n* pl. -S a humorous verse
LIMES	*n* pl. LIMITES a fortified boundary
LIMEY	*n* pl. -EYS a British sailor
LIMIER	comparative of limy
LIMIEST	superlative of limy
LIMINA	a pl. of limen
LIMINAL	*adj* pertaining to the limen
LIMINESS	*n* pl. -ES the state of being limy
LIMING	present participle of lime
LIMIT	*v* -ED, -ING, -S to restrict
LIMITARY	*adj* limiting
LIMITED	*n* pl. -S a train or bus making few stops
LIMITER	*n* pl. -S one that limits
LIMITES	pl. of limes
LIMMER	*n* pl. -S a scoundrel
LIMN	*v* -ED, -ING, -S to depict by painting or drawing
LIMNER	*n* pl. -S one that limns
LIMNETIC	*adj* pertaining to the open water of a lake or pond
LIMNIC	*adj* limnetic
LIMO	*n* pl. LIMOS a limousine
LIMONENE	*n* pl. -S a chemical compound
LIMONITE	*n* pl. -S a major ore of iron
LIMP	*v* -ED, -ING, -S to walk lamely
LIMP	*adj* LIMPER, LIMPEST lacking rigidity
LIMPER	*n* pl. -S one that limps
LIMPET	*n* pl. -S a type of mollusk
LIMPID	*adj* transparent **LIMPIDLY** *adv*
LIMPKIN	*n* pl. -S a wading bird
LIMPLY	*adv* in a limp manner
LIMPNESS	*n* pl. -ES the state of being limp
LIMPSY	*adj* lacking strength or vigor
LIMULOID	*n* pl. -S a horseshoe crab
LIMULUS	*n* pl. -LI a horseshoe crab
LIMY	*adj* LIMIER, LIMIEST resembling or containing lime
LIN	*n* pl. -S linn
LINABLE	*adj* lineable
LINAC	*n* pl. -S a device for imparting high velocities to charged particles
LINAGE	*n* pl. -S the number of lines of printed material
LINALOL	*n* pl. -S linalool
LINALOOL	*n* pl. -S a fragrant alcohol
LINCHPIN	*n* pl. -S a locking pin inserted in the end of a shaft
LINDANE	*n* pl. -S an insecticide
LINDEN	*n* pl. -S a tall forest tree
LINDY	*n* pl. -DIES a lively dance
LINE	*v* LINED, LINING, LINES to mark with lines (slender, continuous marks)
LINEABLE	*adj* lying in a straight line
LINEAGE	*n* pl. -S direct descent from an ancestor
LINEAL	*adj* being directly descended from an ancestor **LINEALLY** *adv*
LINEAR	*adj* of or resembling a straight line **LINEARLY** *adv*
LINEATE	*adj* marked with lines
LINEATED	*adj* lineate
LINEBRED	*adj* produced by interbreeding within a particular line of descent
LINECUT	*n* pl. -S a type of printing plate
LINED	past tense of line
LINELESS	*adj* having no lines
LINELIKE	*adj* resembling a line
LINEMAN	*n* pl. -MEN one who installs or repairs telephone wires
LINEN	*n* pl. -S a fabric woven from the fibers of flax **LINENY** *adj*
LINER	*n* pl. -S a commercial ship or airplane
LINESMAN	*n* pl. -MEN a football official
LINEUP	*n* pl. -S a row of persons
LINEY	*adj* LINIER, LINIEST liny
LING	*n* pl. -S a heath plant
LINGA	*n* pl. -S lingam
LINGAM	*n* pl. -S a Hindu phallic symbol
LINGCOD	*n* pl. -S a marine food fish
LINGER	*v* -ED, -ING, -S to delay leaving
LINGERER	*n* pl. -S one that lingers
LINGERIE	*n* pl. -S women's underwear
LINGIER	comparative of lingy
LINGIEST	superlative of lingy
LINGO	*n* pl. -GOES strange or incomprehensible language
LINGUA	*n* pl. -GUAE the tongue or a tonguelike part

LINGUAL   *n* pl. -S a sound articulated with the tongue

LINGUINE   *n* pl. -S linguini

LINGUINI   *n* pl. -S a type of pasta

LINGUIST   *n* pl. -S a person skilled in several languages

LINGY   *adj* LINGIER, LINGIEST covered with heaths

LINIER   comparative of liny

LINIEST   superlative of liny

LINIMENT   *n* pl. -S a medicinal liquid

LININ   *n* pl. -S a substance in the nucleus of a cell

LINING   *n* pl. -S an inner layer

LINK   *v* -ED, -ING, -S to connect **LINKABLE** *adj*

LINKAGE   *n* pl. -S the act of linking

LINKBOY   *n* pl. -BOYS a man or boy hired to carry a torch to light the way along dark streets

LINKER   *n* pl. -S one that links

LINKMAN   *n* pl. -MEN a linkboy

LINKSMAN   *n* pl. -MEN a golfer

LINKUP   *n* pl. -S something that serves as a linking device

LINKWORK   *n* pl. -S something composed of interlocking rings

LINKY   *adj* full of interlocking rings

LINN   *n* pl. -S a waterfall

LINNET   *n* pl. -S a European songbird

LINO   *n* pl. -NOS linoleum

LINOCUT   *n* pl. -S a print made from a design cut into linoleum

LINOLEUM   *n* pl. -S a durable material used as a floor covering

LINSANG   *n* pl. -S a carnivorous mammal

LINSEED   *n* pl. -S flaxseed

LINSEY   *n* pl. -SEYS a coarse fabric

LINSTOCK   *n* pl. -S a stick having one end divided to hold a match

LINT   *n* pl. -S an accumulation of bits of fiber

LINTEL   *n* pl. -S a horizontal supporting beam

LINTER   *n* pl. -S a machine for removing fibers from cotton seeds

LINTIER   comparative of linty

LINTIEST   superlative of linty

LINTLESS   *adj* free from lint

LINTOL   *n* pl. -S lintel

LINTY   *adj* LINTIER, LINTIEST covered with lint

LINUM   *n* pl. -S a plant of the flax family

LINY   *adj* LINIER, LINIEST resembling a line

LION   *n* pl. -S a large, carnivorous feline mammal

LIONESS   *n* pl. -ES a female lion

LIONFISH   *n* pl. -ES a tropical fish

LIONISE   *v* -ISED, -ISING, -ISES to lionize

LIONISER   *n* pl. -S one that lionises

LIONIZE   *v* -IZED, -IZING, -IZES to treat or regard as a celebrity

LIONIZER   *n* pl. -S one that lionizes

LIONLIKE   *adj* resembling a lion

LIP   *v* LIPPED, LIPPING, LIPS to touch with the lips (the folds of flesh around the mouth)

LIPASE   *n* pl. -S an enzyme

LIPID   *n* pl. -S any of a class of fatty substances **LIPIDIC** *adj*

LIPIDE   *n* pl. -S lipid

LIPIN   *n* pl. -S a lipid

LIPLESS   *adj* having no lips

LIPLIKE   *adj* resembling a lip

LIPOCYTE   *n* pl. -S a fat-producing cell

LIPOID   *n* pl. -S a lipid **LIPOIDAL** *adj*

LIPOMA   *n* pl. -MAS or -MATA a tumor of fatty tissue

LIPPED   past tense of lip

LIPPEN   *v* -ED, -ING, -S to trust

LIPPER   *v* -ED, -ING, -S to ripple

LIPPING   *n* pl. -S a liplike outgrowth of bone

LIPPY   *adj* -PIER, -PIEST impudent

LIPSTICK   *n* pl. -S a cosmetic used to color the lips

LIQUATE   *v* -QUATED, -QUATING, -QUATES to purify metal by heating

LIQUEFY   *v* -FIED, -FYING, -FIES to make or become liquid

LIQUEUR   *n* pl. -S a sweetened alcoholic beverage

LIQUID   *n* pl. -S a substance that flows freely

LIQUIDLY   *adv* in a free-flowing manner

LIQUIFY   *v* -FIED, -FYING, -FIES to liquefy

LIQUOR   v -ED, -ING, -S to intoxicate with liquor (an alcoholic beverage)

LIRA   n pl. LIRE or LIRAS a monetary unit of Italy

LIRA   n pl. LIROTH or LIROT a monetary unit of Israel

LIRIPIPE   n pl. -S a long scarf

LISLE   n pl. -S a fine, tightly twisted cotton thread

LISP   v -ED, -ING, -S to pronounce the letters s and z imperfectly

LISPER   n pl. -S one that lisps

LISSOM   adj lissome **LISSOMLY** adv

LISSOME   adj lithe

LIST   v -ED, -ING, -S to write down in a particular order **LISTABLE** adj

LISTEL   n pl. -S a narrow molding

LISTEN   v -ED, -ING, -S to make conscious use of the sense of hearing

LISTENER   n pl. -S one that listens

LISTER   n pl. -S a type of plow

LISTING   n pl. -S something that is listed

LISTLESS   adj languid

LIT   n pl. -S the litas

LITANY   n pl. -NIES a ceremonial form of prayer

LITAS   n pl. LITAI or LITU a former monetary unit of Lithuania

LITCHI   n pl. -S the edible fruit of a Chinese tree

LITER   n pl. -S a unit of capacity

LITERACY   n pl. -CIES the ability to read and write

LITERAL   n pl. -S a small error in printing or writing

LITERARY   adj of, pertaining to, or having the characteristics of books and writings

LITERATE   n pl. -S one who can read and write

LITERATI   n/pl scholars collectively

LITHARGE   n pl. -S a monoxide of lead

LITHE   adj LITHER, LITHEST bending easily **LITHELY** adv

LITHEMIA   n pl. -S an excess of uric acid in the blood **LITHEMIC** adj

LITHIA   n pl. -S an oxide of lithium

LITHIC   adj pertaining to lithium

LITHIUM   n pl. -S a metallic element

LITHO   n pl. LITHOS a type of print

LITHOID   adj resembling stone

LITHOSOL   n pl. -S a type of soil

LITIGANT   n pl. -S one who is engaged in a lawsuit

LITIGATE   v -GATED, -GATING, -GATES to subject to legal proceedings

LITMUS   n pl. -ES a blue coloring matter

LITORAL   adj pertaining to a coastal region

LITOTES   n pl. LITOTES a figure of speech in which an assertion is made by the negation of its opposite

LITRE   n pl. -S liter

LITTEN   adj lighted

LITTER   v -ED, -ING, -S to scatter rubbish about

LITTERER   n pl. -S one that litters

LITTERY   adj covered with rubbish

LITTLE   adj -TLER, -TLEST small

LITTLE   n pl. -S a small amount

LITTLISH   adj somewhat little

LITTORAL   n pl. -S a coastal region

LITU   a pl. of litas

LITURGY   n pl. -GIES a prescribed system of public worship **LITURGIC** adj

LIVABLE   adj suitable for living in

LIVE   v LIVED, LIVING, LIVES to function as an animal or plant

LIVE   adj LIVER, LIVEST having life

LIVEABLE   adj livable

LIVELONG   adj long in passing

LIVELY   adj -LIER, -LIEST full of energy **LIVELILY** adv

LIVEN   v -ED, -ING, -S to make lively

LIVENER   n pl. -S one that livens

LIVENESS   n pl. -ES the state of being live

LIVER   n pl. -S a secreting organ

LIVERIED   adj wearing a livery

LIVERISH   adj having a liver disorder

LIVERY   n pl. -ERIES a uniform worn by servants

LIVES   pl. of life

LIVEST   superlative of live

LIVETRAP   v -TRAPPED, -TRAPPING, -TRAPS to capture in a type of animal trap

LIVID *adj* having the skin abnormally discolored **LIVIDLY** *adv*

LIVIDITY *n pl.* -TIES the state of being livid

LIVIER *n pl.* -S livyer

LIVING *n pl.* -S a means of subsistence

LIVINGLY *adv* realistically

LIVRE *n pl.* -S a former monetary unit of France

LIVYER *n pl.* -S a permanent resident of Newfoundland

LIXIVIUM *n pl.* -IA or -IUMS a solution obtained by leaching **LIXIVIAL** *adj*

LIZARD *n pl.* -S any of a suborder of reptiles

LLAMA *n pl.* -S a ruminant mammal

LLANO *n pl.* -NOS an open, grassy plain

LO *interj* — used to attract attention or to express surprise

LOACH *n pl.* -ES a freshwater fish

LOAD *v* -ED, -ING, -S to place in or on a means of conveyance

LOADER *n pl.* -S one that loads

LOADING *n pl.* -S a burden

LOADSTAR *n pl.* -S lodestar

LOAF *n pl.* LOAVES a shaped mass of bread

LOAF *v* -ED, -ING, -S to pass time idly

LOAFER *n pl.* -S one that loafs

LOAM *v* -ED, -ING, -S to cover with loam (a type of soil)

LOAMLESS *adj* having no loam

LOAMY *adj* LOAMIER, LOAMIEST resembling loam

LOAN *v* -ED, -ING, -S to lend **LOANABLE** *adj*

LOANER *n pl.* -S one that loans

LOANING *n pl.* -S a lane

LOANWORD *n pl.* -S a word taken from another language

LOATH *adj* unwilling

LOATHE *v* LOATHED, LOATHING, LOATHES to detest greatly

LOATHER *n pl.* -S one that loathes

LOATHFUL *adj* repulsive

LOATHING *n pl.* -S extreme dislike

LOATHLY *adj* repulsive

LOAVES pl. of loaf

LOB *v* LOBBED, LOBBING, LOBS to throw or hit in a high arc

LOBAR *adj* pertaining to a lobe

LOBATE *adj* having lobes **LOBATELY** *adv*

LOBATED *adj* lobate

LOBATION *n pl.* -S the formation of lobes

LOBBED past tense of lob

LOBBING present participle of lob

LOBBY *v* -BIED, -BYING, -BIES to attempt to influence legislators

LOBBYER *n pl.* -S a lobbyist

LOBBYGOW *n pl.* -S an errand boy

LOBBYISM *n pl.* -S the practice of lobbying

LOBBYIST *n pl.* -S one who lobbies

LOBE *n pl.* -S a rounded, projecting anatomical part **LOBED** *adj*

LOBEFIN *n pl.* -S a bony fish

LOBELIA *n pl.* -S a flowering plant

LOBELINE *n pl.* -S a poisonous alkaloid

LOBLOLLY *n pl.* -LIES a pine tree

LOBO *n pl.* -BOS the timber wolf

LOBOTOMY *n pl.* -MIES a type of surgical operation

LOBSTER *n pl.* -S an edible marine crustacean

LOBSTICK *n pl.* -S a tree with its lower branches trimmed

LOBULE *n pl.* -S a small lobe **LOBULAR, LOBULATE, LOBULOSE** *adj*

LOBWORM *n pl.* -S a lugworm

LOCA pl. of locus

LOCAL *n pl.* -S a train or bus making all stops

LOCALE *n pl.* -S a locality

LOCALISE *v* -ISED, -ISING, -ISES to localize

LOCALISM *n pl.* -S a custom or mannerism peculiar to a locality

LOCALIST *n pl.* -S one who is strongly concerned with the matters of a locality

LOCALITE *n pl.* -S a resident of a locality

LOCALITY *n pl.* -TIES an area or neighborhood

LOCALIZE *v* -IZED, -IZING, -IZES to confine to a particular area

LOCALLY *adv* in a particular area

LOCATE   v -CATED, -CATING, -CATES to determine the position of

LOCATER   n pl. -S one that locates

LOCATION   n pl. -S the place where something is at a given moment

LOCATIVE   n pl. -S a type of grammatical case

LOCATOR   n pl. -S locater

LOCH   n pl. -S a lake

LOCHIA   n pl. LOCHIA a vaginal discharge following childbirth **LOCHIAL** adj

LOCI   a pl. of locus

LOCK   v -ED, -ING, -S to secure by means of a mechanical fastening device **LOCKABLE** adj

LOCKAGE   n pl. -S a toll on a ship passing through a canal

LOCKBOX   n pl. -ES a box that locks

LOCKER   n pl. -S an enclosure that may be locked

LOCKET   n pl. -S a small ornamental case

LOCKJAW   n pl. -S a form of tetanus

LOCKNUT   n pl. -S a nut which keeps another from loosening

LOCKOUT   n pl. -S a closing of a business to coerce employees to agree to terms

LOCKRAM   n pl. -S a coarse, linen fabric

LOCKSTEP   n pl. -S a mode of marching in close file

LOCKUP   n pl. -S a jail

LOCO   n pl. -COS or -COES locoweed

LOCO   v -ED, -ING, -S to poison with locoweed

LOCOFOCO   n pl. -COS a type of friction match

LOCOISM   n pl. -S a disease of livestock

LOCOMOTE   v -MOTED, -MOTING, -MOTES to move about

LOCOWEED   n pl. -S a plant that causes poisoning when eaten by livestock

LOCULAR   adj having or divided into loculi

LOCULATE   adj locular

LOCULE   n pl. -S loculus **LOCULED** adj

LOCULUS   n pl. -LI a small, cell-like chamber

LOCUM   n pl. -S a temporary substitute

LOCUS   n pl. LOCI or LOCA a place

LOCUST   n pl. -S a migratory grasshopper

LOCUSTA   n pl. -TAE a spikelet **LOCUSTAL** adj

LOCUTION   n pl. -S a particular form of expression

LOCUTORY   n pl. -RIES a room in a monastery

LODE   n pl. -S a deposit of ore

LODEN   n pl. -S a thick, woolen fabric

LODESTAR   n pl. -S a star used as a point of reference

LODGE   v LODGED, LODGING, LODGES to furnish with temporary quarters

LODGER   n pl. -S one that resides in rented quarters

LODGING   n pl. -S a temporary place to live

LODGMENT   n pl. -S a lodging

LODICULE   n pl. -S a scale at the base of the ovary of a grass

LOESS   n pl. -ES a soil deposit **LOESSAL, LOESSIAL** adj

LOFT   v -ED, -ING, -S to store in a loft (an upper room)

LOFTER   n pl. -S a type of golf club

LOFTILY   adv in a lofty manner

LOFTLESS   adj having no loft

LOFTY   adj LOFTIER, LOFTIEST extending high in the air

LOG   v LOGGED, LOGGING, LOGS to cut down trees for timber

LOGAN   n pl. -S a stone balanced to permit easy movement

LOGBOOK   n pl. -S a record book of a ship or aircraft

LOGE   n pl. -S a small compartment

LOGGATS   n/pl loggets

LOGGED   past tense of log

LOGGER   n pl. -S one that logs

LOGGETS   n/pl an old English throwing game

LOGGIA   n pl. -GIAS or -GIE an open gallery

LOGGING   n pl. -S the business of cutting down trees for timber

LOGGY   adj -GIER, -GIEST logy

LOGIA   a pl. of logion

LOGIC   n pl. -S the science of reasoning

LOGICAL   *adj* pertaining to logic

LOGICIAN   *n pl.* -S one who is skilled in logic

LOGICISE   *v* -CISED, -CISING, -CISES to logicize

LOGICIZE   *v* -CIZED, -CIZING, -CIZES to reason

LOGIER   comparative of logy

LOGIEST   superlative of logy

LOGILY   *adv* in a logy manner

LOGINESS   *n pl.* -ES the state of being logy

LOGION   *n pl.* -GIA or -GIONS a saying attributed to Jesus

LOGISTIC   *n pl.* -S symbolic logic

LOGJAM   *n pl.* -S a tangled mass of logs

LOGO   *n pl.* LOGOS an identifying symbol

LOGOGRAM   *n pl.* -S a symbol used to represent an entire word

LOGOMACH   *n pl.* -S one given to arguing about words

LOGOS   *n pl.* LOGOI the rational principle that governs the universe in ancient Greek philosophy

LOGOTYPE   *n pl.* -S a piece of type bearing a syllable, word, or words

LOGOTYPY   *n pl.* -TYPIES the use of logotypes

LOGROLL   *v* -ED, -ING, -S to obtain passage of by exchanging political favors

LOGWAY   *n pl.* -WAYS a ramp used in logging

LOGWOOD   *n pl.* -S a tropical tree

LOGY   *adj* -GIER, -GIEST sluggish

LOIN   *n pl.* -S a part of the side and back between the ribs and the hipbone

LOITER   *v* -ED, -ING, -S to stand idly about

LOITERER   *n pl.* -S one that loiters

LOLL   *v* -ED, -ING, -S to lounge

LOLLER   *n pl.* -S one that lolls

LOLLIPOP   *n pl.* -S a piece of candy on the end of a stick

LOLLOP   *v* -ED, -ING, -S to loll

LOLLY   *n pl.* -LIES a lollipop

LOLLYGAG   *v* -GAGGED, -GAGGING, -GAGS to lallygag

LOLLYPOP   *n pl.* -S lollipop

LOMENT   *n pl.* -S a type of plant pod

LOMENTUM   *n pl.* -TA or -TUMS loment

LONE   *adj* having no companions

LONELY   *adj* -LIER, -LIEST sad from lack of companionship **LONELILY** *adv*

LONENESS   *n pl.* -ES the state of being lone

LONER   *n pl.* -S one that avoids others

LONESOME   *n pl.* -S self

LONG   *adj* LONGER, LONGEST extending for a considerable distance

LONG   *v* -ED, -ING, -S to desire strongly

LONGAN   *n pl.* -S the edible fruit of a Chinese tree

LONGBOAT   *n pl.* -S the largest boat carried by a sailing vessel

LONGBOW   *n pl.* -S a type of archery bow

LONGE   *v* LONGED, LONGEING, LONGES to guide a horse by means of a long rope

LONGER   *n pl.* -S one that longs

LONGERON   *n pl.* -S a longitudinal support of an airplane

LONGHAIR   *n pl.* -S an intellectual

LONGHAND   *n pl.* -S ordinary handwriting

LONGHEAD   *n pl.* -S a person having a long skull

LONGHORN   *n pl.* -S one of a breed of long-horned cattle

LONGING   *n pl.* -S a strong desire

LONGISH   *adj* somewhat long

LONGLEAF   *n pl.* -LEAVES an evergreen tree

LONGLINE   *n pl.* -S a type of fishing line

LONGLY   *adv* for a considerable distance

LONGNESS   *n pl.* -ES the state of being long

LONGSHIP   *n pl.* -S a medieval ship

LONGSOME   *adj* tediously long

LONGSPUR   *n pl.* -S a long-clawed finch

LONGTIME   *adj* of long duration

LONGUEUR   *n pl.* -S a dull and tedious section

LONGWAYS   *adv* longwise

LONGWISE   *adv* lengthwise

LOO   *v* -ED, -ING, -S to subject to a forfeit at loo (a card game)

LOOBY   *n pl.* -BIES a large, awkward person

LOOEY   *n pl.* -EYS looie

LOOF   *n pl.* -S the palm of the hand

LOOFA   *n pl.* -S loofah

LOOFAH   *n pl.* -S a tropical vine

LOOIE   *n pl.* -S a lieutenant of the armed forces

LOOK   *v* -ED, -ING, -S to use one's eyes in seeing

LOOKDOWN   *n pl.* -S a marine fish

LOOKER   *n pl.* -S one that looks

LOOKOUT   *n pl.* -S one engaged in keeping watch

LOOKUP   *n pl.* -S the process of looking something up

LOOM   *v* -ED, -ING, -S to appear in an enlarged and indistinct form

LOON   *n pl.* -S a diving waterfowl

LOONEY   *adj* -NIER, -NIEST loony

LOONY   *adj* -NIER, -NIEST crazy

LOONY   *n pl.* -NIES a loony person

LOOP   *v* -ED, -ING, -S to form loops (circular or oval openings)

LOOPER   *n pl.* -S one that loops

LOOPHOLE   *v* -HOLED, -HOLING, -HOLES to make small openings in

LOOPY   *adj* LOOPIER, LOOPIEST full of loops

LOOSE   *adj* LOOSER, LOOSEST not firm, taut, or rigid **LOOSELY** *adv*

LOOSE   *v* LOOSED, LOOSING, LOOSES to set free

LOOSEN   *v* -ED, -ING, -S to make looser

LOOSENER   *n pl.* -S one that loosens

LOOSED   past tense of loose

LOOSER   comparative of loose

LOOSEST   superlative of loose

LOOSING   present participle of loose

LOOT   *v* -ED, -ING, -S to plunder

LOOTER   *n pl.* -S one that loots

LOP   *v* LOPPED, LOPPING, LOPS to cut off branches or twigs from

LOPE   *v* LOPED, LOPING, LOPES to run with a steady, easy gait

LOPER   *n pl.* -S one that lopes

LOPPED   past tense of lop

LOPPER   *v* -ED, -ING, -S to curdle

LOPPING   present participle of lop

LOPPY   *adj* -PIER, -PIEST hanging limply

LOPSIDED   *adj* leaning to one side

LOPSTICK   *n pl.* -S lobstick

LOQUAT   *n pl.* -S a small evergreen tree

LORAL   *adj* pertaining to the space between the eye and bill of a bird

LORAN   *n pl.* -S a type of navigational system

LORD   *v* -ED, -ING, -S to invest with the power of a lord (a person having dominion over others)

LORDING   *n pl.* -S a lordling

LORDLESS   *adj* having no lord

LORDLIER   comparative of lordly

LORDLIEST   superlative of lordly

LORDLIKE   *adj* lordly

LORDLING   *n pl.* -S a young or unimportant lord

LORDLY   *adj* -LIER, -LIEST of or befitting a lord

LORDOMA   *n pl.* -S lordosis

LORDOSIS   *n pl.* -DOSES a curvature of the spinal column **LORDOTIC** *adj*

LORDSHIP   *n pl.* -S the power of a lord

LORE   *n pl.* -S traditional knowledge or belief

LOREAL   *adj* loral

LORGNON   *n pl.* -S a pair of eyeglasses with a handle

LORICA   *n pl.* -CAE a protective covering or shell

LORICATE   *n pl.* -S an animal having a lorica

LORIKEET   *n pl.* -S a small parrot

LORIMER   *n pl.* -S a maker of implements for harnesses and saddles

LORINER   *n pl.* -S lorimer

LORIS   *n pl.* -RISES an Asian lemur

LORN   *adj* abandoned

LORNNESS   *n pl.* -ES the state of being lorn

LORRY   *n pl.* -RIES a type of wagon or truck

LORY   *n pl.* -RIES a small parrot

LOSE   *v* LOST, LOSING, LOSES to come to be without and be unable to find **LOSABLE** *adj*

LOSEL   *n pl.* -S a worthless person

LOSER   *n* pl. -S one that loses

LOSING   *n* pl. -S a loss

LOSINGLY   *adv* in a manner characterized by defeat

LOSS   *n* pl. -ES the act of one that loses

LOSSY   *adj* causing dissipation of electrical energy

LOST   *adj* not to be found or recovered

LOSTNESS   *n* pl. -ES the state of being lost

LOT   *v* LOTTED, LOTTING, LOTS to distribute proportionately

LOTA   *n* pl. -S lotah

LOTAH   *n* pl. -S a small water vessel used in India

LOTH   *adj* loath

LOTHARIO   *n* pl. -IOS a seducer of women

LOTHSOME   *adj* repulsive

LOTIC   *adj* pertaining to moving water

LOTION   *n* pl. -S a liquid preparation for external application

LOTOS   *n* pl. -ES lotus

LOTTED   past tense of lot

LOTTERY   *n* pl. -TERIES a type of gambling game

LOTTING   present participle of lot

LOTTO   *n* pl. -TOS a game of chance

LOTUS   *n* pl. -ES an aquatic plant

LOUD   *adj* LOUDER, LOUDEST strongly audible

LOUDEN   *v* -ED, -ING, -S to make or become louder

LOUDISH   *adj* somewhat loud

LOUDLY   *adv* -LIER, -LIEST in a loud manner

LOUDNESS   *n* pl. -ES the quality of being loud

LOUGH   *n* pl. -S a lake

LOUIE   *n* pl. -S looie

LOUIS   *n* pl. LOUIS a former gold coin of France

LOUNGE   *v* LOUNGED, LOUNGING, LOUNGES to recline or lean in a relaxed, lazy manner

LOUNGER   *n* pl. -S one that lounges

LOUNGY   *adj* suitable for lounging

LOUP   *v* LOUPED, LOUPEN, LOUPING, LOUPS to leap

LOUPE   *n* pl. -S a small magnifying glass

LOUR   *v* -ED, -ING, -S to lower

LOURY   *adj* lowery

LOUSE   *n* pl. LICE a parasitic insect

LOUSE   *v* LOUSED, LOUSING, LOUSES to spoil or bungle

LOUSY   *adj* LOUSIER, LOUSIEST mean or contemptible **LOUSILY** *adv*

LOUT   *v* -ED, -ING, -S to bow in respect

LOUTISH   *adj* clumsy

LOUVER   *n* pl. -S a type of window **LOUVERED** *adj*

LOUVRE   *n* pl. -S louver

LOVABLE   *adj* having qualities that attract love **LOVABLY** *adv*

LOVAGE   *n* pl. -S a perennial herb

LOVE   *v* LOVED, LOVING, LOVES to feel great affection for

LOVEABLE   *adj* lovable **LOVEABLY** *adv*

LOVEBIRD   *n* pl. -S a small parrot

LOVED   past tense of love

LOVELESS   *adj* feeling no love

LOVELIER   comparative of lovely

LOVELIES   pl. of lovely

LOVELIEST   superlative of lovely

LOVELILY   *adv* in a lovely manner

LOVELOCK   *n* pl. -S a lock of hair hanging separately

LOVELORN   *adj* not loved

LOVELY   *adj* -LIER, -LIEST beautiful

LOVELY   *n* pl. -LIES a beautiful woman

LOVER   *n* pl. -S one that loves another **LOVERLY** *adj*

LOVESICK   *adj* languishing with love

LOVESOME   *adj* lovely

LOVEVINE   *n* pl. -S a twining herb

LOVING   *adj* affectionate

LOVINGLY   *adv* in a loving manner

LOW   *adj* LOWER, LOWEST having relatively little upward extension

LOW   *v* -ED, -ING, -S to utter the sound characteristic of cattle

LOWBORN   *adj* of humble birth

LOWBOY   *n* pl. -BOYS a low chest of drawers

LOWBRED   *adj* lowborn

LOWBROW   *n* pl. -S an uncultivated person

LOWDOWN   *n* pl. -S the whole truth

LOWE   *v* LOWED, LOWING, LOWES to blaze

LOWER   *v* -ED, -ING, -S to appear dark and threatening

LOWERY   *adj* dark and threatening

LOWING   *n* pl. -S the sound characteristic of cattle

LOWISH   *adj* somewhat low

LOWLAND   *n* pl. -S an area of land lying lower than the adjacent country

LOWLIFE   *n* pl. -S a despicable person

LOWLY   *adj* -LIER, -LIEST low in position or rank

LOWN   *adj* peaceful

LOWNESS   *n* pl. -ES the state of being low

LOWSE   *adj* loose

LOX   *v* -ED, -ING, -ES to supply with lox (liquid oxygen)

LOYAL   *adj* -ALER, -ALEST faithful to one's allegiance

LOYALISM   *n* pl. -S loyalty

LOYALIST   *n* pl. -S one who is loyal

LOYALLY   *adv* in a loyal manner

LOYALTY   *n* pl. -TIES the state of being loyal

LOZENGE   *n* pl. -S a small, often medicated candy

LUAU   *n* pl. -S a Hawaiian feast

LUBBER   *n* pl. -S a clumsy person **LUBBERLY** *adj*

LUBE   *n* pl. -S a lubricant

LUBRIC   *adj* slippery

LUCARNE   *n* pl. -S a type of window

LUCE   *n* pl. -S a freshwater fish

LUCENCE   *n* pl. -S lucency

LUCENCY   *n* pl. -CIES the quality of being lucent

LUCENT   *adj* giving off light **LUCENTLY** *adv*

LUCERN   *n* pl. -S lucerne

LUCERNE   *n* pl. -S alfalfa

LUCES   a pl. of lux

LUCID   *adj* easily understood **LUCIDLY** *adv*

LUCIDITY   *n* pl. -TIES the quality of being lucid

LUCIFER   *n* pl. -S a friction match

LUCK   *v* -ED, -ING, -S to succeed by chance or good fortune

LUCKIE   *n* pl. -S an old woman

LUCKLESS   *adj* unlucky

LUCKY   *adj* LUCKIER, LUCKIEST having good fortune **LUCKILY** *adv*

LUCRE   *n* pl. -S monetary gain

LUCULENT   *adj* lucid

LUES   *n* pl. LUES syphilis

LUETIC   *n* pl. -S one infected with syphilis

LUFF   *v* -ED, -ING, -S to steer a sailing vessel nearer into the wind

LUFFA   *n* pl. -S loofah

LUG   *v* LUGGED, LUGGING, LUGS to carry or pull with effort

LUGE   *n* pl. -S a small sled

LUGGAGE   *n* pl. -S articles containing a traveler's belongings

LUGGED   past tense of lug

LUGGER   *n* pl. -S a small sailing vessel

LUGGIE   *n* pl. -S a small wooden dish or pail

LUGGING   present participle of lug

LUGSAIL   *n* pl. -S a type of sail

LUGWORM   *n* pl. -S a burrowing marine worm

LUKEWARM   *adj* moderately warm

LULL   *v* -ED, -ING, -S to cause to sleep or rest

LULLABY   *v* -BIED, -BYING, -BIES to lull with a soothing song

LULU   *n* pl. -S something remarkable

LUM   *n* pl. -S a chimney

LUMBAGO   *n* pl. -GOS pain in the lower back

LUMBAR   *n* pl. -S an anatomical part situated near the loins

LUMBER   *v* -ED, -ING, -S to cut down and prepare timber for market

LUMBERER   *n* pl. -S one that lumbers

LUMEN   *n* pl. -MENS or -MINA the inner passage of a tubular organ **LUMENAL, LUMINAL** *adj*

LUMINARY   *n* pl. -NARIES a body that gives light

LUMINIST   *n* pl. -S a painter who uses the effects of light

LUMINOUS   *adj* giving off light

LUMMOX   *n* pl. -ES a clumsy person

LUMP v -ED, -ING, -S to make into lumps (shapeless masses)

LUMPEN n pl. -S an uprooted individual

LUMPER n pl. -S a laborer employed to load and unload ships

LUMPFISH n pl. -ES a marine fish

LUMPISH adj stupid

LUMPY adj LUMPIER, LUMPIEST full of lumps LUMPILY adv

LUNA n pl. -S an alchemical designation for silver

LUNACY n pl. -CIES insanity

LUNAR n pl. -S an observation of the moon taken for navigational purposes

LUNARIAN n pl. -S a supposed inhabitant of the moon

LUNATE adj crescent-shaped LUNATELY adv

LUNATED adj lunate

LUNATIC n pl. -S an insane person

LUNATION n pl. -S the interval between two successive new moons

LUNCH v -ED, -ING, -ES to eat a noonday meal

LUNCHEON n pl. -S a noonday meal

LUNCHER n pl. -S one that lunches

LUNE n pl. -S a crescent-shaped figure

LUNET n pl. -S lunette

LUNETTE n pl. -S a crescent-shaped object

LUNG n pl. -S a respiratory organ

LUNGAN n pl. -S longan

LUNGE v LUNGED, LUNGING, LUNGES to make a forceful forward movement

LUNGEE n pl. -S lungi

LUNGER n pl. -S one that lunges

LUNGFISH n pl. -ES a type of fish

LUNGI n pl. -S a loincloth worn by men in India

LUNGING present participle of lunge

LUNGWORM n pl. -S a parasitic worm

LUNGWORT n pl. -S a European herb

LUNGYI n pl. -S lungi

LUNIER comparative of luny

LUNIES pl. of luny

LUNIEST superlative of luny

LUNK n pl. -S a lunkhead

LUNKER n pl. -S a large game fish

LUNKHEAD n pl. -S a stupid person

LUNT v -ED, -ING, -S to emit smoke

LUNULA n pl. -LAE a small crescent-shaped structure LUNULAR, LUNULATE adj

LUNULE n pl. -S lunula

LUNY adj -NIER, -NIEST loony

LUNY n pl. -NIES a loony

LUPANAR n pl. -S a brothel

LUPIN n pl. -S lupine

LUPINE n pl. -S a flowering plant

LUPOUS adj pertaining to lupus

LUPULIN n pl. -S a medicinal powder obtained from the hop plant

LUPUS n pl. -ES a skin disease

LURCH v -ED, -ING, -ES to sway abruptly

LURCHER n pl. -S one that lurks or prowls

LURDAN n pl. -S a lazy or stupid person

LURDANE n pl. -S lurdan

LURE v LURED, LURING, LURES to attract with something desirable

LURER n pl. -S one that lures

LURID adj causing shock or horror LURIDLY adv

LURING present participle of lure

LURK v -ED, -ING, -S to wait in concealment

LURKER n pl. -S one that lurks

LUSCIOUS adj having a very pleasing taste or smell

LUSH adj LUSHER, LUSHEST abounding in vegetation LUSHLY adv

LUSH v -ED, -ING, -ES to drink to excess

LUSHNESS n pl. -ES the state of being lush

LUST v -ED, -ING, -S to have an intense desire

LUSTER v -ED, -ING -S to make or become lustrous

LUSTFUL adj marked by excessive sexual desire

LUSTIER comparative of lusty

LUSTIEST superlative of lusty

LUSTILY adv in a lusty manner

LUSTRA a pl. of lustrum

LUSTRAL *adj* pertaining to a lustrum

LUSTRATE *v* -TRATED, -TRATING, -TRATES to purify ceremonially

LUSTRE *v* -TRED, -TRING, -TRES to luster

LUSTRING *n pl.* -S a glossy silk fabric

LUSTROUS *adj* reflecting light evenly and efficiently

LUSTRUM *n pl.* -TRUMS or -TRA a ceremonial purification of the population in ancient Rome

LUSTY *adj* LUSTIER, LUSTIEST full of vigor

LUSUS *n pl.* -ES an abnormality

LUTANIST *n pl.* -S one who plays the lute

LUTE *v* LUTED, LUTING, LUTES to play a lute (a stringed musical instrument)

LUTEA pl. of luteum

LUTEAL *adj* pertaining to the luteum

LUTECIUM *n pl.* -S lutetium

LUTED past tense of lute

LUTEIN *n pl.* -S a yellow pigment

LUTENIST *n pl.* -S lutanist

LUTEOLIN *n pl.* -S a yellow pigment

LUTEOUS *adj* light to moderate greenish yellow in color

LUTETIUM *n pl.* -S a metallic element

LUTEUM *n pl.* -TEA a hormone-secreting body

LUTHERN *n pl.* -S a type of window

LUTING *n pl.* -S a substance used as a sealant

LUTIST *n pl.* -S a lutanist

LUX *n pl.* LUXES or LUCES a unit of illumination

LUXATE *v* -ATED, -ATING, -ATES to put out of joint

LUXATION *n pl.* -S the act of luxating

LUXE *n pl.* -S luxury

LUXURY *n pl.* -RIES free indulgence in that which affords pleasure or comfort

LYARD *adj* streaked with gray

LYART *adj* lyard

LYASE *n pl.* -S an enzyme

LYCEA a pl. of lyceum

LYCEE *n pl.* -S a French secondary school

LYCEUM *n pl.* -CEUMS or -CEA a hall for public lectures or discussions

LYCHEE *n pl.* -S litchi

LYCHNIS *n pl.* -NISES a flowering plant

LYCOPENE *n pl.* -S a red pigment

LYCOPOD *n pl.* -S an evergreen plant

LYDDITE *n pl.* -S an explosive

LYE *n pl.* -S a solution used in making soap

LYING *n pl.* -S the act of telling lies

LYINGLY *adv* falsely

LYMPH *n pl.* -S a body fluid containing white blood cells **LYMPHOID** *adj*

LYMPHOMA *n pl.* -MAS or -MATA a type of tumor

LYNCEAN *adj* of or resembling a lynx

LYNCH *v* -ED, -ING, -ES to put to death without legal sanction

LYNCHER *n pl.* -S one that lynches

LYNCHING *n pl.* -S the act of one who lynches

LYNX *n pl.* -ES a short-tailed wildcat

LYOPHILE *adj* pertaining to a type of colloid

LYRATE *adj* having the shape of a lyre **LYRATELY** *adv*

LYRATED *adj* lyrate

LYRE *n pl.* -S an ancient harp-like instrument

LYREBIRD *n pl.* -S an Australian bird

LYRIC *n pl.* -S a lyrical poem

LYRICAL *adj* having the form of a song

LYRICISE *v* -CISED, -CISING, -CISES to lyricize

LYRICISM *n pl.* -S the quality of being lyrical

LYRICIST *n pl.* -S one who writes the words for songs

LYRICIZE *v* -CIZED, -CIZING, -CIZES to write lyrically

LYRIFORM *adj* lyrate

LYRISM *n pl.* -S lyricism

LYRIST *n pl.* -S one who plays the lyre

LYSATE *n pl.* -S a product of lysis

LYSE *v* LYSED, LYSING, LYSES to cause to undergo lysis

LYSIN *n pl.* -S a substance capable of disintegrating blood cells or bacteria

LYSINE   *n* pl. -S an amino acid

LYSING   present participle of lyse

LYSIS   *n* pl. LYSES the disintegration of cells by lysins

LYSOGEN   *n* pl. -S a type of antigen

LYSOGENY   *n* pl. -NIES the state of being like a lysogen

LYSOSOME   *n* pl. -S a saclike part of a cell

LYSOZYME   *n* pl. -S an enzyme

LYSSA   *n* pl. -S rabies

LYTIC   *adj* pertaining to lysis

LYTTA   *n* pl. -TAE or -TAS a fibrous band in the tongue of certain carnivorous mammals

MA   *n* pl. -S mother

MAAR   *n* pl. -S a volcanic crater

MAC   *n* pl. -S a raincoat

MACABER   *adj* macabre

MACABRE   *adj* gruesome

MACACO   *n* pl. -COS a lemur

MACADAM   *n* pl. -S a type of pavement

MACAQUE   *n* pl. -S a short-tailed monkey

MACARONI   *n* pl. -NIS or -NIES a tubular pasta

MACAROON   *n* pl. -S a type of cookie

MACAW   *n* pl. -S a large parrot

MACCABAW   *n* pl. -S maccaboy

MACCABOY   *n* pl. -BOYS a type of snuff

MACCHIA   *n* pl. -CHIE a dense growth of small trees and shrubs

MACCOBOY   *n* pl. -BOYS maccaboy

MACE   *v* MACED, MACING, MACES to attack with a clublike weapon

MACER   *n* pl. -S an official who carries a ceremonial staff

MACERATE   *v* -ATED, -ATING, -ATES to soften by soaking in liquid

MACH   *n* pl. -S a number indicating the ratio of the speed of a body to the speed of sound

MACHETE   *n* pl. -S a large, heavy knife

MACHINE   *v* -CHINED, -CHINING, -CHINES to process by machine (a mechanical device)

MACHISMO   *n* pl. -MOS strong masculinity

MACHO   *n* pl. -CHOS a person who exhibits machismo

MACHREE   *n* pl. -S dear

MACHZOR   *n* pl. -ZORIM or -ZORS mahzor

MACING   present participle of mace

MACK   *n* pl. -S mac

MACKEREL   *n* pl. -S a marine food fish

MACKINAW   *n* pl. -S a woolen fabric

MACKLE   *v* -LED, -LING, -LES to blur in printing

MACLE   *n* pl. -S a spot or discoloration in a mineral **MACLED** *adj*

MACRAME   *n* pl. -S a trimming of knotted thread or cord

MACRO   *n* pl. -ROS a type of computer instruction

MACRON   *n* pl. -S a symbol placed over a vowel to show that it has a long sound

MACRURAL   *adj* pertaining to macruran

MACRURAN   *n* pl. -S any of a suborder of crustaceans

MACULA   *n* pl. -LAE or -LAS a spot **MACULAR** *adj*

MACULATE   *v* -LATED, -LATING, -LATES to mark with spots

MACULE   *v* -ULED, -ULING, -ULES to mackle

MAD   *adj* MADDER, MADDEST insane

MAD   *v* MADDED, MADDING, MADS to madden

MADAM   *n* pl. -S a woman who manages a brothel

MADAME   *n* pl. -S madam

MADAME   *n* pl. MESDAMES the French title of respect for a married woman

MADCAP   *n* pl. -S an impulsive person

MADDED past tense of mad

MADDEN v -ED, -ING, -S to make or become mad

MADDER n pl. -S a perennial herb

MADDEST superlative of mad

MADDING present participle of mad

MADDISH adj somewhat mad

MADE past tense of make

MADEIRA n pl. -S a white wine

MADHOUSE n pl. -S an insane asylum

MADLY adv in a mad manner

MADMAN n pl. -MEN a man who is insane

MADNESS n pl. -ES the state of being mad

MADONNA n pl. -S a former Italian title of respect for a woman

MADRAS n pl. -ES a cotton fabric

MADRE n pl. -S mother

MADRIGAL n pl. -S a short lyric poem

MADRONA n pl. -S an evergreen tree

MADRONE n pl. -S a madrona

MADRONO n pl. -NOS madrona

MADURO n pl. -ROS a dark-colored, relatively strong cigar

MADWOMAN n pl. -WOMEN a woman who is insane

MADWORT n pl. -S a flowering plant

MADZOON n pl. -S matzoon

MAE n pl. -S more

MAENAD n pl. -S or -ES a female participant in ancient Greek orgies **MAENADIC** adj

MAESTOSO n pl. -SOS a stately musical passage

MAESTRO n pl. -STROS or -STRI a master of an art

MAFFIA n pl. -S mafia

MAFFICK v -ED, -ING, -S to celebrate boisterously

MAFIA n pl. -S a secret organization operating in opposition to legal authority

MAFIC adj pertaining to minerals rich in magnesium and iron

MAFIOSO n pl. -SI a member of the mafia

MAFTIR n pl. -S the concluding section of a parashah

MAG n pl. -S a magazine

MAGAZINE n pl. -S a type of periodical publication

MAGDALEN n pl. -S a reformed prostitute

MAGE n pl. -S a magician

MAGENTA n pl. -S a red dye

MAGGOT n pl. -S the legless larva of certain insects **MAGGOTY** adj

MAGI pl. of magus

MAGIC v -ICKED, -ICKING, -ICS to affect by magic (sorcery)

MAGICAL adj resembling magic

MAGICIAN n pl. -S one skilled in magic

MAGICKED past tense of magic

MAGICKING present participle of magic

MAGILP n pl. -S megilp

MAGISTER n pl. -S a master or teacher

MAGMA n pl. -MAS or -MATA the molten matter from which igneous rock is formed **MAGMATIC** adj

MAGNATE n pl. -S a powerful or influential person

MAGNESIA n pl. -S a medicinal compound **MAGNESIC** adj

MAGNET n pl. -S a body that possesses the property of attracting iron

MAGNETIC n pl. -S a magnet

MAGNETO n pl. -TOS a type of electric generator

MAGNETON n pl. -S a unit of magnetic moment

MAGNIFIC adj magnificent

MAGNIFY v -FIED, -FYING, -FIES to increase the perceived size of

MAGNOLIA n pl. -S a flowering shrub or tree

MAGNUM n pl. -S a large wine bottle

MAGOT n pl. -S a tailless ape

MAGPIE n pl. -S a corvine bird

MAGUEY n pl. -GUEYS a tropical plant

MAGUS n pl. -GI a magician

MAHARAJA n pl. -S a king or prince in India

MAHARANI n pl. -S the wife of a maharaja

MAHATMA n pl. -S a Hindu sage

MAHJONG n pl. -S a game of Chinese origin

MAHJONGG n pl. -S mahjong

MAHOE n pl. -S a tropical tree

MAHOGANY n pl. -NIES a tropical tree

MAHONIA n pl. -S a flowering shrub

MAHOUT *n* pl. -S the keeper and driver of an elephant

MAHUANG *n* pl. -S an Asian plant

MAHZOR *n* pl. -ZORIM or -ZORS a Jewish prayer book

MAID *n* pl. -S a maiden **MAIDISH** *adj*

MAIDEN *n* pl. -S a young unmarried woman **MAIDENLY** *adj*

MAIDHOOD *n* pl. -S the state of being a maiden

MAIEUTIC *adj* pertaining to a method of eliciting knowledge

MAIGRE *adj* containing neither flesh nor its juices

MAIHEM *n* pl. -S mayhem

MAIL *v* -ED,- ING, -S to send by a governmental postal system. **MAILABLE** *adj*

MAILBAG *n* pl. -S a bag for carrying mail (postal material)

MAILBOX *n* pl. -ES a box for depositing mail

MAILE *n* pl. -S a Pacific island vine

MAILER *n* pl. -S one that mails

MAILING *n* pl. -S a rented farm

MAILL *n* pl. -S a payment

MAILLESS *adj* having no armor

MAILLOT *n* pl. -S a woman's one-piece bathing suit

MAILMAN *n* pl. -MEN a man who carries and delivers mail

MAIM *v* -ED, -ING, -S to injure so as to cause lasting damage

MAIMER *n* pl. -S one that maims

MAIN *n* pl. -S the principal part

MAINLAND *n* pl. -S a principal land mass

MAINLINE *v* -LINED, -LINING, -LINES to inject a narcotic into a major vein

MAINLY *adv* for the most part

MAINMAST *n* pl. -S the principal mast of a vessel

MAINSAIL *n* pl. -S the principal sail of a vessel

MAINSTAY *n* pl. -STAYS a principal support

MAINTAIN *v* -ED, -ING, -S to keep in proper condition

MAINTOP *n* pl. -S a platform at the head of a mainmast

MAIOLICA *n* pl. -S majolica

MAIR *n* pl. -S more

MAIST *n* pl. -S most

MAIZE *n* pl. -S an American cereal grass

MAJAGUA *n* pl. -S a tropical tree

MAJESTIC *adj* having majesty

MAJESTY *n* pl. -TIES regal dignity

MAJOLICA *n* pl. -S a type of pottery

MAJOR *v* -ED, -ING, -S to pursue a specific principal course of study

MAJORITY *n* pl. -TIES the greater number or part

MAKAR *n* pl. -S a poet

MAKE *v* MADE, MAKING, MAKES to cause to exist **MAKABLE, MAKEABLE** *adj*

MAKEBATE *n* pl. -S one that encourages quarrels

MAKEFAST *n* pl. -S an object to which a boat is tied

MAKER *n* pl. -S one that makes

MAKEUP *n* pl. -S the way in which the parts or ingredients of something are put together

MAKIMONO *n* pl. -NOS a Japanese ornamental scroll

MAKING *n* pl. -S material from which something can be developed

MAKO *n* pl. -KOS a large shark

MAKUTA pl. of likuta

MALADY *n* pl. -DIES an illness

MALAISE *n* pl. -S a feeling of vague discomfort

MALAMUTE *n* pl. -S an Alaskan sled dog

MALAPERT *n* pl. -S an impudent person

MALAPROP *n* pl. -S a humorous misuse of a word

MALAR *n* pl. -S the cheekbone

MALARIA *n* pl. -S an infectious disease **MALARIAL, MALARIAN** *adj*

MALARKEY *n* pl. -KEYS nonsense

MALARKY *n* pl. -KIES malarkey

MALAROMA *n* pl. -S a malodor

MALATE *n* pl. -S a chemical salt

MALE *n* pl. -S an individual that begets young by fertilizing the female

MALEATE *n* pl. -S a chemical salt

MALEDICT *v* -ED, -ING, -S to curse

MALEFIC	*adj* producing or causing evil
MALEMIUT	*n pl.* -S malamute
MALEMUTE	*n pl.* -S malamute
MALENESS	*n pl.* -ES the quality of being a male
MALFED	*adj* badly fed
MALGRE	*prep* in spite of
MALIC	*adj* pertaining to apples
MALICE	*n pl.* -S a desire to injure another
MALIGN	*v* -ED, -ING, -S to speak evil of
MALIGNER	*n pl.* -S one that maligns
MALIGNLY	*adv* in an evil manner
MALIHINI	*n pl.* -S a newcomer to Hawaii
MALINE	*n pl.* -S a delicate net used for veils
MALINGER	*v* -ED, -ING, -S to feign illness in order to avoid duty or work
MALISON	*n pl.* -S a curse
MALKIN	*n pl.* -S an untidy woman
MALL	*v* -ED, -ING -S to maul
MALLARD	*n pl.* -S a wild duck
MALLEE	*n pl.* -S an evergreen tree
MALLEI	*pl.* of malleus
MALLEOLI	*n/pl* bony protuberances of the ankle
MALLET	*n pl.* -S a type of hammer
MALLEUS	*n pl.* -LEI a bone of the middle ear
MALLOW	*n pl.* -S a flowering plant
MALM	*n pl.* -S a soft, friable limestone
MALMSEY	*n pl.* -SEYS a white wine
MALMY	*adj* MALMIER, MALMIEST resembling malm
MALODOR	*n pl.* -S an offensive odor
MALPOSED	*adj* being in the wrong position
MALT	*v* -ED, -ING, -S to treat or combine with malt (germinated grain)
MALTASE	*n pl.* -S an enzyme
MALTED	*n pl.* -S a sweet beverage
MALTHA	*n pl.* -S a natural tar
MALTIER	comparative of malty
MALTIEST	superlative of malty
MALTOL	*n pl.* -S a chemical compound
MALTOSE	*n pl.* -S a type of sugar
MALTREAT	*v* -ED, -ING, -S to treat badly
MALTSTER	*n pl.* -S one that makes malt
MALTY	*adj* MALTIER, MALTIEST resembling malt
MALVASIA	*n pl.* -S malmsey
MAMA	*n pl.* -S mother
MAMBA	*n pl.* -S a venomous snake
MAMBO	*v* -ED, -ING, -ES or -S to perform a ballroom dance
MAMELUKE	*n pl.* -S a slave in Muslim countries
MAMEY	*n pl.* -MEYS or -MEYES a tropical tree
MAMIE	*n pl.* -S mamey
MAMLUK	*n pl.* -S mameluke
MAMMA	*n pl.* -S mama
MAMMA	*n pl.* -MAE a milk-secreting organ
MAMMAL	*n pl.* -S any of a class of warm-blooded vertebrates
MAMMARY	*adj* pertaining to the mammae
MAMMATE	*adj* having mammae
MAMMATUS	*n pl.* -TI a type of cloud
MAMMEE	*n pl.* -S mamey
MAMMER	*v* -ED, -ING, -S to hesitate
MAMMET	*n pl.* -S maumet
MAMMEY	*n pl.* -MEYS mamey
MAMMIE	*n pl.* -S mammy
MAMMIES	*pl.* of mammy
MAMMILLA	*n pl.* -LAE a nipple
MAMMITIS	*n pl.* -MITIDES mastitis
MAMMOCK	*v* -ED, -ING, -S to shred
MAMMON	*n pl.* -S material wealth
MAMMOTH	*n pl.* -S an extinct elephant
MAMMY	*n pl.* -MIES mother
MAN	*n pl.* MEN an adult human male
MAN	*v* MANNED, MANNING, MANS to supply with men
MANA	*n pl.* -S a supernatural force in certain Pacific island religions
MANACLE	*v* -CLED, -CLING, -CLES to handcuff
MANAGE	*v* -AGED, -AGING, -AGES to control or direct
MANAGER	*n pl.* -S one that manages
MANAKIN	*n pl.* -S a tropical bird
MANANA	*n pl.* -S tomorrow
MANATEE	*n pl.* -S an aquatic mammal **MANATOID** *adj*

MANCHE *n pl.* -S a heraldic design

MANCHET *n pl.* -S a small loaf of fine white bread

MANCIPLE *n pl.* -S an officer authorized to purchase provisions

MANDALA *n pl.* -S a Hindu or Buddhist graphic symbol of the universe **MANDALIC** *adj*

MANDAMUS *v* -ED, -ING, -ES to command by means of writ issued by a superior court

MANDARIN *n pl.* -S a citrus fruit

MANDATE *v* -DATED, -DATING, -DATES to authorize or decree

MANDATOR *n pl.* -S one that mandates

MANDIBLE *n pl.* -S the bone of the lower jaw

MANDIOCA *n pl.* -S manioc

MANDOLA *n pl.* -S an ancient lute

MANDOLIN *n pl.* -S a stringed musical instrument

MANDRAKE *n pl.* -S a European herb

MANDREL *n pl.* -S a shaft on which a tool is mounted

MANDRIL *n pl.* -S mandrel

MANDRILL *n pl.* -S a large baboon

MANE *n pl.* -S the long hair growing on and about the neck of some animals **MANED, MANELESS** *adj*

MANEGE *n pl.* -S the art of training and riding horses

MANEUVER *v* -ED, -ING, -S to change the position of for a specific purpose

MANFUL *adj* courageous **MANFULLY** *adv*

MANGABEY *n pl.* -BEYS a long-tailed monkey

MANGABY *n pl.* -BIES mangabey

MANGANIC *adj* containing manganese (a metallic element)

MANGE *n pl.* -S a skin disease of domestic animals

MANGEL *n pl.* -S a variety of beet

MANGER *n pl.* -S a trough or box from which horses or cattle eat

MANGEY *adj* **MANGIER, MANGIEST** mangy

MANGIER comparative of mangy

MANGIEST superlative of mangy

MANGILY *adv* in a mangy manner

MANGLE *v* -GLED, -GLING, -GLES to cut, slash, or crush so as to disfigure

MANGLER *n pl.* -S one that mangles

MANGO *n pl.* -GOES or -GOS an edible tropical fruit

MANGOLD *n pl.* -S mangel

MANGONEL *n pl.* -S a medieval military device for hurling stones

MANGROVE *n pl.* -S a tropical tree or shrub

MANGY *adj* **MANGIER, MANGIEST** affected with mange

MANHOLE *n pl.* -S a hole providing entrance to an underground or enclosed structure

MANHOOD *n pl.* -S the state of being a man

MANHUNT *n pl.* -S an intensive search for a person

MANIA *n pl.* -S an excessive interest or enthusiasm

MANIAC *n pl.* -S an insane person **MANIACAL** *adj*

MANIC *n pl.* -S one that is affected with mania

MANICURE *v* -CURED, -CURING, -CURES to trim and polish the fingernails of

MANIFEST *v* -ED, -ING, -S to show clearly

MANIFOLD *v* -ED, -ING, -S to make several copies of

MANIHOT *n pl.* -S a tropical plant

MANIKIN *n pl.* -S an anatomical model of the human body

MANILA *n pl.* -S a strong paper

MANILLA *n pl.* -S manila

MANILLE *n pl.* -S the second highest trump in certain card games

MANIOC *n pl.* -S a tropical plant

MANIOCA *n pl.* -S manioc

MANIPLE *n pl.* -S a silk band worn on the left arm as a vestment

MANITO *n pl.* -TOS manitou

MANITOU *n pl.* -S an Algonquian Indian deity

MANITU *n pl.* -S manitou

MANKIND *n pl.* -MANKIND the human race

MANLESS *adj* destitute of men

MANLIKE *adj* resembling a man

MANLY *adj* -LIER, -LIEST having the qualities of a man **MANLILY** *adv*

MANMADE *adj* made by man

MANNA *n pl.* -S divinely supplied food

MANNAN *n pl.* -S a type of sugar

MANNED past tense of man

MANNER *n pl.* -S a way of acting **MANNERED** *adj*

MANNERLY *adj* polite

MANNIKIN *n pl.* -S manikin

MANNING present participle of man

MANNISH *adj* resembling or characteristic of a man

MANNITE *n pl.* -S mannitol **MANNITIC** *adj*

MANNITOL *n pl.* -S an alcohol

MANNOSE *n pl.* -S a type of sugar

MANO *n pl.* -NOS a stone used for grinding foods

MANOR *n pl.* -S a landed estate or territorial unit **MANORIAL** *adj*

MANPACK *adj* designed to be carried by one person

MANPOWER *n pl.* -S the number of men available for service

MANQUE *adj* frustrated in the fulfillment of one's aspirations

MANROPE *n pl.* -S a rope used as a handrail

MANSARD *n pl.* -S a type of roof

MANSE *n pl.* -S a clergyman's house

MANSION *n pl.* -S a large, impressive house

MANTA *n pl.* -S a cotton fabric

MANTEAU *n pl.* -TEAUS or -TEAUX a loose cloak

MANTEL *n pl.* -S a shelf above a fireplace

MANTELET *n pl.* -S a mobile screen used to protect soldiers

MANTES a pl. of mantis

MANTIC *adj* having powers of prophecy

MANTID *n pl.* -S mantis

MANTILLA *n pl.* -S a woman's scarf

MANTIS *n pl.* -TISES or -TES a predatory insect

MANTISSA *n pl.* -S the decimal part of a logarithm

MANTLE *v* -TLED, -TLING, -TLES to cloak

MANTLET *n pl.* -S mantelet

MANTLING *n pl.* -S an ornamental cloth

MANTRA *n pl.* -S a mystical formula of prayer or incantation in Hinduism

MANTRAP *n pl.* -S a trap for catching men

MANTUA *n pl.* -S a woman's gown

MANUAL *n pl.* -S a small reference book

MANUALLY *adv* by means of the hands

MANUARY *adj* involving the hands

MANUBRIA *n/pl* handle-shaped anatomical parts

MANUMIT *v* -MITTED, -MITTING, -MITS to free from slavery

MANURE *v* -NURED, -NURING, -NURES to fertilize with manure (animal excrement)

MANURER *n pl.* -S one that manures

MANURIAL *adj* of or pertaining to manure

MANURING present participle of manure

MANUS *n pl.* MANUS the end of the forelimb in vertebrates

MANWARD *adv* toward man

MANWARDS *adv* manward

MANWISE *adv* in a manner characteristic of man

MANY *adj* MORE, MOST consisting of or amounting to a large number

MANYFOLD *adv* by many times

MAP *v* MAPPED, MAPPING, MAPS to delineate on a map (a representation of a region)

MAPLE *n pl.* -S a hardwood tree

MAPMAKER *n pl.* -S one that makes maps

MAPPABLE *adj* capable of being mapped

MAPPED past tense of map

MAPPER *n pl.* -S one that maps

MAPPING *n pl.* -S a mathematical correspondence

MAQUETTE *n pl.* -S a small preliminary model

MAQUI *n pl.* -S maquis

MAQUIS *n pl.* MAQUIS a thick underbrush

MAR *v* MARRED, MARRING, MARS to detract from the perfection or wholeness of

MARABOU *n pl.* -S an African stork

MARABOUT *n pl.* -S a marabou

MARACA *n pl.* -S a percussion instrument

MARANTA *n pl.* -S a tropical plant

MARASCA n pl. -S a wild cherry

MARASMUS n pl. -ES a wasting away of the body **MARASMIC** adj

MARATHON n pl. -S a long-distance race

MARAUD v -ED, -ING, -S to rove in search of booty

MARAUDER n pl. -S one that marauds

MARAVEDI n pl. -S a former coin of Spain

MARBLE v -BLED, -BLING, -BLES to give a mottled appearance to

MARBLER n pl. -S one that marbles

MARBLING n pl. -S an intermixture of fat and lean in meat

MARBLY adj -BLIER, -BLIEST mottled

MARC n pl. -S the residue remaining after a fruit has been pressed

MARCEL v -CELLED, -CELLING, -CELS to make a deep, soft wave in the hair

MARCH v -ED, -ING, -ES to walk in a formal military manner

MARCHEN n pl. MARCHEN a folktale

MARCHER n pl. -S one that marches

MARCHESA n pl. -CHESE the wife or widow of a marchese

MARCHESE n pl. -CHESI an Italian nobleman

MARE n pl. -S a mature female horse

MARE n pl. -RIA a dark area on the surface of the moon or Mars

MAREMMA n pl. -REMME a marshy coastal region

MARGARIC adj pearly

MARGARIN n pl. -S a butter substitute

MARGAY n pl. -GAYS a small American wildcat

MARGE n pl. -S a margin

MARGENT v -ED, -ING, -S to margin

MARGIN v -ED, -ING, -S to provide with a margin (a border)

MARGINAL adj of or pertaining to a margin

MARGRAVE n pl. -S the military governor of a medieval German border province

MARIA pl. of mare

MARIACHI n pl. -S a Mexican musical band

MARIGOLD n pl. -S a flowering plant

MARIMBA n pl. -S a percussion instrument

MARINA n pl. -S a docking area for small boats

MARINADE v -NADED, -NADING, -NADES to marinate

MARINARA n pl. -S a seasoned tomato sauce

MARINATE v -NATED, -NATING, -NATES to soak in a seasoned liquid before cooking

MARINE n pl. -S a soldier trained for service at sea and on land

MARINER n pl. -S a sailor

MARIPOSA n pl. -S a flowering plant

MARISH n pl. -ES a marsh

MARITAL adj pertaining to marriage

MARITIME adj pertaining to navigation or commerce on the sea

MARJORAM n pl. -S fragrant herb

MARK v -ED, -ING, -S to make a visible impression on

MARKDOWN n pl. -S a reduction in price

MARKEDLY adv in an evident manner

MARKER n pl. -S one that marks

MARKET v -ED, -ING, -S to offer for sale

MARKETER n pl. -S one that markets

MARKHOOR n pl. -S markhor

MARKHOR n pl. -S a wild goat

MARKING n pl. -S a pattern of marks

MARKKA n pl. -KAA or -KAS a monetary unit of Finland

MARKSMAN n pl. -MEN a person skillful at hitting a target

MARKUP n pl. -S an increase in price

MARL v -ED, -ING, -S to fertilize with marl (an earthy deposit containing lime, clay, and sand)

MARLIER comparative of marly

MARLIEST superlative of marly

MARLIN n pl. -S a marine game fish

MARLINE n pl. -S a rope used on a ship

MARLING n pl. -S marline

MARLITE n pl. -S a type of marl **MARLITIC** adj

MARLY adj MARLIER, MARLIEST abounding with marl

MARMITE n pl. -S a large soup kettle

MARMOSET n pl. -S a small monkey

MARMOT n pl. -S a burrowing rodent

MAROON v -ED, -ING, -S to abandon in an isolated place

MARPLOT *n pl.* -S one that ruins a plan by meddling

MARQUE *n pl.* -S reprisal

MARQUEE *n pl.* -S a rooflike structure projecting over an entrance

MARQUESS *n pl.* -ES marquis

MARQUIS *n pl.* -ES a European nobleman

MARQUISE *n pl.* S the wife or widow of a marquis

MARRAM *n pl.* -S a beach grass

MARRED past tense of mar

MARRER *n pl.* -S one that mars

MARRIAGE *n pl.* -S the legal union of a man and woman

MARRIED *n pl.* -S one who has entered into marriage

MARRIER *n pl.* -S one that marries

MARRIES present 3d person sing. of marry

MARRING present participle of mar

MARRON *n pl.* -S a variety of chestnut

MARROW *v* -ED, -ING, -S to marry

MARROWY *adj* pithy

MARRY *v* -RIED, -RYING, -RIES to enter into marriage

MARSE *n pl.* -S master

MARSH *n pl.* -ES a tract of low, wet land

MARSHAL *v* -ED, -ING, -S to put in proper order

MARSHALL *v* -ED, -ING, -S to marshal

MARSHY *adj* MARSHIER, MARSHIEST resembling a marsh

MARSUPIA *n/pl* abdominal pouches of certain mammals

MART *v* -ED, -ING, -S to market

MARTAGON *n pl.* -S a flowering plant

MARTELLO *n pl.* -LOS a circular fort

MARTEN *n pl.* -S a carnivorous mammal

MARTIAL *adj* pertaining to war

MARTIAN *n pl.* -S a supposed inhabitant of the planet Mars

MARTIN *n pl.* -S a small bird

MARTINET *n pl.* -S one who demands rigid adherence to rules

MARTINI *n pl.* -S an alcoholic beverage

MARTLET *n pl.* -S a martin

MARTYR *v* -ED, -ING, -S to put to death for adhering to a belief

MARTYRLY *adj* resembling a martyr

MARTYRY *n pl.* -TYRIES a shrine erected in honor of a martyred person

MARVEL *v* -VELED, -VELING, -VELLED, -VELLING, -VELS to be filled with wonder or astonishment

MARZIPAN *n pl.* -S an almond candy

MASCARA *n pl.* -S a cosmetic for coloring the eyelashes and eyebrows

MASCON *n pl.* -S a concentration of dense matter beneath the moon's surface

MASCOT *n pl.* -S a person, animal, or object believed to bring good luck

MASER *n pl.* -S a device for amplifying electrical impulses

MASH *v* -ED, -ING, -ES to reduce to a pulpy mass

MASHER *n pl.* -S one that mashes

MASHIE *n pl.* -S a golf club

MASHY *n pl.* MASHIES mashie

MASJID *n pl.* -S a mosque

MASK *v* -ED, -ING, -S to cover with a mask (a covering used to disguise the face) MASKABLE *adj*

MASKEG *n pl.* -S muskeg

MASKER *n pl.* -S one that wears a mask

MASKING *n pl.* -S a piece of scenery used to conceal parts of a stage from the audience

MASKLIKE *adj* suggestive of a mask

MASON *v* -ED, -ING, -S to build with stone or brick

MASONIC *adj* pertaining to masonry

MASONRY *n pl.* -RIES a structure built of stone or brick

MASQUE *n pl.* -S a dramatic entertainment formerly popular in England

MASQUER *n pl.* -S masker

MASS *v* -ED, -ING, -ES to assemble in a mass (a body of coherent matter)

MASSA *n pl.* -S master

MASSACRE *v* -CRED, -CRING, -CRES to kill indiscriminately

MASSAGE *v* -SAGED, -SAGING, -SAGES to manipulate parts of the body for remedial or hygienic purposes

MASSAGER *n pl.* -S one that massages

MASSE *n pl.* -S a type of shot in billiards

MASSEDLY *adv* in a massed manner

MASSETER *n pl.* -S a muscle that raises the lower jaw

MASSEUR *n pl.* -S a man who massages

MASSEUSE *n pl.* -S a woman who massages

MASSICOT *n pl.* -S a yellow pigment

MASSIER comparative of massy

MASSIEST superlative of massy

MASSIF *n pl.* -S a principal mountain mass

MASSIVE *adj* of considerable size

MASSLESS *adj* having no mass

MASSY *adj* MASSIER, MASSIEST massive

MAST *v* -ED, -ING, -S to provide with a mast (a long pole on a ship that supports the sails and rigging)

MASTABA *n pl.* -S an ancient Egyptian tomb

MASTABAH *n pl.* -S mastaba

MASTER *v* -ED, -ING, -S to become skilled in

MASTERLY *adj* very skillful

MASTERY *n pl.* -TERIES superior knowledge or skill

MASTHEAD *v* -ED, -ING, -S to raise to the top of a mast

MASTIC *n pl.* -S an aromatic resin

MASTICHE *n pl.* -S mastic

MASTIFF *n pl.* -S a large, short-haired dog

MASTITIS *n pl.* -TITIDES inflammation of the breast **MASTITIC** *adj*

MASTIX *n pl.* -ES mastic

MASTLESS *adj* having no mast

MASTLIKE *adj* resembling a mast

MASTODON *n pl.* -S an extinct elephant-like mammal

MASTOID *n pl.* -S the rear portion of the temporal bone

MASURIUM *n pl.* -S a metallic element

MAT *v* MATTED, MATTING, MATS to pack down so as to form a dense mass

MATADOR *n pl.* -S the bullfighter who kills the bull in a bullfight

MATCH *v* -ED, -ING, -ES to set in competition or opposition

MATCHBOX *n pl.* -ES a small box

MATCHER *n pl.* -S one that matches

MATE *v* MATED, MATING, MATES to join as mates (partners in a union)

MATELESS *adj* having no mate

MATELOTE *n pl.* -S a fish stew

MATER *n pl.* -TERS or -TRES mother

MATERIAL *n pl.* -S the substance of which anything is or may be composed

MATERIEL *n pl.* -S the aggregate of equipment and supplies used by an organization

MATERNAL *adj* pertaining to a mother

MATESHIP *n pl.* -S the state of being a mate

MATEY *n pl.* -EYS a friend

MATH *n pl.* -S mathematics

MATILDA *n pl.* -S a hobo's bundle

MATIN *n pl.* -S a morning song, as of birds

MATINAL *adj* pertaining to the morning

MATINEE *n pl.* -S a daytime performance

MATINESS *n pl.* -ES friendliness

MATING *n pl.* -S the period during which a seasonal-breeding animal can mate

MATLESS *adj* having no mats (small floor coverings)

MATRASS *n pl.* -ES a long-necked glass vessel

MATRES a pl. of mater

MATRIX *n pl.* -TRICES or -TRIXES something within which something else originates or develops

MATRON *n pl.* -S a married woman of established social position **MATRONAL, MATRONLY** *adj*

MATT *v* -ED, -ING, -S to matte

MATTE *v* MATTED, MATTING, MATTES to produce a dull finish on

MATTED past tense of mat, matt, and matte

MATTEDLY *adv* in a tangled manner

MATTER *v* -ED, -ING, -S to be of importance

MATTERY *adj* producing pus

MATTIN *n pl.* -S matin

MATTING	n pl. -S a woven fabric used as a floor covering
MATTOCK	n pl. -S a digging tool
MATTOID	n pl. -S a mentally unbalanced person
MATTRASS	n pl. -ES matrass
MATTRESS	n pl. -ES a large pad filled with resilient material used on or as a bed
MATURATE	v -RATED, -RATING, -RATES to mature
MATURE	adj -TURER, -TUREST fully developed **MATURELY** adv
MATURE	v -TURED, -TURING, -TURES to make or become mature
MATURITY	n pl. -TIES the state of being mature
MATZA	n pl. -S matzo
MATZAH	n pl. -S matzo
MATZO	n pl. -ZOS, -ZOT, or -ZOTH an unleavened bread
MATZOH	n pl. -S matzo
MATZOON	n pl. -S a food made from milk
MATZOT	a pl. of matzo
MATZOTH	a pl. of matzo
MAUDLIN	adj excessively emotional
MAUGER	prep maugre
MAUGRE	prep in spite of
MAUL	v -ED, -ING, -S to injure by beating
MAULER	n pl. -S one that mauls
MAUMET	n pl. -S an idol
MAUMETRY	n pl. -RIES idolatry
MAUN	v must — MAUN is the only form of this verb; it cannot be conjugated
MAUND	n pl. -S an Asian unit of weight
MAUNDER	v -ED, -ING, -S to talk incoherently
MAUNDY	n pl. -DIES the religious ceremony of washing the feet of the poor
MAUSOLEA	n/pl large, stately tombs
MAUT	n pl. -S malt
MAUVE	n pl. -S a purple color
MAVEN	n pl. -S a mavin
MAVERICK	n pl. -S an unbranded range animal
MAVIE	n pl. -S mavis
MAVIN	n pl. -S an expert

MAVIS	n pl. -VISES a songbird
MAW	v MAWED, MAWN, MAWING, MAWS to mow
MAWKISH	adj offensively sentimental
MAXI	n pl. -S a long skirt or coat
MAXICOAT	n pl. -S a long coat
MAXILLA	n pl. -LAE or -LAS the upper jaw or jawbone
MAXIM	n pl. -S a brief statement of a general truth or principle
MAXIMA	a pl. of maximum
MAXIMAL	n pl. -S an element of a mathematical set that is followed by no other
MAXIMIN	n pl. -S the maximum of a set of minima
MAXIMISE	v -MISED, -MISING, -MISES to maximize
MAXIMITE	n pl. -S a powerful explosive
MAXIMIZE	v -MIZED, -MIZING, -MIZES to make as great as possible
MAXIMUM	n pl. -MUMS or -MA the greatest possible amount, quantity, or degree
MAXIXE	n pl. -S a Brazilian dance
MAXWELL	n pl. -S a unit of magnetic flux
MAY	v present 2d person sing. MAY, MAYEST, or MAYST, past tense MIGHT — used as an auxiliary to express permission
MAY	v -ED, -ING, -S to gather flowers in the spring
MAYA	n pl. -S the power to produce illusions, in Hindu philosophy **MAYAN** adj
MAYAPPLE	n pl. -S a perennial herb
MAYBE	adv possibly
MAYBUSH	n pl. -ES a flowering shrub
MAYDAY	n pl. -DAYS a radio distress call
MAYEST	a present 2d person sing. of may
MAYFLY	n pl. -FLIES a winged insect
MAYHAP	adv maybe
MAYHEM	n pl. -S the offense of willfully maiming a person
MAYING	n pl. -S the gathering of spring flowers
MAYOR	n pl. -S the chief executive official of a city or borough **MAYORAL** adj
MAYORESS	n pl. -ES a female mayor

MAYPOLE n pl. -S a decorated pole used in a spring celebration

MAYPOP n pl. -S a flowering vine

MAYST a present 2d person sing. of may

MAYVIN n pl. -S mavin

MAYWEED n pl. -S a malodorous weed

MAZAEDIA n/pl spore-producing organs of certain lichens

MAZARD n pl. -S the head or face

MAZE v MAZED, MAZING, MAZES to bewilder **MAZEDLY** adv

MAZELIKE adj mazy

MAZER n pl. -S a large drinking bowl

MAZIER comparative of mazy

MAZIEST superlative of mazy

MAZILY adv in a mazy manner

MAZINESS n pl. -ES the quality of being mazy

MAZING present participle of maze

MAZOURKA n pl. -S mazurka

MAZUMA n pl. -S money

MAZURKA n pl. -S a Polish dance

MAZY adj MAZIER, MAZIEST full of confusing turns and passages

MAZZARD n pl. -S a wild cherry

MBIRA n pl. -S an African musical instrument

ME pron the objective case of the pronoun I

MEAD n pl. -S an alcoholic beverage

MEADOW n pl. -S a tract of grassland **MEADOWY** adj

MEAGER adj deficient in quantity or quality **MEAGERLY** adv

MEAGRE adj meager **MEAGRELY** adv

MEAL n pl. -S the food served and eaten in one sitting

MEALIE n pl. -S an ear of corn

MEALIER comparative of mealy

MEALIEST superlative of mealy

MEALLESS adj lacking a meal

MEALTIME n pl. -S the usual time for a meal

MEALWORM n pl. -S the destructive larva of certain beetles

MEALY adj MEALIER, MEALIEST soft, dry, and friable

MEALYBUG n pl. -S a destructive insect

MEAN v MEANT, MEANING, MEANS to intend

MEAN adj MEANER, MEANEST inferior in grade, quality, or character

MEANDER v -ED, -ING, -S to wander

MEANER n pl. -S one that means

MEANEST superlative of mean

MEANIE n pl. -S a nasty person

MEANIES pl. of meany

MEANING n pl. -S something that one intends to convey by language

MEANLY adv in a mean manner

MEANNESS n pl. -ES the state of being mean

MEANT past tense of mean

MEANTIME n pl. -S the intervening time

MEANY n pl. MEANIES meanie

MEASLE n pl. -S a tapeworm larva **MEASLED** adj

MEASLY adj -SLIER, -SLIEST meager

MEASURE v -SURED, -SURING, -SURES to ascertain the dimensions, quantity, or capacity of

MEASURER n pl. -S one that measures

MEAT n pl. -S animal flesh used as food

MEATAL adj pertaining to a meatus

MEATBALL n pl. -S a small ball of chopped meat

MEATHEAD n pl. -S a dolt

MEATIER comparative of meaty

MEATIEST superlative of meaty

MEATILY adv in a meaty manner

MEATLESS adj having no meat

MEATMAN n pl. -MEN a vendor of meat

MEATUS n pl. -ES a natural body passage

MEATY adj MEATIER, MEATIEST full of meat

MECCA n pl. -S a place visited by many people

MECHANIC n pl. -S a person who works with machines

MECONIUM n pl. -S the first fecal excretion of a newborn child

MEDAKA n pl. -S a Japanese fish

MEDAL v -ALED, -ALING, -ALS or -ALLED, -ALLING, -ALS to honor with a medal (a commemorative piece of metal)

MEDALIST   n pl. -S a person to whom a medal has been awarded

MEDALLIC   adj of or pertaining to a medal

MEDALLING   a present participle of medal

MEDDLE   v -DLED, -DLING, -DLES to interest oneself in what is not one's concern

MEDDLER   n pl. -S one that meddles

MEDIA   n pl. -DIAE the middle layer of a blood or lymph vessel

MEDIA   n pl. -S a channel of communication

MEDIACY   n pl. -CIES the act of mediating

MEDIAD   adv toward the middle of a body or part

MEDIAL   n pl. -S a sound, syllable, or letter in the middle of a word

MEDIALLY   adv in a central manner

MEDIAN   n pl. -S a central part

MEDIANLY   adv medially

MEDIANT   n pl. -S a type of musical tone

MEDIATE   v -ATED, -ATING, -ATES to act between disputing parties in order to bring about a settlement

MEDIATOR   n pl. -S one that mediates

MEDIC   n pl. -S one engaged in medical work

MEDICAID   n pl. -S a type of governmental health program

MEDICAL   n pl. -S a physical examination

MEDICARE   n pl. -S a type of governmental health program

MEDICATE   v -CATED, -CATING, -CATES to treat with medicine

MEDICINE   v -CINED, -CINING, -CINES to administer medicine (a substance used in the treatment of disease) to

MEDICK   n pl. -S a flowering plant

MEDICO   n pl. -COS a doctor or medical student

MEDIEVAL   n pl. -S a person belonging to the Middle Ages

MEDII   pl. of medius

MEDIOCRE   adj neither good nor bad

MEDITATE   v -TATED, -TATING, -TATES to ponder

MEDIUM   n pl. -DIA or -DIUMS a surrounding environment in which something functions and thrives

MEDIUS   n pl. -DII the middle finger

MEDLAR   n pl. -S a Eurasian tree

MEDLEY   n pl. -LEYS a mixture

MEDULLA   n pl. -LAS or -LAE the central tissue in the stems of certain plants **MEDULLAR** adj

MEDUSA   n pl. -SAE or -SAS a jellyfish

MEDUSAN   n pl. -S medusa

MEDUSOID   n pl. -S medusa

MEED   n pl. -S a deserved reward

MEEK   adj MEEKER, MEEKEST lacking in spirit and courage **MEEKLY** adv

MEEKNESS   n pl. -ES the quality of being meek

MEET   v MET, MEETING, MEETS to come into the company or presence of

MEETER   n pl. -S one that meets

MEETING   n pl. -S an assembly for a common purpose

MEETLY   adv suitably

MEETNESS   n pl. -ES suitability

MEGABAR   n pl. -S a unit of pressure

MEGABIT   n pl. -S a unit of computer information

MEGABUCK   n pl. -S one million dollars

MEGADYNE   n pl. -S a unit of force

MEGALITH   n pl. -S a huge stone used in prehistoric monuments

MEGAPOD   adj having large feet

MEGAPODE   n pl. -S a large-footed bird

MEGASS   n pl. -ES a bagasse

MEGASSE   n pl. -S megass

MEGATON   n pl. -S a unit of explosive force

MEGAVOLT   n pl. -S a unit of electromotive force

MEGAWATT   n pl. -S a unit of power

MEGILLAH   n pl. -S a long, involved story

MEGILP   n pl. -S a substance with which pigments are mixed in painting

MEGILPH   n pl. -S megilp

MEGOHM   n pl. -S a unit of electrical resistance

MEGRIM   n pl. -S a migraine

MEIKLE   adj large

MEINIE   n pl. -S meiny

MEINY   n pl. -NIES a retinue

MEIOSIS *n* pl. -OSES a type of cell division **MEIOTIC** *adj*

MEL *n* pl. -S honey

MELAMINE *n* pl. -S a chemical compound

MELANGE *n* pl. -S a mixture

MELANIAN *adj* pertaining to dark pigmentation

MELANIC *n* pl. -S one who is affected with melanism

MELANIN *n* pl. -S a dark pigment

MELANISM *n* pl. -S abnormally dark pigmentation of the skin

MELANIST *n* pl. -S a melanic

MELANITE *n* pl. -S a black variety of garnet

MELANIZE *v* -NIZED, -NIZING, -NIZES to make dark

MELANOID *n* pl. -S a dark pigment

MELANOMA *n* pl. -MAS or -MATA a darkly pigmented tumor

MELANOUS *adj* having dark skin and hair

MELD *v* -ED, -ING, -S to blend

MELDER *n* pl. -S the amount of grain ground at one time

MELEE *n* pl. -S a confused struggle

MELIC *adj* pertaining to song

MELILITE *n* pl. -S a mineral group

MELILOT *n* pl. -S a flowering plant

MELINITE *n* pl. -S a powerful explosive

MELISMA *n* pl. -MAS or -MATA melodic embellishment

MELL *v* -ED, -ING, -S to mix

MELLIFIC *adj* producing honey

MELLOW *adj* -LOWER, -LOWEST soft and full-flavored from ripeness **MELLOWLY** *adv*

MELLOW *v* -ED, -ING, -S to make or become mellow

MELODEON *n* pl. -S a musical instrument

MELODIA *n* pl. -S a type of organ stop

MELODIC *adj* pertaining to melody

MELODIES pl. of melody

MELODISE *v* -DISED, -DISING, -DISES to melodize

MELODIST *n* pl. -S a composer of melodies

MELODIZE *v* -DIZED, -DIZING, -DIZES to compose a melody

MELODY *n* pl. -DIES an agreeable succession of musical sounds

MELOID *n* pl. -S a type of beetle

MELON *n* pl. -S any of various gourds

MELT *v* -ED, -ING, -S to change from a solid to a liquid state by heat **MELTABLE** *adj*

MELTAGE *n* pl. -S the process of melting

MELTER *n* pl. -S one that melts

MELTON *n* pl. -S a heavy woolen fabric

MEM *n* pl. -S a Hebrew letter

MEMBER *n* pl. -S a distinct part of a whole **MEMBERED** *adj*

MEMBRANE *n* pl. -S a thin, pliable layer of tissue

MEMENTO *n* pl. -TOS or -TOES something that serves as a reminder of the past

MEMO *n* pl. MEMOS a note designating something to be remembered

MEMOIR *n* pl. -S a biography

MEMORIAL *n* pl. -S something that serves as a remembrance of a person or event

MEMORIZE *v* -RIZED, -RIZING, -RIZES to commit to memory

MEMORY *n* pl. -RIES the mental faculty of retaining and recalling past experience

MEMSAHIB *n* pl. -S a European woman living in colonial India

MEN pl. of man

MENACE *v* -ACED, -ACING, -ACES to theaten

MENACER *n* pl. -S one that menaces

MENAD *n* pl. -S maenad

MENAGE *n* pl. -S a household

MENARCHE *n* pl. -S the first occurrence of menstruation

MEND *v* -ED, -ING, -S to repair **MENDABLE** *adj*

MENDER *n* pl. -S one that mends

MENDIGO *n* pl. -GOS a freshwater fish

MENDING *n* pl. -S an accumulation of articles to be mended

MENFOLK *n/pl* the men of a family or community

MENFOLKS *n/pl* menfolk

MENHADEN *n* pl. -S a marine fish

MENHIR *n* pl. -S a prehistoric monument

MENIAL *n* pl. -S a domestic servant

MENIALLY *adv* in a servile manner

MENINX   *n pl.* -NINGES any of the membranes enclosing the brain and spinal cord

MENISCUS   *n pl.* -CI or -CUSES a crescent-shaped body **MENISCAL** *adj*

MENO   *adv* less — used as a musical direction

MENOLOGY   *n pl.* -GIES an ecclesiastical calendar

MENORAH   *n pl.* -S a candleholder used in Jewish worship

MENSA   *n pl.* -SAS or -SAE the grinding surface of a tooth

MENSAL   *adj* pertaining to or used at the table

MENSCH   *n pl.* MENSCHES or MENSCHEN an admirable person

MENSE   *v* MENSED, MENSING, MENSES to do honor to

MENSEFUL   *adj* proper

MENSTRUA   *n/pl* solvents

MENSURAL   *adj* pertaining to measure

MENSWEAR   *n pl.* -S clothing for men

MENTA   *pl.* of mentum

MENTAL   *adj* pertaining to the mind **MENTALLY** *adv*

MENTHENE   *n pl.* -S a liquid hydrocarbon

MENTHOL   *n pl.* -S an alcohol

MENTION   *v* -ED, -ING, -S to refer to in a casual manner

MENTOR   *n pl.* -S a wise and trusted teacher

MENTUM   *n pl.* -TA the chin

MENU   *n pl.* -S a list of the dishes available in a restaurant

MEOW   *v* -ED, -ING, -S to make the crying sound of a cat

MEPHITIS   *n pl.* -TISES an offensive odor **MEPHITIC** *adj*

MERCAPTO   *adj* containing a particular chemical group

MERCER   *n pl.* -S a dealer in textiles

MERCERY   *n pl.* -CERIES a mercer's shop

MERCHANT   *v* -ED, -ING, -S to buy and sell goods for profit

MERCIES   *pl.* of mercy

MERCIFUL   *adj* full of mercy

MERCURY   *n pl.* -RIES a metallic element **MERCURIC** *adj*

MERCY   *n pl.* -CIES compassion shown to an offender or enemy

MERE   *n pl.* -S a pond or lake

MERE   *adj* MERER, MEREST being nothing more than **MERELY** *adv*

MERENGUE   *n pl.* -S a ballroom dance

MERGE   *v* MERGED, MERGING, MERGES to combine

MERGENCE   *n pl.* -S the act of merging

MERGER   *n pl.* -S the union of two or more businesses into a single enterprise

MERGING   present participle of merge

MERIDIAN   *n pl.* -S a circle around the earth passing through both poles

MERINGUE   *n pl.* -S a topping for pastries

MERINO   *n pl.* -NOS a fine wool

MERISIS   *n pl.* MERISES growth

MERISTEM   *n pl.* -S formative plant tissue

MERISTIC   *adj* made up of segments

MERIT   *v* -ED, -ING, -S to earn

MERK   *n pl.* -S a former coin of Scotland

MERL   *n pl.* -S merle

MERLE   *n pl.* -S a blackbird

MERLIN   *n pl.* -S a European falcon

MERLON   *n pl.* -S the solid part of an indented parapet

MERMAID   *n pl.* -S a legendary marine creature

MERMAN   *n pl.* -MEN a legendary marine creature

MEROPIA   *n pl.* -S partial blindness **MEROPIC** *adj*

MERRY   *adj* -RIER, -RIEST cheerful **MERRILY** *adv*

MESA   *n pl.* -S a land formation having a flat top and steep sides

MESALLY   *adv* medially

MESARCH   *adj* originating in a mesic habitat

MESCAL   *n pl.* -S a cactus

MESDAMES   *pl.* of madame

MESEEMS   *v* past tense MESEEMED it seems to me — MESEEMS is an impersonal verb and is used only in the 3d person sing.

MESH   *v* -ED, -ING, -ES to entangle

MESHWORK   *n pl.* -S a network

MESHY	*adj* MESHIER, MESHIEST netty	**MESTIZO**	*n* pl. -ZOS or -ZOES a person of mixed ancestry
MESIAL	*adj* situated in the middle **MESIALLY** *adv*	**MET**	past tense of meet
MESIAN	*adj* mesial	**META**	*adj* pertaining to positions in a benzene ring separated by one carbon atom
MESIC	*adj* characterized by a medium supply of moisture		
MESMERIC	*adj* pertaining to hypnotism	**METAGE**	*n* pl. -S an official measurement of weight or contents
MESNALTY	*n* pl. -TIES a type of feudal estate	**METAL**	*v* -ALED, -ALING, -ALS or -ALLED, -ALLING, -ALS to cover with metal (any of various ductile, fusible, and lustrous substances)
MESNE	*adj* being between two extremes		
MESOCARP	*n* pl. -S the middle layer of a pericarp		
MESODERM	*n* pl. -S the middle germ layer of an embryo	**METALISE**	*v* -ISED, -ISING, -ISES to metalize
MESOGLEA	*n* pl. -S a gelatinous material in sponges	**METALIST**	*n* pl. -S one who works with metals
MESOMERE	*n* pl. -S an embryonic segment	**METALIZE**	*v* -IZED, -IZING, -IZES to treat with metal
MESON	*n* pl. -S an atomic particle **MESONIC** *adj*	**METALLED**	past tense of metal
MESOPHYL	*n* pl. -S the soft tissue of a leaf	**METALLIC**	*adj* pertaining to or containing a metal
MESOSOME	*n* pl. -S a specialized cellular part	**METALLING**	a present participle of metal
MESOTRON	*n* pl. -S a meson	**METAMER**	*n* pl. -S a type of chemical compound
MESQUIT	*n* pl. -S mesquite	**METAMERE**	*n* pl. -S a somite
MESQUITE	*n* pl. -S a spiny tree or shrub	**METAPHOR**	*n* pl. -S a type of figure of speech
MESS	*v* -ED, -ING, -ES to make dirty or untidy	**METATE**	*n* pl. -S a stone used for grinding grains
MESSAGE	*n* pl. -S an oral, written, or signaled communication	**METAZOAN**	*n* pl. -S any of a major division of multicellular animals **METAZOAL, METAZOIC** *adj*
MESSAN	*n* pl. -S a lapdog		
MESSIAH	*n* pl. -S an expected liberator	**METAZOON**	*n* pl. -ZOA a metazoan
MESSIER	comparative of messy	**METE**	*v* METED, METING, METES to distribute by measure
MESSIEST	superlative of messy	**METEOR**	*n* pl. -S a small celestial body that enters the earth's atmosphere **METEORIC** *adj*
MESSIEURS	pl. of monsieur		
MESSILY	*adv* in a messy manner		
MESSMAN	*n* pl. -MEN a serviceman who works in a dining facility	**METEPA**	*n* pl. -S a chemical compound
		METER	*v* -ED, -ING, -S to measure by mechanical means
MESSMATE	*n* pl. -S a person with whom one eats regularly		
		METERAGE	*n* pl. -S the process of metering
MESSUAGE	*n* pl. -S a dwelling house with its adjacent buildings and land	**METHADON**	*n* pl. -S a narcotic drug
		METHANE	*n* pl. -S a flammable gas
MESSY	*adj* MESSIER, MESSIEST dirty or untidy	**METHANOL**	*n* pl. -S a toxic alcohol
		METHINKS	*v* past tense METHOUGHT it seems to me — METHINKS is an impersonal verb and is used only in the 3d person sing.
MESTEE	*n* pl. -S mustee		
MESTESO	*n* pl. -SOS or -SOES mestizo		
MESTINO	*n* pl. -NOS or -NOES mestizo		
MESTIZA	*n* pl. -S a female mestizo	**METHOD**	*n* pl. -S a means of procedure
		METHODIC	*adj* systematic

METHOUGHT past tense of methinks

METHOXY *adj* containing a certain chemical group

METHOXYL *adj* methoxy

METHYL *n* pl. -S a univalent radical **METHYLIC** *adj*

METHYLAL *n* pl. -S a flammable liquid

METIER *n* pl. -S a vocation

METING present participle of mete

METIS *n* pl. METIS a person of mixed ancestry

METISSE *n* pl. -S a female metis

METONYM *n* pl. -S a word used in metonymy

METONYMY *n* pl. -MIES a type of figure of speech

METOPE *n* pl. -PES or -PAE a space between two triglyphs

METOPIC *adj* pertaining to the forehead

METOPON *n* pl. -S a narcotic drug

METRE *v* -TRED, -TRING, -TRES to meter

METRIC *n* pl. -S a standard of measurement

METRICAL *adj* pertaining to or composed in a system of arranged and measured rhythm

METRIFY *v* -FIED, -FYING, -FIES to compose in metrical form

METRING present participle of metre

METRIST *n* pl. -S one who metrifies

METRITIS *n* pl. -TISES inflammation of the uterus

METRO *n* pl. -ROS a subway

METTLE *n* pl. -S quality of character **METTLED** *adj*

METUMP *n* pl. -S a tumpline

MEUNIERE *adj* cooked in browned butter

MEW *v* -ED, -ING, -S to confine

MEWL *v* -ED, -ING, -S to whimper

MEWLER *n* pl. -S one that mewls

MEZCAL *n* pl. -S mescal

MEZEREON *n* pl. -S a flowering shrub

MEZEREUM *n* pl. -S mezereon

MEZQUIT *n* pl. -S mesquite

MEZQUITE *n* pl. -S mesquite

MEZUZA *n* pl. -S mezuzah

MEZUZAH *n* pl. -ZAHS, -ZOT, or -ZOTH a Judaic scroll

MEZZO *n* pl. -ZOS a female voice of a full, deep quality

MHO *n* pl. MHOS a unit of electrical conductance

MI *n* pl. -S the third tone of the diatonic musical scale

MIAOU *v* -ED, -ING, -S to meow

MIAOW *v* -ED, -ING, -S to meow

MIASM *n* pl. -S miasma

MIASMA *n* pl. -MAS or -MATA a noxious vapor **MIASMAL, MIASMIC** *adj*

MIAUL *v* -ED, -ING, -S to meow

MIB *n* pl. -S a type of playing marble

MICA *n* pl. -S a mineral

MICAWBER *n* pl. -S a person who remains hopeful despite adversity

MICE pl. of mouse

MICELL *n* pl. -S micelle

MICELLA *n* pl. -LAE micelle

MICELLE *n* pl. -S a coherent strand or structure in a fiber **MICELLAR** *adj*

MICK *n* pl. -S an Irishman — an offensive term

MICKEY *n* pl. -EYS a drugged drink

MICKLE *adj* -LER, -LEST large

MICKLE *n* pl. -S a large amount

MICRA a pl. of micron

MICRIFY *v* -FIED, -FYING, -FIES to make small

MICRO *adj* very small

MICROBAR *n* pl. -S a unit of atmospheric pressure

MICROBE *n* pl. -S a minute life form **MICROBIC** *adj*

MICROBUS *n* pl. -BUSES or -BUSSES a small bus

MICROHM *n* pl. -S a unit of electrical resistance

MICROLUX *n* pl. -LUXES or -LUCES a unit of illumination

MICROMHO *n* pl. -S a unit of electrical conductance

MICRON *n* pl. -CRONS or -CRA a unit of length

MICRURGY *n* pl. -GIES the use of minute tools under high magnification

MID *n* pl. -S the middle

MIDAIR *n* pl. -S a region in the middle of the air

MIDBRAIN *n* pl. -S the middle region of the brain

MIDDAY *n* pl. -DAYS the middle of the day

MIDDEN *n* pl. -S a dunghill

MIDDIES pl. of middy

MIDDLE *v* -DLED, -DLING, -DLES to place in the middle (the area or point equidistant from extremes or limits)

MIDDLER *n* pl. -S a student in an intermediate grade

MIDDLING *n* pl. -S a cut of pork

MIDDY *n* pl. -DIES a loosely fitting blouse

MIDFIELD *n* pl. -S the middle portion of a playing field

MIDGE *n* pl. -S a small winged insect

MIDGET *n* pl. -S a very small person

MIDGUT *n* pl. -S the middle part of the embryonic digestive tract

MIDI *n* pl. -S a skirt or coat that extends to the middle of the calf

MIDIRON *n* pl. -S a golf club

MIDLAND *n* pl. -S the middle part of a country

MIDLEG *n* pl. -S the middle of the leg

MIDLINE *n* pl. -S a median line

MIDMONTH *n* pl. -S the middle of the month

MIDMOST *n* pl. -S a part exactly in the middle

MIDNIGHT *n* pl. -S the middle of the night

MIDNOON *n* pl. -S midday

MIDPOINT *n* pl. -S a point at the middle

MIDRANGE *n* pl. -S the middle of a range

MIDRASH *n* pl. -RASHIM an early Jewish interpretation of a biblical text

MIDRIB *n* pl. -S the central vein of a leaf

MIDRIFF *n* pl. -S the middle part of the body

MIDSHIP *adj* pertaining to the middle of a ship

MIDSHIPS *adv* toward the middle of a ship

MIDSPACE *n* pl. -S the middle of a space

MIDST *n* pl. -S the middle

MIDSTORY *n* pl. -RIES the middle of a story

MIDTERM *n* pl. -S an examination given in the middle of an academic semester

MIDTOWN *n* pl. -S the central part of a city

MIDWATCH *n* pl. -ES a watch on a ship between midnight and 4 A.M.

MIDWAY *n* pl. -WAYS an avenue at a fair or carnival for concessions and amusements

MIDWEEK *n* pl. -S the middle of the week

MIDWIFE *v* -WIFED, -WIFING, -WIFES or -WIVED, -WIVING, -WIVES to assist a woman in childbirth

MIDYEAR *n* pl. -S the middle of the year

MIEN *n* pl. -S demeanor

MIFF *v* -ED, -ING, -S to annoy

MIFFY *adj* MIFFIER, MIFFIEST easily annoyed

MIG *n* pl. -S a type of playing marble

MIGG *n* pl. -S mig

MIGGLE *n* pl. -S a mig

MIGHT *n* pl. -S strength

MIGHTY *adj* MIGHTIER, MIGHTIEST strong **MIGHTILY** *adv*

MIGNON *n* pl. -S a cut of beef

MIGNONNE *adj* daintily small

MIGRAINE *n* pl. -S a severe headache

MIGRANT *n* pl. -S one that migrates

MIGRATE *v* -GRATED, -GRATING, -GRATES to move from one region to another

MIGRATOR *n* pl. -S a migrant

MIJNHEER *n* pl. -S mynheer

MIKADO *n* pl. -DOS an emperor of Japan

MIKE *n* pl. -S a microphone

MIKRON *n* pl. -KRONS or -KRA micron

MIKVAH *n* pl. -VAHS or -VOTH a place for ritual bathing by Orthodox Jews

MIKVEH *n* pl. -S mikvah

MIL *n* pl. -S a unit of length

MILADI *n* pl. -S milady

MILADY *n* pl. -DIES an English gentlewoman

MILAGE *n* pl. -S mileage

MILCH *adj* giving milk

MILCHIG *adj* made of or derived from milk

MILD *adj* MILDER, MILDEST not harsh or rough **MILDLY** *adv*

MILDEN *v* -ED, -ING, -S to make or become mild

MILDEW   v -ED, -ING, -S to affect with mildew (a whitish growth produced by fungi)

MILDEWY   adj affected with or resembling mildew

MILDNESS   n pl. -ES the quality of being mild

MILE   n pl. -S a unit of distance

MILEAGE   n pl. -S total distance expressed in miles

MILEPOST   n pl. -S a post indicating distance in miles

MILER   n pl. -S one that runs a mile race

MILESIMO   n pl. -MOS a monetary unit of Chile

MILFOIL   n pl. -S a perennial herb

MILIA   pl. of milium

MILIARIA   n pl. -S a skin disease

MILIARY   adj made up of many small projections

MILIEU   n pl. -LIEUS or -LIEUX environment

MILITANT   n pl. -S a person who is aggressively engaged in a cause

MILITARY   n pl. -TARIES armed forces

MILITATE   v -TATED, -TATING, -TATES to have influence or effect

MILITIA   n pl. -S a citizen army

MILIUM   n pl. -IA a small, whitish lump in the skin

MILK   v -ED, -ING, -S to draw milk (a whitish, nutritious liquid) from the udder of

MILKER   n pl. -S one that milks

MILKFISH   n pl. -ES a marine food fish

MILKIER   comparative of milky

MILKIEST   superlative of milky

MILKILY   adv in a milky manner

MILKMAID   n pl. -S a woman who milks cows

MILKMAN   n pl. -MEN a man who sells or delivers milk

MILKSOP   n pl. -S an effeminate man

MILKWEED   n pl. -S a plant that secretes a milky juice

MILKWOOD   n pl. -S a tropical tree

MILKWORT   n pl. -S a flowering plant

MILKY   adj MILKIER, MILKIEST resembling or suggestive of milk

MILL   v -ED, -ING, -S to grind by mechanical means **MILLABLE** adj

MILLAGE   n pl. -S a type of monetary rate

MILLDAM   n pl. -S a dam built to form a millpond

MILLE   n pl. -S a thousand

MILLEPED   n pl. -S milliped

MILLER   n pl. -S one that mills

MILLET   n pl. -S a cereal grass

MILLIARD   n pl. -S a billion

MILLIARE   n pl. -S a unit of area

MILLIARY   adj marking the distance of a Roman mile

MILLIBAR   n pl. -S a unit of atmospheric pressure

MILLIEME   n pl. -S a coin of Egypt and Libya

MILLIER   n pl. -S a unit of weight

MILLIGAL   n pl. -S a unit of acceleration

MILLILUX   n pl. -LUXES or -LUCES a unit of illumination

MILLIME   n pl. -S a coin of Tunisia

MILLIMHO   n pl. -MHOS a unit of electrical conductance

MILLINE   n pl. -S a unit of advertising space

MILLINER   n pl. -S one who makes or sells women's hats

MILLING   n pl. -S a corrugated edge on a coin

MILLIOHM   n pl. -S a unit of electrical resistance

MILLION   n pl. -S a number

MILLIPED   n pl. -S a multi-legged arthropod

MILLIREM   n pl. -S a quantity of ionizing radiation

MILLPOND   n pl. -S a pond for supplying water to run a mill wheel (a type of waterwheel)

MILLRACE   n pl. -S the current of water that drives a mill wheel

MILLRUN   n pl. -S a millrace

MILLWORK   n pl. -S woodwork produced by milling

MILO   n pl. -LOS a cereal grass

MILORD   n pl. -S an English gentleman

MILPA   n pl. -S a field that is cleared from a jungle for farming purposes

MILREIS   n pl. MILREIS a former monetary unit of Portugal

MILT   v -ED, -ING, -S to impregnate with milt (fish sperm)

MILTER   n pl. -S a male fish at breeding time

MILTY   adj MILTIER, MILTIEST full of milt

MIM   adj primly demure

MIMBAR   n pl. -S a pulpit in a mosque

MIME   v MIMED, MIMING, MIMES to mimic

MIMER   n pl. -S one that mimes

MIMESIS   n pl. -SISES mimicry **MIMETIC** adj

MIMETITE   n pl. -S an ore of lead

MIMIC   v -ICKED, -ICKING, -ICS to imitate closely

MIMICAL   adj of the nature of mimicry

MIMICKER   n pl. -S one that mimics

MIMICKING   present participle of mimic

MIMICRY   n pl. -RIES an instance of mimicking

MIMING   present participle of mime

MIMOSA   n pl. -S a tropical plant

MINA   n pl. -NAS or -NAE an ancient unit of weight and value

MINABLE   adj capable of being mined

MINACITY   n pl. -TIES the state of being threatening

MINARET   n pl. -S a slender tower attached to a mosque

MINATORY   adj threatening

MINCE   v MINCED, MINCING, MINCES to cut into very small pieces

MINCER   n pl. -S one that minces

MINCY   adj MINCIER, MINCIEST affectedly dainty

MIND   v -ED, -ING, -S to heed

MINDER   n pl. -S one that minds

MINDFUL   adj heedful

MINDLESS   adj lacking intelligence

MINE   v MINED, MINING, MINES to dig into for valuable materials

MINEABLE   adj minable

MINER   n pl. -S one that mines

MINERAL   n pl. -S a naturally occurring inorganic substance having a characteristic set of physical properties

MINGIER   comparative of mingy

MINGIEST   superlative of mingy

MINGLE   v -GLED, -GLING, -GLES to mix together

MINGLER   n pl. -S one that mingles

MINGY   adj -GIER, -GIEST mean and stingy

MINI   n pl. -S something distinctively smaller than others of its kind

MINIBIKE   n pl. -S a small motorcycle

MINIBUS   n pl. -BUSES or -BUSSES a small bus

MINICAB   n pl. -S a small taxicab

MINICAR   n pl. -S a small automobile

MINIFY   v -FIED, -FYING, -FIES to make small or smaller

MINIKIN   n pl. -S a small or dainty creature

MINIM   n pl. -S a unit of liquid measure

MINIMA   a pl. of minimum

MINIMAL   n pl. -S an element of a mathematical set that precedes all others

MINIMAX   n pl. -ES the minimum of a set of maxima

MINIMISE   v -MISED, -MISING, -MISES to minimize

MINIMIZE   v -MIZED, -MIZING, -MIZES to make as small as possible

MINIMUM   n pl. -MUMS or -MA the least possible amount, quantity, or degree

MINING   n pl. -S the process or business of working mines (excavations in the earth)

MINION   n pl. -S a servile follower

MINISH   v -ED, -ING, -ES to diminish

MINISTER   v -ED, -ING, -S to give aid or service

MINISTRY   n pl. -TRIES the act of ministering

MINIUM   n pl. -S a red pigment

MINIVER   n pl. -S a white fur

MINK   n pl. -S a carnivorous mammal

MINNOW   n pl. -S a small fish

MINNY   n pl. -NIES minnow

MINOR   v -ED, -ING, -S to pursue a specific subordinate course of study

MINORCA   n pl. -S any of a breed of large domestic fowls

MINORITY *n pl.* -TIES the smaller number or part

MINSTER *n pl.* -S a large or important church

MINSTREL *n pl.* -S a medieval musician

MINT *v* -ED, -ING, -S to produce by stamping metal, as coins

MINTAGE *n pl.* -S the act of minting

MINTER *n pl.* -S one that mints

MINTY *adj* MINTIER, MINTIEST having the flavor mint (an aromatic herb)

MINUEND *n pl.* -S a number from which another is to be subtracted

MINUET *n pl.* -S a slow, stately dance

MINUS *n pl.* -ES a negative quantity

MINUTE *v* -UTED, -UTING, -UTES to make a brief note of

MINUTE *adj* -NUTER, -NUTEST very small **MINUTELY** *adv*

MINUTIA *n pl.* -TIAE a small detail **MINUTIAL** *adj*

MINUTING present participle of minute

MINX *n pl.* -ES a pert girl **MINXISH** *adj*

MINYAN *n pl.* -YANS or -YANIM the minimum number required to be present for the conduct of a Jewish service

MIOSIS *n pl.* -OSES excessive contraction of the pupil of the eye

MIOTIC *n pl.* -S an agent that causes miosis

MIQUELET *n pl.* -S a former Spanish or French soldier

MIR *n pl.* MIRS or MIRI a Russian peasant commune

MIRACLE *n pl.* -S an event ascribed to supernatural or divine origin

MIRADOR *n pl.* -S an architectural feature designed to afford an extensive view

MIRAGE *n pl.* -S a type of optical illusion

MIRE *v* MIRED, MIRING, MIRES to cause to stick in swampy ground

MIREX *n pl.* -ES an insecticide

MIRI a *pl.* of mir

MIRIER comparative of miry

MIRIEST superlative of miry

MIRINESS *n pl.* -ES the state of being miry

MIRING present participle of mire

MIRK *adj* MIRKER, MIRKEST murk

MIRK *n pl.* -S murk

MIRKY *adj* MIRKIER, MIRKIEST murky **MIRKILY** *adv*

MIRROR *v* -ED, -ING, -S to reflect an image of

MIRTH *n pl.* -S spirited gaiety **MIRTHFUL** *adj*

MIRY *adj* MIRIER, MIRIEST swampy

MIRZA *n pl.* -S a Persian title of honor

MISACT *v* -ED, -ING, -S to act badly

MISADAPT *v* -ED, -ING, -S to adapt wrongly

MISADD *v* -ED, -ING, -S to add incorrectly

MISAGENT *n pl.* -S a bad agent

MISAIM *v* -ED, -ING, -S to aim badly

MISALLY *v* -LIED, -LYING, -LIES to ally badly

MISALTER *v* -ED, -ING, -S to alter wrongly

MISAPPLY *v* -PLIED, -PLYING, -PLIES to apply wrongly

MISASSAY *v* -ED, -ING, -S to attempt unsuccessfully

MISATE past tense of miseat

MISATONE *v* -ATONED, -ATONING, -ATONES to atone wrongly

MISAVER *v* -AVERRED, -AVERRING, -AVERS to speak erroneously

MISAWARD *v* -ED, -ING, -S to award wrongly

MISBEGIN *v* -GAN, -GUN, -GINNING, -GINS to begin wrongly

MISBEGOT *adj* born out of wedlock

MISBIAS *v* -ASED, -ASING, -ASES or -ASSED, -ASSING, -ASSES to bias wrongly

MISBILL *v* -ED, -ING, -S to bill wrongly

MISBIND *v* -BOUND, -BINDING, -BINDS to bind imperfectly

MISBRAND *v* -ED, -ING, -S to brand incorrectly

MISBUILD *v* -BUILT, -BUILDING, -BUILDS to build imperfectly

MISCALL *v* -ED, -ING, -S to call by a wrong name

MISCARRY *v* -RIED, -RYING, -RIES to be unsuccessful

MISCAST *v* -CAST, -CASTING, -CASTS to cast in an unsuitable role

MISCHIEF   *n pl.* -S action that causes irritation, harm, or trouble

MISCIBLE   *adj* capable of being mixed

MISCITE   *v* -CITED, -CITING, -CITES to misquote

MISCLAIM   *v* -ED, -ING, -S to claim wrongfully

MISCLASS   *v* -ED, -ING, -ES to put in the wrong class

MISCOIN   *v* -ED, -ING, -S to coin improperly

MISCOLOR   *v* -ED, -ING, -S to color incorrectly

MISCOOK   *v* -ED, -ING, -S to cook badly

MISCOPY   *v* -COPIED, -COPYING, -COPIES to copy incorrectly

MISCOUNT   *v* -ED, -ING, -S to count incorrectly

MISCUE   *v* -CUED, -CUING, -CUES to make a faulty stroke in billiards

MISCUT   *v* -CUT, -CUTTING, -CUTS to cut incorrectly

MISDATE   *v* -DATED, -DATING, -DATES to date incorrectly

MISDEAL   *v* -DEALT, -DEALING, -DEALS to deal cards incorrectly

MISDEED   *n pl.* -S an evil act

MISDEEM   *v* -ED, -ING, -S to judge unfavorably

MISDO   *v* -DID, -DONE, -DOING, -DOES to do wrongly

MISDOER   *n pl.* -S one that misdoes

MISDOING   *n pl.* -S an instance of doing wrong

MISDONE   past participle of misdo

MISDOUBT   *v* -ED, -ING, -S to doubt

MISDRAW   *v* -DREW, -DRAWN, -DRAWING, -DRAWS to draw incorrectly

MISDRIVE   *v* -DROVE, -DRIVEN, -DRIVING, -DRIVES to drive wrongly or improperly

MISE   *n pl.* -S an agreement or settlement

MISEASE   *n pl.* -S discomfort

MISEAT   *v* -ATE, -EATING, -EATS to eat improperly

MISEDIT   *v* -ED, -ING, -S to edit incorrectly

MISENROL   *v* -ROLLED, -ROLLING, -ROLS to misenroll

MISENROLL   *v* -ED, -ING, -S to enroll improperly

MISENTER   *v* -ED, -ING, -S to enter erroneously

MISENTRY   *n pl.* -TRIES an erroneous entry

MISER   *n pl.* -S one who hoards money greedily

MISERERE   *n pl.* -S a part of a church seat

MISERLY   *adj* characteristic of a miser

MISERY   *n pl.* -ERIES a state of great suffering

MISEVENT   *n pl.* -S a mishap

MISFAITH   *n pl.* -S lack of faith; disbelief

MISFIELD   *v* -ED, -ING, -S to field badly

MISFILE   *v* -FILED, -FILING, -FILES to file in the wrong place

MISFIRE   *v* -FIRED, -FIRING, -FIRES to fail to fire

MISFIT   *v* -FITTED, -FITTING, -FITS to fit badly

MISFORM   *v* -ED, -ING, -S to misshape

MISFRAME   *v* -FRAMED, -FRAMING, -FRAMES to frame badly

MISGAUGE   *v* -GAUGED, -GAUGING, -GAUGES to gauge wrongly or inaccurately

MISGIVE   *v* -GAVE, -GIVEN, -GIVING, -GIVES to make doubtful or fearful

MISGRAFT   *v* -ED, -ING, -S to graft wrongly

MISGROW   *v* -GREW, -GROWN, -GROWING, -GROWS to grow abnormally

MISGUESS   *v* -ED, -ING, -ES to guess wrongly

MISGUIDE   *v* -GUIDED, -GUIDING, -GUIDES to guide wrongly

MISHAP   *n pl.* -S an unfortunate accident

MISHEAR   *v* -HEARD, -HEARING, -HEARS to hear incorrectly

MISHIT   *v* -HIT, -HITTING, -HITS to hit poorly

MISHMASH   *n pl.* -ES a confused mixture

MISHMOSH   *n pl.* -ES mishmash

MISINFER   *v* -FERRED, -FERRING, -FERS to infer wrongly

MISINTER   *v* -TERRED, -TERRING, -TERS to inter improperly

MISJOIN   *v* -ED, -ING, -S to join improperly

MISJUDGE   *v* -JUDGED, -JUDGING, -JUDGES to judge wrongly

MISKAL   *n pl.* -S an Oriental unit of weight

MISKEEP   v -KEPT, -KEEPING, -KEEPS to keep wrongly

MISKNOW   v -KNEW, -KNOWN, -KNOWING, -KNOWS to fail to understand or recognize

MISLABEL   v -BELED, -BELING, -BELS or -BELLED, -BELLING, -BELS to label incorrectly or falsely

MISLABOR   v -ED, -ING, -S to labor badly

MISLAIN   past participle of mislie

MISLAY   v -LAID, -LAYING, -LAYS to put in a forgotten place

MISLAYER   n pl. -S one that mislays

MISLEAD   v -LED, -LEADING, -LEADS to lead astray

MISLEARN   v -LEARNED or -LEARNT, -LEARNING, -LEARNS to learn wrongly

MISLIE   v -LAY, -LAIN, -LYING, -LIES to lie in a wrong position

MISLIGHT   v -LIGHTED or -LIT, -LIGHTING, -LIGHTS to lead astray by its light

MISLIKE   v -LIKED, -LIKING, -LIKES to dislike

MISLIKER   n pl. -S one that mislikes

MISLIT   a past tense of mislight

MISLIVE   v -LIVED, -LIVING, -LIVES to live a bad life

MISLODGE   v -LODGED, -LODGING, -LODGES to lodge in a wrong place

MISLYING   present participle of mislie

MISMARK   v -ED, -ING, -S to mark wrongly

MISMATCH   v -ED, -ING, -ES to match badly

MISMATE   v -MATED, -MATING, -MATES to mate unsuitably

MISMEET   v -MET, -MEETING, -MEETS to meet under unfortunate circumstances

MISMOVE   v -MOVED, -MOVING, -MOVES to move wrongly

MISNAME   v -NAMED, -NAMING, -NAMES to call by a wrong name

MISNOMER   n pl. -S a name wrongly used

MISO   n pl. -SOS a type of food paste

MISOGAMY   n pl. -MIES a hatred of marriage

MISOGYNY   n pl. -NIES a hatred of women

MISOLOGY   n pl. -GIES a hatred of debate or reasoning

MISPAGE   v -PAGED, -PAGING, -PAGES to page incorrectly

MISPAINT   v -ED, -ING, -S to paint wrongly

MISPARSE   v -PARSED, -PARSING, -PARSES to parse incorrectly

MISPART   v -ED, -ING, -S to part badly

MISPATCH   v -ED, -ING, -ES to patch badly

MISPEN   v -PENNED, -PENNING, -PENS to write incorrectly

MISPLACE   v -PLACED, -PLACING, -PLACES to put in a wrong place

MISPLANT   v -ED, -ING, -S to plant wrongly

MISPLAY   v -ED, -ING, -S to make a bad play in a game

MISPLEAD   v -PLEADED or -PLED, -PLEADING, -PLEADS to plead wrongly or falsely

MISPOINT   v -ED, -ING, -S to point improperly

MISPOISE   v -POISED, -POISING, -POISES to poise incorrectly

MISPRINT   v -ED, -ING, -S to print incorrectly

MISPRIZE   v -PRIZED, -PRIZING, -PRIZES to despise

MISQUOTE   v -QUOTED, -QUOTING, -QUOTES to quote incorrectly

MISRAISE   v -RAISED, -RAISING, -RAISES to raise wrongly

MISRATE   v -RATED, -RATING, -RATES to rate incorrectly

MISREAD   v -READ, -READING, -READS to read incorrectly

MISREFER   v -FERRED, -FERRING, -FERS to refer incorrectly

MISRELY   v -LIED, -LYING, -LIES to rely wrongly

MISRULE   v -RULED, -RULING, -RULES to rule unwisely or unjustly

MISS   v -ED, -ING, -ES to fail to make contact with

MISSAL   n pl. -S a prayer book

MISSAY   v -SAID, -SAYING, -SAYS to say incorrectly

MISSEAT   v -ED, -ING, -S to seat wrongly

MISSEL   n pl. -S a European thrush

MISSEND   v -SENT, -SENDING, -SENDS to send incorrectly

MISSENSE   n pl. -S a form of genetic mutation

MISSHAPE   v -SHAPED, -SHAPEN, -SHAPING, -SHAPES to shape badly

MISSHOD   adj improperly shod

MISSIES pl. of missy

MISSILE *n* pl. -S an object or weapon that is thrown or projected

MISSILRY *n* pl. -RIES the science of designing and operating guided missiles

MISSION *v* -ED, -ING, -S to send to perform a specific task

MISSIS *n* pl. -SISES a wife

MISSIVE *n* pl. -S a written communication

MISSORT *v* -ED, -ING, -S to sort badly or improperly

MISSOUND *v* -ED, -ING, -S to sound wrongly

MISSOUT *n* pl. -S a losing throw of dice

MISSPACE *v* -SPACED, -SPACING, -SPACES to space incorrectly

MISSPEAK *v* -SPOKE, -SPOKEN, -SPEAKING, -SPEAKS to speak incorrectly

MISSPELL *v* -SPELLED or -SPELT, -SPELLING, -SPELLS to spell incorrectly

MISSPEND *v* -SPENT, -SPENDING, -SPENDS to spend wrongly

MISSPOKE past tense of misspeak

MISSPOKEN past participle of misspeak

MISSTART *v* -ED, -ING, -S to start off badly

MISSTATE *v* -STATED, -STATING, -STATES to state wrongly

MISSTEER *v* -ED, -ING, -S to steer wrongly

MISSTEP *n* pl. -S a false step

MISSTOP *v* -STOPPED, -STOPPING, -STOPS to stop wrongly

MISSTYLE *v* -STYLED, -STYLING, -STYLES to style or call wrongly

MISSUIT *v* -ED, -ING, -S to suit badly

MISSUS *n* pl. -ES missis

MISSY *n* pl. MISSIES a young girl

MIST *v* -ED, -ING, -S to become blurry

MISTAKE *v* -TOOK or -TEUK, -TAKEN, -TAKING, -TAKES to interpret wrongly

MISTAKER *n* pl. -S one that mistakes

MISTBOW *n* pl. -S a fogbow

MISTEACH *v* -TAUGHT, -TEACHING, -TEACHES to teach wrongly or badly

MISTEND *v* -ED, -ING, -S to tend to improperly

MISTER *n* pl. -S sir

MISTERM *v* -ED, -ING, -S to call by a wrong name

MISTEUK a past tense of mistake

MISTHINK *v* -THOUGHT, -THINKING, -THINKS to think wrongly

MISTHROW *v* -THREW, -THROWN, -THROWING, -THROWS to throw errantly

MISTIER comparative of misty

MISTIEST superlative of misty

MISTILY *adv* in a misty manner

MISTIME *v* -TIMED, -TIMING, -TIMES to time wrongly

MISTITLE *v* -TLED, -TLING, -TLES to call by a wrong title

MISTOOK a past tense of mistake

MISTOUCH *v* -ED, -ING, -ES to touch improperly

MISTRACE *v* -TRACED, -TRACING, -TRACES to trace wrongly

MISTRAL *n* pl. -S a cold, dry wind

MISTREAT *v* -ED, -ING, -S to treat badly

MISTRESS *n* pl. -ES a woman in a position of authority

MISTRIAL *n* pl. -S a trial made invalid because of some error in procedure

MISTRUST *v* -ED, -ING, -S to distrust

MISTRYST *v* -ED, -ING, -S to fail to keep an appointment with

MISTUNE *v* -TUNED, -TUNING, -TUNES to tune incorrectly

MISTUTOR *v* -ED, -ING, -S to instruct or bring up badly

MISTY *adj* MISTIER, MISTIEST blurry

MISTYPE *v* -TYPED, -TYPING, -TYPES to type incorrectly

MISUNION *n* pl. -S a bad union

MISUSAGE *n* pl. -S incorrect use

MISUSE *v* -USED, -USING, -USES to use incorrectly

MISUSER *n* pl. -S one that misuses

MISVALUE *v* -UED, -UING, -UES to value incorrectly

MISWORD *v* -ED, -ING, -S to word wrongly

MISWRITE *v* -WROTE or -WRIT, -WRITTEN, -WRITING, -WRITES to write incorrectly

MISYOKE *v* -YOKED, -YOKING, -YOKES to yoke improperly

MITE *n* pl. -S a small arachnid

MITER   *v* -ED, -ING, -S to raise to the rank of a bishop

MITERER   *n* pl. -S one that miters

MITHER   *n* pl. -S mother

MITICIDE   *n* pl. -S a substance used to kill mites

MITIER   comparative of mity

MITIEST   superlative of mity

MITIGATE   *v* -GATED, -GATING, -GATES to make less severe

MITIS   *n* pl. -TISES a type of wrought iron

MITOGEN   *n* pl. -S a substance that induces mitosis

MITOSIS   *n* pl. -TOSES a type of cell division **MITOTIC** *adj*

MITRAL   *adj* pertaining to a valve of the heart

MITRE   *v* -TRED, -TRING, -TRES to miter

MITSVAH   *n* pl. -VAHS or -VOTH mitzvah

MITT   *n* pl. -S a type of baseball glove

MITTEN   *n* pl. -S a type of covering for the hand

MITTIMUS   *n* pl. -ES a warrant committing a person to prison

MITY   *adj* MITIER, MITIEST infested with mites

MITZVAH   *n* pl. -VAHS or -VOTH a commandment of Jewish law

MIX   *v* MIXED or MIXT, MIXING, MIXES to put together into one mass **MIXABLE, MIXIBLE** *adj*

MIXER   *n* pl. -S one that mixes

MIXOLOGY   *n* pl. -GIES the art of making mixed drinks

MIXT   a past tense of mix

MIXTURE   *n* pl. -S something produced by mixing

MIXUP   *n* pl. -S a state of confusion

MIZEN   *n* pl. -S mizzen

MIZZEN   *n* pl. -S a type of sail

MIZZLE   *v* -ZLED, -ZLING, -ZLES to rain in fine droplets

MIZZLY   *adj* characterized by a fine rain

MNEMONIC   *n* pl. -S a device to assist the memory

MOA   *n* pl. -S an extinct flightless bird

MOAN   *v* -ED, -ING, -S to utter a low, mournful sound

MOANFUL   *adj* moaning

MOAT   *v* -ED, -ING, -S to surround with a moat (a water-filled trench)

MOATLIKE   *adj* suggestive of a moat

MOB   *v* MOBBED, MOBBING, MOBS to crowd about

MOBBER   *n* pl. -S one that mobs

MOBBISH   *adj* charaoteristic of a mob (a disorderly crowd of people)

MOBCAP   *n* pl. -S a woman's cap

MOBILE   *n* pl. -S a form of sculpture

MOBILISE   *v* -LISED, -LISING, -LISES to mobilize

MOBILITY   *n* pl. -TIES the ability to move

MOBILIZE   *v* -LIZED, -LIZING, -LIZES to put into movement

MOBOCRAT   *n* pl. -S a supporter of mob rule

MOBSTER   *n* pl. -S a gangster

MOCCASIN   *n* pl. -S a type of shoe

MOCHA   *n* pl. -S a choice, pungent coffee

MOCHILA   *n* pl. -S a leather covering for a saddle

MOCK   *v* -ED, -ING, -S to ridicule **MOCKABLE** *adj*

MOCKER   *n* pl. -S one that mocks

MOCKERY   *n* pl. -ERIES the act of mocking

MOCKUP   *n* pl. -S a full-sized model

MOD   *n* pl. -S one who wears boldly stylish clothes

MODAL   *adj* pertaining to a mode **MODALLY** *adv*

MODALITY   *n* pl. -TIES the state of being modal

MODE   *n* pl. -S a method of doing or acting

MODEL   *v* -ELED, -ELING, -ELS or -ELLED, -ELLING, -ELS to plan or form after a pattern

MODELER   *n* pl. -S one that models

MODELING   *n* pl. -S the treatment of volume in sculpture

MODELLED   a past tense of model

MODELLER   *n* pl. -S modeler

MODELLING   a present participle of model

MODERATE   *v* -ATED, -ATING, -ATES to make less extreme

MODERATO   *n* pl. -TOS a musical passage played at a medium tempo

MODERN *adj* -ERNER, -ERNEST pertaining to present or recent time **MODERNLY** *adv*

MODERN *n* pl. -S a person of modern times or views

MODEST *adj* -ESTER, -ESTEST having a moderate regard for oneself **MODESTLY** *adv*

MODESTY *n* pl. -TIES the quality of being modest

MODI pl. of modus

MODICUM *n* pl. -CA or -CUMS a small amount

MODIFIER *n* pl. -S one that modifies

MODIFY *v* -FIED, -FYING, -FIES to change in form or character

MODIOLUS *n* pl. -LI a bony shaft of the inner ear

MODISH *adj* stylish **MODISHLY** *adv*

MODISTE *n* pl. -S a dealer in stylish women's clothing

MODULAR *adj* pertaining to a module

MODULATE *v* -LATED, -LATING, -LATES to adjust to a certain proportion

MODULE *n* pl. -S a standard of measurement

MODULO *adv* with respect to a modulus

MODULUS *n* pl. -LI a number that produces the same remainder when divided into each of two numbers

MODUS *n* pl. -DI a mode

MOFETTE *n* pl. -S a noxious emanation from a fissure in the earth

MOFFETTE *n* pl. -S mofette

MOG *v* MOGGED, MOGGING, MOGS to move away

MOGUL *n* pl. -S an important person

MOHAIR *n* pl. -S the long, silky hair of the Angora goat

MOHEL *n* pl. -HALIM or -HELS a person who performs Jewish ritual circumcisions

MOHUR *n* pl. -S a former gold coin of India

MOIDORE *n* pl. -S a former gold coin of Portugal

MOIETY *n* pl. -ETIES a half

MOIL *v* -ED, -ING, -S to work hard

MOILER *n* pl. -S one that moils

MOIRA *n* pl. -RAI fate or destiny, in ancient Greek religion

MOIRE *n* pl. -S a fabric having a wavy pattern

MOIST *adj* MOISTER, MOISTEST slightly wet

MOISTEN *v* -ED, -ING, -S to make or become moist

MOISTFUL *adj* moist

MOISTLY *adv* in a moist manner

MOISTURE *n* pl. -S condensed or diffused liquid

MOJARRA *n* pl. -S a marine fish

MOKE *n* pl. -S a donkey

MOL *n* pl. -S mole

MOLA *n* pl. -S a marine fish

MOLAL *adj* pertaining to a mole

MOLALITY *n* pl. -TIES the number of moles of solute per liter of solvent

MOLAR *n* pl. -S a grinding tooth

MOLARITY *n* pl. -TIES the number of moles of solute per liter of solution

MOLASSES *n* pl. -LASSESES a thick syrup

MOLD *v* -ED, -ING, -S to work into a particular shape **MOLDABLE** *adj*

MOLDER *v* -ED, -ING, -S to turn to dust by natural decay

MOLDIER comparative of moldy

MOLDIEST superlative of moldy

MOLDING *n* pl. -S a long, narrow strip used to decorate a surface

MOLDWARP *n* pl. -S a burrowing mammal

MOLDY *adj* MOLDIER, MOLDIEST musty

MOLE *n* pl. -S the quantity of a compound that has a weight equal to the compound's molecular weight

MOLECULE *n* pl. -S the smallest physical unit of an element

MOLEHILL *n* pl. -S a small mold of earth

MOLESKIN *n* pl. -S a cotton fabric

MOLEST *v* -ED, -ING, -S to disturb or annoy

MOLESTER *n* pl. -S one that molests

MOLIES pl. of moly

MOLINE *adj* having arms forked and curved at the ends — used of a heraldic cross

MOLL *n* pl. -S a gangster's girl friend

MOLLAH *n* pl. -S mullah

MOLLIE *n* pl. -S a tropical fish

MOLLIES pl. of molly

MOLLIFY v -FIED, -FYING, -FIES to soothe

MOLLUSC n pl. -S mollusk

MOLLUSK n pl. -S any of a phylum of soft-bodied invertebrates

MOLLY n pl. -LIES mollie

MOLOCH n pl. -S a spiny lizard

MOLT v -ED, -ING, -S to cast off an outer covering

MOLTEN adj made liquid by heat **MOLTENLY** adv

MOLTER n pl. -S one that molts

MOLTO adv very — used in musical directions

MOLY n pl. -LIES a wild garlic

MOLYBDIC adj pertaining to a certain metallic element

MOM n pl. -S mother

MOME n pl. -S a fool

MOMENT n pl. -S a brief period of time

MOMENTA a pl. of momentum

MOMENTLY adv from moment to moment

MOMENTO n pl. -TOS or -TOES memento

MOMENTUM n pl. -TA or -TUMS force of movement

MOMI a pl. of momus

MOMISM n pl. -S an excessive dependence on mothers

MOMMA n pl. -S mother

MOMMY n pl. -MIES mother

MOMUS n pl. -MUSES or -MI a carping person

MON n pl. MEN man

MONACHAL adj pertaining to monks

MONACID n pl. -S monoacid

MONAD n pl. -S a single-celled organism **MONADAL, MONADIC** adj

MONADES pl. of monas

MONADISM n pl. -S a philosophical doctrine

MONANDRY n pl. -DRIES the condition of having one husband at a time

MONARCH n pl. -S an absolute ruler

MONARCHY n pl. -CHIES rule by a monarch

MONARDA n pl. -S an aromatic herb

MONAS n pl. MONADES a monad

MONASTIC n pl. -S a monk

MONAURAL adj pertaining to sound transmission, recording, or reproduction involving a single transmission path

MONAXIAL adj having one axis

MONAZITE n pl. -S a mineral

MONDE n pl. -S the world

MONDO n pl. -DOS a rapid question and answer technique employed in Zen Buddhism

MONECIAN adj having both male and female sex organs in the same individual

MONETARY adj pertaining to money

MONETISE v -TISED, -TISING, -TISES to monetize

MONETIZE v -TIZED, -TIZING, -TIZES to coin into money

MONEY n pl. MONEYS or MONIES an official medium of exchange and measure of value

MONEYBAG n pl. -S a bag for holding money

MONEYED adj having much money

MONEYER n pl. -S one that coins money

MONGEESE a pl. of mongoose

MONGER v -ED, -ING, -S to peddle

MONGO n pl. -GOS mungo

MONGOE n pl. -S mungo

MONGOL n pl. -S a person affected with a form of mental deficiency

MONGOOSE n pl. -GOOSES or -GEESE a carnivorous mammal

MONGREL n pl. -S an animal or plant of mixed breed

MONGST prep amongst

MONICKER n pl. -S moniker

MONIE adj many

MONIED adj moneyed

MONIES a pl. of money

MONIKER n pl. -S a name

MONISH v -ED, -ING, -ES to warn

MONISM n pl. -S a philosophical theory

MONIST n pl. -S an adherent of monism **MONISTIC** adj

MONITION n pl. -S a warning

MONITIVE adj giving warning

MONITOR v -ED, -ING, -S to keep track of

MONITORY n pl. -RIES a letter of warning

MONK   *n* pl. -S a man who is a member of a secluded religious order

MONKERY   *n* pl. -ERIES the mode of life of monks

MONKEY   *v* -ED, -ING, -S to mimic

MONKFISH   *n* pl. -ES a marine fish

MONKHOOD   *n* pl. -S the state of being a monk

MONKISH   *adj* pertaining to monks

MONO   *n* pl. MONOS an infectious disease

MONOACID   *n* pl. -S a type of acid

MONOCARP   *n* pl. -S a plant that yields fruit only once before dying

MONOCLE   *n* pl. -S an eyeglass for one eye **MONOCLED** *adj*

MONOCOT   *n* pl. -S a type of seed plant

MONOCRAT   *n* pl. -S an autocrat

MONOCYTE   *n* pl. -S a type of white blood cell

MONODIST   *n* pl. -S one who writes monodies

MONODY   *n* pl. -DIES an elegy performed by one person **MONODIC** *adj*

MONOECY   *n* pl. -CIES the condition of being monecian

MONOFIL   *n* pl. -S a single filament of synthetic fiber

MONOFUEL   *n* pl. -S a type of rocket propellant

MONOGAMY   *n* pl. -MIES marriage with one person at a time

MONOGENY   *n* pl. -NIES asexual reproduction

MONOGERM   *adj* being a fruit that produces a single plant

MONOGRAM   *v* -GRAMED, -GRAMING, -GRAMS or -GRAMMED, -GRAMMING, -GRAMS to mark with a design of one's initials

MONOGYNY   *n* pl. -NIES the condition of having one wife at a time

MONOLITH   *n* pl. -S a large block of stone

MONOLOG   *n* pl. -S a lengthy speech by one person

MONOLOGY   *n* pl. -GIES the act of uttering a monolog

MONOMER   *n* pl. -S a type of chemical compound

MONOMIAL   *n* pl. -S an algebraic expression consisting of a single term

MONOPODE   *n* pl. -S a creature having one foot

MONOPODY   *n* pl. -DIES a measure consisting of a single metrical foot

MONOPOLE   *n* pl. -S a type of radio antenna

MONOPOLY   *n* pl. -LIES exclusive control of a commodity or service in a particular market

MONORAIL   *n* pl. -S a single rail serving as a track for a wheeled vehicle

MONOSOME   *n* pl. -S a type of chromosome

MONOTINT   *n* pl. -S a painting done in different shades of one color

MONOTONE   *n* pl. -S a vocal utterance in one unvaried tone

MONOTONY   *n* pl. -NIES tedious sameness

MONOTYPE   *n* pl. -S the only representative of its group

MONOXIDE   *n* pl. -S a type of oxide

MONS   *n* pl. MONTES a protuberance of the body

MONSIEUR   *n* pl. MESSIEURS a French title of courtesy for a man

MONSOON   *n* pl. -S a seasonal wind

MONSTER   *n* pl. -S a strange or terrifying creature

MONTAGE   *v* -TAGED, -TAGING, -TAGES to combine into a composite picture

MONTANE   *n* pl. -S the lower vegetation belt of a mountain

MONTE   *n* pl. -S a card game

MONTEITH   *n* pl. -S a large punch bowl

MONTERO   *n* pl. -ROS a type of cap

MONTES   pl. of mons

MONTH   *n* pl. -S a period of approximately 30 days

MONTHLY   *n* pl. -LIES a publication issued once a month

MONUMENT   *n* pl. -S a structure built as a memorial

MONURON   *n* pl. -S an herbicide

MONY   *adj* many

MOO   *v* -ED, -ING, -S to make the deep, moaning sound of a cow

MOOCH   *v* -ED, -ING, -ES to obtain without paying

MOOCHER   *n* pl. -S one that mooches

MOOD   *n* pl. -S a person's emotional state at a particular moment

MOODY *adj* MOODIER, MOODIEST given to changing moods **MOODILY** *adv*

MOOL *n pl.* -S soft soil

MOOLA *n pl.* -S moolah

MOOLAH *n pl.* -S money

MOOLEY *n pl.* -EYS muley

MOON *v* -ED, -ING, -S to spend time idly

MOONBEAM *n pl.* -S a ray of light from the moon (the earth's natural satellite)

MOONBOW *n pl.* -S a rainbow formed by light from the moon

MOONCALF *n pl.* -CALVES a foolish person

MOONEYE *n pl.* -S a freshwater fish

MOONFISH *n pl.* -ES a marine fish

MOONIER comparative of moony

MOONIEST superlative of moony

MOONILY *adv* in a moony manner

MOONISH *adj* fickle

MOONLESS *adj* lacking the light of the moon

MOONLET *n pl.* -S a small satellite

MOONLIKE *adj* resembling the moon

MOONLIT *adj* lighted by the moon

MOONRISE *n pl.* -S the rising of the moon above the horizon

MOONSAIL *n pl.* -S a light, square sail

MOONSEED *n pl.* -S a climbing plant

MOONSET *n pl.* -S the setting of the moon below the horizon

MOONSHOT *n pl.* -S the launching of a spacecraft to the moon

MOONWARD *adv* toward the moon

MOONWORT *n pl.* -S a flowering plant

MOONY *adj* MOONIER, MOONIEST resembling the moon

MOOR *v* -ED, -ING, -S to secure a vessel by means of cables

MOORAGE *n pl.* -S the act of mooring

MOORFOWL *n pl.* -S a game bird

MOORHEN *n pl.* -S an aquatic bird

MOORIER comparative of moory

MOORIEST superlative of moory

MOORING *n pl.* -S a place where a vessel may be moored

MOORISH *adj* marshy

MOORLAND *n pl.* -S a tract of marshy land

MOORWORT *n pl.* -S a marsh plant

MOORY *adj* MOORIER, MOORIEST marshy

MOOSE *n pl.* MOOSE a ruminant mammal

MOOT *v* -ED, -ING, -S to bring up for discussion

MOOTER *n pl.* -S one that moots

MOP *v* MOPPED, MOPPING, MOPS to wipe with a mop (an implement for cleaning floors)

MOPBOARD *n pl.* -S a board at the base of a wall

MOPE *v* MOPED, MOPING, MOPES to act in a dejected or gloomy manner

MOPED *n pl.* -S a type of motorbike

MOPER *n pl.* -S one that mopes

MOPING present participle of mope

MOPINGLY *adv* in a moping manner

MOPISH *adj* given to moping **MOPISHLY** *adv*

MOPOKE *n pl.* -S an Australian bird

MOPPED past tense of mop

MOPPER *n pl.* -S one that mops

MOPPET *n pl.* -S a child

MOPPING present participle of mop

MOQUETTE *n pl.* -S a woolen fabric

MOR *n pl.* -S a forest humus

MORA *n pl.* -RAE or -RAS a unit of metrical time in prosody

MORAINE *n pl.* -S an accumulation of debris deposited by a glacier **MORAINAL, MORAINIC** *adj*

MORAL *adj* pertaining to principles of right and wrong **MORALLY** *adv*

MORALE *n pl.* -S the state of the spirits of an individual or group

MORALISE *v* -ISED, -ISING, -ISES to moralize

MORALISM *n pl.* -S the practice of moralizing

MORALIST *n pl.* -S a teacher of morality

MORALITY *n pl.* -TIES conformity to the rules of right conduct

MORALIZE *v* -IZED, -IZING, -IZES to explain in a moral sense

MORALS *n/pl* rules of conduct with respect to right and wrong

MORASS *n pl.* -ES a marsh **MORASSY** *adj*

MORATORY *adj* authorizing delay of payment

MORAY *n pl.* -RAYS a tropical eel

MORBID *adj* gruesome **MORBIDLY** *adv*

MORBIFIC *adj* causing disease

MORBILLI *n/pl* a virus disease

MORCEAU *n pl.* -CEAUX a short literary or musical composition

MORDANCY *n pl.* -CIES a sarcastic quality

MORDANT *v* -ED, -ING, -S to treat with a caustic substance

MORDENT *n pl.* -S a melodic embellishment

MORE *n pl.* -S a greater amount

MOREEN *n pl.* -S a heavy fabric

MOREL *n pl.* -S an edible mushroom

MORELLE *n pl.* -S a flowering plant

MORELLO *n pl.* -LOS a variety of sour cherry

MOREOVER *adv* in addition

MORESQUE *n pl.* -S an ancient decorative style

MORGEN *n pl.* -S a Dutch unit of land area

MORGUE *n pl.* -S a place where dead bodies are kept for identification

MORIBUND *adj* being about to die

MORION *n pl.* -S a type of helmet

MORN *n pl.* -S morning

MORNING *n pl.* -S the early part of the day

MOROCCO *n pl.* -COS a soft leather

MORON *n pl.* -S a mentally deficient person **MORONIC** *adj*

MORONISM *n pl.* -S the condition of being a moron

MORONITY *n pl.* -TIES moronism

MOROSE *adj* sullen **MOROSELY** *adv*

MOROSITY *n pl.* -TIES the state of being morose

MORPH *n pl.* -S a type of phoneme

MORPHEME *n pl.* -S a linguistic unit

MORPHIA *n pl.* -S morphine

MORPHIC *adj* pertaining to form

MORPHIN *n pl.* -S morphine

MORPHINE *n pl.* -S a narcotic alkaloid

MORPHO *n pl.* -PHOS a tropical butterfly

MORRION *n pl.* -S morion

MORRIS *n pl.* -RISES an English folk dance

MORRO *n pl.* -ROS a rounded elevation

MORROW *n pl.* -S the next day

MORSEL *v* -SELED, -SELING, -SELS or -SELLED, -SELLING, -SELS to divide into small pieces

MORT *n pl.* -S a note sounded on a hunting horn to announce the killing of an animal

MORTAL *n pl.* -S a human being

MORTALLY *adv* fatally

MORTAR *v* -ED, -ING, -S to secure with mortar (a type of cement)

MORTARY *adj* containing or resembling mortar

MORTGAGE *v* -GAGED, -GAGING, -GAGES to pledge to a creditor as security

MORTICE *v* -TICED, -TICING, -TICES to mortise

MORTIFY *v* -FIED, -FYING, -FIES to humiliate

MORTISE *v* -TISED, -TISING, -TISES to join or fasten securely

MORTISER *n pl.* -S one that mortises

MORTMAIN *n pl.* -S perpetual ownership of land

MORTUARY *n pl.* -ARIES a place where dead bodies are kept until burial

MORULA *n pl.* -LAE or -LAS an embryonic mass of cells **MORULAR** *adj*

MOSAIC *v* -ICKED, -ICKING, -ICS to form into a mosaic (a type of inlaid surface decoration)

MOSCHATE *adj* musky

MOSEY *v* -ED, -ING, -S to saunter

MOSHAV *n pl.* -SHAVIM a cooperative settlement of small farms in Israel

MOSK *n pl.* -S mosque

MOSQUE *n pl.* -S a Muslim house of worship

MOSQUITO *n pl.* -TOES or -TOS a winged insect

MOSS *v* -ED, -ING, -ES to cover with moss (a growth of small, leafy-stemmed plants)

MOSSBACK *n pl.* -S a large, old fish

MOSSER *n pl.* -S one that gathers or works with moss

MOSSIER comparative of mossy

MOSSIEST superlative of mossy

MOSSLIKE *adj* resembling moss

MOSSO *adv* rapidly — used as a musical direction

MOSSY *adj* MOSSIER, MOSSIEST covered with moss

MOST *n* pl. -S the greatest amount

MOSTE past tense of mote

MOSTLY *adv* mainly

MOT *n* pl. -S a witty saying

MOTE *v* past tense MOSTE may

MOTE *n* pl. -S a small particle

MOTEL *n* pl. -S a roadside hotel

MOTET *n* pl. -S a type of choral composition

MOTEY *adj* full of motes

MOTH *n* pl. -S a winged insect

MOTHBALL *v* -ED, -ING, -S to put into storage

MOTHER *v* -ED, -ING, -S to give birth to

MOTHERLY *adj* maternal

MOTHERY *adj* slimy

MOTHY *adj* MOTHIER, MOTHIEST full of moths

MOTIF *n* pl. -S a recurring thematic element in an artistic work

MOTILE *n* pl. -S one whose mental imagery consists chiefly of inner feelings of action

MOTILITY *n* pl. -TIES the ability to move

MOTION *v* -ED, -ING, -S to signal by a bodily movement

MOTIONAL *adj* pertaining to movement

MOTIONER *n* pl. -S one that motions

MOTIVATE *v* -VATED, -VATING, -VATES to provide with an incentive

MOTIVE *v* -TIVED, -TIVING, -TIVES to motivate

MOTIVIC *adj* pertaining to a musical motif

MOTIVITY *n* pl. -TIES the ability to move

MOTLEY *adj* -LEYER, -LEYEST or -LIER, -LIEST composed of diverse elements

MOTLEY *n* pl. -LEYS a garment of various colors

MOTMOT *n* pl. -S a tropical bird

MOTOR *v* -ED, -ING, -S to travel by automobile

MOTORBUS *n* pl. -BUSES or -BUSSES a bus

MOTORCAR *n* pl. -S an automobile

MOTORIC *adj* pertaining to muscular movement

MOTORING *n* pl. -S the recreation of traveling by automobile

MOTORISE *v* -ISED, -ISING, -ISES to motorize

MOTORIST *n* pl. -S one who travels by automobile

MOTORIZE *v* -IZED, -IZING, -IZES to equip with motor vehicles

MOTORMAN *n* pl. -MEN one who operates an electric streetcar or subway train

MOTORWAY *n* pl. -WAYS a type of highway

MOTT *n* pl. -S motte

MOTTE *n* pl. -S a small growth of trees on a prairie

MOTTLE *v* -TLED, -TLING, -TLES to mark with spots or streaks of different colors

MOTTLER *n* pl. -S one that mottles

MOTTO *n* pl. -TOES or -TOS a short expression of a guiding principle

MOUCH *v* -ED, -ING, -ES to mooch

MOUCHOIR *n* pl. -S a small handkerchief

MOUE *n* pl. -S a pouting grimace

MOUFFLON *n* pl. -S mouflon

MOUFLON *n* pl. -S a wild sheep

MOUILLE *adj* pronounced with the front of the tongue against the palate

MOUJIK *n* pl. -S muzhik

MOULAGE *n* pl. -S the making of a cast or mold of a mark for use in a criminal investigation

MOULD *v* -ED, -ING, -S to mold

MOULDER *v* -ED, -ING, -S to molder

MOULDING *n* pl. -S molding

MOULDY *adj* MOULDIER, MOULDIEST moldy

MOULIN *n* pl. -S a vertical cavity in a glacier

MOULT *v* -ED, -ING, -S to molt

MOULTER *n* pl. -S molter

MOUND *v* -ED, -ING, -S to pile

MOUNT *v* -ED, -ING, -S to get up on

MOUNTAIN *n* pl. -S a large, natural elevation of the earth's surface

MOUNTER *n* pl. -S one that mounts

MOUNTING	n pl. -S something that provides a backing or appropriate setting for something else	**MOVING**	present participle of move
MOURN	v -ED, -ING, -S to feel or express grief or sorrow	**MOVINGLY**	adv so as to affect the emotions
MOURNER	n pl. -S one that mourns	**MOW**	v MOWED, MOWN, MOWING, MOWS to cut down standing herbage
MOURNFUL	adj -FULLER, -FULLEST expressing grief or sorrow	**MOWER**	n pl. -S one that mows
MOURNING	n pl. -S an outward sign of grief	**MOXA**	n pl. -S a Chinese plant
MOUSE	n pl. MICE a small rodent	**MOXIE**	n pl. -S spirit or courage
MOUSE	v MOUSED, MOUSING, MOUSES to catch mice	**MOZETTA**	n pl. -TAS or -TE mozzetta
MOUSER	n pl. -S an animal that catches mice	**MOZO**	n pl. -ZOS a manual laborer
		MOZZETTA	n pl. -TAS or -TE a hooded cape worn by bishops
MOUSEY	adj MOUSIER, MOUSIEST mousy	**MRIDANGA**	n pl. -S a drum of India
MOUSIER	comparative of mousy	**MU**	n pl. -S a Greek letter
MOUSIEST	superlative of mousy	**MUCH**	n pl. -ES a great amount
MOUSILY	adj in a mousy manner	**MUCHNESS**	n pl. -ES the quality of being great
MOUSING	n pl. -S a wrapping around the shank end of a hook	**MUCID**	adj musty
MOUSSAKA	n pl. -S a Middle Eastern dish of meat and eggplant	**MUCIDITY**	n pl. -TIES the state of being mucid
MOUSSE	n pl. -S a chilled dessert	**MUCILAGE**	n pl. -S an adhesive substance
MOUSY	adj MOUSIER, MOUSIEST resembling a mouse	**MUCIN**	n pl. -S a protein secreted by the mucous membranes **MUCINOID, MUCINOUS** adj
MOUTH	v -ED, -ING, -S to put into the mouth	**MUCK**	v -ED, -ING, -S to fertilize with manure
MOUTHER	n pl. -S a speaker	**MUCKER**	n pl. -S a vulgar person
MOUTHFUL	n pl. -S as much as the mouth can hold	**MUCKIER**	comparative of mucky
		MUCKIEST	superlative of mucky
MOUTHY	adj MOUTHIER, MOUTHIEST very talkative **MOUTHILY** adv	**MUCKILY**	adv in a mucky manner
		MUCKLE	n pl. -S a large amount
MOUTON	n pl. -S sheepskin processed to resemble seal or beaver	**MUCKLUCK**	n pl. -S mukluk
MOVABLE	n pl. -S something that can be moved	**MUCKRAKE**	v -RAKED, -RAKING, -RAKES to search for and expose corruption
MOVABLY	adv so as to be capable of being moved	**MUCKWORM**	n pl. -S a worm found in manure
MOVE	v MOVED, MOVING, MOVES to change from one position to another	**MUCKY**	adj MUCKIER, MUCKIEST filthy
		MUCLUC	n pl. -S mukluk
MOVEABLE	n pl. -S movable	**MUCOID**	n pl. -S a complex protein **MUCOIDAL** adj
MOVEABLY	adv movably		
MOVED	past tense of move	**MUCOR**	n pl. -S a type of fungus
MOVELESS	adj incapable of movement	**MUCOSA**	n pl. -SAE or -SAS a mucous membrane **MUCOSAL** adj
MOVEMENT	n pl. -S the act of moving		
MOVER	n pl. -S one that moves	**MUCOSE**	adj mucous
MOVIE	n pl. -S a motion picture	**MUCOSITY**	n pl. -TIES the state of being mucous
MOVIEDOM	n pl. -S filmdom	**MUCOUS**	adj secreting or containing mucus

MUCRO   *n* pl. -CRONES a sharp point at the end of certain plant and animal organs

MUCUS   *n* pl. -ES a viscid bodily fluid

MUD   *v* MUDDED, MUDDING, MUDS to cover with mud (soft, wet earth)

MUDCAP   *v* -CAPPED, -CAPPING, -CAPS to cover an explosive with mud before detonating

MUDDER   *n* pl. -S a racehorse that runs well on a muddy track

MUDDIED   past tense of muddy

MUDDIER   comparative of muddy

MUDDIES   present 3d person sing. of muddy

MUDDIEST   superlative of muddy

MUDDILY   *adj* in a muddy manner

MUDDING   present participle of mud

MUDDLE   *n* -DLED, -DLING, -DLES to mix in a disordered manner

MUDDLER   *n* pl. -S one that muddles

MUDDY   *adj* -DIER, -DIEST covered or filled with mud

MUDDY   *v* -DIED, -DYING, -DIES to make or become muddy

MUDFISH   *n* pl. -ES a fish found in mud or muddy water

MUDGUARD   *n* pl. -S a fender

MUDLARK   *n* pl. -S a street urchin

MUDPUPPY   *n* pl. -PIES a large salamander

MUDRA   *n* pl. -S a hand gesture in East Indian classical dancing

MUDROCK   *n* pl. -S pelite

MUDROOM   *n* pl. -S a room for shedding muddy clothing or footwear

MUDSILL   *n* pl. -S the lowest supporting timber of a structure

MUDSTONE   *n* pl. -S a type of rock

MUEDDIN   *n* pl. -S muezzin

MUENSTER   *n* pl. -S a mild cheese

MUEZZIN   *n* pl. -S a Muslin crier who calls the faithful to prayer

MUFF   *v* -ED, -ING, -S to bungle

MUFFIN   *n* pl. -S a small, round bread

MUFFLE   *v* -FLED, -FLING, -FLES to wrap with something to deaden sound

MUFFLER   *n* pl. -S a device for deadening sound

MUFTI   *n* pl. -S a judge who interprets Muslim religious law

MUG   *v* MUGGED, MUGGING, MUGS to assault with intent to rob

MUGG   *v* -ED, -ING, -S to make funny faces

MUGGAR   *n* pl. -S mugger

MUGGED   past tense of mug

MUGGER   *n* pl. -S a large Asian crocodile

MUGGIER   comparative of muggy

MUGGIEST   superlative of muggy

MUGGILY   *adv* in a muggy manner

MUGGING   *n* pl. -S a street assault or beating

MUGGINS   *n* pl. MUGGINS a card game

MUGGUR   *n* pl. -S mugger

MUGGY   *adj* -GIER, -GIEST warm and humid

MUGWORT   *n* pl. -S a flowering plant

MUGWUMP   *n* pl. -S a political independent

MUHLY   *n* pl. MUHLIES a perennial grass

MUJIK   *n* pl. -S muzhik

MUKLUK   *n* pl. -S a soft boot worn by Eskimos

MULATTO   *n* pl. -TOES or -TOS the offspring of one white and one black parent

MULBERRY   *n* pl. -RIES a tree bearing an edible, berrylike fruit

MULCH   *v* -ED, -ING, -ES to provide with a protective covering for the soil

MULCT   *v* -ED, -ING, -S to defraud

MULE   *v* MULED, MULING, MULES to strike from dies belonging to two different issues, as a coin

MULETA   *n* pl. -S a red cloth used by a matador

MULETEER   *n* pl. -S one who drives mules (hoofed work animals)

MULEY   *n* pl. -LEYS a hornless cow

MULING   present participle of mule

MULISH   *adj* stubborn MULISHLY *adv*

MULL   *v* -ED, -ING, -S to ponder

MULLA   *n* pl. -S mullah

MULLAH   *n* pl. -S a Muslim religious leader or teacher

MULLEIN   *n* pl. -S a Eurasian herb

MULLEN   *n* pl. -S mullein

MULLER   *n* pl. -S a grinding implement

MULLET   *n* pl. -S an edible fish

MULLEY   *n pl.* -LEYS muley

MULLIGAN   *n pl.* -S a stew of various meats and vegetables

MULLION   *v* -ED, -ING, -S to provide with vertical dividing strips

MULLITE   *n pl.* -S a mineral

MULLOCK   *n pl.* -S waste earth or rock from a mine **MULLOCKY** *adj*

MULTIFID   *adj* divided into many parts

MULTIJET   *adj* having more than two jets

MULTIPED   *n pl.* -S an animal having many feet

MULTIPLE   *n pl.* -S the product of a quantity by an integer

MULTIPLY   *v* -PLIED, -PLYING, -PLIES to increase in number

MULTURE   *n pl.* -S a fee paid to a miller for grinding grain

MUM   *v* MUMMED, MUMMING, MUMS to act in a disguise

MUMBLE   *v* -BLED, -BLING, -BLES to speak unclearly

MUMBLER   *n pl.* -S one that mumbles

MUMM   *v* -ED, -ING, -S to mum

MUMMED   past tense of mum and mumm

MUMMER   *n pl.* -S one that mums

MUMMERY   *n pl.* -MERIES a performance by mummers

MUMMIED   past tense of mummy

MUMMIES   present 3d person sing. of mummy

MUMMIFY   *v* -FIED, -FYING, -FIES to preserve by embalming

MUMMING   present participle of mum

MUMMY   *v* -MIED, -MYING, -MIES to mummify

MUMP   *v* -ED, -ING, -S to beg

MUMPER   *n pl.* -S one that mumps

MUN   *n pl.* -S man; fellow

MUNCH   *v* -ED, -ING, -ES to chew with a crackling sound

MUNCHER   *n pl.* -S one that munches

MUNDANE   *adj* ordinary

MUNDUNGO   *n pl.* -GOS a foul-smelling tobacco

MUNGO   *n pl.* -GOS a low-quality wool

MUNGOOSE   *n pl.* -S mongoose

MUNIMENT   *n pl.* -S a means of defense

MUNITION   *v* -ED, -ING, -S to furnish with war materiel

MUNNION   *n pl.* -S a muntin

MUNSTER   *n pl.* -S muenster

MUNTIN   *n pl.* -S a dividing strip for window panes

MUNTING   *n pl.* -S muntin

MUNTJAC   *n pl.* -S a small Asian deer

MUNTJAK   *n pl.* -S muntjac

MUON   *n pl.* -S an atomic particle **MUONIC** *adj*

MURA   *n pl.* -S a Japanese village

MURAENID   *n pl.* -S a moray

MURAL   *n pl.* -S a painting applied directly to a wall or ceiling

MURALIST   *n pl.* -S a painter of murals

MURDER   *v* -ED, -ING, -S to kill unlawfully with premediated malice

MURDEREE   *n pl.* -S one that is murdered

MURDERER   *n pl.* -S one that murders

MURE   *v* MURED, MURING, MURES to immure

MUREIN   *n pl.* -S a type of polymer

MUREX   *n pl.* -RICES or -REXES a marine mollusk

MURIATE   *n pl.* -S chloride

MURIATED   *adj* pickled

MURICATE   *adj* covered with short, sharp points

MURICES   *a pl.* of murex

MURID   *n pl.* -S a murine

MURINE   *n pl.* -S any of a family of small rodents

MURING   present participle of mure

MURK   *adj* MURKER, MURKEST dark **MURKLY** *adv*

MURK   *n pl.* -S darkness

MURKY   *adj* MURKIER, MURKIEST dark **MURKILY** *adv*

MURMUR   *v* -ED, -ING, -S to speak unclearly

MURMURER   *n pl.* -S one that murmurs

MURPHY   *n pl.* -PHIES a potato

MURR   *n pl.* -S murre

MURRA   *n pl.* -S a substance used to make fine vases and cups in ancient Rome

MURRAIN   *n pl.* -S a disease of cattle

MURRE   *n pl.* -S a diving bird

MURRELET *n pl.* -S a small diving bird

MURREY *n pl.* -REYS a dark purple color

MURRHA *n pl.* -S murra **MURRHINE** *adj*

MURRINE *adj* pertaining to murra

MURRY *n pl.* -RIES a moray

MURTHER *v* -ED, -ING, -S to murder

MUSCA *n pl.* -CAE any of a genus of flies

MUSCADEL *n pl.* -S muscatel

MUSCAT *n pl.* -S a sweet, white grape

MUSCATEL *n pl.* -S a wine made from muscat grapes

MUSCID *n pl.* -S musca

MUSCLE *v* -CLED, -CLING, -CLES to proceed by force

MUSCLY *adj* composed of muscle (tissue that produces bodily movement)

MUSCULAR *adj* pertaining to muscle

MUSE *v* MUSED, MUSING, MUSES to ponder

MUSEFUL *adj* pensive

MUSER *n pl.* -S one that muses

MUSETTE *n pl.* -S a small bagpipe

MUSEUM *n pl.* -S a place where objects of lasting interest or value are cared for and exhibited

MUSH *v* -ED, -ING, -ES to travel over snow with a dog sled

MUSHER *n pl.* -S one that mushes

MUSHROOM *v* -ED, -ING, -S to grow or spread rapidly

MUSHY *adj* MUSHIER, MUSHIEST pulpy **MUSHILY** *adv*

MUSIC *n pl.* -S vocal or instrumental sounds organized to produce a unified composition

MUSICAL *n pl.* -S a play in which dialogue is interspersed with songs and dances

MUSICALE *n pl.* -S a program of music performed at a social gathering

MUSICIAN *n pl.* -S one who performs or composes music

MUSING *n pl.* -S contemplation

MUSINGLY *adv* in a pensive manner

MUSJID *n pl.* -S a mosque

MUSK *n pl.* -S a strongly odorous substance secreted by certain animals

MUSKEG *n pl.* -S a marsh

MUSKET *n pl.* -S a type of firearm

MUSKETRY *n pl.* -RIES the technique of firing small arms

MUSKIE *n pl.* -S a freshwater fish

MUSKIER comparative of musky

MUSKIEST superlative of musky

MUSKILY *adv* in a musky manner

MUSKIT *n pl.* -S mesquite

MUSKRAT *n pl.* -S an aquatic rodent

MUSKY *adj* MUSKIER, MUSKIEST resembling musk

MUSLIN *n pl.* -S a cotton fabric

MUSPIKE *n pl.* -S a freshwater fish

MUSQUASH *n pl.* -ES the muskrat

MUSS *v* -ED, -ING, -ES to mess

MUSSEL *n pl.* -S a bivalve mollusk

MUSSY *adj* MUSSIER, MUSSIEST messy **MUSSILY** *adv*

MUST *v* -ED, -ING, -S to become musty

MUSTACHE *n pl.* -S a growth of hair on the upper lip

MUSTANG *n pl.* -S a wild horse

MUSTARD *n pl.* -S a pungent seasoning

MUSTEE *n pl.* -S an octoroon

MUSTER *v* -ED, -ING, -S to summon or assemble

MUSTH *n pl.* -S a state of frenzy occurring in male elephants

MUSTY *adj* MUSTIER, MUSTIEST having a stale odor **MUSTILY** *adv*

MUT *n pl.* -S mutt

MUTABLE *adj* capable of change **MUTABLY** *adv*

MUTAGEN *n pl.* -S a substance that causes biological mutation

MUTANT *n pl.* -S something that undergoes mutation

MUTASE *n pl.* -S an enzyme

MUTATE *v* -TATED, -TATING, -TATES to undergo mutation

MUTATION *n pl.* -S the act of changing **MUTATIVE** *adj*

MUTCH *n pl.* -ES a close-fitting cap

MUTCHKIN *n pl.* -S a Scottish unit of liquid measure

MUTE *adj* MUTER, MUTEST characterized by an absence of speech **MUTELY** *adv*

MUTE	v MUTED, MUTING, MUTES to deaden the sound of **MUTEDLY** adv
MUTENESS	n pl. -ES the state of being mute
MUTER	comparative of mute
MUTEST	superlative of mute
MUTICOUS	adj lacking a point
MUTILATE	v -LATED, -LATING, -LATES to deprive of a limb or other essential part
MUTINE	v -TINED, -TINING, -TINES to mutiny
MUTINEER	v -ED, -ING, -S to mutiny
MUTING	present participle of mute
MUTINIED	past tense of mutiny
MUTINIES	present 3d person sing. of mutiny
MUTINING	present participle of mutine
MUTINOUS	adj disposed to mutiny
MUTINY	v -NIED, -NYING, -NIES to revolt against constituted authority
MUTISM	n pl. -S muteness
MUTT	n pl. -S a mongrel dog
MUTTER	v -ED, -ING, -S to speak unclearly
MUTTERER	n pl. -S one that mutters
MUTTON	n pl. -S the flesh of sheep used as food **MUTTONY** adj
MUTUAL	adj shared in common **MUTUALLY** adv
MUTUEL	n pl. -S a system of betting on races
MUTULE	n pl. -S an ornamental block used in classical Greek architecture **MUTULAR** adj
MUUMUU	n pl. -S a long, loose dress
MUZHIK	n pl. -S a Russian peasant
MUZJIK	n pl. -S muzhik
MUZZIER	comparative of muzzy
MUZZIEST	superlative of muzzy
MUZZILY	adv in a muzzy manner
MUZZLE	v -ZLED, -ZLING, -ZLES to put a covering over the mouth of to prevent biting or eating
MUZZLER	n pl. -S one that muzzles
MUZZY	adj -ZIER, -ZIEST confused
MY	pron the possessive form of the pronoun I

MYALGIA	n pl. -S muscular pain **MYALGIC** adj
MYASIS	n pl. MYASES myiasis
MYCELE	n pl. -S mycelium
MYCELIUM	n pl. -LIA the vegetive portion of a fungus **MYCELIAL, MYCELIAN, MYCELOID** adj
MYCETOMA	n pl. -MAS or -MATA a fungous infection
MYCOLOGY	n pl. -GIES the branch of botany dealing with fungi
MYCOSIS	n pl. -COSES a disease caused by a fungus **MYCOTIC** adj
MYELIN	n pl. -S a fatty substance that encases certain nerve fibers **MYELINIC** adj
MYELINE	n pl. -S myelin
MYELITIS	n pl. -LITIDES inflammation of the bone marrow
MYELOID	adj pertaining to bone marrow
MYELOMA	n pl. -MAS or -MATA a tumor of the bone marrow
MYIASIS	n pl. MYIASES infestation of human tissue by fly maggots
MYLONITE	n pl. -S a type of rock
MYNA	n pl. -S an Asian bird
MYNAH	n pl. -S myna
MYNHEER	n pl. -S a Dutch title of courtesy for a man
MYOBLAST	n pl. -S a cell capable of giving rise to muscle cells
MYOGENIC	adj originating in muscle tissue
MYOGRAPH	n pl. -S an instrument for recording muscular contractions
MYOID	adj resembling muscle
MYOLOGY	n pl. -GIES the study of muscles **MYOLOGIC** adj
MYOMA	n pl. -MAS or -MATA a tumor composed of muscle tissue
MYOPATHY	n pl. -THIES a disorder of muscle tissue
MYOPE	n pl. -S one who is affected with myopia
MYOPIA	n pl. -S a visual defect **MYOPIC** adj
MYOPY	n pl. -PIES myopia
MYOSCOPE	n pl. -S an instrument for observing muscular contractions
MYOSIN	n pl. -S a protein found in muscle tissue
MYOSIS	n pl. MYOSES miosis

MYOSOTE   *n* pl. -S myosotis

MYOSOTIS   *n* pl. -TISES a flowering plant

MYOTIC   *n* pl. -S miotic

MYOTOME   *n* pl. -S a portion of an embryonic somite

MYOTONIA   *n* pl. -S temporary muscular rigidity **MYOTONIC** *adj*

MYRIAD   *n* pl. -S a very large number

MYRIAPOD   *n* pl. -S a multi-legged arthropod

MYRICA   *n* pl. -S a medicinal tree bark

MYRIOPOD   *n* pl. -S myriapod

MYRMIDON   *n* pl. -S a loyal follower

MYRRH   *n* pl. -S an aromatic gum resin **MYRRHIC** *adj*

MYRTLE   *n* pl. -S an evergreen shrub

MYSELF   *pron* a form of the 1st person sing. pronoun

MYSOST   *n* pl. -S a mild cheese

MYSTAGOG   *n* pl. -S a teacher of religious mysteries

MYSTERY   *n* pl. -TERIES something that is not or cannot be known, understood, or explained

MYSTIC   *n* pl. -S one who professes to have had mystical experiences

MYSTICAL   *adj* spiritually significant or symbolic

MYSTICLY   *adv* in a mystical manner

MYSTIFY   *v* -FIED, -FYING, -FIES to perplex

MYSTIQUE   *n* pl. -S an aura of mystery or mystical power surrounding a particular person or thing

MYTH   *n* pl. -S a type of traditional story

MYTHIC   *adj* mythical

MYTHICAL   *adj* based on or described in a myth

MYTHOS   *n* pl. -THOI a myth

MYXEDEMA   *n* pl. -S a disease caused by decreased activity of the thyroid gland

MYXOCYTE   *n* pl. -S a large cell found in mucous tissue

MYXOID   *adj* containing mucus

MYXOMA   *n* pl. -MAS or -MATA a tumor composed of mucous tissue

NA	*adv* no; not
NAB	*v* NABBED, NABBING, NABS to capture or arrest
NABIS	*n* pl. NABIS a group of French artists
NABOB	*n* pl. -S one who has become rich in India
NABOBERY	*n* pl. -ERIES the state of being a nabob
NABOBESS	*n* pl. -ES a female nabob
NABOBISM	*n* pl. -S great wealth and luxury
NACELLE	*n* pl. -S a shelter on an aircraft
NACRE	*n* pl. -S the pearly internal layer of certain shells NACRED, NACREOUS *adj*
NADIR	*n* pl. -S a point on the celestial sphere NADIRAL *adj*
NAE	*adv* no; not
NAETHING	*n* pl. -S nothing
NAEVUS	*n* pl. -VI nevus NAEVOID *adj*
NAG	*v* NAGGED, NAGGING, NAGS to find fault incessantly
NAGANA	*n* pl. -S a disease of horses in Africa
NAGGER	*n* pl. -S one that nags
NAGGING	present participle of nag
NAIAD	*n* pl. -S or -ES a water nymph
NAIF	*n* pl. -S a naive person
NAIL	*v* -ED, -ING, -S to fasten with a nail (a slender piece of metal)
NAILER	*n* pl. -S one that nails
NAILFOLD	*n* pl. -S a fold of skin around the fingernail
NAILHEAD	*n* pl. -S the top of a nail
NAILSET	*n* pl. -S a steel rod for driving a nail into something
NAINSOOK	*n* pl. -S a cotton fabric
NAIVE	*adj* NAIVER, NAIVEST lacking sophistication NAIVELY *adv*
NAIVE	*n* pl. -S a naive person
NAIVETE	*n* pl. -S the quality of being naive
NAIVETY	*n* pl. -TIES naivete
NAKED	*adj* -KEDER, -KEDEST being without clothing or covering NAKEDLY *adv*
NALED	*n* pl. -S an insecticide
NALOXONE	*n* pl. -S a chemical compound
NAME	*v* NAMED, NAMING, NAMES to give a title to NAMABLE, NAMEABLE *adj*
NAMELESS	*adj* lacking distinction or fame
NAMELY	*adv* that is to say
NAMER	*n* pl. -S one that names
NAMESAKE	*n* pl. -S one who is named after another
NAMING	present participle of name
NANA	*n* pl. -S a grandmother
NANCE	*n* pl. -S an effeminate male
NANDIN	*n* pl. -S an evergreen shrub
NANISM	*n* pl. -S abnormal smallness
NANKEEN	*n* pl. -S a cotton fabric
NANKIN	*n* pl. -S nankeen
NANNIE	*n* pl. -S nanny
NANNY	*n* pl. -NIES a children's nurse
NANOGRAM	*n* pl. -S a unit of mass and weight
NANOWATT	*n* pl. -S a unit of power

NAOS	*n* pl. NAOI an ancient temple
NAP	*v* NAPPED, NAPPING, NAPS to sleep briefly
NAPALM	*v* -ED, -ING, -S to assault with a type of incendiary bomb
NAPE	*n* pl. -S the back of the neck
NAPERY	*n* pl. -PERIES table linen
NAPHTHA	*n* pl. -S a volatile liquid
NAPHTHOL	*n* pl. -S a chemical compound
NAPHTHYL	*adj* containing a certain chemical group
NAPHTOL	*n* pl. -S naphthol
NAPIFORM	*adj* shaped like a turnip
NAPKIN	*n* pl. -S a piece of material used to wipe the hands and mouth
NAPLESS	*adj* threadbare
NAPOLEON	*n* pl. -S a type of pastry
NAPPE	*n* pl. -S a type of rock formation
NAPPED	past tense of nap
NAPPER	*n* pl. -S one that naps
NAPPIE	*n* pl. -S a diaper
NAPPING	present participle of nap
NAPPY	*adj* -PIER, -PIEST kinky
NARC	*n* pl. -S an undercover drug agent
NARCEIN	*n* pl. -S narceine
NARCEINE	*n* pl. -S an opium derivative
NARCISM	*n* pl. -S excessive love of oneself
NARCISSI	*n/pl* bulbous flowering plants
NARCIST	*n* pl. -S one given to narcism
NARCO	*n* pl. -COS narc
NARCOSE	*adj* characterized by stupor
NARCOSIS	*n* pl. -COSES a drug-induced stupor
NARCOTIC	*n* pl. -S a drug that dulls the senses
NARD	*n* pl. -S a fragrant ointment **NARDINE** *adj*
NARES	pl. of naris
NARGHILE	*n* pl. -S a hookah
NARGILE	*n* pl. -S narghile
NARGILEH	*n* pl. -S narghile
NARIS	*n* pl. NARES a nostril **NARIAL**, **NARIC**, **NARINE** *adj*
NARK	*v* -ED, -ING, -S to spy or inform
NARRATE	*v* -RATED, -RATING, -RATES to tell a story

NARRATER	*n* pl. -S narrator
NARRATOR	*n* pl. -S one that narrates
NARROW	*adj* -ROWER, -ROWEST of little width **NARROWLY** *adv*
NARROW	*v* -ED, -ING, -S to make narrow
NARTHEX	*n* pl. -ES a vestibule in a church
NARWAL	*n* pl. -S narwhal
NARWHAL	*n* pl. -S an arctic aquatic mammal
NARWHALE	*n* pl. -S narwhal
NARY	*adj* not one
NASAL	*n* pl. -S a sound uttered through the nose
NASALISE	*v* -ISED, -ISING, -ISES to nasalize
NASALITY	*n* pl. -TIES the quality or an instance of being produced nasally
NASALIZE	*v* -IZED, -IZING, -IZES to produce sounds nasally
NASALLY	*adv* through the nose
NASCENCE	*n* pl. -S nascency
NASCENCY	*n* pl. -CIES birth; origin
NASCENT	*adj* coming into existence
NASION	*n* pl. -S a point in the skull **NASIAL** *adj*
NASTIC	*adj* pertaining to an automatic response of plants
NASTY	*adj* -TIER, -TIEST offensive to the senses **NASTILY** *adv*
NATAL	*adj* pertaining to one's birth
NATALITY	*n* pl. -TIES birth rate
NATANT	*adj* floating or swimming **NATANTLY** *adv*
NATATION	*n* pl. -S the act of swimming
NATATORY	*adj* pertaining to swimming
NATES	*n/pl* the buttocks
NATHLESS	*adv* nevertheless
NATION	*n* pl. -S a politically organized people who share a territory, customs, and history
NATIONAL	*n* pl. -S a citizen of a nation
NATIVE	*n* pl. -S an original inhabitant of an area
NATIVELY	*adv* in an inborn manner
NATIVISM	*n* pl. -S a policy of favoring the interests of native inhabitants
NATIVIST	*n* pl. -S an advocate of nativism

NATIVITY *n* pl. -TIES the process of being born

NATRIUM *n* pl. -S sodium

NATRON *n* pl. -S a chemical compound

NATTER *v* -ED, -ING, -S to chatter

NATTY *adj* -TIER, -TIEST neatly dressed **NATTILY** *adv*

NATURAL *n* pl. -S a type of musical note

NATURE *n* pl. -S the essential qualities of a person or thing **NATURED** *adj*

NAUGHT *n* pl. -S a zero

NAUGHTY *adj* -TIER, -TIEST disobedient

NAUMACHY *n* pl. -CHIES a mock sea battle

NAUPLIUS *n* pl. -PLII a form of certain crustaceans **NAUPLIAL** *adj*

NAUSEA *n* pl. -S a stomach disturbance

NAUSEANT *n* pl. -S an agent that induces nausea

NAUSEATE *v* -ATED, -ATING, -ATES to affect with nausea

NAUSEOUS *adj* affected with nausea

NAUTCH *n* pl. -ES a dancing exhibition in India

NAUTICAL *adj* pertaining to ships

NAUTILUS *n* pl. -LUSES or -LI a spiral-shelled mollusk

NAVAID *n* pl. -S a navigational device

NAVAL *adj* pertaining to ships **NAVALLY** *adv*

NAVAR *n* pl. -S a system of air navigation

NAVE *n* pl. -S the main part of a church

NAVEL *n* pl. -S a depression in the abdomen

NAVETTE *n* pl. -S a gem cut in a pointed oval form

NAVICERT *n* pl. -S a document permitting a vessel passage through a naval blockade

NAVIES pl. of navy

NAVIGATE *v* -GATED, -GATING, -GATES to plan and control the course of

NAVVY *n* pl. -VIES a manual laborer

NAVY *n* pl. -VIES a nation's warships

NAWAB *n* pl. -S a nabob

NAY *n* pl. NAYS a negative vote

NAZI *n* pl. -S a type of fascist

NAZIFY *v* -FIED, -FYING, -FIES to cause to be like a nazi

NEAP *n* pl. -S a tide of lowest range

NEAR *adj* NEARER, NEAREST situated within a short distance

NEAR *v* -ED, -ING, -S to approach

NEARBY *adj* near

NEARLY *adv* -LIER, -LIEST with close approximation

NEARNESS *n* pl. -ES the state of being near

NEAT *adj* NEATER, NEATEST being in a state of cleanliness and order

NEAT *n* pl. -S a bovine

NEATEN *v* -ED, -ING, -S to make neat

NEATH *prep* beneath

NEATHERD *n* pl. -S a cowherd

NEATLY *adv* in a neat manner

NEATNESS *n* pl. -ES the state of being neat

NEB *n* pl. -S the beak of a bird

NEBBISH *n* pl. -ES a meek person

NEBULA *n* pl. -LAS or -LAE a cloud-like interstellar mass **NEBULAR** *adj*

NEBULE *adj* composed of successive short curves

NEBULISE *v* -LISED, -LISING, -LISES to nebulize

NEBULIZE *v* -LIZED, -LIZING, -LIZES to reduce to a fine spray

NEBULOSE *adj* nebulous

NEBULOUS *adj* unclear

NEBULY *adj* nebule

NECK *v* -ED, -ING, -S to kiss and caress in lovemaking

NECKBAND *n* pl. -S a band worn around the neck (the part of the body joining the head to the trunk)

NECKING *n* pl. -S a small molding near the top of a column

NECKLACE *n* pl. -S an ornament worn around the neck

NECKLESS *adj* having no neck

NECKLIKE *adj* resembling the neck

NECKLINE *n* pl. -S the line formed by the neck opening of a garment

NECKTIE *n* pl. -S a strip of fabric worn around the neck

NECKWEAR *n* pl. -S something that is worn around the neck

NECROPSY *v* -SIED, -SYING, -SIES to perform an autopsy on

NECROSE v -CROSED, -CROSING, -CROSES to affect with necrosis

NECROSIS n pl. -CROSES the death of living tissue **NECROTIC** adj

NECTAR n pl. -S a delicious drink

NECTARY n pl. -TARIES a plant gland

NEE adj born with the name of

NEED v -ED, -ING, -S to have an urgent or essential use for

NEEDER n pl. -S one that needs

NEEDFUL n pl. -S something that is needed

NEEDIER comparative of needy

NEEDIEST superlative of needy

NEEDILY adv in a needy manner

NEEDLE v -DLED, -DLING, -DLES to sew with a slender, pointed instrument

NEEDLER n pl. -S one that needles

NEEDLESS adj not necessary

NEEDLING n pl. -S the act of one who needles

NEEDY adj NEEDIER, NEEDIEST in a state of poverty

NEEM n pl. -S an East Indian tree

NEEP n pl. -S a turnip

NEGATE v -GATED, -GATING, -GATES to nullify

NEGATER n pl. -S one that negates

NEGATION n pl. -S the act of negating

NEGATIVE v -TIVED, -TIVING, -TIVES to veto

NEGATON n pl. -S negatron

NEGATOR n pl. -S negater

NEGATRON n pl. -S an electron

NEGLECT v -ED, -ING, -S to fail to pay attention to

NEGLIGE n pl. -S negligee

NEGLIGEE n pl. -S a woman's dressing gown

NEGRO n pl. -GROES a member of the black race of mankind

NEGROID n pl. -S a negro

NEGUS n pl. -ES an alcoholic beverage

NEIF n pl. -S nieve

NEIGH v -ED, -ING, -S to utter the cry of a horse

NEIGHBOR v -ED, -ING, -S to live close to

NEIST adj next

NEITHER adj not one or the other

NEKTON n pl. -S free-swimming marine animals **NEKTONIC** adj

NELSON n pl. -S a wrestling hold

NELUMBO n pl. -BOS an aquatic herb

NEMA n pl. -S a nematode

NEMATIC adj pertaining to a phase of a liquid crystal

NEMATODE n pl. -S a kind of worm

NEMESIS n pl. NEMESES an unbeatable opponent

NENE n pl. NENE a Hawaiian goose

NEOLITH n pl. -S an ancient stone implement

NEOLOGY n pl. -GIES a new word or phrase **NEOLOGIC** adj

NEOMORPH n pl. -S a type of biological structure

NEOMYCIN n pl. -S an antibiotic drug

NEON n pl. -S a gaseous element **NEONED** adj

NEONATE n pl. -S a newborn child **NEONATAL** adj

NEOPHYTE n pl. -S a novice

NEOPLASM n pl. -S a tumor

NEOPRENE n pl. -S a synthetic rubber

NEOTENY n pl. -NIES attainment of sexual maturity in the larval stage **NEOTENIC** adj

NEOTERIC n pl. -S a modern author

NEOTYPE n pl. -S a specimen of a species

NEPENTHE n pl. -S a drug that induces forgetfulness

NEPHEW n pl. -S a son of one's brother or sister

NEPHRIC adj renal

NEPHRISM n pl. -S ill health caused by a kidney disease

NEPHRITE n pl. -S a mineral

NEPHRON n pl. -S an excretory unit of a kidney

NEPOTISM n pl. -S favoritism shown to a relative **NEPOTIC** adj

NEPOTIST n pl. -S one who practices nepotism

NEREID n pl. -S a sea nymph

NEREIS n pl. -REIDES a marine worm

NERITIC adj pertaining to shallow water

NEROL	n pl. -S a fragrant alcohol	**NETTLE**	v -TLED, -TLING, -TLES to make angry
NEROLI	n pl. -S a fragrant oil		
NERTS	interj — used to express defiance or disgust	**NETTLER**	n pl. -S one that nettles
		NETTLY	adj -TLIER, -TLIEST prickly
NERTZ	interj nerts	**NETTY**	adj -TIER, -TIEST resembling a net
NERVATE	adj having veins		
NERVE	v NERVED, NERVING, NERVES to give courage to	**NETWORK**	v -ED, -ING, -S to cover with or as if with crossing lines
NERVIER	comparative of nervy	**NEUM**	n pl. -S neume
NERVIEST	superlative of nervy	**NEUME**	n pl. -S a sign used in musical notation **NEUMATIC, NEUMIC** adj
NERVILY	adv in a nervy manner		
NERVINE	n pl. -S a soothing medicine		
NERVING	n pl. -S a type of veterinary operation	**NEURAL**	adj pertaining to the nervous system **NEURALLY** adv
		NEURAXON	n pl. -S a part of a neuron
NERVOUS	adj easily excited		
NERVULE	n pl. -S nervure	**NEURITIC**	n pl. -S one affected with neuritis
NERVURE	n pl. -S a vascular ridge on a leaf		
		NEURITIS	n pl. -RITIDES or -RITISES inflammation of a nerve
NERVY	adj NERVIER, NERVIEST impudent		
		NEUROID	adj resembling a nerve
NESCIENT	n pl. -S one who is ignorant	**NEUROMA**	n pl. -MAS or -MATA a type of tumor
NESS	n pl. -ES a headland		
NEST	v -ED, -ING, -S to build a nest (a structure for holding bird eggs)	**NEURON**	n pl. -S the basic cellular unit of the nervous system **NEURONAL, NEURONIC** adj
NESTER	n pl. -S one that nests	**NEURONE**	n pl. -S neuron
NESTLE	v -TLED, -TLING, -TLES to lie snugly	**NEUROSIS**	n pl. -ROSES a type of emotional disturbance **NEUROSAL** adj
NESTLER	n pl. -S one that nestles		
NESTLIKE	adj resembling a nest	**NEUROTIC**	n pl. -S one affected with a neurosis
NESTLING	n pl. -S a young bird		
NESTOR	n pl. -S a wise old man	**NEUSTON**	n pl. -S an aggregate of small aquatic organisms
NET	v NETTED, NETTING, NETS to catch in a net (a type of openwork fabric)		
		NEUTER	v -ED, -ING, -S to castrate
		NEUTRAL	n pl. -S one that is impartial
NETHER	adj situated below	**NEUTRINO**	n pl. -NOS an atomic particle
NETLESS	adj having no net	**NEUTRON**	n pl. -S an atomic particle
NETLIKE	adj resembling a net	**NEVE**	n pl. -S a granular snow
NETOP	n pl. -S friend; companion	**NEVER**	adv at no time
NETSUKE	n pl. -S a button-like fixture on Japanese clothing	**NEVUS**	n pl. -VI a birthmark **NEVOID** adj
NETT	v -ED, -ING, -S to net	**NEW**	adj NEWER, NEWEST existing only a short time
NETTABLE	adj capable of being netted		
NETTED	past tense of net, nett	**NEW**	n pl. -S something that is new
NETTER	n pl. -S one that nets	**NEWBORN**	n pl. -S a recently born infant
NETTIER	comparative of netty	**NEWCOMER**	n pl. -S one that has recently arrived
NETTIEST	superlative of netty		
		NEWEL	n pl. -S a staircase support
		NEWFOUND	adj newly found
NETTING	n pl. -S a net	**NEWISH**	adj somewhat new

NEWLY *adv* recently

NEWLYWED *n* pl. -S a person recently married

NEWMOWN *adj* recently mown

NEWNESS *n* pl. -ES the state of being new

NEWS *n/pl* a report of recent events

NEWSBOY *n* pl. -BOYS a boy who delivers or sells newspapers

NEWSCAST *n* pl. -S a news broadcast

NEWSIER comparative of newsy

NEWSIES pl. of newsy

NEWSIEST superlative of newsy

NEWSLESS *adj* having no news

NEWSMAN *n* pl. -MEN a news reporter

NEWSPEAK *n* pl. -S a deliberately ambiguous language

NEWSREEL *n* pl. -S a short movie presenting current events

NEWSROOM *n* pl. -S a room where the news is gathered

NEWSY *adj* NEWSIER, NEWSIEST full of news

NEWSY *n* pl. NEWSIES a newsboy

NEWT *n* pl. -S a small salamander

NEWTON *n* pl. -S a unit of force

NEXT *adj* coming immediately after; adjoining

NEXTDOOR *adj* located in the next building or room

NEXUS *n* pl. -ES a connection or link

NGWEE *n* pl. NGWEE a Zambian unit of currency

NIACIN *n* pl. -S a B vitamin

NIB *v* NIBBED, NIBBING, NIBS to provide with a penpoint

NIBBLE *v* -BLED, -BLING, -BLES to eat with small bites

NIBBLER *n* pl. -S one that nibbles

NIBLICK *n* pl. -S a golf club

NIBLIKE *adj* resembling a penpoint

NICE *adj* NICER, NICEST pleasing to the senses **NICELY** *adv*

NICENESS *n* pl. -ES the quality of being nice

NICETY *n* pl. -TIES a fine point or distinction

NICHE *v* NICHED, NICHING, NICHES to place in a receding space or hollow

NICK *v* -ED, -ING, -S to make a shallow cut in

NICKEL *v* -ELED, -ELING, -ELS or -ELLED, -ELLING, -ELS to plate with nickel (a metallic element)

NICKELIC *adj* pertaining to or containing nickel

NICKER *v* -ED, -ING, -S to neigh

NICKLE *n* pl. -S nickel

NICKNACK *n* pl. -S a trinket

NICKNAME *v* -NAMED, -NAMING, -NAMES to give an alternate name to

NICOL *n* pl. -S a type of prism

NICOTIN *n* pl. -S nicotine

NICOTINE *n* pl. -S a poisonous alkaloid in tobacco

NICTATE *v* -TATED, -TATING, -TATES to wink

NIDAL *adj* pertaining to a nidus

NIDE *v* NIDED, NIDING, NIDES to nest

NIDERING *n* pl. -S a coward

NIDGET *n* pl. -S an idiot

NIDI a pl. of nidus

NIDIFY *v* -FIED, -FYING, -FIES to nest

NIDING present participle of nide

NIDUS *n* pl. NIDI or NIDUSES a nest or breeding place

NIECE *n* pl. -S a daughter of one's brother or sister

NIELLIST *n* pl. -S one that niellos

NIELLO *n* pl. -LI or -LOS a black metallic substance

NIELLO *v* -ED, -ING, -S to decorate with niello

NIEVE *n* pl. -S the fist or hand

NIFFER *v* -ED, -ING, -S to barter

NIFTY *adj* -TIER, -TIEST stylish; pleasing

NIFTY *n* pl. -TIES something that is nifty

NIGGARD *v* -ED, -ING, -S to act stingily

NIGGER *n* pl. -S a black person — an offensive term

NIGGLE *v* -GLED, -GLING, -GLES to worry over petty details

NIGGLER *n* pl. -S one that niggles

NIGGLING *n* pl. -S petty or meticulous work

NIGH *adj* NIGHER, NIGHEST near

NIGH	*v* -ED, -ING, -S to approach
NIGHNESS	*n* pl. -ES the state of being nigh
NIGHT	*n* pl. -S the period from sunset to sunrise
NIGHTCAP	*n* pl. -S a cap worn to bed
NIGHTIE	*n* pl. -S a nightgown
NIGHTIES	pl. of nighty
NIGHTJAR	*n* pl. -S a nocturnal bird
NIGHTLY	*adv* every night; at night
NIGHTY	*n* pl. NIGHTIES nightie
NIGRIFY	*v* -FIED, -FYING, -FIES to make black
NIGROSIN	*n* pl. -S a type of dye
NIHIL	*n* pl. -S nothing
NIHILISM	*n* pl. -S a doctrine that denies traditional values
NIHILIST	*n* pl. -S an adherent of nihilism
NIHILITY	*n* pl. -TIES the state of being nothing
NIL	*n* pl. -S nothing
NILGAI	*n* pl. -S a large antelope
NILGAU	*n* pl. -S nilgai
NILGHAI	*n* pl. -S nilgai
NILGHAU	*n* pl. -S nilgai
NILL	*v* -ED, -ING, -S to be unwilling
NIM	*v* NIMMED, NIMMING, NIMS to steal
NIMBLE	*adj* -BLER, -BLEST agile **NIMBLY** *adv*
NIMBUS	*n* pl. -BI or -BUSES a luminous cloud **NIMBUSED** *adj*
NIMIETY	*n* pl. -ETIES excess **NIMIOUS** *adj*
NIMMED	past tense of nim
NIMMING	present participle of nim
NIMROD	*n* pl. -S a hunter
NINE	*n* pl. -S a number
NINEBARK	*n* pl. -S a flowering shrub
NINEFOLD	*adj* nine times as great
NINEPIN	*n* pl. -S a wooden pin used in a bowling game
NINETEEN	*n* pl. -S a number
NINETY	*n* pl. -TIES a number
NINNY	*n* pl. -NIES a fool **NINNYISH** *adj*
NINON	*n* pl. -S a sheer fabric
NINTH	*n* pl. -S one of nine equal parts
NINTHLY	*adv* in the ninth place

NIOBIUM	*n* pl. -S a metallic element **NIOBIC, NIOBOUS** *adj*
NIP	*v* NIPPED, NIPPING, NIPS to pinch
NIPA	*n* pl. -S a palm tree
NIPPER	*n* pl. -S one that nips
NIPPIER	comparative of nippy
NIPPIEST	superlative of nippy
NIPPILY	*adv* in a nippy manner
NIPPING	present participle of nip
NIPPLE	*n* pl. -S a protuberance on the breast
NIPPY	*adj* -PIER, -PIEST sharp or biting
NIRVANA	*n* pl. -S a blessed state in Buddhism **NIRVANIC** *adj*
NISEI	*n* pl. -S one born in America of immigrant Japanese parents
NISI	*adj* not yet final
NISUS	*n* pl. NISUS an effort
NIT	*n* pl. -S the egg of a parasitic insect
NITCHIE	*n* pl. -S an American Indian — an offensive term
NITER	*n* pl. -S a chemical salt
NITID	*adj* bright
NITON	*n* pl. -S radon
NITPICK	*v* -ED, -ING, -S to fuss over petty details
NITRATE	*v* -TRATED, -TRATING, -TRATES to treat with nitric acid
NITRATOR	*n* pl. -S one that nitrates
NITRE	*n* pl. -S niter
NITRIC	*adj* containing nitrogen
NITRID	*n* pl. -S nitride
NITRIDE	*n* pl. -S a compound of nitrogen
NITRIFY	*v* -FIED, -FYING, -FIES to combine with nitrogen
NITRIL	*n* pl. -S nitrile
NITRILE	*n* pl. -S a chemical compound
NITRITE	*n* pl. -S a salt of nitrous acid
NITRO	*n* pl. -TROS a nitrated product
NITROGEN	*n* pl. -S a gaseous element
NITROLIC	*adj* pertaining to a class of acids
NITROSO	*adj* containing nitrosyl
NITROSYL	*n* pl. -S a univalent radical
NITROUS	*adj* containing nitrogen
NITTY	*adj* -TIER, -TIEST full of nits

NITWIT   *n* pl. -S a stupid person

NIVAL   *adj* pertaining to snow

NIVEOUS   *adj* resembling snow

NIX   *v* -ED, -ING, -ES to veto

NIXIE   *n* pl. -S a female water sprite

NIXY   *n* pl. NIXIES an undeliverable piece of mail

NIZAM   *n* pl. -S a former sovereign of India

NIZAMATE   *n* pl. -S the territory of a nizam

NO   *n* pl. NOS or NOES a negative reply

NOB   *n* pl. -S a wealthy person

NOBBIER   comparative of nobby

NOBBIEST   superlative of nobby

NOBBILY   *adv* in a nobby manner

NOBBLE   *v* -BLED, -BLING, -BLES to disable a racehorse

NOBBLER   *n* pl. -S one that nobbles

NOBBY   *adj* -BIER, -BIEST elegant

NOBELIUM   *n* pl. -S a radioactive element

NOBILITY   *n* pl. -TIES the social class composed of nobles

NOBLE   *adj* -BLER, -BLEST possessing qualities of excellence

NOBLE   *n* pl. -S a person of high birth, rank, or title

NOBLEMAN   *n* pl. -MEN a noble

NOBLER   comparative of noble

NOBLESSE   *n* pl. -S the nobility

NOBLEST   superlative of noble

NOBLY   *adv* in a noble manner

NOBODY   *n* pl. -BODIES an unimportant person

NOCENT   *adj* harmful

NOCK   *v* -ED, -ING, -S to notch a bow or arrow

NOCTUID   *n* pl. -S a night-flying moth **NOCTUOID** *adj*

NOCTULE   *n* pl. -S a large bat

NOCTURN   *n* pl. -S a religious service

NOCTURNE   *n* pl. -S a musical composition

NOCUOUS   *adj* harmful

NOD   *v* NODDED, NODDING, NODS to briefly lower the head forward

NODAL   *adj* of the nature of a node **NODALLY** *adv*

NODALITY   *n* pl. -TIES the state of being nodal

NODDED   past tense of nod

NODDER   *n* pl. -S one that nods

NODDIES   pl. of noddy

NODDING   present participle of nod

NODDLE   *v* -DLED, -DLING, -DLES to nod frequently

NODDY   *n* pl. -DIES a fool

NODE   *n* pl. -S a swollen enlargement

NODI   pl. of nodus

NODICAL   *adj* pertaining to an astronomical point

NODOSE   *adj* having nodes

NODOSITY   *n* pl. -TIES the state of being nodose

NODOUS   *adj* nodose

NODULE   *n* pl. -S a small node **NODULAR, NODULOSE, NODULOUS** *adj*

NODUS   *n* pl. -DI a difficulty

NOEL   *n* pl. -S a Christmas carol

NOESIS   *n* pl. -SISES the process of reason

NOETIC   *adj* pertaining to reason

NOG   *n* pl. -S a strong ale

NOGG   *n* pl. -S nog

NOGGIN   *n* pl. -S a small cup

NOGGING   *n* pl. -S a type of masonry

NOH   *n* pl. NOH the classical drama of Japan

NOHOW   *adv* in no manner

NOIL   *n* pl. -S a kind of short fiber **NOILY** *adj*

NOIR   *adj* black

NOISE   *v* NOISED, NOISING, NOISES to spread as a rumor or report

NOISOME   *adj* disgusting; harmful

NOISY   *adj* NOISIER, NOISIEST making loud sounds **NOISILY** *adv*

NOLO   *n* pl. -LOS a type of legal plea

NOM   *n* pl. -S a name

NOMA   *n* pl. -S a severe inflammation of the mouth

NOMAD   *n* pl. -S a wanderer **NOMADIC** *adj*

NOMADISM   *n* pl. -S the mode of life of a nomad

NOMARCH   *n* pl. -S the head of a nome

NOMARCHY n pl. -ARCHIES a nome

NOMBLES n/pl numbles

NOMBRIL n pl. -S a point on a heraldic shield

NOME n pl. -S a province of modern Greece

NOMEN n pl. -MINA the second name of an ancient Roman

NOMINAL n pl. -S a word functioning as a noun

NOMINATE v -NATED, -NATING, -NATES to name as a candidate

NOMINEE n pl. -S one that is nominated

NOMISM n pl. -S strict adherence to moral law **NOMISTIC** adj

NOMOGRAM n pl. -S a type of graph

NOMOLOGY n pl. -GIES the science of law

NOMOS n pl. NOMOI law

NONA n pl. -S a virus disease

NONACID n pl. -S a substance that is not an acid

NONADULT n pl. -S a person who is not an adult

NONAGE n pl. -S a period of immaturity

NONAGON n pl. -S a nine-sided polygon

NONBANK adj not involving a bank

NONBASIC adj not basic

NONBEING n pl. -S lack of being

NONBOOK n pl. -S a book of little literary merit

NONCASH adj other than cash

NONCE n pl. -S the present occasion

NONCOM n pl. -S a noncommissioned officer

NONDAIRY adj having no milk products

NONE n pl. -S one of seven canonical daily periods for prayer and devotion

NONEGO n pl. -GOS all that is not part of the ego

NONELECT adj not chosen

NONEMPTY adj not empty

NONENTRY n pl. -TRIES the fact of not entering

NONEQUAL n pl. -S one that is not equal

NONESUCH n pl. -ES a person or thing without an equal

NONEVENT n pl. -S an expected event that does not occur

NONFARM adj not pertaining to the farm

NONFAT adj having no fat solids

NONFATAL adj not fatal

NONFLUID n pl. -S a substance that is not a fluid

NONFOCAL adj not focal

NONFOOD adj pertaining to something other than food

NONGAME adj not hunted for food, sport, or fur

NONGREEN adj not green

NONGUILT n pl. -S the absence of guilt

NONHARDY adj not hardy

NONHERO n pl. -ROES an antihero

NONHUMAN adj not human

NONIDEAL adj not ideal

NONIONIC adj not ionic

NONJUROR n pl. -S one who refuses to take a required oath

NONLEGAL adj not legal

NONLIFE n pl. -LIVES the absence of life

NONLOCAL n pl. -S one that is not local

NONMAN n pl. -MEN a being that is not a man

NONMETAL n pl. -S an element that lacks metallic properties

NONMODAL adj not modal

NONMONEY adj not involving money

NONMORAL adj not pertaining to morals

NONNAVAL adj not naval

NONOBESE adj not obese

NONOWNER n pl. -S one who is not the owner

NONPAGAN n pl. -S one who is not a pagan

NONPAPAL adj not papal

NONPAR adj being a stock that has no face value

NONPARTY adj not affiliated with any political party

NONPLUS v -PLUSED, -PLUSING, -PLUSES or -PLUSSED, -PLUSSING, -PLUSSES to baffle

NONPOLAR adj not polar

NONPROS v -PROSSED, -PROSSING, -PROSSES to enter a judgment against a plaintiff who fails to prosecute

NONQUOTA adj not included in or subject to a quota

NONRATED *adj* not rated

NONRIGID *adj* not rigid

NONRIVAL *n pl.* -S an unimportant rival

NONROYAL *adj* not royal

NONRURAL *adj* not rural

NONSENSE *n pl.* -S behavior or language that is meaningless or absurd

NONSKED *n pl.* -S an airline without scheduled flying times

NONSKID *adj* designed to inhibit skidding

NONSKIER *n pl.* -S one that does not ski

NONSLIP *adj* designed to prevent slipping

NONSOLAR *adj* not solar

NONSOLID *n pl.* -S a substance that is not a solid

NONSTICK *adj* allowing of easy removal of cooked food particles

NONSTOP *adj* making no stops

NONSUCH *n pl.* -ES nonsuch

NONSUGAR *n pl.* -S a substance that is not a sugar

NONSUIT *v* -ED, -ING, -S to dismiss the lawsuit of

NONTAX *n pl.* -ES a tax of little consequence

NONTIDAL *adj* not tidal

NONTITLE *adj* pertaining to an athletic contest in which a title is not at stake

NONTOXIC *adj* not toxic

NONTRUMP *adj* not having a trump

NONTRUTH *n pl.* -S something that is not true

NONUNION *n pl.* -S failure of a broken bone to heal

NONUPLE *n pl.* -S a number nine times as great as another

NONURBAN *adj* not urban

NONUSE *n pl.* -S failure to use

NONUSER *n pl.* -S one that is not a user

NONUSING *adj* not using

NONVIRAL *adj* not viral

NONVOCAL *adj* not vocal

NONVOTER *n pl.* -S one that does not vote

NONWHITE *n pl.* -S a person who is not of the white race

NONWOODY *adj* not woody

NONWOVEN *adj* made without weaving

NONZERO *adj* having a value other than zero

NOO *adv* now

NOODLE *v* -DLED, -DLING, -DLES to play idly on a musical instrument

NOOK *n pl.* -S a corner, as in a room **NOOKLIKE** *adj*

NOOKY *n pl.* NOOKIES sexual intercourse — usually considered vulgar

NOON *n pl.* -S midday

NOONDAY *n pl.* -DAYS noon

NOONING *n pl.* -S a meal eaten at noon

NOONTIDE *n pl.* -S noon

NOONTIME *n pl.* -S noon

NOOSE *v* NOOSED, NOOSING, NOOSES to secure with a type of loop

NOOSER *n pl.* -S one that nooses

NOPAL *n pl.* -S a cactus

NOPE *adv* no

NOR *conj* and not

NORIA *n pl.* -S a type of waterwheel

NORITE *n pl.* -S a granular rock **NORITIC** *adj*

NORLAND *n pl.* -S a region in the north

NORM *n pl.* -S a standard regarded as typical for a specific group

NORMAL *n pl.* -S the usual or expected state or form

NORMALCY *n pl.* -CIES conformity with the norm

NORMALLY *adv* as a rule; usually

NORMED *adj* having a norm

NORMLESS *adj* having no norm

NORTH *n pl.* -S a point of the compass

NORTHER *n pl.* -S a wind or storm from the north

NORTHERN *n pl.* -S a person living in the north

NORTHING *n pl.* -S movement toward the north

NOSE *v* NOSED, NOSING, NOSES to sniff with the nose (the organ of smell)

NOSEBAG *n pl.* -S a feedbag

NOSEBAND *n pl.* -S a part of a horse's bridle

NOSED past tense of nose

NOSEGAY *n pl.* -GAYS a bouquet

NOSELESS	adj having no nose
NOSELIKE	adj resembling a nose
NOSEY	adj NOSIER, NOSIEST nosy
NOSH	v -ED, -ING, -ES to eat snacks between meals
NOSHER	n pl. -S one that noshes
NOSIER	comparative of nosy, nosey
NOSIEST	superlative of nosy, nosey
NOSILY	adv in a nosy manner
NOSINESS	n pl. -ES the quality of being nosy
NOSING	n pl. -S a projecting edge
NOSOLOGY	n pl. -GIES a classification of diseases
NOSTOC	n pl. -S a freshwater alga
NOSTRIL	n pl. -S an external opening of the nose
NOSTRUM	n pl. -S a medicine of one's own invention
NOSY	adj NOSIER, NOSIEST unduly curious
NOT	adv in no way
NOTA	pl. of notum
NOTABLE	n pl. -S a person of distinction
NOTABLY	adv in a distinguished manner
NOTAL	adj pertaining to a notum
NOTARIAL	adj pertaining to a notary
NOTARIZE	v -RIZED, -RIZING, -RIZES to certify through a notary
NOTARY	n pl. -RIES a public officer who certifies documents
NOTATE	v -TATED, -TATING, -TATES to put into notation
NOTATION	n pl. -S a system of symbols
NOTCH	v -ED, -ING, -ES to make an angular cut in
NOTCHER	n pl. -S one that notches
NOTE	v NOTED, NOTING, NOTES to write down
NOTEBOOK	n pl. -S a book in which to write
NOTECASE	n pl. -S a billfold
NOTED	past tense of note
NOTEDLY	adv in a famous manner
NOTELESS	adj undistinguished
NOTER	n pl. -S one that notes
NOTHING	n pl. -S the absence of all quantity or magnitude

NOTICE	v -TICED, -TICING, -TICES to become aware of
NOTIFIER	n pl. -S one that notifies
NOTIFY	v -FIED, -FYING, -FIES to inform
NOTING	present participle of note
NOTION	n pl. -S a general idea **NOTIONAL** adj
NOTORNIS	n pl. NOTORNIS a flightless bird
NOTTURNO	n pl. -NI a nocturne
NOTUM	n pl. -TA a part of the thorax of an insect
NOUGAT	n pl. -S a chewy candy
NOUGHT	n pl. -S naught
NOUMENON	n pl. -MENA an object of intellectual intuition **NOUMENAL** adj
NOUN	n pl. -S a word used to denote the name of something **NOUNAL, NOUNLESS** adj **NOUNALLY** adv
NOURISH	v -ED, -ING, -ES to sustain with food
NOUS	n pl. -ES mind, reason, or intellect
NOVA	n pl. -VAS or -VAE a type of star **NOVALIKE** adj
NOVATION	n pl. -S the substitution of a new legal obligation for an old one
NOVEL	n pl. -S a fictional prose narrative
NOVELISE	v -ISED, -ISING, -ISES to novelize
NOVELIST	n pl. -S a writer of novels
NOVELIZE	v -IZED, -IZING, -IZES to put into the form of a novel
NOVELLA	n pl. -LAS or -LE a short novel
NOVELLY	adv in a new or unusual manner
NOVELTY	n pl. -TIES something new or unusual
NOVENA	n pl. -NAS or -NAE a religious devotion lasting nine days
NOVERCAL	adj pertaining to a stepmother
NOVICE	n pl. -S a person new to any field or activity
NOW	n pl. -S the present time
NOWADAYS	adv in these times
NOWAY	adv in no way
NOWAYS	adv noway
NOWHERE	n pl. -S a nonexistent place

NOWISE	adv not at all	**NUDE**	n pl. -S a nude figure
NOWT	n pl. -S naught	**NUDENESS**	n pl. -ES nudity
NOXIOUS	adj harmful to health	**NUDER**	comparative of nude
NOYADE	n pl. -S an execution by drowning	**NUDEST**	superlative of nude
NOZZLE	n pl. -S a projecting spout	**NUDGE**	v NUDGED, NUDGING, NUDGES to push gently
NTH	adj pertaining to an indefinitely large ordinal number	**NUDGER**	n pl. -S one that nudges
NU	n pl. -S a Greek letter	**NUDICAUL**	adj having leafless stems
NUANCE	n pl. -S a slight variation NUANCED adj	**NUDIE**	n pl. -S a movie featuring nude performers
NUB	n pl. -S a protuberance or knob	**NUDISM**	n pl. -S the practice of going nude
NUBBIER	comparative of nubby	**NUDIST**	n pl. -S an advocate of nudism
NUBBIEST	superlative of nubby	**NUDITY**	n pl. -TIES the state of being nude
NUBBIN	n pl. -S an undeveloped fruit	**NUDNICK**	n pl. -S nudnik
NUBBLE	n pl. -S a small nub	**NUDNIK**	n pl. -S an annoying person
NUBBLY	adj -BLIER, -BLIEST having nubbles	**NUGATORY**	adj having no power
NUBBY	adj -BIER, -BIEST having nubs	**NUGGET**	n pl. -S a mass of solid matter NUGGETY adj
NUBIA	n pl. -S a woman's scarf	**NUISANCE**	n pl. -S a source of annoyance
NUBILE	adj suitable for marriage	**NUKE**	n pl. -S a nuclear weapon or power plant
NUBILITY	n pl. -TIES the quality of being nubile	**NULL**	v -ED, -ING, -S to reduce to nothing
NUBILOSE	adj nubilous	**NULLAH**	n pl. -S a ravine
NUBILOUS	adj cloudy	**NULLIFY**	v -FIED, -FYING, -FIES to make useless or ineffective
NUCELLUS	n pl. -LI the essential part of a plant ovule NUCELLAR adj	**NULLITY**	n pl. -TIES something of no legal force
NUCHA	n pl. -CHAE the nape of the neck	**NUMB**	adj NUMBER, NUMBEST lacking sensation
NUCHAL	n pl. -S an anatomical part lying in the region of the nape	**NUMB**	v -ED, -ING, -S to make numb
NUCLEAL	adj nuclear	**NUMBER**	v -ED, -ING, -S to count
NUCLEAR	adj pertaining to a nucleus	**NUMBERER**	n pl. -S one that numbers
NUCLEASE	n pl. -S an enzyme	**NUMBFISH**	n pl. -ES a fish capable of emitting electric shocks
NUCLEATE	v -ATED, -ATING, -ATES to form into a nucleus	**NUMBLES**	n/pl animal entrails
NUCLEI	a pl. of nucleus	**NUMBLY**	adv in a numb manner
NUCLEIN	n pl. -S a protein found in nuclei	**NUMBNESS**	n pl. -ES the state of being numb
NUCLEOLE	n pl. -S a part of a nucleus	**NUMEN**	n pl. -MINA a deity
NUCLEOLI	n/pl nucleoles	**NUMERAL**	n pl. -S a symbol that expresses a number
NUCLEON	n pl. -S an atomic particle	**NUMERARY**	adj pertaining to numbers
NUCLEUS	n pl. -CLEI or -CLEUSES an essential part of a cell	**NUMERATE**	v -ATED, -ATING, -ATES to count
NUCLIDE	n pl. -S a species of atom NUCLIDIC adj	**NUMERIC**	n pl. -S a numeral
NUDE	adj NUDER, NUDEST being without clothing or covering NUDELY adv		

NUMEROUS *adj* many

NUMINA pl. of numen

NUMINOUS *n* pl. -ES the presence or revelation of the numen

NUMMARY *adj* pertaining to coins

NUMMULAR *adj* shaped like a coin

NUMSKULL *n* pl. -S a dunce

NUN *n* pl. -S a woman belonging to a religious order

NUNCIO *n* pl. -CIOS an ambassador from the pope

NUNCLE *n* pl. -S an uncle

NUNLIKE *adj* resembling a nun

NUNNERY *n* pl. -NERIES a religious house for nuns

NUNNISH *adj* of, pertaining to, or characteristic of a nun

NUPTIAL *n* pl. -S a wedding

NURL *n* -ED, -ING, -S to knurl

NURSE *v* NURSED, NURSING, NURSES to care for the sick or infirm

NURSER *n* pl. -S a baby's bottle

NURSERY *n* pl. -ERIES a room for young children

NURSING *n* pl. -S the profession of one who nurses

NURSLING *n* pl. -S an infant

NURTURE *v* -TURED, -TURING, -TURES to nourish

NURTURER *n* pl. -S one that nurtures

NUT *v* NUTTED, NUTTING, NUTS to gather nuts (hard-shelled dry fruits)

NUTANT *adj* drooping

NUTATE *v* -TATED, -TATING, -TATES to exhibit nutation

NUTATION *n* pl. -S an oscillatory movement of the axis of a rotating body

NUTBROWN *adj* of a dark brown

NUTGALL *n* pl. -S a gallnut

NUTGRASS *n* pl. -ES a perennial herb

NUTHATCH *n* pl. -ES a small bird

NUTHOUSE *n* pl. -S an insane asylum

NUTLET *n* pl. -S a small nut

NUTLIKE *adj* resembling a nut

NUTMEAT *n* pl. -S the edible kernel of a nut

NUTMEG *n* pl. -S an aromatic seed used as a spice

NUTPICK *n* pl. -S a device for extracting the kernels from nuts

NUTRIA *n* pl. -S the coypu

NUTRIENT *n* pl. -S a nourishing substance

NUTSEDGE *n* pl. -S nutgrass

NUTSHELL *n* pl. -S the shell of a nut

NUTTED past tense of nut

NUTTER *n* pl. -S one that gathers nuts

NUTTING present participle of nut

NUTTY *adj* -TIER, -TIEST abounding in nuts **NUTTILY** *adv*

NUTWOOD *n* pl. -S a nut-bearing tree

NUZZLE *v* -ZLED, -ZLING, -ZLES to push with the nose

NYALA *n* pl. -S an antelope

NYLGHAI *n* pl. -S nilgai

NYLGHAU *n* pl. -S nilgai

NYLON *n* pl. -S a synthetic material

NYMPH *n* pl. -S a female spirit **NYMPHAL, NYMPHEAN** *adj*

NYMPHA *n* pl. -PHAE a fold of the vulva

NYMPHET *n* pl. -S a young nymph

NYMPHO *n* pl. -PHOS a woman obsessed by sexual desire

OAF   *n* pl. OAFS or OAVES a clumsy, stupid person **OAFISH** *adj* **OAFISHLY** *adv*

OAK   *n* pl. -S a hardwood tree or shrub **OAKEN, OAKLIKE** *adj*

OAKMOSS   *n* pl. -ES a lichen that grows on oak trees

OAKUM   *n* pl. -S loosely twisted hemp fiber

OAR   *v* -ED, -ING, -S to propel with oars (long, broad-bladed poles)

OARFISH   *n* pl. -ES a marine fish

OARLESS   *adj* having no oars

OARLIKE   *adj* resembling an oar

OARLOCK   *n* pl. -S a device for holding an oar in place

OARSMAN   *n* pl. -MEN a person who rows a boat

OASIS   *n* pl. OASES a green area in a desert region

OAST   *n* pl. -S a type of kiln

OAT   *n* pl. -S a cereal grass

OATCAKE   *n* pl. -S a cake made of oatmeal

OATEN   *adj* pertaining to oats

OATER   *n* pl. -S a cowboy movie

OATH   *n* pl. -S a formal declaration or promise to fulfill a pledge

OATLIKE   *adj* resembling oats

OATMEAL   *n* pl. -S meal made from oats

OAVES   a pl. of oaf

OBDURACY   *n* pl. -CIES the quality or an instance of being obdurate

OBDURATE   *adj* stubborn

OBE   *n* pl. -S obeah

OBEAH   *n* pl. -S a form of sorcery of African origin

OBEAHISM   *n* pl. -S the use of obeah

OBEDIENT   *adj* obeying or willing to obey

OBEISANT   *adj* showing reverence or respect

OBELI   pl. of obelus

OBELIA   *n* pl. -S a marine hydroid

OBELISE   *v* -LISED, -LISING, -LISES to obelize

OBELISK   *n* pl. -S a four-sided shaft of stone with a pyramidal top

OBELISM   *n* pl. -S the act of obelizing

OBELIZE   *v* -LIZED, -LIZING, -LIZES to mark with an obelus

OBELUS   *n* pl. -LI a symbol used in ancient manuscripts to indicate a doubtful passage

OBESE   *adj* very fat **OBESELY** *adv*

OBESITY   *n* pl. -TIES the state or condition of being obese

OBEY   *v* -ED, -ING, -S to follow the commands or guidance of **OBEYABLE** *adj*

OBEYER   *n* pl. -S one that obeys

OBI   *n* pl. -S obeah

OBIA   *n* pl. -S obeah

OBIISM   *n* pl. -S obeahism

OBIT   *n* pl. -S an obituary

OBITUARY   *n* pl. -ARIES a published notice of a death

OBJECT   *v* -ED, -ING, -S to argue in opposition

OBJECTOR   *n* pl. -S one that objects

OBLAST n pl. -LASTS or -LASTI an administrative division of the Soviet Union

OBLATE n pl. -S a layman residing in a monastery

OBLATELY adv elliptically

OBLATION n pl. -S the act of making a religious offering **OBLATORY** adj

OBLIGATE v -GATED, -GATING, -GATES to oblige

OBLIGATO n pl. -TI or -TOS an important musical part

OBLIGE v OBLIGED, OBLIGING, OBLIGES to put in one's debt by a favor or service

OBLIGEE n pl. -S one that is obliged

OBLIGER n pl. -S one that obliges

OBLIGING present participle of oblige

OBLIGOR n pl. -S one who places himself under a legal obligation

OBLIQUE v OBLIQUED, OBLIQUING, OBLIQUES to slant

OBLIVION n pl. -S the state of being forgotten; the act of forgetting

OBLONG n pl. -S something that is oblong (elongated)

OBLONGLY adv in an oblong manner

OBLOQUY n pl. -QUIES abusive language

OBOE n pl. -S a woodwind instrument

OBOIST n pl. -S one who plays the oboe

OBOL n pl. -S a coin of ancient Greece

OBOLE n pl. -S a coin of medieval France

OBOLUS n pl. -LI an obol

OBOVATE adj ovate with the narrow end at the base

OBOVOID adj ovoid with the narrow end at the base

OBSCENE adj -SCENER, -SCENEST indecent

OBSCURE adj -SCURER, -SCUREST dark or indistinct

OBSCURE v -SCURED, -SCURING, -SCURES to make obscure

OBSEQUY n pl. -QUIES a funeral rite

OBSERVE v -SERVED, -SERVING, -SERVES to look attentively

OBSERVER n pl. -S one that observes

OBSESS v -ED, -ING, -ES to dominate the thoughts of

OBSESSOR n pl. -S something that obsesses

OBSIDIAN n pl. -S a volcanic glass

OBSOLETE v -LETED, -LETING, -LETES to make out-of-date

OBSTACLE n pl. -S something that obstructs

OBSTRUCT v -ED, -ING, -S to get in the way of

OBTAIN v -ED, -ING, -S to gain possession of

OBTAINER n pl. -S one that obtains

OBTECT adj covered by a hardened secretion

OBTECTED adj obtect

OBTEST v -ED, -ING, -S to beseech

OBTRUDE v -TRUDED, -TRUDING, -TRUDES to thrust forward

OBTRUDER n pl. -S one that obtrudes

OBTUND v -ED, -ING, -S to deaden

OBTURATE v -RATED, -RATING, -RATES to close or stop up

OBTUSE adj -TUSER, -TUSEST dull **OBTUSELY** adv

OBVERSE n pl. -S the side of a coin bearing the main design

OBVERT v -ED, -ING, -S to turn so as to show a different surface

OBVIATE v -ATED, -ATING, -ATES to prevent or eliminate by effective measures **OBVIABLE** adj

OBVIATOR n pl. -S one that obviates

OBVIOUS adj easily perceived or understood

OBVOLUTE adj rolled or tuned in

OCA n pl. -S a South American herb

OCARINA n pl. -S a wind instrument

OCCASION v -ED, -ING, -S to cause

OCCIDENT n pl. -S the west

OCCIPUT n pl. -PITA or -PUTS the back part of the skull

OCCLUDE v -CLUDED, -CLUDING, -CLUDES to close or stop up

OCCLUSAL adj pertaining to the biting surface of a tooth

OCCULT v -ED, -ING, -S to conceal

OCCULTER n pl -S one that occults

OCCULTLY adv secretly

OCCUPANT n pl. -S a resident

OCCUPIER n pl. -S one that occupies

OCCUPY	v -PIED, -PYING, -PIES to engage the attention or energies of
OCCUR	v -CURRED, -CURRING, -CURS to take place
OCEAN	n pl. -S the vast body of salt water that covers most of the earth's surface **OCEANIC** adj
OCELLAR	adj pertaining to an ocellus
OCELLATE	adj having ocelli
OCELLUS	n pl. -LI a minute simple eye
OCELOT	n pl. -S an American wildcat **OCELOID** adj
OCHER	v -ED, -ING, -S to color with ocher (a red or yellow iron ore used as a pigment)
OCHEROUS	adj containing or resembling ocher
OCHERY	adj ocherous
OCHONE	interj — used to express grief
OCHRE	v OCHRED, OCHRING, OCHRES to ocher
OCHREA	n pl. -REAE ocrea
OCHREOUS	adj ocherous
OCHRING	present participle of ochre
OCHROID	adj ocherous
OCHROUS	adj ocherous
OCHRY	adj ochery
OCOTILLO	n pl. -LOS a Mexican shrub
OCREA	n pl. -REAE a sheathing plant part
OCREATE	adj having ocreae
OCTAD	n pl. -S a group of eight **OCTADIC** adj
OCTAGON	n pl. -S an eight-sided polygon
OCTAL	adj pertaining to a number system with a base of eight
OCTANE	n pl. -S a liquid hydrocarbon
OCTANGLE	n pl. -S an octagon
OCTANT	n pl. -S an eighth of a circle **OCTANTAL** adj
OCTARCHY	n pl. -TARCHIES a government by eight persons
OCTAVE	n pl. -S a type of musical interval **OCTAVAL** adj
OCTAVO	n pl. -VOS a page size
OCTET	n pl. -S a group of eight
OCTETTE	n pl. -S octet
OCTONARY	n pl. -NARIES a stanza of eight lines

OCTOPI	a pl. of octopus
OCTOPOD	n pl. -S any of an order of eight-armed mollusks
OCTOPUS	n pl. -PUSES, -PI, or -PODES a nocturnal octopod
OCTOROON	n pl. -S a person of one-eighth black ancestry
OCTROI	n pl. -S a tax on certain articles brought into a city
OCTUPLE	v -PLED, -PLING, -PLES to multiply by eight
OCTUPLET	n pl. -S a group of eight related items
OCTUPLEX	adj being eight times as great
OCTUPLING	present participle of octuple
OCTUPLY	adv to eight times the degree
OCTYL	n pl. -S a univalent radical
OCULAR	n pl. -S an eyepiece
OCULARLY	adv by means of the eyes or sight
OCULIST	n pl. -S a physician who treats diseases of the eye
OD	n pl. -S a hypothetical force of natural power
ODALISK	n pl. -S a female slave in a harem
ODD	adj ODDER, ODDEST unusual
ODD	n pl. -S one that is odd
ODDBALL	n pl. -S an eccentric person
ODDISH	adj somewhat odd
ODDITY	n pl. -TIES one that is odd
ODDLY	adv in an odd manner
ODDMENT	n pl. -S a remnant
ODDNESS	n pl. -ES the state of being odd
ODE	n pl. -S a lyric poem
ODEON	n pl. -S odeum
ODEUM	n pl. ODEA a theater or concert hall
ODIC	adj pertaining to an ode
ODIOUS	adj deserving or causing hatred **ODIOUSLY** adv
ODIUM	n pl. -S hatred
ODOGRAPH	n pl. -S an odometer
ODOMETER	n pl. -S a device for measuring distance traveled
ODOMETRY	n pl. -TRIES the process of using an odometer
ODONATE	n pl. -S any of an order of predacious insects

ODONTOID *n* pl. -S a toothlike vertebral projection

ODOR *n* pl. -S the property of a substance that affects the sense of smell **ODORED, ODORFUL** *adj*

ODORANT *n* pl. -S an odorous substance

ODORIZE *v* -IZED, -IZING, -IZES to make odorous

ODORLESS *adj* having no odor

ODOROUS *adj* having an odor

ODOUR *n* pl. -S odor **ODOURFUL** *adj*

ODYL *n* pl. -S an od

ODYLE *n* pl. -S odyl

ODYSSEY *n* pl. -SEYS a long, wandering journey

OE *n* pl. -S a whirlwind off the Faeroe islands

OECOLOGY *n* pl. -GIES ecology

OEDEMA *n* pl. -MAS or -MATA edema

OEDIPAL *adj* pertaining to the libidinal feelings in a child toward the parent of the opposite sex

OEDIPEAN *adj* oedipal

OEILLADE *n* pl. -S an amorous look

OENOLOGY *n* pl. -GIES the study of wines

OENOMEL *n* pl. -S an ancient Greek beverage of wine and honey

OERSTED *n* pl. -S a unit of magnetic intensity

OESTRIN *n* pl. -S estrin

OESTRIOL *n* pl. -S estriol

OESTRONE *n* pl. -S estrone

OESTROUS *adj* estrous

OESTRUM *n* pl. -S estrum

OESTRUS *n* pl. -ES estrus

OEUVRE *n* pl. -S a work of art

OF *prep* coming from

OFAY *n* pl. OFAYS a white person — usually taken to be offensive

OFF *v* -ED, -ING, -S to go away

OFFAL *n* pl. -S waste material

OFFBEAT *n* pl. -S an unaccented beat in a musical measure

OFFCAST *n* pl. -S a castoff

OFFENCE *n* pl. -S offense

OFFEND *v* -ED, -ING, -S to commit an offense

OFFENDER *n* pl. -S one that offends

OFFENSE *n* pl. -S a violation of a moral or social code

OFFER *v* -ED, -ING, -S to present for acceptance or rejection

OFFERER *n* pl. -S one that offers

OFFERING *n* pl. -S a contribution

OFFEROR *n* pl. -S offerer

OFFHAND *adv* without preparation

OFFICE *n* pl. -S a position of authority

OFFICER *v* -ED, -ING, -S to furnish with officers (persons holding positions of authority)

OFFICIAL *n* pl. -S one that holds a position of authority

OFFING *n* pl. -S the near future

OFFISH *adj* aloof **OFFISHLY** *adv*

OFFLOAD *v* -ED, -ING, -S to unload

OFFPRINT *v* -ED, -ING, -S to reprint an excerpt

OFFSET *v* -SET, -SETTING, -SETS to compensate for

OFFSHOOT *n* pl. -S a lateral shoot from a main stem

OFFSHORE *adv* away from the shore

OFFSIDE *adj* being illegally in front of the ball in football

OFFSTAGE *adj* being on a part of the stage not visible to the audience

OFT *adv* OFTER, OFTEST often

OFTEN *adv* -ENER, -ENEST frequently

OFTTIMES *adv* often

OGAM *n* pl. -S ogham

OGDOAD *n* pl. -S a group of eight

OGEE *n* pl. -S an S-shaped molding

OGHAM *n* pl. -S an Old Irish alphabet **OGHAMIC** *adj*

OGHAMIST *n* pl. -S one who writes in ogham

OGIVE *n* pl. -S a pointed arch **OGIVAL** *adj*

OGLE *v* OGLED, OGLING, OGLES to stare at

OGLER *n* pl. -S one that ogles

OGRE *n* pl. -S a monster

OGREISH *adj* resembling an ogre

OGREISM *n* pl. -S the state of being ogreish

OGRESS *n* pl. -ES a female ogre

OGRISH *adj* ogreish **OGRISHLY** *adv*

OGRISM   *n* pl. -S ogreism

OH   *v* -ED, -ING, -S to exclaim in surprise, pain, or desire

OHIA   *n* pl. -S lehua

OHM   *n* pl. -S a unit of electrical resistance **OHMIC** *adj*

OHMAGE   *n* pl. -S electrical resistance expressed in ohms

OHMMETER   *n* pl. -S an instrument for measuring ohmage

OHO   *interj* — used to express surprise or exultation

OIDIUM   *n* pl. OIDIA a type of fungus

OIL   *v* -ED, -ING, -S to supply with oil (a greasy liquid used for lubrication, fuel, or illumination)

OILBIRD   *n* pl. -S a tropical bird

OILCAMP   *n* pl. -S a living area for workers at an oil well

OILCAN   *n* pl. -S a can for applying lubricating oil

OILCLOTH   *n* pl. -S a waterproof fabric

OILCUP   *n* pl. -S a closed cup for supplying lubricant

OILER   *n* pl. -S one that oils

OILHOLE   *n* pl. -S a hole through which lubricating oil is injected

OILIER   comparative of oily

OILIEST   superlative of oily

OILILY   *adv* in an oily manner

OILINESS   *n* pl. -ES the state of being oily

OILMAN   *n* pl. -MEN one who owns or operates oil wells

OILPAPER   *n* pl. -S a water-resistant paper

OILPROOF   *adj* impervious to oil

OILSEED   *n* pl. -S a seed from which oil is pressed out

OILSKIN   *n* pl. -S a waterproof fabric

OILSTONE   *n* pl. -S a stone for sharpening tools

OILTIGHT   *adj* being so tight as to prevent the passage of oil

OILWAY   *n* pl. -WAYS a channel for the passage of oil

OILY   *adj* OILIER, OILIEST covered or soaked with oil

OINK   *v* -ED, -ING, -S to utter the natural grunt of a hog

OINOLOGY   *n* pl. -GIES oenology

OINOMEL   *n* pl. -S oenomel

OINTMENT   *n* pl. -S a viscous preparation applied to the skin as a medicine or cosmetic

OITICICA   *n* pl. -S a South American tree

OKA   *n* pl. -S a Turkish unit of weight

OKAPI   *n* pl. -S an African ruminant mammal

OKAY   *v* -ED, -ING, -S to approve

OKE   *n* pl. -S oka

OKEH   *n* pl. -S approval

OKEYDOKE   *adj* perfectly all right

OKRA   *n* pl. -S a tall annual herb

OLD   *adj* OLDER, OLDEST or ELDER, ELDEST living or existing for a relatively long time

OLD   *n* pl. -S an individual of a specified age

OLDEN   *adj* pertaining to a bygone era

OLDIE   *n* pl. -S a popular song of an earlier day

OLDISH   *adj* somewhat old

OLDNESS   *n* pl. -ES the state of being old

OLDSTER   *n* pl. -S an old person

OLDSTYLE   *n* pl. -S a style of printing type

OLDWIFE   *n* pl. -WIVES a marine fish

OLE   *n* pl. -S a shout of approval

OLEA   pl. of oleum

OLEANDER   *n* pl. -S a flowering shrub

OLEASTER   *n* pl. -S a flowering shrub

OLEATE   *n* pl. -S a chemical salt

OLEFIN   *n* pl. -S an alkene **OLEFINIC** *adj*

OLEFINE   *n* pl. -S olefin

OLEIC   *adj* pertaining to oil

OLEIN   *n* pl. -S the liquid portion of a fat

OLEINE   *n* pl. -S olein

OLEO   *n* pl. OLEOS margarine

OLEUM   *n* pl. OLEA oil

OLEUM   *n* pl. -S a corrosive liquid

OLIBANUM   *n* pl. -S a fragrant resin

OLIGARCH   *n* pl. -S a ruler in a government by the few

OLIGOMER   *n* pl. -S a type of polymer

OLIO   *n* pl. OLIOS a miscellaneous collection

OLIVARY   *adj* shaped like an olive

OLIVE   *n* pl. -S the small oval fruit of a Mediterranean tree

OLIVINE   *n pl.* -S a mineral **OLIVINIC** *adj*

OLLA   *n pl.* -S a wide-mouthed pot or jar

OLOGIST   *n pl.* -S an expert in a particular ology

OLOGY   *n pl.* -GIES a branch of knowledge

OLYMPIAD   *n pl.* -S a celebration of the Olympic Games

OM   *n pl.* -S a mantra used in contemplation of ultimate reality

OMASUM   *n pl.* -SA the third stomach of a ruminant

OMBER   *n pl.* -S ombre

OMBRE   *n pl.* -S a card game

OMEGA   *n pl.* -S a Greek letter

OMELET   *n pl.* -S a dish of beaten eggs cooked and folded around a filling

OMELETTE   *n pl.* -S omelet

OMEN   *v* -ED, -ING, -S to be an omen (a prophetic sign) of

OMENTUM   *n pl.* -TA or -TUMS a fold in an abdominal membrane **OMENTAL** *adj*

OMER   *n pl.* -S a Hebrew unit of dry measure

OMICRON   *n pl.* -S a Greek letter

OMIKRON   *n pl.* -S omicron

OMINOUS   *adj* portending evil

OMISSION   *n pl.* -S something left undone

OMISSIVE   *adj* marked by omission

OMIT   *v* OMITTED, OMITTING, OMITS to leave out

OMNIARCH   *n pl.* -S an almighty ruler

OMNIBUS   *n pl.* -ES a bus

OMNIFIC   *adj* unlimited in creative power

OMNIFORM   *adj* of all forms

OMNIMODE   *adj* of all modes

OMNIVORA   *n/pl* omnivores

OMNIVORE   *n pl.* -S an animal that eats all kinds of food

OMOPHAGY   *n pl.* -GIES the eating of raw flesh

OMPHALOS   *n pl.* -LI a central point

ON   *n pl.* -S the side of the wicket where a batsman stands in cricket

ONAGER   *n pl.* -GERS or -GRI a wild ass of central Asia

ONANISM   *n pl.* -S coitus deliberately interrupted to prevent insemination

ONANIST   *n pl.* -S one who practices onanism

ONCE   *n pl.* -S one single time

ONCIDIUM   *n pl.* -S a tropical orchid

ONCOLOGY   *n pl.* -GIES the science of tumors

ONCOMING   *n pl.* -S an approach

ONDOGRAM   *n pl.* -S a graph of electric wave forms

ONE   *n pl.* -S a number

ONEFOLD   *adj* constituting a single, undivided whole

ONEIRIC   *adj* pertaining to dreams

ONENESS   *n pl.* -ES unity

ONEROUS   *adj* burdensome or oppressive

ONERY   *adj* -ERIER, -ERIEST ornery

ONESELF   *pron* a person's self

ONETIME   *adj* former

ONGOING   *adj* continuing without interruption

ONION   *n pl.* -S the edible bulb of a cultivated herb

ONIUM   *adj* characterized by a complex cation

ONLOOKER   *n pl.* -S a spectator

ONLY   *adv* with nothing or no one else

ONRUSH   *n pl.* -ES a forward rush or flow

ONSET   *n pl.* -S a beginning

ONSHORE   *adv* toward the shore

ONSIDE   *adj* not offside

ONSTAGE   *adj* being on a part of the stage visible to the audience

ONTIC   *adj* having real being or existence

ONTO   *prep* to a position upon

ONTOGENY   *n pl.* -NIES the development of an individual organism

ONTOLOGY   *n pl.* -GIES the branch of philosophy that deals with being

ONUS   *n pl.* -ES a burden or responsibility

ONWARD   *adv* toward a point ahead or in front

ONWARDS   *adv* onward

ONYX   *n pl.* -ES a variety of quartz

OOCYST   *n pl.* -S a zygote

OOCYTE   *n pl.* -S an egg before maturation

OODLES   *n pl.* OODLES a large amount

OODLINS   *n pl.* OODLINS oodles

OOGAMETE   *n pl.* -S a female gamete of certain protozoa

OOGAMOUS   *adj* having structurally dissimilar gametes

OOGAMY   *n pl.* -MIES the state of being oogamous

OOGENY   *n pl.* -NIES the development of ova

OOGONIUM   *n pl.* -NIA or -NIUMS a female sexual organ in certain algae and fungi OOGONIAL *adj*

OOH   *v* -ED, -ING, -S to exclaim in amazement, joy, or surprise

OOLACHAN   *n pl.* -S eulachon

OOLITE   *n pl.* -S a variety of limestone OOLITIC *adj*

OOLITH   *n pl.* -S oolite

OOLOGIST   *n pl.* -S an expert in oology

OOLOGY   *n pl.* -GIES the study of birds' eggs OOLOGIC *adj*

OOLONG   *n pl.* -S a dark Chinese tea

OOMIAC   *n pl.* -S umiak

OOMIACK   *n pl.* -S umiak

OOMIAK   *n pl.* -S umiak

OOMPH   *n pl.* -S spirited vigor

OOPHYTE   *n pl.* -S a stage of development in certain plants OOPHYTIC *adj*

OOPS   *interj* — used to express mild apology, surprise, or dismay

OORALI   *n pl.* -S curare

OORIE   *adj* ourie

OOSPERM   *n pl.* -S a fertilized egg

OOSPHERE   *n pl.* -S an unfertilized egg within an oogonium

OOSPORE   *n pl.* -S a fertilized egg within an oogonium OOSPORIC *adj*

OOT   *n pl.* -S out

OOTHECA   *n pl.* -CAE an egg case of certain insects OOTHECAL *adj*

OOTID   *n pl.* -S one of the four sections into which a mature ovum divides

OOZE   *v* OOZED, OOZING, OOZES to flow or leak out slowly

OOZINESS   *n pl.* -ES the state of being oozy

OOZY   *adj* OOZIER, OOZIEST containing or resembling soft mud or slime OOZILY *adv*

OP   *n pl.* -S a style of abstract art

OPACIFY   *v* -FIED, -FYING, -FIES to make opaque

OPACITY   *n pl.* -TIES something that is opaque

OPAH   *n pl.* -S a marine fish

OPAL   *n pl.* -S a mineral

OPALESCE   *v* -ESCED, -ESCING, -ESCES to emit an iridescent shimmer of colors

OPALINE   *n pl.* -S an opaque white glass

OPAQUE   *adj* OPAQUER, OPAQUEST impervious to light OPAQUELY *adv*

OPAQUE   *v* OPAQUED, OPAQUING, OPAQUES to make opaque

OPE   *v* OPED, OPING, OPES to open

OPEN   *adj* OPENER, OPENEST affording unobstructed access, passage, or view

OPEN   *v* -ED, -ING, -S to cause to become open OPENABLE *adj*

OPENER   *n pl.* -S one that opens

OPENING   *n pl.* -S a vacant or unobstructed space

OPENLY   *adv* in an open manner

OPENNESS   *n pl.* -ES the state of being open

OPENWORK   *n pl.* -S ornamental or structural work containing numerous openings

OPERA   *n pl.* -S a form of musical drama

OPERABLE   *adj* usable OPERABLY *adv*

OPERAND   *n pl.* -S a quantity on which a mathematical operation is performed

OPERANT   *n pl.* -S one that operates

OPERATE   *v* -ATED, -ATING, -ATES to perform a function

OPERATIC   *n pl.* -S the technique of staging operas

OPERATOR   *n pl.* -S a symbol that represents a mathematical function

OPERCELE   *n pl.* -S opercule

OPERCULA   *n/pl* opercules

OPERCULE   *n pl.* -S an anatomical part that serves as a lid or cover

OPERETTA	*n* pl. -S a light musical drama with spoken dialogue
OPERON	*n* pl. -S a type of gene cluster
OPEROSE	*adj* involving great labor
OPHIDIAN	*n* pl. -S a snake
OPHITE	*n* pl. -S an igneous rock **OPHITIC** *adj*
OPIATE	*v* -ATED, -ATING, -ATES to treat with opium
OPINE	*v* OPINED, OPINING, OPINES to hold or state as an opinion
OPING	present participle of ope
OPINION	*n* pl. -S a conclusion or judgment one holds to be true
OPIUM	*n* pl. -S an addictive narcotic
OPIUMISM	*n* pl. -S opium addiction
OPOSSUM	*n* pl. -S an arboreal mammal
OPPIDAN	*n* pl. -S a townsman
OPPILATE	*v* -LATED, -LATING, -LATES to obstruct **OPPILANT** *adj*
OPPONENT	*n* pl. -S one that opposes another
OPPOSE	*v* -POSED, -POSING, -POSES to be in contention or conflict with
OPPOSER	*n* pl. -S one that opposes
OPPOSITE	*n* pl. -S one that is radically different from another in some related way
OPPRESS	*v* -ED, -ING, -ES to burden by abuse of power or authority
OPPUGN	*v* -ED, -ING, -S to assail with argument
OPPUGNER	*n* pl. -S one that oppugns
OPSIN	*n* pl. -S a type of protein
OPSONIC	*adj* pertaining to opsonin
OPSONIFY	*v* -FIED, -FYING, -FIES to opsonize
OPSONIN	*n* pl. -S an antibody of blood serum
OPSONIZE	*v* -NIZED, -NIZING, -NIZES to form opsonins in
OPT	*v* -ED, -ING, -S to choose
OPTATIVE	*n* pl. -S a mood of verbs that expresses a wish or desire
OPTIC	*n* pl. -S an eye
OPTICAL	*adj* pertaining to sight
OPTICIAN	*n* pl. -S one who makes or deals in optical goods
OPTICIST	*n* pl. -S one engaged in the study of light and vision
OPTIMA	a pl. of optimum
OPTIMAL	*adj* most desirable
OPTIME	*n* pl. -S an honor student in mathematics at Cambridge University
OPTIMISE	*v* -MISED, -MISING, -MISES to optimize
OPTIMISM	*n* pl. -S a disposition to look on the favorable side of things
OPTIMIST	*n* pl. -S one who exhibits optimism
OPTIMIZE	*v* -MIZED, -MIZING, -MIZES to make as perfect, useful, or effective as possible
OPTIMUM	*n* pl. -MA or -MUMS the most favorable condition for obtaining a given result
OPTION	*v* -ED, -ING, -S to grant an option (a right to buy or sell something at a specified price within a specified time) on
OPTIONAL	*n* pl. -S an elective course of study
OPTIONEE	*n* pl. -S one who holds a legal option
OPULENCE	*n* pl. -S wealth
OPULENCY	*n* pl. -CIES opulence
OPULENT	*adj* wealthy
OPUNTIA	*n* pl. -S an American cactus
OPUS	*n* pl. OPERA or OPUSES a literary or musical work
OPUSCULA	*n/pl* opuscules
OPUSCULE	*n* pl. -S a minor work
OQUASSA	*n* pl. -S a small lake trout
OR	*n* pl. -S the heraldic color gold
ORA	pl. of os
ORACH	*n* pl. -ES a cultivated plant
ORACHE	*n* pl. -S orach
ORACLE	*n* pl. -S a person through whom a deity is believed to speak **ORACULAR** *adj*
ORAL	*n* pl. -S an examination requiring spoken answers
ORALITY	*n* pl. -TIES the state of being produced orally
ORALLY	*adv* through the mouth
ORANG	*n* pl. -S a large ape
ORANGE	*n* pl. -S a citrus fruit
ORANGERY	*n* pl. -RIES a place where orange trees are cultivated
ORANGEY	*adj* -ANGIER, -ANGIEST orangy

ORANGISH *adj* of a somewhat orange color

ORANGY *adj* -ANGIER, -ANGIEST resembling or suggestive of an orange

ORATE *v* ORATED, ORATING, ORATES to speak formally

ORATION *n* pl. -S a formal speech

ORATOR *n* pl. -S one that orates

ORATORIO *n* pl. -RIOS a type of musical composition

ORATORY *n* pl. -RIES the art of public speaking

ORATRESS *n* pl. -ES oratrix

ORATRIX *n* pl. -TRICES a female orator

ORB *v* -ED, -ING, -S to form into a circle or sphere

ORBIT *v* -ED, -ING, -S to move or revolve around

ORBITAL *n* pl. -S a subdivision of a nuclear shell

ORBITER *n* pl. -S one that orbits

ORC *n* pl. -S a marine mammal

ORCA *n* pl. -S orc

ORCEIN *n* pl. -S a reddish brown dye

ORCHARD *n* pl. -S an area for the cultivation of fruit trees

ORCHID *n* pl. -S a flowering plant

ORCHIL *n* pl. -S a purple dye

ORCHIS *n* pl. -CHISES an orchid

ORCHITIS *n* pl. -TISES inflammation of the testicle **ORCHITIC** *adj*

ORCIN *n* pl. -S orcinol

ORCINOL *n* pl. -S a chemical compound

ORDAIN *v* -ED, -ING, -S to invest with holy authority

ORDAINER *n* pl. -S one that ordains

ORDEAL *n* pl. -S a severely difficult or painful experience

ORDER *v* -ED, -ING, -S to give a command or instruction to

ORDERER *n* pl. -S one that orders

ORDERLY *n* pl. -LIES a male attendant

ORDINAL *n* pl. -S a number designating position in a series

ORDINAND *n* pl. -S a person about to be ordained

ORDINARY *adj* -NARIER, -NARIEST of a kind to be expected in the normal order of events

ORDINARY *n* pl. -NARIES something that is ordinary

ORDINATE *n* pl. -S a particular geometric coordinate

ORDINES a pl. of ordo

ORDNANCE *n* pl. -S artillery; a cannon

ORDO *n* pl. -DINES or -DOS a calendar of religious directions

ORDURE *n* pl. -S manure

ORE *n* pl. -S a mineral or rock containing a valuable metal

OREAD *n* pl. -S a mountain nymph in Greek mythology

ORECTIC *adj* pertaining to appetites or desires

ORECTIVE *adj* orectic

OREGANO *n* pl. -NOS an aromatic herb used as a seasoning

OREIDE *n* pl. -S oroide

ORFRAY *n* pl. -FRAYS orphrey

ORGAN *n* pl. -S a differentiated part of an organism performing a specific function

ORGANA a pl. of organon and organum

ORGANDIE *n* pl. -S organdy

ORGANDY *n* pl. -DIES a cotton fabric

ORGANIC *n* pl. -S a substance of animal or vegetable origin

ORGANISE *v* -NISED, -NISING, -NISES to organize

ORGANISM *n* pl. -S any form of animal or plant life

ORGANIST *n* pl. -S one who plays the organ (a keyboard musical instrument)

ORGANIZE *v* -NIZED, -NIZING, -NIZES to form into an orderly whole

ORGANON *n* pl. -GANA or -GANONS a system of rules for scientific investigation

ORGANUM *n* pl. -GANA or -GANUMS organon

ORGANZA *n* pl. -S a sheer fabric

ORGASM *n* pl. -S the climax of sexual excitement **ORGASMIC, ORGASTIC** *adj*

ORGEAT *n* pl. -S an almond-flavored syrup

ORGIAC *adj* of the nature of an orgy

ORGIC *adj* orgiac

ORGULOUS *adj* proud

ORGY	*n* pl. -GIES a party marked by unrestrained sexual indulgence	**ORPHICAL**	*adj* orphic
ORIBATID	*n* pl. -S any of a family of eyeless mites	**ORPHREY**	*n* pl. -PHREYS an ornamental band or border
ORIBI	*n* pl. -S an African antelope	**ORPIMENT**	*n* pl. -S a yellow dye
ORIEL	*n* pl. -S a type of projecting window	**ORPIN**	*n* pl. -S orpine
ORIENT	*v* -ED, -ING, -S to adjust in relation to something else	**ORPINE**	*n* pl. -S a perennial herb
		ORRA	*adj* occasional
ORIENTAL	*n* pl. -S an inhabitant of an eastern country	**ORRERY**	*n* pl. -RERIES a mechanical model of the solar system
ORIFICE	*n* pl. -S a mouth or mouthlike opening	**ORRICE**	*n* pl. -S orris
ORIGAMI	*n* pl. -S the Japanese art of paper folding	**ORRIS**	*n* pl. -RISES a flowering plant
		ORT	*n* pl. -S a scrap of food
ORIGAN	*n* pl. -S marjoram	**ORTHICON**	*n* pl. -S a type of television camera tube
ORIGANUM	*n* pl. -S an aromatic herb		
ORIGIN	*n* pl. -S a coming into being	**ORTHO**	*adj* pertaining to reproduction in a photograph of the full range of colors in nature
ORIGINAL	*n* pl. -S the first form of something		
ORINASAL	*n* pl. -S a sound pronounced through both the mouth and nose	**ORTHODOX**	*n* pl. -ES one holding traditional beliefs
		ORTHOEPY	*n* pl. -EPIES the study of correct pronunciation
ORIOLE	*n* pl. -S an American songbird		
ORISON	*n* pl. -S a prayer	**ORTHOTIC**	*adj* pertaining to the bracing of weak joints or muscles
ORLE	*n* pl. -S a heraldic border		
ORLOP	*n* pl. -S the lowest deck of a ship	**ORTOLAN**	*n* pl. -S a European bird
		ORYX	*n* pl. -ES an African antelope
ORMER	*n* pl. -S an abalone	**OS**	*n* pl. ORA an orifice
ORMOLU	*n* pl. -S an alloy used to imitate gold	**OS**	*n* pl. OSSA a bone
		OS	*n* pl. OSAR an esker
ORNAMENT	*v* -ED, -ING, -S to decorate	**OSCINE**	*n* pl. -S any of a family of songbirds **OSCININE** *adj*
ORNATE	*adj* elaborately or excessively ornamented **ORNATELY** *adv*		
		OSCITANT	*adj* yawning
ORNERY	*adj* -NERIER, -NERIEST stubborn and mean-spirited	**OSCULA**	pl. of osculum
		OSCULANT	*adj* adhering closely
ORNIS	*n* pl. ORNITHES avifauna	**OSCULAR**	*adj* pertaining to the mouth
ORNITHIC	*adj* pertaining to birds	**OSCULATE**	*v* -LATED, -LATING, -LATES to kiss
OROGENY	*n* pl. -NIES the process of mountain formation **OROGENIC** *adj*		
		OSCULE	*n* pl. -S osculum
OROIDE	*n* pl. -S an alloy used to imitate gold	**OSCULUM**	*n* pl. -LA an opening in a sponge
		OSE	*n* pl. -S an esker
OROLOGY	*n* pl. -GIES the study of mountains	**OSIER**	*n* pl. -S a European tree
OROMETER	*n* pl. -S a type of barometer	**OSMATIC**	*adj* depending mainly on the sense of smell
OROTUND	*adj* full and clear in sound		
ORPHAN	*v* -ED, -ING, -S to deprive of both parents	**OSMIUM**	*n* pl. -S a metallic element **OSMIC, OSMIOUS** *adj*
		OSMOL	*n* pl. -S a unit of osmotic pressure **OSMOLAL** *adj*
ORPHIC	*adj* mystical		
		OSMOLAR	*adj* osmotic

OSMOSE	v -MOSED, -MOSING, -MOSES to undergo osmosis
OSMOSIS	n pl. -MOSES a form of diffusion of a fluid through a membrane
OSMOTIC	adj pertaining to osmosis
OSMOUS	adj containing osmium
OSMUND	n pl. -S any of a genus of large ferns
OSMUNDA	n pl. -S osmund
OSNABURG	n pl. -S a cotton fabric
OSPREY	n pl. -PREYS an American hawk
OSSA	pl. of os
OSSEIN	n pl. -S a protein substance in bone
OSSEOUS	adj resembling bone
OSSIA	conj or else — used as a musical direction
OSSICLE	n pl. -S a small bone
OSSIFIC	adj pertaining to the formation of bone
OSSIFIER	n pl. -S one that ossifies
OSSIFY	v -FIED, -FYING, -FIES to convert into bone
OSSUARY	n pl. -ARIES a receptacle for the bones of the dead
OSTEAL	adj osseous
OSTEITIS	n pl. -ITIDES inflammation of bone OSTEITIC adj
OSTEOID	n pl. -S uncalcified bone matrix
OSTEOMA	n pl. -MAS or -MATA a tumor of bone tissue
OSTIA	pl. of ostium
OSTIARY	n pl. -ARIES a doorkeeper at a church
OSTINATO	n pl. -TOS a constantly recurring musical phrase
OSTIOLE	n pl. -S a small bodily opening OSTIOLAR adj
OSTIUM	n pl. OSTIA an opening in a bodily organ
OSTLER	n pl. -S hostler
OSTMARK	n pl. -S a monetary unit of East Germany
OSTOMY	n pl. -MIES a type of surgical operation
OSTOSIS	n pl. -TOSES or -TOSISES the formation of bone
OSTRACOD	n pl. -S a minute freshwater crustacean
OSTRICH	n pl. -ES a large, flightless bird
OTALGIA	n pl. -S pain in the ear OTALGIC adj
OTALGY	n pl. -GIES otalgia
OTHER	n pl. -S one that remains of two or more
OTIC	adj pertaining to the ear
OTIOSE	adj lazy OTIOSELY adv
OTIOSITY	n pl. -TIES the state of being otiose
OTITIS	n pl. OTITIDES inflammation of the ear OTITIC adj
OTOCYST	n pl. -S an organ of balance in many invertebrates
OTOLITH	n pl. -S a hard mass that forms in the inner ear
OTOLOGY	n pl. -GIES the science of the ear
OTOSCOPE	n pl. -S an instrument for examining the ear
OTOSCOPY	n pl. -PIES the use of an otoscope
OTTAR	n pl. -S attar
OTTAVA	n pl. -S an octave
OTTER	n pl. -S a carnivorous mammal
OTTO	n pl. -TOS attar
OTTOMAN	n pl. -S a type of sofa
OUABAIN	n pl. -S a cardiac stimulant
OUCH	n pl. -ES a setting for a precious stone
OUD	n pl. -S a stringed instrument of northern Africa
OUGHT	v -ED, -ING, -S to owe
OUISTITI	n pl. -S a South American monkey
OUNCE	n pl. -S a unit of weight
OUPH	n pl. -S ouphe
OUPHE	n pl. -S an elf
OUR	pron a possessive form of the pronoun we
OURANG	n pl. -S orang
OURARI	n pl. -S curare
OUREBI	n pl. -S oribi
OURIE	adj shivering with cold
OURS	pron a possessive form of the pronoun we
OURSELF	pron myself — used in formal or regal contexts
OUSEL	n pl. -S ouzel

OUST *v* -ED, -ING, -S to expel or remove from a position or place

OUSTER *n* pl. -S the act of ousting

OUT *v* -ED, -ING, -S to be revealed

OUTACT *v* -ED, -ING, -S to surpass in acting

OUTADD *v* -ED, -ING, -S to surpass in adding

OUTAGE *n* pl. -S a failure or interruption in use or functioning

OUTARGUE *v* -GUED, -GUING, -GUES to get the better of by arguing

OUTASK *v* -ED, -ING, -S to surpass in asking

OUTATE past tense of outeat

OUTBACK *n* pl. -S isolated rural country

OUTBAKE *v* -BAKED, -BAKING, -BAKES to surpass in baking

OUTBARK *v* -ED, -ING, -S to surpass in barking

OUTBAWL *v* -ED, -ING, -S to surpass in bawling

OUTBEAM *v* -ED, -ING, -S to surpass in beaming

OUTBEG *v* -BEGGED, -BEGGING, -BEGS to surpass in begging

OUTBID *v* -BID, -BIDDEN, -BIDDING, -BIDS to bid higher than

OUTBLAZE *v* -BLAZED, -BLAZING, -BLAZES to surpass in brilliance of light

OUTBLEAT *v* -ED, -ING, -S to surpass in bleating

OUTBLESS *v* -ED, -ING, -ES to surpass in blessing

OUTBLOOM *v* -ED, -ING, -S to surpass in blooming

OUTBLUFF *v* -ED, -ING, -S to surpass in bluffing

OUTBLUSH *v* -ED, -ING, -ES to surpass in blushing

OUTBOARD *n* pl. -S a type of motor

OUTBOAST *v* -ED, -ING, -S to surpass in boasting

OUTBOUND *adj* outward bound

OUTBOX *v* -ED, -ING, -ES to surpass in boxing

OUTBRAG *v* -BRAGGED, -BRAGGING, -BRAGS to surpass in bragging

OUTBRAVE *v* -BRAVED, -BRAVING, -BRAVES to surpass in courage

OUTBREAK *n* pl. -S a sudden eruption

OUTBREED *v* -BRED, -BREEDING, -BREEDS to interbreed relatively unrelated stocks

OUTBRIBE *v* -BRIBED, -BRIBING, -BRIBES to surpass in bribing

OUTBUILD *v* -BUILT, -BUILDING, -BUILDS to surpass in building

OUTBULLY *v* -LIED, -LYING, -LIES to surpass in bullying

OUTBURN *v* -BURNED or -BURNT, -BURNING, -BURNS to burn longer than

OUTBURST *n* pl. -S a sudden and violent outpouring

OUTBY *adv* outdoors

OUTBYE *adv* outby

OUTCAPER *v* -ED, -ING, -S to surpass in capering

OUTCAST *n* pl. -S one that is cast out

OUTCASTE *n* pl. -S a Hindu who has been expelled from his caste

OUTCATCH *v* -CAUGHT, -CATCHING, -CATCHES to surpass in catching

OUTCAVIL *v* -ILED, -ILING, -ILS or -ILLED, -ILLING, -ILS to surpass in caviling

OUTCHARM *v* -ED, -ING, -S to surpass in charming

OUTCHEAT *v* -ED, -ING, -S to surpass in cheating

OUTCHIDE *v* -CHIDED or -CHID, -CHIDDEN, -CHIDING, -CHIDES to surpass in chiding

OUTCLASS *v* -ED, -ING, -ES to surpass so decisively as to appear of a higher class

OUTCLIMB *v* -CLIMBED or -CLOMB, -CLIMBING, -CLIMBS to surpass in climbing

OUTCOME *n* pl. -S a result

OUTCOOK *v* -ED, -ING, -S to surpass in cooking

OUTCRAWL *v* -ED, -ING, -S to surpass in crawling

OUTCRIED past tense of outcry

OUTCRIES present 3d person sing. of outcry

OUTCROP *v* -CROPPED, -CROPPING, -CROPS to protrude above the soil

OUTCROSS *v* -ED, -ING, -ES to cross with a relatively unrelated individual

OUTCROW v -ED, -ING, -S to surpass in crowing

OUTCRY v -CRIED, -CRYING, -CRIES to cry louder than

OUTCURSE v -CURSED, -CURSING, -CURSES to surpass in cursing

OUTCURVE n pl. -S a type of pitch in baseball

OUTDANCE v -DANCED, -DANCING, -DANCES to surpass in dancing

OUTDARE v -DARED, -DARING, -DARES to surpass in daring

OUTDATE v -DATED, -DATING, -DATES to make out-of-date

OUTDO v -DID, -DONE, -DOING, -DOES to exceed in performance

OUTDODGE v -DODGED, -DODGING, -DODGES to surpass in dodging

OUTDOER n pl. -S one that outdoes

OUTDONE past participle of outdo

OUTDOOR adj pertaining to the open air

OUTDOORS adv in the open air

OUTDRANK past tense of outdrink

OUTDRAW v -DREW, -DRAWN, -DRAWING, -DRAWS to attract a larger audience than

OUTDREAM v -DREAMED or -DREAMT, -DREAMING, -DREAMS to surpass in dreaming

OUTDRESS v -ED, -ING, -ES to surpass in dressing

OUTDREW past tense of outdraw

OUTDRINK v -DRANK, -DRUNK, -DRINKING, -DRINKS to surpass in drinking

OUTDRIVE v -DROVE, -DRIVEN, -DRIVING, -DRIVES to drive a golf ball farther than

OUTDROP v -DROPPED, -DROPPING, -DROPS to surpass in dropping

OUTDRUNK past participle of outdrink

OUTEAT v -ATE, -EATEN, -EATING, -EATS to surpass in eating

OUTECHO v -ED, -ING, -ES to surpass in echoing

OUTER n pl. -S a part of a target

OUTFABLE v -BLED, -BLING, -BLES to surpass in fabling

OUTFACE v -FACED, -FACING, -FACES to confront unflinchingly

OUTFALL n pl. -S the outlet of a body of water

OUTFAST v -ED, -ING, -S to surpass in fasting

OUTFAWN v -ED, -ING, -S to surpass in fawning

OUTFEAST v -ED, -ING, -S to surpass in feasting

OUTFEEL v -FELT, -FEELING, -FEELS to surpass in feeling

OUTFIELD n pl. -S a part of a baseball field

OUTFIGHT v -FOUGHT, -FIGHTING, -FIGHTS to defeat

OUTFIND v -FOUND, -FINDING, -FINDS to surpass in finding

OUTFIRE v -FIRED, -FIRING, -FIRES to surpass in firing

OUTFIT v -FITTED, -FITTING, -FITS to equip

OUTFLANK v -ED, -ING, -S to gain a tactical advantage over

OUTFLOW v -ED, -ING, -S to flow out

OUTFLY v -FLEW, -FLOWN, -FLYING, -FLIES to surpass in speed of flight

OUTFOOL v -ED, -ING, -S to surpass in fooling

OUTFOOT v -ED, -ING, -S to surpass in speed

OUTFOUGHT past tense of outfight

OUTFOUND past tense of outfind

OUTFOX v -ED, -ING, -ES to outwit

OUTFROWN v -ED, -ING, -S to frown more than

OUTGAIN v -ED, -ING, -S to gain more than

OUTGAS v -GASSED, -GASSING, -GASSES to remove gas from

OUTGIVE v -GAVE, -GIVEN, -GIVING, -GIVES to give more than

OUTGLARE v -GLARED, -GLARING, -GLARES to surpass in glaring

OUTGLOW v -ED, -ING, -S to surpass in glowing

OUTGNAW v -GNAWED, -GNAWN, -GNAWING, -GNAWS to surpass in gnawing

OUTGO v -WENT, -GONE, -GOING, -GOES to go beyond

OUTGOING n pl. -S a departure

OUTGREW past tense of outgrow

OUTGRIN v -GRINNED, -GRINNING, -GRINS to surpass in grinning

OUTGROUP *n* pl. -S a group of people outside one's own group

OUTGROW *v* -GREW, -GROWN, -GROWING, -GROWS to grow too large for

OUTGUESS *v* -ED, -ING, -ES to anticipate the actions of

OUTGUIDE *v* -GUIDED, -GUIDING, -GUIDES to surpass in guiding

OUTGUN *v* -GUNNED, -GUNNING, -GUNS to surpass in firepower

OUTGUSH *n* pl. -ES a gushing out

OUTHAUL *n* pl. -S a rope for extending a sail along a spar

OUTHEAR *v* -HEARD, -HEARING, -HEARS to surpass in hearing

OUTHIT *v* -HIT, -HITTING, -HITS to get more hits than

OUTHOUSE *n* pl. -S a toilet housed in a small structure

OUTHOWL *v* -ED, -ING, -S to surpass in howling

OUTHUMOR *v* -ED, -ING, -S to surpass in humoring

OUTING *n* pl. -S a short pleasure trip

OUTJINX *v* -ED, -ING, -ES to surpass in jinxing

OUTJUMP *v* -ED, -ING, -S to surpass in jumping

OUTJUT *v* -JUTTED, -JUTTING, -JUTS to stick out

OUTKEEP *v* -KEPT, -KEEPING, -KEEPS to surpass in keeping

OUTKICK *v* -ED, -ING, -S to surpass in kicking

OUTKISS *v* -ED, -ING, -ES to surpass in kissing

OUTLAID past tense of outlay

OUTLAIN past participle of outlie

OUTLAND *n* pl. -S a foreign land

OUTLAST *v* -ED, -ING, -S to last longer than

OUTLAUGH *v* -ED, -ING, -S to surpass in laughing

OUTLAW *v* -ED, -ING, -S to prohibit

OUTLAWRY *n* pl. -RIES habitual defiance of the law

OUTLAY *n* -LAID, -LAYING, -LAYS to pay out

OUTLEAP *v* -LEAPED or -LEAPT, -LEAPING, -LEAPS to surpass in leaping

OUTLEARN *v* -LEARNED or -LEARNT, -LEARNING, -LEARNS to surpass in learning

OUTLET *n* pl. -S a passage for escape or discharge

OUTLIE *v* -LAY, -LAIN, -LYING, -LIES to lie beyond

OUTLIER *n* pl. -S an outlying area or portion

OUTLINE *v* -LINED, -LINING, -LINES to indicate the main features or different parts of

OUTLIVE *v* -LIVED, -LIVING, -LIVES to live longer than

OUTLIVER *n* pl. -S one that outlives

OUTLOOK *n* pl. -S a point of view

OUTLOVE *v* -LOVED, -LOVING, -LOVES to surpass in loving

OUTLYING present participle of outlie

OUTMAN *v* -MANNED, -MANNING, -MANS to surpass in manpower

OUTMARCH *v* -ED, -ING, -ES to surpass in marching

OUTMATCH *v* -ED, -ING, -ES to outdo

OUTMODE *v* -MODED, -MODING, -MODES to outdate

OUTMOST *adj* farthest out

OUTMOVE *v* -MOVED, -MOVING, -MOVES to move faster or farther than

OUTPACE *v* -PACED, -PACING, -PACES to surpass in speed

OUTPAINT *v* -ED, -ING, -S to surpass in painting

OUTPASS *v* -ED, -ING, -ES to excel in passing a football

OUTPITY *v* -PITIED, -PITYING, -PITIES to surpass in pitying

OUTPLAN *v* -PLANNED, -PLANNING, -PLANS to surpass in planning

OUTPLAY *v* -ED, -ING, -S to excel or defeat in a game

OUTPLOD *v* -PLODDED, -PLODDING, -PLODS to surpass in plodding

OUTPOINT *v* -ED, -ING, -S to score more points than

OUTPOLL *v* -ED, -ING, -S to get more votes than

OUTPORT *n* pl. -S a port of export or departure

OUTPOST *n* pl. -S a body of troops stationed at a distance from the main body

OUTPOUR   v -ED, -ING, -S to pour out

OUTPRAY   v -ED, -ING, -S to surpass in praying

OUTPREEN   v -ED, -ING, -S to surpass in preening

OUTPRESS   v -ED, -ING, -ES to surpass in pressing

OUTPRICE   v -PRICED, -PRICING, -PRICES to surpass in pricing

OUTPULL   v -ED, -ING, -S to attract a larger audience or following than

OUTPUSH   v -ED, -ING, -ES to surpass in pushing

OUTPUT   v -PUTTED, -PUTTING, -PUTS to produce

OUTQUOTE   v -QUOTED, -QUOTING, -QUOTES to surpass in quoting

OUTRACE   v -RACED, -RACING, -RACES to run faster or farther than

OUTRAGE   v -RAGED, -RAGING, -RAGES to arouse anger or resentment in

OUTRAISE   v -RAISED, -RAISING, -RAISES to surpass in raising

OUTRAN   past tense of outrun

OUTRANCE   n pl. -S the last extremity

OUTRANG   past tense of outring

OUTRANGE   v -RANGED, -RANGING, -RANGES to surpass in range

OUTRANK   v -ED, -ING, -S to rank higher than

OUTRAVE   v -RAVED, -RAVING, -RAVES to surpass in raving

OUTRE   adj deviating from what is usual or proper

OUTREACH   v -ED, -ING, -ES to reach beyond

OUTREAD   v -READ, -READING, -READS to surpass in reading

OUTRIDE   v -RODE, -RIDDEN, -RIDING, -RIDES to ride faster or better than

OUTRIDER   n pl. -S a mounted attendant who rides before or beside a carriage

OUTRIGHT   adj being without limit or reservation

OUTRING   v -RANG, -RUNG, -RINGING, -RINGS to ring louder than

OUTRIVAL   v -VALED, -VALING, -VALS or -VALLED, -VALLING, -VALS to outdo in a competition or rivalry

OUTROAR   v -ED, -ING, -S to roar louder than

OUTROCK   v -ED, -ING, -S to surpass in rocking

OUTRODE   past tense of outride

OUTROLL   v -ED, -ING, -S to roll out

OUTROOT   v -ED, -ING, -S to pull up by the roots

OUTRUN   v -RAN, -RUNNING, -RUNS to run faster than

OUTRUNG   past participle of outring

OUTRUSH   n pl. -ES a rushing out

OUTSAIL   v -ED, -ING, -S to sail faster than

OUTSANG   past tense of outsing

OUTSAT   past tense of outsit

OUTSAVOR   v -ED, -ING, -S to surpass in a distinctive taste or smell

OUTSAW   past tense of outsee

OUTSCOLD   v -ED, -ING, -S to surpass in scolding

OUTSCORE   v -SCORED, -SCORING, -SCORES to score more points than

OUTSCORN   v -ED, -ING, -S to surpass in scorning

OUTSEE   v -SAW, -SEEN, -SEEING, -SEES to see beyond

OUTSELL   v -SOLD, -SELLING, -SELLS to sell more than

OUTSERT   n pl. -S a folded sheet placed around a folded section of printed matter

OUTSERVE   v -SERVED, -SERVING, -SERVES to surpass in serving

OUTSET   n pl. -S a beginning

OUTSHAME   v -SHAMED, -SHAMING, -SHAMES to surpass in shaming

OUTSHINE   v -SHONE or -SHINED, -SHINING, -SHINES to shine brighter than

OUTSHOOT   v -SHOT, -SHOOTING, -SHOOTS to shoot better than

OUTSHOUT   v -ED, -ING, -S to shout louder than

OUTSIDE   n pl. -S the outer side, surface, or part

OUTSIDER   n pl. -S one that does not belong to a particular group

OUTSIGHT   n pl. -S the power of perceiving external things

OUTSIN   v -SINNED, -SINNING, -SINS to surpass in sinning

OUTSING *v* -SANG, -SUNG, -SINGING, -SINGS to surpass in singing

OUTSIT *v* -SAT, -SITTING, -SITS to remain sitting or in session longer than

OUTSIZE *n* pl. -S an unusual size **OUTSIZED** *adj*

OUTSKIRT *n* pl. -S an outlying area

OUTSLEEP *v* -SLEPT, -SLEEPING, -SLEEPS to sleep later than

OUTSMART *v* -ED, -ING, -S to outwit

OUTSOAR *v* -ED, -ING, -S to soar beyond

OUTSMILE *v* -SMILED, -SMILING, -SMILES to surpass in smiling

OUTSMOKE *v* -SMOKED, -SMOKING, -SMOKES to surpass in smoking

OUTSNORE *v* -SNORED, -SNORING, -SNORES to surpass in snoring

OUTSOLD past tense of outsell

OUTSOLE *n* pl. -S the outer sole of a boot or shoe

OUTSPAN *v* -SPANNED, -SPANNING, -SPANS to unharness a draft animal

OUTSPEAK *v* -SPOKE, -SPOKEN, -SPEAKING, -SPEAKS to outdo in speaking

OUTSPELL *v* -SPELLED or -SPELT, -SPELLING, -SPELLS to surpass in spelling

OUTSPEND *v* -SPENT, -SPENDING, -SPENDS to exceed the limits of in spending

OUTSPOKE past tense of outspeak

OUTSPOKEN past participle of outspeak

OUTSTAND *v* -STOOD, -STANDING, -STANDS to endure beyond

OUTSTARE *v* -STARED, -STARING, -STARES to outface

OUTSTART *v* -ED, -ING, -S to get ahead of at the start

OUTSTATE *v* -STATED, -STATING, -STATES to surpass in stating

OUTSTAY *v* -ED, -ING, -S to surpass in staying power

OUTSTEER *v* -ED, -ING, -S to surpass in steering

OUTSTOOD past tense of outstand

OUTSTRIP *v* -STRIPPED, -STRIPPING, -STRIPS to go faster or farther than

OUTSTUDY *v* -STUDIED, -STUDYING, -STUDIES to surpass in studying

OUTSTUNT *v* -ED, -ING, -S to surpass in stunting

OUTSULK *v* -ED, -ING, -S to surpass in sulking

OUTSUNG past participle of outsing

OUTSWEAR *v* -SWORE or -SWARE, -SWORN, -SWEARING, -SWEARS to surpass in swearing

OUTSWIM *v* -SWAM, -SWUM, -SWIMMING, -SWIMS to swim faster or farther than

OUTTAKE *n* pl. -S a passage outwards

OUTTALK *v* -ED, -ING, -S to surpass in talking

OUTTASK *v* -ED, -ING, -S to surpass in tasking

OUTTELL *v* -TOLD, -TELLING, -TELLS to say openly

OUTTHANK *v* -ED, -ING, -S to surpass in thanking

OUTTHINK *v* -THOUGHT, -THINKING, -THINKS to get the better of by thinking

OUTTHROB *v* -THROBBED, -THROBBING, -THROBS to surpass in throbbing

OUTTHROW *v* -THREW, -THROWN, -THROWING, -THROWS to throw farther or more accurately than

OUTTOLD past tense of outtell

OUTTOWER *v* -ED, -ING, -S to tower above

OUTTRADE *v* -TRADED, -TRADING, -TRADES to get the better of in a trade

OUTTRICK *v* -ED, -ING, -S to get the better of by trickery

OUTTROT *v* -TROTTED, -TROTTING, -TROTS to surpass in trotting

OUTTRUMP *v* -ED, -ING, -S to outplay

OUTTURN *n* pl. -S a quantity produced

OUTVALUE *v* -UED, -UING, -UES to be worth more than

OUTVAUNT *v* -ED, -ING, -S to surpass in vaunting

OUTVOICE *v* -VOICED, -VOICING, -VOICES to surpass in loudness of voice

OUTVOTE *v* -VOTED, -VOTING, -VOTES to defeat by a majority of votes

OUTWAIT *v* -ED, -ING, -S to exceed in patience

OUTWALK *v* -ED, -ING, -S to surpass in walking

OUTWAR *v* -WARRED, -WARRING, -WARS to surpass in warring

OUTWARD *adv* toward the outside

OUTWARDS *adv* outward

OUTWARRED past tense of outwar

OUTWAR-RING present participle of outwar

OUTWASH *n pl.* -ES detritus washed from a glacier

OUTWASTE *v* -WASTED, -WASTING, -WASTES to surpass in wasting

OUTWATCH *v* -ED, -ING, -ES to watch longer than

OUTWEAR *v* -WORE, -WORN, -WEARING, -WEARS to last longer than

OUTWEARY *v* -RIED, -RYING, -RIES to surpass in wearying

OUTWEEP *v* -WEPT, -WEEPING, -WEEPS to weep more than

OUTWEIGH *v* -ED, -ING, -S to weigh more than

OUTWENT past tense of outgo

OUTWEPT past tense of outweep

OUTWHIRL *v* -ED, -ING, -S to surpass in whirling

OUTWILE *v* -WILED, -WILING, -WILES to surpass in wiling

OUTWILL *v* -ED, -ING, -S to surpass in willpower

OUTWIND *v* -ED, -ING, -S to cause to be out of breath

OUTWISH *v* -ED, -ING, -ES to surpass in wishing

OUTWIT *v* -WITTED, -WITTING, -WITS to get the better of by superior cleverness

OUTWORE past tense of outwear

OUTWORK *v* -WORKED or -WROUGHT, -WORKING, -WORKS to work faster or better than

OUTWORN past participle of outwear

OUTWRITE *v* -WROTE or -WRIT, -WRITTEN, -WRITING, -WRITES to write better than

OUT-WROUGHT a past tense of outwork

OUTYELL *v* -ED, -ING, -S to yell louder than

OUTYELP *v* -ED, -ING, -S to surpass in yelping

OUTYIELD *v* -ED, -ING, -S to surpass in yield

OUZEL *n pl.* -S a European bird

OUZO *n pl.* -ZOS a Greek liqueur

OVA pl. of ovum

OVAL *n pl.* -S an oval (egg-shaped) figure or object

OVALITY *n pl.* -TIES ovalness

OVALLY *adv* in the shape of an oval

OVALNESS *n pl.* -ES the state of being oval

OVARIAL *adj* ovarian

OVARIAN *adj* pertaining to an ovary

OVARIES pl. of ovary

OVARIOLE *n pl.* -S one of the tubes of which the ovaries of most insects are composed

OVARITIS *n pl.* -RITIDES inflammation of an ovary

OVARY *n pl.* -RIES a female reproductive gland

OVATE *adj* egg-shaped **OVATELY** *adv*

OVATION *n pl.* -S an expression or demonstration of popular acclaim

OVEN *n pl.* -S an enclosed compartment in which substances are heated **OVENLIKE** *adj*

OVENBIRD *n pl.* -S an American songbird

OVENWARE *n pl.* -S heat resistant dishes for baking and serving food

OVER *v* -ED, -ING, -S to leap above and to the other side of

OVERABLE *adj* excessively able

OVERACT *v* -ED, -ING, -S to act with exaggeration

OVERAGE *n pl.* -S an amount in excess

OVERALL *n pl.* -S a loose outer garment

OVERAPT *adj* excessively apt

OVERARCH *v* -ED, -ING, -ES to form an arch over

OVERARM *adj* done with the arm above the shoulder

OVERATE past tense of overeat

OVERAWE *v* -AWED, -AWING, -AWES to subdue by inspiring awe

OVERBAKE *v* -BAKED, -BAKING, -BAKES to bake too long

OVERBEAR *v* -BORE, -BORNE or -BORN, -BEARING, -BEARS to bring down by superior weight or force

OVERBET *v* -BETTED, -BETTING, -BETS to bet too much

OVERBID *v* -BID, -BIDDEN, -BIDDING, -BIDS to bid higher than

OVERBIG *adj* too big

OVERBITE *n* pl. -S a faulty closure of the teeth

OVERBLOW *v* -BLEW, -BLOWN, -BLOWING, -BLOWS to give excessive importance to

OVERBOLD *adj* excessively bold or forward

OVERBOOK *v* -ED, -ING, -S to issue reservations in excess of the space available

OVERBORE past tense of overbear

OVERBORN a past participle of overbear

OVERBORNE a past participle of overbear

OVERBOUGHT past tense of overbuy

OVERBRED *adj* bred too finely or to excess

OVERBUSY *adj* too busy

OVERBUY *v* -BOUGHT, -BUYING, -BUYS to buy in quantities exceeding need or demand

OVERCALL *v* -ED, -ING, -S to overbid

OVERCAME past tense of overcome

OVERCAST *v* -CAST, -CASTING, -CASTS to become cloudy or dark

OVERCOAT *n* pl. -S a warm coat worn over indoor clothing

OVERCOLD *adj* too cold

OVERCOME *v* -CAME, -COMING, -COMES to get the better of

OVERCOOK *v* -ED, -ING, -S to cook too long

OVERCOOL *v* -ED, -ING, -S to make too cool

OVERCOY *adj* too coy

OVERCRAM *v* -CRAMMED, -CRAMMING, -CRAMS to stuff or cram to excess

OVERCROP *v* -CROPPED, -CROPPING, -CROPS to exhaust the fertility of by cultivating to excess

OVERDARE *v* -DARED, -DARING, -DARES to become too daring

OVERDEAR *adj* too dear; too costly

OVERDECK *v* -ED, -ING, -S to adorn extravagantly

OVERDO *v* -DID, -DONE, -DOING, -DOES to do to excess

OVERDOER *n* pl. -S one that overdoes

OVERDOSE *v* -DOSED, -DOSING, -DOSES to give an excessive dose to

OVERDRAW *v* -DREW, -DRAWN, -DRAWING, -DRAWS to draw checks on in excess of the balance

OVERDRY *adj* too dry

OVERDUE *adj* not paid when due

OVERDYE *v* -DYED, -DYEING, -DYES to dye with too much color

OVEREASY *adj* too easy

OVEREAT *v* -ATE, -EATEN, -EATING, -EATS to eat to excess

OVERFAR *adj* too great in distance, extent, or degree

OVERFAST *adj* too fast

OVERFAT *adj* too fat

OVERFEAR *v* -ED, -ING, -S to fear too much

OVERFEED *v* -FED, -FEEDING, -FEEDS to feed too much

OVERFILL *v* -ED, -ING, -S to fill to overflowing

OVERFISH *v* -ED, -ING, -ES to deplete the supply of fish in an area by fishing to excess

OVERFLOW *v* -FLOWED, -FLOWN, -FLOWING, -FLOWS to flow over the top of

OVERFLY *v* -FLEW, -FLOWN, -FLYING, -FLIES to fly over

OVERFOND *adj* too fond or affectionate

OVERFOUL *adj* too foul

OVERFREE *adj* too free

OVERFULL *adj* too full

OVERGILD *v* -GILDED or -GILT, -GILDING, -GILDS to gild over

OVERGIRD *v* -GIRDED or -GIRT, -GIRDING, -GIRDS to gird to excess

OVERGLAD *adj* too glad

OVERGOAD *v* -ED, -ING, -S to goad too much

OVERGROW *v* -GREW, -GROWN, -GROWING, -GROWS to grow over

OVERHAND *v* -ED, -ING, -S to sew with short, vertical stitches

OVERHANG *v* -HUNG, -HANGING, -HANGS to hang or project over

OVERHARD *adj* too hard

OVERHATE *v* -HATED, -HATING, -HATES to hate to excess

OVERHAUL *v* -ED, -ING, -S to examine carefully for needed repairs

OVERHEAD	n pl. -S the general cost of running a business
OVERHEAP	v -ED, -ING, -S to heap up or accumulate to excess
OVERHEAR	v -HEARD, -HEARING, -HEARS to hear without the speaker's knowledge or intention
OVERHEAT	v -ED, -ING, -S to heat to excess
OVERHIGH	adj too high
OVERHOLD	v -HELD, -HOLDING, -HOLDS to rate too highly
OVERHOLY	adj too holy
OVERHOPE	v -HOPED, -HOPING, -HOPES to hope exceedingly
OVERHOT	adj too hot
OVERHUNG	past tense of overhang
OVERHUNT	v -ED, -ING, -S to deplete the supply of game in an area by hunting to excess
OVERIDLE	adj too idle
OVERJOY	v -ED, -ING, -S to fill with great joy
OVERJUST	adj too just
OVERKEEN	adj too keen
OVERKILL	v -ED, -ING, -S to destroy with more nuclear force than required
OVERKIND	adj too kind
OVERLADE	v -LADED, -LADEN, -LADING, -LADES to load with too great a burden
OVERLAID	past tense of overlay
OVERLAIN	past participle of overlie
OVERLAND	n pl. -S a train or stagecoach that travels over land
OVERLAP	v -LAPPED, -LAPPING, -LAPS to extend over and cover a part of
OVERLATE	adj too late
OVERLAX	adj too lax
OVERLAY	v -LAID, -LAYING, -LAYS to lay over
OVERLEAF	adv on the other side of the page
OVERLEAP	v -LEAPED or -LEAPT, -LEAPING, -LEAPS to leap over
OVERLET	v -LET, -LETTING, -LETS to let to excess
OVERLEWD	adj too lewd
OVERLIE	v -LAY, -LAIN, -LYING, -LIES to lie over
OVERLIVE	v -LIVED, -LIVING, -LIVES to outlive
OVERLOAD	v -ED, -ING, -S to load to excess
OVERLONG	adj too long
OVERLOOK	v -ED, -ING, -S to fail to notice
OVERLORD	v -ED, -ING, -S to rule tyrannically
OVERLOUD	adj too loud
OVERLOVE	v -LOVED, -LOVING, -LOVES to love to excess
OVERLY	adv to an excessive degree
OVERLYING	present participle of overlie
OVERMAN	n pl. -MEN a foreman
OVERMAN	v -MANNED, -MANNING, -MANS to provide with more men than are needed
OVERMANY	adj too many
OVERMEEK	adj excessively meek
OVERMELT	v -ED, -ING, -S to melt too much
OVERMEN	pl. of overman
OVERMILD	adj too mild
OVERMIX	v -ED, -ING, -ES to mix too much
OVERMUCH	n pl. -ES an excess
OVERNEAR	adj too near
OVERNEAT	adj too neat
OVERNEW	adj too new
OVERNICE	adj excessively nice
OVERPASS	v -PASSED or -PAST, -PASSING, -PASSES to pass over
OVERPAY	v -PAID, -PAYING, -PAYS to pay too much
OVERPERT	adj too pert
OVERPLAY	v -ED, -ING, -S to exaggerate
OVERPLUS	n pl. -ES a surplus
OVERPLY	v -PLIED, -PLYING, -PLIES to ply to excess; overwork
OVERRAN	past tense of overrun
OVERRANK	adj too luxuriant in growth
OVERRASH	adj too rash
OVERRATE	v -RATED, -RATING, -RATES to rate too highly
OVERRICH	adj too rich
OVERRIDE	v -RODE, -RIDDEN, -RIDING, -RIDES to ride over
OVERRIFE	adj too rife

OVERRIPE *adj* too ripe

OVERRODE past tense of override

OVERRUDE *adj* excessively rude

OVERRUFF *v* -ED, -ING, -S to trump with a higher trump card than has already been played

OVERRULE *v* -RULED, -RULING, -RULES to disallow the arguments of

OVERRUN *v* -RAN, -RUNNING, -RUNS to spread or swarm over

OVERSAD *adj* excessively sad

OVERSALE *n* pl. -S the act of overselling

OVERSALT *v* -ED, -ING, -S to salt to excess

OVERSAVE *v* -SAVED, -SAVING, -SAVES to save too much

OVERSAW past tense of oversee

OVERSEA *adv* overseas

OVERSEAS *adv* beyond or across the sea

OVERSEE *v* -SAW, -SEEN, -SEEING, -SEES to watch over and direct

OVERSEED *v* -ED, -ING, -S to seed to excess

OVERSEER *n* pl. -S one that oversees

OVERSELL *v* -SOLD, -SELLING, -SELLS to sell more of than can be delivered

OVERSET *v* -SET, -SETTING, -SETS to turn or tip over

OVERSEW *v* -SEWED, -SEWN, -SEWING, -SEWS to overhand

OVERSHOE *n* pl. -S a protective outer shoe

OVERSHOT *n* pl. -S a type of fabric weave

OVERSICK *adj* too sick

OVERSIDE *n* pl. -S the other side of a phonograph record

OVERSIZE *n* pl. -S an unusually large size

OVERSLIP *v* -SLIPPED or -SLIPT, -SLIPPING, -SLIPS to leave out

OVERSLOW *adj* too slow

OVERSOAK *v* -ED, -ING, -S to soak too much

OVERSOFT *adj* too soft

OVERSOLD past tense of oversell

OVERSOON *adv* too soon

OVERSOUL *n* pl. -S a supreme reality or mind in transcendentalism

OVERSPIN *n* pl. -S a forward spin imparted to a ball

OVERSTAY *v* -ED, -ING, -S to stay beyond the limits or duration of

OVERSTEP *v* -STEPPED, -STEPPING, -STEPS to go beyond

OVERSTIR *v* -STIRRED, -STIRRING, -STIRS to stir too much

OVERSUP *v* -SUPPED, -SUPPING, -SUPS to sup to excess

OVERSURE *adj* too sure

OVERT *adj* open to view **OVERTLY** *adv*

OVERTAKE *v* -TOOK, -TAKEN, -TAKING, -TAKES to catch up with

OVERTAME *adj* too tame

OVERTART *adj* too tart

OVERTASK *v* -ED, -ING, -S to task too severely

OVERTAX *v* -ED, -ING, -ES to tax too heavily

OVERTHIN *adj* too thin

OVERTIME *v* -TIMED, -TIMING, -TIMES to exceed the desired timing for

OVERTIRE *v* -TIRED, -TIRING, -TIRES to tire excessively

OVERTOIL *v* -ED, -ING, -S to wear out or exhaust by excessive toil

OVERTONE *n* pl. -S a higher partial tone

OVERTOOK past tense of overtake

OVERTOP *v* -TOPPED, -TOPPING, -TOPS to rise above the top of

OVERTRIM *v* -TRIMMED, -TRIMMING, -TRIMS to trim too much

OVERTURE *v* -TURED, -TURING, -TURES to propose

OVERTURN *v* -ED, -ING, -S to turn over

OVERURGE *v* -URGED, -URGING, -URGES to urge too much

OVERUSE *v* -USED, -USING, -USES to use too much

OVERVIEW *n* pl. -S a summary

OVERVOTE *v* -VOTED, -VOTING, -VOTES to defeat by a majority of votes

OVERWARM *v* -ED, -ING, -S to warm too much

OVERWARY *adj* too wary

OVERWEAK *adj* too weak

OVERWEAR *v* -WORE, -WORN, -WEARING, -WEARS to wear out

OVERWEEN *v* -ED, -ING, -S to be arrogant

OVERWET *v* -WETTED, -WETTING, -WETS to wet too much

OVERWIDE *adj* too wide

OVERWILY *adj* too wily

OVERWIND	*v* -WOUND, -WINDING, -WINDS to wind too much, as a watch
OVERWISE	*adj* too wise
OVERWORD	*n* pl. -S a word or phrase repeated at intervals in a song
OVERWORE	past tense of overwear
OVERWORK	*v* -WORKED or -WROUGHT, -WORKING, -WORKS to cause to work too hard
OVERWORN	past participle of overwear
OVER-WOUND	past tense of overwind
OVER-WROUGHT	a past tense of overwork
OVERZEAL	*n* pl. -S excess of zeal
OVIBOS	*n* pl. OVIBOS a wild ox
OVICIDE	*n* pl. -S an agent that kills eggs **OVICIDAL** *adj*
OVIDUCT	*n* pl. -S a tube through which ova travel from an ovary **OVIDUCAL** *adj*
OVIFORM	*adj* shaped like an egg
OVINE	*n* pl. -S a sheep or a closely related animal
OVIPARA	*n/pl* egg-laying animals
OVIPOSIT	*v* -ED, -ING, -S to lay eggs
OVISAC	*n* pl. -S a sac containing an ovum or ova
OVOID	*n* pl. -S an egg-shaped body **OVOIDAL** *adj*
OVOLO	*n* pl. -LI or -LOS a convex molding
OVONIC	*adj* pertaining to a branch of electronics
OVULATE	*v* -LATED, -LATING, -LATES to produce ova
OVULE	*n* pl. -S a rudimentary seed **OVULAR, OVULARY** *adj*
OVUM	*n* pl. OVA the female reproductive cell of animals
OW	*interj* — used to express sudden pain
OWE	*v* OWED, OWING, OWES to be under obligation to pay or repay
OWL	*n* pl. -S a nocturnal bird
OWLET	*n* pl. -S a young owl
OWLISH	*adj* resembling an owl **OWLISHLY** *adv*
OWLLIKE	*adj* owlish
OWN	*v* -ED, -ING, -S to have as a belonging **OWNABLE** *adj*
OWNER	*n* pl. -S one that owns
OWSE	*n* pl. OWSEN ox
OX	*n* pl. OXEN a hoofed mammal
OX	*n* pl. -ES a clumsy person
OXALATE	*v* -LATED, -LATING, -LATES to treat with an oxalate (a chemical salt)
OXALIS	*n* pl. -ALISES a flowering plant **OXALIC** *adj*
OXAZINE	*n* pl. -S a chemical compound
OXBLOOD	*n* pl. -S a deep red color
OXBOW	*n* pl. -S a U-shaped piece of wood in an ox yoke
OXCART	*n* pl. -S an ox-drawn cart
OXEN	pl. of ox
OXEYE	*n* pl. -S a flowering plant
OXFORD	*n* pl. -S a type of shoe
OXHEART	*n* pl. -S a variety of sweet cherry
OXID	*n* pl. -S oxide
OXIDABLE	*adj* capable of being oxidized
OXIDANT	*n* pl. -S an oxidizing agent
OXIDASE	*n* pl. -S an oxidizing enzyme **OXIDASIC** *adj*
OXIDATE	*v* -DATED, -DATING, -DATES to oxidize
OXIDE	*n* pl. -S a binary compound of oxygen with another element or radical **OXIDIC** *adj*
OXIDISE	*v* -DISED, -DISING, -DISES to oxidize
OXIDISER	*n* pl. -S oxidizer
OXIDIZE	*v* -DIZED, -DIZING, -DIZES to combine with oxygen
OXIDIZER	*n* pl. -S an oxidant
OXIM	*n* pl. -S oxime
OXIME	*n* pl. -S a chemical compound
OXLIP	*n* pl. -S a flowering plant
OXPECKER	*n* pl. -S an African bird
OXTAIL	*n* pl. -S the tail of an ox
OXTER	*n* pl. -S the armpit
OXTONGUE	*n* pl. -S a European herb
OXY	*adj* containing oxygen
OXYACID	*n* pl. -S an acid that contains oxygen
OXYGEN	*n* pl. -S a gaseous element **OXYGENIC** *adj*

OXYMORON	*n* pl. -MORA a combination of contradictory or incongruous words
OXYPHIL	*n* pl. -S oxyphile
OXYPHILE	*n* pl. -S an organism that thrives in a relatively acid environment
OXYSALT	*n* pl. -S of an oxyacid
OXYSOME	*n* pl. -S a structural unit of cellular cristae
OXYTOCIC	*n* pl. -S a drug that hastens the process of childbirth
OXYTOCIN	*n* pl. -S a pituitary hormone
OXYTONE	*n* pl. -S a word having heavy stress on the last syllable
OY	*interj* — used to express dismay or pain
OYER	*n* pl. -S a type of legal writ
OYES	*n* pl. OYESSES oyez
OYEZ	*n* pl. OYESSES a cry used to introduce the opening of a court of law
OYSTER	*v* -ED, -ING, -S to gather oysters (edible mollusks)
OYSTERER	*n* pl. -S one that gathers or sells oysters
OZONE	*n* pl. -S a form of oxygen **OZONIC** *adj*
OZONIDE	*n* pl. -S a compound of ozone
OZONISE	*v* -ISED, -ISING, -ISES to ozonize
OZONIZE	*v* -IZED, -IZING, -IZES to convert into ozone
OZONIZER	*n* pl. -S a device for converting oxygen into ozone
OZONOUS	*adj* pertaining to ozone

PA   *n* pl. -S a father

PABULUM   *n* pl. -S food **PABULAR** *adj*

PAC   *n* pl. -S a shoe patterned after a moccasin

PACA   *n* pl. -S a large rodent

PACE   *v* PACED, PACING, PACES to walk with a regular step

PACER   *n* pl. -S a horse whose gait is a pace

PACHA   *n* pl. -S pasha

PACHADOM   *n* pl. -S pashadom

PACHALIC   *n* pl. -S pashalik

PACHISI   *n* pl. -S a board game of India

PACHOULI   *n* pl. -S an East Indian herb

PACHUCO   *n* pl. -COS a flashy Mexican-American youth

PACIFIC   *adj* peaceful

PACIFIED   past tense of pacify

PACIFIER   *n* pl. -S one that pacifies

PACIFIES   present 3d person sing. of pacify

PACIFISM   *n* pl. -S opposition to war or violence

PACIFIST   *n* pl. -S an advocate of pacifism

PACIFY   *v* -FIED, -FYING, -FIES to make peaceful

PACING   present participle of pace

PACK   *v* -ED, -ING, -S to put into a receptacle for transportation or storage **PACKABLE** *adj*

PACKAGE   *v* -AGED, -AGING, -AGES to make into a package (a wrapped or boxed object)

PACKAGER   *n* pl. -S one that packages

PACKER   *n* pl. -S one that packs

PACKET   *v* -ED, -ING, -S to make into a small package

PACKING   *n* pl. -S material used to pack

PACKLY   *adv* intimately

PACKMAN   *n* pl. -MEN a peddler

PACKNESS   *n* pl. -ES intimacy

PACKSACK   *n* pl. -S a carrying bag to be worn on the back

PACKWAX   *n* pl. -ES paxwax

PACT   *n* pl. -S an agreement

PACTION   *n* pl. -S a pact

PAD   *v* PADDED, PADDING, PADS to line or stuff with soft material

PADAUK   *n* pl. -S a tropical tree

PADDIES   pl. of paddy

PADDING   *n* pl. -S material with which to pad

PADDLE   *v* -DLED, -DLING, -DLES to propel with a broad-bladed implement

PADDLER   *n* pl. -S one that paddles

PADDLING   *n* pl. -S the act of one who paddles

PADDOCK   *v* -ED, -ING, -S to confine in an enclosure for horses

PADDY   *n* pl. -DIES a rice field

PADISHAH   *n* pl. -S a sovereign

PADLE   *n* pl. -S a hoe

PADLOCK   *v* -ED, -ING, -S to secure with a type of lock

PADNAG   *n* pl. -S a horse that moves along at an easy pace

PADOUK   *n* pl. -S padauk

PADRE   *n* pl. PADRES or PADRI a Christian clergyman

PADRONE   *n* pl. -NES or -NI a master

PADSHAH   *n* pl. -S padishah

PADUASOY   *n* pl. -SOYS a strong silk fabric

PAEAN   *n* pl. -S a song of joy

PAEANISM   *n* pl. -S the chanting of a paean

PAELLA   *n* pl. -S a saffron-flavored stew

PAEON   *n* pl. -S a metrical foot of four syllables

PAGAN   *n* pl. -S an irreligious person

PAGANDOM   *n* pl. -S the realm of pagans

PAGANISE   *v* -ISED, -ISING, -ISES to paganize

PAGANISH   *adj* resembling a pagan

PAGANISM   *n* pl. -S an irreligious attitude

PAGANIST   *n* pl. -S a pagan

PAGANIZE   *v* -IZED, -IZING, -IZES to make irreligious

PAGE   *v* PAGED, PAGING, PAGES to summon by calling out the name of

PAGEANT   *n* pl. -S an elaborate public spectacle

PAGEBOY   *n* pl. -BOYS a woman's hairstyle

PAGED   past tense of page

PAGINAL   *adj* pertaining to the pages of a book

PAGINATE   *v* -NATED, -NATING, -NATES to number the pages of

PAGING   present participle of page

PAGOD   *n* pl. -S pagoda

PAGODA   *n* pl. -S a Far Eastern temple

PAGURIAN   *n* pl. -S a hermit crab

PAGURID   *n* pl. -S pagurian

PAH   *interj* — used as an exclamation of disgust

PAHLAVI   *n* pl. -S a coin of Iran

PAID   a past tense of pay

PAIK   *v* -ED, -ING, -S to beat or strike

PAIL   *n* pl. -S a watertight cylindrical container

PAILFUL   *n* pl. -PAILFULS or PAILSFUL as much as a pail will hold

PAIN   *v* -ED, -ING, -S to cause pain (suffering or distress)

PAINCH   *n* pl. -ES paunch

PAINFUL   *adj* -FULLER, -FULLEST causing pain

PAINLESS   *adj* not causing pain

PAINT   *v* -ED, -ING, -S to make a representation of with paints (coloring substances)

PAINTER   *n* pl. -S one that paints

PAINTING   *n* pl. -S a picture made with paints

PAINTY   *adj* PAINTIER, PAINTIEST covered with paint

PAIR   *v* -ED, -ING, -S to arrange in sets of two

PAISA   *n* pl. PAISE or PAISAS a coin of Pakistan

PAISAN   *n* pl. -S paisano

PAISANO   *n* pl. -NOS a fellow countryman

PAISE   a pl. of paisa

PAISLEY   *n* pl. -LEYS a patterned wool fabric

PAJAMA   *n* pl. -S a garment for sleeping or lounging

PAL   *v* PALLED, PALLING, PALS to associate as friends

PALABRA   *n* pl. -S a word

PALACE   *n* pl. -S a royal residence
PALACED *adj*

PALADIN   *n* pl. -S a knightly champion

PALAIS   *n* pl. PALAIS a palace

PALATAL   *n* pl. -S a bone of the palate

PALATE   *n* pl. -S the roof of the mouth

PALATIAL   *adj* resembling a palace

PALATINE   *n* pl. -S a high officer of an empire

PALAVER   *v* -ED, -ING, -S to chatter

PALAZZO   *n* pl. -ZI an impressive building

PALE   *adj* PALER, PALEST lacking intensity of color

PALE   *v* PALED, PALING, PALES to make or become pale

PALEA   *n* pl. -LEAE a small bract
PALEAL *adj*

PALEFACE   *n* pl. -S a white person

PALELY   *adv* in a pale manner

PALENESS   *n* pl. -ES the quality of being pale

PALER   comparative of pale

PALEST   superlative of pale

PALESTRA   *n* pl. -TRAS or -TRAE a school for athletics in ancient Greece

PALET   *n* pl. -S a palea

PALETOT   *n* pl. -S a loose overcoat

PALETTE   *n* pl. -S a board on which an artist mixes colors

PALEWAYS   *adv* palewise

PALEWISE   *adv* vertically

PALFREY   *n* pl. -FREYS a riding horse

PALIER   comparative of paly

PALIEST   superlative of paly

PALIKAR   *n* pl. -S a Greek soldier

PALING   *n* pl. -S a picket fence

PALINODE   *n* pl. -S a formal retraction

PALISADE   *v* -SADED, -SADING, -SADES to fortify with a heavy fence

PALISH   *adj* somewhat pale

PALL   *v* -ED, -ING, -S to become insipid

PALLADIA   *n/pl* safeguards

PALLADIC   *adj* pertaining to the metallic element palladium

PALLED   past tense of pal

PALLET   *n* pl. -S a bed or mattress of straw

PALLETTE   *n* pl. -S a piece of armor protecting the armpit

PALLIA   a pl. of pallium

PALLIAL   *adj* pertaining to a part of the brain

PALLIATE   *v* -ATED, -ATING, -ATES to conceal the seriousness of

PALLID   *adj* pale **PALLIDLY** *adv*

PALLIER   comparative of pally

PALLIEST   superlative of pally

PALLING   present participle of pal

PALLIUM   *n* pl. -LIA or -LIUMS a cloak worn in ancient Rome

PALLOR   *n* pl. -S paleness

PALLY   *adj* -LIER, -LIEST marked by close friendship

PALM   *v* -ED, -ING, -S to touch with the palm (inner surface) of the hand

PALMAR   *adj* pertaining to the palm

PALMARY   *adj* worthy of praise

PALMATE   *adj* resembling an open hand

PALMATED   *adj* palmate

PALMER   *n* pl. -S a religious pilgrim

PALMETTE   *n* pl. -S a type of ornament

PALMETTO   *n* pl. -TOS or -TOES a tropical tree

PALMIER   comparative of palmy

PALMIEST   superlative of palmy

PALMIST   *n* pl. -S a fortune-teller

PALMITIN   *n* pl. -S a chemical compound

PALMLIKE   *adj* resembling a palm tree

PALMY   *adj* PALMIER, PALMIEST marked by prosperity

PALMYRA   *n* pl. -S a tropical tree

PALOMINO   *n* pl. -NOS a slender-legged horse

PALOOKA   *n* pl. -S an inferior boxer

PALP   *n* pl. -S a palpus

PALPABLE   *adj* capable of being felt **PALPABLY** *adv*

PALPAL   *adj* pertaining to a palpus

PALPATE   *v* -PATED, -PATING, -PATES to examine by touch

PALPATOR   *n* pl. -S one that palpates

PALPEBRA   *n* pl. -BRAE an eyelid

PALPUS   *n* pl. -PI a sensory organ of an arthropod

PALSY   *v* -SIED, -SYING, -SIES to paralyze

PALTER   *v* -ED, -ING, -S to talk or act insincerely

PALTERER   *n* pl. -S one that palters

PALTRY   *adj* -TRIER, -TRIEST petty **PALTRILY** *adv*

PALUDAL   *adj* pertaining to a marsh

PALUDISM   *n* pl. -S malaria

PALY   *adj* PALIER, PALIEST somewhat pale

PAM   *n* pl. -S the jack of clubs in certain card games

PAMPA   *n* pl. -S a grassland of South America

PAMPEAN   *n* pl. -S a native of the pampas

PAMPER   *v* -ED, -ING, -S to treat with extreme or excessive indulgence

PAMPERER   *n* pl. -S one that pampers

PAMPERO   *n* pl. -ROS a cold, dry wind

PAMPHLET   *n* pl. -S a printed work with a paper cover

PAN   *v* PANNED, PANNING, PANS to criticize harshly

PANACEA   *n* pl. -S a remedy for all diseases or ills **PANACEAN** *adj*

PANACHE   *n* pl. -S an ornamental tuft of feathers

PANADA *n* pl. -S a thick sauce

PANAMA *n* pl. -S a lightweight hat

PANATELA *n* pl. -S a long, slender cigar

PANCAKE *v* -CAKED, -CAKING, -CAKES to land an airplane in a certain manner

PANCHAX *n* pl. -ES a tropical fish

PANCREAS *n* pl. -ES a large gland

PANDA *n* pl. -S a carnivorous mammal

PANDANUS *n* pl. -NI or -NUSES a tropical plant

PANDECT *n* pl. -S a complete body of laws

PANDEMIC *n* pl. -S a widespread disease

PANDER *v* -ED, -ING, -S to provide gratification for others' desires

PANDERER *n* pl. -S one that panders

PANDIED past tense of pandy

PANDIES present 3d person sing. of pandy

PANDIT *n* pl. -S a wise or learned man in India

PANDOOR *n* pl. -S pandour

PANDORA *n* pl. -S bandore

PANDORE *n* pl. -S bandore

PANDOUR *n* pl. -S a marauding soldier

PANDOWDY *n* pl. -DIES an apple dessert

PANDURA *n* pl. -S bandore

PANDY *v* -DIED, -DYING, -DIES to punish by striking the hand

PANE *n* pl. -S a sheet of glass for a window **PANED** *adj*

PANEL *v* -ELED, -ELING, -ELS or -ELLED, -ELLING, -ELS to decorate with thin sheets of material

PANELING *n* pl. -S material with which to panel

PANELIST *n* pl. -S a member of a discussion or advisory group

PANELLED past tense of panel

PANELLING a present participle of panel

PANETELA *n* pl. -S panatela

PANFISH *n* pl. -ES any small fish that can be fried whole

PANFUL *n* pl. -S as much as a pan will hold

PANG *v* -ED, -ING, -S to cause to have spasms of pain

PANGA *n* pl. -S a large knife

PANGEN *n* pl. -S a hypothetical heredity-controlling particle of proto-plasm

PANGOLIN *n* pl. -S a toothless mammal

PANHUMAN *adj* pertaining to all humanity

PANIC *v* -ICKED, -ICKING, -ICS to be overwhelmed by fear

PANICKY *adj* -ICKIER, -ICKIEST tending to panic

PANICLE *n* pl. -S a loosely branched flower cluster **PANICLED** *adj*

PANICUM *n* pl. -S a grass

PANIER *n* pl. -S pannier

PANMIXIA *n* pl. -S random mating within a breeding population

PANNE *n* pl. -S a lustrous velvet

PANNED past tense of pan

PANNIER *n* pl. -S a large basket

PANNIKIN *n* pl. -S a small saucepan

PANNING present participle of pan

PANOCHA *n* pl. -S a coarse Mexican sugar

PANOCHE *n* pl. -S panocha

PANOPLY *n* pl. -PLIES a suit of armor

PANOPTIC *adj* including everything visible in one view

PANORAMA *n* pl. -S a complete view

PANPIPE *n* pl. -S a musical instrument

PANSOPHY *n* pl. -PHIES universal knowledge

PANSY *n* pl. -SIES a flowering plant

PANT *v* -ED, -ING, -S to breathe quickly and with difficulty

PANTHEON *n* pl. -S a temple dedicated to all the gods

PANTHER *n* pl. -S a leopard

PANTIE *n* pl. -S a woman's or child's undergarment

PANTIES pl. of panty

PANTILE *n* pl. -S a roofing tile **PANTILED** *adj*

PANTOFLE *n* pl. -S a slipper

PANTOUM *n* pl. -S a verse form

PANTRY *n* pl. -TRIES a closet or room for storing kitchen utensils

PANTSUIT *n* pl. -S a type of woman's suit

PANTY *n* pl. PANTIES pantie

PANZER *n* pl. -S an armored combat vehicle

PAP *n* pl. -S a soft food for infants

PAPA *n* pl. -S a father

PAPACY *n* pl. -CIES the office of the pope

PAPAIN *n* pl. -S an enzyme

PAPAL *adj* pertaining to the pope **PAPALLY** *adv*

PAPAW *n* pl. -S a fleshy fruit

PAPAYA *n* pl. -S a melon-like fruit **PAPAYAN** *adj*

PAPER *v* -ED, -ING, -S to cover or wrap with paper (a thin sheet material made of cellulose pulp)

PAPERBOY *n* pl. -BOYS a newsboy

PAPERER *n* pl. -S one that papers

PAPERY *adj* resembling paper

PAPHIAN *n* pl. -S a prostitute

PAPILLA *n* pl. -LAE a nipple-like projection **PAPILLAR** *adj*

PAPILLON *n* pl. -S a small dog

PAPIST *n* pl. -S a Roman Catholic — usually used disparagingly **PAPISTIC** *adj*

PAPISTRY *n* pl. -TRIES the Roman Catholic religion — usually used disparagingly

PAPOOSE *n* pl. -S an American Indian baby

PAPPI a pl. of pappus

PAPPIER comparative of pappy

PAPPIES pl. of pappy

PAPPIEST superlative of pappy

PAPPOOSE *n* pl. -S papoose

PAPPUS *n* pl. -PI a tuft of bristles on the achene of certain plants **PAPPOSE, PAPPOUS** *adj*

PAPPY *adj* -PIER, -PIEST resembling pap

PAPPY *n* pl. -PIES a father

PAPRICA *n* pl. -S paprika

PAPRIKA *n* pl. -S a seasoning made from red peppers

PAPULA *n* pl. -LAE papule

PAPULE *n* pl. -S a pimple **PAPULAN, PAPULAR, PAPULOSE** *adj*

PAPYRUS *n* pl. -RUSES or -RI a tall aquatic plant **PAPYRAL, PAPYRIAN, PAPYRINE** *adj*

PAR *v* PARRED, PARRING, PARS to shoot in a standard number of strokes in golf

PARA *n* pl. -S a monetary unit of Yugoslavia

PARABLE *n* pl. -S a simple story conveying a moral or religious lesson

PARABOLA *n* pl. -S a conic section

PARACHOR *n* pl. -S a mathematical constant that relates molecular volume to surface tension

PARADE *v* -RADED, -RADING, -RADES to march in a public procession

PARADER *n* pl. -S one that parades

PARADIGM *n* pl. -S a pattern or example

PARADING present participle of parade

PARADISE *n* pl. -S a place of extreme beauty or delight

PARADOS *n* pl. -ES a protective embankment

PARADOX *n* pl. -ES a statement seemingly contradictory or absurd yet perhaps true

PARADROP *v* -DROPPED, -DROPPING, -DROPS to deliver by parachute

PARAFFIN *v* -ED, -ING, -S to coat with a waxy substance

PARAFORM *n* pl. -S a substance used as an antiseptic

PARAGOGE *n* pl. -S the addition of a sound or sounds at the end of a word

PARAGON *v* -ED, -ING, -S to compare with

PARAKEET *n* pl. -S a small parrot

PARALLAX *n* pl. -ES an apparent optical displacement of an object

PARALLEL *v* -LELED, -LELING, -LELS or -LELLED, -LELLING, -LELS to be similar or analogous to

PARALYSE *v* -LYSED, -LYSING, -LYSES to paralyze

PARALYZE *v* -LYZED, -LYZING, -LYZES to render incapable of movement

PARAMENT *n* pl. -MENTS or -MENTA an ornamental vestment

PARAMO *n* pl. -MOS a plateau region of South America

PARAMOUR *n* pl. -S an illicit lover

PARANG *n* pl. -S a heavy knife

PARANOEA *n* pl. -S paranoia

PARANOIA *n* pl. -S a mental disorder

PARANOID *n* pl. -S one affected with paranoia

PARAPET *n* pl. -S a protective wall

PARAPH *n pl.* -S a flourish at the end of a signature

PARAQUAT *n pl.* -S a weed killer

PARAQUET *n pl.* -S parakeet

PARASANG *n pl.* -S a Persian unit of distance

PARASHAH *n pl.* -SHOTH or -SHIOTH a passage in Jewish scripture

PARASITE *n pl.* -S an organism that lives and feeds on or in another organism

PARASOL *n pl.* -S a small, light umbrella

PARAVANE *n pl.* -S an underwater device used to cut cables

PARBOIL *v* -ED, -ING, -S to cook partially by boiling for a short time

PARCEL *v* -CELED, -CELING, -CELS or -CELLED, -CELLING, -CELS to divide into parts or shares

PARCENER *n pl.* -S a joint heir

PARCH *v* -ED, -ING, -ES to make very dry

PARD *n pl.* -S a leopard

PARDAH *n pl.* -S purdah

PARDEE *interj* pardi

PARDI *interj* — used as a mild oath

PARDIE *interj* pardi

PARDINE *adj* pertaining to a leopard

PARDNER *n pl.* -S chum; friend

PARDON *v* -ED, -ING, -S to release from liability for an offense

PARDONER *n pl.* -S one that pardons

PARDY *interj* pardi

PARE *v* PARED, PARING, PARES to cut off the outer covering of

PARECISM *n pl.* -S the state of having the male and female sexual organs beside or near each other

PAREIRA *n pl.* -S a medicinal plant root

PARENT *v* -ED, -ING, -S to exercise the functions of a parent (a father or mother)

PARENTAL *adj* pertaining to a parent

PARER *n pl.* -S one that pares

PARESIS *n pl.* -RESES partial loss of the ability to move

PARETIC *n pl.* -S one affected with paresis

PAREU *n pl.* -S a Polynesian garment

PAREVE *adj* parve

PARFAIT *n pl.* -S a frozen dessert

PARFLESH *n pl.* -ES a rawhide smoked in lye to remove the hair and dried

PARFOCAL *adj* having lenses with the corresponding focal points in the same plane

PARGE *v* PARGED, PARGING, PARGES to parget

PARGET *v* -GETED, -GETING, -GETS or -GETTED, -GETTING, -GETS to cover with plaster

PARGO *n pl.* -GOS a food fish

PARHELIA *n/pl* bright circular spots appearing on a solar halo

PARHELIC *adj* pertaining to parhelia

PARIAH *n pl.* -S a social outcast

PARIAN *n pl.* -S a hard, white porcelain

PARIES *n pl.* PARIETES the wall of an organ

PARIETAL *n pl.* -S a bone of the skull

PARING *n pl.* -S something pared off

PARIS *n pl.* -ISES a European herb

PARISH *n pl.* -ES an ecclesiastical district

PARITY *n pl.* -TIES equality

PARK *v* -ED, -ING, -S to leave a vehicle in a location for a time

PARKA *n pl.* -S a hooded garment

PARKER *n pl.* -S one that parks

PARKING *n pl.* -S an area in which vehicles may be left

PARKLAND *n pl.* -S a grassland region with isolated or grouped trees

PARKLIKE *adj* resembling an outdoor recreational area

PARKWAY *n pl.* -WAYS a wide highway

PARLANCE *n pl.* -S a manner of speaking

PARLANDO *adj* sung in a manner suggestive of speech

PARLANTE *adj* parlando

PARLAY *v* -ED, -ING, -S to bet an original wager and its subsequent winnings on a subsequent event

PARLE *v* PARLED, PARLING, PARLES to parley

PARLEY *v* -LEYED, -LEYING, -LEYS to discuss terms with an enemy

PARLEYER *n pl.* -S one that parleys

PARLING present participle of parle

PARLOR	n pl. -S a room for the entertainment of visitors
PARLOUR	n pl. -S parlor
PARLOUS	adj dangerous
PARODIC	adj comically imitative
PARODIED	past tense of parody
PARODIES	present 3d person sing. of parody
PARODIST	n pl. -S one who parodies
PARODOS	n pl. -DOI an ode sung in ancient Greek drama
PARODY	v -DIED, -DYING, -DIES to imitate a serious literary work for comic effect
PAROL	n pl. -S an utterance
PAROLE	v -ROLED, -ROLING, -ROLES to release from prison before completion of the imposed sentence
PAROLEE	n pl. -S one who is paroled
PARONYM	n pl. -S a word having the same root as another
PAROQUET	n pl. -S parakeet
PAROTIC	adj situated near the ear
PAROTID	n pl. -S a salivary gland
PAROTOID	n pl. -S a gland of certain toads and frogs
PAROUS	adj having produced offspring
PAROXYSM	n pl. -S a sudden fit or attack
PARQUET	v -ED, -ING, -S to furnish with a floor of inlaid design
PARR	n pl. -S a young salmon
PARRAL	n pl. -S parrel
PARRED	past tense of par
PARREL	n pl. -S a sliding loop of rope or chain used on a ship
PARRIDGE	n pl. -S porridge
PARRIED	past tense of parry
PARRIES	present 3d person sing. of parry
PARRING	present participle of par
PARRITCH	n pl. -ES porridge
PARROKET	n pl. -S parakeet
PARROT	v -ED, -ING, -S to repeat or imitate without thought or understanding
PARROTER	n pl. -S one that parrots
PARROTY	adj resembling a parrot (a hook-billed tropical bird)

PARRY	v -RIED, -RYING, -RIES to ward off a blow
PARSE	v PARSED, PARSING, PARSES to describe and analyze grammatically **PARSABLE** adj
PARSEC	n pl. -S a unit of astronomical distance
PARSER	n pl. -S one that parses
PARSING	present participle of parse
PARSLEY	n pl. -LEYS a cultivated herb
PARSNIP	n pl. -S a European herb
PARSON	n pl. -S a clergyman **PARSONIC** adj
PART	v -ED, -ING, -S to divide or break into separate parts
PARTAKE	v -TOOK, -TAKEN, -TAKING, -TAKES to participate
PARTAKER	n pl. -S one that partakes
PARTAN	n pl. -S an edible crab
PARTERRE	n pl. -S a section of a theater
PARTIAL	n pl. -S a simple component of a complex tone
PARTIBLE	adj divisible
PARTICLE	n pl. -S a very small piece or part
PARTIED	past tense of party
PARTIES	present 3d person sing. of party
PARTING	n pl. -S a division or separation
PARTISAN	n pl. -S a firm supporter of a person, party, or cause
PARTITA	n pl. -S a set of related instrumental pieces
PARTITE	adj divided into parts
PARTIZAN	n pl. -S partisan
PARTLET	n pl. -S a woman's garment
PARTLY	adv in some measure or degree
PARTNER	v -ED, -ING, -S to associate with in some activity of common interest
PARTON	n pl. -S a hypothetical atomic particle
PARTOOK	past tense of partake
PARTWAY	adv to some extent
PARTY	v -TIED, -TYING, -TIES to attend a social gathering
PARURA	n pl. -S parure
PARURE	n pl. -S a set of matched jewelry
PARVE	adj made without milk or meat

PARVENU *n pl.* -S one who has suddenly risen above his class

PARVENUE *adj* characteristic of a parvenu

PARVIS *n pl.* -VISES an enclosed area in front of a church

PARVISE *n pl.* -S parvis

PARVOLIN *n pl.* -S an oily liquid obtained from fish

PAS *n pl.* PAS a dance step

PASCHAL *n pl.* -S a candle used in certain religious ceremonies

PASE *n pl.* -S a movement of a matador's cape

PASEO *n pl.* -SEOS a leisurely stroll

PASH *v* -ED, -ING, -ES to strike violently

PASHA *n pl.* -S a former Turkish high official

PASHADOM *n pl.* -S the rank of a pasha

PASHALIC *n pl.* -S pashalik

PASHALIK *n pl.* -S the territory of a pasha

PASQUIL *n pl.* -S a satire or lampoon

PASS *v* -ED, -ING, -ES to go by

PASSABLE *adj* fairly good or acceptable **PASSABLY** *adv*

PASSADE *n pl.* -S a turn of a horse backward or forward on the same ground

PASSADO *n pl.* -DOS or -DOES a forward thrust in fencing

PASSAGE *v* -SAGED, -SAGING, -SAGES to make a voyage

PASSANT *adj* walking with the farther forepaw raised — used of a heraldic animal

PASSBAND *n pl.* -S a frequency band that permits transmission with maximum efficiency

PASSBOOK *n pl.* -S a bankbook

PASSE *adj* outmoded

PASSEE *adj* passe

PASSEL *n pl.* -S a large quantity or number

PASSER *n pl.* -S one that passes

PASSERBY *n pl.* PASSERSBY one who passes by

PASSIBLE *adj* capable of feeling or suffering

PASSIM *adv* here and there

PASSING *n pl.* -S a death

PASSION *n pl.* -S an intense emotion

PASSIVE *n pl.* -S a verb form

PASSKEY *n pl.* -KEYS a key that opens several different locks

PASSLESS *adj* incapable of being traveled over or through

PASSOVER *n pl.* -S the lamb eaten at the feast of a Jewish holiday

PASSPORT *n pl.* -S a document allowing travel from one country to another

PASSUS *n pl.* -ES a section of a story or poem

PASSWORD *n pl.* -S a secret word that must be spoken to gain admission

PAST *n pl.* -S time gone by

PASTA *n pl.* -S a food made of dough

PASTE *v* PASTED, PASTING, PASTES to fasten with a sticky mixture

PASTEL *n pl.* -S a soft, delicate hue

PASTER *n pl.* -S one that pastes

PASTERN *n pl.* -S a part of a horse's foot

PASTICCI *n/pl* pastiches

PASTICHE *n pl.* -S an artistic work made of fragments from various sources

PASTIER comparative of pasty

PASTIES pl. of pasty

PASTIEST superlative of pasty

PASTIL *n pl.* -S pastille

PASTILLE *n pl.* -S a lozenge

PASTIME *n pl.* -S a recreational activity

PASTINA *n pl.* -S a type of macaroni

PASTING present participle of paste

PASTNESS *n pl.* -ES the state of being past or gone by

PASTOR *v* -ED, -ING, -S to serve as the spiritual overseer of

PASTORAL *n pl.* -S a literary or artistic work that depicts country life

PASTRAMI *n pl.* -S a highly seasoned smoked beef

PASTROMI *n pl.* -S pastrami

PASTRY *n pl.* -TRIES a sweet baked food

PASTURAL *adj* pertaining to a pasture

PASTURE *v* -TURED, -TURING, -TURES to put in a pasture (a grazing area)

PASTURER *n pl.* -S one that pastures livestock

PASTY	*adj* PASTIER, PASTIEST pale and unhealthy in appearance
PASTY	*n pl.* PASTIES a meat pie
PAT	*v* PATTED, PATTING, PATS to touch lightly
PATACA	*n pl.* -S a monetary unit of Macao
PATAGIUM	*n pl.* -GIA a wing membrane of a bat
PATAMAR	*n pl.* -S a sailing vessel
PATCH	*v* -ED, -ING, -ES to mend or cover a hole or weak spot in
PATCHER	*n pl.* -S one that patches
PATCHY	*adj* PATCHIER, PATCHIEST uneven in quality PATCHILY *adv*
PATE	*n pl.* -S the top of the head PATED *adj*
PATELLA	*n pl.* -LAE or -LAS the flat movable bone at the front of the knee PATELLAR *adj*
PATEN	*n pl.* -S a plate
PATENCY	*n pl.* -CIES the state of being obvious
PATENT	*v* -ED, -ING, -S to obtain a patent (a government grant protecting the rights of an inventor) on
PATENTEE	*n pl.* -S one that holds a patent
PATENTLY	*adv* obviously
PATENTOR	*n pl.* -S one that grants a patent
PATER	*n pl.* -S a father
PATERNAL	*adj* pertaining to a father
PATH	*n pl.* -S a trodden way or track
PATHETIC	*adj* arousing pity
PATHLESS	*adj* having no path
PATHOGEN	*n pl.* -S any disease-producing organism
PATHOS	*n pl.* -ES a quality that arouses feelings of pity or compassion
PATHWAY	*n pl.* -WAYS a path
PATIENCE	*n pl.* -S the quality of being patient
PATIENT	*adj* -TIENTER, -TIENTEST able to endure disagreeable circumstances without complaint
PATIENT	*n pl.* -S one who is under medical treatment
PATIN	*n pl.* -S paten
PATINA	*n pl.* -NAE or -NAS a green film that forms on bronze
PATINE	*v* -TINED, -TINING, -TINES to cover with a patina
PATIO	*n pl.* -TIOS an outdoor paved area adjoining a house
PATLY	*adv* suitably
PATNESS	*n pl.* -ES suitability
PATOIS	*n pl.* PATOIS a dialect
PATRIOT	*n pl.* -S one who loves his country
PATROL	*v* -TROLLED, -TROLLING, -TROLS to pass through an area for the purposes of observation or security
PATRON	*n pl.* -S a regular customer PATRONAL, PATRONLY *adj*
PATROON	*n pl.* -S a landowner granted manorial rights under old Dutch law
PATSY	*n pl.* -SIES a person who is easily fooled
PATTAMAR	*n pl.* -S patamar
PATTED	past tense of pat
PATTEE	*adj* paty
PATTEN	*n pl.* -S a shoe having a thick wooden sole
PATTER	*v* -ED, -ING, -S to talk glibly or rapidly
PATTERER	*n pl.* -S one that patters
PATTERN	*v* -ED, -ING, -S to make according to a prescribed design
PATTIE	*n pl.* -S patty
PATTING	present participle of pat
PATTY	*n pl.* -TIES a small, flat cake of chopped food
PATTYPAN	*n pl.* -S a pan in which patties are baked
PATULENT	*adj* patulous
PATULOUS	*adj* spreading; open
PATY	*adj* formee
PAUCITY	*n pl.* -TIES smallness of number or quantity
PAUGHTY	*adj* arrogant
PAULDRON	*n pl.* -S a piece of armor for the shoulder
PAULIN	*n pl.* -S a sheet of waterproof material
PAUNCH	*n pl.* -ES the belly or abdomen PAUNCHED *adj*
PAUNCHY	*adj* PAUNCHIER, PAUNCHIEST having a protruding belly

PAUPER   *v* -ED, -ING, -S to reduce to poverty

PAUSAL   *adj* pertaining to a break or rest in speaking or writing

PAUSE   *v* PAUSED, PAUSING, PAUSES to stop temporarily

PAUSER   *n* pl. -S one that pauses

PAVAN   *n* pl. -S a slow, stately dance

PAVANE   *n* pl. -S pavan

PAVE   *v* PAVED, PAVING, PAVES to cover with material that forms a firm, level surface

PAVEMENT   *n* pl. -S a paved surface

PAVER   *n* pl. -S one that paves

PAVID   *adj* timid

PAVILION   *v* -ED, -ING, -S to cover with a large tent

PAVIN   *n* pl. -S pavan

PAVING   *n* pl. -S pavement

PAVIOR   *n* pl. -S a paver

PAVIOUR   *n* pl. -S a paver

PAVIS   *n* pl. -ISES a large medieval shield

PAVISE   *n* pl. -S pavis

PAVISER   *n* pl. -S a soldier carrying a pavis

PAVONINE   *adj* resembling a peacock

PAW   *v* -ED, -ING, -S to strike or scrape with a beating motion

PAWER   *n* pl. -S one that paws

PAWKY   *adj* PAWKIER, PAWKIEST sly **PAWKILY** *adv*

PAWL   *n* pl. -S a hinged mechanical part

PAWN   *v* -ED, -ING, -S to give as security for something borrowed **PAWNABLE** *adj*

PAWNAGE   *n* pl. -S an act of pawning

PAWNEE   *n* pl. -S one to whom something is pawned

PAWNER   *n* pl. -S one that pawns something

PAWNOR   *n* pl. -S pawner

PAWNSHOP   *n* pl. -S a place where things are pawned

PAWPAW   *n* pl. -S papaw

PAX   *n* pl. -ES a ceremonial embrace given to signify Christian love and unity

PAXWAX   *n* pl. -ES the nuchal ligament of a quadruped

PAY   *v* PAID or PAYED, PAYING, PAYS to give money or something of value in exchange for goods or services

PAYABLE   *adj* profitable **PAYABLY** *adv*

PAYCHECK   *n* pl. -S a check in payment of wages or salary

PAYDAY   *n* pl. -DAYS the day on which wages are paid

PAYEE   *n* pl. -S one to whom money is paid

PAYER   *n* pl. -S one that pays

PAYLOAD   *n* pl. -S the part of a cargo producing income

PAYMENT   *n* pl. -S something that is paid

PAYNIM   *n* pl. -S a pagan

PAYOFF   *n* pl. -S the act of distributing gains

PAYOLA   *n* pl. -S a secret payment for favors

PAYOR   *n* pl. -S payer

PAYROLL   *n* pl. -S a list of employees entitled to payment

PE   *n* pl. -S a Hebrew letter

PEA   *n* pl. -S the edible seed of an annual herb

PEACE   *v* PEACED, PEACING, PEACES to be or become silent

PEACEFUL   *adj* -FULLER, -FULLEST undisturbed; calm

PEACH   *v* -ED, -ING, -ES to inform against someone

PEACHER   *n* pl. -S one that peaches

PEACHY   *adj* PEACHIER, PEACHIEST dandy

PEACING   present participle of peace

PEACOAT   *n* pl. -S a heavy woolen jacket

PEACOCK   *v* -ED, -ING, -S to strut vainly

PEACOCKY   *adj* -COCKIER, -COCKIEST vain

PEAFOWL   *n* pl. -S a large pheasant

PEAG   *n* pl. -S wampum

PEAGE   *n* pl. -S peag

PEAHEN   *n* pl. -S a female peafowl

PEAK   *v* -ED, -ING, -S to reach a maximum

PEAKIER   comparative of peaky

PEAKIEST   superlative of peaky

PEAKISH   *adj* somewhat sickly

PEAKLESS	*adj* having no peak (a pointed top)
PEAKLIKE	*adj* resembling a peak
PEAKY	*adj* PEAKIER, PEAKIEST sickly
PEAL	*v* -ED, -ING, -S to ring out
PEALIKE	*adj* resembling a pea
PEAN	*n* pl. -S paean
PEANUT	*n* pl. -S the nutlike seed or pod of an annual vine
PEAR	*n* pl. -S a fleshy fruit
PEARL	*v* -ED, -ING, -S to adorn with pearls (smooth, rounded masses formed in certain mollusks)
PEARLASH	*n* pl. -ES an alkaline compound
PEARLER	*n* pl. -S one that dives for pearls
PEARLITE	*n* pl. -S a cast-iron alloy
PEARLY	*adj* PEARLIER, PEARLIEST resembling a pearl
PEARMAIN	*n* pl. -S a variety of apple
PEART	*adj* PEARTER, PEARTEST lively **PEARTLY** *adv*
PEASANT	*n* pl. -S a person of inferior social rank
PEASCOD	*n* pl. -S peasecod
PEASE	*n* pl. PEASEN or PEASES a pea
PEASECOD	*n* pl. -S a pea pod
PEAT	*n* pl. -S a substance composed of partially decayed vegetable matter
PEATY	*adj* PEATIER, PEATIEST resembling or containing peat
PEAVEY	*n* pl. -VEYS a lever used to move logs
PEAVY	*n* pl. -VIES peavey
PEBBLE	*v* -BLED, -BLING, -BLES to cover with pebbles (small, rounded stones)
PEBBLY	*adj* -BLIER, -BLIEST resembling pebbles
PECAN	*n* pl. -S a nut-bearing tree
PECCABLE	*adj* liable to sin
PECCANCY	*n* pl. -CIES the state of being peccant
PECCANT	*adj* sinful
PECCARY	*n* pl. -RIES a hoofed mammal
PECCAVI	*n* pl. -S a confession of sin
PECH	*v* -ED, -ING, -S to pant
PECHAN	*n* pl. -S the stomach
PECK	*v* -ED, -ING, -S to strike with the beak or something pointed
PECKER	*n* pl. -S one that pecks
PECKY	*adj* PECKIER, PECKIEST marked by decay caused by fungi
PECTASE	*n* pl. -S an enzyme
PECTATE	*n* pl. -S a chemical salt
PECTEN	*n* pl. -TENS or -TINES a comblike anatomical part
PECTIN	*n* pl. -S a carbohydrate derivative **PECTIC** *adj*
PECTIZE	*v* -TIZED, -TIZING, -TIZES to change into a jelly
PECTORAL	*n* pl. -S something worn on the breast
PECULATE	*v* -LATED, -LATING, -LATES to embezzle
PECULIAR	*n* pl. -S something belonging exclusively to a person
PECULIUM	*n* pl. -LIA private property
PED	*n* pl. -S a natural soil aggregate
PEDAGOG	*n* pl. -S a teacher
PEDAGOGY	*n* pl. -GIES the work of a teacher
PEDAL	*v* -ALED, -ALING, -ALS or -ALLED, -ALLING, -ALS to operate by means of foot levers
PEDALFER	*n* pl. -S a type of soil
PEDALIER	*n* pl. -S the pedal keyboard of an organ
PEDALLED	past tense of pedal
PEDALLING	present participle of pedal
PEDANT	*n* pl. -S one who flaunts his knowledge **PEDANTIC** *adj*
PEDANTRY	*n* pl. -RIES ostentatious display of knowledge
PEDATE	*adj* resembling a foot **PEDATELY** *adv*
PEDDLE	*v* -DLED, -DLING, -DLES to travel about selling wares
PEDDLER	*n* pl. -S one that peddles
PEDDLERY	*n* pl. -RIES the trade of a peddler
PEDDLING	present tense of peddle
PEDERAST	*n* pl. -S a man who engages in sexual activities with boys
PEDES	pl. of pes
PEDESTAL	*v* -TALED, -TALING, -TALS or -TALLED, -TALLING, -TALS to provide with an architectural support or base

PEDICAB   *n* pl. -S a passenger vehicle that is pedaled

PEDICEL   *n* pl. -S a slender basal part of an organism

PEDICLE   *n* pl. -S pedicel **PEDICLED** *adj*

PEDICURE   *v* -CURED, -CURING, -CURES to administer a cosmetic treatment to the feet and toenails

PEDIFORM   *adj* shaped like a foot

PEDIGREE   *n* pl. -S a line of ancestors

PEDIMENT   *n* pl. -S a triangular architectural part

PEDIPALP   *n* pl. -S an appendage of an arachnid

PEDLAR   *n* pl. -S a peddler

PEDLARY   *n* pl. -LARIES peddlery

PEDLER   *n* pl. -S a peddler

PEDOCAL   *n* pl. -S a type of soil

PEDOLOGY   *n* pl. -GIES the scientific study of the behavior and development of children

PEDRO   *n* pl. -DROS a card game

PEDUNCLE   *n* pl. -S a flower stalk

PEE   *v* PEED, PEEING, PEES to urinate — sometimes considered vulgar

PEEBEEN   *n* pl. -S an evergreen tree

PEEK   *v* -ED, -ING, -S to look furtively or quickly

PEEKABOO   *n* pl. -BOOS a children's game

PEEL   *v* -ED, -ING, -S to strip off an outer covering of **PEELABLE** *adj*

PEELER   *n* pl. -S one that peels

PEELING   *n* pl. -S a piece or strip that has been peeled off

PEEN   *v* -ED, -ING, -S to beat with the non-flat end of a hammerhead

PEEP   *v* -ED, -ING, -S to utter a short, shrill cry

PEEPER   *n* pl. -S one that peeps

PEEPHOLE   *n* pl. -S a small opening through which one may look

PEEPSHOW   *n* pl. -S an exhibition viewed through a small opening

PEEPUL   *n* pl. -S pipal

PEER   *v* -ED, -ING, -S to look narrowly or searchingly

PEERAGE   *n* pl. -S the rank of a nobleman

PEERESS   *n* pl. -ES a noblewoman

PEERIE   *n* pl. -S peery

PEERLESS   *adj* having no equal

PEERY   *n* pl. PEERIES a child's toy

PEESWEEP   *n* pl. -S a lapwing

PEETWEET   *n* pl. -S a wading bird

PEEVE   *v* PEEVED, PEEVING, PEEVES to annoy

PEEVISH   *adj* irritable

PEEWEE   *n* pl. -S an unusually small person or thing

PEEWIT   *n* pl. -S pewit

PEG   *v* PEGGED, PEGGING, PEGS to fasten with a peg (a wooden pin)

PEGBOARD   *n* pl. -S a board with holes for pegs

PEGBOX   *n* pl. -ES a part of a stringed instrument

PEGGED   past tense of peg

PEGGING   present participle of peg

PEGLESS   *adj* lacking a peg

PEGLIKE   *adj* resembling a peg

PEIGNOIR   *n* pl. -S a woman's gown

PEIN   *v* -ED, -ING, -S to peen

PEISE   *v* PEISED, PEISING, PEISES to weigh

PEKAN   *n* pl. -S a carnivorous mammal

PEKE   *n* pl. -S a small, long-haired dog

PEKIN   *n* pl. -S a silk fabric

PEKOE   *n* pl. -S a black tea

PELAGE   *n* pl. -S the coat or covering of a mammal **PELAGIAL** *adj*

PELAGIC   *adj* oceanic

PELE   *n* pl. -S a medieval fortified tower

PELERINE   *n* pl. -S a woman's cape

PELF   *n* pl. -S money or wealth

PELICAN   *n* pl. -S a large, web-footed bird

PELISSE   *n* pl. -S a long outer garment

PELITE   *n* pl. -S a rock composed of fine fragments **PELITIC** *adj*

PELLAGRA   *n* pl. -S a niacin-deficiency disease

PELLET   *v* -ED, -ING, -S to strike with pellets (small rounded masses)

PELLETAL   *adj* resembling a pellet

PELLICLE   *n* pl. -S a thin skin or film

PELLMELL   *n* pl. -S a jumbled mass

PELLUCID   *adj* transparent

PELON	*adj* hairless
PELORIA	*n pl.* -S abnormal regularity of a flower form **PELORIAN, PELORIC** *adj*
PELORUS	*n pl.* -ES a navigational instrument
PELOTA	*n pl.* -S a court game of Spanish origin
PELT	*v* -ED, -ING, -S to strike repeatedly with blows or missiles
PELTAST	*n pl.* -S a soldier of ancient Greece
PELTATE	*adj* shaped like a shield
PELTER	*n pl.* -S one that pelts
PELTRY	*n pl.* -RIES an animal skin
PELVIC	*n pl.* -S a bone of the pelvis
PELVIS	*n pl.* -VES or -VISES a part of the skeleton
PEMBINA	*n pl.* -S a variety of cranberry
PEMICAN	*n pl.* -S pemmican
PEMMICAN	*n pl.* -S a food prepared by North American Indians
PEMOLINE	*n pl.* -S a drug used experimentally to improve memory
PEMPHIX	*n pl.* -ES a skin disease
PEN	*v* PENNED, PENNING, PENS to write with a pen (an instrument for writing with fluid ink)
PENAL	*adj* pertaining to punishment
PENALISE	*v* -ISED, -ISING, -ISES to penalize
PENALITY	*n pl.* -TIES liability to punishment
PENALIZE	*v* -IZED, -IZING, -IZES to subject to a penalty
PENALLY	*adv* in a penal manner
PENALTY	*n pl.* -TIES a punishment imposed for violation of a law, rule, or agreement
PENANCE	*v* -ANCED, -ANCING, -ANCES to impose a type of punishment upon
PENANG	*n pl.* -S a cotton fabric
PENATES	*n/pl* the Roman gods of the household
PENCE	a *pl.* of penny
PENCEL	*n pl.* -S a small flag
PENCHANT	*n pl.* -S a strong liking for something
PENCIL	*v* -CILED, -CILING, -CILS or -CILLED, -CILLING, -CILS to produce by using a pencil (a writing and drawing implement)
PENCILER	*n pl.* -S one that pencils
PEND	*v* -ED, -ING, -S to remain undecided or unsettled
PENDANT	*n pl.* -S a hanging ornament
PENDENCY	*n pl.* -CIES a pending state
PENDENT	*n pl.* -S pendant
PENDULUM	*n pl.* -S a type of free swinging body **PENDULAR** *adj*
PENES	a *pl.* of penis
PENGO	*n pl.* -GOS a former monetary unit of Hungary
PENGUIN	*n pl.* -S a flightless, aquatic bird
PENICIL	*n pl.* -S a small tuft of hairs
PENIS	*n pl.* -NES or -NISES the male organ of copulation **PENIAL, PENILE** *adj*
PENITENT	*n pl.* -S a person who repents his sins
PENKNIFE	*n pl.* -KNIVES a small pocketknife
PENLIGHT	*n pl.* -S a small flashlight
PENLITE	*n pl.* -S penlight
PENMAN	*n pl.* -MEN an author
PENNA	*n pl.* -NAE any of the feathers that determine a bird's shape
PENNAME	*n pl.* -S a name used by an author instead of his real name
PENNANT	*n pl.* -S a long, narrow flag
PENNATE	*adj* having wings or feathers
PENNATED	*adj* pennate
PENNED	past tense of pen
PENNER	*n pl.* -S one that pens
PENNI	*n pl.* -NIA or -NIS a Finnish coin
PENNIES	a *pl.* of penny
PENNINE	*n pl.* -S a mineral
PENNING	present participle of pen
PENNON	*n pl.* -S a pennant **PENNONED** *adj*
PENNY	*n pl.* PENNIES or PENCE a coin of the United Kingdom
PENOCHE	*n pl.* -S penuche
PENOLOGY	*n pl.* -GIES the science of the punishment of crime
PENONCEL	*n pl.* -S a small pennon
PENPOINT	*n pl.* -S the point of a pen

PENSEE	n pl. -S a thought
PENSIL	n pl. -S pencel
PENSILE	adj hanging loosely
PENSION	v -ED, -ING, -S to grant a retirement allowance to
PENSIONE	n pl. -S a boarding house
PENSIVE	adj engaged in deep thought
PENSTER	n pl. -S a writer
PENSTOCK	n pl. - S a conduit for conveying water to a waterwheel
PENT	adj confined
PENTACLE	n pl. -S a five-pointed star
PENTAD	n pl. -S a group of five
PENTAGON	n pl. -S a five-sided polygon
PENTANE	n pl. -S a volatile liquid
PENTARCH	n pl. -S one of five joint rulers
PENTOMIC	adj made up of five battle groups
PENTOSAN	n pl. -S a complex carbohydrate
PENTOSE	n pl. -S a sugar having five carbon atoms per molecule
PENTYL	n pl. -S amyl
PENUCHE	n pl. -S a fudge-like candy
PENUCHI	n pl. -S penuche
PENUCHLE	n pl. -S pinochle
PENUCKLE	n pl. -S pinochle
PENULT	n pl. -S the next to last syllable in a word
PENUMBRA	n pl. -BRAE or -BRAS a partial shadow
PENURY	n pl. -RIES extreme poverty
PEON	n pl. -S or -ES an unskilled laborer
PEONAGE	n pl. -S the condition of being a peon
PEONISM	n pl. -S peonage
PEONY	n pl. -NIES a flowering plant
PEOPLE	v -PLED, -PLING, -PLES to furnish with inhabitants
PEOPLER	n pl. -S one that peoples
PEP	v, PEPPED, PEPPING, PEPS to fill with energy
PEPERONI	n pl. -S a highly seasoned sausage
PEPLOS	n pl. -ES a garment worn by women in ancient Greece
PEPLUM	n pl. -LUMS or -LA a short section attached to the waistline of a garment PEPLUMED adj
PEPLUS	n pl. -ES peplos
PEPO	n pl. -POS a fruit having a fleshy interior and a hard rind
PEPONIDA	n pl. -S pepo
PEPONIUM	n pl. -S pepo
PEPPED	past tense of pep
PEPPER	v -ED, -ING, -S to season with pepper (a pungent condiment)
PEPPERER	n pl. -S one that peppers
PEPPERY	adj resembling pepper
PEPPING	present participle of pep
PEPPY	adj -PIER, -PIEST full of energy PEPPILY adv
PEPSIN	n pl. -S a digestive enzyme of the stomach
PEPSINE	n pl. -S pepsin
PEPTIC	n pl. -S a substance that promotes digestion
PEPTID	n pl. -S peptide
PEPTIDE	n pl. -S a combination of amino acids PEPTIDIC adj
PEPTIZE	v -TIZED, -TIZING, -TIZES to increase the colloidal dispersion of
PEPTIZER	n pl. -S one that peptizes
PEPTONE	n pl. -S a protein compound PEPTONIC adj
PER	prep for each
PERACID	n pl. -S a type of acid
PERCALE	n pl. -S a cotton fabric
PERCEIVE	v -CEIVED, -CEIVING, -CEIVES to become aware of through the senses
PERCENT	n pl. -S one part in a hundred
PERCEPT	n pl. -S something that is perceived
PERCH	v -ED, -ING, -ES to sit or rest on an elevated place
PERCHER	n pl. -S one that perches
PERCOID	n pl. -S a spiny-finned fish
PERCUSS	v -ED, -ING, -ES to strike with force
PERDIE	interj pardi
PERDU	n pl. -S a soldier sent on a dangerous mission
PERDUE	n pl. -S perdu
PERDY	interj pardi
PERE	n pl. -S a father
PEREGRIN	n pl. -S a swift falcon much used in falconry

PERFECT _adj_ -FECTER, -FECTEST lacking fault or defect; of an extreme kind

PERFECT _v_ -ED, -ING, -S to make perfect

PERFECTA _n pl._ -S a system of betting

PERFECTO _n pl._ -TOS a medium-sized cigar

PERFIDY _n pl._ -DIES deliberate breach of faith or trust

PERFORCE _adj_ of necessity

PERFORM _v_ -ED, -ING, -S to begin and carry through to completion

PERFUME _v_ -FUMED, -FUMING, -FUMES to fill with a fragrant odor

PERFUMER _n pl._ -S one that perfumes

PERFUSE _v_ -FUSED, -FUSING, -FUSES to spread over or through something

PERGOLA _n pl._ -S a shaded shelter or passageway

PERHAPS _n pl._ -ES something open to doubt or conjecture

PERI _n pl._ -S a supernatural being of Persian mythology

PERIANTH _n pl._ -S an outer covering of a flower

PERIAPT _n pl._ -S an amulet

PERIBLEM _n pl._ -S a region of plant tissue

PERICARP _n pl._ -S the wall of a ripened plant ovary or fruit

PERICOPE _n pl._ -PES or -PAE a selection from a book

PERIDERM _n pl._ -S an outer layer of plant tissue

PERIDIUM _n pl._ -IA the covering of the spore-bearing organ in many fungi **PERIDIAL** _adj_

PERIDOT _n pl._ -S a mineral

PERIGEE _n pl._ -S the point in the orbit of a celestial body which is nearest to the earth **PERIGEAL, PERIGEAN** _adj_

PERIGON _n pl._ -S an angle equal to 360 degrees

PERIGYNY _n pl._ -NIES the state of being situated on a cuplike organ surrounding the pistil

PERIL _v_ -ILED, -ILING, -ILS or -ILLED, -ILLING, -ILS to imperil

PERILLA _n pl._ -S an Asian herb

PERILOUS _adj_ dangerous

PERILUNE _n pl._ -S the point in the orbit of a celestial body which is nearest to the moon

PERINEUM _n pl._ -NEA a region of the body at the lower end of the trunk **PERINEAL** _adj_

PERIOD _n pl._ -S a portion of time

PERIODIC _adj_ recurring at regular intervals

PERIODID _n pl._ -S an iodide

PERIOTIC _adj_ surrounding the ear

PERIPETY _n pl._ -TIES a sudden change in a course of events

PERIPTER _n pl._ -S a structure with a row of columns around all sides

PERIQUE _n pl._ -S a dark tobacco

PERISARC _n pl._ -S a protective covering of certain hydrozoans

PERISH _v_ -ED, -ING, -ES to die

PERIWIG _n pl._ -S a wig

PERJURE _v_ -JURED, -JURING, -JURES to make a perjurer of

PERJURER _n pl._ -S one guilty of perjury

PERJURY _n pl._ -RIES the willful giving of false testimony under oath in a judicial proceeding

PERK _v_ -ED, -ING, -S to carry oneself jauntily

PERKISH _adj_ somewhat perky

PERKY _adj_ PERKIER, PERKIEST jaunty **PERKILY** _adv_

PERLITE _n pl._ -S a volcanic glass **PERLITIC** _adj_

PERM _n pl._ -S a long-lasting hair setting

PERMEASE _n pl._ -S a catalyzing agent

PERMEATE _v_ -ATED, -ATING, -ATES to spread through

PERMIT _v_ -MITTED, -MITTING, -MITS to allow

PERMUTE _v_ -MUTED, -MUTING, -MUTES to change the order of

PERONEAL _adj_ pertaining to the fibula

PERORAL _adj_ occurring through the mouth

PERORATE _v_ -RATED, -RATING, -RATES to make a lengthy speech

PEROXID _n pl._ -S peroxide

PEROXIDE _v_ -IDED, -IDING, -IDES to treat with peroxide (a bleaching agent)

PERPEND _v_ -ED, -ING, -S to ponder

PERPENT _n pl._ -S a large building stone

PERPLEX *v* -ED, -ING, -ES to make mentally uncertain

PERRON *n* pl. -S an outdoor stairway

PERRY *n* pl. -RIES a beverage of pear juice often fermented

PERSALT *n* pl. -S a chemical salt

PERSE *n* pl. -S a blue color

PERSIST *v* -ED, -ING, -S to continue resolutely in some activity

PERSON *n* pl. -S a human being

PERSONA *n* pl. -NAE a character in a literary work

PERSONA *n* pl. -S the public role that a person assumes

PERSONAL *n* pl. -S a brief, private notice in a newspaper

PERSPIRE *v* -SPIRED, -SPIRING, -SPIRES to give off moisture through the pores of the skin **PERSPIRY** *adj*

PERSUADE *v* -SUADED, -SUADING, -SUADES to cause to do something by means of argument, reasoning, or entreaty

PERT *adj* PERTER, PERTEST impudent **PERTLY** *adv*

PERTAIN *v* -ED, -ING, -S to have reference or relation

PERTNESS *n* pl. -ES the quality of being pert

PERTURB *v* -ED, -ING, -S to disturb greatly

PERUKE *n* pl. -S a wig

PERUSAL *n* pl. -S the act of perusing

PERUSE *v* -RUSED, -RUSING, -RUSES to read

PERUSER *n* pl. -S one that peruses

PERVADE *v* -VADED, -VADING, -VADES to spread through every part of

PERVADER *n* pl. -S one that pervades

PERVERSE *adj* willfully deviating from desired or expected conduct

PERVERT *v* -ED, -ING, -S to turn away from the right course of action

PERVIOUS *adj* capable of being penetrated

PES *n* pl. PEDES a foot or footlike part

PESADE *n* pl. -S the position of a horse when rearing

PESETA *n* pl. -S a monetary unit of Spain

PESEWA *n* pl. -S a monetary unit of Ghana

PESKY *adj* -KIER, -KIEST annoying **PESKILY** *adv*

PESO *n* pl. -SOS a monetary unit of various Spanish-speaking countries

PESSARY *n* pl. -RIES a contraceptive device worn in the vagina

PEST *n* pl. -S an annoying person or thing

PESTER *v* -ED, -ING, -S to bother

PESTERER *n* pl. -S one that pesters

PESTHOLE *n* pl. -S a place liable to epidemic disease

PESTLE *v* -TLED, -TLING, -TLES to crush with a club-shaped hand tool

PET *v* PETTED, PETTING, PETS to caress with the hand

PETAL *n* pl. -S a leaflike part of a corolla **PETALED, PETALLED** *adj*

PETALINE *adj* resembling a petal

PETALODY *n* pl. -DIES the metamorphosis of various floral organs into petals

PETALOID *adj* resembling a petal

PETALOUS *adj* having petals

PETARD *n* pl. -S an explosive device

PETASOS *n* pl. -ES petasus

PETASUS *n* pl. -ES a broad-brimmed hat worn in ancient Greece

PETCOCK *n* pl. -S a small valve or faucet

PETECHIA *n* pl. -CHIAE a small hemorrhagic spot on a body surface

PETER *v* -ED, -ING, -S to diminish gradually

PETIOLAR *adj* pertaining to a petiole

PETIOLE *n* pl. -S the stalk of a leaf **PETIOLED** *adj*

PETIT *adj* small; minor

PETITE *n* pl. -S a clothing size for short women

PETITION *v* -ED, -ING, -S to make a formal request

PETREL *n* pl. -S a small seabird

PETRIFY *v* -FIED, -FYING, -FIES to convert into stone or a stony substance

PETROL *n* pl. -S gasoline

PETROLIC *adj* derived from petroleum

PETRONEL *n* pl. -S a portable firearm

PETROSAL	*adj* petrous
PETROUS	*adj* resembling stone in hardness
PETTED	past tense of pet
PETTEDLY	*adv* peevishly
PETTER	*n* pl. -S one that pets
PETTI	pl. of petto
PETTIER	comparative of petty
PETTIEST	superlative of petty
PETTIFOG	*v* -FOGGED, -FOGGING, -FOGS to quibble
PETTILY	*adv* in a petty manner
PETTING	present participle of pet
PETTISH	*adj* peevish
PETTLE	*v* -TLED, -TLING, -TLES to caress
PETTO	*n* pl. -TI the breast
PETTY	*adj* -TIER, -TIEST insignificant
PETULANT	*adj* peevish
PETUNIA	*n* pl. -S a tropical herb
PETUNTSE	*n* pl. -S a mineral
PETUNTZE	*n* pl. -S petuntse
PEW	*n* pl. -S a bench for seating people in church
PEWEE	*n* pl. -S a small bird
PEWIT	*n* pl. -S the lapwing
PEWTER	*n* pl. -S a tin alloy
PEWTERER	*n* pl. -S one that makes articles of pewter
PEYOTE	*n* pl. -S a cactus
PEYOTL	*n* pl. -S peyote
PEYTRAL	*n* pl. -S a piece of armor for the breast of a horse
PEYTREL	*n* pl. -S peytral
PFENNIG	*n* pl. -NIGS or -NIGE a bronze coin of Germany
PHAETON	*n* pl. -S a light carriage
PHAGE	*n* pl. -S an organism that destroys bacteria
PHALANGE	*n* pl. -S any bone of a finger or toe
PHALANX	*n* pl. -ES a formation of infantry in ancient Greece
PHALLI	a pl. of phallus
PHALLIC	*adj* pertaining to a phallus
PHALLISM	*n* pl. -S worship of the phallus as symbolic of nature's creative power

PHALLIST	*n* pl. -S one who practices phallism
PHALLUS	*n* pl. -LI or -LUSES the penis
PHANTASIED	past tense of phantasy
PHANTASIES	present 3d person sing. of phantasy
PHANTASM	*n* pl. -S a creation of the imagination
PHANTAST	*n* pl. -S fantast
PHANTASY	*v* -SIED, -SYING, -SIES to fantasy
PHANTOM	*n* pl. -S something existing in appearance only
PHARAOH	*n* pl. -S a ruler of ancient Egypt
PHARISEE	*n* pl. -S a hypocritically self-righteous person
PHARMACY	*n* pl. -CIES a drugstore
PHAROS	*n* pl. -ES a lighthouse or beacon to guide seamen
PHARYNX	*n* pl. -YNGES or -YNXES a section of the digestive tract
PHASE	*v* PHASED, PHASING, PHASES to plan or carry out by phases (distinct stages of development) PHASEAL, PHASIC *adj*
PHASEOUT	*n* pl. -S a gradual stopping of operations
PHASIS	*n* pl. PHASES a phase
PHASMID	*n* pl. -S a tropical insect
PHAT	*adj* susceptible of easy and rapid typesetting
PHATIC	*adj* sharing feelings rather than ideas
PHEASANT	*n* pl. -S a large, long-tailed bird
PHELLEM	*n* pl. -S a layer of plant cells
PHELONIA	*n/pl* liturgical vestments
PHENAZIN	*n* pl. -S a chemical compound
PHENETIC	*adj* pertaining to a type of classificatory system
PHENETOL	*n* pl. -S a volatile liquid
PHENIX	*n* pl. -ES phoenix
PHENOL	*n* pl. -S a caustic compound
PHENOLIC	*n* pl. -S a synthetic resin
PHENOM	*n* pl. -S a person of extraordinary ability or promise
PHENYL	*n* pl. -S a univalent chemical radical PHENYLIC *adj*
PHEW	*interj* — used to express relief, fatigue, or disgust
PHI	*n* pl. -S a Greek letter

PHIAL	n pl. -S a vial	**PHONY**	adj -NIER, -NIEST not genuine or real
PHILABEG	n pl. -S filibeg		
PHILIBEG	n pl. -S filibeg	**PHONY**	n pl. -NIES one that is phony
PHILOMEL	n pl. -S a songbird	**PHOOEY**	interj — used as an exclamation of disgust or contempt
PHILTER	v -ED, -ING, -S to put under the spell of a love potion	**PHORATE**	n pl. -S an insecticide
PHILTRE	v -TRED, -TRING, -TRES to philter	**PHOSGENE**	n pl. -S a poisonous gas
		PHOSPHID	n pl. -S a chemical compound
PHIMOSIS	n pl. -MOSES the abnormal constriction of the opening of the prepuce **PHIMOTIC** adj	**PHOSPHIN**	n pl. -S a poisonous gas
		PHOSPHOR	n pl. -S a substance that will emit light when exposed to radiation
PHIZ	n pl. -ES a face or facial expression		
PHLEGM	n pl. -S a thick mucus secreted in the air passages	**PHOT**	n pl. -S a unit of illumination
		PHOTIC	adj pertaining to light
PHLEGMY	adj PHLEGMIER, PHLEGMIEST resembling phlegm	**PHOTICS**	n/pl the science of light
		PHOTO	v -ED, -ING, -S to photograph
PHLOEM	n pl. -S a complex plant tissue	**PHOTOG**	n pl. -S one who takes photographs
PHLOX	n pl. -ES a flowering plant		
PHOBIA	n pl. -S an obsessive or irrational fear **PHOBIC** adj	**PHOTOMAP**	v -MAPPED, -MAPPING, -MAPS to map by means of aerial photography
PHOCINE	adj pertaining to seals		
PHOEBE	n pl. -S a small bird	**PHOTON**	n pl. -S a quantum of radiant energy **PHOTONIC** adj
PHOENIX	n pl. -ES a mythical bird		
PHON	n pl. -S a unit of loudness	**PHOTOPIA**	n pl. -S vision in bright light **PHOTOPIC** adj
PHONAL	adj pertaining to speech sounds		
PHONATE	v -NATED, -NATING, -NATES to produce speech sounds	**PHOTOSET**	v -SET, -SETTING, -SETS to prepare for printing by photographic means
PHONE	v PHONED, PHONING, PHONES to telephone	**PHPHT**	interj pht
PHONEME	n pl. -S a unit of speech **PHONEMIC** adj	**PHRASAL**	adj pertaining to a group of two or more associated words
		PHRASE	v PHRASED, PHRASING, PHRASES to express in words
PHONETIC	adj pertaining to speech sounds		
PHONEY	adj -NIER, -NIEST phony	**PHRASING**	n pl. -S manner or style of verbal expression
PHONEY	n pl. -NEYS a phony		
PHONIC	adj pertaining to the nature of sound	**PHRATRY**	n pl. -TRIES a tribal unit among primitive peoples **PHRATRAL, PHRATRIC** adj
PHONICS	n/pl the science of sound		
PHONIER	comparative of phoney and phony	**PHREATIC**	adj pertaining to underground waters
		PHRENIC	adj pertaining to the mind
PHONIES	pl. of phony	**PHRENSY**	v -SIED, -SYING, -SIES to frenzy
PHONIEST	superlative of phoney and phony	**PHT**	interj — used as an expression of mild anger or annoyance
PHONILY	adv in a phony manner		
PHONING	present participle of phone	**PHTHALIC**	adj pertaining to a certain acid
PHONO	n pl. -NOS a record player	**PHTHALIN**	n pl. -S a chemical compound
PHONON	n pl. -S a quantum of vibrational energy	**PHTHISIC**	n pl. -S phthisis
		PHTHISIS	n pl. PHTHISES a disease of the lungs
		PHYLA	pl. of phylon and phylum

PHYLAE pl. of phyle

PHYLAR *adj* pertaining to a phylum

PHYLAXIS *n* pl. -AXISES an inhibiting of infection by the body

PHYLE *n* pl. -LAE a political subdivision in ancient Greece **PHYLIC** *adj*

PHYLESIS *n* pl. -LESES or -LESISES the course of evolutionary development **PHYLETIC** *adj*

PHYLLARY *n* pl. -RIES a bract of certain plants

PHYLLITE *n* pl. -S a foliated rock

PHYLLODE *n* pl. -S a flattened petiole that serves as a leaf

PHYLLOID *n* pl. -S a leaflike plant part

PHYLLOME *n* pl. -S a leaf of a plant

PHYLON *n* pl. -LA a genetically related group

PHYLUM *n* pl. -LA a taxonomic division

PHYSES pl. of physis

PHYSIC *v* -ICKED, -ICKING, -ICS to treat with medicine

PHYSICAL *n* pl. -S a medical examination of the body

PHYSIQUE *n* pl. -S the form or structure of the body

PHYSIS *n* pl. PHYSES the principle of growth or change in nature

PHYTANE *n* pl. -S a chemical compound

PHYTIN *n* pl. -S a chemical salt

PHYTOID *adj* resembling a plant

PHYTON *n* pl. -S a structural unit of a plant **PHYTONIC** *adj*

PI *n* pl. -S a Greek letter

PI *v* PIED, PIEING or PIING, PIES to jumble or disorder

PIA *n* pl. -S a membrane of the brain

PIACULAR *adj* atoning

PIAFFE *v* PIAFFED, PIAFFING, PIAFFES to perform a piaffer

PIAFFER *n* pl. -S a movement in horsemanship

PIAL *adj* pertaining to a pia

PIAN *n* pl. -S a tropical disease **PIANIC** *adj*

PIANISM *n* pl. -S performance on the piano

PIANIST *n* pl. -S one who plays the piano

PIANO *n* pl. -NOS a musical instrument

PIASABA *n* pl. -S piassava

PIASAVA *n* pl. -S piassava

PIASSABA *n* pl. -S piassava

PIASSAVA *n* pl. -S a coarse, stiff fiber

PIASTER *n* pl. -S a monetary unit of several Arab countries

PIASTRE *n* pl. -S piaster

PIAZZA *n* pl. -ZAS or -ZE a public square in an Italian town

PIBROCH *n* pl. -S a musical piece played on the bagpipe

PIC *n* pl. -S a photograph

PICA *n* pl. -S a craving for unnatural food

PICACHO *n* pl. -CHOS an isolated peak of a hill

PICADOR *n* pl. -ES or -S a horseman in a bullfight

PICAL *adj* resembling a pica

PICARA *n* pl. -S a female picaro

PICARO *n* pl. -ROS a vagabond

PICAROON *v* -ED, -ING, -S to act as a pirate

PICAYUNE *n* pl. -S a former Spanish-American coin

PICCOLO *n* pl. -LOS a small flute

PICE *n* pl. PICE a former coin of India and Pakistan

PICEOUS *adj* glossy-black in color

PICK *v* -ED, -ING, -S to select

PICKADIL *n* pl. -S a type of collar

PICKAX *v* -ED, -ING, -ES to use a pickax (a tool for breaking hard surfaces)

PICKAXE *v* -AXED, -AXING, -AXES to pickax

PICKEER *v* -ED, -ING, -S to skirmish in advance of an army

PICKER *n* pl. -S one that picks

PICKEREL *n* pl. -S a freshwater fish

PICKET *v* -ED, -ING, -S to stand outside of some location, as a business, to publicize one's grievances against it

PICKETER *n* pl. -S one who pickets

PICKIER comparative of picky

PICKIEST superlative of picky

PICKING *n* pl. -S the act of one that picks

PICKLE	v -LED, -LING, -LES to preserve or flavor in a solution of brine or vinegar	**PIER**	n pl. -S a structure extending from land out over water
PICKLOCK	n pl. -S a tool for opening locks	**PIERCE**	v PIERCED, PIERCING, PIERCES to cut or pass into or through
PICKOFF	n pl. -S a play in baseball	**PIERCER**	n pl. -S one that pierces
PICKUP	n pl. -S a small truck	**PIERROT**	n pl. -S a clown
PICKWICK	n pl. -S a device for raising wicks in oil lamps	**PIETA**	n pl. -S a representation of the Virgin Mary mourning over the body of Christ
PICKY	adj PICKIER, PICKIEST fussy		
PICLORAM	n pl. -S an herbicide	**PIETIES**	pl. of piety
PICNIC	v -NICKED, -NICKING, -NICS to go on a picnic (an outdoor excursion with food)	**PIETISM**	n pl. -S piety
		PIETIST	n pl. -S a pious person
		PIETY	n pl. -TIES the quality or state of being pious
PICNICKY	adj pertaining to a picnic		
PICOGRAM	n pl. -S one trillionth of a gram	**PIFFLE**	v -FLED, -FLING, -FLES to babble
PICOLIN	n pl. -S picoline		
PICOLINE	n pl. -S a chemical compound	**PIG**	v PIGGED, PIGGING, PIGS to bear pigs (cloven-hoofed mammals)
PICOT	v -ED, -ING, -S to edge with ornamental loops		
PICOTEE	n pl. -S a variety of carnation	**PIGBOAT**	n pl. -S a submarine
PICQUET	n pl. -S piquet	**PIGEON**	n pl. -S a short-legged bird
PICRATE	n pl. -S a chemical salt PICRATED adj	**PIGFISH**	n pl. -ES a marine fish
		PIGGED	past tense of pig
PICRIC	adj having a very bitter taste	**PIGGERY**	n pl. -GERIES a pigpen
PICRITE	n pl. -S an igneous rock	**PIGGIE**	n pl. -S piggy
PICTURE	v -TURED, -TURING, -TURES to make a visual representation of	**PIGGIES**	pl. of piggy
		PIGGIN	n pl. -S a small wooden pail
PICUL	n pl. -S an Asian unit of weight	**PIGGING**	present participle of pig
PIDDLE	v -DLED, -DLING, -DLES to waste time	**PIGGISH**	adj greedy or dirty
		PIGGY	n pl. -GIES a small pig
PIDDLER	n pl. -S one that piddles	**PIGLET**	n pl. -S a small pig
PIDDOCK	n pl. -S a bivalve mollusk	**PIGMENT**	v -ED, -ING, -S to add a coloring matter to
PIDGIN	n pl. -S a mixed language		
PIE	v PIED, PIEING, PIES to pi	**PIGMY**	n pl. -MIES pygmy
PIEBALD	n pl. -S a spotted animal	**PIGNUS**	n pl. -NORA property held as security for a debt
PIECE	v PIECED, PIECING, PIECES to join into a whole		
		PIGNUT	n pl. -S a hickory nut
PIECER	n pl. -S one that pieces	**PIGPEN**	n pl. -S a place where pigs are kept
PIECING	n pl. -S material to be sewn together		
		PIGSKIN	n pl. -S the skin of a pig
PIECRUST	n pl. -S the crust of a pie	**PIGSNEY**	n pl. -NEYS a darling
PIED	past tense of pie	**PIGSTICK**	v -ED, -ING, -S to hunt for wild boar
PIEDFORT	n pl. -S piefort		
PIEDMONT	n pl. -S an area lying at the foot of a mountain	**PIGSTY**	n pl. -STIES a pigpen
		PIGTAIL	n pl. -S a tight braid of hair
PIEFORT	n pl. -S an unusually thick coin	**PIGWEED**	n pl. -S a weedy plant
PIEING	a present participle of pi	**PIKA**	n pl. -S a small mammal
PIEPLANT	n pl. -S a rhubarb	**PIKAKE**	n pl. -S an East Indian vine

PIKE   v PIKED, PIKING, PIKES to pierce with a pike (a long spear)

PIKEMAN   n pl. -MEN a soldier armed with a pike

PIKER   n pl. -S a stingy person

PIKING   present participle of pike

PILAF   n pl. -S a dish made of seasoned rice and often meat

PILAFF   n pl. -S pilaf

PILAR   adj pertaining to hair

PILASTER   n pl. -S a rectangular column

PILAU   n pl. -S pilaf

PILAW   n pl. -S pilaf

PILCHARD   n pl. -S a small marine fish

PILE   v PILED, PILING, PILES to lay one upon the other

PILEA   pl. of pileum

PILEATE   adj having a pileus

PILEATED   adj pileate

PILED   past tense of pile

PILEI   pl. of pileus

PILEOUS   adj pilose

PILEUM   n pl. -LEA the top of a bird's head

PILEUP   n pl. -S a collision involving several motor vehicles

PILEUS   n pl. -LEI the umbrella-shaped portion of a mushroom

PILEWORT   n pl. -S a medicinal plant

PILFER   v -ED, -ING, -S to steal

PILFERER   n pl. -S one that pilfers

PILGRIM   n pl. -S a traveler or wanderer

PILI   n pl. -S a Philippine tree

PILIFORM   adj resembling a hair

PILING   n pl. -S a structure of building supports

PILL   v -ED, -ING, -S to dose with pills (small, rounded masses of medicine)

PILLAGE   v -LAGED, -LAGING, -LAGES to plunder

PILLAGER   n pl. -S one that pillages

PILLAR   v -ED, -ING, -S to provide with vertical building supports

PILLBOX   n pl. -ES a small box for pills

PILLION   n pl. -S a pad or cushion for an extra rider on a horse or motorcycle

PILLORY   v -RIED, -RYING, -RIES to expose to public ridicule or abuse

PILLOW   v -ED, -ING, -S to rest on a pillow (a cushion for the head)

PILLOWY   adj resembling a pillow

PILOSE   adj covered with hair

PILOSITY   n pl. -TIES the state of being pilose

PILOT   v -ED, -ING, -S to control the course of

PILOTAGE   n pl. -S the act of piloting

PILOTING   n pl. -S a branch of navigation

PILOUS   adj pilose

PILSENER   n pl. -S pilsner

PILSNER   n pl. -S a light beer

PILULE   n pl. -S a small pill PILULAR adj

PILUS   n pl. -LI a hair or hairlike structure

PILY   adj divided into a number of wedge-shaped heraldic designs

PIMA   n pl. -S a strong, high-grade cotton

PIMENTO   n pl. -TOS pimiento

PIMIENTO   n pl. -TOS a sweet pepper

PIMP   v -ED, -ING, -S to solicit clients for a prostitute

PIMPLE   n pl. -S an inflamed swelling of the skin PIMPLED adj

PIMPLY   adj -PLIER, -PLIEST covered with pimples

PIN   v PINNED, PINNING, PINS to fasten with a pin (a slender, pointed piece of metal)

PINA   n pl. -S a pineapple

PINAFORE   n pl. -S a child's apron

PINANG   n pl. -S a palm tree

PINASTER   n pl. -S a pine tree

PINATA   n pl. -S a pottery jar used in a Mexican game

PINBALL   n pl. -S an electric game

PINBONE   n pl. -S the hipbone

PINCER   n pl. -S one of the two pivoted parts of a grasping tool

PINCH   v -ED, -ING, -ES to squeeze between two edges or surfaces

PINCHBUG   n pl. -S a large beetle

PINCHECK   n pl. -S a fabric design

PINCHER   n pl. -S one that pinches

PINDER *n* pl. -S an official who formerly impounded stray animals

PINDLING *adj* puny or sickly

PINE *v* PINED, PINING, PINES to yearn intensely

PINEAL *adj* shaped like a pinecone

PINECONE *n* pl. -S a cone-shaped fruit of a pine tree

PINED past tense of pine

PINELIKE *adj* resembling a pine (an evergreen tree)

PINENE *n* pl. -S the main constituent of turpentine

PINERY *n* pl. -ERIES an area where pineapples are grown

PINESAP *n* pl. -S a fragrant herb

PINETUM *n* pl. -TA a plantation of pine trees

PINEWOOD *n* pl. -S the wood of a pine tree

PINEY *adj* PINIER, PINIEST piny

PINFISH *n* pl. -ES a small marine fish

PINFOLD *v* -ED, -ING, -S to confine in an enclosure for stray animals

PING *v* -ED, -ING, -S to produce a brief, high-pitched sound

PINGER *n* pl. -S a device for producing pulses of sound

PINGO *n* pl. -GOS a hill forced up by the effects of frost

PINGRASS *n* pl. -ES a European weed

PINGUID *adj* greasy

PINHEAD *n* pl. -S the head of a pin

PINHOLE *n* pl. -S a small hole made by a pin

PINIER comparative of piney and piny

PINIEST superlative of piney and piny

PINING present participle of pine

PINION *v* -ED, -ING, -S to remove or bind the wing feathers of to prevent flight

PINITE *n* pl. -S a mineral

PINK *adj* PINKER, PINKEST of a pale reddish hue

PINK *v* -ED, -ING, -S to stab with a pointed weapon

PINKEYE *n* pl. -S an inflammation of the eye

PINKIE *n* pl. -S the little finger

PINKIES pl. of pinky

PINKING *n* pl. -S a method of cutting or decorating

PINKISH *adj* somewhat pink

PINKLY *adv* with a pink hue

PINKNESS *n* pl. -ES the state of being pink

PINKO *n* pl. PINKOS or PINKOES a person who holds somewhat radical political views

PINKROOT *n* pl. -S a medicinal plant root

PINKY *n* pl. PINKIES pinkie

PINNA *n* pl. -NAE or -NAS a feather, wing, or winglike part

PINNACE *n* pl. -S a small sailing ship

PINNACLE *v* -CLED, -CLING, -CLES to place on a summit

PINNAE a pl. of pinna

PINNAL *adj* pertaining to a pinna

PINNATE *adj* resembling a feather

PINNATED *adj* pinnate

PINNED past tense of pin

PINNER *n* pl. -S one that pins

PINNING present participle of pin

PINNIPED *n* pl. -S a mammal with limbs modified into flippers

PINNULA *n* pl. -LAE pinnule **PINNULAR** *adj*

PINNULE *n* pl. -S a pinnate part or organ

PINOCHLE *n* pl. -S a card game

PINOCLE *n* pl. -S pinochle

PINOLE *n* pl. -S a finely ground flour

PINON *n* pl. -S or -ES a pine tree

PINPOINT *v* -ED, -ING, -S to locate precisely

PINPRICK *v* -ED, -ING, -S to puncture with a pin

PINSCHER *n* pl. -S a large, short-haired dog

PINT *n* pl. -S a liquid and dry measure of capacity

PINTA *n* pl. -S a skin disease

PINTADA *n* pl. -S pintado

PINTADO *n* pl. -DOS or -DOES a large food fish

PINTAIL *n* pl. -S a river duck

PINTANO *n* pl. -NOS a tropical fish

PINTLE *n* pl. -S a pin on which something turns

PINTO *n* pl. -TOS or -TOES a spotted horse

PINTSIZE   *adj* small

PINUP   *n pl.* -S a picture that may be pinned up on a wall

PINWALE   *n pl.* -S a type of fabric

PINWEED   *n pl.* -S a perennial herb

PINWHEEL   *n pl.* -S a child's toy resembling a windmill

PINWORK   *n pl.* -S a type of embroidery

PINWORM   *n pl.* -S a parasitic worm

PINY   *adj* PINIER, PINIEST suggestive of or covered with pine trees

PINYON   *n pl.* -S pinon

PIOLET   *n pl.* -S an ice ax

PION   *n pl.* -S an atomic particle **PIONIC** *adj*

PIONEER   *v* -ED, -ING, -S to take part in the beginnings of

PIOSITY   *n pl.* -TIES an excessive show of piety

PIOUS   *adj* marked by religious reverence **PIOUSLY** *adv*

PIP   *v* PIPPED, PIPPING, PIPS to break through the shell of an egg

PIPAGE   *n pl.* -S a system of pipes

PIPAL   *n pl.* -S a fig tree of India

PIPE   *v* PIPED, PIPING, PIPES to convey by means of a pipe (a hollow cylinder)

PIPEAGE   *n pl.* -S pipage

PIPEFISH   *n pl.* -ES a slender fish

PIPEFUL   *n pl.* -S a quantity sufficient to fill a tobacco pipe

PIPELESS   *adj* having no pipe

PIPELIKE   *adj* resembling a pipe

PIPELINE   *v* -LINED, -LINING, -LINES to convey by a line of pipe

PIPER   *n pl.* -S one that plays on a tubular musical instrument

PIPERINE   *n pl.* -S a chemical compound

PIPESTEM   *n pl.* -S the stem of a tobacco pipe

PIPET   *v* -PETTED, -PETTING, -PETS to pipette

PIPETTE   *v* -PETTED, -PETTING, -PETTES to measure liquid with a calibrated tube

PIPIER   comparative of pipy

PIPIEST   superlative of pipy

PIPING   *n pl.* -S a system of pipes

PIPINGLY   *adv* shrilly

PIPIT   *n pl.* -S a songbird

PIPKIN   *n pl.* -S a small pot

PIPPED   past tense of pip

PIPPIN   *n pl.* -S any of several varieties of apple

PIPPING   present participle of pip

PIPY   *adj* PIPIER, PIPIEST shrill

PIQUANCY   *n pl.* -CIES the quality of being piquant

PIQUANT   *adj* having an agreeably sharp taste

PIQUE   *v* PIQUED, PIQUING, PIQUES to arouse anger or resentment in

PIQUET   *n pl.* -S a card game

PIRACY   *n pl.* -CIES robbery on the high seas

PIRAGUA   *n pl.* -S a dugout canoe

PIRANA   *n pl.* -S piranha

PIRANHA   *n pl.* -S a voracious fish

PIRARUCU   *n pl.* -S a large food fish

PIRATE   *v* -RATED, -RATING, -RATES to commit piracy

PIRATIC   *adj* pertaining to piracy

PIRAYA   *n pl.* -S piranha

PIRN   *n pl.* -S a spinning-wheel bobbin

PIROG   *n pl.* -ROGEN, -ROGHI or -ROGI a large Russian pastry

PIROGUE   *n pl.* -S piragua

PIROQUE   *n pl.* -S piragua

PIROZHOK   *n pl.* -ROZHKI, -ROSHKI or -ROJKI a small Russian pastry

PISCARY   *n pl.* -RIES a place for fishing

PISCATOR   *n pl.* -S a fisherman

PISCINA   *n pl.* -NAE or -NAS a basin used in certain church ceremonies **PISCINAL** *adj*

PISCINE   *adj* pertaining to fish

PISH   *v* -ED, -ING, -ES to express contempt

PISIFORM   *n pl.* -S a small bone of the wrist

PISMIRE   *n pl.* -S an ant

PISOLITE   *n pl.* -S a limestone

PISS   *v* -ED, -ING, -ES to urinate — sometimes considered vulgar

PISSANT   *n pl.* -S an ant

PISSOIR   *n pl.* -S a public urinal

PISTACHE *n pl.* -S a shade of green

PISTIL *n pl.* -S the seed-bearing organ of flowering plants

PISTOL *v* -TOLED, -TOLING, -TOLS or -TOLLED, -TOLLING, -TOLS to shoot with a small firearm

PISTOLE *n pl.* -S a former European gold coin

PISTON *n pl.* -S a part of an engine

PIT *v* PITTED, PITTING, PITS to mark with cavities or depressions

PITA *n pl.* -S a strong fiber

PITAPAT *v* -PATTED, -PATTING, -PATS to make a repeated tapping sound

PITCH *v* -ED, -ING, -ES to throw

PITCHER *n pl.* -S a container for holding and pouring liquids

PITCHIER comparative of pitchy

PITCHIEST superlative of pitchy

PITCHILY *adv* in a very dark manner

PITCHMAN *n pl.* -MEN a salesman of small wares

PITCHOUT *n pl.* -S a type of pitch in baseball

PITCHY *adj* PITCHIER, PITCHIEST tarry

PITEOUS *adj* pitiful

PITFALL *n pl.* -S a hidden danger or difficulty

PITH *v* -ED, -ING, -S to sever the spinal cord of

PITHEAD *n pl.* -S a mine entrance

PITHLESS *adj* lacking force

PITHY *adj* PITHIER, PITHIEST concise **PITHILY** *adv*

PITIABLE *adj* pitiful **PITIABLY** *adv*

PITIED past tense of pity

PITIER *n pl.* -S one that pities

PITIES present 3d person sing. of pity

PITIFUL *adj* -FULLER, -FULLEST arousing pity

PITILESS *adj* having no pity

PITMAN *n pl.* -MEN a mine worker

PITMAN *n pl.* -S a connecting rod

PITON *n pl.* -S a metal spike used in mountain climbing

PITSAW *n pl.* -S a large saw for cutting logs

PITTANCE *n pl.* -S a small allowance of money

PITTED past tense of pit

PITTING *n pl.* -S an arrangement of cavities or depressions

PITY *v* PITIED, PITYING, PITIES to feel pity (sorrow aroused by another's misfortune)

PIU *adv* more — used as a musical direction

PIVOT *v* -ED, -ING, -S to turn on a shaft or rod

PIVOTAL *adj* critically important

PIX *n pl.* -ES pyx

PIXIE *n pl.* -S pixy **PIXIEISH** *adj*

PIXINESS *n pl.* -ES the state of being playfully mischievous

PIXY *n pl.* PIXIES a playfully mischievous fairy or elf **PIXYISH** *adj*

PIZAZZ *n pl.* -ES the quality of being exciting or attractive

PIZZA *n pl.* -S an Italian open pie

PIZZERIA *n pl.* -S a place where pizzas are made and sold

PIZZLE *n pl.* -S the penis of an animal

PLACABLE *adj* capable of being placated **PLACABLY** *adv*

PLACARD *v* -ED, -ING, -S to publicize by means of posters

PLACATE *v* -CATED, -CATING, -CATES to soothe or mollify

PLACATER *n pl.* -S one that placates

PLACE *v* PLACED, PLACING, PLACES to set in a particular position

PLACEBO *n pl.* -BOS or -BOES a substance containing no medication that is given for its psychological effect

PLACEMAN *n pl.* -MEN a political appointee to a public office

PLACENTA *n pl.* -TAS or -TAE a vascular organ in most mammals

PLACER *n pl.* -S one that places

PLACET *n pl.* -S a vote of assent

PLACID *adj* calm or peaceful **PLACIDLY** *adv*

PLACING present participle of place

PLACK *n pl.* -S a former coin of Scotland

PLACKET *n pl.* -S a slit in a garment

PLACOID *n pl.* -S a fish having platelike scales

PLAFOND	*n* pl. -S an elaborately decorated ceiling
PLAGAL	*adj* designating a medieval musical mode
PLAGE	*n* pl. -S a bright region on the sun
PLAGIARY	*n* pl. -RIES the act of passing off another's work as one's own
PLAGUE	*v* PLAGUED, PLAGUING, PLAGUES to harass or torment
PLAGUER	*n* pl. -S one that plagues
PLAGUEY	*adj* plaguy
PLAGUING	present participle of plague
PLAGUY	*adj* troublesome **PLAGUILY** *adv*
PLAICE	*n* pl. -S a European flatfish
PLAID	*n* pl. -S a woolen scarf of a checkered pattern **PLAIDED** *adj*
PLAIN	*adj* PLAINER, PLAINEST evident **PLAINLY** *adv*
PLAIN	*v* -ED, -ING, -S to complain
PLAINT	*n* pl. -S a complaint
PLAISTER	*v* -ED, -ING, -S to plaster
PLAIT	*v* -ED, -ING, -S to braid
PLAITER	*n* pl. -S one that plaits
PLAITING	*n* pl. -S something that is plaited
PLAN	*v* PLANNED, PLANNING, PLANS to formulate a plan (a method for achieving an end)
PLANAR	*adj* flat
PLANARIA	*n* pl. -S an aquatic flatworm
PLANATE	*adj* having a flat surface
PLANCH	*n* pl. -ES a plank
PLANCHE	*n* pl. -S planch
PLANCHET	*n* pl. -S a flat piece of metal for stamping into a coin
PLANE	*v* PLANED, PLANING, PLANES to make smooth or even
PLANER	*n* pl. -S one that planes
PLANET	*n* pl. -S a celestial body
PLANFORM	*n* pl. -S the contour of an object as viewed from above
PLANGENT	*adj* resounding loudly
PLANING	present participle of plane
PLANISH	*v* -ED, -ING, -ES to toughen and smooth by hammering lightly
PLANK	*v* -ED, -ING, -S to cover with planks (long, flat pieces of lumber)

PLANKING	*n* pl. -S covering made of planks
PLANKTER	*n* pl. -S any organism that is an element of plankton
PLANKTON	*n* pl. -S the minute animal and plant life of a body of water
PLANLESS	*adj* having no plan
PLANNED	past tense of plan
PLANNER	*n* pl. -S one that plans
PLANNING	*n* pl. -S the establishment of goals or policies
PLANOSOL	*n* pl. -S a type of soil
PLANT	*v* -ED, -ING, -S to place in the ground for growing
PLANTAIN	*n* pl. -S a short-stemmed herb
PLANTAR	*adj* pertaining to the sole of the foot
PLANTER	*n* pl. -S one that plants
PLANTING	*n* pl. -S an area where plants are grown
PLANULA	*n* pl. -LAE the free-swimming larva of certain organisms **PLANULAR** *adj*
PLAQUE	*n* pl. -S an ornamental plate or disk
PLASH	*v* -ED, -ING, -ES to weave together
PLASHER	*n* pl. -S one that plashes
PLASHY	*adj* PLASHIER, PLASHIEST marshy
PLASM	*n* pl. -S plasma
PLASMA	*n* pl. -S the liquid part of blood **PLASMIC** *adj*
PLASMID	*n* pl. -S a hereditary structure of a cell
PLASMIN	*n* pl. -S an enzyme
PLASMOID	*n* pl. -S a type of high energy particle
PLASMON	*n* pl. -S a determinant of inheritance believed to exist in cells
PLASTER	*v* -ED, -ING, -S to cover with plaster (a mixture of lime, sand, and water)
PLASTERY	*adj* resembling plaster
PLASTIC	*n* pl. -S any of a group of synthetic or natural moldable materials
PLASTID	*n* pl. -S a structure in plant cells
PLASTRON	*n* pl. -S a part of the shell of a turtle **PLASTRAL** *adj*

PLASTRUM   n pl. -S plastron

PLAT   v PLATTED, PLATTING, PLATS to plait

PLATAN   n pl. -S a large tree

PLATANE   n pl. -S platan

PLATE   v PLATED, PLATING, PLATES to coat with a thin layer of metal

PLATEAU   n pl. -TEAUS or -TEAUX a level stretch of elevated land

PLATEAU   v -ED, -ING, -S to reach a period or condition of stability

PLATED   past tense of plate

PLATEFUL   n pl. PLATEFULS or PLATESFUL the quantity that fills a plate (a shallow dish)

PLATELET   n pl. -S a small, flattened body

PLATEN   n pl. -S the roller of a typewriter

PLATER   n pl. -S one that plates

PLATESFUL   a pl. of plateful

PLATFORM   n pl. -S a raised floor or flat surface

PLATIER   comparative of platy

PLATIES   a pl. of platy

PLATIEST   superlative of platy

PLATINA   n pl. -S platinum

PLATING   n pl. -S a thin layer of metal

PLATINIC   adj pertaining to platinum

PLATINUM   n pl. -S a metallic element

PLATONIC   adj purely spiritual and free from sensual desire

PLATOON   v -ED, -ING, -S to alternate with another player at the same position

PLATTED   past tense of plat

PLATTER   n pl. -S a large, shallow dish

PLATTING   present participle of plat

PLATY   adj PLATIER, PLATIEST split into thin, flat pieces

PLATY   n pl. PLATYS or PLATIES a small tropical fish

PLATYPUS   n pl. -PUSES or -PI an aquatic mammal

PLAUDIT   n pl. -S an expression of praise

PLAUSIVE   adj expressing praise

PLAY   v -ED, -ING, -S to engage in amusement or sport PLAYABLE adj

PLAYA   n pl. -S the bottom of a desert basin

PLAYACT   v -ED, -ING, -S to take part in a theatrical performance

PLAYBACK   n pl. -S the act of replaying a newly made recording

PLAYBILL   n pl. -S a program for a theatrical performance

PLAYBOOK   n pl. -S a book containing one or more literary works for the stage

PLAYBOY   n pl. -BOYS a man devoted to pleasurable activities

PLAYDAY   n pl. -DAYS a holiday

PLAYDOWN   n pl. -S a playoff

PLAYER   n pl. -S one that plays

PLAYFUL   adj frolicsome

PLAYGIRL   n pl. -S a female playboy

PLAYGOER   n pl. -S one who attends the theater

PLAYLAND   n pl. -S a recreational area

PLAYLESS   adj lacking playfulness

PLAYLET   n pl. -S a short theatrical performance

PLAYLIKE   adj resembling a theatrical performance

PLAYMATE   n pl. -S a companion in play

PLAYOFF   n pl. -S a series of games played to determine a championship

PLAYPEN   n pl. -S an enclosure in which a young child may play

PLAYROOM   n pl. -S a recreation room

PLAYSUIT   n pl. -S a sports outfit for women and children

PLAYTIME   n pl. -S a time for play or amusement

PLAYWEAR   n pl. -S clothing worn for leisure activities

PLAZA   n pl. -S a public square

PLEA   n pl. -S an entreaty

PLEACH   v -ED, -ING, -ES to weave together

PLEAD   v PLEADED or PLED, PLEADING, PLEADS to ask for earnestly

PLEADER   n pl. -S one that pleads

PLEADING   n pl. -S an allegation in a legal action

PLEASANT   adj -ANTER, -ANTEST pleasing

PLEASE   v PLEASED, PLEASING, PLEASES to give enjoyment or satisfaction to

PLEASER *n* pl. -S one that pleases

PLEASURE *v* -SURED, -SURING, -SURES to please

PLEAT *v* -ED, -ING, -S to fold in an even manner

PLEATER *n* pl. -S one that pleats

PLEB *n* pl. -S a commoner

PLEBE *n* pl. -S a freshman at a military or naval academy

PLEBEIAN *n* pl. -S a commoner

PLECTRON *n* pl. -TRONS or -TRA plectrum

PLECTRUM *n* pl. -TRUMS or -TRA an implement used to pluck the strings of a stringed instrument

PLED a past tense of plead

PLEDGE *v* PLEDGED, PLEDGING, PLEDGES to give as security for something borrowed

PLEDGEE *n* pl. -S one to whom something is pledged

PLEDGEOR *n* pl. -S pledger

PLEDGER *n* pl. -S one that pledges something

PLEDGET *n* pl. -S a pad of absorbent cotton

PLEDGING present participle of pledge

PLEDGOR *n* pl. -S pledger

PLEIAD *n* pl. -S or -ES a group of seven illustrious persons

PLENA a pl. of plenum

PLENARY *adj* complete in every respect

PLENISH *v* -ED, -ING, -ES to fill up

PLENISM *n* pl. -S the doctrine that space is fully occupied by matter

PLENIST *n* pl. -S an advocate of plenism

PLENTY *n* pl. -TIES a sufficient or abundant amount

PLENUM *n* pl. -NUMS or -NA space considered as fully occupied by matter

PLEONASM *n* pl. -S the use of needless words

PLEOPOD *n* pl. -S an appendage of crustaceans

PLESSOR *n* pl. -S plexor

PLETHORA *n* pl. -S an excess

PLEURA *n* pl. -RAE or -RAS a membrane that envelops the lungs **PLEURAL** *adj*

PLEURISY *n* pl. -SIES inflammation of the pleura

PLEURON *n* pl. -RA a part of a thoracic segment of an insect

PLEUSTON *n* pl. -S aquatic vegetation

PLEXOR *n* pl. -S a small, hammer-like medical instrument

PLEXUS *n* pl. -ES an interlacing of parts

PLIABLE *adj* easily bent **PLIABLY** *adv*

PLIANCY *n* pl. -CIES the quality of being pliant

PLIANT *adj* easily bent **PLIANTLY** *adv*

PLICA *n* pl. -CAE a fold of skin **PLICAL** *adj*

PLICATE *adj* pleated

PLICATED *adj* plicate

PLIE *n* pl. -S a movement in ballet

PLIED past tense of ply

PLIER *n* pl. -S one that plies

PLIES present 3d person sing. of ply

PLIGHT *v* -ED, -ING, -S to promise or bind by a solemn pledge

PLIGHTER *n* pl. -S one that plights

PLIMSOL *n* pl. -S plimsoll

PLIMSOLE *n* pl. -S plimsoll

PLIMSOLL *n* pl. -S a rubber-soled cloth shoe

PLINK *v* -ED, -ING, -S to shoot at random targets

PLINKER *n* pl. -S one that plinks

PLINTH *n* pl. -S a stone or slab upon which a column or pedestal rests

PLISKIE *n* pl. -S a practical joke

PLISKY *n* pl. -KIES pliskie

PLISSE *n* pl. -S a puckered texture of cloth

PLOD *v* PLODDED, PLODDING, PLODS to walk heavily

PLODDER *n* pl. -S one that plods

PLOIDY *n* pl. -DIES the extent of repetition of the basic number of chromosomes

PLONK *v* -ED, -ING, -S to plunk

PLOP *v* PLOPPED, PLOPPING, PLOPS to drop or fall heavily

PLOSION *n* pl. -S a release of breath after the articulation of certain consonants

PLOSIVE *n* pl. -S a sound produced by plosion

PLOT   v PLOTTED, PLOTTING, PLOTS to plan secretly

PLOTLESS   adj planless

PLOTTAGE   n pl. -S an area of land

PLOTTED   past tense of plot

PLOTTER   n pl. -S one that plots

PLOTTIER   comparative of plotty

PLOTTIES   pl. of plotty

PLOTTING   present participle of plot

PLOTTY   adj -TIER, -TIEST full of intrigue, as a novel

PLOTTY   n pl. -TIES a hot, spiced beverage

PLOUGH   v -ED, -ING, -S to plow

PLOUGHER   n pl. -S one that ploughs

PLOVER   n pl. -S a shore bird

PLOW   v -ED, -ING, -S to turn up land with a plow (a farm implement) PLOWABLE adj

PLOWBACK   n pl. -S a reinvestment of profits in a business

PLOWBOY   n pl. -BOYS a boy who leads a plow team

PLOWER   n pl. -S one that plows

PLOWHEAD   n pl. -S the clevis of a plow

PLOWLAND   n pl. -S land suitable for cultivation

PLOWMAN   n pl. -MEN a man who plows

PLOY   v -ED, -ING, -S to move from a line into column

PLUCK   v -ED, -ING, -S to pull out or off

PLUCKER   n pl. -S one that plucks

PLUCKY   adj PLUCKIER, PLUCKIEST brave and spirited PLUCKILY adv

PLUG   v PLUGGED, PLUGGING, PLUGS to seal or close with a plug (a piece of material used to fill a hole)

PLUGGER   n pl. -S one that plugs

PLUGLESS   adj having no plug

PLUGUGLY   n pl. -LIES a hoodlum

PLUM   n pl. -S a fleshy fruit

PLUMAGE   n pl. -S the feathers of a bird PLUMAGED adj

PLUMATE   adj resembling a feather

PLUMB   v -ED, -ING, -S to determine the depth of

PLUMBAGO   n pl. -GOS graphite

PLUMBER   n pl. -S one who installs and repairs plumbing

PLUMBERY   n pl. -ERIES the work of a plumber

PLUMBIC   adj containing lead

PLUMBING   n pl. -S the pipe system of a building

PLUMBISM   n pl. -S lead poisoning

PLUMBOUS   adj containing lead

PLUMBUM   n pl. -S lead

PLUME   v PLUMED, PLUMING, PLUMES to cover with feathers

PLUMELET   n pl. -S a small feather

PLUMIER   comparative of plumy

PLUMIEST   superlative of plumy

PLUMING   present participle of plume

PLUMIPED   n pl. -S a bird having feathered feet

PLUMLIKE   adj resembling a plum

PLUMMET   v -ED, -ING, -S to drop straight down

PLUMMY   adj -MIER, -MIEST full of plums

PLUMOSE   adj having feathers

PLUMP   adj PLUMPER, PLUMPEST well-rounded and full in form

PLUMP   v -ED, -ING, -S to make plump

PLUMPEN   v -ED, -ING, -S to plump

PLUMPER   n pl. -S a heavy fall

PLUMPISH   adj somewhat plump

PLUMPLY   adv in a plump way

PLUMULE   n pl. -S the primary bud of a plant embryo PLUMULAR adj

PLUMY   adj PLUMIER, PLUMIEST covered with feathers

PLUNDER   v -ED, -ING, -S to rob of goods by force

PLUNGE   v PLUNGED, PLUNGING, PLUNGES to throw or thrust suddenly or forcibly into something

PLUNGER   n pl. -S one that plunges

PLUNK   v -ED, -ING, -S to fall or drop heavily

PLUNKER   n pl. -S one that plunks

PLURAL   n pl. -S a word that expresses more than one

PLURALLY   adv in a manner or form that expresses more than one

PLUS   n pl. PLUSES or PLUSSES an additional quantity

PLUSH	*adj* PLUSHER, PLUSHEST luxurious **PLUSHLY** *adv*
PLUSH	*n* pl. -ES a fabric with a long pile
PLUSHY	*adj* PLUSHIER, PLUSHIEST luxurious **PLUSHILY** *adv*
PLUSSAGE	*n* pl. -S an amount over and above another
PLUSSES	a pl. of plus
PLUTON	*n* pl. -S a formation of igneous rock **PLUTONIC** *adj*
PLUVIAL	*n* pl. -S a prolonged period of wet climate
PLUVIOSE	*adj* pluvious
PLUVIOUS	*adj* pertaining to rain
PLY	*v* PLIED, PLYING, PLIES to supply with or offer repeatedly **PLYINGLY** *adv*
PLYER	*n* pl. -S plier
PLYWOOD	*n* pl. -S a building material
PNEUMA	*n* pl. -S the soul or spirit
POACEOUS	*adj* pertaining to plants of the grass family
POACH	*v* -ED, -ING, -ES to trespass for the purpose of taking game or fish
POACHER	*n* pl. -S one that poaches
POACHY	*adj* POACHIER, POACHIEST swampy
POCHARD	*n* pl. -S a sea duck
POCK	*v* -ED, -ING, -S to mark with pocks (pustules caused by an eruptive disease)
POCKET	*v* -ED, -ING, -S to place in a pouch sewed into a garment
POCKETER	*n* pl. -S one that pockets
POCKMARK	*v* -ED, -ING, -S to mark with scars caused by an eruptive disease
POCKY	*adj* POCKIER, POCKIEST covered with pocks **POCKILY** *adv*
POCO	*adv* a little — used as a musical direction
POCOSIN	*n* pl. -S an upland swamp
POD	*v* PODDED, PODDING, PODS to produce seed vessels
PODAGRA	*n* pl. -S gout in the foot **PODAGRAL, PODAGRIC** *adj*
PODESTA	*n* pl. -S an Italian magistrate
PODGY	*adj* PODGIER, PODGIEST pudgy **PODGILY** *adv*

PODIA	a pl. of podium
PODIATRY	*n* pl. -TRIES the study and treatment of the human foot
PODITE	*n* pl. -S a limb segment of an arthropod **PODITIC** *adj*
PODIUM	*n* pl. -DIUMS or -DIA a small platform
PODOMERE	*n* pl. -S a podite
PODSOL	*n* pl. -S podzol **PODSOLIC** *adj*
PODZOL	*n* pl. -S an infertile soil **PODZOLIC** *adj*
POECHORE	*n* pl. -S a semiarid region
POEM	*n* pl. -S a composition in verse
POESY	*n* pl. -ESIES poetry
POET	*n* pl. -S one who writes poems
POETESS	*n* pl. -ES a female poet
POETIC	*adj* pertaining to poetry
POETICAL	*adj* poetic
POETICS	*n/pl* poetic theory or practice
POETISE	*v* -ISED, -ISING, -ISES to poetize
POETISER	*n* pl. -S poetizer
POETIZE	*v* -IZED, -IZING, -IZES to write poetry
POETIZER	*n* pl. -S one that poetizes
POETLESS	*adj* lacking a poet
POETLIKE	*adj* resembling a poet
POETRY	*n* pl. -RIES literary work in metrical form
POGEY	*n* pl. -GEYS any form of government relief
POGIES	pl. of pogy
POGONIA	*n* pl. -S a small orchid
POGONIP	*n* pl. -S a dense fog of suspended ice particles
POGROM	*v* -ED, -ING, -S to massacre systematically
POGY	*n* pl. -GIES a marine fish
POH	*interj* — used to express disgust
POI	*n* pl. -S a Hawaiian food
POIGNANT	*adj* emotionally distressing
POILU	*n* pl. -S a French soldier
POIND	*v* -ED, -ING, -S to seize and sell the property of to satisfy a debt
POINT	*v* -ED, -ING, -S to indicate direction with the finger
POINTE	*n* pl. -S a ballet position
POINTER	*n* pl. -S one that points

POINTMAN *n* pl. -MEN a certain player in hockey

POINTY *adj* POINTIER, POINTIEST coming to a sharp, tapering end

POISE *v* POISED, POISING, POISES to hold in a state of equilibrium

POISER *n* pl. -S one that poises

POISON *v* -ED, -ING, -S to administer a harmful substance to

POISONER *n* pl. -S one that poisons

POITREL *n* pl. -S peytral

POKE *v* POKED, POKING, POKES to push or prod

POKER *n* pl. -S one that pokes

POKEROOT *n* pl. -S pokeweed

POKEWEED *n* pl. -S a perennial herb

POKEY *n* pl. -KEYS poky

POKIER comparative of poky

POKIES pl. of poky

POKIEST superlative of poky

POKILY *adv* in a poky manner

POKINESS *n* pl. -ES the state of being poky

POKING present participle of poke

POKY *n* pl. POKIES a jail

POKY *adj* POKIER, POKIEST slow

POL *n* pl. -S a politician

POLAR *n* pl. -S a straight line related to a point

POLARISE *v* -ISED, -ISING, -ISES to polarize

POLARITY *n* pl. -TIES the possession of two opposite qualities

POLARIZE *v* -IZED, -IZING, -IZES to give polarity to

POLARON *n* pl. -S a type of electron

POLDER *n* pl. -S a tract of low land reclaimed from a body of water

POLE *v* POLED, POLING, POLES to propel with a pole (a long, thin piece of wood or metal)

POLEAX *v* -ED, -ING, -ES to strike with an axlike weapon

POLEAXE *v* -AXED, -AXING, -AXES to poleax

POLECAT *n* pl. -S a carnivorous mammal

POLED past tense of pole

POLEIS pl. of polis

POLELESS *adj* having no pole

POLEMIC *n* pl. -S a controversial argument

POLEMIST *n* pl. -S one who engages in polemics

POLEMIZE *v* -MIZED, -MIZING, -MIZES to engage in polemics

POLENTA *n* pl. -S a thick mush of cornmeal

POLER *n* pl. -S one that poles

POLESTAR *n* pl. -S a guiding principle

POLEWARD *adv* in the direction of either extremity of the earth's axis

POLEYN *n* pl. -S a protective piece of leather for the knee

POLICE *v* -LICED, -LICING, -LICES to make clean or orderly

POLICY *n* pl. -CIES an action or a procedure considered with reference to prudence or expediency

POLING present participle of pole

POLIO *n* pl. -LIOS an infectious virus disease

POLIS *n* pl. -LEIS an ancient Greek city-state

POLISH *v* -ED, -ING, -ES to make smooth and lustrous by rubbing

POLISHER *n* pl. -S one that polishes

POLITE *adj* -LITER, -LITEST showing consideration for others POLITELY *adv*

POLITIC *adj* shrewd

POLITICK *v* -ED, -ING, -S to engage in politics

POLITICO *n* pl. -COS or -COES one who politicks

POLITICS *n/pl* the art or science of government

POLITY *n* pl. -TIES a form or system of government

POLKA *v* -ED, -ING, -S to perform a lively dance

POLL *v* -ED, -ING, -S to question for the purpose of surveying public opinion

POLLACK *n* pl. -S a marine food fish

POLLARD *v* -ED, -ING, -S to cut the top branches of a tree back to the trunk

POLLEE *n* pl. -S one who is polled

POLLEN   *v* -ED, -ING, -S to convey pollen (the fertilizing element in a seed plant) to

POLLER   *n* pl. -S one that polls

POLLEX   *n* pl. -LICES the innermost digit of the forelimb **POLLICAL** *adj*

POLLINIA   *n/pl* masses of pollen grains

POLLINIC   *adj* pertaining to pollen

POLLIST   *n* pl. -S a poller

POLLIWOG   *n* pl. -S a tadpole

POLLOCK   *n* pl. -S pollack

POLLSTER   *n* pl. -S a poller

POLLUTE   *v* -LUTED, -LUTING, -LUTES to make unclean or impure

POLLUTER   *n* pl. -S one that pollutes

POLLYWOG   *n* pl. -S polliwog

POLO   *n* pl. -LOS a game played on horseback

POLOIST   *n* pl. -S a polo player

POLONIUM   *n* pl. -S a radioactive element

POLTROON   *n* pl. -S a base coward

POLY   *n* pl. POLYS a type of white blood cell

POLYBRID   *n* pl. -S a type of hybrid plant

POLYCOT   *n* pl. -S a type of plant

POLYENE   *n* pl. -S a chemical compound **POLYENIC** *adj*

POLYGALA   *n* pl. -S a flowering plant

POLYGAMY   *n* pl. -MIES the condition of having more than one spouse at the same time

POLYGENE   *n* pl. -ES a type of gene

POLYGLOT   *n* pl. -S one that speaks or writes several languages

POLYGON   *n* pl. -S a closed plane figure bounded by straight lines

POLYGONY   *n* pl. -NIES an herb

POLYGYNY   *n* pl. -NIES the condition of having more than one wife at the same time

POLYMATH   *n* pl. -S a person of great and varied learning

POLYMER   *n* pl. -S a complex chemical compound

POLYNYA   *n* pl. -S an area of open water surrounded by sea ice

POLYP   *n* pl. -S an invertebrate

POLYPARY   *n* pl. -ARIES the common supporting structure of a polyp colony

POLYPI   a pl. of polypus

POLYPIDE   *n* pl. -S a polyp

POLYPNEA   *n* pl. -S rapid breathing

POLYPOD   *n* pl. -S a many-footed organism

POLYPODY   *n* pl. -DIES a fern

POLYPOID   *adj* resembling a polyp

POLYPORE   *n* pl. -S a type of fungus

POLYPOUS   *adj* pertaining to a polyp

POLYPUS   *n* pl. -PI or -PUSES a growth protruding from the mucous lining of an organ

POLYSEMY   *n* pl. -MIES diversity of meanings

POLYSOME   *n* pl. -S a cluster of protein particles

POLYTENE   *adj* having chromosomes of a certain type

POLYTENY   *n* pl. -NIES the state of being polytene

POLYTYPE   *n* pl. -S a crystal structure

POLYURIA   *n* pl. -S excessive urination **POLYURIC** *adj*

POLYZOAN   *n* pl. -S a bryozoan

POLYZOIC   *adj* composed of many zooids

POMACE   *n* pl. -S the pulpy residue of crushed fruits

POMADE   *v* -MADED, -MADING, -MADES to apply a perfumed hair dressing to

POMANDER   *n* pl. -S a mixture of aromatic substances

POMATUM   *n* pl. -S a perfumed hair dressing

POME   *n* pl. -S a fleshy fruit with a core

POMELO   *n* pl. -LOS a grapefruit

POMMEE   *adj* having arms with knoblike ends — used of a heraldic cross

POMMEL   *v* -MELED, -MELING, -MELS or -MELLED, -MELLING, -MELS to strike with the fists

POMOLOGY   *n* pl. -GIES the study of fruits

POMP   *n* pl. -S stately or splendid display

POMPANO   *n* pl. -NOS a marine food fish

POMPOM   *n* pl. -S an antiaircraft cannon

POMPON   *n* pl. -S an ornamental tuft or ball

POMPOUS   *adj* marked by exaggerated self-importance

PONCE	*n* pl. -S a man who solicits clients for a prostitute
PONCHO	*n* pl. -CHOS a type of cloak
POND	*n* pl. -S a body of water smaller than a lake
PONDER	*v* -ED, -ING, -S to consider something deeply and thoroughly
PONDERER	*n* pl. -S one that ponders
PONDWEED	*n* pl. -S an aquatic plant
PONE	*n* pl. -S a corn bread
PONENT	*adj* affirmative
PONGEE	*n* pl. -S a type of silk
PONGID	*n* pl. -S an anthropoid ape
PONIARD	*v* -ED, -ING, -S to stab with a dagger
PONIED	past tense of pony
PONIES	present 3d person sing. of pony
PONS	*n* pl. PONTES a band of nerve fibers in the brain
PONTIFEX	*n* pl. -FICES an ancient Roman priest
PONTIFF	*n* pl. -S a pope or bishop
PONTIFIC	*adj* pertaining to a pope or bishop
PONTIFICES	pl. of pontifex
PONTIL	*n* pl. -S a punty
PONTINE	*adj* pertaining to bridges
PONTON	*n* pl. -S pontoon
PONTOON	*n* pl. -S a flat-bottomed boat
PONY	*v* -NIED, -NYING, -NIES to prepare lessons with the aid of a literal translation
PONYTAIL	*n* pl. -S a hairstyle
POOCH	*n* pl. -ES a dog
POOD	*n* pl. -S a Russian unit of weight
POODLE	*n* pl. -S a heavy-coated dog
POOH	*v* -ED, -ING, -S to express contempt for
POOL	*v* -ED, -ING, -S to combine in a common fund
POOLHALL	*n* pl. -S a poolroom
POOLROOM	*n* pl. -S an establishment for the playing of billiards
POON	*n* pl. -S an East Indian tree
POOP	*v* -ED, -ING, -S to tire out

POOR	*adj* POORER, POOREST lacking the means of support
POORI	*n* pl. -S a light, flat wheat cake
POORISH	*adj* somewhat poor
POORLY	*adv* in a poor manner
POORNESS	*n* pl. -ES the state of being poor
POORTITH	*n* pl. -S poverty
POP	*v* POPPED, POPPING, POPS to make a sharp, explosive sound
POPCORN	*n* pl. -S a variety of corn
POPE	*n* pl. -S the head of the Roman Catholic Church **POPELESS, POPELIKE** *adj*
POPEDOM	*n* pl. -S the office of a pope
POPERY	*n* pl. -ERIES Roman Catholicism — usually used disparagingly
POPEYED	*adj* having bulging eyes
POPGUN	*n* pl. -S a toy gun
POPINJAY	*n* pl. -JAYS a vain person
POPISH	*adj* pertaining to the Roman Catholic Church — usually used disparagingly **POPISHLY** *adv*
POPLAR	*n* pl. -S a fast-growing tree
POPLIN	*n* pl. -S a durable fabric
POPLITIC	*adj* pertaining to the part of the leg behind the knee
POPOVER	*n* pl. -S a very light egg muffin
POPPA	*n* pl. -S papa
POPPED	past tense of pop
POPPER	*n* pl. -S one that pops
POPPET	*n* pl. -S a mechanical valve
POPPIED	*adj* covered with poppies
POPPIES	pl. of poppy
POPPING	present participle of pop
POPPLE	*v* -PLED, -PLING, -PLES to move in a bubbling or rippling manner
POPPY	*n* pl. -PIES a flowering plant
POPULACE	*n* pl. -S the common people
POPULAR	*adj* liked by many people
POPULATE	*v* -LATED, -LATING, -LATES to inhabit
POPULISM	*n* pl. -S populists' doctrines
POPULIST	*n* pl. -S a member of a party which represents the common people
POPULOUS	*adj* containing many inhabitants

PORCH   *n* pl. -ES a covered structure at the entrance to a building

PORCINE   *adj* pertaining to swine

PORE   *v* PORED, PORING, PORES to gaze intently

PORGY   *n* pl. -GIES a marine food fish

PORISM   *n* pl. -S a type of mathematical proposition

PORK   *n* pl. -S the flesh of swine used as food

PORKER   *n* pl. -S a pig

PORKIER   comparative of porky

PORKIES   pl. of porky

PORKIEST   superlative of porky

PORKPIE   *n* pl. -S a man's hat

PORKWOOD   *n* pl. -S a tropical tree

PORKY   *adj* PORKIER, PORKIEST resembling pork

PORKY   *n* pl. -KIES a porcupine

PORN   *n* pl. -S pornography

PORNO   *n* pl. -NOS pornography

POROSE   *adj* porous

POROSITY   *n* pl. -TIES the state of being porous

POROUS   *adj* having minute openings **POROUSLY** *adv*

PORPHYRY   *n* pl. -RIES an igneous rock

PORPOISE   *n* pl. -S an aquatic mammal

PORRECT   *adj* extended forward

PORRIDGE   *n* pl. -S a soft food

PORT   *v* -ED, -ING, -S to shift to the left side

PORTABLE   *n* pl. -S something that can be carried

PORTABLY   *adv* so as to be capable of being carried

PORTAGE   *v* -TAGED, -TAGING, -TAGES to transport from one navigable waterway to another

PORTAL   *n* pl. -S a door, gate, or entrance **PORTALED** *adj*

PORTANCE   *n* pl. -S demeanor

PORTEND   *v* -ED, -ING, -S to serve as an omen of

PORTENT   *n* pl. -S an omen

PORTER   *n* pl. -S a person employed to carry luggage

PORTHOLE   *n* pl. -S a small window in a ship's side

PORTICO   *n* pl. -COS or -COES a type of porch

PORTIERE   *n* pl. -S a curtain for a doorway

PORTION   *v* -ED, -ING, -S to divide into shares for distribution

PORTLESS   *adj* having no place for ships to load or unload

PORTLY   *adj* -LIER, -LIEST rather heavy or fat

PORTRAIT   *n* pl. -S a likeness of a person

PORTRAY   *v* -ED, -ING, -S to represent pictorially

PORTRESS   *n* pl. -ES a female doorkeeper

POSADA   *n* pl. -S an inn

POSE   *v* POSED, POSING, POSES to assume a fixed position

POSER   *n* pl. -S one that poses

POSEUR   *n* pl. -S an affected or insincere person

POSH   *adj* POSHER, POSHEST stylish or elegant

POSIES   pl. of posy

POSING   present participle of pose

POSINGLY   *adv* in a posing manner

POSIT   *v* -ED, -ING, -S to place

POSITION   *v* -ED, -ING, -S to put in a particular location

POSITIVE   *adj* -TIVER, -TIVEST certain

POSITIVE   *n* pl. -S a quantity greater than zero

POSITRON   *n* pl. -S an atomic particle

POSOLOGY   *n* pl. -GIES a branch of medicine that deals with drug dosages

POSSE   *n* pl. -S a body of men summoned to aid a peace officer

POSSESS   *v* -ED, -ING, -ES to have as property

POSSET   *n* pl. -S a hot, spiced drink

POSSIBLE   *adj* -BLER, -BLEST capable of happening or proving true **POSSIBLY** *adv*

POSSUM   *n* pl. -S an opossum

POST   *v* -ED, -ING, -S to affix in a public place

POSTAGE   *n* pl. -S the charge for mailing an item

POSTAL   *n* pl. -S a postcard

POSTALLY   *adv* in a manner pertaining to the mails

POSTANAL — *adj* situated behind the anus
POSTBAG — *n* pl. -S a mailbag
POSTBOX — *n* pl. -ES a mailbox
POSTBOY — *n* pl. -BOYS a boy who carries mail
POSTCARD — *n* pl. -S a card for use in the mail
POSTCAVA — *n* pl. -VAE a vein in higher vertebrates
POSTDATE — *v* -DATED, -DATING, -DATES to give a date later than the actual date to
POSTEEN — *n* pl. -S an Afghan outer garment
POSTER — *n* pl. -S a printed or written notice for posting
POSTERN — *n* pl. -S a rear door or date
POSTFACE — *n* pl. -S a brief note placed at the end of a publication
POSTFIX — *v* -ED, -ING, -ES to affix at the end of something
POSTFORM — *v* -ED, -ING, -S to shape subsequently
POSTHOLE — *n* pl. -S a hole dug to secure a fence post
POSTICHE — *n* pl. -S an imitation
POSTIN — *n* pl. -S posteen
POSTING — *n* pl. -S the act of transferring to a ledger
POSTIQUE — *n* pl. -S postiche
POSTLUDE — *n* pl. -S a closing musical piece
POSTMAN — *n* pl. -MEN a mailman
POSTMARK — *v* -ED, -ING, -S to stamp mail with an official mark
POSTORAL — *adj* situated behind the mouth
POSTPAID — *adv* with the postage prepaid
POSTPONE — *v* -PONED, -PONING, -PONES to put off to a future time
POSTURAL — *adj* pertaining to the position of the body
POSTURE — *v* -TURED, -TURING, -TURES to assume a particular position
POSTURER — *n* pl. -S one that postures
POSTWAR — *adj* occurring or existing after a war
POSY — *n* pl. -SIES a flower or bouquet
POT — *v* POTTED, POTTING, POTS to put in a pot (a round, fairly deep container)
POTABLE — *n* pl. -S a liquid suitable for drinking

POTAGE — *n* pl. -S a thick soup
POTAMIC — *adj* pertaining to rivers
POTASH — *n* pl. -ES an alkaline compound
POTASSIC — *adj* pertaining to potassium (a metallic element)
POTATION — *n* pl. -S the act of drinking
POTATO — *n* pl. -TOES the edible tuber of a cultivated plant
POTATORY — *adj* pertaining to drinking
POTBELLY — *n* pl. -LIES a protruding abdominal region
POTBOIL — *v* -ED, -ING, -S to produce a literary or artistic work of poor quality
POTBOY — *n* pl. -BOYS a boy who serves customers in a tavern
POTEEN — *n* pl. -S Irish whiskey that is distilled unlawfully
POTENCE — *n* pl. -S potency
POTENCY — *n* pl. -CIES the quality of being potent
POTENT — *adj* powerful POTENTLY *adv*
POTFUL — *n* pl. -S as much as a pot can hold
POTHEAD — *n* pl. -S one who smokes marijuana
POTHEEN — *n* pl. -S poteen
POTHER — *v* -ED, -ING, -S to trouble
POTHERB — *n* pl. -S any herb used as a food or seasoning
POTHOLE — *n* pl. -S a deep hole in a road POTHOLED *adj*
POTHOOK — *n* pl. -S a hook for lifting or hanging pots
POTHOUSE — *n* pl. -S a tavern
POTICHE — *n* pl. -S a type of vase
POTION — *n* pl. -S a magical or medicinal drink
POTLACH — *n* pl. -ES a ceremonial feast
POTLACHE — *n* pl. -S potlach
POTLATCH — *v* -ED, -ING, -ES to hold a ceremonial feast for
POTLIKE — *adj* resembling a pot
POTLUCK — *n* pl. -S food which is incidentally available
POTMAN — *n* pl. -MEN a man who serves customers in a tavern
POTPIE — *n* pl. -S a deep-dish pie containing meat and vegetables
POTSHARD — *n* pl. -S potsherd

POTSHERD   *n* pl. -S a fragment of broken pottery

POTSHOT   *v* -SHOT, -SHOTTING, -SHOTS to shoot randomly at

POTSIE   *n* pl. -S potsy

POTSTONE   *n* pl. -S a variety of steatite

POTSY   *n* pl. -SIES a children's game

POTTAGE   *n* pl. -S a thick soup

POTTED   past tense of pot

POTTEEN   *n* pl. -S poteen

POTTER   *v* -ED, -ING, -S to putter

POTTERER   *n* pl. -S one that potters

POTTERY   *n* pl. -TERIES ware molded from clay and hardened by heat

POTTIER   comparative of potty

POTTIES   pl. of potty

POTTIEST   superlative of potty

POTTING   present participle of pot

POTTLE   *n* pl. -S a drinking vessel

POTTO   *n* pl. -TOS a lemur of tropical Africa

POTTY   *adj* -TIER, -TIEST of little importance

POTTY   *n* pl. -TIES a small toilet seat

POUCH   *v* -ED, -ING, -ES to put in a pouch (a small, flexible receptacle)

POUCHY   *adj* POUCHIER, POUCHIEST resembling a pouch

POUF   *n* pl. -S a loose roll of hair POUFED *adj*

POUFF   *n* pl. -S pouf POUFFED *adj*

POUFFE   *n* pl. -S pouf

POULARD   *n* pl. -S a spayed hen

POULARDE   *n* pl. -S poulard

POULT   *n* pl. -S a young domestic fowl

POULTICE   *v* -TICED, -TICING, -TICES to apply a healing substance to

POULTRY   *n* pl. -TRIES domestic fowls kept for eggs or meat

POUNCE   *v* POUNCED, POUNCING, POUNCES to make a sudden assault or approach

POUNCER   *n* pl. -S one that pounces

POUND   *v* -ED, -ING, -S to strike heavily and repeatedly

POUNDAGE   *n* pl. -S the act of impounding

POUNDAL   *n* pl. -S a unit of force

POUNDER   *n* pl. -S one that pounds

POUR   *v* -ED, -ING, -S to cause to flow POURABLE *adj*

POURER   *n* pl. -S one that pours

POUSSIE   *n* pl. -S pussy

POUT   *v* -ED, -ING, -S to protrude the lips in ill humor

POUTER   *n* pl. -S one that pouts

POUTFUL   *adj* pouty

POUTY   *adj* POUTIER, POUTIEST tending to pout

POVERTY   *n* pl. -TIES the state of being poor

POW   *n* pl. -S an explosive sound

POWDER   *v* -ED, -ING, -S to reduce to powder (matter in a finely divided state)

POWDERER   *n* pl. -S one that powders

POWDERY   *adj* resembling powder

POWER   *v* -ED, -ING, -S to provide with means of propulsion

POWERFUL   *adj* possessing great force

POWTER   *n* pl. -S a domestic pigeon

POWWOW   *v* -ED, -ING, -S to hold a conference

POX   *v* -ED, -ING, -ES to infect with syphilis

POXVIRUS   *n* pl. -ES a type of virus

POYOU   *n* pl. -S an armadillo of Argentina

POZZOLAN   *n* pl. -S a finely divided material used to make cement

PRAAM   *n* pl. -S pram

PRACTIC   *adj* practical

PRACTICE   *v* -TICED, -TICING, -TICES to perform often so as to acquire skill

PRACTISE   *v* -TISED, -TISING, -TISES to practice

PRAECIPE   *n* pl. -S a legal writ

PRAEDIAL   *adj* pertaining to land

PRAEFECT   *n* pl. -S prefect

PRAELECT   *v* -ED, -ING, -S to prelect

PRAETOR   *n* pl. -S an ancient Roman magistrate

PRAHU   *n* pl. -S prau

PRAIRIE   *n* pl. -S a tract of grassland

PRAISE   *v* PRAISED, PRAISING, PRAISES to express approval or admiration of

PRAISER   *n* pl. -S one that praises

PRALINE *n pl.* -S a confection made of nuts cooked in sugar

PRAM *n pl.* -S a flat-bottomed boat

PRANCE *v* PRANCED, PRANCING, PRANCES to spring forward on the hind legs

PRANCER *n pl.* -S one that prances

PRANDIAL *adj* pertaining to a meal

PRANG *v* -ED, -ING, -S to cause to crash

PRANK *v* -ED, -ING, -S to adorn gaudily

PRANKISH *adj* mischievous

PRAO *n pl.* PRAOS prau

PRASE *n pl.* -S a mineral

PRAT *n pl.* -S the buttocks

PRATE *v* PRATED, PRATING, PRATES to chatter

PRATER *n pl.* -S one that prates

PRATFALL *n pl.* -S a fall on the buttocks

PRATING present participle of prate

PRATIQUE *n pl.* -S clearance given a ship by the health authority of a port

PRATTLE *v* -TLED, -TLING, -TLES to babble

PRATTLER *n pl.* -S one that prattles

PRAU *n pl.* -S a swift Malaysian sailing vessel

PRAWN *v* -ED, -ING, -S to fish for prawns (edible shellfishes)

PRAWNER *n pl.* -S one that prawns

PRAXIS *n pl.* PRAXISES or PRAXES practical use of a branch of learning

PRAY *v* -ED, -ING, -S to address prayers to

PRAYER *n pl.* -S a devout petition to a deity

PREACH *v* -ED, -ING, -ES to advocate or recommend urgently

PREACHER *n pl.* -S one that preaches

PREACHY *adj* PREACHIER, PREACHIEST tending to preach

PREACT *v* -ED, -ING, -S to act beforehand

PREADAPT *v* -ED, -ING, -S to adapt beforehand

PREADMIT *v* -MITTED, -MITTING, -MITS to admit beforehand

PREADOPT *v* -ED, -ING, -S to adopt beforehand

PREADULT *adj* preceding adulthood

PREAGED *adj* previously aged

PREALLOT *v* -LOTTED, -LOTTING, -LOTS to allot beforehand

PREAMBLE *n pl.* -S an introductory statement

PREAMP *n pl.* -S an amplifier

PREANAL *adj* situated in front of the anus

PREARM *v* -ED, -ING, -S to arm beforehand

PREAVER *v* -VERRED, -VERRING, -VERS to aver or assert beforehand

PREAXIAL *adj* situated in front of an axis

PREBASAL *adj* situated in front of a base

PREBEND *n pl.* -S a clergyman's stipend

PREBILL *v* -ED, -ING, -S to bill beforehand

PREBIND *v* -BOUND, -BINDING, -BINDS to bind in durable materials for library use

PREBLESS *v* -ED, -ING, -ES to bless beforehand

PREBOIL *v* -ED, -ING, -S to boil beforehand

PREBOUND past tense of prebind

PRECAST *v* -CAST, -CASTING, -CASTS to cast and finish before placing in position

PRECAVA *n pl.* -VAE a vein in higher vertebrates **PRECAVAL** *adj*

PRECEDE *v* -CEDED, -CEDING, -CEDES to go before

PRECENT *v* -ED, -ING, -S to lead a church choir in singing

PRECEPT *n pl.* -S a rule of conduct

PRECESS *v* -ED, -ING, -ES to rotate with a complex motion

PRECHECK *v* -ED, -ING, -S to check beforehand

PRECHILL *v* -ED, -ING, -S to chill beforehand

PRECIEUX *adj* excessively refined

PRECINCT *n pl.* -S a subdivision of a city or town

PRECIOUS *n pl.* -ES a darling

PRECIPE *n pl.* -S praecipe

PRECIS *v* -ED, -ING, -ES to make a concise summary of

PRECISE *adj* -CISER, -CISEST sharply and clearly defined or stated

PRECITED	adj previously cited	**PREFOCUS**	v -CUSED, -CUSING, -CUSES or -CUSSED, -CUSSING, -CUSSES to focus beforehand
PRECLEAN	v -ED, -ING, -S to clean beforehand		
PRECLUDE	v -CLUDED, -CLUDING, -CLUDES to make impossible by previous action	**PREFORM**	v -ED, -ING, -S to form beforehand
		PREFRANK	v -ED, -ING, -S to frank beforehand
PRECOOK	v -ED, -ING, -S to cook beforehand	**PREGAME**	adj preceding a game
PRECOOL	v -ED, -ING, -S to cool beforehand	**PREGNANT**	adj carrying a developing fetus in the uterus
PRECURE	v -CURED, -CURING, -CURES to cure beforehand	**PREHEAT**	v -ED, -ING, -S to heat beforehand
PREDATE	v -DATED, -DATING, -DATES to date before the actual or a specified time	**PREHUMAN**	n pl. -S a prototype of man
		PREJUDGE	v -JUDGED, -JUDGING, -JUDGES to judge beforehand
PREDATOR	n pl. -S one that plunders	**PRELACY**	n pl. -CIES the office of a prelate
PREDAWN	n pl. -S the time just before dawn		
		PRELATE	n pl. -S a high-ranking clergyman **PRELATIC** adj
PREDIAL	adj praedial		
PREDICT	v -ED, -ING, -S to tell of or about in advance	**PRELECT**	v -ED, -ING, -S to lecture
		PRELEGAL	adj occurring before the commencement of studies in law
PREDUSK	n pl. -S the time just before dusk		
		PRELIM	n pl. -S a minor match preceding the main event
PREE	v PREED, PREEING, PREES to test by tasting		
		PRELIMIT	v -ED, -ING, -S to limit beforehand
PREELECT	v -ED, -ING, -S to elect or choose beforehand	**PRELUDE**	v -LUDED, -LUDING, -LUDES to play a musical introduction
PREEMIE	n pl. -S an infant born prematurely		
		PRELUDER	n pl. -S one that preludes
PREEMPT	v -ED, -ING, -S to acquire by prior right	**PREMAN**	n pl. -MEN a hypothetical ancestor of man
PREEN	v -ED, -ING, -S to smooth or clean with the beak or tongue	**PREMED**	n pl. -S a student preparing for the study of medicine
PREENACT	v -ED, -ING, -S to enact beforehand	**PREMEDIC**	n pl. -S a premed
PREENER	n pl. -S one that preens	**PREMEN**	pl. of preman
PREEXIST	v -ED, -ING, -S to exist before	**PREMIE**	n pl. -S preemie
PREFAB	v -FABBED, -FABBING, FABS to construct beforehand	**PREMIER**	n pl. -S a prime minister
		PREMIERE	v -MIERED, -MIERING, -MIERES to present publicly for the first time
PREFACE	v -ACED, -ACING, -ACES to provide with an introductory statement		
		PREMISE	v -MISED, -MISING, -MISES to state in advance
PREFACER	n pl. -S one that prefaces		
PREFECT	n pl. -S an ancient Roman official	**PREMISS**	n pl. -ES a proposition in logic
		PREMIUM	n pl. -S an additional payment
PREFER	v -FERRED, -FERRING, -FERS to hold in higher regard or esteem	**PREMIX**	v -ED, -ING, -ES to mix before use
		PREMOLAR	n pl. -S a tooth
PREFIX	v -ED, -ING, -ES to add as a prefix (a form affixed to the beginning of a root word)	**PREMORSE**	adj ending abruptly, as if bitten off
		PREMUNE	adj resistant to a disease
PREFIXAL	adj pertaining to or being a prefix	**PRENAME**	n pl. -S a forename

PRENATAL *adj* prior to birth

PRENOMEN *n* pl. -MENS or -MINA the first name of an ancient Roman

PRENTICE *v* -TICED, -TICING, -TICES to place with an employer for instruction in a trade

PREP *v* PREPPED, PREPPING, PREPS to attend a preparatory school

PREPACK *v* -ED, -ING, -S to package before retail distribution

PREPAID past tense of prepay

PREPARE *v* -PARED, -PARING, -PARES to put in proper condition or readiness

PREPARER *n* pl. -S one that prepares

PREPAY *v* -PAID, -PAYING, -PAYS to pay in advance

PREPENSE *adj* planned in advance

PREPLACE *v* -PLACED, -PLACING, -PLACES to place beforehand

PREPLAN *v* -PLANNED, -PLANNING, -PLANS to plan in advance

PREPLANT *adj* occurring before planting

PREPPED past tense of prep

PREPPIE *n* pl. -S one who preps

PREPPING present participle of prep

PREPRINT *v* -ED, -ING, -S to print in advance

PREPUCE *n* pl. -S a fold of skin covering the penis

PREPUNCH *v* -ED, -ING, -ES to punch in advance

PRERENAL *adj* situated in front of the kidney

PRESA *n* pl. -SE a musical symbol

PRESAGE *v* -SAGED, -SAGING, -SAGES to foretell

PRESAGER *n* pl. -S one that presages

PRESCIND *v* -ED, -ING, -S to consider separately

PRESCORE *v* -SCORED, -SCORING, -SCORES to record the sound of before filming

PRESE pl. of presa

PRESELL *v* -SOLD, -SELLING, -SELLS to promote a product not yet being sold to the public

PRESENCE *n* pl. -S close proximity

PRESENT *v* -ED, -ING, -S to bring into the presence of someone

PRESERVE *v* -SERVED, -SERVING, -SERVES to keep free from harm or danger

PRESET *v* -SET, -SETTING, -SETS to set beforehand

PRESHAPE *v* -SHAPED, -SHAPING, -SHAPES to shape beforehand

PRESHOW *v* -SHOWED, -SHOWN, -SHOWING, -SHOWS to show beforehand

PRESIDE *v* -SIDED, -SIDING, -SIDES to occupy the position of authority

PRESIDER *n* pl. -S one that presides

PRESIDIA *n/pl* Soviet executive committees

PRESIDIO *n* pl. -DIOS a Spanish fort

PRESIFT *v* -ED, -ING, -S to sift beforehand

PRESOAK *v* -ED, -ING, -S to soak beforehand

PRESOLD past tense of presell

PRESS *v* -ED, -ING, -ES to act upon with steady force

PRESSER *n* pl. -S one that presses

PRESSMAN *n* pl. -MEN a printing press operator

PRESSOR *adj* causing an increase in blood pressure

PRESSRUN *n* pl. -S a continuous operation of a printing press

PRESSURE *v* -SURED, -SURING, -SURES to apply force to

PREST *n* pl. -S a loan

PRESTAMP *v* -ED, -ING, -S to stamp beforehand

PRESTER *n* pl. -S a priest

PRESTIGE *n* pl. -S distinction or reputation in the eyes of people

PRESTO *n* pl. -TOS a musical passage played in rapid tempo

PRESUME *v* -SUMED, -SUMING, -SUMES to take for granted

PRESUMER *n* pl. -S one that presumes

PRETASTE *v* -TASTED, -TASTING, -TASTES to taste beforehand

PRETAX *adj* existing before provision for taxes

PRETEEN *n* pl. -S a child under the age of thirteen

PRETENCE *n* pl. -S pretense

PRETEND *v* -ED, -ING, -S to assume or display a false appearance of

PRETENSE	*n* pl. -S the act of pretending
PRETERIT	*n* pl. -S a past tense in grammar
PRETEST	*v* -ED, -ING, -S to give a preliminary test to
PRETEXT	*v* -ED, -ING, -S to allege as an excuse
PRETOR	*n* pl. -S praetor
PRETREAT	*v* -ED, -ING, -S to treat beforehand
PRETTIED	past tense of pretty
PRETTIER	comparative of pretty
PRETTIES	present 3d person sing. of pretty
PRETTIEST	superlative of pretty
PRETTIFY	*v* -FIED, -FYING, -FIES to make pretty
PRETTY	*v* -TIED, -TYING, -TIES to make pretty
PRETTY	*adj* -TIER, -TIEST pleasing to the eye **PRETTILY** *adv*
PRETZEL	*n* pl. -S a glazed, salted cracker
PREUNION	*n* pl. -S a union beforehand
PREUNITE	*v* -UNITED, -UNITING, -UNITES to unite beforehand
PREVAIL	*v* -ED, -ING, -S to triumph
PREVENT	*v* -ED, -ING, -S to keep from happening
PREVIEW	*v* -ED, -ING, -S to view or exhibit in advance
PREVIOUS	*adj* coming or occurring before in time or order
PREVISE	*v* -VISED, -VISING, -VISES to foresee
PREVISOR	*n* pl. -S one that previses
PREVUE	*v* -VUED, -VUING, -VUES to preview
PREWAR	*adj* occurring or existing before a war
PREWARM	*v* -ED, -ING, -S to warm beforehand
PREWARN	*v* -ED, -ING, -S to warn in advance
PREWASH	*v* -ED, -ING, -ES to wash beforehand
PREWRAP	*v* -WRAPPED, -WRAPPING, -WRAPS to wrap beforehand
PREX	*n* pl. -ES prexy
PREXY	*n* pl. PREXIES a president
PREY	*v* -ED, -ING, -S to seize and devour animals for food

PREYER	*n* pl. -S one that preys
PRIAPEAN	*adj* priapic
PRIAPI	a pl. of priapus
PRIAPIC	*adj* phallic
PRIAPISM	*n* pl. -S a persistent erection of the penis
PRIAPUS	*n* pl. -PUSES or -PI a representation of the phallus
PRICE	*v* PRICED, PRICING, PRICES to set a value on
PRICER	*n* pl. -S one that prices
PRICEY	*adj* PRICIER, PRICIEST expensive
PRICIER	comparative of pricey and pricy
PRICIEST	superlative of pricey and pricy
PRICING	present participle of price
PRICK	*v* -ED, -ING, -S to puncture slightly
PRICKER	*n* pl. -S one that pricks
PRICKET	*n* pl. -S a spike for holding a candle upright
PRICKIER	comparative of pricky
PRICKIEST	superlative of pricky
PRICKLE	*v* -LED, -LING, -LES to prick
PRICKLY	*adj* -LIER, -LIEST having many sharp points
PRICKY	*adj* PRICKIER, PRICKIEST prickly
PRICY	*adj* PRICIER, PRICIEST pricey
PRIDE	*v* PRIDED, PRIDING, PRIDES to feel pride (a feeling of self-esteem)
PRIDEFUL	*adj* full of pride
PRIED	past tense of pry
PRIEDIEU	*n* pl. -DIEUS or -DIEUX a piece of furniture for kneeling on during prayer
PRIER	*n* pl. -S one that pries
PRIES	present 3d person sing. of pry
PRIEST	*v* -ED, -ING, -S to ordain as a priest (one authorized to perform religious rites)
PRIESTLY	*adj* -LIER, -LIEST characteristic of or befitting a priest
PRIG	*v* PRIGGED, PRIGGING, PRIGS to steal
PRIGGERY	*n* pl. -GERIES priggism
PRIGGISH	*adj* marked by priggism
PRIGGISM	*n* pl. -S prim adherence to convention

PRILL v -ED, -ING, -S to convert into pellets

PRIM adj PRIMMER, PRIMMEST formally precise or proper

PRIM v PRIMMED, PRIMMING, PRIMS to give a prim expression to

PRIMA n pl. -S

PRIMACY n pl. -CIES the state of being first

PRIMAGE n pl. -S an amount paid as an addition to freight charges

PRIMAL adj being at the beginning or foundation

PRIMARY n pl. -RIES a preliminary election

PRIMATE n pl. -S any of an advanced order of mammals **PRIMATAL** adj

PRIME v PRIMED, PRIMING, PRIMES to make ready

PRIMELY adv excellently

PRIMER n pl. -S a book that covers the basics of a subject

PRIMERO n pl. -ROS a card game

PRIMEVAL adj pertaining to the earliest ages

PRIMI a pl. of primo

PRIMINE n pl. -S the outer covering of an ovule

PRIMING n pl. -S the act of one that primes

PRIMLY adv in a prim manner

PRIMMED past tense of prim

PRIMMER comparative of prim

PRIMMEST superlative of prim

PRIMMING present participle of prim

PRIMNESS n pl. -ES the state of being prim

PRIMO n pl. -MOS or -MI the main part in a musical piece

PRIMP v -ED, -ING, -S to dress or adorn carefully

PRIMROSE n pl. -S a perennial herb

PRIMSIE adj prim

PRIMULA n pl. -S primrose

PRIMUS n pl. -ES the head bishop of Scotland

PRINCE n pl. -S a non-reigning male member of a royal family

PRINCELY adj -LIER, -LIEST of or befitting a prince

PRINCESS n pl. -ES a non-reigning female member of a royal family

PRINCIPE n pl. -PI a prince

PRINCOCK n pl. -S a coxcomb

PRINCOX n pl. -ES princock

PRINK v -ED, -ING, -S to dress or adorn in a showy manner

PRINKER n pl. -S one that prinks

PRINT v -ED, -ING, -S to produce by pressed type on a surface

PRINTER n pl. -S one that prints

PRINTERY n pl. -ERIES a place where printing is done

PRINTING n pl. -S a reproduction from a printing surface

PRINTOUT n pl. -S the printed output of a computer

PRIOR n pl. -S an officer in a monastery

PRIORATE n pl. -S the office of a prior

PRIORESS n pl. -ES a nun corresponding in rank to a prior

PRIORIES pl. of priory

PRIORITY n pl. -TIES precedence established by importance

PRIORLY adv previously

PRIORY n pl. -RIES a religious house

PRISE v PRISED, PRISING, PRISES to raise or force with a lever

PRISERE n pl. -S a succession of vegetational stages

PRISM n pl. -S a solid which disperses light into a spectrum

PRISMOID n pl. -S a geometric solid

PRISON v -ED, -ING, -S to imprison

PRISONER n pl. -S one that is imprisoned

PRISS n pl. -ES a prissy

PRISSY adj -SIER, -SIEST excessively or affectedly proper **PRISSILY** adv

PRISSY n pl. -SiES one who is prissy

PRISTANE n pl. -S a chemical compound

PRISTINE adj pertaining to the earliest time or state

PRITHEE interj — used to express a wish or request

PRIVACY n pl. -CIES the state of being private

PRIVATE adj -VATER, -VATEST secluded from the sight, presence, or intrusion of others

PRIVATE	n pl. -S a soldier of lower rank
PRIVET	n pl. -S an ornamental shrub
PRIVIER	comparative of privy
PRIVIES	pl. of privy
PRIVITY	n pl. -TIES private knowledge
PRIVY	adj PRIVIER, PRIVIEST private **PRIVILY** adv
PRIVY	n pl. PRIVIES an outhouse
PRIZE	v PRIZED, PRIZING, PRIZES to value highly
PRIZER	n pl. -S one who vies for a reward
PRO	n pl. PROS an argument or vote in favor of something
PROA	n pl. -S prau
PROBABLE	adj likely to occur or prove true **PROBABLY** adv
PROBAND	n pl. -S one whose reactions or responses are studied
PROBANG	n pl. -S a surgical rod
PROBATE	v -BATED, -BATING, -BATES to establish the validity of
PROBE	v PROBED, PROBING, PROBES to investigate or examine thoroughly
PROBER	n pl. -S one that probes
PROBIT	n pl. -S a unit of statistical probability
PROBITY	n pl. -TIES complete and confirmed integrity
PROBLEM	n pl. -S a perplexing question or situation
PROCAINE	n pl. -S a compound used as a local anesthetic
PROCARP	n pl. -S a female sexual organ in certain algae
PROCEED	v -ED, -ING, -S to go forward or onward
PROCESS	v -ED, -ING, -ES to treat or prepare by a special method
PROCHAIN	adj prochein
PROCHEIN	adj nearest in time, relation, or degree
PROCLAIM	v -ED, -ING, -S to make known publicly or officially
PROCTOR	v -ED, -ING, -S to supervise
PROCURAL	n pl. -S the act of procuring
PROCURE	v -CURED, -CURING, -CURES to obtain by effort
PROCURER	n pl. -S one that procures

PROD	v PRODDED, PRODDING, PRODS to jab with something pointed
PRODDER	n pl. -S one that prods
PRODIGAL	n pl. -S one who spends lavishly and foolishly
PRODIGY	n pl. -GIES a child having exceptional talent or ability
PRODROME	n pl. -DROMES or -DROMATA a sign of impending disease
PRODUCE	v -DUCED, -DUCING, -DUCES to bring into existence
PRODUCER	n pl. -S one that produces
PRODUCT	n pl. -S something produced by labor or effort
PROEM	n pl. -S an introductory statement **PROEMIAL** adj
PROETTE	n pl. -S a female professional athlete
PROF	n pl. -S a professor
PROFANE	v -FANED, -FANING, -FANES to treat with irreverence or abuse
PROFANER	n pl. -S one that profanes
PROFESS	v -ED, -ING, -ES to affirm openly
PROFFER	v -ED, -ING, -S to present for acceptance
PROFILE	v -FILED, -FILING, -FILES to draw an outline of
PROFILER	n pl. -S one that profiles
PROFIT	v -ED, -ING, -S to gain an advantage or benefit
PROFITER	n pl. -S one that profits
PROFOUND	adj -FOUNDER, -FOUNDEST intellectually deep and penetrating
PROFOUND	n pl. -S something that is very deep
PROFUSE	adj pouring forth generously
PROG	v PROGGED, PROGGING, PROGS to prowl about for food or plunder
PROGENY	n pl. -NIES a descendant or offspring
PROGGER	n pl. -S one that progs
PROGGING	present participle of prog
PROGNOSE	v -NOSED, -NOSING, -NOSES to forecast the probable course of a disease
PROGRADE	adj pertaining to the orbital motion of a body

PROGRAM *v* -GRAMED, -GRAMING, -GRAMS or -GRAMMED, -GRAMMING, -GRAMS to arrange in a plan of proceedings

PROGRESS *v* -ED, -ING, -ES to move forward or onward

PROHIBIT *v* -ED, -ING, -S to forbid by authority

PROJECT *v* -ED, -ING, -S to extend outward

PROJET *n pl.* -S a plan or outline

PROLABOR *adj* favoring organized labor

PROLAMIN *n pl.* -S a simple protein

PROLAN *n pl.* -S a sex hormone

PROLAPSE *v* -LAPSED, -LAPSING, -LAPSES to fall or slip out of place

PROLATE *adj* extended lengthwise

PROLE *n pl.* -S a member of the working class

PROLEG *n pl.* -S an abdominal leg of certain insect larvae

PROLIFIC *adj* producing abundantly

PROLINE *n pl.* -S an amino acid

PROLIX *adj* tediously long and wordy **PROLIXLY** *adv*

PROLOG *v* -ED, -ING, -S to prologue

PROLOGUE *v* -LOGUED, -LOGUING, -LOGUES to preface

PROLONG *v* -ED, -ING, -S to lengthen in duration

PROLONGE *n pl.* -S a rope used for pulling a gun carriage

PROM *n pl.* -S a formal dance

PROMISE *v* -ISED, -ISING, -ISES to make a declaration of assurance

PROMISEE *n pl.* -S one who is promised something

PROMISER *n pl.* -S promisor

PROMISING present participle of promise

PROMISOR *n pl.* -S one that promises

PROMOTE *v* -MOTED, -MOTING, -MOTES to contribute to the progress of

PROMOTER *n pl.* -S one that promotes

PROMPT *adj* PROMPTER, PROMPTEST quick to act or respond

PROMPT *v* -ED, -ING, -S to induce to action

PROMPTER *n pl.* -S one that prompts

PROMPTLY *adv* in a prompt manner

PROMULGE *v* -MULGED, -MULGING, -MULGES to proclaim

PRONATE *v* -NATED, -NATING, -NATES to turn the palm downward or backward

PRONATOR *n pl.* -S or -ES a forearm or forelimb muscle

PRONE *adj* lying with the front or face downward **PRONELY** *adv*

PRONG *v* -ED, -ING, -S to pierce with a pointed projection

PRONOTUM *n pl.* -NOTA a hard outer plate of an insect

PRONOUN *n pl.* -S a word that may be used in place of a noun

PRONTO *adv* quickly

PROOF *v* -ED, -ING, -S to examine for errors

PROOFER *n pl.* -S one that proofs

PROP *v* PROPPED, PROPPING, PROPS to keep from falling

PROPANE *n pl.* -S a flammable gas

PROPEL *v* -PELLED, -PELLING, -PELS to cause to move forward or onward

PROPEND *v* -ED, -ING, -S to have a tendency toward

PROPENE *n pl.* -S a flammable gas

PROPENOL *n pl.* -S a flammable liquid

PROPENSE *adj* tending toward

PROPENYL *adj* pertaining to a certain chemical group

PROPER *adj* -ERER, -EREST suitable **PROPERLY** *adv*

PROPER *n pl.* -S a portion of the Mass

PROPERTY *n pl.* -TIES something owned

PROPHAGE *n pl.* -S a form of virus

PROPHASE *n pl.* -S the first stage in mitosis

PROPHECY *n pl.* -CIES a prediction

PROPHESY *v* -SIED, -SYING, -SIES to predict

PROPHET *n pl.* -S one who predicts

PROPINE *v* -PINED, -PINING, -PINES to offer as a gift

PROPJET *n pl.* -S a type of airplane

PROPMAN *n pl.* -MEN a man in charge of stage properties

PROPOLIS *n pl.* -LISES a resinous substance used as a cement by bees

PROPONE   *v* -PONED, -PONING, -PONES to propose

PROPOSAL   *n* pl. -S something that is proposed

PROPOSE   *v* -POSED, -POSING, -POSES to put forward for consideration or acceptance

PROPOSER   *n* pl. -S one that proposes

PROPOUND   *v* -ED, -ING, -S to propose

PROPPED   past tense of prop

PROPPING   present participle of prop

PROPYL   *n* pl. -S a univalent radical **PROPYLIC** *adj*

PROPYLON   *n* pl. -LA an entrance to a temple

PRORATE   *v* -RATED, -RATING, -RATES to divide proportionately

PROROGUE   *v* -ROGUED, -ROGUING, -ROGUES to discontinue a session of

PROSAIC   *adj* pertaining to prose

PROSAISM   *n* pl. -S a prosaic style

PROSAIST   *n* pl. -S a writer of prose

PROSE   *v* PROSED, PROSING, PROSES to write prose (writing without metrical structure)

PROSECT   *v* -ED, -ING, -S to dissect

PROSER   *n* pl. -S a prosaist

PROSIER   comparative of prosy

PROSIEST   superlative of prosy

PROSILY   *adv* in a prosy manner

PROSING   present participle of prose

PROSIT   *interj* — used as a drinking toast

PROSO   *n* pl. -SOS millet

PROSODY   *n* pl. -DIES the study of poetical forms **PROSODIC** *adj*

PROSOMA   *n* pl. -S the front region of the body of an invertebrate **PROSOMAL** *adj*

PROSPECT   *v* -ED, -ING, -S to explore for mineral deposits

PROSPER   *v* -ED, -ING, -S to be successful or fortunate

PROST   *interj* prosit

PROSTATE   *n* pl. -S a gland in male mammals

PROSTYLE   *n* pl. -S a building having a row of columns across the front only

PROSY   *adj* PROSIER, PROSIEST prosaic

PROTAMIN   *n* pl. -S a simple protein

PROTASIS   *n* pl. -ASES the introductory part of a classical drama **PROTATIC** *adj*

PROTEA   *n* pl. -S an evergreen shrub

PROTEAN   *adj* readily taking on different shapes or forms

PROTEASE   *n* pl. -S an enzyme

PROTECT   *v* -ED, -ING, -S to keep from harm, attack, or injury

PROTEGE   *n* pl. -S one whose career is promoted by an influential person

PROTEGEE   *n* pl. -S a female protege

PROTEI   pl. of proteus

PROTEID   *n* pl. -S protein

PROTEIDE   *n* pl. -S proteid

PROTEIN   *n* pl. -S a nitrogenous organic compound

PROTEND   *v* -ED, -ING, -S to extend

PROTEOSE   *n* pl. -S a water-soluble protein

PROTEST   *v* -ED, -ING, -S to express strong objection

PROTEUS   *n* pl. -TEI any of a genus of aerobic bacteria

PROTIST   *n* pl. -S any of a group of unicellular organisms

PROTIUM   *n* pl. -S an isotope of hydrogen

PROTOCOL   *v* -COLED, -COLING, -COLS or -COLLED, -COLLING, -COLS to form a preliminary draft of an official document

PROTON   *n* pl. -S an atomic particle **PROTONIC** *adj*

PROTOPOD   *n* pl. -S a part of a crustacean appendage

PROTOXID   *n* pl. -S an oxide

PROTOZOA   *n/pl* unicellular microscopic organisms

PROTRACT   *v* -ED, -ING, -S to prolong

PROTRUDE   *v* -TRUDED, -TRUDING, -TRUDES to extend beyond the main portion

PROTYL   *n* pl. -S protyle

PROTYLE   *n* pl. -S a hypothetical substance from which all the elements are supposedly derived

PROUD   *adj* PROUDER, PROUDEST having or displaying pride **PROUDLY** *adv*

PROUDFUL   *adj* prideful

PROUNION	*adj* favoring labor unions
PROVE	*v* PROVED, PROVEN, PROVING, PROVES to establish the truth or validity of **PROVABLE** *adj* **PROVABLY** *adv*
PROVENLY	*adv* without doubt
PROVER	*n* pl. -S one that proves
PROVERB	*v* -ED, -ING, -S to make a byword of
PROVIDE	*v* -VIDED, -VIDING, -VIDES to supply
PROVIDER	*n* pl. -S one that provides
PROVINCE	*n* pl. -S an administrative division of a country
PROVING	present participle of prove
PROVIRUS	*n* pl. -ES a form of virus **PROVIRAL** *adj*
PROVISO	*n* pl. -SOS or -SOES a clause in a document introducing a condition or restriction
PROVOKE	*v* -VOKED, -VOKING, -VOKES to incite to anger or resentment
PROVOKER	*n* pl. -S one that provokes
PROVOST	*n* pl. -S a high-ranking university official
PROW	*n* pl. -S the forward part of a ship
PROW	*adj* PROWER, PROWEST brave
PROWAR	*adj* favoring war
PROWESS	*n* pl. -ES exceptional ability
PROWL	*v* -ED, -ING, -S to move about stealthily
PROWLER	*n* pl. -S one that prowls
PROXEMIC	*adj* pertaining to a branch of environmental study
PROXIES	pl. of proxy
PROXIMAL	*adj* located near the point of origin
PROXIMO	*adj* of or occurring in the following month
PROXY	*n* pl. PROXIES a person authorized to act for another
PRUDE	*n* pl. -S a prudish person
PRUDENCE	*n* pl. -S the quality of being prudent
PRUDENT	*adj* having, showing, or exercising good judgment
PRUDERY	*n* pl. -ERIES excessive regard for propriety, modesty, or morality
PRUDISH	*adj* marked by prudery

PRUINOSE	*adj* having a powdery covering
PRUNE	*v* PRUNED, PRUNING, PRUNES to cut off branches or parts from **PRUNABLE** *adj*
PRUNELLA	*n* pl. -S a strong woolen fabric
PRUNELLE	*n* pl. -S a plum-flavored liqueur
PRUNELLO	*n* pl. -LOS prunella
PRUNER	*n* pl. -S one that prunes
PRUNING	present participle of prune
PRURIENT	*adj* having lustful thoughts or desires
PRURIGO	*n* pl. -GOS a skin disease
PRURITUS	*n* pl. -ES intense itching **PRURITIC** *adj*
PRUSSIC	*adj* pertaining to a type of acid
PRUTA	*n* pl. PRUTOT prutah
PRUTAH	*n* pl. PRUTOTH a monetary unit of Israel
PRY	*v* PRIED, PRYING, PRIES to inquire impertinently into private matters **PRYINGLY** *adv*
PRYER	*n* pl. -S prier
PRYTHEE	*interj* prithee
PSALM	*v* -ED, -ING, -S to praise in psalms (sacred songs)
PSALMIC	*adj* of or pertaining to a psalm
PSALMIST	*n* pl. -S a writer of psalms
PSALMODY	*n* pl. -DIES the use of psalms in worship
PSALTER	*n* pl. -S a book of psalms
PSALTERY	*n* pl. -TERIES an ancient stringed musical instrument
PSALTRY	*n* pl. -TRIES psaltery
PSAMMITE	*n* pl. -S a fine-grained rock
PSCHENT	*n* pl. -S a crown worn by ancient Egyptian kings
PSEPHITE	*n* pl. -S a rock composed of small pebbles
PSEUDO	*adj* false or counterfeit
PSHAW	*v* -ED, -ING, -S to utter an expression of disapproval
PSI	*n* pl. -S a Greek letter
PSILOSIS	*n* pl. -LOSES a tropical disease **PSILOTIC** *adj*
PSOAS	*n* pl. PSOAI or PSOAE a muscle of the loin
PSOCID	*n* pl. -S a minute winged insect
PSORALEA	*n* pl. -S a plant of the bean family

PSST *interj* — used to attract someone's attention

PSYCH *v* -ED, -ING, -S to put into the proper frame of mind

PSYCHE *n* pl. -S the mental structure of a person

PSYCHIC *n* pl. -S one sensitive to extrasensory phenomena

PSYCHO *n* pl. -CHOS a mentally unstable person

PSYLLA *n* pl. -S any of various plant lice

PSYLLID *n* pl. -S psylla

PTERIN *n* pl. -S a chemical compound

PTEROPOD *n* pl. -S a type of mollusk

PTERYLA *n* pl. -LAE a feathered area on the skin of a bird

PTISAN *n* pl. -S a tea of herbs or barley

PTOMAIN *n* pl. -S ptomaine

PTOMAINE *n* pl. -S a compound produced by the decomposition of protein

PTOSIS *n* pl. PTOSES a drooping of the upper eyelid **PTOTIC** *adj*

PTYALIN *n* pl. -S a salivary enzyme

PTYALISM *n* pl. -S an excessive flow of saliva

PUB *n* pl. -S a tavern

PUBERTY *n* pl. -TIES a period of sexual maturation **PUBERAL, PUBERTAL** *adj*

PUBES *n* pl. PUBES the lower part of the abdomen

PUBIC *adj* pertaining to the pubes or pubis

PUBIS *n* pl. PUBES the forward portion of either of the hipbones

PUBLIC *n* pl. -S the community or the people as a whole

PUBLICAN *n* pl. -S one who owns or manages a pub

PUBLICLY *adv* by the public

PUBLISH *v* -ED, -ING, -ES to print and issue to the public

PUCCOON *n* pl. -S an herb that yields a red dye

PUCE *n* pl. -S a dark red color

PUCK *n* pl. -S a rubber disk used in ice hockey

PUCKA *adj* pukka

PUCKER *v* -ED, -ING, -S to gather into small wrinkles or folds

PUCKERER *n* pl. -S one that puckers

PUCKERY *adj* -ERIER, -ERIEST having a tendency to pucker

PUCKISH *adj* impish

PUD *n* pl. -S pudding

PUDDING *n* pl. -S a thick, soft dessert

PUDDLE *v* -DLED, -DLING, -DLES to strew with puddles (small pools of water)

PUDDLER *n* pl. -S one who subjects iron to puddling

PUDDLING *n* pl. -S the process of converting pig iron to wrought iron

PUDDLY *adj* -DLIER, -DLIEST full of puddles

PUDENCY *n* pl. -CIES modesty

PUDENDUM *n* pl. -DA the external genital organs of a woman **PUDENDAL** *adj*

PUDGY *adj* PUDGIER, PUDGIEST short and fat **PUDGILY** *adv*

PUDIC *adj* pertaining to the pudendum

PUEBLO *n* pl. -LOS a communal dwelling of certain Indian tribes

PUERILE *adj* childish

PUFF *v* -ED, -ING, -S to blow in short gusts

PUFFBALL *n* pl. -S any of various globular fungi

PUFFER *n* pl. -S one that puffs

PUFFERY *n* pl. -ERIES excessive public praise

PUFFIN *n* pl. -S a sea bird

PUFFY *adj* -FIER, -FIEST swollen **PUFFILY** *adv*

PUG *v* PUGGED, PUGGING, PUGS to fill in with clay or mortar

PUGAREE *n* pl. -S pugree

PUGGAREE *n* pl. -S pugree

PUGGED past tense of pug

PUGGIER comparative of puggy

PUGGIEST superlative of puggy

PUGGING present participle of pug

PUGGISH *adj* somewhat stubby

PUGGREE *n* pl. -S pugree

PUGGRY *n* pl. -GRIES pugree

PUGGY *adj* -GIER, -GIEST puggish

PUGH *interj* — used to express disgust

PUGILISM *n pl.* -S the art or practice of fighting with the fists

PUGILIST *n pl.* -S one who fights with his fists

PUGMARK *n pl.* -S a footprint

PUGREE *n pl.* -S a cloth band wrapped around a hat

PUISNE *n pl.* -S one of lesser rank

PUISSANT *adj* powerful

PUKE *v* PUKED, PUKING, PUKES to vomit

PUKKA *adj* genuine

PUL *n pl.* PULS or PULI a coin of Afghanistan

PULE *v* PULED, PULING, PULES to whine

PULER *n pl.* -S one that pules

PULI *n pl.* -LIK or -LIS a long-haired sheepdog

PULICENE *adj* pertaining to fleas

PULICIDE *n pl.* -S an agent used for destroying fleas

PULIK a *pl.* of puli

PULING *n pl.* -S a plaintive cry

PULINGLY *adv* in a whining manner

PULL *v* -ED, -ING, -S to exert force in order to cause motion toward the force

PULLBACK *n pl.* -S a restraint or drawback

PULLER *n pl.* -S one that pulls

PULLET *n pl.* -S a young hen

PULLEY *n pl.* -LEYS a device used for lifting weight

PULLMAN *n pl.* -S a railroad sleeping car

PULLOUT *n pl.* -S a withdrawal

PULLOVER *n pl.* -S a garment that is put on by being drawn over the head

PULMONIC *adj* pertaining to the lungs

PULMOTOR *n pl.* -S a respiratory device

PULP *v* -ED, -ING, -S to reduce to pulp (a soft, moist mass of matter)

PULPAL *adj* pertaining to pulp **PULPALLY** *adv*

PULPER *n pl.* -S one that pulps

PULPIER comparative of pulpy

PULPIEST superlative of pulpy

PULPILY *adv* in a pulpy manner

PULPIT *n pl.* -S a platform in a church **PULPITAL** *adj*

PULPLESS *adj* having no pulp

PULPOUS *adj* pulpy

PULPWOOD *n pl.* -S soft wood used in making paper

PULPY *adj* PULPIER, PULPIEST resembling pulp

PULQUE *n pl.* -S a fermented Mexican beverage

PULSANT *adj* pulsating

PULSAR *n pl.* -S a celestial source of radio waves

PULSATE *v* -SATED, -SATING, -SATES to expand and contract rhythmically

PULSATOR *n pl.* -S something that pulsates

PULSE *v* PULSED, PULSING, PULSES to pulsate

PULSEJET *n pl.* -S a type of engine

PULSER *n pl.* -S a device that causes pulsations

PULSING present participle of pulse

PULSION *n pl.* -S propulsion

PULSOJET *n pl.* -S pulsejet

PULVILLI *n/pl* pads between the claws of an insect's foot

PULVINUS *n pl.* -NI a swelling at the base of a leaf **PULVINAR** *adj*

PUMA *n pl.* -S a cougar

PUMELO *n pl.* -LOS pomelo

PUMICE *v* -ICED, -ICING, -ICES to polish with a porous volcanic rock

PUMICER *n pl.* -S one that pumices

PUMICITE *n pl.* -S a porous volcanic rock

PUMMEL *v* -MELED, -MELING, -MELS or -MELLED, -MELLING, -MELS to pommel

PUMP *v* -ED, -ING, -S to cause to flow by means of a pump (a device for moving fluids)

PUMPER *n pl.* -S one that pumps

PUMPKIN *n pl.* -S a large, edible fruit

PUMPLESS *adj* lacking a pump

PUMPLIKE *adj* resembling a pump

PUN *v* PUNNED, PUNNING, PUNS to make a pun (a play on words)

PUNA *n pl.* -S a cold, arid plateau

PUNCH *v* -ED, -ING, -ES to perforate with a type of tool

PUNCHEON *n pl.* -S a vertical supporting timber

PUNCHER *n* pl. -S one that punches

PUNCHY *adj* PUNCHIER, PUNCHIEST dazed

PUNCTATE *adj* covered with dots

PUNCTUAL *adj* being on time

PUNCTURE *v* -TURED, -TURING, -TURES to pierce with a pointed object

PUNDIT *n* pl. -S a Hindu scholar **PUNDITIC** *adj*

PUNDITRY *n* pl. -RIES the learning of pundits

PUNG *n* pl. -S a box-shaped sleigh

PUNGENCY *n* pl. -CIES the state of being pungent

PUNGENT *adj* sharply affecting the organs of taste or smell

PUNIER comparative of puny

PUNIEST superlative of puny

PUNILY *adv* in a puny manner

PUNINESS *n* pl. -ES the state of being puny

PUNISH *v* -ED, -ING, -ES to impose a penalty on in requital for wrongdoing

PUNISHER *n* pl. -S one that punishes

PUNITION *n* pl. -S the act of punishing; punishment

PUNITIVE *adj* inflicting punishment

PUNITORY *adj* punitive

PUNK *n* pl. -S dry, decayed wood used as tinder

PUNK *adj* PUNKER, PUNKEST of inferior quality

PUNKA *n* pl. -S a ceiling fan used in India

PUNKAH *n* pl. -S punka

PUNKEY *n* pl. -KEYS punkie

PUNKIE *n* pl. -S a biting gnat

PUNKIN *n* pl. -S pumpkin

PUNKY *adj* PUNKIER, PUNKIEST resembling punk

PUNNED past tense of pun

PUNNER *n* pl. -S a punster

PUNNING present participle of pun

PUNNY *adj* -NIER, -NIEST being or involving a pun

PUNSTER *n* pl. -S one who is given to punning

PUNT *v* -ED, -ING, -S to propel through water with a pole

PUNTER *n* pl. -S one that punts

PUNTO *n* pl. -TOS a hit or thrust in fencing

PUNTY *n* pl. -TIES an iron rod used in glassmaking

PUNY *adj* PUNIER, PUNIEST of inferior size, strength, or significance

PUP *v* PUPPED, PUPPING, PUPS to give birth to puppies

PUPA *n* pl. -PAS or -PAE an intermediate stage of a metamorphic insect **PUPAL** *adj*

PUPARIUM *n* pl. -IA a pupal shell **PUPARIAL** *adj*

PUPATE *v* -PATED, -PATING, -PATES to pass through the pupal stage

PUPATION *n* pl. -S the act of pupating

PUPFISH *n* pl. -ES a small, freshwater fish

PUPIL *n* pl. -S a student under the close supervision of a teacher

PUPILAGE *n* pl. -S the state of being a pupil

PUPILAR *adj* pertaining to a part of the eye

PUPILARY *adj* pupilar

PUPPED past tense of pup

PUPPET *n* pl. -S a small figure, as of a person or animal, manipulated by the hand

PUPPETRY *n* pl. -RIES the art of making or manipulating puppets

PUPPING present participle of pup

PUPPY *n* pl. -PIES a young dog **PUPPYISH** *adj*

PUPPYDOM *n* pl. -S the world of puppies

PUR *v* PURRED, PURRING, PURS to purr

PURANA *n* pl. -S a Hindu scripture **PURANIC** *adj*

PURBLIND *adj* partially blind

PURCHASE *v* -CHASED, -CHASING, -CHASES to acquire by the payment of money

PURDA *n* pl. -S purdah

PURDAH *n* pl. -S a curtain used in India to seclude women

PURE *adj* PURER, PUREST free from anything different, inferior, or contaminating

PUREBRED *n* pl. -S an animal of unmixed stock

PUREE   v -REED, -REEING, -REES to reduce to a thick pulp by cooking and sieving

PURELY   adv in a pure manner

PURENESS   n pl. -ES the quality of being pure

PURER   comparative of pure

PUREST   superlative of pure

PURFLE   v -FLED, -FLING, -FLES to decorate the border of

PURFLING   n pl. -S an ornamental border

PURGE   v PURGED, PURGING, PURGES to purify

PURGER   n pl. -S one that purges

PURGING   n pl. -S the act of purifying

PURI   n pl. -S poori

PURIFIER   n pl. -S one that purifies

PURIFY   v -FIED, -FYING, -FIES to free from impurities

PURIN   n pl. -S purine

PURINE   n pl. -S a chemical compound

PURISM   n pl. -S strict adherence to traditional correctness

PURIST   n pl. -S one who practices purism **PURISTIC** adj

PURITAN   n pl. -S a rigorously moral or religious person

PURITY   n pl. -TIES the quality of being pure

PURL   v -ED, -ING, -S to knit with a particular stitch

PURLIEU   n pl. -S an outlying or neighboring area

PURLIN   n pl. -S a horizontal supporting timber

PURLINE   n pl. -S purlin

PURLOIN   v -ED, -ING, -S to steal

PURPLE   adj -PLER, -PLEST of a color intermediate between red and blue

PURPLE   v -PLED, -PLING, -PLES to make purple

PURPLISH   adj somewhat purple

PURPLY   adj purplish

PURPORT   v -ED, -ING, -S to profess or claim

PURPOSE   v -POSED, -POSING, -POSES to resolve to perform or accomplish

PURPURA   n pl. -S a disease characterized by purple spots on the skin

PURPURE   n pl. -S the heraldic color purple

PURPURIC   adj pertaining to purpura

PURPURIN   n pl. -S a reddish dye

PURR   v -ED, -ING, -S to utter a low, vibrant sound

PURRED   past tense of pur and purr

PURRING   present participle of pur and purr

PURSE   v PURSED, PURSING, PURSES to pucker

PURSER   n pl. -S an officer in charge of a ship's accounts

PURSIER   comparative of pursy

PURSIEST   superlative of pursy

PURSILY   adv in a pursy manner

PURSING   present participle of purse

PURSLANE   n pl. -S a common garden herb

PURSUANT   adv in accordance

PURSUE   v -SUED, -SUING, -SUES to follow in order to overtake or capture

PURSUER   n pl. -S one that pursues

PURSUIT   n pl. -S the act of pursuing

PURSY   adj PURSIER, PURSIEST short of breath

PURULENT   adj secreting pus

PURVEY   v -ED, -ING, -S to supply

PURVEYOR   n pl. -S one that purveys

PURVIEW   n pl. -S the extent of operation, authority, or concern

PUS   n pl. -ES a viscous fluid formed in infected tissue

PUSH   v -ED, -ING, -ES to exert force in order to cause motion away from the force

PUSHBALL   n pl. -S a type of ball game

PUSHCART   n pl. -S a light cart pushed by hand

PUSHDOWN   n pl. -S a store of computer data

PUSHER   n pl. -S one that pushes

PUSHFUL   adj pushy

PUSHIER   comparative of pushy

PUSHIEST   superlative of pushy

PUSHILY   adv in a pushy manner

PUSHOVER   n pl. -S an easily defeated person or team

PUSHPIN   n pl. -S a large-headed pin

PUSHUP   n pl. -S a type of exercise

PUSHY   adj PUSHIER, PUSHIEST offensively aggressive

PUSLEY   n pl. -LEYS pussley

PUSLIKE   adj resembling pus

PUSS   n pl. -ES a cat

PUSSIER   comparative of pussy

PUSSIES   pl. of pussy

PUSSIEST   superlative of pussy

PUSSLEY   n pl. -LEYS purslane

PUSSLIKE   adj catlike

PUSSLY   n pl. -LIES pussley

PUSSY   n pl. PUSSIES a cat

PUSSY   adj -SIER, -SIEST full of pus

PUSSYCAT   n pl. -S a cat

PUSTULE   n pl. -S a small elevation of the skin containing pus PUSTULAR, PUSTULED adj

PUT   v PUT, PUTTING, PUTS to place in a particular position

PUTAMEN   n pl. -MINA the hard covering of the kernel of certain fruits

PUTATIVE   adj generally regarded as such

PUTLOG   n pl. -S a horizontal supporting timber

PUTOFF   n pl. -S an excuse

PUTON   n pl. -S a hoax or deception

PUTOUT   n pl. -S an act of causing an out in baseball

PUTREFY   v -FIED, -FYING, -FIES to make or become putrid

PUTRID   adj being in a decomposed, foul-smelling state PUTRIDLY adv

PUTSCH   n pl. -ES a suddenly executed attempt to overthrow a government

PUTT   v -ED, -ING, -S to hit with a light stroke in golf

PUTTEE   n pl. -S a strip of cloth wound around the leg

PUTTER   v -ED, -ING, -S to occupy oneself in a leisurely or ineffective manner

PUTTERER   n pl. -S one that putters

PUTTIED   past tense of putty

PUTTIER   n pl. -S one that putties

PUTTING   present participle of put

PUTTY   v -TIED, -TYING, -TIES to fill with a type of cement

PUZZLE   v -ZLED, -ZLING, -ZLES to cause uncertainty and indecision in

PUZZLER   n pl. -S something that puzzles

PYA   n pl. -S a copper coin of Burma

PYAEMIA   n pl. -S pyemia PYAEMIC adj

PYCNIDIA   n/pl spore-bearing organs of certain fungi

PYE   n pl. -S a book of ecclesiastical rules in the pre-Reformation English church

PYELITIS   n pl. -TISES inflammation of the pelvis or the kidney PYELITIC adj

PYEMIA   n pl. -S the presence of pus in the blood PYEMIC adj

PYGIDIUM   n pl. -IA the posterior region of certain invertebrates PYGIDIAL adj

PYGMY   n pl. -MIES a small person PYGMAEAN, PYGMEAN, PYGMOID, PYGMYISH adj

PYGMYISM   n pl. -S a stunted or dwarfish condition

PYIC   adj pertaining to pus

PYIN   n pl. -S a protein compound contained in pus

PYJAMAS   n pl. PYJAMAS pajamas

PYKNIC   n pl. -S a person having a broad, stocky build

PYLON   n pl. -S a tall structure marking an entrance or approach

PYLORUS   n pl. -RI or -RUSES the opening between the stomach and the duodenum PYLORIC adj

PYODERMA   n pl. -S a pus-causing skin disease

PYOGENIC   adj producing pus

PYOID   adj puslike

PYORRHEA   n pl. -S a discharge of pus

PYOSIS   n pl. -OSES the formation of pus

PYRALID   n pl. -S a long-legged moth

PYRAMID   v -ED, -ING, -S to raise or increase by adding amounts gradually

PYRAN   n pl. -S a chemical compound PYRANOID adj

PYRANOSE   n pl. -S a simple sugar

PYRE   n pl. -S a pile of combustible material

PYRENE   n pl. -S a putamen

PYRENOID	n pl. -S a protein body of certain lower organisms	**PYROPE**	n pl. -S a variety of garnet
PYRETIC	adj pertaining to fever	**PYROSIS**	n pl. -SISES heartburn
PYREXIA	n pl. -S fever **PYREXIAL, PYREXIC** adj	**PYROSTAT**	n pl. -S a thermostat
PYRIC	adj pertaining to burning	**PYROXENE**	n pl. -S any of a group of minerals common in igneous rocks
PYRIDINE	n pl. -S a flammable liquid **PYRIDIC** adj	**PYRRHIC**	n pl. -S a type of metrical foot
PYRIFORM	adj pear-shaped	**PYRROL**	n pl. -S pyrrole
PYRITE	n pl. -S a metallic sulfide **PYRITIC, PYRITOUS** adj	**PYRROLE**	n pl. -S a chemical compound **PYRROLIC** adj
PYROGEN	n pl. -S a substance that produces fever	**PYRUVATE**	n pl. -S a chemical salt
PYROLA	n pl. -S a perennial herb	**PYTHON**	n pl. -S a large snake **PYTHONIC** adj
PYROLOGY	n pl. -GIES the scientific examination of materials by heat	**PYURIA**	n pl. -S the presence of pus in the urine
PYROLYZE	v -LYZED, -LYZING, -LYZES to affect compounds by the application of heat	**PYX**	n pl. -ES a container in which the eucharistic bread is kept
		PYXIDES	pl. of pyxis
PYRONE	n pl. -S a chemical compound	**PYXIDIUM**	n pl. -IA a type of seed vessel
PYRONINE	n pl. -S a dye	**PYXIE**	n pl. -S an evergreen shrub
		PYXIS	n pl. PYXIDES a pyxidium

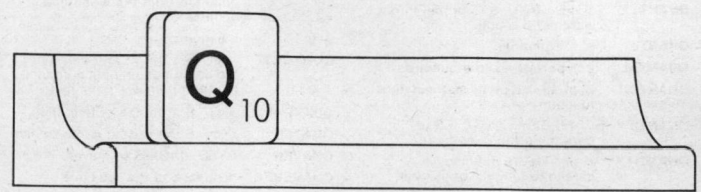

QAID	*n* pl. -S caid
QINDAR	*n* pl. -S qintar
QINTAR	*n* pl. -S a monetary unit of Albania
QIVIUT	*n* pl. -S the wool of a musk-ox
QOPH	*n* pl. -S koph
QUA	*adv* in the capacity of
QUACK	*v* -ED, -ING, -S to utter the characteristic cry of a duck
QUACKERY	*n* pl. -ERIES fraudulent practice
QUACKISH	*adj* fraudulent
QUACKISM	*n* pl. -S quackery
QUAD	*v* QUADDED, QUADDING, QUADS to space out by means of quadrats
QUADRANS	*n* pl. -RANTES an ancient Roman coin
QUADRANT	*n* pl. -S a quarter section of a circle
QUADRAT	*n* pl. -S a piece of type metal used for filling spaces
QUADRATE	*v* -RATED, -RATING, -RATES to correspond or agree
QUADRIC	*n* pl. -S a type of geometric surface
QUADRIGA	*n* pl. -GAE a chariot drawn by four horses
QUADROON	*n* pl. -S a person of one-quarter black ancestry
QUAERE	*n* pl. -S a question
QUAESTOR	*n* pl. -S an ancient Roman magistrate
QUAFF	*v* -ED, -ING, -S to drink deeply
QUAFFER	*n* pl. -S one that quaffs
QUAG	*n* pl. -S a quagmire

QUAGGA	*n* pl. -S an extinct zebralike mammal
QUAGGY	*adj* -GIER, -GIEST marshy
QUAGMIRE	*n* pl. -S an area of marshy ground
QUAGMIRY	*adj* -MIRIER, -MIRIEST marshy
QUAHAUG	*n* pl. -S quahog
QUAHOG	*n* pl. -S an edible clam
QUAI	*n* pl. -S quay
QUAICH	*n* pl. -ES or -S a small drinking vessel
QUAIGH	*n* pl. -S quaich
QUAIL	*v* -ED, -ING, -S to cower
QUAINT	*adj* QUAINTER, QUAINTEST pleasingly old-fashioned or unfamiliar **QUAINTLY** *adv*
QUAKE	*v* QUAKED, QUAKING, QUAKES to shake or vibrate
QUAKER	*n* pl. -S one that quakes
QUAKY	*adj* QUAKIER, QUAKIEST tending to quake **QUAKILY** *adv*
QUALE	*n* pl. -LIA a property considered apart from things having the property
QUALIFY	*v* -FIED, -FYING, -FIES to make suitable or capable
QUALITY	*n* pl. -TIES a characteristic or attribute
QUALM	*n* pl. -S a feeling of doubt or misgiving
QUALMISH	*adj* having qualms
QUALMY	*adj* QUALMIER, QUALMIEST qualmish
QUAMASH	*n* pl. -ES camass
QUANDANG	*n* pl. -S quandong

QUANDARY *n* pl. -RIES a dilemma

QUANDONG *n* pl. -S an Australian tree

QUANT *v* -ED, -ING, -S to propel through water with a pole

QUANTA pl. of quantum

QUANTAL *adj* pertaining to a quantum

QUANTIC *n* pl. -S a type of mathematical function

QUANTIFY *v* -FIED, -FYING, -FIES to determine the quantity of

QUANTITY *n* pl. -TIES a specified or indefinite amount or number

QUANTIZE *v* -TIZED, -TIZING, -TIZES to limit the possible values of to a discrete set

QUANTONG *n* pl. -S quandong

QUANTUM *n* pl. -TA a fundamental unit of energy

QUARE *adj* queer

QUARK *n* pl. -S a hypothetical atomic particle

QUARREL *v* -RELED, -RELING, -RELS or -RELLED, -RELLING, -RELS to engage in an angry dispute

QUARRIER *n* pl. -S one that quarries

QUARRY *v* -RIED, -RYING, -RIES to dig stone from an excavation

QUART *n* pl. -S a liquid measure of capacity

QUARTAN *n* pl. -S a recurrent malarial fever

QUARTE *n* pl. -S a fencing thrust

QUARTER *v* -ED, -ING, -S to divide into four equal parts

QUARTERN *n* pl. -S one-fourth of something

QUARTET *n* pl. -S a group of four

QUARTIC *n* pl. -S a type of mathematical function

QUARTILE *n* pl. -S a portion of a frequency distribution

QUARTO *n* pl. -TOS the size of a piece of paper cut four from a sheet

QUARTZ *n* pl. -ES a mineral

QUASAR *n* pl. -S a distant celestial object emitting strong radio waves

QUASH *v* -ED, -ING, -ES to suppress completely

QUASI *adj* similar but not exactly the same

QUASS *n* pl. -ES kvass

QUASSIA *n* pl. -S a tropical tree

QUASSIN *n* pl. -S a medicinal compound obtained from the wood of a quassia

QUATE *adj* quiet

QUATORZE *n* pl. -S a set of four cards of the same denomination scoring fourteen points

QUATRAIN *n* pl. -S a stanza of four lines

QUATRE *n* pl. -S the four at cards or dice

QUAVER *v* -ED, -ING, -S to quiver

QUAVERER *n* pl. -S one that quavers

QUAVERY *adj* quivery

QUAY *n* pl. QUAYS a wharf **QUAYLIKE** *adj*

QUAYAGE *n* pl. -S a charge for the use of a quay

QUAYSIDE *n* pl. -S the area adjacent to a quay

QUEAN *n* pl. -S a harlot

QUEASY *adj* -SIER, -SIEST easily nauseated **QUEASILY** *adv*

QUEAZY *adj* -ZIER, -ZIEST queasy

QUEEN *v* -ED, -ING, -S to make a queen (a female monarch) of

QUEENLY *adj* -LIER, -LIEST of or befitting a queen

QUEER *adj* QUEERER, QUEEREST deviating from the expected or normal

QUEER *v* -ED, -ING, -S to spoil the effect or success of

QUEERISH *adj* somewhat queer

QUEERLY *adv* in a queer manner

QUELL *v* -ED, -ING, -S to suppress

QUELLER *n* pl. -S one that quells

QUENCH *v* -ED, -ING, -ES to put out or extinguish

QUENCHER *n* pl. -S one that quenches

QUENELLE *n* pl. -S a type of dumpling

QUERCINE *adj* pertaining to oaks

QUERIDA *n* pl. -S a female sweetheart

QUERIED past tense of query

QUERIER *n* pl. -S a querist

QUERIES present 3d person sing. of query

QUERIST *n* pl. -S one who queries

QUERN *n* pl. -S a hand-turned grain mill

QUERY *v* -RIED, -RYING, -RIES to question

QUEST   *v* -ED, -ING, -S to make a search

QUESTER   *n pl.* -S one that quests

QUESTION   *v* -ED, -ING, -S to put a question (an inquiry) to

QUESTOR   *n pl.* -S quaestor

QUETZAL   *n pl.* -S or -ES a tropical bird

QUEUE   *v* QUEUED, QUEUING or QUEUEING, QUEUES to line up

QUEUER   *n pl.* -S one that queues

QUEY   *n pl.* QUEYS a young cow

QUEZAL   *n pl.* -S or -ES quetzal

QUIBBLE   *v* -BLED, -BLING, -BLES to argue over trivialities

QUIBBLER   *n pl.* -S one that quibbles

QUICHE   *n pl.* -S a custard-filled pastry

QUICK   *adj* QUICKER, QUICKEST acting or capable of acting with speed

QUICK   *n pl.* -S a sensitive area of flesh

QUICKEN   *v* -ED, -ING, -S to speed up

QUICKIE   *n pl.* -S something done quickly

QUICKLY   *adv* in a quick manner

QUICKSET   *n pl.* -S a plant suitable for hedges

QUID   *n pl.* -S a portion of something to be chewed

QUIDDITY   *n pl.* -TIES the true nature of a thing

QUIDNUNC   *n pl.* -S a nosy person

QUIET   *adj* -ETER, -ETEST making little or no noise

QUIET   *v* -ED, -ING, -S to cause to be quiet

QUIETEN   *v* -ED, -ING, -S to quiet

QUIETER   *n pl.* -S one that quiets

QUIETISM   *n pl.* -S a form of religious mysticism

QUIETIST   *n pl.* -S an advocate of quietism

QUIETLY   *adv* in a quiet manner

QUIETUDE   *n pl.* -S a state of tranquillity

QUIETUS   *n pl.* -ES a final settlement

QUIFF   *n pl.* -S a forelock

QUILL   *v* -ED, -ING, -S to press small ridges in

QUILLAI   *n pl.* -S an evergreen tree

QUILLET   *n pl.* -S a trivial distinction

QUILT   *v* -ED, -ING, -S to stitch together with padding in between

QUILTER   *n pl.* -S one that quilts

QUILTING   *n pl.* -S material that is used for making quilts

QUINARY   *n pl.* -RIES a group of five

QUINATE   *adj* arranged in groups of five

QUINCE   *n pl.* -S an apple-like fruit

QUINCUNX   *n pl.* -ES an arrangement of five objects

QUINELLA   *n pl.* -S a type of bet in horse racing

QUINIC   *adj* pertaining to quinine

QUINIELA   *n pl.* -S quinella

QUININ   *n pl.* -S quinine

QUININA   *n pl.* -S quinine

QUININE   *n pl.* -S a medicinal alkaloid

QUINNAT   *n pl.* -S a food fish

QUINOA   *n pl.* -S a weedy plant

QUINOID   *n pl.* -S a chemical compound

QUINOL   *n pl.* -S a chemical compound

QUINOLIN   *n pl.* -S a chemical compound

QUINONE   *n pl.* -S a chemical compound

QUINSY   *n pl.* -SIES an inflammation of the tonsils

QUINT   *n pl.* -S a group of five

QUINTAIN   *n pl.* -S an object used as a target in a medieval sport

QUINTAL   *n pl.* -S a unit of weight

QUINTAN   *n pl.* -S a recurrent fever

QUINTAR   *n pl.* -S qintar

QUINTET   *n pl.* -S a group of five

QUINTIC   *n pl.* -S a type of mathematical function

QUINTILE   *n pl.* -S a portion of a frequency distribution

QUINTIN   *n pl.* -S a fine linen

QUIP   *v* QUIPPED, QUIPPING, QUIPS to make witty remarks

QUIPPISH   *adj* witty

QUIPPU   *n pl.* -S quipu

QUIPSTER   *n pl.* -S one that quips

QUIPU   *n pl.* -S an ancient calculating device

QUIRE   *v* QUIRED, QUIRING, QUIRES to arrange sheets of paper in sets of twenty-four

QUIRK   *v* -ED, -ING, -S to twist

QUIRKY   *adj* QUIRKIER, QUIRKIEST tricky **QUIRKILY** *adv*

QUIRT   *v* -ED, -ING, -S to strike with a riding whip

QUISLING   *n* pl. -S a traitor who aids the invaders of his country

QUIT   *v* QUITTED, QUITTING, QUITS to end one's engagement in or occupation with

QUITCH   *n* pl. -ES a perennial grass

QUITE   *adv* to the fullest extent

QUITRENT   *n* pl. -S a fixed rent due from a socage tenant

QUITTED   past tense of quit

QUITTER   *n* pl. -S one that quits

QUITTING   present participle of quit

QUITTOR   *n* pl. -S an inflammation of an animal's hoof

QUIVER   *v* -ED, -ING, -S to shake with a slight but rapid motion

QUIVERER   *n* pl. -S one that quivers

QUIVERY   *adj* marked by quivering

QUIXOTE   *n* pl. -S a quixotic person

QUIXOTIC   *adj* extremely idealistic

QUIXOTRY   *n* pl. -TRIES quixotic action or thought

QUIZ   *v* QUIZZED, QUIZZING, QUIZZES to test the knowledge of by asking questions

QUIZZER   *n* pl. -S one that quizzes

QUOD   *n* pl. -S a prison

QUOIN   *v* -ED, -ING, -S to secure with a type of wedge

QUOIT   *v* -ED, -ING, -S to play a throwing game similar to ringtoss

QUOMODO   *n* pl. -DOS a means or manner

QUONDAM   *adj* that once was

QUORUM   *n* pl. -S a particularly chosen group

QUOTA   *n* pl. -S a proportional part or share

QUOTE   *v* QUOTED, QUOTING, QUOTES to repeat the words of QUOTABLE *adj* QUOTABLY *adv*

QUOTER   *n* pl. -S one that quotes

QUOTH   *v* said — QUOTH is the only accepted form of this verb; it cannot be conjugated

QUOTHA   *interj* — used to express surprise or sarcasm

QUOTIENT   *n* pl. -S the number resulting from the division of one number by another

QUOTING   present participle of quote

QURSH   *n* pl. -ES a monetary unit of Saudi Arabia

QURUSH   *n* pl. -ES qursh

RABATO *n* pl. -TOS a wide, lace-edged collar

RABBET *v* -ED, -ING, -S to cut a groove in

RABBI *n* pl. -S or -ES a Jewish spiritual leader

RABBIN *n* pl. -S rabbi

RABBINIC *adj* pertaining to rabbis

RABBIT *v* -ED, -ING, -S to hunt rabbits (rodent-like mammals)

RABBITER *n* pl. -S one that rabbits

RABBITRY *n* pl. -RIES a place where rabbits are kept

RABBLE *v* -BLED, -BLING, -BLES to mob

RABBLER *n* pl. -S an iron bar used in puddling

RABBONI *n* pl. -S master; teacher — used as a Jewish title of respect

RABIC *adj* pertaining to rabies

RABID *adj* affected with rabies **RABIDLY** *adv*

RABIDITY *n* pl. -TIES the state of being rabid

RABIES *n* pl. RABIES an infectious virus disease **RABIETIC** *adj*

RACCOON *n* pl. -S a carnivorous mammal

RACE *v* RACED, RACING, RACES to compete in a contest of speed

RACEMATE *n* pl. -S a chemical salt

RACEME *n* pl. -S a mode of arrangement of flowers along an axis **RACEMED** *adj*

RACEMIC *adj* constituting a chemical compound that is optically inactive

RACEMISM *n* pl. -S the state of being racemic

RACEMIZE *v* -MIZED, -MIZING, -MIZES to convert into a racemic compound

RACEMOID *adj* pertaining to a raceme

RACEMOSE *adj* having the form of a raceme

RACEMOUS *adj* racemose

RACER *n* pl. -S one that races

RACEWAY *n* pl. -WAYS a channel for conducting water

RACHET *n* pl. -S ratchet

RACHIS *n* pl. -CHISES or -CHIDES the spinal column **RACHIAL** *adj*

RACHITIS *n* pl. -TIDES rickets **RACHITIC** *adj*

RACIAL *adj* pertaining to an ethnic group **RACIALLY** *adv*

RACIER comparative of racy

RACIEST superlative of racy

RACILY *adv* in a racy manner

RACINESS *n* pl. -ES the quality of being racy

RACING *n* pl. -S the sport of engaging in contests of speed

RACISM *n* pl. -S a doctrine of racial superiority

RACIST *n* pl. -S an advocate of racism

RACK *v* -ED, -ING, -S to place in a type of framework

RACKER *n* pl. -S one that racks

RACKET *v* -ED, -ING, -S to make a loud noise

RACKETY *adj* -ETIER, -ETIEST noisy

RACKLE *adj* impetuous; rash

RACKWORK *n* pl. -S a type of mechanism

RACLETTE *n* pl. -S a cheese dish

RACON *n* pl. -S a type of radar transmitter

RACOON *n* pl. -S raccoon

RACQUET *n* pl. -S a lightweight implement used in various ball games

RACY *adj* RACIER, RACIEST bordering on impropriety or indecency

RAD *v* RADDED, RADDING, RADS to fear

RADAR *n* pl. -S an electronic locating device

RADDLE *v* -DLED, -DLING, -DLES to weave together

RADIABLE *adj* capable of radiating

RADIAL *n* pl. -S a part diverging from a center

RADIALE *n* pl. -LIA a bone of the carpus

RADIALLY *adv* in a diverging manner

RADIAN *n* pl. -S a unit of angular measure

RADIANCE *n* pl. -S brightness

RADIANCY *n* pl. -CIES radiance

RADIANT *n* pl. -S a point from which rays are emitted

RADIATE *v* -ATED, -ATING, -ATES to emit rays

RADIATOR *n* pl. -S a heating device

RADICAL *n* pl. -S a group of atoms that acts as a unit in chemical compounds

RADICAND *n* pl. -S a quantity in mathematics

RADICATE *v* -CATED, -CATING, -CATES to cause to take root

RADICEL *n* pl. -S a rootlet

RADICES a pl. of radix

RADICLE *n* pl. -S a part of a plant embryo

RADII a pl. of radius

RADIO *v* -ED, -ING, -S to transmit by radio (an apparatus for wireless communication)

RADIOMAN *n* pl. -MEN a radio operator or technician

RADISH *n* pl. -ES a pungent, edible root

RADIUM *n* pl. -S a radioactive element

RADIUS *n* pl. -DII or -DIUSES a straight line from the center of a circle to the circumference

RADIX *n* pl. -DICES or -DIXES the root of a plant

RADOME *n* pl. -S a domelike device used to shelter a radar antenna

RADON *n* pl. -S a radioactive element

RADULA *n* pl. -LAE or -LAS a tonguelike organ of mollusks **RADULAR** *adj*

RAFF *n* pl. -S riffraff

RAFFIA *n* pl. -S a palm tree

RAFFISH *adj* tawdry

RAFFLE *v* -FLED, -FLING, -FLES to dispose of by a form of lottery

RAFFLER *n* pl. -S one that raffles

RAFT *v* -ED, -ING, -S to transport on a raft (a type of buoyant structure)

RAFTER *n* pl. -S a supporting beam

RAFTSMAN *n* pl. -MEN one who manages a raft

RAG *v* RAGGED, RAGGING, RAGS to scold

RAGA *n* pl. -S a Hindu musical form

RAGBAG *n* pl. -S a bag for storing scraps of cloth

RAGE *v* RAGED, RAGING, RAGES to act or speak with violent anger

RAGEE *n* pl. -S ragi

RAGGED *adj* -GEDER, -GEDEST tattered **RAGGEDLY** *adv*

RAGGEDY *adj* somewhat ragged

RAGGING present participle of rag

RAGGLE *n* pl. -S a groove cut in masonry

RAGGY *n* pl. -GIES ragi

RAGI *n* pl. -S an East Indian cereal grass

RAGING present participle of rage

RAGINGLY *adv* in a furious manner

RAGLAN *n* pl. -S a type of overcoat

RAGMAN *n* pl. -MEN one who gathers and sells scraps of cloth

RAGOUT *v* -ED, -ING, -S to make into a highly seasoned stew

RAGTAG *n* pl. -S riffraff

RAGTIME *n* pl. -S a style of American dance music

RAGWEED *n* pl. -S a weedy herb

RAGWORT *n* pl. -S a flowering plant

RAH *interj* — used to cheer on a team or player

RAIA	*n* pl. -S rayah	**RAJA**	*n* pl. -S rajah
RAID	*v* -ED, -ING, -S to make a sudden assault on	**RAJAH**	*n* pl. -S a king or prince in India
RAIDER	*n* pl. -S one that raids	**RAKE**	*v* RAKED, RAKING, RAKES to gather with a toothed implement
RAIL	*v* -ED, -ING, -S to scold in abusive or insolent language	**RAKEE**	*n* pl. -S raki
RAILBIRD	*n* pl. -S a racing enthusiast	**RAKEHELL**	*n* pl. -S a man lacking in moral restraint
RAILER	*n* pl. -S one that rails	**RAKEOFF**	*n* pl. -S a share of profits
RAILHEAD	*n* pl. -S the end of a railroad line	**RAKER**	*n* pl. -S one that rakes
RAILING	*n* pl. -S a fence-like barrier	**RAKI**	*n* pl. -S a Turkish liqueur
RAILLERY	*n* pl. -LERIES good-natured teasing	**RAKING**	present participle of rake
		RAKISH	*adj* dapper **RAKISHLY** *adv*
RAILROAD	*v* -ED, -ING, -S to transport by railroad (a type of road on which locomotives are run)	**RALE**	*n* pl. -S an abnormal respiratory sound
		RALLIED	past tense of rally
RAILWAY	*n* pl. -WAYS a railroad	**RALLIER**	*n* pl. -S one that rallies
RAIMENT	*n* pl. -S clothing	**RALLINE**	*adj* pertaining to a family of marsh birds
RAIN	*v* -ED, -ING, -S to fall like rain (drops of water condensed from atmospheric vapor)	**RALLY**	*v* -LIED, -LYING, -LIES to call together for a common purpose
RAINBAND	*n* pl. -S a dark band in the solar spectrum	**RALLYE**	*n* pl. -S a type of automobile race
RAINBIRD	*n* pl. -S a type of bird	**RALLYING**	*n* pl. -S the sport of driving in rallyes
RAINBOW	*n* pl. -S an arc of spectral colors formed in the sky	**RALLYIST**	*n* pl. -S a participant in a rallye
RAINCOAT	*n* pl. -S a waterproof coat	**RAM**	*v* RAMMED, RAMMING, RAMS to strike with great force
RAINDROP	*n* pl. -S a drop of rain	
RAINFALL	*n* pl. -S a fall of rain	**RAMATE**	*adj* having branches
RAINIER	comparative of rainy	**RAMBLE**	*v* -BLED, -BLING, -BLES to wander
RAINIEST	superlative of rainy	
RAINILY	*adv* in a rainy manner	**RAMBLER**	*n* pl. -S one that rambles
RAINLESS	*adj* having no rain	**RAMBUTAN**	*n* pl. -S the edible fruit of a Malayan tree
RAINOUT	*n* pl. -S atomic fallout occurring in precipitation	**RAMEE**	*n* pl. -S ramie
RAINWASH	*n* pl. -ES the washing away of material by rain	**RAMEKIN**	*n* pl. -S a cheese dish
		RAMENTUM	*n* pl. -TA a scale formed on the surface of leaves
RAINWEAR	*n* pl. -S waterproof clothing	**RAMEQUIN**	*n* pl. -S ramekin
RAINY	*adj* RAINIER, RAINIEST marked by rain	**RAMET**	*n* pl. -S an independent member of a clone
RAISE	*v* RAISED, RAISING, RAISES to move to a higher position **RAISABLE** *adj*	**RAMI**	pl. of ramus
		RAMIE	*n* pl. -S an Asian shrub
RAISER	*n* pl. -S one that raises	**RAMIFORM**	*adj* shaped like a branch
RAISIN	*n* pl. -S a dried grape **RAISINY** *adj*	**RAMIFY**	*v* -FIED, -FYING, -FIES to divide into branches
RAISING	*n* pl. -S an elevation	**RAMILIE**	*n* pl. -S ramillie
RAISONNE	*adj* arranged systematically	**RAMILLIE**	*n* pl. -S a type of wig
RAJ	*n* pl. -ES dominion; sovereignty	**RAMJET**	*n* pl. -S a type of engine

RAMMED past tense of ram

RAMMER *n* pl. -S one that rams

RAMMIER comparative of rammy

RAMMIEST superlative of rammy

RAMMING present participle of ram

RAMMISH *adj* resembling a ram (a male sheep)

RAMMY *adj* -MIER, -MIEST rammish

RAMOSE *adj* having many branches RAMOSELY *adv*

RAMOSITY *n* pl. -TIES the state of being ramose

RAMOUS *adj* ramose

RAMP *v* -ED, -ING, -S to rise or stand on the hind legs

RAMPAGE *v* -PAGED, -PAGING, -PAGES to move about wildly or violently

RAMPAGER *n* pl. -S one that rampages

RAMPANCY *n* pl. -CIES the state of being rampant

RAMPANT *adj* unrestrained

RAMPART *v* -ED, -ING, -S to furnish with a fortifying embankment

RAMPIKE *n* pl. -S a standing dead tree

RAMPION *n* pl. -S a European plant

RAMPOLE *n* pl. -S rampike

RAMROD *n* pl. -S a rod used in loading a firearm

RAMSHORN *n* pl. -S a snail used as an aquarium scavenger

RAMSON *n* pl. -S a broad-leaved garlic

RAMTIL *n* pl. -S a tropical plant

RAMULOSE *adj* having many small branches

RAMULOUS *adj* ramulose

RAMUS *n* pl. -MI a branch-like part of a structure

RAN past tense of run and rin

RANCE *n* pl. -S a variety of marble

RANCH *v* -ED, -ING, -ES to work on a ranch (an establishment for raising livestock)

RANCHER *n* pl. -S one that owns or works on a ranch

RANCHERO *n* pl. -ROS a rancher

RANCHMAN *n* pl. -MEN a rancher

RANCHO *n* pl. -CHOS a ranch

RANCID *adj* having an unpleasant odor or taste

RANCOR *n* pl. -S bitter and vindictive enmity RANCORED *adj*

RANCOUR *n* pl. -S rancor

RAND *n* pl. -S a strip of leather at the heel of a shoe

RANDAN *n* pl. -S a boat rowed by three persons

RANDIES pl. of randy

RANDOM *n* pl. -S a haphazard course

RANDOMLY *adv* in a haphazard manner

RANDY *n* pl. RANDIES a rude person

RANEE *n* pl. -S rani

RANG past tense of ring

RANGE *v* RANGED, RANGING, RANGES to place in a particular order

RANGER *n* pl. -S an officer supervising the care of a forest

RANGY *adj* RANGIER, RANGIEST tall and slender

RANI *n* pl. -S the wife of a rajah

RANID *n* pl. -S any of a large family of frogs

RANK *v* -ED, -ING, -S to determine the relative position of

RANK *adj* RANKER, RANKEST strong and disagreeable in odor or taste

RANKER *n* pl. -S an enlisted soldier

RANKISH *adj* somewhat rank

RANKLE *v* -KLED, -KLING, -KLES to cause irritation or resentment in

RANKLY *adv* in a rank manner

RANKNESS *n* pl. -ES the state of being rank

RANPIKE *n* pl. -S rampike

RANSACK *v* -ED, -ING, -S to search thoroughly

RANSOM *v* -ED, -ING, -S to obtain the release of by paying a demanded price

RANSOMER *n* pl. -S one that ransoms

RANT *v* -ED, -ING, -S to speak in a loud or vehement manner

RANTER *n* pl. -S one that rants

RANULA *n* pl. -S a cyst formed under the tongue

RAP *v* RAPPED, RAPPING, RAPS to strike sharply

RAPACITY *n* pl. -TIES the quality of being ravenous

RAPE   v RAPED, RAPING, RAPES to force to submit to sexual intercourse

RAPER   n pl. -S a rapist

RAPESEED   n pl. -S the seed of a European herb

RAPHE   n pl. RAPHAE or RAPHES a seamlike ridge between two halves of an organ or part

RAPHIA   n pl. -S raffia

RAPHIDE   n pl. -S a needle-shaped crystal occurring in plant cells

RAPHIS   n pl. -PHIDES raphide

RAPID   adj -IDER, -IDEST moving or acting with great speed **RAPIDLY** adv

RAPID   n pl. -S a fast-moving part of a river

RAPIDITY   n pl. -TIES the state of being rapid

RAPIER   n pl. -S a long, slender sword **RAPIERED** adj

RAPINE   n pl. -S the taking of property by force

RAPING   present participle of rape

RAPIST   n pl. -S one who rapes

RAPPAREE   n pl. -S a plunderer

RAPPED   past tense of rap

RAPPEE   n pl. -S a strong snuff

RAPPEL   v -PELLED, -PELLING, -PELS to descend from a steep height by means of a rope

RAPPEN   n pl. RAPPEN a Swiss coin

RAPPER   n pl. -S one that raps

RAPPING   present participle of rap

RAPPINI   n/pl immature turnip plants

RAPPORT   n pl. -S a harmonious relationship

RAPT   adj deeply engrossed **RAPTLY** adv

RAPTNESS   n pl. -ES the state of being rapt

RAPTOR   n pl. -S a bird of prey

RAPTURE   v -TURED, -TURING, -TURES to fill with great joy

RARE   adj RARER, RAREST occurring infrequently

RAREBIT   n pl. -S a cheese dish

RAREFIER   n pl. -S one that rarefies

RAREFY   v -EFIED, -EFYING, -EFIES to make less dense

RARELY   adv not often

RARENESS   n pl. -ES the quality of being rare

RARER   comparative of rare

RARERIPE   n pl. -S a fruit that ripens early

RAREST   superlative of rare

RARIFY   v -FIED, -FYING, -FIES to rarefy

RARING   adj full of enthusiasm

RARITY   n pl. -TIES rareness

RAS   n pl. -ES an Ethiopian prince

RASBORA   n pl. -S a tropical fish

RASCAL   n pl. -S an unscrupulous or dishonest person

RASCALLY   adj characteristic of a rascal

RASE   v RASED, RASING, RASES to raze

RASER   n pl. -S one that rases

RASH   adj RASHER, RASHEST acting without due caution or forethought

RASH   n pl. -ES a skin eruption **RASHLIKE** adj

RASHER   n pl. -S a thin slice of meat

RASHLY   adv in a rash manner

RASHNESS   n pl. -ES the state of being rash

RASING   present participle of rase

RASORIAL   adj habitually scratching the ground for food

RASP   v -ED, -ING, -S to rub with something rough

RASPER   n pl. -S one that rasps

RASPISH   adj irritable

RASPY   adj RASPIER, RASPIEST rough

RASSLE   v -SLED, -SLING, -SLES to wrestle

RASTER   n pl. -S the area reproducing images on the picture tube of a television set

RASURE   n pl. -S erasure

RAT   v RATTED, RATTING, RATS to hunt rats (long-tailed rodents)

RATABLE   adj capable of being rated **RATABLY** adv

RATAFEE   n pl. -S ratafia

RATAFIA   n pl. -S an almond-flavored liqueur

RATAL   n pl. -S an amount on which rates are assessed

RATAN   n pl. -S rattan

RATANY   *n* pl. -NIES rhatany

RATAPLAN   *v* -PLANNED, -PLANNING, -PLANS to make a rapidly repeating sound

RATATAT   *n* pl. -S a quick, sharp rapping sound

RATCH   *n* pl. -ES a ratchet

RATCHET   *n* pl. -S a mechanism which allows motion in one direction only

RATE   *v* RATED, RATING, RATES to estimate the value of

RATEABLE   *adj* ratable **RATEABLY** *adv*

RATEL   *n* pl. -S a carnivorous mammal

RATER   *n* pl. -S one that rates

RATFINK   *n* pl. -S a contemptible person

RATFISH   *n* pl. -ES a marine fish

RATH   *adj* rathe

RATHE   *adj* appearing or ripening early

RATHER   *adv* preferably

RATHOLE   *n* pl. -S a hole made by a rat

RATICIDE   *n* pl. -S a substance for killing rats

RATIFIER   *n* pl. -S one that ratifies

RATIFY   *v* -FIED, -FYING, -FIES to approve and sanction formally

RATINE   *n* pl. -S a heavy fabric

RATING   *n* pl. -S relative estimate or evaluation

RATIO   *n* pl. -TIOS a proportional relationship

RATION   *v* -ED, -ING, -S to distribute in fixed portions

RATIONAL   *n* pl. -S a number that can be expressed as a quotient of integers

RATITE   *n* pl. -S a flightless bird

RATLIKE   *adj* resembling a rat

RATLIN   *n* pl. -S ratline

RATLINE   *n* pl. -S one of the ropes forming the steps of a rope ladder on a ship

RATO   *n* pl. -TOS a rocket-assisted airplane takeoff

RATOON   *v* -ED, -ING, -S to sprout from a root planted the previous year

RATOONER   *n* pl. -S a plant that ratoons

RATSBANE   *n* pl. -S rat poison

RATTAIL   *n* pl. -S a marine fish

RATTAN   *n* pl. -S a palm tree

RATTED   past tense of rat

RATTEEN   *n* pl. -S a coarse woolen fabric

RATTEN   *v* -ED, -ING, -S to harass

RATTENER   *n* pl. -S one that rattens

RATTER   *n* pl. -S an animal used for catching rats

RATTIER   comparative of ratty

RATTIEST   superlative of ratty

RATTING   present participle of rat

RATTISH   *adj* ratlike

RATTLE   *v* -TLED, -TLING, -TLES to make a quick succession of short, sharp sounds

RATTLER   *n* pl. -S one that rattles

RATTLING   *n* pl. -S ratline

RATTLY   *adj* tending to rattle

RATTON   *n* pl. -S a rat

RATTOON   *v* -ED, -ING, -S to ratoon

RATTRAP   *n* pl. -S a trap for catching rats

RATTY   *adj* -TIER, -TIEST infested with rats

RAUCITY   *n* pl. -TIES the state of being raucous

RAUCOUS   *adj* loud and unruly

RAUNCHY   *adj* -CHIER, -CHIEST slovenly

RAVAGE   *v* -AGED, -AGING, -AGES to destroy

RAVAGER   *n* pl. -S one that ravages

RAVE   *v* RAVED, RAVING, RAVES to speak irrationally or incoherently

RAVEL   *v* -ELED, -ELING, -ELS or -ELLED, -ELLING, -ELS to separate the threads of

RAVELER   *n* pl. -S one that ravels

RAVELIN   *n* pl. -S a type of fortification

RAVELING   *n* pl. -S a loose thread

RAVELLED   a past tense of ravel

RAVELLER   *n* pl. -S raveler

RAVELLING   *n* pl. -S raveling

RAVELLY   *adj* tangled

RAVEN   *v* -ED, -ING, -S to eat in a ravenous manner

RAVENER   *n* pl. -S one that ravens

RAVENING   *n* pl. -S rapacity

RAVENOUS   *adj* extremely hungry

RAVER   *n* pl. -S one that raves

RAVIGOTE   *n* pl. -S a spiced vinegar sauce

RAVIN	v -ED, -ING, -S to raven
RAVINE	n pl. -S a narrow, steep-sided valley
RAVING	n pl. -S irrational, incoherent speech
RAVINGLY	adv in a delirious manner
RAVIOLI	n pl. -S an Italian dish
RAVISH	v -ED, -ING, -ES to seize and carry off by force
RAVISHER	n pl. -S one that ravishes
RAW	adj RAWER, RAWEST uncooked
RAW	n pl. -S a sore or irritated spot
RAWBONED	adj having little flesh
RAWHIDE	v -HIDED, -HIDING, -HIDES to beat with a type of whip
RAWISH	adj somewhat raw
RAWLY	adv in a raw manner
RAWNESS	n pl. -ES the state of being raw
RAX	v -ED, -ING, -ES to stretch out
RAY	v -ED, -ING, -S to emit rays (narrow beams of light)
RAYA	n pl. -S rayah
RAYAH	n pl. -S a non-Muslim inhabitant of Turkey
RAYGRASS	n pl. -ES ryegrass
RAYLESS	adj having no rays
RAYON	n pl. -S a synthetic fiber
RAZE	v RAZED, RAZING, RAZES to tear down or demolish
RAZEE	v -ZEED, -ZEEING, -ZEES to make lower by removing the upper deck, as a ship
RAZER	n pl. -S one that razes
RAZING	present participle of raze
RAZOR	v -ED, -ING, -S to shave or cut with a sharp-edged instrument
RAZZ	v -ED, -ING, -ES to deride
RE	n pl. -S the second tone of the diatonic musical scale

Following is a list of self-explanatory verbs containing the prefix RE- (again):

REABSORB	v -ED, -ING, -S
REACCEDE	v -CEDED, -CEDING, -CEDES
REACCENT	v -ED, -ING, -S

REACCEPT	v -ED, -ING, -S
REACCUSE	v -CUSED, -CUSING, -CUSES
READAPT	v -ED, -ING, -S
READD	v -ED, -ING, -S
READDICT	v -ED, -ING, -S
READJUST	v -ED, -ING, -S
READMIT	v -MITTED, -MITTING, -MITS
READOPT	v -ED, -ING, -S
READORN	v -ED, -ING, -S
REAFFIRM	v -ED, -ING, -S
REAFFIX	v -ED, -ING, -ES
REALIGN	v -ED, -ING, -S
REALLOT	v -LOTTED, -LOTTING, -LOTS
REALTER	v -ED, -ING, -S
REANNEX	v -ED, -ING, -ES
REANOINT	v -ED, -ING, -S
REAPPEAR	v -ED, -ING, -S
REAPPLY	v -PLIED, -PLYING, -PLIES
REARGUE	v -GUED, -GUING, -GUES
REARM	v -ED, -ING, -S
REAROUSE	v -AROUSED, -AROUSING, -AROUSES
REARREST	v -ED, -ING, -S
REASCEND	v -ED, -ING, -S
REASSAIL	v -ED, -ING, -S
REASSERT	v -ED, -ING, -S
REASSESS	v -ED, -ING, -ES
REASSIGN	v -ED, -ING, -S
REASSORT	v -ED, -ING, -S
REASSUME	v -SUMED, -SUMING, -SUMES
REASSURE	v -SURED, -SURING, -SURES
REATTACH	v -ED, -ING, -ES
REATTACK	v -ED, -ING, -S
REATTAIN	v -ED, -ING, -S
REAVOW	v -ED, -ING, -S
REAWAKE	v -AWAKED or -AWOKE, -AWOKEN, -AWAKING, -AWAKES
REAWAKEN	v -ED, -ING, -S
REBAIT	v -ED, -ING, -S
REBID	v -BID, -BIDDEN, -BIDDING, -BIDS
REBILL	v -ED, -ING, -S
REBIND	v -BOUND, -BINDING, -BINDS
REBLOOM	v -ED, -ING, -S
REBOARD	v -ED, -ING, -S
REBOIL	v -ED, -ING, -S
REBOUND	past tense of rebind
REBUILD	v -BUILT or -BUILDED, -BUILDING, -BUILDS
REBURY	v -BURIED, -BURYING, -BURIES
REBUTTON	v -ED, -ING, -S
RECANE	v -CANED, -CANING, -CANES
RECARRY	v -RIED, -RYING, -RIES
RECAST	v -CAST, -CASTING, -CASTS

RECHANGE	v -CHANGED, -CHANGING, -CHANGES	**REEJECT**	v -ED, -ING, -S
RECHARGE	v -CHARGED, -CHARGING, -CHARGES	**REELECT**	v -ED, -ING, -S
		REEMBARK	v -ED, -ING, -S
RECHART	v -ED, -ING, -S	**REEMBODY**	v -BODIED, -BODYING, -BODIES
RECHECK	v -ED, -ING, -S	**REEMERGE**	v -EMERGED, -EMERGING, -EMERGES
RECHOOSE	v -CHOSE, -CHOSEN, -CHOOSING, -CHOOSES	**REEMIT**	v -EMITTED, -EMITTING, -EMITS
RECIRCLE	v -CLED, -CLING, -CLES	**REEMPLOY**	v -ED, -ING, -S
RECLAD	a past tense of reclothe	**REENACT**	v -ED, -ING, -S
RECLASP	v -ED, -ING, -S	**REENDOW**	v -ED, -ING, -S
RECLEAN	v -ED, -ING, -S	**REENGAGE**	v -GAGED, -GAGING, -GAGES
RECLOTHE	v -CLOTHED or -CLAD, -CLOTHING, -CLOTHES	**REENJOY**	v -ED, -ING, -S
		REENLIST	v -ED, -ING, -S
RECOAL	v -ED, -ING, -S	**REENTER**	v -ED, -ING, -S
RECOCK	v -ED, -ING, -S	**REEQUIP**	v -EQUIPPED, -EQUIPPING, -EQUIPS
RECODIFY	v -FIED, -FYING, -FIES	**REERECT**	v -ED, -ING, -S
RECOIN	v -ED, -ING, -S	**REEVOKE**	v -EVOKED, -EVOKING, -EVOKES
RECOLOR	v -ED, -ING, -S	**REEXPEL**	v -PELLED, -PELLING, -PELS
RECOMB	v -ED, -ING, -S	**REEXPORT**	v -ED, -ING, -S
RECOMMIT	v -MITTED, -MITTING, -MITS	**REFALL**	v -FELL, -FALLEN, -FALLING, -FALLS
RECOOK	v -ED, -ING, -S	**REFASTEN**	v -ED, -ING, -S
RECOPY	v -COPIED, -COPYING, -COPIES	**REFEED**	v -FED, -FEEDING, -FEEDS
RECOUPLE	v -PLED, -PLING, -PLES	**REFELL**	past tense of refall
RECRATE	v -CRATED, -CRATING, -CRATES	**REFIGHT**	v -FOUGHT, -FIGHTING, -FIGHTS
RECROSS	v -ED, -ING, -ES	**REFIGURE**	v -URED, -URING, -URES
RECROWN	v -ED, -ING, -S	**REFILE**	v -FILED, -FILING, -FILES
RECUT	v -CUT, -CUTTING, -CUTS	**REFILL**	v -ED, -ING, -S
REDATE	v -DATED, -DATING, -DATES	**REFILM**	v -ED, -ING, -S
REDEFEAT	v -ED, -ING, -S	**REFILTER**	v -ED, -ING, -S
REDEFINE	v -FINED, -FINING, -FINES	**REFIND**	v -FOUND, -FINDING, -FINDS
REDEFY	v -FIED, -FYING, -FIES	**REFIRE**	v -FIRED, -FIRING, -FIRES
REDEMAND	v -ED, -ING, -S	**REFIX**	v -ED, -ING, -ES
REDENY	v -NIED, -NYING, -NIES	**REFLEW**	past tense of refly
REDEPLOY	v -ED, -ING, -S	**REFLIES**	present 3d person sing. of refly
REDESIGN	v -ED, -ING, -S	**REFLOAT**	v -ED, -ING, -S
REDID	past tense of redo	**REFLOOD**	v -ED, -ING, -S
REDIGEST	v -ED, -ING, -S	**REFLOW**	v -ED, -ING, -S
REDIP	v -DIPPED or -DIPT, -DIPPING, -DIPS	**REFLOWER**	v -ED, -ING, -S
REDIVIDE	v -VIDED, -VIDING, -VIDES	**REFLY**	v -FLEW, -FLOWN, -FLYING, -FLIES
REDO	v -DID, -DONE, -DOING, -DOES	**REFOCUS**	v -CUSED, -CUSING, -CUSES or -CUSSED, -CUSSING, -CUSSES
REDOCK	v -ED, -ING, -S		
REDRAW	v -DREW, -DRAWN, -DRAWING, -DRAWS	**REFOLD**	v -ED, -ING, -S
		REFORGE	v -FORGED, -FORGING, -FORGES
REDRIED	past tense of redry	**REFORMAT**	v -MATTED, -MATTING, -MATS
REDRIES	present 3d person sing. of redry	**REFOUGHT**	past tense of refight
REDRILL	v -ED, -ING, -S	**REFOUND**	v -ED, -ING, -S
REDRIVE	v -DROVE, -DRIVEN, -DRIVING, -DRIVES	**REFRAME**	v -FRAMED, -FRAMING, -FRAMES
		REFREEZE	v -FROZE, -FROZEN, -FREEZING, -FREEZES
REDRY	v -DRIED, -DRYING, -DRIES		
REDYE	v -DYED, -DYEING, -DYES	**REFRONT**	v -ED, -ING, -S
REEARN	v -ED, -ING, -S	**REFRY**	v -FRIED, -FRYING, -FRIES
REECHO	v -ED, -ING, -ES	**REFUEL**	v -ELED, -ELING, -ELS or -ELLED, -ELLING, -ELS
REEDIT	v -ED, -ING, -S		

REGAIN	v -ED, -ING, -S
REGATHER	v -ED, -ING, -S
REGAUGE	v -GAUGED, -GAUGING, -GAUGES
REGAVE	past tense of regive
REGEAR	v -ED, -ING, -S
REGILD	v -GILDED or -GILT, -GILDING, -GILDS
REGIVE	v -GAVE, -GIVEN, -GIVING, -GIVES
REGLAZE	v -GLAZED, -GLAZING, -GLAZES
REGLOSS	v -ED, -ING, -ES
REGLOW	v -ED, -ING, -S
REGLUE	v -GLUED, -GLUING, -GLUES
REGRADE	v -GRADED, -GRADING, -GRADES
REGRAFT	v -ED, -ING, -S
REGRANT	v -ED, -ING, -S
REGREW	past tense of regrow
REGRIND	v -GROUND, -GRINDING, -GRINDS
REGROOVE	v -GROOVED, -GROOVING, -GROOVES
REGROUP	v -ED, -ING, -S
REGROW	v -GREW, -GROWN, -GROWING, -GROWS
REHAMMER	v -ED, -ING, -S
REHANDLE	v -DLED, -DLING, -DLES
REHANG	v -HUNG or -HANGED, -HANGING, -HANGS
REHARDEN	v -ED, -ING, -S
REHASH	v -ED, -ING, -ES
REHEAR	v -HEARD, -HEARING, -HEARS
REHEAT	v -ED, -ING, -S
REHEEL	v -ED, -ING, -S
REHEM	v -HEMMED, -HEMMING, -HEMS
REHINGE	v -HINGED, -HINGING, -HINGES
REHIRE	v -HIRED, -HIRING, -HIRES
REHUNG	a past tense of rehang
REIGNITE	v -NITED, -NITING, -NITES
REIMAGE	v -AGED, -AGING, -AGES
REIMPORT	v -ED, -ING, -S
REIMPOSE	v -POSED, -POSING, -POSES
REINCITE	v -CITED, -CITING, -CITES
REINCUR	v -CURRED, -CURRING, -CURS
REINDEX	v -ED, -ING, -ES
REINDUCE	v -DUCED, -DUCING, -DUCES
REINDUCT	v -ED, -ING, -S
REINFECT	v -ED, -ING, -S
REINFORM	v -ED, -ING, -S
REINFUSE	v -FUSED, -FUSING, -FUSES
REINJURE	v -JURED, -JURING, -JURES
REINSERT	v -ED, -ING, -S
REINSURE	v -SURED, -SURING, -SURES
REINTER	v -TERRED, -TERRING, -TERS
REINVENT	v -ED, -ING, -S
REINVEST	v -ED, -ING, -S
REINVITE	v -VITED, -VITING, -VITES
REINVOKE	v -VOKED, -VOKING, -VOKES
REISSUE	v -SUED, -SUING, -SUES
REJOIN	v -ED, -ING, -S
REJUDGE	v -JUDGED, -JUDGING, -JUDGES
REKEY	v -ED, -ING, -S
REKINDLE	v -DLED, -DLING, -DLES
REKNIT	v -KNITTED, -KNITTING, -KNITS
RELABEL	v -BELED, -BELING, -BELS or -BELLED, -BELLING, -BELS
RELACE	v -LACED, -LACING, -LACES
RELAUNCH	v -ED, -ING, -ES
RELAY	v -LAID, -LAYING, -LAYS
RELEARN	v -LEARNED or -LEARNT, -LEARNING, -LEARNS
RELEND	v -LENT, -LENDING, -LENDS
RELET	v -LET, -LETTING, -LETS
RELETTER	v -ED, -ING, -S
RELIGHT	v -LIGHTED or -LIT, -LIGHTING, -LIGHTS
RELINE	v -LINED, -LINING, -LINES
RELIST	v -ED, -ING, -S
RELIT	a past tense of relight
RELOAD	v -ED, -ING, -S
RELOAN	v -ED, -ING, -S
REMAIL	v -ED, -ING, -S
REMAKE	v -MADE, -MAKING, -MAKES
REMAP	v -MAPPED, -MAPPING, -MAPS
REMARRY	v -RIED, -RYING, -RIES
REMATCH	v -ED, -ING, -ES
REMEET	v -MET, -MEETING, -MEETS
REMELT	v -ED, -ING, -S
REMEND	v -ED, -ING, -S
REMERGE	v -MERGED, -MERGING, -MERGES
REMET	past tense of remeet
REMIX	v -MIXED or -MIXT, -MIXING, -MIXES
REMODIFY	v -FIED, -FYING, -FIES
REMOLD	v -ED, -ING, -S
REMOUNT	v -ED, -ING, -S
RENAME	v -NAMED, -NAMING, -NAMES
RENOTIFY	v -FIED, -FYING, -FIES
RENUMBER	v -ED, -ING, -S
REOBJECT	v -ED, -ING, -S
REOBTAIN	v -ED, -ING, -S
REOCCUPY	v -PIED, -PYING, -PIES
REOCCUR	v -CURRED, -CURRING, -CURS
REOIL	v -ED, -ING, -S
REOPEN	v -ED, -ING, -S
REOPPOSE	v -POSED, -POSING, -POSES
REORDAIN	v -ED, -ING, -S
REORDER	v -ED, -ING, -S
REORIENT	v -ED, -ING, -S
REPACIFY	v -FIED, -FYING, -FIES
REPACK	v -ED, -ING, -S
REPAINT	v -ED, -ING, -S

REPAPER	v -ED, -ING, -S
REPASS	v -ED, -ING, -ES
REPAVE	v -PAVED, -PAVING, -PAVES
REPEOPLE	v -PLED, -PLING, -PLES
REPERK	v -ED, -ING, -S
REPHRASE	v -PHRASED, -PHRASING, -PHRASES
REPIN	v -PINNED, -PINNING, -PINS
REPLAN	v -PLANNED, -PLANNING, -PLANS
REPLANT	v -ED, -ING, -S
REPLATE	v -PLATED, -PLATING, -PLATES
REPLAY	v -ED, -ING, -S
REPLEDGE	v -PLEDGED, -PLEDGING, -PLEDGES
REPLUNGE	v -PLUNGED, -PLUNGING, -PLUNGES
REPOLISH	v -ED, -ING, -ES
REPOUR	v -ED, -ING, -S
REPOWER	v -ED, -ING, -S
REPRICE	v -PRICED, -PRICING, -PRICES
REPRINT	v -ED, -ING, -S
REPROBE	v -PROBED, -PROBING, -PROBES
REPURIFY	v -FIED, -FYING, -FIES
REPURSUE	v -SUED, -SUING, -SUES
REREAD	v -READ, -READING, -READS
RERECORD	v -ED, -ING, -S
RERISE	v -ROSE, -RISEN, -RISING, -RISES
REROLL	v -ED, -ING, -S
REROUTE	v -ROUTED, -ROUTING, -ROUTES
RESADDLE	v -DLED, -DLING, -DLES
RESAID	past tense of resay
RESAIL	v -ED, -ING, -S
RESALUTE	v -LUTED, -LUTING, -LUTES
RESAMPLE	v -PLED, -PLING, -PLES
RESAW	v -SAWED, -SAWN, -SAWING, -SAWS
RESAY	v -SAID, -SAYING, -SAYS
RESCORE	v -SCORED, -SCORING, -SCORES
RESCREEN	v -ED, -ING, -S
RESEAL	v -ED, -ING, -S
RESEAT	v -ED, -ING, -S
RESEE	v -SAW, -SEEN, -SEEING, -SEES
RESEED	v -ED, -ING, -S
RESEEK	v -SOUGHT, -SEEKING, -SEEKS
RESEEN	past participle of resee
RESEIZE	v -SEIZED, -SEIZING, -SEIZES
RESELL	v -SOLD, -SELLING, -SELLS
RESEND	v -SENT, -SENDING, -SENDS
RESET	v -SET, -SETTING, -SETS
RESETTLE	v -TLED, -TLING, -TLES
RESEW	v -SEWED, -SEWN, -SEWING, -SEWS
RESHAPE	v -SHAPED, -SHAPING, -SHAPES
RESHIP	v -SHIPPED, -SHIPPING, -SHIPS
RESHOE	v -SHOD, -SHOEING, -SHOES

RESHOOT	v -SHOT, -SHOOTING, -SHOOTS
RESHOW	v -SHOWED, -SHOWN, -SHOWING, -SHOWS
RESIFT	v -ED, -ING, -S
RESILVER	v -ED, -ING, -S
RESIZE	v -SIZED, -SIZING, -SIZES
RESMELT	v -ED, -ING, -S
RESMOOTH	v -ED, -ING, -S
RESOLD	past tense of resell
RESOLDER	v -ED, -ING, -S
RESOLE	v -SOLED, -SOLING, -SOLES
RESOUGHT	past tense of reseek
RESOW	v -SOWED, -SOWN, -SOWING, -SOWS
RESPELL	v -SPELLED or -SPELT, -SPELLING, -SPELLS
RESPREAD	v -SPREAD, -SPREADING, -SPREADS
RESPRING	v -SPRANG or -SPRUNG, -SPRINGING, -SPRINGS
RESTACK	v -ED, -ING, -S
RESTAFF	v -ED, -ING, -S
RESTAGE	v -STAGED, -STAGING, -STAGES
RESTAMP	v -ED, -ING, -S
RESTART	v -ED, -ING, -S
RESTATE	v -STATED, -STATING, -STATES
RESTOCK	v -ED, -ING, -S
RESTRIKE	v -STRUCK, -STRICKEN, -STRIKING, -STRIKES
RESTRING	v -STRUNG, -STRINGING, -STRINGS
RESTRIVE	v -STROVE, -STRIVEN, -STRIVING, -STRIVES
RESTRUCK	past tense of restrike
RESTRUNG	past tense of restring
RESTUDY	v -STUDIED, -STUDYING, -STUDIES
RESTUFF	v -ED, -ING, -S
RESTYLE	v -STYLED, -STYLING, -STYLES
RESUBMIT	v -MITTED, -MITTING, -MITS
RESUMMON	v -ED, -ING, -S
RESUPPLY	v -PLIED, -PLYING, -PLIES
RESURVEY	v -ED, -ING, -S
RETAILOR	v -ED, -ING, -S
RETASTE	v -TASTED, -TASTING, -TASTES
RETEACH	v -TAUGHT, -TEACHING, -TEACHES
RETELL	v -TOLD, -TELLING, -TELLS
RETEST	v -ED, -ING, -S
RETHINK	v -THOUGHT, -THINKING, -THINKS
RETHREAD	v -ED, -ING, -S
RETIE	v -TIED, -TYING, -TIES
RETIME	v -TIMED, -TIMING, -TIMES
RETINT	v -ED, -ING, -S
RETITLE	v -TLED, -TLING, -TLES
RETOLD	past tense of retell
RETRACK	v -ED, -ING, -S
RETRAIN	v -ED, -ING, -S

RETRIM	v -TRIMMED, -TRIMMING, -TRIMS
RETRY	v -TRIED, -TRYING, -TRIES
RETUNE	v -TUNED, -TUNING, -TUNES
RETWIST	v -ED, -ING, -S
RETYING	present participle of retie
RETYPE	v -TYPED, -TYPING, -TYPES
REUNIFY	v -FIED, -FYING, -FIES
REUNITE	v -UNITED, -UNITING, -UNITES
REUSE	v -USED, -USING, -USES
REUTTER	v -ED, -ING, -S
REVALUE	v -UED, -UING, -UES
REVERIFY	v -FIED, -FYING, -FIES
REVEST	v -ED, -ING, -S
REVIEW	v -ED, -ING, -S
REVISIT	v -ED, -ING, -S
REVOICE	v -VOICED, -VOICING, -VOICES
REWAKE	v -WAKED or -WOKE, -WOKEN, -WAKING, -WAKES
REWAKEN	v -ED, -ING, -S
REWAN	a past tense of rewin
REWARM	v -ED, -ING, -S
REWASH	v -ED, -ING, -ES
REWAX	v -ED, -ING, -ES
REWEAVE	v -WOVE or -WEAVED, -WOVEN, -WEAVING, -WEAVES
REWEIGH	v -ED, -ING, -S
REWELD	v -ED, -ING, -S
REWIDEN	v -ED, -ING, -S
REWIN	v -WON or -WAN, -WINNING, -WINS
REWIND	v -WOUND or -WINDED, -WINDING, -WINDS
REWIRE	v -WIRED, -WIRING, -WIRES
REWOKE	a past tense of rewake
REWOKEN	past participle of rewake
REWON	a past tense of rewin
REWORK	v -WORKED or -WROUGHT, -WORKING, -WORKS
REWOUND	a past tense of rewind
REWOVE	a past tense of reweave
REWOVEN	past participle of reweave
REWRAP	v -WRAPPED, or -WRAPT, -WRAPPING, -WRAPS
REWRITE	v -WROTE, -WRITTEN, -WRITING, -WRITES
REWROUGHT	a past tense of rework
REZONE	v -ZONED, -ZONING, -ZONES
REACH	v -ED, -ING, -ES to stretch out or put forth
REACHER	n pl. -S one that reaches
REACT	v -ED, -ING, -S to respond to a stimulus

REACTANT	n pl. -S one that reacts
REACTION	n pl. -S the act of reacting
REACTIVE	adj tending to react
REACTOR	n pl. -S one that reacts
READ	v READ, READING, READS to look at so as to take in the meaning of, as something written or printed **READABLE** adj **READABLY** adv
READER	n pl. -S one that reads
READIED	past tense of ready
READIER	comparative of ready
READIES	present 3d person sing. of ready
READIEST	superlative of ready
READILY	adv in a ready manner
READING	n pl. -S material that is read
READOUT	n pl. -S a presentation of computer data
READY	adj READIER, READIEST prepared
READY	v READIED, READYING, READIES to make ready
REAGENT	n pl. -S a substance used in a chemical reaction to ascertain the nature or composition of another
REAGIN	n pl. -S a type of antibody **REAGINIC** adj
REAL	adj REALER, REALEST having actual existence
REAL	n pl. -S or -ES a former monetary unit of Spain
REAL	n pl. REIS a former monetary unit of Portugal and Brazil
REALGAR	n pl. -S a mineral
REALIA	n/pl objects used by a teacher to illustrate everyday living
REALISE	v -ISED, -ISING, -ISES to realize
REALISER	n pl. -S one that realises
REALISM	n pl. -S concern with fact or reality
REALIST	n pl. -S one who is concerned with fact or reality
REALITY	n pl. -TIES something that is real
REALIZE	v -IZED, -IZING, -IZES to understand completely
REALIZER	n pl. -S one that realizes
REALLY	adv actually
REALM	n pl. -S a kingdom

REALNESS *n* pl. -ES the state of being real

REALTY *n* pl. -TIES property in buildings and land

REAM *v* -ED, -ING, -S to enlarge with a reamer

REAMER *n* pl. -S a tool used to enlarge holes

REAP *v* -ED, -ING, -S to cut for harvest **REAPABLE** *adj*

REAPER *n* pl. -S one that reaps

REAPHOOK *n* pl. -S an implement used in reaping

REAR *v* -ED, -ING, -S to lift upright

REARER *n* pl. -S one that rears

REARMICE *n/pl* reremice

REARMOST *adj* coming or situated last

REARWARD *n* pl. -S the rearmost division of an army

REASCENT *n* pl. -S a new or second ascent

REASON *v* -ED, -ING, -S to derive inferences or conclusions from known or presumed facts

REASONER *n* pl. -S one that reasons

REATA *n* pl. -S riata

REAVE *v* REAVED or REFT, REAVING, REAVES to plunder

REAVER *n* pl. -S one that reaves

REB *n* pl. -S a Confederate soldier

REBATE *v* -BATED, -BATING, -BATES to deduct or return from a payment or bill

REBATER *n* pl. -S one that rebates

REBATO *n* pl. -TOS rabato

REBBE *n* pl. -S a rabbi

REBEC *n* pl. -S an ancient stringed instrument

REBECK *n* pl. -S rebec

REBEL *v* -BELLED, -BELLING, -BELS to oppose the established government of one's land

REBELDOM *n* pl. -S an area controlled by rebels

REBIRTH *n* pl. -S a new or second birth

REBOANT *adj* resounding loudly

REBOP *n* pl. -S a type of music

REBORN *adj* born again

REBOUND *v* -ED, -ING, -S to spring back

REBOZO *n* pl. -ZOS a long scarf

REBRANCH *v* -ED, -ING, -ES to form secondary branches

REBUFF *v* -ED, -ING, -S to reject or refuse curtly

REBUKE *v* -BUKED, -BUKING, -BUKES to criticize sharply

REBUKER *n* pl. -S one that rebukes

REBURIAL *n* pl. -S a second burial

REBUS *n* pl. -ES a type of puzzle

REBUT *v* -BUTTED, -BUTTING, -BUTS to refute

REBUTTAL *n* pl. -S argument or proof that rebuts

REBUTTER *n* pl. -S one that rebuts

REBUTTING present participle of rebut

REC *n* pl. -S recreation

RECALL *v* -ED, -ING, -S to call back

RECALLER *n* pl. -S one that recalls

RECANT *v* -ED, -ING, -S to make a formal retraction or disavowal of

RECANTER *n* pl. -S one that recants

RECAP *v* -CAPPED, -CAPPING, -CAPS to review by a brief summary

RECEDE *v* -CEDED, -CEDING, -CEDES to move back or away

RECEIPT *v* -ED, -ING, -S to mark as having been paid

RECEIVE *v* -CEIVED, -CEIVING, -CEIVES to come into possession of

RECEIVER *n* pl. -S one that receives

RECENCY *n* pl. -CIES the state of being recent

RECENT *adj* -CENTER, -CENTEST of or pertaining to a time not long past **RECENTLY** *adv*

RECEPT *n* pl. -S a type of mental image

RECEPTOR *n* pl. -S a nerve ending specialized to receive stimuli

RECESS *v* -ED, -ING, -ES to place in a receding space or hollow

RECHEAT *n* pl. -S a hunting call

RECIPE *n* pl. -S a set of instructions for making something

RECISION *n* pl. -S a cancellation

RECITAL *n* pl. -S a detailed account

RECITE *v* -CITED, -CITING, -CITES to declaim or say from memory

RECITER *n* pl. -S one that recites

RECK *v* -ED, -ING, -S to be concerned about

RECKLESS	*adj* foolishly heedless of danger	**RECTUS**	*n* pl. -TI a straight muscle
RECKON	*v* -ED, -ING, -S to count or compute	**RECUR**	*v* -CURRED, -CURRING, -CURS to happen again
RECKONER	*n* pl. -S one that reckons	**RECURVE**	*v* -CURVED, -CURVING, -CURVES to curve backward or downward
RECLAIM	*v* -ED, -ING, -S to make suitable for cultivation or habitation		
RECLAME	*n* pl. -S publicity	**RECUSANT**	*n* pl. -S one who refuses to accept established authority
RECLINE	*v* -CLINED, -CLINING, -CLINES to lean or lie back	**RECUSE**	*v* -CUSED, -CUSING, -CUSES to disqualify or challenge as judge in a particular case
RECLINER	*n* pl. -S one that reclines		
RECLUSE	*n* pl. -S one who lives in solitude and seclusion	**RECYCLE**	*v* -CLED, -CLING, -CLES to process in order to extract useful materials
RECOIL	*v* -ED, -ING, -S to draw back in fear or disgust	**RED**	*adj* REDDER, REDDEST of the color of blood
RECOILER	*n* pl. -S one that recoils		
RECON	*n* pl. -S a preliminary survey	**RED**	*v* REDDED, REDDING, REDS to redd
RECONVEY	*v* -ED, -ING, -S to convey back to a previous position	**REDACT**	*v* -ED, -ING, -S to prepare for publication
RECORD	*v* -ED, -ING, -S to set down for preservation	**REDACTOR**	*n* pl. -S one that redacts
RECORDER	*n* pl. -S one that records	**REDAN**	*n* pl. -S a type of fortification
RECOUNT	*v* -ED, -ING, -S to relate in detail	**REDARGUE**	*v* -GUED, -GUING, -GUES to disprove
RECOUP	*v* -ED, -ING, -S to get back the equivalent of	**REDBAIT**	*v* -ED, -ING, -S to denounce as Communist
RECOUPE	*adj* divided twice	**REDBAY**	*n* pl. -BAYS a small tree
RECOURSE	*n* pl. -S a turning or applying to someone or something for aid	**REDBIRD**	*n* pl. -S a bird with red plummage
RECOVER	*v* -ED, -ING, -S to obtain again after losing	**REDBONE**	*n* pl. -S a hunting dog
RECOVERY	*n* pl. -ERIES an economic upturn	**REDBRICK**	*adj* pertaining to modern British universities
RECREANT	*n* pl. -S a coward	**REDBUD**	*n* pl. -S a small tree
RECREATE	*v* -ATED, -ATING, -ATES to refresh mentally or physically	**REDBUG**	*n* pl. -S a chigger
RECRUIT	*v* -ED, -ING, -S to engage for military service	**REDCAP**	*n* pl. -S a porter
		REDCOAT	*n* pl. -S a British soldier during the American Revolution
RECTA	a pl. of rectum		
RECTAL	*adj* pertaining to the rectum **RECTALLY** *adv*	**REDD**	*v* -ED, -ING, -S to put in order
		REDDED	past tense of red and redd
RECTI	pl. of rectus	**REDDEN**	*v* -ED, -ING, -S to make or become red
RECTIFY	*v* -FIED, -FYING, -FIES to correct		
		REDDER	*n* pl. -S one that redds
RECTO	*n* pl. -TOS a right-hand page of a book	**REDDEST**	superlative of red
RECTOR	*n* pl. -S a clergyman in charge of a parish	**REDDING**	present participle of red and redd
RECTORY	*n* pl. -RIES a rector's dwelling	**REDDISH**	*adj* somewhat red
RECTRIX	*n* pl. -TRICES a feather of a bird's tail	**REDDLE**	*v* -DLED, -DLING, -DLES to ruddle
RECTUM	*n* pl. -TUMS or -TA the terminal portion of the large intestine	**REDE**	*v* REDED, REDING, REDES to advise
		REDEAR	*n* pl. -S a common sunfish

REDEEM v -ED, -ING, -S to buy back

REDEEMER n pl. -S one that redeems

REDEYE n pl. -S a railroad danger signal

REDFIN n pl. -S a freshwater fish

REDFISH n pl. -ES an edible rockfish

REDHEAD n pl. -S a person with red hair

REDHORSE n pl. -S a freshwater fish

REDIA n pl. -DIAE or -DIAS the larva of certain flatworms **REDIAL** adj

REDING present participle of rede

REDIRECT v -ED, -ING, -S to change the course or direction of

REDLEG n pl. -S a bird with red legs

REDLY adv with red color

REDNECK n pl. -S one that redraws of the southern United States

REDNESS n pl. -ES the state of being red

REDO n pl. -DOS something that is done again

REDOLENT adj fragrant

REDOUBLE v -BLED, -BLING, -BLES to double

REDOUBT n pl. -S an enclosed fortification

REDOUND v -ED, -ING, -S to have an effect or consequence

REDOUT n pl. -S a condition in which blood is driven to the head

REDOWA n pl. -S a lively dance

REDOX n pl. -ES a type of chemical reaction

REDPOLL n pl. -S a small finch

REDRAFT v -ED, -ING, -S to make a revised copy of

REDRAWER n pl. -S one that redraws

REDRESS v -ED, -ING, -ES to set right

REDROOT n pl. -S a perennial herb

REDSHANK n pl. -S a shore bird

REDSHIRT v -ED, -ING, -S to keep a college athlete out of varsity play in order to extend his eligibility

REDSKIN n pl. -S a North American Indian

REDSTART n pl. -S a small songbird

REDTOP n pl. -S a type of grass

REDUCE v -DUCED, -DUCING, -DUCES to diminish

REDUCER n pl. -S one that reduces

REDUVIID n pl. -S a bloodsucking insect

REDWARE n pl. -S an edible seaweed

REDWING n pl. -S a European thrush

REDWOOD n pl. -S a very tall evergreen tree

REE n pl. -S the female Eurasian sandpiper

REED v -ED, -ING, -S to fasten with reeds (the stalks of tall grasses)

REEDBIRD n pl. -S the bobolink

REEDBUCK n pl. -S an African antelope

REEDIER comparative of reedy

REEDIEST superlative of reedy

REEDIFY v -FIED, -FYING, -FIES to rebuild

REEDING n pl. -S a convex molding

REEDLING n pl. -S a marsh bird

REEDY adj REEDIER, REEDIEST abounding in reeds

REEF v -ED, -ING, -S to reduce the area of a sail

REEFER n pl. -S one that reefs

REEFY adj REEFIER, REEFIEST abounding in ridges of rock

REEK v -ED, -ING, -S to give off a strong, unpleasant odor

REEKER n pl. -S one that reeks

REEKY adj REEKIER, REEKIEST reeking

REEL v -ED, -ING, -S to wind on a type of rotary device **REELABLE** adj

REELER n pl. -S one that reels

REENTRY n pl. -TRIES a new or second entry

REEST v -ED, -ING, -S to balk

REEVE v REEVED or ROVE, ROVEN, REEVING, REEVES to fasten by passing through or around something

REF v REFFED, REFFING, REFS to referee

REFACE v -FACED, -FACING, -FACES to repair the outer surface of

REFECT v -ED, -ING, -S to refresh with food and drink

REFEL v -FELLED, -FELLING, -FELS to reject

REFER v -FERRED, -FERRING, -FERS to direct to a source for help or information

REFEREE   v -EED, -EEING, -EES to supervise the play in certain sports

REFERENT   n pl. -S something referred to

REFERRAL   n pl. -S one that is referred

REFERRED   past tense of refer

REFERRER   n pl. -S one that refers

REFERRING   present participle of refer

REFFED   past tense of ref

REFFING   present participle of ref

REFINE   v -FINED, -FINING, -FINES to free from impurities

REFINER   n pl. -S one that refines

REFINERY   n pl. -ERIES a place where crude material is refined

REFINING   present participle of refine

REFINISH   v -ED, -ING, -ES to give a new surface to

REFIT   v -FITTED, -FITTING, -FITS to prepare and equip for additional use

REFLATE   v -FLATED, -FLATING, -FLATES to inflate again

REFLECT   v -ED, -ING, -S to turn or throw back from a surface

REFLET   n pl. -S special brilliance of surface

REFLEX   v -ED, -ING, -ES to bend back

REFLEXLY   adv in a reflexed manner

REFLUENT   adj flowing back

REFLUX   v -ED, -ING, -ES to cause to flow back

REFOREST   v -ED, -ING, -S to replant with trees

REFORM   v -ED, -ING, -S to change to a better state

REFORMER   n pl. -S one that reforms

REFRACT   v -ED, -ING, -S to deflect in a particular manner, as a ray of light

REFRAIN   v -ED, -ING, -S to keep oneself back

REFRESH   v -ED, -ING, -ES to restore the well-being and vigor of

REFT   a past tense of reave

REFUGE   v -UGED, -UGING, -UGES to give or take shelter

REFUGEE   n pl. -S one who flees for safety

REFUGIUM   n pl. -GIA a stable area during a period of continental climactic change

REFUND   v -ED, -ING, -S to give back

REFUNDER   n pl. -S one that refunds

REFUSAL   n pl. -S the act of refusing

REFUSE   v -FUSED, -FUSING, -FUSES to express oneself as unwilling to accept, do, or comply with

REFUSER   n pl. -S one that refuses

REFUTAL   n pl. -S the act of refuting

REFUTE   v -FUTED, -FUTING, -FUTES to prove to be false or erroneous

REFUTER   n pl. -S one that refutes

REGAINER   n pl. -S one that regains

REGAL   adj of or befitting a king

REGALE   v -GALED, -GALING, -GALES to delight

REGALIA   n/pl the rights and privileges of a king

REGALITY   n pl. -TIES regal authority

REGALLY   adv in a regal manner

REGARD   v -ED, -ING, -S to look upon with a particular feeling

REGATTA   n pl. -S a boat race

REGELATE   v -LATED, -LATING, -LATES to refreeze ice by reducing the pressure

REGENCY   n pl. -CIES the office of a regent

REGENT   n pl. -S one who rules in the place of a sovereign **REGENTAL** adj

REGES   pl. of rex

REGICIDE   n pl. -S the killing of a king

REGIME   n pl. -S a system of government

REGIMEN   n pl. -S a systematic plan

REGIMENT   v -ED, -ING, -S to form into military units

REGINA   n pl. -NAE or -NAS queen **REGINAL** adj

REGION   n pl. -S an administrative area or division

REGIONAL   n pl. -S something that serves as a region

REGISTER   v -ED, -ING, -S to record officially

REGISTRY   n pl. -TRIES the act of registering

REGIUS   adj holding a professorship founded by the sovereign

REGLET   n pl. -S a flat, narrow molding

REGMA   n pl. -MATA a type of fruit

REGNA   pl. of regnum

REGNAL   *adj* pertaining to a king or his reign

REGNANCY   *n* pl. -CIES the state of being regnant

REGNANT   *adj* reigning

REGNUM   *n* pl. -NA dominion

REGOLITH   *n* pl. -S a layer of loose rock

REGORGE   *v* -GORGED, -GORGING, -GORGES to vomit

REGOSOL   *n* pl. -S a type of soil

REGRATE   *v* -GRATED, -GRATING, -GRATES to buy up in order to sell for a higher price in the same area

REGREET   *v* -ED, -ING, -S to greet in return

REGRESS   *v* -ED, -ING, -ES to go back

REGRET   *v* -GRETTED, -GRETTING, -GRETS to look back upon with sorrow or remorse

REGROWTH   *n* pl. -S a new or second growth

REGULAR   *n* pl. -S an habitual customer

REGULATE   *v* -LATED, -LATING, -LATES to control according to rule

REGULUS   *n* pl. -LI or -LUSES a mass that forms beneath the slag in a furnace REGULINE *adj*

REHEARSE   *v* -HEARSED, -HEARSING, -HEARSES to practice in preparation for a public appearance

REHEATER   *n* pl. -S one that reheats

REHOUSE   *v* -HOUSED, -HOUSING, -HOUSES to establish in a new housing unit

REI   *n* pl. -S an erroneous English form for a former Portuguese coin

REIF   *n* pl. -S robbery

REIFIER   *n* pl. -S one that reifies

REIFY   *v* -IFIED, -IFYING, -IFIES to regard as real or concrete

REIGN   *v* -ED, -ING, -S to exercise sovereign power

REIN   *v* -ED, -ING, -S to restrain

REINDEER   *n* pl. -S a large deer

REINLESS   *adj* unrestrained

REINSMAN   *n* pl. -MEN a skilled rider of horses

REIS   pl. of real

REISSUER   *n* pl. -S one that reissues

REITBOK   *n* pl. -S the reedbuck

REIVE   *v* REIVED, REIVING, REIVES to plunder

REIVER   *n* pl. -S one that reives

REJECT   *v* -ED, -ING, -S to refuse to accept, consider, or make use of

REJECTEE   *n* pl. -S one that is rejected

REJECTER   *n* pl. -S one that rejects

REJECTOR   *n* pl. -S rejecter

REJIGGER   *v* -ED, -ING, -S to alter

REJOICE   *v* -JOICED, -JOICING, -JOICES to feel joyful

REJOICER   *n* pl. -S one that rejoices

RELAPSE   *v* -LAPSED, -LAPSING, -LAPSES to fall or slip back into a former state

RELAPSER   *n* pl. -S one that relapses

RELATE   *v* -LATED, -LATING, -LATES to give an account of

RELATER   *n* pl. -S one that relates

RELATION   *n* pl. -S a significant association between two or more things

RELATIVE   *n* pl. -S one who is connected with another by blood or marriage

RELATOR   *n* pl. -S relater

RELAX   *v* -ED, -ING, -ES to make less tense or rigid

RELAXANT   *n* pl. -S a drug that relieves muscular tension

RELAXER   *n* pl. -S one that relaxes

RELAXIN   *n* pl. -S a female hormone

RELAY   *v* -ED, -ING, -S to send along by using fresh sets to replace tired ones

RELEASE   *v* -LEASED, -LEASING, -LEASES to set free

RELEASER   *n* pl. -S one that releases

RELEGATE   *v* -GATED, -GATING, -GATES to assign

RELENT   *v* -ED, -ING, -S to become less severe

RELEVANT   *adj* pertaining to the matter at hand

RELIABLE   *adj* suitable to be relied on RELIABLY *adv*

RELIANCE   *n* pl. -S confident or trustful dependence

RELIANT   *adj* showing reliance

RELIC	n pl. -S a surviving memorial of something past
RELICT	n pl. -S an organism surviving in a changed environment
RELIED	past tense of rely
RELIEF	n pl. -S aid in the form of money or necessities
RELIER	n pl. -S one that relies
RELIES	present 3d person sing. of rely
RELIEVE	v -LIEVED, -LIEVING, -LIEVES to lessen or free from pain or discomfort
RELIEVER	n pl. -S one that relieves
RELIEVO	n pl. -VOS the projection of figures or forms from a flat background
RELIGION	n pl. -S the worship of a god or the supernatural
RELIQUE	n pl. -S relic
RELISH	v -ED, -ING, -ES to enjoy
RELIVE	v -LIVED, -LIVING, -LIVES to experience again
RELOADER	n pl. -S one that reloads
RELOCATE	v -CATED, -CATING, -CATES to establish in a new place
RELUCENT	adj reflecting light
RELUCT	v -ED, -ING, -S to show opposition
RELUME	v -LUMED, -LUMING, -LUMES to light again
RELUMINE	v -MINED, -MINING, -MINES to relume
RELY	v -LIED, -LYING, -LIES to place trust or confidence
REM	n pl. -S a quantity of ionizing radiation
REMAIN	v -ED, -ING, -S to continue in the same state
REMAN	v -MANNED, -MANNING, -MANS to furnish with a fresh supply of men
REMAND	v -ED, -ING, -S to send back
REMANENT	adj remaining
REMANNED	past tense of reman
REMANNING	present participle of reman
REMARK	v -ED, -ING, -S to say or write briefly or casually
REMARKER	n pl. -S one that remarks
REMARQUE	n pl. -S a mark made in the margin of an engraved plate

REMEDIAL	adj intended to correct something
REMEDY	v -DIED, -DYING, -DIES to relieve or cure
REMEMBER	v -ED, -ING, -S to bring to mind again
REMEX	n pl. REMIGES a flight feather of a bird's wing **REMIGIAL** adj
REMIND	v -ED, -ING, -S to cause to remember
REMINDER	n pl. -S one that reminds
REMINT	v -ED, -ING, -S to melt down and make into new coin
REMISE	v -MISED, -MISING, -MISES to give up a claim to
REMISS	adj careless **REMISSLY** adv
REMIT	v -MITTED, -MITTING, -MITS to send money in payment
REMITTAL	n pl. -S the act of remitting
REMITTER	n pl. -S one that remits
REMITTING	present participle of remit
REMITTOR	n pl. -S remitter
REMNANT	n pl. -S something remaining
REMODEL	v -ELED, -ELING, -ELS or -ELLED, -ELLING, -ELS to make over
REMOLADE	n pl. -S a piquant sauce
REMORA	n pl. -S a type of marine fish **REMORID** adj
REMORSE	n pl. -S deep anguish caused by a sense of guilt
REMOTE	adj -MOTER, -MOTEST situated far away **REMOTELY** adv
REMOTION	n pl. -S the act of removing
REMOVAL	n pl. -S the act of removing
REMOVE	v -MOVED, -MOVING, -MOVES to take or move away
REMOVER	n pl. -S one that removes
REMUDA	n pl. -S a herd of horses
RENAL	adj pertaining to the kidneys
RENATURE	v -TURED, -TURING, -TURES to restore natural qualities
REND	v RENT or RENDED, RENDING, RENDS to tear apart forcibly
RENDER	v -ED, -ING, -S to cause to be or become
RENDERER	n pl. -S one that renders
RENDIBLE	adj capable of being rent
RENDZINA	n pl. -S a type of soil

RENEGADE v -GADED, -GADING, -GADES to become a traitor

RENEGADO n pl. -DOS or -DOES a traitor

RENEGE v -NEGED, -NEGING, -NEGES to fail to carry out a promise or commitment

RENEGER n pl. -S one that reneges

RENEW v -ED, -ING, -S to make new or as if new again

RENEWAL n pl. -S the act of renewing

RENEWER n pl. -S one that renews

RENIFORM adj kidney-shaped

RENIG v -NIGGED, -NIGGING, -NIGS to renege

RENIN n pl. -S an enzyme

RENITENT adj resisting physical pressure

RENNASE n pl. -S rennin

RENNET n pl. -S a lining membrane in the stomach of certain young animals

RENNIN n pl. -S an enzyme

RENOGRAM n pl. -S a photographic depiction of the course of renal excretion

RENOUNCE v -NOUNCED, -NOUNCING, -NOUNCES to disown

RENOVATE v -VATED, -VATING, -VATES to make like new

RENOWN v -ED, -ING, -S to make famous

RENT v -ED, -ING, -S to obtain temporary use of in return for compensation **RENTABLE** adj

RENTAL n pl. -S an amount paid or collected as rent

RENTE n pl. -S annual income under French law

RENTER n pl. -S one that rents

RENTIER n pl. -S one that receives a fixed income

RENVOI n pl. -S the expulsion by a government of an alien

REOFFER v -ED, -ING, -S to offer for public sale

REOVIRUS n pl. -ES a type of virus

REP n pl. -S a cross-ribbed fabric

REPAID past tense of repay

REPAIR v -ED, -ING, -S to restore to good condition

REPAIRER n pl. -S one that repairs

REPAND adj having a wavy margin **REPANDLY** adv

REPARTEE n pl. -S a quick, witty reply

REPAST v -ED, -ING, -S to eat or feast

REPAY v -PAID, -PAYING, -PAYS to pay back

REPEAL v -ED, -ING, -S to revoke

REPEALER n pl. -S one that repeals

REPEAT v -ED, -ING, -S to say or do again

REPEATER n pl. -S one that repeats

REPEL v -PELLED, -PELLING, -PELS to drive back

REPELLER n pl. -S one that repels

REPENT v -ED, -ING, -S to feel remorse or self-reproach for a past action

REPENTER n pl. -S one that repents

REPETEND n pl. -S a phrase or sound that is repeated

REPINE v -PINED, -PINING, -PINES to express discontent

REPINER n pl. -S one that repines

REPLACE v -PLACED, -PLACING, -PLACES to take the place of

REPLACER n pl. -S one that replaces

REPLETE adj abundantly supplied

REPLEVIN v -ED, -ING, -S to replevy

REPLEVY v -PLEVIED, -PLEVYING, -PLEVIES to regain possession of by legal action

REPLICA n pl. -S a close copy or reproduction

REPLIER n pl. -S one that replies

REPLY v -PLIED, -PLYING, -PLIES to answer

REPORT v -ED, -ING, -S to give an account of

REPORTER n pl. -S one that reports

REPOSAL n pl. -S the act of reposing

REPOSE v -POSED, -POSING, -POSES to lie at rest

REPOSER n pl. -S one that reposes

REPOSIT v -ED, -ING, -S to put away

REPOUSSE n pl. -S a raised design hammered in metal

REPP n pl. -S rep

REPPED adj resembling rep

REPRESS v -ED, -ING, -ES to keep under control

REPRIEVE — *v* -PRIEVED, -PRIEVING, -PRIEVES to postpone the punishment of

REPRISAL — *n* pl. -S an act of retaliation

REPRISE — *v* -PRISED, -PRISING, -PRISES to take back by force

REPRO — *n* pl. -PROS a trial ohoot of printed material suitable for photographic reproduction

REPROACH — *v* -ED, -ING, -ES to find fault with

REPROOF — *n* pl. -S criticism for a fault

REPROVAL — *n* pl. -S reproof

REPROVE — *v* -PROVED, -PROVING, -PROVES to rebuke

REPROVER — *n* pl. -S one that reproves

REPTANT — *adj* creeping or crawling

REPTILE — *n* pl. -S any of a class of cold-blooded, air-breathing verte-brates

REPUBLIC — *n* pl. -S a constitutional form of government

REPUGN — *v* -ED, -ING, -S to oppose

REPULSE — *v* -PULSED, -PULSING, -PULSES to drive back

REPULSER — *n* pl. -S one that repulses

REPUTE — *v* -PUTED, -PUTING, -PUTES to consider to be as specified

REQUEST — *v* -ED, -ING, -S to express a desire for

REQUIEM — *n* pl. -S a musical composition for the dead

REQUIN — *n* pl. -S a voracious shark

REQUIRE — *v* -QUIRED, -QUIRING, -QUIRES to have need of

REQUIRER — *n* pl. -S one that requires

REQUITAL — *n* pl. -S something given in return, compensation, or retaliation

REQUITE — *v* -QUITED, -QUITING, -QUITES to make equivalent return for

REQUITER — *n* pl. -S one that requites

RERAN — past tense of rerun

REREDOS — *n* pl. -ES an ornamental screen behind an altar

REREMICE — *n/pl* bats (flying mammals)

REREWARD — *n* pl. -S rearward

REROLLER — *n* pl. -S one that rerolls

RERUN — *v* -RAN, -RUNNING, -RUNS to present a repetition of a recorded performance

RES — *n* pl. RES a particular thing or matter

RESALE — *n* pl. -S the act of selling again

RESCALE — *v* -SCALED, -SCALING, -SCALES to plan on a new scale

RESCIND — *v* -ED, -ING, -S to annul

RESCRIPT — *n* pl. -S something rewritten

RESCUE — *v* -CUED, -CUING, -CUES to free from danger

RESCUER — *n* pl. -S one that rescues

RESEARCH — *v* -ED, -ING, -ES to investigate thoroughly

RESEAU — *n* pl. -SEAUS or -SEAUX a filter screen for making color films

RESECT — *v* -ED, -ING, -S to excise part of an organ or structure surgically

RESEDA — *n* pl. -S a flowering plant

RESELLER — *n* pl. -S one that resells

RESEMBLE — *v* -BLED, -BLING, -BLES to be similar to

RESENT — *v* -ED, -ING, -S to feel or express annoyance or ill will at

RESERVE — *v* -SERVED, -SERVING, -SERVES to keep back for future use

RESERVER — *n* pl. -S one that reserves

RESETTER — *n* pl. -S one that resets

RESH — *n* pl. -ES a Hebrew letter

RESHAPER — *n* pl. -S one that reshapes something

RESID — *n* pl. -S a type of fuel oil

RESIDE — *v* -SIDED, -SIDING, -SIDES to dwell permanently or continu-ously

RESIDENT — *n* pl. -S one who resides

RESIDER — *n* pl. -S a resident

RESIDUA — a pl. of residuum

RESIDUAL — *n* pl. -S something left over

RESIDUE — *n* pl. -S something remaining after the removal of a part

RESIDUUM — *n* pl. -SIDUA or -SIDUUMS residue

RESIGN — *v* -ED, -ING, -S to give up one's office or position

RESIGNER — *n* pl. -S one that resigns

RESILE — *v* -SILED, -SILING, -SILES to spring back

RESIN — *v* -ED, -ING, -S to treat with resin (a viscous substance obtained from certain plants)

RESINATE   v -ATED, -ATING, -ATES to resin

RESINIFY   v -FIED, -FYING, -FIES to convert into resin

RESINOID   n pl. -S a resinous substance

RESINOUS   adj resembling resin

RESINY   adj resinous

RESIST   v -ED, -ING, -S to strive against

RESISTER   n pl. -S one that resists

RESISTOR   n pl. -S a device in an electric circuit

RESOJET   n pl. -S a pulsejet

RESOLUTE   adj -LUTER, -LUTEST characterized by firmness or determination

RESOLUTE   n pl. -S one who is resolute

RESOLVE   v -SOLVED, -SOLVING, -SOLVES to make a firm decision about

RESOLVER   n pl. -S one that resolves

RESONANT   n pl. -S a resounding sound

RESONATE   v -NATED, -NATING, -NATES to resound

RESORB   v -ED, -ING, -S to absorb again

RESORCIN   n pl. -S a chemical compound

RESORT   v -ED, -ING, -S to go frequently or habitually

RESORTER   n pl. -S one that resorts

RESOUND   v -ED, -ING, -S to make a loud, long, or echoing sound

RESOURCE   n pl. -S an available supply

RESPECT   v -ED, -ING, -S to have a high regard for

RESPIRE   v -SPIRED, -SPIRING, -SPIRES to breathe

RESPITE   v -SPITED, -SPITING, -SPITES to relieve temporarily

RESPOND   v -ED, -ING, -S to say or act in return

RESPONSA   n/pl written rabbinic decisions

RESPONSE   n pl. -S a reply or reaction

REST   v -ED, -ING, -S to refresh oneself by ceasing work or activity

RESTER   n pl. -S one that rests

RESTFUL   adj -FULLER, -FULLEST tranquil

RESTIVE   adj difficult to control

RESTLESS   adj unable or disinclined to remain at rest

RESTORAL   n pl. -S the act of restoring

RESTORE   v -STORED, -STORING, -STORES to bring back to a former or original condition

RESTORER   n pl. -S one that restores

RESTRAIN   v -ED, -ING, -S to hold back from action

RESTRICT   v -ED, -ING, -S to keep within certain boundaries

RESULT   v -ED, -ING, -S to occur as a consequence

RESUME   v -SUMED, -SUMING, -SUMES to take up again after interruption

RESUMER   n pl. -S one that resumes

RESUPINE   adj lying on the back

RESURGE   v -SURGED, -SURGING, -SURGES to rise again

RET   v RETTED, RETTING, RETS to soak in order to loosen the fiber from the woody tissue

RETABLE   n pl. -S a raised shelf above an altar

RETAIL   v -ED, -ING, -S to sell in small quantities

RETAILER   n pl. -S one that retails

RETAIN   v -ED, -ING, -S to keep possession of

RETAINER   n pl. -S one that retains

RETAKE   v -TOOK, -TAKEN, -TAKING, -TAKES to take back

RETAKER   n pl. -S one that retakes

RETARD   v -ED, -ING, -S to slow the progress of

RETARDER   n pl. -S one that retards

RETCH   v -ED, -ING, -ES to make an effort to vomit

RETE   n pl. -TIA an anatomical mesh or network

RETEM   n pl. -S a desert shrub

RETENE   n pl. -S a chemical compound

RETIA   pl. of rete

RETIAL   adj pertaining to a rete

RETIARII   n/pl ancient Roman gladiators

RETIARY   adj resembling a net

RETICENT   adj tending to be silent

RETICLE   n pl. -S a network of lines in the eyepiece of an optical instrument

RETICULA   n/pl netlike structures

RETICULE   n pl. -S a woman's handbag

RETIFORM	adj arranged like a net	RETURNEE	n pl. -S one that has returned
RETINA	n pl. -NAS or -NAE a membrane of the eye	RETURNER	n pl. -S one that returns
		RETUSE	adj having a rounded apex with a shallow notch — used of leaves
RETINAL	n pl. -S retinene		
RETINENE	n pl. -S a pigment in the retina	REUNION	n pl. -S a reuniting of persons after separation
RETINITE	n pl. -S a fossil resin		
RETINOL	n pl. -S a liquid hydrocarbon	REUNITER	n pl. -S one that reunites
RETINUE	n pl. -S a group of attendants RETINUED adj	REUSABLE	adj capable of being used again
		REV	v REVVED, REVVING, REVS to increase the speed of
RETINULA	n pl. -LAE or -LAS a neural receptor of an arthropod's eye		
		REVAMP	v -ED, -ING, -S to make over
RETIRANT	n pl. -S a retiree	REVAMPER	n pl. -S one that revamps
RETIRE	v -TIRED, -TIRING, -TIRES to go away or withdraw	REVANCHE	n pl. -S a political policy designed to regain lost territory
RETIREE	n pl. -S one who has retired from his vocation	REVEAL	v -ED, -ING, -S to make known
		REVEALER	n pl. -S one that reveals
RETIRER	n pl. -S one that retires	REVEHENT	adj carrying back
RETIRING	adj shy	REVEILLE	n pl. -S a morning bugle call
RETOOK	past tense of retake	REVEL	v -ED, -ELING, -ELS or -ELLED, -ELLING, -ELS to engage in revelry
RETOOL	v -ED, -ING, -S to reequip with tools		
RETORT	v -ED, -ING, -S to answer back	REVELER	n pl. -S one that revels
RETORTER	n pl. -S one that retorts	REVELLER	n pl. -S a reveler
RETOUCH	v -ED, -ING, -ES to add new details or touches to	REVELRY	n pl. -RIES noisy merrymaking
		REVENANT	n pl. -S one that returns
RETRACE	v -TRACED, -TRACING, -TRACES to go back over	REVENGE	v -VENGED, -VENGING, -VENGES to inflict injury in return for
RETRACT	v -ED, -ING, -S to take back		
RETRAIN	v -ED, -ING, -S to train again	REVENGER	n pl. -S one that revenges
RETRAL	adj situated toward the back RETRALLY adv	REVENUE	n pl. -S the income of a government REVENUAL, REVENUED adj
RETREAD	v -ED, -ING, -S to furnish with a new tread		
		REVENUER	n pl. -S a revenue officer
RETREAT	v -ED, -ING, -S to go back or backward	REVERB	n pl. -S an echo effect in recorded music
RETRENCH	v -ED, -ING, -ES to curtail		
RETRIAL	n pl. -S a second trial	REVERE	v -VERED, -VERING, -VERES to regard with great respect
RETRIEVE	v -TRIEVED, -TRIEVING, -TRIEVES to get back		
		REVEREND	n pl. -S a clergyman
RETROACT	v -ED, -ING, -S to act in return	REVERENT	adj deeply respectful
RETROFIT	v -FITTED, -FITTING, -FITS to furnish with new parts not originally available	REVERER	n pl. -S one that reveres
		REVERIE	n pl. -S a daydream
		REVERIES	pl. of revery
RETRORSE	adj bent backward	REVERING	present participle of revere
RETSINA	n pl. -S a Greek wine	REVERS	n pl. REVERS a part of a garment turned back to show the inside
RETTED	past tense of ret		
RETTING	present participle of ret		
RETURN	v -ED, -ING, -S to come or go back		
		REVERSAL	n pl. -S the act of reversing

REVERSE *v* -VERSED, -VERSING, -VERSES to turn or move in the opposite direction

REVERSER *n pl.* -S one that reverses

REVERSO *n pl.* -VERSOS verso

REVERT *v* -ED, -ING, -S to return to a former state

REVERTER *n pl.* -S one that reverts

REVERY *n pl.* -ERIES reverie

REVET *v* -VETTED, -VETTING, -VETS to face with masonry

REVIEWAL *n pl.* -S the act of reviewing

REVIEWER *n pl.* -S one that reviews

REVILE *v* -VILED, -VILING, -VILES to denounce with abusive language

REVILER *n pl.* -S one that reviles

REVISAL *n pl.* -S a revision

REVISE *v* -VISED, -VISING, -VISES to make a new or improved version of

REVISER *n pl.* -S one that revises

REVISION *n pl.* -S a revised version

REVISOR *n pl.* -S reviser

REVISORY *adj* pertaining to revision

REVIVAL *n pl.* -S renewed attention to or interest in something

REVIVE *v* -VIVED, -VIVING, -VIVES to bring back to life or consciousness

REVIVER *n pl.* -S one that revives

REVIVIFY *v* -FIED, -FYING, -FIES to give new life to

REVIVING present participle of revive

REVOKE *v* -VOKED, -VOKING, -VOKES to annul by taking back

REVOKER *n pl.* -S one that revokes

REVOLT *v* -ED, -ING, -S to rise up against authority

REVOLTER *n pl.* -S one that revolts

REVOLUTE *adj* rolled backward or downward

REVOLVE *v* -VOLVED, -VOLVING, -VOLVES to turn about an axis

REVOLVER *n pl.* -S a type of handgun

REVUE *n pl.* -S a type of musical show

REVUIST *n pl.* -S a writer of revues

REVULSED *adj* affected with revulsion

REVVED past tense of rev

REVVING present participle of rev

REWARD *v* -ED, -ING, -S to give recompense to for worthy behavior

REWARDER *n pl.* -S one that rewards

REWINDER *n pl.* -S one that rewinds

REWORD *v* -ED, -ING, -S to state again in other words

REWRITER *n pl.* -S one that rewrites

REX *n pl.* REGES king

REX *n pl.* -ES an animal with a single wavy layer of hair

REYNARD *n pl.* -S a fox

RHABDOM *n pl.* -S a rodlike structure in the retinula

RHABDOME *n pl.* -S rhabdom

RHACHIS *n pl.* -CHISES or -CHIDES rachis

RHAMNOSE *n pl.* -S a sugar found in plants

RHAMNUS *n pl.* -ES a thorny tree or shrub

RHAPHE *n pl.* -PHAE or -PHES raphe

RHAPSODE *n pl.* -S a reciter of epic poetry in ancient Greece

RHAPSODY *n pl.* -DIES an exalted expression of feeling

RHATANY *n pl.* -NIES a South American shrub

RHEA *n pl.* -S a flightless bird

RHEBOK *n pl.* -S a large antelope

RHEMATIC *adj* pertaining to a verb

RHENIUM *n pl.* -S a metallic element

RHEOBASE *n pl.* -S the smallest amount of electricity required to stimulate a nerve

RHEOLOGY *n pl.* -GIES the study of matter in the fluid state

RHEOPHIL *adj* living in flowing water

RHEOSTAT *n pl.* -S a resistor used to control electric current

RHESUS *n pl.* -ES an Asian monkey

RHETOR *n pl.* -S a teacher of rhetoric

RHETORIC *n pl.* -S the study of effective speech and writing

RHEUM *n pl.* -S a watery discharge from the eyes or nose **RHEUMIC** *adj*

RHEUMY *adj* RHEUMIER, RHEUMIEST marked by rheum

RHINAL *adj* pertaining to the nose

RHINITIS *n pl.* RHINITIDES inflammation of the mucous membranes of the nose

RHINO *n pl.* -NOS a rhinoceros

RHIZOBIA — *n/pl* rod-shaped bacteria

RHIZOID — *n pl.* -S a rootlike structure

RHIZOMA — *n pl.* -MATA rhizome

RHIZOME — *n pl.* -S a rootlike, underground stem **RHIZOMIC** *adj*

RHIZOPOD — *n pl.* -S any of a class of protozoans

RHIZOPUS — *n pl.* -PI or -PUSES any of a genus of mold fungi

RHO — *n pl.* RHOS a Greek letter

RHODAMIN — *n pl.* -S a red dye

RHODIUM — *n pl.* -S a metallic element **RHODIC** *adj*

RHODORA — *n pl.* -S a flowering shrub

RHOMB — *n pl.* -S a rhombus

RHOMBI — a pl. of rhombus

RHOMBIC — *adj* having the shape of a rhombus

RHOMBOID — *n pl.* -S a type of geometric figure

RHOMBUS — *n pl.* -BUSES or -BI a type of geometric figure

RHONCHUS — *n pl.* -CHI a rattling respiratory sound **RHONCHAL** *adj*

RHUBARB — *n pl.* -S a perennial herb

RHUMB — *n pl.* -S a point of the mariner's compass

RHUMBA — *v* -ED, -ING, -S to rumba

RHUS — *n pl.* -ES any of a genus of shrubs and trees

RHYME — *v* RHYMED, RHYMING, RHYMES to compose verse with corresponding terminal sounds

RHYMER — *n pl.* -S one that rhymes

RHYOLITE — *n pl.* -S a volcanic rock

RHYTA — pl. of rhyton

RHYTHM — *n pl.* -S movement or procedure with uniform recurrence of strong and weak elements

RHYTHMIC — *n pl.* -S the science of rhythm

RHYTON — *n pl.* -TA an ancient Greek drinking horn

RIAL — *n pl.* -S a monetary unit of Iran

RIALTO — *n pl.* -TOS a marketplace

RIANT — *adj* cheerful **RIANTLY** *adv*

RIATA — *n pl.* -S a lasso

RIB — *v* RIBBED, RIBBING, RIBS to poke fun at

RIBALD — *n pl.* -S one who uses crude language

RIBALDLY — *adv* crudely

RIBALDRY — *n pl.* -RIES crude language

RIBAND — *n pl.* -S a ribbon

RIBBAND — *n pl.* -S a long, narrow strip used in shipbuilding

RIBBED — past tense of rib

RIBBER — *n pl.* -S one that ribs

RIBBIER — comparative of ribby

RIBBIEST — superlative of ribby

RIBBING — *n pl.* -S the act of one that ribs

RIBBON — *v* -ED, -ING, -S to decorate with ribbons (narrow strips of fine fabric)

RIBBONY — *adj* resembling ribbon

RIBBY — *adj* -BIER, -BIEST marked by prominent ribs (curved bony rods in the body)

RIBES — *n pl.* RIBES a flowering shrub

RIBGRASS — *n pl.* -ES a weedy plant

RIBLESS — *adj* having no ribs

RIBLET — *n pl.* -S the rib end in a breast of lamb or veal

RIBLIKE — *adj* resembling a rib

RIBOSE — *n pl.* -S a pentose sugar

RIBOSOME — *n pl.* -S a particle composed of protein and ribonucleic acid

RIBWORT — *n pl.* -S ribgrass

RICE — *v* RICED, RICING, RICES to press through a ricer

RICEBIRD — *n pl.* -S the bobolink

RICER — *n pl.* -S a kitchen utensil consisting of a container perforated with small holes

RICERCAR — *n pl.* -S an instrumental composition

RICH — *adj* RICHER, RICHEST having wealth

RICHEN — *v* -ED, -ING, -S to make rich

RICHES — *n/pl* wealth

RICHLY — *adv* in a rich manner

RICHNESS — *n pl.* -ES the state of being rich

RICHWEED — *n pl.* -S a flowering plant

RICIN — *n pl.* -S a poisonous protein

RICING — present participle of rice

RICINUS — *n pl.* -ES a large-leaved plant

RICK — *v* -ED, -ING, -S to pile hay in stacks

RICKETS n/pl a disease resulting from vitamin D deficiency

RICKETY adj -ETIER, -ETIEST likely to fall or collapse

RICKEY n pl. -EYS an alcoholic beverage containing lime juice, sugar, and soda water

RICKRACK n pl. -S a flat braid used as a trimming

RICKSHA n pl. -S rickshaw

RICKSHAW n pl. -S a small, two-wheeled passenger vehicle

RICOCHET v -CHETED, -CHETING, -CHETS or -CHETTED, -CHETTING, -CHETS to rebound from a surface

RICOTTA n pl. -S an Italian cheese

RICRAC n pl. -S rickrack

RICTUS n pl. -ES the expanse of the open mouth **RICTAL** adj

RID v RID or RIDDED, RIDDING, RIDS to free from something objectionable

RIDABLE adj capable of being ridden

RIDDANCE n pl. -S deliverance

RIDDED past tense of rid

RIDDEN past participle of ride

RIDDER n pl. -S one that rids

RIDDING present participle of rid

RIDDLE v -DLED, -DLING, -DLES to pierce with many holes

RIDDLER n pl. -S one that riddles

RIDE v RODE, RIDDEN, RIDING, RIDES to sit on, control, and be conveyed by an animal or machine

RIDEABLE adj ridable

RIDENT adj laughing

RIDER n pl. -S one that rides

RIDGE v RIDGED, RIDGING, RIDGES to form into ridges (long, narrow elevations)

RIDGEL n pl. -S a ridgling

RIDGIER comparative of ridgy

RIDGIEST superlative of ridgy

RIDGIL n pl. -S a ridgling

RIDGING present participle of ridge

RIDGLING n pl. -S a male animal with undescended testicles

RIDGY adj RIDGIER, RIDGIEST having ridges

RIDICULE v -CULED, -CULING, -CULES to make fun of

RIDING n pl. -S the act of one that rides

RIDLEY n pl. -LEYS a sea turtle

RIDOTTO n pl. -TOS a public musical entertainment in 18th century England

RIEL n pl. -S a monetary unit of Cambodia

RIEVER n pl. -S reaver

RIFE adj RIFER, RIFEST abundant **RIFELY** adv

RIFENESS n pl. -ES the state of being rife

RIFF v -ED, -ING, -S to riffle

RIFFLE v -FLED, -FLING, -FLES to flip through hastily

RIFFLER n pl. -S a filing and scraping tool

RIFFRAFF n pl. -S the disreputable element of society

RIFLE v -FLED, -FLING, -FLES to search through and rob

RIFLEMAN n pl. -MEN a soldier armed with a rifle (a type of firearm)

RIFLER n pl. -S one that rifles

RIFLERY n pl. -RIES the practice of shooting at targets with a rifle

RIFLING n pl. -S the system of grooves in a gun barrel

RIFT v -ED, -ING, -S to form rifts (clefts)

RIFTLESS adj having no rift

RIG v RIGGED, RIGGING, RIGS to put in proper condition for use

RIGADOON n pl. -S a lively dance

RIGATONI n pl. -S a tubular pasta

RIGAUDON n pl. -S rigadoon

RIGGED past tense of rig

RIGGER n pl. -S one that rigs

RIGGING n pl. -S the system of lines, chains, and tackle used aboard a ship

RIGHT adj RIGHTER, RIGHTEST being in accordance with what is good, proper, or just

RIGHT v -ED, -ING, -S to put in proper order or condition

RIGHTER n pl. -S one that rights

RIGHTFUL adj just or proper

RIGHTIES pl. of righty

RIGHTISM *n* pl. -S a conservative political philosophy

RIGHTIST *n* pl. -S an advocate of rightism

RIGHTLY *adv* in a right manner

RIGHTO *interj* — used to express cheerful consent

RIGHTY *n* pl. RIGHTIES a right-handed person

RIGID *adj* not flexible

RIGIDIFY *v* -FIED, -FYING, -FIES to make rigid

RIGIDITY *n* pl. -TIES the state of being rigid

RIGIDLY *adv* in a rigid manner

RIGOR *n* pl. -S strictness or severity

RIGORISM *n* pl. -S strictness or severity in conduct or attitude

RIGORIST *n* pl. -S one that professes rigorism

RIGOROUS *adj* characterized by rigor

RIGOUR *n* pl. -S rigor

RIKISHA *n* pl. -S rickshaw

RIKSHAW *n* pl. -S rickshaw

RILE *v* RILED, RILING, RILES to anger

RILEY *adj* angry

RILIEVO *n* pl. -VI relievo

RILING present participle of rile

RILL *v* -ED, -ING, -S to flow like a rill (a small brook)

RILLE *n* pl. -S a valley on the moon's surface

RILLET *n* pl. -S a small rill

RIM *v* RIMMED, RIMMING, RIMS to provide with a rim (an outer edge)

RIME *v* RIMED, RIMING, RIMES to rhyme

RIMER *n* pl. -S one that rimes

RIMESTER *n* pl. -S a rimer

RIMFIRE *adj* designed for the use of certain cartridges

RIMIER comparative of rimy

RIMIEST superlative of rimy

RIMING present participle of rime

RIMLAND *n* pl. -S an outlying area

RIMLESS *adj* having no rim

RIMMED past tense of rim

RIMMER *n* pl. -S a reamer

RIMMING present participle of rim

RIMOSE *adj* marked by cracks **RIMOSELY** *adv*

RIMOSITY *n* pl. -TIES the state of being rimose

RIMOUS *adj* rimose

RIMPLE *v* -PLED, -PLING, -PLES to wrinkle

RIMROCK *n* pl. -S a type of rock formation

RIMY *adj* RIMIER, RIMIEST frosty

RIN *v* RAN, RINNING, RINS to run or melt

RIND *n* pl. -S a thick and firm outer covering **RINDED** *adj*

RING *v* -ED, -ING, -S to form a ring (a circular band) around

RING *v* RANG, RUNG, RINGING, RINGS to give forth a clear, resonant sound

RINGBARK *v* -ED, -ING, -S to make an encircling cut through the bark of

RINGBOLT *n* pl. -S a type of eyebolt

RINGBONE *n* pl. -S a bony growth on a horse's foot

RINGDOVE *n* pl. -S a European pigeon

RINGENT *adj* having open liplike parts

RINGER *n* pl. -S one that rings

RINGHALS *n* pl. -ES a venomous snake

RINGLET *adj* a small ring

RINGLIKE *adj* resembling a ring

RINGNECK *n* pl. -S a bird having a ring of color around the neck

RINGSIDE *n* pl. -S the area just outside a boxing or wrestling ring (a square enclosure)

RINGTAIL *n* pl. -S an animal having a tail with ringlike markings

RINGTAW *n* pl. -S a game of marbles

RINGTOSS *n* pl. -ES a game in which the object is to toss a ring onto an upright stick

RINGWORM *n* pl. -S a skin disease

RINK *n* pl. -S a surface of ice for skating

RINNING present participle of rin

RINSE *v* RINSED, RINSING, RINSES to cleanse with clear water **RINSABLE, RINSIBLE** *adj*

RINSER *n* pl. -S one that rinses

RINSING	*n* pl. -S the act of one that rinses	**RISIBLE**	*adj* inclined to laugh **RISIBLY** *adv*
RIOT	*v* -ED, -ING, -S to take part in a violent public disturbance	**RISIBLES**	*n/pl* a sense of the ridiculous
		RISING	*n* pl. -S the act of one that rises
RIOTER	*n* pl. -S one that riots	**RISK**	*v* -ED, -ING, -S to expose to a chance of injury or loss
RIOTOUS	*adj* characterized by rioting		
RIP	*v* RIPPED, RIPPING, RIPS to tear or cut apart roughly	**RISKER**	*n* pl. -S one that risks
		RISKY	*adj* RISKIER, RISKIEST dangerous **RISKILY** *adv*
RIPARIAN	*adj* pertaining to the bank of a river		
		RISOTTO	*n* pl. -TOS a rice dish
RIPCORD	*n* pl. -S a cord pulled to release a parachute	**RISQUE**	*adj* bordering on impropriety or indecency
RIPE	*adj* RIPER, RIPEST fully developed **RIPELY** *adv*	**RISSOLE**	*n* pl. -S a small roll filled with meat or fish
RIPE	*v* RIPED, RIPING, RIPES to cleanse	**RISUS**	*n* pl. -ES a grin or laugh
RIPEN	*v* -ED, -ING, -S to become ripe	**RITARD**	*n* pl. -S a musical passage with a gradual slackening in tempo
RIPENER	*n* pl. -S one that ripens		
RIPENESS	*n* pl. -ES the state of being ripe	**RITE**	*n* pl. -S a ceremonial act or procedure
RIPER	comparative of ripe	**RITTER**	*n* pl. -S a knight
RIPEST	superlative of ripe	**RITUAL**	*n* pl. -S a system of rites
RIPIENO	*n* pl. -NI or -NOS tutti	**RITUALLY**	*adv* ceremonially
RIPING	present participle of ripe	**RITZ**	*n* pl. -ES pretentious display
RIPOST	*v* -ED, -ING, -S to riposte	**RITZY**	*adj* RITZIER, RITZIEST elegant **RITZILY** *adv*
RIPOSTE	*v* -POSTED, -POSTING, -POSTES to make a return thrust in fencing		
		RIVAGE	*n* pl. -S a coast, shore, or bank
		RIVAL	*v* -VALED, -VALING, -VALS or -VALLED, -VALLING, -VALS to strive to equal or surpass
RIPPABLE	*adj* capable of being ripped		
RIPPED	past tense of rip		
RIPPER	*n* pl. -S one that rips	**RIVALRY**	*n* pl. -RIES competition
RIPPING	*adj* excellent	**RIVE**	*v* RIVED, RIVEN, RIVING, RIVES to tear apart
RIPPLE	*v* -PLED, -PLING, -PLES to form ripples (small waves)		
		RIVER	*n* pl. -S a large, natural stream of water
RIPPLER	*n* pl. -S a toothed tool for cleaning flax fiber	**RIVERBED**	*n* pl. -S the area covered or once covered by a river
RIPPLET	*n* pl. -S a small ripple		
RIPPLING	present participle of ripple	**RIVERINE**	*adj* pertaining to a river
RIPPLY	*adj* -PLIER, -PLIEST marked by ripples	**RIVET**	*v* -ETED, -ETING, -ETS or -ETTED, -ETTING, -ETS to fasten with a type of metal bolt
RIPRAP	*v* -RAPPED, -RAPPING, -RAPS to strengthen with a foundation of broken stones		
		RIVETER	*n* pl. -S one that rivets
		RIVIERA	*n* pl. -S a coastal resort area
RIPSAW	*n* pl. -S a type of saw	**RIVIERE**	*n* pl. -S a necklace of precious stones
RIPTIDE	*n* pl. -S a tide that opposes other tides		
		RIVING	present participle of rive
RISE	*v* ROSE, RISEN, RISING, RISES to move upward	**RIVULET**	*n* pl. -S a small stream
		RIYAL	*n* pl. -S a monetary unit of Saudi Arabia
RISER	*n* pl. -S one that rises		
RISHI	*n* pl. -S a Hindu sage	**ROACH**	*v* -ED, -ING, -ES to cause to arch

ROAD   *n* pl. -S an open way for public passage

ROADBED   *n* pl. -S the foundation for a railroad track

ROADLESS   *adj* having no roads

ROADSIDE   *n* pl. -S the area along the side of a road

ROADSTER   *n* pl. -S a light, open automobile

ROADWAY   *n* pl. -WAYS a road

ROADWORK   *n* pl. -S outdoor running as a form of physical conditioning

ROAM   *v* -ED, -ING, -S to move about without purpose or plan

ROAMER   *n* pl. -S one that roams

ROAN   *n* pl. -S an animal having a coat sprinkled with white or gray

ROAR   *v* -ED, -ING, -S to utter a loud, deep sound

ROARER   *n* pl. -S one that roars

ROARING   *n* pl. -S a loud, deep sound

ROAST   *v* -ED, -ING, -S to cook with dry heat

ROASTER   *n* pl. -S one that roasts

ROB   *v* ROBBED, ROBBING, ROBS to take property from illegally

ROBALO   *n* pl. -LOS a marine food fish

ROBAND   *n* pl. -S a piece of yarn used to fasten a sail

ROBBED   past tense of rob

ROBBER   *n* pl. -S one that robs

ROBBERY   *n* pl. -BERIES the act of one who robs

ROBBIN   *n* pl. -S a roband

ROBBING   present participle of rob

ROBE   *v* ROBED, ROBING, ROBES to cover with a robe (a long, loose outer garment)

ROBIN   *n* pl. -S a songbird

ROBLE   *n* pl. -S an oak tree

ROBORANT   *n* pl. -S an invigorating drug

ROBOT   *n* pl. -S a humanlike machine that performs various functions

ROBOTICS   *n/pl* a field of interest concerned with robots

ROBOTISM   *n* pl. -S the state of being a robot

ROBOTIZE   *v* -IZED, -IZING, -IZES to make automatic

ROBOTRY   *n* pl. -RIES the science of robots

ROBUST   *adj* -BUSTER, -BUSTEST strong and healthy **ROBUSTLY** *adv*

ROC   *n* pl. -S a lengendary bird of prey

ROCHET   *n* pl. -S a linen vestment

ROCK   *v* -ED, -ING, -S to move back and forth

ROCKABY   *n* pl. -BIES a song used to lull a child to sleep

ROCKABYE   *n* pl. -S rockaby

ROCKAWAY   *n* pl. -WAYS a light carriage

ROCKER   *n* pl. -S a rocking chair

ROCKERY   *n* pl. -ERIES a rock garden

ROCKET   *v* -ED, -ING, -S to convey by means of a rocket (a device propelled by the reaction of escaping gases)

ROCKETER   *n* pl. -S one that designs or launches rockets

ROCKETRY   *n* pl. -RIES the science of rockets

ROCKFALL   *n* pl. -S a mass of fallen rocks

ROCKFISH   *n* pl. -ES a fish living around rocks

ROCKIER   comparative of rocky

ROCKIEST   superlative of rocky

ROCKLESS   *adj* having no rocks

ROCKLIKE   *adj* resembling a rock (a large mass of stone)

ROCKLING   *n* pl. -S a marine fish

ROCKOON   *n* pl. -S a small rocket

ROCKROSE   *n* pl. -S a flowering plant

ROCKWEED   *n* pl. -S a brown seaweed

ROCKWORK   *n* pl. -S a natural mass of rocks

ROCKY   *adj* ROCKIER, ROCKIEST unsteady

ROCOCO   *n* pl. -COS a style of architecture and decoration

ROD   *v* RODDED, RODDING, RODS to provide with a rod (a straight, slender piece of wood, metal, or other material)

RODE   past tense of ride

RODENT   *n* pl. -S a gnawing mammal

RODEO   *n* pl. -DEOS a public exhibition of cowboy skills

RODLESS   *adj* having no rod

RODLIKE   *adj* resembling a rod

RODMAN   *n* pl. -MEN a surveyor's assistant

RODSMAN *n* pl. -MEN rodman

ROE *n* pl. -S the mass of eggs within a female fish

ROEBUCK *n* pl. -S the male of a small Eurasian deer

ROENTGEN *n* pl. -S a unit of radiation dosage

ROGATION *n* pl. -S the proposal of a law in ancient Rome

ROGATORY *adj* requesting information

ROGER *n* pl. -S the pirate flag bearing the skull and crossbones

ROGUE *v* ROGUED, ROGUEING or ROGUING, ROGUES to defraud

ROGUERY *n* pl. -ERIES roguish conduct

ROGUISH *adj* dishonest

ROIL *v* -ED, -ING, -S to make muddy

ROILY *adj* ROILIER, ROILIEST muddy

ROISTER *v* -ED, -ING, -S to revel

ROLAMITE *n* pl. -S a nearly frictionless mechanical device

ROLE *n* pl. -S a part played by an actor

ROLL *v* -ED, -ING, -S to move along by repeatedly turning over

ROLLAWAY *adj* mounted on rollers for easy movement

ROLLBACK *n* pl. -S a return to a lower level of prices or wages

ROLLER *n* pl. -S a cylindrical device that rolls or rotates

ROLLICK *v* -ED, -ING, -S to frolic

ROLLICKY *adj* given to rollicking

ROLLING *n* pl. -S the act of one that rolls

ROLLMOP *n* pl. -S a fillet of herring

ROLLOUT *n* pl. -S a type of play in football

ROLLOVER *n* pl. -S a motor vehicle accident in which the vehicle overturns

ROLLTOP *adj* having a flexible, sliding cover

ROLLWAY *n* pl. -WAYS an incline for rolling logs

ROMAINE *n* pl. -S a variety of lettuce

ROMAN *n* pl. -S a metrical narrative of medieval France

ROMANCE *v* -MANCED, -MANCING, -MANCES to woo

ROMANCER *n* pl. -S one that romances

ROMANIZE *v* -IZED, -IZING, -IZES to write in the Roman alphabet

ROMANO *n* pl. -NOS an Italian cheese

ROMANTIC *n* pl. -S a fanciful person

ROMAUNT *n* pl. -S a long, medieval narrative

ROMP *v* -ED, -ING, -S to play boisterously

ROMPER *n* pl. -S one that romps

ROMPISH *adj* inclined to romp

RONDEAU *n* pl. -DEAUX a short poem of fixed form

RONDEL *n* pl. -S a rondeau of 14 lines

RONDELET *n* pl. -S a rondeau of 5 or 7 lines

RONDELLE *n* pl. -S rondel

RONDO *n* pl. -DOS a type of musical composition

RONDURE *n* pl. -S a circle or sphere

RONION *n* pl. -S a mangy animal or person

RONNEL *n* pl. -S an insecticide

RONTGEN *n* pl. -S roentgen

RONYON *n* pl. -S ronion

ROOD *n* pl. -S a crucifix

ROOF *v* -ED, -ING, -S to provide with a roof (the external upper covering of a building)

ROOFER *n* pl. -S one that builds or repairs roofs

ROOFING *n* pl. -S material for a roof

ROOFLESS *adj* having no roof

ROOFLIKE *adj* resembling a roof

ROOFLINE *n* pl. -S the profile of a roof

ROOFTOP *n* pl. -S a roof

ROOFTREE *n* pl. -S a horizontal timber in a roof

ROOK *v* -ED, -ING, -S to swindle

ROOKERY *n* pl. -ERIES a colony of rooks (European crows)

ROOKIE *n* pl. -S a novice

ROOKY *adj* ROOKIER, ROOKIEST abounding in rooks

ROOM *v* -ED, -ING, -S to occupy a room (a walled space within a building)

ROOMER *n* pl. -S a lodger

ROOMETTE *n* pl. -S a small room

ROOMFUL *n* pl. -S as much as a room will hold

ROOMMATE *n* pl. -S one with whom a room is shared

ROOMY *adj* ROOMIER, ROOMIEST spacious **ROOMILY** *adv*

ROORBACK *n* pl. -S a false story used for political advantage

ROOSE *v* ROOSED, ROOSING, ROOSES to praise

ROOSER *n* pl. -S one that rooses

ROOST *v* -ED, -ING, -S to settle down for rest or sleep

ROOSTER *n* pl. -S a male chicken

ROOT *v* -ED, -ING, -S to put forth a root (an underground portion of a plant)

ROOTAGE *n* pl. -S a system of roots

ROOTER *n* pl. -S one that gives encouragement or support

ROOTHOLD *n* pl. -S the embedding of a plant to soil through the growing of roots

ROOTIER comparative of rooty

ROOTIEST superlative of rooty

ROOTLESS *adj* having no roots

ROOTLET *n* pl. -S a small root

ROOTLIKE *adj* resembling a root

ROOTY *adj* ROOTIER, ROOTIEST full of roots

ROPE *v* ROPED, ROPING, ROPES to bind with a rope (a thick line of twisted fibers) **ROPABLE** *adj*

ROPER *n* pl. -S one that ropes

ROPERY *n* pl. -ERIES a place where ropes are made

ROPEWALK *n* pl. -S a long path where ropes are made

ROPEWAY *n* pl. -WAYS an aerial cable used to transport freight

ROPIER comparative of ropy

ROPIEST superlative of ropy

ROPILY *adv* in a ropy manner

ROPINESS *n* pl. -ES the quality of being ropy

ROPING present participle of rope

ROPY *adj* ROPIER, ROPIEST resembling a rope or ropes

ROQUE *n* pl. -S a form of croquet

ROQUET *v* -ED, -ING, -S to cause one's own ball to hit another in croquet

RORQUAL *n* pl. -S a large whale

ROSARIA a pl. of rosarium

ROSARIAN *n* pl. -S a cultivator of roses

ROSARIUM *n* pl. -IA or -IUMS a rose garden

ROSARY *n* pl. -RIES a series of prayers in the Roman Catholic Church

ROSCOE *n* pl. -S a pistol

ROSE *v* ROSED, ROSING, ROSES to make the color of a rose (a reddish flower)

ROSEATE *adj* rose-colored

ROSEBAY *n* pl. -BAYS an evergreen shrub

ROSEBUD *n* pl. -S the bud of a rose

ROSEBUSH *n* pl. -ES a shrub that bears roses

ROSED past tense of rose

ROSEFISH *n* pl. -ES a marine food fish

ROSELIKE *adj* resembling a rose

ROSELLE *n* pl. -S a tropical plant

ROSEMARY *n* pl. -MARIES an evergreen shrub

ROSEOLA *n* pl. -S a rose-colored skin rash **ROSEOLAR** *adj*

ROSEROOT *n* pl. -S a perennial herb

ROSERY *n* pl. -ERIES a place where roses are grown

ROSET *n* pl. -S resin

ROSETTE *n* pl. -S an ornament resembling a rose

ROSEWOOD *n* pl. -S a tropical tree

ROSIER comparative of rosy

ROSIEST superlative of rosy

ROSILY *adv* in a rosy manner

ROSIN *v* -ED, -ING, -S to treat with rosin (a brittle resin)

ROSINESS *n* pl. -ES the state of being rosy

ROSING present participle of rose

ROSINOUS *adj* resembling rosin

ROSINY *adj* rosinous

ROSOLIO *n* pl. -LIOS a liqueur made from raisins and brandy

ROSTELLA *n/pl* small, beaklike structures

ROSTER *n* pl. -S a list of names

ROSTRA a pl. of rostrum

ROSTRAL *adj* pertaining to a rostrum

ROSTRATE *adj* having a rostrum

ROSTRUM *n* pl. -TRA or -TRUMS a beaklike process or part

ROSULATE *adj* arranged in the form of a rosette

ROSY *adj* ROSIER, ROSIEST rose-colored

ROT *v* ROTTED, ROTTING, ROTS to decompose

ROTA *n pl.* -S a roster

ROTARY *n pl.* -RIES a rotating part or device

ROTATE *v* -TATED, -TATING, -TATES to turn about an axis

ROTATION *n pl.* -S the act or an instance of rotating **ROTATIVE** *adj*

ROTATOR *n pl.* -S one that rotates

ROTATOR *n pl.* -ES a muscle serving to rotate a part of the body

ROTATORY *adj* pertaining to rotation

ROTCH *n pl.* -ES rotche

ROTCHE *n pl.* -S a seabird

ROTE *n pl.* -S mechanical routine

ROTENONE *n pl.* -S an insecticide

ROTGUT *n pl.* -S inferior liquor

ROTIFER *n pl.* -S a microscopic aquatic organism

ROTIFORM *adj* shaped like a wheel

ROTL *n pl.* ROTLS or ARTAL a unit of weight in Muslim countries

ROTO *n pl.* -TOS a type of printing process

ROTOR *n pl.* -S a rotating part of a machine

ROTOTILL *v* -ED, -ING, -S to till soil with a type of farming implement

ROTTED past tense of rot

ROTTEN *adj* -TENER, -TENEST being in a state of decay **ROTTENLY** *adv*

ROTTER *n pl.* -S a scoundrel

ROTTING present participle of rot

ROTUND *adj* marked by roundness **ROTUNDLY** *adv*

ROTUNDA *n pl.* -S a round building

ROTURIER *n pl.* -S a commoner

ROUBLE *n pl.* -S ruble

ROUCHE *n pl.* -S ruche

ROUE *n pl.* -S a lecherous man

ROUEN *n pl.* -S any of a breed of domestic ducks

ROUGE *v* ROUGED, ROUGING, ROUGES to color with a red cosmetic

ROUGH *adj* ROUGHER, ROUGHEST having an uneven surface

ROUGH *v* -ED, -ING, -S to make rough

ROUGHAGE *n pl.* -S coarse, bulky food

ROUGHDRY *v* -DRIED, -DRYING, -DRIES to dry without ironing, as washed clothes

ROUGHEN *v* -ED, -ING, -S to make rough

ROUGHER *n pl.* -S one that roughs

ROUGHHEW *v* -HEWED, -HEWN, -HEWING, -HEWS to shape roughly

ROUGHISH *adj* somewhat rough

ROUGHLEG *n pl.* -S a large hawk

ROUGHLY *adv* in a rough manner

ROUGING present participle of rouge

ROULADE *n pl.* -S a musical embellishment

ROULEAU *n pl.* -LEAUX or -LEAUS a roll of coins wrapped in paper

ROULETTE *v* -LETTED, -LETTING, -LETTES to make tiny slits in

ROUND *adj* ROUNDER, ROUNDEST shaped like a sphere

ROUND *v* -ED, -ING, -S to make round

ROUNDEL *n pl.* -S a round figure or object

ROUNDER *n pl.* -S a tool for rounding

ROUNDISH *adj* somewhat round

ROUNDLET *n pl.* -S a small circle

ROUNDLY *adv* in a round manner

ROUNDUP *n pl.* -S the driving together of cattle scattered over a range

ROUP *v* -ED, -ING, -S to auction

ROUPET *adj* roupy

ROUPY *adj* ROUPIER, ROUPIEST hoarse **ROUPILY** *adv*

ROUSE *v* ROUSED, ROUSING, ROUSES to bring out of a state of sleep or inactivity

ROUSER *n pl.* -S one that rouses

ROUSSEAU *n pl.* -S fried pemmican

ROUST *v* -ED, -ING, -S to arouse and drive out

ROUSTER *n pl.* -S a wharf laborer and deckhand

ROUT *v* -ED, -ING, -S to defeat overwhelmingly

ROUTE *v* ROUTED, ROUTING, ROUTES to send on a particular course

ROUTEMAN *n pl.* -MEN one who conducts business on a customary course

ROUTER   *n* pl. -S a scooping tool

ROUTEWAY   *n* pl. -WAYS an established course of travel

ROUTH   *n* pl. -S an abundance

ROUTINE   *n* pl. -S a regular course of procedure

ROUTING   present participle of route

ROUX   *n* pl. ROUX a mixture of butter and flour

ROVE   *v* ROVED, ROVING, ROVES to roam

ROVEN   a past participle of reeve

ROVER   *n* pl. -S one that roves

ROVING   *n* pl. -S a roll of textile fibers

ROVINGLY   *adv* in a roving manner

ROW   *v* -ED, -ING, -S to propel by means of oars **ROWABLE** *adj*

ROWAN   *n* pl. -S a Eurasian tree

ROWBOAT   *n* pl. -S a small boat designed to be rowed

ROWDY   *adj* -DIER, -DIEST disorderly in behavior **ROWDILY** *adv*

ROWDY   *n* pl. -DIES a rowdy person

ROWDYISH   *adj* tending to be rowdy

ROWDYISM   *n* pl. -S disorderly behavior

ROWEL   *v* -ELED, -ELING, -ELS or -ELLED, -ELLING, -ELS to prick with a spiked wheel in order to urge forward

ROWEN   *n* pl. -S a second growth of grass

ROWER   *n* pl. -S one that rows

ROWING   *n* pl. -S the sport of racing in light, long, and narrow rowboats

ROWLOCK   *n* pl. -S an oarlock

ROWTH   *n* pl. -S routh

ROYAL   *n* pl. -S a size of printing paper

ROYALISM   *n* pl. -S support of a monarch or monarchy

ROYALIST   *n* pl. -S a supporter of a monarch or monarchy

ROYALLY   *adv* in a kingly manner

ROYALTY   *n* pl. -TIES the status or power of a monarch

ROYSTER   *v* -ED, -ING, -S to roister

ROZZER   *n* pl. -S a policeman

RUB   *v* RUBBED, RUBBING, RUBS to move along the surface of a body with pressure

RUBABOO   *n* pl. -BOOS a type of soup

RUBACE   *n* pl. -S rubasse

RUBAIYAT   *n* pl. RUBAIYAT four-lined stanzas in Persian poetry

RUBASSE   *n* pl. -S a variety of quartz

RUBATO   *n* pl. -TOS a fluctuation of speed within a musical phrase

RUBBABOO   *n* pl. -BOOS rubaboo

RUBBED   past tense of rub

RUBBER   *n* pl. -S an elastic substance **RUBBERY** *adj*

RUBBING   *n* pl. -S an image produced by rubbing

RUBBISH   *n* pl. -ES worthless, unwanted matter **RUBBISHY** *adj*

RUBBLE   *v* -BLED, -BLING, -BLES to reduce to rubble (broken pieces)

RUBBLY   *adj* -BLIER, -BLIEST abounding in rubble

RUBDOWN   *n* pl. -S a brisk rubbing of the body

RUBE   *n* pl. -S a rustic

RUBELLA   *n* pl. -S a virus disease

RUBEOLA   *n* pl. -S a virus disease **RUBEOLAR** *adj*

RUBICUND   *adj* ruddy

RUBIDIUM   *n* pl. -S a metallic element **RUBIDIC** *adj*

RUBIED   past tense of ruby

RUBIER   comparative of ruby

RUBIES   present 3d person sing. of ruby

RUBIEST   superlative of ruby

RUBIGO   *n* pl. -GOS red iron oxide

RUBIOUS   *adj* ruby-colored

RUBLE   *n* pl. -S a monetary unit of the Soviet Union

RUBRIC   *n* pl. -S a part of a manuscript or book that appears in red **RUBRICAL** *adj*

RUBUS   *n* pl. RUBUS a plant of the rose family

RUBY   *v* -BIED, -BYING, -BIES to tint with the color of a ruby (a deep-red precious stone)

RUBY   *adj* -BIER, -BIEST of a deep-red color

RUBYLIKE   *adj* resembling a ruby

RUCHE   *n* pl. -S a pleated strip of fine fabric

RUCHING   *n* pl. -S a ruche

RUCK *v* -ED, -ING, -S to wrinkle or crease

RUCKSACK *n pl.* -S a knapsack

RUCKUS *n pl.* -ES a noisy disturbance

RUCTION *n pl.* -S a ruckus

RUCTIOUS *adj* quarrelsome

RUDD *n pl.* -S a freshwater fish

RUDDER *n pl.* -S a vertical blade used to direct the course of a vessel

RUDDIER comparative of ruddy

RUDDIEST superlative of ruddy

RUDDILY *adv* in a ruddy manner

RUDDLE *v* -DLED, -DLING, -DLES to color with a red dye

RUDDOCK *n pl.* -S a European bird

RUDDY *adj* -DIER, -DIEST having a healthy, reddish color

RUDE *adj* RUDER, RUDEST discourteous or impolite **RUDELY** *adv*

RUDENESS *n pl.* -ES the quality of being rude

RUDERAL *n pl.* -S a plant growing in poor land

RUDESBY *n pl.* -BIES a rude person

RUDEST superlative of rude

RUDIMENT *n pl.* -S a basic principle or element

RUE *v* RUED, RUING, RUES to feel sorrow or remorse for

RUEFUL *adj* feeling sorrow or remorse **RUEFULLY** *adv*

RUER *n pl.* -S one that rues

RUFF *v* -ED, -ING, -S to trump

RUFFE *n pl.* -S a freshwater fish

RUFFIAN *n pl.* -S a tough, lawless person

RUFFLE *v* -FLED, -FLING, -FLES to destroy the smoothness of

RUFFLER *n pl.* -S one that ruffles

RUFFLIKE *adj* resembling a ruff (a pleated collar)

RUFFLING present participle of ruffle

RUFFLY *adj* not smooth

RUFOUS *adj* reddish

RUG *v* RUGGED, RUGGING, RUGS to tear roughly

RUGA *n pl.* -GAE an anatomical fold or wrinkle **RUGAL, RUGATE** *adj*

RUGBY *n pl.* -BIES a form of football

RUGGED *adj* -GEDER, -GEDEST having an uneven surface **RUGGEDLY** *adv*

RUGGER *n pl.* -S rugby

RUGGING present participle of rug

RUGLIKE *adj* resembling a rug (a thick fabric used as a floor covering)

RUGOSE *adj* full of wrinkles **RUGOSELY** *adv*

RUGOSITY *n pl.* -TIES the state of being rugose

RUGOUS *adj* rugose

RUGULOSE *adj* having small wrinkles

RUIN *v* -ED, -ING, -S to destroy **RUINABLE** *adj*

RUINATE *v* -ATED, -ATING, -ATES to ruin

RUINER *n pl.* -S one that ruins

RUING present participle of rue

RUINOUS *adj* destructive

RULE *v* RULED, RULING, RULES to exercise control over **RULABLE** *adj*

RULELESS *adj* not restrained or regulated by law

RULER *n pl.* -S one that rules

RULING *n pl.* -S an authoritative decision

RUM *n pl.* -S an alcoholic liquor

RUM *adj* RUMMER, RUMMEST odd

RUMBA *v* -ED, -ING, -S to perform a ballroom dance

RUMBLE *v* -BLED, -BLING, -BLES to make a deep, thunderous sound

RUMBLER *n pl.* -S one that rumbles

RUMBLING *n pl.* -S a deep, thunderous sound

RUMBLY *adj* tending to rumble

RUMEN *n pl.* -MINA or -MENS a part of the stomach of a ruminant **RUMINAL** *adj*

RUMINANT *n pl.* -S a hoofed, even-toed mammal

RUMINATE *v* -NATED, -NATING, -NATES to chew again

RUMMAGE *v* -MAGED, -MAGING, -MAGES to search thoroughly through

RUMMAGER *n pl.* -S one that rummages

RUMMER *n pl.* -S a large drinking glass

RUMMEST superlative of rum

RUMMY *n pl.* -MIES a card game

RUMMY	*adj* -MIER, -MIEST odd
RUMOR	*v* -ED, -ING, -S to spread by hearsay
RUMOUR	*v* -ED, -ING, -S to rumor
RUMP	*n* pl. -S the lower and back part of the trunk **RUMPLESS** *adj*
RUMPLE	*v* -PLED, -PLING, -PLES to wrinkle
RUMPLY	*adj* -PLIER, -PLIEST rumpled
RUMPUS	*n* pl. -ES a noisy disturbance
RUN	*v* RAN, RUNNING, RUNS to move by rapid steps
RUNABOUT	*n* pl. -S a small, open auto
RUNAGATE	*n* pl. -S a deserter
RUNAWAY	*n* pl. -AWAYS one that runs away
RUNBACK	*n* pl. -S a type of run in football
RUNDLE	*n* pl. -S a rung
RUNDLET	*n* pl. -S a small barrel
RUNDOWN	*n* pl. -S a summary
RUNE	*n* pl. -S a letter of an ancient alphabet **RUNELIKE** *adj*
RUNG	*n* pl. -S a crosspiece forming a step of a ladder **RUNGLESS** *adj*
RUNIC	*adj* pertaining to a rune
RUNKLE	*v* -KLED, -KLING, -KLES to wrinkle
RUNLESS	*adj* scoring no runs in baseball
RUNLET	*n* pl. -S a small stream
RUNNEL	*n* pl. -S a small stream
RUNNER	*n* pl. -S one that runs
RUNNING	*n* pl. -S a race
RUNNY	*adj* -NIER, -NIEST tending to drip
RUNOFF	*n* pl. -S rainfall that is not absorbed by the soil
RUNOUT	*n* pl. -S the end of a film strip
RUNOVER	*n* pl. -S matter for publication that exceeds the allotted space
RUNROUND	*n* pl. -S evasive action
RUNT	*n* pl. -S a small person or animal **RUNTISH** *adj*
RUNTY	*adj* RUNTIER, RUNTIEST small
RUNWAY	*n* pl. -WAYS a landing and takeoff strip for aircraft
RUPEE	*n* pl. -S a monetary unit of India
RUPIAH	*n* pl. -S a monetary unit of Indonesia

RUPTURE	*v* -TURED, -TURING, -TURES to burst
RURAL	*adj* pertaining to the country
RURALISE	*v* -ISED, -ISING, -ISES to ruralize
RURALISM	*n* pl. -S the state of being rural
RURALIST	*n* pl. -S one who lives in the country
RURALITE	*n* pl. -S a ruralist
RURALITY	*n* pl. -TIES the state of being rural
RURALIZE	*v* -IZED, -IZING, -IZES to make rural
RURALLY	*adv* in a rural manner
RURBAN	*adj* partially rural and urban
RUSE	*n* pl. -S a deception
RUSH	*v* -ED, -ING, -ES to move swiftly
RUSHEE	*n* pl. -S a college student seeking admission to a fraternity or sorority
RUSHER	*n* pl. -S one that rushes
RUSHIER	comparative of rushy
RUSHIEST	superlative of rushy
RUSHING	*n* pl. -S yardage gained in football by running plays
RUSHLIKE	*adj* resembling a rush (a grasslike marsh plant)
RUSHY	*adj* RUSHIER, RUSHIEST abounding in rushes
RUSINE	*adj* pertaining to a genus of deer
RUSK	*n* pl. -S a sweetened biscuit
RUSSET	*n* pl. -S a reddish or yellowish brown color **RUSSETY** *adj*
RUSSIFY	*v* -FIED, -FYING, -FIES to make Russian
RUST	*v* -ED, -ING, -S to form rust (a reddish coating that forms on iron) **RUSTABLE** *adj*
RUSTIC	*n* pl. -S one who lives in the country **RUSTICAL** *adj*
RUSTICLY	*adv* in a rural manner
RUSTIER	comparative of rusty
RUSTIEST	superlative of rusty
RUSTILY	*adv* in a rusty manner
RUSTLE	*v* -TLED, -TLING, -TLES to make a succession of slight, soft sounds
RUSTLER	*n* pl. -S one that rustles
RUSTLESS	*adj* free from rust
RUSTLING	present participle of rustle

RUSTY	*adj* RUSTIER, RUSTIEST covered with rust
RUT	*v* RUTTED, RUTTING, RUTS to make ruts (grooves) in
RUTABAGA	*n* pl. -S a plant having a thick, edible root
RUTH	*n* pl. -S compassion
RUTHENIC	*adj* pertaining to a rare, metallic element
RUTHFUL	*adj* full of compassion
RUTHLESS	*adj* having no compassion
RUTILANT	*adj* having a reddish glow
RUTILE	*n* pl. -S a mineral
RUTTED	past tense of rut
RUTTIER	comparative of rutty

RUTTIEST	superlative of rutty
RUTTILY	*adv* in a rutty manner
RUTTING	present participle of rut
RUTTISH	*adj* lustful
RUTTY	*adj* -TIER, -TIEST marked by ruts
RYA	*n* pl. -S a Scandinavian handwoven rug
RYE	*n* pl. -S a cereal grass
RYEGRASS	*n* pl. -ES a European grass
RYKE	*v* RYKED, RYKING, RYKES to reach
RYND	*n* pl. -S an iron support
RYOT	*n* pl. -S a tenant farmer in India

SAB	*v* SABBED, SABBING, SABS to sob
SABATON	*n pl.* -S a piece of armor for the foot
SABBAT	*n pl.* -S an assembly of demons and witches
SABBATH	*n pl.* -S sabbat
SABBATIC	*adj* bringing a period of rest
SABBED	past tense of sab
SABBING	present participle of sab
SABE	*v* SABED, SABEING, SABES to savvy
SABER	*v* -ED, -ING, -S to strike with a saber (a type of sword)
SABIN	*n pl.* -S a unit of sound absorption
SABINE	*n pl.* -S savin
SABIR	*n pl.* -S a French-based pidgin language
SABLE	*n pl.* -S a carnivorous mammal
SABOT	*n pl.* -S a wooden shoe
SABOTAGE	*v* -TAGED, -TAGING, -TAGES to destroy maliciously
SABOTEUR	*n pl.* -S one who sabotages
SABRA	*n pl.* -S a native Israeli
SABRE	*v* -BRED, -BRING, -BRES to saber
SABULOSE	*adj* sabulous
SABULOUS	*adj* sandy
SAC	*n pl.* -S a pouchlike structure in an animal or plant
SACATON	*n pl.* -S a perennial grass
SACBUT	*n pl.* -S sackbut

SACCADE	*n pl.* -S a rapid, jerky movement of the eye **SACCADIC** *adj*
SACCATE	*adj* having a sac
SACCULAR	*adj* resembling a sac
SACCULE	*n pl.* -S a small sac
SACCULUS	*n pl.* -LI saccule
SACHEM	*n pl.* -S a North American Indian chief **SACHEMIC** *adj*
SACHET	*n pl.* -S a small bag containing perfumed powder **SACHETED** *adj*
SACK	*v* -ED, -ING, -S to put into a sack (a large bag)
SACKBUT	*n pl.* -S a medieval trombone
SACKER	*n pl.* -S one that sacks
SACKFUL	*n pl.* SACKFULS or SACKSFUL as much as a sack will hold
SACKING	*n pl.* -S material for making sacks
SACKLIKE	*adj* resembling a sack
SACKSFUL	a *pl.* of sackful
SACLIKE	*adj* resembling a sac
SACQUE	*n pl.* -S a loose-fitting dress
SACRA	*pl.* of sacrum
SACRAL	*n pl.* -S a vertebra or nerve situated near the sacrum
SACRARIA	*n/pl* ancient Roman shrines
SACRED	*adj* dedicated to or set apart for the worship of a deity **SACREDLY** *adv*
SACRIST	*n pl.* -S a person in charge of a sacristy
SACRISTY	*n pl.* -TIES a room in which sacred vessels and vestments are kept

SACRUM	n pl. -CRA a bone of the pelvis	**SAGAMORE**	n pl. -S an Algonquian Indian chief
SAD	adj SADDER, SADDEST unhappy	**SAGANASH**	n pl. -ES a white man — an Algonquian Indian term
SADDEN	v -ED, -ING, -S to make sad	**SAGBUT**	n pl. -S sackbut
SADDHU	n pl. -S sadhu	**SAGE**	adj SAGER, SAGEST wise SAGELY adv
SADDLE	v -DLED, -DLING, -DLES to put a saddle (a leather seat for a rider) on	**SAGE**	n pl. -S an aromatic herb used as seasoning
SADDLER	n pl. -S one that makes, repairs, or sells saddles	**SAGENESS**	n pl. -ES wisdom
SADDLERY	n pl. -DLERIES the shop of a saddler	**SAGER**	comparative of sage
		SAGEST	superlative of sage
SADDLING	present participle of saddle	**SAGGAR**	v -ED, -ING, -S to bake in a saggar (a protective clay casing)
SADE	n pl. -S a Hebrew letter		
SADHE	n pl. -S sade	**SAGGARD**	n pl. -S a saggar
SADHU	n pl. -S a Hindu holy man	**SAGGED**	past tense of sag
SADI	n pl. -S sade	**SAGGER**	v -ED, -ING, -S to saggar
SADIRON	n pl. -S a heavy flatiron	**SAGGING**	present participle of sag
SADISM	n pl. -S a tendency to take delight in inflicting pain	**SAGIER**	comparative of sagy
		SAGIEST	superlative of sagy
SADIST	n pl. -S one marked by sadism SADISTIC adj	**SAGITTAL**	adj resembling an arrow or arrowhead
SADLY	adv in a sad manner	**SAGO**	n pl. -GOS a tropical tree
SADNESS	n pl. -ES the state of being sad	**SAGUARO**	n pl. -ROS a tall cactus
SAE	adv so	**SAGUM**	n pl. -GA a cloak worn by ancient Roman soldiers
SAFARI	v -ED, -ING, -S to go on a hunting expedition	**SAGY**	adj SAGIER, SAGIEST flavored with sage
SAFE	adj SAFER, SAFEST free from danger SAFELY adv	**SAHIB**	n pl. -S sir; master — used as a term of respect in colonial India
SAFE	n pl. -S a metal receptacle for storing valuables	**SAHIWAL**	n pl. -S any of a breed of humped dairy cattle
SAFENESS	n pl. -ES the quality of being safe	**SAHUARO**	n pl. -ROS saguaro
SAFER	comparative of safe	**SAICE**	n pl. -S syce
SAFEST	superlative of safe	**SAID**	n pl. -S sayyid
SAFETY	v -TIED, -TYING, -TIES to protect against failure, breakage, or accident	**SAIGA**	n pl. -S a small antelope
		SAIL	v -ED, -ING, -S to move across the surface of water by the action of wind SAILABLE adj
SAFFRON	n pl. -S a flowering plant		
SAFRANIN	n pl. -S a red dye	**SAILBOAT**	n pl. -S a boat that sails
SAFROL	n pl. -S safrole	**SAILER**	n pl. -S a vessel that sails
SAFROLE	n pl. -S a poisonous liquid	**SAILFISH**	n pl. -ES a large marine fish
SAG	v SAGGED, SAGGING, SAGS to bend or sink downward from weight or pressure	**SAILING**	n pl. -S the act of one that sails
		SAILOR	n pl. -S a member of a ship's crew SAILORLY adj
SAGA	n pl. -S a medieval Scandinavian narrative	**SAIN**	v -ED, -ING, -S to make the sign of the cross on
SAGACITY	n pl. -TIES wisdom		
SAGAMAN	n pl. -MEN a writer of sagas	**SAINFOIN**	n pl. -S a perennial herb

SAINT   *v* -ED, -ING, -S to declare to be a saint (a person of exceptional holiness)

SAINTDOM   *n pl.* -S the condition of being a saint

SAINTLY   *adj* -LIER, -LIEST of or befitting a saint

SAITH   a present 3d person sing. of say

SAITHE   *n pl.* SAITHE a marine food fish

SAIYID   *n pl.* -S sayyid

SAJOU   *n pl.* -S a capuchin

SAKE   *n pl.* -S benefit, interest, or advantage

SAKER   *n pl.* -S a Eurasian falcon

SAKI   *n pl.* -S a Japanese liquor

SAL   *n pl.* -S salt

SALAAM   *v* -ED, -ING, -S to greet with a low bow

SALABLE   *adj* capable of being or fit to be sold **SALABLY** *adv*

SALACITY   *n pl.* -TIES lewdness

SALAD   *n pl.* -S a dish of green, raw vegetables

SALADANG   *n pl.* -S a wild ox

SALAMI   *n pl.* -S a seasoned sausage

SALARIAT   *n pl.* -S the class of salaried persons

SALARY   *v* -RIED, -RYING, -RIES to pay a periodic, fixed compensation to

SALE   *n pl.* -S the act or an instance of selling

SALEABLE   *adj* salable **SALEABLY** *adv*

SALEP   *n pl.* -S a starchy meal ground from the roots of certain orchids

SALEROOM   *n pl.* -S a room in which goods are displayed for sale

SALESMAN   *n pl.* -MEN a man who sells merchandise

SALIC   *adj* pertaining to a group of igneous rocks

SALICIN   *n pl.* -S a chemical compound

SALICINE   *n pl.* -S salicin

SALIENCE   *n pl.* -S a projecting feature or detail

SALIENCY   *n pl.* -CIES salience

SALIENT   *n pl.* -S the part of a fortification projecting closest to the enemy

SALIFY   *v* -FIED, -FYING, -FIES to combine with a salt

SALINA   *n pl.* -S a pond, marsh, or lake containing salt water

SALINE   *n pl.* -S a salt solution

SALINITY   *n pl.* -TIES a concentration of salt

SALINIZE   *v* -NIZED, -NIZING, -NIZES to treat with salt

SALIVA   *n pl.* -S a fluid secreted by the glands of the mouth **SALIVARY** *adj*

SALIVATE   *v* -VATED, -VATING, -VATES to secrete saliva

SALL   *v* shall — SALL is the only form of this verb; it cannot be conjugated

SALLET   *n pl.* -S a light medieval helmet

SALLIED   past tense of sally

SALLIER   *n pl.* -S one that sallies

SALLIES   present 3d person sing. of sally

SALLOW   *adj* -LOWER, -LOWEST of a sickly yellowish color **SALLOWLY** *adv*

SALLOW   *v* -ED, -ING, -S to make sallow

SALLOWY   *adj* abounding in willow trees

SALLY   *v* -LIED, -LYING, -LIES to rush out suddenly

SALMI   *n pl.* -S a dish of roasted game birds

SALMON   *n pl.* -S a food fish

SALMONID   *n pl.* -S a fish of the salmon family

SALOL   *n pl.* -S a chemical compound

SALON   *n pl.* -S a large room in which guests are received

SALOON   *n pl.* -S a tavern

SALOOP   *n pl.* -S a hot drink made from an infusion of aromatic herbs

SALP   *n pl.* -S salpa

SALPA   *n pl.* -PAE or -PAS a free-swimming tunicate

SALPIAN   *n pl.* -S salpa

SALPID   *n pl.* -S salpa

SALPINX   *n pl.* -PINGES an anatomical tube

SALSIFY   *n pl.* -FIES a European herb

SALSILLA   *n pl.* -S a tropical plant

SALT   *v* -ED, -ING, -S to treat with salt (a crystalline compound used as a seasoning and preservative)

SALT   *adj* SALTER, SALTEST salty

SALTANT *adj* jumping or dancing

SALTBOX *n* pl. -ES a type of house

SALTBUSH *n* pl. -ES a salt-tolerant plant

SALTER *n* pl. -S one that salts

SALTERN *n* pl. -S a place where salt is produced

SALTIE *n* pl. -S a deep-sea vessel sailing the Great Lakes

SALTIER *n* pl. -S saltire

SALTIEST superlative of salty

SALTILY *adv* in a salty manner

SALTINE *n* pl. -S a salted cracker

SALTIRE *n* pl. -S a heraldic design

SALTISH *adj* somewhat salty

SALTLESS *adj* having no salt

SALTLIKE *adj* resembling salt

SALTNESS *n* pl. -ES the state of being salty

SALTPAN *n* pl. -S a large pan for making salt by evaporation

SALTWORK *n* pl. -S a saltern

SALTWORT *n* pl. -S a seaside herb

SALTY *adj* SALTIER, SALTIEST tasting of or containing salt

SALUKI *n* pl. -S a tall, slender dog

SALUTARY *adj* producing a beneficial effect

SALUTE *v* -LUTED, -LUTING, -LUTES to greet with a sign of welcome or respect

SALUTER *n* pl. -S one that salutes

SALVABLE *adj* capable of being saved SALVABLY *adv*

SALVAGE *v* -VAGED, -VAGING, -VAGES to save from loss or destruction

SALVAGEE *n* pl. -S one in whose favor salvage has been effected

SALVAGER *n* pl. -S one that salvages

SALVAGING present participle of salvage

SALVE *v* SALVED, SALVING, SALVES to soothe

SALVER *n* pl. -S a tray or serving platter

SALVIA *n* pl. -S a flowering plant

SALVIFIC *adj* having the power to save

SALVING present participle of salve

SALVO *v* -ED, -ING, -S or -ES to discharge firearms simultaneously

SALVOR *n* pl. -S a salvager

SAMARA *n* pl. -S a dry, one-seeded fruit

SAMARIUM *n* pl. -S a metallic element

SAMBA *v* -ED, -ING, -S to perform a Brazilian dance

SAMBAR *n* pl. -S a large Asian deer

SAMBHAR *n* pl. -S sambar

SAMBHUR *n* pl. -S sambar

SAMBO *n* pl. -BOS a Latin American of mixed black and Indian ancestry

SAMBUCA *n* pl. -S an ancient stringed instrument

SAMBUKE *n* pl. -S sambuca

SAMBUR *n* pl. -S sambar

SAME *adj* resembling in every relevant respect

SAMECH *n* pl. -S samek

SAMEK *n* pl. -S a Hebrew letter

SAMEKH *n* pl. -S samek

SAMENESS *n* pl. -ES lack of change or variety

SAMIEL *n* pl. -S the simoom

SAMISEN *n* pl. -S a Japanese stringed instrument

SAMITE *n* pl. -S a silk fabric

SAMLET *n* pl. -S a young salmon

SAMOVAR *n* pl. -S a metal urn for heating water

SAMP *n* pl. -S coarsely ground corn

SAMPAN *n* pl. -S a flat-bottomed Chinese skiff

SAMPHIRE *n* pl. -S a European herb

SAMPLE *v* -PLED, -PLING, -PLES to test a representative portion of a whole

SAMPLER *n* pl. -S one that samples

SAMPLING *n* pl. -S a small part selected for analysis

SAMSARA *n* pl. -S the cycle of birth, death, and rebirth in Buddhism

SAMSHU *n* pl. -S a Chinese liquor

SAMURAI *n* pl. -S a Japanese warrior

SANATIVE *adj* having the power to cure or heal

SANCTA a pl. of sanctum

SANCTIFY *v* -FIED, -FYING, -FIES to make holy

SANCTION *v* -ED, -ING, -S to authorize

SANCTITY *n* pl. -TIES holiness

SANCTUM n pl. -TUMS or -TA a sacred place

SAND v -ED, -ING, -S to cover with sand (a loose, granular rock material)

SANDAL v -DALED, -DALING, -DALS or -DALLED, -DALLING, -DALS to provide with sandals (light, open shoes)

SANDARAC n pl. -S an aromatic resin

SANDBAG v -BAGGED, -BAGGING, -BAGS to surround with bags of sand

SANDBANK n pl. -S a large mass of sand

SANDBAR n pl. -S a ridge of sand formed in a river or sea

SANDBOX n pl. -ES a box containing sand for children to play in

SANDBUR n pl. -S an annual herb

SANDBURR n pl. -S sandbur

SANDER n pl. -S one that sands

SANDFISH n pl. -ES a marine fish

SANDFLY n pl. -FLIES a biting fly

SANDHI n pl. -S a process of phonetic modification

SANDHOG n pl. -S a worker who digs or works in sand

SANDIER comparative of sandy

SANDIEST superlative of sandy

SANDLIKE adj resembling sand

SANDLING n pl. -S a marine fish

SANDLOT n pl. -S a vacant lot

SANDMAN n pl. -MEN a mythical person who makes children sleepy by sprinkling sand in their eyes

SANDPEEP n pl. -S a wading bird

SANDPILE n pl. -S a pile of sand

SANDPIT n pl. -S a pit dug in sandy soil

SANDSOAP n pl. -S a type of soap

SANDWICH v -ED, -ING, -ES to place between two layers or objects

SANDWORM n pl. -S a sand-dwelling worm

SANDWORT n pl. -S a flowering plant

SANDY adj SANDIER, SANDIEST containing or covered with sand

SANE adj SANER, SANEST mentally sound SANELY adv

SANE v SANED, SANING, SANES to sain

SANENESS n pl. -ES sanity

SANER comparative of sane

SANEST superlative of sane

SANG past tense of sing

SANGA n pl. -S sangar

SANGAR n pl. -S a temporary fortification for two or three men

SANGAREE n pl. -S an alcoholic beverage

SANGER n pl. -S sangar

SANGH n pl. -S an association promoting unity between the different groups in Hinduism

SANGRIA n pl. -S an alcoholic beverage

SANGUINE n pl. -S a red color

SANICLE n pl. -S a medicinal herb

SANIES n pl. SANIES a fluid discharged from wounds SANIOUS adj

SANING present participle of sane

SANITARY n pl. -TARIES a public urinal

SANITATE v -TATED, -TATING, -TATES to sanitize

SANITIES pl. of sanity

SANITISE v -TISED, -TISING, -TISES to sanitize

SANITIZE v -TIZED, -TIZING, -TIZES to guard against infection or disease by cleaning or sterilizing

SANITY n pl. -TIES the state of being sane

SANJAK n pl. -S an administrative district of Turkey

SANK past tense of sink

SANNOP n pl. -S sannup

SANNUP n pl. -S a married male American Indian

SANNYASI n pl. -S a Hindu monk

SANS prep without

SANSAR n pl. -S sarsar

SANSEI n pl. -S a grandchild of Japanese immigrants to the United States

SANSERIF n pl. -S a typeface without serifs

SANTALIC adj pertaining to sandalwood

SANTIMS n pl. -TIMI a former coin of Latvia

SANTIR n pl. -S a Persian dulcimer

SANTOL n pl. -S a tropical tree

SANTONIN n pl. -S a chemical compound

SANTOUR n pl. -S santir

SAP	v SAPPED, SAPPING, SAPS to deplete or weaken gradually	**SARCASM**	n pl. -S a sharply mocking or contemptuous remark
SAPAJOU	n pl. -S a capuchin	**SARCENET**	n pl. -S a silk fabric
SAPHEAD	n pl. -S a foolish, stupid, or gullible person	**SARCOID**	n pl. -S a disease of horses
SAPHENA	n pl. -NAE a vein of the leg	**SARCOMA**	n pl. -MAS or -MATA a type of tumor
SAPID	adj pleasant to the taste	**SARCOUS**	adj composed of flesh or muscle
SAPIDITY	n pl. -TIES the state of being sapid	**SARD**	n pl. -S a variety of quartz
SAPIENCE	n pl. -S wisdom	**SARDAR**	n pl. -S sirdar
SAPIENCY	n pl. -CIES sapience	**SARDINE**	n pl. -S a small food fish
SAPIENS	adj pertaining to recent man	**SARDIUS**	n pl. -ES sard
SAPIENT	adj wise	**SARDONIC**	adj mocking
SAPLESS	adj lacking vitality	**SARDONYX**	n pl. -ES a variety of quartz
SAPLING	n pl. -S a young tree	**SAREE**	n pl. -S sari
SAPONIFY	v -FIED, -FYING, -FIES to convert into soap	**SARGASSO**	n pl. -GASSOS a brownish seaweed
SAPONIN	n pl. -S a soapy substance obtained from plants	**SARGE**	n pl. -S sergeant
SAPONINE	n pl. -S saponin	**SARI**	n pl. -S an outer garment worn by Hindu women
SAPONITE	n pl. -S a mineral found in veins and cavities of rocks	**SARIN**	n pl. -S a toxic gas
SAPOR	n pl. -S flavor SAPOROUS adj	**SARK**	n pl. -S a shirt
SAPOTA	n pl. -S an evergreen tree	**SARMENT**	n pl. -S a type of plant stem
SAPOUR	n pl. -S sapor	**SARMENTA**	n/pl sarments
SAPPED	past tense of sap	**SAROD**	n pl. -S a lute of northern India
SAPPER	n pl. -S a military engineer	**SARODE**	n pl. -S sarod
SAPPHIC	n pl. -S a type of verse form	**SARODIST**	n pl. -S one who plays the sarod
SAPPHIRE	n pl. -S a blue gem	**SARONG**	n pl. -S an outer garment worn in the Pacific islands
SAPPHISM	n pl. -S lesbianism	**SARSAR**	n pl. -S a cold, whistling wind
SAPPHIST	n pl. -S a lesbian	**SARSEN**	n pl. -S a large sandstone block
SAPPING	present participle of sap	**SARSENET**	n pl. -S sarcenet
SAPPY	adj -PIER, -PIEST silly SAPPILY adv	**SARTOR**	n pl. -S a tailor
SAPREMIA	n pl. -S a form of blood poisoning SAPREMIC adj	**SARTORII**	n/pl flat, narrow thigh muscles
SAPROBE	n pl. -S an organism that derives its nourishment from decaying organic matter SAPROBIC adj	**SASH**	v -ED, -ING, -ES to furnish with a frame in which glass is set
SAPROPEL	n pl. -S mud consisting chiefly of decaying organic matter	**SASHAY**	v -ED, -ING, -S to flounce
SAPSAGO	n pl. -GOS a hard green cheese	**SASHIMI**	n pl. -S a Japanese dish of sliced raw fish
SAPWOOD	n pl. -S the newly formed outer wood of a tree	**SASIN**	n pl. -S an antelope of India
SARABAND	n pl. -S a stately Spanish dance	**SASS**	v -ED, -ING, -ES to talk impudently to
SARAPE	n pl. -S serape	**SASSABY**	n pl. -BIES an African antelope
		SASSIER	comparative of sassy
		SASSIEST	superlative of sassy
		SASSILY	adv in a sassy manner

SASSWOOD n pl. -S an African tree

SASSY n pl. -SIES sasswood

SASSY adj SASSIER, SASSIEST impudent

SASTRUGA n pl. -GI a ridge of snow formed by the wind in polar regions

SAT past tense of sit

SATANG n pl. -S a monetary unit of Thailand

SATANIC adj extremely evil

SATANISM n pl. -S worship of the powers of evil

SATANIST n pl. -S one who practices satanism

SATARA n pl. -S a woolen fabric

SATCHEL n pl. -S a small carrying bag

SATE v SATED, SATING, SATES to satiate

SATEEN n pl. -S a cotton fabric

SATEM adj pertaining to a group of Indo-European languages

SATI n pl. -S suttee

SATIABLE adj capable of being satiated SATIABLY adv

SATIATE v -ATED, -ATING, -ATES to satisfy to or beyond capacity

SATIETY n pl. -ETIES the state of being satiated

SATIN n pl. -S a smooth fabric

SATINET n pl. -S a thin satin

SATING present participle of sate

SATINPOD n pl. -S a flowering plant

SATINY adj resembling satin

SATIRE n pl. -S the use of derisive wit to attack folly or wickedness SATIRIC adj

SATIRISE v -RISED, -RISING, -RISES to satirize

SATIRIST n pl. -S one who satirizes

SATIRIZE v -RIZED, -RIZING, -RIZES to subject to satire

SATISFY v -FIED, -FYING, -FIES to provide fully with what is desired, expected, or needed

SATORI n pl. -S the illumination of spirit sought by Zen Buddhists

SATRAP n pl. -S a governor of a province in ancient Persia

SATRAPY n pl. -PIES the territory of a satrap

SATURANT n pl. -S a substance used to saturate

SATURATE v -RATED, -RATING, -RATES to fill completely with something that permeates

SATYR n pl. -S a woodland deity of Greek mythology SATYRIC adj

SATYRID n pl. -S a brownish butterfly

SAU n pl. SAU xu

SAUCE v SAUCED, SAUCING, SAUCES to season with sauce (a flavorful liquid dressing)

SAUCEBOX n pl. -ES a saucy person

SAUCEPAN n pl. -S a cooking utensil

SAUCER n pl. -S a small, shallow dish

SAUCH n pl. -S saugh

SAUCING present participle of sauce

SAUCY adj SAUCIER, SAUCIEST impudent SAUCILY adv

SAUGER n pl. -S a freshwater fish

SAUGH n pl. -S a willow tree SAUGHY adj

SAUL n pl. -S soul

SAULT n pl. -S a waterfall

SAUNA n pl. -S a Finnish steam bath

SAUNTER v -ED, -ING, -S to walk in a leisurely manner

SAUREL n pl. -S a marine fish

SAURIAN n pl. -S any of a suborder of reptiles

SAUROPOD n pl. -S any of a suborder of large dinosaurs

SAURY n pl. -RIES a marine fish

SAUSAGE n pl. -S finely chopped and seasoned meat stuffed into a casing

SAUTE v -TEED or -TED, -TEING, -TES to fry in a small amount of fat

SAUTERNE n pl. -S a sweet white wine

SAUTOIR n pl. -S a saltire

SAUTOIRE n pl. -S sautoir

SAVABLE adj capable of being saved

SAVAGE adj -AGER, -AGEST fierce SAVAGELY adv

SAVAGE v -AGED, -AGING, -AGES to attack or treat brutally

SAVAGERY n pl. -RIES the quality of being savage

SAVAGEST superlative of savage

SAVAGING present participle of savage

SAVAGISM   *n* pl. -S savagery

SAVANNA   *n* pl. -S a flat, treeless grassland

SAVANNAH   *n* pl. -S savanna

SAVANT   *n* pl. -S a man of profound learning

SAVATE   *n* pl. -S a pugilistic sport

SAVE   *v* SAVED, SAVING, SAVES to rescue from danger, injury, or loss **SAVEABLE** *adj*

SAVELOY   *n* pl. -LOYS a highly seasoned sausage

SAVER   *n* pl. -S one that saves

SAVIN   *n* pl. -S an evergreen shrub

SAVINE   *n* pl. -S savin

SAVING   *n* pl. -S the act or an instance of saving

SAVINGLY   *adv* in a thrifty manner

SAVIOR   *n* pl. -S one that saves

SAVIOUR   *n* pl. -S savior

SAVOR   *v* -ED, -ING, -S to taste or smell with pleasure

SAVORER   *n* pl. -S one that savors

SAVORIER   comparative of savory

SAVORIES   pl. of savory

SAVOROUS   *adj* savory

SAVORY   *adj* -VORIER, -VORIEST pleasant to the taste or smell **SAVORILY** *adv*

SAVORY   *n* pl. -VORIES a savory dish served before or after a meal

SAVOUR   *v* -ED, -ING, -S to savor

SAVOURER   *n* pl. -S savorer

SAVOURY   *adj* -VOURIER, -VOURIEST savory

SAVOURY   *n* pl. -VOURIES a savory

SAVOY   *n* pl. -VOYS a variety of cabbage

SAVVY   *v* -VIED, -VYING, -VIES to understand

SAW   *v* SAWED, SAWN, SAWING, SAWS to cut or divide with a saw (a type of cutting tool)

SAWBILL   *n* pl. -S a tropical bird

SAWBONES   *n* pl. -BONESES a surgeon

SAWBUCK   *n* pl. -S a sawhorse

SAWDUST   *n* pl. -S small particles of wood produced in sawing

SAWER   *n* pl. -S one that saws

SAWFISH   *n* pl. -ES a marine fish

SAWFLY   *n* pl. -FLIES a winged insect

SAWHORSE   *n* pl. -S a rack used to support a piece of wood being sawed

SAWLIKE   *adj* resembling a saw

SAWLOG   *n* pl. -S a log large enough to saw into boards

SAWMILL   *n* pl. -S a place where logs are sawed

SAWN   a past participle of saw

SAWNEY   *n* pl. -NEYS a foolish person

SAWTOOTH   *n* pl. -TEETH a cutting edge on a saw

SAWYER   *n* pl. -S one that saws wood for a living

SAX   *n* pl. -ES a saxophone

SAXATILE   *adj* living or growing among rocks

SAXHORN   *n* pl. -S a brass wind instrument

SAXONY   *n* pl. -NIES a woolen fabric

SAXTUBA   *n* pl. -S a bass saxhorn

SAY   *v* SAID, SAYING, present sing. 2d person SAY, SAYEST, or SAYST, 3d person SAYS or SAITH to utter **SAYABLE** *adj*

SAYER   *n* pl. -S one that says

SAYID   *n* pl. -S sayyid

SAYING   *n* pl. -S a maxim

SAYONARA   *n* pl. -S goodby

SAYST   a present 2d person sing. of say

SAYYID   *n* pl. -S lord; sir — used as a title of respect for a Muslim dignitary

SCAB   *v* SCABBED, SCABBING, SCABS to become covered with a scab (a crust that forms over a healing wound)

SCABBARD   *v* -ED, -ING, -S to put into a sheath, as a sword

SCABBLE   *v* -BLED, -BLING, -BLES to shape roughly

SCABBY   *adj* -BIER, -BIEST covered with scabs **SCABBILY** *adv*

SCABIES   *n* pl. SCABIES a skin disease

SCABIOSA   *n* pl. -S scabious

SCABIOUS   *n* pl. -ES a flowering plant

SCABLIKE   *adj* resembling a scab

SCABROUS   *adj* roughened with small projections

SCAD   *n* pl. -S a marine fish

SCAFFOLD   *v* -ED, -ING, -S to provide with a scaffold (a temporary platform for workmen)

SCAG   *n* pl. -S heroin

SCALABLE   *adj* capable of being scaled **SCALABLY** *adv*

SCALADE   *n* pl. -S an act of scaling the walls of a fortification

SCALADO   *n* pl. -DOS scalade

SCALAGE   *n* pl. -S a percentage deduction to compensate for shrinkage

SCALAR   *n* pl. -S a mathematical quantity possessing only magnitude

SCALARE   *n* pl. -S a tropical fish

SCALAWAG   *n* pl. -S a rascal

SCALD   *v* -ED, -ING, -S to burn with hot liquid or steam

SCALDIC   *adj* skaldic

SCALE   *v* SCALED, SCALING, SCALES to climb up or over

SCALENE   *adj* designating a triangle having no two sides equal

SCALENUS   *n* pl. -NI a muscle of the neck

SCALEPAN   *n* pl. -S a pan on a weighing scale

SCALER   *n* pl. -S one that scales

SCALIER   comparative of scaly

SCALIEST   superlative of scaly

SCALING   present participle of scale

SCALL   *n* pl. -S a scaly eruption of the skin

SCALLION   *n* pl. -S an onion-like plant

SCALLOP   *v* -ED, -ING, -S to bake in a sauce topped with bread crumbs

SCALP   *v* -ED, -ING, -S to remove an upper part from

SCALPEL   *n* pl. -S a small surgical knife

SCALPER   *n* pl. -S one that scalps

SCALY   *adj* SCALIER, SCALIEST peeling off in flakes

SCAMMONY   *n* pl. -NIES a climbing plant

SCAM   *n* pl. -S a swindle

SCAMP   *v* -ED, -ING, -S to perform in a hasty or careless manner

SCAMPER   *v* -ED, -ING, -S to run playfully about

SCAMPI   *n* pl. SCAMPI large shrimp used in Italian cooking

SCAMPISH   *adj* rascally

SCAN   *v* SCANNED, SCANNING, SCANS to examine closely

SCANDAL   *v* -DALED, -DALING, -DALS or -DALLED, -DALLING, -DALS to defame

SCANDENT   *adj* climbing, as a plant

SCANDIA   *n* pl. -S an oxide of scandium

SCANDIUM   *n* pl. -S a metallic element **SCANDIC** *adj*

SCANNED   past tense of scan

SCANNER   *n* pl. -S one that scans

SCANNING   *n* pl. -S close examination

SCANSION   *n* pl. -S the analysis of verse into metrical feet and rhythm patterns

SCANT   *adj* SCANTER, SCANTEST meager

SCANT   *v* -ED, -ING, -S to provide with a meager portion

SCANTIER   comparative of scanty

SCANTIES   *n/pl* brief panties for women

SCANTLY   *adv* in a scant manner

SCANTY   *adj* SCANTIER, SCANTIEST meager **SCANTILY** *adv*

SCAPE   *v* SCAPED, SCAPING, SCAPES to escape

SCAPHOID   *n* pl. -S a bone of the wrist

SCAPOSE   *adj* bearing a leafless stalk

SCAPULA   *n* pl. -LAE or -LAS a bone of the shoulder

SCAPULAR   *n* pl. -S a sleeveless outer garment worn by monks

SCAR   *v* SCARRED, SCARRING, SCARS to form a scar (a mark left by the healing of injured tissue)

SCARAB   *n* pl. -S a large, black beetle

SCARCE   *adj* SCARCER, SCARCEST infrequently seen or found

SCARCELY   *adv* by a narrow margin

SCARCITY   *n* pl. -TIES the quality of being scarce

SCARE   *v* SCARED, SCARING, SCARES to frighten

SCARER   *n* pl. -S one that scares

SCAREY   *adj* SCARIER, SCARIEST scary

SCARF   *n* pl. SCARFS or SCARVES a piece of cloth worn for warmth or protection

SCARF   *v* -ED, -ING, -S to cover with a scarf

SCARFPIN   *n* pl. -S a tiepin

SCARIER   comparative of scarey and scary

SCARIEST   superlative of scarey and scary

SCARIFY   *v* -FIED, -FYING, -FIES to make superficial cuts in

SCARING   present participle of scare

SCARIOSE   *adj* scarious

SCARIOUS   *adj* thin, dry, and membranous

SCARLESS   *adj* having no scars

SCARLET   *n* pl. -S a red color

SCARP   *v* -ED, -ING, -S to cut or make into a steep slope

SCARPER   *v* -ED, -ING, -S to flee

SCARPH   *v* -ED, -ING, -S to unite by means of a type of joint

SCARRED   past tense of scar

SCARRING   present participle of scar

SCARRY   *adj* -RIER, -RIEST marked with scars

SCART   *v* -ED, -ING, -S to scratch

SCARVES   a pl. of scarf

SCARY   *adj* SCARIER, SCARIEST frightening

SCAT   *v* SCATTED, SCATTING, SCATS to leave hastily

SCATBACK   *n* pl. -S a type of player in football

SCATHE   *v* SCATHED, SCATHING, SCATHES to criticize severely

SCATT   *n* pl. -S a tax

SCATTED   past tense of scat

SCATTER   *v* -ED, -ING, -S to go or send in various directions

SCATTING   present participle of scat

SCATTY   *adj* -TIER, -TIEST crazy

SCAUP   *n* pl. -S a sea duck

SCAUPER   *n* pl. -S an engraving tool

SCAUR   *n* pl. -S a protruding, isolated rock

SCAVENGE   *v* -ENGED, -ENGING, -ENGES to search through rubbish for usable items

SCENA   *n* pl. -S an elaborate composition for a single voice

SCENARIO   *n* pl. -IOS a summary of the plot of a dramatic work

SCEND   *v* -ED, -ING, -S to rise upward, as a ship on a wave

SCENE   *n* pl. -S the place where some action or event occurs

SCENERY   *n* pl. -ERIES a picturesque landscape or view

SCENIC   *adj* pertaining to scenery

SCENICAL   *adj* scenic

SCENT   *v* -ED, -ING, -S to fill with an odor

SCEPTER   *v* -ED, -ING, -S to invest with royal authority

SCEPTIC   *n* pl. -S skeptic

SCEPTRAL   *adj* pertaining to royal authority

SCEPTRE   *v* -TRED, -TRING, -TRES to scepter

SCHAPPE   *n* pl. -S a silk fabric

SCHAV   *n* pl. -S a chilled soup

SCHEDULE   *v* -ULED, -ULING, -ULES to assign to a certain date or time

SCHEMA   *n* pl. -MATA a generalized diagram or plan

SCHEME   *v* SCHEMED, SCHEMING, SCHEMES to plan or plot

SCHEMER   *n* pl. -S one that schemes

SCHERZO   *n* pl. -ZOS or -ZI a lively musical movement

SCHILLER   *n* pl. -S a brownish luster occurring on certain minerals

SCHISM   *n* pl. -S a division into opposing parties

SCHIST   *n* pl. -S a rock that readily splits into parallel layers

SCHIZO   *n* pl. SCHIZOS a schizoid

SCHIZOID   *n* pl. -S a person affected with a type of psychotic disorder

SCHIZONT   *n* pl. -S an organism that reproduces by a form of asexual reproduction

SCHLEP   *v* SCHLEPPED, SCHLEPPING, SCHLEPS to lug or drag

SCHLEPP   *v* -ED, -ING, -S to schlep

SCHLOCK   *n* pl. -S inferior merchandise

SCHMALTZ   *n* pl. -ES excessive sentimentality

SCHMALZ   *n* pl. -ES schmaltz

SCHMALZY   *adj* SCHMALZIER, SCHMALZIEST characterized by schmaltz

SCHMEER   *v* -ED, -ING, -S to bribe

SCHMELZE   *n* pl. -S a type of decorative glass

SCHMO   *n* pl. SCHMOES a stupid person

SCHMOE   *n* pl. -S schmo

SCHMOOS   *v* -ED, -ING, -ES to schmooze

SCHMOOSE   *v* SCHMOOSED, SCHMOOSING, SCHMOOSES to schmooze

SCHMOOZE   *v* SCHMOOZED, SCHMOOZING, SCHMOOZES to gossip

SCHMUCK   *n* pl. -S a foolish or clumsy person

SCHNAPPS   *n* pl. SCHNAPPS a strong liquor

SCHNAPS   *n* pl. SCHNAPS schnapps

SCHNECKE   *n* pl. -KEN a sweet roll

SCHNOOK   *n* pl. -S an easily deceived person

SCHOLAR   *n* pl. -S a learned person

SCHOLIUM   *n* pl. -LIA or -LIUMS an explanatory marginal note

SCHOOL   *v* -ED, -ING, -S to educate in an institution of learning

SCHOONER   *n* pl. -S a sailing vessel

SCHORL   *n* pl. -S a mineral

SCHRIK   *n* pl. -S sudden fright

SCHTICK   *n* pl. -S shtick

SCHUIT   *n* pl. -S a Dutch sailing vessel

SCHUL   *n* pl. SCHULN shul

SCHUSS   *v* -ED, -ING, -ES to make a fast, straight run in skiing

SCHWA   *n* pl. -S a type of vowel sound

SCIAENID   *n* pl. -S a carnivorous fish

SCIATIC   *n* pl. -S a nerve, vein, or artery situated near the hip

SCIATICA   *n* pl. -S a painful disorder of the hip and adjoining areas

SCIENCE   *n* pl. -S a department of systematized knowledge

SCILICET   *adv* namely

SCILLA   *n* pl. -S a flowering plant

SCIMETAR   *n* pl. -S scimitar

SCIMITAR   *n* pl. -S a curved Oriental sword

SCIMITER   *n* pl. -S scimitar

SCINCOID   *n* pl. -S one of a family of smooth, short-limbed lizards

SCIOLISM   *n* pl. -S superficial knowledge

SCIOLIST   *n* pl. -S one whose knowledge is superficial

SCION   *n* pl. -S a child or descendant

SCIROCCO   *n* pl. -COS sirocco

SCIRRHUS   *n* pl. -RHI or -RHUSES a hard tumor

SCISSILE   *adj* capable of being cut or split easily

SCISSION   *n* pl. -S the act of cutting or splitting

SCISSOR   *v* -ED, -ING, -S to cut with a two-bladed cutting implement

SCISSURE   *n* pl. -S a lengthwise cut

SCIURINE   *n* pl. -S a rodent of the squirrel family

SCIUROID   *adj* resembling a squirrel

SCLAFF   *v* -ED, -ING, -S to strike the ground with the club before hitting the ball in golf

SCLAFFER   *n* pl. -S one that sclaffs

SCLERA   *n* pl. -RAS or -RAE the white, fibrous outer coat of the eyeball **SCLERAL** *adj*

SCLEREID   *n* pl. -S a type of plant cell

SCLERITE   *n* pl. -S one of the hard plates forming the outer covering of an arthropod

SCLEROID   *adj* sclerous

SCLEROMA   *n* pl. -MATA a hardened patch of cellular tissue

SCLEROSE   *v* -ROSED, -ROSING, -ROSES to become hard, as tissue

SCLEROUS   *adj* hardened

SCOFF   *v* -ED, -ING, -S to express rude doubt or derision

SCOFFER   *n* pl. -S one that scoffs

SCOFFLAW   *n* pl. -S an habitual law violator

SCOLD   *v* -ED, -ING, -S to rebuke harshly

SCOLDER   *n* pl. -S one that scolds

SCOLDING   *n* pl. -S a harsh reproof

SCOLEX   *n* pl. -LECES or -LICES the knoblike head of a tapeworm

SCOLIOMA   *n* pl. -S abnormal curvature of the spine

SCOLLOP   *v* -ED, -ING, -S to scallop

SCONCE   *v* SCONCED, SCONCING, SCONCES to fine

SCONE   *n* pl. -S a flat, round cake

SCOOP   *v* -ED, -ING, -S to take up with a scoop (a spoonlike utensil)

SCOOPER   *n* pl. -S one that scoops

SCOOPFUL   *n* pl. SCOOPFULS or SCOOPSFUL as much as a scoop will hold

SCOOT   *v* -ED, -ING, -S to go quickly

SCOOTER   *n* pl. -S a two-wheeled vehicle

SCOP	*n* pl. -S an Old English poet	**SCOUTING**	*n* pl. -S the act of one that scouts
SCOPE	*n* pl. -S extent		
SCOPULA	*n* pl. -LAE or -LAS a dense tuft of hairs	**SCOW**	*v* -ED, -ING, -S to transport by scow (a flat-bottomed boat)
SCORCH	*v* -ED, -ING, -ES to burn slightly so as to alter the color or taste	**SCOWDER**	*v* -ED, -ING, -S to scouther
		SCOWL	*v* -ED, -ING, -S to frown angrily
SCORCHER	*n* pl. -S one that scorches	**SCOWLER**	*n* pl. -S one that scowls
SCORE	*v* SCORED, SCORING, SCORES to make a point in a game or contest	**SCRABBLE**	*v* -BLED, -BLING, -BLES to claw or grope about frantically
		SCRABBLY	*adj* raspy
SCOREPAD	*n* pl. -S a pad on which scored points are recorded	**SCRAG**	*v* SCRAGGED, SCRAGGING, SCRAGS to wring the neck of
SCORER	*n* pl. -S one that scores		
SCORIA	*n* pl. -RIAE the refuse of a smelted metal or ore	**SCRAGGLY**	*adj* -GLIER, -GLIEST uneven
		SCRAGGY	*adj* -GIER, -GIEST scrawny
SCORIFY	*v* -FIED, -FYING, -FIES to reduce to scoria	**SCRAICH**	*v* -ED, -ING, -S to utter a shrill cry
SCORING	present participle of score	**SCRAIGH**	*v* -ED, -ING, -S to scraich
SCORN	*v* -ED, -ING, -S to treat or regard with contempt	**SCRAM**	*v* SCRAMMED, SCRAMMING, SCRAMS to leave quickly
SCORNER	*n* pl. -S one that scorns	**SCRAMBLE**	*v* -BLED, -BLING, -BLES to move or climb hurriedly
SCORNFUL	*adj* feeling or expressing contempt	**SCRANNEL**	*n* pl. -S a thin person
SCORPION	*n* pl. -S a stinging arachnid	**SCRAP**	*v* SCRAPPED, SCRAPPING, SCRAPS to discard
SCOT	*n* pl. -S a tax		
SCOTCH	*v* -ED, -ING, -ES to put a definite end to	**SCRAPE**	*v* SCRAPED, SCRAPING, SCRAPES to rub so as to remove an outer layer
SCOTER	*n* pl. -S a sea duck		
SCOTIA	*n* pl. -S a concave molding	**SCRAPER**	*n* pl. -S one that scrapes
SCOTOMA	*n* pl. -MAS or -MATA a blind spot in the field of vision	**SCRAPIE**	*n* pl. -S a disease of sheep
		SCRAPING	*n* pl. -S something scraped off
SCOTOPIA	*n* pl. -S vision in dim light **SCOTOPIC** *adj*	**SCRAPPED**	past tense of scrap
		SCRAPPER	*n* pl. -S a fighter
SCOTTIE	*n* pl. -S a short-legged terrier	**SCRAPPIER**	comparative of scrappy
SCOUR	*v* -ED, -ING, -S to cleanse or polish by hard rubbing	**SCRAPPIEST**	superlative of scrappy
		SCRAPPING	present participle of scrap
SCOURER	*n* pl. -S one that scours	**SCRAPPLE**	*n* pl. -S a seasoned mixture of ground meat and cornmeal
SCOURGE	*v* SCOURGED, SCOURGING, SCOURGES to punish severely		
		SCRAPPY	*adj* -PIER, -PIEST marked by fighting spirit
SCOURGER	*n* pl. -S one that scourges		
SCOURING	*n* pl. -S material removed by scouring	**SCRATCH**	*v* -ED, -ING, -ES to make a thin, shallow cut or mark on
SCOUSE	*n* pl. -S a type of meat stew	**SCRATCHY**	*adj* SCRATCHIER, SCRATCHIEST uneven in quality
SCOUT	*v* -ED, -ING, -S to observe for the purpose of obtaining information	**SCRAWL**	*v* -ED, -ING, -S to write hastily or illegibly
		SCRAWLER	*n* pl. -S one that scrawls
SCOUTER	*n* pl. -S one that scouts	**SCRAWLY**	*adj* SCRAWLIER, SCRAWLIEST written hastily or illegibly
SCOUTH	*n* pl. -S plenty		
SCOUTHER	*v* -ED, -ING, -S to scorch	**SCRAWNY**	*adj* -NIER, -NIEST extremely thin

SCREAK	v -ED, -ING, -S to screech	**SCROOGE**	n pl. -S a miserly person
SCREAKY	adj screechy	**SCROOP**	v -ED, -ING, -S to make a harsh, grating sound
SCREAM	v -ED, -ING, -S to utter a prolonged, piercing cry	**SCROTUM**	n pl. -TA or -TUMS the pouch of skin that contains the testes **SCROTAL** adj
SCREAMER	n pl. -S one that screams		
SCREE	n pl. -S a mass of rocks at the foot of a slope	**SCROUGE**	v SCROUGED, SCROUGING, SCROUGES to crowd
SCREECH	v -ED, -ING, -ES to utter a harsh, shrill cry	**SCROUNGE**	v SCROUNGED, SCROUNGING, SCROUNGES to gather by foraging
SCREECHY	adj SCREECHIER, SCREECHIEST screeching	**SCROUNGY**	adj SCROUNGIER, SCROUNGIEST dirty
SCREED	v -ED, -ING, -S to shred		
SCREEN	v -ED, -ING, -S to provide with a screen (a device designed to divide, conceal, or protect)	**SCRUB**	v SCRUBBED, SCRUBBING, SCRUBS to rub hard in order to clean
SCREENER	n pl. -S one that screens	**SCRUBBER**	n pl. -S one that scrubs
SCREW	v -ED, -ING, -S to attach with a screw (a type of metal fastener)	**SCRUBBY**	adj -BIER, -BIEST inferior in size or quality
SCREWER	n pl. -S one that screws	**SCRUFF**	n pl. -S the back of the neck
SCREWY	adj SCREWIER, SCREWIEST crazy	**SCRUFFY**	adj -FIER, -FIEST shabby
		SCRUM	n pl. -S a formation around the ball in rugby
SCRIBAL	adj pertaining to a public clerk or secretary		
SCRIBBLE	v -BLED, -BLING, -BLES to write hastily or carelessly	**SCRUNCH**	v -ED, -ING, -ES to crush
		SCRUPLE	v -PLED, -PLING, -PLES to hesitate because of ethical considerations
SCRIBE	v SCRIBED, SCRIBING, SCRIBES to mark with a scriber		
SCRIBER	n pl. -S a pointed instrument used for marking off material to be cut	**SCRUTINY**	n pl. -NIES a close examination
		SCUBA	n pl. -S an underwater breathing device
SCRIEVE	v SCRIEVED, SCRIEVING, SCRIEVES to move along swiftly and smoothly	**SCUD**	v SCUDDED, SCUDDING, SCUDS to run or move swiftly
SCRIM	n pl. -S a cotton fabric	**SCUDO**	n pl. -DI a former Italian coin
SCRIMP	v -ED, -ING, -S to be very or overly thrifty	**SCUFF**	v -ED, -ING, -S to walk without lifting the feet
SCRIMPIT	adj meager	**SCUFFLE**	v -FLED, -FLING, -FLES to struggle in a rough, confused manner
SCRIMPY	adj SCRIMPIER, SCRIMPIEST meager		
SCRIP	n pl. -S a small piece of paper	**SCUFFLER**	n pl. -S one that scuffles
SCRIPT	v -ED, -ING, -S to prepare a written text for, as a play or motion picture	**SCULK**	v -ED, -ING, -S to skulk
		SCULKER	n pl. -S skulker
		SCULL	v -ED, -ING, -S to propel with a type of oar
SCRIVE	v SCRIVED, SCRIVING, SCRIVES to engrave		
		SCULLER	n pl. -S one that sculls
SCROD	n pl. -S a young cod	**SCULLERY**	n pl. -LERIES a room in which kitchen utensils are cleaned and stored
SCROFULA	n pl. -S a disease of the lymph glands		
SCROGGY	adj -GIER, -GIEST of stunted growth	**SCULLION**	n pl. -S a kitchen servant who does menial work
SCROLL	n pl. -S a roll of parchment or paper with writing on it	**SCULP**	v -ED, -ING, -S to sculpt
		SCULPIN	n pl. -S a freshwater fish

SCULPT	v -ED, -ING, -S to form an image or representation of from solid material	**SCUTTER**	v -ED, -ING, -S to scurry
SCULPTOR	n pl. -S one that sculpts	**SCUTTLE**	v -TLED, -TLING, -TLES to scurry
SCUM	v SCUMMED, SCUMMING, SCUMS to remove the scum (impure or extraneous matter) from	**SCUTUM**	n pl. -TA scute
		SCYPHATE	adj shaped like a cup
SCUMBLE	v -BLED, -BLING, -BLES to soften the outlines or colors of by rubbing lightly	**SCYTHE**	v SCYTHED, SCYTHING, SCYTHES to cut with a scythe (a single-bladed cutting implement)
SCUMLIKE	adj resembling scum	**SEA**	n pl. -S the ocean
SCUMMED	past tense of scum	**SEABAG**	n pl. -S a bag used by a sailor
SCUMMER	n pl. -S one that scums	**SEABEACH**	n pl. -ES a beach lying along the sea
SCUMMING	present participle of scum		
SCUMMY	adj -MIER, -MIEST covered with scum	**SEABED**	n pl. -S a seafloor
		SEABIRD	n pl. -S a bird frequenting the ocean or seacoast
SCUNNER	v -ED, -ING, -S to feel loathing or disgust	**SEABOARD**	n pl. -S the seacoast
SCUP	n pl. -S a marine food fish	**SEABOOT**	n pl. -S a waterproof boot
SCUPPAUG	n pl. -S scup	**SEABORNE**	adj carried on or over the sea
SCUPPER	v -ED, -ING, -S to ambush	**SEACOAST**	n pl. -S land bordering on the sea
SCURF	n pl. -S scaly or shredded dry skin		
		SEACOCK	n pl. -S a valve in a ship's hull
SCURFY	adj SCURFIER, SCURFIEST covered with scurf	**SEACRAFT**	n pl. -S skill in sea navigation
		SEADOG	n pl. -S a fogbow
SCURRIED	past tense of scurry	**SEADROME**	n pl. -S an airport in the sea
SCURRIES	present 3d person sing. of scurry	**SEAFARER**	n pl. -S a sailor
		SEAFLOOR	n pl. -S the bottom of a sea
SCURRIL	adj scurrile	**SEAFOOD**	n pl. -S edible fish or shellfish from the sea
SCURRILE	adj expressed in coarse and abusive language		
		SEAFOWL	n pl. -S a seabird
SCURRY	v -RIED, -RYING, -RIES to move hurriedly	**SEAFRONT**	n pl. -S an area along the edge of the sea
SCURVY	adj -VIER, -VIEST base or contemptible **SCURVILY** adv	**SEAGIRT**	adj surrounded by the sea
		SEAGOING	adj designed for use on the sea
SCURVY	n pl. -VIES a disease resulting from vitamin C deficiency	**SEAL**	v -ED, -ING, -S to close or make secure against access, leakage, or passage **SEALABLE** adj
SCUT	n pl. -S a short tail, as of a rabbit		
		SEALANT	n pl. -S a sealing agent
SCUTA	pl. of scutum	**SEALER**	n pl. -S one that seals
SCUTAGE	n pl. -S a tax exacted by a feudal lord in lieu of military service	**SEALERY**	n pl. -ERIES the occupation of hunting seals
		SEALLIKE	adj resembling a seal (an aquatic mammal)
SCUTATE	adj shaped like a shield		
SCUTCH	v -ED, -ING, -ES to separate the woody fiber from by beating	**SEALSKIN**	n pl. -S the skin of a seal
		SEAM	v -ED, -ING, -S to join with a seam (a line formed by sewing two pieces of fabric together)
SCUTCHER	n pl. -S one that scutches		
SCUTE	n pl. -S a horny plate or scale		
SCUTELLA	n/pl small, scutate organs or parts	**SEAMAN**	n pl. -MEN a sailor **SEAMANLY** adj

SEAMARK   n pl. -S a landmark serving as a navigational guide to mariners

SEAMER   n pl. -S one that seams

SEAMIER   comparative of seamy

SEAMIEST   superlative of seamy

SEAMLESS   adj having no seam

SEAMLIKE   adj resembling a seam

SEAMOUNT   n pl. -S an undersea mountain

SEAMSTER   n pl. -S a person whose occupation is sewing

SEAMY   adj SEAMIER, SEAMIEST unpleasant

SEANCE   n pl. -S a meeting of persons seeking spiritualistic messages

SEAPIECE   n pl. -S a seascape

SEAPLANE   n pl. -S an airplane designed to take off from or land on the water

SEAPORT   n pl. -S a harbor or town accessible to seagoing ships

SEAQUAKE   n pl. -S an undersea earthquake

SEAR   adj SEARER, SEAREST sere

SEAR   v -ED, -ING, -S to burn the surface of

SEARCH   v -ED, -ING, -ES to look through or over carefully in order to find something

SEARCHER   n pl. -S one that searches

SEARER   comparative of sear

SEAREST   superlative of sear

SEASCAPE   n pl. -S a picture of the sea

SEASCOUT   n pl. -S a boy scout trained in water activities

SEASHELL   n pl. -S the shell of a marine mollusk

SEASHORE   n pl. -S land bordering on the sea

SEASICK   adj affected with nausea caused by the motion of a vessel at sea

SEASIDE   n pl. -S the seashore

SEASON   v -ED, -ING, -S to heighten or improve the flavor of by adding savory ingredients

SEASONAL   adj occurring at a certain time of the year

SEASONER   n pl. -S one that seasons

SEAT   v -ED, -ING, -S to place on a seat (something on which one sits)

SEATER   n pl. -S one that seats

SEATING   n pl. -S material for covering seats

SEATLESS   adj having no seat

SEATMATE   n pl. -S one with whom one shares a seat

SEATRAIN   n pl. -S a ship equipped to carry railroad cars

SEATWORK   n pl. -S work done at one's seat

SEAWALL   n pl. -S a wall to protect a shoreline from erosion

SEAWAN   n pl. -S wampum

SEAWANT   n pl. -S seawan

SEAWARD   n pl. -S the direction toward the open sea

SEAWARE   n pl. -S seaweed used as fertilizer

SEAWATER   n pl. -S water from the sea

SEAWAY   n pl. -WAYS the headway made by a ship

SEAWEED   n pl. -S a plant growing in the sea

SEBACIC   adj derived from a certain acid

SEBASIC   adj sebacic

SEBUM   n pl. -S a fatty matter secreted by certain glands of the skin

SEC   n pl. -S secant

SECANT   n pl. -S a trigonometric function of an angle

SECANTLY   adv in an intersecting manner

SECATEUR   n pl. -S a pruning tool

SECCO   n pl. -COS the art of painting on dry plaster

SECEDE   v -CEDED, -CEDING, -CEDES to withdraw formally from an alliance or association

SECEDER   n pl. -S one that secedes

SECERN   v -ED, -ING, -S to discern as separate

SECLUDE   v -CLUDED, -CLUDING, -CLUDES to remove or set apart from others

SECOND   v -ED, -ING, -S to give support or encouragement to

SECONDE   n pl. -S a position in fencing

SECONDER   n pl. -S one that seconds

SECONDLY   adv in the next place after the first

SECONDO   n pl. -DI the lower part in a piano duet

SECPAR *n pl.* -S a parsec

SECRECY *n pl.* -CIES the condition of being secret

SECRET *adj* -CRETER, -CRETEST kept from knowledge or view

SECRET *n pl.* -S something kept from the knowledge of others

SECRETE *v* -CRETED, -CRETING, -CRETES to generate and separate out from cells or bodily fluids

SECRETIN *n pl.* -S a hormone

SECRETLY *adv* in a secret manner

SECRETOR *n pl.* -S one that secretes

SECT *n pl.* -S a group of people united by common beliefs or interests

SECTARY *n pl.* -RIES a member of a sect

SECTILE *adj* capable of being cut smoothly

SECTION *v* -ED, -ING, -S to divide into sections (distinct parts)

SECTOR *v* -ED, -ING, -S to divide into sectors (sections)

SECTORAL *adj* of or pertaining to a sector

SECULAR *n pl.* -S a layman

SECUND *adj* having the parts or organs arranged on one side only **SECUNDLY** *adv*

SECUNDUM *adv* according to

SECURE *adj* -CURER, -CUREST free from danger **SECURELY** *adv*

SECURE *v* -CURED, -CURING, -CURES to make firm or tight

SECURER *n pl.* -S one that secures

SECUREST superlative of secure

SECURING present participle of secure

SECURITY *n pl.* -TIES the state of being secure

SEDAN *n pl.* -S a type of automobile

SEDARIM a pl. of seder

SEDATE *adj* -DATER, -DATEST calm **SEDATELY** *adv*

SEDATE *v* -DATED, -DATING, -DATES to administer a sedative to

SEDATION *n pl.* -S the reduction of stress or excitement by the use of sedatives

SEDATIVE *n pl.* -S a drug that induces a calm state

SEDER *n pl.* -DARIM or -DERS a Jewish ceremonial dinner

SEDERUNT *n pl.* -S a prolonged sitting

SEDGE *n pl.* -S a marsh plant

SEDGY *adj* SEDGIER, SEDGIEST abounding in sedge

SEDILE *n pl.* -LIA one of the seats in a church for the use of the officiating clergy

SEDILIUM *n pl.* -LIA sedile

SEDIMENT *v* -ED, -ING, -S to settle to the bottom of a liquid

SEDITION *n pl.* -S incitement of rebellion against a government

SEDUCE *v* -DUCED, -DUCING, -DUCES to lead astray **SEDUCIVE** *adj*

SEDUCER *n pl.* -S one that seduces

SEDULITY *n pl.* -TIES the state of being sedulous

SEDULOUS *adj* diligent

SEDUM *n pl.* -S a flowering plant

SEE *v* SAW, SEEN, SEEING, SEES to perceive with the eyes **SEEABLE** *adj*

SEECATCH *n pl.* -CATCHIE an adult male fur seal

SEED *v* -ED, -ING, -S to plant seeds (propagative plant structures) in

SEEDBED *n pl.* -S land prepared for seeding

SEEDCAKE *n pl.* -S a sweet cake containing aromatic seeds

SEEDCASE *n pl.* -S a pericarp

SEEDER *n pl.* -S one that seeds

SEEDIER comparative of seedy

SEEDIEST superlative of seedy

SEEDILY *adv* in a seedy manner

SEEDLESS *adj* having no seeds

SEEDLIKE *adj* resembling a seed

SEEDLING *n pl.* -S a young plant

SEEDMAN *n pl.* -MEN seedsman

SEEDPOD *n pl.* -S a type of seed vessel

SEEDSMAN *n pl.* -MEN a dealer in seeds

SEEDTIME *n pl.* -S the season for sowing seeds

SEEDY *adj* SEEDIER, SEEDIEST containing seeds; inferior in condition or quality

SEEING *n pl.* -S the act of one that sees

SEEK *v* SOUGHT, SEEKING, SEEKS to go in search of

SEEKER *n pl.* -S one that seeks

SEEL	v -ED, -ING, -S to stitch closed the eyes of, as a falcon during training
SEELY	adj frail
SEEM	v -ED, -ING, -S to give the impression of being
SEEMER	n pl. -S one that seems
SEEMING	n pl. -S outward appearance
SEEMLY	adj -LIER, -LIEST of pleasing appearance
SEEN	past participle of see
SEEP	v -ED, -ING, -S to pass slowly through small openings
SEEPAGE	n pl. -S the quantity of fluid that has seeped
SEEPY	adj SEEPIER, SEEPIEST soaked or oozing with water
SEER	n pl. -S a prophet
SEERESS	n pl. -ES a female seer
SEESAW	v -ED, -ING, -S to move up and down or back and forth
SEETHE	v SEETHED, SEETHING, SEETHES to surge or foam as if boiling
SEGETAL	adj growing in fields of grain
SEGGAR	n pl. -S a saggar
SEGMENT	v -ED, -ING, -S to divide into sections
SEGNO	n pl. -GNI or -GNOS a musical sign
SEGO	n pl. -GOS a perennial herb
SEGUE	v -GUED, -GUEING, -GUES to proceed without pause from one musical theme to another
SEI	n pl. -S a rorqual
SEICENTO	n pl. -TOS the seventeenth century
SEICHE	n pl. -S an oscillation of the surface of a lake or landlocked sea
SEIDEL	n pl. -S a large beer glass
SEIGNEUR	n pl. -S seignior
SEIGNIOR	n pl. -S a feudal lord
SEIGNORY	n pl. -GNORIES the power of a seignior
SEINE	v SEINED, SEINING, SEINES to catch fish with a large, vertically hanging net
SEINER	n pl. -S one that seines
SEISE	v SEISED, SEISING, SEISES to seize **SEISABLE** adj
SEISER	n pl. -S seizer
SEISIN	n pl. -S seizin
SEISING	n pl. -S seizing
SEISM	n pl. -S an earthquake **SEISMAL, SEISMIC** adj
SEISMISM	n pl. -S the natural activity involved in earthquakes
SEISOR	n pl. -S seizor
SEISURE	n pl. -S seizure
SEIZE	v SEIZED, SEIZING, SEIZES to take hold of suddenly and forcibly **SEIZABLE** adj
SEIZER	n pl. -S one that seizes
SEIZIN	n pl. -S legal possession of land
SEIZING	n pl. -S the act of one that seizes
SEIZOR	n pl. -S one that takes seizin
SEIZURE	n pl. -S the act of seizing
SEJANT	adj represented in a sitting postion — used of a heraldic animal
SEJEANT	adj sejant
SEL	n pl. -S self
SELADANG	n pl. -S saladang
SELAH	n pl. -S a word of unknown meaning often marking the end of a verse in the Psalms
SELAMLIK	n pl. -S the portion of a Turkish house reserved for men
SELCOUTH	adj unusual
SELDOM	adj infrequent **SELDOMLY** adv
SELECT	v -ED, -ING, -S to choose
SELECTEE	n pl. -S one that is selected
SELECTLY	adv by selection
SELECTOR	n pl. -S one that selects
SELENATE	n pl. -S a chemical salt
SELENIC	adj pertaining to selenium
SELENIDE	n pl. -S a compound of selenium
SELENITE	n pl. -S a variety of gypsum
SELENIUM	n pl. -S a nonmetallic element **SELENOUS** adj
SELF	n pl. SELVES the total, essential, or particular being of one person
SELF	v -ED, -ING, -S to inbreed
SELFDOM	n pl. -S selfhood
SELFHEAL	n pl. -S a perennial herb

SELFHOOD *n* pl. -S the state of being an individual person

SELFISH *adj* concerned chiefly or only with oneself

SELFLESS *adj* unselfish

SELFNESS *n* pl. -ES selfhood

SELFSAME *adj* identical

SELFWARD *adv* toward oneself

SELL *v* SOLD, SELLING, SELLS to give up to another for money or other valuable consideration **SELLABLE** *adj*

SELLE *n* pl. -S a saddle

SELLER *n* pl. -S one that sells

SELLOUT *n* pl. -S a performance for which all seats have been sold

SELSYN *n* pl. -S a type of remote-control device

SELTZER *n* pl. -S carbonated mineral water

SELVAGE *n* pl. -S the edge of a woven fabric finished to prevent raveling **SELVAGED** *adj*

SELVEDGE *n* pl. -S selvage

SELVES pl. of self

SEMANTIC *adj* pertaining to meaning

SEMATIC *adj* serving as a warning

SEME *n* pl. -S a type of ornamental pattern

SEMEME *n* pl. -S the meaning of a morpheme

SEMEN *n* pl. -MINA or -MENS a fluid produced in the male reproductive organs

SEMESTER *n* pl. -S a period constituting half of an academic year

SEMI *n* pl. -S a freight trailer

SEMIARID *adj* characterized by light rainfall

SEMIBALD *adj* partly bald

SEMICOMA *n* pl. -S a coma from which a person can be aroused

SEMIDEAF *adj* partly deaf

SEMIDOME *n* pl. -S a half dome

SEMIDRY *adj* moderately dry

SEMIFIT *adj* conforming somewhat to the lines of the body

SEMIGALA *adj* somewhat gala

SEMIHARD *adj* moderately hard

SEMIHIGH *adj* moderately high

SEMIHOBO *n* pl. -BOS or -BOES a person having some of the characteristics of a hobo

SEMILOG *adj* having one scale logarithmic and the other arithmetic

SEMIMAT *adj* having a slight luster

SEMIMATT *adj* semimat

SEMIMUTE *adj* having partially lost the faculty of speech

SEMINA a pl. of semen

SEMINAL *adj* pertaining to semen

SEMINAR *n* pl. -S an advanced study group at a college or university

SEMINARY *n* pl. -NARIES a school for the training of priests, ministers, or rabbis

SEMINUDE *adj* partly nude

SEMIOSIS *n* pl. -OSES a process in which something functions as a sign to an organism

SEMIOTIC *n* pl. -S a general theory of signs and symbolism

SEMIPRO *n* pl. -PROS one who is engaged in some field or sport for pay on a part-time basis

SEMIRAW *adj* somewhat raw

SEMIS *n* pl. -MISES a coin of ancient Rome

SEMISOFT *adj* moderately soft

SEMITIST *n* pl. -S one who favors Jewish interests

SEMITONE *n* pl. -S a type of musical tone

SEMIWILD *adj* somewhat wild

SEMOLINA *n* pl. -S a granular product of wheat used for pasta

SEMPLE *adj* of humble birth

SEMPLICE *adj* simple — used as a musical direction

SEMPRE *adv* in the same manner throughout — used as a musical direction

SEN *n* pl. SEN a monetary unit of Japan

SENARIUS *n* pl. -NARII a Greek or Latin verse consisting of six metrical feet

SENARY *adj* pertaining to the number six

SENATE *n* pl. -S an assembly having high deliberative and legislative functions

SENATOR *n* pl. -S a member of a senate

SEND   v SENT, SENDING, SENDS to cause to go SENDABLE adj

SENDAL   n pl. -S a silk fabric

SENDER   n pl. -S one that sends

SENDOFF   n pl. -S a farewell celebration

SENECA   n pl. -S senega

SENECIO   n pl. -CIOS a flowering plant

SENEGA   n pl. -S a medicinal plant root

SENGI   n pl. SENGI a monetary unit of Zaire

SENHOR   n pl. -S or -ES a Portuguese or Brazilian gentleman

SENHORA   n pl. -S a married Portuguese or Brazilian woman

SENILE   n pl. -S one who exhibits senility

SENILELY   adv in a senile manner

SENILITY   n pl. -TIES mental and physical infirmity due to old age

SENIOR   n pl. -S a person who is older than another

SENITI   n pl. SENITI a monetary unit of Tonga

SENNA   n pl. -S a medicinal plant

SENNET   n pl. -S a call sounded on a trumpet signaling the entrance or exit of actors

SENNIGHT   n pl. -S a week

SENNIT   n pl. -S braided straw used in making hats

SENOPIA   n pl. -S an improvement of near vision

SENOR   n pl. -S or -ES a Spanish gentleman

SENORA   n pl. -S a married Spanish woman

SENORITA   n pl. -S an unmarried Spanish girl or woman

SENSA   pl. of sensum

SENSATE   v -SATED, -SATING, -SATES to sense

SENSE   v SENSED, SENSING, SENSES to perceive by the senses (any of certain agencies through which an individual receives impressions of the external world)

SENSEFUL   adj sensible

SENSIBLE   adj -BLER, -BLEST having or showing good judgment SENSIBLY adv

SENSIBLE   n pl. -S something that can be sensed

SENSILLA   n/pl simple sense organs

SENSING   present participle of sense

SENSOR   n pl. -S a device that receives and responds to a stimulus

SENSORIA   n/pl the parts of the brain concerned with the reception and interpretation of sensory stimuli

SENSORY   adj pertaining to the senses or sensation

SENSUAL   adj pertaining to the physical senses

SENSUM   n pl. -SA an object of perception or sensation

SENSUOUS   adj pertaining to or derived from the senses

SENT   past tense of send

SENTENCE   v -TENCED, -TENCING, -TENCES to declare judicially the extent of punishment to be imposed

SENTI   n pl. SENTI a monetary unit of Tanzania

SENTIENT   n pl. -S a person or thing capable of sensation

SENTINEL   v -NELED, -NELING, -NELS or -NELLED, -NELLING, -NELS to stand guard

SENTRY   n pl. -TRIES one who stands guard

SEPAL   n pl. -S one of the individual leaves of a calyx SEPALED, SEPALINE, SEPALLED, SEPALOID, SEPALOUS adj

SEPARATE   v -RATED, -RATING, -RATES to set or keep apart

SEPIA   n pl. -S a brown pigment SEPIC adj

SEPOY   n pl. -POYS a native of India serving in the British army

SEPPUKU   n pl. -S a Japanese form of suicide

SEPSIS   n pl. SEPSES bacterial invasion of the body

SEPT   n pl. -S a clan

SEPTA   pl. of septum

SEPTAL   adj pertaining to a septum

SEPTARIA   n/pl limestone nodules

SEPTATE   adj having a septum

SEPTET   n pl. -S a group of seven

SEPTETTE   n pl. -S septet

SEPTIC   *n* pl. -S an agent producing sepsis **SEPTICAL** *adj*

SEPTIME   *n* pl. -S a position in fencing

SEPTUM   *n* pl. -TA a dividing membrane or partition

SEPTUPLE   *v* -PLED, -PLING, -PLES to make seven times as great

SEQUEL   *n* pl. -S something that follows and serves as a continuation

SEQUELA   *n* pl. -QUELAE an abnormal condition resulting from a preceding disease

SEQUENCE   *v* -QUENCED, -QUENCING, -QUENCES to arrange in consecutive order

SEQUENCY   *n* pl. -CIES the following of one thing after another

SEQUENT   *n* pl. -S something that follows

SEQUIN   *n* pl. -S a shiny ornamental disk **SEQUINED** *adj*

SEQUITUR   *n* pl. -S the conclusion of an inference

SEQUOIA   *n* pl. -S a large evergreen tree

SER   *n* pl. -S a unit of weight of India

SERA   a pl. of serum

SERAC   *n* pl. -S a large mass of ice broken off of a glacier

SERAGLIO   *n* pl. -GLIOS a harem

SERAI   *n* pl. -S a Turkish palace

SERAIL   *n* pl. -S a seraglio

SERAL   *adj* pertaining to a series of ecological changes

SERAPE   *n* pl. -S a colorful woolen shawl

SERAPH   *n* pl. -APHS, -APHIM, or -APHIN a winged celestial being **SERAPHIC** *adj*

SERAPHIM   *n* pl. -S seraph

SERDAB   *n* pl. -S a chamber within an ancient Egyptian tomb

SERE   *adj* SERER, SEREST withered; dry

SERE   *v* SERED, SERING, SERES to sear

SEREIN   *n* pl. -S a fine rain falling from an apparently clear sky

SERENADE   *v* -NADED, -NADING, -NADES to perform an honorific evening song for

SERENATA   *n* pl. -TAS or -TE a dramatic cantata

SERENE   *adj* SERENER, SERENEST calm; tranquil **SERENELY** *adv*

SERENE   *n* pl. -S a serene condition or expanse

SERENITY   *n* pl. -TIES the state of being serene

SERER   comparative of sere

SEREST   superlative of sere

SERF   *n* pl. -S a feudal slave

SERFAGE   *n* pl. -S serfdom

SERFDOM   *n* pl. -S the state of being a serf

SERFHOOD   *n* pl. -S serfdom

SERFISH   *adj* characteristic of a serf

SERFLIKE   *adj* serfish

SERGE   *n* pl. -S a twilled fabric

SERGEANT   *n* pl. -S a noncommissioned military officer

SERGING   *n* pl. -S a process of finishing the raw edges of a fabric

SERIAL   *n* pl. -S a literary or dramatic work presented in successive installments

SERIALLY   *adv* in the manner or form of a serial

SERIATE   *v* -ATED, -ATING, -ATES to put into a series

SERIATIM   *adv* serially

SERICIN   *n* pl. -S a kind of protein

SERIEMA   *n* pl. -S a Brazilian bird

SERIES   *n* pl. SERIES an arrangement of one after another

SERIF   *n* pl. -S a fine line used to finish off the main stroke of a letter

SERIN   *n* pl. -S a European finch

SERINE   *n* pl. -S an amino acid

SERING   present participle of sere

SERINGA   *n* pl. -S a Brazilian tree

SERIOUS   *adj* thoughtful or subdued in appearance or manner

SERJEANT   *n* pl. -S sergeant

SERMON   *n* pl. -S a religious discourse **SERMONIC** *adj*

SEROLOGY   *n* pl. -GIES the science of serums

SEROSA   *n* pl. -SAS or -SAE a thin membrane lining certain bodily cavities **SEROSAL** *adj*

SEROSITY   *n* pl. -TIES the quality or state of being serous

SEROTINE   *n* pl. -S a European bat

SEROTYPE *n* pl. -S a group of closely related organisms distinguished by a common set of antigens

SEROUS *adj* of or resembling serum

SEROW *n* pl. -S an Asian antelope

SERPENT *n* pl. -S a snake

SERPIGO *n* pl. -GOES or -GINES a spreading skin eruption

SERRANID *n* pl. -S a marine fish

SERRATE *v* -RATED, -RATING, -RATES to furnish with toothlike projections

SERRY *v* -RIED, -RYING, -RIES to crowd together

SERUM *n* pl. -RUMS or -RA the watery portion of whole blood
SERUMAL *adj*

SERVABLE *adj* capable of serving or being served

SERVAL *n* pl. -S an African wildcat

SERVANT *n* pl. -S one that serves others

SERVE *v* SERVED, SERVING, SERVES to work for

SERVER *n* pl. -S one that serves another

SERVICE *v* -VICED, -VICING, -VICES to repair

SERVICER *n* pl. -S one that services

SERVILE *adj* slavishly submissive

SERVING *n* pl. -S a portion of food

SERVITOR *n* pl. -S a male servant

SERVO *n* pl. -VOS an automatic device used to control another mechanism

SESAME *n* pl. -S an East Indian plant

SESAMOID *n* pl. -S a nodular mass of bone or cartilage

SESSILE *adj* permanently attached

SESSION *n* pl. -S a meeting of a legislative or judicial body for the transaction of business

SESSPOOL *n* pl. -S cesspool

SESTERCE *n* pl. -S a coin of ancient Rome

SESTET *n* pl. -S a stanza of six lines

SESTINA *n* pl. -S a type of verse form

SESTINE *n* pl. -S sestina

SET *v* SET, SETTING, SETS to put in a particular position

SETA *n* pl. -TAE a coarse, stiff hair
SETAL *adj*

SETBACK *n* pl. -S a defeat

SETIFORM *adj* having the form of a seta

SETLINE *n* pl. -S a strong fishing line

SETOFF *n* pl. -S something that offsets something else

SETON *n* pl. -S a type of surgical thread

SETOSE *adj* covered with setae

SETOUS *adj* setose

SETOUT *n* pl. -S a display

SETSCREW *n* pl. -S a type of screw

SETTEE *n* pl. -S a long seat with a high back

SETTER *n* pl. -S one that sets

SETTING *n* pl. -S the scenery used in a dramatic production

SETTLE *v* -TLED, -TLING, -TLES to place in a desired state or order

SETTLER *n* pl. -S one that settles

SETTLING *n* pl. -S sediment

SETTLOR *n* pl. -S one that makes a legal settlement

SETULOSE *adj* covered with seta

SETULOUS *adj* setulose

SETUP *n* pl. -S the way something is arranged

SEVEN *n* pl. -S a number

SEVENTH *n* pl. -S one of seven equal parts

SEVENTY *n* pl. -TIES a number

SEVER *v* -ED, -ING, -S to divide or cut into parts

SEVERAL *n* pl. -S a few persons or things

SEVERE *adj* -VERER, -VEREST unsparing in the treatment of others
SEVERELY *adv*

SEVERITY *n* pl. -TIES the quality or state of being severe

SEW *v* SEWED, SEWN, SEWING, SEWS to mend or fasten with a needle and thread

SEWAGE *n* pl. -S the waste matter carried off by sewers

SEWAN *n* pl. -S seawan

SEWAR *n* pl. -S a medieval servant

SEWER *n* pl. -S an underground conduit for carrying off liquid and solid waste

SEWERAGE *n* pl. -S sewage

SEWING *n* pl. -S material that has been or is to be sewed

SEWN a past participle of sew

SEX v -ED, -ING, -ES to determine the sex (the property by which organisms are classified according to reproductive functions) of

SEXIER comparative of sexy

SEXIEST superlative of sexy

SEXILY adv in a sexy manner

SEXINESS n pl. -ES the quality or state of being sexy

SEXISM n pl. -S prejudice or discrimination against women

SEXIST n pl. -S one that practices sexism

SEXLESS adj lacking sexual characteristics

SEXOLOGY n pl. -GIES the study of human sexual behavior

SEXPOT n pl. -S a sexually attractive woman

SEXT n pl. -S one of seven canonical daily periods for prayer and devotion

SEXTAIN n pl. -S a stanza of six lines

SEXTAN n pl. -S a recurrent malarial fever

SEXTANT n pl. -S an instrument for measuring angular distances

SEXTARII n/pl ancient Roman units of liquid measure

SEXTET n pl. -S a group of six

SEXTETTE n pl. -S sextet

SEXTILE n pl. -S the position of two celestial bodies when they are sixty degrees apart

SEXTO n pl. -TOS sixmo

SEXTON n pl. -S a maintenance worker of a church

SEXTUPLE v -PLED, -PLING, -PLES to make six times as great

SEXTUPLY adv to six times as much or as many

SEXUAL adj pertaining to sex **SEXUALLY** adv

SEXY adj SEXIER, SEXIEST arousing sexual desire

SFERICS n/pl an electronic detector of storms

SFORZATO n pl. -TOS the playing of a tone or chord with sudden force

SFUMATO n pl. -TOS a technique used in painting

SH interj — used to urge silence

SHABBY adj -BIER, -BIEST ragged **SHABBILY** adv

SHACK n pl. -S a shanty

SHACKLE v -LED, -LING, -LES to confine with metal fastenings placed around the wrists or ankles

SHACKLER n pl. -S one that shackles

SHACKO n pl. -KOS or -KOES shako

SHAD n pl. -S a food fish

SHADBLOW n pl. -S a shadbush

SHADBUSH n pl. -ES a flowering tree or shrub

SHADCHAN n pl. -CHANIM or -CHANS a Jewish marriage broker

SHADDOCK n pl. -S a citrus fruit

SHADE v SHADED, SHADING, SHADES to screen from light or heat

SHADER n pl. -S one that shades

SHADFLY n pl. -FLIES a winged insect

SHADIER comparative of shady

SHADIEST superlative of shady

SHADILY adv in a shady manner

SHADING n pl. -S protection against light or heat

SHADOOF n pl. -S a device used in Egypt for raising water for irrigation

SHADOW v -ED, -ING, -S to make dark or gloomy

SHADOWER n pl. -S one that shadows

SHADOWY adj -OWIER, -OWIEST dark

SHADRACH n pl. -S a mass of unfused material in the hearth of a blast furnace

SHADUF n pl. -S shadoof

SHADY adj SHADIER, SHADIEST shaded

SHAFT v -ED, -ING, -S to push or propel with a pole

SHAFTING n pl. -S a system of rods for transmitting motion or power

SHAG v SHAGGED, SHAGGING, SHAGS to make shaggy

SHAGBARK n pl. -S a hardwood tree

SHAGGY adj -GIER, -GIEST covered with long, coarse hair **SHAGGILY** adv

SHAGREEN n pl. -S the rough skin of certain sharks

SHAH n pl. -S an Iranian ruler

SHAHDOM	n pl. -S the territory ruled by a shah
SHAIRD	n pl. -S shard
SHAIRN	n pl. -S sharn
SHAITAN	n pl. -S an evil spirit
SHAKE	v SHOOK, SHAKEN, SHAKING, SHAKES to move to and fro with short, rapid movements SHAKABLE adj
SHAKEOUT	n pl. -S a minor economic recession
SHAKER	n pl. -S one that shakes
SHAKEUP	n pl. -S a total reorganization
SHAKIER	comparative of shaky
SHAKIEST	superlative of shaky
SHAKILY	adv in a shaky manner
SHAKING	present participle of shake
SHAKO	n pl. -KOS or -KOES a type of military hat
SHAKY	adj SHAKIER, SHAKIEST shaking
SHALE	n pl. -S a fissile rock
SHALED	adj having a shell or husk
SHALIER	comparative of shaly
SHALIEST	superlative of shaly
SHALL	v present sing. 2d person SHALL or SHALT, past sing. 2d person SHOULD, SHOULDST, or SHOULDEST — used as an auxiliary to express futurity, inevitability, or command
SHALLOON	n pl. -S a woolen fabric
SHALLOP	n pl. -S a small, open boat
SHALLOT	n pl. -S a plant resembling an onion
SHALLOW	adj -LOWER, -LOWEST having little depth
SHALLOW	v -ED, -ING, -S to make shallow
SHALOM	interj peace — used as a Jewish greeting and farewell
SHALT	a present 2d person sing. of shall
SHALY	adj SHALIER, SHALIEST resembling shale
SHAM	v SHAMMED, SHAMMING, SHAMS to feign
SHAMABLE	adj capable of being shamed
SHAMAN	n pl. -S a medicine man among certain North American Indians SHAMANIC adj

SHAMBLE	v -BLED, -BLING, -BLES to walk awkwardly
SHAME	v SHAMED, SHAMING, SHAMES to cause to feel a painful sense of guilt or degradation
SHAMEFUL	adj disgraceful
SHAMES	n pl. -MOSIM shammes
SHAMING	present participle of shame
SHAMMAS	n pl. -MASIM shammes
SHAMMASH	n pl. -MASHIM shammes
SHAMMED	past tense of sham
SHAMMER	n pl. -S one that shams
SHAMMES	n pl. -MOSIM a minor official of a synagogue
SHAMMIED	past tense of shammy
SHAMMIES	present 3d person sing. of shammy
SHAMMING	present participle of sham
SHAMMOS	n pl. -MOSIM shammes
SHAMMOSIM	pl. of shammes
SHAMMY	v -MIED, -MYING, -MIES to chamois
SHAMOIS	n pl. SHAMOIS chamois
SHAMOSIM	pl. of shames
SHAMOY	v -ED, -ING, -S to chamois
SHAMPOO	v -ED, -ING, -S to cleanse with a special preparation
SHAMROCK	n pl. -S a three-leaved plant
SHAMUS	n pl. -ES a private detective
SHANDY	n pl. -DIES an alcoholic drink
SHANGHAI	v -ED, -ING, -S to kidnap for service aboard a ship
SHANK	v -ED, -ING, -S to hit sharply to the right, as a golf ball
SHANTEY	n pl. -TEYS chantey
SHANTI	n pl. -S peace
SHANTIES	pl. of shanty
SHANTIH	n pl. -S shanti
SHANTUNG	n pl. -S a silk fabric
SHANTY	n pl. -TIES a small, crudely built dwelling
SHAPE	v SHAPED, SHAPEN, SHAPING, SHAPES to give shape (outward form) to SHAPABLE adj
SHAPELY	adj -LIER, -LIEST having a pleasing shape
SHAPER	n pl. -S one that shapes
SHAPEUP	n pl. -S a system of hiring a work crew

SHAPING present participle of shape

SHARD n pl. -S a fragment of broken pottery

SHARE v SHARED, SHARING, SHARES to have, get, or use in common with another or others SHARABLE adj

SHARER n pl. -S one that shares

SHARIF n pl. -S sherif

SHARING present participle of share

SHARK v -ED, -ING, -S to live by trickery

SHARKER n pl. -S one that sharks

SHARN n pl. -S cow dung SHARNY adj

SHARP adj SHARPER, SHARPEST suitable for or capable of cutting or piercing

SHARP v -ED, -ING, -S to raise in pitch, as a musical tone

SHARPEN v -ED, -ING, -S to make or become sharp

SHARPER n pl. -S a swindler

SHARPIE n pl. -S a very alert person

SHARPLY adv in a sharp manner

SHARPY n pl. SHARPIES sharpie

SHASHLIK n pl. -S kabob

SHASLIK n pl. -S shashlik

SHAT a past tense of shit

SHATTER v -ED, -ING, -S to break into pieces

SHAUGH n pl. -S a thicket

SHAUL v -ED, -ING, -S to shoal

SHAVE v SHAVED, SHAVEN, SHAVING, SHAVES to sever the hair close to the roots SHAVABLE adj

SHAVER n pl. -S one that shaves

SHAVIE n pl. -S a trick or prank

SHAVING n pl. -S something shaved off

SHAW v SHAWED, SHAWN, SHAWING, SHAWS to show

SHAWL v -ED, -ING, -S to wrap in a shawl (a piece of cloth worn as a covering)

SHAWM n pl. -S an early woodwind instrument

SHAWN past participle of shaw

SHAY n pl. SHAYS a chaise

SHE n pl. -S a female person

SHEA n pl. -S an African tree

SHEAF v -ED, -ING, -S to sheave

SHEAL n pl. -S shealing

SHEALING n pl. -S a shepherd's hut

SHEAR v SHEARED or SHORE, SHORN, SHEARING, SHEARS to cut the hair from

SHEARER n pl. -S one that shears

SHEATH v -ED, -ING, -S to sheathe

SHEATHE v SHEATHED, SHEATHING, SHEATHES to put into a protective case

SHEATHER n pl. -S one that sheathes

SHEAVE v SHEAVED, SHEAVING, SHEAVES to gather into a bundle

SHEBANG n pl. -S a situation, organization, or matter

SHEBEAN n pl. -S shebeen

SHEBEEN n pl. -S a place where liquor is sold illegally

SHED v SHEDDED, SHEDDING, SHEDS to house in a shed (a small, low structure)

SHEDABLE adj capable of being cast off

SHEDDER n pl. -S one that casts off something

SHEDDING present participle of shed

SHEEN v -ED, -ING, -S to shine

SHEENEY n pl. -NEYS sheenie

SHEENFUL adj shining

SHEENIE n pl. -S a Jew — an offensive term

SHEENY adj SHEENIER, SHEENIEST shining

SHEEP n pl. SHEEP a ruminant mammal

SHEEPDOG n pl. -S a dog trained to guard and herd sheep

SHEEPISH adj embarrassed

SHEEPMAN n pl. -MEN a person who raises sheep

SHEER v -ED, -ING, -S to deviate from a course

SHEER adj SHEERER, SHEEREST of very thin texture SHEERLY adv

SHEET v -ED, -ING, -S to cover with a sheet (a thin, rectangular piece of material)

SHEETER n pl. -S one that sheets

SHEETFED adj pertaining to a type of printing press

SHEETING *n* pl. -S material in the form of sheets

SHEEVE *n* pl. -S a grooved pulley wheel

SHEGETZ *n* pl. SHKOTZIM a non-Jewish boy or young man

SHEIK *n* pl. -S an Arab chief

SHEIKDOM *n* pl. -S the area ruled by a sheik

SHEIKH *n* pl. -S sheik

SHEITAN *n* pl. -S shaitan

SHEKEL *n* pl. -S an ancient unit of weight and money

SHELDUCK *n* pl. -S a European duck

SHELF *n* pl. SHELVES a flat rigid structure used to support articles

SHELFFUL *n* pl. -S as much as a shelf can hold

SHELL *v* -ED, -ING, -S to divest of a shell (a hard outer covering)

SHELLAC *v* -LACKED, -LACKING, -LACS to cover with a thin varnish

SHELLACK *v* -ED, -ING, -S to shellac

SHELLER *n* pl. -S one that shells

SHELLY *adj* SHELLIER, SHELLIEST abounding in seashells

SHELTER *v* -ED, -ING, -S to provide cover or protection for

SHELTIE *n* pl. -S a small, shaggy pony

SHELTY *n* pl. -TIES sheltie

SHELVE *v* SHELVED, SHELVING, SHELVES to place on a shelf

SHELVER *n* pl. -S one that shelves

SHELVES pl. of shelf

SHELVING *n* pl. -S material for shelves

SHELVY *adj* SHELVIER, SHELVIEST inclining gradually

SHEND *v* SHENT, SHENDING, SHENDS to disgrace

SHEOL *n* pl. -S hell

SHEPHERD *v* -ED, -ING, -S to watch over carefully

SHERBERT *n* pl. -S sherbet

SHERBET *n* pl. -S a frozen fruit-flavored mixture

SHERD *n* pl. -S shard

SHEREEF *n* pl. -S sherif

SHERIF *n* pl. -S an Arab ruler

SHERIFF *n* pl. -S a law-enforcement officer of a county

SHERLOCK *n* pl. -S a detective

SHEROOT *n* pl. -S cheroot

SHERRIS *n* pl. -RISES sherry

SHERRY *n* pl. -RIES a type of wine

SHETLAND *n* pl. -S a wool yarn

SHEUCH *n* pl. -S sheugh

SHEUGH *n* pl. -S a ditch

SHEW *v* SHEWED, SHEWN, SHEWING, SHEWS to show

SHEWER *n* pl. -S one that shews

SHH *interj* sh

SHIBAH *n* pl. -S shiva

SHICKSA *n* pl. -S shiksa

SHIED past tense of shy

SHIEL *n* pl. -S shieling

SHIELD *v* -ED, -ING, -S to provide with a protective cover or shelter

SHIELDER *n* pl. -S one that shields

SHIELING *n* pl. -S shealing

SHIER *n* pl. -S a horse having a tendency to shy

SHIES present 3d person sing. of shy

SHIEST a superlative of shy

SHIFT *v* -ED, -ING, -S to move from one position to another

SHIFTER *n* pl. -S one that shifts

SHIFTY *adj* SHIFTIER, SHIFTIEST tricky **SHIFTILY** *adv*

SHIGELLA *n* pl. -LAE or -LAS any of a genus of aerobic bacteria

SHIKAR *v* -KARRED, -KARRING, -KARS to hunt

SHIKAREE *n* pl. -S a big game hunter

SHIKARI *n* pl. -S shikaree

SHIKARRED past tense of shikar

SHIKARRING present participle of shikar

SHIKSA *n* pl. -S a non-Jewish girl or young woman

SHIKSE *n* pl. -S shiksa

SHILINGI *n* pl. SHILINGI a monetary unit of Tanzania

SHILL *v* -ED, -ING, -S to act as a decoy

SHILLALA *n* pl. -S a short, thick club

SHILLING *n* pl. -S a former monetary unit of Great Britain

SHILPIT *adj* sickly

SHILY *adv* in a shy manner

SHIM	*v* SHIMMED, SHIMMING, SHIMS to fill out or level by inserting a thin wedge
SHIMMER	*v* -ED, -ING, -S to glimmer
SHIMMERY	*adj* shimmering
SHIMMING	present participle of shim
SHIMMY	*v* -MIED, -MYING, -MIES to vibrate or wobble
SHIN	*v* SHINNED, SHINNING, SHINS to climb by gripping and pulling alternately with the hands and legs
SHINBONE	*n pl.* -S the tibia
SHINDIG	*n pl.* -S an elaborate dance or party
SHINDY	*n pl.* -DYS or -DIES a shindig
SHINE	*v* SHONE or SHINED, SHINING, SHINES to emit light
SHINER	*n pl.* -S one that shines
SHINGLE	*v* -GLED, -GLING, -GLES to cover with shingles (thin, oblong pieces of building material)
SHINGLER	*n pl.* -S one that shingles
SHINGLY	*adj* covered with small, loose stones
SHINIER	comparative of shiny
SHINIEST	superlative of shiny
SHINILY	*adv* in a shiny manner
SHINING	*adj* emitting or reflecting light
SHINLEAF	*n pl.* -LEAFS or -LEAVES a perennial herb
SHINNED	past of shin
SHINNERY	*n pl.* -NERIES a dense growth of small trees
SHINNEY	*n pl.* -NEYS a form of hockey
SHINNING	present participle of shin
SHINNY	*v* -NIED, -NYING, -NIES to shin
SHINY	*adj* SHINIER, SHINIEST filled with shine
SHIP	*v* SHIPPED, SHIPPING, SHIPS to transport by ship (a vessel suitable for navigation in deep water)
SHIPLAP	*n pl.* -S an overlapping joint used in carpentry
SHIPLOAD	*n pl.* -S as much as a ship can carry
SHIPMAN	*n pl.* -MEN a sailor
SHIPMATE	*n pl.* -S a fellow sailor
SHIPMENT	*n pl.* -S something that is shipped
SHIPPED	past tense of ship
SHIPPEN	*n pl.* -S a cowshed
SHIPPER	*n pl.* -S one that ships
SHIPPING	*n pl.* -S the business of one that ships
SHIPPON	*n pl.* -S shippen
SHIPSIDE	*n pl.* -S the area alongside a ship
SHIPWAY	*n pl.* -WAYS a canal deep enough to serve ships
SHIPWORM	*n pl.* -S a wormlike marine mollusk
SHIPYARD	*n pl.* -S a place where ships are built or repaired
SHIRE	*n pl.* -S a territorial division of Great Britain
SHIRK	*v* -ED, -ING, -S to avoid work or duty
SHIRKER	*n pl.* -S one that shirks
SHIRR	*v* -ED, -ING, -S to draw into three or more parallel rows, as cloth
SHIRRING	*n pl.* -S a shirred arrangement of cloth
SHIRT	*n pl.* -S a garment for the upper part of the body
SHIRTING	*n pl.* -S fabric used for making shirts
SHIRTY	*adj* SHIRTIER, SHIRTIEST angry
SHIST	*n pl.* -s schist
SHIT	*v* SHITTED or SHAT, SHITTING, SHITS to defecate — usually considered vulgar
SHITTAH	*n pl.* -S a hardwood tree
SHITTIM	*n pl.* -S the wood of the shittah
SHITTING	present participle of shit
SHIV	*n pl.* -S a knife
SHIVA	*n pl.* -S a period of mourning
SHIVAH	*n pl.* -S shiva
SHIVAREE	*v* -REED, -REEING, -REES to chivaree
SHIVE	*n pl.* -S a thin fragment
SHIVER	*v* -ED, -ING, -S to tremble with fear or cold
SHIVERER	*n pl.* -S one that shivers
SHIVERY	*adj* shivering
SHKOTZIM	pl. of shegetz
SHLEMIEL	*n pl.* -S an unlucky bungler
SHLOCK	*n pl.* -S schlock

SHMO — *n* pl. SHMOES schmo

SHNAPS — *n* pl. SHNAPS schnapps

SHOAL — *adj* SHOALER, SHOALEST shallow

SHOAL — *v* -ED, -ING, -S to become shallow

SHOALY — *adj* SHOALIER, SHOALIEST full of shallow areas

SHOAT — *n* pl. -S a young hog

SHOCK — *v* -ED, -ING, -S to strike with great surprise, horror, or disgust

SHOCKER — *n* pl. -S one that shocks

SHOD — a past tense of shoe

SHODDEN — a past participle of shoe

SHODDY — *adj* -DIER, -DIEST of inferior quality SHODDILY *adv*

SHODDY — *n* pl. -DIES a low-quality wool

SHOE — *n* pl. SHOES or SHOON a covering for the foot

SHOE — *v* SHOD or SHOED, SHODDEN, SHOEING, SHOES to provide with shoes

SHOEBILL — *n* pl. -S a wading bird

SHOEHORN — *v* -ED, -ING, -S to force into a small space

SHOELACE — *n* pl. -S a lace for fastening a shoe

SHOEPAC — *n* pl. -S a waterproof boot

SHOEPACK — *n* pl. -S shoepac

SHOER — *n* pl. -S one that shoes horses

SHOETREE — *n* pl. -S a device shaped like a foot that is inserted into a shoe to preserve its shape

SHOFAR — *n* pl. SHOFARS or SHOFROTH a ram's-horn trumpet blown in certain Jewish rituals

SHOG — *v* SHOGGED, SHOGGING, SHOGS to move along

SHOGUN — *n* pl. -S a former military leader of Japan SHOGUNAL *adj*

SHOJI — *n* pl. -S a paper screen used as a partition or door in a Japanese house

SHOLOM — *interj* shalom

SHONE — a past tense of shine

SHOO — *v* -ED, -ING, -S to drive away

SHOOFLY — *n* pl. -FLIES a child's rocker

SHOOK — *n* pl. -S a set of parts for assembling a barrel or packing

SHOOL — *v* -ED, -ING, -S to shovel

SHOON — a pl. of shoe

SHOOT — *v* SHOT, SHOOTING, SHOOTS to hit, wound, or kill with a missile discharged from a weapon

SHOOTER — *n* pl. -S one that shoots

SHOOTING — *n* pl. -S the act of one that shoots

SHOP — *v* SHOPPED, SHOPPING, SHOPS to examine goods with intent to buy

SHOPBOY — *n* pl. -BOYS a salesclerk

SHOPGIRL — *n* pl. -S a salesgirl

SHOPHAR — *n* pl. -PHARS or -PHROTH shofar

SHOPLIFT — *v* -ED, -ING, -S to steal goods from a store

SHOPMAN — *n* pl. -MEN one who owns or operates a small store

SHOPPE — *n* pl. -S a small store

SHOPPED — past tense of shop

SHOPPER — *n* pl. -S one that shops

SHOPPING — *n* pl. -S the act of one that shops

SHOPTALK — *n* pl. -S conversation concerning one's business or occupation

SHOPWORN — *adj* worn out from being on display in a store

SHORAN — *n* pl. -S a type of navigational system

SHORE — *v* SHORED, SHORING, SHORES to prop with a supporting timber

SHORING — *n* pl. -S a system of supporting timbers

SHORL — *n* pl. -S schorl

SHORN — a past participle of shear

SHORT — *adj* SHORTER, SHORTEST having little length

SHORT — *v* -ED, -ING, -S to cause a type of electrical malfunction in

SHORTAGE — *n* pl. -S an insufficient supply or amount

SHORTCUT — *n* pl. -S a shorter or quicker way

SHORTEN — *v* -ED, -ING, -S to make or become shorter

SHORTIA — *n* pl. -S a perennial herb

SHORTIE — *n* pl. -S shorty

SHORTIES — pl. of shorty

SHORTISH — *adj* somewhat short

SHORTLY — *adv* in a short time

SHORTY   *n* pl. SHORTIES one that is short

SHOT   *v* SHOTTED, SHOTTING, SHOTS to load with shot (small lead or steel pellets)

SHOTE   *n* pl. -S shoat

SHOTGUN   *v* -GUNNED, -GUNNING, -GUNS to shoot with a type of gun

SHOTT   *n* pl. -S chott

SHOTTED   past tense of shot

SHOTTEN   *adj* having spawned — used of a fish

SHOTTING   present participle of shot

SHOULD   past tense of shall

SHOULDER   *v* -ED, -ING, -S to assume the burden or responsibility of

SHOULDEST   a 2d person sing. past tense of shall

SHOULDST   a 2d person sing. past tense of shall

SHOUT   *v* -ED, -ING, -S to utter loudly

SHOUTER   *n* pl. -S one that shouts

SHOVE   *v* SHOVED, SHOVING, SHOVES to push roughly

SHOVEL   *v* -ELED, -ELING, -ELS or -ELLED, -ELLING, -ELS to take up with a shovel (a digging implement)

SHOVELER   *n* pl. -S one that shovels

SHOVER   *n* pl. -S one that shoves

SHOVING   present participle of shove

SHOW   *v* SHOWED, SHOWN, SHOWING, SHOWS to cause or permit to be seen

SHOWBOAT   *n* pl. -S a boat on which theatrical performances are given

SHOWCASE   *v* -CASED, -CASING, -CASES to exhibit

SHOWDOWN   *n* pl. -S an event that forces the conclusion of an issue

SHOWER   *v* -ED, -ING, -S to fall in a brief, heavy rain

SHOWERY   *adj* showering

SHOWGIRL   *n* pl. -S a chorus girl

SHOWIER   comparative of showy

SHOWIEST   superlative of showy

SHOWILY   *adv* in a showy manner

SHOWING   *n* pl. -S an exhibition or display

SHOWMAN   *n* pl. -MEN a theatrical producer

SHOWN   past participle of show

SHOWOFF   *n* pl. -S one given to pretentious display

SHOWROOM   *n* pl. -S a room used for the display of merchandise

SHOWY   *adj* SHOWIER, SHOWIEST making a great or brilliant display

SHRANK   past tense of shrink

SHRAPNEL   *n* pl. SHRAPNEL fragments from an exploding bomb, mine, or shell

SHRED   *v* SHREDDED, SHREDDING, SHREDS to tear into small strips

SHREDDER   *n* pl. -S one that shreds

SHREW   *v* -ED, -ING, -S to curse

SHREWD   *adj* SHREWDER, SHREWDEST having keen insight **SHREWDLY** *adv*

SHREWISH   *adj* ill-tempered

SHRI   *n* pl. -S sri

SHRIEK   *v* -ED, -ING, -S to utter a shrill cry

SHRIEKER   *n* pl. -S one that shrieks

SHRIEKY   *adj* SHRIEKIER, SHRIEKIEST shrill

SHRIEVAL   *adj* pertaining to a sheriff

SHRIEVE   *v* SHRIEVED, SHRIEVING, SHRIEVES to shrive

SHRIFT   *n* pl. -S the act of shriving

SHRIKE   *n* pl. -S a predatory bird

SHRILL   *adj* SHRILLER, SHRILLEST having a high-pitched and piercing quality **SHRILLY** *adv*

SHRILL   *v* -ED, -ING, -S to utter a shrill sound

SHRIMP   *v* -ED, -ING, -S to catch shrimps (small marine decapods)

SHRIMPER   *n* pl. -S a shrimp fisher

SHRIMPY   *adj* SHRIMPIER, SHRIMPIEST abounding in shrimp

SHRINE   *v* SHRINED, SHRINING, SHRINES to place in a shrine (a receptacle for sacred relics)

SHRINK   *v* SHRANK, SHRUNK or SHRUNKEN, SHRINKING, SHRINKS to contract or draw back

SHRINKER   *n* pl. -S one that shrinks

SHRIVE   *v* SHROVE or SHRIVED, SHRIVEN, SHRIVING, SHRIVES to hear the confession of and grant absolution to

SHRIVEL   *v* -ELED, -ELING, -ELS or -ELLED, -ELLING, -ELS to contract into wrinkles

SHRIVER   *n* pl. -S one that shrives

SHRIVING   present participle of shrive

SHROFF   *v* -ED, -ING, -S to test the genuineness of, as a coin

SHROUD   *v* -ED, -ING, -S to wrap in burial clothing

SHROVE   a past tense of shrive

SHRUB   *n* pl. -S a low, woody plant

SHRUBBY   *adj* -BIER, -BIEST covered with shrubs

SHRUG   *v* SHRUGGED, SHRUGGING, SHRUGS to raise and contract the shoulders

SHRUNK   a past tense of shrink

SHRUNKEN   a past participle of shrink

SHTETEL   *n* pl. SHTETLACH a Jewish village

SHTETL   *n* pl. SHTETLACH shtetel

SHTICK   *n* pl. -S an entertainment routine

SHUCK   *v* -ED, -ING, -S to remove the husk or shell from

SHUCKER   *n* pl. -S one that shucks

SHUCKING   *n* pl. -S the act of one that shucks

SHUDDER   *v* -ED, -ING, -S to tremble

SHUDDERY   *adj* shuddering

SHUFFLE   *v* -FLED, -FLING, -FLES to walk without lifting the feet

SHUFFLER   *n* pl. -S one that shuffles

SHUL   *n* pl. SHULN or SHULS a synagogue

SHUN   *v* SHUNNED, SHUNNING, SHUNS to avoid

SHUNNER   *n* pl. -S one that shuns

SHUNPIKE   *n* pl. -S a side road taken to avoid paying tolls

SHUNT   *v* -ED, -ING, -S to turn aside

SHUNTER   *n* pl. -S one that shunts

SHUSH   *v* -ED, -ING, -ES to silence

SHUT   *v* SHUT, SHUTTING, SHUTS to close

SHUTDOWN   *n* pl. -S a temporary closing of an industrial plant

SHUTE   *v* SHUTED, SHUTING, SHUTES to chute

SHUTEYE   *n* pl. -S sleep

SHUTOFF   *n* pl. -S a device that shuts something off

SHUTOUT   *n* pl. -S a game in which one team fails to score

SHUTTER   *v* -ED, -ING, -S to provide with shutters (hinged window covers)

SHUTTING   present participle of shut

SHUTTLE   *v* -TLED, -TLING, -TLES to move or travel back and forth

SHWANPAN   *n* pl. -S swanpan

SHY   *adj* SHIER, SHIEST or SHYER, SHYEST timid

SHY   *v* SHIED, SHYING, SHIES to move suddenly back or aside, as in fear

SHYER   *n* pl. -S shier

SHYLOCK   *v* -ED, -ING, -S to lend money at high interest rates

SHYLY   *adv* in a shy manner

SHYNESS   *n* pl. -ES the state of being shy

SHYSTER   *n* pl. -S an unscrupulous lawyer or politician

SI   *n* pl. -S ti

SIAL   *n* pl. -S a type of rock formation SIALIC *adj*

SIALOID   *adj* resembling saliva

SIAMANG   *n* pl. -S a large, black gibbon

SIAMESE   *n* pl. -S a water pipe with a connection for two hoses

SIB   *n* pl. -S a sibling

SIBB   *n* pl. -S sib

SIBILANT   *n* pl. -S a speech sound produced by the fricative passage of breath through a narrow orifice

SIBILATE   *v* -LATED, -LATING, -LATES to hiss

SIBLING   *n* pl. -S one having the same parents as another

SIBYL   *n* pl. -S a female prophet SIBYLIC, SIBYLLIC *adj*

SIC   *v* SICCED, SICCING, SICS to urge to attack

SICCAN   *adj* such

SICE   *n* pl. -S syce

SICK | adj SICKER, SICKEST affected with disease or ill health

SICK | v -ED, -ING, -S to sic

SICKBAY | n pl. -BAYS a ship's hospital

SICKBED | n pl. -S a sick person's bed

SICKEN | v -ED, -ING, -S to make sick

SICKENER | n pl. -S one that sickens

SICKERLY | adv securely

SICKISH | adj somewhat sick

SICKLE | v -LED, -LING, -LES to cut with an agricultural implement having a single blade

SICKLY | adj -LIER, -LIEST appearing as if sick SICKLILY adv

SICKLY | v -LIED, -LYING, -LIES to make sickly

SICKNESS | n pl. -ES the state of being sick

SICKROOM | n pl. -S a room occupied by a sick person

SIDDUR | n pl. -DURIM or -DURS a Jewish prayer book

SIDE | v SIDED, SIDING, SIDES to agree with or support

SIDEARM | adj thrown with a sideways sweep of the arm

SIDEBAND | n pl. -S a band of radio frequencies

SIDECAR | n pl. -S a passenger car attached to a motorcycle

SIDED | past tense of side

SIDEHILL | n pl. -S a hillside

SIDEKICK | n pl. -S a close friend

SIDELINE | v -LINED, -LINING, -LINES to put out of action

SIDELING | adj sloping

SIDELONG | adj directed to one side

SIDEMAN | n pl. -MEN a member of a jazz band

SIDEREAL | adj pertaining to the stars

SIDERITE | n pl. -S a mineral

SIDESHOW | n pl. -S a small show offered in addition to a main attraction

SIDESLIP | v -SLIPPED, -SLIPPING, -SLIPS to slip to one side

SIDESPIN | n pl. -S a type of spin imparted to a ball

SIDESTEP | v -STEPPED, -STEPPING, -STEPS to step to one side

SIDEWALK | n pl. -S a paved walk for pedestrians

SIDEWALL | n pl. -S a side surface of a tire

SIDEWARD | adv toward one side

SIDEWAY | adv sideways

SIDEWAYS | adv toward or from one side

SIDEWISE | adv sideways

SIDING | n pl. -S material used for surfacing a frame building

SIDLE | v -DLED, -DLING, -DLES to move sideways

SIDLER | n pl. -S one that sidles

SIEGE | v SIEGED, SIEGING, SIEGES to attempt to capture or gain

SIEMENS | n pl. SIEMENS a unit of electrical conductance

SIENITE | n pl. -S syenite

SIENNA | n pl. -S a brown pigment

SIEROZEM | n pl. -S a type of soil

SIERRA | n pl. -S a mountain range SIERRAN adj

SIESTA | n pl. -S an afternoon nap or rest

SIEUR | n pl. -S an old French title of respect for a man

SIEVE | v SIEVED, SIEVING, SIEVES to pass through a sieve (a utensil for separating the coarse parts from the fine parts of loose matter)

SIFFLEUR | n pl. -S an animal that makes a whistling noise

SIFT | v -ED, -ING, -S to sieve

SIFTER | n pl. -S one that sifts

SIFTING | n pl. -S the work of a sifter

SIGANID | n pl. -S any of a family of fishes

SIGH | v -ED, -ING, -S to let out a sigh (a deep, audible breath)

SIGHER | n pl. -S one that sighs

SIGHLESS | adj uttering no sigh

SIGHLIKE | adj resembling a sigh

SIGHT | v -ED, -ING, -S to observe or notice

SIGHTER | n pl. -S one that sights

SIGHTLY | adj -LIER, -LIEST pleasing to look at

SIGHTSEE | v -SAW, -SEEN, -SEEING, -SEES to visit and view places of interest

SIGIL | n pl. -S an official seal

SIGLOS | n pl. -LOI an ancient Persian coin

SIGMA   *n* pl. -S a Greek letter **SIGMATE** *adj*

SIGMOID   *n* pl. -S an S-shaped curve in a bodily part

SIGN   *v* -ED, -ING, -S to write one's name on

SIGNAL   *v* -NALED, -NALING, -NALS or -NALLED, -NALLING, -NALS to notify by a means of communication

SIGNALER   *n* pl. -S one that signals

SIGNALLY   *adv* notably

SIGNER   *n* pl. -S one that signs

SIGNET   *v* -ED, -ING, -S to mark with an official seal

SIGNIFY   *v* -FIED, -FYING, -FIES to make known

SIGNIOR   *n* pl. -GNIORI or -GNIORS signor

SIGNIORY   *n* pl. -GNIORIES signory

SIGNOR   *n* pl. -GNORI or -GNORS an Italian title of courtesy for a man

SIGNORA   *n* pl. -GNORE or -GNORAS an Italian title of courtesy for a married woman

SIGNORE   *n* pl. -GNORI signor

SIGNORY   *n* pl. -GNORIES seignory

SIGNPOST   *v* -ED, -ING, -S to provide with signposts (posts bearing signs)

SIKE   *n* pl. -S syke

SIKER   *adj* secure

SILAGE   *n* pl. -S fodder that has been preserved in a silo

SILANE   *n* pl. -S a chemical compound

SILD   *n* pl. -S a young herring

SILENCE   *v* -LENCED, -LENCING, -LENCES to make silent

SILENCER   *n* pl. -S one that silences

SILENI   pl. of silenus

SILENT   *adj* -LENTER, -LENTEST making no sound or noise **SILENTLY** *adv*

SILENTS   *n/pl* silent movies

SILENUS   *n* pl. -NI a woodland deity of Greek mythology

SILESIA   *n* pl. -S a cotton fabric

SILEX   *n* pl. -ES silica

SILICA   *n* pl. -S a form of silicon

SILICATE   *n* pl. -S a chemical salt

SILICIC   *adj* pertaining to silicon

SILICIDE   *n* pl. -S a silicon compound

SILICIFY   *v* -FIED, -FYING, -FIES to convert into silica

SILICIUM   *n* pl. -S silicon

SILICLE   *n* pl. -S a short, flat silique

SILICON   *n* pl. -S a nonmetallic element

SILICONE   *n* pl. -S a silicon compound

SILIQUA   *n* pl. -QUAE silique

SILIQUE   *n* pl. -LIQUES a type of seed vessel

SILK   *v* -ED, -ING, -S to cover with silk (a soft, lustrous fabric)

SILKEN   *adj* made of silk

SILKIER   comparative of silky

SILKIEST   superlative of silky

SILKILY   *adv* in a silky manner

SILKLIKE   *adj* resembling silk

SILKWEED   *n* pl. -S milkweed

SILKWORM   *n* pl. -S a caterpillar that spins a cocoon of silk fibers

SILKY   *adj* SILKIER, SILKIEST resembling silk

SILL   *n* pl. -S the horizontal piece that bears the upright portion of a frame

SILLABUB   *n* pl. -S an alcoholic beverage or dessert

SILLER   *n* pl. -S silver

SILLIBUB   *n* pl. -S sillabub

SILLY   *adj* -LIER, -LIEST showing a lack of good sense **SILLILY** *adv*

SILLY   *n* pl. -LIES a silly person

SILO   *v* -ED, -ING, -S to store in a silo (a tall, cylindrical structure)

SILOXANE   *n* pl. -S a chemical compound

SILT   *v* -ED, -ING, -S to fill with silt (a sedimentary material)

SILTY   *adj* SILTIER, SILTIEST full of silt

SILURID   *n* pl. -S any of a family of catfishes

SILUROID   *n* pl. -S a silurid

SILVA   *n* pl. -VAS or -VAE sylva

SILVAN   *n* pl. -S sylvan

SILVER   *v* -ED, -ING, -S to cover with silver (a metallic element)

SILVERER   *n* pl. -S one that silvers

SILVERLY   *adv* with a silvery appearance

SILVERN   *adj* silvery

SILVERY   *adj* resembling silver

SILVICAL   *adj* pertaining to silvics

SILVICS   *n/pl* the study of forest trees

SIM   *n* pl. -S simulation

SIMA   *n* pl. -S an igneous rock

SIMAR   *n* pl. -S a woman's light jacket or robe

SIMARUBA   *n* pl. -S a tropical tree

SIMAZINE   *n* pl. -S an herbicide

SIMIAN   *n* pl. -S an ape or monkey

SIMILAR   *adj* being like but not completely identical to

SIMILE   *n* pl. -S a figure of speech

SIMIOID   *adj* simious

SIMIOUS   *adj* pertaining to simians

SIMITAR   *n* pl. -S scimitar

SIMLIN   *n* pl. -S cymling

SIMMER   *v* -ED, -ING, -S to cook below or just at the boiling point

SIMNEL   *n* pl. -S a crisp bread

SIMOLEON   *n* pl. -S a dollar

SIMONIAC   *n* pl. -S one who practices simony

SIMONIES   pl. of simony

SIMONIST   *n* pl. -S a simoniac

SIMONIZE   *v* -NIZED, -NIZING, -NIZES to polish with wax

SIMONY   *n* pl. -NIES the buying or selling of a church office

SIMOOM   *n* pl. -S a hot, dry desert wind

SIMOON   *n* pl. -S simoom

SIMP   *n* pl. -S a foolish person

SIMPER   *v* -ED, -ING, -S to smile in a silly manner

SIMPERER   *n* pl. -S one that simpers

SIMPLE   *adj* SIMPLER, SIMPLEST not complex or complicated

SIMPLE   *n* pl. -S something that is simple

SIMPLEX   *n* pl. -PLEXES, -PLICES, or -PLICIA a simple word

SIMPLIFY   *v* -FIED, -FYING, -FIES to make simple

SIMPLISM   *n* pl. -S the tendency to oversimplify an issue or problem

SIMPLY   *adv* in a simple manner

SIMULANT   *n* pl. -S one that simulates

SIMULAR   *n* pl. -S a simulant

SIMULATE   *v* -LATED, -LATING, -LATES to take on the appearance of

SIN   *v* SINNED, SINNING, SINS to commit a sin (an offense against religious or moral law)

SINAPISM   *n* pl. -S a pasty mixture applied to an irritated part of the body

SINCE   *adv* from then until now

SINCERE   *adj* -CERER, -CEREST free from hypocrisy or falseness

SINCIPUT   *n* pl. -CIPUTS or -CIPITA the forehead

SINE   *n* pl. -S a trigonometric function of an angle

SINECURE   *n* pl. -S an office or position requiring little or no work

SINEW   *v* -ED, -ING, -S to strengthen

SINEWY   *adj* lean and muscular

SINFONIA   *n* pl. -NIE a symphony

SINFUL   *adj* marked by sin **SINFULLY** *adv*

SING   *v* SANG, SUNG, SINGING, SINGS to utter with musical inflections of the voice **SINGABLE** *adj*

SINGE   *v* SINGED, SINGEING, SINGES to burn slightly

SINGER   *n* pl. -S one that sings

SINGLE   *v* -GLED, -GLING, -GLES to select from a group

SINGLET   *n* pl. -S a man's undershirt or jersey

SINGLY   *adv* without the company of others

SINGSONG   *n* pl. -S monotonous cadence in speaking or reading

SINGULAR   *n* pl. -S a word form that denotes one person or thing

SINH   *n* pl. -S a hyperbolic function of an angle

SINICIZE   *v* -CIZED, -CIZING, -CIZES to modify by Chinese influence

SINISTER   *adj* threatening or portending evil

SINK   *v* SANK, SUNK or SUNKEN, SINKING, SINKS to move to a lower level **SINKABLE** *adj*

SINKAGE   *n* pl. -S the act, process, or degree of sinking

SINKER   *n* pl. -S one that sinks

SINKHOLE   *n* pl. -S a natural depression in a land surface

SINLESS   *adj* free from sin

SINNED   past tense of sin

SINNER	*n* pl. -S one that sins
SINNING	present participle of sin
SINOLOGY	*n* pl. -GIES the study of the Chinese
SINOPIA	*n* pl. -PIAS or -PIE a red pigment
SINSYNE	*adv* since
SINTER	*v* -ED, -ING, -S to make cohesive by the combined action of heat and pressure
SINUATE	*v* -ATED, -ATING, -ATES to curve in and out
SINUOUS	*adj* characterized by curves, bends, or turns
SINUS	*n* pl. -ES a cranial cavity
SINUSOID	*n* pl. -S a mathematical curve
SIP	*v* SIPPED, SIPPING, SIPS to drink in small quantities
SIPE	*v* SIPED, SIPING, SIPES to seep
SIPHON	*v* -ED, -ING, -S to draw off through a siphon (a type of tube)
SIPHONAL	*adj* of or pertaining to a siphon
SIPHONIC	*adj* siphonal
SIPING	present participle of sipe
SIPPED	past tense of sip
SIPPER	*n* pl. -S one that sips
SIPPET	*n* pl. -S a small piece of bread soaked in gravy
SIPPING	present participle of sip
SIR	*n* pl. -S a respectful form of address used to a man
SIRDAR	*n* pl. -S a person of rank in India
SIRE	*v* SIRED, SIRING, SIRES to beget
SIREE	*n* pl. -S sirree
SIREN	*n* pl. -S a device that produces a penetrating warning sound
SIRENIAN	*n* pl. -S any of an order of aquatic mammals
SIRING	present participle of sire
SIRLOIN	*n* pl. -S a cut of beef
SIROCCO	*n* pl. -COS a hot, dry wind
SIRRA	*n* pl. -S sirrah
SIRRAH	*n* pl. -S a form of address used to inferiors
SIRREE	*n* pl. -S sir
SIRUP	*n* pl. -S syrup **SIRUPY** *adj*
SIRVENTE	*n* pl. -S a satirical medieval song or poem
SIS	*n* pl. SISES sister
SISAL	*n* pl. -S a strong fiber used for rope
SISKIN	*n* pl. -S a Eurasian finch
SISSY	*n* pl. -SIES an effeminate man or boy
SISSY	*adj* SISSIER, SISSIEST sissyish
SISSYISH	*adj* resembling a sissy
SISTER	*v* -ED, -ING, -S to treat like a sister (a female sibling)
SISTERLY	*adj* of or resembling a sister
SISTRA	a pl. of sistrum
SISTROID	*adj* included between the convex sides of two intersecting curves
SISTRUM	*n* pl. -TRUMS or -TRA an ancient Egyptian percussion instrument
SIT	*v* SAT, SITTEN, SITTING, SITS to rest on the buttocks
SITAR	*n* pl. -S a lute of India
SITARIST	*n* pl. -S one who plays the sitar
SITE	*v* SITED, SITING, SITES to place in position for operation
SITH	*adv* since
SITHENCE	*adv* since
SITHENS	*adv* since
SITI	a pl. of situs
SITING	present participle of site
SITOLOGY	*n* pl. -GIES the science of nutrition and diet
SITTEN	a past participle of sit
SITTER	*n* pl. -S one that sits
SITTING	*n* pl. -S a meeting or session
SITUATE	*v* -ATED, -ATING, -ATES to place in a certain position
SITUS	*n* pl. -TI or -TUSES a position or location
SITZMARK	*n* pl. -S a mark left in the snow by a skier who has fallen backward
SIVER	*n* pl. -S a sewer
SIX	*n* pl. -ES a number
SIXFOLD	*adj* being six times as great as
SIXMO	*n* pl. -MOS a paper size
SIXPENCE	*n* pl. -S a British coin worth six pennies

SIXPENNY *adj* worth sixpence

SIXTE *n pl.* -S a fencing parry

SIXTEEN *n pl.* -S a number

SIXTH *n pl.* -S one of six equal parts

SIXTHLY *adv* in the sixth place

SIXTIETH *n pl.* -S one of sixty equal parts

SIXTY *n pl.* -TIES a number

SIZABLE *adj* of considerable size **SIZABLY** *adv*

SIZAR *n pl.* -S a British student who receives financial assistance from his college

SIZE *v* SIZED, SIZING, SIZES to arrange according to size (physical proportions)

SIZEABLE *adj* sizable **SIZEABLY** *adv*

SIZER *n pl.* -S sizar

SIZIER comparative of sizy

SIZIEST superlative of sizy

SIZINESS *n pl.* -ES the quality or state of being sizy

SIZING *n pl.* -S a substance used as a glaze or filler for porous materials

SIZY *adj* SIZIER, SIZIEST viscid

SIZZLE *v* -ZLED, -ZLING, -ZLES to burn or fry with a hissing sound

SIZZLER *n pl.* -S a very hot day

SKAG *n pl.* -S heroin

SKALD *n pl.* -S an ancient Scandinavian poet **SKALDIC** *adj*

SKAT *n pl.* -S a card game

SKATE *v* SKATED, SKATING, SKATES to glide over ice or the ground on skates (shoes fitted with runners or wheels)

SKATER *n pl.* -S one that skates

SKATING *n pl.* -S the sport of gliding on skates

SKATOL *n pl.* -S skatole

SKATOLE *n pl.* -S a chemical compound

SKEAN *n pl.* -S a type of dagger

SKEANE *n pl.* -S a length of yarn wound in a loose coil

SKEE *v* SKEED, SKEEING, SKEES to ski

SKEEN *n pl.* -S skean

SKEET *n pl.* -S the sport of shooting at clay pigeons hurled in the air by spring traps

SKEETER *n pl.* -S a skeet shooter

SKEG *n pl.* -S a timber that connects the keel and sternpost of a ship

SKEIGH *adj* proud

SKEIN *v* -ED, -ING, -S to wind into long, loose coils

SKELETON *n pl.* -S the supporting or protective framework of a human or animal body **SKELETAL** *adj*

SKELLUM *n pl.* -S a rascal

SKELP *v* SKELPED or SKELPIT, SKELPING, SKELPS to slap

SKELTER *v* -ED, -ING, -S to scurry

SKENE *n pl.* -S skean

SKEP *n pl.* -S a beehive

SKEPSIS *n pl.* -SISES the attitude or outlook of a skeptic

SKEPTIC *n pl.* -S a person who doubts generally accepted ideas

SKERRY *n pl.* -RIES a small, rocky island

SKETCH *v* -ED, -ING, -ES to make a rough, hasty drawing of

SKETCHER *n pl.* -S one that sketches

SKETCHY *adj* SKETCHIER, SKETCHIEST lacking in completeness or clearness

SKEW *v* -ED, -ING, -S to turn aside

SKEWBACK *n pl.* -S a sloping surface against which the end of an arch rests

SKEWBALD *n pl.* -S a horse having patches of brown and white

SKEWER *v* -ED, -ING, -S to pierce with a long pin, as meat

SKEWNESS *n pl.* -ES lack of symmetry

SKI *v* -ED, -ING, -S to travel on skis (long, narrow strips of wood or metal)

SKIABLE *adj* capable of being skied over

SKIAGRAM *n pl.* -S a picture made up of shadows or outlines

SKIBOB *n pl.* -S a vehicle used for traveling over snow

SKID *v* SKIDDED, SKIDDING, SKIDS to slide sideways as a result of a loss of traction

SKIDDER *n pl.* -S one that skids

SKIDDOO *v* -ED, -ING, -S to go away

SKIDDY *adj* -DIER, -DIEST likely to cause skidding

SKIDOO   v -ED, -ING, -S to skiddoo

SKIDWAY   n pl. -WAYS a platform on which logs are piled for loading or sawing

SKIED   past tense of ski and sky

SKIER   n pl. -S one that skis

SKIES   present 3d person sing. of sky

SKIEY   adj skyey

SKIFF   n pl. -S a small, open boat

SKIFFLE   v -FLED, -FLING, -FLES to play a particular style of music

SKIING   n pl. -S the sport of traveling on skis

SKIJORER   n pl. -S a skier who is drawn over snow by a horse or vehicle

SKILFUL   adj skillful

SKILL   n pl. -S the ability to do something well **SKILLED** adj

SKILLESS   adj having no skill

SKILLET   n pl. -S a frying pan

SKILLFUL   adj having skill

SKILLING   n pl. -S a former coin of Scandinavian countries

SKIM   v SKIMMED, SKIMMING, SKIMS to remove floating matter from the surface of

SKIMMER   n pl. -S one that skims

SKIMMING   n pl. -S something that is skimmed from a liquid

SKIMO   n pl. -MOS an Eskimo

SKIMP   v -ED, -ING, -S to scrimp

SKIMPY   adj SKIMPIER, SKIMPIEST scanty **SKIMPILY** adv

SKIN   v SKINNED, SKINNING, SKINS to strip or deprive of skin (the membranous tissue covering the body of an animal)

SKINFUL   n pl. -S as much as a skin container can hold

SKINHEAD   n pl. -S one whose hair is cut very short

SKINK   v -ED, -ING, -S to pour out or serve, as liquor

SKINKER   n pl. -S one that skinks

SKINLESS   adj having no skin

SKINLIKE   adj resembling skin

SKINNED   past tense of skin

SKINNER   n pl. -S one that skins

SKINNING   present participle of skin

SKINNY   adj -NIER, -NIEST very thin

SKINT   adj having no money

SKIORING   n pl. -S a form of skiing

SKIP   v SKIPPED, SKIPPING, SKIPS to move with light springing steps

SKIPJACK   n pl. -S a marine fish

SKIPLANE   n pl. -S an airplane designed to take off from or land on snow

SKIPPED   past tense of skip

SKIPPER   v -ED, -ING, -S to act as master or captain of

SKIPPET   n pl. -S a small box for protecting an official seal

SKIPPING   present participle of skip

SKIRL   v -ED, -ING, -S to produce a shrill sound

SKIRMISH   v -ED, -ING, -ES to engage in a minor battle

SKIRR   v -ED, -ING, -S to move rapidly

SKIRRET   n pl. -S an Asian herb

SKIRT   v -ED, -ING, -S to go or pass around

SKIRTER   n pl. -S one that skirts

SKIRTING   n pl. -S a board at the base of a wall

SKIT   n pl. -S a short dramatic scene

SKITE   v SKITED, SKITING, SKITES to move away quickly

SKITTER   v -ED, -ING, -S to move lightly or rapidly along a surface

SKITTERY   adj -TERIER, -TERIEST skittish

SKITTISH   adj easily frightened

SKITTLE   n pl. -S a wooden pin used in a bowling game

SKIVE   v SKIVED, SKIVING, SKIVES to pare

SKIVER   n pl. -S one that skives

SKIVVY   n pl. -VIES a female servant

SKIWEAR   n pl. -S clothing suitable for wear while skiing

SKLENT   v -ED, -ING, -S to slant

SKOAL   v -ED, -ING, -S to drink to the health of

SKOOKUM   adj excellent

SKREEGH   v -ED, -ING, -S to screech

SKREIGH   v -ED, -ING, -S to screech

SKUA   n pl. -S a predatory seabird

SKULK   v -ED, -ING, -S to move about stealthily

SKULKER   n pl. -S one that skulks

SKULL	*n* pl. -S the framework of the head **SKULLED** *adj*
SKULLCAP	*n* pl. -S a close-fitting cap
SKUNK	*v* -ED, -ING, -S to defeat overwhelmingly
SKY	*v* SKIED or SKYED, SKYING, SKIES to hit or throw toward the sky (the upper atmosphere)
SKYBORNE	*adj* airborne
SKYCAP	*n* pl. -S a porter at an airport
SKYDIVE	*v* -DIVED or -DOVE, -DIVING, -DIVES to parachute from an airplane for sport
SKYDIVER	*n* pl. -S one that skydives
SKYEY	*adj* resembling the sky
SKYHOOK	*n* pl. -S a hook conceived as being suspended from the sky
SKYJACK	*v* -ED, -ING, -S to hijack an airplane
SKYLARK	*v* -ED, -ING, -S to frolic
SKYLIGHT	*n* pl. -S a window in a roof or ceiling
SKYLINE	*n* pl. -S the horizon
SKYMAN	*n* pl. -MEN an aviator
SKYPHOS	*n* pl. -PHOI a drinking vessel used in ancient Greece
SKYSAIL	*n* pl. -S a type of sail
SKYWARD	*adv* toward the sky
SKYWARDS	*adv* skyward
SKYWAY	*n* pl. -WAYS an elevated highway
SKYWRITE	*v* -WROTE, -WRITTEN, -WRITING, -WRITES to write in the sky by releasing a visible vapor from an airplane
SLAB	*v* SLABBED, SLABBING, SLABS to cover with slabs (broad, flat pieces of solid material)
SLABBER	*v* -ED, -ING, -S to slobber
SLABBERY	*adj* slobbery
SLABBING	present participle of slab
SLACK	*adj* SLACKER, SLACKEST not tight or taut
SLACK	*v* -ED, -ING, -S to slacken
SLACKEN	*v* -ED, -ING, -S to make less tight or taut
SLACKER	*n* pl. -S a shirker
SLACKLY	*adv* in a slack manner
SLAG	*v* SLAGGED, SLAGGING, SLAGS to convert into slag (the fused residue of a smelted ore)

SLAGGY	*adj* -GIER, -GIEST resembling slag
SLAIN	past participle of slay
SLAKE	*v* SLAKED, SLAKING, SLAKES to quench **SLAKABLE** *adj*
SLAKER	*n* pl. -S one that slakes
SLALOM	*v* -ED, -ING, -S to ski in a zigzag course
SLAM	*v* SLAMMED, SLAMMING, SLAMS to shut forcibly and noisily
SLANDER	*v* -ED, -ING, -S to defame
SLANG	*v* -ED, -ING, -S to assail with harsh or coarse language
SLANGY	*adj* SLANGIER, SLANGIEST given to vulgarity **SLANGILY** *adv*
SLANK	a past tense of slink
SLANT	*v* -ED, -ING, -S to deviate from the horizontal or vertical
SLAP	*v* SLAPPED, SLAPPING, SLAPS to strike with the open hand
SLAPDASH	*n* pl. -ES careless work
SLAPJACK	*n* pl. -S a pancake
SLAPPED	past tense of slap
SLAPPER	*n* pl. -S one that slaps
SLAPPING	present participle of slap
SLASH	*v* -ED, -ING, -ES to cut with violent sweeping strokes
SLASHER	*n* pl. -S one that slashes
SLASHING	*n* pl. -S the act of one that slashes
SLAT	*v* SLATTED, SLATTING, SLATS to provide with slats (narrow strips of wood or metal)
SLATCH	*n* pl. -ES a calm between breaking waves
SLATE	*v* SLATED, SLATING, SLATES to cover with slate (a roofing material)
SLATER	*n* pl. -S one that slates
SLATHER	*v* -ED, -ING, -S to spread thickly
SLATIER	comparative of slaty
SLATIEST	superlative of slaty
SLATING	*n* pl. -S the act of one that slates
SLATTED	past tense of slat
SLATTERN	*n* pl. -S a slovenly woman
SLATTING	present participle of slat
SLATY	*adj* SLATIER, SLATIEST resembling slate

SLAVE *v* SLAVED, SLAVING, SLAVES to work like a slave (one who is owned by another)

SLAVER *v* -ED, -ING, -S to drool

SLAVERER *n pl.* -S one that slavers

SLAVERY *n pl.* -ERIES ownership of one person by another

SLAVEY *n pl.* -EYS a female servant

SLAVING present participle of slave

SLAVISH *adj* pertaining to or characteristic of a slave

SLAW *n pl.* -S coleslaw

SLAY *v* SLEW, SLAIN, SLAYING, SLAYS to kill violently

SLAYER *n pl.* -S one that slays

SLEAVE *v* SLEAVED, SLEAVING, SLEAVES to separate into filaments

SLEAZY *adj* SLEAZIER, SLEAZIEST shoddy **SLEAZILY** *adv*

SLED *v* SLEDDED, SLEDDING, SLEDS to convey on a sled (a vehicle for carrying people or loads over snow or ice)

SLEDDER *n pl.* -S one that sleds

SLEDDING *n pl.* -S the act of one that sleds

SLEDGE *v* SLEDGED, SLEDGING, SLEDGES to convey on a type of sled

SLEEK *adj* SLEEKER, SLEEKEST smooth and glossy

SLEEK *v* -ED, -ING, -S to make sleek

SLEEKEN *v* -ED, -ING, -S to sleek

SLEEKIER comparative of sleeky

SLEEKIEST superlative of sleeky

SLEEKIT *adj* sleek

SLEEKLY *adv* in a sleek manner

SLEEKY *adj* SLEEKIER, SLEEKIEST sleek

SLEEP *v* SLEPT, SLEEPING, SLEEPS to be in a natural, periodic state of rest

SLEEPER *n pl.* -S one that sleeps

SLEEPING *n pl.* -S the act of one that sleeps

SLEEPY *adj* SLEEPIER, SLEEPIEST ready or inclined to sleep **SLEEPILY** *adv*

SLEET *v* -ED, -ING, -S to shower sleet (frozen rain)

SLEETY *adj* SLEETIER, SLEETIEST resembling sleet

SLEEVE *v* SLEEVED, SLEEVING, SLEEVES to furnish with a sleeve (the part of a garment covering the arm)

SLEIGH *v* -ED, -ING, -S to ride in a sled

SLEIGHER *n pl.* -S one that sleighs

SLEIGHT *n pl.* -S deftness

SLENDER *adj* -DERER, -DEREST thin

SLEPT past tense of sleep

SLEUTH *v* -ED, -ING, -S to act as a detective

SLEW *v* -ED, -ING, -S to slue

SLICE *v* SLICED, SLICING, SLICES to cut into thin, flat pieces

SLICER *n pl.* -S one that slices

SLICK *adj* SLICKER, SLICKEST smooth and slippery

SLICK *v* -ED, -ING, -S to make slick

SLICKER *n pl.* -S an oilskin raincoat

SLICKLY *adv* in a slick manner

SLIDE *v* SLID, SLIDDEN, SLIDING, SLIDES to move smoothly along a surface **SLIDABLE** *adj*

SLIDER *n pl.* -S one that slides

SLIDEWAY *n pl.* -WAYS a route along which something slides

SLIDING present participle of slide

SLIER a comparative of sly

SLIEST a superlative of sly

SLIGHT *adj* SLIGHTER, SLIGHTEST small in size or amount **SLIGHTLY** *adv*

SLIGHT *v* -ED, -ING, -S to treat with disregard

SLILY *adv* in a sly manner

SLIM *adj* SLIMMER, SLIMMEST slender

SLIM *v* SLIMMED, SLIMMING, SLIMS to make slim

SLIME *v* SLIMED, SLIMING, SLIMES to cover with slime (viscous mud)

SLIMIER comparative of slimy

SLIMIEST superlative of slimy

SLIMILY *adv* in a slimy manner

SLIMING present participle of slime

SLIMLY *adv* in a slim manner

SLIMMED past tense of slim

SLIMMER	comparative of slim
SLIMMEST	superlative of slim
SLIMMING	present participle of slim
SLIMNESS	n pl. -ES the state of being slim
SLIMPSY	adj -SIER, -SIEST slimsy
SLIMSY	adj -SIER, -SIEST flimsy
SLIMY	adj SLIMIER, SLIMIEST resembling slime
SLING	v SLUNG, SLINGING, SLINGS to throw with a sudden motion
SLINGER	n pl. -S one that slings
SLINK	v SLUNK or SLANK, SLINKING, SLINKS to move stealthily
SLINKY	adj SLINKIER, SLINKIEST stealthy **SLINKILY** adv
SLIP	v SLIPPED or SLIPT, SLIPPING, SLIPS to slide suddenly and accidentally
SLIPCASE	n pl. -S a protective box for a book
SLIPE	v SLIPED, SLIPING, SLIPES to peel
SLIPFORM	v -ED, -ING, -S to construct with the use of a mold in which concrete is placed to set
SLIPKNOT	n pl. -S a type of knot
SLIPLESS	adj free from errors
SLIPOUT	n pl. -S an insert in a newspaper
SLIPOVER	n pl. -S a pullover
SLIPPAGE	n pl. -S a falling off from a standard or level
SLIPPED	a past tense of slip
SLIPPER	n pl. -S a light, low shoe
SLIPPERY	adj -PERIER, -PERIEST causing or tending to cause slipping
SLIPPING	present participle of slip
SLIPPY	adj -PIER, -PIEST slippery
SLIPSHOD	adj carelessly done or made
SLIPSLOP	n pl. -S watery food
SLIPSOLE	n pl. -S a thin insole
SLIPT	a past tense of slip
SLIPUP	n pl. -S a mistake
SLIPWARE	n pl. -S a type of pottery
SLIPWAY	n pl. -WAYS an area sloping toward the water in a shipyard
SLIT	v SLITTED, SLITTING, SLITS to make a slit (a long, narrow cut) in
SLITHER	v -ED, -ING, -S to slide from side to side
SLITHERY	adj slippery
SLITLESS	adj having no slits
SLITTED	past tense of slit
SLITTER	n pl. -S one that slits
SLITTING	present participle of slit
SLIVER	v -ED, -ING, -S to cut into long, thin pieces
SLIVERER	n pl. -S one that slivers
SLIVOVIC	n pl. -S a plum brandy
SLOB	n pl. -S a slovenly or boorish person
SLOBBER	v -ED, -ING, -S to drool
SLOBBERY	adj slobbering
SLOBBISH	adj resembling a slob
SLOE	n pl. -S a plumlike fruit
SLOG	v SLOGGED, SLOGGING, SLOGS to plod
SLOGAN	n pl. -S a motto adopted by a group
SLOGGER	n pl. -S one that slogs
SLOGGING	present participle of slog
SLOID	n pl. -S sloyd
SLOJD	n pl. -S sloyd
SLOOP	n pl. -S a type of sailing vessel
SLOP	v SLOPPED, SLOPPING, SLOPS to spill or splash
SLOPE	v SLOPED, SLOPING, SLOPES to slant
SLOPER	n pl. -S one that slopes
SLOPPED	past tense of slop
SLOPPING	present participle of slop
SLOPPY	adj -PIER, -PIEST messy **SLOPPILY** adv
SLOPWORK	n pl. -S the manufacture of cheap clothing
SLOSH	v -ED, -ING, -ES to move with a splashing motion
SLOSHY	adj SLOSHIER, SLOSHIEST slushy
SLOT	v SLOTTED, SLOTTING, SLOTS to cut a long, narrow opening in
SLOTBACK	n pl. -S a type of football player
SLOTH	n pl. -S a slow-moving arboreal mammal
SLOTHFUL	adj sluggish
SLOTTED	past tense of slot

SLOTTING present participle of slot

SLOUCH *v* -ED, -ING, -ES to sit, stand, or move with a drooping posture

SLOUCHER *n* pl. -S one that slouches

SLOUCHY *adj* SLOUCHIER, SLOUCHIEST slouching

SLOUGH *v* -ED, -ING, -S to cast off

SLOUGHY *adj* SLOUGHIER, SLOUGHIEST miry

SLOVEN *n* pl. -S a slovenly person

SLOVENLY *adj* -LIER, -LIEST habitually untidy or unclean

SLOW *adj* SLOWER, SLOWEST moving with little speed

SLOW *v* -ED, -ING, -S to lessen the speed of

SLOWDOWN *n* pl. -S a lessening of pace

SLOWISH *adj* somewhat slow

SLOWLY *adv* in a slow manner

SLOWNESS *n* pl. -ES the state of being slow

SLOWPOKE *n* pl. -S a slow individual

SLOWWORM *n* pl. -S a European lizard having no legs

SLOYD *n* pl. -S a Swedish system of manual training

SLUB *v* SLUBBED, SLUBBING, SLUBS to draw out and twist slightly

SLUBBER *v* -ED, -ING, -S to stain or dirty

SLUBBING *n* pl. -S a slightly twisted roll of textile fibers

SLUDGE *n* pl. -S a muddy deposit

SLUDGY *adj* SLUDGIER, SLUDGIEST covered with sludge

SLUE *v* SLUED, SLUING, SLUES to cause to move sideways

SLUFF *v* -ED, -ING, -S to discard a card or cards

SLUG *v* SLUGGED, SLUGGING, SLUGS to strike heavily

SLUGABED *n* pl. -S one inclined to stay in bed out of laziness

SLUGFEST *n* pl. -S a vigorous fight

SLUGGARD *n* pl. -S an habitually lazy person

SLUGGED past tense of slug

SLUGGER *n* pl. -S one that slugs

SLUGGING present participle of slug

SLUGGISH *adj* displaying little movement or activity

SLUICE *v* SLUICED, SLUICING, SLUICES to wash with a sudden flow of water

SLUICY *adj* falling in streams

SLUING present participle of slue

SLUM *v* SLUMMED, SLUMMING, SLUMS to visit slums (squalid urban areas)

SLUMBER *v* -ED, -ING, -S to sleep

SLUMBERY *adj* sleepy

SLUMGUM *n* pl. -S the residue remaining after honey is extracted from a honeycomb

SLUMLORD *n* pl. -S a landlord of slum property

SLUMMED past tense of slum

SLUMMER *n* pl. -S one that slums

SLUMMING present participle of slum

SLUMMY *adj* -MIER, -MIEST resembling a slum

SLUMP *v* -ED, -ING, -S to fall or sink suddenly

SLUNG past tense of sling

SLUNK a past tense of slink

SLUR *v* SLURRED, SLURRING, SLURS to pass over lightly or carelessly

SLURB *n* pl. -S a poorly planned suburban area **SLURBAN** *adj*

SLURP *v* -ED, -ING, -S to eat or drink noisily

SLURRED past tense of slur

SLURRING present participle of slur

SLURRY *v* -RIED, -RYING, -RIES to convert into a type of watery mixture

SLUSH *v* -ED, -ING, -ES to splash with slush (partly melted snow)

SLUSHY *adj* SLUSHIER, SLUSHIEST resembling slush **SLUSHILY** *adv*

SLUT *n* pl. -S a slovenly woman **SLUTTISH** *adj*

SLY *adj* SLIER, SLIEST or SLYER, SLYEST crafty **SLYLY** *adv*

SLYBOOTS *n* pl. SLYBOOTS a sly person

SLYNESS *n* pl. -ES the quality or state of being sly

SLYPE *n* pl. -S a narrow passage in an English cathedral

SMACK *v* -ED, -ING, -S to strike sharply

SMACKER *n* pl. -S one that smacks

SMALL   adj SMALLER, SMALLEST of limited size or quantity

SMALL   n pl. -S a small part

SMALLAGE   n pl. -S a wild celery

SMALLISH   adj somewhat small

SMALLPOX   n pl. -ES a virus disease

SMALT   n pl. -S a blue pigment

SMALTI   a pl. of smalto

SMALTINE   n pl. -S smaltite

SMALTITE   n pl. -S a mineral

SMALTO   n pl. -TOS or -TI colored glass used in mosaics

SMARAGD   n pl. -S an emerald

SMARAGDE   n pl. -S smaragd

SMARM   n pl. -S trite sentimentality

SMARMY   adj SMARMIER, SMARMIEST marked by excessive flattery

SMART   v -ED, -ING, -S to cause a sharp, stinging pain

SMART   adj SMARTER, SMARTEST characterized by mental acuity

SMARTEN   v -ED, -ING, -S to improve in appearance

SMARTIE   n pl. -S smarty

SMARTLY   adv in a smart manner

SMARTY   n pl. SMARTIES an obnoxiously conceited person

SMASH   v -ED, -ING, -ES to shatter violently

SMASHER   n pl. -S one that smashes

SMASHUP   n pl. -S a collision of motor vehicles

SMATTER   v -ED, -ING, -S to speak with little knowledge

SMAZE   n pl. -S an atmospheric mixture of smoke and haze

SMEAR   v -ED, -ING, -S to spread with a sticky, greasy, or dirty substance

SMEARER   n pl. -S one that smears

SMEARY   adj SMEARIER, SMEARIEST smeared

SMECTIC   adj pertaining to a phase of a liquid crystal

SMEDDUM   n pl. -S ground malt powder

SMEEK   v -ED, -ING, -S to smoke

SMEGMA   n pl. -S sebum

SMELL   v SMELLED or SMELT, SMELLING, SMELLS to perceive by means of the olfactory nerves

SMELLER   n pl. -S one that smells

SMELLY   adj SMELLIER, SMELLIEST having an unpleasant odor

SMELT   v -ED, -ING, -S to melt or fuse, as ores

SMELTER   n pl. -S one that smelts

SMELTERY   n pl. -ERIES a place for smelting

SMERK   v -ED, -ING, -S to smirk

SMEW   n pl. -S a Eurasian duck

SMIDGEN   n pl. -S a very small amount

SMIDGEON   n pl. -S smidgen

SMIDGIN   n pl. -S smidgen

SMILAX   n pl. -ES a twining plant

SMILE   v SMILED, SMILING, SMILES to upturn the corners of the mouth in pleasure

SMILER   n pl. -S one that smiles

SMIRCH   v -ED, -ING, -ES to soil

SMIRK   v -ED, -ING, -S to smile in an affected or smug manner

SMIRKER   n pl. -S one that smirks

SMIRKY   adj SMIRKIER, SMIRKIEST smirking

SMITE   v SMOTE, SMIT or SMITTEN, SMITING, SMITES to strike heavily

SMITER   n pl. -S one that smites

SMITH   n pl. -S a worker in metals

SMITHERY   n pl. -ERIES the trade of a smith

SMITHY   n pl. SMITHIES the workshop of a smith

SMITING   present participle of smite

SMITTEN   a past participle of smite

SMOCK   v -ED, -ING, -S to furnish with a smock (a loose outer garment)

SMOCKING   n pl. -S a type of embroidery

SMOG   n pl. -S an atmospheric mixture of smoke and fog **SMOGLESS** adj

SMOGGY   adj -GIER, -GIEST filled with smog

SMOKE   v SMOKED, SMOKING, SMOKES to emit smoke (the gaseous product of burning materials) **SMOKABLE** adj

SMOKEPOT *n* pl. -S a container for giving off smoke

SMOKER *n* pl. -S one that smokes

SMOKEY *adj* SMOKIER, SMOKIEST smoky

SMOKING present participle of smoke

SMOKY *adj* SMOKIER, SMOKIEST filled with smoke **SMOKILY** *adv*

SMOLDER *v* -ED, -ING, -S to burn with no flame

SMOLT *n* pl. -S a young salmon

SMOOCH *v* -ED, -ING, -ES to kiss

SMOOCHY *adj* smudgy

SMOOTH *adj* SMOOTHER, SMOOTHEST having a surface that is free from irregularities

SMOOTH *v* -ED, -ING, -S to make smooth

SMOOTHEN *v* -ED, -ING, -S to smooth

SMOOTHER *n* pl. -S one that smooths

SMOOTHIE *n* pl. -S a person with polished manners

SMOOTHLY *adv* in a smooth manner

SMOOTHY *n* pl. SMOOTHIES smoothie

SMOTE past tense of smite

SMOTHER *v* -ED, -ING, -S to prevent from breathing

SMOTHERY *adj* tending to smother

SMOULDER *v* -ED, -ING, -S to smolder

SMUDGE *v* SMUDGED, SMUDGING, SMUDGES to smear or dirty

SMUDGY *adj* SMUDGIER, SMUDGIEST smudged **SMUDGILY** *adv*

SMUG *adj* SMUGGER, SMUGGEST highly self-satisfied

SMUGGLE *v* -GLED, -GLING, -GLES to import or export illicitly

SMUGGLER *n* pl. -S one that smuggles

SMUGLY *adv* in a smug manner

SMUGNESS *n* pl. -ES the quality or state of being smug

SMUT *v* SMUTTED, SMUTTING, SMUTS to soil

SMUTCH *v* -ED, -ING, -ES to smudge

SMUTCHY *adj* SMUTCHIER, SMUTCHIEST smudgy

SMUTTED past tense of smut

SMUTTING present participle of smut

SMUTTY *adj* -TIER, -TIEST obscene **SMUTTILY** *adv*

SNACK *v* -ED, -ING, -S to eat a light meal

SNAFFLE *v* -FLED, -FLING, -FLES to obtain by devious means

SNAFU *v* -ED, -ING, -S to bring into a state of confusion

SNAG *v* SNAGGED, SNAGGING, SNAGS to catch on a snag (a jagged protuberance)

SNAGGY *adj* -GIER, -GIEST full of snags

SNAGLIKE *adj* resembling a snag

SNAIL *v* -ED, -ING, -S to move slowly

SNAKE *v* SNAKED, SNAKING, SNAKES to move like a snake (a limbless reptile)

SNAKY *adj* SNAKIER, SNAKIEST resembling a snake **SNAKILY** *adv*

SNAP *v* SNAPPED, SNAPPING, SNAPS to make a sharp cracking sound

SNAPBACK *n* pl. -S a sudden rebound or recovery

SNAPLESS *adj* lacking a snap (a type of fastening device)

SNAPPED past tense of snap

SNAPPER *n* pl. -S one that snaps

SNAPPIER comparative of snappy

SNAPPIEST superlative of snappy

SNAPPILY *adv* in a snappy manner

SNAPPING present participle of snap

SNAPPISH *adj* tending to speak in an impatient or irritable manner

SNAPPY *adj* -PIER, -PIEST snappish

SNAPSHOT *v* -SHOTTED, -SHOTTING, -SHOTS to photograph informally and quickly

SNAPWEED *n* pl. -S a flowering plant

SNARE *v* SNARED, SNARING, SNARES to trap

SNARER *n* pl. -S one that snares

SNARK *n* pl. -S an imaginary animal

SNARL *v* -ED, -ING, -S to growl viciously

SNARLER *n* pl. -S one that snarls

SNARLY *adj* SNARLIER, SNARLIEST tangled

SNASH *n* pl. -ES abusive language

SNATCH *v* -ED, -ING, -ES to seize suddenly

SNATCHER *n* pl. -S one that snatches

SNATCHY	*adj* SNATCHIER, SNATCHIEST occurring irregularly
SNATH	*n pl.* -S the handle of a scythe
SNATHE	*n pl.* -S snath
SNAW	*v* -ED, -ING, -S to snow
SNAZZY	*adj* -ZIER, -ZIEST very stylish
SNEAK	*v* SNEAKED or SNUCK, SNEAKING, SNEAKS to move stealthily
SNEAKER	*n pl.* -S one that sneaks
SNEAKY	*adj* SNEAKIER, SNEAKIEST deceitful **SNEAKILY** *adv*
SNEAP	*v* -ED, -ING, -S to chide
SNECK	*n pl.* -S a latch
SNED	*v* SNEDDED, SNEDDING, SNEDS to prune
SNEER	*v* -ED, -ING, -S to curl the lip in contempt
SNEERER	*n pl.* -S one that sneers
SNEERFUL	*adj* given to sneering
SNEESH	*n pl.* -ES snuff
SNEEZE	*v* SNEEZED, SNEEZING, SNEEZES to make a sudden, involuntary expiration of breath
SNEEZER	*n pl.* -S one that sneezes
SNEEZY	*adj* SNEEZIER, SNEEZIEST tending to sneeze
SNELL	*n pl.* -S a short line by which a fishhook is attached to a longer line
SNELL	*adj* SNELLER, SNELLEST keen
SNIB	*v* SNIBBED, SNIBBING, SNIBS to latch
SNICK	*v* -ED, -ING, -S to nick
SNICKER	*v* -ED, -ING, -S to utter a partly stifled laugh
SNICKERY	*adj* tending to snicker
SNIDE	*adj* SNIDER, SNIDEST maliciously derogatory **SNIDELY** *adv*
SNIFF	*v* -ED, -ING, -S to inhale audibly through the nose
SNIFFER	*n pl.* -S one that sniffs
SNIFFIER	comparative of sniffy
SNIFFIEST	superlative of sniffy
SNIFFILY	*adv* in a sniffy manner
SNIFFISH	*adj* haughty
SNIFFLE	*v* -FLED, -FLING, -FLES to sniff repeatedly
SNIFFLER	*n pl.* -S one that sniffles
SNIFFY	*adj* -FIER, -FIEST sniffish
SNIFTER	*n pl.* -S a pear-shaped liquor glass
SNIGGER	*v* -ED, -ING, -S to snicker
SNIGGLE	*v* -GLED, -GLING, -GLES to fish for eels
SNIGGLER	*n pl.* -S one that sniggles
SNIP	*v* SNIPPED, SNIPPING, SNIPS to cut with a short, quick stroke
SNIPE	*v* SNIPED, SNIPING, SNIPES to shoot at individuals from a concealed place
SNIPER	*n pl.* -S one that snipes
SNIPPED	past tense of snip
SNIPPER	*n pl.* -S one that snips
SNIPPET	*n pl.* -S a small piece snipped off
SNIPPETY	*adj* -PETIER, -PETIEST snippy
SNIPPING	present participle of snip
SNIPPY	*adj* -PIER, -PIEST snappish **SNIPPILY** *adv*
SNIT	*n pl.* -S a state of agitation
SNITCH	*v* -ED, -ING, -ES to tattle
SNITCHER	*n pl.* -S one that snitches
SNIVEL	*v* -ELED, -ELING, -ELS or -ELLED, -ELLING, -ELS to cry or whine with sniffling
SNIVELER	*n pl.* -S one that snivels
SNOB	*n pl.* -S one who tends to avoid or rebuff those regarded as inferior
SNOBBERY	*n pl.* -BERIES snobbish behavior
SNOBBIER	comparative of snobby
SNOBBIEST	superlative of snobby
SNOBBILY	*adv* in a snobby manner
SNOBBISH	*adj* characteristic of a snob
SNOBBISM	*n pl.* -S snobbery
SNOBBY	*adj* -BIER, -BIEST snobbish
SNOOD	*v* -ED, -ING, -S to secure with a snood (a net or fabric cap for the hair)
SNOOK	*v* -ED, -ING, -S to sniff
SNOOKER	*n pl.* -S a pocket billiards game
SNOOL	*v* -ED, -ING, -S to yield meekly
SNOOP	*v* -ED, -ING, -S to pry about
SNOOPER	*n pl.* -S one that snoops
SNOOPY	*adj* SNOOPIER, SNOOPIEST given to snooping **SNOOPILY** *adv*

SNOOT   *v* -ED, -ING, -S to treat with disdain

SNOOTY   *adj* SNOOTIER, SNOOTIEST snobbish **SNOOTILY** *adv*

SNOOZE   *v* SNOOZED, SNOOZING, SNOOZES to sleep lightly

SNOOZER   *n* pl. -S one that snoozes

SNOOZLE   *v* -ZLED, -ZLING, -ZLES to nuzzle

SNOOZY   *adj* SNOOZIER, SNOOZIEST drowsy

SNORE   *v* SNORED, SNORING, SNORES to breathe loudly while sleeping

SNORER   *n* pl. -S one that snores

SNORKEL   *v* -ED, -ING, -S to swim underwater with a type of breathing device

SNORT   *v* -ED, -ING, -S to exhale noisily through the nostrils

SNORTER   *n* pl. -S one that snorts

SNOT   *n* pl. -S nasal mucus

SNOTTY   *adj* -TIER, -TIEST arrogant **SNOTTILY** *adv*

SNOUT   *v* -ED, -ING, -S to provide with a nozzle

SNOUTISH   *adj* snouty

SNOUTY   *adj* SNOUTIER, SNOUTIEST resembling a long, projecting nose

SNOW   *v* -ED, -ING, -S to fall as snow (precipitation in the form of ice crystals)

SNOWBALL   *v* -ED, -ING, -S to increase at a rapidly accelerating rate

SNOWBANK   *n* pl. -S a mound of snow

SNOWBELL   *n* pl. -S a flowering shrub

SNOWBIRD   *n* pl. -S a small bird

SNOWBUSH   *n* pl. -ES a flowering shrub

SNOWCAP   *n* pl. -S a covering of snow

SNOWDROP   *n* pl. -S a European herb

SNOWFALL   *n* pl. -S a fall of snow

SNOWIER   comparative of snowy

SNOWIEST   superlative of snowy

SNOWILY   *adv* in a snowy manner

SNOWLAND   *n* pl. -S an area marked by a great amount of snow

SNOWLESS   *adj* having no snow

SNOWLIKE   *adj* resembling snow

SNOWMAN   *n* pl. -MEN a figure of a person that is made of snow

SNOWMELT   *n* pl. -S water produced by the melting of snow

SNOWPACK   *n* pl. -S an accumulation of packed snow

SNOWPLOW   *v* -ED, -ING, -S to execute a type of skiing maneuver

SNOWSHED   *n* pl. -S a structure built to provide protection against snow

SNOWSHOE   *v* -SHOED, -SHOEING, -SHOES to walk on snowshoes (oval frames that allow a person to walk on deep snow)

SNOWSUIT   *n* pl. -S a child's garment for winter wear

SNOWY   *adj* SNOWIER, SNOWIEST abounding in snow

SNUB   *v* SNUBBED, SNUBBING, SNUBS to treat with contempt or neglect

SNUBBER   *n* pl. -S one that snubs

SNUBBY   *adj* -BIER, -BIEST blunt

SNUBNESS   *n* pl. -ES bluntness

SNUCK   a past tense of sneak

SNUFF   *v* -ED, -ING, -S to use or inhale snuff (powdered tobacco)

SNUFFBOX   *n* pl. -ES a box for holding snuff

SNUFFER   *n* pl. -S one that snuffs

SNUFFIER   comparative of snuffy

SNUFFIEST   superlative of snuffy

SNUFFILY   *adv* in a snuffy manner

SNUFFLE   *v* -FLED, -FLING, -FLES to sniffle

SNUFFLER   *n* pl. -S one that snuffles

SNUFFLY   *adj* -FLIER, -FLIEST tending to snuffle

SNUFFY   *adj* SNUFFIER, SNUFFIEST dingy

SNUG   *adj* SNUGGER, SNUGGEST warmly comfortable

SNUG   *v* SNUGGED, SNUGGING, SNUGS to make snug

SNUGGERY   *n* pl. -GERIES a snug place

SNUGGEST   superlative of snug

SNUGGING   present participle of snug

SNUGGLE   *v* -GLED, -GLING, -GLES to lie or press closely

SNUGLY   *adv* in a snug manner

SNUGNESS   *n* pl. -ES the quality or state of being snug

SNYE   *n* pl. -S a side channel in a river or creek

SO	*n pl.* SOS sol		**SOCIETY**	*n pl.* -ETIES an organized group of persons **SOCIETAL** *adj*
SOAK	*v* -ED, -ING, -S to saturate thoroughly in liquid		**SOCK**	*n pl.* SOCKS or SOX a knitted or woven covering for the foot
SOAKAGE	*n pl.* -S the act of soaking		**SOCK**	*v* -ED, -ING, -S to strike forcefully
SOAKER	*n pl.* -S one that soaks			
SOAP	*v* -ED, -ING, -S to treat with soap (a cleansing agent)		**SOCKET**	*v* -ED, -ING, -S to furnish with a socket (an opening for receiving something)
SOAPBARK	*n pl.* -S a tropical tree		**SOCKEYE**	*n pl.* -S a food fish
SOAPBOX	*n pl.* -ES a box for soap		**SOCKMAN**	*n pl.* -MEN socman
SOAPIER	comparative of soapy		**SOCLE**	*n pl.* -S a block used as a base for a column or pedestal
SOAPIEST	superlative of soapy		**SOCMAN**	*n pl.* -MEN a socager
SOAPILY	*adv* in a soapy manner		**SOD**	*v* SODDED, SODDING, SODS to cover with sod (turf)
SOAPLESS	*adj* having no soap			
SOAPLIKE	*adj* resembling soap		**SODA**	*n pl.* -S a type of chemical compound **SODALESS** *adj*
SOAPSUDS	*n/pl* suds (soapy water)		**SODALIST**	*n pl.* -S a member of a sodality
SOAPWORT	*n pl.* -S a perennial herb		**SODALITE**	*n pl.* -S a mineral
SOAPY	*adj* SOAPIER, SOAPIEST containing or resembling soap		**SODALITY**	*n pl.* -TIES a society
			SODAMIDE	*n pl.* -S a chemical compound
SOAR	*v* -ED, -ING, -S to fly at a great height		**SODDED**	past tense of sod
SOARER	*n pl.* -S one that soars		**SODDEN**	*v* -ED, -ING, -S to make soggy
SOARING	*n pl.* -S the sport of flying in a heavier-than-air craft without power		**SODDENLY**	*adv* in a soggy manner
			SODDING	present participle of sod
			SODDY	*n pl.* -DIES a house built of sod
SOAVE	*n pl.* -S an Italian wine		**SODIUM**	*n pl.* -S a metallic element **SODIC** *adj*
SOB	*v* SOBBED, SOBBING, SOBS to cry with a convulsive catching of the breath			
			SODOMITE	*n pl.* -S one who practices sodomy
SOBBER	*n pl.* -S one that sobs		**SODOMY**	*n pl.* -OMIES unnatural copulation
SOBEIT	*conj* provided that			
SOBER	*adj* SOBERER, SOBEREST having control of one's faculties		**SOEVER**	*adv* at all
			SOFA	*n pl.* -S a long, upholstered seat
SOBER	*v* -ED, -ING, -S to make sober		**SOFAR**	*n pl.* -S a system for locating underwater explosions
SOBERIZE	*v* -IZED, -IZING, -IZES to sober			
SOBERLY	*adv* in a sober manner		**SOFFIT**	*n pl.* -S the underside of an architectural structure
SOBFUL	*adj* given to sobbing		**SOFT**	*adj* SOFTER, SOFTEST yielding readily to pressure
SOBRIETY	*n pl.* -ETIES the quality or state of being sober			
			SOFT	*n pl.* -S a soft object or part
SOCAGE	*n pl.* -S a form of feudal land tenure		**SOFTA**	*n pl.* -S a Muslim theological student
SOCAGER	*n pl.* -S a tenant by socage			
SOCCAGE	*n pl.* -S socage		**SOFTBACK**	*n pl.* -S a book bound in a flexible paper cover
SOCCER	*n pl.* -S a type of ball game		**SOFTBALL**	*n pl.* -S a type of ball
SOCIABLE	*n pl.* -S a social		**SOFTEN**	*v* -ED, -ING, -S to make soft
SOCIABLY	*adv* in a friendly manner		**SOFTENER**	*n pl.* -S one that softens
SOCIAL	*n pl.* -S a friendly gathering			
SOCIALLY	*adv* with respect to society			

SOFTHEAD *n* pl. -S a foolish person

SOFTIE *n* pl. -S softy

SOFTIES pl. of softy

SOFTLY *adv* in a soft manner

SOFTNESS *n* pl. -ES the quality or state of being soft

SOFTWARE *n* pl. -S written or printed data used in computer operations

SOFTWOOD *n* pl. -S the soft wood of various trees

SOFTY *n* pl. SOFTIES a sentimental person

SOGGED *adj* soggy

SOGGY *adj* -GIER, -GIEST heavy with moisture **SOGGILY** *adv*

SOIGNE *adj* carefully done

SOIGNEE *adj* soigne

SOIL *v* -ED, -ING, -S to make dirty

SOILAGE *n* pl. -S green crops for feeding animals

SOILLESS *adj* carried on without soil (finely divided rock mixed with organic matter)

SOILURE *n* pl. -S a stain or smudge

SOIREE *n* pl. -S an evening party

SOJA *n* pl. -S the soybean

SOJOURN *v* -ED, -ING, -S to stay temporarily

SOKE *n* pl. -S a feudal right to administer justice within a certain territory

SOKEMAN *n* pl. -MEN socman

SOL *n* pl. -S the fifth tone of the diatonic musical scale

SOLA a pl. of solum

SOLACE *v* -LACED, -LACING, -LACES to console

SOLACER *n* pl. -S one that solaces

SOLAN *n* pl. -S a gannet

SOLAND *n* pl. -S solan

SOLANDER *n* pl. -S a protective box for library materials

SOLANIN *n* pl. -S solanine

SOLANINE *n* pl. -S a poisonous alkaloid

SOLANO *n* pl. -NOS a strong, hot wind

SOLANUM *n* pl. -S any of a genus of herbs and shrubs

SOLAR *adj* pertaining to the sun

SOLARIA a pl. of solarium

SOLARISE *v* -ISED, -ISING, -ISES to solarize

SOLARISM *n* pl. -S an interpretation of folk tales as concepts of the nature of the sun

SOLARIUM *n* pl. -IA or -IUMS a room exposed to the sun

SOLARIZE *v* -IZED, -IZING, -IZES to expose to sunlight

SOLATE *v* -ATED, -ATING, -ATES to change to a fluid colloidal system

SOLATIA pl. of solatium

SOLATION *n* pl. -S the act of solating

SOLATIUM *n* pl. -TIA a compensation given for damage to the feelings

SOLD past tense of sell

SOLDAN *n* pl. -S a Muslim ruler

SOLDER *v* -ED, -ING, -S to join closely together

SOLDERER *n* pl. -S one that solders

SOLDI pl. of soldo

SOLDIER *v* -ED, -ING, -S to perform military service

SOLDIERY *n* pl. -DIERIES the military profession

SOLDO *n* pl. -DI a former coin of Italy

SOLE *v* SOLED, SOLING, SOLES to furnish with a sole (the bottom surface of a shoe or boot)

SOLECISE *v* -CISED, -CISING, -CISES to solecize

SOLECISM *n* pl. -S an ungrammatical combination of words in a sentence

SOLECIST *n* pl. -S one who solecizes

SOLECIZE *v* -CIZED, -CIZING, -CIZES to use solecisms

SOLED past tense of sole

SOLELESS *adj* having no sole

SOLELY *adv* singly

SOLEMN *adj* -EMNER, -EMNEST serious **SOLEMNLY** *adv*

SOLENESS *n* pl. -ES the state of being the only one

SOLENOID *n* pl. -S a type of electric coil

SOLERET *n* pl. -S solleret

SOLFEGE *n* pl. -S a type of singing exercise

SOLFEGGI *n/pl* solfeges

SOLGEL *adj* involving some changes in the state of a colloidal system

SOLI a pl. of solo

SOLICIT *v* -ED, -ING, -S to ask for earnestly

SOLID *adj* -IDER, -IDEST having definite shape and volume

SOLID *n* pl. -S a solid substance

SOLIDAGO *n* pl. -GOS a flowering plant

SOLIDARY *adj* united

SOLIDI pl. of solidus

SOLIDIFY *v* -FIED, -FYING, -FIES to make solid

SOLIDITY *n* pl. -TIES the quality or state of being solid

SOLIDLY *adv* in a solid manner

SOLIDUS *n* pl. -DI a coin of ancient Rome

SOLING present participle of sole

SOLION *n* pl. -S an electronic detecting and amplifying device

SOLIQUID *n* pl. -S a fluid colloidal system

SOLITARY *n* pl. -TARIES one who lives alone

SOLITUDE *n* pl. -S the state of being alone

SOLLERET *n* pl. -S a sabaton

SOLO *n* pl. -LOS or -LI a musical composition for a single voice or instrument

SOLO *v* -ED, -ING, -S to perform alone

SOLOIST *n* pl. -S one that performs a solo

SOLON *n* pl. -S a wise lawgiver

SOLONETS *n* pl. -ES solonetz

SOLONETZ *n* pl. -ES a type of soil

SOLSTICE *n* pl. -S the time of the year when the sun is at its greatest distance from the celestial equator

SOLUBLE *n* pl. -S something that is soluble (capable of being dissolved)

SOLUBLY *adv* in a soluble manner

SOLUM *n* pl. -LA or -LUMS a soil layer

SOLUS *adj* alone

SOLUTE *n* pl. -S a dissolved substance

SOLUTION *n* pl. -S a homogenous liquid mixture

SOLVABLE *adj* capable of being solved

SOLVATE *v* -VATED, -VATING, -VATES to convert into a type of ion

SOLVE *v* SOLVED, SOLVING, SOLVES to find the answer or explanation for

SOLVENCY *n* pl. -CIES the ability to pay all debts

SOLVENT *n* pl. -S a substance capable of dissolving others

SOLVER *n* pl. -S one that solves

SOLVING present participle of solve

SOMA *n* pl. -MATA or -MAS the body of an organism SOMATIC *adj*

SOMBER *adj* gloomy SOMBERLY *adv*

SOMBRE *adj* somber SOMBRELY *adv*

SOMBRERO *n* pl. -ROS a broad-brimmed hat

SOMBROUS *adj* somber

SOME *adj* being an unspecified number or part

SOMEBODY *n* pl. -BODIES an important person

SOMEDAY *adv* at some future time

SOMEDEAL *adv* to some degree

SOMEHOW *adv* by some means

SOMEONE *n* pl. -S a somebody

SOMERSET *v* -SETED, -SETING, -SETS or -SETTED, -SETTING, -SETS to roll the body in a complete circle, head over heels

SOMETIME *adv* at some future time

SOMEWAY *adv* somehow

SOMEWAYS *adv* someway

SOMEWHAT *n* pl. -S an unspecified number or part

SOMEWHEN *adv* sometime

SOMEWISE *adv* somehow

SOMITE *n* pl. -S a longitudinal segment of the body of some animals SOMITAL, SOMITIC *adj*

SON *n* pl. -S a male child

SONANCE *n* pl. -S sound

SONANT *n* pl. -S a sound uttered with vibration of the vocal cords SONANTAL, SONANTIC *adj*

SONAR *n* pl. -S an underwater locating device

SONARMAN *n* pl. -MEN a person who operates sonar equipment

SONATA *n* pl. -S a type of musical composition

SONATINA *n* pl. -TINAS or -TINE a short sonata

SONDE   *n* pl. -S a device for observing atmospheric phenomena

SONDER   *n* pl. -S a class of small yachts

SONE   *n* pl. -S a unit of loudness

SONG   *n* pl. -S a musical composition written or adapted for singing

SONGBIRD   *n* pl. -S a bird that utters a musical call

SONGBOOK   *n* pl. -S a book of songs

SONGFEST   *n* pl. -S an informal gathering for group singing

SONGFUL   *adj* melodious

SONGLESS   *adj* incapable of singing

SONGLIKE   *adj* resembling a song

SONGSTER   *n* pl. -S a singer

SONIC   *adj* pertaining to sound

SONICATE   *v* -CATED, -CATING, -CATES to disrupt with sound waves

SONICS   *n/pl* the science dealing with the practical applications of sound

SONLESS   *adj* having no son

SONLIKE   *adj* resembling a son

SONLY   *adj* pertaining to a son

SONNET   *v* -NETED, -NETING, -NETS or -NETTED, -NETTING, -NETS to compose a sonnet (a type of poem)

SONNY   *n* pl. -NIES a small boy

SONORANT   *n* pl. -S a type of voiced sound

SONORITY   *n* pl. -TIES the quality or state of being sonorous

SONOROUS   *adj* characterized by a full and loud sound

SONOVOX   *n* pl. -ES a sound effects device

SONSHIP   *n* pl. -S the state of being a son

SONSIE   *adj* -SIER, -SIEST sonsy

SONSY   *adj* -SIER, -SIEST comely

SOOCHONG   *n* pl. -S souchong

SOOEY   *interj* — used in calling pigs

SOON   *adv* SOONER, SOONEST in the near future

SOONER   *n* pl. -S one who settles on government land before it is officially opened for settlement

SOOT   *v* -ED, -ING, -S to cover with soot (a black substance produced by combustion)

SOOTH   *adj* SOOTHER, SOOTHEST true

SOOTH   *n* pl. -S truth

SOOTHE   *v* SOOTHED, SOOTHING, SOOTHES to restore to a quiet or normal state

SOOTHER   *n* pl. -S one that soothes

SOOTHEST   superlative of sooth

SOOTHING   present participle of soothe

SOOTHLY   *adv* in truth

SOOTHSAY   *v* -SAID, -SAYING, -SAYS to predict

SOOTY   *adj* SOOTIER, SOOTIEST covered with soot **SOOTILY** *adv*

SOP   *v* SOPPED, SOPPING, SOPS to dip or soak in a liquid

SOPH   *n* pl. -S a sophomore

SOPHIES   pl. of sophy

SOPHISM   *n* pl. -S a plausible but fallacious argument

SOPHIST   *n* pl. -S one that uses sophisms

SOPHY   *n* pl. -PHIES a ruler of Persia

SOPITE   *v* -PITED, -PITING, -PITES to put to sleep

SOPOR   *n* pl. -S an abnormally deep sleep

SOPPED   past tense of sop

SOPPING   *adj* very wet

SOPPY   *adj* -PIER, -PIEST very wet

SOPRANO   *n* pl. -NOS or -NI the highest singing voice

SORA   *n* pl. -S a marsh bird

SORB   *v* -ED, -ING, -S to take up and hold by absorption or adsorption **SORBABLE** *adj*

SORBATE   *n* pl. -S a sorbed substance

SORBENT   *n* pl. -S a substance that sorbs

SORBET   *n* pl. -S sherbet

SORBIC   *adj* pertaining to a type of fruit

SORBITOL   *n* pl. -S a chemical compound

SORBOSE   *n* pl. -S a type of sugar

SORCERER   *n* pl. -S one who practices sorcery

SORCERY   *n* pl. -CERIES alleged use of supernatural powers

SORD   *n* pl. -S a flight of mallards

SORDID   *adj* filthy **SORDIDLY** *adv*

SORDINE   *n* pl. -S a device used to muffle the tone of a musical instrument

SORDINO   *n* pl. -NI sordine

SORE   *adj* SORER, SOREST painfully sensitive to the touch

SORE	*n* pl. -S a sore area on the body
SOREHEAD	*n* pl. -S a person who is easily angered or offended
SOREL	*n* pl. -S sorrel
SORELY	*adv* in a sore manner
SORENESS	*n* pl. -ES the quality or state of being sore
SORER	comparative of sore
SOREST	superlative of sore
SORGHO	*n* pl. -GHOS sorgo
SORGHUM	*n* pl. -S a cereal grass
SORGO	*n* pl. -GOS a variety of sorghum
SORI	pl. of sorus
SORICINE	*adj* belonging to the shrew family of mammals
SORITES	*n* pl. SORITES a type of argument used in logic **SORITIC** *adj*
SORN	*v* -ED, -ING, -S to force oneself on others for food and lodging
SORNER	*n* pl. -S one that sorns
SOROCHE	*n* pl. -S mountain sickness
SORORAL	*adj* sisterly
SORORATE	*n* pl. -S the marriage of a man usually with his deceased wife's sister
SORORITY	*n* pl. -TIES a social club for women
SOROSIS	*n* pl. -ROSES or -ROSISES a women's club or society
SORPTION	*n* pl. -S the act or process of sorbing **SORPTIVE** *adj*
SORREL	*n* pl. -S a reddish brown color
SORRIER	comparative of sorry
SORRIEST	superlative of sorry
SORRILY	*adv* in a sorry manner
SORROW	*v* -ED, -ING, -S to grieve
SORROWER	*n* pl. -S one that sorrows
SORRY	*adj* -RIER, -RIEST feeling grief or penitence
SORT	*v* -ED, -ING, -S to arrange according to kind, class, or size **SORTABLE** *adj* **SORTABLY** *adv*
SORTER	*n* pl. -S one that sorts
SORTIE	*v* -TIED, -TIEING, -TIES to attack suddenly from a defensive position
SORUS	*n* pl. -RI a cluster of plant reproductive bodies
SOT	*n* pl. -S an habitual drunkard
SOTH	*n* pl. -S sooth
SOTOL	*n* pl. -S a flowering plant
SOTTISH	*adj* resembling a sot
SOU	*n* pl. -S a former French coin
SOUARI	*n* pl. -S a tropical tree
SOUBISE	*n* pl. -S a sauce of onions and butter
SOUCAR	*n* pl. -S a Hindu banker
SOUCHONG	*n* pl. -S a Chinese tea
SOUDAN	*n* pl. -S soldan
SOUFFLE	*n* pl. -S a light, baked dish
SOUGH	*v* -ED, -ING, -S to make a moaning or sighing sound
SOUGHT	past tense of seek
SOUL	*n* pl. -S the spiritual aspect of human beings **SOULED, SOULLESS, SOULLIKE** *adj*
SOULFUL	*adj* full of emotion
SOUND	*adj* **SOUNDER, SOUNDEST** being in good health or condition
SOUND	*v* -ED, -ING, -S to make a sound (something that stimulates the auditory receptors)
SOUNDBOX	*n* pl. -ES a resonant cavity in a musical instrument
SOUNDER	*n* pl. -S one that sounds
SOUNDING	*n* pl. -S a sampling or test of opinions
SOUNDLY	*adv* in a sound manner
SOUP	*v* -ED, -ING, -S to increase the power or efficiency of
SOUPCON	*n* pl. -S a minute amount
SOUPY	*adj* **SOUPIER, SOUPIEST** foggy
SOUR	*adj* **SOURER, SOUREST** sharp or biting to the taste
SOUR	*v* -ED, -ING, -S to make or become sour
SOURBALL	*n* pl. -S a sour candy
SOURCE	*n* pl. -S a point of origin
SOURDINE	*n* pl. -S sordine
SOURISH	*adj* somewhat sour
SOURLY	*adv* in a sour manner
SOURNESS	*n* pl. -ES the quality or state of being sour
SOURPUSS	*n* pl. -ES a grouchy person
SOURSOP	*n* pl. -S a tropical tree
SOURWOOD	*n* pl. -S a flowering tree

SOUSE   v SOUSED, SOUSING, SOUSES to immerse

SOUTACHE   n pl. -S a flat, narrow braid

SOUTANE   n pl. -S a cassock

SOUTER   n pl. -S a shoemaker

SOUTH   v -ED, -ING, -S to move toward the south (a cardinal point of the compass)

SOUTHER   n pl. -S a wind or storm from the south

SOUTHERN   n pl. -S a person living in the south

SOUTHING   n pl. -S movement toward the south

SOUTHPAW   n pl. -S a left-handed person

SOUTHRON   n pl. -S a southern

SOUVENIR   n pl. -S a memento

SOVIET   n pl. -S a legislative body in a Communist country

SOVKHOZ   n pl. -KHOZES or -KHOZY a state-owned farm in the Soviet Union

SOVRAN   n pl. -S a monarch

SOVRANLY   adv supremely

SOVRANTY   n pl. -TIES a monarchy

SOW   v SOWED, SOWN, SOWING, SOWS to scatter over land for growth, as seed **SOWABLE** adj

SOWANS   n pl. SOWANS sowens

SOWAR   n pl. -S a mounted native soldier in India

SOWBELLY   n pl. -LIES pork cured in salt

SOWBREAD   n pl. -S a flowering plant

SOWCAR   n pl. -S a soucar

SOWENS   n pl. SOWENS porridge made from oat husks

SOWER   n pl. -S one that sows

SOWN   past participle of sow

SOX   a pl. of sock

SOY   n pl. SOYS the soybean

SOYA   n pl. -S soy

SOYBEAN   n pl. -S the seed of a cultivated Asian herb

SOZIN   n pl. -S a type of protein

SOZINE   n pl. -S sozin

SPA   n pl. -S a mineral spring

SPACE   v SPACED, SPACING, SPACES to set some distance apart

SPACEMAN   n pl. -MEN an astronaut

SPACER   n pl. -S one that spaces

SPACIAL   adj spatial

SPACING   n pl. -S the distance between any two objects

SPACIOUS   adj vast or ample in extent

SPADE   v SPADED, SPADING, SPADES to take up with a spade (a digging implement)

SPADEFUL   n pl. -S as much as a spade can hold

SPADER   n pl. -S one that spades

SPADICES   pl. of spadix

SPADILLE   n pl. -S the highest trump in certain card games

SPADING   present participle of spade

SPADIX   n pl. -DICES a flower cluster

SPADO   n pl. -DONES a castrated man or animal

SPAE   v SPAED, SPAEING, SPAES to foretell

SPAEING   n pl. -S the act of foretelling

SPAGYRIC   n pl. -S a person skilled in alchemy

SPAHEE   n pl. -S spahi

SPAHI   n pl. -S a Turkish cavalryman

SPAIL   n pl. -S spale

SPAIT   n pl. -S spate

SPAKE   a past tense of speak

SPALE   n pl. -S a splinter or chip

SPALL   v -ED, -ING, -S to break up into fragments

SPALLER   n pl. -S one that spalls

SPALPEEN   n pl. -S a rascal

SPAN   v SPANNED, SPANNING, SPANS to extend over or across

SPANCEL   v -CELED, -CELING, -CELS or -CELLED, -CELLING, -CELS to bind or fetter with a rope

SPANDREL   n pl. -S a space between two adjoining arches

SPANDRIL   n pl. -S spandrel

SPANG   adv directly

SPANGLE   v -GLED, -GLING, -GLES to adorn with spangles (bits of sparkling metal)

SPANGLY   adj -GLIER, -GLIEST covered with spangles

SPANIEL   n pl. -S a dog with silky hair

SPANK   v -ED, -ING, -S to slap on the buttocks

SPANKER   n pl. -S one that spanks

SPANKING   n pl. -S the act of one that spanks

SPANLESS   adj having no extent

SPANNED   past tense of span

SPANNER   n pl. -S one that spans

SPANNING   present participle of span

SPANWORM   n pl. -S an inchworm

SPAR   v SPARRED, SPARRING, SPARS to provide with spars (stout poles used to support rigging)

SPARABLE   n pl. -S a type of nail

SPARE   v SPARED, SPARING, SPARES to refrain from punishing, harming, or destroying

SPARE   adj SPARER, SPAREST meager SPARELY adv

SPARER   n pl. -S one that spares

SPARERIB   n pl. -S a cut of pork

SPAREST   adj superlative of spare

SPARGE   v SPARGED, SPARGING, SPARGES to sprinkle

SPARGER   n pl. -S one that sparges

SPARID   n pl. -S any of a family of marine fishes

SPARING   present participle of spare

SPARK   v -ED, -ING, -S to give off sparks (small fiery particles)

SPARKER   n pl. -S something that sparks

SPARKIER   comparative of sparky

SPARKIEST   superlative of sparky

SPARKILY   adv in a lively manner

SPARKISH   adj jaunty

SPARKLE   v -KLED, -KLING, -KLES to give off or reflect flashes of light

SPARKLER   n pl. -S something that sparkles

SPARKY   adj SPARKIER, SPARKIEST lively

SPARLIKE   adj resembling a spar

SPARLING   n pl. -S a young herring

SPAROID   n pl. -S a sparid

SPARRED   past tense of spar

SPARRIER   comparative of sparry

SPARRIEST   superlative of sparry

SPARRING   present participle of spar

SPARROW   n pl. -S a small bird

SPARRY   adj -RIER, -RIEST resembling spar (a lustrous mineral)

SPARSE   adj SPARSER, SPARSEST thinly distributed SPARSELY adv

SPARSITY   n pl. -S the quality or state of being sparse

SPASM   n pl. -S an abnormal, involuntary muscular contraction

SPASTIC   n pl. -S one suffering from spastic paralysis (a paralysis with muscle spasms)

SPAT   v SPATTED, SPATTING, SPATS to strike lightly

SPATE   n pl. -S a freshet

SPATHE   n pl. -S a leaflike organ of certain plants SPATHAL, SPATHED, SPATHOSE adj

SPATHIC   adj sparry

SPATIAL   adj of or pertaining to space

SPATTED   past tense of spat

SPATTER   v -ED, -ING, -S to scatter in drops

SPATTING   present participle of spat

SPATULA   n pl. -S a mixing implement SPATULAR adj

SPAVIE   n pl. -S spavin SPAVIET adj

SPAVIN   n pl. -S a disease of horses SPAVINED adj

SPAWN   v -ED, -ING, -S to deposit eggs

SPAWNER   n pl. -S one that spawns

SPAY   v -ED, -ING, -S to remove the ovaries of

SPEAK   v SPOKE or SPAKE, SPOKEN, SPEAKING, SPEAKS to utter words

SPEAKER   n pl. -S one that speaks

SPEAKING   n pl. -S a speech or discourse

SPEAN   v -ED, -ING, -S to wean

SPEAR   v -ED, -ING, -S to pierce with a spear (a long, pointed weapon)

SPEARER   n pl. -S one that spears

SPEARMAN   n pl. -MEN a person armed with a spear

SPECIAL   adj -CIALER, -CIALEST of a distinct or particular kind or character

SPECIAL   n pl. -S a special person or thing

SPECIATE   v -ATED, -ATING, -ATES to undergo a type of evolutionary process

SPECIE   *n* pl. -S coined money

SPECIFIC   *n* pl. -S a remedy intended for a particular disease

SPECIFY   *v* -FIED, -FYING, -FIES to state in detail

SPECIMEN   *n* pl. -S a part or individual representative of a group or whole

SPECIOUS   *adj* having a false look of truth or authenticity

SPECK   *v* -ED, -ING, -S to mark with small spots

SPECKLE   *v* -LED, -LING, -LES to speck

SPECS   *n/pl* eyeglasses

SPECTATE   *v* -TATED, -TATING, -TATES to attend and view

SPECTER   *n* pl. -S a visible disembodied spirit

SPECTRA   a pl. of spectrum

SPECTRAL   *adj* resembling a specter

SPECTRE   *n* pl. -S specter

SPECTRUM   *n* pl. -TRA or -TRUMS an array of the components of a light wave

SPECULUM   *n* pl. -LA or -LUMS a medical instrument **SPECULAR** *adj*

SPED   a past tense of speed

SPEECH   *n* pl. -ES the faculty or act of speaking

SPEED   *v* SPED or SPEEDED, SPEEDING, SPEEDS to move swiftly

SPEEDER   *n* pl. -S one that speeds

SPEEDIER   comparative of speedy

SPEEDIEST   superlative of speedy

SPEEDILY   *adv* in a speedy manner

SPEEDING   *n* pl. -S the act of driving faster than the law allows

SPEEDUP   *n* pl. -S an acceleration of production without an increase in pay

SPEEDWAY   *n* pl. -WAYS a road designed for rapid travel

SPEEDY   *adj* SPEEDIER, SPEEDIEST swift

SPEEL   *v* -ED, -ING, -S to climb

SPEER   *v* -ED, -ING, -S to inquire

SPEERING   *n* pl. -S inquiry

SPEIL   *v* -ED, -ING, -S to speel

SPEIR   *v* -ED, -ING, -S to speer

SPEISE   *n* pl. -S speiss

SPEISS   *n* pl. -ES a metallic mixture obtained in smelting certain ores

SPELAEAN   *adj* spelean

SPELEAN   *adj* living in caves

SPELL   *v* SPELLED or SPELT, SPELLING, SPELLS to name or write the letters of in order

SPELLER   *n* pl. -S one that spells words

SPELLING   *n* pl. -S a sequence of letters composing a word

SPELT   *n* pl. -S a variety of wheat

SPELTER   *n* pl. -S zinc in the form of ingots

SPELTZ   *n* pl. -ES spelt

SPELUNK   *v* -ED, -ING, -S to explore caves

SPENCE   *n* pl. -S a pantry

SPENCER   *n* pl. -S a trysail

SPEND   *v* SPENT, SPENDING, SPENDS to pay out

SPENDER   *n* pl. -S one that spends

SPENT   past tense of spend

SPERM   *n* pl. -S a male gamete **SPERMIC** *adj*

SPERMARY   *n* pl. -RIES an organ in which sperms are formed

SPERMINE   *n* pl. -S a chemical compound

SPERMOUS   *adj* resembling or made up of sperms

SPEW   *v* -ED, -ING, -S to vomit

SPEWER   *n* pl. -S one that spews

SPHAGNUM   *n* pl. -S a grayish moss

SPHENE   *n* pl. -S a mineral

SPHENIC   *adj* shaped like a wedge

SPHENOID   *n* pl. -S a bone of the skull

SPHERAL   *adj* of, pertaining to, or having the form of a sphere

SPHERE   *v* SPHERED, SPHERING, SPHERES to form into a sphere (a type of geometric solid)

SPHERIC   *adj* spheral

SPHERICS   *n/pl* the geometry of figures on the surface of a sphere

SPHERIER   comparative of sphery

SPHERIEST   superlative of sphery

SPHERING   present participle of sphere

SPHEROID   *n* pl. -S a type of geometric solid

SPHERULE   *n* pl. -S a small sphere

SPHERY	*adj* SPHERIER, SPHERIEST resembling a sphere
SPHINGES	a pl. of sphinx
SPHINGID	*n* pl. -S the hawkmoth
SPHINX	*n* pl. SPHINXES or SPHINGES a figure of a creature of Egyptian mythology
SPHYGMUS	*n* pl. -ES the pulse **SPHYGMIC** *adj*
SPIC	*n* pl. -S a Spanish-American person — an offensive term
SPICA	*n* pl. -CAE or -CAS an ear of grain **SPICATE, SPICATED** *adj*
SPICCATO	*n* pl. -TOS a method of playing a stringed instrument
SPICE	*v* SPICED, SPICING, SPICES to season with a spice (an aromatic vegetable substance)
SPICER	*n* pl. -S one that spices
SPICERY	*n* pl. -ERIES a spicy quality
SPICEY	*adj* SPICIER, SPICIEST spicy
SPICIER	comparative of spicy
SPICIEST	superlative of spicy
SPICILY	*adv* in a spicy manner
SPICING	present participle of spice
SPICK	*n* pl. -S spic
SPICULA	*n* pl. -LAE spicule **SPICULAR** *adj*
SPICULE	*n* pl. -S a small, needlelike structure
SPICULUM	*n* pl. -LA spicule
SPICY	*adj* SPICIER, SPICIEST containing spices
SPIDER	*n* pl. -S a type of arachnid
SPIDERY	*adj* -DERIER, -DERIEST resembling a spider
SPIED	past tense of spy
SPIEGEL	*n* pl. -S a type of cast iron
SPIEL	*v* -ED, -ING, -S to talk at length
SPIELER	*n* pl. -S one that spiels
SPIER	*v* -ED, -ING, -S to speer
SPIES	present 3d person sing. of spy
SPIFFING	*adj* spiffy
SPIFFY	*adj* -FIER, -FIEST stylish **SPIFFILY** *adv*
SPIGOT	*n* pl. -S a faucet
SPIK	*n* pl. -S spic

SPIKE	*v* SPIKED, SPIKING, SPIKES to fasten with a spike (a long, thick nail)
SPIKELET	*n* pl. -S a type of flower cluster
SPIKER	*n* pl. -S one that spikes
SPIKING	present participle of spike
SPIKY	*adj* SPIKIER, SPIKIEST resembling a spike **SPIKILY** *adv*
SPILE	*v* SPILED, SPILING, SPILES to stop up with a wooden plug
SPILIKIN	*n* pl. -S a strip of wood used in a game
SPILING	*n* pl. -S a piling
SPILL	*v* SPILLED or SPILT, SPILLING, SPILLS to cause to run out of a container
SPILLAGE	*n* pl. -S something that is spilled
SPILLER	*n* pl. -S one that spills
SPILLWAY	*n* pl. -WAYS a channel for surplus water in a reservoir
SPILT	a past tense of spill
SPILTH	*n* pl. -S spillage
SPIN	*v* SPUN, SPINNING, SPINS to draw out and twist into threads
SPINACH	*n* pl. -ES a cultivated herb
SPINAGE	*n* pl. -S spinach
SPINAL	*n* pl. -S an injection of an anesthetic into the spinal cord
SPINALLY	*adv* with respect to the spine
SPINATE	*adj* bearing thorns
SPINDLE	*v* -DLED, -DLING, -DLES to impale on a slender rod
SPINDLER	*n* pl. -S one that spindles
SPINDLY	*adj* -DLIER, -DLIEST long and slender
SPINE	*n* pl. -S the vertebral column **SPINED** *adj*
SPINEL	*n* pl. -S a mineral
SPINELLE	*n* pl. -S spinel
SPINET	*n* pl. -S a small piano
SPINIER	comparative of spiny
SPINIEST	superlative of spiny
SPINIFEX	*n* pl. -ES an Australian grass
SPINLESS	*adj* having no rotation
SPINNER	*n* pl. -S one that spins
SPINNERY	*n* pl. -NERIES a spinning mill
SPINNEY	*n* pl. -NEYS a thicket

SPINNING *n* pl. -S the act of one that spins

SPINNY *n* pl. -NIES spinney

SPINOFF *n* pl. -S a new application or incidental result

SPINOR *n* pl. -S a type of mathematical vector

SPINOSE *adj* spiny

SPINOUS *adj* spiny

SPINOUT *n* pl. -S a rotational skid by an automobile

SPINSTER *n* pl. -S an unmarried woman who is past the usual age for marrying

SPINULA *n* pl. -LAE spinule

SPINULE *n* pl. -S a small thorn

SPINY *adj* SPINIER, SPINIEST bearing or covered with thorns

SPIRACLE *n* pl. -S an orifice through which breathing occurs

SPIRAEA *n* pl. -S spirea

SPIRAL *v* -RALED, -RALING, -RALS or -RALLED, -RALLING, -RALS to move like a spiral (a type of plane curve)

SPIRALLY *adv* in a spiral manner

SPIRANT *n* pl. -S a speech sound produced by the forcing of breath through a narrow passage

SPIRE *v* SPIRED, SPIRING, SPIRES to rise in a tapering manner

SPIREA *n* pl. -S a flowering shrub

SPIREM *n* pl. -S spireme

SPIREME *n* pl. -S a filament forming part of a cell nucleus during mitosis

SPIRILLA *n/pl* spirally twisted, aerobic bacteria

SPIRING present participle of spire

SPIRIT *v* -ED, -ING, -S to carry off secretly

SPIROID *adj* resembling a spiral

SPIRT *v* -ED, -ING, -S to spurt

SPIRULA *n* pl. -LAE or -LAS a spiral-shelled mollusk

SPIRY *adj* tall, slender, and tapering

SPIT *v* SPITTED, SPITTING, SPITS to impale on a spit (a pointed rod on which meat is turned)

SPITAL *n* pl. -S a hospital

SPITBALL *n* pl. -S a type of pitch in baseball

SPITE *v* SPITED, SPITING, SPITES to treat with malice

SPITEFUL *adj* -FULLER, -FULLEST malicious

SPITFIRE *n* pl. -S a quick-tempered person

SPITING present participle of spite

SPITTED past tense of spit

SPITTER *n* pl. -S a spitball

SPITTING present participle of spit

SPITTLE *n* pl. -S saliva

SPITTOON *n* pl. -S a receptacle for saliva

SPITZ *n* pl. -ES a dog having a heavy coat

SPIV *n* pl. -S a petty criminal

SPLAKE *n* pl. -S a freshwater fish

SPLASH *v* -ED, -ING, -ES to scatter a liquid about

SPLASHER *n* pl. -S one that splashes

SPLASHY *adj* SPLASHIER, SPLASHIEST showy

SPLAT *n* pl. -S a piece of wood forming the middle of a chair back

SPLATTER *v* -ED, -ING, -S to spatter

SPLAY *v* -ED, -ING, -S to spread out

SPLEEN *n* pl. -S a ductless organ of the body

SPLEENY *adj* SPLEENIER, SPLEENIEST peevish

SPLENDID *adj* -DIDER, -DIDEST magnificent

SPLENDOR *n* pl. -S magnificence

SPLENIA pl. of splenium

SPLENIAL *adj* pertaining to the splenius

SPLENIC *adj* pertaining to the spleen

SPLENIUM *n* pl. -NIA a surgical bandage

SPLENIUS *n* pl. -NII a muscle of the neck

SPLENT *n* pl. -S a splint

SPLICE *v* SPLICED, SPLICING, SPLICES to join at the ends

SPLICER *n* pl. -S one that splices

SPLINE *v* SPLINED, SPLINING, SPLINES to provide with a spline (a key that connects two rotating mechanical parts)

SPLINT *v* -ED, -ING, -S to brace with a splint (a thin piece of wood)

SPLINTER   v -ED, -ING, -S to split into sharp, slender pieces

SPLIT   v SPLIT, SPLITTING, SPLITS to separate lengthwise

SPLITTER   n pl. -S one that splits

SPLORE   n pl. -S a carousal

SPLOSH   v -ED, -ING, -ES to splash

SPLOTCH   v -ED, -ING, -ES to mark with large, irregular spots

SPLOTCHY   adj SPLOTCHIER, SPLOTCHIEST splotched

SPLURGE   v SPLURGED, SPLURGING, SPLURGES to spend money lavishly

SPLURGY   adj SPLURGIER, SPLURGIEST tending to splurge

SPLUTTER   v -ED, -ING, -S to speak rapidly and confusedly

SPODE   n pl. -S a fine china

SPOIL   v SPOILED or SPOILT, SPOILING, SPOILS to impair the value or quality of

SPOILAGE   n pl. -S something that is spoiled or wasted

SPOILER   n pl. -S one that spoils

SPOILT   a past tense of spoil

SPOKE   v SPOKED, SPOKING, SPOKES to provide with spokes (rods that support the rim of a wheel)

SPOKEN   past participle of speak

SPOLIATE   v -ATED, -ATING, -ATES to plunder

SPONDAIC   n pl. -S a spondee

SPONDEE   n pl. -S a type of metrical foot

SPONGE   v SPONGED, SPONGING, SPONGES to wipe with a sponge (a mass of absorbent material)

SPONGER   n pl. -S one that sponges

SPONGIER   comparative of spongy

SPONGIEST   superlative of spongy

SPONGILY   adv in a spongy manner

SPONGIN   n pl. -S a fibrous material

SPONGING   present participle of sponge

SPONGY   adj SPONGIER, SPONGIEST resembling a sponge

SPONSAL   adj pertaining to marriage

SPONSION   n pl. -S the act of sponsoring

SPONSON   n pl. -S a projection from the side of a ship

SPONSOR   v -ED, -ING, -S to make oneself responsible for

SPONTOON   n pl. -S a spear-like weapon

SPOOF   v -ED, -ING, -S to hoax

SPOOK   v -ED, -ING, -S to scare

SPOOKISH   adj spooky

SPOOKY   adj SPOOKIER, SPOOKIEST scary SPOOKILY adv

SPOOL   v -ED, -ING, -S to wind on a small cylinder

SPOON   v -ED, -ING, -S to take up with a spoon (a type of eating utensil)

SPOONEY   adj SPOONIER, SPOONIEST spoony

SPOONEY   n pl. -EYS a spoony

SPOONFUL   n pl. SPOONFULS or SPOONSFUL as much as a spoon will hold

SPOONIER   comparative of spooney

SPOONIES   pl. of spoony

SPOONIEST   superlative of spooney

SPOONING   present participle of spoon

SPOONY   adj SPOONIER, SPOONIEST overly sentimental SPOONILY adv

SPOONY   n pl. SPOONIES a spoony person

SPOOR   v -ED, -ING, -S to track

SPORADIC   adj occurring at irregular intervals

SPORAL   adj of, pertaining to, or resembling a spore

SPORE   v SPORED, SPORING, SPORES to produce spores (asexual, usually single-celled reproductive bodies)

SPOROID   adj resembling a spore

SPORRAN   n pl. -S a large purse worn by Scottish Highlanders

SPORT   v -ED, -ING, -S to frolic

SPORTER   n pl. -S one that sports

SPORTFUL   adj sportive

SPORTIVE   adj playful

SPORTY   adj SPORTIER, SPORTIEST showy SPORTILY adv

SPORULE   n pl. -S a small spore SPORULAR adj

SPOT   v SPOTTED, SPOTTING, SPOTS to mark with spots (small, roundish discolorations)

SPOTLESS   adj perfectly clean

SPOTTER *n* pl. -S one that spots

SPOTTING present participle of spot

SPOTTY *adj* -TIER, -TIEST marked with spots **SPOTTILY** *adv*

SPOUSAL *n* pl. -S marriage

SPOUSE *v* SPOUSED, SPOUSING, SPOUSES to marry

SPOUT *v* -ED, -ING, -S to eject in a rapid stream

SPOUTER *n* pl. -S one that spouts

SPRADDLE *v* -DLED, -DLING, -DLES to straddle

SPRAG *n* pl. -S a device used to prevent a vehicle from rolling backward

SPRAIN *v* -ED, -ING, -S to weaken by a sudden and violent twisting or wrenching

SPRANG a past tense of spring

SPRAT *n* pl. -S a small herring

SPRATTLE *v* -TLED, -TLING, -TLES to struggle

SPRAWL *v* -ED, -ING, -S to stretch out ungracefully

SPRAWLER *n* pl. -S one that sprawls

SPRAWLY *adj* SPRAWLIER, SPRAWLIEST tending to sprawl

SPRAY *v* -ED, -ING, -S to disperse in fine particles

SPRAYER *n* pl. -S one that sprays

SPREAD *v* SPREAD, SPREADING, SPREADS to open or expand over a larger area

SPREADER *n* pl. -S one that spreads

SPREE *n* pl. -S an unrestrained indulgence in an activity

SPRENT *adj* sprinkled over

SPRIER a comparative of spry

SPRIEST a superlative of spry

SPRIG *v* SPRIGGED, SPRIGGING, SPRIGS to fasten with small, thin nails

SPRIGGER *n* pl. -S one that sprigs

SPRIGGY *adj* -GIER, -GIEST having small branches

SPRIGHT *n* pl. -S sprite

SPRING *v* SPRANG or SPRUNG, SPRINGING, SPRINGS to move upward suddenly and swiftly

SPRINGAL *n* pl. -S a young man

SPRINGE *v* SPRINGED, SPRINGEING, SPRINGES to catch with a type of snare

SPRINGER *n* pl. -S one that springs

SPRINGY *adj* SPRINGIER, SPRINGIEST resilient

SPRINKLE *v* -KLED, -KLING, -KLES to scatter drops or particles on

SPRINT *v* -ED, -ING, -S to run at top speed

SPRINTER *n* pl. -S one that sprints

SPRIT *n* pl. -S a ship's spar

SPRITE *n* pl. -S an elf or fairy

SPROCKET *n* pl. -S a toothlike projection that engages with the links of a chain

SPROUT *v* -ED, -ING, -S to begin to grow

SPRUCE *adj* SPRUCER, SPRUCEST neat and trim in appearance **SPRUCELY** *adv*

SPRUCE *v* SPRUCED, SPRUCING, SPRUCES to make spruce

SPRUCY *adj* SPRUCIER, SPRUCIEST spruce

SPRUE *n* pl. -S a tropical disease

SPRUG *n* pl. -S a sparrow

SPRUNG a past tense of spring

SPRY *adj* SPRYER, SPRYEST or SPRIER, SPRIEST nimble **SPRYLY** *adv*

SPRYNESS *n* pl. -ES the quality or state of being spry

SPUD *v* SPUDDED, SPUDDING, SPUDS to remove with a spade-like tool

SPUDDER *n* pl. -S a tool for removing bark from trees

SPUE *v* SPUED, SPUING, SPUES to spew

SPUME *v* SPUMED, SPUMING, SPUMES to foam

SPUMIER comparative of spumy

SPUMIEST superlative of spumy

SPUMING present participle of spume

SPUMONE *n* pl. -S an Italian ice cream

SPUMONI *n* pl. -S spumone

SPUMOUS *adj* spumy

SPUMY *adj* SPUMIER, SPUMIEST foamy

SPUN past tense of spin

SPUNK *v* -ED, -ING, -S to begin to burn

SPUNKIE *n* pl. -S a light caused by the combustion of marsh gas

SPUNKY *adj* SPUNKIER, SPUNKIEST plucky **SPUNKILY** *adv*

SPUR *v* SPURRED, SPURRING, SPURS to urge on with a spur (a horseman's goad)

SPURGALL *v* -ED, -ING, -S to injure with a spur

SPURGE *n* pl. -S a tropical plant

SPURIOUS *adj* not genuine

SPURN *v* -ED, -ING, -S to reject with contempt

SPURNER *n* pl. -S one that spurns

SPURRED past tense of spur

SPURRER *n* pl. -S one that spurs

SPURREY *n* pl. -REYS spurry

SPURRIER *n* pl. -S one that makes spurs

SPURRING present participle of spur

SPURRY *n* pl. -RIES a European weed

SPURT *v* -ED, -ING, -S to gush forth

SPURTLE *n* pl. -S a stick for stirring porridge

SPUTA pl. of sputum

SPUTNIK *n* pl. -S a Soviet artificial earth satellite

SPUTTER *v* -ED, -ING, -S to eject particles in short bursts

SPUTUM *n* pl. -TA saliva

SPY *v* SPIED, SPYING, SPIES to watch secretly

SPYGLASS *n* pl. -ES a small telescope

SQUAB *n* pl. -S a young pigeon

SQUABBLE *v* -BLED, -BLING, -BLES to quarrel

SQUABBY *adj* -BIER, -BIEST short and fat

SQUAD *v* SQUADDED, SQUADDING, SQUADS to form into squads (small, organized groups)

SQUADRON *v* -ED, -ING, -S to arrange in squadrons (units of military organization)

SQUALENE *n* pl. -S a chemical compound

SQUALID *adj* -IDER, -IDEST marked by filthiness caused by neglect or poverty

SQUALL *v* -ED, -ING, -S to cry or scream loudly

SQUALLER *n* pl. -S one that squalls

SQUALLY *adj* SQUALLIER, SQUALLIEST gusty

SQUALOR *n* pl. -S the quality or state of being squalid

SQUAMA *n* pl. -MAE a scale **SQUAMATE, SQUAMOSE, SQUAMOUS** *adj*

SQUANDER *v* -ED, -ING, -S to spend wastefully

SQUARE *adj* SQUARER, SQUAREST having four equal sides and four right angles

SQUARE *v* SQUARED, SQUARING, SQUARES to make square

SQUARELY *adv* in a direct manner

SQUARER *n* pl. -S one that squares

SQUAREST superlative of square

SQUARING present participle of square

SQUARISH *adj* somewhat square

SQUASH *v* -ED, -ING, -ES to press into a pulp or flat mass

SQUASHER *n* pl. -S one that squashes

SQUASHY *adj* SQUASHIER, SQUASHIEST soft and moist

SQUAT *v* SQUATTED, SQUATTING, SQUATS to sit on one's heels

SQUAT *adj* SQUATTER, SQUATTEST short and thick **SQUATLY** *adv*

SQUATTER *v* -ED, -ING, -S to move through water

SQUATTING present participle of squat

SQUATTY *adj* -TIER, -TIEST squat

SQUAW *n* pl. -S an American Indian woman

SQUAWK *v* -ED, -ING, -S to utter a loud, harsh cry

SQUAWKER *n* pl. -S one that squawks

SQUEAK *v* -ED, -ING, -S to make a sharp, high-pitched sound

SQUEAKER *n* pl. -S one that squeaks

SQUEAKY *adj* SQUEAKIER, SQUEAKIEST tending to squeak

SQUEAL *v* -ED, -ING, -S to utter a sharp, shrill cry

SQUEALER *n* pl. -S one that squeals

SQUEEGEE *v* -GEED, -GEEING, -GEES to wipe with a squeegee (an implement for removing water from a surface)

SQUEEZE *v* SQUEEZED, SQUEEZING, SQUEEZES to press hard upon

SQUEEZER	n pl. -S one that squeezes		**SQUISHY**	adj SQUISHIER, SQUISHIEST squashy
SQUEG	v SQUEGGED, SQUEGGING, SQUEGS to oscillate in an irregular manner		**SQUOOSH**	v -ED, -ING, -ES to squash
			SQUUSH	v -ED, -ING, -ES to squash
SQUELCH	v -ED, -ING, -ES to squash		**SRADDHA**	n pl. -S sradha
SQUELCHY	adj SQUELCHIER, SQUELCHIEST squashy		**SRADHA**	n pl. -S a Hindu ceremonial offering
SQUIB	v SQUIBBED, SQUIBBING, SQUIBS to lampoon		**SRI**	n pl. -S mister; sir — used as a Hindu title of respect
SQUID	v SQUIDDED, SQUIDDING, SQUIDS to fish for squid (ten-armed marine mollusks)		**STAB**	v STABBED, STABBING, STABS to pierce with a pointed weapon
SQUIFFED	adj drunk		**STABBER**	n pl. -S one that stabs
SQUIFFY	adj squiffed		**STABILE**	n pl. -S a stationary abstract sculpture
SQUIGGLE	v -GLED, -GLING, -GLES to wriggle		**STABLE**	adj -BLER, -BLEST resistant to sudden change or position or condition
SQUIGGLY	adj -GLIER, -GLIEST wriggly			
SQUILGEE	v -GEED, -GEEING, -GEES to squeegee		**STABLE**	v -BLED, -BLING, -BLES to put in a stable (a shelter for domestic animals)
SQUILL	n pl. -S a Eurasian herb			
SQUILLA	n pl. -LAS or -LAE a burrowing crustacean		**STABLER**	n pl. -S one that keeps a stable
SQUINCH	v -ED, -ING, -ES to squint		**STABLEST**	superlative of stable
SQUINNY	v -NIED, -NYING, -NIES to squint		**STABLING**	n pl. -S accommodation for animals in a stable
SQUINNY	adj -NIER, -NIEST squinty		**STABLISH**	v -ED, -ING, -ES to establish
SQUINT	adj SQUINTER, SQUINTEST cross-eyed		**STABLY**	adv in a stable manner
SQUINT	v -ED, -ING, -S to look with the eyes partly closed		**STACCATO**	n pl. -TOS or -TI a musical passage marked by the short, clear-cut playing of tones
SQUINTER	n pl. -S one that squints		**STACK**	v -ED, -ING, -S to pile
SQUINTY	adj SQUINTIER, SQUINTIEST marked by squinting		**STACKER**	n pl. -S one that stacks
SQUIRE	v SQUIRED, SQUIRING, SQUIRES to serve as a squire (an escort)		**STACTE**	n pl. -S a spice used by the ancient Jews in making incense
			STADDLE	n pl. -S a platform on which hay is stacked
SQUIREEN	n pl. -S an owner of a small estate		**STADE**	n pl. -S an ancient Greek unit of length
SQUIRISH	adj of, resembling, or befitting a squire		**STADIA**	n pl. -S a method of surveying distances
SQUIRM	v -ED, -ING, -S to wriggle		**STADIUM**	n pl. -S a structure in which athletic events are held
SQUIRMER	n pl. -S one that squirms			
SQUIRMY	adj SQUIRMIER, SQUIRMIEST wriggly		**STAFF**	v -ED, -ING, -S to provide with a staff (a body of assistants)
SQUIRREL	v -RELED, -RELING, -RELS or -RELLED, -RELLING, -RELS to store up for future use		**STAFFER**	n pl. -S a member of a staff
			STAG	v STAGGED, STAGGING, STAGS to attend a social function without a female companion
SQUIRT	v -ED, -ING, -S to eject in a thin, swift stream		**STAGE**	v STAGED, STAGING, STAGES to produce for public view
SQUIRTER	n pl. -S one that squirts		**STAGER**	n pl. -S an experienced person
SQUISH	v -ED, -ING, -ES to squash		**STAGEY**	adj STAGIER, STAGIEST stagy

STAGGARD *n* pl. -S a full-grown male red deer

STAGGART *n* pl. -S staggard

STAGGED past tense of stag

STAGGER *v* -ED, -ING, -S to walk or stand unsteadily

STAGGERY *adj* unsteady

STAGGIE *n* pl. -S a colt

STAGGING present participle of stag

STAGGY *adj* -GIER, -GIEST having the appearance of a mature male

STAGIER comparative of stagey and stagy

STAGIEST superlative of stagey and stagy

STAGILY *adv* in a stagy manner

STAGING *n* pl. -S a temporary platform

STAGNANT *adj* not moving or flowing

STAGNATE *v* -NATED, -NATING, -NATES to become stagnant

STAGY *adj* STAGIER, STAGIEST having a theatrical quality

STAID *adj* STAIDER, STAIDEST sober and sedate **STAIDLY** *adv*

STAIG *n* pl. -S a colt

STAIN *v* -ED, -ING, -S to discolor or dirty

STAINER *n* pl. -S one that stains

STAIR *n* pl. -S a rest for the foot used in going from one level to another

STAIRWAY *n* pl. -WAYS a flight of stairs

STAKE *v* STAKED, STAKING, STAKES to fasten with a stake (a pointed piece of wood or metal)

STAKEOUT *n* pl. -S a surveillance of an area especially by the police

STALAG *n* pl. -S a German prisoner-of-war camp

STALE *adj* STALER, STALEST not fresh **STALELY** *adv*

STALE *v* STALED, STALING, STALES to become stale

STALK *v* -ED, -ING, -S to pursue stealthily

STALKER *n* pl. -S one that stalks

STALKY *adj* STALKIER, STALKIEST long and slender **STALKILY** *adv*

STALL *v* -ED, -ING, -S to stop the progress of

STALLION *n* pl. -S an uncastrated male horse

STALWART *n* pl. -S an unwavering partisan

STAMEN *n* pl. -S the pollen-bearing organ of flowering plants

STAMINA *n* pl. -S endurance **STAMINAL** *adj*

STAMMEL *n* pl. -S a red color

STAMMER *v* -ED, -ING, -S to speak with involuntary breaks and pauses

STAMP *v* -ED, -ING, -S to bring the foot down heavily

STAMPEDE *v* -PEDED, -PEDING, -PEDES to cause to run away in headlong panic

STAMPER *n* pl. -S one that stamps

STANCE *n* pl. -S a manner of standing

STANCH *adj* STANCHER, STANCHEST staunch

STANCH *v* -ED, -ING, -ES to stop the flow of blood from

STANCHER *n* pl. -S one that stanches

STANCHLY *adv* in a stanch manner

STAND *v* STOOD, STANDING, STANDS to assume or maintain an upright position

STANDARD *n* pl. -S an established measure of comparison

STANDBY *n* pl. -BYS one that can be relied on

STANDEE *n* pl. -S one who stands because of the lack of seats

STANDER *n* pl. -S one that stands

STANDING *n* pl. -S a position or condition in society

STANDISH *n* pl. -ES a receptacle for pens and ink

STANDOFF *n* pl. -S a tie or draw, as in a game

STANDOUT *n* pl. -S one that shows marked superiority

STANDPAT *adj* resisting or opposing change

STANDUP *adj* having an upright position

STANE *v* STANED, STANING, STANES to stone

STANG *v* -ED, -ING, -S to sting

STANHOPE *n* pl. -S a light, open carriage

STANING present participle of stane

STANK *n* pl. -S a pond

STANNARY *n* pl. -RIES a tin-mining region

STANNIC *adj* pertaining to tin

STANNITE _n_ pl. -S an ore of tin

STANNOUS _adj_ pertaining to tin

STANNUM _n_ pl. -S tin

STANZA _n_ pl. -S a division of a poem **STANZAED, STANZAIC** _adj_

STAPEDES pl. of stapes

STAPELIA _n_ pl. -S an African plant

STAPES _n_ pl. -PEDES a bone of the middle ear

STAPH _n_ pl. -S any of various spherical bacteria

STAPLE _v_ -PLED, -PLING, -PLES to fasten by means of a U-shaped metal loop

STAPLER _n_ pl. -S a stapling device

STAR _v_ STARRED, STARRING, STARS to shine as a star (a natural luminous body visible in the sky)

STARCH _v_ -ED, -ING, -ES to treat with starch (a solid carbohydrate)

STARCHY _adj_ STARCHIER, STARCHIEST containing starch

STARDOM _n_ pl. -S the status of a preeminent performer

STARDUST _n_ pl. -S a romantic quality

STARE _v_ STARED, STARING, STARES to gaze fixedly

STARER _n_ pl. -S one that stares

STARETS _n_ pl. STARTSY a spiritual adviser in the Eastern Orthodox Church

STARFISH _n_ pl. -ES a star-shaped marine animal

STARGAZE _v_ -GAZED, -GAZING, -GAZES to gaze at the stars

STARING present participle of stare

STARK _adj_ STARKER, STARKEST harsh in appearance **STARKLY** _adv_

STARLESS _adj_ having no stars

STARLET _n_ pl. -S a small star

STARLIKE _adj_ resembling a star

STARLING _n_ pl. -S a European bird

STARLIT _adj_ lighted by the stars

STARNOSE _n_ pl. -S a burrowing mammal

STARRED past tense of star

STARRING present participle of star

STARRY _adj_ -RIER, -RIEST abounding with stars

START _v_ -ED, -ING, -S to set out

STARTER _n_ pl. -S one that starts

STARTLE _v_ -TLED, -TLING, -TLES to frighten or surprise suddenly

STARTLER _n_ pl. -S one that startles

STARTSY pl. of starets

STARVE _v_ STARVED, STARVING, STARVES to die from lack of food

STARVER _n_ pl. -S one that starves

STARWORT _n_ pl. -S a flowering plant

STASES pl. of stasis

STASH _v_ -ED, -ING, -ES to store in a secret place

STASIMON _n_ pl. -MA a choral ode in ancient Greek drama

STASIS _n_ pl. STASES a stoppage of the normal flow of bodily fluids

STATABLE _adj_ capable of being stated

STATAL _adj_ pertaining to a national government

STATANT _adj_ standing with all feet on the ground — used of a heraldic animal

STATE _v_ STATED, STATING, STATES to set forth in words

STATEDLY _adv_ regularly

STATELY _adj_ -LIER, -LIEST dignified

STATER _n_ pl. -S one that states

STATIC _n_ pl. -S random noise produced in a radio or television receiver **STATICAL** _adj_

STATICE _n_ pl. -S a flowering plant

STATING present participle of state

STATION _v_ -ED, -ING, -S to assign to a position

STATISM _n_ pl. -S a theory of government

STATIST _n_ pl. -S an adherent of statism

STATIVE _n_ pl. -S a verb that expresses a condition

STATOR _n_ pl. -S the part of a machine about which the rotor revolves

STATUARY _n_ pl. -ARIES a group of statues

STATUE _n_ pl. -S a three-dimensional work of art **STATUED** _adj_

STATURE _n_ pl. -S the natural height of a human or animal body

STATUS _n_ pl. -ES relative position

STATUTE _n_ pl. -S a law enacted by the legislative branch of a government

STAUMREL _n_ pl. -S a dolt

STAUNCH *adj* STAUNCHER, STAUNCHEST firm and dependable

STAUNCH *v* -ED, -ING, -ES to stanch

STAVE *v* STAVED or STOVE, STAVING, STAVES to drive or thrust away

STAW a past tense of steal

STAY *v* STAYED or STAID, STAYING, STAYS to continue in a place or condition

STAYER *n pl.* -S one that stays

STAYSAIL *n pl.* -S a type of sail

STEAD *v* -ED, -ING, -S to be of advantage to

STEADIED past tense of steady

STEADIER *n pl.* -S one that steadies

STEADIES present 3d person sing. of steady

STEADING *n pl.* -S a small farm

STEADY *adj* STEADIER, STEADIEST firm in position **STEADILY** *adv*

STEADY *v* STEADIED, STEADYING, STEADIES to make steady

STEAK *n pl.* -S a slice of meat

STEAL *v* STOLE or STAW, STOLEN, STEALING, STEALS to take without right or permission

STEALAGE *n pl.* -S theft

STEALER *n pl.* -S one that steals

STEALING *n pl.* -S the act of one that steals

STEALTH *n pl.* -S stealthy procedure

STEALTHY *adj* STEALTHIER, STEALTHIEST intended to escape observation

STEAM *v* -ED, -ING, -S to expose to steam (water in the form of vapor)

STEAMER *v* -ED, -ING, -S to travel by steamship

STEAMY *adj* STEAMIER, STEAMIEST marked by steam **STEAMILY** *adv*

STEAPSIN *n pl.* -S an enzyme

STEARATE *n pl.* -S a chemical salt

STEARIN *n pl.* -S the solid portion of a fat **STEARIC** *adj*

STEARINE *n pl.* -S stearin

STEATITE *n pl.* -S a variety of talc

STEDFAST *adj* staunch

STEED *n pl.* -S a horse

STEEK *v* -ED, -ING, -S to shut

STEEL *v* -ED, -ING, -S to cover with steel (a tough iron alloy)

STEELIE *n pl.* -S a steel playing marble

STEELY *adj* STEELIER, STEELIEST resembling steel

STEENBOK *n pl.* -S an African antelope

STEEP *adj* STEEPER, STEEPEST inclined sharply

STEEP *v* -ED, -ING, -S to soak in a liquid

STEEPEN *v* -ED, -ING, -S to make steep

STEEPER *n pl.* -S one that steeps

STEEPLE *n pl.* -S a tapering structure on a church tower **STEEPLED** *adj*

STEEPLY *adv* in a steep manner

STEER *v* -ED, -ING, -S to direct the course of

STEERAGE *n pl.* -S the act of steering

STEERER *n pl.* -S one that steers

STEEVE *v* STEEVED, STEEVING, STEEVES to stow in the hold of a ship

STEEVING *n pl.* -S the angular elevation of a bowsprit from a ship's keel

STEGODON *n pl.* -S an extinct elephant-like mammal

STEIN *n pl.* -S a beer mug

STEINBOK *n pl.* -S steenbok

STELA *n pl.* -LAE or -LAI an inscribed slab used as a monument **STELAR, STELENE** *adj*

STELE *n pl.* -S the central portion of vascular tissue in a plant stem **STELIC** *adj*

STELLA *n pl.* -S a former coin of the United States

STELLAR *adj* pertaining to the stars

STELLATE *adj* shaped like a star

STELLIFY *v* -FIED, -FYING, -FIES to convert into a star

STEM *v* STEMMED, STEMMING, STEMS to remove stems (ascending axes of a plant) from

STEMLESS *adj* having no stem

STEMLIKE *adj* resembling a stem

STEMMA *n pl.* -MAS or -MATA a scroll recording the genealogy of a family in ancient Rome

STEMMED past tense of stem

STEMMER *n pl.* -S one that removes stems

STEMMERY n pl. -MERIES a place where tobacco leaves are stripped

STEMMING present participle of stem

STEMMY adj -MIER, -MIEST abounding in stems

STEMSON n pl. -S a supporting timber of a ship

STEMWARE n pl. -S a type of glassware

STENCH n pl. -ES a foul odor

STENCHY adj STENCHIER, STENCHIEST having a stench

STENCIL v -CILED, -CILING, -CILS or -CILLED, -CILLING, -CILS to mark by means of a perforated sheet of material

STENGAH n pl. -S a mixed drink

STENO n pl. STENOS a stenographer

STENOSED adj affected with stenosis

STENOSIS n pl. -NOSES a narrowing of a bodily passage **STENOTIC** adj

STENTOR n pl. -S a person having a very loud voice

STEP v STEPPED, STEPPING, STEPS to move by lifting the foot and setting it down in another place

STEPDAME n pl. -S a stepmother

STEPLIKE adj resembling a stair

STEPPE n pl. -S a vast treeless plain

STEPPED past tense of step

STEPPER n pl. -S one that steps

STEPPING present participle of step

STEPSON n pl. -S a son of one's spouse by a former marriage

STEPWISE adj marked by a gradual progression

STERE n pl. -S a unit of volume

STEREO v -ED, -ING, -S to make a type of printing plate

STERIC adj pertaining to the spatial relationships of atoms in a molecule

STERICAL adj steric

STERIGMA n pl. -MAS or -MATA a spore-bearing stalk of certain fungi

STERILE adj incapable of producing offspring

STERLET n pl. -S a small sturgeon

STERLING n pl. -S British money

STERN adj STERNER, STERNEST unyielding

STERN n pl. -S the rear part of a ship

STERNA a pl. of sternum

STERNAL adj pertaining to the sternum

STERNITE n pl. -S a somitic sclerite

STERNLY adv in a stern manner

STERNSON n pl. -S a reinforcing post of a ship

STERNUM n pl. -NA or -NUMS a long, flat supporting bone of most vertebrates

STERNWAY n pl. -WAYS the backward movement of a vessel

STEROID n pl. -S a type of chemical compound

STEROL n pl. -S a type of solid alcohol

STERTOR n pl. -S a deep snoring sound

STET v STETTED, STETTING, STETS to cancel a previously made printing correction

STETSON n pl. -S a broad-brimmed hat

STEW v -ED, -ING, -S to cook by boiling slowly

STEWARD v -ED, -ING, -S to manage

STEWBUM n pl. -S a drunken bum

STEWPAN n pl. -S a pan used for stewing

STEY adj steep

STHENIA n pl. -S excessive energy **STHENIC** adj

STIBIAL adj pertaining to stibium

STIBINE n pl. -S a poisonous gas

STIBIUM n pl. -S antimony

STIBNITE n pl. -S an ore of antimony

STICH n pl. -S a line of poetry **STICHIC** adj

STICK v -ED, -ING, -S to support with slender pieces of wood

STICK v STUCK, STICKING, STICKS to pierce with a pointed object

STICKER n pl. -S an adhesive label

STICKFUL n pl. -S an amount of set type

STICKIER comparative of sticky

STICKIEST superlative of sticky

STICKILY adv in a sticky manner

STICKIT adj unsuccessful

STICKLE v -LED, -LING, -LES to argue stubbornly

STICKLER n pl. -S one that stickles

STICKMAN n pl. -MEN one who supervises the play at a dice table

STICKOUT   *n* pl. -S one that is conspicuous

STICKPIN   *n* pl. -S a decorative tiepin

STICKUM   *n* pl. -S a substance that causes adhesion

STICKUP   *n* pl. -S a robbery at gunpoint

STICKY   *adj* STICKIER, STICKIEST tending to adhere

STIED   a past tense of sty

STIES   present 3d person sing. of sty

STIFF   *adj* STIFFER, STIFFEST difficult to bend or stretch

STIFF   *n* pl. -S a corpse

STIFFEN   *v* -ED, -ING, -S to make stiff

STIFFISH   *adj* somewhat stiff

STIFFLY   *adv* in a stiff manner

STIFLE   *v* -FLED, -FLING, -FLES to smother

STIFLER   *n* pl. -S one that stifles

STIGMA   *n* pl. -MAS or -MATA a mark of disgrace STIGMAL *adj*

STILBENE   *n* pl. -S a chemical compound

STILBITE   *n* pl. -S a mineral

STILE   *n* pl. -S a series of steps for passing over a fence or wall

STILETTO   *v* -ED, -ING, -S or -ES to stab with a short dagger

STILL   *adj* STILLER, STILLEST free from sound or motion

STILL   *v* -ED, -ING, -S to make still

STILLMAN   *n* pl. -MEN one who operates a distillery

STILLY   *adj* STILLIER, STILLIEST still

STILT   *v* -ED, -ING, -S to raise on stilts (long, slender poles)

STIME   *n* pl. -S a glimpse

STIMULUS   *n* pl. -LI something that causes a response

STIMY   *v* -MIED, -MYING, -MIES to stymie

STING   *v* STUNG, STINGING, STINGS to prick painfully

STINGER   *n* pl. -S one that stings

STINGIER   comparative of stingy

STINGIEST   superlative of stingy

STINGILY   *adv* in a stingy manner

STINGO   *n* pl. -GOS a strong ale or beer

STINGRAY   *n* pl. -RAYS a flat-bodied marine fish

STINGY   *adj* -GIER, -GIEST unwilling to spend or give

STINK   *v* STANK or STUNK, STINKING, STINKS to emit a foul odor

STINKARD   *n* pl. -S a despicable person

STINKBUG   *n* pl. -S an insect that emits a foul odor

STINKER   *n* pl. -S one that stinks

STINKIER   comparative of stinky

STINKIEST   superlative of stinky

STINKO   *adj* drunk

STINKPOT   *n* pl. -S a jar containing foul-smelling combustibles formerly used in warfare

STINKY   *adj* STINKIER, STINKIEST emitting a foul odor

STINT   *v* -ED, -ING, -S to limit

STINTER   *n* pl. -S one that stints

STIPE   *n* pl. -S a slender supporting part of a plant STIPED *adj*

STIPEL   *n* pl. -S a small stipule

STIPEND   *n* pl. -S a fixed sum of money paid periodically

STIPES   *n* pl. STIPITES a stipe

STIPPLE   *v* -PLED, -PLING, -PLES to draw, paint, or engrave by means of dots or short touches

STIPPLER   *n* pl. -S one that stipples

STIPULE   *n* pl. -S an appendage at the base of a leaf in certain plants STIPULAR, STIPULED *adj*

STIR   *v* STIRRED, STIRRING, STIRS to pass an implement through in circular motions

STIRK   *n* pl. -S a young cow

STIRP   *n* pl. -S lineage

STIRPS   *n* pl. STIRPES a family or branch of a family

STIRRED   past tense of stir

STIRRER   *n* pl. -S one that stirs

STIRRING   present participle of stir

STIRRUP   *n* pl. -S a support for the foot of a horseman

STITCH   *v* -ED, -ING, -ES to join by making in-and-out movements with a threaded needle

STITCHER   *n* pl. -S one that stitches

STITHY   *v* STITHIED, STITHYING, STITHIES to forge on an anvil

STIVER   *n* pl. -S a former Dutch coin

STOA   *n* pl. STOAE, STOAI, or STOAS an ancient Greek covered walkway

STOAT   *n* pl. -S a weasel with a black-tipped tail

STOB   *v* STOBBED, STOBBING, STOBS to stab

STOCCADO   *n* pl. -DOS a thrust with a rapier

STOCCATA   *n* pl. -S stoccado

STOCK   *v* -ED, -ING, -S to keep for future sale or use

STOCKADE   *v* -ADED, -ADING, -ADES to build a type of protective fence around

STOCKCAR   *n* pl. -S a boxcar for carrying livestock

STOCKER   *n* pl. -S a young animal suitable for being fattened for market

STOCKIER   comparative of stocky

STOCKIEST   superlative of stocky

STOCKILY   *adv* in a stocky manner

STOCKING   *n* pl. -S a knitted or woven covering for the foot and leg

STOCKISH   *adj* stupid

STOCKIST   *n* pl. -S one who stocks goods

STOCKMAN   *n* pl. -MEN one who owns or raises livestock

STOCKPOT   *n* pl. -S a pot in which broth is prepared

STOCKY   *adj* STOCKIER, STOCKIEST having a short, thick body

STODGE   *v* STODGED, STODGING, STODGES to stuff full with food

STODGY   *adj* STODGIER, STODGIEST boring **STODGILY** *adv*

STOGEY   *n* pl. -GEYS stogy

STOGIE   *n* pl. -S stogy

STOGY   *n* pl. -GIES a long, slender cigar

STOIC   *n* pl. -S one who is indifferent to pleasure or pain **STOICAL** *adj*

STOICISM   *n* pl. -S indifference to pleasure or pain

STOKE   *v* STOKED, STOKING, STOKES to supply a furnace with fuel

STOKER   *n* pl. -S one that stokes

STOKESIA   *n* pl. -S a perennial herb

STOKING   present participle of stoke

STOLE   *n* pl. -S a long-wide scarf **STOLED** *adj*

STOLEN   past participle of steal

STOLID   *adj* -IDER, -IDEST showing little or no emotion **STOLIDLY** *adv*

STOLLEN   *n* pl. -S a sweet bread

STOLON   *n* pl. -S a type of plant stem **STOLONIC** *adj*

STOMA   *n* pl. -MAS or -MATA a minute opening in the epidermis of a plant organ

STOMACH   *v* -ED, -ING, -S to tolerate

STOMACHY   *adj* paunchy

STOMAL   *adj* stomatal

STOMATA   a pl. of stoma

STOMATAL   *adj* pertaining to a stoma

STOMATE   *n* pl. -S a stoma

STOMATIC   *adj* pertaining to the mouth

STOMODEA   *n/pl* embryonic oral cavities

STOMP   *v* -ED, -ING, -S to tread heavily

STOMPER   *n* pl. -S one that stomps

STONE   *v* STONED, STONING, STONES to pelt with stones (pieces of concreted earthy or mineral matter) **STONABLE** *adj*

STONEFLY   *n* pl. -FLIES a winged insect

STONER   *n* pl. -S one that stones

STONEY   *adj* STONIER, STONIEST stony

STONIER   comparative of stony

STONIEST   superlative of stony

STONILY   *adv* in a stony manner

STONING   present participle of stone

STONISH   *v* -ED, -ING, -ES to astonish

STONY   *adj* STONIER, STONIEST abounding in stones

STOOD   past tense of stand

STOOGE   *v* STOOGED, STOOGING, STOOGES to act as a comedian's straight man

STOOK   *v* -ED, -ING, -S to stack upright in a field for drying, as bundles of grain

STOOKER   *n* pl. -S one that stooks

STOOL   *v* -ED, -ING, -S to defecate

STOOLIE   *n* pl. -S an informer

STOOP   *v* -ED, -ING, -S to bend the body forward and down

STOOPER   *n* pl. -S one that stoops

STOP   *v* STOPPED or STOPT, STOPPING, STOPS to discontinue the progress or motion of

STOPCOCK	*n* pl. -S a type of faucet	**STOUTLY**	*adv* in a stout manner
STOPE	*v* STOPED, STOPING, STOPES to excavate in layers, as ore	**STOVE**	*n* pl. -S a heating apparatus
		STOVER	*n* pl. -S coarse food for cattle
STOPER	*n* pl. -S one that stopes	**STOW**	*v* -ED, -ING, -S to pack **STOWABLE** *adj*
STOPGAP	*n* pl. -S a temporary substitute		
STOPING	present participle of stope	**STOWAGE**	*n* pl. -S goods in storage
STOPOVER	*n* pl. -S a brief stop in the course of a journey	**STOWAWAY**	*n* pl. -AWAYS one who hides aboard a conveyance to obtain free passage
STOPPAGE	*n* pl. -S the act of stopping		
STOPPED	a past tense of stop	**STOWP**	*n* pl. -S stoup
STOPPER	*v* -ED, -ING, -S to plug	**STRADDLE**	*v* -DLED, -DLING, -DLES to sit, stand, or walk with the legs wide apart
STOPPING	present participle of stop		
STOPPLE	*v* -PLED, -PLING, -PLES to stopper		
		STRAFE	*v* STRAFED, STRAFING, STRAFES to attack with machine-gun fire from an airplane
STOPT	a past tense of stop		
STORABLE	*n* pl. -S something that can be stored		
STORAGE	*n* pl. -S a place for storing	**STRAFER**	*n* pl. -S one that strafes
STORAX	*n* pl. -ES a fragrant resin	**STRAGGLE**	*v* -GLED, -GLING, -GLES to stray
STORE	*v* STORED, STORING, STORES to put away for future use		
		STRAGGLY	*adj* -GLIER, -GLIEST irregularly spread out
STOREY	*n* pl. -REYS a horizontal division of a building **STOREYED** *adj*		
		STRAIGHT	*adj* STRAIGHTER, STRAIGHTEST extending uniformly in one direction without bends or irregularities
STORIED	past tense of story		
STORIES	present 3d person sing. of story		
		STRAIGHT	*v* -ED, -ING, -S to make straight
STORING	present participle of store	**STRAIN**	*v* -ED, -ING, -S to exert to the utmost
STORK	*n* pl. -S a wading bird		
STORM	*v* -ED, -ING, -S to blow violently	**STRAINER**	*n* pl. -S a utensil used to separate liquids from solids
STORMY	*adj* STORMIER, STORMIEST storming **STORMILY** *adv*		
		STRAIT	*n* pl. -S a narrow waterway connecting two larger bodies of water
STORY	*v* -RIED, -RYING, -RIES to relate as a story (an account of an event or series of events)		
		STRAIT	*adj* STRAITER, STRAITEST narrow **STRAITLY** *adv*
STOSS	*adj* facing the direction from which a glacier moves	**STRAITEN**	*v* -ED, -ING, -S to make strait
STOTINKA	*n* pl. -KI a monetary unit of Bulgaria	**STRAKE**	*n* pl. -S a line of planking extending along a ship's hull **STRAKED** *adj*
STOUND	*v* -ED, -ING, -S to ache		
STOUP	*n* pl. -S a basin for holy water	**STRAMASH**	*n* pl. -ES an uproar
STOUR	*n* pl. -S dust	**STRAMONY**	*n* pl. -NIES a poisonous weed
STOURE	*n* pl. -S stour	**STRAND**	*v* -ED, -ING, -S to leave in an unfavorable situation
STOURIE	*adj* stoury		
STOURY	*adj* dusty	**STRANDER**	*n* pl. -S a machine that twists fibers into rope
STOUT	*adj* STOUTER, STOUTEST fat		
STOUT	*n* pl. -S a strong, dark ale	**STRANG**	*adj* strong
STOUTEN	*v* -ED, -ING, -S to make stout	**STRANGE**	*adj* STRANGER, STRANGEST unusual or unfamiliar
STOUTISH	*adj* somewhat stout	**STRANGER**	*v* -ED, -ING, -S to estrange
		STRANGLE	*v* -GLED, -GLING, -GLES to choke to death

STRAP   v STRAPPED, STRAPPING, STRAPS to fasten with a strap (a narrow strip of flexible material)

STRAPPER   n pl. -S one that straps

STRASS   n pl. -ES a brilliant glass used in making imitation gems

STRATA   n pl. a stratum

STRATAL   adj pertaining to a stratum

STRATEGY   n pl. -GIES a plan for obtaining a specific goal

STRATH   n pl. -S a wide river valley

STRATI   pl. of stratus

STRATIFY   v -FIED, -FYING, -FIES to form or arrange in layers

STRATOUS   adj stratal

STRATUM   n pl. -TA or -TUMS a layer of material

STRATUS   n pl. -TI a type of cloud

STRAVAGE   v -VAGED, -VAGING, -VAGES to stroll

STRAVAIG   v -ED, -ING, -S to stravage

STRAW   v -ED, -ING, -S to cover with straw (stalks of threshed grain)

STRAWHAT   adj pertaining to a summer theater situated in a resort area

STRAWY   adj STRAWIER, STRAWIEST resembling straw

STRAY   v -ED, -ING, -S to wander from the proper area or course

STRAYER   n pl. -S one that strays

STREAK   v -ED, -ING, -S to cover with streaks (long, narrow marks)

STREAKER   n pl. -S one that streaks

STREAKY   adj STREAKIER, STREAKIEST covered with streaks

STREAM   v -ED, -ING, -S to flow in a steady current

STREAMER   n pl. -S a long, narrow flag

STREAMY   adj STREAMIER, STREAMIEST streaming

STREEK   v -ED, -ING, -S to stretch

STREEKER   n pl. -S one that streeks

STREET   n pl. -S a public thoroughfare

STRENGTH   n pl. -S capacity for exertion or endurance

STREP   n pl. -S any of various spherical or oval bacteria

STRESS   v -ED, -ING, -ES to place emphasis on

STRESSOR   n pl. -S a type of stimulus

STRETCH   v -ED, -ING, -ES to draw out or open to full length

STRETCHY   adj STRETCHIER, STRETCHIEST having a tendency to stretch

STRETTA   n pl. -TE or -TAS stretto

STRETTO   n pl. -TI or -TOS a concluding musical passage played at a faster tempo

STREUSEL   n pl. -S a topping for coffee cakes

STREW   v STREWED, STREWN, STREWING, STREWS to scatter about

STREWER   n pl. -S one that strews

STRIA   n pl. STRIAE a thin groove, stripe, or streak

STRIATE   v -ATED, -ATING, -ATES to mark with striae

STRICK   n pl. -S a bunch of flax fibers

STRICKEN   adj strongly affected or afflicted

STRICKLE   v -LED, -LING, -LES to shape or smooth with a strickle (an instrument for leveling off grain)

STRICT   adj STRICTER, STRICTEST kept within narrow and specific limits **STRICTLY** adv

STRIDE   v STRODE or STRID, STRIDDEN, STRIDING, STRIDES to walk with long steps

STRIDENT   adj shrill

STRIDER   n pl. -S one that strides

STRIDING   present participle of stride

STRIDOR   n pl. -S a strident sound

STRIFE   n pl. -S bitter conflict or dissension

STRIGIL   n pl. -S a scraping instrument

STRIGOSE   adj covered with short, stiff hairs

STRIKE   v STRUCK or STROOK, STRICKEN or STRUCKEN, STRIKING, STRIKES to come or cause to come into contact with

STRIKER   n pl. -S one that strikes

STRING   v STRUNG or STRINGED, STRINGING, STRINGS to provide with strings (slender cords)

STRINGER   n pl. -S one that strings

STRINGY   adj STRINGIER, STRINGIEST resembling a string or strings

STRIP *v* STRIPPED or STRIPT, STRIPPING, STRIPS to remove the outer covering from

STRIPE *v* STRIPED, STRIPING, STRIPES to mark with stripes (long, distinct bands)

STRIPER *n pl.* -S a food and game fish

STRIPIER comparative of stripy

STRIPIEST superlative of stripy

STRIPING *n pl.* -S the stripes marked or painted on something

STRIPPED a past tense of strip

STRIPPER *n pl.* -S one that strips

STRIPPING present participle of strip

STRIPT a past tense of strip

STRIPY *adj* STRIPIER, STRIPIEST marked with stripes

STRIVE *v* STROVE or STRIVED, STRIVEN, STRIVING, STRIVES to exert much effort or energy

STRIVER *n pl.* -S one that strives

STROBE *n pl.* -S a device that produces brief, high-intensity flashes of light

STROBIC *adj* spinning

STROBIL *n pl.* -S strobile

STROBILA *n pl.* -LAE the entire body of a tapeworm

STROBILE *n pl.* -S the conical, multiple fruit of certain trees

STROBILI *n/pl* strobiles

STRODE a past tense of stride

STROKE *v* STROKED, STROKING, STROKES to rub gently

STROKER *n pl.* -S one that strokes

STROLL *v* -ED, -ING, -S to walk in a leisurely manner

STROLLER *n pl.* -S one that strolls

STROMA *n pl.* -MATA the substance that forms the framework of an organ or cell **STROMAL** *adj*

STRONG *adj* STRONGER, STRONGEST having great strength **STRONGLY** *adv*

STRONGYL *n pl.* -S a parasitic worm

STRONTIA *n pl.* -S a chemical compound **STRONTIC** *adj*

STROOK a past tense of strike

STROP *v* STROPPED, STROPPING, STROPS to sharpen on a strip of leather

STROPHE *n pl.* -S a part of an ancient Greek choral ode **STROPHIC** *adj*

STROUD *n pl.* -S a coarse woolen blanket

STROVE a past tense of strive

STROW *v* STROWED, STROWN, STROWING, STROWS to strew

STROY *v* -ED, -ING, -S to destroy

STROYER *n pl.* -S one that stroys

STRUCK a past tense of strike

STRUCKEN a past participle of strike

STRUDEL *n pl.* -S a type of pastry

STRUGGLE *v* -GLED, -GLING, -GLES to make strenuous efforts against opposition

STRUM *v* STRUMMED, STRUMMING, STRUMS to play a stringed instrument by running the fingers lightly across the strings

STRUMA *n pl.* -MAE or -MAS scrofula

STRUMMER *n pl.* -S one that strums

STRUMMING present participle of strum

STRUMOSE *adj* having a struma

STRUMOUS *adj* having or pertaining to a struma

STRUMPET *n pl.* -S a prostitute

STRUNG a past tense of string

STRUNT *v* -ED, -ING, -S to strut

STRUT *v* STRUTTED, STRUTTING, STRUTS to walk with a pompous air

STRUTTER *n pl.* -S one that struts

STUB *v* STUBBED, STUBBING, STUBS to strike accidentally against a projecting object

STUBBIER comparative of stubby

STUBBIEST superlative of stubby

STUBBILY *adv* in a stubby manner

STUBBING present participle of stub

STUBBLE *n pl.* -S a short, rough growth of beard **STUBBLED** *adj*

STUBBLY *adj* -BLIER, -BLIEST covered with stubble

STUBBORN *adj* unyielding

STUBBY *adj* -BIER, -BIEST short and thick

STUCCO *v* -ED, -ING, -ES or -S to coat with a type of plaster

STUCCOER *n pl.* -S one that stuccoes

STUCK past tense of stick

STUD v STUDDED, STUDDING, STUDS to set thickly with small projections

STUDBOOK n pl. -S a record of the pedigree of purebred animals

STUDDIE n pl. -S an anvil

STUDDING n pl. -S the framework of a wall

STUDENT n pl. -S a person formally engaged in learning

STUDFISH n pl. -ES a freshwater fish

STUDIED past tense of study

STUDIER n pl. -S one that studies

STUDIES present 3d person sing. of study

STUDIO n pl. -DIOS an artist's workroom

STUDIOUS adj given to study

STUDWORK n pl. -S studding

STUDY v STUDIED, STUDYING, STUDIES to apply the mind to the acquisition of knowledge

STUFF v -ED, -ING, -S to fill or pack tightly

STUFFER n pl. -S one that stuffs

STUFFING n pl. -S material with which something is stuffed

STUFFY adj STUFFIER, STUFFIEST poorly ventilated **STUFFILY** adv

STUIVER n pl. -S stiver

STULL n pl. -S a supporting timber in a mine

STULTIFY v -FIED, -FYING, -FIES to cause to appear absurd

STUM v STUMMED, STUMMING, STUMS to increase the fermentation of by adding grape juice

STUMBLE v -BLED, -BLING, -BLES to miss one's step in walking or running

STUMBLER n pl. -S one that stumbles

STUMMED past tense of stum

STUMMING present participle of stum

STUMP v -ED, -ING, -S to baffle

STUMPAGE n pl. -S uncut marketable timber

STUMPER n pl. -S a baffling question

STUMPY adj STUMPIER, STUMPIEST short and thick

STUN v STUNNED, STUNNING, STUNS to render senseless or incapable of action

STUNG past tense of sting

STUNK a past tense of stink

STUNNED past tense of stun

STUNNER n pl. -S one that stuns

STUNNING adj strikingly beautiful or attractive

STUNSAIL n pl. -S a type of sail

STUNT v -ED, -ING, -S to hinder the normal growth of

STUPA n pl. -S a Buddhist shrine

STUPE n pl. -S a medicated cloth to be applied to a wound

STUPEFY v -FIED, -FYING, -FIES to dull the senses of

STUPID adj -PIDER, -PIDEST mentally slow **STUPIDLY** adv

STUPID n pl. -S a stupid person

STUPOR n pl. -S a state of reduced sensibility

STURDY adj -DIER, -DIEST strong and durable **STURDILY** adv

STURDY n pl. -DIES a disease of sheep **STURDIED** adj

STURGEON n pl. -S an edible fish

STURT n pl. -S contention

STUTTER v -ED, -ING, -S to speak with spasmodic repetition

STY v STIED or STYED, STYING, STIES to keep in a pigpen

STYE n pl. -S an inflamed swelling of the eyelid

STYGIAN adj gloomy

STYLAR adj pertaining to a stylus

STYLATE adj bearing a stylet

STYLE v STYLED, STYLING, STYLES to name

STYLER n pl. -S one that styles

STYLET n pl. -S a small, stiff organ or appendage of certain animals

STYLI a pl. of stylus

STYLING n pl. -S the way in which something is styled

STYLISE v -ISED, -ISING, -ISES to stylize

STYLISER n pl. -S one that stylises

STYLISH adj fashionable

STYLISING present participle of stylise

STYLIST n pl. -S one who is a master of a literary or rhetorical style

STYLITE n pl. -S an early Christian ascetic **STYLITIC** adj

STYLIZE   *v* -IZED, -IZING, -IZES to make conventional

STYLIZER   *n pl.* -S one that stylizes

STYLOID   *adj* slender and pointed

STYLUS   *n pl.* -LI or -LUSES a pointed instrument for writing, marking, or engraving

STYMIE   *v* -MIED, -MIEING, -MIES to thwart

STYMY   *v* -MIED, -MYING, -MIES to stymie

STYPSIS   *n pl.* -SISES the use of a styptic

STYPTIC   *n pl.* -S a substance used to check bleeding

STYRAX   *n pl.* -ES storax

STYRENE   *n pl.* -S a liquid hydrocarbon

SUABLE   *adj* capable of being sued SUABLY *adv*

SUASION   *n pl.* -S persuasion SUASIVE, SUASORY *adj*

SUAVE   *adj* SUAVER, SUAVEST smoothly affable and polite SUAVELY *adv*

SUAVITY   *n pl.* -TIES the state of being suave

SUB   *v* SUBBED, SUBBING, SUBS to act as a substitute

SUBA   *n pl.* -S subah

SUBABBOT   *n pl.* -S a subordinate abbot

SUBACID   *adj* slightly sour

SUBACRID   *adj* somewhat acrid

SUBACUTE   *adj* somewhat acute

SUBADAR   *n pl.* -S subahdar

SUBADULT   *n pl.* -S an individual approaching adulthood

SUBAGENT   *n pl.* -S a subordinate agent

SUBAH   *n pl.* -S a province of India

SUBAHDAR   *n pl.* -S a governor of a subah

SUBALAR   *adj* somewhat alar

SUBAREA   *n pl.* -S a subdivision of an area

SUBARID   *adj* somewhat arid

SUBATOM   *n pl.* -S a component of an atom

SUBAXIAL   *adj* somewhat axial

SUBBASE   *n pl.* -S the lowest part of a base

SUBBASS   *n pl.* -ES a pedal stop producing the lowest tones of an organ

SUBBED   past tense of sub

SUBBING   *n pl.* -S a thin coating on the support of a photographic film

SUBBREED   *n pl.* -S a distinguishable strain within a breed

SUBCAUSE   *n pl.* -S a subordinate cause

SUBCELL   *n pl.* -S a subdivision of a cell

SUBCHIEF   *n pl.* -S a subordinate chief

SUBCLAN   *n pl.* -S a subdivision of a clan

SUBCLASS   *v* -ED, -ING, -ES to place in a subdivision of a class

SUBCLERK   *n pl.* -S a subordinate clerk

SUBCOOL   *v* -ED, -ING, -S to cool below the freezing point without solidification

SUBCUTIS   *n pl.* -CUTES or -CUTISES the deeper part of the dermis

SUBDEAN   *n pl.* -S a subordinate dean

SUBDEB   *n pl.* -S a girl the year before she becomes a debutante

SUBDEPOT   *n pl.* -S a military depot that operates under the jurisdiction of another depot

SUBDUAL   *n pl.* -S the act of subduing

SUBDUCE   *v* -DUCED, -DUCING, -DUCES to take away

SUBDUCT   *v* -ED, -ING, -S to subduce

SUBDUE   *v* -DUED, -DUING, -DUES to bring under control

SUBDUER   *n pl.* -S one that subdues

SUBECHO   *n pl.* -ECHOES an inferior echo

SUBEDIT   *v* -ED, -ING, -S to act as the assistant editor of

SUBENTRY   *n pl.* -TRIES an entry made under a more general entry

SUBEPOCH   *n pl.* -S a subdivision of an epoch

SUBER   *n pl.* -S phellem

SUBERECT   *adj* nearly erect

SUBERIC   *adj* pertaining to cork

SUBERIN   *n pl.* -S a substance found in cork cells

SUBERISE   *v* -ISED, -ISING, -ISES to suberize

SUBERIZE   *v* -IZED, -IZING, -IZES to convert into cork tissue

SUBEROSE   *adj* corky

SUBEROUS   *adj* suberose

SUBFIELD   *n pl.* -S a subset of a mathematical field that is itself a field

SUBFIX   *n* pl. -ES a distinguishing symbol or letter written below another character

SUBFLOOR   *n* pl. -S a rough floor laid as a base for a finished floor

SUBFLUID   *adj* somewhat fluid

SUBFUSC   *adj* dark in color

SUBGENUS   *n* pl. -GENERA or -GENUSES a subdivision of a genus

SUBGRADE   *n* pl. -S a surface on which a pavement is placed

SUBGROUP   *n* pl. -S a distinct group within a group

SUBGUM   *adj* prepared with mixed vegetables

SUBHEAD   *n* pl. -S the heading of a subdivision

SUBHUMAN   *n* pl. -S one that is less than human

SUBHUMID   *adj* somewhat humid

SUBIDEA   *n* pl. -S an inferior idea

SUBINDEX   *n* pl. -DEXES or -DICES a subfix

SUBITEM   *n* pl. -S an item that forms a subdivision of a larger topic

SUBITO   *adv* quickly — used as a musical direction

SUBJECT   *v* -ED, -ING, -S to cause to experience

SUBJOIN   *v* -ED, -ING, -S to add at the end

SUBLATE   *v* -LATED, -LATING, -LATES to cancel

SUBLEASE   *v* -LEASED, -LEASING, -LEASES to sublet

SUBLET   *v* -LET, -LETTING, -LETS to rent leased property to another

SUBLEVEL   *n* pl. -S a lower level

SUBLIME   *adj* -LIMER, -LIMEST of elevated or noble quality

SUBLIME   *v* -LIMED, -LIMING, -LIMES to make sublime

SUBLIMER   *n* pl. -S one that sublimes

SUBLIMEST   superlative of sublime

SUBLIMING   present participle of sublime

SUBMERGE   *v* -MERGED, -MERGING, -MERGES to place below the surface of a liquid

SUBMERSE   *v* -MERSED, -MERSING, -MERSES to submerge

SUBMISS   *adj* inclined to submit

SUBMIT   *v* -MITTED, -MITTING, -MITS to yield to the power of another

SUBNASAL   *adj* situated under the nose

SUBNODAL   *adj* situated under a node

SUBOPTIC   *adj* situated under the eyes

SUBORAL   *adj* situated under the mouth

SUBORDER   *n* pl. -S a category of related families within an order

SUBORN   *v* -ED, -ING, -S to induce to commit perjury

SUBORNER   *n* pl. -S one that suborns

SUBOVAL   *adj* nearly oval

SUBOVATE   *adj* nearly ovate

SUBOXIDE   *n* pl. -S an oxide containing relatively little oxygen

SUBPAR   *adj* below par

SUBPART   *n* pl. -S a subdivision of a part

SUBPENA   *v* -ED, -ING, -S to subpoena

SUBPHYLA   *n/pl* divisions within a phylum

SUBPLOT   *n* pl. -S a secondary literary plot

SUBPOENA   *v* -ED, -ING, -S to summon with a type of judicial writ

SUBPOLAR   *adj* situated just outside the polar circles

SUBPUBIC   *adj* situated under the pubis

SUBRACE   *n* pl. -S a subdivision of a race

SUBRENT   *n* pl. -S rent from a subtenant

SUBRING   *n* pl. -S a subset of a mathematical ring that is itself a ring

SUBRULE   *n* pl. -S a subordinate rule

SUBSALE   *n* pl. -S a resale of purchased goods

SUBSECT   *n* pl. -S a sect directly derived from another

SUBSERE   *n* pl. -S a type of ecological succession

SUBSERVE   *v* -SERVED, -SERVING, -SERVES to serve to promote

SUBSET   *n* pl. -S a mathematical set contained within a larger set

SUBSHAFT   *n* pl. -S a shaft that is beneath another shaft

SUBSHRUB   *n* pl. -S a low shrub

SUBSIDE   *v* -SIDED, -SIDING, -SIDES to sink to a lower or normal level

SUBSIDER   *n* pl. -S one that subsides

SUBSIDY   *n* pl. -DIES a grant or contribution of money

SUBSIST   v -ED, -ING, -S to continue to exist

SUBSOIL   v -ED, -ING, -S to plow so as to turn up the subsoil (the layer of earth beneath the surface soil)

SUBSOLAR   adj situated directly beneath the sun

SUBSONIC   adj moving at a speed less than that of sound

SUBSPACE   n pl. -S a subset of a mathematical space

SUBSTAGE   n pl. -S a part of a microscope for supporting accessories

SUBSUME   v -SUMED, -SUMING, -SUMES to classify within a larger category

SUBTEEN   n pl. -S a person approaching the teenage years

SUBTEND   v -ED, -ING, -S to extend under or opposite to

SUBTEXT   n pl. -S written or printed matter under a more general text

SUBTILE   adj -TILER, -TILEST subtle

SUBTILTY   n pl. -TIES subtlety

SUBTITLE   v -TLED, -TLING, -TLES to give a secondary title to

SUBTLE   adj -TLER, -TLEST so slight as to be difficult to detect **SUBTLY** adj

SUBTLETY   n pl. -TIES the state of being subtle

SUBTONE   n pl. -S a low or subdued tone

SUBTONIC   n pl. -S a type of musical tone

SUBTOPIC   n pl. -S a secondary topic

SUBTOTAL   v -TALED, -TALING, -TALS or -TALLED, -TALLING, -TALS to total a portion of

SUBTRACT   v -ED, -ING, -S to take away

SUBTRIBE   n pl. -S a subdivision of a tribe

SUBTUNIC   n pl. -S a tunic worn under another tunic

SUBTYPE   n pl. -S a type that is subordinate to or included in another type

SUBULATE   adj slender and tapering to a point

SUBUNIT   n pl. -S a unit that is a part of a larger unit

SUBURB   n pl. -S a residential area adjacent to a city **SUBURBED** adj

SUBURBAN   n pl. -S one who lives in a suburb

SUBURBIA   n pl. -S the suburbs of a city

SUBVENE   v -VENED, -VENING, -VENES to arrive or occur as a support or relief

SUBVERT   v -ED, -ING, -S to destroy completely

SUBVICAR   n pl. -S a subordinate vicar

SUBVIRAL   adj pertaining to a part of a virus

SUBVOCAL   adj mentally formulated as words

SUBWAY   n pl. -WAYS an underground railroad

SUBZONE   n pl. -S a subdivision of a zone

SUCCAH   n pl. -CAHS or -COTH sukkah

SUCCEED   v -ED, -ING, -S to accomplish something desired or intended

SUCCESS   n pl. -ES the attainment of something desired or intended

SUCCINCT   adj -CINCTER, -CINCTEST clearly expressed in few words

SUCCINIC   adj pertaining to amber

SUCCINYL   n pl. -S a univalent radical

SUCCOR   v -ED, -ING, -S to go to the aid of

SUCCORER   n pl. -S one that succors

SUCCORY   n pl. -RIES chicory

SUCCOTH   a pl. of succah

SUCCOUR   v -ED, -ING, -S to succor

SUCCUBA   n pl. -BAE a succubus

SUCCUBUS   n pl. -BI or -BUSES a female demon

SUCCUMB   v -ED, -ING, -S to yield to superior force

SUCCUSS   v -ED, -ING, -ES to shake violently

SUCH   adj of that kind

SUCHLIKE   adj of a similar kind

SUCHNESS   n pl. -ES essential or characteristic quality

SUCK   v -ED, -ING, -S to draw in by establishing a partial vacuum

SUCKER   v -ED, -ING, -S to strip of lower shoots or branches

SUCKFISH   n pl. -ES a remora

SUCKLE   v -LED, -LING, -LES to give milk to from the breast

SUCKLER   n pl. -S one that suckles

SUCKLESS   adj having no juice

SUCKLING   *n* pl. -S a young mammal that has not been weaned

SUCRASE   *n* pl. -S an enzyme

SUCRE   *n* pl. -S a monetary unit of Ecuador

SUCROSE   *n* pl. -S a type of sugar

SUCTION   *n* pl. -S the act of sucking

SUDARIUM   *n* pl. -IA a cloth for wiping the face

SUDARY   *n* pl. -RIES sudarium

SUDATION   *n* pl. -S excessive sweating

SUDATORY   *n* pl. -RIES a hot-air bath for inducing sweating

SUDD   *n* pl. -S a floating mass of vegetation

SUDDEN   *adj* happening quickly and without warning **SUDDENLY** *adv*

SUDDEN   *n* pl. -S a sudden occurrence

SUDOR   *n* pl. -S sweat **SUDORAL** *adj*

SUDS   *v* -ED, -ING, -ES to wash in soapy water

SUDSER   *n* pl. -S one that sudses

SUDSLESS   *adj* having no suds

SUDSY   *adj* SUDSIER, SUDSIEST foamy

SUE   *v* SUED, SUING, SUES to institute legal proceedings against

SUEDE   *v* SUEDED, SUEDING, SUEDES to finish leather with a soft, napped surface

SUER   *n* pl. -S one that sues

SUET   *n* pl. -S the hard, fatty tissue around the kidneys of cattle and sheep **SUETY** *adj*

SUFFARI   *n* pl. -S a safari

SUFFER   *v* -ED, -ING, -S to feel pain or distress

SUFFERER   *n* pl. -S one that suffers

SUFFICE   *v* -FICED, -FICING, -FICES to be adequate

SUFFICER   *n* pl. -S one that suffices

SUFFIX   *v* -ED, -ING, -ES to add as a suffix (a form affixed to the end of a root word)

SUFFIXAL   *adj* pertaining to or being a suffix

SUFFLATE   *v* -FLATED, -FLATING, -FLATES to inflate

SUFFRAGE   *n* pl. -S the right to vote

SUFFUSE   *v* -FUSED, -FUSING, -FUSES to spread through or over

SUGAR   *v* -ED, -ING, -S to cover with sugar (a sweet carbohydrate)

SUGARY   *adj* -ARIER, -ARIEST containing or resembling sugar

SUGGEST   *v* -ED, -ING, -S to bring or put forward for consideration

SUGH   *v* -ED, -ING, -S to sough

SUICIDAL   *adj* self-destructive

SUICIDE   *v* -CIDED, -CIDING, -CIDES to kill oneself intentionally

SUING   present participle of sue

SUINT   *n* pl. -S a natural grease found in the wool of sheep

SUIT   *v* -ED, -ING, -S to be appropriate to

SUITABLE   *adj* appropriate **SUITABLY** *adv*

SUITCASE   *n* pl. -S a flat, rectangular piece of luggage

SUITE   *n* pl. -S a series of things forming a unit

SUITING   *n* pl. -S fabric for making suits

SUITLIKE   *adj* resembling a suit (a set of garments)

SUITOR   *n* pl. -S one that is courting a woman

SUKIYAKI   *n* pl. -S a Japanese dish

SUKKAH   *n* pl. -KAHS or -KOTH a temporary shelter in which meals are eaten during a Jewish festival

SULCATE   *adj* having long, narrow furrows

SULCATED   *adj* sulcate

SULCUS   *n* pl. -CI furrow

SULDAN   *n* pl. -S soldan

SULFA   *n* pl. -S a bacteria-inhibiting drug

SULFATE   *v* -FATED, -FATING, -FATES to treat with sulfuric acid

SULFID   *n* pl. -S sulfide

SULFIDE   *n* pl. -S a sulfur compound

SULFINYL   *n* pl. -S a bivalent radical

SULFITE   *n* pl. -S a chemical salt **SULFITIC** *adj*

SULFO   *adj* sulfonic

SULFONAL   *n* pl. -S a sulfone used as a sedative

SULFONE   *n* pl. -S a sulfur compound

SULFONIC   *adj* containing a certain univalent radical

SULFONYL   *n* pl. -S a bivalent radical

SULFUR *v* -ED, -ING, -S to treat with sulfur (a nonmetallic element)

SULFURET *v* -RETED, -RETING, -RETS or -RETTED, -RETTING, -RETS to treat with sulfur

SULFURIC *adj* pertaining to sulfur

SULFURY *adj* resembling sulfur

SULFURYL *n* pl. -S sulfonyl

SULK *v* -ED, -ING, -S to be sulky

SULKER *n* pl. -S one that sulks

SULKY *adj* SULKIER, SULKIEST sullenly aloof or withdrawn **SULKILY** *adv*

SULKY *n* pl. SULKIES a light horse-drawn vehicle

SULLAGE *n* pl. -S sewage

SULLEN *adj* -LENER, -LENEST showing a brooding ill humor or resentment **SULLENLY** *adv*

SULLY *v* -LIED, -LYING, -LIES to soil

SULPHA *n* pl. -S sulfa

SULPHATE *v* -PHATED, -PHATING, -PHATES to sulfate

SULPHID *n* pl. -S sulfide

SULPHIDE *n* pl. -S sulfide

SULPHITE *n* pl. -S sulfite

SULPHONE *n* pl. -S sulfone

SULPHUR *v* -ED, -ING, -S to sulfur

SULPHURY *adj* sulfury

SULTAN *n* pl. -S the ruler of a Muslim country **SULTANIC** *adj*

SULTANA *n* pl. -S a sultan's wife

SULTRY *adj* -TRIER, -TRIEST very hot and humid **SULTRILY** *adv*

SUM *v* SUMMED, SUMMING, SUMS to add into one total

SUMAC *n* pl. -S a flowering tree or shrub

SUMACH *n* pl. -S sumac

SUMLESS *adj* too large for calculation

SUMMA *n* pl. -MAE or -MAS a comprehensive work covering a specific subject

SUMMABLE *adj* capable of being summed

SUMMAND *n* pl. -S an addend

SUMMARY *n* pl. -RIES a condensation of the substance of a larger work

SUMMATE *v* -MATED, -MATING, -MATES to sum

SUMMED past tense of sum

SUMMER *v* -ED, -ING, -S to pass the summer (the warmest season of the year)

SUMMERLY *adj* summery

SUMMERY *adj* -MERIER, -MERIEST characteristic of summer

SUMMING present participle of sum

SUMMIT *n* pl. -S the highest point **SUMMITAL** *adj*

SUMMITRY *n* pl. -RIES the use of conferences between chiefs of state for international negotiation

SUMMON *v* -ED, -ING, -S to order to appear

SUMMONER *n* pl. -S one that summons

SUMMONS *v* -ED, -ING, -ES to summon with a court order

SUMO *n* pl. -MOS a Japanese form of wrestling

SUMP *n* pl. -S a low area serving as a drain or receptacle for liquids

SUMPTER *n* pl. -S a pack animal

SUMPWEED *n* pl. -S a marsh plant

SUN *v* SUNNED, SUNNING, SUNS to expose to the sun (the star around which the earth revolves)

SUNBACK *adj* cut low to expose the back to sunlight

SUNBAKED *adj* baked by the sun

SUNBATH *n* pl. -S an exposure to sunlight

SUNBATHE *v* -BATHED, -BATHING, -BATHES to take a sunbath

SUNBEAM *n* pl. -S a beam of sunlight

SUNBIRD *n* pl. -S a tropical bird

SUNBOW *n* pl. -S an arc of spectral colors formed by the sun shining through a mist

SUNBURN *v* -BURNED or -BURNT, -BURNING, -BURNS to burn or discolor from exposure to the sun

SUNBURST *n* pl. -S a burst of sunlight

SUNDAE *n* pl. -S a dish of ice cream served with a topping

SUNDER *v* -ED, -ING, -S to break apart

SUNDERER *n* pl. -S one that sunders

SUNDEW *n* pl. -S a marsh plant

SUNDIAL *n* pl. -S a type of time-telling device

SUNDOG *n* pl. -S a small rainbow

SUNDOWN   n pl. -S sunset

SUNDRIES   n/pl miscellaneous items

SUNDROPS   n pl. SUNDROPS a flowering plant

SUNDRY   adj miscellaneous

SUNFAST   adj resistant to fading by the sun

SUNFISH   n pl. -ES a marine fish

SUNG   past participle of sing

SUNGLASS   n pl. -ES a lens for concentrating the sun's rays in order to produce heat

SUNGLOW   n pl. -S a glow in the sky caused by the sun

SUNK   a past participle of sink

SUNKEN   a past participle of sink

SUNKET   n pl. -S a tidbit

SUNLAMP   n pl. -S a lamp that radiates ultraviolet rays

SUNLAND   n pl. -S an area marked by a great amount of sunshine

SUNLESS   adj having no sunlight

SUNLIGHT   n pl. -S the light of the sun

SUNLIKE   adj resembling the sun

SUNLIT   adj lighted by the sun

SUNN   n pl. -S an East Indian shrub

SUNNA   n pl. -S the body of traditional Muslim law

SUNNED   past tense of sun

SUNNING   present participle of sun

SUNNY   adj -NIER, -NIEST filled with sunlight **SUNNILY** adv

SUNRISE   n pl. -S the ascent of the sun above the horizon in the morning

SUNROOF   n pl. -S an automobile roof having an openable panel

SUNROOM   n pl. -S a room built to admit a great amount of sunlight

SUNSCALD   n pl. -S an injury of woody plants caused by the sun

SUNSET   n pl. -S the descent of the sun below the horizon in the evening

SUNSHADE   n pl. -S something used as a protection from the sun

SUNSHINE   n pl. -S the light of the sun **SUNSHINY** adj

SUNSPOT   n pl. -S a dark spot on the surface of the sun

SUNSTONE   n pl. -S a variety of quartz

SUNSUIT   n pl. -S an outfit worn for sunbathing

SUNTAN   n pl. -S a brown color on the skin produced by exposure to the sun

SUNUP   n pl. -S sunrise

SUNWARD   adv toward the sun

SUNWARDS   adv sunward

SUNWISE   adv from left to right

SUP   v SUPPED, SUPPING, SUPS to eat supper

SUPE   n pl. -S an actor without a speaking part

SUPER   v -ED, -ING, -S to reinforce with a thin cotton mesh, as a book

SUPERADD   n pl. -ED, -ING, -S to add further

SUPERB   adj -PERBER, -PERBEST of excellent quality **SUPERBLY** adv

SUPEREGO   n pl. -EGOS a part of the psyche

SUPERFIX   n. pl. -ES a recurrent pattern of stress in speech

SUPERIOR   n pl. -S one of higher rank, quality, or authority than another

SUPERJET   n pl. -S a type of jet airplane

SUPERLIE   v -LAY, -LAIN, -LYING, -LIES to lie above

SUPERMAN   n pl. -MEN a hypothetical superior man

SUPERNAL   adj pertaining to the sky

SUPERSEX   n pl. -ES a type of sterile organism

SUPERTAX   n pl. -ES an additional tax

SUPINATE   v -NATED, -NATING, -NATES to turn so that the palm is facing upward

SUPINE   n pl. -S a Latin verbal noun

SUPINELY   adv in an inactive manner

SUPPED   past tense of sup

SUPPER   n pl. -S an evening meal

SUPPING   present participle of sup

SUPPLANT   v -ED, -ING, -S to take the place of

SUPPLE   adj -PLER, -PLEST pliant **SUPPLELY** adv

SUPPLE   v -PLED, -PLING, -PLES to make supple

SUPPLIER   n pl. -S one that supplies

SUPPLY   v -PLIED, -PLYING, -PLIES to furnish with what is needed

SUPPORT *v* -ED, -ING, -S to hold up or add strength to

SUPPOSAL *n* pl. -S something supposed

SUPPOSE *v* -POSED, -POSING, -POSES to assume to be true

SUPPOSER *n* pl. -S one that supposes

SUPPRESS *v* -ED, -ING, -ES to put an end to forcibly

SUPRA *adv* above

SUPREME *adj* -PREMER, -PREMEST highest in power or authority

SURA *n* pl. -S a chapter of the Koran

SURAH *n* pl. -S a silk fabric

SURAL *adj* pertaining to the calf of the leg

SURBASE *n* pl. -S a molding or border above the base of a structure **SURBASED** *adj*

SURCEASE *v* -CEASED, -CEASING, -CEASES to cease

SURCOAT *n* pl. -S an outer coat or cloak

SURD *n* pl. -S a voiceless speech sound

SURE *adj* SURER, SUREST free from doubt

SUREFIRE *adj* sure to meet expectations

SURELY *adv* certainly

SURENESS *n* pl. -ES the state of being sure

SURER comparative of sure

SUREST superlative of sure

SURETY *n* pl. -TIES sureness

SURF *v* -ED, -ING, -S to ride breaking waves on a long, narrow board **SURFABLE** *adj*

SURFACE *v* -FACED, -FACING, -FACES to apply an outer layer to

SURFACER *n* pl. -S one that surfaces

SURFBIRD *n* pl. -S a shore bird

SURFBOAT *n* pl. -S a strong rowboat

SURFEIT *v* -ED, -ING, -S to supply to excess

SURFER *n* pl. -S one that surfs

SURFFISH *n* pl. -ES a marine fish

SURFIER comparative of surfy

SURFIEST superlative of surfy

SURFING *n* pl. -S the act or sport of riding the surf (breaking waves)

SURFLIKE *adj* resembling breaking waves

SURFY *adj* SURFIER, SURFIEST abounding in breaking waves

SURGE *v* SURGED, SURGING, SURGES to move in a swelling manner

SURGEON *n* pl. -S one who practices surgery

SURGER *n* pl. -S one that surges

SURGERY *n* pl. -GERIES the treatment of medical problems by operation

SURGICAL *adj* pertaining to surgery

SURGING present participle of surge

SURGY *adj* surging

SURICATE *n* pl. -S a burrowing mammal

SURLY *adj* -LIER, -LIEST sullenly rude **SURLILY** *adv*

SURMISE *v* -MISED, -MISING, -MISES to infer with little evidence

SURMISER *n* pl. -S one that surmises

SURMOUNT *v* -ED, -ING, -S to get over or across

SURNAME *v* -NAMED, -NAMING, -NAMES to give a family name to

SURNAMER *n* pl. -S one that surnames

SURPASS *v* -ED, -ING, -ES to go beyond

SURPLICE *n* pl. -S a loose-fitting vestment

SURPLUS *n* pl. -ES an excess

SURPRINT *v* -ED, -ING, -S to print over something already printed

SURPRISE *v* -PRISED, -PRISING, -PRISES to come upon suddenly and unexpectedly

SURPRIZE *v* -PRIZED, -PRIZING, -PRIZES to surprise

SURRA *n* pl. -S a disease of domestic animals

SURREAL *adj* having dreamlike qualities

SURREY *n* pl. -REYS a light carriage

SURROUND *v* -ED, -ING, -S to extend completely around

SURROYAL *n* pl. -S the topmost prong of a stag's antler

SURTAX *v* -ED, -ING, -ES to assess with an extra tax

SURTOUT *n* pl. -S a close-fitting overcoat

SURVEIL *v* -ED, -ING, -S to watch closely

SURVEY *v* -ED, -ING, -S to determine the boundaries, area, or elevations of by measuring angles and distances

SURVEYOR *n* pl. -S one that surveys land

SURVIVAL   *n* pl. -S a living or continuing longer than another person or thing

SURVIVE   *v* -VIVED, -VIVING, -VIVES to remain in existence

SURVIVER   *n* pl. -S survivor

SURVIVOR   *n* pl. -S one that survives

SUSLIK   *n* pl. -S a Eurasian rodent

SUSPECT   *v* -ED, -ING, -S to think guilty on slight evidence

SUSPEND   *v* -ED, -ING, -S to cause to stop for a period

SUSPENSE   *n* pl. -S a state of mental uncertainty or excitement

SUSPIRE   *v* -PIRED, -PIRING, -PIRES to sigh

SUSTAIN   *v* -ED, -ING, -S to maintain by providing with food and drink

SUSURRUS   *n* pl. -ES a soft rustling sound

SUTLER   *n* pl. -S one that peddles goods to soldiers

SUTRA   *n* pl. -S a Hindu aphorism

SUTTA   *n* pl. -S sutra

SUTTEE   *n* pl. -S a Hindu widow cremated on her husband's funeral pile to show her devotion to him

SUTURAL   *adj* pertaining to the line of junction between two bones

SUTURE   *v* -TURED, -TURING, -TURES to unite by sewing

SUZERAIN   *n* pl. -S a feudal lord

SVARAJ   *n* pl. -ES swaraj

SVEDBERG   *n* pl. -S a unit of time

SVELTE   *adj* SVELTER, SVELTEST gracefully slender **SVELTELY** *adv*

SWAB   *v* SWABBED, SWABBING, SWABS to clean with a large mop

SWABBER   *n* pl. -S one that swabs

SWABBIE   *n* pl. -S a sailor

SWABBING   present participle of swab

SWABBY   *n* pl. -BIES swabbie

SWADDLE   *v* -DLED, -DLING, -DLES to wrap in bandages

SWAG   *v* SWAGGED, SWAGGING, SWAGS to sway

SWAGE   *v* SWAGED, SWAGING, SWAGES to shape with a hammering tool

SWAGER   *n* pl. -S one that swages

SWAGGED   past tense of swag

SWAGGER   *v* -ED, -ING, -S to walk with a pompous air

SWAGGING   present participle of swag

SWAGING   present participle of swage

SWAGMAN   *n* pl. -MEN a hobo

SWAIL   *n* pl. -S swale

SWAIN   *n* pl. -S a country boy **SWAINISH** *adj*

SWALE   *n* pl. -S a tract of low, marshy ground

SWALLOW   *v* -ED, -ING, -S to take through the mouth and esophagus into the stomach

SWAM   past tense of swim

SWAMI   *n* pl. -S a Hindu religious teacher

SWAMIES   pl. of swamy

SWAMP   *v* -ED, -ING, -S to inundate

SWAMPER   *n* pl. -S one that lives in a swampy area

SWAMPISH   *adj* swampy

SWAMPY   *adj* SWAMPIER, SWAMPIEST marshy

SWAMY   *n* pl. -MIES swami

SWAN   *v* SWANNED, SWANNING, SWANS to swear

SWANG   a past tense of swing

SWANHERD   *n* pl. -S one who tends swans (large aquatic birds)

SWANK   *adj* SWANKER, SWANKEST imposingly elegant

SWANK   *v* -ED, -ING, -S to swagger

SWANKY   *adj* SWANKIER, SWANKIEST swank **SWANKILY** *adv*

SWANLIKE   *adj* resembling a swan

SWANNED   past tense of swan

SWANNERY   *n* pl. -NERIES a place where swans are raised

SWANNING   present participle of swan

SWANPAN   *n* pl. -S a Chinese abacus

SWANSKIN   *n* pl. -S the skin of a swan

SWAP   *v* SWAPPED, SWAPPING, SWAPS to trade

SWAPPER   *n* pl. -S one that swaps

SWARAJ   *n* pl. -ES self-government in British India

SWARD   *v* -ED, -ING, -S to cover with turf

SWARE	a past tense of swear	**SWEEP**	v SWEPT, SWEEPING, SWEEPS to clear or clean with a brush or broom
SWARF	n pl. -S material removed by a cutting tool		
SWARM	v -ED, -ING, -S to move in a large group	**SWEEPER**	n pl. -S one that sweeps
		SWEEPING	n pl. -S the act of one that sweeps
SWARMER	n pl. -S one that swarms		
SWART	adj swarthy	**SWEEPY**	adj SWEEPIER, SWEEPIEST of wide range or scope
SWARTH	n pl. -S turf		
SWARTHY	adj -THIER, -THIEST having a dark complexion	**SWEER**	adj lazy
		SWEET	adj SWEETER, SWEETEST pleasing to the taste
SWARTY	adj swarthy		
SWASH	v -ED, -ING, -ES to swagger	**SWEET**	n pl. -S something that is sweet
SWASHER	n pl. -S one that swashes	**SWEETEN**	v -ED, -ING, -S to make sweet
SWASTICA	n pl. -S swastika	**SWEETIE**	n pl. -S darling
SWASTIKA	n pl. -S a geometrical figure used as a symbol or ornament	**SWEETING**	n pl. -S a sweet apple
		SWEETISH	adj somewhat sweet
SWAT	v SWATTED, SWATTING, SWATS to hit sharply	**SWEETLY**	adv in a sweet manner
		SWEETSOP	n pl. -S a tropical tree
SWATCH	n pl. -ES a sample piece of cloth	**SWELL**	v SWELLED, SWOLLEN, SWELLING, SWELLS to increase in size or volume
SWATH	n pl. -S a row of cut grass or grain		
		SWELL	adj SWELLER, SWELLEST stylish
SWATHE	v SWATHED, SWATHING, SWATHES to wrap in bandages		
		SWELLING	n pl. -S something that is swollen
SWATHER	n pl. -S one that swathes		
SWATTED	past tense of swat	**SWELTER**	v -ED, -ING, -S to suffer from oppressive heat
SWATTER	n pl. -S one that swats		
SWATTING	present participle of swat	**SWELTRY**	adj -TRIER, -TRIEST oppressively hot
SWAY	v -ED, -ING, -S to move slowly back and forth **SWAYABLE** adj		
		SWEPT	past tense of sweep
SWAYBACK	n pl. -S an abnormal sagging of the back	**SWERVE**	v SWERVED, SWERVING, SWERVES to turn aside suddenly from a straight course
SWAYER	n pl. -S one that sways	**SWERVER**	n pl. -S one that swerves
SWAYFUL	adj capable of influencing	**SWEVEN**	n pl. -S a dream or vision
SWEAR	v SWORE or SWARE, SWORN, SWEARING, SWEARS to utter a solemn oath	**SWIFT**	adj SWIFTER, SWIFTEST moving with a great rate of motion
SWEARER	n pl. -S one that swears	**SWIFT**	n pl. -S a fast-flying bird
SWEAT	v -ED, -ING, -S to perspire	**SWIFTER**	n pl. -S a rope on a ship
SWEATBOX	n pl. -ES a small enclosure in which one is made to sweat	**SWIFTLY**	adv in a swift manner
		SWIG	v SWIGGED, SWIGGING, SWIGS to drink deeply or rapidly
SWEATER	n pl. -S a knitted outer garment		
SWEATY	adj SWEATIER, SWEATIEST covered with perspiration **SWEATILY** adv	**SWIGGER**	n pl. -S one that swigs
		SWILL	v -ED, -ING, -S to swig
		SWILLER	n pl. -S one that swills
SWEDE	n pl. -S a rutabaga	**SWIM**	v SWAM, SWUM, SWIMMING, SWIMS to propel oneself in water by natural means
SWEENY	n pl. -NIES atrophy of the shoulder muscles in horses		
		SWIMMER	n pl. -S one that swims

SWIMMING   *n* pl. -S the act of one that swims

SWIMMY   *adj* -MIER, -MIEST dizzy
SWIMMILY *adv*

SWIMSUIT   *n* pl. -S a bathing suit

SWINDLE   *v* -DLED, -DLING, -DLES to take money or property from by fraudulent means

SWINDLER   *n* pl. -S one that swindles

SWINE   *n* pl. SWINE a domestic pig

SWINEPOX   *n* pl. -ES a disease of swine

SWING   *v* SWUNG or SWANG, SWINGING, SWINGS to move freely back and forth

SWINGE   *v* SWINGED, SWINGEING, SWINGES to flog

SWINGER   *n* pl. -S one that swings

SWINGLE   *v* -GLED, -GLING, -GLES to scutch

SWINGY   *adj* SWINGIER, SWINGIEST marked by swinging

SWINISH   *adj* resembling or befitting swine

SWINK   *v* -ED, -ING, -S to toil

SWINNEY   *n* pl. -NEYS sweeny

SWIPE   *v* SWIPED, SWIPING, SWIPES to strike with a sweeping blow

SWIPLE   *n* pl. -S a part of a threshing device

SWIPPLE   *n* pl. -S swiple

SWIRL   *v* -ED, -ING, -S to move with a whirling motion

SWIRLY   *adj* SWIRLIER, SWIRLIEST swirling

SWISH   *v* -ED, -ING, -ES to move with a prolonged hissing sound

SWISHER   *n* pl. -S one that swishes

SWISHY   *adj* SWISHIER, SWISHIEST swishing

SWISS   *n* pl. -ES a cotton fabric

SWITCH   *v* -ED, -ING, -ES to beat with a flexible rod

SWITCHER   *n* pl. -S one that switches

SWITH   *adv* quickly

SWITHE   *adv* swith

SWITHER   *v* -ED, -ING, -S to doubt

SWITHLY   *adv* swith

SWIVE   *v* SWIVED, SWIVING, SWIVES to copulate with

SWIVEL   *v* -ELED, -ELING, -ELS or -ELLED, -ELLING, -ELS to turn on a pivoted support

SWIVET   *n* pl. -S a state of nervous excitement

SWIVING   present participle of swive

SWIZZLE   *v* -ZLED, -ZLING, -ZLES to drink excessively

SWIZZLER   *n* pl. -S one that swizzles

SWOB   *v* SWOBBED, SWOBBING, SWOBS to swab

SWOBBER   *n* pl. -S swabber

SWOLLEN   past participle of swell

SWOON   *v* -ED, -ING, -S to faint

SWOONER   *n* pl. -S one that swoons

SWOOP   *v* -ED, -ING, -S to make a sudden descent

SWOOPER   *n* pl. -S one that swoops

SWOOSH   *v* -ED, -ING, -ES to move with a rustling sound

SWOP   *v* SWOPPED, SWOPPING, SWOPS to swap

SWORD   *n* pl. -S a weapon having a long blade for cutting or thrusting

SWORDMAN   *n* pl. -MEN one skilled in the use of a sword

SWORE   a past tense of swear

SWORN   past participle of swear

SWOT   *v* SWOTTED, SWOTTING, SWOTS to swat

SWOTTER   *n* pl. -S one that swots

SWOUN   *v* -ED, -ING, -S to swoon

SWOUND   *v* -ED, -ING, -S to swoon

SWUM   past participle of swim

SWUNG   a past tense of swing

SYBARITE   *n* pl. -S a person devoted to pleasure and luxury

SYBO   *n* pl. -BOES the cibol

SYCAMINE   *n* pl. -S the mulberry tree

SYCAMORE   *n* pl. -S a North American tree

SYCE   *n* pl. -S a male servant in India

SYCEE   *n* pl. -S fine uncoined silver formerly used in China as money

SYCOMORE   *n* pl. -S sycamore

SYCONIUM   *n* pl. -NIA a fleshy multiple fruit

SYCOSIS   *n* pl. -COSES an inflammatory disease of the hair follicles

SYENITE   *n* pl. -S an igneous rock
SYENITIC *adj*

SYKE	*n* pl. -S a small stream
SYLLABI	a pl. of syllabus
SYLLABIC	*n* pl. -S a speech sound of high sonority
SYLLABLE	*v* -BLED, -BLING, -BLES to pronounce syllables (units of spoken language)
SYLLABUB	*n* pl. -S sillabub
SYLLABUS	*n* pl. -BI or -BUSES an outline of a course of study
SYLPH	*n* pl. -S a slender, graceful girl or woman **SYLPHIC, SYLPHISH, SYLPHY** *adj*
SYLPHID	*n* pl. -S a young sylph
SYLVA	*n* pl. -VAS or -VAE the forest trees of an area
SYLVAN	*n* pl. -S one that lives in a forest
SYLVATIC	*adj* pertaining to a forest
SYLVIN	*n* pl. -S sylvite
SYLVINE	*n* pl. -S sylvite
SYLVITE	*n* pl. -S an ore of potassium
SYMBION	*n* pl. -S symbiont
SYMBIONT	*n* pl. -S an organism living in close association with another
SYMBIOT	*n* pl. -S symbiont
SYMBIOTE	*n* pl. -S symbiont
SYMBOL	*v* -BOLED, -BOLING, -BOLS or -BOLLED, -BOLLING, -BOLS to serve as a symbol (a representation) of
SYMBOLIC	*adj* pertaining to a symbol
SYMMETRY	*n* pl. -TRIES an exact correspondence between the opposite halves of a figure
SYMPATHY	*n* pl. -THIES a feeling of compassion for another's suffering
SYMPATRY	*n* pl. -RIES the state of occupying the same area without loss of identity from interbreeding
SYMPHONY	*n* pl. -NIES an orchestral composition
SYMPODIA	*n/pl* plant stems made up of a series of superposed branches
SYMPOSIA	*n/pl* conferences for the purpose of discussion
SYMPTOM	*n* pl. -S an indication of something
SYN	*adv* syne

SYNAGOG	*n* pl. -S a building for Jewish worship
SYNAPSE	*v* -APSED, -APSING, -APSES to come together in synapsis
SYNAPSIS	*n* pl. -APSES the point at which a nervous impulse passes from one neuron to another **SYNAPTIC** *adj*
SYNC	*v* -ED, -ING, -S to cause to operate in unison
SYNCARP	*n* pl. -S a fleshy multiple fruit
SYNCARPY	*n* pl. -PIES the state of being a syncarp
SYNCH	*v* -ED, -ING, -S to sync
SYNCHRO	*n* pl. -CHROS a selsyn
SYNCLINE	*n* pl. -S a type of rock formation
SYNCOM	*n* pl. -S a type of communications satellite
SYNCOPE	*n* pl. -S the contraction of a word by omitting one or more sounds from the middle **SYNCOPAL, SYNCOPIC** *adj*
SYNCYTIA	*n/pl* masses of protoplasm resulting from cell fusion
SYNDESIS	*n* pl. -DESES or -DESISES synapsis
SYNDET	*n* pl. -S a synthetic detergent
SYNDETIC	*adj* serving to connect
SYNDIC	*n* pl. -S a business agent **SYNDICAL** *adj*
SYNDROME	*n* pl. -S a group of symptoms that characterize a particular disorder
SYNE	*adv* since
SYNECTIC	*adj* pertaining to a system of problem solving
SYNERGIA	*n* pl. -S synergy
SYNERGID	*n* pl. -S a cell found in the embryo sac of a seed plant
SYNERGY	*n* pl. -GIES combined action **SYNERGIC** *adj*
SYNESIS	*n* pl. -SISES a type of grammatical construction
SYNGAMY	*n* pl. -MIES the union of two gametes **SYNGAMIC** *adj*
SYNOD	*n* pl. -S a church council **SYNODAL, SYNODIC** *adj*
SYNONYM	*n* pl. -S a word having the same meaning as another
SYNONYME	*n* pl. -S synonym
SYNONYMY	*n* pl. -MIES equivalence of meaning

SYNOPSIS   *n* pl. -OPSES a summary **SYNOPTIC** *adj*

SYNOVIA   *n* pl. -S a lubricating fluid secreted by certain membranes **SYNOVIAL** *adj*

SYNTAX   *n* pl. -ES the way in which words are put together to form phrases and sentences

SYNTONY   *n* pl. -NIES the tuning of transmitters and receivers with each other **SYNTONIC** *adj*

SYNURA   *n* pl. -RAE any of a genus of protozoa

SYPHER   *v* -ED, -ING, -S to overlap so as to make an even surface, as beveled plank edges

SYPHILIS   *n* pl. -LISES a venereal disease

SYPHON   *v* -ED, -ING, -S to siphon

SYREN   *n* pl. -S siren

SYRINGA   *n* pl. -S an ornamental shrub

SYRINGE   *v* -RINGED, -RINGING, -RINGES to cleanse or treat with injected fluid

SYRINX   *n* pl. -INGES or -INXES the vocal organ of a bird

SYRPHIAN   *n* pl. -S syrphid

SYRPHID   *n* pl. -S a winged insect

SYRUP   *n* pl. -S a thick, sweet liquid **SYRUPY** *adj*

SYSTEM   *n* pl. -S a group of interacting elements forming a unified whole

SYSTEMIC   *n* pl. -S a type of pesticide

SYSTOLE   *n* pl. -S the normal rhythmic contraction of the heart **SYSTOLIC** *adj*

SYZYGY   *n* pl. -GIES the configuration of the earth, moon, and sun lying in a straight line **SYZYGAL, SYZYGIAL** *adj*

TA	*n* pl. -S an expression of gratitude	**TABLOID**	*n* pl. -S a small newspaper
TAB	*v* TABBED, TABBING, TABS to name or designate	**TABOO**	*v* -ED, -ING, -S to exclude from use, approach, or mention
TABANID	*n* pl. -S a bloodsucking insect	**TABOR**	*v* -ED, -ING, -S to beat on a small drum
TABARD	*n* pl. -S a sleeveless outer garment **TABARDED** *adj*	**TABORER**	*n* pl. -S one that tabors
TABARET	*n* pl. -S a silk fabric	**TABORET**	*n* pl. -S a small drum
TABBED	past tense of tab	**TABORIN**	*n* pl. -S taborine
TABBIED	past tense of tabby	**TABORINE**	*n* pl. -S a taboret
TABBIES	present 3d person sing. of tabby	**TABOUR**	*v* -ED, -ING, -S to tabor
TABBING	present participle of tab	**TABOURER**	*n* pl. -S taborer
TABBIS	*n* pl. -BISES a silk fabric	**TABOURET**	*n* pl. -S taboret
TABBY	*v* -BIED, -BYING, -BIES to give a wavy appearance to	**TABU**	*v* -ED, -ING, -S to taboo
TABER	*v* -ED, -ING, -S to tabor	**TABULAR**	*adj* of or pertaining to a list
TABES	*n* pl. TABES a syphilitic disease	**TABULATE**	*v* -LATED, -LATING, -LATES to arrange in a list
TABETIC	*n* pl. -S one affected with tabes	**TACE**	*n* pl. -S tasse
TABID	*adj* affected with tabes	**TACET**	*interj* be silent — used as a musical direction
TABLA	*n* pl. -S a small drum	**TACH**	*n* pl. -S a device for indicating speed of rotation
TABLE	*v* -BLED, -BLING, -BLES to place on a table (a piece of furniture having a flat upper surface)	**TACHE**	*n* pl. -S a clasp or buckle
TABLEAU	*n* pl. -LEAUX or -LEAUS a picture	**TACHINID**	*n* pl. -S a grayish fly
		TACHISM	*n* pl. -S action painting
TABLEFUL	*n* pl. TABLEFULS or TABLESFUL as much as a table can hold	**TACHIST**	*n* pl. -S an action painter
		TACHISTE	*n* pl. -S tachist
		TACIT	*adj* unspoken **TACITLY** *adv*
TABLET	*v* -LETED, -LETING, -LETS or -LETTED, -LETTING, -LETS to inscribe on a small, flat surface	**TACITURN**	*adj* habitually silent
		TACK	*v* -ED, -ING, -S to fasten with tacks (short, sharp-pointed nails)
TABLETOP	*n* pl. -S the top of a table	**TACKER**	*n* pl. -S one that tacks
TABLING	present participle of table	**TACKET**	*n* pl. -S a hobnail

TACKEY *adj* TACKIER, TACKIEST tacky

TACKIER comparative of tacky

TACKIEST superlative of tacky

TACKIFY *v* -FIED, -FYING, -FIES to make tacky

TACKILY *adv* in a tacky manner

TACKLE *v* -LED, -LING, -LES to seize and throw to the ground

TACKLER *n pl.* -S one that tackles

TACKLESS *adj* having no tacks

TACKLING *n pl.* -S equipment

TACKY *adj* TACKIER, TACKIEST adhesive

TACNODE *n pl.* -S a point of contact between two curves

TACO *n pl.* -COS a tortilla folded around a filling

TACONITE *n pl.* -S a low-grade iron ore

TACT *n pl.* -S skill in dealing with delicate situations

TACTFUL *adj* having tact

TACTIC *n pl.* -S a maneuver for gaining an objective TACTICAL *adj*

TACTILE *adj* pertaining to the sense of touch

TACTION *n pl.* -S the act of touching

TACTLESS *adj* lacking tact

TACTUAL *adj* tactile

TAD *n pl.* -S a small boy

TADPOLE *n pl.* -S the aquatic larva of an amphibian

TAE *prep* to

TAEL *n pl.* -S a Chinese unit of weight

TAENIA *n pl.* -NIAE or -NIAS a headband worn in ancient Greece

TAFFAREL *n pl.* -S taffrail

TAFFEREL *n pl.* -S taffrail

TAFFETA *n pl.* -S a lustrous fabric

TAFFIA *n pl.* -S tafia

TAFFRAIL *n pl.* -S a rail around the stern of a ship

TAFFY *n pl.* -FIES a chewy candy

TAFIA *n pl.* -S an inferior rum

TAG *v* TAGGED, TAGGING, TAGS to provide with a tag (an identifying marker)

TAGALONG *n pl.* -S one that follows another

TAGBOARD *n pl.* -S a material for making shipping tags

TAGGED past tense of tag

TAGGER *n pl.* -S one that tags

TAGGING present participle of tag

TAGLIKE *adj* resembling a tag

TAGMEME *n pl.* -S the smallest unit of meaningful grammatical relation

TAGRAG *n pl.* -S riffraff

TAHR *n pl.* -S a goatlike mammal

TAHSIL *n pl.* -S a district in India

TAIGA *n pl.* -S a subarctic evergreen forest

TAIGLACH *n pl.* TAIGLACH teiglach

TAIL *v* -ED, -ING, -S to provide with a tail (a hindmost part)

TAILBACK *n pl.* -S a member of the backfield in some football formations

TAILBONE *n pl.* -S the coccyx

TAILCOAT *n pl.* -S a man's coat

TAILER *n pl.* -S one that secretly follows another

TAILGATE *v* -GATED, -GATING, -GATES to drive dangerously close behind another vehicle

TAILING *n pl.* -S the part of a projecting stone or brick that is inserted into a wall

TAILLE *n pl.* -S a former French tax

TAILLESS *adj* having no tail

TAILLIKE *adj* resembling a tail

TAILOR *v* -ED, -ING, -S to fit with clothes

TAILPIPE *n pl.* -S an exhaust pipe

TAILRACE *n pl.* -S a part of a millrace

TAILSKID *n pl.* -S a support on which the tail of an airplane rests

TAILSPIN *n pl.* -S the spiral descent of a stalled airplane

TAILWIND *n pl.* -S a wind coming from behind a moving vehicle

TAIN *n pl.* -S a thin plate

TAINT *v* -ED, -ING, -S to touch or affect slightly with something bad

TAIPAN *n pl.* -S a venomous snake

TAJ *n pl.* -ES a tall, conical cap worn in Muslim countries

TAKAHE *n pl.* -S a flightless bird

TAKE	v TOOK, TAKEN, TAKING, TAKES to get possession of **TAKABLE, TAKEABLE** adj
TAKEDOWN	n pl. -S an article that can be taken apart easily
TAKEOFF	n pl. -S the act of rising in flight
TAKEOUT	n pl. -S the act of removing
TAKEOVER	n pl. -S the act of assuming control
TAKER	n pl. -S one that takes
TAKIN	n pl. -S a goatlike mammal
TAKING	n pl. -S a seizure
TAKINGLY	adv in an attractive manner
TALA	n pl. -S a traditional rhythmic pattern of music in India
TALAPOIN	n pl. -S a small African monkey
TALAR	n pl. -S a long cloak
TALARIA	n/pl winged sandals worn by various figures of classical mythology
TALC	v TALCKED, TALCKING, TALCS or TALCED, TALCING, TALCS to treat with talc (a soft mineral with a soapy texture) **TALCKY, TALCOSE, TALCOUS** adj
TALCUM	n pl. -S a powder made from talc
TALE	n pl. -S a story
TALENT	n pl. -S a special natural ability **TALENTED** adj
TALER	n pl. -S a former German coin
TALESMAN	n pl. -MEN a person summoned to fill a vacancy on a jury
TALEYSIM	a pl. of tallith
TALI	pl. of talus
TALION	n pl. -S a retaliation for a crime
TALIPED	n pl. -S a person afflicted with clubfoot
TALIPES	n pl. TALIPES clubfoot
TALIPOT	n pl. -S a tall palm tree
TALISMAN	n pl. -S an object believed to possess magical powers
TALK	v -ED, -ING, -S to communicate by speaking
TALKABLE	adj able to be talked about
TALKER	n pl. -S one that talks
TALKIE	n pl. -S a moving picture with synchronized sound
TALKING	n pl. -S conversation

TALKY	adj TALKIER, TALKIEST tending to talk a great deal
TALL	adj TALLER, TALLEST having great height
TALLAGE	v -LAGED, -LAGING, -LAGES to tax
TALLAISIM	a pl. of tallith
TALLBOY	n pl. -BOYS a highboy
TALLIED	past tense of tally
TALLIER	n pl. -S one that tallies
TALLIES	present 3d person sing. of tally
TALLISH	adj somewhat tall
TALLITH	n pl. TALLITHES, TALLITHIM, TALLITOTH, TALEYSIM, or TALLAISIM a Jewish prayer shawl
TALLNESS	n pl. -ES the state of being tall
TALLOL	n pl. -S a resinous liquid
TALLOW	v -ED, -ING, -S to smear with tallow (a mixture of animal fats)
TALLOWY	adj resembling tallow
TALLY	v -LIED, -LYING, -LIES to count
TALLYHO	v -ED, -ING, -S to make an encouraging shout to hunting hounds
TALLYMAN	n pl. -MEN a person who tallies
TALMUDIC	adj pertaining to the body of Jewish civil and religious law
TALON	n pl. -S a claw of a bird of prey **TALONED** adj
TALOOKA	n pl. -S taluk
TALUK	n pl. -S an estate in India
TALUKA	n pl. -S taluk
TALUS	n pl. -LI a bone of the foot
TALUS	n pl. -ES a slope formed by an accumulation of rock debris
TAM	n pl. -S a tight-fitting Scottish cap
TAMABLE	adj capable of being tamed
TAMAL	n pl. -S tamale
TAMALE	n pl. -S a Mexican dish
TAMANDU	n pl. -S tamandua
TAMANDUA	n pl. -S an arboreal anteater
TAMARACK	n pl. -S a timber tree
TAMARAO	n pl. -RAOS tamarau
TAMARAU	n pl. -S a small buffalo of the Philippines
TAMARIN	n pl. -S a South American monkey

TAMARIND   *n pl.* -S a tropical tree

TAMARISK   *n pl.* -S an evergreen shrub

TAMASHA   *n pl.* -S a public entertainment in India

TAMBAC   *n pl.* -S tombac

TAMBALA   *n pl.* -S a monetary unit of Malawi

TAMBOUR   *v* -ED, -ING, -S to embroider on a round wooden frame

TAMBOURA   *n pl.* -S tambura

TAMBUR   *n pl.* -S tambura

TAMBURA   *n pl.* -S a stringed instrument

TAME   *adj* TAMER, TAMEST gentle or docile

TAME   *v* TAMED, TAMING, TAMES to make tame

TAMEABLE   *adj* tamable

TAMEIN   *n pl.* -S a garment worn by Burmese women

TAMELESS   *adj* not capable of being tamed

TAMELY   *adv* in a tame manner

TAMENESS   *n pl.* -ES the state of being tame

TAMER   *n pl.* -S one that tames

TAMEST   superlative of tame

TAMING   present participle of tame

TAMIS   *n pl.* -ISES a strainer made of cloth mesh

TAMMIE   *n pl.* -S tammy

TAMMY   *n pl.* -MIES a fabric of mixed fibers

TAMP   *v* -ED, -ING, -S to pack down by tapping

TAMPALA   *n pl.* -S an annual herb

TAMPAN   *n pl.* -S a biting insect

TAMPER   *v* -ED, -ING, -S to interfere in a harmful manner

TAMPERER   *n pl.* -S one that tampers

TAMPION   *n pl.* -S a plug for the muzzle of a cannon

TAMPON   *v* -ED, -ING, -S to plug with a cotton pad

TAN   *v* TANNED, TANNING, TANS to convert hide into leather by soaking in chemicals

TAN   *adj* TANNER, TANNEST brown from the sun's rays

TANAGER   *n pl.* -S a brightly colored bird

TANBARK   *n pl.* -S a tree bark used as a source of tannin

TANDEM   *n pl.* -S a bicycle built for two

TANG   *v* -ED, -ING, -S to provide with a pungent flavor

TANGELO   *n pl.* -LOS a citrus fruit

TANGENCE   *n pl.* -S tangency

TANGENCY   *n pl.* -CIES the state of being in immediate physical contact

TANGENT   *n pl.* -S a straight line in contact with a curve at one point

TANGIBLE   *n pl.* -S something palpable

TANGIBLY   *adv* palpably

TANGIER   comparative of tangy

TANGIEST   superlative of tangy

TANGLE   *v* -GLED, -GLING, -GLES to bring together in intricate confusion

TANGLER   *n pl.* -S one that tangles

TANGLY   *adj* -GLIER, -GLIEST tangled

TANGO   *v* -ED, -ING, -S to perform a Latin-American dance

TANGRAM   *n pl.* -S a Chinese puzzle

TANGY   *adj* TANGIER, TANGIEST pungent

TANIST   *n pl.* -S the heir apparent to a Celtic chief

TANISTRY   *n pl.* -RIES the system of electing a tanist

TANK   *v* -ED, -ING, -S to store in a tank (a container usually for liquids)

TANKA   *n pl.* -S a Japanese verse form

TANKAGE   *n pl.* -S the capacity of a tank

TANKARD   *n pl.* -S a tall drinking vessel

TANKER   *n pl.* -S a ship designed to transport liquids

TANKFUL   *n pl.* -S the amount a tank can hold

TANKSHIP   *n pl.* -S a tanker

TANNABLE   *adj* capable of being tanned

TANNAGE   *n pl.* -S the process of tanning

TANNATE   *n pl.* -S a chemical salt

TANNED   past tense of tan

TANNER   *n pl.* -S one that tans

TANNERY   *n pl.* -NERIES a place where hides are tanned

TANNEST   superlative of tan

TANNIC   *adj* pertaining to tannin

TANNIN   *n pl.* -S a chemical compound used in tanning

TANNING *n* pl. -S the process of converting hides into leather

TANNISH *adj* somewhat tan

TANREC *n* pl. -S tenrec

TANSY *n* pl. -SIES a perennial herb

TANTALUM *n* pl. -S a metallic element **TANTALIC** *adj*

TANTALUS *n* pl. -ES a case for wine bottles

TANTARA *n* pl. -S the sound of a trumpet or horn

TANTIVY *n* pl. -TIVIES a hunting cry

TANTO *adv* so much — used as a musical direction

TANTRA *n* pl. -S one of a class of Hindu religious writings **TANTRIC** *adj*

TANTRUM *n* pl. -S a fit of rage

TANYARD *n* pl. -S the section of a tannery containing the vats

TAO *n* pl. -S the path of virtuous conduct according to a Chinese philosophy

TAP *v* TAPPED, TAPPING, TAPS to strike gently

TAPA *n* pl. -S a cloth made from tree bark

TAPADERA *n* pl. -S a part of a saddle

TAPADERO *n* pl. -ROS tapadera

TAPALO *n* pl. -LOS a scarf worn in Latin-American countries

TAPE *v* TAPED, TAPING, TAPES to fasten with tape (a long, narrow strip or band)

TAPELESS *adj* being without tape

TAPELIKE *adj* resembling tape

TAPELINE *n* pl. -S a tape for measuring distances

TAPER *v* -ED, -ING, -S to become gradually narrower toward one end

TAPERER *n* pl. -S one that carries a candle in a religious procession

TAPESTRY *v* -TRIED, -TRYING, -TRIES to decorate with woven wall hangings

TAPETUM *n* pl. -TA a layer of cells in some plants **TAPETAL** *adj*

TAPEWORM *n* pl. -S a parasitic worm

TAPHOLE *n* pl. -S a hole in a blast furnace

TAPHOUSE *n* pl. -S a tavern

TAPING present participle of tape

TAPIOCA *n* pl. -S a starchy food

TAPIR *n* pl. -S a hoofed mammal

TAPIS *n* pl. -PISES material used for wall hangings and floor coverings

TAPPED past tense of tap

TAPPER *n* pl. -S one that taps

TAPPET *n* pl. -S a sliding rod that causes another part of a mechanism to move

TAPPING *n* pl. -S the process or means by which something is tapped

TAPROOM *n* pl. -S a barroom

TAPROOT *n* pl. -S the main root of a plant

TAPSTER *n* pl. -S one that dispenses liquor in a barroom

TAR *v* TARRED, TARRING, TARS to cover with tar (a black viscous liquid)

TARANTAS *n* pl. -ES a Russian carriage

TARBOOSH *n* pl. -ES a cap worn by Muslim men

TARBUSH *n* pl. -ES tarboosh

TARDIER comparative of tardy

TARDIES pl. of tardy

TARDO *adj* slow — used as a musical direction

TARDY *adj* TARDIER, TARDIEST late **TARDILY** *adv*

TARDY *n* pl. -DIES an instance of being late

TARE *v* TARED, TARING, TARES to determine the weight of a container holding goods

TARGE *n* pl. -S a small, round shield

TARGET *v* -ED, -ING, -S to make a goal of

TARIFF *v* -ED, -ING, -S to tax imported or exported goods

TARING present participle of tare

TARLATAN *n* pl. -S a cotton fabric

TARLETAN *n* pl. -S tarlatan

TARMAC *n* pl. -S an asphalt road

TARN *n* pl. -S a small mountain lake

TARNAL *adj* damned **TARNALLY** *adv*

TARNISH *v* -ED, -ING, -ES to dull the luster of

TARO *n* pl. -ROS a tropical plant

TAROC *n* pl. -S tarok

TAROK *n* pl. -S a card game

TAROT	*n pl.* -S any of a set of playing cards used for fortune-telling
TARP	*n pl.* -S a protective canvas covering
TARPAN	*n pl.* -S an Asian wild horse
TARPAPER	*n pl.* -S a heavy paper coated with tar
TARPON	*n pl.* -S a marine game fish
TARRAGON	*n pl.* -S a perennial herb
TARRE	*v* TARRED, TARRING, TARRES to urge to action
TARRED	past tense of tar
TARRIED	past tense of tarry
TARRIER	*n pl.* -S one that tarries
TARRIES	present 3d person sing. of tarry
TARRIEST	superlative of tarry
TARRING	present participle of tar and tarre
TARRY	*v* -RIED, -RYING, -RIES to delay or be slow in acting or doing
TARRY	*adj* -RIER, -RIEST resembling tar
TARSAL	*n pl.* -S a bone of the foot
TARSI	pl. of tarsus
TARSIA	*n pl.* -S intarsia
TARSIER	*n pl.* -S a nocturnal primate
TARSUS	*n pl.* TARSI a part of the foot
TART	*adj* TARTER, TARTEST having a sharp, sour taste
TART	*v* -ED, -ING, -S to dress up
TARTAN	*n pl.* -S a patterned woolen fabric
TARTANA	*n pl.* -S a Mediterranean sailing vessel
TARTAR	*n pl.* -S a crust on the teeth TARTARIC *adj*
TARTISH	*adj* somewhat tart
TARTLET	*n pl.* -S a small pie
TARTLY	*adv* in a tart manner
TARTNESS	*n pl.* -ES the state of being tart
TARTRATE	*n pl.* -S a chemical salt
TARTUFE	*n pl.* -S tartuffe
TARTUFFE	*n pl.* -S a hypocrite
TARWEED	*n pl.* -S a flowering plant
TARZAN	*n pl.* -S a person of superior strength and agility
TASK	*v* -ED, -ING, -S to assign a job to

TASKWORK	*n pl.* -S hard work
TASS	*n pl.* -ES a drinking cup
TASSE	*n pl.* -S tasset
TASSEL	*v* -SELED, -SELING, -SELS or -SELLED, -SELLING, -SELS to adorn with dangling ornaments
TASSET	*n pl.* -S a piece of plate armor for the upper thigh
TASSIE	*n pl.* -S tass
TASTE	*v* TASTED, TASTING, TASTES to perceive the flavor of by taking into the mouth TASTABLE *adj*
TASTEFUL	*adj* tasty
TASTER	*n pl.* -S one that tastes
TASTING	present participle of taste
TASTY	*adj* TASTIER, TASTIEST pleasant to the taste TASTILY *adv*
TAT	*v* TATTED, TATTING, TATS to make tatting
TATAMI	*n pl.* -S straw matting used as a floor covering
TATE	*n pl.* -S a tuft of hair
TATER	*n pl.* -S a potato
TATOUAY	*n pl.* -AYS a South American armadillo
TATTED	past tense of tat
TATTER	*v* -ED, -ING, -S to become torn and worn
TATTIER	comparative of tatty
TATTIEST	superlative of tatty
TATTING	*n pl.* -S delicate handmade lace
TATTLE	*v* -TLED, -TLING, -TLES to reveal the activities of another
TATTLER	*n pl.* -S one that tattles
TATTOO	*v* -ED, -ING, -S to mark the skin with indelible pigments
TATTOOER	*n pl.* -S one that tattoos
TATTY	*adj* -TIER, -TIEST shabby
TAU	*n pl.* -S a Greek letter
TAUGHT	past tense of teach
TAUNT	*v* -ED, -ING, -S to challenge or reproach sarcastically
TAUNTER	*n pl.* -S one that taunts
TAUPE	*n pl.* -S a dark gray color
TAURINE	*n pl.* -S a chemical compound
TAUT	*adj* TAUTER, TAUTEST fully stretched, so as not to be slack
TAUT	*v* -ED, -ING, -S to tangle

TAUTAUG *n* pl. -S tautog

TAUTEN *v* -ED, -ING, -S to make taut

TAUTLY *adv* in a taut manner

TAUTNESS *n* pl. -ES the state of being taut

TAUTOG *n* pl. -S a marine fish

TAUTOMER *n* pl. -S a type of chemical compound

TAUTONYM *n* pl. -S a type of taxonomic designation

TAV *n* pl. -S a Hebrew letter

TAVERN *n* pl. -S a place where liquor is sold to be drunk on the premises

TAVERNER *n* pl. -S one that runs a tavern

TAW *v* -ED, -ING, -S to convert into white leather by the application of minerals

TAWDRY *adj* -DRIER, -DRIEST gaudy **TAWDRILY** *adv*

TAWDRY *n* pl. -DRIES gaudy finery

TAWER *n* pl. -S one that taws

TAWIE *adj* docile

TAWNEY *n* pl. -NEYS tawny

TAWNY *adj* -NIER, -NIEST light brown **TAWNILY** *adv*

TAWNY *n* pl. -NIES a light brown color

TAWPIE *n* pl. -S a foolish young person

TAWSE *v* TAWSED, TAWSING, TAWSES to flog

TAX *v* -ED, -ING, -ES to place a tax (a charge imposed by authority for public purposes) on

TAXA a pl. of taxon

TAXABLE *adj* subject to tax **TAXABLY** *adv*

TAXABLE *n* pl. -S a taxable item

TAXATION *n* pl. -S the process of taxing

TAXEME *n* pl. -S a minimum grammatical feature of selection **TAXEMIC** *adj*

TAXER *n* pl. -S one that taxes

TAXI *v* TAXIED, TAXIING or TAXYING, TAXIS or TAXIES to travel in a taxicab

TAXICAB *n* pl. -S an automobile for hire

TAXIMAN *n* pl. -MEN the operator of a taxicab

TAXINGLY *adv* in an onerous manner

TAXITE *n* pl. -S a volcanic rock **TAXITIC** *adj*

TAXIWAY *n* pl. -WAYS a paved strip at an airport

TAXLESS *adj* free from taxation

TAXMAN *n* pl. -MEN one who collects taxes

TAXON *n* pl. TAXA or TAXONS a unit of scientific classification

TAXONOMY *n* pl. -MIES the study of scientific classification

TAXPAID *adj* paid for by taxes

TAXPAYER *n* pl. -S one that pays taxes

TAXUS *n* pl. TAXUS an evergreen tree or shrub

TAXWISE *adj* pertaining to taxes

TAXYING a present participle of taxi

TAZZA *n* pl. -ZAS or -ZE an ornamental bowl

TEA *n* pl. -S a beverage made by infusing dried leaves in boiling water

TEABERRY *n* pl. -RIES a North American shrub

TEABOARD *n* pl. -S a tray for serving tea

TEABOWL *n* pl. -S a teacup having no handle

TEABOX *n* pl. -ES a box for tea leaves

TEACAKE *n* pl. -S a small cake served with tea

TEACART *n* pl. -S a wheeled table used in serving tea

TEACH *v* TAUGHT, TEACHING, TEACHES to impart knowledge or skill to

TEACHER *n* pl. -S one that teaches

TEACHING *n* pl. -S a doctrine

TEACUP *n* pl. -S a cup in which tea is served

TEAHOUSE *n* pl. -S a public establishment serving tea

TEAK *n* pl. -S an East Indian tree

TEAKWOOD *n* pl. -S the wood of the teak

TEAL *n* pl. -S a river duck

TEAM *v* -ED, -ING, -S to form a team (a group of persons associated in a joint action)

TEAMAKER *n* pl. -S one that makes tea

TEAMMATE *n* pl. -S a member of the same team

TEAMSTER *n* pl. -S a truck driver

TEAMWORK *n* pl. -S cooperative effort to achieve a common goal

TEAPOT n pl. -S a vessel used in making and serving tea

TEAPOY n pl. -POYS a small table used in serving tea

TEAR v -ED, -ING, -S to emit tears (drops of saline liquid secreted by a gland of the eye)

TEAR v TORE, TORN, TEARING, TEARS to pull apart or into pieces **TEARABLE** adj

TEARDOWN n pl. -S the process of disassembling

TEARDROP n pl. -S a tear

TEARER n pl. -S one that tears or rips

TEARFUL adj full of tears

TEARGAS v -GASSED, -GASSING, -GASES or -GASSES to subject to a gas that irritates the eyes

TEARIER comparative of teary

TEARIEST superlative of teary

TEARILY adv in a teary manner

TEARLESS adj being without tears

TEAROOM n pl. -S a restaurant serving tea

TEARY adj TEARIER, TEARIEST tearful

TEASE v TEASED, TEASING, TEASES to make fun of

TEASEL v -SELED, -SELING, -SELS or -SELLED, -SELLING, -SELS to raise a soft surface on fabric with a bristly flower head

TEASELER n pl. -S one that teasels

TEASER n pl. -S one that teases

TEASHOP n pl. -S a tearoom

TEASING present participle of tease

TEASPOON n pl. -S a small spoon

TEAT n pl. -S a mammary gland **TEATED** adj

TEATIME n pl. -S the customary time for tea

TEAWARE n pl. -S a tea service

TEAZEL v -ZELED, -ZELING, -ZELS or -ZELLED, -ZELLING, -ZELS to teasel

TEAZLE v -ZLED, -ZLING, -ZLES to teasel

TECHED adj crazy

TECHNIC n pl. -S technique

TECHY adj TECHIER, TECHIEST tetchy **TECHILY** adj

TECTA pl. of tectum

TECTAL adj pertaining to a tectum

TECTONIC adj pertaining to construction

TECTRIX n pl. -TRICES a small feather of a bird's wing

TECTUM n pl. -TA a bodily structure resembling or serving as a roof

TED v TEDDED, TEDDING, TEDS to spread for drying

TEDDER n pl. -S one that teds

TEDDY n pl. -DIES a woman's undergarment

TEDIOUS adj causing weariness

TEDIUM n pl. -S the state of being tedious

TEE v TEED, TEEING, TEES to place a golf ball on a small peg

TEEM v -ED, -ING, -S to be full to overflowing

TEEMER n pl. -S one that teems

TEEN n pl. -S a teenager

TEENAGE adj pertaining to teenagers

TEENAGED adj teenage

TEENAGER n pl. -S a person between the ages of thirteen and nineteen

TEENER n pl. -S a teenager

TEENFUL adj filled with grief

TEENSY adj -SIER, -SIEST tiny

TEENTSY adj -SIER, -SIEST tiny

TEENY adj -NIER, -NIEST tiny

TEEPEE n pl. -S tepee

TEETER v -ED, -ING, -S to move unsteadily

TEETH pl. of tooth

TEETHE v TEETHED, TEETHING, TEETHES to cut teeth

TEETHER n pl. -S an object for a baby to bite on during teething

TEETHING n pl. -S the first growth of teeth

TEETOTAL v -TALED, -TALING, -TALS or -TALLED, -TALLING, -TALS to abstain completely from alcoholic beverages

TEETOTUM n pl. -S a spinning toy

TEFF n pl. -S a cereal grass

TEG n pl. -S a yearling sheep

TEGMEN n pl. -MINA a covering

TEGMENTA n/pl anatomical coverings

TEGMINAL adj pertaining to a tegmen

TEGUA n pl. -S a type of moccasin

TEGULAR	*adj* resembling a tile	**TELFER**	*v* -ED, -ING, -S to telpher
TEGUMEN	*n* pl. -MINA tegmen	**TELFORD**	*n* pl. -S a road made of stones
TEGUMENT	*n* pl. -S a covering	**TELIA**	pl. of telium
TEIGLACH	*n* pl. TEIGLACH a confection consisting of balls of dough boiled in honey	**TELIAL**	*adj* pertaining to a telium
		TELIC	*adj* directed toward a goal
TEIID	*n* pl. -S a tropical American lizard	**TELIUM**	*n* pl. -LIA a sorus on the host plant of a rust fungus
TEIND	*n* pl. -S a tithe	**TELL**	*v* TOLD, TELLING, TELLS to give a detailed account of **TELLABLE** *adj*
TEKTITE	*n* pl. -S a glassy body believed to be of meteoritic origin **TEKTITIC** *adj*		
		TELLER	*n* pl. -S a bank employee who receives and pays out money
TELA	*n* pl. -LAE an anatomical tissue		
TELAMON	*n* pl. -ES a male figure used as a supporting column	**TELLIES**	pl. of telly
		TELLTALE	*n* pl. -S a tattler
TELE	*n* pl. -S a television set	**TELLURIC**	*adj* pertaining to the earth
TELECAST	*v* -ED, -ING, -S to broadcast by television	**TELLY**	*n* pl. -LIES a television set
		TELOME	*n* pl. -S a structural unit of a vascular plant **TELOMIC** *adj*
TELEDU	*n* pl. -S a carnivorous mammal		
TELEFILM	*n* pl. -S a motion picture made for television	**TELOS**	*n* pl. TELOI an ultimate end
		TELPHER	*v* -ED, -ING, -S to transport by a system of aerial cable cars
TELEGA	*n* pl. -S a Russian wagon		
TELEGONY	*n* pl. -NIES the supposed influence of a previous sire on the offspring of later matings of the mother with other males	**TELSON**	*n* pl. -S the terminal segment of an arthropod **TELSONIC** *adj*
		TEMBLOR	*n* pl. -S or -ES an earthquake
		TEMERITY	*n* pl. -TIES foolish boldness
TELEGRAM	*v* -GRAMMED, -GRAMMING, -GRAMS to send a message by telegraph	**TEMPEH**	*n* pl. -S an Asian food
		TEMPER	*v* -ED, -ING, -S to moderate by adding a counterbalancing agent
TELEMAN	*n* pl. -MEN a naval officer		
TELEMARK	*n* pl. -S a type of turn in skiing	**TEMPERA**	*n* pl. -S a technique of painting
TELEOST	*n* pl. -S a bony fish	**TEMPERER**	*n* pl. -S one that tempers
TELEPLAY	*n* pl. -PLAYS a play written for television	**TEMPEST**	*v* -ED, -ING, -S to agitate violently
TELEPORT	*v* -ED, -ING, -S to transport by a process that involves no physical means	**TEMPI**	a pl. of tempo
		TEMPLAR	*n* pl. -S a lawyer or student of law in London
TELERAN	*n* pl. -S a system of air navigation	**TEMPLATE**	*n* pl. -S a pattern used as a guide in making something
TELESIS	*n* pl. TELESES planned progress	**TEMPLE**	*n* pl. -S a house of worship **TEMPLED** *adj*
TELETHON	*n* pl. -S a fund-raising television program	**TEMPLET**	*n* pl. -S template
		TEMPO	*n* pl. -PI or -POS the rate of speed of a musical piece
TELEVIEW	*v* -ED, -ING, -S to observe by means of television		
		TEMPORAL	*n* pl. -S a bone of the skull
TELEVISE	*v* -VISED, -VISING, -VISES to broadcast by television (an electronic system of transmitting images and sound)	**TEMPT**	*v* -ED, -ING, -S to entice to commit an unwise or immoral act
		TEMPTER	*n* pl. -S one that tempts
TELEX	*v* -ED, -ING, -ES to send a message by a type of telegraphic system	**TEMPURA**	*n* pl. -S a Japanese dish

TEN	n pl. -S a number
TENABLE	adj capable of being held **TENABLY** adv
TENACE	n pl. -S a combination of two high cards in some card games
TENACITY	n pl. -TIES perseverance or persistence
TENACULA	n/pl hooked surgical instruments
TENAIL	n pl. -S tenaille
TENAILLE	n pl. -S an outer defense
TENANCY	n pl. -CIES the temporary occupancy of something that belongs to another
TENANT	v -ED, -ING, -S to inhabit
TENANTRY	n pl. -RIES tenancy
TENCH	n pl. -ES a freshwater fish
TEND	v -ED, -ING, -S to be disposed or inclined
TENDANCE	n pl. -S watchful care
TENDENCE	n pl. -S tendance
TENDENCY	n pl. -CIES an inclination to act or think in a particular way
TENDER	adj -DERER, -DEREST soft or delicate
TENDER	v -ED, -ING, -S to present for acceptance
TENDERER	n pl. -S one that tenders
TENDERLY	adv in a tender manner
TENDON	n pl. -S a band of tough, fibrous tissue
TENDRIL	n pl. -S a leafless organ of climbing plants
TENEBRAE	n/pl a religious service
TENEMENT	n pl. -S an apartment house
TENESMUS	n pl. -ES an urgent but ineffectual effort to defecate or urinate **TENESMIC** adj
TENET	n pl. -S a principle, belief, or doctrine held to be true
TENFOLD	n pl. -S an amount ten times as great as a given unit
TENIA	n pl. -NIAE or -NIAS a tapeworm
TENIASIS	n pl. -SISES infestation with tapeworms
TENNER	n pl. -S a ten-dollar bill
TENNIS	n pl. -NISES an outdoor ball game
TENNIST	n pl. -S a tennis player

TENON	v -ED, -ING, -S to unite by means of a tenon (a projection on the end of a piece of wood)
TENONER	n pl. -S one that tenons
TENOR	n pl. -S a high male singing voice
TENORITE	n pl. -S a mineral
TENOTOMY	n pl. -MIES the surgical division of a tendon
TENOUR	n pl. -S tenor
TENPENCE	n pl. -S the sum of ten pennies
TENPENNY	adj worth tenpence
TENPIN	n pl. -S a bowling pin
TENREC	n pl. -S a mammal that feeds on insects
TENSE	adj TENSER, TENSEST taut **TENSELY** adv
TENSE	v TENSED, TENSING, TENSES to make tense
TENSIBLE	adj capable of being stretched **TENSIBLY** adv
TENSILE	adj tensible
TENSING	present participle of tense
TENSION	v -ED, -ING, -S to make tense
TENSITY	n pl. -TIES the state of being tense
TENSIVE	adj causing tensity
TENSOR	n pl. -S a muscle that stretches a body part
TENT	v -ED, -ING, -S to live in a tent (a type of portable shelter)
TENTACLE	n pl. -S an elongated, flexible appendage of some animals
TENTAGE	n pl. -S a supply of tents
TENTER	v -ED, -ING, -S to stretch on a type of frame
TENTH	n pl. -S one of ten equal parts
TENTHLY	adv in the tenth place
TENTIE	adj TENTIER, TENTIEST tenty
TENTIER	comparative of tenty
TENTIEST	superlative of tenty
TENTLESS	adj having no tent
TENTLIKE	adj resembling a tent
TENTY	adj TENTIER, TENTIEST watchful
TENUIS	n pl. -UES a voiceless phonetic stop
TENUITY	n pl. -ITIES lack of substance or strength

TENUOUS *adj* having little substance or strength

TENURE *n* pl. -S the holding of something **TENURED, TENURIAL** *adj*

TENUTO *n* pl. -TI or -TOS a musical note or chord held longer than its normal duration

TEOCALLI *n* pl. -S an Aztec temple

TEOPAN *n* pl. -S a teocalli

TEOSINTE *n* pl. -S an annual grass

TEPA *n* pl. -S a chemical compound

TEPAL *n* pl. -S a division of a perianth

TEPEE *n* pl. -S a conical tent of some North American Indians

TEPEFY *v* -FIED, -FYING, -FIES to make tepid

TEPHRA *n* pl. -S solid material ejected from a volcano

TEPHRITE *n* pl. -S a volcanic rock

TEPID *adj* moderately warm **TEPIDLY** *adv*

TEPIDITY *n* pl. -TIES the state of being tepid

TEQUILA *n* pl. -S a Mexican liquor

TERAI *n* pl. -S a sun hat with a wide brim

TERAOHM *n* pl. -S one trillion ohms

TERAPH *n* pl. -APHIM an image of a Semitic household god

TERATISM *n* pl. -S a malformed fetus **TERATOID** *adj*

TERATOMA *n* pl. -MAS or -MATA a type of tumor

TERBIA *n* pl. -S an oxide of terbium

TERBIUM *n* pl. -S a metallic element **TERBIC** *adj*

TERCE *n* pl. -S tierce

TERCEL *n* pl. -S a male falcon

TERCELET *n* pl. -S tercel

TERCET *n* pl. -S a group of three lines of verse

TEREBENE *n* pl. -S a mixture of terpenes

TEREBIC *adj* pertaining to an acid derived from oil of turpentine

TEREDO *n* pl. -DOS or -DINES a bivalve mollusk

TEREFAH *adj* tref

TERETE *adj* cylindrical and slightly tapering

TERGA pl. of tergum

TERGAL *adj* pertaining to a tergum

TERGITE *n* pl. -S a tergum

TERGUM *n* pl. -GA a back part of a segment of an arthropod

TERIYAKI *n* pl. -S a Japanese food

TERM *v* -ED, -ING, -S to give a name to

TERMER *n* pl. -S a prisoner serving a specified sentence

TERMINAL *n* pl. -S an end or extremity

TERMINUS *n* pl. -NI or -NUSES a terminal

TERMITE *n* pl. -S an insect resembling an ant **TERMITIC** *adj*

TERMLESS *adj* having no limits

TERMLY *adv* periodically

TERMOR *n* pl. -S one that holds land for a certain number of years

TERMTIME *n* pl. -S the time when a school or court is in session

TERN *n* pl. -S a seabird

TERNARY *n* pl. -RIES a group of three

TERNATE *adj* arranged in groups of three

TERNE *n* pl. -S an alloy of lead and tin

TERNION *n* pl. -S a group of three

TERPENE *n* pl. -S a chemical compound **TERPENIC** *adj*

TERPINOL *n* pl. -S a fragrant liquid

TERRA *n* pl. -RAE earth; land

TERRACE *v* -RACED, -RACING, -RACES to provide with a terrace (a raised embankment)

TERRAIN *n* pl. -S a tract of land

TERRANE *n* pl. -S a rock formation

TERRAPIN *n* pl. -S a North American tortoise

TERRARIA *n/pl* glass enclosures for plants or small animals

TERRAS *n* pl. -ES trass

TERRAZZO *n* pl. -ZOS a mosaic flooring

TERREEN *n* pl. -S terrine

TERRELLA *n* pl. -S a spherical magnet

TERRENE *n* pl. -S a land area

TERRET *n* pl. -S a metal ring on a harness

TERRIBLE *adj* very bad **TERRIBLY** *adv*

TERRIER *n* pl. -S a small, active dog

TERRIES pl. of terry

TERRIFIC   adj very good; fine

TERRIFY   v -FIED, -FYING, -FIES to fill with terror

TERRINE   n pl. -S an earthenware jar

TERRIT   n pl. -S terret

TERROR   n pl. -S intense fear

TERRY   n pl. -RIES an absorbent fabric

TERSE   adj TERSER, TERSEST succinct **TERSELY** adv

TERTIAL   n pl. -S a flight feather of a bird's wing

TERTIAN   n pl. -S a recurrent fever

TERTIARY   n pl. -ARIES a tertial

TESLA   n pl. -S a unit of magnetic induction

TESSERA   n pl. -SERAE a small square used in mosaic work

TEST   v -ED, -ING, -S to subject to an examination **TESTABLE** adj

TESTA   n pl. -TAE the hard outer coating of a seed

TESTACY   n pl. -CIES the state of being testate

TESTATE   adj having made a valid will before death

TESTATOR   n pl. -S one that makes a will

TESTEE   n pl. -S one that is tested

TESTER   n pl. -S one that tests

TESTES   pl. of testis

TESTICLE   n pl. -S a testis

TESTIER   comparative of testy

TESTIEST   superlative of testy

TESTIFY   v -FIED, -FYING, -FIES to make a declaration of truth under oath

TESTILY   adv in a testy manner

TESTING   present participle of test

TESTIS   n pl. TESTES a male reproductive gland

TESTON   n pl. -S a former French coin

TESTOON   n pl. -S teston

TESTUDO   n pl. -DINES or -DOS a portable screen used as a shield by the ancient Romans

TESTY   adj TESTIER, TESTIEST irritable

TETANAL   adj pertaining to tetanus

TETANIC   n pl. -S a drug capable of causing convulsions

TETANIES   pl. of tetany

TETANISE   v -NISED, -NISING, -NISES to tetanize

TETANIZE   v -NIZED, -NIZING, -NIZES to affect with convulsions

TETANUS   n pl. -ES an infectious disease **TETANOID** adj

TETANY   n pl. -NIES a condition marked by painful muscular spasms

TETCHED   adj crazy

TETCHY   adj TETCHIER, TETCHIEST irritable **TETCHILY** adv

TETH   n pl. -S a Hebrew letter

TETHER   v -ED, -ING, -S to fasten to a fixed object with a rope

TETOTUM   n pl. -S teetotum

TETRA   n pl. -S a tropical fish

TETRACID   n pl. -S a type of acid

TETRAD   n pl. -S a group of four **TETRADIC** adj

TETRAGON   n pl. -S a four-sided polygon

TETRAMER   n pl. -S a type of polymer

TETRAPOD   n pl. -S a four-footed animal

TETRARCH   n pl. -S one of four joint rulers

TETRODE   n pl. -S a type of electron tube

TETROXID   n pl. -S a type of oxide

TETRYL   n pl. -S a chemical compound

TETTER   n pl. -S a skin disease

TEUCH   adj teugh

TEUGH   adj tough **TEUGHLY** adv

TEW   v -ED, -ING, -S to work hard

TEXAS   n pl. -ES the uppermost structure on a steamboat

TEXT   n pl. -S the main body of a written or printed work

TEXTBOOK   n pl. -S a book used in the study of a subject

TEXTILE   n pl. -S a woven fabric

TEXTLESS   adj having no text

TEXTUAL   adj pertaining to a text

TEXTUARY   n pl. -ARIES a specialist in the study of the Scriptures

TEXTURE   v -TURED, -TURING, -TURES to make by weaving

TEXTURAL   adj pertaining to the surface characteristics of something

THACK   v -ED, -ING, -S to thatch

THAE   adj these; those

THAIRM   n pl. -S tharm

THALAMUS *n* pl. -MI a part of the brain **THALAMIC** *adj*

THALER *n* pl. -S taler

THALLIUM *n* pl. -S a metallic element **THALLIC, THALLOUS** *adj*

THALLUS *n* pl. -LI or -LUSES a plant body without true root, stem, or leaf **THALLOID** *adj*

THAN *conj* — used to introduce the second element of a comparison

THANAGE *n* pl. -S the land held by a thane

THANATOS *n* pl. -ES an instinctual desire for death

THANE *n* pl. -S a man holding land by military service in Anglo-Saxon England

THANK *v* -ED, -ING, -S to express gratitude to

THANKER *n* pl. -S one that thanks

THANKFUL *adj* -FULLER, -FULLEST feeling gratitude

THARM *n* pl. -S the belly

THAT *pron* pl. THOSE the one indicated

THATAWAY *adv* in that direction

THATCH *v* -ED, -ING, -ES to cover with thatch (plant stalks or foliage)

THATCHER *n* pl. -S one that thatches

THATCHY *adj* resembling thatch

THAW *v* -ED, -ING, -S to melt

THAWER *n* pl. -S one that thaws

THAWLESS *adj* never thawing

THE *definite article* — used to specify or make particular

THEARCHY *n* pl. -CHIES rule by a god

THEATER *n* pl. -S a building for dramatic presentations **THEATRIC** *adj*

THEATRE *n* pl. -S theater

THEBAINE *n* pl. -S a poisonous alkaloid

THECA *n* pl. -CAE a protective anatomical covering **THECAL, THECATE** *adj*

THEE *pron* the objective case of the pronoun thou

THEELIN *n* pl. -S estrone

THEELOL *n* pl. -S estriol

THEFT *n* pl. -S the act of stealing

THEGN *n* pl. -S thane **THEGNLY** *adj*

THEIN *n* pl. -S theine

THEINE *n* pl. -S caffeine

THEIR *pron* a possessive form of the pronoun they

THEIRS *pron* a possessive form of the pronoun they

THEISM *n* pl. -S belief in the existence of a god

THEIST *n* pl. -S one who belives in the existence of a god **THEISTIC** *adj*

THELITIS *n* pl. -TISES inflammation of the nipple

THEM *pron* the objective case of the pronoun they

THEMATIC *adj* pertaining to a theme

THEME *n* pl. -S a subject discussed in speech or writing

THEN *n* pl. -S that time

THENAGE *n* pl. -S thanage

THENAL *adj* pertaining to the palm of the hand

THENAR *n* pl. -S the palm of the hand

THENCE *adv* from that place

THEOCRAT *n* pl. -S a person who rules as a representative of a god

THEODICY *n* pl. -CIES a defense of God's goodness in respect to the existence of evil

THEOGONY *n* pl. -NIES an account of the origin of the gods

THEOLOG *n* pl. -S a student of theology

THEOLOGY *n* pl. -GIES the study of religion

THEONOMY *n* pl. -MIES rule by a god

THEORBO *n* pl. -BOS an ancient lute

THEOREM *n* pl. -S a proposition that is demonstrably true or is assumed to be so

THEORIES pl. of theory

THEORISE *v* -RISED, -RISING, -RISES to theorize

THEORIST *n* pl. -S one that theorizes

THEORIZE *v* -RIZED, -RIZING, -RIZES to form theories

THEORY *n* pl. -RIES a group of propositions used to explain a class of phenomena

THERAPY *n* pl. -PIES the treatment of illness or disability

THERE *n* pl. -S that place

THEREAT *adv* at that place or time

THEREBY *adv* by that means

THEREFOR *adv* for that

THEREIN *adv* in that place

THEREMIN *n* pl. -S a musical instrument

THEREOF *adv* of that

THEREON *adv* on that

THERETO *adv* to that

THERIAC *n* pl. -S molasses

THERIACA *n* pl. -S theriac

THERM *n* pl. -S a unit of quantity of heat

THERMAE *n/pl* hot springs

THERMAL *n* pl. -S a rising mass of warm air

THERME *n* pl. -S therm

THERMEL *n* pl. -S a device for temperature measurement

THERMIC *adj* pertaining to heat

THERMION *n* pl. -S an ion emitted by a heated body

THERMIT *n* pl. -S thermite

THERMITE *n* pl. -S a metallic mixture that produces intense heat when ignited

THERMOS *n* pl. -ES a container used to keep liquids either hot or cold

THEROID *adj* resembling a beast

THEROPOD *n* pl. -S a carnivorous dinosaur

THESAURI *n/pl* dictionaries of synonyms and antonyms

THESE pl. of this

THESIS *n* pl. THESES a proposition put forward for discussion

THESPIAN *n* pl. -S an actor or actress

THETA *n* pl. -S a Greek letter

THETIC *adj* arbitrary

THETICAL *adj* thetic

THEURGY *n* pl. -GIES divine intervention in human affairs **THEURGIC** *adj*

THEW *n* pl. -S a well-developed muscle **THEWY** *adj*

THEWLESS *adj* weak

THEY *pron* the 3d person pl. pronoun in the nominative case

THIAMIN *n* pl. -S thiamine

THIAMINE *n* pl. -S a B vitamin

THIAZIDE *n* pl. -S a drug used to treat high blood pressure

THIAZIN *n* pl. -S thiazine

THIAZINE *n* pl. -S a chemical compound

THIAZOL *n* pl. -S thiazole

THIAZOLE *n* pl. -S a chemical compound

THICK *adj* THICKER, THICKEST having relatively great extent from one surface to its opposite

THICK *n* pl. -S the thickest part

THICKEN *v* -ED, -ING, -S to make thick

THICKET *n* pl. -S a dense growth of shrubs or small trees **THICKETY** *adj*

THICKISH *adj* somewhat thick

THICKLY *adv* in a thick manner

THICKSET *n* pl. -S a thicket

THIEF *n* pl. THIEVES one that steals

THIEVE *v* THIEVED, THIEVING, THIEVES to steal

THIEVERY *n* pl. -ERIES the act or practice of stealing

THIEVES pl. of thief

THIEVING present participle of thieve

THIEVISH *adj* given to stealing

THIGH *n* pl. -S a part of the leg **THIGHED** *adj*

THILL *n* pl. -S a shaft of a vehicle

THIMBLE *n* pl. -S a cap used to protect the fingertip during sewing

THIN *adj* THINNER, THINNEST having relatively little density or thickness

THIN *v* THINNED, THINNING, THINS to make thin

THINCLAD *n* pl. -S a runner on a track team

THINDOWN *n* pl. -S a lessening in the number of atomic particles and cosmic rays passing through the earth's atmosphere

THINE *pron* a possessive form of the pronoun thou

THING *n* pl. -S an inanimate object

THINK *v* THOUGHT, THINKING, THINKS to formulate in the mind

THINKER *n* pl. -S one that thinks

THINKING *n* pl. -S an opinion or judgment

THINLY *adv* in a thin manner

THINNED past tense of thin

THINNER *n* pl. -S one that thins

THINNESS *n* pl. -ES the quality or state of being thin

THINNEST	superlative of thin
THINNING	present participle of thin
THINNISH	*adj* somewhat thin
THIO	*adj* containing sulfur
THIOL	*n* pl. -S a sulfur compound **THIOLIC** *adj*
THIONATE	*n* pl. -S a chemical salt
THIONIC	*adj* pertaining to sulfur
THIONIN	*n* pl. -S a violet dye
THIONINE	*n* pl. -S thionin
THIONYL	*n* pl. -S sulfinyl
THIOPHEN	*n* pl. -S a chemical compound
THIOTEPA	*n* pl. -S a chemical compound
THIOUREA	*n* pl. -S a chemical compound
THIR	*pron* these
THIRAM	*n* pl. -S a chemical compound
THIRD	*n* pl. -S one of three equal parts
THIRDLY	*adv* in the third place
THIRL	*v* -ED, -ING, -S to thrill
THIRLAGE	*n* pl. -S an obligation requiring feudal tenants to grind grain at a certain mill
THIRST	*v* -ED, -ING, -S to feel a desire or need to drink
THIRSTER	*n* pl. -S one that thirsts
THIRSTY	*adj* THIRSTIER, THIRSTIEST feeling a desire or need to drink
THIRTEEN	*n* pl. -S a number
THIRTY	*n* pl. -TIES a number
THIS	*pron* pl. THESE the person or thing just mentioned
THISTLE	*n* pl. -S a prickly plant **THISTLY** *adj*
THITHER	*adv* in that direction
THO	*conj* though
THOLE	*v* THOLED, THOLING, THOLES to endure
THOLEPIN	*n* pl. -S a pin that serves as an oarlock
THOLOS	*n* pl. -LOI a circular, underground tomb
THONG	*n* pl. -S a narrow strip of leather used for binding **THONGED** *adj*
THORAX	*n* pl. -RACES or -RAXES the part of the body between the neck and the abdomen **THORACAL, THORACIC** *adj*
THORIA	*n* pl. -S an oxide of thorium
THORIC	*adj* pertaining to thorium
THORITE	*n* pl. -S a thorium ore
THORIUM	*n* pl. -S a metallic element
THORN	*v* -ED, -ING, -S to prick with a thorn (a sharp, rigid projection on a plant)
THORNY	*adj* THORNIER, THORNIEST full of thorns **THORNILY** *adv*
THORO	*adj* thorough
THORON	*n* pl. -S a radioactive isotope of radon
THOROUGH	*adj* -OUGHER, -OUGHEST complete in all respects
THORP	*n* pl. -S a small village
THORPE	*n* pl. -S thorp
THOSE	pl. of that
THOU	*v* -ED, -ING, -S to address as "thou" (the 2d person sing. pronoun in the nominative case)
THOUGH	*conj* despite the fact that
THOUGHT	*n* pl. -S a product of thinking
THOUSAND	*n* pl. -S a number
THOWLESS	*adj* listless
THRALDOM	*n* pl. -S servitude
THRALL	*v* -ED, -ING, -S to enslave
THRASH	*v* -ED, -ING, -ES to beat
THRASHER	*n* pl. -S one that thrashes
THRAVE	*n* pl. -S a unit of measure for grain
THRAW	*v* -ED, -ING, -S to twist
THRAWART	*adj* stubborn
THRAWN	*adj* twisted **THRAWNLY** *adv*
THREAD	*v* -ED, -ING, -S to pass a thread (a very slender cord) through
THREADER	*n* pl. -S one that threads
THREADY	*adj* THREADIER, THREADIEST resembling a thread
THREAP	*v* -ED, -ING, -S to dispute
THREAPER	*n* pl. -S one that threaps
THREAT	*v* -ED, -ING, -S to threaten
THREATEN	*v* -ED, -ING, -S to be a source of danger to
THREE	*n* pl. -S a number
THREEP	*v* -ED, -ING, -S to threap
THRENODE	*n* pl. -S a threnody
THRENODY	*n* pl. -DIES a song of lamentation
THRESH	*v* -ED, -ING, -ES to separate the grain or seeds from a plant mechanically

THRESHER	*n* pl. -S one that threshes	**THRUST**	*v* -ED, -ING, -S to push forcibly
THREW	past tense of throw	**THRUSTER**	*n* pl. -S one that thrusts
THRICE	*adv* three times	**THRUSTOR**	*n* pl. -S thruster
THRIFT	*n* pl. -S care and wisdom in the management of one's resources	**THRUWAY**	*n* pl. -WAYS an express highway
THRIFTY	*adj* THRIFTIER, THRIFTIEST displaying thrift	**THUD**	*v* THUDDED, THUDDING, THUDS to make a dull, heavy sound
THRILL	*v* -ED, -ING, -S to excite greatly	**THUG**	*n* pl. -S a brutal ruffian or assassin
THRILLER	*n* pl. -S one that thrills	**THUGGEE**	*n* pl. -S thuggery in India
THRIP	*n* pl. -S a British coin	**THUGGERY**	*n* pl. -GERIES thuggish behavior
THRIVE	*v* THROVE or THRIVED, THRIVEN, THRIVING, THRIVES to grow vigorously	**THUGGISH**	*adj* characteristic of a thug
		THUJA	*n* pl. -S an evergreen tree or shrub
THRIVER	*n* pl. -S one that thrives	**THULIA**	*n* pl. -S an oxide of thulium
THRO	*prep* through	**THULIUM**	*n* pl. -S a metallic element
THROAT	*v* -ED, -ING, -S to utter in a hoarse voice	**THUMB**	*v* -ED, -ING, -S to leaf through with the thumb (the short, thick digit of the human hand)
THROATY	*adj* THROATIER, THROATIEST hoarse	**THUMBKIN**	*n* pl. -S a screw that is turned by the thumb and fingers
THROB	*v* THROBBED, THROBBING, THROBS to pulsate	**THUMBNUT**	*n* pl. -S a nut that is turned by the thumb and fingers
THROBBER	*n* pl. -S one that throbs	**THUMP**	*v* -ED, -ING, -S to strike so as to make a dull, heavy sound
THROE	*n* pl. -S a violent spasm of pain	**THUMPER**	*n* pl. -S one that thumps
THROMBIN	*n* pl. -S an enzyme	**THUNDER**	*v* -ED, -ING, -S to produce a loud, resounding sound
THROMBUS	*n* pl. -BI a clot occluding a blood vessel	**THUNDERY**	*adj* accompanied with thunder
THRONE	*v* THRONED, THRONING, THRONES to place on a throne (a royal chair)	**THURIBLE**	*n* pl. -S a censer
		THURIFER	*n* pl. -S one who carries a thurible in a religious ceremony
THRONG	*v* -ED, -ING, -S to crowd into	**THURL**	*n* pl. -S the hip joint in cattle
THROSTLE	*n* pl. -S a songbird	**THUS**	*adv* in this manner
THROTTLE	*v* -TLED, -TLING, -TLES to strangle	**THUSLY**	*adv* thus
THROUGH	*prep* by way of	**THUYA**	*n* pl. -S thuja
THROVE	a past tense of thrive	**THWACK**	*v* -ED, -ING, -S to strike with something flat
THROW	*v* THREW, THROWN, THROWING, THROWS to propel through the air with a movement of the arm	**THWACKER**	*n* pl. -S one that thwacks
		THWART	*v* -ED, -ING, -S to prevent the accomplishment of
THROWER	*n* pl. -S one that throws	**THWARTER**	*n* pl. -S one that thwarts
THRU	*prep* through	**THWARTLY**	*adv* athwart
THRUM	*v* THRUMMED, THRUMMING, THRUMS to play a stringed instrument idly or monotonously	**THY**	*pron* a possessive form of the pronoun thou
		THYME	*n* pl. -S an aromatic herb
THRUMMER	*n* pl. -S one that thrums	**THYMEY**	*adj* THYMIER, THYMIEST thymy
THRUMMY	*adj* -MIER, -MIEST shaggy	**THYMI**	a pl. of thymus
THRUPUT	*n* pl. -S the amount of raw material processed within a given time	**THYMIC**	*adj* pertaining to thyme
THRUSH	*n* pl. -ES a songbird		

THYMIER comparative of thymey and thymy

THYMIEST superlative of thymey and thymy

THYMINE n pl. -S a chemical compound

THYMOL n pl. -S a chemical compound

THYMUS n pl. -MI or -MUSES a glandular structure in the body

THYMY adj THYMIER, THYMIEST abounding in thyme

THYREOID adj pertaining to the thyroid

THYROID n pl. -S an endocrine gland

THYROXIN n pl. -S an amino acid

THYRSE n pl. -S thyrsus

THYRSUS n pl. -SI a type of flower cluster **THYRSOID** adj

THYSELF pron yourself

TI n pl. -S the seventh tone of the diatonic musical scale

TIARA n pl. -S a jeweled headpiece worn by women **TIARAED** adj

TIBIA n pl. -IAE or -IAS a bone of the leg **TIBIAL** adj

TIC n pl. -S an involuntary muscular contraction

TICAL n pl. -S a former Thai unit of weight

TICK v -ED, -ING, -S to make a recurrent clicking sound

TICKER n pl. -S one that ticks

TICKET v -ED, -ING, -S to attach a tag to

TICKING n pl. -S a strong cotton fabric

TICKLE v -LED, -LING, -LES to touch lightly so as to produce a tingling sensation

TICKLER n pl. -S one that tickles

TICKLISH adj sensitive to tickling

TICKSEED n pl. -S a flowering plant

TICKTACK v -ED, -ING, -S to ticktock

TICKTOCK v -ED, -ING, -S to make the ticking sound of a clock

TICTAC v -TACKED, -TACKING, -TACS to ticktack

TICTOC v -TOCKED, -TOCKING, -TOCS to ticktock

TIDAL adj pertaining to the tides **TIDALLY** adv

TIDBIT n pl. -S a choice bit of food

TIDDLY adj slightly drunk

TIDE v TIDED, TIDING, TIDES to flow like the tide (the rise and fall of the ocean's waters)

TIDELAND n pl. -S land alternately covered and uncovered by the tide

TIDELESS adj lacking a tide

TIDELIKE adj resembling a tide

TIDEMARK n pl. -S a mark showing the highest or lowest point of a tide

TIDERIP n pl. -S a riptide

TIDEWAY n pl. -WAYS a tidal channel

TIDIED past tense of tidy

TIDIER comparative of tidy

TIDIES present 3d person sing. of tidy

TIDIEST superlative of tidy

TIDILY adv in a tidy manner

TIDINESS n pl. -ES the state of being tidy

TIDING n pl. -S a piece of news

TIDY adj -DIER, -DIEST neat and orderly

TIDY v -DIED, -DYING, -DIES to make tidy

TIDYTIPS n pl. TIDYTIPS an annual herb

TIE v TIED, TYING or TIEING, TIES to fasten with a cord or rope

TIEBACK n pl. -S a loop for holding a curtain back to one side

TIECLASP n pl. -S a clasp for securing a necktie

TIED past tense of tie

TIEPIN n pl. -S a pin for securing a necktie

TIER v -ED, -ING, -S to arrange in tiers (rows placed one above another)

TIERCE n pl. -S one of seven canonical daily periods for prayer and devotion

TIERCED adj divided into three equal parts

TIERCEL n pl. -S tercel

TIFF v -ED, -ING, -S to have a petty quarrel

TIFFANY n pl. -NIES a thin, mesh fabric

TIFFIN v -ED, -ING, -S to lunch

TIGER n pl. -S a large feline mammal

TIGEREYE n pl. -S a gemstone

TIGERISH adj resembling a tiger

TIGHT *adj* TIGHTER, TIGHTEST firmly or closely fixed in place **TIGHTLY** *adv*

TIGHTEN *v* -ED, -ING, -S to make tight

TIGHTS *n/pl* a close-fitting garment

TIGHTWAD *n* pl. -S a miser

TIGLON *n* pl. -S the offspring of a male tiger and a female lion

TIGON *n* pl. -S tiglon

TIGRESS *n* pl. -ES a female tiger

TIGRISH *adj* tigerish

TIKE *n* pl. -S tyke

TIKI *n* pl. -S a wood or stone image of a Polynesian god

TIL *n* pl. -S the sesame plant

TILAPIA *n* pl. -S an African fish

TILBURY *n* pl. -BURIES a carriage having two wheels

TILDE *n* pl. -S a mark placed over a letter to indicate its sound

TILE *v* TILED, TILING, TILES to cover with tiles (thin slabs of baked clay)

TILEFISH *n* pl. -ES a marine food fish

TILELIKE *adj* resembling a tile

TILER *n* pl. -S one that tiles

TILING *n* pl. -S a surface of tiles

TILL *v* -ED, -ING, -S to prepare land for crops by plowing **TILLABLE** *adj*

TILLAGE *n* pl. -S cultivated land

TILLER *v* -ED, -ING, -S to put forth stems from a root

TILT *v* -ED, -ING, -S to cause to slant **TILTABLE** *adj*

TILTER *n* pl. -S one that tilts

TILTH *n* pl. -S tillage

TILTYARD *n* pl. -S an area for jousting contests

TIMARAU *n* pl. -S tamarau

TIMBAL *n* pl. -S a large drum

TIMBALE *n* pl. -S a pastry shell shaped like a drum

TIMBER *v* -ED, -ING, -S to furnish with timber (wood used as a building material)

TIMBRE *n* pl. -S the quality given to a sound by its overtones

TIMBREL *n* pl. -S a percussion instrument

TIME *v* TIMED, TIMING, TIMES to determine the speed or duration of

TIMECARD *n* pl. -S a card for recording an employee's times of arrival and departure

TIMELESS *adj* having no beginning or end

TIMELY *adj* -LIER, -LIEST occurring at the right moment

TIMEOUS *adj* timely

TIMEOUT *n* pl. -S a brief suspension of activity

TIMER *n* pl. -S one that times

TIMEWORK *n* pl. -S work paid for by the hour or by the day

TIMEWORN *adj* showing the effects of long use or wear

TIMID *adj* -IDER, -IDEST lacking courage or self-confidence **TIMIDLY** *adv*

TIMIDITY *n* pl. -TIES the quality of being timid

TIMING *n* pl. -S the selection of the proper moment for doing something

TIMOROUS *adj* fearful

TIMOTHY *n* pl. -THIES a European grass

TIMPANO *n* pl. -NI a kettledrum

TIMPANUM *n* pl. -NA or -NUMS tympanum

TIN *v* TINNED, TINNING, TINS to coat with tin (a metallic element)

TINAMOU *n* pl. -S a South American game bird

TINCAL *n* pl. -S crude borax

TINCT *v* -ED, -ING, -S to tinge

TINCTURE *v* -TURED, -TURING, -TURES to tinge

TINDER *n* pl. -S readily combustible material **TINDERY** *adj*

TINE *v* TINED, TINING, TINES to lose

TINEA *n* pl. -S a fungous skin disease **TINEAL** *adj*

TINEID *n* pl. -S one of a family of moths

TINFOIL *n* pl. -S a thin metal sheeting

TINFUL *n* pl. -S as much as a tin container can hold

TING *v* -ED, -ING, -S to emit a high-pitched metallic sound

TINGE *v* TINGED, TINGEING or TINGING, TINGES to apply a trace of color to

TINGLE	v -GLED, -GLING, -GLES to cause a prickly, stinging sensation	**TINTLESS**	adj lacking color
		TINTYPE	n pl. -S a kind of photograph
TINGLER	n pl. -S one that tingles	**TINWARE**	n pl. -S articles made of tinplate
TINGLY	adj -GLIER, -GLIEST tingling	**TINWORK**	n pl. -S something made of tin
TINHORN	n pl. -S a showily pretentious person	**TINY**	adj TINIER, TINIEST very small
		TIP	v TIPPED, TIPPING, TIPS to tilt
TINIER	comparative of tiny	**TIPCART**	n pl. -S a type of cart
TINIEST	superlative of tiny	**TIPCAT**	n pl. -S a game resembling baseball
TINILY	adv in a tiny manner		
TININESS	n pl. -ES the quality of being tiny	**TIPI**	n pl. -S tepee
		TIPLESS	adj having no point or extremity
TINING	present participle of tine	**TIPOFF**	n pl. -S a hint or warning
TINKER	v -ED, -ING, -S to repair in an unskilled or experimental manner	**TIPPABLE**	adj capable of being tipped
		TIPPED	past tense of tip
TINKERER	n pl. -S one that tinkers	**TIPPER**	n pl. -S one that tips
TINKLE	v -KLED, -KLING, -KLES to make slight, sharp, metallic sounds	**TIPPET**	n pl. -S a covering for the shoulders
		TIPPIER	comparative of tippy
TINKLING	n pl. -S the sound made by something that tinkles	**TIPPIEST**	superlative of tippy
		TIPPING	present participle of tip
TINKLY	adj -KLIER, -KLIEST producing a tinkling sound	**TIPPLE**	v -PLED, -PLING, -PLES to drink alcoholic beverages
TINLIKE	adj resembling tin	**TIPPLER**	n pl. -S one that tipples
TINMAN	n pl. -MEN a tinsmith	**TIPPY**	adj -PIER, -PIEST unsteady
TINNED	past tense of tin	**TIPSIER**	comparative of tipsy
TINNER	n pl. -S a tin miner	**TIPSIEST**	superlative of tipsy
TINNIER	comparative of tinny	**TIPSILY**	adv in a tipsy manner
TINNIEST	superlative of tinny	**TIPSTAFF**	n pl. -STAFFS or -STAVES an attendant in a court of law
TINNILY	adv in a tinny manner		
TINNING	present participle of tin	**TIPSTER**	n pl. -S one that sells information to gamblers
TINNITUS	n pl. -ES a ringing sound in the ears	**TIPSTOCK**	n pl. -S a part of a gun
TINNY	adj -NIER, -NIEST of or resembling tin	**TIPSY**	adj -SIER, -SIEST slightly drunk
		TIPTOE	v -TOED, -TOEING, -TOES to walk on the tips of one's toes
TINPLATE	n pl. -S thin sheet iron coated with tin	**TIPTOP**	n pl. -S the highest point
TINSEL	v -SELED, -SELING, -SELS or -SELLED, -SELLING, -SELS to give a showy or gaudy appearance to	**TIRADE**	n pl. -S a long, vehement speech
		TIRE	v TIRED, TIRING, TIRES to grow tired
TINSELLY	adj cheaply gaudy	**TIRED**	adj TIREDER, TIREDEST sapped of strength **TIREDLY** adv
TINSMITH	n pl. -S one who works with tin		
TINSTONE	n pl. -S a tin ore	**TIRELESS**	adj seemingly incapable of tiring
TINT	v -ED, -ING, -S to color slightly or delicately	**TIRESOME**	adj tedious
		TIRING	present participle of tire
TINTER	n pl. -S one that tints	**TIRL**	v -ED, -ING, -S to make a vibrating sound
TINTING	n pl. -S the process of one that tints		

TIRO	*n* pl. -ROS tyro
TIRRIVEE	*n* pl. -S a tantrum
TISANE	*n* pl. -S a ptisan
TISSUAL	*adj* pertaining to tissue
TISSUE	*v* -SUED, -SUING, -SUES to weave into tissue (a fine sheer fabric)
TISSUEY	*adj* resembling tissue
TIT	*n* pl. -S a small bird
TITAN	*n* pl. -S a person of great size
TITANATE	*n* pl. -S a chemical salt
TITANESS	*n* pl. -ES a female titan
TITANIA	*n* pl. -S a mineral
TITANIC	*adj* of great size
TITANISM	*n* pl. -S revolt against social conventions
TITANITE	*n* pl. -S a mineral
TITANIUM	*n* pl. -S a metallic element
TITANOUS	*adj* pertaining to titanium
TITBIT	*n* pl. -S tidbit
TITER	*n* pl. -S the strength of a chemical solution
TITHABLE	*adj* subject to the payment of tithes
TITHE	*v* TITHED, TITHING, TITHES to pay a tithe (a small tax)
TITHER	*n* pl. -S one that tithes
TITHING	*n* pl. -S the act of levying tithes
TITHONIA	*n* pl. -S a tall herb
TITI	*n* pl. -S an evergreen shrub or tree
TITIAN	*n* pl. -S a reddish brown color
TITIVATE	*v* -VATED, -VATING, -VATES to dress smartly
TITLARK	*n* pl. -S a songbird
TITLE	*v* -TLED, -TLING, -TLES to furnish with a title (a distinctive appellation)
TITLIST	*n* pl. -S a sports champion
TITMAN	*n* pl. -MEN the smallest of a litter of pigs
TITMOUSE	*n* pl. -MICE a small bird
TITRABLE	*adj* capable of being titrated
TITRANT	*n* pl. -S the reagent used in titration
TITRATE	*v* -TRATED, -TRATING, -TRATES to determine the strength of a solution by adding a reagent until a desired reaction occurs
TITRATOR	*n* pl. -S one that titrates

TITRE	*n* pl. -S titer
TITTER	*v* -ED, -ING, -S to utter a restrained, nervous laugh
TITTERER	*n* pl. -S one that titters
TITTIE	*n* pl. -S a sister
TITTIES	pl. of titty
TITTLE	*n* pl. -S a very small mark in writing or printing
TITTUP	*v* -TUPED, -TUPING, -TUPS or -TUPPED, -TUPPING, -TUPS to move in a lively manner
TITTUPPY	*adj* shaky; unsteady
TITTY	*n* pl. -TIES a teat
TITULAR	*n* pl. -S one who holds a title
TITULARY	*n* pl. -LARIES a titular
TIVY	*adv* with great speed
TIZZY	*n* pl. -ZIES a state of nervous confusion
TMESIS	*n* pl. TMESES the separation of the parts of a compound word by an intervening word or words
TO	*prep* in the direction of
TOAD	*n* pl. -S a tailless, jumping amphibian
TOADFISH	*n* pl. -ES a marine fish
TOADFLAX	*n* pl. -ES a perennial herb
TOADIED	past tense of toady
TOADIES	present 3d person sing. of toady
TOADISH	*adj* resembling a toad
TOADLESS	*adj* having no toads
TOADLIKE	*adj* resembling a toad
TOADY	*v* TOADIED, TOADYING, TOADIES to engage in servile flattering
TOADYISH	*adj* characteristic of one that toadies
TOADYISM	*n* pl. -S toadyish behavior
TOAST	*v* -ED, -ING, -S to brown by exposure to heat
TOASTER	*n* pl. -S a device for toasting
TOASTY	*adj* TOASTIER, TOASTIEST comfortably warm
TOBACCO	*n* pl. -COS or -COES an annual herb cultivated for its leaves
TOBOGGAN	*v* -ED, -ING, -S to ride on a long, narrow sled
TOBY	*n* pl. -BIES a type of drinking mug

TOCCATA   *n* pl. -TAS or -TE a musical composition usually for an organ

TOCHER   *v* -ED, -ING, -S to give a dowry to

TOCOLOGY   *n* pl. -GIES the branch of medicine dealing with childbirth

TOCSIN   *n* pl. -S an alarm sounded on a bell

TOD   *n* pl. -S a British unit of weight

TODAY   *n* pl. -DAYS the present day

TODDIES   pl. of toddy

TODDLE   *v* -DLED, -DLING, -DLES to walk unsteadily

TODDLER   *n* pl. -S one that toddles

TODDY   *n* pl. -DIES an alcoholic beverage

TODY   *n* pl. -DIES a West Indian bird

TOE   *v* TOED, TOEING, TOES to touch with the toe (one of the terminal members of the foot)

TOECAP   *n* pl. -S a covering for the tip of a shoe or boot

TOEHOLD   *n* pl. -S a space that supports the toes in climbing

TOELESS   *adj* having no toes

TOELIKE   *adj* resembling a toe

TOENAIL   *v* -ED, -ING, -S to fasten with obliquely driven nails

TOEPIECE   *n* pl. -S a piece of a shoe designed to cover the toes

TOEPLATE   *n* pl. -S a metal tab attached to the tip of a shoe

TOESHOE   *n* pl. -S a dance slipper without a heel

TOFF   *n* pl. -S a dandy

TOFFEE   *n* pl. -S a chewy candy

TOFFY   *n* pl. -FIES toffee

TOFT   *n* pl. -S a hillock

TOFU   *n* pl. -S a soft Oriental cheese made from soybean milk

TOG   *v* TOGGED, TOGGING, TOGS to clothe

TOGA   *n* pl. -GAS or -GAE an outer garment worn in ancient Rome **TOGAED** *adj*

TOGATE   *adj* pertaining to ancient Rome

TOGATED   *adj* wearing a toga

TOGETHER   *adv* into a union or relationship

TOGGED   past tense of tog

TOGGERY   *n* pl. -GERIES clothing

TOGGING   present participle of tog

TOGGLE   *v* -GLED, -GLING, -GLES to fasten with a type of pin or short rod

TOGGLER   *n* pl. -S one that toggles

TOGUE   *n* pl. -S a freshwater fish

TOIL   *v* -ED, -ING, -S to work strenuously

TOILE   *n* pl. -S a sheer linen fabric

TOILER   *n* pl. -S one that toils

TOILET   *v* -ED, -ING, -S to dress and groom oneself

TOILETRY   *n* pl. -TRIES an article used in dressing and grooming oneself

TOILETTE   *n* pl. -S the act of dressing and grooming oneself

TOILFUL   *adj* toilsome

TOILSOME   *adj* demanding much exertion

TOILWORN   *adj* worn by toil

TOIT   *v* -ED, -ING, -S to saunter

TOKAY   *n* pl. -KAYS a Malaysian gecko

TOKE   *n* pl. -S a puff on a marijuana cigarette

TOKEN   *v* -ED, -ING, -S to serve as a sign of

TOKENISM   *n* pl. -S the policy of making only a superficial effort

TOKOLOGY   *n* pl. -GIES tocology

TOKONOMA   *n* pl. -S a small alcove in a Japanese house

TOLA   *n* pl. -S a unit of weight used in India

TOLAN   *n* pl. -S a chemical compound

TOLANE   *n* pl. -S tolan

TOLBOOTH   *n* pl. -S a prison

TOLD   past tense of tell

TOLE   *v* TOLED, TOLING, TOLES to allure

TOLEDO   *n* pl. -DOS a finely tempered sword

TOLERANT   *adj* inclined to tolerate

TOLERATE   *v* -ATED, -ATING, -ATES to allow without active opposition

TOLIDIN   *n* pl. -S tolidine

TOLIDINE   *n* pl. -S a chemical compound

TOLING   present participle of tole

TOLL — *v* -ED, -ING, -S to collect or impose a toll (a fixed charge for a service or privilege)

TOLLAGE — *n* pl. -S a toll

TOLLBAR — *n* pl. -S a tollgate

TOLLER — *n* pl. -S a collector of tolls

TOLLGATE — *n* pl. -S a gate where a toll is collected

TOLLMAN — *n* pl. -MEN a toller

TOLLWAY — *n* pl. -WAYS a road on which tolls are collected

TOLU — *n* pl. -S a fragrant resin

TOLUATE — *n* pl. -S a chemical salt

TOLUENE — *n* pl. -S a flammable liquid

TOLUIC — *adj* pertaining to any of four isomeric acids derived from toluene

TOLUID — *n* pl. -S toluide

TOLUIDE — *n* pl. -S an amide

TOLUIDIN — *n* pl. -S an amine

TOLUOL — *n* pl. -S toluene

TOLUOLE — *n* pl. -S toluol

TOLUYL — *n* pl. -S a univalent chemical radical

TOLYL — *n* pl. -S a univalent chemical radical

TOM — *n* pl. -S the male of various animals

TOMAHAWK — *v* -ED, -ING, -S to strike with a light ax

TOMALLEY — *n* pl. -LEYS the liver of a lobster

TOMAN — *n* pl. -S a coin of Iran

TOMATO — *n* pl. -TOES the fleshy, edible fruit of a perennial plant

TOMB — *v* -ED, -ING, -S to place in a tomb (a burial vault or chamber)

TOMBAC — *n* pl. -S an alloy of copper and zinc

TOMBACK — *n* pl. -S tombac

TOMBAK — *n* pl. -S tombac

TOMBAL — *adj* pertaining to a tomb

TOMBLESS — *adj* having no tomb

TOMBLIKE — *adj* resembling a tomb

TOMBOLO — *n* pl. -LOS a sandbar connecting an island to the mainland

TOMBOY — *n* pl. -BOYS a girl who prefers boyish activities

TOMCAT — *n* pl. -S a male cat

TOMCOD — *n* pl. -S a marine fish

TOME — *n* pl. -S a large book

TOMENTUM — *n* pl. -TA a network of small blood vessels

TOMFOOL — *n* pl. -S a foolish person

TOMMY — *n* pl. -MIES a loaf of bread

TOMMYROT — *n* pl. -S nonsense

TOMOGRAM — *n* pl. -S a photograph made with X rays

TOMORROW — *n* pl. -S the day following today

TOMPION — *n* pl. -S tampion

TOMTIT — *n* pl. -S a small bird

TON — *n* pl. -S a unit of weight

TONAL — *adj* pertaining to tone **TONALLY** *adv*

TONALITY — *n* pl. -TIES a system of tones

TONDO — *n* pl. -DI a circular painting

TONE — *v* TONED, TONING, TONES to give a particular tone (a sound of definite pitch and vibration) to

TONELESS — *adj* lacking in tone

TONEME — *n* pl. -S a tonal unit of speech **TONEMIC** *adj*

TONER — *n* pl. -S one that tones

TONETICS — *n/pl* the phonetic study of tone in language **TONETIC** *adj*

TONETTE — *n* pl. -S a simple flute

TONG — *v* -ED, -ING, -S to lift with a type of grasping device

TONGA — *n* pl. -S a light cart used in India

TONGER — *n* pl. -S one that tongs

TONGMAN — *n* pl. -MEN a member of a Chinese secret society

TONGUE — *v* TONGUED, TONGUING, TONGUES to touch with the tongue (an organ of the mouth)

TONGUING — *n* pl. -S the use of the tongue in articulating notes on a wind instrument

TONIC — *n* pl. -S something that invigorates or refreshes

TONICITY — *n* pl. -TIES normal, healthy bodily condition

TONIER — comparative of tony

TONIEST — superlative of tony

TONIGHT — *n* pl. -S the present night

TONING — present participle of tone

TONISH — *adj* stylish **TONISHLY** *adv*

TONLET — *n* pl. -S a skirt of plate armor

TONNAGE   *n* pl. -S total weight in tons

TONNE   *n* pl. -S a unit of weight

TONNEAU   *n* pl. -NEAUS or -NEAUX the rear seating compartment of an automobile

TONNER   *n* pl. -S an object having a specified tonnage

TONNISH   *adj* tonish

TONSIL   *n* pl. -S a lymphoid organ **TONSILAR** *adj*

TONSURE   *v* -SURED, -SURING, -SURES to shave the head of

TONTINE   *n* pl. -S a form of collective life insurance

TONUS   *n* pl. -ES a normal state of tension in muscle tissue

TONY   *adj* TONIER, TONIEST stylish

TOO   *adv* in addition

TOOK   past tense of take

TOOL   *v* -ED, -ING, -S to form or finish with a tool (an implement used in manual work)

TOOLBOX   *n* pl. -ES a box for tools

TOOLER   *n* pl. -S one that tools

TOOLHEAD   *n* pl. -S a part of a machine

TOOLING   *n* pl. -S ornamentation done with tools

TOOLLESS   *adj* having no tools

TOOLROOM   *n* pl. -S a room where tools are stored

TOOLSHED   *n* pl. -S a building where tools are stored

TOOM   *adj* empty

TOON   *n* pl. -S an East Indian tree

TOOT   *v* -ED, -ING, -S to sound a horn or whistle in short blasts

TOOTER   *n* pl. -S one that toots

TOOTH   *n* pl. TEETH one of the hard structures attached in a row to each jaw

TOOTH   *v* -ED, -ING, -S to furnish with toothlike projections

TOOTHY   *adj* TOOTHIER, TOOTHIEST having or showing prominent teeth **TOOTHILY** *adv*

TOOTLE   *v* -TLED, -TLING, -TLES to toot softly or repeatedly

TOOTLER   *n* pl. -S one that tootles

TOOTS   *n* pl. -ES a woman or girl — usually used as a form of address

TOOTSIE   *n* pl. -S tootsy

TOOTSY   *n* pl. -SIES a foot

TOP   *v* TOPPED, TOPPING, TOPS to cut off the top (the highest part, point, or surface) of

TOPAZ   *n* pl. -ES a mineral **TOPAZINE** *adj*

TOPCOAT   *n* pl. -S a lightweight overcoat

TOPCROSS   *n* pl. -ES a cross between a purebred male and inferior female stock

TOPE   *v* TOPED, TOPING, TOPES to drink liquor to excess

TOPEE   *n* pl. -S topi

TOPER   *n* pl. -S one that topes

TOPFUL   *adj* topfull

TOPFULL   *adj* full to the top

TOPH   *n* pl. -S tufa

TOPHE   *n* pl. -S tufa

TOPHUS   *n* pl. -PHI a deposit of urates in the tissue around a joint

TOPI   *n* pl. -S a sun helmet

TOPIARY   *n* pl. -ARIES the art of trimming shrubs into shapes

TOPIC   *n* pl. -S a subject of discourse **TOPICAL** *adj*

TOPING   present participle of tope

TOPKICK   *n* pl. -S a first sergeant

TOPKNOT   *n* pl. -S an ornament for the hair

TOPLESS   *adj* having no top

TOPLOFTY   *adj* -LOFTIER, -LOFTIEST haughty

TOPMAST   *n* pl. -S a mast of a ship

TOPMOST   *adj* highest

TOPNOTCH   *adj* excellent

TOPOI   pl. of topos

TOPOLOGY   *n* pl. -GIES a branch of mathematics

TOPONYM   *n* pl. -S the name of a place

TOPONYMY   *n* pl. -MIES the study of toponyms

TOPOS   *n* pl. -POI a stock rhetorical theme

TOPOTYPE   *n* pl. -S a specimen selected from a locality typical of a species

TOPPED   past tense of top

TOPPER   *n* pl. -S one that tops

TOPPING *n* pl. -S something that forms a top

TOPPLE *v* -PLED, -PLING, -PLES to fall forward

TOPSAIL *n* pl. -S a sail of a ship

TOPSIDE *n* pl. -S the upper portion of a ship

TOPSOIL *v* -ED, -ING, -S to remove the surface layer of soil from

TOPSTONE *n* pl. -S the stone at the top of a structure

TOPWORK *v* -ED, -ING, -S to graft scions of another variety of plant on the main branches of

TOQUE *n* pl. -S a close-fitting woman's hat

TOQUET *n* pl. -S toque

TOR *n* pl. -S a high, craggy hill

TORA *n* pl. -S torah

TORAH *n* pl. -S the body of Jewish law

TORC *n* pl. -S a metal collar or necklace

TORCH *v* -ED, -ING, -ES to set on fire

TORCHERE *n* pl. -S a type of electric lamp

TORCHIER *n* pl. -S torchere

TORCHON *n* pl. -S a coarse lace

TORE *n* pl. -S a torus

TOREADOR *n* pl. -S a bullfighter

TORERO *n* pl. -ROS a bullfighter

TOREUTIC *adj* pertaining to a type of metalwork

TORI pl. of torus

TORIC *adj* pertaining to a torus

TORIES pl. of tory

TORII *n* pl. TORII the gateway of a Japanese temple

TORMENT *v* -ED, -ING, -S to inflict with great bodily or mental suffering

TORN past participle of tear

TORNADO *n* pl. -DOES or -DOS a violent windstorm **TORNADIC** *adj*

TORNILLO *n* pl. -LOS a flowering shrub

TORO *n* pl. -ROS a bull

TOROID *n* pl. -S a type of geometric surface **TOROIDAL** *adj*

TOROSE *adj* cylindrical and swollen at intervals

TOROSITY *n* pl. -TIES the quality or state of being torose

TOROUS *adj* torose

TORPEDO *v* -ED, -ING, -ES or -S to damage or sink with an underwater missile

TORPID *n* pl. -S a racing boat

TORPIDLY *adv* in a sluggish manner

TORPOR *n* pl. -S mental or physical inactivity

TORQUATE *adj* having a torques

TORQUE *v* TORQUED, TORQUING, TORQUES to cause to twist

TORQUER *n* pl. -S one that torques

TORQUES *n* pl. -QUESES a band of feathers, hair, or coloration around the neck

TORQUING present participle of torque

TORR *n* pl. TORR a unit of pressure

TORREFY *v* -FIED, -FYING, -FIES to subject to intense heat

TORRENT *n* pl. -S a rapid stream of water

TORRID *adj* -RIDER, -RIDEST extremely hot **TORRIDLY** *adv*

TORRIFY *v* -FIED, -FYING, -FIES to torrefy

TORSADE *n* pl. -S a twisted cord

TORSE *n* pl. -S a wreath of twisted silks

TORSI a pl. of torso

TORSION *n* pl. -S the act of twisting

TORSK *n* pl. -S a marine food fish

TORSO *n* pl. -SI or -SOS the trunk of the human body

TORT *n* pl. -S a civil wrong

TORTE *n* pl. TORTEN or TORTES a rich cake

TORTILE *adj* twisted; coiled

TORTILLA *n* pl. -S a round, flat cake of unleavened cornmeal

TORTIOUS *adj* of the nature of a tort

TORTOISE *n* pl. -S any of an order of reptiles having the body enclosed in a bony shell

TORTONI *n* pl. -S a type of ice cream

TORTRIX *n* pl. -ES a small moth

TORTUOUS *adj* marked by repeated turns or bends

TORTURE *v* -TURED, -TURING, -TURES to subject to severe physical pain

TORTURER *n* pl. -S one that tortures

TORULA *n* pl. -LAE or -LAS a type of fungus

TORUS	*n* pl. -RI a large convex molding
TORY	*n* pl. -RIES a political conservative
TOSH	*n* pl. -ES nonsense
TOSS	*v* TOSSED or TOST, TOSSING, TOSSES to throw lightly
TOSSER	*n* pl. -S one that tosses
TOSSPOT	*n* pl. -S a drunkard
TOSSUP	*n* pl. -S an even choice or chance
TOST	a past tense of toss
TOT	*v* TOTTED, TOTTING, TOTS to total
TOTABLE	*adj* capable of being toted
TOTAL	*v* -TALED, -TALING, -TALS or -TALLED, -TALLING, -TALS to ascertain the entire amount of
TOTALISE	*v* -ISED, -ISING, -ISES to totalize
TOTALISM	*n* pl. -S centralized control by an autocratic authority
TOTALITY	*n* pl. -TIES the quality or state of being complete
TOTALIZE	*v* -IZED, -IZING, -IZES to make complete
TOTALLED	a past tense of total
TOTALLING	a present participle of total
TOTALLY	*adv* completely
TOTE	*v* TOTED, TOTING, TOTES to carry by hand
TOTEM	*n* pl. -S a natural object serving as the emblem of a family or clan **TOTEMIC** *adj*
TOTEMISM	*n* pl. -S a system of tribal division according to totems
TOTEMIST	*n* pl. -S a specialist in totemism
TOTEMITE	*n* pl. -S a totemist
TOTER	*n* pl. -S one that totes
TOTHER	*pron* the other
TOTING	present participle of tote
TOTTED	past tense of tot
TOTTER	*v* -ED, -ING, -S to walk unsteadily
TOTTERER	*n* pl. -S one that totters
TOTTERY	*adj* shaky
TOTTING	present participle of tot
TOUCAN	*n* pl. -S a tropical bird
TOUCH	*v* -ED, -ING, -ES to be in or come into contact with
TOUCHE	*interj* — used to acknowledge a hit in fencing
TOUCHER	*n* pl. -S one that touches
TOUCHUP	*n* pl. -S an act of finishing by adding minor improvements
TOUCHY	*adj* TOUCHIER, TOUCHIEST overly sensitive **TOUCHILY** *adv*
TOUGH	*adj* TOUGHER, TOUGHEST strong and resilient
TOUGH	*n* pl. -S a rowdy
TOUGHEN	*v* -ED, -ING, -S to make tough
TOUGHIE	*n* pl. -S a tough
TOUGHIES	pl. of toughy
TOUGHISH	*adj* somewhat tough
TOUGHLY	*adv* in a tough manner
TOUGHY	*n* pl. TOUGHIES toughie
TOUPEE	*n* pl. -S a wig worn to cover a bald spot
TOUR	*v* -ED, -ING, -S to travel from place to place
TOURACO	*n* pl. -COS an African bird
TOURER	*n* pl. -S a large, open automobile
TOURING	*n* pl. -S cross-country skiing for pleasure
TOURISM	*n* pl. -S the practice of touring for pleasure
TOURIST	*n* pl. -S one who tours for pleasure **TOURISTY** *adj*
TOURNEY	*v* -ED, -ING, -S to compete in a tournament
TOUSE	*v* TOUSED, TOUSING, TOUSES to tousle
TOUSLE	*v* -SLED, -SLING, -SLES to dishevel
TOUT	*v* -ED, -ING, -S to solicit brazenly
TOUTER	*n* pl. -S one that touts
TOUZLE	*v* -ZLED, -ZLING, -ZLES to tousle
TOVARICH	*n* pl. -ES comrade
TOVARISH	*n* pl. -ES tovarich
TOW	*v* -ED, -ING, -S to pull by means of a rope or chain
TOWAGE	*n* pl. -S the price paid for towing
TOWARD	*prep* in the direction of
TOWARDLY	*adj* favorable
TOWARDS	*prep* toward
TOWAWAY	*n* pl. -AWAYS the act of towing away a vehicle

TOWBOAT *n* pl. -S a tugboat

TOWEL *v* -ELED, -ELING, -ELS or -ELLED, -ELLING, -ELS to wipe with a towel (an absorbent cloth)

TOWELING *n* pl. -S material used for towels

TOWER *v* -ED, -ING, -S to rise to a great height

TOWERY *adj* -ERIER, -ERIEST very tall

TOWHEAD *n* pl. -S a head of light blond hair

TOWHEE *n* pl. -S a common finch

TOWIE *n* pl. -S a form of contract bridge for three players

TOWLINE *n* pl. -S a line used in towing

TOWMOND *n* pl. -S a year

TOWMONT *n* pl. -S towmond

TOWN *n* pl. -S a center of population smaller than a city

TOWNEE *n* pl. -S a townsman

TOWNFOLK *n/pl* the inhabitants of a town

TOWNIE *n* pl. -S a nonstudent who lives in a college town

TOWNIES pl. of towny

TOWNISH *adj* characteristic of a town

TOWNLESS *adj* having no towns

TOWNLET *n* pl. -S a small town

TOWNSHIP *n* pl. -S an administrative division of a county

TOWNSMAN *n* pl. -MEN a resident of a town

TOWNWEAR *n* pl. -S apparel that is suitable for wear in the city

TOWNY *n* pl. TOWNIES townie

TOWPATH *n* pl. -S a path along a river that is used by animals towing boats

TOWROPE *n* pl. -S a rope used in towing

TOWY *adj* resembling coarse hemp or flax fiber

TOXAEMIA *n* pl. -S toxemia **TOXAEMIC** *adj*

TOXEMIA *n* pl. -S the condition of having toxins in the blood **TOXEMIC** *adj*

TOXIC *adj* pertaining to a toxin

TOXICAL *adj* toxic

TOXICANT *n* pl. -S a poisonous substance

TOXICITY *n* pl. -TIES the quality of being poisonous

TOXIN *n* pl. -S a poisonous substance

TOXINE *n* pl. -S toxin

TOXOID *n* pl. -S a type of toxin

TOY *v* -ED, -ING, -S to amuse oneself as if with a toy (a child's plaything)

TOYER *n* pl. -S one that toys

TOYISH *adj* frivolous

TOYLESS *adj* having no toy

TOYLIKE *adj* resembling a toy

TOYO *n* pl. -YOS a smooth straw used in making hats

TOYON *n* pl. -S an evergreen shrub

TRABEATE *adj* constructed with horizontal beams

TRACE *v* TRACED, TRACING, TRACES to follow the course of

TRACER *n* pl. -S one that traces

TRACERY *n* pl. -ERIES ornamental work of interlaced lines

TRACING present participle of trace

TRACHEA *n* pl. -CHEAE or -CHEAS the passage for conveying air to the lungs **TRACHEAL** *adj*

TRACHEID *n* pl. -S a long, tubular plant cell

TRACHLE *v* -LED, -LING, -LES to draggle

TRACHOMA *n* pl. -S a disease of the eye

TRACHYTE *n* pl. -S an igneous rock

TRACING *n* pl. -S something that is traced

TRACK *v* -ED, -ING, -S to follow the marks left by an animal, a person, or a vehicle

TRACKAGE *n* pl. -S the track system of a railroad

TRACKER *n* pl. -S one that tracks

TRACKING *n* pl. -S the placement of students within a curriculum

TRACKMAN *n* pl. -MEN a railroad worker

TRACT *n* pl. -S an expanse of land

TRACTATE *n* pl. -S a treatise

TRACTILE *adj* capable of being drawn out in length

TRACTION *n* pl. -S the act of pulling or drawing over a surface **TRACTIVE** *adj*

TRACTOR *n* pl. -S a motor vehicle used in farming

TRAD *adj* traditional

TRADE *v* TRADED, TRADING, TRADES to give in exchange for another commodity **TRADABLE** *adj*

TRADER *n* pl. -S one that trades

TRADITOR *n pl.* -ES a traitor among the early Christians

TRADUCE *v* -DUCED, -DUCING, -DUCES to defame

TRADUCER *n pl.* -S one that traduces

TRAFFIC *v* -FICKED, -FICKING, -FICS to engage in buying and selling

TRAGEDY *n pl.* -DIES a disastrous event

TRAGI *pl.* of tragus

TRAGIC *adj* of the nature of a tragedy

TRAGICAL *adj* tragic

TRAGOPAN *n pl.* -S an Asian pheasant

TRAGUS *n pl.* -GI a part of the external opening of the ear

TRAIK *v* -ED, -ING, -S to trudge

TRAIL *v* -ED, -ING, -S to drag along a surface

TRAILER *v* -ED, -ING, -S to transport by means of a trailer (a vehicle drawn by another)

TRAIN *v* -ED, -ING, -S to instruct systematically

TRAINEE *n pl.* -S a person receiving training

TRAINER *n pl.* -S one that trains

TRAINFUL *n pl.* -S as much as a railroad train will hold

TRAINING *n pl.* -S systematic instruction

TRAINMAN *n pl.* -MEN a railroad employee

TRAINWAY *n pl.* -WAYS a railway

TRAIPSE *v* TRAIPSED, TRAIPSING, TRAIPSES to walk about in an idle or aimless manner

TRAIT *n pl.* -S a distinguishing characteristic

TRAITOR *n pl.* -S one who betrays another

TRAJECT *v* -ED, -ING, -S to transmit

TRAM *v* TRAMMED, TRAMMING, TRAMS to convey in a tramcar

TRAMCAR *n pl.* -S a streetcar

TRAMEL *v* -ELED, -ELING, -ELS or -ELLED, -ELLING, -ELS to trammel

TRAMELL *v* -ED, -ING, -S to trammel

TRAMLESS *adj* having no tramcar

TRAMLINE *n pl.* -S a streetcar line

TRAMMED past tense of tram

TRAMMEL *v* -MELED, -MELING, -MELS or -MELLED, -MELLING, -MELS to hinder

TRAMMING present participle of tram

TRAMP *v* -ED, -ING, -S to walk with a firm, heavy step

TRAMPER *n pl.* -S one that tramps

TRAMPISH *adj* resembling a vagabond

TRAMPLE *v* -PLED, -PLING, -PLES to tread on heavily

TRAMPLER *n pl.* -S one that tramples

TRAMROAD *n pl.* -S a railway in a mine

TRAMWAY *n pl.* -WAYS a tramline

TRANCE *v* TRANCED, TRANCING, TRANCES to put into a trance (a semiconscious state)

TRANGAM *n pl.* -S a gewgaw

TRANQUIL *adj* -QUILER, -QUILEST or -QUILLER, -QUILLEST free from disturbance

TRANS *adj* characterized by the arrangement of different atoms on opposite sides of the molecule

TRANSACT *v* -ED, -ING, -S to carry out

TRANSECT *v* -ED, -ING, -S to cut across

TRANSEPT *n pl.* -S a major transverse part of the body of a church

TRANSFER *v* -FERRED, -FERRING, -FERS to convey from one source to another

TRANSFIX *v* -FIXED or -FIXT, -FIXING, -FIXES to impale

TRANSHIP *v* -SHIPPED, -SHIPPING, -SHIPS to transfer from one conveyance to another

TRANSIT *v* -ED, -ING, -S to pass across or through

TRANSMIT *v* -MITTED, -MITTING, -MITS to send from one place or person to another

TRANSOM *n pl.* -S a small window above a door or another window

TRANSUDE *v* -SUDED, -SUDING, -SUDES to pass through a membrane

TRAP *v* TRAPPED or TRAPT, TRAPPING, TRAPS to catch in a trap (a device for capturing and holding animals)

TRAPAN *v* -PANNED, -PANNING, -PANS to trepan

TRAPBALL *n pl.* -S a type of ball game

TRAPDOOR *n pl.* -S a lifting or sliding door covering an opening

TRAPES *v* -ED, -ING, -ES to traipse

TRAPEZE *n pl.* -S a gymnastic apparatus

TRAPEZIA *n/pl* four-sided polygons having no parallel sides

TRAPLIKE *adj* resembling a trap

TRAPNEST *v* -ED, -ING, -S to determine the productivity of hens with a type of nest

TRAPPEAN *adj* pertaining to traprock

TRAPPED a past tense of trap

TRAPPER *n pl.* -S one that traps

TRAPPING *n pl.* -S a covering for a horse

TRAPPOSE *adj* trappean

TRAPPOUS *adj* trappean

TRAPROCK *n pl.* -S an igneous rock

TRAPT a past tense of trap

TRAPUNTO *n pl.* -TOS a decorative quilted design

TRASH *v* -ED, -ING, -ES to free from trash (worthless or waste matter)

TRASHMAN *n pl.* -MEN a person who removes trash

TRASHY *adj* TRASHIER, TRASHIEST resembling trash **TRASHILY** *adv*

TRASS *n pl.* -ES a volcanic rock

TRAUCHLE *v* -LED, -LING, -LES to trachle

TRAUMA *n pl.* -MAS or -MATA a severe emotional shock

TRAVAIL *v* -ED, -ING, -S to toil

TRAVE *n pl.* -S a frame for confining a horse

TRAVEL *v* -ELED, -ELING, -ELS or -ELLED, -ELLING, -ELS to go from one place to another

TRAVELER *n pl.* -S one that travels

TRAVELOG *n pl.* -S a lecture or film on traveling

TRAVERSE *v* -VERSED, -VERSING, -VERSES to pass across or through

TRAVESTY *v* -TIED, -TYING, -TIES to parody

TRAVOIS *n pl.* -ES a type of sled

TRAVOISE *n pl.* -S travois

TRAWL *v* -ED, -ING, -S to fish by dragging a net along the sea bottom

TRAWLER *n pl.* -S a boat used for trawling

TRAWLEY *n pl.* -LEYS a small truck or car for conveying material

TRAY *n pl.* TRAYS a flat, shallow receptacle

TRAYFUL *n pl.* -S as much as a tray will hold

TREACLE *n pl.* -S molasses **TREACLY** *adj*

TREAD *v* TROD, TRODE, or TREADED, TRODDEN, TREADING, TREADS to walk on, over, or along

TREADER *n pl.* -S one that treads

TREADLE *v* -LED, -LING, -LES to work a foot lever

TREADLER *n pl.* -S one that treadles

TREASON *n pl.* -S violation of allegiance toward one's country

TREASURE *v* -URED, -URING, -URES to value highly

TREASURY *n pl.* -URIES a place where funds are received, kept, and disbursed

TREAT *v* -ED, -ING, -S to behave in a particular way toward

TREATER *n pl.* -S one that treats

TREATISE *n pl.* -S a formal and systematic written account of a subject

TREATY *n pl.* -TIES a formal agreement between two or more nations

TREBLE *v* -BLED, -BLING, -BLES to triple

TREBLY *adv* triply

TRECENTO *n pl.* -TOS the fourteenth century

TREDDLE *v* -DLED, -DLING, -DLES to treadle

TREE *v* TREED, TREEING, TREES to drive up a tree (a tall, woody plant)

TREELESS *adj* having no tree

TREELIKE *adj* resembling a tree

TREENAIL *n pl.* -S a wooden peg used for fastening timbers

TREETOP *n pl.* -S the top of a tree

TREF *adj* unfit for use according to Jewish law

TREFAH *adj* tref

TREFOIL *n pl.* -S a plant having ternate leaves

TREHALA *n pl.* -S a sweet, edible substance forming the pupal case of certain weevils

TREK	v TREKKED, TREKKING, TREKS to make a slow or arduous journey	**TREY**	n pl. TREYS a three in cards, dice, or dominoes
TREKKER	n pl. -S one that treks	**TRIABLE**	adj subject to judicial examination
TRELLIS	v -ED, -ING, -ES to provide with a trellis (a frame used as a support for climbing plants)	**TRIACID**	n pl. -S a type of acid
		TRIAD	n pl. -S a group of three
TREMBLE	v -BLED, -BLING, -BLES to shake involuntarily	**TRIADIC**	n pl. -S a member of a triad
TREMBLER	n pl. -S one that trembles	**TRIADISM**	n pl. -S the quality or state of being a triad
TREMBLY	adj -BLIER, -BLIEST marked by trembling	**TRIAGE**	n pl. -S a system of treating disaster victims
TREMOLO	n pl. -LOS a vibrating musical effect	**TRIAL**	n pl. -S a judicial examination
TREMOR	n pl. -S a shaking movement	**TRIANGLE**	n pl. -S a polygon having three sides
TRENAIL	n pl. -S treenail	**TRIARCHY**	n pl. -CHIES government by three persons
TRENCH	v -ED, -ING, -ES to dig a long, narrow excavation in the ground		
TRENCHER	n pl. -S a wooden platter for serving food	**TRIAXIAL**	adj having three axes
TREND	v -ED, -ING, -S to take a particular course	**TRIAZIN**	n pl. -S triazine
		TRIAZINE	n pl. -S a chemical compound
TRENDY	adj TRENDIER, TRENDIEST very fashionable **TRENDILY** adv	**TRIAZOLE**	n pl. -S a chemical compound
		TRIBADE	n pl. -S a lesbian **TRIBADIC** adj
TREPAN	v -PANNED, -PANNING, -PANS to trephine	**TRIBAL**	adj pertaining to a tribe **TRIBALLY** adv
TREPANG	n pl. -S a marine animal	**TRIBASIC**	adj having three replaceable hydrogen atoms
TREPHINE	v -PHINED, -PHINING, -PHINES to operate on with a surgical saw	**TRIBE**	n pl. -S a group of people sharing a common ancestry, language, and culture
TREPID	adj timorous		
TRESPASS	v -ED, -ING, -ES to enter upon the land of another unlawfully	**TRIBRACH**	n pl. -S a type of metrical foot
		TRIBUNAL	n pl. -S a court of justice
TRESS	n pl. -ES a long lock of hair **TRESSED** adj	**TRIBUNE**	n pl. -S a defender of the rights of the people
TRESSEL	n pl. -S trestle	**TRIBUTE**	n pl. -S something given to show respect, gratitude, or admiration
TRESSIER	comparative of tressy		
TRESSIEST	superlative of tressy	**TRICE**	v TRICED, TRICING, TRICES to haul up with a rope
TRESSOUR	n pl. -S tressure		
TRESSURE	n pl. -S a type of heraldic design	**TRICEPS**	n pl. -ES an arm muscle
		TRICHINA	n pl. -NAE or -NAS a parasitic worm
TRESSY	adj TRESSIER, TRESSIEST abounding in tresses	**TRICHITE**	n pl. -S a minute mineral body found in volcanic rocks
TRESTLE	n pl. -S a framework for supporting a bridge	**TRICHOID**	adj hairlike
		TRICHOME	n pl. -S a hairlike outgrowth
TRET	n pl. -S an allowance formerly paid to purchasers for waste incurred in transit	**TRICING**	present participle of trice
		TRICK	v -ED, -ING, -S to deceive
		TRICKER	n pl. -S one that tricks
TREVET	n pl. -S trivet	**TRICKERY**	n pl. -ERIES deception
TREWS	n/pl close-fitting tartan trousers	**TRICKIE**	adj TRICKIER, TRICKIEST tricky

TRICKIER	comparative of tricky	**TRIGGEST**	superlative of trig
TRICKIEST	superlative of tricky	**TRIGGING**	present participle of trig
TRICKILY	adv in a tricky manner	**TRIGLY**	adv in a trig manner
TRICKISH	adj tricky	**TRIGLYPH**	n pl. -S an architectural ornament
TRICKLE	v -LED, -LING, -LES to flow or fall in drops	**TRIGNESS**	n pl. -ES the quality or state of being trig
TRICKLY	adj -LIER, -LIEST marked by trickling	**TRIGO**	n pl. -GOS wheat
TRICKSY	adj -SIER, -SIEST mischievous	**TRIGON**	n pl. -S an ancient stringed instrument
TRICKY	adj TRICKIER, TRICKIEST characterized by deception	**TRIGONAL**	adj shaped like a triangle
TRICLAD	n pl. -S an aquatic flatworm	**TRIGRAPH**	n pl. -S a group of three letters representing one sound
TRICOLOR	n pl. -S a flag having three colors	**TRIHEDRA**	n/pl figures having three plane surfaces meeting at a point
TRICORN	n pl. -S a hat with the brim turned up on three sides	**TRIJET**	n pl. -S an airplane powered by three jet engines
TRICORNE	n pl. -S tricorn		
TRICOT	n pl. -S a knitted fabric	**TRILBY**	n pl. -BIES a soft felt hat
TRICTRAC	n pl. -S a form of backgammon	**TRILL**	v -ED, -ING, -S to sing or play with a vibrating effect
TRICYCLE	n pl. -S a vehicle having three wheels		
		TRILLER	n pl. -S one that trills
TRIDENT	n pl. -S a spear having three prongs	**TRILLION**	n pl. -S a number
		TRILLIUM	n pl. -S a flowering plant
TRIDUUM	n pl. -S a period of three days of prayer	**TRILOBAL**	adj trilobed
		TRILOBED	adj having three lobes
TRIED	past tense of try	**TRILOGY**	n pl. -GIES a group of three related literary works
TRIENE	n pl. -S a type of chemical compound		
		TRIM	adj TRIMMER, TRIMMEST neat and orderly
TRIENNIA	n/pl periods of three years		
TRIENS	n pl. -ENTES a coin of ancient Rome	**TRIM**	v TRIMMED, TRIMMING, TRIMS to make trim by cutting
		TRIMARAN	n pl. -S a sailing vessel
TRIER	n pl. -S one that tries	**TRIMER**	n pl. -S a type of chemical compound
TRIES	present 3d person sing. of try		
TRIETHYL	adj containing three ethyl groups	**TRIMETER**	n pl. -S a verse of three metrical feet
		TRIMLY	adv in a trim manner
TRIFID	adj divided into three parts	**TRIMMED**	past tense of trim
TRIFLE	v -FLED, -FLING, -FLES to waste time	**TRIMMER**	n pl. -S one that trims
		TRIMMEST	superlative of trim
TRIFLER	n pl. -S one that trifles	**TRIMMING**	n pl. -S something added as a decoration
TRIFLING	n pl. -S a waste of time		
TRIFOCAL	n pl. -S a type of lens	**TRIMNESS**	n pl. -ES the state of being trim
TRIFOLD	adj having three parts	**TRIMORPH**	n pl. -S a substance existing in three forms
TRIFORIA	n/pl galleries in a church		
TRIFORM	adj having three forms	**TRIMOTOR**	n pl. -S an airplane powered by three engines
TRIG	adj TRIGGER, TRIGGEST neat		
TRIG	v TRIGGED, TRIGGING, TRIGS to make trig	**TRINAL**	adj having three parts
		TRINARY	adj consisting of three parts
TRIGGER	v -ED, -ING, -S to actuate		

TRINDLE v -DLED, -DLING, -DLES to trundle

TRINE v TRINED, TRINING, TRINES to place in a particular astrological position

TRINITY n pl. -TIES a group of three

TRINKET v -ED, -ING, -S to deal secretly

TRINKUMS n/pl small ornaments

TRINODAL adj having three nodes

TRIO n pl. TRIOS a group of three

TRIODE n pl. -S a type of electron tube

TRIOL n pl. -S a type of chemical compound

TRIOLET n pl. -S a short poem of fixed form

TRIOSE n pl. -S a simple sugar

TRIOXID n pl. -S trioxide

TRIOXIDE n pl. -S a type of oxide

TRIP v TRIPPED, TRIPPING, TRIPS to stumble

TRIPACK n pl. -S a type of film pack

TRIPART adj divided into three parts

TRIPE n pl. -S a part of the stomach of a ruminant that is used as food

TRIPEDAL adj having three feet

TRIPHASE adj having three phases

TRIPLANE n pl. -S a type of airplane

TRIPLE v -PLED, -PLING, -PLES to make three times as great

TRIPLET n pl. -S a group of three of one kind

TRIPLEX n pl. -ES an apartment having three floors

TRIPLING present participle of triple

TRIPLITE n pl. -S a mineral

TRIPLOID n pl. -S a cell having a chromosome number that is three times the basic number

TRIPLY adv in a triple degree, manner, or number

TRIPOD n pl. -S a stand having three legs TRIPODAL, TRIPODIC adj

TRIPODY n pl. -DIES a verse of three metrical feet

TRIPOLI n pl. -S a soft, friable rock

TRIPOS n pl. -ES a tripod

TRIPPED past tense of trip

TRIPPER n pl. -S one that trips

TRIPPET n pl. -S a part of a mechanism designed to strike another part

TRIPPING n pl. -S the act of one that trips

TRIPTANE n pl. -S a chemical compound

TRIPTYCA n pl. -S a triptych

TRIPTYCH n pl. -S an ancient writing table

TRIREME n pl. -S an ancient Greek or Roman warship

TRISCELE n pl. -S triskele

TRISECT v -ED, -ING, -S to divide into three equal parts

TRISEME n pl. -S a type of metrical foot TRISEMIC adj

TRISKELE n pl. -S a figure consisting of three branches radiating from a center

TRISMUS n pl. -ES lockjaw TRISMIC adj

TRISOME n pl. -S an organism having one chromosome in addition to the usual diploid number

TRISOMIC n pl. -S a trisome

TRISOMY n pl. -MIES the condition of being a trisome

TRISTATE adj pertaining to an area made up of three adjoining states

TRISTE adj sad

TRISTEZA n pl. -S a disease of citrus trees

TRISTFUL adj sad

TRISTICH n pl. -S a stanza of three lines

TRITE adj TRITER, TRITEST used so often as to be made commonplace TRITELY adv

TRITHING n pl. -S an administrative division in England

TRITICUM n pl. -S a cereal grass

TRITIUM n pl. -S an isotope of hydrogen

TRITOMA n pl. -S an African herb

TRITON n pl. -S a marine mollusk

TRITONE n pl. -S a musical interval of three whole tones

TRIUMPH v -ED, -ING, -S to be victorious

TRIUMVIR n pl. -VIRS or -VIRI one of a ruling body of three in ancient Rome

TRIUNE n pl. -S a trinity

TRIUNITY n pl. -TIES a trinity

TRIVALVE n pl. -S a type of shell

TRIVET n pl. -S a small stand having three legs

TRIVIA	*n/pl* insignificant matters	**TROMMEL**	*n* pl. -S a screen used for sifting rock, ore, or coal
TRIVIAL	*adj* insignificant	**TROMP**	*v* -ED, -ING, -S to tramp
TRIVIUM	*n* pl. -IA a group of studies in medieval schools	**TROMPE**	*n* pl. -S a device used for supplying air to a furnace
TROAK	*v* -ED, -ING, -S to troke	**TRONA**	*n* pl. -S a mineral
TROCAR	*n* pl. -S a surgical instrument	**TRONE**	*n* pl. -S a weighing device
TROCHAIC	*n* pl. -S a trochee	**TROOP**	*v* -ED, -ING, -S to move or gather in crowds
TROCHAL	*adj* shaped like a wheel		
TROCHAR	*n* pl. -S trocar	**TROOPER**	*n* pl. -S a cavalryman
TROCHE	*n* pl. -S a medicated lozenge	**TROOPIAL**	*n* pl. -S troupial
TROCHEE	*n* pl. -S a type of metrical foot	**TROOZ**	*n/pl* trews
TROCHIL	*n* pl. -S an African bird	**TROP**	*adv* too much
TROCHILI	*n/pl* trochils	**TROPE**	*n* pl. -S the figurative use of a word
TROCHLEA	*n* pl. -LEAE or -LEAS an anatomical structure resembling a pulley	**TROPHIC**	*adj* pertaining to nutrition
		TROPHY	*v* -PHIED, -PHYING, -PHIES to honor with a trophy (a symbol of victory)
TROCHOID	*n* pl. -S a type of geometric curve		
TROCK	*v* -ED, -ING, -S to troke	**TROPIC**	*n* pl. -S either of two circles of the celestial sphere on each side of the equator **TROPICAL** *adj*
TROD	a past tense of tread		
TRODDEN	past participle of tread		
TRODE	a past tense of tread	**TROPIN**	*n* pl. -S tropine
TROFFER	*n* pl. -S a fixture for fluorescent lighting	**TROPINE**	*n* pl. -S a poisonous alkaloid
		TROPISM	*n* pl. -S the involuntary response of an organism to an external stimulus
TROGON	*n* pl. -S a tropical bird		
TROIKA	*n* pl. -S a Russian carriage		
TROILITE	*n* pl. -S a mineral	**TROT**	*v* TROTTED, TROTTING, TROTS to go at a gait between a walk and a run
TROILUS	*n* pl. -ES a large butterfly		
TROIS	*n* pl. TROIS the number three		
TROKE	*v* TROKED, TROKING, TROKES to exchange	**TROTH**	*v* -ED, -ING, -S to betroth
		TROTLINE	*n* pl. -S a strong fishing line
TROLAND	*n* pl. -S a unit of measurement of retinal response to light	**TROTTED**	past tense of trot
		TROTTER	*n* pl. -S a horse that trots
TROLL	*n* pl. -S a dwarf or giant of Teutonic folklore	**TROTTING**	present participle of trot
		TROTYL	*n* pl. -S an explosive
TROLL	*v* -ED, -ING, -S to fish with a slowly trailing line	**TROUBLE**	*v* -BLED, -BLING, -BLES to distress
TROLLER	*n* pl. -S one that trolls	**TROUBLER**	*n* pl. -S one that troubles
TROLLEY	*v* -ED, -ING, -S to convey by streetcar	**TROUGH**	*n* pl. -S a long, narrow receptacle
TROLLIED	past tense of trolly	**TROUNCE**	*v* TROUNCED, TROUNCING, TROUNCES to beat severely
TROLLIES	present 3d person sing. of trolly		
TROLLING	*n* pl. -S the act of one that trolls	**TROUPE**	*v* TROUPED, TROUPING, TROUPES to tour with a theatrical company
TROLLOP	*n* pl. -S a prostitute **TROLLOPY** *adj*		
		TROUPER	*n* pl. -S a member of a theatrical company
TROLLY	*v* -LIED, -LYING, -LIES to trolley		
TROMBONE	*n* pl. -S a brass wind instrument	**TROUPIAL**	*n* pl. -S a tropical bird

TROUPING present participle of troupe

TROUSER adj pertaining to trousers

TROUSERS n/pl a garment for the lower part of the body

TROUT n pl. -S a freshwater fish

TROUTY adj TROUTIER, TROUTIEST abounding in trout

TROUVERE n pl. -S a medieval poet

TROUVEUR n pl. -S trouvere

TROVE n pl. -S a valuable discovery

TROVER n pl. -S a type of legal action

TROW v -ED, -ING, -S to suppose

TROWEL v -ELED, -ELING, -ELS or -ELLED, -ELLING, -ELS to smooth with a trowel (a hand tool having a flat blade)

TROWELER n pl. -S one that trowels

TROWSERS n/pl trousers

TROWTH n pl. -S truth

TROY n pl. TROYS a system of weights

TRUANCY n pl. -CIES an act of truanting

TRUANT v -ED, -ING, -S to stay out of school without permission

TRUANTRY n pl. -RIES truancy

TRUCE v TRUCED, TRUCING, TRUCES to suspend hostilities by mutual agreement

TRUCK v -ED, -ING, -S to transport by truck (an automotive vehicle designed to carry loads)

TRUCKAGE n pl. -S transportation of goods by trucks

TRUCKER n pl. -S a truck driver

TRUCKING n pl. -S truckage

TRUCKLE v -LED, -LING, -LES to yield weakly

TRUCKLER n pl. -S one that truckles

TRUCKMAN n pl. -MEN a trucker

TRUDGE v TRUDGED, TRUDGING, TRUDGES to walk tiredly

TRUDGEN n pl. -S a swimming stroke

TRUDGEON n pl. -S trudgen

TRUDGER n pl. -S one that trudges

TRUDGING present participle of trudge

TRUE adj TRUER, TRUEST consistent with fact or reality

TRUE v TRUED, TRUING or TRUEING, TRUES to bring to conformity with a standard or requirement

TRUEBLUE n pl. -S a person of unwavering loyalty

TRUEBORN adj genuinely such by birth

TRUED past tense of true

TRUELOVE n pl. -S a sweetheart

TRUENESS n pl. -ES the quality or state of being true

TRUER comparative of true

TRUEST superlative of true

TRUFFE n pl. -S truffle

TRUFFLE n pl. -S an edible fungus **TRUFFLED** adj

TRUING a present participle of true

TRUISM n pl. -S an obvious truth **TRUISTIC** adj

TRULL n pl. -S a prostitute

TRULY adv in conformity with fact or reality

TRUMEAU n pl. -MEAUX a column supporting part of a doorway

TRUMP v -ED, -ING, -S to outdo

TRUMPERY n pl. -ERIES worthless finery

TRUMPET v -ED, -ING, -S to sound on a trumpet (a brass wind instrument)

TRUNCATE v -CATED, -CATING, -CATES to shorten by cutting off a part

TRUNDLE v -DLED, -DLING, -DLES to propel by causing to rotate

TRUNDLER n pl. -S one that trundles

TRUNK n pl. -S the main stem of a tree **TRUNKED** adj

TRUNNEL n pl. -S treenail

TRUNNION n pl. -S a pin or pivot on which something can be rotated

TRUSS v -ED, -ING, -ES to secure tightly

TRUSSER n pl. -S one that trusses

TRUSSING n pl. -S the framework of a structure

TRUST v -ED, -ING, -S to place confidence in

TRUSTEE v -TEED, -TEEING, -TEES to commit to the care of an administrator

TRUSTER n pl. -S one that trusts

TRUSTFUL adj inclined to trust

TRUSTY adj TRUSTIER, TRUSTIEST worthy of trust **TRUSTILY** adv

TRUSTY	*n pl.* TRUSTIES one worthy of trust
TRUTH	*n pl.* -S conformity to fact or reality
TRUTHFUL	*adj* telling the truth
TRY	*v* TRIED, TRYING, TRIES to attempt
TRYINGLY	*adv* in a distressing manner
TRYMA	*n pl.* -MATA a type of nut
TRYOUT	*n pl.* -S a test of ability
TRYPSIN	*n pl.* -S an enzyme **TRYPTIC** *adj*
TRYSAIL	*n pl.* -S a type of sail
TRYST	*v* -ED, -ING, -S to agree to meet
TRYSTE	*n pl.* -S a market
TRYSTER	*n pl.* -S one that trysts
TRYWORKS	*n/pl* a type of furnace
TSADE	*n pl.* -S sade
TSADI	*n pl.* -S sade
TSAR	*n pl.* -S czar
TSARDOM	*n pl.* -S czardom
TSAREVNA	*n pl.* -S czarevna
TSARINA	*n pl.* -S czarina
TSARISM	*n pl.* -S czarism
TSARIST	*n pl.* -S czarist
TSARITZA	*n pl.* -S czaritza
TSETSE	*n pl.* -S an African fly
TSIMMES	*n pl.* TSIMMES tzimmes
TSK	*v* -ED, -ING, -S to utter an exclamation of annoyance
TSKTSK	*v* -ED, -ING, -S to tsk
TSUBA	*n pl.* TSUBA a part of a Japanese sword
TSUNAMI	*n pl.* -S a very large ocean wave **TSUNAMIC** *adj*
TSURIS	*n pl.* TSURIS a series of misfortunes
TUATARA	*n pl.* -S a large reptile
TUATERA	*n pl.* -S tuatara
TUB	*v* TUBBED, TUBBING, TUBS to wash in a tub (a round, open vessel)
TUBA	*n pl.* -BAS or -BAE a brass wind instrument
TUBAL	*adj* pertaining to a tube
TUBATE	*adj* tubular
TUBBABLE	*adj* suitable for washing in a tub
TUBBED	past tense of tub

TUBBER	*n pl.* -S one that tubs
TUBBING	present participle of tub
TUBBY	*adj* -BIER, -BIEST short and fat
TUBE	*v* TUBED, TUBING, TUBES to provide with a tube (a long, hollow cylinder)
TUBELESS	*adj* having no tube
TUBELIKE	*adj* resembling a tube
TUBER	*n pl.* -S a thick underground stem
TUBERCLE	*n pl.* -S a small, rounded swelling
TUBEROID	*adj* pertaining to a tuber
TUBEROSE	*n pl.* -S a Mexican herb
TUBEROUS	*adj* pertaining to a tuber
TUBEWORK	*n pl.* -S tubing
TUBFUL	*n pl.* -S as much as a tub will hold
TUBIFEX	*n pl.* -ES an aquatic worm
TUBIFORM	*adj* tubular
TUBING	*n pl.* -S material in the form of a tube
TUBLIKE	*adj* resembling a tub
TUBULAR	*adj* shaped like a tube
TUBULATE	*v* -LATED, -LATING, -LATES to form into a tube
TUBULE	*n pl.* -S a small tube
TUBULOSE	*adj* tubular
TUBULOUS	*adj* tubular
TUBULURE	*n pl.* -S a short tubular opening
TUCHUN	*n pl.* -S a Chinese military governor
TUCK	*v* -ED, -ING, -S to fold under
TUCKAHOE	*n pl.* -S the edible root of certain arums
TUCKER	*v* -ED, -ING, -S to weary
TUCKET	*n pl.* -S a trumpet fanfare
TUFA	*n pl.* -S a porous limestone
TUFF	*n pl.* -S a volcanic rock
TUFFET	*n pl.* -S a clump of grass
TUFT	*v* -ED, -ING, -S to form into tufts (clusters of flexible outgrowths attached at the base)
TUFTER	*n pl.* -S one that tufts
TUFTY	*adj* TUFTIER, TUFTIEST abounding in tufts **TUFTILY** *adv*
TUG	*v* TUGGED, TUGGING, TUGS to pull with force

TUGBOAT   *n* pl. -S a boat built for towing

TUGGER   *n* pl. -S one that tugs

TUGGING   present participle of tug

TUGLESS   *adj* being without a rope or chain with which to pull

TUGRIK   *n* pl. -S a Mongolian unit of currency

TUI   *n* pl. -S a bird of New Zealand

TUILLE   *n* pl. -S a tasset

TUITION   *n* pl. -S a fee for instruction

TULADI   *n* pl. -S a freshwater fish

TULE   *n* pl. -S a tall marsh plant

TULIP   *n* pl. -S a flowering plant

TULLE   *n* pl. -S a silk material

TULLIBEE   *n* pl. -S a freshwater fish

TUMBLE   *v* -BLED, -BLING, -BLES to fall or roll end over end

TUMBLER   *n* pl. -S one that tumbles

TUMBLING   *n* pl. -S the sport of gymnastics

TUMBREL   *n* pl. -S a type of cart

TUMBRIL   *n* pl. -S tumbrel

TUMEFY   *v* -FIED, -FYING, -FIES to swell

TUMID   *adj* swollen **TUMIDLY** *adv*

TUMIDITY   *n* pl. -TIES the quality or state of being tumid

TUMMY   *n* pl. -MIES the stomach

TUMOR   *n* pl. -S an abnormal swelling **TUMORAL, TUMOROUS** *adj*

TUMOUR   *n* pl. -S tumor

TUMP   *n* pl. -S tumpline

TUMPLINE   *n* pl. -S a strap for supporting a load on the back

TUMULAR   *adj* having the form of a mound

TUMULI   a pl. of tumulus

TUMULOSE   *adj* full of mounds

TUMULOUS   *adj* tumulose

TUMULT   *n* pl. -S a great din and commotion

TUMULUS   *n* pl. -LI or -LUSES a mound over a grave

TUN   *v* TUNNED, TUNNING, TUNS to store in a large cask

TUNA   *n* pl. -S a marine food fish

TUNABLE   *adj* capable of being tuned **TUNABLY** *adv*

TUNDISH   *n* pl. -ES a receptacle for molten metal

TUNDRA   *n* pl. -S a level, treeless expanse of arctic land

TUNE   *v* TUNED, TUNING, TUNES to put into the proper pitch

TUNEABLE   *adj* tunable **TUNEABLY** *adv*

TUNEFUL   *adj* melodious

TUNELESS   *adj* not tuneful

TUNER   *n* pl. -S one that tunes

TUNG   *n* pl. -S a Chinese tree

TUNGSTEN   *n* pl. -S a metallic element **TUNGSTIC** *adj*

TUNIC   *n* pl. -S a loose-fitting garment

TUNICA   *n* pl. -CAE an enveloping membrane or layer of body tissue

TUNICATE   *n* pl. -S a small marine animal

TUNICLE   *n* pl. -S a type of vestment

TUNING   present participle of tune

TUNNAGE   *n* pl. -S tonnage

TUNNED   past tense of tun

TUNNEL   *v* -NELED, -NELING, -NELS or -NELLED, -NELLING, -NELS to dig a tunnel (an underground passageway)

TUNNELER   *n* pl. -S one that tunnels

TUNNING   present participle of tun

TUNNY   *n* pl. -NIES a tuna

TUP   *v* TUPPED, TUPPING, TUPS to copulate with a ewe

TUPELO   *n* pl. -LOS a softwood tree

TUPIK   *n* pl. -S an Eskimo tent

TUPPED   past tense of tup

TUPPENCE   *n* pl. -S twopence

TUPPING   present participle of tup

TUPPENNY   *adj* twopenny

TUQUE   *n* pl. -S a knitted woolen cap

TURACO   *n* pl. -COS touraco

TURACOU   *n* pl. -S touraco

TURBAN   *n* pl. -S a head covering worn by Muslims **TURBANED** *adj*

TURBARY   *n* pl. -RIES a place where peat can be dug

TURBETH   *n* pl. -S turpeth

TURBID   *adj* thick or opaque with roiled sediment **TURBIDLY** *adv*

TURBINAL   *n* pl. -S a bone of the nasal passage

TURBINE   *n* pl. -S a type of engine

TURBIT   *n* pl. -S a domestic pigeon

TURBITH   *n* pl. -S turpeth

TURBO   *n* pl. -BOS a turbine

TURBOCAR   *n* pl. -S an auto powered by a gas turbine

TURBOFAN   *n* pl. -S a type of jet engine

TURBOJET   *n* pl. -S a type of jet engine

TURBOT   *n* pl. -S a European flatfish

TURD   *n* pl. -S a piece of dung

TURDINE   *adj* belonging to a large family of singing birds

TUREEN   *n* pl. -S a large, deep bowl

TURF   *n* pl. TURFS or TURVES a surface layer of earth containing a dense growth of grass and its roots

TURF   *v* -ED, -ING, -S to cover with turf

TURFIER   comparative of turfy

TURFIEST   superlative of turfy

TURFLESS   *adj* having no turf

TURFLIKE   *adj* resembling turf

TURFMAN   *n* pl. -MEN a person who is devoted to horse racing

TURFSKI   *n* pl. -S a type of ski

TURFY   *adj* TURFIER, TURFIEST covered with turf

TURGENCY   *n* pl. -CIES turgor

TURGENT   *adj* turgid

TURGID   *adj* swollen **TURGIDLY** *adv*

TURGITE   *n* pl. -S an iron ore

TURGOR   *n* pl. -S the quality or state of being turgid

TURKEY   *n* pl. -KEYS a large American bird

TURKOIS   *n* pl. -ES turquois

TURMERIC   *n* pl. -S an East Indian herb

TURMOIL   *v* -ED, -ING, -S to throw into an uproar

TURN   *v* -ED, -ING, -S to move around a central point **TURNABLE** *adj*

TURNCOAT   *n* pl. -S a traitor

TURNDOWN   *n* pl. -S a rejection

TURNER   *n* pl. -S one that turns

TURNERY   *n* pl. -ERIES the process of shaping articles on a lathe

TURNHALL   *n* pl. -S a building where gymnasts practice

TURNING   *n* pl. -S a rotation about an axis

TURNIP   *n* pl. -S an edible plant root

TURNKEY   *n* pl. -KEYS a person who has charge of a prison's keys

TURNOFF   *n* pl. -S a road that branches off from a larger one

TURNOUT   *n* pl. -S an assemblage of people

TURNOVER   *n* pl. -S an upset or overthrow

TURNPIKE   *n* pl. -S a highway on which tolls are collected

TURNSOLE   *n* pl. -S a plant that turns with the sun

TURNSPIT   *n* pl. -S one that turns a roasting spit

TURNUP   *n* pl. -S a part of a garment that is turned up

TURPETH   *n* pl. -S a medicinal plant root

TURPS   *n* pl. TURPS turpentine

TURQUOIS   *n* pl. -ES a greenish blue gem

TURRET   *n* pl. -S a small tower **TURRETED** *adj*

TURRICAL   *adj* resembling a turret

TURTLE   *v* -TLED, -TLING, -TLES to catch turtles (tortoises)

TURTLER   *n* pl. -S one that turtles

TURTLING   *n* pl. -S the act of one that turtles

TURVES   a pl. of turf

TUSCHE   *n* pl. -S a liquid used in lithography

TUSH   *v* -ED, -ING, -ES to tusk

TUSK   *v* -ED, -ING, -S to gore with a tusk (a long, pointed tooth extending outside of the mouth)

TUSKER   *n* pl. -S an animal with tusks

TUSKLESS   *adj* having no tusk

TUSKLIKE   *adj* resembling a tusk

TUSSAH   *n* pl. -S an Asian silkworm

TUSSAL   *adj* pertaining to a cough

TUSSAR   *n* pl. -S tussah

TUSSEH   *n* pl. -S tussah

TUSSER   *n* pl. -S tussah

TUSSIS   *n* pl. -SISES a cough **TUSSIVE** *adj*

TUSSLE   *v* -SLED, -SLING, -SLES to struggle

TUSSOCK   *n* pl. -S a clump of grass **TUSSOCKY** *adj*

TUSSOR   *n* pl. -S tussah

TUSSORE *n* pl. -S tussah

TUSSUCK *n* pl. -S tussock

TUSSUR *n* pl. -S tussah

TUT *v* TUTTED, TUTTING, TUTS to utter an exclamation of impatience

TUTEE *n* pl. -S one who is being tutored

TUTELAGE *n* pl. -S the act of tutoring

TUTELAR *n* pl. -S a tutelary

TUTELARY *n* pl. -LARIES one who has the power to protect

TUTOR *v* -ED, -ING, -S to instruct privately

TUTORAGE *n* pl. -S tutelage

TUTORESS *n* pl. -ES a female who tutors

TUTORIAL *n* pl. -S a session of tutoring

TUTOYER *v* -TOYERED or -TOYED, -TOYERING, -TOYERS to address familiarly

TUTTED past tense of tut

TUTTI *n* pl. -S a musical passage performed by all the performers

TUTTING present participle of tut

TUTTY *n* pl. -TIES an impure zinc oxide

TUTU *n* pl. -S a short ballet skirt

TUX *n* pl. -ES a tuxedo

TUXEDO *n* pl. -DOES or -DOS a man's semiformal dinner coat

TUYER *n* pl. -S tuyere

TUYERE *n* pl. -S a pipe through which air is forced into a blast furnace

TWA *n* pl. -S two

TWADDLE *v* -DLED, -DLING, -DLES to talk foolishly

TWADDLER *n* pl. -S one that twaddles

TWAE *n* pl. -S two

TWAIN *n* pl. -S a set of two

TWANG *v* -ED, -ING, -S to make a sharp, vibrating sound

TWANGIER comparative of twangy

TWANGIEST superlative of twangy

TWANGLE *v* -GLED, -GLING, -GLES to twang

TWANGLER *n* pl. -S one that twangles

TWANGY *adj* TWANGIER, TWANGIEST twanging

TWANKY *n* pl. -KIES a variety of green tea

TWASOME *n* pl. -S twosome

TWAT *n* pl. -S the vulva — usually considered vulgar

TWATTLE *v* -TLED, -TLING, -TLES to twaddle

TWEAK *v* -ED, -ING, -S to pinch and twist sharply

TWEAKY *adj* TWEAKIER, TWEAKIEST twitchy

TWEED *n* pl. -S a coarse woolen fabric

TWEEDLE *v* -DLED, -DLING, -DLES to perform casually on a musical instrument

TWEEDY *adj* TWEEDIER, TWEEDIEST resembling tweed

TWEEN *prep* between

TWEET *v* -ED, -ING, -S to chirp

TWEETER *n* pl. -S a loudspeaker designed to reproduce high-pitched sounds

TWEEZE *v* TWEEZED, TWEEZING, TWEEZES to pluck with a tweezer

TWEEZER *n* pl. -S a pincerlike tool

TWELFTH *n* pl. -S the number twelve in a series

TWELVE *n* pl. -S a number

TWELVEMO *n* pl. -MOS a page size

TWENTY *n* pl. -TIES a number

TWERP *n* pl. -S a small, impudent person

TWIBIL *n* pl. -S a battle-ax with two cutting edges

TWIBILL *n* pl. -S twibil

TWICE *adv* two times

TWIDDLE *v* -DLED, -DLING, -DLES to play idly with something

TWIDDLER *n* pl. -S one that twiddles

TWIER *n* pl. -S tuyere

TWIG *v* TWIGGED, TWIGGING, TWIGS to observe

TWIGGEN *adj* made of twigs (small branches)

TWIGGY *adj* -GIER, -GIEST twiglike

TWIGLESS *adj* having no twigs

TWIGLIKE *adj* resembling a twig

TWILIGHT *n* pl. -S the early evening light

TWILIT *adj* lighted by twilight

TWILL *v* -ED, -ING, -S to weave so as to produce a diagonal pattern

TWILLING   *n* pl. -S a twilled fabric

TWIN   *v* TWINNED, TWINNING, TWINS to bring together in close association

TWINBORN   *adj* born at the same birth

TWINE   *v* TWINED, TWINING, TWINES to twist together

TWINER   *n* pl. -S one that twines

TWINGE   *v* TWINGED, TWINGING, TWINGES to affect with a sharp pain

TWINIER   comparative of twiny

TWINIEST   superlative of twiny

TWINIGHT   *adj* pertaining to a baseball doubleheader that begins in the late afternoon

TWINING   present participle of twine

TWINKLE   *v* -KLED, -KLING, -KLES to shine with a flickering or sparkling light

TWINKLER   *n* pl. -S one that twinkles

TWINKLY   *adj* twinkling

TWINNED   past tense of twin

TWINNING   *n* pl. -S the bearing of two children at the same birth

TWINSHIP   *n* pl. -S close similarity or association

TWINY   *adj* TWINIER, TWINIEST resembling twine (a strong string)

TWIRL   *v* -ED, -ING, -S to rotate rapidly

TWIRLER   *n* pl. -S one that twirls

TWIRLY   *adj* TWIRLIER, TWIRLIEST curved

TWIRP   *n* pl. -S a twerp

TWIST   *v* -ED, -ING, -S to combine by winding together

TWISTER   *n* pl. -S one that twists

TWISTING   *n* pl. -S a form of trickery used in selling life insurance

TWIT   *v* TWITTED, TWITTING, TWITS to ridicule

TWITCH   *v* -ED, -ING, -ES to move or pull with a sudden motion

TWITCHER   *n* pl. -S one that twitches

TWITCHY   *adj* TWITCHIER, TWITCHIEST fidgety

TWITTED   past tense of twit

TWITTER   *v* -ED, -ING, -S to utter a succession of chirping sounds

TWITTERY   *adj* nervously agitated

TWITTING   present participle of twit

TWIXT   *prep* between

TWO   *n* pl. TWOS a number

TWOFER   *n* pl. -S something sold at the rate of two for the price of one

TWOFOLD   *n* pl. -S an amount twice as great as a given unit

TWOPENCE   *n* pl. -S a British coin worth two pennies

TWOPENNY   *adj* worth twopence

TWOSOME   *n* pl. -S a group of two

TWYER   *n* pl. -S tuyere

TYCOON   *n* pl. -S a wealthy and powerful business person

TYE   *n* pl. -S a chain on a ship

TYEE   *n* pl. -S a food fish

TYING   a present participle of tie

TYKE   *n* pl. -S a small child

TYMBAL   *n* pl. -S timbal

TYMPAN   *n* pl. -S a drum

TYMPANA   a pl. of tympanum

TYMPANAL   *adj* tympanic

TYMPANI   *n/pl* kettledrums

TYMPANIC   *adj* pertaining to the tympanum

TYMPANUM   *n* pl. -NA or -NUMS the middle ear

TYMPANY   *n* pl. -NIES a swelling of the abdomen

TYNE   *v* TYNED, TYNING, TYNES to tine

TYPAL   *adj* typical

TYPE   *v* TYPED, TYPING, TYPES to write with a typewriter **TYPEABLE** *adj*

TYPEBAR   *n* pl. -S a part of a typewriter

TYPECASE   *n* pl. -S a tray for holding printing type

TYPECAST   *v* -CAST, -CASTING, -CASTS to cast in an acting role befitting one's own nature

TYPED   past tense of type

TYPEFACE   *n* pl. -S the face of printing type

TYPESET   *v* -SET, -SETTING, -SETS to set in type

TYPEY   *adj* TYPIER, TYPIEST typy

TYPHOID   *n* pl. -S an infectious disease

TYPHON   *n* pl. -S a type of signal horn

TYPHOON   *n* pl. -S a tropical hurricane **TYPHONIC** *adj*

TYPHOSE	*adj* pertaining to typhoid
TYPHUS	*n* pl. -ES an infectious disease **TYPHOUS** *adj*
TYPIC	*adj* typical
TYPICAL	*adj* having the nature of a representative specimen
TYPIER	comparative of typey and typy
TYPIEST	superlative of typey and typy
TYPIFIER	*n* pl. -S one that typifies
TYPIFY	*v* -FIED, -FYING, -FIES to serve as a typical example of
TYPING	present participle of type
TYPIST	*n* pl. -S one who types
TYPO	*n* pl. -POS a typographical error
TYPOLOGY	*n* pl. -GIES the study of classification according to common characteristics
TYPP	*n* pl. -S a unit of yarn size
TYPY	*adj* TYPIER, TYPIEST characterized by strict conformance to the characteristics of a group
TYRAMINE	*n* pl. -S a chemical compound
TYRANNIC	*adj* characteristic of a tyrant
TYRANNY	*n* pl. -NIES the rule of a tyrant
TYRANT	*n* pl. -S an absolute ruler
TYRE	*v* TYRED, TYRING, TYRES to furnish with a covering for a wheel
TYRO	*n* pl. -ROS a beginner **TYRONIC** *adj*
TYROSINE	*n* pl. -S an amino acid
TYTHE	*v* TYTHED, TYTHING, TYTHES to tithe
TZADDIK	*n* pl. -DIKIM zaddik
TZAR	*n* pl. -S czar
TZARDOM	*n* pl. -S czardom
TZAREVNA	*n* pl. -S czarevna
TZARINA	*n* pl. -S czarina
TZARISM	*n* pl. -S czarism
TZARIST	*n* pl. -S czarist
TZARITZA	*n* pl. -S czaritza
TZETZE	*n* pl. -S tsetse
TZIGANE	*n* pl. -S a gypsy
TZIMMES	*n* pl. TZIMMES a vegetable stew
TZITZIS	*n* pl. TZITZIS zizith
TZITZITH	*n* pl. TZITZITH zizith
TZURIS	*n* pl. TZURIS tsuris

UBIETY	*n* pl. -ETIES the state of having a definite location
UBIQUE	*adv* everywhere
UBIQUITY	*n* pl. -TIES the state of being everywhere at the same time
UDDER	*n* pl. -S a mammary gland
UDO	*n* pl. UDOS a Japanese herb
UDOMETER	*n* pl. -S a rain gauge
UDOMETRY	*n* pl. -TRIES the measurement of rain
UGH	*n* pl. -S the sound of a cough or grunt
UGLIER	comparative of ugly
UGLIEST	superlative of ugly
UGLIFIER	*n* pl. -S one that uglifies
UGLIFY	*v* -FIED, -FYING, -FIES to make ugly
UGLINESS	*n* pl. -ES the state of being ugly
UGLY	*adj* -LIER, -LIEST displeasing to the sight **UGLILY** *adv*
UGSOME	*adj* disgusting
UHLAN	*n* pl. -S one of a body of Prussian cavalry
UINTAITE	*n* pl. -S a variety of asphalt
UIT	*prep* out of
UKASE	*n* pl. -S an edict
UKE	*n* pl. -S ukelele
UKELELE	*n* pl. -S ukulele
UKULELE	*n* pl. -S a small guitar-like instrument
ULAMA	*n* pl. -S ulema
ULAN	*n* pl. -S uhlan
ULCER	*v* -ED, -ING, -S to affect with an ulcer (a type of lesion)

ULCERATE	*v* -ATED, -ATING, -ATES to ulcer
ULCEROUS	*adj* being or affected with an ulcer
ULEMA	*n* pl. -S a Muslim scholar
ULEXITE	*n* pl. -S a mineral
ULLAGE	*n* pl. -S the amount that a container lacks of being full **ULLAGED** *adj*
ULNA	*n* pl. -NAE or -NAS a bone of the forearm **ULNAR** *adj*
ULSTER	*n* pl. -S a long, loose overcoat
ULTERIOR	*adj* more remote
ULTIMA	*n* pl. -S the last syllable of a word
ULTIMACY	*n* pl. -CIES an ultimate
ULTIMATA	*n/pl* final proposals
ULTIMATE	*n* pl. -S something final or fundamental
ULTIMO	*adj* of or occurring in the preceding month
ULTRA	*n* pl. -S an ultraist
ULTRAISM	*n* pl. -S advocacy of extreme measures
ULTRAIST	*n* pl. -S an advocate of extreme measures
ULTRARED	*n* pl. -S infrared
ULULANT	*adj* howling
ULULATE	*v* -LATED, -LATING, -LATES to howl
ULVA	*n* pl. -S an edible seaweed
UMBEL	*n* pl. -S a type of flower cluster **UMBELED, UMBELLAR, UMBELLED** *adj*
UMBELLET	*n* pl. -S a small umbel

UMBER   *v* -ED, -ING, -S to color with a brown pigment

UMBILICI   *n/pl* navels

UMBLES   *n/pl* the entrails of a deer

UMBO   *n* pl. -BONES or -BOS the rounded elevation at the center of a shield **UMBONAL, UMBONATE, UMBONIC** *adj*

UMBRA   *n* pl. -BRAE or -BRAS a dark area **UMBRAL** *adj*

UMBRAGE   *n* pl. -S resentment

UMBRELLA   *v* -ED, -ING, -S to provide with an umbrella (a portable cover for protection from rain or sun)

UMBRETTE   *n* pl. -S a wading bird

UMIAC   *n* pl. -S umiak

UMIACK   *n* pl. -S umiak

UMIAK   *n* pl. -S an open Eskimo boat

UMLAUT   *v* -ED, -ING, -S to modify a vowel sound by partial assimilation to a succeeding sound

UMP   *v* -ED, -ING, -S to umpire

UMPIRAGE   *n* pl. -S the function of an umpire

UMPIRE   *v* -PIRED, -PIRING, -PIRES to act as umpire (a person appointed to rule on the plays in a game)

UMPTEEN   *adj* indefinitely numerous

UMTEENTH   *adj* being the last in an indefinitely numerous series

UN   *pron* pl. -S one

U₁	N₁

Following is a list of self-explanatory adjectives and adverbs containing the prefix UN- (not):

UNABATED   *adj*
UNABLE   *adj*
UNABUSED   *adj*
UNACTED   *adj*
UNAFRAID   *adj*
UNAGED   *adj*
UNAGEING   *adj*
UNAGILE   *adj*
UNAGING   *adj*
UNAIDED   *adj*
UNAIMED   *adj*
UNAIRED   *adj*

UNALIKE   *adj*
UNALLIED   *adj*
UNAMUSED   *adj*
UNANELED   *adj*
UNAPT   *adj*
UNAPTLY   *adv*
UNARGUED   *adj*
UNARTFUL   *adj*
UNASKED   *adj*
UNATONED   *adj*
UNAVOWED   *adj*
UNAWAKED   *adj*
UNAWARE   *adj*
UNAWED   *adj*
UNBACKED   *adj*
UNBAKED   *adj*
UNBARBED   *adj*
UNBASED   *adj*
UNBEATEN   *adj*
UNBENIGN   *adj*
UNBIASED   *adj*
UNBITTED   *adj*
UNBLAMED   *adj*
UNBLEST   *adj*
UNBLOODY   *adj*
UNBONED   *adj*
UNBORN   *adj*
UNBOUGHT   *adj*
UNBOWED   *adj*
UNBRED   *adj*
UNBROKE   *adj*
UNBROKEN   *adj*
UNBURIED   *adj*
UNBURNED   *adj*
UNBURNT   *adj*
UNCALLED   *adj*
UNCANDID   *adj*
UNCARING   *adj*
UNCASHED   *adj*
UNCAUGHT   *adj*
UNCAUSED   *adj*
UNCHARY   *adj*
UNCHASTE   *adj*
UNCHEWED   *adj*
UNCHIC   *adj*
UNCHOSEN   *adj*
UNCIVIL   *adj*
UNCLEAN   *adj* -CLEANER, -CLEANEST
UNCLEAR   *adj* -CLEARER, -CLEAREST
UNCLOYED   *adj*
UNCOATED   *adj*
UNCOINED   *adj*
UNCOMBED   *adj*

UNCOMELY	adj		UNFORCED	adj
UNCOMIC	adj		UNFORGED	adj
UNCOMMON	adj -MONER, -MONEST		UNFORKED	adj
UNCOOKED	adj		UNFORMED	adj
UNCOOL	adj		UNFOUGHT	adj
UNCOUTH	adj		UNFOUND	adj
UNCURED	adj		UNFRAMED	adj
UNCURSED	adj		UNFUNDED	adj
UNCUT	adj		UNFUNNY	adj
UNDAMPED	adj		UNFUSED	adj
UNDARING	adj		UNFUSSY	adj
UNDATED	adj		UNGALLED	adj
UNDECKED	adj		UNGENIAL	adj
UNDENIED	adj		UNGENTLE	adj
UNDEVOUT	adj		UNGENTLY	adv
UNDIMMED	adj		UNGIFTED	adj
UNDREAMT	adj		UNGLAZED	adj
UNDRIED	adj		UNGOWNED	adj
UNDULLED	adj		UNGRACED	adj
UNDYED	adj		UNGRADED	adj
UNEAGER	adj		UNGREEDY	adj
UNEARNED	adj		UNGUIDED	adj
UNEATEN	adj		UNHAILED	adj
UNEDIBLE	adj		UNHALVED	adj
UNEDITED	adj		UNHAPPY	adj -PIER, -PIEST
UNENDED	adj		UNHARMED	adj
UNENDING	adj		UNHASTY	adj
UNENVIED	adj		UNHEALED	adj
UNERASED	adj		UNHEARD	adj
UNERRING	adj		UNHEATED	adj
UNEVADED	adj		UNHEEDED	adj
UNEVEN	adj -EVENER, -EVENEST		UNHELPED	adj
UNEVENLY	adv		UNHEROIC	adj
UNEXOTIC	adj		UNHEWN	adj
UNEXPERT	adj		UNHIP	adj
UNFADED	adj		UNHIRED	adj
UNFADING	adj		UNHOLILY	adv
UNFAIR	adj -FAIRER, -FAIREST		UNHOLY	adj -LIER, -LIEST
UNFAIRLY	adv		UNHUMAN	adj
UNFALLEN	adj		UNHUNG	adj
UNFANCY	adj		UNHURT	adj
UNFAZED	adj		UNIDEAL	adj
UNFEARED	adj		UNIMBUED	adj
UNFED	adj		UNIRONED	adj
UNFELT	adj		UNISSUED	adj
UNFILIAL	adj		UNJADED	adj
UNFILLED	adj		UNJOINED	adj
UNFILMED	adj		UNJOYFUL	adj
UNFIRED	adj		UNJUDGED	adj
UNFISHED	adj		UNJUST	adj
UNFLEXED	adj		UNJUSTLY	adv
UNFOILED	adj		UNKEPT	adj
UNFOND	adj		UNKIND	adj -KINDER, -KINDEST

UNKINDLY	adv -LIER, -LIEST	UNPARTED	adj
UNKINGLY	adj	UNPAVED	adj
UNKISSED	adj	UNPAYING	adj
UNKOSHER	adj	UNPITIED	adj
UNLAWFUL	adj	UNPLACED	adj
UNLEASED	adj	UNPLAYED	adj
UNLED	adj	UNPLIANT	adj
UNLETHAL	adj	UNPLOWED	adj
UNLETTED	adj	UNPOETIC	adj
UNLEVIED	adj	UNPOISED	adj
UNLICKED	adj	UNPOLITE	adj
UNLIKE	adj	UNPOLLED	adj
UNLIKELY	adj -LIER, -LIEST	UNPOSED	adj
UNLINED	adj	UNPOSTED	adj
UNLISTED	adj	UNPRETTY	adj
UNLIT	adj	UNPRICED	adj
UNLIVELY	adj	UNPRIMED	adj
UNLOBED	adj	UNPRIZED	adj
UNLOVED	adj	UNPROBED	adj
UNLOVELY	adj -LIER, -LIEST	UNPROVED	adj
UNLOVING	adj	UNPROVEN	adj
UNLUCKY	adj -LUCKIER, -LUCKIEST	UNPRUNED	adj
UNMANFUL	adj	UNPURE	adj
UNMANLY	adj	UNPURGED	adj
UNMAPPED	adj	UNQUIET	adj -ETER, -ETEST
UNMARKED	adj	UNRAISED	adj
UNMARRED	adj	UNRAKED	adj
UNMATED	adj	UNRANKED	adj
UNMATTED	adj	UNRATED	adj
UNMEANT	adj	UNRAZED	adj
UNMELLOW	adj	UNREAD	adj
UNMELTED	adj	UNREADY	adj -READIER, -READIEST
UNMENDED	adj	UNREAL	adj
UNMET	adj	UNREALLY	adv
UNMILLED	adj	UNRENTED	adj
UNMIXED	adj	UNREPAID	adj
UNMIXT	adj	UNRESTED	adj
UNMODISH	adj	UNRHYMED	adj
UNMOLTEN	adj	UNRIFLED	adj
UNMOVED	adj	UNRIMED	adj
UNMOVING	adj	UNRINSED	adj
UNMOWN	adj	UNRISEN	adj
UNNAMED	adj	UNROUGH	adj
UNNEEDED	adj	UNRULED	adj
UNNOISY	adj	UNRUSHED	adj
UNNOTED	adj	UNSAFE	adj
UNOILED	adj	UNSAFELY	adv
UNOPEN	adj	UNSALTED	adj
UNOPENED	adj	UNSATED	adj
UNORNATE	adj	UNSAVED	adj
UNOWNED	adj	UNSAVORY	adj
UNPAID	adj	UNSAWED	adj
UNPAIRED	adj	UNSAWN	adj

UNSCALED	adj		UNSTUNG	adj
UNSEARED	adj		UNSUBTLE	adj
UNSEEDED	adj		UNSUITED	adj
UNSEEING	adj		UNSUNG	adj
UNSEEMLY	adj -LIER, -LIEST		UNSUNK	adj
UNSEEN	adj		UNSURE	adj
UNSEIZED	adj		UNSURELY	adv
UNSENT	adj		UNSWAYED	adj
UNSERVED	adj		UNSWEPT	adj
UNSEXUAL	adj		UNTAGGED	adj
UNSHADED	adj		UNTAKEN	adj
UNSHAKEN	adj		UNTAME	adj
UNSHAMED	adj		UNTAMED	adj
UNSHAPED	adj		UNTANNED	adj
UNSHAPEN	adj		UNTAPPED	adj
UNSHARED	adj		UNTASTED	adj
UNSHARP	adj		UNTAXED	adj
UNSHAVED	adj		UNTENDED	adj
UNSHAVEN	adj		UNTESTED	adj
UNSHED	adj		UNTHAWED	adj
UNSHOD	adj		UNTIDILY	adv
UNSHORN	adj		UNTIDY	adj -DIER, -DIEST
UNSHRUNK	adj		UNTILLED	adj
UNSHUT	adj		UNTILTED	adj
UNSIFTED	adj		UNTIMELY	adj -LIER, -LIEST
UNSIGNED	adj		UNTINGED	adj
UNSILENT	adj		UNTIRED	adj
UNSINFUL	adj		UNTIRING	adj
UNSIZED	adj		UNTITLED	adj
UNSLAKED	adj		UNTOLD	adj
UNSMOKED	adj		UNTRACED	adj
UNSOAKED	adj		UNTRIED	adj
UNSOBER	adj		UNTRUE	adj -TRUER, -TRUEST
UNSOCIAL	adj		UNTRULY	adv
UNSOILED	adj		UNTRUSTY	adj
UNSOLD	adj		UNTUFTED	adj
UNSOLID	adj		UNTURNED	adj
UNSOLVED	adj		UNUNITED	adj
UNSORTED	adj		UNURGED	adj
UNSOUGHT	adj		UNUSABLE	adj
UNSOUND	adj -SOUNDER, -SOUNDEST		UNUSED	adj
UNSOURED	adj		UNUSUAL	adj
UNSOWED	adj		UNVALUED	adj
UNSOWN	adj		UNVARIED	adj
UNSPENT	adj		UNVEINED	adj
UNSPILT	adj		UNVERSED	adj
UNSPLIT	adj		UNVEXED	adj
UNSPOILT	adj		UNVEXT	adj
UNSPRUNG	adj		UNVIABLE	adj
UNSPUN	adj		UNVOCAL	adj
UNSTABLE	adj -BLER, -BLEST		UNWALLED	adj
UNSTABLY	adv		UNWANTED	adj
UNSTEADY	adj -STEADIER, -STEADIEST		UNWARIER	comparative of unwary

UNWARIEST	superlative of unwary
UNWARILY	adv
UNWARMED	adj
UNWARNED	adj
UNWARPED	adj
UNWARY	adj -WARIER, -WARIEST
UNWASTED	adj
UNWAXED	adj
UNWEANED	adj
UNWEARY	adj
UNWED	adj
UNWEDDED	adj
UNWEEDED	adj
UNWELDED	adj
UNWELL	adj
UNWEPT	adj
UNWETTED	adj
UNWIELDY	adj -WIELDIER, -WIELDIEST
UNWIFELY	adj
UNWILLED	adj
UNWISE	adj -WISER, -WISEST
UNWISELY	adv
UNWON	adj
UNWOODED	adj
UNWOOED	adj
UNWORKED	adj
UNWORN	adj
UNWORTHY	adj -THIER, -THIEST
UNWRUNG	adj
UNZONED	adj

UNAI	n pl. -S unau
UNANCHOR	v -ED, -ING, -S to loosen from an anchor
UNARM	v -ED, -ING, -S to disarm
UNARY	adj consisting of a single element
UNAU	n pl. -S a two-toed sloth
UNAWARES	adv without warning
UNBAR	v -BARRED, -BARRING, -BARS to remove a bar from
UNBATED	adj unabated
UNBE	v to cease to have being — UNBE is the only accepted form of this verb; it cannot be conjugated
UNBEAR	v -BEARED, -BEARING, -BEARS to free from the pressure of a rein
UNBELIEF	n pl. -S lack of belief

UNBELT	v -ED, -ING, -S to remove the belt of
UNBEND	v -BENT or -BENDED, -BENDING, -BENDS to make or allow to become straight
UNBID	adj unbidden
UNBIDDEN	adj not invited
UNBIND	v -BOUND, -BINDING, -BINDS to free from bindings
UNBLOCK	v -ED, -ING, -S to free from being blocked
UNBODIED	adj having no body
UNBOLT	v -ED, -ING, -S to open by withdrawing a bolt (a metal bar)
UNBONNET	v -ED, -ING, -S to uncover the head
UNBOSOM	v -ED, -ING, -S to reveal
UNBOUND	past tense of unbind
UNBOX	v -ED, -ING, -ES to remove from a box
UNBRACE	v -BRACED, -BRACING, -BRACES to free from braces
UNBRAID	v -ED, -ING, -S to separate the strands of
UNBREECH	v -ED, -ING, -ES to remove the breeches of
UNBRIDLE	v -DLED, -DLING, -DLES to set loose
UNBUCKLE	v -LED, -LING, -LES to loosen a buckle
UNBUILD	v -BUILT, -BUILDING, -BUILDS to demolish
UNBUNDLE	v -DLED, -DLING, -DLES to price separately
UNBURDEN	v -ED, -ING, -S to free from a burden
UNBUTTON	v -ED, -ING, -S to unfasten the buttons of
UNCAGE	v -CAGED, -CAGING, -CAGES to release from a cage
UNCAKE	v -CAKED, -CAKING, -CAKES to break up a cake (a block of compacted matter)
UNCANNY	adj -NIER, -NIEST strange and inexplicable
UNCAP	v -CAPPED, -CAPPING, -CAPS to remove the cap from
UNCASE	v -CASED, -CASING, -CASES to remove from a case
UNCHAIN	v -ED, -ING, -S to free by removing a chain
UNCHANCY	adj unlucky

UNCHARGE v -CHARGED, -CHARGING, -CHARGES to acquit

UNCHOKE v -CHOKED, -CHOKING, -CHOKES to free from obstruction

UNCHURCH v -ED, -ING, -ES to expel from a church

UNCI pl. of uncus

UNCIA n pl. -CIAE a coin of ancient Rome

UNCIAL n pl. -S a style of writing

UNCIALLY adv in the uncial style

UNCIFORM n pl. -S a bone of the wrist

UNCINAL adj uncinate

UNCINATE adj bent at the end like a hook

UNCINUS n pl. -NI an uncinate structure

UNCLAD a past tense of unclothe

UNCLAMP v -ED, -ING, -S to free from a clamp

UNCLASP v -ED, -ING, -S to free from a clasp

UNCLE n pl. -S the brother of one's father or mother

UNCLENCH v -ED, -ING, -ES to open from a clenched position

UNCLINCH v -ED, -ING, -ES to unclench

UNCLOAK v -ED, -ING, -S to remove a cloak from

UNCLOG v -CLOGGED, -CLOGGING, -CLOGS to free from a difficulty or obstruction

UNCLOSE v -CLOSED, -CLOSING, -CLOSES to open

UNCLOTHE v -CLOTHED or -CLAD, -CLOTHING, -CLOTHES to divest of clothing

UNCLOUD v -ED, -ING, -S to free from clouds

UNCO n pl. -COS a stranger

UNCOCK v -ED, -ING, -S to remove from a cocked position

UNCOFFIN v -ED, -ING, -S to remove from a coffin

UNCOIL v -ED, -ING, -S to release from a coiled position

UNCORK v -ED, -ING, -S to draw the cork from

UNCOUPLE v -PLED, -PLING, -PLES to disconnect

UNCOVER v -ED, -ING, -S to remove the covering from

UNCRATE v -CRATED, -CRATING, -CRATES to remove from a crate

UNCREATE v -ATED, -ATING, -ATES to deprive of existence

UNCROSS v -ED, -ING, -ES to change from a crossed position

UNCROWN v -ED, -ING, -S to deprive of a crown

UNCTION n pl. -S the act of anointing

UNCTUOUS adj greasy

UNCURB v -ED, -ING, -S to remove restraints from

UNCURL v -ED, -ING, -S to straighten the curls of

UNCUS n pl. -CI a hook-shaped anatomical part

UNDE adj wavy

UNDEE adj unde

UNDER prep in a lower position than

UNDERACT v -ED, -ING, -S to act subtly and with restraint

UNDERAGE n pl. -S a shortage

UNDERARM n pl. -S the armpit

UNDERATE past tense of undereat

UNDERBID v -BID, -BIDDING, -BIDS to bid lower than

UNDERBUD v -BUDDED, -BUDDING, -BUDS to bud from beneath

UNDERBUY v -BOUGHT, -BUYING, -BUYS to buy at a lower price than

UNDERCUT v -CUT, -CUTTING, -CUTS to cut under

UNDERDO v -DID, -DONE, -DOING, -DOES to do insufficiently

UNDERDOG n pl. -S one who is expected to lose

UNDEREAT v -ATE, -EATEN, -EATING, -EATS to eat an insufficient amount

UNDERFED adj fed an insufficient amount

UNDERFUR n pl. -S the thick, soft fur beneath the outer coat of certain mammals

UNDERGO v -WENT, -GONE, -GOING, -GOES to be subjected to

UNDERGOD n pl. -S a lesser god

UNDERJAW n pl. -S the lower jaw

UNDERLAIN past participle of underlie

UNDERLAP v -LAPPED, -LAPPING, -LAPS to extend partly under

UNDERLAY v -LAID, -LAYING, -LAYS to place under

UNDERLET v -LET, -LETTING, -LETS to lease at less than the usual value

UNDERLIE v -LAY, -LAIN, -LYING, -LIES to lie under

UNDERLIP n pl. -S the lower lip

UNDERLIT adj lacking adequate light

UNDERLYING present participle of underlie

UNDERPAY v -PAID, -PAYING, -PAYS to pay less than is deserved

UNDERPIN v -PINNED, -PINNING, -PINS to support from below

UNDERRUN v -RAN, -RUNNING, -RUNS to pass or extend under

UNDERSEA adv beneath the surface of the sea

UNDERSET n pl. -S a current below the surface of the ocean

UNDERTAX v -ED, -ING, -ES to tax less than the usual amount

UNDERTOW n pl. -S the seaward pull of receding waves breaking on a shore

UNDERWAY adv in progress

UNDERWENT past tense of undergo

UNDID past tense of undo

UNDIES n/pl underwear

UNDINE n pl. -S a female water spirit

UNDO v -DID, -DONE, -DOING, -DOES to bring to ruin

UNDOCK v -ED, -ING, -S to move away from a dock

UNDOER n pl. -S one that undoes

UNDOING n pl. -S a cause of ruin

UNDONE past participle of undo

UNDOUBLE v -BLED, -BLING, -BLES to unfold

UNDRAPE v -DRAPED, -DRAPING, -DRAPES to strip of drapery

UNDRAW v -DREW, -DRAWN, -DRAWING, -DRAWS to draw open

UNDRESS v -DRESSED or -DREST, -DRESSING, -DRESSES to remove one's clothing

UNDRUNK adj not swallowed

UNDUE adj exceeding what is appropriate or normal

UNDULANT adj undulating

UNDULATE v -LATED, -LATING, -LATES to move with a wavelike motion

UNDULY adv in an undue manner

UNDY adj unde

UNDYING adj not subject to death

UNEARTH v -ED, -ING, -S to dig up

UNEASE n pl. -S mental or physical discomfort

UNEASY adj -EASIER, -EASIEST marked by mental or physical discomfort **UNEASILY** adv

UNEQUAL n pl. -S one that is not equal to another

UNFAITH n pl. -S lack of faith

UNFASTEN v -ED, -ING, -S to release from fastenings

UNFENCE v -FENCED, -FENCING, -FENCES to remove a fence from

UNFETTER v -ED, -ING, -S to free from fetters

UNFIT v -FITTED, -FITTING, -FITS to make unsuitable

UNFITLY adv in an unsuitable manner

UNFIX v -FIXED or -FIXT, -FIXING, -FIXES to unfasten

UNFOLD v -ED, -ING, -S to open something that is folded

UNFOLDER n pl. -S one that unfolds

UNFORGOT adj not forgotten

UNFREE v -FREED, -FREEING, -FREES to deprive of freedom

UNFREEZE v -FROZE, -FROZEN, -FREEZING, -FREEZES to cause to thaw

UNFROCK v -ED, -ING, -S to divest of ecclesiastical authority

UNFURL v -ED, -ING, -S to unroll

UNGAINLY adj -LIER, -LIEST awkward

UNGIRD v -GIRDED or -GIRT, -GIRDING, -GIRDS to remove a belt from

UNGLOVE v -GLOVED, -GLOVING, -GLOVES to uncover by removing a glove

UNGLUE v -GLUED, -GLUING, -GLUES to disjoin

UNGODLY adj -LIER, -LIEST impious

UNGOT adj ungotten

UNGOTTEN adj not obtained

UNGUAL adj pertaining to an unguis

UNGUARD *v* -ED, -ING, -S to leave unprotected

UNGUENT *n pl.* -S an ointment

UNGUIS *n pl.* -GUES a nail, claw, or hoof

UNGULA *n pl.* -LAE an unguis **UNGULAR** *adj*

UNGULATE *n pl.* -S a hoofed mammal

UNHAIR *v* -ED, -ING, -S to remove the hair from

UNHALLOW *v* -ED, -ING, -S to profane

UNHAND *v* -ED, -ING, -S to remove the hand from

UNHANDY *adj* -HANDIER, -HANDIEST difficult to handle

UNHANG *v* -HUNG or -HANGED, -HANGING, -HANGS to detach from a hanging support

UNHAT *v* -HATTED, -HATTING, -HATS to remove one's hat

UNHELM *v* -ED, -ING, -S to remove the helmet from

UNHINGE *v* -HINGED, -HINGING, -HINGES to remove from hinges

UNHITCH *v* -ED, -ING, -ES to free from being hitched

UNHOOD *v* -ED, -ING, -S to remove a hood from

UNHOOK *v* -ED, -ING, -S to remove from a hook

UNHOPED *adj* not hoped for or expected

UNHORSE *v* -HORSED, -HORSING, -HORSES to cause to fall from a horse

UNHOUSE *v* -HOUSED, -HOUSING, -HOUSES to deprive of a protective shelter

UNHUSK *v* -ED, -ING, -S to remove the husk from

UNIALGAL *adj* pertaining to a single algal cell

UNIAXIAL *adj* having one axis

UNICOLOR *adj* of one color

UNICORN *n pl.* -S a mythical horselike creature

UNICYCLE *n pl.* -S a one-wheeled vehicle

UNIDEAED *adj* lacking ideas

UNIFACE *n pl.* -S a coin having a design on only one side

UNIFIC *adj* unifying

UNIFIED past tense of unify

UNIFIER *n pl.* -S one that unifies

UNIFIES present 3d person sing. of unify

UNIFILAR *adj* having only one thread, wire, or fiber

UNIFORM *adj* -FORMER, -FORMEST unchanging

UNIFORM *v* -ED, -ING, -S to make uniform

UNIFY *v* -FIED, -FYING, -FIES to make into a coherent whole

UNILOBED *adj* having one lobe

UNION *n pl.* -S a number of persons, parties, or political entities united for a common purpose

UNIONISE *v* -ISED, -ISING, -ISES to unionize

UNIONISM *n pl.* -S the principle of forming a union

UNIONIST *n pl.* -S an advocate of unionism

UNIONIZE *v* -IZED, -IZING, -IZES to form into a union

UNIPOD *n pl.* -S a one-legged support

UNIPOLAR *adj* showing only one kind of polarity

UNIQUE *adj* UNIQUER, UNIQUEST existing as the only one of its kind; very unusual **UNIQUELY** *adv*

UNIQUE *n pl.* -S something that is unique

UNISEX *n pl.* -ES the condition of not being distinguishable as to sex

UNISON *n pl.* -S complete agreement **UNISONAL** *adj*

UNIT *n pl.* -S a specific quantity used as a standard of measurement

UNITAGE *n pl.* -S amount in units

UNITARY *adj* pertaining to a unit

UNITE *v* UNITED, UNITING, UNITES to bring together so as to form a whole **UNITEDLY** *adv*

UNITER *n pl.* -S one that unites

UNITIES pl. of unity

UNITIVE *adj* serving to unite

UNITIZE *v* -IZED, -IZING, -IZES to divide into units

UNITY *n pl.* -TIES the state of being one single entity

UNIVALVE *n pl.* -S a mollusk having a single shell

UNIVERSE *n pl.* -S the totality of all existing things

UNIVOCAL *n* pl. -S a word having only one meaning

UNKEMPT *adj* untidy

UNKEND *adj* unkenned

UNKENNED *adj* not known or recognized

UNKENNEL *v* -NELED, -NELING, -NELS or -NELLED, -NELLING, -NELS to release from a kennel

UNKENT *adj* unkenned

UNKNIT *v* -KNITTED, -KNITTING, -KNITS to unravel

UNKNOT *v* -KNOTTED, -KNOTTING, -KNOTS to undo a knot in

UNKNOWN *n* pl. -S one that is not known

UNLACE *v* -LACED, -LACING, -LACES to unfasten the laces of

UNLADE *v* -LADED, -LADEN, -LADING, -LADES to unload

UNLAID past tense of unlay

UNLASH *v* -ED, -ING, -ES to untie the lashing (a type of binding) of

UNLATCH *v* -ED, -ING, -ES to open by lifting the latch (a fastening device)

UNLAY *v* -LAID, -LAYING, -LAYS to untwist

UNLEAD *v* -ED, -ING, -S to remove the lead from

UNLEARN *v* -LEARNED or -LEARNT, -LEARNING, -LEARNS to put out of one's knowledge or memory

UNLEASH *v* -ED, -ING, -ES to free from a leash

UNLESS *conj* except on the condition that

UNLET *adj* not rented

UNLEVEL *v* -ELED, -ELING, -ELS or -ELLED, -ELLING, -ELS to make uneven

UNLIMBER *v* -ED, -ING, -S to prepare for action

UNLINK *v* -ED, -ING, -S to unfasten the links (connecting devices) of

UNLIVE *v* -LIVED, -LIVING, -LIVES to live so as to make amends for

UNLOAD *v* -ED, -ING, -S to remove the load or cargo from

UNLOADER *n* pl. -S one that unloads

UNLOCK *v* -ED, -ING, -S to unfasten the lock of

UNLOOSE *v* -LOOSED, -LOOSING, -LOOSES to set free

UNLOOSEN *v* -ED, -ING, -S to unloose

UNMAKE *v* -MADE, -MAKING, -MAKES to destroy

UNMAKER *n* pl. -S one that unmakes

UNMAN *v* -MANNED, -MANNING, -MANS to deprive of courage

UNMASK *v* -ED, -ING, -S to remove a mask from

UNMASKER *n* pl. -S one that unmasks

UNMEET *adj* improper **UNMEETLY** *adv*

UNMEW *v* -ED, -ING, -S to set free

UNMINGLE *v* -GLED, -GLING, -GLES to separate things that are mixed

UNMITER *v* -ED, -ING, -S to depose from the rank of bishop

UNMITRE *v* -TRED, -TRING, -TRES to unmiter

UNMOLD *v* -ED, -ING, -S to remove from a mold

UNMOOR *v* -ED, -ING, -S to release from moorings

UNMORAL *adj* amoral

UNMUFFLE *v* -FLED, -FLING, -FLES to free from something that muffles

UNMUZZLE *v* -ZLED, -ZLING, -ZLES to remove a muzzle from

UNNAIL *v* -ED, -ING, -S to remove the nails from

UNNERVE *v* -NERVED, -NERVING, -NERVES to deprive of courage

UNPACK *v* -ED, -ING, -S to remove the contents of

UNPACKER *n* pl. -S one that unpacks

UNPAGED *adj* having no page numbers

UNPEG *v* -PEGGED, -PEGGING, -PEGS to remove the pegs from

UNPEN *v* -PENNED or -PENT, -PENNING, -PENS to release from confinement

UNPEOPLE *v* -PLED, -PLING, -PLES to remove people from

UNPERSON *n* pl. -S one who is removed completely from recognition

UNPICK *v* -ED, -ING, -S to remove the stitches from

UNPILE *v* -PILED, -PILING, -PILES to take or disentangle from a pile

UNPIN *v* -PINNED, -PINNING, -PINS to remove the pins from

UNPLAIT *v* -ED, -ING, -S to undo the plaits of

UNPLUG   *v* -PLUGGED, -PLUGGING, -PLUGS to take a plug out of

UNPUCKER   *v* -ED, -ING, -S to remove the wrinkles from

UNPUZZLE   *v* -ZLED, -ZLING, -ZLES to work out the obscured meaning of

UNQUIET   *n* pl. -S a state of unrest

UNQUOTE   *v* -QUOTED, -QUOTING, -QUOTES to close a quotation

UNRAVEL   *v* -ELED, -ELING, -ELS or -ELLED, -ELLING, -ELS to separate the threads of

UNREASON   *v* -ED, -ING, -S to disrupt the sanity of

UNREEL   *v* -ED, -ING, -S to unwind from a reel

UNREELER   *n* pl. -S one that unreels

UNREEVE   *v* -REEVED or -ROVE, -ROVEN, -REEVING, -REEVES to withdraw a rope from an opening

UNRENT   *adj* not torn

UNREPAIR   *n* pl. -S lack of repair

UNREST   *n* pl. -S a disturbed or uneasy state

UNRIDDLE   *v* -DLED, -DLING, -DLES to solve

UNRIG   *v* -RIGGED, -RIGGING, -RIGS to divest of rigging

UNRIP   *v* -RIPPED, -RIPPING, -RIPS to rip open

UNRIPE   *adj* -RIPER, -RIPEST not ripe
UNRIPELY *adv*

UNROBE   *v* -ROBED, -ROBING, -ROBES to undress

UNROLL   *v* -ED, -ING, -S to open something that is rolled up

UNROOF   *v* -ED, -ING, -S to strip off the roof of

UNROOT   *v* -ED, -ING, -S to uproot

UNROUND   *v* -ED, -ING, -S to articulate without rounding the lips

UNROVE   a past tense of unreeve

UNROVEN   a past participle of unreeve

UNRULY   *adj* -LIER, -LIEST difficult to control

UNSADDLE   *v* -DLED, -DLING, -DLES to remove the saddle from

UNSAFETY   *n* pl. -TIES lack of safety

UNSAY   *v* -SAID, -SAYING, -SAYS to retract something said

UNSCREW   *v* -ED, -ING, -S to remove the screws from

UNSEAL   *v* -ED, -ING, -S to remove the seal of

UNSEAM   *v* -ED, -ING, -S to open the seams of

UNSEAT   *v* -ED, -ING, -S to remove from a seat

UNSET   *v* -SET, -SETTING, -SETS to unsettle

UNSETTLE   *v* -TLED, -TLING, -TLES to make unstable

UNSEW   *v* -SEWED, -SEWN, -SEWING, -SEWS to undo the sewing of

UNSEX   *v* -ED, -ING, -ES to deprive of sexual power

UNSHELL   *v* -ED, -ING, -S to remove the shell from

UNSHIFT   *v* -ED, -ING, -S to release the shift key on a typewriter

UNSHIP   *v* -SHIPPED, -SHIPPING, -SHIPS to unload from a ship

UNSICKER   *adj* unreliable

UNSIGHT   *v* -ED, -ING, -S to prevent from seeing

UNSLING   *v* -SLUNG, -SLINGING, -SLINGS to remove from a slung position

UNSNAP   *v* -SNAPPED, -SNAPPING, -SNAPS to undo the snaps (fastening devices) of

UNSNARL   *v* -ED, -ING, -S to untangle

UNSOLDER   *v* -ED, -ING, -S to separate

UNSONCY   *adj* unsonsie

UNSONSIE   *adj* unlucky

UNSONSY   *adj* unsonsie

UNSPEAK   *v* -SPOKE, -SPOKEN, -SPEAKING, -SPEAKS to unsay

UNSPHERE   *v* -SPHERED, -SPHERING, -SPHERES to remove from a sphere

UNSTACK   *v* -ED, -ING, -S to remove from a stack

UNSTATE   *v* -STATED, -STATING, -STATES to deprive of status

UNSTEADY   *v* -STEADIED, -STEADYING, -STEADIES to make unsteady

UNSTEEL   *v* -ED, -ING, -S to make soft

UNSTEP   *v* -STEPPED, -STEPPING, -STEPS to remove from a socket

UNSTICK   *v* -ED, -ING, -S to disjoin

UNSTOP   *v* -STOPPED, -STOPPING, -STOPS to remove a stopper from

UNSTRAP   v -STRAPPED, -STRAPPING, -STRAPS to remove a strap from

UNSTRESS   n pl. -ES a syllable having relatively weak stress

UNSTRING   v -STRUNG, -STRINGING, -STRINGS to remove from a string

UNSWATHE   v -SWATHED, -SWATHING, -SWATHES to unbind

UNSWEAR   v -SWORE, -SWORN, -SWEARING, -SWEARS to retract something sworn

UNTACK   v -ED, -ING, -S to remove a tack from

UNTANGLE   v -GLED, -GLING, -GLES to free from tangles

UNTEACH   v -TAUGHT, -TEACHING, -TEACHES to cause to unlearn something

UNTETHER   v -ED, -ING, -S to free from a tether

UNTHINK   v -THOUGHT, -THINKING, -THINKS to dismiss from the mind

UNTHREAD   v -ED, -ING, -S to remove the thread from

UNTHRONE   v -THRONED, -THRONING, -THRONES to remove from a throne

UNTIDY   v -DIED, -DYING, -DIES to make untidy

UNTIE   v -TIED, -TYING, -TIES to free from something that ties

UNTIL   prep up to the time of

UNTO   prep to

UNTOWARD   adj unruly

UNTREAD   v -TROD, -TRODDEN, -TREADING, -TREADS to retrace

UNTRIM   v -TRIMMED, -TRIMMING, -TRIMS to strip of trimming

UNTRUSS   v -ED, -ING, -ES to free from a truss

UNTRUTH   n pl. -S something that is untrue

UNTUCK   v -ED, -ING, -S to release from being tucked up

UNTUNE   v -TUNED, -TUNING, -TUNES to put out of tune

UNTWINE   v -TWINED, -TWINING, -TWINES to separate the twisted or tangled parts of

UNTWIST   v -ED, -ING, -S to untwine

UNTYING   present participle of untie

UNVEIL   v -ED, -ING, -S to remove a covering from

UNVOICE   v -VOICED, -VOICING, -VOICES to deprive of voice or vocal quality

UNWASHED   n pl. -S an ignorant or underprivileged group

UNWEAVE   v -WOVE, -WOVEN, -WEAVING, -WEAVES to undo something woven

UNWEIGHT   v -ED, -ING, -S to reduce the weight of

UNWIND   v -WOUND, -WINDING, -WINDS to reverse the winding of

UNWINDER   n pl. -S one that unwinds

UNWISDOM   n pl. -S lack of wisdom

UNWISH   v -ED, -ING, -ES to cease to wish for

UNWIT   v -WITTED, -WITTING, -WITS to make insane

UNWONTED   adj unusual

UNWORTHY   n pl. -THIES an unworthy person

UNWOUND   past tense of unwind

UNWOVE   past tense of unweave

UNWOVEN   past participle of unweave

UNWRAP   v -WRAPPED, -WRAPPING, -WRAPS to remove the wrapping from

UNYEANED   adj unborn

UNYOKE   v -YOKED, -YOKING, -YOKES to free from a yoke

UNZIP   v -ZIPPED, -ZIPPING, -ZIPS to open the zipper of

UP   v UPPED, UPPING, UPS to raise

UPAS   n pl. -ES an Asian tree

UPBEAR   v -BORE, -BORNE, -BEARING, -BEARS to raise aloft

UPBEARER   n pl. -S one that upbears

UPBEAT   n pl. -S an unaccented beat in a musical measure

UPBIND   v -BOUND, -BINDING, -BINDS to bind completely

UPBOIL   v -ED, -ING, -S to boil up

UPBORE   past tense of upbear

UPBORNE   past participle of upbear

UPBOUND   past tense of upbind

UPBRAID   v -ED, -ING, -S to reproach severely

UPBUILD   v -BUILT, -BUILDING, -BUILDS to build up

UPBY   *adv* upbye

UPBYE   *adv* a little farther on

UPCAST   *v* -CAST, -CASTING, -CASTS to cast up

UPCHUCK   *v* -ED, -ING, -S to vomit

UPCLIMB   *v* -ED, -ING, -S to climb up

UPCOIL   *v* -ED, ING, S to coil up

UPCOMING   *adj* about to happen or appear

UPCURL   *v* -ED, -ING, -S to curl up

UPCURVE   *v* -CURVED, -CURVING, -CURVES to curve upward

UPDART   *v* -ED, -ING, -S to dart up

UPDATE   *v* -DATED, -DATING, -DATES to bring up to date

UPDATER   *n* pl. -S one that updates

UPDIVE   *v* -DIVED or -DOVE, -DIVING, -DIVES to spring upward

UPDO   *n* pl. -DOS an upswept hairdo

UPDRAFT   *n* pl. -S an upward movement of air

UPDRY   *v* -DRIED, -DRYING, -DRIES to dry completely

UPEND   *v* -ED, -ING, -S to set or stand on end

UPFIELD   *adv* into the part of the field toward which the offensive team is going

UPFLING   *v* -FLUNG, -FLINGING, -FLINGS to fling up

UPFLOW   *v* -ED, -ING, -S to flow up

UPFOLD   *v* -ED, -ING, -S to fold up

UPGATHER   *v* -ED, -ING, -S to gather up

UPGAZE   *v* -GAZED, -GAZING, -GAZES to gaze up

UPGIRD   *v* -GIRDED or -GIRT, -GIRDING, -GIRDS to gird completely

UPGOING   *adj* going up

UPGRADE   *v* -GRADED, -GRADING, -GRADES to raise to a higher grade or standard

UPGROW   *v* -GREW, -GROWN, -GROWING, -GROWS to grow up

UPGROWTH   *n* pl. -S the process of growing up

UPHEAP   *v* -ED, -ING, -S to heap up

UPHEAVAL   *n* pl. -S the act of upheaving

UPHEAVE   *v* -HEAVED or -HOVE, -HEAVING, -HEAVES to heave up

UPHEAVER   *n* pl. -S one that upheaves

UPHELD   past tense of uphold

UPHILL   *n* pl. -S an upward slope

UPHOARD   *v* -ED, -ING, -S to hoard up

UPHOLD   *v* -HELD, -HOLDING, -HOLDS to hold aloft

UPHOLDER   *n* pl. -S one that upholds

UPHOVE   a past tense of upheave

UPHROE   *n* pl. -S euphroe

UPKEEP   *n* pl. -S the cost of maintaining something in good condition

UPLAND   *n* pl. -S the higher land of a region

UPLANDER   *n* pl. -S an inhabitant of an upland

UPLEAP   *v* -LEAPED or -LEAPT, -LEAPING, -LEAPS to leap up

UPLIFT   *v* -ED, -ING, -S to lift up

UPLIFTER   *n* pl. -S one that uplifts

UPLIGHT   *v* -LIGHTED or -LIT, -LIGHTING, -LIGHTS to light to a higher degree

UPMOST   *adj* highest

UPO   *prep* upon

UPON   *prep* on

UPPED   past tense of up

UPPER   *n* pl. -S the part of a boot or shoe above the sole

UPPERCUT   *v* -CUT, -CUTTING, -CUTS to strike an upward blow

UPPILE   *v* -PILED, -PILING, -PILES to pile up

UPPING   *n* pl. -S the process of marking young swans for identification purposes

UPPISH   *adj* uppity **UPPISHLY** *adv*

UPPITY   *adj* tending to be snobbish and arrogant

UPPROP   *v* -PROPPED, -PROPPING, -PROPS to prop up

UPRAISE   *v* -RAISED, -RAISING, -RAISES to raise up

UPRAISER   *n* pl. -S one that upraises

UPREACH   *v* -ED, -ING, -ES to reach up

UPREAR   *v* -ED, -ING, -S to upraise

UPRIGHT   *v* -ED, -ING, -S to make vertical

UPRISE   *v* -ROSE, -RISEN, -RISING, -RISES to rise up

UPRISER   *n* pl. -S one that uprises

UPRISING   *n* pl. -S a revolt

UPRIVER   *n* pl. -S an area lying toward the source of a river

UPROAR *n pl.* -S a state of noisy excitement and confusion

UPROOT *v* -ED, -ING, -S to pull up by the roots

UPROOTAL *n pl.* -S the act of uprooting

UPROOTER *n pl.* -S one that uproots

UPROSE past tense of uprise

UPROUSE *v* -ROUSED, -ROUSING, -ROUSES to rouse up

UPRUSH *v* -ED, -ING, -ES to rush up

UPSEND *v* -SENT, -SENDING, -SENDS to send upward

UPSET *v* -SET, -SETTING, -SETS to overturn

UPSETTER *n pl.* -S one that upsets

UPSHIFT *v* -ED, -ING, -S to shift an automotive vehicle into a higher gear

UPSHOOT *v* -SHOT, -SHOOTING, -SHOOTS to shoot upward

UPSHOT *n pl.* -S the final result

UPSIDE *n pl.* -S the upper side

UPSILON *n pl.* -S a Greek letter

UPSOAR *v* -ED, -ING, -S to soar upward

UPSPRING *v* -SPRANG or -SPRUNG, -SPRINGING, -SPRINGS to spring up

UPSTAGE *v* -STAGED, -STAGING, -STAGES to outdo theatrically

UPSTAIR *adj* pertaining to an upper floor

UPSTAIRS *adv* up the stairs

UPSTAND *v* -STOOD, -STANDING, -STANDS to stand up on one's feet

UPSTARE *v* -STARED, -STARING, -STARES to stare upward

UPSTART *v* -ED, -ING, -S to spring up suddenly

UPSTATE *n pl.* -S the northern region of a state

UPSTATER *n pl.* -S an inhabitant of an upstate region

UPSTEP *v* -STEPPED, -STEPPING, -STEPS to step up

UPSTIR *v* -STIRRED, -STIRRING, -STIRS to stir up

UPSTOOD past tense of upstand

UPSTREAM *adv* toward the source of a stream

UPSTROKE *n pl.* -S an upward stroke

UPSURGE *v* -SURGED, -SURGING, -SURGES to surge up

UPSWEEP *v* -SWEPT, -SWEEPING, -SWEEPS to sweep upward

UPSWELL *v* -SWELLED, -SWOLLEN, -SWELLING, -SWELLS, to swell up

UPSWING *v* -SWUNG, -SWINGING, -SWINGS to swing upward

UPTAKE *n pl.* -S an upward ventilating shaft

UPTEAR *v* -TORE, -TORN, -TEARING, -TEARS to tear out by the roots

UPTHROW *v* -THREW, -THROWN, -THROWING, -THROWS to throw upward

UPTHRUST *v* -THRUST, -THRUSTING, -THRUSTS to thrust up

UPTIGHT *adj* nervous

UPTILT *v* -ED, -ING, -S to tilt upward

UPTIME *n pl.* -S the time during which machinery is functioning

UPTORE past tense of uptear

UPTORN past participle of uptear

UPTOSS *v* -ED, -ING, -ES to toss upward

UPTOWN *n pl.* -S the upper part of a city

UPTOWNER *n pl.* -S one that lives uptown

UPTREND *n pl.* -S a tendency upward or toward growth

UPTURN *v* -ED, -ING, -S to turn up or over

UPWAFT *v* -ED, -ING, -S to waft upward

UPWARD *adv* toward a higher place or position **UPWARDLY** *adv*

UPWARDS *adv* upward

UPWELL *v* -ED, -ING, -S to well up

UPWIND *n pl.* -S a wind that blows against one's course

URACIL *n pl.* -S a chemical compound

URAEI a *pl.* of uraeus

URAEMIA *n pl.* -S uremia **URAEMIC** *adj*

URAEUS *n pl.* URAEI or URAEUSES the figure of the sacred serpent on the headdress of ancient Egyptian rulers

URALITE *n pl.* -S a mineral **URALITIC** *adj*

URANIC *adj* pertaining to uranium

URANIDE *n pl.* -S uranium

URANISM *n pl.* -S homosexuality

URANITE *n pl.* -S a mineral **URANITIC** *adj*

URANIUM   *n* pl. -S a radioactive element

URANOUS   *adj* pertaining to uranium

URANYL   *n* pl. -S a bivalent radical **URANYLIC** *adj*

URARE   *n* pl. -S curare

URARI   *n* pl. -S curare

URASE   *n* pl. -S urease

URATE   *n* pl. -S a chemical salt **URATIC** *adj*

URBAN   *adj* pertaining to a city

URBANE   *adj* -BANER, -BANEST refined and elegant **URBANELY** *adv*

URBANISE   *v* -ISED, -ISING, -ISES to urbanize

URBANISM   *n* pl. -S the life-style of city dwellers

URBANIST   *n* pl. -S a specialist in city planning

URBANITE   *n* pl. -S one who lives in a city

URBANITY   *n* pl. -TIES the quality of being urbane

URBANIZE   *v* -IZED, -IZING, -IZES to cause to take on urban characteristics

URCHIN   *n* pl. -S a mischievous boy

URD   *n* pl. -S an annual bean grown in India

UREA   *n* pl. -S a chemical compound **UREAL** *adj*

UREASE   *n* pl. -S an enzyme

UREDIA   pl. of uredium

UREDIAL   *adj* pertaining to a uredium

UREDINIA   *n/pl* uredia

UREDIUM   *n* pl. -DIA a spore-producing organ of certain fungi

UREDO   *n* pl. -DOS a skin irritation

UREIC   *adj* pertaining to urea

UREIDE   *n* pl. -S a chemical compound

UREMIA   *n* pl. -S an abnormal condition of the blood **UREMIC** *adj*

URETER   *n* pl. -S the duct that conveys urine from the kidney to the bladder **URETERAL, URETERIC** *adj*

URETHAN   *n* pl. -S urethane

URETHANE   *n* pl. -S a chemical compound

URETHRA   *n* pl. -THRAE or -THRAS the duct through which urine is discharged from the bladder **URETHRAL** *adj*

URETIC   *adj* pertaining to urine

URGE   *v* URGED, URGING, URGES to force forward

URGENCY   *n* pl. -CIES the quality of being urgent

URGENT   *adj* requiring immediate attention **URGENTLY** *adv*

URGER   *n* pl. -S one that urges

URGING   present participle of urge

URGINGLY   *adv* in an urging manner

URIC   *adj* pertaining to urine

URIDINE   *n* pl. -S a chemical compound

URINAL   *n* pl. -S a fixture used for urinating

URINARY   *n* pl. -NARIES a urinal

URINATE   *v* -NATED, -NATING, -NATES to discharge urine

URINE   *n* pl. -S a liquid containing body wastes

URINEMIA   *n* pl. -S uremia **URINEMIC** *adj*

URINOSE   *adj* pertaining to urine

URINOUS   *adj* pertaining to urine

URN   *n* pl. -S a type of vase **URNLIKE** *adj*

UROCHORD   *n* pl. -S a rodlike structure in certain lower vertebrates

URODELE   *n* pl. -S a type of amphibian

UROLITH   *n* pl. -S a concretion in the urinary tract

UROLOGY   *n* pl. -GIES the branch of medicine dealing with the urinary tract **UROLOGIC** *adj*

UROPOD   *n* pl. -S an abdominal limb of an arthropod **UROPODAL** *adj*

UROSCOPY   *n* pl. -PIES analysis of the urine as a means of diagnosis

UROSTYLE   *n* pl. -S a part of the vertebral column of frogs and toads

URSA   *n* pl. -SAE a female bear

URSIFORM   *adj* having the form of a bear

URSINE   *adj* pertaining to a bear

URTICANT   *n* pl. -S an urticating substance

URTICATE   *v* -CATED, -CATING, -CATES to cause itching or stinging

URUS   *n* pl. -ES an extinct European ox

URUSHIOL   *n* pl. -S a toxic liquid

US   *pron* the objective case of the pronoun we

USABLE   *adj* capable of being used **USABLY** *adv*

USAGE	*n pl.* -S a firmly established and generally accepted practice or procedure
USANCE	*n pl.* -S usage
USAUNCE	*n pl.* -S usance
USE	*v* USED, USING, USES to put into service
USEABLE	*adj* usable **USEABLY** *adv*
USEFUL	*adj* serving a purpose **USEFULLY** *adv*
USELESS	*adj* serving no purpose
USER	*n pl.* -S one that uses
USHER	*v* -ED, -ING, -S to conduct to a place
USING	present participle of use
USNEA	*n pl.* -S any of a genus of lichens
USQUABAE	*n pl.* -S usquebae
USQUE	*n pl.* -S usquebae
USQUEBAE	*n pl.* -S whiskey
USTULATE	*adj* scorched
USUAL	*n pl.* -S something that is usual (ordinary)
USUALLY	*adv* ordinarily
USUFRUCT	*n pl.* -S the legal right to use another's property so long as it is not damaged or altered
USURER	*n pl.* -S one that practices usury
USURIES	pl. of usury
USURIOUS	*adj* practicing usury
USURP	*v* -ED, -ING, -S to seize and hold without legal authority
USURPER	*n pl.* -S one that usurps
USURY	*n pl.* -RIES the lending of money at an exorbitant interest rate
UT	*n pl.* -S the musical tone C in the French solmization system now replaced by do
UTA	*n pl.* -S any of a genus of large lizards
UTENSIL	*n pl.* -S a useful implement

UTERUS	*n pl.* UTERI or UTERUSES an organ of female mammals **UTERINE** *adj*
UTILE	*adj* useful
UTILIDOR	*n pl.* -S an insulated system of pipes for use in arctic regions
UTILISE	*v* -LISED, -LISING, -LISES to utilize
UTILISER	*n pl.* -S utilizer
UTILITY	*n pl.* -TIES the quality of being useful
UTILIZE	*v* -LIZED, -LIZING, -LIZES to make use of
UTILIZER	*n pl.* -S one who utilizes
UTMOST	*n pl.* -S the greatest degree or amount
UTOPIA	*n pl.* -S a place of ideal perfection
UTOPIAN	*n pl.* -S one who believes in the perfectibility of human society
UTOPISM	*n pl.* -S the body of ideals or principles of a utopian
UTOPIST	*n pl.* -S a utopian
UTRICLE	*n pl.* -S a saclike cavity in the inner ear
UTRICULI	*n/pl* utricles
UTTER	*v* -ED, -ING, -S to give audible expression to
UTTERER	*n pl.* -S one that utters
UTTERLY	*adv* totally
UVEA	*n pl.* -S a layer of the eye **UVEAL** *adj*
UVEITIS	*n pl.* -ITISES inflammation of the uvea **UVEITIC** *adj*
UVEOUS	*adj* pertaining to the uvea
UVULA	*n pl.* -LAE or -LAS the pendent, fleshy portion of the soft palate
UVULAR	*n pl.* -S a uvularly produced sound
UVULARLY	*adv* with the use of the uvula
UVULITIS	*n pl.* -TISES inflammation of the uvula
UXORIAL	*adj* pertaining to a wife
UXORIOUS	*adj* excessively submissive or devoted to one's wife

VACANCY *n* pl. -CIES the quality or state of being vacant

VACANT *adj* empty **VACANTLY** *adv*

VACATE *v* -CATED, -CATING, -CATES to make vacant

VACATION *v* -ED, -ING, -S to take a vacation (a period of time devoted to rest and relaxation)

VACCINA *n* pl. -S vaccinia

VACCINE *n* pl. -S a preparation given to produce immunity to a specific disease **VACCINAL** *adj*

VACCINIA *n* pl. -S cowpox

VACUA a pl. of vacuum

VACUITY *n* pl. -ITIES an empty space

VACUOLE *n* pl. -S a small cavity in organic tissue **VACUOLAR** *adj*

VACUOUS *adj* empty

VACUUM *n* pl. VACUUMS or VACUA a space entirely devoid of matter

VACUUM *v* -ED, -ING, -S to use a device that cleans by suction

VADOSE *adj* located above the permanent groundwater level

VAGABOND *v* -ED, -ING, -S to live like a vagabond (a vagrant)

VAGAL *adj* pertaining to the vagus nerve **VAGALLY** *adv*

VAGARY *n* pl. -RIES a whim

VAGI pl. of vagus

VAGILE *adj* free to move about

VAGILITY *n* pl. -TIES freedom of movement

VAGINA *n* pl. -NAE or -NAS the passage leading from the uterus to the vulva **VAGINAL** *adj*

VAGINATE *adj* enclosed in a sheath

VAGOTOMY *n* pl. -MIES surgical division of the vagus nerve

VAGRANCY *n* pl. -CIES the state of being a vagrant

VAGRANT *n* pl. -S a wanderer with no apparent means of support

VAGROM *adj* wandering

VAGUE *adj* VAGUER, VAGUEST not clearly expressed or understood **VAGUELY** *adv*

VAGUS *n* pl. -GI a cranial nerve

VAHINE *n* pl. -S wahine

VAIL *v* -ED, -ING, -S to lower

VAIN *adj* VAINER, VAINEST filled with undue admiration for oneself **VAINLY** *adv*

VAINNESS *n* pl. -ES the quality or state of being vain

VAIR *n* pl. -S a fur used for lining and trimming medieval garments

VAKEEL *n* pl. -S a native lawyer in India

VAKIL *n* pl. -S vakeel

VALANCE *v* -LANCED, -LANCING, -LANCES to furnish with a short drapery

VALE *n* pl. -S a valley

VALENCE *n* pl. -S the degree of combining power of an element or radical

VALENCIA *n* pl. -S a woven fabric

VALENCY *n* pl. -CIES valence

VALERATE *n* pl. -S a chemical salt

VALERIAN *n* pl. -S a perennial herb **VALERIC** *adj*

VALET   v -ED, -ING, -S to act as a personal servant to

VALGUS   n pl. -ES the position of a joint that is abnormally turned outward **VALGOID** adj

VALIANCE   n pl. -S valor

VALIANCY   n pl. -CIES valor

VALIANT   n pl. -S a courageous person

VALID   adj based on evidence that can be supported

VALIDATE   v -DATED, -DATING, -DATES to give legal force to

VALIDITY   n pl. -TIES the quality or state of being valid

VALIDLY   adv in a valid manner

VALINE   n pl. -S an amino acid

VALISE   n pl. -S a small piece of hand luggage

VALKYR   n pl. -S valkyrie

VALKYRIE   n pl. -S a maiden in Norse mythology

VALLATE   adj bordered by a raised edge

VALLEY   n pl. -LEYS a depression of the earth's surface

VALONIA   n pl. -S a substance obtained from dried acorn cups and used in tanning and dyeing

VALOR   n pl. -S courage

VALORISE   v -ISED, -ISING, -ISES to valorize

VALORIZE   v -IZED, -IZING, -IZES to establish and maintain the price of by governmental action

VALOROUS   adj courageous

VALOUR   n pl. -S valor

VALSE   n pl. -S a concert waltz

VALUABLE   n pl. -S a possession of value

VALUABLY   adv with value

VALUATE   v -ATED, -ATING, -ATES to appraise

VALUATOR   n pl. -S one that valuates

VALUE   v -UED, -UING, -UES to estimate the value (the quality that renders a thing useful or desirable) of

VALUER   n pl. -S one that values

VALUTA   n pl. -S the agreed or exchange value of a currency

VALVAL   adj resembling or pertaining to a valve

VALVAR   adj valval

VALVATE   adj having valves or parts resembling valves

VALVE   v VALVED, VALVING, VALVES to provide with a valve (a device for controlling the flow of a liquid or gas)

VALVELET   n pl. -S a small valve

VALVULA   n pl. -LAE valvule

VALVULAR   adj pertaining to a valve

VALVULE   n pl. -S a small valve

VAMBRACE   n pl. -S a piece of armor for the forearm

VAMOOSE   v -MOOSED, -MOOSING, -MOOSES to leave quickly

VAMOSE   v -MOSED, -MOSING, -MOSES to vamoose

VAMP   v -ED, -ING, -S to repair or patch

VAMPER   n pl. -S one that vamps

VAMPIRE   n pl. -S a reanimated corpse believed to feed on sleeping persons' blood **VAMPIRIC** adj

VAMPISH   adj seductive

VAN   n pl. -S a large motor vehicle

VANADATE   n pl. -S a chemical salt

VANADIUM   n pl. -S a metallic element **VANADIC, VANADOUS** adj

VANDA   n pl. -S a tropical orchid

VANDAL   n pl. -S one who willfully destroys or defaces property **VANDALIC** adj

VANDYKE   n pl. -S a short, pointed beard **VANDYKED** adj

VANE   n pl. -S a device for showing the direction of the wind **VANED** adj

VANG   n pl. -S a rope on a ship

VANGUARD   n pl. -S the forefront of a movement

VANILLA   n pl. -S a flavoring extract **VANILLIC** adj

VANILLIN   n pl. -S a chemical compound used in flavoring

VANISH   v -ED, -ING, -ES to disappear

VANISHER   n pl. -S one that vanishes

VANITY   n pl. -TIES inflated pride in oneself **VANITIED** adj

VANMAN   n pl. -MEN a person who drives a van

VANQUISH   v -ED, -ING, -ES to defeat in battle

VANTAGE   *n* pl. -S superiority over a competitor

VANWARD   *adv* toward the front

VAPID   *adj* insipid **VAPIDLY** *adv*

VAPIDITY   *n* pl. -TIES the quality or state of being vapid

VAPOR   *v* -ED, -ING, -S to emit vapor (visible floating moisture)

VAPORER   *n* pl. -S one that vapors

VAPORING   *n* pl. -S boastful talk

VAPORISE   *v* -ISED, -ISING, -ISES to vaporize

VAPORISH   *adj* resembling vapor

VAPORIZE   *v* -IZED, -IZING, -IZES to convert into vapor

VAPOROUS   *adj* vaporish

VAPORY   *adj* vaporish

VAPOUR   *v* -ED, -ING, -S to vapor

VAPOURER   *n* pl. -S a vaporer

VAPOURY   *adj* vapory

VAQUERO   *n* pl. -ROS a cowboy

VARA   *n* pl. -S a Spanish unit of length

VARIA   *n/pl* a collection of various literary works

VARIABLE   *n* pl. -S something that varies

VARIABLY   *adv* in a varying manner

VARIANCE   *n* pl. -S a license to perform an act contrary to the usual rule

VARIANT   *n* pl. -S a variable

VARIATE   *v* -ATED, -ATING, -ATES to vary

VARICES   pl. of varix

VARICOSE   *adj* abnormally swollen or dilated

VARIED   past tense of vary

VARIEDLY   *adv* in a varied manner

VARIER   *n* pl. -S one that varies

VARIES   present 3d person sing. of vary

VARIETY   *n* pl. -ETIES something differing from others of the same general kind **VARIETAL** *adj*

VARIFORM   *adj* having various forms

VARIOLA   *n* pl. -S smallpox **VARIOLAR** *adj*

VARIOLE   *n* pl. -S a foveola

VARIORUM   *n* pl. -S an edition containing various versions of a text

VARIOUS   *adj* of diverse kinds

VARISTOR   *n* pl. -S a type of electrical resistor

VARIX   *n* pl. VARICES a varicose vein

VARLET   *n* pl. -S a knave

VARLETRY   *n* pl. -RIES a group of common people

VARMENT   *n* pl. -S varmint

VARMINT   *n* pl. -S an animal considered to be a pest

VARNA   *n* pl. -S any of the four main Hindu social classes

VARNISH   *v* -ED, -ING, -ES to give a glossy appearance to

VARNISHY   *adj* glossy

VARSITY   *n* pl. -TIES the principal team representing a university, college, or school in any activity

VARUS   *n* pl. -ES a malformation of a bone or joint

VARVE   *n* pl. -S a deposit of sedimentary material **VARVED** *adj*

VARY   *v* VARIED, VARYING, VARIES to become or make different

VAS   *n* pl. VASA an anatomical duct **VASAL** *adj*

VASCULAR   *adj* pertaining to ducts that convey body liquids

VASCULUM   *n* pl. -LA or -LUMS a box used to hold plant specimens

VASE   *n* pl. -S a rounded, decorative container **VASELIKE** *adj*

VASIFORM   *adj* having the form of a vase

VASSAL   *n* pl. -S a person granted the use of land by a feudal lord in return for homage and allegiance

VAST   *adj* VASTER, VASTEST of great extent or size

VAST   *n* pl. -S a vast space

VASTIER   comparative of vasty

VASTIEST   superlative of vasty

VASTITY   *n* pl. -TIES vastness

VASTLY   *adv* to a vast extent or degree

VASTNESS   *n* pl. -ES the quality or state of being vast

VASTY   *adj* VASTIER, VASTIEST vast

VAT   *v* VATTED, VATTING, VATS to put into a vat (a large container for holding liquids)

VATFUL   *n* pl. -S as much as a vat will hold

VATIC   *adj* pertaining to a prophet

VATICAL	*adj* vatic
VATICIDE	*n* pl. -S the killing of a prophet
VATTED	past tense of vat
VATTING	present participle of vat
VAU	*n* pl. -S vav
VAULT	*v* -ED, -ING, -S to provide with a vault (an arched ceiling)
VAULTER	*n* pl. -S one that leaps
VAULTING	*n* pl. -S the structure forming a vault
VAULTY	*adj* VAULTIER, VAULTIEST resembling a vault
VAUNT	*v* -ED, -ING, -S to brag
VAUNTER	*n* pl. -S one that vaunts
VAUNTFUL	*adj* boastful
VAUNTIE	*adj* boastful
VAUNTY	*adj* vauntie
VAV	*n* pl. -S a Hebrew letter
VAVASOR	*n* pl. -S a high-ranking vassal
VAVASOUR	*n* pl. -S vavasor
VAVASSOR	*n* pl. -S vavasor
VAW	*n* pl. -S vav
VAWARD	*n* pl. -S the foremost part
VAWNTIE	*adj* vaunty
VEAL	*v* -ED, -ING, -S to kill and prepare a calf for food
VEALER	*n* pl. -S a calf raised for food
VEALY	*adj* VEALIER, VEALIEST immature
VECTOR	*v* -ED, -ING, -S to guide in flight by means of radioed directions
VEDALIA	*n* pl. -S an Australian ladybug
VEDETTE	*n* pl. -S a small boat used for scouting
VEE	*n* pl. -S the letter V
VEENA	*n* pl. -S vina
VEEP	*n* pl. -S a vice-president
VEEPEE	*n* pl. -S veep
VEER	*v* -ED, -ING, -S to change direction
VEERY	*n* pl. -RIES a songbird
VEG	*n* pl. VEG a vegetable
VEGAN	*n* pl. -S one that eats only plant products
VEGANISM	*n* pl. -S the practice of eating only plant products
VEGETAL	*adj* pertaining to plants

VEGETANT	*adj* characteristic of plant life
VEGETATE	*v* -TATED, -TATING, -TATES to grow in the manner of a plant
VEGETE	*adj* healthy
VEGETIST	*n* pl. -S one that eats only plant products
VEGETIVE	*adj* growing or capable of growing
VEHEMENT	*adj* ardent
VEHICLE	*n* pl. -S a device used as a means of conveyance
VEIL	*v* -ED, -ING, -S to provide with a veil (a piece of sheer fabric worn over the face)
VEILEDLY	*adv* in a disguised manner
VEILER	*n* pl. -S one that veils
VEILING	*n* pl. -S a veil
VEILLIKE	*adj* resembling a veil
VEIN	*v* -ED, -ING, -S to fill with veins (tubular blood vessels)
VEINAL	*adj* of or pertaining to the veins
VEINER	*n* pl. -S a tool used in wood carving
VEINIER	comparative of veiny
VEINIEST	superlative of veiny
VEINING	*n* pl. -S a network of veins
VEINLESS	*adj* having no veins
VEINLET	*n* pl. -S a small vein
VEINLIKE	*adj* resembling a vein
VEINULE	*n* pl. -S venule
VEINULET	*n* pl. -S venule
VEINY	*adj* VEINIER, VEINIEST full of veins
VELA	pl. of velum
VELAMEN	*n* pl. -MINA a velum
VELAR	*n* pl. -S a kind of speech sound
VELARIUM	*n* pl. -IA an awning over an ancient Roman theater
VELARIZE	*v* -IZED, -IZING, -IZES to pronounce with the back of the tongue touching the soft palate
VELATE	*adj* having a velum
VELD	*n* pl. -S veldt
VELDT	*n* pl. -S a grassland of southern Africa
VELIGER	*n* pl. -S a larval stage of certain mollusks

VELITES   *n/pl* foot soldiers of ancient Rome

VELLEITY   *n* pl. -ITIES a very low degree of desire

VELLUM   *n* pl. -S a fine parchment

VELOCE   *adv* rapidly — used as a musical direction

VELOCITY   *n* pl. -TIES rapidity of motion

VELOUR   *n* pl. -S a fabric resembling velvet

VELOUTE   *n* pl. -S a type of sauce

VELUM   *n* pl. -LA a thin membranous covering or partition

VELURE   *v* -LURED, -LURING, -LURES to smooth with a velvet or silk pad, as a hat

VELVERET   *n* pl. -S a fabric resembling velvet

VELVET   *n* pl. -S a soft, smooth fabric **VELVETED, VELVETY** *adj*

VENA   *n* pl. -NAE a vein

VENAL   *adj* open to bribery **VENALLY** *adv*

VENALITY   *n* pl. -TIES the quality or state of being venal

VENATIC   *adj* pertaining to hunting

VENATION   *n* pl. -S an arrangement of veins

VEND   *v* -ED, -ING, -S to sell **VENDABLE** *adj*

VENDACE   *n* pl. -S a European fish

VENDEE   *n* pl. -S a buyer

VENDER   *n* pl. -S a vendor

VENDETTA   *n* pl. -S a feud between two families

VENDIBLE   *n* pl. -S a salable article

VENDIBLY   *adv* salably

VENDOR   *n* pl. -S a seller

VENDUE   *n* pl. -S a public sale

VENEER   *v* -ED, -ING, -S to overlay with thin layers of material

VENEERER   *n* pl. -S one that veneers

VENENATE   *v* -NATED, -NATING, -NATES to poison

VENENOSE   *adj* poisonous

VENERATE   *v* -ATED, -ATING, -ATES to revere

VENEREAL   *adj* involving the genital organs

VENERY   *n* pl. -ERIES sexual intercourse

VENETIAN   *n* pl. -S a flexible window screen

VENGE   *v* VENGED, VENGING, VENGES to avenge

VENGEFUL   *adj* seeking to avenge

VENIAL   *adj* easily excused or forgiven **VENIALLY** *adv*

VENIN   *n* pl. -S a toxin found in snake venom

VENINE   *n* pl. -S venin

VENIRE   *n* pl. -S a type of judicial writ

VENISON   *n* pl. -S the edible flesh of a deer

VENOM   *v* -ED, -ING, -S to inject with venom (a poisonous secretion of certain animals)

VENOMER   *n* pl. -S one that venoms

VENOMOUS   *adj* poisonous

VENOSE   *adj* venous

VENOSITY   *n* pl. -TIES the quality of state of being venous

VENOUS   *adj* full of veins **VENOUSLY** *adv*

VENT   *v* -ED, -ING, -S to provide with a vent (an opening for the escape of gas or liquid)

VENTAGE   *n* pl. -S a small opening

VENTAIL   *n* pl. -S the adjustable front of a medieval helmet

VENTER   *n* pl. -S the abdomen

VENTLESS   *adj* having no vent

VENTRAL   *n* pl. -S a fin located on the underside of a fish

VENTURE   *v* -TURED, -TURING, -TURES to risk

VENTURER   *n* pl. -S one that ventures

VENTURI   *n* pl. -S a device for measuring the flow of a fluid

VENTURING   present participle of venture

VENUE   *n* pl. -S the locale of an event

VENULE   *n* pl. -S a small vein **VENULAR, VENULOSE, VENULOUS** *adj*

VERA   *adj* very

VERACITY   *n* pl. -TIES conformity to truth

VERANDA   *n* pl. -S a type of porch

VERANDAH   *n* pl. -S veranda

VERATRIA   *n* pl. -S veratrin

VERATRIN   *n* pl. -S a poisonous mixture of alkaloids

VERATRUM   *n* pl. -S a poisonous herb

VERB   *n* pl. -S a word used to express an act, occurrence, or mode of being

VERBAL   n pl. -S a word derived from a verb

VERBALLY   adv in a spoken manner

VERBATIM   adv word for word

VERBENA   n pl. -S a flowering plant

VERBIAGE   n pl. -S an excess of words

VERBID   n pl. -S a verbal

VERBIFY   v -FIED, -FYING, -FIES to use as a verb

VERBILE   n pl. -S one whose mental imagery consists of words

VERBLESS   adj lacking a verb

VERBOSE   adj wordy

VERBOTEN   adj forbidden

VERDANCY   n pl. -CIES the quality or state of being verdant

VERDANT   adj green with vegetation

VERDERER   n pl. -S an officer in charge of the royal forests of England

VERDEROR   n pl. -S verderer

VERDICT   n pl. -S the decision of a jury at the end of a legal proceeding

VERDIN   n pl. -S a small bird

VERDITER   n pl. -S a blue or green pigment

VERDURE   n pl. -S green vegetation **VERDURED** adj

VERECUND   adj shy

VERGE   v VERGED, VERGING, VERGES to come near

VERGENCE   n pl. -S a movement of one eye in relation to the other

VERGER   n pl. -S a church official

VERGING   present participle of verge

VERGLAS   n pl. -ES a thin coating of ice on rock

VERIDIC   adj truthful

VERIER   comparative of very

VERIEST   superlative of very

VERIFIER   n pl. -S one that verifies

VERIFY   v -FIED, -FYING, -FIES to prove to be true

VERILY   adv in truth

VERISM   n pl. -S realism in art or literature

VERISMO   n pl. -MOS verism

VERIST   n pl. -S one who practices verism **VERISTIC** adj

VERITAS   n pl. -TATES truth

VERITY   n pl. -TIES truth

VERJUICE   n pl. -S the juice of sour or unripe fruit

VERMEIL   n pl. -S a red color

VERMES   pl. of vermis

VERMIAN   adj pertaining to worms

VERMIN   n pl. VERMIN small, common, harmful, or objectionable animals

VERMIS   n pl. -MES a part of the brain

VERMOULU   adj eaten by worms

VERMOUTH   n pl. -S a liqueur

VERMUTH   n pl. -S vermouth

VERNACLE   n pl. -S vernicle

VERNAL   adj pertaining to spring **VERNALLY** adv

VERNICLE   n pl. -S veronica

VERNIER   n pl. -S an auxiliary scale used with a main scale to obtain fine measurements

VERNIX   n pl. -ES a fatty substance covering the skin of a fetus

VERONICA   n pl. -S a handkerchief bearing the image of Christ's face

VERRUCA   n pl. -CAE a wart

VERSAL   adj entire

VERSANT   n pl. -S the slope of a mountain or mountain chain

VERSE   v VERSED, VERSING, VERSES to versify

VERSEMAN   n pl. -MEN one who versifies

VERSER   n pl. -S a verseman

VERSET   n pl. -S a versicle

VERSICLE   n pl. -S a short line of metrical writing

VERSIFY   v -FIED, -FYING, -FIES to change from prose into metrical form

VERSINE   n pl. -S a trigonometric function of an angle

VERSING   present participle of verse

VERSION   n pl. -S an account or description from a particular point of view

VERSO   n pl. -SOS a left-hand page of a book

VERST   n pl. -S a Russian measure of distance

VERSTE   n pl. -S verst

VERSUS   prep against

VERT *n* pl. -S the heraldic color green

VERTEBRA *n* pl. -BRAE or -BRAS any of the bones or segments forming the spinal column

VERTEX *n* pl. -TEXES or -TICES the highest point of something

VERTICAL *n* pl. -S something that is vertical (extending up and down)

VERTICIL *n* pl. -S a circular arrangement, as of flowers or leaves, about a point on an axis

VERTIGO *n* pl. -GOES, -GOS, or -GINES a disordered state in which the individual or his surroundings seem to whirl dizzily

VERTU *n* pl. -S virtu

VERVAIN *n* pl. -S a flowering plant

VERVE *n* pl. -S vivacity

VERVET *n* pl. -S an African monkey

VERY *adj* VERIER, VERIEST absolute

VESICA *n* pl. -CAE a bladder **VESICAL** *adj*

VESICANT *n* pl. -S a chemical warfare agent that induces blistering

VESICATE *v* -CATED, -CATING, -CATES to blister

VESICLE *n* pl. -S a small bladder

VESICULA *n* pl. -LAE a vesicle

VESPER *n* pl. -S an evening service, prayer, or song

VESPERAL *n* pl. -S a covering for an altar cloth

VESPIARY *n* pl. -ARIES a nest of wasps

VESPID *n* pl. -S a wasp

VESPINE *adj* pertaining to wasps

VESSEL *n* pl. -S a craft for traveling on water **VESSELED** *adj*

VEST *v* -ED, -ING, -S to place in the control of

VESTA *n* pl. -S a short friction match

VESTAL *n* pl. -S a chaste woman

VESTALLY *adv* chastely

VESTEE *n* pl. -S a garment worn under a woman's jacket or blouse

VESTIARY *n* pl. -ARIES a dressing room

VESTIGE *n* pl. -S a visible sign of something that is no longer in existence

VESTIGIA *n/pl* vestiges

VESTING *n* pl. -S the right of an employee to share in and withdraw from a pension fund without penalty

VESTLESS *adj* being without a vest

VESTLIKE *adj* resembling a vest (a short, sleeveless garment)

VESTMENT *n* pl. -S one of the ceremonial garments of the clergy

VESTRY *n* pl. -TRIES a room in which vestments are kept **VESTRAL** *adj*

VESTURAL *adj* pertaining to clothing

VESTURE *v* -TURED, -TURING, -TURES to clothe

VESUVIAN *n* pl. -S a mineral

VET *v* VETTED, VETTING, VETS to treat animals medically

VETCH *n* pl. -ES a climbing plant

VETERAN *n* pl. -S a former member of the armed forces

VETIVER *n* pl. -S an Asian grass

VETO *v* -ED, -ING, -ES to forbid or prevent action

VETOER *n* pl. -S one that vetoes

VETTED past tense of vet

VETTING present participle of vet

VEX *v* VEXED or VEXT, VEXING, VEXES to annoy

VEXATION *n* pl. -S a cause of trouble

VEXEDLY *adv* in a vexed manner

VEXER *n* pl. -S one that vexes

VEXIL *n* pl. -S vexillum

VEXILLUM *n* pl. -LA the web or vane of a feather **VEXILLAR** *adj*

VEXINGLY *adv* in a vexing manner

VEXT a past tense of vex

VIA *prep* by way of

VIABLE *adj* capable of living **VIABLY** *adv*

VIADUCT *n* pl. -S a type of bridge

VIAL *v* VIALED, VIALING, VIALS or VIALLED, VIALLING, VIALS to put in a vial (a small container for liquids)

VIAND *n* pl. -S an article of food

VIATIC *adj* pertaining to traveling

VIATICAL *adj* viatic

VIATICUM *n* pl. -CA or -CUMS an allowance for traveling expenses

VIATOR   *n pl.* -ES or -S a traveler

VIBES   *n/pl* a percussion instrument

VIBIST   *n pl.* -S one who plays the vibes

VIBRANCE   *n pl.* -S vibrancy

VIBRANCY   *n pl.* -CIES the quality or state of being vibrant

VIBRANT   *n pl.* -S a sonant

VIBRATE   *v* -BRATED, -BRATING, -BRATES to move back and forth rapidly

VIBRATO   *n pl.* -TOS a tremulous or pulsating musical effect

VIBRATOR   *n pl.* -S something that vibrates

VIBRIO   *n pl.* -RIOS any of a genus of bacteria shaped like a comma **VIBRIOID** *adj*

VIBRION   *n pl.* -S vibrio

VIBRISSA   *n pl.* -SAE one of the stiff hairs growing about the mouth of certain mammals

VIBURNUM   *n pl.* -S a flowering shrub

VICAR   *n pl.* -S a church official

VICARAGE   *n pl.* -S the office of a vicar

VICARATE   *n pl.* -S vicarage

VICARIAL   *adj* pertaining to a vicar

VICARLY   *adj* vicarial

VICE   *v* VICED, VICING, VICES to vise

VICELESS   *adj* having no immoral habits

VICENARY   *adj* pertaining to the number twenty

VICEROY   *n pl.* -ROYS one who rules as the representative of a sovereign

VICHY   *n pl.* -CHIES a type of mineral water

VICINAGE   *n pl.* -S vicinity

VICINAL   *adj* nearby

VICING   present participle of vice

VICINITY   *n pl.* -TIES the region near or about a place

VICIOUS   *adj* dangerously aggressive

VICOMTE   *n pl.* -S a French nobleman

VICTIM   *n pl.* -S one who suffers from a destructive or injurious action

VICTOR   *n pl.* -S one who defeats an adversary

VICTORIA   *n pl.* -S a light carriage

VICTORY   *n pl.* -RIES a successful outcome in a contest or struggle

VICTRESS   *n pl.* -ES a female victor

VICTUAL   *v* -UALED, -UALING, -UALS or -UALLED, -UALLING, -UALS to provide with food

VICUGNA   *n pl.* -S vicuna

VICUNA   *n pl.* -S a ruminant mammal

VIDE   *v* see — used to direct a reader to another item; VIDE is the only form of this verb; it cannot be conjugated

VIDEO   *n pl.* -EOS television

VIDETTE   *n pl.* -S vedette

VIDICON   *n pl.* -S a type of television camera tube

VIDUITY   *n pl.* -ITIES the quality or state of being a widow

VIE   *v* VIED, VYING, VIES to strive for superiority

VIER   *n pl.* -S one that vies

VIEW   *v* -ED, -ING, -S to look at **VIEWABLE** *adj*

VIEWER   *n pl.* -S one that views

VIEWIER   comparative of viewy

VIEWIEST   superlative of viewy

VIEWING   *n pl.* -S an act of seeing, watching, or looking

VIEWLESS   *adj* having no opinions

VIEWY   *adj* VIEWIER, VIEWIEST showy

VIGIL   *n pl.* -S a period of watchfulness maintained during normal sleeping hours

VIGILANT   *adj* watchful

VIGNETTE   *v* -GNETTED, -GNETTING, -GNETTES to describe briefly

VIGOR   *n pl.* -S active strength or force

VIGORISH   *n pl.* -ES a charge paid to a bookie on a bet

VIGOROSO   *adv* with emphasis and spirit — used as a musical direction

VIGOROUS   *adj* full of vigor

VIGOUR   *n pl.* -S vigor

VIKING   *n pl.* -S a Scandinavian pirate

VILAYET   *n pl.* -S an administrative division of Turkey

VILE   *adj* VILER, VILEST physically repulsive **VILELY** *adv*

VILENESS   *n pl.* -ES the state of being vile

VILIFIER   *n pl.* -S one that vilifies

VILIFY   *v* -FIED, -FYING, -FIES to defame

VILIPEND   *v* -ED, -ING, -S to vilify

VILL   *n* pl. -S a village

VILLA   *n* pl. -LAE or -LAS an agricultural estate of ancient Rome

VILLADOM   *n* pl. -S the world constituted by suburban residences and their occupants

VILLAGE   *n* pl. -S a small community in a rural area

VILLAGER   *n* pl. -S one who lives in a village

VILLAIN   *n* pl. -S a cruelly malicious person

VILLAINY   *n* pl. -LAINIES conduct characteristic of a villain

VILLATIC   *adj* rural

VILLEIN   *n* pl. -S a type of serf

VILLUS   *n* pl. -LI one of the hairlike projections found on certain membranes **VILLOSE, VILLOUS** *adj*

VIM   *n* pl. -S energy

VIMEN   *n* pl. -MINA a long, flexible branch of a plant **VIMINAL** *adj*

VIN   *n* pl. -S wine

VINA   *n* pl. -S a stringed instrument of India

VINAL   *n* pl. -S a synthetic textile fiber

VINASSE   *n* pl. -S a residue left after the distillation of liquor

VINCA   *n* pl. -S a flowering plant

VINCIBLE   *adj* capable of being conquered

VINCULUM   *n* pl. -LA or -LUMS a unifying bond

VINE   *v* VINED, VINING, VINES to grow like a vine (a climbing plant)

VINEAL   *adj* vinous

VINEGAR   *n* pl. -S a sour liquid used as a condiment or preservative **VINEGARY** *adj*

VINERY   *n* pl. -ERIES a place in which grapevines are grown

VINEYARD   *n* pl. -S an area planted with grapevines

VINIC   *adj* derived from wine

VINIER   comparative of viny

VINIEST   superlative of viny

VINIFERA   *n* pl. -S a European grape

VINING   present participle of vine

VINO   *n* pl. -NOS wine

VINOSITY   *n* pl. -TIES the character of a wine

VINOUS   *adj* pertaining to wine **VINOUSLY** *adv*

VINTAGE   *n* pl. -S a season's yield of wine from a vineyard

VINTAGER   *n* pl. -S one that harvests wine grapes

VINTNER   *n* pl. -S a wine merchant

VINY   *adj* VINIER, VINIEST covered with vines

VINYL   *n* pl. -S a type of plastic **VINYLIC** *adj*

VIOL   *n* pl. -S a stringed instrument

VIOLA   *n* pl. -S a stringed instrument

VIOLABLE   *adj* capable of being violated **VIOLABLY** *adv*

VIOLATE   *v* -LATED, -LATING, -LATES to break or disregard the terms or requirements of

VIOLATER   *n* pl. -S violator

VIOLATOR   *n* pl. -S one that violates

VIOLENCE   *n* pl. -S violent action

VIOLENT   *adj* marked by intense physical force or roughness

VIOLET   *n* pl. -S a flowering plant

VIOLIN   *n* pl. -S a stringed instrument

VIOLIST   *n* pl. -S one who plays the viol or viola

VIOLONE   *n* pl. -S a stringed instrument

VIOMYCIN   *n* pl. -S an antibiotic

VIPER   *n* pl. -S a venomous snake **VIPERINE, VIPERISH, VIPEROUS** *adj*

VIRAGO   *n* pl. -GOES or -GOS a noisy, domineering woman

VIRAL   *adj* pertaining to or caused by a virus **VIRALLY** *adv*

VIRELAI   *n* pl. -S virelay

VIRELAY   *n* pl. -LAYS a medieval French verse form

VIREMIA   *n* pl. -S the presence of a virus in the blood **VIREMIC** *adj*

VIREO   *n* pl. -EOS a small bird

VIRES   pl. of vis

VIRGA   *n* pl. -S wisps of precipitation evaporating before reaching ground

VIRGATE   *n* pl. -S an early English measure of land area

VIRGIN   *n* pl. -S a person who has never had sexual intercourse

VIRGINAL   *n* pl. -S a musical instrument

VIRGULE   *n* pl. -S a diagonal printing mark used to separate alternatives

VIRICIDE   *n* pl. -S a substance that destroys viruses

VIRID   *adj* verdant

VIRIDIAN   *n* pl. -S a bluish-green pigment

VIRIDITY   *n* pl. -TIES verdancy

VIRILE   *adj* having masculine vigor

VIRILISM   *n* pl. -S the development of male secondary sex characteristics in a female

VIRILITY   *n* pl. -TIES the quality or state of being virile

VIRION   *n* pl. -S a virus particle

VIRL   *n* pl. -S a metal ring or cap put around a shaft to prevent splitting

VIROLOGY   *n* pl. -GIES the study of viruses

VIROSIS   *n* pl. -ROSES infection with a virus

VIRTU   *n* pl. -S a love or taste for the fine arts

VIRTUAL   *adj* having the effect but not the actual form of what is specified

VIRTUE   *n* pl. -S moral excellence

VIRTUOSA   *n* pl. -SAS or -SE a female virtuoso

VIRTUOSO   *n* pl. -SOS or -SI a highly skilled artistic performer

VIRTUOUS   *adj* characterized by virtue

VIRUCIDE   *n* pl. -S viricide

VIRULENT   *adj* extremely poisonous

VIRUS   *n* pl. -ES any of a class of submicroscopic pathogens

VIS   *n* pl. VIRES force or power

VISA   *v* -ED, -ING, -S to put an official endorsement on, as a passport

VISAGE   *n* pl. -S the face or facial expression of a person **VISAGED** *adj*

VISARD   *n* pl. -S vizard

VISCACHA   *n* pl. -S a burrowing rodent

VISCERA   pl. of viscus

VISCERAL   *adj* pertaining to the internal organs

VISCID   *adj* thick and adhesive **VISCIDLY** *adv*

VISCOID   *adj* somewhat viscid

VISCOSE   *n* pl. -S a viscous solution

VISCOUNT   *n* pl. -S a British nobleman

VISCOUS   *adj* having relatively high resistance to flow

VISCUS   *n* pl. -CERA an internal organ

VISE   *v* VISED, VISING, VISES to hold in a vise (a clamping device)

VISE   *v* VISEED, VISEING, VISES to visa

VISELIKE   *adj* resembling a vice

VISIBLE   *adj* capable of being seen **VISIBLY** *adv*

VISING   present participle of vise

VISION   *v* -ED, -ING, -S to imagine

VISIONAL   *adj* imaginary

VISIT   *v* -ED, -ING, -S to go or come to see someone or something

VISITANT   *n* pl. -S a visitor

VISITER   *n* pl. -S visitor

VISITOR   *n* pl. -S one that visits

VISIVE   *adj* visible

VISOR   *v* -ED, -ING, -S to provide with a visor (a projecting brim)

VISTA   *n* pl. -S a distant view **VISTAED** *adj*

VISUAL   *adj* pertaining to the sense of sight **VISUALLY** *adv*

VITA   *n* pl. -TAE a brief, autobiographical sketch

VITAL   *adj* necessary to life

VITALISE   *v* -ISED, -ISING, -ISES to vitalize

VITALISM   *n* pl. -S a philosophical doctrine

VITALIST   *n* pl. -S an advocate of vitalism

VITALITY   *n* pl. -TIES exuberant physical strength or mental vigor

VITALIZE   *v* -IZED, -IZING, -IZES to give life to

VITALLY   *adv* in a vital manner

VITALS   *n/pl* vital organs

VITAMER   *n* pl. -S a type of chemical compound

VITAMIN   *n* pl. -S any of various organic substances essential to proper nutrition

VITAMINE   *n* pl. -S vitamin

VITELLIN   *n* pl. -S a protein found in egg yolk

VITELLUS   *n* pl. -ES the yolk of an egg

VITESSE *n* pl. -S speed

VITIATE *v* -ATED, -ATING, ATES to impair the value or quality of **VITIABLE** *adj*

VITIATOR *n* pl. -S one that vitiates

VITILIGO *n* pl. -GOS a skin disease

VITREOUS *adj* resembling glass

VITRIC *adj* pertaining to glass

VITRIFY *v* -FIED, -FYING, -FIES to convert into glass

VITRINE *n* pl. -S a glass showcase for art objects

VITRIOL *v* -OLED, -OLING, -OLS or -OLLED, -OLLING, -OLS to treat with sulfuric acid

VITTA *n* pl. -TAE a streak or band of color **VITTATE** *adj*

VITTLE *v* -TLED, -TLING, -TLES to victual

VITULINE *adj* pertaining to a calf

VIVA *n* pl. -S a shout or cry used to express approval

VIVACE *adj* lively — used as a musical direction

VIVACITY *n* pl. -TIES the quality or state of being lively

VIVARIUM *n* pl. -IA or -IUMS a place for raising and keeping live animals

VIVARY *n* pl. -RIES vivarium

VIVE *interj* — used as an exclamation of approval

VIVERRID *n* pl. -S any of a family of small carnivorous mammals

VIVERS *n/pl* food

VIVID *adj* -IDER, -IDEST strikingly bright or intense **VIVIDLY** *adv*

VIVIFIC *adj* vivifying

VIVIFIER *n* pl. -S one that vivifies

VIVIFY *v* -FIED, -FYING, -FIES to give life to

VIVIPARA *n/pl* animals that bring forth living young

VIVISECT *v* -ED, -ING, -S to dissect the living body of

VIXEN *n* pl. -S a shrewish woman **VIXENISH, VIXENLY** *adj*

VIZARD *n* pl. -S a mask **VIZARDED** *adj*

VIZCACHA *n* pl. -S a viscacha

VIZIER *n* pl. -S a high official in some Muslim countries

VIZIR *n* pl. -S vizier **VIZIRIAL** *adj*

VIZIRATE *n* pl. -S the office of a vizir

VIZOR *v* -ED, -ING, -S to visor

VIZSLA *n* pl. -S a Hungarian breed of dog

VOCABLE *n* pl. -S a word

VOCABLY *adv* in a manner that may be voiced aloud

VOCAL *n* pl. -S a sound produced with the voice

VOCALIC *n* pl. -S a vowel sound

VOCALISE *v* -ISED, -ISING, -ISES to vocalize

VOCALISM *n* pl. -S the act of vocalizing

VOCALIST *n* pl. -S a singer

VOCALITY *n* pl. -TIES possession or exercise of vocal powers

VOCALIZE *v* -IZED, -IZING, -IZES to produce with the voice

VOCALLY *adv* with the voice

VOCATION *n* pl. -S the work in which a person is regularly employed

VOCATIVE *n* pl. -S a grammatical case used in some languages

VOCES pl. of vox

VOCODER *n* pl. -S an electronic device used in transmitting speech signals

VODKA *n* pl. -S a liquor

VODUM *n* pl. -S a primitive religion of the West Indies

VOE *n* pl. -S a small bay, creek, or inlet

VOGIE *adj* vain

VOGUE *n* pl. -S the current trend or style **VOGUISH** *adj*

VOICE *v* VOICED, VOICING, VOICES to express or utter

VOICEFUL *adj* sonorous

VOICER *n* pl. -S one that voices

VOICING present participle of voice

VOID *v* -ED, -ING, -S to make void (of no legal force or effect) **VOIDABLE** *adj*

VOIDANCE *n* pl. -S the act or process of voiding

VOIDER *n* pl. -S one that voids

VOIDNESS *n* pl. -ES the quality or state of being void

VOILE *n* pl. -S a sheer fabric

VOLANT *adj* flying or capable of flying

VOLANTE   *adj* moving with light rapidity — used as a musical direction

VOLAR   *adj* pertaining to flight

VOLATILE   *n* pl. -S a winged creature

VOLCANIC   *n* pl. -S a rock produced by a volcano

VOLCANO   *n* pl. -NOES or -NOS an opening in the earth's crust through which molten rock and gases are ejected

VOLE   *v* VOLED, VOLING, VOLES to win all the tricks in a card game

VOLERY   *n* pl. -ERIES a large birdcage

VOLITANT   *adj* volant

VOLITION   *n* pl. -S the power of choosing or determining

VOLITIVE   *adj* pertaining to volition

VOLLEY   *v* -ED, -ING, -S to return a tennis ball before it touches the ground

VOLLEYER   *n* pl. -S one that volleys

VOLOST   *n* pl. -S an administrative district in Russia

VOLPLANE   *v* -PLANED, -PLANING, -PLANES to glide in an airplane

VOLT   *n* pl. -S a unit of electromotive force

VOLTA   *n* pl. -TE a turning

VOLTAGE   *n* pl. -S electromotive force expressed in volts

VOLTAISM   *n* pl. -S electricity produced by chemical action VOLTAIC *adj*

VOLTE   *n* pl. -S a fencing movement

VOLTI   *interj* — used to direct musicians to turn the page

VOLUBLE   *adj* talkative VOLUBLY *adv*

VOLUME   *v* -UMED, -UMING, -UMES to send or give out in large quantities

VOLUTE   *n* pl. -S a spiral architectural ornament VOLUTED *adj*

VOLUTIN   *n* pl. -S a granular substance that is common in microorganisms

VOLUTION   *n* pl. -S a spiral

VOLVA   *n* pl. -S a membranous sac that encloses certain immature mushrooms VOLVATE *adj*

VOLVOX   *n* pl. -ES any of a genus of freshwater protozoa

VOLVULUS   *n* pl. -LI or -LUSES a twisting of the intestine that causes obstruction

VOMER   *n* pl. -S a bone of the skull VOMERINE *adj*

VOMICA   *n* pl. -CAE a cavity in the body containing pus

VOMIT   *v* -ED, -ING, -S to eject the contents of the stomach through the mouth

VOMITER   *n* pl. -S one that vomits

VOMITIVE   *n* pl. -S an emetic

VOMITO   *n* pl. -TOS the black vomit of yellow fever

VOMITORY   *n* pl. -RIES an emetic

VOMITOUS   *adj* pertaining to vomiting

VOMITUS   *n* pl. -ES vomited matter

VON   *prep* of; from — used in some surnames

VOODOO   *v* -ED, -ING, -S to hex

VORACITY   *n* pl. -TIES the quality or state of being ravenous

VORLAGE   *n* pl. -S a position in skiing

VORTEX   *n* pl. -TEXES or -TICES a whirling mass of fluid VORTICAL *adj*

VOTABLE   *adj* capable of being voted on

VOTARESS   *n* pl. -ES a female votary

VOTARIST   *n* pl. -S a votary

VOTARY   *n* pl. -RIES a person who is bound by religious vows

VOTE   *v* VOTED, VOTING, VOTES to cast a vote (a formal expression of will or opinion)

VOTEABLE   *adj* votable

VOTELESS   *adj* having no vote

VOTER   *n* pl. -S one that votes

VOTING   present participle of vote

VOTIVE   *adj* performed in fullfillment of a vow VOTIVELY *adv*

VOTRESS   *n* pl. -ES votaress

VOUCH   *v* -ED, -ING, -ES to give one's personal assurance or guarantee

VOUCHEE   *n* pl. -S one for whom another vouches

VOUCHER   *v* -ED, -ING, -S to establish the authenticity of

VOUSSOIR   *n* pl. -S a wedge-shaped building stone

VOW   *v* -ED, -ING, -S to make a vow (a solemn promise)

VOWEL   *n* pl. -S a type of speech sound

VOWELIZE   *v* -IZED, -IZING, -IZES to provide with symbols used to indicate vowels

VOWER   *n* pl. -S one that vows

VOWLESS   *adj* having made no vow

VOX   *n* pl. VOCES voice

VOYAGE   *v* -AGED, -AGING, -AGES to travel

VOYAGER   *n* pl. -S one that voyages

VOYAGEUR   *n* pl. -S a person employed by a fur company to transport goods between distant stations

VOYEUR   *n* pl. -S one who is sexually gratified by looking at sexual objects or acts

VROOM   *v* -ED, -ING, -S to run an engine at high speed

VROUW   *n* pl. -S a Dutch woman

VROW   *n* pl. -S vrouw

VUG   *n* pl. -S a small cavity in a rock or lode **VUGGY** *adj*

VUGG   *n* pl. -S vug

VUGH   *n* pl. -S vug

VULCANIC   *adj* pertaining to a volcano

VULGAR   *adj* -GARER, -GAREST crude **VULGARLY** *adv*

VULGAR   *n* pl. -S a common person

VULGATE   *n* pl. -S the common speech of a people

VULGO   *adv* commonly

VULGUS   *n* pl. -ES an exercise in Latin formerly required of pupils in some English public schools

VULPINE   *adj* pertaining to a fox

VULTURE   *n* pl. -S a bird of prey

VULVA   *n* pl. -VAE or -VAS the external genital organs of a female **VULVAL, VULVAR, VULVATE** *adj*

VULVITIS   *n* pl. -TISES inflammation of the vulva

VYING   present participle of vie

VYINGLY   *adv* in a vying manner

WAB	n pl. -S a web		**WADING**	present participle of wade
WABBLE	v -BLED, -BLING, -BLES to wobble		**WADMAAL**	n pl. -S wadmal
			WADMAL	n pl. -S a thick woolen fabric
WABBLER	n pl. -S one that wabbles		**WADMEL**	n pl. -S wadmal
WABBLY	adj -BLIER, -BLIEST wobbly		**WADMOL**	n pl. -S wadmal
WACK	n pl. -S a wacky person		**WADMOLL**	n pl. -S wadmal
WACKE	n pl. -S a type of basaltic rock		**WADSET**	v -SETTED, -SETTING, -SETS to mortgage
WACKY	adj WACKIER, WACKIEST very irrational **WACKILY** adv		**WADY**	n pl. -DIES wadi
			WAE	n pl. -S woe
WAD	v WADDED, WADDING, WADS to form into a wad (a small mass of soft material)		**WAEFU**	adj waeful
			WAEFUL	adj woeful
			WAENESS	n pl. -ES woeness
WADABLE	adj wadeable		**WAESUCK**	interj waesucks
WADDER	n pl. -S one that wads		**WAESUCKS**	interj — used to express pity
WADDIE	n pl. -S a cowboy		**WAFER**	v -ED, -ING, -S to seal with an adhesive disk
WADDIED	past tense of waddy		
WADDIES	present 3d person sing. of waddy		**WAFERY**	adj resembling a wafer (a thin, crisp biscuit)
WADDING	n pl. -S a wad		**WAFF**	v -ED, -ING, -S to wave
WADDLE	v -DLED, -DLING, -DLES to walk with short, swaying steps		**WAFFIE**	n pl. -S a vagabond
			WAFFLE	v -FLED, -FLING, -FLES to talk foolishly
WADDLER	n pl. -S one that waddles		
WADDLY	adj having or being a waddling gait		**WAFT**	v -ED, -ING, -S to carry lightly over air or water
WADDY	v -DIED, -DYING, -DIES to strike with a thick club		
			WAFTAGE	n pl. -S the act of wafting
WADE	v WADED, WADING, WADES to walk through water		**WAFTER**	n pl. -S one that wafts
			WAFTURE	n pl. -S waftage
WADEABLE	adj capable of being passed through by wading		**WAG**	v WAGGED, WAGGING, WAGS to move briskly up and down or to and fro
WADER	n pl. -S one that wades		
WADI	n pl. -S the bed of a usually dry watercourse		**WAGE**	v WAGED, WAGING, WAGES to engage in or carry on
WADIES	pl. of wady		

WAGELESS   *adj* unpaid

WAGER   *v* -ED, -ING, -S to risk on an uncertain outcome

WAGERER   *n* pl. -S one that wagers

WAGGED   past tense of wag

WAGGER   *n* pl. -S one that wags

WAGGERY   *n* pl. -GERIES waggish behavior

WAGGING   present participle of wag

WAGGISH   *adj* playfully humorous

WAGGLE   *v* -GLED, -GLING, -GLES to wag

WAGGLY   *adj* waggling

WAGGON   *v* -ED, -ING, -S to wagon

WAGGONER   *n* pl. -S wagoner

WAGING   present participle of wage

WAGON   *v* -ED, -ING, -S to convey by wagon (a four-wheeled, horse-drawn vehicle)

WAGONAGE   *n* pl. -S conveyance by wagon

WAGONER   *n* pl. -S one who drives a wagon

WAGSOME   *adj* waggish

WAGTAIL   *n* pl. -S a songbird

WAHCONDA   *n* pl. -S wakanda

WAHINE   *n* pl. -S a Hawaiian woman

WAHOO   *n* pl. -HOOS a flowering shrub

WAIF   *v* -ED, -ING, -S to throw away

WAIL   *v* -ED, -ING, -S to utter a long, mournful cry

WAILER   *n* pl. -S one that wails

WAILFUL   *adj* mournful

WAILSOME   *adj* wailful

WAIN   *n* pl. -S a large, open wagon

WAINSCOT   *v* -SCOTED, -SCOTING, -SCOTS or -SCOTTED, -SCOTTING, -SCOTS to line the walls of with wooden paneling

WAIR   *v* -ED, -ING, -S to spend

WAIST   *n* pl. -S the part of the body between the ribs and the hips WAISTED *adj*

WAISTER   *n* pl. -S a seaman stationed in the middle section of a ship

WAISTING   *n* pl. -S a type of dressmaking material

WAIT   *v* -ED, -ING, -S to stay in expectation of

WAITER   *n* pl. -S one who serves food in a restaurant

WAITING   *n* pl. -S the act of one who waits

WAITRESS   *n* pl. -ES a woman who serves food in a restaurant

WAIVE   *v* WAIVED, WAIVING, WAIVES to give up intentionally

WAIVER   *n* pl. -S the act of waiving something

WAKANDA   *n* pl. -S a supernatural force in Sioux beliefs

WAKE   *v* WAKED or WOKE, WOKEN, WAKING, WAKES to rouse from sleep

WAKEFUL   *adj* not sleeping or able to sleep

WAKELESS   *adj* unbroken — used of sleep

WAKEN   *v* -ED, -ING, -S to wake

WAKENER   *n* pl. -S one that wakens

WAKENING   *n* pl. -S the act of one that wakens

WAKER   *n* pl. -S one that wakes

WAKERIFE   *adj* wakeful

WAKIKI   *n* pl. -S shell money of the South Sea Islands

WAKING   present participle of wake

WALE   *v* WALED, WALING, WALES to mark with welts

WALER   *n* pl. -S an Australian-bred saddle horse

WALIES   pl. of waly

WALING   present participle of wale

WALK   *v* -ED, -ING, -S to advance on foot WALKABLE *adj*

WALKAWAY   *n* pl. -AWAYS an easy victory

WALKER   *n* pl. -S one that walks

WALKING   *n* pl. -S the act of one that walks

WALKOUT   *n* pl. -S a strike by workers

WALKOVER   *n* pl. -S a walkaway

WALKUP   *n* pl. -S an apartment house having no elevator

WALKWAY   *n* pl. -WAYS a passage for walking

WALKYRIE   *n* pl. -S valkyrie

WALL   *v* -ED, -ING, -S to provide with a wall (an upright structure built to enclose an area)

WALLA   *n* pl. -S wallah

WALLABY   *n* pl. -BIES a small kangaroo

WALLAH   *n* pl. -S a person engaged in a particular occupation or activity

WALLAROO   *n* pl. -ROOS a large kangaroo

WALLET   n pl. -S a flat folding case

WALLEYE   n pl. -S an eye having a white cornea **WALLEYED** adj

WALLIE   n pl. -S a valet

WALLIES   pl. of wally

WALLOP   v -ED, -ING, -S to beat soundly

WALLOPER   n pl. -S one that wallops

WALLOW   v -ED, -ING, -S to roll about

WALLOWER   n pl. -S one that wallows

WALLY   n pl. -LIES waly

WALNUT   n pl. -S an edible nut

WALRUS   n pl. -ES a marine mammal

WALTZ   v -ED, -ING, -ES to perform a ballroom dance

WALTZER   n pl. -S one that waltzes

WALY   n pl. WALIES something visually pleasing

WAMBLE   v -BLED, -BLING, -BLES to move unsteadily

WAMBLY   adj -BLIER, -BLIEST unsteady

WAME   n pl. -S the belly

WAMEFOU   n pl. -S a bellyful

WAMEFUL   n pl. -S wamefou

WAMMUS   n pl. -ES wamus

WAMPISH   v -ED, -ING, -ES to throw about

WAMPUM   n pl. -S a form of currency formerly used by North American Indians

WAMPUS   n pl. -ES wamus

WAMUS   n pl. -ES a heavy outer jacket

WAN   adj WANNER, WANNEST unnaturally pale

WAN   v WANNED, WANNING, WANS to become wan

WAND   n pl. -S a slender rod

WANDER   v -ED, -ING, -S to move about with no destination or purpose

WANDERER   n pl. -S one that wanders

WANDEROO   n pl. -ROOS an Asian monkey

WANDLE   adj supple

WANE   v WANED, WANING, WANES to decrease in size or extent

WANEY   adj WANIER, WANIEST wany

WANGAN   n pl. -S wanigan

WANGLE   v -GLED, -GLING, -GLES to obtain or accomplish by contrivance

WANGLER   n pl. -S one that wangles

WANGUN   n pl. -S wanigan

WANIER   comparative of waney and wany

WANIEST   superlative of waney and wany

WANIGAN   n pl. -S a supply chest used in a logging camp

WANING   present participle of wane

WANION   n pl. -S vengeance

WANLY   adv in a wan manner

WANNED   past tense of wan

WANNER   comparative of wan

WANNESS   n pl. -ES the quality of being wan

WANNEST   superlative of wan

WANNIGAN   n pl. -S wanigan

WANNING   present participle of wan

WANT   v -ED, -ING, -S to have a desire for

WANTAGE   n pl. -S something that is lacking

WANTER   n pl. -S one that wants

WANTON   v -ED, -ING, -S to behave immorally

WANTONER   n pl. -S one that wantons

WANTONLY   adv immorally

WANY   adj WANIER, WANIEST waning in some parts

WAP   v WAPPED, WAPPING, WAPS to wrap

WAPITI   n pl. -S a large deer

WAR   v WARRED, WARRING, WARS to engage in war (a state of open, armed conflict)

WARBLE   v -BLED, -BLING, -BLES to sing with melodic embellishments

WARBLER   n pl. -S one that warbles

WARCRAFT   n pl. -S the art of war

WARD   v -ED, -ING, -S to turn aside

WARDEN   n pl. -S the chief officer of a prison

WARDENRY   n pl. -RIES the office of a warden

WARDER   n pl. -S a person who guards something

WARDRESS   n pl. -ES a female warden

WARDROBE   n pl. -S a collection of garment

WARDROOM   n pl. -S a recreation area on a warship

WARDSHIP   *n* pl. -S the state of being under a guardian

WARE   *v* WARED, WARING, WARES to beware of

WAREROOM   *n* pl. -S a room in which goods are displayed for sale

WARFARE   *n* pl. -S the act of engaging in war

WARFARIN   *n* pl. -S a chemical compound

WARHEAD   *n* pl. -S the front part of a missile containing the explosive

WARIER   comparative of wary

WARIEST   superlative of wary

WARILY   *adv* in a wary manner

WARINESS   *n* pl. -ES the state of being wary

WARING   present participle of ware

WARISON   *n* pl. -S a call to attack

WARK   *v* -ED, -ING, -S to endure pain

WARLESS   *adj* free from war

WARLIKE   *adj* disposed to engage in war

WARLOCK   *n* pl. -S a sorcerer

WARLORD   *n* pl. -S a military leader of a warlike nation

WARM   *adj* WARMER, WARMEST moderately hot

WARM   *v* -ED, -ING, -S to make warm

WARMAKER   *n* pl. -S one that wars

WARMER   *n* pl. -S one that warms

WARMISH   *adj* somewhat warm

WARMLY   *adv* in a warm manner

WARMNESS   *n* pl. -ES the state of being warm

WARMOUTH   *n* -S a freshwater fish

WARMTH   *n* pl. -S warmness

WARMUP   *n* pl. -S a preparatory exercise or procedure

WARN   *v* -ED, -ING, -S to make aware of impending or possible danger

WARNER   *n* pl. -S one that warns

WARNING   *n* pl. -S something that warns

WARP   *v* -ED, -ING, -S to turn or twist out of shape

WARPAGE   *n* pl. -S the act of warping

WARPATH   *n* pl. -S the route taken by attacking American Indians

WARPER   *n* pl. -S one that warps

WARPLANE   *n* pl. -S an airplane armed for combat

WARPOWER   *n* pl. -S the power to make war

WARPWISE   *adv* in a vertical direction

WARRAGAL   *n* pl. -S warrigal

WARRANT   *v* -ED, -ING, -S to give authority to

WARRANTY   *n* pl. -TIES the act of warranting

WARRED   past tense of war

WARREN   *n* pl. -S a place where rabbits live and breed

WARRENER   *n* pl. -S the keeper of a warren

WARRIGAL   *n* pl. -S a dingo

WARRING   present participle of war

WARRIOR   *n* pl. -S one engaged or experienced in warfare

WARSAW   *n* pl. -S a marine fish

WARSHIP   *n* pl. -S a ship armed for combat

WARSLE   *v* -SLED, -SLING, -SLES to wrestle

WARSLER   *n* pl. -S a wrestler

WARSTLE   *v* -TLED, -TLING, -TLES to wrestle

WARSTLER   *n* pl. -S a wrestler

WART   *n* pl. -S a protuberance on the skin WARTED *adj*

WARTHOG   *n* pl. -S an African wild hog

WARTIER   comparative of warty

WARTIEST   superlative of warty

WARTIME   *n* pl. -S a time of war

WARTLIKE   *adj* resembling a wart

WARTY   *adj* WARTIER, WARTIEST covered with warts

WARWORK   *n* pl. -S work done during a war

WARWORN   *adj* showing the effects of war

WARY   *adj* WARIER, WARIEST watchful

WAS   1st and 3d person sing. past indicative of be

WASH   *v* -ED, -ING, -ES to cleanse by immersing in or applying a liquid

WASHABLE   *adj* capable of being washed without damage

WASHBOWL   *n* pl. -S a bowl used for washing oneself

WASHDAY   *n* pl. -DAYS a day set aside for washing clothes

WASHER   *n* pl. -S one that washes

WASHIER   comparative of washy

WASHIEST   superlative of washy

WASHING *n* pl. -S articles washed or to be washed

WASHOUT *n* pl. -S an erosion of earth by the action of water

WASHRAG *n* pl. -S a small cloth used for washing oneself

WASHROOM *n* pl. -S a lavatory

WASHTUB *n* pl. -S a tub used for washing clothes

WASHY *adj* WASHIER, WASHIEST overly diluted

WASP *n* pl. -S a stinging insect **WASPISH, WASPLIKE** *adj*

WASPY *adj* WASPIER, WASPIEST resembling a wasp **WASPILY** *adv*

WASSAIL *v* -ED, -ING, -S to drink to the health of

WAST *n* pl. -S west

WASTABLE *adj* capable of being wasted

WASTAGE *n* pl. -S something that is wasted

WASTE *v* WASTED, WASTING, WASTES to use thoughtlessly

WASTEFUL *adj* tending to waste

WASTELOT *n* pl. -S a vacant lot

WASTER *n* pl. -S one that wastes

WASTERIE *n* pl. -S wastry

WASTERY *n* pl. -RIES wastry

WASTEWAY *n* pl. -WAYS a channel for excess water

WASTING present participle of waste

WASTREL *n* pl. -S one that wastes

WASTRIE *n* pl. -S wastry

WASTRY *n* pl. -RIES reckless extravagance

WAT *adj* WATTER, WATTEST wet

WAT *n* pl. -S a hare

WATAP *n* pl. -S a thread made from the roots of various trees

WATAPE *n* pl. -S watap

WATCH *v* -ED, -ING, -ES to observe carefully

WATCHCRY *n* pl. -CRIES a password

WATCHDOG *v* -DOGGED, -DOGGING, -DOGS to act as a guardian for

WATCHER *n* pl. -S one that watches

WATCHEYE *n* pl. -S a walleye

WATCHFUL *adj* closely observant or alert

WATCHMAN *n* pl. -MEN a man employed to stand guard

WATCHOUT *n* pl. -S the act of looking out for something

WATER *v* -ED, -ING, -S to sprinkle with water (a transparent, odorless, tasteless liquid)

WATERAGE *n* pl. -S the conveyance of goods by water

WATERBED *n* pl. -S a bed whose mattress is a plastic bag filled with water

WATERDOG *n* pl. -S a large salamander

WATERER *n* pl. -S one that waters

WATERIER comparative of watery

WATERIEST superlative of watery

WATERILY *adv* in a watery manner

WATERING *n* pl. -S the act of one that waters

WATERISH *adj* watery

WATERLOG *v* -LOGGED, -LOGGING, -LOGS to soak with water

WATERLOO *n* pl. -LOOS a decisive defeat

WATERMAN *n* pl. -MEN a boatman

WATERWAY *n* pl. -WAYS a navigable body of water

WATERY *adj* -TERIER, -TERIEST containing water

WATT *n* pl. -S a unit of power

WATTAGE *n* pl. -S an amount of power in terms of watts

WATTAPE *n* pl. -S watap

WATTER comparative of wat

WATTEST superlative of wat

WATTHOUR *n* pl. -S a unit of energy

WATTLE *v* -TLED, -TLING, -TLES to weave into a network

WATTLESS *adj* denoting a type of electric current

WAUCHT *v* -ED, -ING, -S to waught

WAUGH *adj* damp

WAUGHT *v* -ED, -ING, -S to drink deeply

WAUK *v* -ED, -ING, -S to wake

WAUL *v* -ED, -ING, -S to cry like a cat

WAUR *adj* worse

WAVE *v* WAVED, WAVING, WAVES to move freely back and forth or up and down

WAVEBAND *n* pl. -S a range of radio frequencies

WAVEFORM *n* pl. -S a type of mathematical graph

WAVELESS *adj* having no waves (moving ridges on the surface of a liquid)

WAVELET *n* pl. -S a small wave

WAVELIKE *adj* resembling a wave

WAVEOFF *n* pl. -S the act of denying landing permission to an approaching aircraft

WAVER *v* -ED, -ING, -S to move back and forth

WAVERER *n* pl. -S one that wavers

WAVERY *adj* wavering

WAVEY *n* pl. -VEYS the snow goose

WAVIER comparative of wavy

WAVIES present 3d person sing. of wavy

WAVIEST superlative of wavy

WAVILY *adv* in a wavy manner

WAVINESS *n* pl. -ES the state of being wavy

WAVING present participle of wave

WAVY *adj* WAVIER, WAVIEST full of waves

WAVY *n* pl. -VIES wavey

WAW *n* pl. -S vav

WAWL *v* -ED, -ING, -S to waul

WAX *v* -ED, -ING, -ES to coat with wax (a natural, heat-sensitive substance)

WAXBERRY *n* pl. -RIES a berry with a waxy coating

WAXBILL *n* pl. -S a tropical bird

WAXEN *adj* covered with wax

WAXER *n* pl. -S one that waxes

WAXIER comparative of waxy

WAXIEST superlative of waxy

WAXILY *adv* in a waxy manner

WAXINESS *n* pl. -ES the quality of being waxy

WAXING *n* pl. -S the act of one that waxes

WAXLIKE *adj* resembling wax

WAXPLANT *n* pl. -S a tropical plant

WAXWEED *n* pl. -S an annual herb

WAXWING *n* pl. -S a type of bird

WAXWORK *n* pl. -S an effigy made of wax

WAXWORM *n* pl. -S a moth that infests beehives

WAXY *adj* WAXIER, WAXIEST resembling wax

WAY *n* pl. WAYS a method of doing something

WAYBILL *n* pl. -S a list of goods relative to a shipment

WAYFARER *n* pl. -S a traveler

WAYGOING *n* pl. -S the act of leaving

WAYLAY *v* -LAID, -LAYING, -LAYS to ambush

WAYLAYER *n* pl. -S one that waylays

WAYLESS *adj* having no road or path

WAYSIDE *n* pl. -S the side of a road

WAYWARD *adj* willful

WAYWORN *adj* fatigued by travel

WE *pron* 1st person pl. pronoun in the nominative case

WEAK *adj* WEAKER, WEAKEST lacking strength

WEAKEN *v* -ED, -ING, -S to make weak

WEAKENER *n* pl. -S one that weakens

WEAKFISH *n* pl. -ES a marine fish

WEAKISH *adj* somewhat weak

WEAKLING *n* pl. -S a weak person

WEAKLY *adj* -LIER, -LIEST weak and sickly

WEAKNESS *n* pl. -ES the state of being weak

WEAL *n* pl. -S a welt

WEALD *n* pl. -S a woodland

WEALTH *n* pl. -S a great quantity of valuable material

WEALTHY *adj* WEALTHIER, WEALTHIEST having wealth

WEAN *v* -ED, -ING, -S to withhold mother's milk from and substitute other nourishment

WEANER *n* pl. -S one that weans

WEANLING *n* pl. -S a recently weaned child or animal

WEAPON *v* -ED, -ING, -S to supply with a weapon (an instrument used in combat)

WEAPONRY *n* pl. -RIES an aggregate of weapons

WEAR *v* WORE, WORN, WEARING, WEARS to have on one's person

WEARABLE *n* pl. -S a garment

WEARER *n* pl. -S one that wears something

WEARIED	past tense of weary	**WEDGY**	*adj* WEDGIER, WEDGIEST resembling a wedge
WEARIER	comparative of weary	**WEDLOCK**	*n pl.* -S the state of being married
WEARIES	present 3d person sing. of weary		
WEARIEST	superlative of weary	**WEE**	*adj* WEER, WEEST very small
WEARIFUL	*adj* tiresome	**WEE**	*n pl.* -S a short time
WEARISH	*adj* tasteless	**WEED**	*v* -ED, -ING, -S to remove weeds (undesirable plants)
WEARY	*adj* -RIER, -RIEST tired **WEARILY** *adv*	**WEEDER**	*n pl.* -S one that weeds
WEARY	*v* -RIED, -RYING, -RIES to make or become weary	**WEEDIER**	comparative of weedy
		WEEDIEST	superlative of weedy
WEASAND	*n pl.* -S the throat	**WEEDILY**	*adv* in a weedy manner
WEASEL	*v* -ED, -ING, -S to act evasively	**WEEDLESS**	*adj* having no weeds
WEASON	*n pl.* -S weasand	**WEEDLIKE**	*adj* resembling a weed
WEATHER	*v* -ED, -ING, -S to expose to atmospheric conditions	**WEEDY**	*adj* WEEDIER, WEEDIEST resembling a weed
WEAVE	*v* WOVE or WEAVED, WOVEN, WEAVING, WEAVES to form by interlacing threads	**WEEK**	*n pl.* -S a period of seven days
		WEEKDAY	*n pl.* -DAYS any day of the week except Sunday
WEAVER	*n pl.* -S one that weaves	**WEEKEND**	*v* -ED, -ING, -S to spend the weekend (the end of the week)
WEAZAND	*n pl.* -S weasand		
WEB	*v* WEBBED, WEBBING, WEBS to provide with a web (an interlaced fabric or structure)	**WEEKLONG**	*adj* continuing for a week
		WEEKLY	*n pl.* -LIES a publication issued once a week
WEBBING	*n pl.* -S a woven strip of fiber	**WEEL**	*adj* well
WEBBY	*adj* -BIER, -BIEST weblike	**WEEN**	*v* -ED, -ING, -S to suppose
WEBER	*n pl.* -S a unit of magnetic flux	**WEENIE**	*n pl.* -S a wiener
WEBFED	*adj* pertaining to a type of printing press	**WEENSY**	*adj* -SIER, -SIEST tiny
		WEENY	*adj* -NIER, -NIEST tiny
WEBFOOT	*n pl.* -FEET a foot having the toes joined by a membrane	**WEEP**	*v* WEPT, WEEPING, WEEPS to express sorrow by shedding tears
WEBLESS	*adj* having no webs		
WEBLIKE	*adj* resembling a web	**WEEPER**	*n pl.* -S one that weeps
WEBSTER	*n pl.* -S a weaver	**WEEPY**	*adj* WEEPIER, WEEPIEST tending to weep
WEBWORM	*n pl.* -S a web-spinning caterpillar		
		WEER	comparative of wee
WECHT	*n pl.* -S weight	**WEEST**	superlative of wee
WED	*v* WEDDED, WEDDING, WEDS to marry	**WEET**	*v* -ED, -ING, -S to know
		WEEVER	*n pl.* -S a marine fish
WEDDER	*n pl.* -S one that weds	**WEEVIL**	*n pl.* -S a small beetle **WEEVILED, WEEVILLY, WEEVILY** *adj*
WEDDING	*n pl.* -S a marriage ceremony		
WEDEL	*v* -ED, -ING, -S to perform a wedeln	**WEEWEE**	*v* -WEED, -WEEING, -WEES to urinate
WEDELN	*n pl.* -S a skiing technique	**WEFT**	*n pl.* -S a woven fabric or garment
WEDGE	*v* WEDGED, WEDGING, WEDGES to force apart with a wedge (a tapering piece of wood or metal)		
		WEFTWISE	*adv* in a horizontal direction
		WEIGELA	*n pl.* -S a flowering shrub
WEDGIE	*n pl.* -S a type of woman's shoe	**WEIGELIA**	*n pl.* -S weigela

WEIGH   v -ED, -ING, -S to determine the weight of

WEIGHER   n pl. -S one that weighs

WEIGHMAN   n pl. -MEN one whose occupation is weighing goods

WEIGHT   v -ED, -ING, -S to add weight (heaviness) to

WEIGHTER   n pl. -S one that weights

WEIGHTY   adj WEIGHTIER, WEIGHTIEST having great weight

WEINER   n pl. -S wiener

WEIR   n pl. -S a fence placed in a stream to catch fish

WEIRD   adj WEIRDER, WEIRDEST mysteriously strange

WEIRD   n pl. -S destiny

WEIRDIE   n pl. -S a very strange person

WEIRDIES   pl. of weirdy

WEIRDLY   adv in a weird manner

WEIRDO   n pl. WEIRDOES or WEIRDOS weirdie

WEIRDY   n pl. WEIRDIES weirdie

WEKA   n pl. -S a flightless bird

WELCH   v -ED, -ING, -ES to welsh

WELCHER   n pl. -S one that welshes

WELCOME   v -COMED, -COMING, -COMES to greet cordially

WELCOMER   n pl. -S one that welcomes

WELD   v -ED, -ING, -S to join by applying heat **WELDABLE** adj

WELDER   n pl. -S one that welds

WELDLESS   adj having no welded joints

WELDMENT   n pl. -S a unit composed of welded pieces

WELDOR   n pl. -S welder

WELFARE   n pl. -S general well-being

WELKIN   n pl. -S the sky

WELL   v -ED, -ING, -S to rise to the surface and flow forth

WELLADAY   n pl. -DAYS wellaway

WELLAWAY   n pl. -WAYS an expression of sorrow

WELLBORN   adj of good birth or ancestry

WELLCURB   n pl. -S the stone ring around a well (a hole dug in the ground to obtain water)

WELLDOER   n pl. -S a doer of good deeds

WELLHEAD   n pl. -S the source of a spring or stream

WELLHOLE   n pl. -S the shaft of a well

WELLNESS   n pl. -ES the state of being healthy

WELLSITE   n pl. -S a mineral

WELSH   v -ED, -ING, -ES to fail to pay a debt

WELSHER   n pl. -S one that welshes

WELT   v -ED, -ING, -S to mark with welts (ridges or lumps raised on the skin)

WELTER   v -ED, -ING, -S to roll about

WELTING   n pl. -S a cord or strip used to reinforce a seam

WEN   n pl. -S a benign tumor of the skin

WENCH   v -ED, -ING, -ES to consort with prostitutes

WENCHER   n pl. -S one that wenches

WEND   v -ED, -ING, -S to proceed along

WENDIGO   n pl. -GOS windigo

WENNISH   adj wenny

WENNY   adj -NIER, -NIEST resembling a wen

WENT   past tense of go

WEPT   past tense of weep

WERE   a pl. and 2d person sing. past indicative, and past subjunctive of be

WEREGILD   n pl. -S wergeld

WEREWOLF   n pl. -WOLVES a person capable of assuming the form of a wolf

WERGELD   n pl. -S a price paid for the taking of a man's life in Anglo-Saxon law

WERGELT   n pl. -S wergeld

WERGILD   n pl. -S wergeld

WERT   a 2d person sing. past tense of be

WERWOLF   n pl. -WOLVES werewolf

WESKIT   n pl. -S a vest

WESSAND   n pl. -S weasand

WEST   n pl. -S a cardinal point of the compass

WESTER   v -ED, -ING, -S to move toward the west

WESTERLY   n pl. -LIES a wind from the west

WESTERN   n pl. -S one who lives in the west

WESTING   n pl. -S a shifting west

WESTMOST *adj* farthest west

WESTWARD *n pl.* -S a direction toward the west

WET *adj* WETTER, WETTEST covered or saturated with a liquid

WET *v* WETTED, WETTING, WETS to make wet

WETBACK *n pl.* -S a Mexican who enters the United States illegally

WETHER *n pl.* -S a gelded male sheep

WETLAND *n pl.* -S land containing much soil moisture

WETLY *adv* in a wet manner

WETNESS *n pl.* -ES the state of being wet

WETPROOF *adj* waterproof

WETTABLE *adj* capable of being wetted

WETTED past tense of wet

WETTER *n pl.* -S one that wets

WETTEST superlative of wet

WETTING *n pl.* -S a liquid used in moistening something

WETTISH *adj* somewhat wet

WHA *pron* who

WHACK *v* -ED, -ING, -S to strike sharply

WHACKER *n pl.* -S one that whacks

WHACKY *adj* WHACKIER, WHACKIEST wacky

WHALE *v* WHALED, WHALING, WHALES to engage in the hunting of whales (large marine mammals)

WHALEMAN *n pl.* -MEN a whaler

WHALER *n pl.* -S a person engaged in whaling

WHALING *n pl.* -S the industry of capturing and processing whales

WHAM *v* WHAMMED, WHAMMING, WHAMS to hit with a loud impact

WHAMMY *n pl.* -MIES a supernatural spell bringing bad luck

WHANG *v* -ED, -ING, -S to beat with a whip

WHANGEE *n pl.* -S an Asian grass

WHAP *v* WHAPPED, WHAPPING, WHAPS to whop

WHAPPER *n pl.* -S whopper

WHARF *v* -ED, -ING, -S to moor to a wharf (a landing place for vessels)

WHARFAGE *n pl.* -S the use of a wharf

WHARVE *n pl.* -S a round piece of wood used in spinning thread

WHAT *n pl.* -S the true nature of something

WHATEVER *adj* being what or who it may be

WHATNOT *n pl.* -S an ornamental set of shelves

WHAUP *n pl.* -S a European bird

WHEAL *n pl.* -S a welt

WHEAT *n pl.* -S a cereal grass

WHEATEAR *n pl.* -S a small bird of northern regions

WHEATEN *adj* pertaining to wheat

WHEE *interj* — used to express delight

WHEEDLE *v* -DLED, -DLING, -DLES to attempt to persuade by flattery

WHEEDLER *n pl.* -S one that wheedles

WHEEL *v* -ED, -ING, -S to convey on wheels (circular frames designed to turn on an axis)

WHEELER *n pl.* -S one that wheels

WHEELIE *n pl.* -S a maneuver made on a wheeled vehicle

WHEELING *n pl.* -S the condition of a road for vehicles

WHEELMAN *n pl.* -MEN a helmsman

WHEEN *n pl.* -S a fairly large amount

WHEEP *v* -ED, -ING, -S to wheeple

WHEEPLE *v* -PLED, -PLING, -PLES to give forth a prolonged whistle

WHEEZE *v* WHEEZED, WHEEZING, WHEEZES to breathe with a whistling sound

WHEEZER *n pl.* -S one that wheezes

WHEEZY *adj* WHEEZIER, WHEEZIEST characterized by wheezing **WHEEZILY** *adv*

WHELK *n pl.* -S a pustule

WHELKY *adj* WHELKIER, WHELKIEST marked with whelks

WHELM *v* -ED, -ING, -S to cover with water

WHELP *v* -ED, -ING, -S to give birth to

WHEN *n pl.* -S the time in which something is done or occurs

WHENAS *conj* at which time

WHENCE *adv* from what place

WHENEVER *adv* at whatever time

WHERE *n* pl. -S the place at or in which something is located or occurs

WHEREAS *n* pl. -ES an introductory statement of a formal document

WHEREAT *adv* at what

WHEREBY *adv* by what

WHEREIN *adv* in what

WHEREOF *adv* of what

WHEREON *adv* on what

WHERETO *adv* to what

WHEREVER *adv* in or to whatever place

WHERRY *v* -RIED, -RYING, -RIES to transport in a light rowboat

WHERVE *n* pl. -S wharve

WHET *v* WHETTED, WHETTING, WHETS to sharpen by friction

WHETHER *conj* if it be the case that

WHETTER *n* pl. -S one that whets

WHETTING present participle of whet

WHEW *n* pl. -S a whistling sound

WHEY *n* pl. WHEYS the watery part of milk **WHEYEY, WHEYISH** *adj*

WHEYFACE *n* pl. -S a pale, sallow face

WHICH *pron* what particular one or ones

WHICKER *v* -ED, -ING, -S to whinny

WHID *v* WHIDDED, WHIDDING, WHIDS to move rapidly and quietly

WHIDAH *n* pl. -S whydah

WHIFF *v* -ED, -ING, -S to blow or convey with slight gusts of air

WHIFFER *n* pl. -S one that whiffs

WHIFFET *n* pl. -S an insignificant person

WHIFFLE *v* -FLED, -FLING, -FLES to move or think erratically

WHIFFLER *n* pl. -S one that whiffles

WHILE *v* WHILED, WHILING, WHILES to cause to pass pleasantly

WHILOM *adv* formerly

WHILST *conj* during the time that

WHIM *n* pl. -S an impulsive idea

WHIMBREL *n* pl. -S a shore bird

WHIMPER *v* -ED, -ING, -S to cry with plaintive, broken sounds

WHIMSEY *n* pl. -SEYS whimsy

WHIMSY *n* pl. -SIES a whim **WHIMSIED** *adj*

WHIN *n* pl. -S furze

WHINCHAT *n* pl. -S a songbird

WHINE *v* WHINED, WHINING, WHINES to utter a plaintive, high-pitched sound

WHINER *n* pl. -S one that whines

WHINEY *adj* WHINIER, WHINIEST whiny

WHINIER comparative of whiny

WHINIEST superlative of whiny

WHINING present participle of whine

WHINNY *v* -NIED, -NYING, -NIES to neigh in a low or gentle manner

WHINNY *adj* -NIER, -NIEST abounding in whin

WHINY *adj* WHINIER, WHINIEST tending to whine

WHIP *v* WHIPPED or WHIPT, WHIPPING, WHIPS to strike with a whip (an instrument for administering corporal punishment)

WHIPCORD *n* pl. -S a strong, twisted cord

WHIPLASH *n* pl. -ES the lash of a whip

WHIPLIKE *adj* resembling a whip

WHIPPED a past tense of whip

WHIPPER *n* pl. -S one that whips

WHIPPET *n* pl. -S a small, swift dog

WHIPPIER comparative of whippy

WHIPPIEST superlative of whippy

WHIPPING *n* pl. -S material used to whip

WHIPPY *adj* -PIER, -PIEST pertaining to or resembling a whip

WHIPRAY *n* pl. -RAYS a stingray

WHIPSAW *v* -SAWED, -SAWN, -SAWING, -SAWS to cut with a narrow, tapering saw

WHIPT a past tense of whip

WHIPTAIL *n* pl. -S a lizard having a long, slender tail

WHIPWORM *n* pl. -S a parasitic worm

WHIR *v* WHIRRED, WHIRRING, WHIRS to move with a buzzing sound

WHIRL *v* -ED, -ING, -S to revolve rapidly

WHIRLER *n* pl. -S one that whirls

WHIRLY *adj* WHIRLIER, WHIRLIEST marked by a whirling motion

WHIRLY *n* pl. WHIRLIES a small tornado

WHIRR *v* -ED, -ING, -S to whir

WHIRRED past tense of whir

WHIRRING present participle of whir

WHIRRY v -RIED, -RYING, -RIES to hurry

WHISH v -ED, -ING, -ES to move with a hissing sound

WHISHT v -ED, -ING, -S to hush

WHISK v -ED, -ING, -S to move quickly and easily

WHISKER n pl. -S a hair on a man's face **WHISKERY** adj

WHISKEY n pl. -KEYS a liquor

WHISKY n pl. -KIES whiskey

WHISPER v -ED, -ING, -S to speak softly

WHISPERY adj resembling a whisper

WHIST v -ED, -ING, -S to hush

WHISTLE v -TLED, -TLING, -TLES to make a shrill, clear musical sound

WHISTLER n pl. -S one that whistles

WHIT n pl. -S a particle

WHITE adj WHITER, WHITEST of the color of pure snow

WHITE v WHITED, WHITING, WHITES to whiten

WHITECAP n pl. -S a wave with a crest of foam

WHITEFLY n pl. -FLIES a small whitish insect

WHITELY adv in a white manner

WHITEN v -ED, -ING, -S to make white

WHITENER n pl. -S one that whitens

WHITEOUT n pl. -S an arctic weather condition

WHITER comparative of white

WHITEST superlative of white

WHITEY n pl. -EYS a white man — an offensive term

WHITHER adv to what place

WHITIES pl. of whity

WHITING n pl. -S a marine food fish

WHITISH adj somewhat white

WHITLOW n pl. -S an inflammation of the finger or toe

WHITRACK n pl. -S a weasel

WHITTER n pl. -S a large draft of liquor

WHITTLE v -TLED, -TLING, -TLES to cut or shave bits from

WHITTLER n pl. -S one that whittles

WHITTRET n pl. -S a weasel

WHITY n pl. WHITIES whitey

WHIZ v WHIZZED, WHIZZING, WHIZZES to move with a buzzing or hissing sound

WHIZBANG n pl. -S a type of explosive shell

WHIZZ v -ED, -ING, -ES to whiz

WHIZZED past tense of whiz

WHIZZER n pl. -S one that whizzes

WHIZZES present 3d person sing. of whiz

WHIZZING present participle of whiz

WHO pron what or which person or persons

WHOA interj — used to command an animal to stop

WHODUNIT n pl. -S a mystery story

WHOEVER pron whatever person

WHOLE n pl. -S all the parts or elements entering into and making up a thing

WHOLISM n pl. -S holism

WHOLLY adv totally

WHOM pron the objective case of who

WHOMEVER pron the objective case of whoever

WHOMP v -ED, -ING, -S to defeat decisively

WHOMSO pron the objective case of whoso

WHOOP v -ED, -ING, -S to utter loud cries

WHOOPEE n pl. -S boisterous fun

WHOOPER n pl. -S one that whoops

WHOOPLA n pl. -S a noisy commotion

WHOOSH v -ED, -ING, -ES to move with a hissing sound

WHOOSIS n pl. -SISES an object or person whose name is not known

WHOP v WHOPPED, WHOPPING, WHOPS to strike forcibly

WHOPPER n pl. -S something unusually large

WHORE v WHORED, WHORING, WHORES to consort with prostitutes

WHOREDOM n pl. -S prostitution

WHORESON n pl. -S a bastard

WHORING present participle of whore

WHORISH adj lewd

WHORL n pl. -S a circular arrangement of similar parts **WHORLED** adj

WHORT n pl. -S an edible berry

WHORTLE   n pl. -S whort

WHOSE   pron the possessive case of who

WHOSEVER   pron the possessive case of whoever

WHOSIS   n pl. -SISES whoosis

WHOSO   pron whoever

WHUMP   v -ED, -ING, -S to thump

WHY   n pl. WHYS the reason or cause of something

WHYDAH   n pl. -S an African bird

WICH   n pl. -ES wych

WICK   n pl. -S a bundle of loosely twisted fibers in a candle or oil lamp

WICKAPE   n pl. -S wicopy

WICKED   adj -EDER, -EDEST evil **WICKEDLY** adv

WICKER   n pl. -S a slender, pliant twig or branch

WICKET   n pl. -S a small door or gate

WICKING   n pl. -S material for wicks

WICKIUP   n pl. -S an American Indian hut

WICKYUP   n pl. -S wickiup

WICOPY   n pl. -PIES a flowering shrub

WIDDER   n pl. -S a widow

WIDDIE   n pl. -S widdy

WIDDLE   v -DLED, -DLING, -DLES to wriggle

WIDDY   n pl. -DIES a hangman's noose

WIDE   adj WIDER, WIDEST having great extent from side to side **WIDELY** adv

WIDE   n pl. -S a type of bowled ball in cricket

WIDEN   v -ED, -ING, -S to make wide or wider

WIDENER   n pl. -S one that widens

WIDENESS   n pl. -ES the state of being wide

WIDER   comparative of wide

WIDEST   superlative of wide

WIDGEON   n pl. -S a river duck

WIDGET   n pl. -S a gadget

WIDISH   adj somewhat wide

WIDOW   v -ED, -ING, -S to deprive of a husband

WIDOWER   n pl. -S a man whose wife has died and who has not remarried

WIDTH   n pl. -S extent from side to side

WIDTHWAY   adv from side to side

WIELD   v -ED, -ING, -S to handle or use effectively

WIELDER   n pl. -S one that wields

WIELDY   adj WIELDIER, WIELDIEST easily wielded

WIENER   n pl. -S a frankfurter

WIENIE   n pl. -S a wiener

WIFE   n pl. WIVES a woman married to a man

WIFE   v WIFED, WIFING, WIFES to wive

WIFEDOM   n pl. -S the status or function of a wife

WIFEHOOD   n pl. -S the state of being a wife

WIFELESS   adj having no wife

WIFELIKE   adj wifely

WIFELY   adj -LIER, -LIEST of or befitting a wife

WIFING   present participle of wife

WIG   v WIGGED, WIGGING, WIGS to provide with a wig (an artificial covering of hair for the head)

WIGAN   n pl. -S a stiff fabric

WIGEON   n pl. -S widgeon

WIGGED   past tense of wig

WIGGERY   n pl. -GERIES a wig

WIGGING   n pl. -S a scolding

WIGGLE   v -GLED, -GLING, -GLES to move with short, quick movements from side to side

WIGGLER   n pl. -S one that wiggles

WIGGLY   adj -GLIER, -GLIEST tending to wiggle

WIGHT   n pl. -S a living being

WIGLESS   adj having no wig

WIGLET   n pl. -S a small wig

WIGLIKE   adj resembling a wig

WIGMAKER   n pl. -S one that makes wigs

WIGWAG   v -WAGGED, -WAGGING, -WAGS to move back and forth

WIGWAM   n pl. -S an American Indian dwelling

WIKIUP   n pl. -S wickiup

WILCO   interj — used to indicate that a message received will be complied with

WILD   adj WILDER, WILDEST living in a natural state

WILD n pl. -S an uninhabited or uncultivated area

WILDCAT v -CATTED, -CATTING, -CATS to search for oil in an area of doubtful productivity

WILDER v -ED, -ING, -S to bewilder

WILDFIRE n pl. -S a raging, destructive fire

WILDFOWL n pl. -S a wild game bird

WILDING n pl. -S a wild plant or animal

WILDISH adj somewhat wild

WILDLIFE n pl. WILDLIFE wild animals and vegetation

WILDLING n pl. -S a wilding

WILDLY adv in a wild manner

WILDNESS n pl. -ES the state of being wild

WILDWOOD n pl. -S natural forest land

WILE v WILED, WILING, WILES to entice

WILFUL adj willful WILFULLY adv

WILIER comparative of wily

WILIEST superlative of wily

WILILY adv in a wily manner

WILINESS n pl. -ES the quality of being wily

WILING present participle of wile

WILL v -ED, -ING, -S to decide upon WILLABLE adj

WILL v past sing. 2d person WOULD, WOULDEST, or WOULDST — used as an auxiliary followed by a simple infinitive to express futurity, inclination, likelihood, or requirement

WILLER n pl. -S one that wills

WILLET n pl. -S a shore bird

WILLFUL adj bent on having one's own way

WILLIED past tense of willy

WILLIES present 3d person sing. of willy

WILLING adj -INGER, -INGEST inclined or favorably disposed in mind

WILLIWAU n pl. -S williwaw

WILLIWAW n pl. -S a violent gust of cold wind

WILLOW v -ED, -ING, -S to clean textile fibers with a certain machine

WILLOWER n pl. -S one that willows

WILLOWY adj -LOWIER, -LOWIEST pliant

WILLY v -LIED, -LYING, -LIES to willow

WILLYARD adj willful

WILLYART adj willyard

WILLYWAW n pl. -S williwaw

WILT v -ED, -ING, -S to become limp

WILY adj WILIER, WILIEST crafty

WIMBLE v -BLED, -BLING, -BLES to bore with a hand tool

WIMPLE v -PLED, -PLING, -PLES to pleat

WIN v WON or WAN, WINNING, WINS to be victorious

WIN v WINNED, WINNING, WINS to winnow

WINCE v WINCED, WINCING, WINCES to flinch

WINCER n pl. -S one that winces

WINCEY n pl. -CEYS a type of fabric

WINCH v -ED, -ING, -ES to raise with a winch (a hoisting machine)

WINCHER n pl. -S one that winches

WINCING present participle of wince

WIND v WOUND or WINDED, WINDING, WINDS to pass around an object or fixed center WINDABLE adj

WINDAGE n pl. -S the effect of the wind (air in natural motion) on a projectile

WINDBAG n pl. -S a talkative person

WINDBURN v -BURNED or -BURNT, -BURNING, -BURNS to be affected with skin irritation caused by exposure to the wind

WINDER n pl. -S one that winds

WINDFALL n pl. -S a sudden and unexpected gain

WINDFLAW n pl. -S a gust of wind

WINDGALL n pl. -S a swelling on a horse's leg

WINDIER comparative of windy

WINDIEST superlative of windy

WINDIGO n pl. -GOS an evil demon in Algonquian mythology

WINDILY adv in a windy manner

WINDING n pl. -S material wound about an object

WINDLASS v -ED, -ING, -ES to raise with a windlass (a hoisting machine)

WINDLE v -DLED, -DLING, -DLES to wind

WINDLESS adj being without wind

WINDLING n pl. -S a bundle of straw

WINDMILL v -ED, -ING, -S to rotate solely under the force of a passing airstream

WINDOW v -ED, -ING, -S to provide with a window (an opening in a wall to admit light and air)

WINDPIPE n pl. -S the trachea

WINDROW v -ED, -ING, -S to arrange in long rows, as hay or grain

WINDSOCK n pl. -S a device used to indicate wind direction

WINDUP n pl. -S a conclusion

WINDWARD n pl. -S the direction from which the wind blows

WINDWAY n pl. -WAYS a passage for air

WINDY adj WINDIER, WINDIEST marked by strong wind

WINE v WINED, WINING, WINES to provide with wine (the fermented juice of the grape)

WINELESS adj having no wine

WINERY n pl. -ERIES an establishment for making wine

WINESHOP n pl. -S a shop where wine is sold

WINESKIN n pl. -S a goatskin bag for holding wine

WINESOP n pl. -S a food sopped in wine

WINEY adj WINIER, WINIEST winy

WING v -ED, -ING, -S to travel by means of wings (organs of flight)

WINGBACK n pl. -S a certain player in football

WINGBOW n pl. -S a mark on the wing of a domestic fowl

WINGDING n pl. -S a lively party

WINGEDLY adv swiftly

WINGER n pl. -S a certain player in soccer

WINGIER comparative of wingy

WINGIEST superlative of wingy

WINGLESS adj having no wings

WINGLET n pl. -S a small wing

WINGLIKE adj resembling a wing

WINGMAN n pl. -MEN a pilot behind the leader of a flying formation

WINGOVER n pl. -S a flight maneuver

WINGSPAN n pl. -S the distance from the tip of one of a pair of wings to that of the other

WINGY adj WINGIER, WINGIEST swift

WINIER comparative of winey and winy

WINIEST superlative of winey and winy

WINING present participle of wine

WINISH adj winy

WINK v ED, ING, -S to close and open one eye quickly

WINKER n pl. -S one that winks

WINKLE v -KLED, -KLING, -KLES to displace, extract, or evict from a position

WINNABLE adj able to be won

WINNED past tense of win (to winnow)

WINNER n pl. -S one that wins

WINNING n pl. -S money won in a game or competition

WINNOCK n pl. -S a window

WINNOW v -ED, -ING, -S to free grain from impurities

WINNOWER n pl. -S one that winnows

WINO n pl. WINOES or WINOS one who is habitually drunk on wine

WINSOME adj -SOMER, -SOMEST charming

WINTER v -ED, -ING, -S to pass the winter (the coldest season of the year)

WINTERER n pl. -S one that winters

WINTERLY adj wintry

WINTERY adj -TERIER, -TERIEST wintry

WINTLE v -TLED, -TLING, -TLES to stagger

WINTRY adj -TRIER, -TRIEST characteristic of winter **WINTRILY** adv

WINY adj WINIER, WINIEST having the taste or qualities of wine

WINZE n pl. -S a steeply inclined mine shaft

WIPE v WIPED, WIPING, WIPES to rub lightly in order to clean or dry

WIPEOUT n pl. -S a fall from a surfboard

WIPER n pl. -S one that wipes

WIPING present participle of wipe

WIRE v WIRED, WIRING, WIRES to fasten with wire (a slender rod, strand, or thread of ductile metal) **WIRABLE** adj

WIREDRAW v -DREW, -DRAWN, -DRAWING, -DRAWS to draw into wire

WIREHAIR *n pl.* -S a dog having a wiry coat

WIRELESS *v* -ED, -ING, -ES to radio

WIRELIKE *adj* resembling wire

WIREMAN *n pl.* -MEN one who makes or works with wire

WIRER *n pl.* -S one that wires

WIRETAP *v* -TAPPED, -TAPPING, -TAPS to intercept messages by means of a concealed monitoring device

WIREWAY *n pl.* -WAYS a tube for protecting electric wires

WIREWORK *n pl.* -S an article made of wire

WIREWORM *n pl.* -S a wirelike worm

WIRIER comparative of wiry

WIRIEST superlative of wiry

WIRILY *adv* in a wiry manner

WIRINESS *n pl.* -ES the quality of being wiry

WIRING *n pl.* -S a system of electric wires

WIRRA *interj* — used to express sorrow

WIRY *adj* WIRIER, WIRIEST resembling wire

WIS *v* past tense WIST to know — WIS and WIST are the only accepted forms of this verb; it cannot be conjugated further

WISDOM *n pl.* -S the power of true and right discernment

WISE *v* WISED, WISING, WISES to become aware or informed

WISE *adj* WISER, WISEST having wisdom

WISEACRE *n pl.* -S a pretentiously wise person

WISED past tense of wise

WISELY *adv* -LIER, -LIEST in a wise manner

WISENESS *n pl.* -ES wisdom

WISENT *n pl.* -S a European bison

WISER comparative of wise

WISEST superlative of wise

WISH *v* -ED, -ING, -ES to feel an impulse toward attainment or possession of something

WISHA *interj* — used to express surprise

WISHBONE *n pl.* -S a forked bone in front of a bird's breastbone

WISHER *n pl.* -S one that wishes

WISHFUL *adj* desirous

WISHLESS *adj* not wishful

WISING present participle of wise

WISP *v* -ED, -ING, -S to twist into a wisp (a small bunch or bundle)

WISPIER comparative of wispy

WISPIEST superlative of wispy

WISPILY *adv* in a wispy manner

WISPISH *adj* wispy

WISPLIKE *adj* wispy

WISPY *adj* WISPIER, WISPIEST resembling a wisp

WISS *v* -ED, -ING, -ES to wish

WIST *v* -ED, -ING, -S to know

WISTARIA *n pl.* -S wisteria

WISTERIA *n pl.* -S a flowering shrub

WISTFUL *adj* yearning

WIT *n pl.* -S intelligence

WIT *v* WIST, WITING or WITTING, present sing. 1st person WOT, 2d WOST or WOSTTETH, 3d WOT or WOTTETH, present pl. WITE or WITEN to know

WITAN *n/pl* the members of a national council in Anglo-Saxon England

WITCH *v* -ED, -ING, -ES to bewitch

WITCHERY *n pl.* -ERIES sorcery

WITCHING *n pl.* -S sorcery

WITCHY *adj* WITCHIER, WITCHIEST malicious

WITE *v* WITED, WITING, WITES to blame

WITEN a present pl. of wit

WITH *prep* in the company of

WITHAL *adv* in addition

WITHDRAW *v* -DREW, -DRAWN, -DRAWING, -DRAWS to move back or away

WITHE *v* WITHED, WITHING, WITHES to bind with flexible twigs

WITHER *v* -ED, -ING, -S to dry up and wilt

WITHERER *n pl.* -S one that withers

WITHHOLD *v* -HELD, -HOLDING, -HOLDS to hold back

WITHIER comparative of withy

WITHIES pl. of withy

WITHIEST superlative of withy

WITHIN	*n* pl. -S an interior place or area
WITHING	present participle of withe
WITHOUT	*n* pl. -S an exterior place or area
WITHY	*n* pl. WITHIES a flexible twig
WITHY	*adj* WITHIER, WITHIEST flexible and tough
WITING	present participle of wit and wite
WITLESS	*adj* lacking intelligence
WITLING	*n* pl. -S one who considers himself witty
WITLOOF	*n* pl. -S chicory
WITNESS	*v* -ED, -ING, -ES to see or know by personal experience
WITNEY	*n* pl. -NEYS a heavy woolen fabric
WITTED	*adj* having intelligence
WITTIER	comparative of witty
WITTIEST	superlative of witty
WITTILY	*adv* in a witty manner
WITTING	*n* pl. -S knowledge
WITTOL	*n* pl. -S a man who tolerates his wife's infidelity
WITTY	*adj* -TIER, -TIEST humorously clever
WIVE	*v* WIVED, WIVING, WIVES to marry a woman
WIVER	*n* pl. -S wivern
WIVERN	*n* pl. -S a two-legged dragon
WIVES	pl. of wife
WIVING	present participle of wive
WIZ	*n* pl. -ES a very clever or skillful person
WIZARD	*n* pl. -S a sorcerer **WIZARDLY** *adj*
WIZARDRY	*n* pl. -RIES sorcery
WIZEN	*v* -ED, -ING, -S to shrivel
WIZZEN	*n* pl. -S weasand
WO	*n* pl. WOS woe
WOAD	*n* pl. -S a blue dye **WOADED** *adj*
WOADWAX	*n* pl. -ES an ornamental shrub
WOALD	*n* pl. -S a yellow pigment
WOBBLE	*v* -BLED, -BLING, -BLES to move unsteadily
WOBBLER	*n* pl. -S one that wobbles
WOBBLY	*adj* -BLIER, -BLIEST unsteady

WOBBLY	*n* pl. -BLIES a member of the Industrial Workers of the World
WOBEGONE	*adj* affected with woe
WOE	*n* pl. -S tremendous grief
WOEFUL	*adj* -FULLER, -FULLEST full of woe **WOEFULLY** *adv*
WOENESS	*n* pl. -ES sadness
WOESOME	*adj* woeful
WOFUL	*adj* woeful **WOFULLY** *adv*
WOK	*n* pl. -S a cooking utensil
WOKE	a past tense of wake
WOKEN	a past participle of wake
WOLD	*n* pl. -S an elevated tract of open land
WOLF	*n* pl. WOLVES a carnivorous mammal
WOLF	*v* -ED, -ING, -S to devour voraciously
WOLFER	*n* pl. -S one who hunts wolves
WOLFFISH	*n* pl. -ES a marine fish
WOLFISH	*adj* wolflike
WOLFLIKE	*adj* resembling a wolf
WOLFRAM	*n* pl. -S tungsten
WOLVER	*n* pl. -S wolfer
WOLVES	pl. of wolf
WOMAN	*n* pl. WOMEN an adult human female
WOMAN	*v* -ED, -ING, -S to play the part of a woman
WOMANISE	*v* -ISED, -ISING, -ISES to womanize
WOMANISH	*adj* characteristic of a woman
WOMANIZE	*v* -IZED, -IZING, -IZES to make effeminate
WOMANLY	*adj* -LIER, -LIEST having the qualities of a woman
WOMB	*n* pl. -S the uterus **WOMBED** *adj*
WOMBAT	*n* pl. -S a nocturnal mammal
WOMBY	*adj* WOMBIER, WOMBIEST hollow
WOMEN	pl. of woman
WOMERA	*n* pl. -S a device used to propel spears
WOMMERA	*n* pl. -S womera
WON	*v* WONNED, WONNING, WONS to dwell
WONDER	*v* -ED, -ING, -S to have a feeling of curiosity or doubt

WONDERER *n pl.* -S one that wonders

WONDROUS *adj* marvelous

WONKY *adj* -KIER, -KIEST unsteady

WONNED past tense of won

WONNER *n pl.* -S a prodigy

WONNING present participle of won

WONT *v* -ED, -ING, -S to make accustomed to

WONTEDLY *adv* in a usual manner

WONTON *n pl.* -S a pork-filled dumpling used in Chinese cooking

WOO *v* -ED, -ING, -S to seek the affection of

WOOD *v* -ED, -ING, -S to furnish with wood (the hard, fibrous substance beneath the bark of a tree or shrub)

WOODBIN *n pl.* -S a bin for holding firewood

WOODBIND *n pl.* -S woodbine

WOODBINE *n pl.* -S a European shrub

WOODBOX *n pl.* -ES a woodbin

WOODCHAT *n pl.* -S a European shrike

WOODCOCK *n pl.* -S a game bird

WOODCUT *n pl.* -S an engraved block of wood

WOODEN *adj* -ENER, -ENEST resembling wood in stiffness **WOODENLY** *adv*

WOODHEN *n pl.* -S the weka

WOODIER comparative of woody

WOODIEST superlative of woody

WOODLAND *n pl.* -S land covered with trees

WOODLARK *n pl.* -S a songbird

WOODLESS *adj* having no wood

WOODLORE *n pl.* -S knowledge of the forest

WOODLOT *n pl.* -S an area restricted to the growing of forest trees

WOODMAN *n pl.* -MEN woodsman

WOODNOTE *n pl.* -S a song or call of a forest bird

WOODPILE *n pl.* -S a pile of wood

WOODRUFF *n pl.* -S an aromatic herb

WOODSHED *v* -SHEDDED, -SHEDDING, -SHEDS to practice on a musical instrument

WOODSIA *n pl.* -S a small fern

WOODSMAN *n pl.* -MEN one who works or lives in the forest

WOODSY *adj* WOODSIER, WOODSIEST suggestive of a forest

WOODWAX *n pl.* -ES woadwax

WOODWIND *n pl.* -S a musical wind instrument

WOODWORK *n pl.* -S work made of wood

WOODWORM *n pl.* -S a wood-boring worm

WOODY *adj* WOODIER, WOODIEST containing or resembling wood

WOOER *n pl.* -S one that woos

WOOF *v* -ED, -ING, -S to utter a gruff barking sound

WOOFER *n pl.* -S a loudspeaker designed to reproduce low-pitched sounds

WOOINGLY *adv* attractively

WOOL *n pl.* -S the dense, soft hair forming the coat of certain mammals **WOOLED** *adj*

WOOLEN *n pl.* -S a fabric made of wool

WOOLER *n pl.* -S a domestic animal raised for its wool

WOOLFELL *n pl.* -S woolskin

WOOLIE *n pl.* -S a woolly

WOOLIER comparative of wooly

WOOLIES pl. of wooly

WOOLIEST superlative of wooly

WOOLLEN *n pl.* -S woolen

WOOLLIER comparative of woolly

WOOLLIES pl. of woolly

WOOLLIEST superlative of woolly

WOOLLIKE *adj* resembling wool

WOOLLY *adj* -LIER, -LIEST consisting of or resembling wool

WOOLLY *n pl.* -LIES a garment made of wool

WOOLMAN *n pl.* -MEN a dealer in wool

WOOLPACK *n pl.* -S a bag for packing a bale of wool

WOOLSACK *n pl.* -S a sack of wool

WOOLSHED *n pl.* -S a building in which sheep are sheared

WOOLSKIN *n pl.* -S a sheepskin with the wool still on it

WOOLY *adj* WOOLIER, WOOLIEST woolly

WOOLY *n pl.* WOOLIES a woolly

WOOMERA *n pl.* -S womera

WOOPS *interj* oops

WOORALI *n pl.* -S curare

WOORARI *n pl.* -S curare

WOOSH *v* -ED, -ING, -ES to whoosh

WOOZY *adj* -ZIER, -ZIEST dazed
WOOZILY *adv*

WOP *n pl.* -S an Italian — an offensive term

WORD *v* -ED, -ING, -S to express in words (speech sounds that communicate meaning)

WORDAGE *n pl.* -S the number of words used

WORDBOOK *n pl.* -S a dictionary

WORDIER comparative of wordy

WORDIEST superlative of wordy

WORDILY *adv* in a wordy manner

WORDING *n pl.* -S the act or style of expressing in words

WORDLESS *adj* being without words

WORDPLAY *n pl.* -PLAYS a witty exchange of words

WORDY *adj* WORDIER, WORDIEST using many or too many words

WORE past tense of wear

WORK *v* WORKED or WROUGHT, WORKING, WORKS to exert one's powers of body or mind for some purpose

WORKABLE *adj* capable of being done

WORKADAY *adj* everyday

WORKBAG *n pl.* -S a bag for holding work instuments and materials

WORKBOAT *n pl.* -S a boat used for commercial purposes

WORKBOOK *n pl.* -S an exercise book for a student

WORKBOX *n pl.* -ES a box for holding work instruments and materials

WORKDAY *n pl.* -DAYS a day on which work is done

WORKER *n pl.* -S one that works

WORKFOLK *n/pl* manual laborers

WORKING *n pl.* -S a mining excavation

WORKLESS *adj* unemployed

WORKLOAD *n pl.* -S the amount of work assigned to an employee

WORKMAN *n pl.* -MEN a male worker

WORKOUT *n pl.* -S a period of physical exercise

WORKROOM *n pl.* -S a room in which work is done

WORKSHOP *n pl.* -S a workroom

WORKUP *n pl.* -S an intensive diagnostic study

WORKWEEK *n pl.* -S the number of hours worked in a week

WORLD *n pl.* -S the earth and all its inhabitants

WORLDLY *adj* -LIER, -LIEST pertaining to the world

WORM *v* -ED, -ING, -S to rid of worms (small, limbless invertebrates)

WORMER *n pl.* -S one that worms

WORMHOLE *n pl.* -S a hole made by a burrowing worm

WORMIER comparative of wormy

WORMIEST superlative of wormy

WORMIL *n pl.* -S a lump in the skin of an animal's back

WORMISH *adj* wormlike

WORMLIKE *adj* resembling a worm

WORMROOT *n pl.* -S pinkroot

WORMSEED *n pl.* -S a tropical plant

WORMWOOD *n pl.* -S a European herb

WORMY *adj* WORMIER, WORMIEST infested with worms

WORN *adj* affected by wear or use

WORNNESS *n pl.* -ES the state of being worn

WORRIED past tense of worry

WORRIER *n pl.* -S one that worries

WORRIT *v* -ED, -ING, -S to worry

WORRY *v* -RIED, -RYING, -RIES to feel anxious and uneasy about something

WORSE *n pl.* -S something that is worse (bad in a greater degree)

WORSEN *v* -ED, -ING, -S to make or become worse

WORSER *adj* worse

WORSET *n pl.* -S worsted

WORSHIP *v* -SHIPED, -SHIPING, -SHIPS or -SHIPPED, -SHIPPING, -SHIPS to honor and love as a divine being

WORST *v* -ED, -ING, -S to defeat

WORSTED *n pl.* -S a woolen yarn

WORT *n pl.* -S a plant, herb, or vegetable

WORTH *v* -ED, -ING, -S to befall

WORTHFUL *adj* worthy

WORTHY	*adj* -THIER, -THIEST having value or merit **WORTHILY** *adv*
WORTHY	*n pl.* -THIES a worthy person
WOST	a present 2d person sing. of wit
WOSTTETH	a present 2d person sing. of wit
WOT	*v* WOTTED, WOTTING, WOTS to know
WOTTETH	a present 3d person sing. of wit
WOULD	past tense of will
WOULDEST	a 2d person sing. past tense of will
WOULDST	a 2d person sing. past tense of will
WOUND	*v* -ED, -ING, -S to inflict an injury upon
WOVE	a past tense of weave
WOVEN	past participle of weave
WOW	*v* -ED, -ING, -S to excite to enthusiastic approval
WOWSER	*n pl.* -S a puritanical person
WRACK	*v* -ED, -ING, -S to wreck
WRACKFUL	*adj* destructive
WRAITH	*n pl.* -S a ghost
WRANG	*n pl.* -S a wrong
WRANGLE	*v* -GLED, -GLING, -GLES to argue noisily
WRANGLER	*n pl.* -S one that wrangles
WRAP	*v* WRAPPED or WRAPT, WRAPPING, WRAPS to enclose in something wound or folded about
WRAPPER	*n pl.* -S one that wraps
WRAPPING	*n pl.* -S the material in which something is wrapped
WRAPT	a past tense of wrap
WRASSE	*n pl.* -S a marine fish
WRASTLE	*v* -TLED, -TLING, -TLES to wrestle
WRATH	*v* -ED, -ING, -S to make wrathful
WRATHFUL	*adj* extremely angry
WRATHY	*adj* WRATHIER, WRATHIEST wrathful **WRATHILY** *adv*
WREAK	*v* -ED, -ING, -S to inflict
WREAKER	*n pl.* -S one that wreaks
WREATH	*n pl.* -S a band of flowers **WREATHY** *adj*
WREATHE	*v* WREATHED, WREATHEN, WREATHING, WREATHES to shape into a wreathe
WRECK	*v* -ED, -ING, -S to cause the ruin of
WRECKAGE	*n pl.* -S the act of wrecking
WRECKER	*n pl.* -S one that wrecks
WRECKFUL	*adj* destructive
WRECKING	*n pl.* -S the occupation of salvaging wrecked objects
WREN	*n pl.* -S a small songbird
WRENCH	*v* -ED, -ING, -ES to twist suddenly and forcibly
WREST	*v* -ED, -ING, -S to take away by force
WRESTER	*n pl.* -S one that wrests
WRESTLE	*v* -TLED, -TLING, -TLES to engage in a type of hand-to-hand contest
WRESTLER	*n pl.* -S one that wrestles
WRETCH	*n pl.* -ES a wretched person
WRETCHED	*adj* -EDER, -EDEST extremely unhappy
WRIED	past tense of wry
WRIER	a comparative of wry
WRIES	present 3d person sing. of wry
WRIEST	a superlative of wry
WRIGGLE	*v* -GLED, -GLING, -GLES to turn or twist in a sinuous manner
WRIGGLER	*n pl.* -S one that wriggles
WRIGGLY	*adj* -GLIER, -GLIEST wriggling
WRIGHT	*n pl.* -S one who constructs or creates
WRING	*v* WRUNG or WRINGED, WRINGING, WRINGS to twist so as to compress
WRINGER	*n pl.* -S one that wrings
WRINKLE	*v* -KLED, -KLING, -KLES to make wrinkles (small ridges or furrows) in
WRINKLY	*adj* -KLIER, -KLIEST having wrinkles
WRIST	*n pl.* -S the junction between the hand and forearm
WRISTLET	*n pl.* -S a band worn around the wrist
WRISTY	*adj* WRISTIER, WRISTIEST using much wrist action
WRIT	*n pl.* -S a written legal order

WRITE	*v* WROTE, WRITTEN, WRITING, WRITES to form characters or symbols on a surface with an instrument **WRITABLE** *adj*
WRITER	*n* pl. -S one that writes
WRITHE	*v* WRITHED, WRITHING, WRITHES to squirm or twist in pain
WRITHEN	*adj* twisted
WRITHER	*n* pl. -S one that writhes
WRITHING	present participle of writhe
WRITING	*n* pl. -S a written composition
WRITTEN	past participle of write
WRONG	*adj* WRONGER, WRONGEST not according to what is right, proper, or correct
WRONG	*v* -ED, -ING, -S to treat injuriously or unjustly
WRONGER	*n* pl. -S one that wrongs
WRONGFUL	*adj* wrong
WRONGLY	*adv* in a wrong manner
WROTE	past tense of write
WROTH	*adj* very angry
WROTHFUL	*adj* wroth
WROUGHT	a past tense of work
WRUNG	a past tense of wring
WRY	*adj* WRIER, WRIEST or WRYER, WRYEST contorted **WRYLY** *adv*
WRY	*v* WRIED, WRYING, WRIES to contort
WRYNECK	*n* pl. -S a European bird
WRYNESS	*n* pl. -ES the state of being wry
WUD	*adj* insane
WURST	*n* pl. -S sausage
WURZEL	*n* pl. -S a variety of beet
WYCH	*n* pl. -ES a European elm
WYE	*n* pl. -S the letter Y
WYLE	*v* WYLED, WYLING, WYLES to beguile
WYND	*n* pl. -S a narrow street
WYNN	*n* pl. -S the rune for W
WYTE	*v* WYTED, WYTING, WYTES to wite
WYVERN	*n* pl. -S wivern

XANTHATE	*n* pl. -S a chemical salt
XANTHEIN	*n* pl. -S the water-soluble part of the coloring matter in yellow flowers
XANTHENE	*n* pl. -S a chemical compound
XANTHIC	*adj* tending to have a yellow color
XANTHIN	*n* pl. -S a yellow pigment
XANTHINE	*n* pl. -S a chemical compound
XANTHOMA	*n* pl. -MAS or -MATA a skin disease
XANTHONE	*n* pl. -S a chemical compound
XANTHOUS	*adj* yellow
XEBEC	*n* pl. -S a Mediterranean sailing vessel
XENIA	*n* pl. -S the effect of pollen on certain plant structures **XENIAL** *adj*
XENIC	*adj* pertaining to a type of culture medium
XENOGAMY	*n* pl. -MIES the transfer of pollen from one plant to another
XENOGENY	*n* pl. -NIES the supposed production of offspring totally different from the parent
XENOLITH	*n* pl. -S a rock fragment included in another rock
XENON	*n* pl. -S a gaseous element
XERARCH	*adj* developing in a dry area
XERIC	*adj* requiring only a small amount of moisture
XEROSERE	*n* pl. -S a dry-land sere

XEROSIS	*n* pl. -ROSES abnormal dryness of a body part or tissue **XEROTIC** *adj*
XERUS	*n* pl. -ES an African ground squirrel
XI	*n* pl. -S a Greek letter
XIPHOID	*n* pl. -S a part of the sternum
XU	*n* pl. XU a monetary unit of Vietnam
XYLAN	*n* pl. -S a substance found in cell walls of plants
XYLEM	*n* pl. -S a complex plant tissue
XYLENE	*n* pl. -S a flammable hydrocarbon
XYLIDIN	*n* pl. -S xylidine
XYLIDINE	*n* pl. -S a chemical compound
XYLOCARP	*n* pl. -S a hard, woody fruit
XYLOID	*adj* resembling wood
XYLOL	*n* pl. -S xylene
XYLOSE	*n* pl. -S a type of sugar
XYLOTOMY	*n* pl. -MIES the preparation of sections of wood for microscopic examination
XYLYL	*n* pl. -S a univalent radical
XYST	*n* pl. -S xystus
XYSTER	*n* pl. -S a surgical instrument fo scraping bones
XYSTOS	*n* pl. -TOI xystus
XYSTUS	*n* pl. -TI a roofed area where athletes trained in ancient Greece

YA	*pron* you	**YANQUI**	*n* pl. -S a United States citizen
YABBER	*v* -ED, -ING, -S to jabber	**YAP**	*v* YAPPED, YAPPING, YAPS to bark shrilly
YACHT	*v* -ED, -ING, -S to sail in a yacht (a vessel used for pleasure cruising or racing)	**YAPOCK**	*n* pl. -S an aquatic mammal
		YAPOK	*n* pl. -S yapock
YACHTER	*n* pl. -S one who sails a yacht	**YAPON**	*n* pl. -S yaupon
YACHTING	*n* pl. -S the sport of sailing in yachts	**YAPPED**	past tense of yap
		YAPPER	*n* pl. -S one that yaps
YACHTMAN	*n* pl. -MEN a yachter	**YAPPING**	present participle of yap
YACK	*v* -ED, -ING, -S to yak	**YAR**	*adj* yare
YAFF	*v* -ED, -ING, -S to bark	**YARD**	*v* -ED, -ING, -S to put in a yard (a tract of ground adjacent to a building)
YAGER	*n* pl. -S jaeger		
YAGI	*n* pl. -S a type of shortwave antenna	**YARDAGE**	*n* pl. -S the use of an enclosure for livestock at a railroad station
YAH	*interj* — used as an exclamation of disgust	**YARDARM**	*n* pl. -S either end of a ship's spar
YAHOO	*n* pl. -HOOS a coarse, uncouth person	**YARDBIRD**	*n* pl. -S an army recruit
		YARDMAN	*n* pl. -MEN a man employed to do outdoor work
YAHOOISM	*n* pl. -S coarse, uncouth behavior	**YARDWAND**	*n* pl. -S a measuring stick
YAIRD	*n* pl. -S a garden	**YARE**	*adj* YARER, YAREST nimble
YAK	*v* YAKKED, YAKKING, YAKS to chatter	**YARELY** *adv*	
		YARMELKE	*n* pl. -S yarmulke
YALD	*adj* yauld	**YARMULKE**	*n* pl. -S a skullcap worn by Jewish males
YAM	*n* pl. -S a plant having an edible root		
YAMEN	*n* pl. -S the residence of a Chinese public official	**YARN**	*v* -ED, -ING, -S to tell a long story
YAMMER	*v* -ED, -ING, -S to whine or complain peevishly	**YARROW**	*n* pl. -S a perennial herb
		YASHMAC	*n* pl. -S yashmak
YAMMERER	*n* pl. -S one that yammers	**YASHMAK**	*n* pl. -S a veil worn by Muslim women
YAMUN	*n* pl. -S yamen		
YANG	*n* pl. -S the masculine active principle in Chinese cosmology	**YASMAK**	*n* pl. -S yashmak
YANK	*v* -ED, -ING, -S to pull suddenly	**YATAGAN**	*n* pl. -S yataghan

YATAGHAN	*n* pl. -S a Turkish sword
YAUD	*n* pl. -S an old mare
YAULD	*adj* vigorous
YAUP	*v* -ED, -ING, -S to yawp
YAUPER	*n* pl. -S one that yaups
YAUPON	*n* pl. -S an evergreen shrub
YAW	*v* -ED, -ING, -S to deviate from an intended course
YAWL	*v* -ED, -ING, -S to yowl
YAWMETER	*n* pl. -S an instrument in an aircraft
YAWN	*v* -ED, -ING, -S to open the mouth wide with a deep inhalation of air
YAWNER	*n* pl. -S one that yawns
YAWP	*v* -ED, -ING, -S to utter a loud, harsh cry
YAWPER	*n* pl. -S one that yawps
YAWPING	*n* pl. -S a loud, harsh cry
YAY	*adv* to this extent
YCLEPED	*adj* yclept
YCLEPT	*adj* called; named
YE	*pron* you
YEA	*n* pl. -S an affirmative vote
YEAH	*adv* yes
YEALING	*n* pl. -S a person of the same age
YEAN	*v* -ED, -ING, -S to bear young
YEANLING	*n* pl. -S the young of a sheep or goat
YEAR	*n* pl. -S a period of time consisting of 365 or 366 days
YEARBOOK	*n* pl. -S a book published each year by a graduating class
YEARLIES	pl. of yearly
YEARLING	*n* pl. -S an animal past its first year and not yet two years old
YEARLONG	*adj* lasting through a year
YEARLY	*n* pl. -LIES a publication appearing once a year
YEARN	*v* -ED, -ING, -S to have a stong or deep desire
YEARNER	*n* pl. -S one that yearns
YEARNING	*n* pl. -S a strong or deep desire
YEAST	*v* -ED, -ING, -S to foam
YEASTY	*adj* YEASTIER, YEASTIEST foamy **YEASTILY** *adv*
YEELIN	*n* pl. -S yealing

YEGG	*n* pl. -S a burglar
YEGGMAN	*n* pl. -MEN a yegg
YEH	*adv* yeah
YELD	*adj* not giving milk
YELK	*n* pl. -S yolk
YELL	*v* -ED, -ING, -S to cry out loudly
YELLER	*n* pl. -S one that yells
YELLOW	*adj* -LOWER, -LOWEST of a bright color like that of ripe lemons **YELLOWLY** *adv*
YELLOW	*v* -ED, -ING, -S to make or become yellow
YELLOWY	*adj* somewhat yellow
YELP	*v* -ED, -ING, -S to utter a sharp, shrill cry
YELPER	*n* pl. -S one that yelps
YEN	*v* YENNED, YENNING, YENS to yearn
YENTA	*n* pl. -S a gossipy woman
YEOMAN	*n* pl. -MEN an independent farmer **YEOMANLY** *adj*
YEOMANRY	*n* pl. -RIES the collective body of yeomen
YEP	*adv* yes
YERBA	*n* pl. -S a South American beverage resembling tea
YERK	*v* -ED, -ING, -S to beat vigorously
YES	*v* YESSED, YESSING, YESSES or YESES to give an affirmative reply to
YESHIVA	*n* pl. -VAS or -VOTH an orthodox Jewish school
YESHIVAH	*n* pl. -S yeshiva
YESSED	past tense of yes
YESSES	a 3d person sing. of yes
YESSING	present participle of yes
YESTER	*adj* pertaining to yesterday
YESTERN	*adj* yester
YESTREEN	*n* pl. -S the previous evening
YET	*adv* up to now
YETI	*n* pl. -S the abominable snowman
YETT	*n* pl. -S a gate
YEUK	*v* -ED, -ING, -S to itch
YEUKY	*adj* itchy
YEW	*n* pl. -S an evergreen tree or shrub

YID	*n* pl. -S a Jew — an offensive term
YIELD	*v* -ED, -ING, -S to give up
YIELDER	*n* pl. -S one that yields
YILL	*n* pl. -S ale
YIN	*n* pl. -S the feminine passive principle in Chinese cosmology
YINCE	*adv* once
YIP	*v* YIPPED, YIPPING, YIPS to yelp
YIPE	*interj* — used to express fear or surprise
YIPES	*interj* yipe
YIPPED	past tense of yip
YIPPEE	*interj* — used to express joy
YIPPIE	*n* pl. -S a politically radical hippie
YIPPING	present participle of yip
YIRD	*n* pl. -S earth
YIRR	*v* -ED, -ING, -S to snarl
YIRTH	*n* pl. -S yird
YOD	*n* pl. -S a Hebrew letter
YODEL	*v* -DELED, -DELING, -DELS or -DELLED, -DELLING, -DELS to sing with a fluctuating voice
YODELER	*n* pl. -S one that yodels
YODELLER	*n* pl. -S yodeler
YODH	*n* pl. -S yod
YODLE	*v* -DLED, -DLING, -DLES to yodel
YODLER	*n* pl. -S yodeler
YOGA	*n* pl. -S a Hindu philosophy involving physical and mental disciplines
YOGEE	*n* pl. -S yogi
YOGH	*n* pl. -S a Middle English letter
YOGHOURT	*n* pl. -S yogurt
YOGHURT	*n* pl. -S yogurt
YOGI	*n* pl. -S a person who practices yoga
YOGIC	*adj* pertaining to yoga
YOGIN	*n* pl. -S yogi
YOGINI	*n* pl. -S a female yogi
YOGURT	*n* pl. -S a food made from milk
YOICKS	*interj* — used to encourage hunting hounds

YOKE	*v* YOKED, YOKING, YOKES to fit with a yoke (a wooden frame for joining together draft animals)
YOKEL	*n* pl. -S a naive or gullible rustic
YOKELESS	*adj* having no yoke
YOKELISH	*adj* resembling a yokel
YOKEMATE	*n* pl. -S a companion in work
YOKING	present participle of yoke
YOLK	*n* pl. -S the yellow portion of an egg YOLKED *adj*
YOLKY	*adj* YOLKIER, YOLKIEST resembling a yolk
YOM	*n* pl. YOMIM day
YON	*adv* yonder
YOND	*adv* yonder
YONDER	*adv* over there
YONI	*n* pl. -S a symbol for the vulva in Hindu religion
YONKER	*n* pl. -S younker
YORE	*n* pl. -S time past
YOU	*pron* the 2d person sing. or pl. pronoun
YOUNG	*adj* YOUNGER, YOUNGEST being in the early period of life or growth
YOUNG	*n* pl. -S offspring
YOUNGER	*n* pl. -S an inferior in age
YOUNGISH	*adj* somewhat young
YOUNKER	*n* pl. -S a young gentleman
YOUPON	*n* pl. -S yaupon
YOUR	*adj* a possessive form of the pronoun you
YOURN	*pron* yours
YOURS	*pron* a possessive form of the pronoun you
YOURSELF	*pron* pl. -SELVES a form of the 2d person pronoun
YOUSE	*pron* you
YOUTH	*n* pl. -S a young person
YOUTHEN	*v* -ED, -ING, -S to make youthful
YOUTHFUL	*adj* young
YOW	*v* -ED, -ING, -S to yowl
YOWE	*n* pl. -S a ewe
YOWIE	*n* pl. -S a small ewe
YOWL	*v* -ED, -ING, -S to utter a loud, long, mournful cry
YOWLER	*n* pl. -S one that yowls

YPERITE	*n* pl. -S a poisonous gas	**YULAN**	*n* pl. -S a Chinese tree
YTTERBIA	*n* pl. -S a chemical compound **YTTERBIC** *adj*	**YULE**	*n* pl. -S Christmas time
YTTRIA	*n* pl. -S a chemical compound	**YULETIDE**	*n* pl. -S yule
YTTRIUM	*n* pl. -S a metallic element **YTTRIC** *adj*	**YUMMY**	*adj* -MIER, -MIEST delicious
YUAN	*n* pl. -S a monetary unit of China	**YUMMY**	*n* pl. -MIES something delicious
		YUP	*adv* yep
YUCCA	*n* pl. -S a tropical plant	**YUPON**	*n* pl. -S yaupon
YUGA	*n* pl. -S an age of time in Hinduism	**YURT**	*n* pl. YURTA or YURTS a portable tent
YUK	*v* YUKKED, YUKKING, YUKS to laugh loudly	**YWIS**	*adv* iwis

ZABAIONE   *n* pl. -S a dessert resembling custard

ZABAJONE   *n* pl. -S zabaione

ZACATON   *n* pl. -S a Mexican grass

ZADDIK   *n* pl. -DIKIM a virtuous person by Jewish religious standards

ZAFFAR   *n* pl. -S zaffer

ZAFFER   *n* pl. -S a blue ceramic coloring

ZAFFIR   *n* pl. -S zaffer

ZAFFRE   *n* pl. -S zaffer

ZAFTIG   *adj* full-bosomed

ZAG   *v* ZAGGED, ZAGGING, ZAGS to turn sharply

ZAIBATSU   *n* pl. ZAIBATSU a powerful family combine in Japan

ZAIRE   *n* pl. -S a monetary unit of Zaire

ZAMARRA   *n* pl. -S a sheepskin coat

ZAMARRO   *n* pl. -ROS zamarra

ZAMIA   *n* pl. -S a tropical plant

ZAMINDAR   *n* pl. -S a tax collector in precolonial India

ZANANA   *n* pl. -S zenana

ZANDER   *n* pl. -S a freshwater fish

ZANIER   comparative of zany

ZANIES   pl. of zany

ZANINESS   *n* pl. -ES the quality or state of being zany

ZANY   *adj* ZANIER, ZANIEST ludicrously comical **ZANILY** *adv*

ZANY   *n* pl. -NIES a zany person

ZANYISH   *adj* somewhat zany

ZANZA   *n* pl. -S an African musical instrument

ZAP   *v* ZAPPED, ZAPPING, ZAPS to kill or destroy

ZAPATEO   *n* pl. -TEOS a Spanish dance

ZAPTIAH   *n* pl. -S a Turkish policeman

ZAPTIEH   *n* pl. -S zaptiah

ZARATITE   *n* pl. -S a chemical compound

ZAREBA   *n* pl. -S an improvised stockade

ZAREEBA   *n* pl. -S zareba

ZARF   *n* pl. -S a metal holder for a coffee cup

ZARIBA   *n* pl. -S zareba

ZARZUELA   *n* pl. -S a Spanish operetta

ZASTRUGA   *n* pl. -GI sastruga

ZAX   *n* pl. -ES a tool for cutting roof slates

ZAYIN   *n* pl. -S a Hebrew letter

ZEAL   *n* pl. -S enthusiastic devotion

ZEALOT   *n* pl. -S one who is zealous

ZEALOTRY   *n* pl. -RIES excessive zeal

ZEALOUS   *adj* filled with zeal

ZEATIN   *n* pl. -S a chemical compound found in maize

ZEBEC   *n* pl. -S xebec

ZEBECK   *n* pl. -S xebec

ZEBRA   *n* pl. -S an African mammal that is related to the horse **ZEBRAIC** *adj*

ZEBRASS   *n* pl. -ES the offspring of a zebra and an ass

ZEBRINE   *adj* pertaining to a zebra

ZEBROID   *adj* zebrine

ZEBU   *n* pl. -S an Asian ox

ZECCHIN   *n* pl. -S zecchino

ZECCHINO	*n pl.* -NI or -NOS a former gold coin of Italy
ZECHIN	*n pl.* -S zecchino
ZED	*n pl.* -S the letter Z
ZEDOARY	*n pl.* -ARIES the medicinal root of a tropical plant
ZEE	*n pl.* -S the letter Z
ZEIN	*n pl.* -S a simple protein
ZELKOVA	*n pl.* -S a Japanese tree
ZEMINDAR	*n pl.* -S zamindar
ZEMSTVO	*n pl.* -VOS an elective council in czarist Russia
ZENANA	*n pl.* -S the section of a house in India reserved for women
ZENITH	*n pl.* -S the highest point **ZENITHAL** *adj*
ZEOLITE	*n pl.* -S a mineral **ZEOLITIC** *adj*
ZEPHYR	*n pl.* -S a gentle breeze
ZEPPELIN	*n pl.* -S a long, rigid airship
ZERO	*v* -ED, -ING, -ES or -S to aim at the exact center of a target
ZEST	*v* -ED, -ING, -S to fill with zest (invigorating excitement)
ZESTFUL	*adj* full of zest
ZESTY	*adj* ZESTIER, ZESTIEST marked by zest
ZETA	*n pl.* -S a Greek letter
ZEUGMA	*n pl.* -S the use of a word to modify or govern two or more words, while applying to each in a different sense
ZIBELINE	*n pl.* -S a soft fabric
ZIBET	*n pl.* -S an Asian civet
ZIBETH	*n pl.* -S zibet
ZIG	*v* ZIGGED, ZIGGING, ZIGS to turn sharply
ZIGGURAT	*n pl.* -S an ancient Babylonian temple tower
ZIGZAG	*v* -ZAGGED, -ZAGGING, -ZAGS to proceed on a course marked by sharp turns
ZIKKURAT	*n pl.* -S ziggurat
ZIKURAT	*n pl.* -S ziggurat
ZILCH	*n pl.* -ES nothing
ZILLAH	*n pl.* -S an administrative district in India
ZILLION	*n pl.* -S an indeterminately large number
ZINC	*v* ZINCED, ZINCING, ZINCS or ZINCKED, ZINCKING, ZINCS to coat with zinc (a metallic element)
ZINCATE	*n pl.* -S a chemical salt
ZINCIC	*adj* pertaining to zinc
ZINCIFY	*v* -FIED, -FYING, -FIES to coat with zinc
ZINCITE	*n pl.* -S an ore of zinc
ZINCKED	a past tense of zinc
ZINCKING	a present participle of zinc
ZINCKY	*adj* resembling zinc
ZINCOID	*adj* zincic
ZINCOUS	*adj* zincic
ZINCY	*adj* zincky
ZING	*v* -ED, -ING, -S to move with a high-pitched humming sound
ZINGANO	*n pl.* -NI zingaro
ZINGARA	*n pl.* -RE a female gypsy
ZINGARO	*n pl.* -RI a gypsy
ZINGY	*adj* ZINGIER, ZINGIEST enjoyably exciting
ZINKIFY	*v* -FIED, -FYING, -FIES to zincify
ZINKY	*adj* zincky
ZINNIA	*n pl.* -S a tropical plant
ZIP	*v* ZIPPED, ZIPPING, ZIPS to move with speed and vigor
ZIPPER	*v* -ED, -ING, -S to fasten with a zipper (a fastener consisting of two rows of interlocking teeth)
ZIPPY	*adj* -PIER, -PIEST full of energy
ZIRAM	*n pl.* -S a chemical salt
ZIRCON	*n pl.* -S a mineral
ZIRCONIA	*n pl.* -S a chemical compound
ZIRCONIC	*adj* pertaining to a certain metallic element
ZITHER	*n pl.* -S a stringed instrument
ZITHERN	*n pl.* -S zither
ZITI	*n pl.* -S a tubular pasta
ZIZITH	*n/pl* the tassels on the four corners of a Jewish prayer shawl
ZIZZLE	*v* -ZLED, -ZLING, -ZLES to sizzle
ZLOTY	*n pl.* ZLOTYS a monetary unit of Poland
ZOA	a *pl.* of zoon
ZOARIUM	*n pl.* -IA a colony of bryozoans **ZOARIAL** *adj*

ZODIAC *n pl.* -S an imaginary belt encircling the celestial sphere **ZODIACAL** *adj*

ZOEA *n pl.* ZOEAE or ZOEAS a larval form of certain crustaceans **ZOEAL** *adj*

ZOFTIG *adj* zaftig

ZOIC *adj* pertaining to animals or animal life

ZOISITE *n pl.* -S a mineral

ZOMBI *n pl.* -S a snake god of voodoo cults in West Africa

ZOMBIE *n pl.* -S zombi

ZOMBIISM *n pl.* -S the system of beliefs connected with zombis

ZONAL *adj* pertaining to a zone **ZONALLY** *adv*

ZONARY *adj* zonal

ZONATE *adj* arranged in zones

ZONATED *adj* zonate

ZONATION *n pl.* -S arrangement in zones

ZONE *v* ZONED, ZONING, ZONES to arrange in zones (areas distinguished from other adjacent areas)

ZONELESS *adj* having no zone or belt

ZONER *n pl.* -S one that zones

ZONETIME *n pl.* -S standard time used at sea

ZONING present participle of zone

ZONKED *adj* under the influence of alcohol or a drug

ZONULA *n pl.* -LAE or -LAS zonule

ZONULE *n pl.* -S a small zone **ZONULAR** *adj*

ZOO *n pl.* ZOOS a place where animals are kept for public exhibition

ZOOCHORE *n pl.* -S a plant dispersed by animals

ZOOGENIC *adj* caused by animals or their activities

ZOOGLEA *n pl.* -GLEAE or -GLEAS a jellylike mass of bacteria **ZOOGLEAL** *adj*

ZOOGLOEA *n pl.* -GLOEAE or -GLOEAS zooglea

ZOOID *n pl.* -S an organic cell or body capable of independent movement **ZOOIDAL** *adj*

ZOOKS *interj* — used as a mild oath

ZOOLATER *n pl.* -S one that worships animals

ZOOLATRY *n pl.* -TRIES the worship of animals

ZOOLOGY *n pl.* -GIES the science that deals with animals **ZOOLOGIC** *adj*

ZOOM *v* -ED, -ING, -S to move with a loud humming sound

ZOOMANIA *n pl.* -S an excessive interest in animals

ZOOMETRY *n pl.* -TRIES the measurement of animals or animal parts

ZOOMORPH *n pl.* -S something in the form of an animal

ZOON *n pl.* ZOA or ZOONS the whole product of one fertilized egg **ZOONAL** *adj*

ZOONOSIS *n pl.* -NOSES a disease that can be transmitted from animals to man **ZOONOTIC** *adj*

ZOOPHILE *n pl.* -S a lover of animals

ZOOPHYTE *n pl.* -S an invertebrate animal

ZOOSPERM *n pl.* -S the male fertilizing element of an animal

ZOOSPORE *n pl.* -S a type of spore

ZOOTOMY *n pl.* -MIES the dissection of animals **ZOOTOMIC** *adj*

ZORI *n pl.* ZORI a type of sandal

ZORIL *n pl.* -S a small African mammal

ZORILLA *n pl.* -S zoril

ZORILLE *n pl.* -S zoril

ZORILLO *n pl.* -LOS zoril

ZOSTER *n pl.* -S a virus disease

ZOUAVE *n pl.* -S a French infantryman

ZOUNDS *interj* — used as a mild oath

ZOWIE *interj* — used to express surprise or pleasure

ZOYSIA *n pl.* -S a perennial grass

ZUCCHINI *n pl.* -S a vegetable

ZWIEBACK *n pl.* -S a sweetened bread

ZYGOMA *n pl.* -MAS or -MATA the cheekbone

ZYGOSIS *n pl.* -GOSES the union of two gametes **ZYGOSE** *adj*

ZYGOSITY *n pl.* -TIES the makeup of a particular zygote

ZYGOTE *n pl.* -S a cell formed by the union of two gametes **ZYGOTIC** *adj*

ZYGOTENE *n pl.* -S a stage in meiosis

ZYMASE *n* pl. -S an enzyme

ZYME *n* pl. -S an enzyme

ZYMOGEN *n* pl. -S a substance that develops into an enzyme when suitably activated

ZYMOGENE *n* pl. -S zymogen

ZYMOLOGY *n* pl. -GIES the science of fermentation

ZYMOSIS *n* pl. -MOSES fermentation **ZYMOTIC** *adj*

ZYMURGY *n* pl. -GIES a branch of chemistry dealing with fermentation

ZYZZYVA *n* pl. -S a tropical weevil